ISBN 978-0-282-88523-6
PIBN 10871584

1 MONTH OF FREE READING

at

www.ForgottenBooks.com

By purchasing this book you are eligible for one month membership to ForgottenBooks.com, giving you unlimited access to our entire collection of over 1,000,000 titles via our web site and mobile apps.

To claim your free month visit:

www.forgottenbooks.com/free871584

Britannia having chained the Demon of War receives in gratitude the announcement of Peace with all Europe.

THE

HISTORY OF THE WAR,

FROM THE

Commencement

OF THE

FRENCH REVOLUTION

TO THE

PRESENT TIME.

By HEWSON CLARKE, Esq.
LATE OF EMANUEL COLLEGE, CAMBRIDGE.

EMBELLISHED WITH BEAUTIFUL ENGRAVINGS

VOL. I.

LONDON:

PUBLISHED BY T. KINNERSLEY, ACTON PLACE, KINGSLAND ROAD.

STEREOTYPED AND PRINTED BY COCK AND M'GOWAN,
16, GREAT WINDMILL STREET

1816

CONTENTS

OF THE

FIRST VOLUME.

a

HISTORY, &c.

INTRODUCTION.

IN tracing the annals of Europe during the eventful period of the last twenty-five years, the first attention of the historian is naturally directed to the origin and progress of that momentous revolution, which in its immediate effects, and in its remoter consequences, has so materially contributed to decide the fate of nations, and to influence the happiness of mankind. It will be necessary therefore at the commencement of the present work, to enter into a preliminary examination of the internal situation of France immediately previous to the actual commencement of revolutionary measures : to detail the grievances and oppressions by which the dissatisfaction of the people was excited, and to expatiate as fully as is consistent with the limits of an Introduction, on the moral influence of the manners of the court, and the writings of pretended philosophers.

The immediate and most effective causes of the revolution must be referred to the distresses of the people, and the embarassments of the government, occasioned by the enormous expences of the war in which France supported the independence of the American colonies. The profligacy of the court; the dissentions of the clergy ; the gradual progress of general intelligence; the dissemination of revolutionary principles occasioned by the American contest, and the long-established oppressions to which the mass of the people were subjected ; all contributed to the same effect, but in a subordinate degree. It was not till the court and the ministers were reduced to the most desperate expedients of finance, and compelled to court the favour, while they insulted the distresses of the nation, that the latent dissatisfaction of the people was excited to activity, and terminated in the fury of revolutionary enthusiasm.

When the unhappy contest occurred between Great Britain and her colonies, it was conceived by the court of France, that a favourable occasion was now presented of avenging the late inglorious war, and destroying the effects of the peace of 1763. The capture of Burgoyne was accordingly regarded as a propitious opportunity for the declaration of hostilities ; and the descendant of so many absolute monarchs did not regard it as impolitic, or unjust, to acknowledge and assist the exertions of a people struggling for independence.

M. de Vergennes directed the department of foreign affairs with acknowledged ability. M. de Sartine restored the navy ; while Neckar, a foreigner, a protestant, and a banker, in whose favour so many prejudices were resigned, and of whose talents the most exalted expectations had been formed, regulated the revenues as comptroller-general. A skilful financier rather than an able minister, he raised loans on the annual savings obtained by a reduction of the public expenses, and attempted the brilliant, but impossible paradox of conducting an expensive war, without oppressing the people by additional taxes.

The present was the only conflict with England during more than three centuries, that did not prove inglorious to France; for, although England displayed her antient valour and superiority on the sea, yet she failed in the object of the contest: while the alliance of the American States, the temporary humiliation of her antient rival, and the triumph attendant on success, gratified the vanity of the French people, and the ambition of the court.

But it was not difficult to conceive that a free intercourse and intimate connection between individuals, who had been hitherto in a great measure strangers to each other, should produce a mutual communication of sentiments; and as prejudice and error subsided an exchange of opinions. It was scarcely possible that many thousand Frenchmen should live for several years in America, under all the vicissitudes of a common and dangerous war, and in all the ease and festivity of an unexpected peace, without becoming, in a considerable degree, American. On the other hand, the rigid sectaries of Boston, forgetting their former aversion to popery, were so much gratified by the society of their new friends and guests, that they not only permitted, but attended their solemn service for the dead, which they had before considered as an abomination, scarcely inferior to idolatry.

It was to the honour of the French gentlemen who served by sea and land, that they were disposed to examine, and to apply the new objects which came within their immediate observation. Many were employed in civil, diplomatic, and mercantile affairs; curiosity, pleasure, and private connections influenced the habits of others; and some who were professedly philosophers, went thither with the intention to speculate upon, and to explore a new world and new orders of mankind. It was impossible that these individuals should not have been impressed with the excellence of that original constitution, of which the emanations diffused at so great a distance, so many examples of equality, security, and prosperity.

The intercourse which for several years had been continually increasing between France and England; the frequent visits paid by individuals of the first rank and talents from the former to the latter; and more than both, the passion for reading the works of the first English writers, upon the great subjects of government and philosophy; and on those of a lighter nature, combined to produce a singular revolution, not only among men of learning and the lovers of speculation, but in the tide of popular opinion. The predominance of England in the affairs of Europe, the former success of our arms, and extension of our dominion, by fixing the attention and exciting the admiration of other nations, gave rise to a spirit of imitation, which led them to copy us in all things, but principally in that by which we were most distinguished, the form of our government. In France subjects were openly and eagerly discussed which were before regarded as too dangerous for inquiry; or, which it was imagined, a people so vain and frivolous, would not take the trouble to investigate. The principles upon which governments were originally founded, the ultimate objects of their institution, the relative rights and duties of the governors and the governed, became the subjects of common conversation among common men. But above all, the personal security afforded by the English constitution, and the right which every man possessed of appealing publicly to the laws and to the world, in all cases of injury, or oppression by power, were generally admired and envied, while *lettres de cachet*, and every other mode of punishment, without legal trial and legal condemnation, were universally execrated.

This disposition of the people might have been easily repressed in its infancy, had not the American war effectually provided for its nurture and advancement. The minds of men became attached to those principles which the cause they had espoused required them to maintain ; and as the necessity of referring to the rights of government during the American contest, may, in some degree, have enfeebled the spirit of liberty in England, the French nation having more frequent occasion to appeal to provisions and principles by which the abuses of power are corrected, than to those by which its energy is maintained, imbibed a love of freedom, scarcely compatible with loyalty.

But it was owing to a still more important cause, that the American war became instrumental to the revolution. It involved the crown in such difficulties and distresses, as compelled it to cast itself on the indulgence and support of the people ; affording them an opportunity of thinking, acting, and speaking, which they had not enjoyed since the conclusion of the civil wars.

The public debts of the kingdom had been insupportably oppressive ; and its finances involved in the utmost embarassment. The intolerable burdens to which war and ambition had subjected the nation, were continually encreased by the enormous expenses of the crown, and the profusion that prevailed during the unequalled length of the two last reigns. But the weight and amount of the public debts were only part of the national misfortune. The whole system of finances was to the last degree faulty and ruinous : the taxes were injudiciously imposed, and arbitrarily levied. The farmers of the revenues who made immense fortunes, were almost the only untitled members of the community who lived in splendor ; while the greater and more valuable part of the nation was groaning beneath the pressure of hopeless poverty.

The American war commenced in this situation of affairs, and the people in their zeal to support their sovereign, forgot their debts and their taxes. The ostensible causes, and the private motives of the war, as far as they were understood, were highly alluring and captivating to the imaginations of a generous, brave, and commercial nation. It appeared great and heroic to rescue an oppressed people who were gallantly contending for their rights, from inevitable ruin : it bore the impressions of skilful policy to reduce the power and humble the pride of a great and haughty rival ; the disasters sustained in the preceding war with England, could not be forgotten ; and, notwithstanding, the wounds inflicted were partially healed by a favourable peace, they still rankled in the breast of every Frenchman. Nothing, therefore, could be more flattering to the national pride, than to seize the opportunity now arrived, of erasing the disgrace attached to that unfortunate period. As it was universally supposed that the loss of America would prove an incurable, if not a mortal wound to England ; it was equally expected, that the power of the Gallic throne would be established by that event, on foundations so permanent, as never to be shaken by the vicissitudes of fortune. To complete the prospect of glory and advantage, commercial benefits before unknown, and an accession of naval strength that should command the seas, were to be derived from the new alliance and connection with America. These speculations ended only in surprize and disappointment ; but the nation entered into the war with unexampled eagerness, and a common hand, directed by a common heart, appeared in its execution.

Though the American war failed in producing the desired and expected results in favour of France, it left behind it consequences of a less pleasing nature. Through various causes, particularly from the novel manner in which it was conducted ; its operations being chiefly naval, and extended to the remotest quarters of the world ; from the extreme poverty and urgent necessity of the Americans, and the prevailing spirit of the time, which led to the most unbounded supplies, under the persuasion that the money so laid out would be amply repaid : the American war became the most expensive in proportion to the time of its continuance, of any

B 2

in which France had been engaged. This expense was the more ruinous in its effect, from the circumstance that a great part of the money expended, was sunk at a distance from home, or laid out in commodities so perishable, that there was little hope of its recovery. From this war therefore, a new debt, of immense amount, was superadded to the old ; and the accumulation became so vast, as to swell beyond the common bounds of examination and inquiry.

It is the misfortune of every hereditary sovereign, in a despotic government, that he cannot indulge the natural benevolence of his disposition, nor endeavour to ameliorate, even at the expense of his own convenience, the political situation of his people, without endangering the existence of his crown, and hazarding the occurrence of a long and lamentable series of turbulence and bloodshed. In proportion to the rigour by which the energies of the public mind are repressed, will be the elasticity of their revulsion, when the hand of power relaxes its pressure. The eagerness of the people to take advantage of every concession from the sovereign, will be in proportion to the severity of the humiliations and privations to which they have been formerly subjected ; and who shall limit the excesses of a nation intoxicated by the possession of unexpected freedom, and the prospect of blessings in which it had not hoped to participate ? Whoever compares the bloodless and tranquil revolutions of England, when those revolutions were rational in their object, and patriotic in their formation, with the miseries attendant upon resistance to the French monarchy ; a resistance creditable to the people at large, and to its principal agents, will regard it as one of the strongest arguments against the establishment of a despotic government, that it not only entails upon the people the misfortunes and privations of its own existence and exercise, but exposes them in its future downfall to all the horrors of sanguinary turbulence. They become the prey of those atrocious individuals, who, in every state, endeavour to convert the errors and in-

fatuation of the people, to the exaltation of their desperate fortunes, or the gratifica tion of their ferocious and unprincipled ambition.

The depravation of the public mind, immediately previous to the assembling of the states-general, on the 5th of May, 1789, had been completed by the tendency of a variety of causes, of which the ultimate effect was as decisive as the progress was conspicuous. The advancement of Marie Antoinette in impolicy and indiscretion had been open and regular. Continuing, with equal folly and weakness, to brood over an affront received from the duchesses at the court ball upon the occasion of her marriagè, she removed those ladies from her household who were distinguished by their rank, the reputation of their families, and their attachment to the antient usages of the house of Bourbou. The French ceremonial, one of the sources of the majesty of the throne, became the object of her constant raillery. She entrusted the education of her children to a woman of no character or consideration at court, and consequently excited the discontent of those respectable families who usually aspired at such employments. The more state and authority she assumed, the more the aunts of the king and her two sisters-in-law contrived to oppose her, and to procure her the hatred of the courtly circle. The sisters of the late Dauphin, warmly attached to the memory of that prince, considered her as the protector of the party of the duke de Choiseul, who had deprived them by poison, of a brother so lately beloved. From the castle of Bellevue and of Mendon, the retreat of the malcontent princes since the period of the gloomy and discontented demeanours of the only son of Lewis the XV. the sarcasm was propagated, that an Austrian occupied the place of the queen of France. The royal family accused her of a desire to assume a superiority over the house of Bourbon, and place the princes of Lorraine on a level with the princes of the blood. They charged her with an intention to degrade the great persons of the state, and to raise from the dust, at the expense of the public treasure, her favourites of both sexes, and particularly the house of Polignæ.

The clamours and complaints from Versailles and Bellevue, were imported into the capital, and disseminated among all classes of the people. The haughty tone which the queen observed in the decline of her credit, gradually diminished the respectful affection with which she had hitherto been regarded. Marie Antoinette was no longer the dauphiness, young, charming, and adored, indulging only in the amusements suited to her age. In the eyes of the daughters of Lewis XV. who considered themselves as having happily escaped from the poison of Choiseul, she was regarded in no other light than as an archduchess of Austria, an enemy of the French, arrived from Vienna to rule over their country.

The virulence of the public resentment increased from this time; and was carried to such a degree, that doubts of the legitimacy of the dauphin were intimated, both in conversation and in writings: doubts which she never condescended to refute by adopting a reserved or discreet behaviour. Lewis XIV. from a motive of policy, had fixed his ordinary residence at a distance from the capital, lest his authority might be diminished by rendering his person familiar to the eyes of the people: the queen, on the contrary, purchased St. Cloud, and moved nearer to Paris, when the concourse of nobility had declined at Versailles. Her private life was the object of public and malicious satire; yet she still affected periodical retreats to Trianon, which her enemies regarded as a suspicious residence. The people proceeding in their injustice began to attribute to her influence, the selection of obnoxious ministers, and the design of unsuccessful measures. They spoke freely of the acquisition of St. Cloud, the orgies of Trianon, the terrace of Versailles, and the nocturnal revels of the park. The count D'Artois, the duke de Coigny, the count de Fersen, the handsome Dillon, and the officers of the life guards, were sarcastically mentioned, and pleasures were recited

of a nature which history has only recorded of periods of the most extreme depravity. The people depreciated the royal dignity with a warmth which nothing could restrain.

It was at this moment that the reputation of the queen sustained a wound from which it was never able to recover; the circumstances of the singular event which excited the indignation of the people of Paris, have never been consistently related, or minutely developed. It may be collected, however, from the multitude of partial and contradictory accounts, that the cardinal de Rohan, anxious to retrieve his fortune, which he had exhausted by extravagance, became the dupe of the countess de la Motte, a titled prostitute, who shared the favour of the queen. A diamond necklace of very considerable value, having been exhibited by the jewellers in the courtly circles, the countess intimated to the cardinal de Rohan, that the queen had taken a fancy to the jewels, and produced a paper, to which was the signature, Marie Antoinette of France, as a security to the jewellers for the payment by instalments, of the stipulated price. The cardinal, determined to purloin some of the most valuable stones of the necklace as it passed through his hand, believing the representations of the countess, and well acquainted with the motives of the queen for the most inviolable secrecy, readily pledged himself to the merchants for the amount of their demand. When the first instalment became due, the queen disclaimed all knowledge of the transaction, and both the culprits were sentenced to deserved, but arbitrary punishment. That the queen was innocent there can be no reason to doubt; but the effects of this transaction on the public mind were extensively pernicious. The people beheld with indignation, the names of the most notorious adventurers, swindlers, and women of dubious character, associated with that of the queen of France: while in consequence of de Rohan's trial and conviction, the whole ecclesiastical body partook of the infamy of the bishop of Strasburg.

The active interference of the French cabinet in the affairs of Russia, America,

levities of the court, and the imbecility and licentiousness of the clergy, corrupted the public mind, and diffused a general indifference to the duties of religion and the habits of morality. The theoretical sophistries of the philosophers, co-operating with the practical conviction and experience of the people, contributed to confirm their scepticism, to give new confidence to their licentiousness, and to render more acute and more severe, their scrutiny of the conduct of their superiors. The effect of the rapid progress of public opinion was apparent immediately after the accession of Lewis XVI. It compelled him to restore the antient parliaments ; and the alleviation of the miseries of the people bécame the object of anxious attention on the part of the government ; jurisprudence was rendered more mild by the abolition of the *question* by torture ; the inferior clergy were inspired with courage to resist the encroachments of the superior ; and the unfortunate protestants were animated by the hope of no longer enduring the rigour of intolerance. In return for the important privilege of exemption from taxation, the government of France frequently exacted from the clergy a contribution, which from a regard to the delicacy and dignity of the church, was denominated a *free-gift*. The mode of raising this free gift was extremely unequal, and the inferior clergy were compelled to furnish so large a proportion, that the burden of expense on the superior was comparatively trifling. The inferior clergy long sustained the oppression with patient endurance, and it was not till after the commencement of the reign of Lewis XVI. that they began to complain. Their complaints made a deep impression on the minds of the people : they were received by the bishops with all the rage and rancour of bigotry, but the curés were not discouraged ; the conduct of their oppressors did not surprise them ; and the popular approbation and support excited them to more vigorous exertions.

The cures of the province of Dauphiny presented a powerful example to the other provinces. The disproportion between the revenues of the superior and inferior clergy was greater in Dauphiny than in any other province : the latter therefore resolved to petition the king for an augmentation of their income. Yet cautious in their address, and respectful even towards their oppressors, they requested from the bishops permission to assemble. A rude refusal was returned. The parliament, however, granted its permission, and they drew up an eloquent and faithful representation of the miseries of their condition. The representation was conveyed to the king, whose answer was returned in the form of an order to the deputies to retire to their province. The parliament of Paris was also prevailed on to register an edict against the assemblies of the curés, without the permission of their diocesans. Yet amidst all these difficulties, amidst this indifference on the part of the monarch, and this oppression on the part of the bishops, the confederacy of the curés increased in number and in courage, and though the voice of their distresses did not reach the throne, it was heard with respectful attention by the people. The sentiments which they delivered from the pulpit took a complexion from their wrongs ; and men who smarted beneath the scourge of a despotic government, felt little inclination to recommend the doctrines of passive obedience and nonresistance.

In proportion to the gloom of ignorance, and the rancour of the prejudices which darkened the highest and lowest ranks of society, was the diffusion of information through the intermediate classes. France was not deficient in well-informed men, but information was confined to families of the first nobility, who were kept at a distance from the seat of folly and depravity, by a taste for independence and domestic life ; to a small portion of that secondary nobility who were excluded from court by the mediocrity of their fortune, and the etiquette of vanity ; or, above all, to the numerous class of citizens in easy circumstances called the *haut tiers etat*, which in itself supplied more than three-fourths of the magistrates and clergy ; and of which the individuals being unqualified to avail themselves of the equivocal merit of ancestry, had no other means of recommending themselves than undisputed personal merit.

The great body of the army, hitherto the bulwark of the monarchy and the scourge of the people, participated in the general dissatisfaction. During the administration of the count de St. Germain, who had served many years abroad, Lewis XVI was persuaded to adopt the military punishments of Prussia, Austria, and Russia. Since the days of Turenne and Conde, the French troops had been flattered into obedience, and the *principle of honour* substituted in the place of harshness and rigour. When it was unwisely attempted, therefore, to subdue the refined sense of delicacy, of which the French soldier had always boasted, and to overcome his vanity by subjecting him to the degrading discipline of the sabre, many preferred a voluntary death to such a degradation. The clamours of the people, the disorders of the court, the derangement of the finances, the tyranny 1788. of an arbitrary government, odious even to soldiers, and the hopes derived from the convocation of the states-general, had awakened feelings responsive to those of the religious and civil orders of the community. They could not behold, without indignation, the selection of foreign troops as the peculiar objects of courtly favour. The individuals who had served in America, remembered the cause in which they had been already victorious, and those who resided in the capital had begun to adopt the manners and opinions of the inhabitants. Dazzled with gold, gratified with women, intoxicated with wine, inflamed by patriotism, it was impossible that they should resist so many allurements: and the troops of the capital decided the fate of the most general conspiracy Europe had hitherto witnessed against the despotism of a throne, supported by a powerful clergy and nobility, surrounded by numerous armies, accustomed to implicit obedience, and strengthened and supported by the inveteracy of custom, and the prejudices of ages.

The burdens sustained by the people were great and numerous. A multitude of grievances existed: crimes of the greatest enormity had long been perpetrated with impunity, and the various abuses were so numerous as to extend to every department of the state, and every province of the empire. The Bastile and many subordinate prisons had always opened their dungeons at the voice of a resolute prince; a free press was still unknown, and *lettres de cachet* had been granted during the early part of the present reign with the most shameless impunity. Nor were the grievances of the people confined to the injuries sustained from the exercise of the regal functions. The administration of justice was a source of continual censure and universal despair. The magistrates reimbursed themselves by fees and perquisites, and by the sale of their decisions; and females, distinguished by the appellation of *Les soliciteuses*, were employed to supplicate the favour and corrupt the integrity of the courts. The rigors of the feudal system still degraded the law and practice of the nation. The game-laws were enforced with barbarous and unrelenting oppression; the death of a partridge was not unfrequently expiated by slavery in the galleys; the right of *free-warren* was carried to such an extent, that the peasant beheld the rabbit and the pigeon devouring the fruits of his labour with impunity, while the scanty remnant of his harvest was to be ground at the mill of his lord alone, after being still farther diminished by ecclesiastical exactions.

While the bulk of the people were exhausted and distressed by the rigor of taxation, offices, conferring nobility, were the objects of public barter. The contributions of the clergy were voluntary, under the name of a benevolence; and the nobility were exempt from the operation of imposts. The occupations of the merchant and the farmer were viewed with contempt; the profession of arms was consecrated to the enjoyment of a particular race, and to command a regiment, or any vessel above the rate of a frigate, it was necessary to be a noble.

Exhausted by oppression, irritated by the continual presence of insulting tyranny and unblushing licentiousness, excited to resentment of their wrongs, and instructed in the knowledge of their rights, by the diffusion of enthusiastic sentiments, in favour of religious scepticism and civil freedom, the people of France were, at length, awakened to one universal spirit of complaint and resistance. The cry of liberty resounded from the capital to the frontiers, and was reverberated to the Alps, the Pyrennees, the plains of Flanders, the borders of the Channel, and the shores of the Mediterranean and the Atlantic. Like all sudden and violent alterations in corrupt states, the explosion was accompanied by evils and atrocities, before which the crimes and the miseries of the antient despotism faded into insignificance ; yet the motives of the first agitators of the French revolution, were consistent with the noblest principles of patriotism and of virtue ; nor can they justly be chargeable with subsequent actions and events, over which they retained no personal control, and which eluded the prospective sagacity of the most virtuous and able members of the European community.

HISTORY OF THE WAR.

CHAP. I.

AT the close of the year 1788, France exhibited one melancholy scene of commercial embarrassment and domestic distress. The taxes, numerous as they were, and ruinous to the people, were totally unequal to the supply of the current expenses of the state, and to the discharge of the interest and annuities arising from the various funds. The whole amount of the revenues fell short, by several millions sterling, of the demand in each year. New funds could not be raised, but the exigencies of the state must be supplied, and no means appeared so well calculated to accomplish this purpose as withholding the payment of the annuities to the public creditors for a sum equivalent to the amount of the deficiency. A measure so ruinous, unjust, and arbitrary, could not fail to involve the people in the greatest distress and calamity; and to excite the most clamorous discontent at the undue preference supposed to be given to those individuals whose payments were not suspended.

In this disastrous state of public affairs while financier succeeded financier, and projects multiplied upon projects, each new minister attributed the public evils to the faults of his predecessor, and produced his own favourite scheme of arrangement. This occasioned a cessation of the murmurs of the people while the short sunshine of hope lasted; but only tended to redouble their grief and indignation, when

they perceived that every attempt at elucidation only contributed to render obscurity more impervious, and that every hope of redress terminated in the aggravation of evil. The crown, with respect to all that lay within its own immediate cognizance and power, acted the noblest part during this state of public embarrassment and distress. Incapable of comprehending the complicated details and the perplexed situation of the national finances, the king endeavoured to alleviate the distresses of the people by curtailing the expenses of his court and household. But though these reductions were so extensive as to trench deeply upon the established splendor of the crown, and though the savings were considerable, yet they failed to answer the patriotic and generous purpose of the monarch. The free gifts granted by the clergy and other public bodies, produced as little permanent effect, and amidst the multitude of demands could scarcely afford relief to any pecuniary pressure of the government.

The clamor and discontent excited by these circumstances placed the crown in a situation extremely favourable to the wishes of a people, who began to burn with impatience for some opportunity of recovering their antient privileges. The monarch, wearied out by the repeated failure and disappointments which he had experienced from the promises and speculations of the

c 2

ministers, and finding that his difficulties were becoming every day more dangerous and insupportable, determined to throw himself upon the wisdom and affection of the nation for succour and advice.

The disgrace of Neckar bereaved the state of a minister whose integrity acquired the confidence of the monied men, and. Calonne, his rival and enemy, who affected a felicitous union of business and pleasure, succeeded to the administration of the finances. Bold, original, and daring, he projected gigantic plans which endangered the happiness of the people, while his pliant temper and subservient manners, rendered him the favourite of the noblesse. By his advice, amidst the wreck of public credit, Rambouillet and St. Cloud were purchased for the royal family, and the debts of the king's brothers were discharged. To accomplish these objects, some of the domains of the crown were mortgaged, loans were once more recurred to, a variety of taxes were devised ; and such was the presumption of the new minister, that he pledged himself to pay off the whole national debt within the period of twenty years. But the plans of Calonne were as unsuccessful as they were enterprising ; his imposts were regarded with abhorrence, his pecuniary schemes became inefficient ; and the king, exhausted by difficulties and delays, at length determined that no new loans nor taxes should be demanded. The new financier, ever fertile in resources, determined therefore to have recourse to an expedient which had often been adopted during the reigns of Francis I. and Henry IV. Although so much time had elapsed since the convocation of the states-general, and these assemblies were almost obsolete, yet the French nation never entirely lost sight of that remnant of the antient constitution. Their wisest patriots, and the most spirited of their governors, often looked back to a measure which in former times had been attended with the most salutary effects. In that period of alternate insurrection, tyranny, and foreign glory, which distinguished the administration of cardinal Richelieu, the nation was never reduced to the necessity of deliberating in common,

nor qualified so to do by its temper and its intelligence. During the troubles which attended the minority of Lewis XIV. the queen regent frequently announced her intention of calling together the states-general. During the splendid vicissitudes and the final disasters of that reign, the power of the monarch was too absolute to permit even the apparent interference of any subordinate legislative body. The duke of Burgundy, the pupil of the author of Telemachus, to whom his grandfather had begun to delegate a portion of his authority, to whom the fondest hopes of the nation had been directed, and who promised to unite the qualities of the Christian, the philosopher, and the king, had formed a design among many other projects, for the advantage of the kingdom and the relief of his people, to convene the states. This amiable and intelligent prince dying immaturely, the sovereign power on the demise of Lewis XIV. devolved to feebler and polluted hands. It is not improbable that the veneration in which the character of this prince remained in the memory of the French, and particularly of his family, infused similar sentiments into the mind of the dauphin (son of Lewis XV. and father of Lewis XVI.) who formed himself on the model of the duke of Burgundy. The reverence, approaching to adoration, which Lewis XVI. entertained for the opinions and attachments of his father, were the ruling principles of his character and his conduct. It is therefore a curious and not improbable speculation to suppose, that the approximation to the body of the nation, and the partiality to public councils, which distinguished the present reign, derived their origin from these remote and successive causes.

It became, however, a question of difficulty, in what manner to obtain the sense or aid of the nation in the present exigence. The antient assemblies of the states of the kingdom had been so long disused, that not only their forms were forgotten, but the extent of their rights and power was so much unknown, that all information on the subject was to be sought amidst the rubbish of the antiquarian, or in the obscure and faithless pages of vague and ignorant historians. It was generally known, however, that the antient assemblies of the states resembled the English parliaments in the most important points of their institution : of which, the first was the power of granting the public money for the public service, or of withholding it, if the purpose for which it was required by the crown did not appear advantageous or necessary to the welfare of the kingdom.

In this state of darkness and uncertainty, the first effort made by the court, for the accomplishment of its purpose, was to summon a convention of principal persons from the different classes of the people, and from all parts of the kingdom, who were to receive from the king a communication of his intentions for the relief of his subjects, and information respecting the present state of the finances, and provide the most efficacious remedies against several abuses. The members of this assembly were distinguished by the appellation of notables, being the name of a convention of the same nature which had been held in the year 1626.

The notables were accordingly summoned by means of a circular letter signed by the king, in which he appointed to meet them at Versailles ; but the meeting was prorogued in consequence of the death of Vergennes. At length his majesty repaired to the place where they were solemnly assembled, accompanied by the princes of the blood, and attended by all the ministers and principal officers of the royal household. On this occasion M. de Calonne displayed his usual address by descanting on the deplorable state of the finances previous to his entrance into office : he also alluded to the immense expenditure occasioned by a glorious and successful war, the creation of a fleet, and the great naval works carrying on at Havre, Rochelle, Dunkirk, and Cherburg. To supply the deficiency of the revenue, it was recommended that neither the clergy nor the nobility should be any longer exempted from the territorial impost, or landtax ; all the domains of the crown were to be mortgaged and it was intended that the landed property of the church should be subject to certain regulations in aid of the public burdens. Notwithstanding M. de Calonne had employed every means of conciliation to gain the assembly, *Monsieur* the king's brother, strenuously opposed the propositions ; M. de Brienne, archbishop of Thoulouse attacked all his plans, and the attorney-general of Provence contended that neither the notables, the parliament, nor the king himself, could assess the proposed imposts in the province which he represented ; such imposts being expressly in violation of the specific and indefeasible rights of the people. This assembly, from whose labours the nation had the mortification of learning the alarming deficiency in the old taxes, to the amount of 110,000,000 of livres, and the scandalous and vexatious manner in which all the imposts were levied, was dissolved on the 25th of May, 1787 ; soon after which the projector himself was dismissed, and found it advisable to repair to England, where he might shelter himself from the vengeance of the parliament.

M. de Brienne, who had so decidedly opposed the plans of Calonne, now succeeded to his office, and in some degree adopted the very measures which he had so vehemently reprobated. It was proposed to raise money by virtue of the king's edict alone, and the doubling of the landtax, the re-establishment of a third twentieth, and a stamp-duty were immediately proposed. To render these effective, it was absolutely necessary that they should be registered by the parliament of Paris. That body strenuously opposed the measures adopted, and insisted that a true account of the state of the finances, and of the purposes to which the sums intended to be levied were applied, should be presented before they acceded to the king's request. No sooner was Lewis informed that the parliament had refused to register the edict than he had recourse to a *bed of justice*. On this occasion the duke of Orleans contributed to exasperate that hatred which he had already provoked by his shameless and public immoralities. He informed the parliament, that if he were monarch, the members should be forced to comply. "If you were monarch," replied the president, "I should repeat what I have now asserted: my heart is the people's, my understanding is my own, and my head is the king's." It was one of the great misfortunes of Lewis XVI. that the resentment which he provoked by unjust severity, he encouraged to insulting triumph by premature retractation or obvious indecision. In a few days, after receiving a protest from the parliament against the edict, he ordered the hall in which they sat, to be surrounded by a body of troops, and banished the members to Troyes; yet, in consequence of their vehement and energetic remonstrance, he was intimidated into their recal, and withdrew the unpopular edicts relative to the stamp-duty and the land-tax. While the public mind was thus agitated by successive hopes and fears, the king was persuaded by the ministers to visit, at nine o'clock in the morning, the parliament of Paris, and produce two edicts which were required to be enforced; one of which demanded a new loan to the amount of 450,000,000 of livres. After a speech of considerable length, in which his majesty, departing from his accustomed moderation, claimed the exercise of the royal prerogative, with a zeal unsuitable to the times, he added, that he had paid them a visit on purpose to hear any objections that might be made in opposition to his will. Permission being thus given, a debate ensued in the royal presence, which continued during nine hours, at the end of which period the king suddenly arose and commanded the edicts to be immediately registered. This singular and injudicious mode of conduct excited the indignation of the assembly, and the duke of Orleans having protested against the proceedings, as rendered null by the unprecedented conduct of the sovereign, the parliament was encouraged by his example, remained firm, and declared the business of the day to have been conducted with irregularity, and to convey no pledge of the opinions or intentions of the parliament.

The duke of Orleans was immediately sent into exile; a circumstance which would have excited the general exultation of the people of Paris, had not the impolitic conduct of the sovereign elevated him to some degree of temporary popularity. *Lettres de cachet* were issued against two other members, and several arbitrary proceedings on the part of the monarch produced the most spirited remonstrances from the parliament. They claimed not the indulgence of their sovereign but his justice, which was subject, they asserted, to regulations independent of the will of men; and they concluded with observing, that his glorious ancestor, Henry IV. acknowledged his subjection to two sovereigns, "God and the laws." The answer of the king, that they could not demand from his justice what solely depended upon his will, tended only to irritate the members, who, recurring to the antient principles of the constitution, at length declared, that it was not in their power, in that of the crown, nor of both united, to grant or to levy any new taxes upon the people.

The affairs of the kingdom were now in such a situation that the crown was subjected to the absolute necessity of proceeding to extremities in support of its authority; or of resigning for ever the power of raising money on any occasion, however immediate or urgent, without the consent of the parliament. No prince could have found it easy to surrender an authority which had been so long exercised by his predecessors. Paris, since the commencement of the disputes, had been so filled with troops, that it carried more the appearance of a military camp, under military law, than that of a great and peaceable capital, under the government of a civil magistrate and its own municipal laws. All the avenues to the palais, where the different chambers of parliament held their meetings, were perpetually and continually occupied by soldiers; and the members had the mortification of passing through rows of bayonets in the way to and from their dwelling-houses. The Parisians afforded, in some degree, a colour to this measure, by the extraordinary license which they assumed in words, in writing, and in acting on public and political affairs. The interest which they now displayed on subjects of this nature was so great, that a stranger might well have supposed himself to be surrounded by republicans. This licence was carried to such an extremity by the populace, that even a military force could not protect the count D'Artois from meeting with the strongest indications of public indignation and animadversion: at the same time Monsieur, the next brother to the king, by pursuing a different line of conduct, was loaded with the benedictions and the eulogies of the populace.

Commotions of the most serious kind, and a repetition of similar proceedings, at length alarmed the feelings of the court, and completed the triumph of the people. M. de Brienne was reluctantly dismissed, and was enabled to console himself with the archbishopric of Sens, a cardinal's hat, and a retreat in Italy.

The public, disappointed in their hopes, again cast their eyes on Mr. Neckar. The prime minister himself advised his recal. He wished to place him under his own direction in the department of the finances. The pride of Neckar, however, which suffered no equal near him, could not accept a master. Convinced that necessity would restore him to undivided power, he would listen to no alternative.

He had not deceived himself. He received a complimentary letter from the queen, informing him that the king had placed him at the head of the finances. From that moment his ambition knew no bounds. The readiness of the queen to convince him that she was deeply interested in his return, his warm reception on his arrival at Versailles, the general applause of the court, the capital, and the provinces, all conspired to elevate his hopes, and confirm his confidence.

Neckar, a native of Geneva, the most turbulent of republics, a cashier in Thelluson's banking-house, afterwards his partner, and a banker himself, had, by his skill in the management of money, early acquired a brilliant fortune. Several pamphlets, and among others the panygeric on Colbert, gained him the reputation of superior talents in finance and in government. At the

moment of his first elevation to the direction of the finances, his introduction into the ministry, as he was a Calvinist, required the utmost circumspection, and he was elevated to office under the title of Director of the Royal Treasury. He was appointed, as we have seen, minister of the finances, and the administration was confided to him alone.

The king, who disliked M. Neckar personally, yielded to the pressure of circumstances, without feeling any change of sentiment in his favour. Of this antipathy Neckar was aware. Hence originated his project of attempting to be nominated by the nation as the nation's minister: hence his intrigues to divide, and, if possible, disorganize the orders of the clergy and nobility, and to ruin the parliaments. Hence the invariable principle of using every means to enervate the royal power, to strengthen the pretensions of the *tiers etat*, to render himself, through the influence of the public opinion, and the positive will of the nation, sufficiently powerful to defy the jealousy of the court, and to change the government at his pleasure.

At the earnest entreaty of the new minister of finance, his majesty reluctantly consented to the convocation of the states-general, which had been promised by Brienne. They were called for by the clergy, the princes of the blood, the privileged provinces, the parliament of Paris, and all the sovereign courts. Neckar, fearless of the consequences, hastened the convocation of the states. He caused it to be announced for the year 1789. The notables, again called together, were consulted on the formation of these states, and on the mode of their deliberation. The opinions of the members were various, and terminated in no effectual and authoritative decision. The present Lewis XVIII. observed, that the laws had determined nothing on this important question, "The letters of convocation have always been silent on this subject; if my reason condemns me, my heart absolves me." At length the king issued a declaration, in which he announced to his people, that having heard the report made to his council by the minister o his finances, relative to the approaching convocation of the states-general, his majesty had so far adopted its objects and its principles, as to command that the number of the deputies in the approaching states-general, should be at least a thousand ; that this number should be formed as nearly as possible in proportion to the amount of the contributions of each bailiwick, and that the number of the deputies of the *tiers etat*, should be equal to the number from the other two orders together. The decision thus promulgated by the king obtained M. Neckar the most extensive popularity. In the capital, and in the provinces he had numerous partizans, by some of whom he was almost worshipped. He was regarded by the people as their only protector against the oppression of the court, and the persecution of the law ; as the destined harbinger of liberty, and the deliverer from pecuniary distress.

The meeting of this celebrated assembly being at length announced to take place on the first of May, 1789, the nation appeared to be electrified. The city of Paris was divided into districts for the elections, and the deputies began to draw up their instructions for the reformation of a multitude of antient and grievous abuses. A variety of pamphlets, all of them favourable to liberty, made their appearance at this period ; one of the most celebrated of these " The Ultimatum of a Citizen of the *tiers etat*," was burnt by the hands of the common hangman, while another written by the abbe Sieyes, " What are the *tiers etat ?*" was so fortunate as to receive the suffrage of the Parisians.

On the first of May, 1789, after an interval of 175 years, the states-general of France met for the first time. The king, addressing the members in a speech adapted to the occasion, after declaring his resolution to maintain the constitution inviolate, concluded, by observing, that they might and ought to confide in his attachment to the national happiness ; a declaration perfectly corresponding with his general conduct, which, though it discovered in some instances the most cul-

pable timidity, was distinguished by goodness of heart and by a sincere regard to the public welfare. The speech of the monarch was succeeded by the more diffuse orations of Monsieur Barentin, keeper of the seals, and Monsieur Neckar, which were rather calculated to dispose the different orders to mutual concession, than to gratify the curiosity or guide the opinions of the nation, anxious as it was to ascertain their sentiments respecting the various points in dispute.

It was soon discovered that the assembly was divided into various descriptions of delegates, marshalled under their respective chiefs, and ready to combat their antagonists on the field of political warfare. The strenuous aristocrats, who insisted on the separation of the assembly into three chambers, each of which should have a veto on the other, acknowledged for their leaders Messieurs d'Epresmenil and Cazales among the nobles, and the abbé Maury among the clergy : individuals who were supposed to be connected with the favourites of her majesty,—the count d'Artois, the Polignæs, the princes of Condé and Conti. Their opponents were ranged under the banners of Mirabeau, the bishop of Autun, the curate Gregoire, Chapelier, Barnave, Rabaut, de St. Etienne, Petion, Lameth, and Roberspierre ; all of whom were patronized by the duke of Orleans. The moderate party was composed of Monnier, Bergasse, Malouet, Lally, Tolendal, the count de Clermont, Topnere, and the bishop of Langre. It was the object of this latter party to frame and establish a constitution resembling that of England ; their numbers and political importance were as magnificent as their virtues and integrity were exemplary, but they were subsequently overpowered by the united intolerance and turbulence of the opposing factions. In the verification of the writs of return, the nobles and dignified clergy maintained the distinction of chambers as essential to a monarchic constitution. The commons, on the contrary, inflexibly insisted on a union of chambers. After repeated conferences, and much altercation, being joined by a considerable number of the clergy, they assumed the legislative power under the title of the National Assembly, and proceeded to engage in the important business of financial regulation without the concurrence of the nobles. The intentions of this assembly were evinced in their first proceedings. After pronouncing that the contributions, " as they are now levied in the kingdom, not having been consented to by the nation, are all illegal, and consequently null," the assembly declares, that "it consents provisionally for the nation, that the taxes and contributions, though illegally established and levied, shall continue to be exacted in the same manner, until the day of the separation of this assembly only." When the minister heard this language spoken in the assembly, and observed that the populace grew daily more tumultuous, he advised the monarch to hold a royal session in the hall of the states-general, which, by assembling, would prevent the meeting of that body. The king agreed to follow this advice, and on the 20th of June he issued a proclamation, appointing the 22nd of the month for that purpose. The majority having now agreed to join the commons, the members of the third estate repaired to the hall. The king having appointed the same day for the royal session, the guards were ordered to keep that apartment clear till the arrival of his majesty. As the members of the assembly arrived, they were refused admittance by the soldiers. An apprehension that the states were about to be dissolved instantly prevailing, the commons retired to an old tennis-court, where they bound themselves by a common oath never to part until the constitution was completed. The occupation of the hall of assembly had the effect usually produced by the appearance of persecution, and a majority of the clergy, chiefly curés, many of whom were warmly attached to the popular party, united themselves with the tiers etat, and were received with open arms, and loud acclamations, by that body from which they were soon to experience the most atrocious ingratitude.

On the day appointed the three orders were assembled by the king's command,

and the court appeared with more than usual splendour. After lamenting the disputes which had occurred, his majesty insisted on maintaining the distinction of orders, and on annulling the celebrated decree by which the commons had assumed the title of the National Assembly. At the same time he promised to establish no new tax, nor to prolong an old impost beyond the term assigned by the laws. He renounced the right of borrowing money, unless with the approbation of the states : he consented that there should be an end of pecuniary exemptions, and that lettres de cachet should cease, with some modifications. He concluded by declaring, that none of the laws established by the present states-general should ever be altered, but by the free consent of future states-general. On the other hand he decided, that all titles and feudal rents should be accounted property, and therefore regarded as sacred, and that the states should be assembled in three chambers instead of one. He commanded the members of the session to separate, and to meet the next day in the halls of their respective orders. His majesty was immediately followed by the nobles and the minority of the clergy, but the commons remained motionless, while the workmen, who had received orders to take down the throne and the other decorations, being appalled by their presence, desisted from their labours. Amidst the awful silence that ensued, M. de Brezé, grand master of the ceremonies, approached, and intimated the king's orders to retire ; but he, in his turn, was struck with awe, and withdrew, after receiving a severe rebuke from the count de Mirabeau, who already began to distinguish himself by the strength and promptitude of his eloquence. When the king was retired, and the assembly delayed compliance with his demand, an officer was commissioned to remind them of their neglect. The president replied, that the national assembly received orders from no man. Mirabeau seized the favourable moment to confirm himself in the affections of the people by treating the royal mandate with scorn. " Go and tell those who sent you," said he, "that we are here assembled by the will of the French people, and that nothing but the point of the bayonet will drive us hence." Camus, Barnave, Gregoire, and Petion, individuals intimately connected with subsequent events, inveighed with vehemence against the aggression committed upon the representatives of the nation, and it was instantly and unanimously decreed that they persist in their former resolutions.

The measures adopted by the court to defeat the designs of its adversaries, and accomplish its own, were planned without judgment and enforced without energy. Eleven of the foot-guards were prosecuted for disobedience to orders, and were liberated by the populace without incurring the infliction of punishment for so outrageous a violation of the peace. The disorderly state of the metropolis and the unfitness of the guards for re-establishing tranquillity, were advanced as ostensible reasons for collecting in the neighbourhood of the capital a considerable body of troops from various parts of the kingdom. On the 10th of July the National Assembly presented strong remonstrances to the king, on the unexpected approach of the forces. He replied, that he was influenced in the adoption of this measure by no other motive than his anxiety to maintain and establish good order in the capital. He assured them that he was so far from pretending to interrupt the proceedings of the assembly, that if the presence of the military gave them umbrage, he was not unwilling to transfer the *states-general* to Noyon or Soisson, and repair himself to some place in its vicinity, where he could retain a ready communication with the legislative body. The moderate members were inclined to acquiesce in this proposal, but the popular leaders, who depended chiefly for their support on the inhabitants of the capital, circulated a report that a plot was formed by the court to crush the nascent liberties of Frenchmen. The partizans of the antient monarchy severely reprobated the conduct of Neckar, to whose republican sentiments and councils they imputed the degradation of the royal authority, and strongly urged the king to discharge a servant, who, from

design or imprudence, had endangered the monarchy. Accordingly, on the 11th of July, M. Neckar was dismissed the administration and ordered to quit the kingdom. The consternation which ensued among the Parisians on receiving intelligence of the dismissal of a minister whom they regarded as the only protector of their freedom, can scarcely be imagined. Riot and tumult pervaded every quarter of the city. The rashness of the prince de Lambese, who, endeavouring to disperse a riotous body of the populace, wounded with his own hand, an inactive and inoffensive spectator, increased the violence and exasperated the irritation of the people. The mob, with clubs, spits, and such weapons as they could procure, rushed upon Lambese's troops and put them to flight. From this period the proceedings of the malcontents, though equally violent, wore a greater appearance of regularity. The citizens determined to co-operate with the National Assembly in the establishment of a free government in opposition to the military force brought against them, formed themselves into a regular militia, classed according to their several sections, and amounting to 48,000 men. Some unknown individual, on the morning of the 14th of July, after attracting the attention of the citizens, exclaimed, "Let us take the Bastile." The name of this fortress, which recalled to the memory of the people every thing hateful and oppressive in the antient despotism, operated with immediate and irresistible effect. The cry of "To the Bastile," resounded from rank to rank, from street to street, and from the Palais Royal to the suburbs of St. Antoine. An army composed of citizens and soldiers provided with pikes forged during the night, and with muskets procured at the Invalids, was immediately formed. The French guards were prevailed upon to join this motley crew, and the close order of their march, their shining firelocks, their military appearance, and their cannon, while they exhibited a striking contrast to their party-coloured allies, afforded the only reasonable hope of reducing a fortress hitherto terrible to the Parisians, and which since the time of Lewis XI. had been accustomed to receive the victims of royal despotism. Deputations from the Hotel de Ville, an astonishing crowd in motion from the vicinity, a body of armed men in front, and forces marching to their support from all parts of an immense capital, equally intimidated and perplexed de Launey the governor, who sometimes parleyed and sometimes fought with the assailants. To the astonishment of all military men, the Bastile, defended by ditches apparently impassable, and to the towers and battlements of which there seemed no access, was carried by storm after an assault of two hours. De Launey the governor, was conveyed to the *place de Greve*, and instantly massacred. M. de Losme the mayor, a man of great humanity, unhappily shared a similar fate. The marquis of Pelleport was so deeply penetrated with the kindness which the mayor had shewn him while a prisoner in the Bastile, that ardently clasping him in his arms, he implored the people, in the most pathetic manner, to spare the life of a friend to whom he was so deeply indebted. But his supplications were unavailing. The mayor's head was inhumanly severed from his body, and it was with great difficulty that the generous marquis, a young nobleman of rank and merit, escaped the same unmerited doom. Regnart, a subaltern officer, who had prevented the governor from setting fire to the powder magazine, was also killed, and the whole garrison would have been sacrificed by the populace, had it not been for the generous interposition of the French guards, who implored and obtained mercy. The populace now proceeded to insult and mutilate the remains of the dead, and exhibited their heads on pikes, to the gaze of insulting multitudes. The victorious Parisians · exploring the gloomy dungeons of oppression, in expectation of delivering numbers of unfortunate victims, found only seven captives, four of whom were confined for forgery: so little was this engine of tyranny employed under the mild and humane sway of the reigning monarch.

When intelligence of these outrages was brought to Versailles, the king could no longer be kept in ignorance of the real state of the public mind. At midnight, the duke de Liencour, master of the wardrobe, forced his way into his majesty's apartment and informed him of the circumstances which had just occurred. No other resource presenting itself, unconditional submission was determined upon. The king repaired to the National Assembly early in the morning, unattended by guards, and declared his willingness that the troops should be instantly withdrawn, and that Neckar should be recalled. He implored the assembly to save the state, and by that act of condescension virtually resigned the sovereignty to *them*. The Parisians, however, being still afraid of sieges and blockades, proceeded with preparations for defence. They appointed M. La Fayette commander of their armed corps, on which they conferred the title of the National Guards. The capital was now a great republic, and soon became so sensible of its power, as to give the law not only to the unfortunate sovereign, but to the legislature and to the whole people. The National Assembly sent to the capital a deputation of 84 members, not to demand peace, but to implore it. The session of the states at Versailles may be regarded as the cause of this, and of many other evils; for had the assembly been placed beyond the reach of the turbulent metropolis, it is by no means probable that they would have submitted to so humiliating and so dangerous an act of subservience to the people. The Parisians received the deputies with every mark of respect and applause, but expressed a desire that the king himself should visit the capital. This degrading and impolitic measure his majesty carried into execution on the 17th of July, under a full conviction that he encountered the peril of instant assassination. On his procession towards the city, no cry of *vive le roi* was heard, to cheer his spirits. He was met at Seve by the marquis de la Fayette, commander of the national guards, at the head of 25,000 men, and by him escorted to Paris, amidst loud acclamations of *vive le nation*. At the barrier he was received by Bailly, now mayor of Paris, and was conducted to the hotel de Ville, where, after declaring his affection for his subjects, and receiving their testimonies of loyalty, he shewed himself at the window with the national cockade in his hat, and was at last greeted with the cry of *vive le roi*. This conciliatory measure of the king was followed by the return of Neckar, who made his triumphant entry into Paris amidst the acclamations of the people, and resumed the administration assisted by Montmorin and others, who had shared in his disgrace. He laudably endeavoured to convert his popularity to the advantage of others, and he requested the people of Paris to send orders for the release of several imprisoned individuals, and to set the glorious example of a general pardon as the best means of restoring peace and tranquillity to a distracted nation. But the rectitude of his intentions only excited the disappointment of the populace, and the displeasure of the National Assembly. He addressed the electors of Paris as a legal body, though the multitude no longer regarded their privilege of nominating representatives but with distrust and jealousy; and by appealing to the people for the liberation of several accused individuals, he insulted the dignity and violated the rights of the assembly, whose exclusive functions of inflicting and remitting punishment, he encouraged his auditors to usurp.

The count d'Artois, the presumptive heir of the throne, having been informed that a price was set upon his head, had escaped with his two sons previous to the arrival of Neckar, and deemed himself fortunate in having eluded the vengeance of his countrymen. The marshal de Broglio retreated with part of his army now on its march to the frontiers, and every where assailed with stones and menaces by the people. Beneath the protection of his troops, he at length found refuge in the dominions of the house of Austria. Breteuil, who had enjoyed the confidence of the queen, and occupied an important situation in the government, secretly fled. The princes of Condé and Conti followed his example, and were immediately suc-

ceeded by the dukes de Luxemburgh and Vauguion, by the abbés de Calonne, Maury, Cazales, and d'Epresmenil; the three last of whom were intercepted and obliged to return. It was in vain that Foulon, an unpopular contractor, had recourse to a supposititious burial, with the view of concealment. The place of his retreat was discovered by his own tenants, and he was conducted to Paris with his neck encircled by a collar of nettles, a bunch of thistles, in the form of a nosegay, placed in his bosom, and a truss of hay fastened to his back. Notwithstanding the entreaties of Bailly and La Fayette, he was put to death by a frantic mob, while his son-in-law Berthier, became a sacrifice to the vengeance of an exasperated individual.

The electors of Paris endeavoured to secure their own safety by an instant resignation of their privileges, as they perceived that they would soon be treated as usurpers. The whole government of the city was then vested in a body, which received the appellation of the Representative Assembly of the Commons of Paris, M. Bailly, the mayor, being placed at its head. The mention of a general pardon had inflamed the resentment of the districts of Paris to such a degree, that a deputation was sent by them to the National Assembly, to complain of the attempt, and to guard them against sanctioning its adoption. The assembly declared that a tribunal should be instituted for bringing the late ministers and other delinquents to trial, a committee being appointed in the mean time to examine the charges brought against them. It was decreed that Bezenval, a commander of the Swiss corps, who had incurred the hatred of the Parisians, in consequence of his having advised the governor of the Bastile to defend it to the last extremity, should be kept under a strong guard at Brie Comte Robert, the place where he was now confined. This to him was the most favourable circumstance that could possibly have occurred, for 30,000 Parisians, absolutely frantic, had waited for him a whole day at the place de Greve, having all the instruments of torture and of death prepared for his reception. To such a height of turbulence and inhumanity had the feelings of the French people been excited, that neither liberty, property, nor life, were any longer secure, and the same ferocious and sanguinary disposition extended to the most retired villages and the remotest provinces.

A short and deceitful interval of tranquillity having been established at Paris by the arrival of M. Neckar, the National Assembly proceeded to the formation of a new constitution. As the foundation of their edifice, they began by forming a declaration of rights. This manifesto was introduced by a remark tending to shew that the ignorance, neglect, or contempt of human rights, are the sole causes of public misfortune, and that to avoid these evils it was necessary to define and explain those rights. The declaration contains the outlines of the doctrines afterwards supported by the various revolutionists, and enforces the principle that legitimate government is founded upon, the natural rights of man. Their mode of announcing these principles, was, however, too abstract and too indefinite. Were the moral character and the intellectual endowments of mankind on a level of perfect equality; were all men moderately wise, and incorruptibly virtuous, the right of every individual to share in common the fruits of the earth, and the products of general industry, would be as obvious as that no distinction of rank or office could arise. It is well observed by the bishop of Landaff, that in the existing state of human nature, it would be impossible for a small company of mariners to be cast upon a rock, without the ultimate election of some one individual to decide disputed claims, and direct the conduct of his fellow sufferers. The *rights of man* imply only the possession of such privileges, on the part of every individual as is consistent with the happiness of the whole community.

In the debates which ensued subsequent to the declaration of rights, the attention of the National Assembly was directed to the establishment of a constitution conformable with the prevailing political principles. After violent contention, several conditions were adopted for the basis of the intended system of government. It was determined that all power proceeds from the nation, that the constitution should be monarchical, the crown hereditary, the king's person sacred, and his ministers responsible. That the National Assembly should be continued by successive legislatures, each of which should continue two years, and to consist of one chamber ; the right of making laws and imposing taxes was to reside in the legislature, and a power was vested in the king of suspending for two years, any proposition sanctioned by its authority. His majesty gave the royal assent to these articles, but insisted on a stipulation, that the executive power should have its entire effect in the hands of the monarch, and by this condition gave great offence to the violent democrats, who flattered the duke of Orleans with the prospect of ascending the throne in case of the deposition of Lewis. They availed themselves of that nobleman's aversion to the queen, his influence, and his wealth, to propagate sedition, and to expose the people to insurrection ; to resist the efforts of the remaining court partizans, and counteract the good intentions of the advocates of moderate measures.

At this critical moment the public mind was in a state of extreme irritation; each party was suspected by its adversaries of designs upon the public welfare ; the adherents of the duke of Orleans of a project to raise that prince to the throne, the republicans of intentions to subvert the monarchy and establish a democratic government ; and the court party of a plan for conveying the king to Metz. The regiment of Flanders having been ordered to Versailles for the greater security of his majesty and the royal family, an entertainment was given them by the king's body guards. Their majesties and the dauphin visiting them after dinner, they were received with rapturous demonstrations of joy ; and among other expressions of loyalty a favourite ballad was sung, beginning with the words " *O Richard, O mon roi, l'univers t'abandonne!*—"Oh! Richard, oh!

my sovereign, thou art deserted by the world." These trifling incidents, which at any other time would have passed unnoticed, served to confirm the populace in their suspicion, that a project was in agitation to convey the royal family to Metz, where they might unite with the refugee princes in an attempt to restore the antient government. Impressed with these ideas, and exasperated by the prevailing dearth of bread, a mob of frantic *poissardes*, (fishwomen) among whom were several agents of the democratic leaders in disguise, having seized on a magazine of arms, hurried away to Versailles to demand bread of their sovereign, and to take vengeance on the *garde de corps*. The king, informed of their arrival, gave them present sustenance, and assured them that every means should be employed to alleviate their distress. It was now that Mirabeau betrayed the inveteracy of his hatred towards the queen. In a debate on the subject of the new constitution, when, after an inflammatory harangue, some one asked him if he meant to impeach any particular person, he arose, and with looks full of rage, exclaimed, " Declare that the person of the king alone is sacred, and I myself will bring forward the impeachment." It was at this moment of impending danger that her majesty displayed the greatness of mind, which atoned for many of her private intrigues and casual indiscretions. The marquis de la Fayette had followed the national guards and the poissardes, to Versailles, and had sworn fidelity to the king and to the laws. But even this favorite champion of liberty could not restrain the fury of the mob. When the whole court was impressed with dismay, and the poissardes were heard to breathe vengeance against her majesty, the king entreated her to retire to some place of safety. She nobly refused, declaring that she would sooner stay and die at the feet of the king. In the midst of this scene of confusion and of horror, she went with much composure to rest. It was not till these frantic wretches had actually broke into her palace, at the ensuing dawn, and pursued her with horrid threats and

imprecations, that she at last cried out to the guard as she was flying from room to room, Oh ! my friends, save my life, save my children ! Being assembled round the king, when their fury was in some measure exhausted, he presented himself to the populace at a balcony, attended by her majesty, bearing the dauphin in her arms. A temporary calm then ensued, which was suddenly succeeded by a cry of " To Paris, to Paris." No resistance could be made. Had they hesitated even la Fayette could not have secured their lives. The king, in compliance with their wishes, took his leave of Versailles, with the royal family and his court, and proceeded in solemn and mournful procession to the capital ; escorted by la Fayette, and attended by the ruffian bands of poissardes and their associates, bearing on pikes the bloody hands of the king's own guards, whom they had murdered in savage triumph, and endeavouring by these inhuman orgies, by expressions of vengeance, and by their ferocious looks, to exasperate the present afflictions of the royal family by the anticipation of their future sufferings.

This event has been ascribed to the machinations of two opposing factions. The republicans, whose design was to abolish monarchy, or to render the monarch an insignificant instrument of their views, were desirous of moving the king to Paris, that they might have him completely in their power. The cabal of the duke of Orleans, whose principal object it was to invest that prince with the sovereign power, wished to preserve the monarchy entire, and they hoped to prepare the way to the execution of their plot, by impressing the mind of the king with the most excruciating terrors, and compelling him to fly the kingdom in the hope of safety. The democrats succeeded. A vote was passed that the National Assembly was inseparable from the king. This vote was succeeded by many resolutions indicative of determined hostility to the sovereign, and the president, Mounier, one of the most disinterested patriots in the assembly, foreseeing that from that moment the assembly must lose its independence, and become the instrument of a tumultuous populace, actuated by a desperate faction, immediately seceded and was accompanied by Tolendal and other partizans of a free, but limited, monarchy.

The two factions had hitherto co-operated from their common desire to subvert the existing system. Their respective views now became obvious to each other. The republicans were the favorites of the populace, and having no further occasion for the pecuniary support of the duke of Orleans, were anxious to sacrifice his views upon the throne to their private plans of interest and ambition. La Fayette had supplanted Mirabeau in his popularity. He employed his ascendency with the Parisians to destroy the power of the duke, which involved in its termination the fate of Mirabeau. Availing himself of the present propitious concurrence of circumstances, he informed the duke that the name of Orleans was made the pretext for the most atrocious disturbances, and that he must immediately leave the kingdom. The duke was deficient in eloquence and courage. He was equally unable to influence the passions of the populace and unwilling to sustain their resentment. Being furnished with an ostensible mission to England, he immediately repaired to London. Mirabeau, despising a prince who had the villany of a usurper, without the courage to usurp, and who thus tamely deserted his own cause, when the schemes he had planned in his favour were ripe for execution, expressed his contempt in very pointed language; and despairing of being enabled to govern the state, as the minister of that flagitious and despicable prince, made overtures to the court that he might be introduced into the administration. But the republican party, fearing the effects of his intrigues, voted a resolution that no member of the National Assembly should accept a place in the ministry. Finding himself precluded from the object of his ambition by this self-denying ordinance, he once more devoted his time and talents to the people.

The National Assembly had now acquired an unlimited ascendency over the Parisians, and its popularity was daily extending to the provinces; nor can it be denied, that many of their most important measures were patriotic and judicious. They issued a decree, authorizing the magistrates to require military aid in case of riots; *lettres de cachet* were abolished, the parliaments were suspended from their functions, and a new bank was established by the name of *Caisse d'Extraordinaire*, for the purpose of restoring trade and reviving the public credit. But these wise and advantageous changes were unfortunately counteracted by innovations of a tendency equally unjust, and destructive to the prosperity and happiness of the nation. The licentiousness of the populace, and the hatred of superior rank and salutary authority, were encouraged and exasperated by the abolition of every hereditary and political distinction; the clergy and the monastics were despoiled of their estates, estimated at 150,000,000 of livres, which were decreed to be national property, and the local attachments, and most amiable prejudices of the lower orders of the people were effaced or extinguished by the division of the kingdom into eighty-three departments, subdivided into districts and cantons, each having its assembly for the purpose of legislative government. Of all these measures the confiscation of the property of the clergy was the most vigorously and generally opposed. It was regarded as an act of extreme ingratitude, to a body, which had recently given the nobles an example of willingness, to join the *tiers etat* in one chamber, and to unite with them in their plans of reform. There have been ages when such a violation of the property of the church would have excited a religious war, but at the present juncture temporal considerations were seen to predominate over regard for the interests of the church, and reverence for the priesthood.

Notwithstanding, Mounier, Lally, Tolendal, and a number of other distinguished leaders, who had zealously supported the party of the king, on observing the violence of these proceedings and the alternate severity and irresolution of the monarch, retired from the assembly. That body continued during the remainder of the year, to proceed with vigor and dispatch in the formation of a constitution. Rigorous measures were adopted against sedition, which produced the subsequent massacre of the *Champ de Mars*, and led to the disgrace of la Fayette, and the death of Bailly.

The practical operation of the principles adopted by the assembly was displayed in the licentiousness of the press, which even exceeded the licentiousness of the mob, and which powerfully prompted its atrocity. Twenty thousand literary men were daily and hourly employed in exhorting and stimulating the people to every description of brutal and sanguinary outrage. Never was intellectual superiority more disgracefully debased by the venal panegyrists of corrupted courts, or the hired encomiast of titled stupidity and insignificance, than by these flatterers of an infuriate populace. Even in the promotion of anarchy and disorder, the inventive, bold, and ready genius of Frenchmen was conspicuous. A confederacy was formed, which, in its institution and effects, exhibited a new phenomenon in the history of political establishments. A combination had been formed of literary men, who determined to associate under the name of a club, with the intention of concerting measures for guiding the conduct of the mob, and influencing, by the dread of popular turbulence, the decrees of the National Assembly, and the acts of the municipal, judicial, and executive bodies. These demagogues invited into their society, such of the populace as they conceived likely to become useful instruments of their designs, exhorted them to construct other clubs in Paris and throughout the provinces, and determined that such meetings should be *affiliated* together. One of the clubs meeting in a convent formerly belonging to the Dominicans, (who were distinguished by the title of *Jacobins*) assumed the name of the *Jacobin* club, a name which afterwards predominated throughout all other societies of the same description. In the first deliberations of the National Assembly these

societies, guided by literary demagogues, and directing the populace, obtained a powerful influence. Many of the lawgivers themselves were members of these new institutions, and those who were most inimical to the existing establishments, and to rank and property were held in the highest estimation. Various in detail as were the precepts of these innovators, in principle and object they were simple and uniform. Their lessons of instruction and exhortations to practice, may be compressed into a few words. Religion is folly, every establishment is contrary to natural right, order is an encroachment on natural freedom, property is an infringement on natural equality. Such was the system generally received in the enthusiasm of reform, by a powerful and populous nation, distinguished for promptitude and fertility of genius, for boldness and activity of character, and by its very virtues rendering its errors more extensively pernicious.

While the minds of the populace were influenced by delusive representations, and the circulation of the most pernicious opinions, the financial department occupied the attention of the National Assembly. The objects were promoted 1790. by the sale of lands belonging to the church and to the monastic orders. These, together with a small addition to the territorial taxes, enabled it to abolish the gabelle on salt, and other imposts oppressive to the lower orders. The satisfaction excited by these proceedings was more than counterbalanced by the publication of the *red* book, containing an account of the money issued from the treasury in pensions and gifts, during the present and the two last reigns. From this catalogue, which was published by a committee appointed to examine it, and was descanted on with extreme severity by the National Assembly, it appeared, that the pensions and gratuities granted by the crown, made a material part of the burdens so oppressive to the people, and that his majesty's brothers were among the principal receivers. More striking proof cannot be adduced of the culpable ductility of temper, which was the chief cause of the king's misfortunes, than was afforded by these pecuniary disclosures. While he was rigidly economical in what related to his own person, he was easily prevailed upon to sanction, with his own hand, these enormous and extravagant grants to his brothers.

Reports having been circulated that his majesty regarded the proceedings of the assembly with distrust and aversion, he repaired voluntarily and unexpectedly to their place of meeting, and declared his assent to the principles of the constitution, a measure that disconcerted for a while the machinations of his enemies; but while it gratified the democratic party, whose intention it was to render the sovereign subservient to the legislature, it filled with dismay that respectable minority which had still hoped to see the dignity of the crown restored, under limitations consistent with the liberty and security of the people. He lost the attachment of the partizans of monarchy without obtaining the confidence of the democrats. The assembly taking advantage of the king's condescension, passed a decree, enjoining every member to take a new civil oath, under the penalty of being excluded from giving his vote on any occasion. By this oath each individual pledged himself to the nation, to the law, and to the king, to maintain, with all his power, the constitution decreed by the National Assembly and accepted by the monarch. The attachment between his majesty and the representatives which this oath apparently secured, excited the most unfeigned rejoicing among the well disposed members of the community, and it was determined to celebrate its enactment by a public confederation. The day already distinguished as the anniversary of the capture of the Bastile, was selected for that purpose, and the president, and inhabitants of the country around Versailles, laboured with indefatigable industry to prepare a grand amphitheatre in the *Champ de Mars*, near the city. In that plain, where but one year before a formidable assemblage of troops had menaced the capital with ruin, appeared deputations

from the national guards, and from all the regular troops, infantry, cavalry, marines, and foreign soldiers in the kingdom, in addition to 300,000 spectators of both sexes. The genius of the nation was observable in the manner of conducting the preparations, in which gaiety and mirth were blended with labour. The king, the representatives, 2000 musicians, 200 priests clothed in white surplices, ornamented with tri-coloured ribbands, and preceded by the popular bishop of Autun, dressed in his episcopal robes, tended not a little to add to the grandeur of this imposing scene: at the close of which the monarch, the National Assembly, and the armed citizens, took a solemn oath to maintain the constitution.

The spirit of anarchy and disorganization which had overspread the kingdom, and extended to the army and navy, at length reached the colonies. It was well observed in the National Assembly by M. Barnave, an able and distinguished leader of the revolution, that unfortunately their rights of men could not apply to the West Indies; that if they endeavoured to make the application they would lose their colonies, and impoverish their trading and manufacturing towns, until the common people, grown desperate by the disappointment of their hopes, would be ready to sell themselves to the enemies of the revolution. In St. Domingo the free mulattoes, who composed a large portion of the population, relying on the hopes held out by the assembly, began to consider themselves as men, and even to aspire to the rights of citizens. The white inhabitants, struck with horror at the idea of an equality of rights on the part of a race which they had hitherto regarded as merely brutal, and whose relatives by the female side were still subjected to the most rigorous bondage, denied them a participation in the elections. Both of them sent deputies to the mother country, and the pride of the planters and the pertinacity of men of colour, at length reduced the most flourishing colony belonging to Europe, to desolation and depair.

The members of the legislature experienced in their own persons many inconveniences from the diffusion of their favorite doctrines. They had found it necessary to idolize the mob, and to declaim on the majesty of the people. In proportion to the zeal and success with which they circulated their opinions, meetings, clubs, parties, and individuals, regarded themselves collectively and separately as rulers of the empire. The populace and the soldiers conceived that by their political regeneration, they were entitled, without restraint, to gratify every passion. The most active of the revolutionary leaders had spared no pains to banish from the people every remaining impression of Christianity. A great portion of the vulgar, both civil and military, were confirmed infidels. From the utter destitution of religious feeling in every class of society, the most serious iniquity was perpetrated with all the hilarity of inoffensive merriment, acts of the most atrocious inhumanity were committed, not only with impunity, but with exultation; neither the most atrocious guilt nor the most abandoned licentiousness, contributed to render the individuals, in whom they were united, odious or unpopular.

Previous to the celebration of the fête in the *Champs de Mars*, the credulity of the people was strikingly exemplified in the reception of Anacharsis Clootz, a Prussian malcontent, an individual anxious to communicate to France, the knowledge of that liberty which he durst not venture to propagate at home. He was one of those extraordinary individuals who could never have emerged into notice but by the perpetration of some enormous crime, nor under any circumstances in any country but France. He supposed himself to excel chiefly in philosophy, declamation, and infidelity; but in the exhibition of his eloquence, he unexpectedly failed to attract that notice on which he had calculated with some degree of certainty. Infidelity was too common, either to attract by its novelty, or to captivate by the language in which it was conveyed. Though oratory and infidelity failed, he shrewdly suspected that extravagance might succeed. Collecting a great number of his companions

and other vagabonds who swarmed about the streets, and hiring all the foreign and grotesque dresses from the opera and playhouses, he bedecked his retinue, and, proceeding to the National Assembly, introduced his followers as strangers arrived from every quarter of the globe, disposed to enter into fraternity with France, and be rescued from the fangs of despotism. That Clootz might exhibit a full display of his talents for oratory, he delivered a speech in the name of his dumb crew of ambassadors, declaring that those citizens were the real representatives of all mankind, who had desired him to obtain them places at the ensuing confederation. This deputation, to the utter degradation and the indelible disgrace of the individuals present, was graciously received by the assembly, of which it being the evening sitting, the few members present were in a condition suited to a frolic; in the impulse of the moment the resolution I have already noticed for the abolition of titles, and the degradation of the nobility was passed, and it was decreed that the figure of chained slaves, intended as emblems of prostrate and vanquished nations, surrounding the statue of Lewis XIV. should be removed or destroyed. The last of these measures was regarded with satisfaction by the virtuous and intelligent inhabitants of the metropolis. Had it not been for the enforcement of the assembly's decree, it might have long remained a disgraceful memorial of the insufferable vanity and unjustifiable arrogance of that haughty despot.

It happened contrary to expectation that no mischief occurred on the day of confederation. The oath administered on the *Champs de Mars*, was imposed on the same day throughout the kingdom, but the licentiousness of the troops was too prevalent to be corrected by oaths; they claimed great merit to themselves for redressing the grievances of the nation, and presumed that they were endowed with authority to redress their own. They pretended that they were cheated by their officers, and different regiments under that pretence plundered their military chests. They were actively engaged in all the tumults and disorders which were constantly occurring. The marquis de Bouille commanded the troops at Metz, and received an order from the National Assembly to suppress the insurgents at Nancy by force of arms; an order which was repented of as soon as given, for Bouille was suspected to be an aristocrat who might employ his army for the purpose of effecting a counter-revolution. The marquis appeared before Nancy; he found· the insurgents in a state of readiness to receive him, and determined on a vigorous defence. A bloody conflict ensued, in which both sides suffered severely, but the insurgents were reduced. The rage of the people of Paris was beyond description at the sacrifice of so many individuals, to whom they attributed the virtues and the principles of genuine patriots, nor was the National Assembly less dissatisfied with the result of its own indiscretion. The populace surrounded the hall of the assembly and demanded the head of Bouille, whom they denominated a murdering aristocrat. The most alarming consequences were only prevented by the resolution and firmness of the national guards.

This event hastened the resignation of M. Neckar, and his final departure from France. This once favourite minister of the people received on the night of the tumult a friendly intimation that he was destined to fall a victim to the rage of the mob; in consequence of which he fled from his house, passing several hours in the fields near Paris, agitated by the most gloomy apprehensions. He had declined from his former importance into the tool of a party, who no longer wanted, and therefore no longer valued, his services. This neglect preyed deeply on his spirit, and he instantly set out for Switzerland. He was stopped at the little town of Arcis-sur-Aube, by the national guard, who resolved that a minister of finance should not quit the country till he had made a proper settlement of his affairs. On these principles he was made a prisoner, and was reduced to the mortification of applying to the assembly, assuring them that more than £100,000 of his property was lodged in the French

funds; a sum abundantly sufficient to compensate any trivial error which might be found in his accounts. The assembly returned a cold and laconic answer, but he was ordered to be liberated, and arrived in safety in his own country. Whatever might be the errors of Neckar as a minister, his exile was occasioned by the exemplary rectitude of his political views and his personal conduct. His integrity as a statesman, and his honesty and virtue as an individual, rendered him the object of hatred and of jealousy to every private profligate, and every official manager or agent of political deception.

The remainder of the year was distinguished by many acts of the most flagrant injustice on the part of the National Assembly. They ejected from their livings the refractory priests who would not swear contrary to their belief and conscience, and filled their places with more complaisant pastors, who were willing to submit to "the powers that be;" and in a few months the country was committed to the guidance of a new body of spiritual teachers, ardently attached, to the revolution, to which they were indebted for their benefices. Besides this body of auxiliaries, the National Assembly, by robbing the church, procured another class of active assistants in the holders of assignments. These were a kind of revolutionary pawn-brokers who advanced money on plundered effects and depended for payment on the stability of the new system. By the spiritual influence of these elected clergy, and the temporal influence of the brokers, the people became still more attached to the revolution, and its engine, the National Assembly. This body of legislators finding confiscation so productive a source of revenue, deemed it unwise to confine it to the possessions of the church. They extended their system to the property of foreigners. Several German princes, secular and ecclesiastical, held valuable possessions in Alsace, by tenures repeatedly ratified under the most solemn treaties and guaranteed by the great neighbouring powers. Yet these rights the National Assembly overthrew, by an act of lawless robbery. This open and unjustifiable aggression on the rights of independent powers, not only excited the indignant resentment of the princes who were actually despoiled, but the displeasure and apprehension of others. The emperor remonstrated on the violation of existing treaties, requiring compensation for the past, and security for the future. The National Assembly imputed this requisition to hostile intentions, and affirmed that there was a concert of foreign sovereigns, French princes, and aristocrats, to effect a counter-revolution. They asserted that Lewis had acceded to this confederation, and was preparing to escape from France.

The king, though invested by the constitution, with no inconsiderable share of power, might be considered from the time of his arrival at Paris, as in the virtual custody of the National Assembly. The Thuilleries was both his palace and his prison ; and the troops, by which he was surrounded, were rather spies on his actions than the guards of his person. Under these circumstances a plan was formed for setting the king at liberty, and by conveying him to some place on the German frontiers, where he might place himself at the head of a strong body of troops to enable him to dictate reasonable terms to the assembly. The marquis de Bouille, governor of Metz, was prepared to become the chief agent in the enterprise, but he wanted an able colleague in the capital. Mirabeau, whose talents and address peculiarly qualified him for such a task, was now no more. La Fayette was too enthusiastic and too eagerly desirous of popular applause to be entrusted with the execution of a scheme so important and so difficult ; and the king was too irresolute and possessed too little firmness of mind to bear his part in the transaction, even beneath the conduct of others.

On the 18th of April his majesty intended to repair with his family to St. Cloud, a palace about three miles from the city. In the morning, as the family were stepping into their carriages, they were surrounded by an immense crowd, who compelled them to return. The marquis de la Fayette

in vain interposed to procure him a passage, and was so much insensed at the disregard shewn to his admonitions, that he instantly resigned the command of the national troops, and was with difficulty persuaded to resume it. His majesty, repairing to the assembly, laid before it his complaints of the insult offered to his person, which were coolly received. After giving and receiving assurances of fidelity and loyalty to the state, and formally notifying to foreign powers his acceptance of the constitution, he proceeded with his family to St. Cloud. The interruption of his visit to that place proved very unfavourable to the execution of his project of escape, as it increased the vigilance of the populace. But the mortification which he suffered from being despoiled of his prerogatives, was so much aggravated by the humiliating thraldom to which he was reduced, that he resolved to attempt his own extrication at any hazard, and in defiance of every obstacle. Montmedi, a fortress on the borders of Luxemburg, was chosen as the place of his majesty's residence ; and the marquis de Bouille had prepared to facilitate his escape, by placing relays of horses at proper places, and had secured his protection in case of resistance, by posting parties of dragoons under various pretexts, on the road. On the 18th of June the Russian ambassador procured a passport for a Russian lady, whom he described as about to set out for Germany with a specified number of attendants and 1791. two children. On the 20th, the royal party left Paris about midnight, having escaped the vigilance of the guard, and took the road of Chalons sur Marne, and St. Menehond. At the latter of these places the postillion, recognizing Lewis from his resemblance to his picture, informed the postmaster, who dispatched his son to Varennes the next stage, to inform the magistrates. He was there detained till some of the national guards could be assembled, by the preconcerted overturning of a waggon loaded with furniture, upon a bridge which led towards Montmedi. Parties of dragoons were stationed at St. Menehond and Varennes, but were seduced from their duty. On information of the disaster, de Bouille used all possible dispatch to rescue his sovereign; hastening with a regiment of dragoons to Varennes for that purpose. But he arrived too late; his majesty had been placed under an arrest, and was instantly carried back to Paris, under an escort of the national guards. The king's flight having been discovered about eight in the morning, filled the city with the greatest consternation. To overtake him was impracticable, as Paris was not 200 miles from the frontiers, and he must have already effected one third of his journey. It was universally believed that measures had been concerted between the king and his partizans on the frontiers of the kingdom, where he was to collect all the force which he could assemble and invade France. The National Assembly having met, directed that the people should take up arms to repel the expected attempts of the king's party. Lewis had left particular directions that no use should be made of the seals of office during his absence; but the assembly decreed that the king, having absented himself, the business of the nation ought, notwithstanding, to proceed, and that the seals of the state should, in virtue of their authority as representatives of the nation, be affixed as usual to their decrees by the chief minister. On the following day intelligence arriving of the king's detention excited the most general exultation. After investigating the conduct of various suspected persons, the assembly at last determined to subject the sovereign himself to judicial examination. A deputation of three members was appointed to receive his deposition. He refused to answer any interrogatories, but avowed his willingness to disclose the motives of his departure. He declared that he was induced to leave his capital by his apprehension of danger to the royal family, especially her majesty, excited by the insults of the populace, and the threats conveyed in various inflammatory pamphlets which were circulated with impunity; that he meant not to leave the kingdom, but only to repair to Montmedi, where he would have been better situated

than at the capital for opposing the attempts of foreign powers; that he wished to ascertain by his absence from Paris the real wishes of the nation respecting the constitution, and that he wished to prove to France and to Europe that he was at liberty and not a prisoner, as was believed by many.

The majority of the people were of opinion that the king having abandoned them, could no longer claim their attachment or obedience, and ought to be tried and punished for his violation of his public duty: but the assembly acted upon this occasion with unusual magnanimity, and passed an act of oblivion. In order to prevent farther tumult, it declared that the revolution was complete. The committee for compiling and digesting their decrees, was enabled to produce the new constitutional code on the fourth day of August. Each article having been separately debated in the assembly, the code was presented to his majesty, and consecrated by his acceptance, accompanied by an oath that he would employ the powers vested in him, for the maintenance of the constitution and the due execution of the law. Soon after the occurrence of this solemnity the constituent assembly, having accomplished the objects of its mission, dissolved itself on the 30th of September, after a session of two years and four months. From this moment the balance of power among the several parties of the state was entirely lost. The most violent measures of the majority in the National Assembly had been modified in their tendency, or counteracted in their object, by the influence of several enlightened and independent members; but on the dissolution of that body nothing was wanting to the success, and the predominance of the partizans of unlimited democracy. The democrats were favoured by the proceedings of the foreign princes, whose rights the assembly had invaded and whose property they had sequestrated. The congresses held at Mantua and at Pilnitz, to consider of the most effectual measures by which restitution might be obtained, excited a suspicion that their secret objects were the invasion of France, the suoversion of its new constitution, and the dismemberment of the kingdom.

It is impossible to retrace the events of the preceding year without lamenting the untimely fate of the accomplished but unprincipled Mirabeau. Possessing the most commanding eloquence, a gift derived from nature alone, he exhibited the rare example of a man, without any previous study, displaying all the promptitude, the boldness, the variety, and the graces of a veteran and accomplished orator. Born a noble but excluded by his own order, he became a deputy from the *third estate*, and for some time sustained the popular cause with a fluency that charmed, with a genius that astonished, with an enthusiasm that animated and enraptured the minds of his hearers. Such was the magic of his oratory, that while he spoke his auditory forgot the scandalous immrality of his life; such was his good fortune, that, a few short intervals excepted, he retained his celebrity, even after he had been corrupted by the court; and such his confidence in his own powers, that with a voice enfeebled by disease, and in the agonies of death, he bequeathed his opinions on the formation of a new constitution, as his last and most valuable legacy to a mourning and applauding people.

As an author he exhibited more zeal than genius, and more industry than talent; he declaimed rather than argued, he surprised rather than convinced. Though his time had been devoted to licentious pleasures, his writings were always dedicated to the cause of honour, humanity, and virtue. It was as an orator alone, however, that he stood unrivalled. To conceive a just idea of the effects he produced, it would have been necessary to witness the lofty and continued flights of his eloquence on great occasions, or the majestic cadence of his language, and the varied intonations of his voice on unimportant subjects. Nor were the features of his countenance or the gesticulations of his person, although the one was devoid of elegance, and the other of beauty, deficient in interest or unsuitable to his purpose; the frown upon his ample forehead, the lightning of his eye, and the thunder of his voice, well accorded with the other characteristics of his eloquence, and impressed with involuntary admiration the individuals who detested his private vices, and suspected his public principles.

HISTORY OF THE WAR.

CHAP. II.

THE important revolution which had occurred in France could not but be viewed with anxiety by the neighbouring nations. Some men, actuated by the love of novelty or an aversion to legal restraint, hailed the approach of those days when mankind would be blest with the full enjoyment of liberty ; and others, from interested motives, were desirous of any change that might afford them an opportunity of improving their condition, or repairing their broken fortunes. Many were affrighted by the progress of principles, which gave to the people the power of new modelling their forms of government, while in England the sincere well-wishers to the established constitution, looked forward to the result of the changes in France with extreme solicitude ; apprehensive that the glorious system of government under which the British people had so long flourished, might be undermined in its principles by designing men, or might be reduced to ruin amidst the crash of empires. Those who considered France as the rival of our commercial prosperity and political grandeur, who had observed with regret the struggles made by that kingdom to augment its naval force, even during its decline, and thought, with Mr. Burke, that the works constructed at Cherburg, for the security of that fortress and the accommodation of their navy, were more vast in their

design than the pyramids of Egypt, were relieved from their apprehensions, when they saw that powerful rival disabled from contending with England by her domestic troubles. Among the British subjects who declared themselves the friends of liberty, there were undoubtedly a few who wished for a republican government, and others who were inflamed with a spirit of violent Jacobinism ; but no man of candor will deny that many of them were sincerely attached to the principles of that constitution which was improved and secured under the sway of William III. Individuals of these different descriptions celebrated the anniversary of the French revolution in convivial meetings at London, Norwich, Manchester, Liverpool, and other towns. At Birmingham a similar meeting took place but did not end without disturbances. An appeal had been previously made to the people in a printed bill, complaining, in strong terms, of political abuses and general grievances, yet recommending order and forbearance till the majority should be disposed to resist oppression. As a riot appears to have been preconcerted, some zealous partizans of the civil and religious establishment might have circulated this paper, that, being regarded as the production of the discontented party, it might excite odium against them ; but this is merely the cursory surmise of a partial historian, and cannot be stated as an historical fact.

The populace assembling near the hotel at which the festive party dined, gave various signs of disapprobation. After the celebrators of the anniversary had retired, the windows of the house were broken, and the rioters proceeded to more serious mischief. They set the new meeting-house on fire, nearly demolished the old one, and destroyed the house, library, and philosophical apparatus of Dr. Priestley, who was particularly obnoxious to these turbulent champions of church and state. Several other houses near the town were burned, because they belonged to dissenters, and in one of these some of the incendiaries lost their lives. The civil power being unable to prevent the continuance of tumult, depredation, and havoc, troops were sent into the town and ordered to scour the country. Four of the offenders were condemned at Warwick, two were hanged, and the county, being sued by Dr. Priestley and others who had suffered the loss of property, compensation was awarded by the jury.

The malice of party was exercised on this occasion in various animadversions. Some accused the magistrates of having connived at the proceedings of the rioters against individuals, who were suspected of a want of attachment to the government. Others affirmed with equal injustice, that the dissenters and their friends deserved these attacks for presuming to express their joy at the triumph of the French revolutionists. The former party were of opinion that too few were punished for delinquency so outrageous, while the latter seemed to consider it as an act of cruelty to put any of the rioters to death.

The contrast of sentiment on the subject of the French revolution, was manifested in the speeches of several members of the lower house of parliament in the present and preceding year. When a report respecting the military estimates was made from the committee on the 9th of February, 1790, a further debate occurred, in which Mr. Fox expressed his ardent admiration of the revolutionists. Mr.

Burke replied by adverting with considerable vehemence to the internal state of France. That country, he observed, from the single circumstance of its vicinity, ought to call forth our vigilence in the first instance, not merely on account of her actual power, but on account of her influence and example, which once had been and might yet become, more dangerous than her determined hostility. He mentioned the more early part of the reign of Lewis XIV. and with what difficulty the patriots of that day struggled in our country against the influence of an example, of which the success and splendor not only captivated our kings, Charles and James, but made some impression on all ranks and denominations of people. The danger in the last age arose from 1790. an example of despotism in government and intolerance in religion ; but the present disease was of a character directly opposite, and still more likely to be contagious. On the side of religion it was atheism, and anarchy with respect to government. We were in danger of being led to imitate the excesses of an irrational, unprincipled, plundering, ferocious, and tyrannical democracy, through a foolish admiration of successful fraud and violence. He considered the late assumption of citizenship by the army as the worst part of the example set by France, and in animadverting on the sentiments of Mr. Fox, so contrary to his own, expressed his regret in differing from his valuable friend. Having pronounced a beautiful panygeric on his superior talents, and having borne testimony to the natural moderation, disinterestedness and benevolence of his disposition, he entreated the house, from his coming forward to notice an expression or two of his best friend, to judge of his extreme anxiety to prevent the contagion of French principles from the slightest diffusion in Great Britain, where he well knew that some wicked persons had ardently wished to recommend an imitation of the French spirit of reform ; so strongly would he oppose the least tendency towards the means of introducing a democracy like theirs, as well as the end itself, that he would forsake his best friends and unite with his bitterest enemies, in order to oppose both the means and the end.

Mr. Burke then took a cursory survey of the recent transactions in France. That nation, he said, had gloried, (and some in Great Britain had thought proper to share in the glory) in bringing about a revolution, as if revolutions were beneficial in themselves. All the crimes and horrors which led to the French revolution, which marked its progress and might virtually attend its establishment, were nothing thought of by the lovers of revolutions. The French had made their way to a bad constitution through the destruction of their country, when they were in possession of a good one. Of this they were in possession on the very day in which the states-general met in separate orders. Their business, had they possessed either virtue or wisdom, was to secure the independence of the states, according to those orders under the monarch on the throne, and that purpose being accomplished, *then*, and not till then, it was their duty to proceed to the redress of grievances.

Instead, however, of acting in this laudable manner, and improving the fabric of the state, an object for which they had been called by their sovereign, and deputed by their country, they pursued a course entirely different. They first destroyed all the balances that tended to confirm the stability of the state, and framed and recorded a digest of anarchy, denominated the Rights of Man, exhibiting a pedantic prostitution of elementary principles that would disgrace an English school-boy. It was, however, much worse than trifling and pedantry in them, for they systematically destroyed every hold, civil or religious on the public mind. The most pernicious effect of all their proceedings was upon the military. Were it the question whether soldiers were to forget that they were citizens as an abstract principle, he would not quarrel respecting it; but if applied to the events which had taken place in France, where the abstract principle was clothed with its circumstances, he hoped his friend Mr. Fox would coincide with

him in opinion, that the occurrences in that country were no ground for exultation, whether we considered the act or the example. It was not the mere circumstance of an army under the respectable and patriotic citizens, embodied for the purpose of resisting tyranny, but the case of common soldiers abandoning their officers to unite with a furious and licentious rabble. He was deeply concerned that this strange thing, denominated the French Revolution, should be put in the balance with that glorious event usually called the Revolution in England, and the behaviour of the soldiery on that occasion, compared with the conduct of some of the French troops in the present instance. At that time the prince of Orange, one of the blood-royal of England, was called in by the flower of the aristocratical party to defend the antient constitution, but by no means to level all distinctions. To this prince so invited, the aristocratical party, who commanded the troops, went over in bodies with their different corps, as the saviours of their country. The *object* of military obedience was changed, but the *principle* of military obedience was not interrupted for a single moment.

If the conduct of the English armies was different, so also was that of the whole English nation at that memorable period. In fact the circumstances of our revolution and that of France, are exactly the reverse of each other, in almost every particular, as well as in the whole spirit of the transaction. What we did was in truth and substance, and in a constitutional point of view, not to cause a revolution but to prevent it. We did not impair but strengthen the monarchy, and we did not injure or degrade the church. We made no change in the fundamental parts of our constitution, and the nation preserved the same ranks, privileges, and securities for property. The church and state were the same after as before the revolution, but we may venture to maintain that in every part they were much better secured.

The result of all this was, that the state flourished. Instead of lying, as if dead, in a species of trance, or exposed like some others in an epileptic fit to the pity or scorn of the world, for her wild convulsive movements unfit for every purpose but that of dashing out her brains, Great Britain rose above the standard even of her former self. A period thus commenced of a more improved domestic prosperity, and still continues not only unimpaired, but in every part much better secured.

It was in reply to this oration, that Mr. Fox, after expressing his esteem and veneration for Burke, declared that if he were to put all the information he had gained from books, all that he had learned from science, or that the knowledge of the world and affairs had taught him into one scale, and the improvement he had derived from Mr. Burke's conversation in the other, the latter would preponderate. Still, however, he could not agree with the opinion of his friend respecting the French revolution, at which he rejoiced as an emancipation from despotism. He declared himself as much an enemy to democratical as to aristocratical or monarchical despotism, but he did not apprehend that the new constitution of France would degenerate into that description of tyranny. He was a friend only to a mixed government like our own, in which if the aristocracy or any of the three branches were destroyed, the good effects of the whole and the happiness derived under it would in his mind be at an end.

Mr. Sheridan expressed his disapprobation of the remarks and reasonings of Burke, much more strongly than Mr. Fox. He thought them utterly inconsistent with the general principles and conduct of so constant and powerful a friend of liberty, and one who so highly valued the British government and revolution. Indignation and abhorrence of the French revolution, he regarded as inconsistent with admiration of that of England. Detesting the cruelties that had been committed, he imputed them to the natural resentment of a populace, for long-suffered and long-felt oppression. He praised the National Assembly as the dispensers of good to their own country and to other nations. Its members had

exerted a firmness and perseverance hitherto unexampled, which had secured the liberty of France, and vindicated the cause of mankind. Which of their actions could authorise the appellation of a bloody, ferocious, and tyrannical democracy? Burke, perceiving the views of Sheridan to be totally different from his own, disapproving in particular of the opinion that there was a resemblance between the principles of the two revolutions in France and England, and impressed with the persuasion that the construction of his observations was uncandid and unjust, declared that Mr. Sheridan and he were from that time separated for ever in politics. "Mr. Sheridan (he said) has sacrificed my friendship in exchange for the applause of clubs and associations. I assure him he will find the acquisition too insignificant to be worth the price at which it is purchased."

Mr. Burke had many correspondents at Paris of different nations, abilities, and sentiments. Through them he completed his acquaintance with the French system. While attending to its progress and its operation within the country which it more immediately affected, he directed his views to the impressions which it had made in his own country. The promulgation of Dr. Price's political opinions in a printed sermon, animated Mr. Burke to convince mankind that the French revolution did not tend to ameliorate but to deprave the human character. To establish his position he analized the principles on which the revolutionists reasoned, the religious, moral, and political system on which they acted, and the natural and necessary consequences of their doctrines. Profound wisdom, solid and beneficial philosophy, enforced by all the power of Mr. Burke's eloquence, produced an important change in the public opinion. From this time many men of talents, learning, and political eminence, openly declared sentiments decidedly inimical to the French revolution. The nobility, with few exceptions, were apprehensive of the dangers which awaited their order if French principles became prevalent in Great Britain. The public opinion, which had been at first so extremely favourable, was at the end of 1790 greatly divided.

In expressing his opinions of the Rights of Man, Mr. Burke was equally distinguished by the profundity of his views and the splendor of his eloquence. " Far," he exclaimed, " am I from denying in theory, far is it from my heart, from withholding in practice, if I were of power to give or to withhold, the *real* rights of men. In denying their false claims of right, I do not wish to injure those which are *real*, and such as their pretended rights would totally destroy. If civil society be made for the advantage of man, all the advantages for which it is made became his right; it is an institution of beneficence, and law itself is only beneficence acting by rule. Men have a right to live by that rule. They have a right to justice as between their fellows, whether their fellows are employed in political functions or in ordinary occupation. They have a right to the fruits of their industry, and to the means of rendering their industry fruitful. They have a right to the acquisitions of their parents, to the nourishment and improvement of their offspring, to instruction in life and consolation in death. Whatever each man can separately do without trespassing on others, he has a right to for himself, and he has a right to a fair portion of all which society, with its combination of skill and force, can do in his favor. In this partnership all men have equal rights, but not to equal things: He that has but five shillings in the partnership, has as good a right to it as he that has five hundred has to his larger proportion, but he has not a right to an equal dividend in the product of the joint estate; and as to the share of power, authority, and direction, which each individual ought to have in the management of the state, *that* I must deny to be amongst the direct original rights of man in civil society, for I have in my contemplation, the civil social man, and no other. It is a thing to be settled by convention.

" If civil society be the offspring of convention, that convention must be its law. That convention must limit and modify all the descriptions of constitution which are formed under it. Every sort of legislative, judicial, and executory power, are its creatures. They can have no being in any other state of things; and how can any man claim, under the conventions of civil society, rights which do not so much as suppose its existence.

" Government is not made in virtue of natural rights which may and do exist in total independence of it, and exist in much greater clearness and in a much greater degree of abstract perfection; but their abstract perfection is their practical defect. By having a right to every thing, they want every thing. Government is a contrivance of human wisdom, to provide for human wants. Men have a right that these wants should be provided for by this wisdom. Among these wants is to be reckoned, the want, out of civil society, of a sufficient restraint upon their passions. Society requires, not only that the passions of individuals should be subjected, but that even in the mass and body, as well as in the individuals, the inclination of men should frequently be thwarted, their will controlled, and their passions brought into subjection. This can only be done by a power distinct from themselves, and not in the exercise of its function subject to that will, and those passions which it is its office to bridle and to subdue. In this sense the restraints on men, as well as their liberties, are to be reckoned among their rights. But as the liberty and the restrictions vary with time and circumstances, and admit of infinite modification, they cannot be settled by any abstract rule, and nothing is so foolish as to discuss them upon that principle."

In 1791 a bill was proposed for the government of Canada. In discussing it Mr. Burke entered upon the general principles of legislation, considered the doctrine of the rights of man, proceeded to its offspring, the constitution of France, and expressed his conviction that a design had been formed in this country for the subversion of the monarch's authority, and for the corruption of the legislative bodies.

Mr. Burke being called to order, Mr. Fox, in order to remove the imputation on his conduct and opinion, conveyed by the speech of his friend and by the previous observations of Mr. Pitt, declared his conviction that the British constitution, though defective in theory, was in practice excellently adapted to this country. He repeated, however, his praises of the French revolution ; he thought it, on the whole, one of the most glorious events in the history of mankind, and proceeded to express his dissent from Burke's opinion on the subject, as inconsistent with just views of the inherent rights of mankind, and with that gentleman's former principles. Mr. Burke replied in the following language. " Mr. Fox has treated me with harshness and malignity ; after having harassed with his light troops in the skirmishes of order, he brought the heavy artillery of his own great abilities to bear on me." He maintained that the constitution and general system of the French, were replete with anarchy, impiety, vice, and misery. He denied the charge of inconsistency ; his opinions on government, he insisted, had been the same during the whole career of his political life. He said Mr. Fox and he had often differed, and there had been no loss of friendship between them, but " there is something in the cursed French constitution which envenoms every thing." Fox whispered " there is no loss of friendship between us." Burke answered, " There is—I know the price of my conduct ; our friendship is at an end." He concluded by exhorting the two great men who headed the opposite parties, whether they should move in the political hemisphere as two blazing stars in opposite orbits, or walk together as brethren, that they would preserve the British constitution, and guard it against innovation. For his own part he gave up private friendship and party support, and separated from those he esteemed most highly. This country, he trusted, would estimate the sincerity of his avowals, and the importance of his warnings by the price which they had cost himself. He was far from imputing to Mr. Fox a wish for the practical adoption in this country of the revolutionary doctrines, but thinking and feeling as Mr. Fox and he now did, their intercourse must terminate. With great emotion Mr. Fox deprecated the renunciation of Mr. Burke's friendship, and tears for several minutes interrupted his utterance. When the first ebullitions of sensibility had subsided, he expressed the highest esteem, affection, and gratitude, for Mr. Burke, whom, notwithstanding his harshness, he must still continue to love. Proceeding, for some time, in a strain of plaintive tenderness, he gradually recovered his usual firmness, and afterwards displayed considerable asperity. He renewed the accusation of inconsistency against Mr. Burke, and this repetition of the charge effaced the impression of his respectful and affectionate language and behaviour ; the breach was irreparable, and from this time Mr. Fox and Mr. Burke never resumed their former friendship. In this discussion the impartial examiner cannot discover a single sentence or phrase of Mr. Fox, which was not highly in favor of the British constitution, so that the political differences between these illustrious men, arose entirely from their opposite opinions of the French revolution. Burke had already conceived such an abhorrence of the Gallic system that he could not endure any expression of satisfaction at a change, which he regarded as destructive to the best interests of society.

Among the subjects of anxiety bequeathed by the constituent assembly to their successors, was the report of an intended invasion by several great continental powers, united to support the claims of the emigrant nobles and prelates, and to invade and dismember the French territory. It could not be expected that the other branches of the house of Bourbon, would, without indignation, behold the chief of their line detained in unmerited captivity by his own subjects, and the princes of the blood seeking shelter and soliciting precarious protection in foreign courts, or that the emperor, who boasted of deriving his origin from the Cæsars, could listen, without impatience, to the report of the intolerable indignities offered by the lowest of mankind to his own sister. A plan had been projected by M. Montmorin, for combining the various princes whom blood or interest called into such an alliance, in a mock attack on France, not for the purpose of terrifying the legislature or the people into any particular mode of conduct, but of gaining for the king the command of an army, which might contribute to the restoration of his authority, and render him beloved by his subjects as the restorer of peace. The plan was impolitic and trifling. A sagacious politician would not have expected that so many powers would incur the expense and trouble of marching armies towards a foreign frontier without seeking an indemnity, or raising some topic of dispute among themselves, in which the monarch, for whose benefit they were ostensibly armed, must become a party, and to which a portion of his dominions might fall an unexpected sacrifice. Some of the potentates, however, on whose assistance the projector of the plan chiefly relied, agreed to the proposal, but no view of personal aggrandizement had yet entered their minds, as they desisted from arming after the acceptance of the constitution by Lewis, and would not approach the frontier, though the prospect of success was extremely favorable, and motives of aggression were abundant.

The emperor, however, did not abandon the cause of his august relatives. Count Alphonso Durfort, a confidential person, employed after the 18th of April to make the count d'Artois acquainted with the situation of the king and queen, was entrusted at Florence with a new plan proposed by the emperor, and finally arranged on the 20th of May, between him, the count d'Artois, M. de Calonne, and M. d'Escars, at Mantua. It was in substance that the emperor, the Swiss circles, and the kings of Spain and of Sardinia, should raise a force of 500,000 men, to march in five columns in due proportions towards the contiguous frontiers, where they were to be joined by the loyal regiments, and by the royalists. Prussia was not to interfere, and the neutrality of England was stated as a momentous acquisition. The sovereigns

were to issue, at an appointed period, a joint proclamation, founded on a declaration in which all the members of the house of Bourbon were previously to concur; and, lest the queen should suffer from the fury of the French populace, they were to take the lead; though the emperor was avowedly the soul of the compact. The parliaments of France were to be restored as necessary to the re-establishment of forms; the king and queen were recommended to increase their popularity, in hopes that the people, alarmed by the approach of foreign armies, would fly for safety to the mediation of the monarch, and submit to his authority. It is not necessary to discuss the faults or merits of this project, for terrifying the French nation by a force of one hundred thousand men, scattered over five points of their frontier, since it was rejected both by Lewis and the queen. The king objected to assembling the parliaments in any but a judicial capacity; both concurred in the necessity of quitting Paris, and refused to recal the orders given to M. de Bouille. The emperor's plan was therefore relinquished, nor were the particulars divulged till more than two years after the death of the king.

Though the enemies of the court had been unable to obtain intelligence respecting these unexecuted projects, they imputed to the sovereigns of the houses of Bourbon and Austria, and to the emigrants, numerous other designs. They accused the king of authorising the count d'Artois to levy troops in his name, and they rendered their motions against the emigrants more popular, by continually reporting to the assembly the most improbable narratives respecting the formidable force which they described as assembling on the frontiers. Such futile intimations of general danger could not produce much permanent effect; a bolder scheme was therefore tried by publishing as authentic, the substance of a pretended treaty concluded at Pavia, in July 1791, between Austria, Russia, Prussia, and Spain, for dismembering France, and dividing among the contracting powers a large proportion of her territory. Although every circumstance respecting the relative situations of the parties to this pretended compact, the terms of their agreement, and even the inaccurate manner in which the names of monarchs and ministers are affixed to the paper, gave internal evidence of its fabrication ; and though it was ascertained that at the time of its supposed execution not one of the subscribers was at Pavia, yet the forgery was the subject of general declamation in the political societies of Paris, and served as a theme of declamation to the advocates of the French cause in other countries.

The temporary credit with which this document was received, was augmented by an incident involved in obscurity and only partially avowed. A conference was held at the castle of Pilnitz, in Saxony, between the emperor Leopold and the king of Prussia, at which some conspicuous emigrants were present, and the affairs of France were minutely discussed. At the request of the brothers of Lewis XVI. the imperial and Prussian sovereigns took into consideration their representations on the state of their native country, and its probable effects on the other states of Europe. The two monarchs speedily arranged the compact which had occasioned the interview, but differed entirely on the measures to be pursued respecting France. Frederic William was eager for hostilities, but Leopold, considering the danger of his sister and her family, and influenced probably by other considerations, was anxious for the adoption of pacific measures. Both, however, concurred in viewing with jealousy, the preparations of the king of Sweden, who was employed in raising a force to succour the French monarch. Amidst such a diversity of views no extensive operation could be agreed on ; but the baron de Spielman, the emperor's ambassador, M. de Bischofswerder, for the king of Prussia, and M. de Calonne, on behalf of the French princes, drew up a declaration which was sanctioned after long debates. The princes obtained nothing more from the conference than this paper, and a secret convention that the emperor and the king of Prussia should each provide 12,000 men on the frontiers of the Rhine to support the army of the emigrants, to demonstrate unequivocally their protection of the French princes, and to urge the commerce of other powers. In this paper signed by themselves and delivered to the count d'Artois, Leopold and Frederick William declared their opinion that the situation of the king of France was an object of common interest to all the sovereigns of Europe. They hoped, that this interest would be recognized by other powers, who would not refuse to employ in conjunction with them, the most efficacious means of enabling Lewis to establish the foundations of a monarchical government equally agreeable to the rights of sovereigns and the welfare of the French ; *then, and in that case,* their majesties were determined to act promptly with the forces necessary to the end proposed, and in the mean time their troops were ordered to be in readiness. The conditional terms *then and in that case* prove that this declaration was dependent for its effect on the concurrence of other powers. It was dated the 27th of August, and had a copy reached Lewis XVI. in time to prevent his pure and unconditional acceptance of the constitution, it might have produced the most beneficial results. But the vigilance of La Fayette impeded all access to the king, and the princes, baffled in all their endeavours, published the declaration in the gazettes. This step was in every respect imprudent ; the king had already accepted the constitution, and the declaration therefore could not influence his conduct or that of the legislature. His acceptance being pure, unconditional, and apparently free, deprived the foreign powers of a pretence for interference. The paper had no other effect than that of exciting alarm among the sovereigns of the house of Bourbon, flattering the emigrants with hopes which could not be realized, and exasperating the violence of their persecutors. It gave to the democratic party an opportunity of calumniating the persons, cause, and conduct of the continental sovereigns, and representing themselves as the defenders of a country, devoted to plunder and partition, for having dared to legislate for itself. These sentiments were rendered more prevalent by the shameless contrivance of blending the avowed declaration of Pilnitz with the imaginary treaty of Pavia, and by the assertion that the king was perfectly free when he accepted the constitution, and the nation extremely generous when they permitted him on any terms to retain his crown. Under these inauspicious circumstances, Lewis XVI. opened the second, denominated the *Legislative* Assembly, on the 12th of October, 1791. At their first meeting the constitutional act was introduced with great ceremony, and every deputy in succession ascending the rostrum and placing his hand on the original, swore to maintain the constitution decreed during the years 1789, 1790, 1791. Previously to the appearance of the king, the mode in which he was to be received and addressed underwent a long discussion, and it was determined that the expression of " Sire," should be omitted as partaking of the feudal forms, and that of " majesty," as incompatible with a limited monarchy. The sentiment of decorum and respect was not yet so entirely extinguished, but that the nation expressed its resentment at the endeavours of the new legislature to degrade the chief magistrate without assigning a cause, or proposing a benefit. Their feelings were the more ardent when they considered of whom the assembly was composed. The majority of the legislative assembly were among the lowest classes of society except that of criminals. The refuse of the colleges and the monasteries, the discarded servants of printers and booksellers, bankrupt tradesmen and the lowest class of literati, formed the majority of those legislators, who, reinforced by Condorcet, Brissot, and other leaders of the republican party, were encouraged and supported by the most violent of the Jacobin partizans, and by the most inconsiderate and ambitious of an agitated populace. The king, averse to a constitution to which he had reluctantly sworn, intrigued both at home and abroad to produce a counter-revolution. Around the royal standard appeared to be assembled a remnant of the national nobility, and all these devoted by place, sentiment,

attachment, or prejudice, to the interests of the crown. The ascendency of the metropolis, now become the joint residence of the assembly and the king, contributed to give a decided preponderance to the patriots, while the powerful influence of the press scarcely admitted of calculation. Every printing-house in the capital teemed with productions, and in addition to innumerable bills, journals, placards, and regular periodical works, it has been estimated that during the first years of the revolution, no fewer than 250 pamphlets issued daily from the shops of the booksellers. Mirabeau had been one of the first agents of the people who had resorted to this obvious mode of promoting the interests of his party. It was afterwards attempted without success by Robespierre; but the writings of Condorcet, Cerutti, Brissot, Merci, and Carra, obtained an irresistible influence over the public mind, and it must be allowed that their compositions were far superior to those of their antagonists.

In addition to various other causes, by means of which the public opinion was continually agitated, one of the most powerful engines employed during the whole revolutionary warfare, still presented itself to the contemplation of the enemies of the French revolution, under the title of Jacobins.

LANGUINAIS, a deputy to the states-general and a president of the National Assembly, was the founder of that celebrated political sect, which, like the Rota, during the protectorate of Cromwell, discussed a variety of important questions, and investigated the means of ensuring the safety and prosperity of the state. It originated in 1789, under the denomination of the Breton Club, in consequence of having been first established by the representatives of Brittany. The most celebrated orators, patriots, and politicians, considered this society as an admirable engine for the support of the public cause. It became at length the first and most prominent of those assemblies designated by the appellation of the Jacobin Clubs. Yet, although its power has greatly increased, its character was on the decline The

incendiary motions, the outrageous proceedings, and the equivocal characters
of many of the ruling members, had cast an
indelible stain on a society, which, after
counterbalancing the influence of the court,
and efficaciously supporting the public
cause, was likely, at no distant period, to endanger the fabric of national liberty, by its
unqualified violence. The majority of the
deputies and some respectable private
members had accordingly withdrawn,
while the names of many individuals, conspicuous for their virtue, patriotism, and
oratorical powers, were erased from the list.
The committees were now regulated, and
the chair occupied according to the secret
suggestions of two or three ambitious and
aspiring individuals.

Maximilian Robespierre, a native of
Arras, and by profession an advocate,
might, even at this period, be esteemed the
principal leader. He had sat in the states-
general as a representative of the third
estate of the province in which he was
born; and though unable to acquire celebrity by his eloquence, he found means to
render himself conspicuous, by the steadiness of his opposition to every deviation
from principle, and every abuse of authority.
Such was the extent of his hypocrisy, that
when the articles of the criminal code were
discussed, this man, doomed hereafter to
make the blood of his fellow-citizens flow
in torrents, by the hands of the executioner,
expressed the most decided antipathy to
the infliction of death, and declared for the
immediate abolition of so cruel, so useless,
and so sanguinary, a punishment. On the
revision of the constitution he persisted in
his former sentiments with an uniformity
the more remarkable, as many of the other
deputies had been prevailed upon to relinquish their principles in consequence of
the bribes and promises of the court. This
circumstance alone tended not a little to his
celebrity, and as he was never distinguished
by the love of lucre or by rapacity, he began to acquire and in some measure to deserve the title of "incorruptible." An
altar erected by "public gratitude" was
inscribed with his name, and on the dissolution of the National Assembly, a triumph

resembling the antient oration was decreed
to him by popular esteem. When he and
Petion left the hall, they were placed in
an open carriage crowned with oak; and
conducted home amidst the acclamations
of an applauding multitude.

He was soon afterwards nominated to
the responsible office of "public accuser,"
but he suddenly resigned that situation
and dedicated the whole of his time to the
organization of the Jacobin society. When
that institution was abandoned by most
of the other deputies, Robespierre, one of
the six who remained, acted frequently as
president, and at length acquired a complete ascendency. Gloomy, vindictive,
and ferocious; at once replete with cowardice and malignity, such was his matchless
hypocrisy, that he concealed his real
character while he had triumphed over his
enemies, and such his unabating envy, that
he regarded, with malignant hatred, every
individual whose talents and virtues entitled them to the public esteem. His reputation had been hitherto unstained by
crimes, but even now he secretly contemplated an original and monstrous species
of dominion before unknown, in any age
or country, and equally alarming for its
novelty and its atrocity. The Jacobins
where the instruments by which he proposed to execute the suggestions of a
gloomy ambition, and crimes which a Nero,
or a Caligula, would scarcely have dared
to perpetrate, though invested with the imperial purple and surrounded by the
satellites of despotism, were at length
achieved with facility by a private individual, in the name of liberty.

DANTON, first the associate, afterwards
the victim, of Robespierre, and like him,
an advocate by profession, was born at
Arien-sur-Aube, in 1759. He seemed designed by nature for the turbulent period
in which he lived, and the bold and decisive
character which he assumed. His figure
was tall and athletic; he possessed a
stentorian voice, which kept alive the attention of the most numerous assembly,
and a bold and specious eloquence admirably calculated to impose upon the
multitude. Not contented with acting

a conspicuous part in the Jacobin society, he instituted a club denominated the *Cordeliers*, and became at once their founder and their chief. Open, daring, generous, and unreserved, his good qualities were obscured by the violence of his temper, and the ardor of unprincipled ambition.

MARAT was born at Geneva in 1745, and was surgeon to the regiment of the count d'Artois. He was the creature of Robespierre and Danton, who not unfrequently protected him from punishment, and directed his personal and literary conduct. A dwarf in stature, with a head disproportionate to his body; nature seemed to have marked him from his birth with the seal of reprobation. As an author he circulated the most immoral and ferocious principles, in language at once obscure, inflated, and intemperate; to use the language of Junius, masks, hatchets, files, and vipers, danced through his pages, in all the mazes of metaphorical confusion. His oratory was of the same character with his literary efforts; and his future notoriety can only be attributed to the influence of his patrons, and the concurrence of unexpected opportunities.

Such were the present leaders of that famous club destined in a short time to decide the fate of the empire, and ultimately of Europe. While they were supported by a multitude of dangerous and daring adventurers, collected from every part of France and Europe, whose names had been lately enrolled in the books of the society, they were hailed as the friends of their country by a crowd of honest but deluded followers; yet they would not have been enabled to acquire a fatal pre-eminence had it not been for the open hostility of the queen to the new constitution, the wavering and suspicious conduct of Lewis, the impolitic and insulting interference on the part of foreign powers, and the commencement of a war, equally hostile and repugnant to the pride, freedom, and independence of a great nation.

While the present leaders of the Jacobins scarcely concealed their wishes to dethrone the king, and erect a republic on the ruins of the monarchy, a rival society existed, of which the members entitling themselves constitutionalists, were desirous of a legislature consisting of two houses. Many of these individuals were devoted to the court, and had made their peace with it. In consequence of a schism among the Jacobins, Talleyrand, bishop of Autun, Emery, a member of the assembly, the dukes de Rochefoucault, and Liancourt, the two Lameths, la Fayette, and many others, had left that celebrated society and determined to found another. They at first assembled in a magnificent hotel, and when they became more numerous assumed the appellation of the club of 1789, but were afterwards distinguished by the appellation of *Feuillans*, a name derived from that of the convent to which they removed the scene of their debates.

The *Girondists*, so called from the department whence they were deputed, possessed considerable influence in the legislative body, and were equally celebrated for their talents and integrity. Of these one of the most conspicuous was Verginaux, a native of Limoges, and one of the representatives for Bourdeaux. He had been bred to the bar, but was better calculated by nature to obtain ascendency in popular assemblies. Devoted to the cause of liberty and of his country, he was resolute and able, but indolent. He disputed the palm of eloquence with the most celebrated orators of the second assembly, and of all his countrymen was inferior to Mirabeau alone. *Gensonné* and *Guadet* were neither destitute of talents nor of virtue.

Brissot, the chairman of the Girondist society, was the son of a pastry-cook, and was educated for the bar, but he applied himself solely to writing, and published several works on criminal jurisprudence, which are rendered more interesting by the abhorrence of injustice, which they uniformly display, than by extent of research or profundity of thought. In the beginning of 1784, he visited London with the intention of establishing an academy, and took a house for that purpose in Newman-street, Oxford-street. In June, 1784,

Mr. Cox, printer of the *Courier de l'Europe*, arrested him for the expenses of printing a Journal of Arts and Sciences. He was liberated in a few hours upon paying half the sum, and faithfully promising to discharge the remainder of the demand; but, instead of fulfilling his engagement, he immediately escaped to France, where, in consequence of his friend Lefit comte Pelport having been arrested some time before, and a letter of Brissot being found upon him, he also was imprisoned in the Bastile, but was liberated through the interest of the duke de Chartres.

Condorcet, one of the forty members of the royal academy, was equally distinguished as a man of letters and a politician. Though born a noble, he was an active and determined enemy of nobility. His name conferred a lustre on the party, and his writings greatly contributed to the changes that ensued.

The triumph of the Jacobins, however, over every rival society, and their influence on the public mind and on the conduct of the monarch, was decisive and conspicuous. The king, though decidedly adverse to a change of ministers, found it necessary to consult their wishes relative to the formation of a new cabinet. The place of minister of justice was conferred on Duranton, an advocate of Bourdeaux; the administration of the finances was again committed to a banker and a citizen of Geneva, in the person of Claviere.

Roland, the minister of the home department, united an intimate knowledge of commerce with a devotion to literary pursuits. He had acted at the same time as inspector-general of the manufactures of Arras; a writer in the Encyclopædia, and a member of all the learned societies in the south of France. His talents were respectable, his views moderate, and his habits simple and austere. It was his fortune to be united to a female of singular accomplishments, who, after assisting him in his academical pursuits, became at once his amanuensis and his adviser.

Dumouriez, the minister for foreign affairs, had been a soldier of fortune; he was employed in 1757 as a commissary at war,

in the army of M. d'Etrees, and having conceived an attachment to a military life, procured a cornetcy of horse, and was wounded at the battle of Emstetten. After having obtained the rank of a captain, he was dismissed, at the end of the war, with the cross of St. Lewis, which he had merited by his bravery, and a pension, which remained unpaid. Of a restless temper and in embarrassed circumstances, he repaired to Italy, where he offered his sword and his services to any state or party that would employ him. His offers being rejected by Paoli and the Genoese, who were fighting for the possession of Corsica, he returned home and visited Spain and Portugal, the latter of which he was secretly commissioned to survey, by the French minister, with a view to a future invasion. Having been recalled and employed in the reduction of Corsica, with the rank of colonel, he was afterwards sent to Poland, and assisted the confederation at Bar, sometimes with his advice and sometimes by his personal services. In consequence of a change in the ministry, he was seized and confined in the Bastile, but on the death of Lewis XV. regained his freedom. He was successively promoted commandant of Cherburgh, governor of Lower Normandy, and major-general. At the commencement of the revolution he displayed his enthusiasm in favour of the king, and drew up a plan for the preservation of the Bastile and the subjection of Paris. On learning the flight of Lewis, he transmitted a letter to Barrere, then president of the assembly, stating his attachment to that body and his determination to defend it, by hastening to its assistance with a considerable force. While Dumouriez commanded in la Vendée, he formed an intimacy with Gensonné, and being introduced by him to the patriots of the legislative assembly, they procured his nomination to the office of foreign affairs, vacant by the confinement of his predecessor Delessart, who had been sent a prisoner to Orleans. By the introduction of Dumouriez into one of the first offices of the state, and the other changes which accompanied his accession, Lewis consented to deprive himself of every minister in whom he placed his confidence. But the effects of these sacrifices were lost in the eyes of the nation, who were more strongly impressed by the suggestions of his enemies than by his professions of attachment to the constitution, and would probably have respected him more for his firm and intrepid resistance than for his temporizing policy. Deserted by those on whom he had heaped his favors, deprived of his faithful guards, and insulted by the populace, this virtuous and benevolent monarch exhibited a striking example of the unhappy effects arising from the want of firmness, vigor, and decision.

After Dumouriez was chosen minister, he received orders to wait upon the queen. He found her majesty alone, and in a state of great agitation. Approaching the minister she appeared to be much irritated, and addressed him in the following words. " Sir, you are all-powerful at this moment, but it is through the favor of the people who soon demolish their idols. Your situation depends upon your conduct. It is said that you possess great talents. You ought to know that neither the king nor myself will suffer the prevailing novelties, or the constitution. I declare it frankly to you. Choose therefore the part you are to act." M. Dumouriez represented how necessary it was that the king should give his cordial concurrence in establishing the constitution ; to which the queen passionately replied, in a still louder tone, " It will not last, therefore take care of yourself." Thus did the infatuated Marie Antoinette rush on with blindness and precipitation in the very path which led to destruction.

The emperor Leopold II. died suddenly on the 1st of March, 1792, of a malignant fever, and was succeeded by his son Francis II. under the appellation of king of Hungary. No sooner had he ascended the throne, than he informed the court of Berlin, that he was fully resolved to adhere most scrupulously to the terms of the convention of Pilnitz, so that his coronation produced no change, except by adding fresh violence to the system of Austrian policy.

The ultimate objects of the court of Vienna were the establishment of monarchy, in conformity to the royal session of Lewis XVI. which was held on the 23rd of June, 1789, and the re-establishment of the nobility and clergy, as distinct orders. The restitution of the property of the clergy, of the lands in Alsace to the German princes, and of every right of sovereignty and feudal power, as well as the possession of Avignon and the Venaissin. It is remarked by M. Dumouriez, that if the court of Vienna had remained in a torpid state during the thirty-three months which had passed away since the royal session, and dictated this note on the resumption of activity, it could not have proposed any terms more inimical to the spirit of the revolution. Every hope of reconciliation appeared to be terminated ; and, although the new administration were sincere lovers of peace, they found it prudent to yield to the clamours of their friends the democrats, and in virtue of a message from the king, war was declared against Austria on the 20th of April. They found it necessary to employ all their efforts in rendering an accommodation with Francis, the successor of Leopold, impossible ; they treated his dispatches as evasive, and submitting them, without discrimination, to the assembly, and through them to the press, occasioned such a series of intemperate reflections on his conduct and sentiments, that they found themselves, in a month after their nomination, enabled to issue a declaration of war with the approbation of the people and the enthusiastic support of their adherents.

This measure was utterly repugnant to the inclinations of the king. He had issued his orders and employed his entreaties to prevent the emigrants from committing any act of hostility, and expressed, in the strongest terms, his disapprobation at the arming of the French nobles. Even after the declaration of war, he was so apprehensive that his subjects should suffer from the incursions of the enemy, that he sent a message to the emperor and the king of Prussia, requesting that they would not act offensively against France, without the most imperious necessity, and that even then they would not invade the country without publishing an auxiliary manifesto, distinguishing the king and the people from a faction who were careless about the ruin of both.

At the period when France was thus eager to rush into war, without any immediate motive or ulterior object, the state of the kingdom required the utmost caution and prudence, to prevent the total dissolution of all social order. Anarchy prevailed in every department of the state and every class of society. The members of the assembly disgraced their sittings by tumultuous debates, unmanly reproaches, and manual contentions. Unaccustomed to the manners or feelings of polished life, they indulged in the unlimited licence of vulgar brutality; and, "Silence that bell!" "Off with your hat, Mr. President!" were among the frequent exclamations in the hall. The tumultuous senators were themselves beneath the influence of the galleries; for, as they aimed only at popular acclamation, without any expectation of respect, they were obliged to submit, without resistance, to all the caprices of the mob, who, without ceremony or constraint, overawed, controlled, and interrupted their proceedings. The clubs and the multitude, knowing themselves to be the sources of political influence and popularity, and dignified by the ludicrous epithet of the sovereign people, knew no bounds to their insolence. They were subject only to the mandates of a few factious leaders, who, by the distribution of money and liquor, knew how to move, impel, and govern them. The payment of taxes was entirely superseded, convoys of grain and specie destined for the supply of distant parts were stopped and plundered, to satisfy the exigencies of those who had been formerly relieved by the bounty of the great. The freedom of worship was every where violated; several constituted authorities shut up the churches, though the king had not sanctioned the decree against the priests, while the injured individuals, who applied to the constitution for protection, found no resource but in flight, and numbers were daily added to the list of emigrants. The assignants or government securities issued on the credit of the lands of the church, already circulated at a loss of forty per cent; business stagnated for want of capital and encouragement, and every impartial observer, who speculated on the state of France, was convinced that nothing less than madness could impel a declaration of war amidst domestic weakness, insolvency, and distress.

HISTORY OF THE WAR.

CHAP. III.

IMMEDIATELY after the declaration of war the troops of France proceeded to their respective places of destination. Of four armies, the first was assembled on the northern confines of France, under the command of the marshal de Rochambeau, an experienced officer, who had served in the French armies during the American war. This force was destined to cover the frontier towards the Austrian Netherlands, from the German Ocean at Dunkirk, to Maubeuge in French Hainault, with their right extending to the Meuse. The marquis de la Fayette, appointed to command the second army, fixed his head quarters at Metz, and occupied Nancy, Thionville, and Luneville. The cordon, or line of communication, was thus extended from the banks of the Meuse to the Moselle, and retained in check the important fortress of Luxemburgh. The third army was formed on the Rhine under Luckner, and extended from Landau by Strasburg, towards Mont Belliard, and the pass of Porentrui into Switzerland. The possession of this important defile, aided by the favourable positions of the mountains of Jura, rendered the extensive frontier of Franche Compte perfectly secure. A fourth army was assembled on the side of Savoy, to watch the motions of the king of Sardinia, who was expected to join the hostile confederacy. The army of the north, commanded by Rochambeau, amounted to 15,000 men; the army of the centre, commanded by la Fayette, to 17,000; the army of the Rhine, under Luckner, to 23,000; and the army of observation to 12,000 men. The plan of the campaign was to penetrate into the Austrian Low Countries, before the emperor was prepared for defence, and capture his fortresses by surprise. The war was begun by an attack on the cities of Mons and Tournay, but the soldiers being impressed with a persuasion that they were betrayed by their generals, retreated in great confusion; in the blindness of their rage they murdered several officers, and among the rest Dillon, their lieutenant-general. They trampled upon his body, and, having lighted a fire, threw the corpse into the flames. The infuriated soldiers danced around the remains of their commander, so ferocious and brutal had they become; Rochambeau resigned in disgust, and Luckner, removed to the command of the army of the north, found the troops in a situation much more turbulent and insubordinate than they had been represented by his predecessor. La Fayette made the same complaints of the unprovided state of the forces, as deficient in camp-equipage, stores, ammunition, and artillery. The equipment of the armies was so incomplete that their distresses were attributed to the treachery of the government, an imputation which the ministers endeavoured to efface, by the promptitude of their exertions in the transmission of supplies and the formation of magazines. It was found necessary, in the mean time, to postpone the operations of the campaign till these arrangements were completed; and the weakness and tardiness of the Austrians permitted them to extend and mature their preparations for decisive hostility.

While the war against foreign powers was conducted with such conspicuous imbecility, that which the Jacobins were waging against the king and constitution was attended with more encouraging results. A fiction was invented of a secret committee, composed of members of the royal family, priests, and ex-nobles, to concert the ruin of the constitution, and the re-establishment of the antient system. These calumnies continually exasperated the fury of the populace; execration of the king and queen was not confined to select parties, or even to promiscuous meetings, but their very residence was selected as the fittest spot for the utterance of the grossest abuse, and for insulting the adherents of the royal family. These atrocities were feelingly described by the queen in conversation with Dumouriez. "I am," said she, "quite disconsolate. I dare no longer approach the windows that look into the garden. Yesterday evening when I appeared at that opposite court, to breathe a little fresh air, a cannonier of the national guard seized the opportunity to overwhelm me with insults; adding, by way of conclusion, *What pleasure would it give me to have your head stuck upon the point of my bayonet.*" In this frightful garden you see in one place a man mounted on a chair, and reading the most horrible calumnies against us in a loud voice; in another you perceive an officer or an abbé dragged towards a bason of water, and overwhelmed with injuries and blows, while the spectators play at foot-ball, or walk about without the least concern. What a habitation! What a people!" Prud'homme, a Jacobin journalist and bookseller, after disseminating the most profane and insulting libels, under the title of the *Crimes of Sovereigns* and

the *Crimes of Popes*, announced, by posting bills at the entrance of the legislative assembly, that he would speedily publish a work entitled, "The Crimes of the Queens of France, from the earliest times down to Marie Antoinette inclusive." A complaint against this audacious advertisement met with little notice from the assembly. The sufferings of the royal family were not confined to insults from the savage licentiousness of the multitude: they were prevented from receiving, in their own apartments, the visits of their most welcome friends, and compelled to endure the presence of persons employed as spies, who were not even endowed with sufficient address to conceal their odious mission.

Nor were the inferior orders of society less exhorbitant in their demands, than ferocious in their habits. The meanest citizens sought a more general equalization of property, and assumed the supreme executive authority. A ragged coat was deemed an honourable testimony of the wearer's political principles, and the lowest rabble, denominated, from their want of decent covering, *sans culottes*, took a lead in public affairs. The turbulence and malignity of the people were gratified by a new and more severe decree against the nonjuring priests. The national guards having lately displayed unusual moderation; the Jacobin club, the sans culottes, and the Jacobins of every kind, determined that an army should be formed, composed of 20,000 men, under the walls of Paris. Their wishes were gratified by the assembly. It would have been prudent on the part of the king, to have yielded to a stream which he had not strength to resist; but on this occasion he did not choose to temporize. From motives of honour and conscience he refused his sanction to the decree for banishing the ecclesiastics who had adhered to him, and to that for assembling an army near the capital, which was justly termed by the queen, A decree for embodying an army of 20,000 banditti to govern Paris. The clamour excited by the firmness of the king, could no longer be repressed by the utmost exertions of the ministry; and madame Roland, in her zeal for liberty, having composed a letter to his majesty in her husband's name, admonishing him to withdraw his veto, it was regarded as a menace rather than an admonition, and was immediately followed by the dismission of Roland, Servan, and Claviere. Dumouriez, who had incurred disgrace by the councils, which he was supposed to have given to his majesty, ostensibly advised him at this moment to yield to a torrent, which must otherwise overwhelm himself and his family, and by this manœuvre he for awhile defeated the purposes of his opponents, being continued in office as minister of war and prime minister.

In the mean time general Luckner endeavoured to re-establish the offensive system of warfare in the Low Countries. He advanced into the Austrian territories, and seized on Apres, Courtrai, and Menin; but having heard that Dumouriez himself had resigned his office, he determined to return. Previously to his departure, he ordered, without provocation or necessity, the town of Courtrai to be burnt, within an hour before its evacuation. As it was the obvious interest of France to conciliate the good opinion of the inhabitants of the Austrian Netherlands, this act of imprudence was formally reprobated by the assembly, and the commander-in-chief was consigned, first to obscurity. and afterwards to punishment, while an adequate compensation was voted to the sufferers.

A defensive system was once more adopted, and the army of the north having returned to its former station, occupied the entrenched camp of Famars. This position was objectionable in many points of view, and its proximity to Valenciennes facilitated the debauchery of the troops; nor was it adapted to a formidable defence, or an expeditious and secure retreat. In front was the Ronelle, which might be crossed with facility, while its elevated bank presented a formal position to the enemy's artillery; in the rear flowed the Scheldt, which could not be forded, and was only to be passed by three bridges, two of which might have been seized upon

by a judicious assailant. There were two other entrenched camps, one at Maubeuge and the other at Maulde; the former was commanded by lieutenant-general Lanoue, the latter by Dumouriez, who, immediately after his resignation, had resumed the profession of arms.

The approach of the allies to the frontiers of France, was at this moment announced to the French people, and contributed to favor the designs of the republicans by the alarm which it excited. While the friends of the king determined to support his prerogatives, the various factions in opposition forgetting their private quarrels, united their efforts to accelerate the crisis of popular violence. The irritation of all parties was still further inflamed by a letter from de la Fayette to the assembly, dictated by ill-directed zeal, in which he unveiled the criminal designs of the Jacobin club, and imputed to them a great part of the public calamities. Headed by Santerre and St. Hurugne, their revolutionary chiefs, an armed multitude presented themselves in the hall of the assembly on the 20th of June, 1792, and peremptorily called upon the deputies to enforce their decrees. They were a motley and squalid band, drawn from all the receptacles of infamy and idleness in Paris; armed with pikes, rusty swords, scythes, pitchforks, bludgeons, pickaxes, and clubs. They carried ensigns with these inscriptions, "Tyrants tremble or be just; and restore the liberties of the people!" "Lewis! the people are tired of suffering!" "Tremble tyrant! thy hour is come!" One man supported a reeking heart stuck on a pike, inscribed, "The heart of an aristocrat." Ragged breeches were suspended with the inscription, "Libre and sans culottes." After a tumultuous debate they were admitted. The orator at the head of the deputation indulged in a long and violent speech against the king and the conduct of the court, and as soon as he had concluded, the whole party marched through the hall. The procession lasted two hours; and at its conclusion M. Santerre presented the president with a banner, which was graciously received.

Proceeding to the Thuilleries, this motley

assemblage were prepared to break open the door of the apartment in which the royal family were assembled. There was stationed in the palace a sufficient force of troops of the line and of national guards to have defended it against every attack; but respect for the lives of the deluded multitude induced the king to forbear from repelling force by force. At four o'clock in the afternoon the mob amounted to about 40,000, and the gates of the Thuilleries were thrown open to them. At the moment of their entrance the royal family was at dinner, and on their attempting to break open the door of their apartment, the king rose to prevent the guards from making resistance, and said calmly, "I will go to them." On the instant that the door was opened, a pike, which had been thrust against it to force it open, would have killed the king, but a chasseur turned the weapon aside with his hand. His friends fearing that he would be borne down by the violence and rapidity of the rabble, placed him in the recess of a window where he leaned on M. Acloque, while a few grenadiers formed round him to resist the torrent. The mob was so numerous and poured in so rapidly, that no one could effect any premeditated purpose. Yet many pointed insults were offered. One of the mob advanced and insisted that the king should wear a red cap, the ensign of the Jacobins; another presented him a bottle, and desired him to drink the health of the nation. Some of the attendants offered to bring a glass, but the sovereign refused the offer, and immediately drank out of the bottle. Petion, the mayor of Paris, was unaccountably absent during these disgraceful scenes; but, arriving at the end of three hours, prevailed on the tumultuous mob to retire. Great part of the popular rage was, as usual, directed against the queen. She was stopped in the council room with the dauphin in her arms, by general Whitingof and the minister Lajarre, who formed a feeble rampart of the council table, behind which they placed the queen, the dauphin, the princess royal, and all the ladies who refused to quit her side. This table was defended by a double line of national guards, and in that situation the queen was obliged to remain a helpless hearer of the incendiary and obscene reproaches which men and women of the lowest class were unwearied in repeating. Marie Antoinette displayed the same contempt of danger which distinguished the king, but her fortitude was almost overpowered, when Santerre forced his way into her presence, and snatching the red or revolutionary cap which the infant dauphin had been compelled to wear, exclaimed, "The child is smothered! Why is this cap left on her head?" and then in a low but distinct voice, added to the queen, "You have very awkward friends madam; I know those who would serve you much better."

These proceedings at the capital decided the fate of the marquis de la Fayette. This general, who was hated by the court as one of the chief causes of the revolution, had now incurred the aversion of the republicans as a warm advocate of monarchy. Consistently with his ardent character, on becoming acquainted with the transactions at the Thuilleries, he hastened to the capital to protect his sovereign by his influence, and prevent the fall of royalty. Presenting himself in the hall of the National Assembly, he declared the sentiments of indignation excited in his troops by the late violences on the king's liberty and safety, and boldly demanded the maintenance of the constitution against a faction which were meditating its destruction. It was not to be expected that such an exhortation would be received with satisfaction or indifference. After some altercation the president coolly replied to his address, that the assembly had sworn to maintain the laws, and knew how to defend them: De la Fayette then retired, and perceiving with mortification how completely he had lost his popularity, thought it expedient to leave Paris on the same night, and return to his camp. He was severely censured by the Jacobins and the Girondists, for leaving the army without permission; commissioners were sent from the assembly to arrest him; he gave orders to have the deputies apprehended, but finding no disposition in his army to afford him support, withdrew in the night to Liege, where, falling into the hands of the enemy, and refusing to join the standard of the French princes, he was sent a prisoner to Namur.

The events of the twentieth of June were an evident prelude to the downfal of monarchy. From this moment all respect to authority, all order and subordination were at an end : a momentary shame indeed appeared at first to restrain the outrages of the Parisians, and the directory of the department of Paris, at the head of whom was M. Rochefoucault and the former bishop of Autun. M. Talleyrand determined to take every step for the prevention of similar outrages. The conduct on this occasion of M. Petion, could not be viewed without suspicion. One of the first steps of the department was to publish a declaration, that the events of the 20th could not have occurred had the laws in being, and particularly those relating to the public force, been better known to the citizens, and better observed by the magistrates. To this declaration M. Petion returned a very voluminous answer, calling upon them to commence a prosecution and protesting his innocence. The department next published an advertisement to the people, exhorting them to peace and subordination, and intimating that there existed a secret connection between the external and the internal foes of the public tranquillity.

On the 5th of July the king informed the assembly of his determination to celebrate the anniversary of the confederation. The approach of this festival was rendered alarming by the arrival of numerous bands of *federés* from the departments, who were selected from the numerous votaries of the clubs, and presented petitions of the most inflammatory and unconstitutional tendency. A plot of Santerre to murder the queen was betrayed, and the assassin arrested, but rescued by his party. The ceremony of the confederation, however, was, upon the whole, quiet and orderly. The royal family were placed in a balcony covered with crimson velvet, which gave rise to some petulant observations ; but the king, having descended to take the

Vol. I.

oath on the altar instead of remaining in his place, completely gratified the populace, and he quitted the *Champs de Mars* amidst loud and general acclamations.

The convention had proclaimed on the first of July, that the country was in danger. " Your constitution, citizens, restores the principles of eternal justice. A league of kings is formed to destroy it. Their battalions are advancing." On the third of July the duke of Brunswick arrived at Coblentz with the first division of the Prussian army, and being joined by fresh troops in the course of the month, proceeded to commence the campaign. His serene highness, with very considerable talents, the greatest military skill, and eminent political abilities, was extremely diffident. He frequently treated inferior capacities with excessive deference, and did not maintain, with sufficient vigor, the dictates of his own excellent understanding. In concerting the plan of the campaign of 1792, he left its formation chiefly to Francis and Frederic William. These princes were impressed with an opinion naturally adopted, and studiously propagated by the emigrants, that the greater number of Frenchmen were attached to the old government, and would join the standard of monarchy if they found themselves properly supported. On this supposition they formed the plan of the campaign. It was proposed that the duke of Brunswick should set out from Coblentz with an army, of Prussians, fifty thousand strong, and march by Treves and Luxemburg to Longwy. After reducing this fortress, and, if possible, that of Montmedi, the next object was to establish magazines, continue the march, and invest Verdun. The court of Vienna engaged to bring into the field two armies ; the one to act between the Rhine and the Moselle, which should, be of sufficient strength to menace Landau, and Saar Lewis, and to carry on the siege of Thionville ; while the other, of much superior force, should be stationed in the Low Countries. Their positions were to, be as near the Meuse as possible. Should the expectation of a general rise in France be disappointed, the duke of Brunswick,

H

was not to cross the river with his main body, but to detach a considerable portion of his army to co-operate with the Austrians, in French Hainault, in reducing Verdun, Sedan, and Meziers. By this arrangement the allies, establishing themselves upon the French frontier would be able to winter in security, and commence the following campaign with great advantage. To oppose this invading force, I have before observed that the entrenched camp at Maubeuge, and another at Maulde, with the fortress of Valenciennes, formed the principle points of defence on the part of the French. It is evident from the very outline of the campaign that the invading monarchs must have viewed the prospect of partitioning France, even had they entertained that wish, as too distant and chimerical to be attempted. Their whole policy was directed to co-operation with the people, and the deliverance of the king; and the accomplishment of the first of these objects, absolutely necessary as it was to their first successes, would have effectually prevented their ulterior design.

The emperor and king of Prussia published energetic and judicious declarations of their motives for engaging in hostilities, but on the armies being put in motion, a manifesto was issued in the name of the duke of Brunswick, to which may unfortunately be ascribed the successful resistance of France and the long duration of the miseries of Europe.

Declaration of the reigning Duke of Brunswick Lunenburgh, Commander of the combined Armies of the Emperor and King of Prussia, to the Inhabitants of France.

Their majesties the emperor and the king of Prussia, having entrusted me with the command of the combined armies, assembled on the frontiers of France, I think it my duty to inform the inhabitants of that kingdom of the motives which have influenced the conduct of the two sovereigns, and of the principles by which they are guided.

After arbitrarily suppressing the rights,

and invading the possessions; of the German princes in Alsace and Lorrain ; after having disturbed and overthrown in the interior part of the kingdom all order and lawful government ; after having been guilty of the most daring attacks, and having had recourse to the most violent measures, which are still daily renewed against the sacred person of the king, and against his august family; those who have seized on the reins of government have, at length, filled the measure of their guilt, by declaring an unjust war against his majesty the emperor, and by invading his provinces of the Low Countries. Some of the possessions belonging to the German empire have been equally exposed to the same oppression, and many others have only avoided the danger by yielding to the imperious threats of the domineering party and of their emissaries.

His majesty the king of Prussia, united with his imperial majesty in the bands of the strictest defensive alliance, and as a preponderant member himself of the Germanic body, could not refuse marching to the assistance of his ally and of his co-estates. It is under this double relation, that he undertakes the defence of that monarch and of Germany.

To these high interests is added another important object, and which both the sovereigns have most cordially in view ; which is, to put an end to that anarchy which prevails in the interior parts of France, to put a stop to the attacks made on the throne and the altar, to restore the king to his legitimate power, to liberty, and to safety, of which he is now deprived, and to place him in such a situation, that he may exercise that legitimate authority to which he is entitled.

Convinced that the sober part of the nation detest the excesses of a faction which has enslaved them, and that the majority of the inhabitants wait with impatience the moment when succours shall arrive, to declare themselves openly against the odious enterprises of their oppressors ; his majesty the emperor, and his majesty the king of Prussia, earnestly invite them to return without delay into the paths of reason and of justice, of order and peace. It is with this view that I, the underwritten, general commandant in chief of the two armies, do declare,

1st, That, drawn into the present war by irresistible circumstances, the two allied courts have no other object in .view than the welfare of France, without any pretence to enrich themselves by making conquests.

2nd, That they do not mean to meddle with the internal government of France, but that.they simply intend to deliver the king, the queen, and the royal family, from their captivity, and to insure to his most Christian majesty that safety which is necessary for his making, without danger and without obstacles, such convocations as he shall judge proper, and for endeavouring to insure the welfare of his subjects, according to his promises, and to the utmost of his power.

3rd, That the combined armies shall protect the towns, burghs, and villages, as well as the persons and property of all those who shall submit to the king ; and that they will concur in the immediate restoration of order and police throughout all France.

4th, That the national guards are called upon to preserve, provisionally, tranquillity in towns and in the country, to provide for the personal safety and property of all Frenchmen until the arrival of the troops belonging to their imperial and royal majesties, or until orders be given to the contrary, on pain of being personally responsible : that, on the contrary, such national guards as shall fight against the troops of the. two allied courts, and who shall be. taken with arms in their hands, shall be treated as enemies, and punished as rebels to their king, and as disturbers of the public peace.

5th, That the general officers, the subalterns, and soldiers of the regular French troops, are equally called upon to return to their former allegiance, and to submit imme diately to the king, their legitimate sovereign.

6th, That the members of departments, districts, and municipalities, shall be equally responsible, on pain of losing their heads and estates, for all the conflagrations, for all the murders, and for all the pillage which they shall suffer to take place, and which they shall not have, in a public manner, attempted to prevent within their respective territories ; that they shall also be obliged to continue their functions, until his most Christian majesty, when set at full liberty, shall make farther arrangements, or until further orders be given in his name.

7th, That the inhabitants of towns, burghs, and villages, who shall dare to defend themselves against the troops of their imperial and royal majesties, and to fire upon them, either in open country, or through half open doors or windows of their houses, shall be punished instantly, according to the rigorous rules of war, or their houses shall be demolished or burned. On the contrary, all the inhabitants of the said towns, burghs, and villages, who shall readily submit to their king, by opening their gates to the troops belonging to their majesties, shall be immediately under their safeguard and protection ; and their estates, their property, and their persons, shall be secured by the laws, and each and all of them shall be in full safety.

8th, The city of Paris and all its inhabitants, without distinction, shall be called upon to submit instantly and without delay to the king, to set that prince at full liberty; and to ensure to his and to. all royal persons that inviolability and respect which are due, by the laws of nature and of nations, to sovereigns ; their imperial and royal majesties, making personally responsible for all events, on pain of losing their heads, pursuant to military trials, without hopes of pardon, all the members of the National Assembly, of the department, of the district, of the municipality, and of the national guards of Paris, justices of the peace, and others whom it may concern : and their imperial and royal majesties farther declare, on their faith and word of emperor and king, that if the palace of the Thuilleries be forced or insulted, if the least violence be offered, the least outrage done to their majesties, the king, queen, and the royal family, if they be not immediately placed in safety and set at liberty, they will inflict on those who shall deserve it, the most exemplary and ever-memorable avenging punishments, by giving up the city of Paris to military execution, and exposing it to total destruction ; and the rebels who shall be guilty of illegal resistance, shall suffer the punishments which they shall have deserved. Their imperial and royal majesties promise, on the contrary, to all the inhabitants of the city of Paris, to employ their good offices with his most Christian majesty, to obtain for them a pardon for their insults and errors, and to adopt the most vigorous measures for the security of their persons and property, provided they speedily and strictly conform to the above injunctions.

Finally, Their majesties, not being at liberty to acknowledge any other laws in France except those which shall be derived from the king, when at full liberty, protest beforehand against the authenticity of all kinds of declarations which may be issued in the name of the king, so long as his sacred person, and that of the queen, the princes, and of the whole royal family, shall not be in full safety : and with this view, their imperial and royal majesties invite and intreat his most christian majesty to name a town in his kingdom, nearest to the frontiers, to which he would wish to remove, together with the queen, and the royal family, under a strong and safe escort, which shall be sent for that purpose : so that his most Christian majesty may, in perfect safety, send for such ministers and counsellors as he shall be pleased to name, order such convocation as he shall think proper, and provide for the restoration of order and the regular administration of his kingdom.

In fine, I declare and promise, in my own individual name, and in my above quality, to cause to be observed, every where, by the troops under my command, good and strict discipline, promising to treat with mildness and moderation, those well-disposed subjects who shall submit peaceably and quietly, and to employ force against those only who shall be guilty of resistance or of manifest evil intentions.

I therefore call upon and expect all the inhabitants of the kingdom, in the most earnest and forcible manner, not to make any opposition to the troops under my command, but rather to suffer them every where to enter the kingdom freely, and to afford them all the assistance, and shew them all the benevolence which circumstances may require.

Given at general quarters at Coblentz, July 25, 1792.

CHARLES GUILLAUME FERDINAND, DUC DE BRUNSWICK LUNENBOURG.

This insulting and sanguinary manifesto was signed in a moment of weakness by the duke of Brunswick, who had not been consulted in its composition. It was calculated to have the very worst effect upon the Parisian populace, it left no middle party in the nation ; all who wished to preserve a government in any degree popular, all who conceived that a limitation of the supreme authority was an object worthy of contention, were thrown by this measure into the hands of the avowed republicans, and felt themselves compelled to give way to the madness of that sanguinary party, or at once accede to the destruction of liberty by the army of the duke of Brunswick. A fatal alternative which rendered it almost impossible to be at once the advocate of order and the friend of liberty.

The unfortunate Lewis did not dare to present this declaration to the assembly as an authentic paper. The very letter which submitted it to the inspection of the legislature questioned its authenticity, and though the royal message was replete with the strongest, and probably the most sincere expressions of patriotism ; the proposal of printing it for the use of the departments was rejected, and M. Isnard, in commenting on the declaration of his majesty, that he questioned the authenticity of the manifesto, remarked that " the king had asserted what was not true." The republican party acquired new accessions of vigor and of authority ; and on the third of August the fatal die was cast, when M. Petion, at the head of the factions of Paris, appeared at the bar of the assembly to demand the deposition of the sovereign. The proposal was heard with indignation by all good patriots, but it was followed by others of the same nature. A petition had laid for eight days on the altar of the *Champs de Mars*, and was presented on the 6th by a countless multitude, who were preceded by a pike supporting the Jacobin ensign, the red cap of liberty, inscribed with " The deposition of the king."

In compliance with these repeated requisitions, the assembly at length determined to come to a decision on this difficult and dangerous subject ; and the fatal 10th of August was appointed for the discussion. The assembly, however, had exhibited some proofs of caution and temperance which did not coincide with the impetuosity of the Jacobins and the urgency of their cause. The *federés* had been detained under various pretences in the metropolis, and even if their stay could be protracted, the leaders of the revolutionary party were doubtful whether harmony could long exist between them and the mob of Paris : the passions of the people were now inflamed, but the French are versatile, and a change of opinion might succeed. The Jacobin party distrusting therefore the motives of the assembly, and the duration of the enthusiasm of the people, determined to take immediate advantage of the existing turbulence, to effect those objects which they despaired of obtaining through the medium of the constituted powers. Regular notice was given to several foreigners by the Jacobin party, who were afraid of their interference, to absent themselves on the day of discussion, and one of the most active in the conspiracy was heard to observe, " If we cannot provoke the people to rise by the 10th, we are lost." While such were the evident designs of the adverse party, the king was not uninformed of their proceedings, and as no alternative now appeared but to repel force by force, preparations were made for defending the Thuilleries. The dreadful Rubicon was now passed, and no hope of the return of harmony or peace remained A solemn gloom

overspread the palace, and superseded the native gaiety of the French nation. Amidst his accumulated misfortunes a small and firm band retained their attachment to the king, and from different motives devoted themselves to his defence. Among these might be numbered some of the remnants of the antient aristocracy, who made this last sacrifice to their principles, and whose errors, when accompanied by such disinterested virtue, became respectable. Some had been among the most forward of those who united in the first efforts to meliorate the condition of their countrymen ; but equally averse to anarchy and despotism now dreaded the evils which impended from a total alteration of government. Some were the personal friends of the fallen majesty of France, some were influenced by gratitude, some by prejudice : and some, in the frenzy of despair, crowded around the tottering standard of royalty. Among these brave and gallant men none were more respectable than the Swiss guards. By repeated decrees of the assembly this body of troops had been considerably reduced, and on the 7th of August the king had been obliged to dismiss 300 of them. The departure of the whole from Paris had been formally decreed, but the king had delayed the execution of the decree, and the number which remained in the Thuilleries previous to the 10th of August, was about 700. On these the court party placed their strongest reliance for the defence of the palace. Besides the Swiss, the number of gentlemen and others who repaired to the palace on this melancholy occasion, is said to have amounted to twelve or fourteen hundred men. As these however were not considered as sufficient, the commander of the national guards, M. Mandat, a man of integrity and attached to the constitution, having represented to the mayor the apprehensions he entertained for the safety of the royal family, had obtained from that magistrate a written order to defend the palace with all his forces, and to repel the attack of any invader. The detachments of national guards which M. Mandat had ordered to the palace on this occasion, are stated at about 2400 men with 12 pieces of cannon, and to these may be added a body of cavalry, amounting to about one thousand. Unfortunately many of the individuals on whom the monarch most firmly relied, entailed disrepute upon the court by their aristocratic principles, without contributing much to its defence, and the national guards were shaken in their fidelity by the reproaches and insinuations of the advocates of liberty. The Marsellois, on the other hand, on whom the republicans chiefly relied, did not exceed 800 men, but their intrepid and ferocious character compensated for the inferiority of numbers, and rendered victory more easy by the terror which it spread before them.

The tocsin sounding at midnight before the 10th of August, the deputies of the different sections of the city who were in the plot flew to the *commune*, and having deposed the municipal officers, assumed their places. They then requested the presence of M. Mandat by a message sent to the palace, and causing him to be murdered as he was leaving their hall of assembly, appointed the ruffian Santerre in his room, who immediately removed from the Pont-neuf the battalions placed by his predecessor, to prevent the junction of the insurjents from the opposite side of the river, and scattered all the troops who were attached to the king, in such a manner that their exertions would be vain. The Marsellois had now pointed their artillery against the Thuilleries and were prepared for the assault. Could Lewis for a moment have exchanged the virtues of a saint for those of a hero, had he in compliance with the queen's entreaties drawn his sword and placed himself at the head of the Swiss guards, the valor which his conduct would have inspired might even now have given him the victory. In passive courage he was not deficient; but he had not the active courage which his situation demanded, nor could surrounding perils arouse him to decided and immediate action. On receiving information that the assailants had broken into the palace, he escaped with the royal family to the hall of the National Asssembly, and addressing the

deputies in confusion exclaimed, "I am come hither to prevent a great crime—among you gentlemen I believe myself safe." He was scarcely seated in the midst of the assembly, trembling for their own safety, and dreading the consequences of affording him protection, before the noise of artillery announced that the battle was begun, and the melancholy intelligence soon arrived that the national guards had deserted their posts, and that the brave Swiss, after a desperate resistance, were overpowered, and nearly all cut in pieces. The banditti, enraged instead of being interested by their gallantry and fidelity, had pursued the fugitives with the rancour of savages, and the victory was converted into a massacre. The national guards, not contented with deserting the cause of their sovereign, united with the populace in the extermination of those whom just before they had regarded as their fellow-soldiers. A small party of 17 of the Swiss had taken refuge in the vestry-room of the chapel, and as they had not been engaged from the first, they imagined that they might secure the clemency of their victors, by surrendering at discretion, and shouting "*Vive la nation!*" but they no sooner laid down their arms than they were put to death. The gentlemen who remained in the palace saw no alternative but to remain and be destroyed, or to make their way, if possible, to the National Assembly. The only passable road was through the queen's gate, they rallied all the Swiss whom they found dispersed in their way, and as many of the national guard as still retained their fidelity. The number of the fugitives might amount to 500, but as only one person could pass through the gate at a time, they were exposed to a continual fire from several battalions stationed at the distance of about 30 yards. As the red uniform of the Swiss attracted particular notice, these devoted strangers were still the greatest sufferers.

The defenceless victims who were found in the palace were involved in one promiscuous massacre. The gentlemen ushers, the pages, all who were employed in the lowest and most servile offices, were slaughtered without discrimination. Streams of blood defiled the edifice of the Thuilleries from the roof to the foundations. The massacre was followed by a general pillage of the palace. A few chests only, containing papers, assignets, and some of the royal plate, were taken from the plunderers, and brought into the hall of the National Assembly.

The king, immediately after his entrance, was required to retire to a part of the hall called the Logographic Lodge, that the business of the assembly might not be interrupted by his presence. As soon as the members were recovered from their terror, they passed a decree in nine articles, of which the most material were these. " The French people are invited to form a national convention.—The executive power is provisionally suspended from this moment until the national convention shall have decreed the measures necessary to be pursued for preserving national independence.—The king and royal family are under the safeguard of the law, and their defence is entrusted to the national guard of Paris." The convention appointed to meet on the 20th of the ensuing month, September, and the ministers nominated by the king were declared to have forfeited the confidence of the nation. A new executive council was appointed, and consisted of M. Roland for the home department, M. Servan for that of war, and M. Claviere for the finance, M. le Brun was nominated minister for foreign affairs, M. Danton minister of justice, and M. Monge of the marine.

After much deliberation, the hotel of the minister of justice was chosen as the habitation of the fallen monarch and his unfortunate family; but on the representation of M. Manuel, who stated that under circumstances of confinement so limited, the municipality could not charge themselves with being responsible for the person of the king, the place of confinement was changed to the temple. It cannot be doubted indeed, that many of the restraints and the suspicions to which the monarch was subjected, were occasioned by the remembrance of his flight to Varennes. and it is not improbable, that, uninfluenced

by the prejudice occasioned by that event, the people, and the revolutionists surrounding him, might have yielded him the facilities of daily intercourse, and enabled him by many acts of conciliation from which he had been debarred, to confirm his friends, and propitiate his enemies.

After the passions of the Jacobin mob were gratified by revenge, after the tempest was assuaged, some time elapsed before its violence entirely subsided; and even then it was not the calm of domestic peace and good order which prevailed, but the sullen stillness which succeeds a storm and presages a renewal of its rage. Legal authority was annihilated: the grief of the royal family was continually aggravated by hearing that murder was committed on some of their most faithful friends, and that others had with difficulty escaped to foreign countries: punishments were inflicted, not according to judicial rules, but agreeably to the will of the leaders of the multitude of Paris, who had wrested the chief power from the hands of the legislative assembly. It may appear extraordinary that a country thus paralyzed by anarchy, and depressed by democratic tyranny, should have displayed the most exemplary energy in its military operations; that the emigrants should have been disappointed in the hopes which they had founded on the disorganization of the state, and the discord which prevailed among the factions contending for power. But this will be accounted for if we reflect that all parties but that of the monarch were chiefly actuated by a dread of the re-establishment of the old government: that opposition to this attempt and resistance to the invading armies of whom it was the avowed object, served as a common principle of action in combining and stimulating them to exertion during the impending danger.

The confusion which the transactions we have just narrated had produced, encouraged the combined armies to advance, and the first conquest they atchieved was that of Longwy. On the 21st of August general Clairfait presented himself with an army of 60,000 men before that fortress. The siege lasted during fourteen hours, during which time the enemy kept up a continual and heavy fire of bombs and artillery. The commandant reported, that the magistrates and citizens, terrified by the bombardment, had insisted on a surrender, and that he had only complied with their requisition; on the other hand it was suspected that nothing less than treachery in a commander could compel a garrison of 3,500 men, well appointed, in a place strongly fortified, defended with 75 pieces of cannon and excellent casemates, to surrender after so short a siege. On further inquiry these suspicions were confirmed, and M. de Lavergne, the governor, was ordered to be tried by a court-martial. The capture of Verdun almost immediately succeeded that of Longwy, and the allies already anticipated their entrance into Paris, and the restoration of the monarch to his original authority.

The number and singularity of the occurrences connected with the revolution during the remainder of the year, and more particularly the progress and vicissitudes of the campaign, will require the utmost attention of the reader, and can only be intelligible in a minute and connected narrative. It will be necessary therefore, before I proceed to record the subsequent atrocities of the Parisians, and the splendid and unexpected succession of military exploits, to exhibit a rapid but not unimportant sketch of the corresponding policy of England, and of the principal events which at a period so momentous, may be regarded as worthy of historical commemoration.

Immediately previous to the declaration of war against Austria, the French monarch addressed a letter to his Britannic majesty, in which he made the most eager advances towards the establishment of a treaty of friendship and alliance. "Between our countries," said Lewis, "new connections ought to take place. I think I see the remains of that rivalship which has done so much mischief to both, daily wearing away. It becomes two kings who have distinguished their reigns by a constant desire to promote the happiness of their people, to connect APRIL, 1792. themselves by such ties as will appear to be durable in proportion as the two nations shall have clearer views of their own interests. I consider the success of the alliance, in which I wish you to concur with as much zeal as I do, as of the highest importance; I consider it as necessary to the stability of the respective constitutions; and I will add that our union ought to command peace to Europe." As this letter produced no sensible effect, an application was made in due form by M. Chauvelin, on the part of the king of France to the king of Great Britain, "to oppose, and by his wisdom and influence to avert, while it is still time, the progress of the confederacy formed against France, and which threatened the peace, the liberty, and the happiness of Europe." An answer was returned on the 8th of July, that "in the existing circumstances of the war begun, the intervention of his Britannic majesty's councils or good offices, could not be of use unless they were desired by all the parties interested." A wise neutrality was therefore all that could be expected by the French patriots from the British government; and, while they suspected the views of the English monarch, they confided in the apparent moderation of the minister.

In the mean time the diffusion of revolutionary principles among the people of Great Britain, was rapid and general. In the metropolis, besides individuals of genius and learning, well affected to the French revolution, there was a numerous class of adventurers in politics and literature, who espoused and circulated its principles. If learning be not more profound in the present than in former ages, it is certainly spread over a wider surface. The commercial opulence of the country encourages the sale and manufacture of literary commodities of every value and denomination. The demand extending to a vast variety of productions which require neither profound learning nor vigorous genius, the number of authors multiplies in proportion to the moderate qualifications that are necessary. All these down to translators of German novels, and collectors of paragraphs for the daily papers, deemed themselves persons of genius and erudition and members of the republic o. letters. In France the influence of literary men was great and extensive, and many of this class in England conceived that if the same system were established here, they might rise to the same distinction in the new order of things. There were in the literary, as in other classes, persons, who, deluded by the benevolence of their enthusiasm, exulted in the prospect that vice and misery would be extirpated by the influence of the French constitution, and by the diffusion of the principles on which it was established. Among the most conspicuous advocates of the revolution were the worshippers of sensibility, who regarded the restraints of religion, morality, and political regulation, as harsh, tyrannical, and absurd, because they frequently contradicted the impulse of sentimental feeling. In this class were to be ranked several female votaries of literature, and at their head Mary Anne Wollstonecraft, who produced as a counterpart to Paine's *Rights of Man*, a performance entitled the Rights of Woman ; vindicating the exemption of the sex from every moral and decorous restriction, and claiming the free and full indulgence of every gratification which fancy could suggest or passion stimulate. Besides these classes there was a great and multiplying variety of clubs, to which resorted many mechanics, tradesmen, and others, from a desire extremely prevalent among the English, of distinguishing themselves as *spokesmen*. After hearing or delivering speeches and reading pamphlets, they assumed the importance of politicians and philosophers, and hastened in consequence of their recent discoveries, to abandon the prejudices of education, and to sacrifice religion, patriotism, and loyalty, at the shrine of vanity. From so many causes and through so many agents, the revolutionary doctrines were widely disseminated. To facilitate the circulation of their opinions, the opulent votaries of acobinism, published cheap editions of the most inflammatory works, and more particularly of the *Rights of Man.* The seditious proceedings of several

societies and individuals were carried to such an extent, that his majesty was induced before the prorogation of parliament, to issue a proclamation, solemnly warning his subjects against all such attempts as aimed at the subversion of good government, and were inconsistent with the peace and good order of society. The French convention had notoriously endeavoured to cherish in this kingdom a spirit of sedition by its correspondence with societies which were known to be inimical to the established government. It had insulted Great Britain by declaring its design and its right to open the Scheldt, in opposition to treaties of which the crown of England was a guarantee. On the 19th of November, when its arms had been successful in the Netherlands, in the exultation inspired by success, it had issued a decree, declaring that the convention would "grant fraternity and assistance to all those people who wish to procure liberty ;" and charging their generals " to give assistance to such people, and to defend such citizens, as have suffered or are now suffering in the cause of liberty." The general term, liberty, being applicable to every mode of free government, the manifesto might have been understood as addressed to the subjects of despotic states, had not such a conclusion been contradicted by the late violent proceedings in France, the declaration of many members of the convention, and the general tenor of its conduct, which had an evident tendency to the subversion of all established governments. Its unprovoked violence towards the pope in the seizure of Avignon without a pretext, sufficiently proved, that, notwithstanding its pacific professions, the interests of the republic would be the sole standard of its policy. It was not necessary, however, for Great Britain to justify her future proceedings by asserting the commission of injury or of insult towards herself, or by alledging the legitimacy of the motives by which the continental powers were actuated in their hostile demonstrations against France. Under whatever pretences or circumstances the war between France and the most formidable of the combined powers commenced, it was obviously the interest of Britain to make a common cause with the opponents of an enemy whose views were evidently hostile, and to become a participator in the contest, while exertion and union might yet be effectual. Whatever might be the disasters, the misfortunes, and the errors of the continental powers, it cannot be doubted that their alliance with England mitigated their distresses, and relieved their misfortunes, while it counteracted the triumphs and impeded the progress of the enemy. Had we persevered in the defensive system recommended by superficial politicians, we should first have witnessed the downfall of Austria and Prussia, and have been compelled to struggle single-handed, with the violence and the augmented power of an inveterate and triumphant enemy.

I have hitherto only considered the *expedience* of a war with France : in forming our opinions respecting the *justice* of our cause, we shall be assisted by reflecting on some events and transactions which preceded the commencement of the war. In proof of the pacific disposition of the British government before it had experienced extreme provocation from that of France, we may adduce the words of the emperor Leopold to the marquis de Bouillé, after the conferences at Pilnitz. Speaking of the invitation given to Spain, Russia, England, and the principal cities of Italy, to unite with him and the king of Prussia, he said, " I am assured of the co-operation of all these powers with the exception of England, which is resolved to preserve the most strict neutrality." As a further testimony of the same disposition, his majesty so lately as the beginning of the current year, in his address to the two houses of parliament, proposed a reduction of the naval and military establishments. A yet stronger proof that the English government had not by any overt act discovered an hostile disposition towards France, till after the dreadful events of the 10th of August, is found in the words of Brissot himself, who acknowledged " that England had observed the most strict neutrality till that *immortal day*." The national convention itself

admitted that England had persevered in this line of conduct till the beginning of the present year.

Great Britain had indeed more than negative merit to plead in its conduct towards France. It had the merit of displaying the most generous friendship in return for the injuries she had so frequently received. When the negroes of St. Domingo were in a state of insurrection, when Blanchelande the governor, was in a state of extreme distress, and the planters would gladly have passed into the hands of the English to save them from impending ruin, lord Effingham, governor of Jamaica, in compliance with Blanchelande's request, immediately dispatched two frigates to their relief, laden with necessaries and provisions. The words with which the president closed his address of thanks are deserving of notice. " We will avail ourselves of your benevolence, but the days you preserve to us will not be sufficient to manifest our gratitude ; our children shall keep it in remembrance. Regenerated France, unapprised that such calamities might befal us, has taken no measures to protect us against their effects. With what admiration will she learn, that, without your assistance, we should no longer exist as a dependency to any nation." That France, though regenerated, had not yet learned to be grateful, appeared from her behaviour on this occasion. For when the British ambassador at Paris, in the month of November, 1791, as a testimony of his sovereign's amity, notified his approbation of lord Effingham's conduct, a motion was coldly passed in the National Assembly, that its thanks should be given neither to the British government nor to the government of Jamaica, but to the *British nation*." Nor was this the only testimony of amity shewn by the crown of England to regenerated France. When Lewis in the late autumn, wrote letters to the different courts of Europe, intimating his acceptance of the new constitution, his Britannic majesty immediately returned an answer in terms of great respect. When Chauvelin notified the French declaration of war against the king of Hungary and Bohemia, and demanded that conformably with the treaty of 1786, his majesty should prohibit his subjects from committing hostilities against the French ships, he instantly complied by issuing a declaration to that effect; and so well satisfied was the French government with this conduct on the part of Great-Britain, that Chauvelin was instructed to assure his majesty of " the sense which the French king entertained of the friendly dispositions, and of the sentiments of humanity, of justice, and of peace, which are so clearly manifested in his answer."

It may be fairly deduced from the transactions of the convention, and from the language of its leading members, that they regarded the commencement of hostilities as necessary to the success of their ambitious designs. So early as the close of the year 1791, Brissot declared in the assembly that war was a real benefit to the nation, and that the only evil which they had reason to dread was the absence of war. A few days after, Isnard announced to the assembly that war was about to be kindled—" war which is indispensible to the completion of the revolution." "Peace" exclaimed Roland, "is out of the question. We have 300,000 men in arms; we must make them march as far as their legs will carry them, or they will return and cut our throats." But it was not merely war on which they were so resolutely bent; it was war with royalty, the destruction of which the Jacobin party contemplated as the first object of their ambition. "It was," said Brissot, "the abolition of royalty which I had in view, when I provoked the declaration of war."—Let it be remembered that these declarations were unaccompanied by any offers of accomodation with the other continental powers; that the object specified is not the defence of their own territory or their own security, but the overthrow of every existing monarchy, and arbitrary interference with the rights and condition of every contemporary people. That the republican partizans were influenced by designs of hostility against Great Britain in particular, long before that crown had offended them by the recal of its ambassador: immediately after our

friendly offices in the West Indies, and while Great Britain was reducing her naval and military establishments, is proved by the report of Lameth de- M_{ARCH} 18, 1792. livered to the National Assembly in the name of the committee for naval affairs, importing that " about 80,000 sailors would be necessary to man the vessels now at the disposition of the state, and which the honour of the nation as well as the interests of its commerce did not permit the assembly to reduce." A subsequent report of the minister of marine expressly declares, that so early as September 22nd, 21 ships of the line, 30 frigates, 10 vessels armed en flute, and 42 smaller vessels of war, were actually at sea; and that 34 ships of the line in addition to these were in a state to be commissioned, that 19 more were capable of being refitted, and that 7 were rebuilding: preparations which could only be designed against the two maratime powers, England, and Holland her ally.

The hostility of the government of France to that of England was still further exemplified, in the friendly intercourse subsisting between the republican partizans in France, and the malcontent societies of Great Britain. The addresses of the latter were received after the tenth of August by the convention itself, and every possible encouragement was given the addressers to rebel against the government. " What is liberty? Where are our rights?" said an address from the united English societies. " Frenchmen, you are already free, and Englishmen are preparing to become so." To which the president of the convention replied, " Citizens of the world! principles are waging war against tyranny, which will fall under the blows of philosophy. Royalty in Europe is destroyed, or is perishing on the ruins of feudality; and the declaration of rights placed by the side of thrones is a devouring fire which will consume them. Worthy republicans, congratulate yourselves on thinking that the festival you have celebrated in honour of the French revolution is the prelude to the festival of nations." Even Dumouriez himself, confesses that it required all the imprudence of Brissot, all the petulance of the national convention, and the murder of Lewis XVI. as atrocious as impolitic to drive the English from their system of neutrality, and to plunge them into an expensive war, which gave them momentary advantages, balanced by great losses and enormous subsidies, without an assurance of preserving their conquests." But the danger to be apprehended from the diffusion of French principles and from the rapidity of their military progress ; the influence of just indignation against open insult and secret machination ; and the obvious necessity of combining vigorous precaution with every demonstration of anxiety for the continuance of peace, at length induced the king of England to embody his militia, and to augment his naval and military forces. He assembled the parliament on the 13th of December, 1792, and addressed them in a speech explanatory of the measures he had adopted. He observed that, notwithstanding the strict neutrality which he had uniformly observed in the war now raging on the continent, he could not, without concern, observe the strong indications of an intention, on the part of the French, to excite disturbances in other countries ; to pursue views of conquest and aggrandisement, inconsistent with the balance of Europe ; to disregard the rights of neutral powers, and to adopt towards his allies, the states-general, measures neither conformable to the public law, nor to the positive articles of existing treaties. He had therefore found it necessary to make some augmentation of his army and navy : these exertions were demanded by the present state of affairs, to maintain internal tranquillity, and render a firm but temperate conduct effectual for preserving the blessings of peace.

While so many important objects divided the attention of the British government, the war in India attracted a considerable share of the public interest. The peace of Mangalore endured no longer than the weakness of Tippoo Saib continued. Inheriting the views and passions of his father, he sought the empire of India, and as a step to its attainment, the expulsion of the English, his most powerful rivals. For several years he had been collecting and disciplining large armies, and, though hopeless of assistance from France or the native powers, was not afraid singly to provoke England to war. Lord Cornwallis being sent out to India in the spring of 1786, with the double appointment of governor-general and commander-in-chief, arrived in September at Calcutta, and found the different presidencies in a state of rising prosperity. He availed himself with moderation, firmness, and temper, of the best arrangements of his predecessors, and introduced several new regulations that contributed still further to the public welfare, and to the security and happiness of the natives. In Madras and Bombay affairs were proportionally flourishing, and the British presidencies were secured by a powerful military force. The Nizam and the Mahrattas, as well as less considerable powers in the southern parts of the Peninsula, were in alliance with the English. Such was the state of India when Tippoo Saib commenced hostilities by attacking our ally, the Rajah of Travancore, to whom the English had guaranteed the possession of his dominions. Early in the year 1790 some attempts were made by the government of Madras, to effect an accomodation between Tippoo and the Rajah, but they were attended with the ill success which might reasonably be expected from the duplicity and faithlessness of the sultan's character : and the council of Bengal found it necessary to issue against him a declaration of war. In June, general Meadows, from the Carnatic, invaded Tippoo's dominions, while general Abercrombie from the west, having conquered Cananore, advanced towards Seringapatam. Tippoo, with masterly skill, eluded all the efforts of Meadows, to bring him to battle, and after a long and tiresome succession of marches and counter-marches, the English general was obliged, by the rainy season, to return to Madras. Nor were the exertions of Abercrombie, after the reduction of Cananore, during the first campaign, attended with any decisive effects. Though the campaign in all its operations very honourably displayed the valor and conduct of the British, it did not answer expectation, and lord Cornwallis found it expedient to take the field in person in the course of the following year. In March 1791, he proceeded to Mysore by the eastern Gauts, and having surmounted the passes, attacked Bangalore, the second city of the Mysorean empire. Tippoo marched to its relief, and for an object so important, ventured a pitched battle. He was defeated, and the town taken by storm. Lord Cornwallis now proceeded towards the capital of Mysore, whither Abercrombie was advancing with the western army. In the month of May he arrived in the neighbourhood of Seringapatam, where he found Tippoo very strongly posted, and protected in front and flank by swamps and mountains. Not deterred by these difficulties, the British general attacked the enemy, and though the Mysoreans made a gallant resistance, entirely defeated them, and compelled them to seek shelter under the guns of the capital. The sun was about to set when the victorious English, pursuing the enemy, first beheld the city of Seringapatam, rising upon an island in all the splendor of eastern magnificence, decorated with sumptuous buildings, encircled by beautiful and extensive gardens, and defended by strong and extensive fortifications. The grand object of their pursuit now appeared to the English within their immediate grasp, but unexpected disasters obstructed its attainment. They had experienced the inclemency of the weather, and the season of the year led them to expect its continuance. They had occasion for a covering army, not only to facilitate the means of procuring a regular supply of provisions, but to protect the besiegers. When lord Cornwallis set out on this expedition, he had trusted to the co-operation of the Mahrattas, but was disappointed. Continuing to expect the arrival of general Abercrombie, he marched up the Cavery to secure and facilitate the advance of the western army; but the unexpected swelling of the river rendered the junction of the two armies impracticable. The troops from Bombay

reluctantly yielding to necessity, departed for the western coast, exposed to all the fury of the monsoon, which was then raging on the Malabar side of the mountains. Cornwallis having halted some days to cover the retreat of the other army, deemed it expedient to defer the siege of Seringapatam till the following campaign, and spent the remainder of the season in reducing the interjacent country and forts, securing communication with the allies, preparing plentiful supplies of provision, and making other dispositions for commencing the investment as soon as the monsoon should be over. The most difficult and important acquisitions during the remainder of the campaign were Nundydroog, the capital of a rich district, and Savendroog, or the Rock of Death, a fortress which commanded a great part of the country between Bangalore and Seringapatam.

Early in 1792 the Nizam and the Mahrattas joined the British army, now on its march, and on the 5th of February the British troops, the auxiliary Nizamates, and the Mahrattas who still remained with him, moved under Cornwallis to Seringapatam. Every attempt to convey just ideas of the several bodies which composed this huge mass must fall miserably short of the original. Regular columns of infantry ready to act on the appearance of an enemy, extended (to use the words of captain Mackenzie) along the front and left flank, wherever danger was to be apprehended. The train and heavy carriages of every description, moved on better ground to the right of the infantry, in general at the distance of 100 yards. Stores, suttling vehicles, and private carriages of various kinds, advanced on a third road to the right of the other two, and elephants, camels, buffaloes, bullocks, and asses, with myriads of followers that defy description, kept pace with these lines on the baggage flank. In the rear and to the right were large bodies of horse from the army of Nizam Ally, connected with powerful divisions from Hurry Punt. These in their turn, co-operating with the cavalry of colonel Floyd, extended to the infantry in front. One immense chain of cavalry and infantry embracing the whole mass, afforded complete protection to the several component parts. From this moving world swarms of irregular horse branched out in every direction as far as the eye could reach. The capital of Mysore, besides the natural strength which it derived from its insular situation in the Cavery, was secured by batteries placed along the banks of that river. The position which Tippoo had taken for its defence on its north side was fortified by six well-constructed redoubts, and was guarded by the river Lockani, which covered part of his front, and by ravines and marshy ground in other quarters.

The commander-in-chief having encamped within eight miles of the island, formed his British forces into three divisions: the centre, commanded under himself by Stuart, the right by Meadows, and the left by Maxwell. The artillery corps was commanded by Montague, and the defence of the camp was committed to Duff. They moved from the camp in the dusk of the evening, a full moon affording them light, and the stillness of night adding to the solemnity of the scene.

Maxwell's division began its operations before midnight by an assault on one of the enemy's redoubts. It was guarded by a double breast-work; but the assailants bore down all resistance, and, driving the enemy before them, they entered the sultan's lines, and formed a junction with the centre division. The successive assaults were furious and attended with prodigious slaughter, and besides those who perished by the sword, multitudes were driven into the Cavery. A body of troops under Stuart, Maxwell, Knox, and Baird, fording the river, made a lodgment on the island; and the sultan, when light returned, had the mortification of beholding the grounds adjacent to his capital, and a great part of the island of Seringapatam, in possession of his enemy.

The enemy having quitted every post on the north side of the river, the camp was advanced on the succeeding days as near to the bound hedge as the guns of the fort would permit, and a chain of posts connecting along the northern and eastern faces of the fort, were formed, so as strongly to invest the capital of Mysore on its two principal sides.

Thus pressed by the invaders in every quarter; his palace and beautiful gardens in the possession of the enemy, and his whole power reduced within the narrow limits of a citadel, the possession of which was even uncertain, the hitherto unsubdued spirit of the sultan seems to have given way with his tottering fortunes; and peace, almost upon any terms, appeared a desirable acquisition. As a preliminary step towards an accommodation, he determined to release lieutenants Chalmers and Nash, who had been captured at Coimbettore. On the evening of the 8th of February these officers were introduced into the sultan's presence. They found him in a small tent on the south glacis of the fort, very plainly dressed, and with few attendants. After acquainting them with their release, he asked Mr. Chalmers, if on going to the camp he was likely to see lord Cornwallis; and on being answered in the affirmative, he requested that he would take charge of a letter to his lordship on the subject of peace. He affirmed solemnly that it never had been his wish or intention to break with the English; that from the first commencement of hostilities he had been extremely anxious for the restoration of peace. He expressed a wish that Mr. Chalmers would return with the answer; and concluded, by presenting him with two shawls and 500 rupees. Lieutenants Chalmers and Nash had been remarkably well treated while detained by Tippoo.

While the sultan was thus anxiously endeavouring to restore tranquillity to his exhausted country, his mind was still fertile in the expedients and stratagems of war. By one master-stroke of policy, that of capturing the commander-in-chief, he hoped to effect his purpose in a shorter and more honourable mode than by the slow and precarious method of negotiation. On the 8th and 9th of February, small parties of his cavalry were observed to cross the Cavery at the ford near Arrakerry (the station which lord Cornwallis had occupied in the preceding campaign;) and on the morning of the 10th a considerable body of them got round the left wing undiscovered, and entered between the British camp and that of the Nizam. The allies, not suspecting these horsemen to be enemies, suffered them to pass on quietly; and on their asking some of the camp-followers for the Burra Saib, or commander, these persons, supposing that the horsemen only wished to communicate some intelligence to colonel Duff, the commanding officer of artillery, pointed to his tent. The horsemen then drew their sabres and galloped to the tent, but being fortunately perceived by a party of seapoy drafts and recruits, who were encamped in the rear of the artillery park, and who formed with singular alacrity, and faced the enemy with undaunted firmness, they were soon dispersed, and the attempt proved abortive.

On the 16th of February the Bombay army under general Abercrombie, after a fatiguing march, and after having been in some degree harassed by detached parties of the enemy during their progress, joined lord Cornwallis, and afforded a reinforcement of about 2,000 Europeans, and 4,000 native troops fit for duty. Preparations therefore were vigorously made on the 18th, for the attack of the fort, not on the island side, which was deemed the strongest, but on the quarter facing the north, which appeared to lord Cornwallis most assailable; and trenches were immediately ordered to be opened, and batteries to be constructed with all expedition on that side.

As it was proper, however, to draw off the attention of the enemy as much as possible from these operations, on the 19th a diversion was ordered to be made from the island, and an assault was projected on the enemy's cavalry, which was encamped on the south side of the river.

Major Dalrymple and captain Robertson, with the 71st regiment and the 13th battalion of Bengal seapoys, were sent upon this enterprise. Captain Robertson with a party entered the camp undiscovered, and with the bayonet killed upward of 100 troopers, and double that number of horses,

and retired without molestation, and without the loss of a man.

While this affair was transacting, a much more important operation was carried on during the night of the 19th, a parallel and redoubt having been completed within a small distance of the walls of the fort, from which it was only separated by the river. Day-light revealed to the sultan these formidable arrangements; and he lost no time in endeavouring to defeat their effect. He opened every gun he could bring to bear on the parallel, and sent continual parties of infantry to harass the troops and interrupt the work. Finding these exertions to be in vain, Tippoo next endeavoured to deprive the camp of its supply of water, by altering the course and evacuating a large canal, from which it had been hitherto supplied: to counteract this injurious operation therefore, a party was detached under the command of captain Wahab, with pioneers to repair the embankment. They soon dislodged the enemy from their station, and as they had not been able to destroy much of the embankment, the damage was presently repaired, and the water restored to its accustomed channel.

On the 19th, the grand operation of the siege commenced by the opening of the trenches, and a heavy discharge from all the batteries; in the mean time, the Bombay army crossed the river in order to invest the western side of the capital. Some little resistance was made to general Abercrombie's establishing himself on that side of the river; but towards evening the party which opposed him was dispersed. General Abercrombie's force on the south side of the river consisted of three regiments of Europeans, and six battalions of seapoys. His camp, strongly situated on the heights, was pitched just beyond the gunshot of the fort.

In consequence of the application through lieutenant Chalmers, lord Cornwallis agreed to receive vakeels or convoys to treat of peace. On the 15th, 16th, 19th, and 21st, sir John Kennaway and Mr. Cherry, assisted by vakeels from the Nizam's sou and Harry Punt, the Mahratta chief, met the agents of the sultan, but apparently little progress was made in the negotiation.

The siege still continued without intermission, and on the 22nd, general Abercrombie conceiving it necessary to take possession of an evacuated redoubt and a grove, situated between his camp and the fort, the possession was warmly disputed by a detachinent, chiefly consisting of dismounted cavalry ; and though the British were in the end victorious, it was not till after the loss of 104 men killed and wounded.

During the nights of the 22nd and 23rd of February, new works were erected ; and two breaching batteries, one of 20 and the other of 12 guns, would have been ready to open on the 1st of March. The Mahratta army commanded by Purseram Bhow, and consisting of 20,000 horse, a body of several thousand infantry, and 30 pieces of cannon, was expected daily to join, as well as major Cuppage from the Coimbettore country, with 400 Europeans and three battalions of seapoys. In the mean time, Tippoo had been compelled to send off all his cavalry, as well as his workmen and camp followers, to Mysore. The British army was well supplied with every necessary, and that of the sultan in want of every thing.

In this hopeless situation the monarch of Mysore was compelled to accept of whatever terms were offered by the British commander. Lord Cornwallis in this instance is supposed to have been actuated by motives of policy, rather than by any doubt of success in capitulating with Tippoo. The best informed persons on the politics of India, have been averse to the annihilation of the Mysorean power ; and it is generally supposed that the governor-general rather wished it to be humbled than destroyed. However this may be, preliminaries of peace were signed on the evening of the 23rd of February, and on the following day there was an entire cessation of hostilities. The substance of the treaty was—

1st, That Tippoo was to cede one half of his dominions to the allied powers. 2nd, That he was to pay three crores and 30 lacks of rupees. 3rd, That all prisoners were to be restored. 4th, That two of the sultan's three eldest sons were to become hostages for the due performance of the treaty.

On the 26th the two princes, each mounted on an elephant, richly caparisoned, proceeded from the fort to lord Cornwallis's camp, where they were received by his lordship with his staff. The eldest, Abdul Kalick, was about ten, the youngest, Mooza-ud-Deen, about eight years of age. The princes were dressed in long white muslin gowns, with red turbans richly adorned with pearls. Educated from infancy with the utmost care, the spectators were astonished to behold in these children all the reserve, the politeness and attention of maturer years. The kindness with which they were received by the British commander appeared to afford them visible satisfaction. Some presents were exchanged on both sides ; and the scene is described by an eye-witness as highly interesting.

It was the 19th of March before the definitive treaty was finally adjusted. The allies were exorbitant in their demands, and Tippoo and his courtiers appear to have exerted their utmost abilities, in artfully endeavouring to gain time and to mitigate the terms of submission. Tippoo however at length gave a reluctant consent to 'the terms prescribed by lord Cornwallis ; and the definitive treaty was delivered by the young princes with great solemnity into the hands of his lordship and the allies.

Such was the termination of a war that must be considered as the most beneficial, and the most glorious of any which the English company or government had waged in India. By the terms of peace the Mysorean monarch was punished for his injustice and his violation of the public peace ; he was deprived of the ascendency which had enabled him to tyrannize over the powers of Hindostan, which might at some future period have enabled him to confederate with France for the purpose of expelling the English from the Peninsula ;

Pub by T. Kinnersly May 12, 1812.

Lord Cornwallis receiving the Sons of Tippoo Saib.

and the balance of Indian power was re-established and secured.

At the commencement of the present year the hostile demonstrations of Gustavus Adolphus, in concert with the marquis de Bouille, and in favour of the king of France, awakened the discontent of his people, and commanded the interest of the other states of Europe. He was preparing for his enterprise regardless of the evils arising from an arbitrary and ill-digested government, when the kingdom was saved from the embarrassments incident on war, by the commission of an act which spread throughout his kingdom the utmost terror and consternation. A conspiracy was formed against him by a number of individuals who agreed to murder him amidst the confusion of a masked ball. Lilien Horn, one of the conspirators, stung with remorse, and desirous to save his sovereign's life without betraying his accomplices, advised him by a note not to attend the entertainment, where the bloody deed was to be perpetrated : and some of his majesty's confidential friends warmly recommended an attention to this friendly admonition. But he affected to regard it with contempt, and to consider it as an insult to his courage to attempt to deter him from enjoying his evening's entertainment. It was late before he entered the ball-room ; but after some time he sat down in a box with count de Essen, and observed that he was not deceived in his contempt of the letter, since had there been any design against his life, no time could be more propitious than that moment. He then mingled, without apprehension, among the crowd, and, just as he was preparing to retire, in company with the Prussian ambassador, he was surrounded by several persons in masks, one of whom fixed a pistol at the back of the king, and lodged the contents in his body. A scene of dreadful confusion immediately ensued. The conspirators, amidst the general tumult and alarm, had time to retire to other parts of the room, but one of them had previously dropt his pistols and a dagger at the feet of the wounded king. A general order was given for all the company.

to unmask, and the doors were immediately closed, but no person appeared with any particular marks of guilt. The king was immediately conveyed to his apartment, and the surgeon, after extracting a ball and some slugs, gave favourable hopes of his majesty's recovery. He languished from the 17th to the 29th of March. On the 28th, a mortification was found to have taken place, which terminated his existence in a few hours. On opening his body, a square piece of lead and two rusty nails, were found unextracted within the ribs. In the last awful scene of his life, the king displayed the cool intrepidity which had distinguished his character in every preceding part of it. Being apprized by his own feelings that his death was certain, he prepared for it with manly fortitude : and his son being a minor, he committed the regency of the kingdom to his brother, the duke of Sudermania. Gustavus Adolphus II. was only thirteen years of age when he ascended the throne ; and it may be esteemed one of the happiest circumstances attending the Swedish state and nation at this eventful period, that the reins of government were committed to a prince, who, with the accomplishments of a soldier, and an enlightened and vigorous understanding, was enabled to perceive the errors of his brother's policy, and was induced by his prudence, to preserve to the nation over which he presided, the blessings of peace. The first object of the regent was to investigate and punish the assassination of his brother. Suspicion immediately fell on such of the nobles as had been notorious for their opposition to the court. An order was issued directing all the armourers, gunsmiths, and cutlers in Stockholm, to give every information in their power to the officers of justice, respecting the weapons left behind by the assassins. A gunsmith who had repaired the pistols, readily recognized them to be the same which he had repaired for a nobleman of the name of Ankerstrom, a captain in the army ; and the cutler who had made the dagger, referred, without hesitation, to the same individual. Having confessed his crime, Ankerstrom was tried, condemned to die, and executed. Baron Beilke, the king's private secretary, was arrested on suspicion, but had evaded the vengeance of the law by swallowing poison; and two other accomplices were sentenced to share the fate of the principal assassin. The regent, however, in order to impress the public with a conviction of his clemency, or to sooth the passions of the conspirators, who were powerfully supported, commuted their expected punishment for that of exile.

The kingdom of Poland was at this period destined to fall a sacrifice to the ambition and injustice of the empress Catharine. On the 21st of April the diet received the first notification from the king, of the inimical and unjust intentions of Russia. He informed them, that without the shadow of pretence, this avowed enemy of the rights of mankind had determined to invade the territory of the republic with an army of 60,000 men. This formidable banditti, commanded by generals Soltikof, Michelson, and Kosakofski, was afterward to be supported by corps amounting to 20,000 men, and by the troops then acting in Moldavia, amounting to 70,000. The diet and nation arose as one man to assert their independence. All private animosities were obliterated; all private interests were sacrificed. The spirit manifested by the nobles was truly honourable. Some of them delivered their plate to the mint. Prince Radzvil engaged voluntarily to furnish 10,000 stand of arms, and a train of artillery. Prince Poniatofsky, nephew to the king, was appointed commander-in-chief; and, notwithstanding the great inferiority of his force, made a noble stand. On the 24th of May, the enemy's cossacks were repulsed, and pursued by the public patroles to their entrenchments. On the 26th the picquets discovered a large body of Don cossacks approaching the outposts, and a squadron of cavalry, commanded by lieutenant Kwasniefski, supported by lieutenant Golejofski, with two squadrons more, in all about 300, marched out to

meet them. They attacked the cossacks with success, but pursued them with more valour than prudence, to the side of a wood, where they found themselves drawn into an ambuscade and surrounded by 2000 horse, two battalions of chasseurs, and six pieces of cannon. The intrepid Poles bravely fought their way through the Russian line, and killed upwards of 200 of the enemy. The Poles in this engagement lost 100 men and two officers, one of whom, lieutenant Kwasniefski, was wounded and made prisoner. The remainder of the detachment reached their quarters in safety.

Perhaps the history of man, previous to the atrocities of Buonaparte, can scarcely furnish an instance of perfidy, meanness, and duplicity, more flagrant, than the conduct of the king of Prussia on this occasion. By the treaty of defensive alliance solemnly contracted between the republic of Poland and the king of Prussia, and ratified on the 23rd of April, 1790, it was expressly stipulated, "That the contracting parties shall do all in their power to guarantee and preserve to each other reciprocally, the whole of the territories which they respectively possess: that in case of menace or invasion from any foreign power, they shall assist each other with their whole force if necessary: and that if any foreign power, on any pretence whatever, shall presume to interfere in the internal affairs of Poland, his Prussian majesty shall consider this as a case falling within the meaning of the alliance, and shall assist the republic." Yet on the application of the Poles to the court of Berlin, for the succours thus solemnly stipulated, they received for answer, "That the treaty was dated previous to the new constitution; and that constitution, establishing a new order of things, his Prussian majesty held himself absolved from his engagement." Of such value are treaties in the eyes of despotic monarchs. The enormity of the king of Prussia's conduct was aggravated by the circumstances that many of the obnoxious acts of which the empress complained in her declaration against the Poles, were done by the influence and advice of Prussia : that when the constitution was proposed, the king of Prussia never gave the smallest intimation that the new order of things would dissolve the alliance ; and that on the 17th of May, 1791, M. Goltz chargé d'Affaires, from the court of Berlin, formally announced his sovereign's approbation of the new arrangement.

The duchy of Lithuania was the great scene of action at the beginning of the war, but the Russians had made little progress till the middle of the month of June. The army of Poniatofski distinguished itself by the most heroic feats of valour, skill, and intrepidity. After several conflicts between detachments in which the Poles displayed their courage, without obtaining any decided advantage, the two armies approached each other near Zielimc. A pitched battle ensued, in which, after a conflict of ten hours, victory at last declared for the patriots : the Russians leaving 4000 men dead upon the field.

Notwithstanding this advantage, the Poles were compelled to retire before the numerous and disciplined armies of their invaders. Nieffez, Wilna, Minsk, and several other places of less consequence, fell into their hands one after the other. On a truce being proposed to the Russian general Kochofski, the proposal was haughtily rejected, while the desertion of brigadier Rudnicki, and several others who preferred dishonour to personal danger, proclaimed a tottering cause.

This unequal contest was prematurely terminated. The king, whose benevolent intentions were overpowered by his mental imbecility, and whose age and infirmities rendered him unequal to the difficulties and dangers which attend a protracted war, instead of appearing according to his first resolve at the head of his army, determined to surrender at discretion. Deceived by the friendly professions of Catharine, he mispent the precious moments in fruitless negotiations which ought to have been employed in unremitted and vigorous resistance. He called a meeting of the different provinces, in order to deliberate on the measures to be adopted, and obtained a decree that his subjects should lay down their arms. Yet the whole of the Polish nobles did not acquiesce in the surrender of their country's rights and independence. Count Malachouski, and the princes Radzivil and Sapieha, placed their names at the head of a protest against the proceedings of he confederation, and were rewarded by the attachment of their countrymen, and the benevolent support of the people of England, who had already transmitted considerable sums intended to assist the struggle of the Poles for independence, and were afterwards equally liberal in relieving their misfortunes. It cannot be doubted that the example presented by Russia to the other powers of Europe, materially contributed to many future acts of oppression and atrocity. The growing happiness of a respectable nation had been sacrificed to the personal ambition of three despotic sovereigns : the citizens of a free republic were reduced to the most abject subjection; and the balance of power so necessary to the permanent welfare of Europe, was sacrificed to private and selfish views ; while the nations, who on former occasions had devoted to its preservation millions of lives, and enormous treasures, viewed with frigid tranquillity, the violation of every acknowledged principle of the law of nations, and the triumph and fatal increase of despotic authority.

HISTORY OF THE WAR.

CHAP. IV.

THE apprehensions excited in the city of Paris by the capture of Longwy and Verdun, were increased by a report which had been industriously circulated, that a rapid march of a few hours would bring the duke of Brunswick to the vicinity of Paris. Alarm and melancholy were painted in every countenance, when the minister of justice, M. Danton, proposed a measure which revived the courage of the people, and converted despair into presumption. He declared that there could not be less than 80,000 stand of arms in the metropolis, in the possession of private individuals, with which he proposed to equip an army of volunteers, not merely to protect Paris from any sudden assault, but to march against the enemy on the shortest notice, and intercept their progress. His plan was enthusiastically adopted; and a decree of the assembly ordered all citizens to keep themselves in readiness for the worst that could happen, if they were not disqualified by bodily distress or the infirmities of age. To render the measure still more efficacious, it was ordered that no person should be permitted to appear in arms who was suspected of enmity to the republican interest.

Robespierre was a member of the first constituent assembly; for which reason, in consequence of their rash and voluntary act, he could not be admitted as a member of the second, but he had filled the office of public accuser with indefatigable diligence and attention. He had acquired so complete an ascendency over the Jacobins by the violence of his principles, and the sanguinary ferocity of his temper, that he became their ostensible leader. He and the infamous journalist Marat, were in habits of the strictest intimacy with the minister of justice. The duplicity of Petion, uncertain to which party he should devote his unlimited services, diminished his popularity, and in proportion as his reputation began to decline that of Robespierre continued to increase. Of a fiery temper and destitute of erudition, his eloquence was of that species which captivated the vulgar, because it never soared above their comprehension, and inculcated nothing but what perfectly accorded with their sentiments. In the Jacobin club he had been unremittingly clamorous for the trial of the state prisoners, and by his endeavours to satiate the barbarous revenge of the populace he gained their affections.

Whether from a concerted plan to produce a general massacre, or with a view to excite the ardor of the people in defence of the country, the measures pursued by the commune of Paris on the 2nd of September, were pregnant with danger to the tranquillity of the city. Instead of directing the enrolment of volunteers to

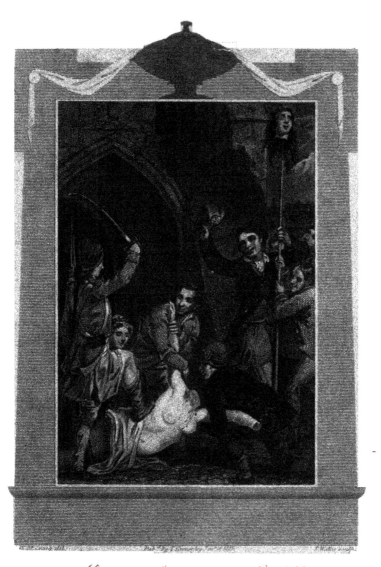

Murder of the Princess de Lamballe

be made in their respective section with order and quietness, they commanded the alarm guns to be fired at two o'clock ; the country was declared to be in danger, and the people were invited to assemble in the *Champs de Mars*, from whence it was announced that they were immediately to march against the common enemy. The people accordingly assembled, not to defend their country, but to embrue their hands in the blood of their countrymen. This, at least, was the intention of calling them together ; but instead of going to the *Champs de Mars*, as was intended, they went to their respective districts and had their names enrolled. Multitudes, however, were easily collected, who made no scruple to perpetrate the most horrid enormities. When Danton, the minister of justice, was applied to, that his authority might put an effectual stop to these atrocities, he made this shameful reply, "When the people have done their part, I will perform mine." In conformity with the declaration of the minister, numbers were heard to declare, that they were ready to devote themselves to the service of their country, and to march against their foreign enemies, but they must first purge themselves of their domestic foes. Under the influence of this sanguinary disposition, they repaired to the monastery of Carmelites, where they found that a number of nonjuring clergymen were confined till a favourable opportunity should occur for their transportation beyond the sea. These unhappy men were sacrificed in cold blood, and the pleas of innocence and of age were of no avail. From the Carmelites they proceeded to the Abbey prison, in which were confined the Swiss officers, and those arrested for treasonable offences against the French nation on the 10th of August. The murderers proceeded in their crimes with an appearance of method. They impannelled a jury, of whom nine were Italian assassins, and three were Frenchmen of obscure or disreputable character. Before these self-constituted judges the wretched prisoners underwent a summary examination. The watchword that pronounced the prisoner guilty was, "*Il faut*

le largir," " he must be set at liberty ," when the victim was precipitated from the door, to pass through a defile of miscreants variously armed, and was cut to pieces with sabres, or pierced through with innumerable pikes. A few they acquitted, and these were declared under the protection of the nation, and accompanied to their respective homes by some of the banditti. The assassins continued the whole night of the 2nd at the abbey and the prison of the Chatelet, whence they proceeded to the prison of La Force, where the ladies of the court, arrested on the 10th of August, had been confined. Among these was the princess de Lamballe, the confidant of the queen, a woman of exquisite beauty and varied accomplishments. When summoned to appear before this self-constituted tribunal, she was indulging herself in that repose which her melancholy situation too often denied her. She was informed by the person who delivered the message, that it was only intended to remove her to the abbey. She begged, in return, to remain undisturbed, since to her one prison was as acceptable as another. Being informed that she must immediately appear before the tribunal, she dressed in haste and obeyed the summons. During her examination, she was strongly urged to bring forward some accusation against the royal family ; and it is believed that even her sanguinary judges intended to acquit her. She fell a victim, however, to the savage rage of the populace. As she was conducted out of the prison, stupified by the spectacle of the dead bodies, over which she had to pass, she received a blow on her head from the edge of a sabre, which produced a violent effusion of blood. In this situation she was supported by two men, who, seizing her arms, compelled her to continue her progress over the dead bodies. As she fainted every moment from loss of blood, she was solicitous to fall in a decent attitude ; and when at last she became so enfeebled as to be able to proceed no further, her head was severed from her body. The mangled corpse was exposed to every description of indignity, and the head, fixed upon a pike, was purposely shewn to the queen, who, on beholding the proofs of so dreadful an act of inhumanity, experienced a temporary suspension of the functions of life. It was afterwards carried in triumph through the streets of Paris, and particularly to the Palais Royal, where it was recognized by her brutal relatives. These dreadful massacres lasted during the whole of the 2nd and 3rd of September. At the Abbey prison 159 were massacred, exclusive of M. M. D'Angremont, Rosoy, and de la Porte, who had been previously beheaded; at the seminary of St. Firman 92 unfortunate victims suffered; at the Carmelites, 141; at the Hotel de la Force, 168; at the Chatelat, 214; at the Conciergerie, 85; at the Bicetre, 153; at the cloister of the Bernardins, 73; in all amounting to 1085: among whom must be estimated a small number of felons, who had been guilty of forging assignats, and were condemned to death.

The rapid advance of the allied armies after the reduction of Longwy and Verdun, gave general alarm. Dumouriez displayed no common share of ability and activity in the exercise of the new and important employment with which he was now entrusted. On the 30th of August he deemed it absolutely necessary to call a council of war at Sedan, that the most vigorous and effectual measures might be adopted for the safety of the nation. He collected the general officers in the neighbourhood, and invited M. Dillon from Valenciennes to obtain his advice. He represented to the council the melancholy situation of the French army, the prodigious force of the combined powers, the brilliance of their late victories, and the strong probability, from existing circumstances, that they would soon attempt the reduction of Montmedi. The Prussian army was supposed to amount to more than 55,000 disciplined troops, besides 16,000 men under the command of Clairfait, who was stationed at Chiers. It was ascertained that numerous reinforcements of Hessians and Austrians were on their march. From a consideration of all these circumstances, it was determined to be highly imprudent to hazard an engagement with numbers so decidedly superior, as no hopes of victory could be entertained, but there was every reason to anticipate defeat and disgrace.

During this dilemma, M. Dumouriez dispatched general Galbaud to support Verdun, with two battalions of infantry; but in the present situation of the enemy it was not to be expected that his endeavours would be effectual. He believed it impossible to prevent the enemy from crossing the Meuse, which, according to his calculation, was passable at no fewer than sixty-nine places within the distance from Verdun to Stenay, a space of twenty-seven miles. On the last day of August the enemy, having effected the passage of this river, took possession of Stenay; a circumstance which obliged the national guards at that place to retreat, and unite themselves with the forces of Dillon, then commanding the vanguard, which consisted of no more than five battalions of infantry and fourteen squadrons of light horse. The whole effective force of the French commander-in-chief, at this period, did not equal that under the immediate authority of general Clairfait; so that this officer must have been totally unacquainted with the actual strength of Dumouriez, or he could not have failed to attack him, in the certainty of obtaining a decisive victory. Taking advantage of the first inadvertence of his enemy, Dumouriez afterwards, by skilful movements and well chosen positions, postponed a general action until he was reinforced. " Verdun," said he, in a confidential letter, " surrendered on the 2nd, and had I been opposed by Frederic the Great, I should on the 3rd have been driven back as far as Chalons. But my friends, the Prussians, no longer know how to make war. Their great army appeared on the 10th, and in five days I beat them in all their attacks on my posts." With less than 25,000 men under himself and Dillon, he opposed the enemy at the defiles which lead to the forest of Argonne, in Champagne, during several days. That which he occupied himself was forced, recovered, forced again, and his rear was turned by 20,000 men. In this perilous situation he displayed all his address by a retreat, notwithstanding the murmurs of his troops, to the strong position of St. Menehould, a town situated about twenty-six miles W. S. W. of Verdun. The Austrians in disputing the pass, lost a considerable number of men, and among the rest Charles, the prince de Ligne. By the possession of this place he intercepted the progress of the enemy to Chalons and Paris, and drew him into extreme embarrassment. Happily for him, Dillon at this moment gave the Austrians a repulse at the pass of Biesme, which obliged the duke of Brunswick to take a long circuit in order to reach Champagne, during which Kellerman effected his junction with 22,000 men, and Bournonville with 11,000. With this force amounting to more than 60,000 men, they presented an undaunted front to the confederates; and, being attacked by them immediately after their conjunction, Kellerman's division, supported by Dumouriez, repulsed them on the 20th of September, after an action of fourteen hours, which enabled them to establish themselves firmly in this position.

General Clairfait, who did not arrive until the morning after the engagement, assumed a position near Valmy, having on his left wing the Prussian camp of Hans, and on his right the advanced guard, now stationed on the road leading to Chalons, and within four leagues of that town. The prince of Hohenlohe occupied the heights of Gizencourt and the post of La Lune, while the emigrants were placed in the rear. On the other hand, the French, under Dumouriez, still retained their original camp, with the right inclining to Islettes, and the left strengthened by a strong redoubt provided with 18 pieces of cannon of large dimensions.

The late action completely dissipated the illusions of Frederic William II. who, after seeing the hopes of the emigrants in some measure realized after the surrender of Longwy and Verdun, expected the immediate flight or surrender of the French forces; but their intrepidity not only disappointed his hopes, but gave a new turn to the war. The king began to reflect seriously on the critical situation to which he was reduced. He had neglected the opinion of the duke of Brunswick, who insisted soon after the commencement of the campaign, that, in consequence of the changes which had occurred in Paris, it was necessary to give a systematic direction to the operations of the combined armies; and, sensible of his imprudence in disregarding this advice, he was still further alarmed by the prevalence in his camp of famine and disease. The French exulted in the daily expectation of fresh succours. General d'Harville was assembling troops at Rheims, and general Sparre at Chalons. Paris, Soissons, Epernai, Troyes, and Vitri, were pouring forth swarms of volunteers; unacquainted with discipline and impatient of restraint, but zealous to shed their blood for their country, and acquire glory and liberty for themselves. The forces of the allied courts, on the contrary, deceived with respect to the opposition they were likely to experience, became dispirited and dejected. They found themselves entangled amidst the fastnesses of a sterile province, destitute of water, forage, and provisions, with a resolute enemy in front, to join which additional levies were arriving from all quarters, and their own resources daily dimishing. The garrisons of Thionville, Sedan, and Montmedi, at the same time harassed and cut off their convoys, which arrived but slowly, in consequence of the circuit they were obliged to make, by Grandprey, Longwy, and Verdun. The autumn was wet and cold; the troops were enervated by disease; the roads became nearly impracticable; and it was at length almost equally difficult to advance or to retire. A disgraceful retreat had now become inevitable. Dumouriez was equally aware of his own superiority, and of the critical situation of the enemy. Though the combined forces were posted between him and the capital, and the immediate communication with his own magazines was cut off, he asserted, with great confidence, that his Prussian majesty would not be able to penetrate much further into Champagne; and that within the short

space of ten days his once formidable army
would be compelled to retreat through
the same defiles, by which it had entered
France. Not contented with this predic-
tion which was speedily realized, he assured the Parisians that he should have
time to march to the succour of Lisle, now
menaced by the duke of Saxe Teschen,
and demanded as the recompence of
his services, that. he might be permitted
to make Brussels his head-quarters during
the winter, as he intended to arrive there
by the 15th of November.

In this melancholy situation of affairs
the commander-in-chief of the confederates
proposed an armistice, which was acceded
to. Conferences of a pacific nature were
opened between Dumouriez and Manstein,
a Prussian general, who was sent to treat
respecting a cartel. But these approaches
to amity were suddenly retracted on intelligence arriving of the abolition of
royalty of France, and another manifesto
conched in terms equally vindictive and insulting with the former, was published by
the duke of Brunswick.

Those who judged from the nature of
this manifesto, and the successes with
which the allies had commenced the campaign, were astonished when they heard
that the duke of Brunswick, instead of
attempting to force his way to Paris, or to
bring Dumouriez to a battle, had begun
his retreat. It has been suspected that
the mistress and ministers of Frederic had
been influenced by secret and liberal
bribes to produce an event so propitious
to the interests of France, but no evidence
has been adduced to confirm this supposition, and it is reasonable to believe,
that the flight of the duke of Brunswick
was dictated by the impossibility of accomplishing his enterprise, and the necessity of immediate retreat. During the
progress of the negotiation for an armistice,
the duke confessed to Dumouriez the embarrassment to which he was reduced.
" Make Lewis your king," said he, " under
the strictest limits. Do not content yourself by circumscribing his power, like that
of the king of England—make him a king
of Mahrattas, make him a stadtholder,

make him the principal tax-gatherer of
the country,—give him only a place, that is
all we ask, and then we have a pretext for
retiring." Indeed the general tenor of the
diplomatic correspondence, exhibited on
the part of the Prussians a striking contrast
to the tone of their two manifestoes ; the
one drawn up and circulated in the moment
of presumptuous success, and the other
issued immediately subsequent to the most
humiliating concessions. It might have
been expected that the mortifications to
which they had been subjected, from the
comparison between the boasts of their
first manifesto and their performances,
would have prevented them from issuing
a second equally violent, immediately after
imploring forbearance in the most servile
language of supplication.

The example of the Prussians was followed by the troops of Austria and Hesse
Cassel. On abandoning the strong en-
campments on the heights of La Lune,
they left behind them 300 horses, which
were half devoured ; so dreadfully destitute
were the soldiers of provisions. The retreat of the allies was slow, encumbered
as they were with the sick and those
wasted by want and fatigue. At Verdun
the Prussian commander assured generals
Dillon and Galbaud, that the manifestoes
were issued contrary to his advice, and
without his sanction, a declaration, that
if it exculpates him from the charge of
cruelty and presumption, entails upon his
character the disgrace of subservient imbecility. The manifestoes were signed by
his own hand and circulated in his presence.

On his first determination to retreat,
the king reproached in the severest terms
the French princes, and the Austrian general Clairfait. He declared that they had
deceived him grossly, and that he would
remember it to the end of his existence.
His resentment, whether just or capricious,
exasperated him to the commission of an
act equally impolitic and atrocious. In
the stipulations for a cartel, a distinction
was made between the Prussian soldiers
and the emigrants. By the exception of
these brave and unfortunate men, several
of them became the prey of revolutionary.

vengeance, and were executed as rebels. It is equally difficult to dicover any reasonable foundation for the vague complaints of his Prussian majesty, and any adequate motive for the sacrifice of the virtuous, but perhaps mistaken individuals, who had fought beneath his banner. The sacrifice of the emigrant prisoners was by no means ardently insisted on, and might have been evaded by the slightest demonstration of firmness or address.

After the French had retaken Verdun, they followed up their conquest by the recapture of Longwy on the 22nd of October, and the territories of France being evacuated by the allied armies, the country was decreed by the assembly to be no longer in danger. It cannot be asserted that the conduct of the Austrians or the Prussians was consistent with justice or with humanity, while they occupied the territories of France. The most flagrant acts of robbery and plunder were committed by the Hessians, but the barbarity and rapine of the soldiers were forgotten in the injustice of the commander-in-chief, who levied contributions on the credit of notes, which were made payable by the king of France, whenever he should be restored to the *absolute* enjoyment of his power: a mode of obtaining money and supplies which combined all the evils of deliberate insult, open extortion, offensive interference with the internal administration of the kingdom, and an avowal of the arbitrary and despotic principles, by which the invaders were actuated in their attempts to restore the monarchy.

In a military point of view the conduct of the duke of Brunswick was frequently characterized by the indecision and timidity consequent upon his subservience to the wishes and caprices of his master. He neglected to avail himself of the confusion and disorganization that prevailed in the French army on Fayette's defection, by immediately bringing Dumouriez to action; he suffered himself to be detained by fruitless sieges, while Dumouriez was recruiting his army instead of pressing forward to the ultimate object of his enterprise, while his enemy was unprepared for resistance;

and he took no advantage of his superior force to possess himself of the defiles leading to the forest of Argonne. He deserves, however, some commendation for having conducted a retreat through a hostile country, in the face of an enemy stronger than himself, with an inconsiderable loss of men. It is probable, that, during the more favourable period of his advance, and while a march to Paris was not yet impossible, he submitted to the dictates or the wishes of his superiors, but that in the confusion and disgrace of a retreat, he was left to rely on the resources of his own talent and experience.

At Rhetel two battalions of Parisian volunteers disgraced their reputation by an act of lawless barbarity, which the commander-in-chief did not fail to visit with exemplary punishment. A quarrel having ensued between some of the volunteers and four deserters who had relinquished the Prussian cause, it was instantly reported that they were spies and emigrants, intending to betray the interest of France. In a moment of passion they murdered these four men, notwithstanding they had been previously received by the French officers. Dumouriez deprived the regiment of their uniforms and weapons for this flagrant outrage, and compelled them to deliver up to justice those of their number who had been most eminently guilty.

Thionville, situated about forty-two miles east of Verdun, was in the mean time besieged by the Austrians: but it resisted, during the campaign, all their attempts to reduce it. This small, but strongly fortified place, was commanded by the brave and intrepid general Wrinpfen, who, on being summoned by the Austrian general to surrender, replied, "You may destroy the fortress and not leave one stone upon another, but you cannot burn the ramparts." The inhabitants having procured in one of their sallies, a quantity of forage, they fabricated a wooden horse for the inspection of the enemy, with a box suspended from his neck filled with hay, bearing this inscription, "When this horse has eat his hay the city of Thionville will surrender." The besieging force amounted to 28,000 men, but were frequently repulsed, and numbers of them were hourly destroyed by the sallies of the garrison. They were at length relieved by the retreat of the combined armies, and Wrinpfen and his gallant troops received those testimonies of gratitude and admiration to which they were entitled by their meritorious conduct. The siege of Lisle was not less fatal to the invaders, than honourable to the intrepidity of those entrusted with its defence. It was besieged about the beginning of September, and on the 23rd of that month the assembly received a declaration from its defenders, that they would be buried under the ruins of the town rather than abandon their post. Six days after this solemn declaration, (September 29th,) the city was summoned to surrender, by the duke of Saxe Teschen, who received from the council-general this spirited reply. "We have just renewed our oath to be faithful to the nation, and to maintain liberty and equality, or die at our post. We will not perjure ourselves." It was easy to foresee the consequences of this declaration. The Austrian batteries were immediately opened on the city, and levelled with dreadful fury for the space of a week, against that quarter of the town which was inhabited by the lower orders of the community, with a view to render them rebellious on account of their sufferings, and to obtain a capitulation as soon as the furious populace should become superior to their magistrates. After a prodigious waste, however, of ammunition, occasioned by an excessive fire continued for a whole weeek, the duke had the mortification to find that the body of the people were not less attached to the "existing order of things, than their superiors." So far were they from discovering any symptoms of mutiny, as the duke expected, that the keys of the city were suspended on the tree of liberty, in the middle of the great square, accompanied with a solemn oath, that the first person who should take them down with a view to capitulate, should be punished with death. The ferocity of the besiegers was exasperated by the obstinacy of the besieged; and the duke of Saxe Teschen's sister applied the match

with her own hands to some of the instruments of death with which the city was assailed. Finding that no distresses, however extreme, no attacks, however formidable, could induce them to surrender, the Austrians, equally affected by shame and anger, raised the siege, and retired on the 8th of October from before the city, after having thrown 6000 bombs and 30,000 red hot balls into this important fortress.

While the allies were thus sustaining the natural results of their own injustice and impolicy, the election of the members of the national convention, conformably with the decree of the 10th of August, proceeded with rapidity. A circular letter from the municipality of Paris, countersigned by Danton, had been sent to all the other municipalities, requiring the approbation of the people to the recent massacres, and recommending them to imitation. Under such control the election proceeded. The clergy were banished; the highest and most honourable of the nobility had fled, or had fallen by the hands of the assassins: the royal family in prison, resigned themselves to despair: all who favoured royalty or distinction of rank, were held in abhorrence, and the citizens were declared to be eligible to all the offices of state. The convention was chiefly chosen from the most violent and desperate republicans. The members assembled on the 20th of September, and established the law previously introduced for the abolition of royalty.

After the retreat of the allied armies Dumouriez repaired to Paris, to concert with the executive council a plan for the prosecution of the war. He found the state more than ever distracted by the factions of the Jacobins and Girondists, allied with the Rolandists: the former employing their ascendancy with the Girondists to establish their power; the latter desirous to render the disorders which prevailed in the metropolis a plea for translating the convention and the royal family to some place beyond the Loire, where they might be less influenced and endangered by the Jacobin mob, yet too jealous of Dumouriez to avail themselves of his influence among the troops, though it presented the only possible means of accomplishing their wishes. Having been gratified by the plaudits of the people, and obtained an approval of his design from the Jacobin ministry, who, though they dreaded him for his abilities and hated him for his popularity, dared not to dismiss him, he returned October 26th, to his army, near Valenciennes, where he received the welcome intelligence that Pache, a Girondist and confidant of Roland, had succeeded Servan, as minister of war.

The preliminary measures of the French convention were directed to the means of confiscation, and the convertibility of the objects seized into gold and silver, which they found more current than the assignats. Agents were sent to London, Amsterdam, and other opulent cities with orders to negotiate bills on Paris, payable in assignats. These bills being discounted in foreign countries, the value in specie was transmitted to France. When they became due they were paid according to the course of exchange, but before the checques could be converted into cash, assassins were hired to patrole the streets and threaten the sellers of gold and silver, who were stationed at that period in the public places, for the purpose of bargaining with the holders of paper money. The payers were therefore obliged to take their paper money, or a much less sum in coin than that which had been remitted from the discount. By every operation of this kind the quantity of specie in France was increased. The convention with much ease amassed immense quantities of gold and silver, and equally replenished the public treasury and their private coffers.

The evacuation of France was soon discovered to have materially injured the cause of the allies. The flight of the enemy after their extravagant hopes of uninterrupted success, operating on the susceptibility of the French character, elevated their spirits, and turned the military energy which defence had excited, to offence and invasion. Dumouriez made rapid and effective preparations in men, provisions, and artillery. The state of the French

army evinced the resources of the country and the national energy. Montesquiou, with above 20,000 men posted near Lyons, was ordered to invade Savoy. Biron, with 25,000 men, was stationed on the Upper Rhine, and was instructed to co-operate with general Custine, who was destined with 22,000 men commanded by himself, and 12,000 under Meusnie, to oppose the movements of the Austrians, Bavarians, and Imperialists, in Suabia, Franconia, and the Palatinate. Bournonville, who had succeeded Kellerman in his command, was opposed to the Prussians on the Lower Rhine, to prevent them from aiding the Austrians during the intended invasion of the Netherlands, and was supported by 10,000 men under general Chazot. A strong body of troops called the army of Ardennes, assembled at Givet under the command of Valence, who had been appointed in the room of general Dillon, was destined to co-operate with the grand army, with which Dumouriez was to invade the Low Countries.

That general, in the beginning of November, having issued a proclamation, declaring to the people that he came among them as a friend, wishing to assert their rights, without any intention to interfere in the organization of their government, penetrated the Austrian Netherlands from Valenciennes. After a successful encounter at Bossu, he advanced against the Austrian grand army, commanded by the duke of Saxe Teschen. According to the statement of Dumouriez himself, the French amounted to 28,000 men, and the enemy to 20,000 ; but according to the report of the latter, 60,000 French were opposed to 15,000 Austrians. It is probable that calculating the number of useless individuals, induced by enthusiasm or impelled by hunger, to join the French army, the effective numbers were nearly equal.

On the 5th of November in the morning, Dumouriez reconnoitred the position of the enemy. The Austrian right extended to the village of Jemappe, near Mons, and their left towards Mont Palidel. They were posted in all this length on a woody hill, where they had placed, as in an

L 2

amphitheatre, three tiers of redoubts furnished with twenty pieces of heavy artillery, twenty field pieces, in addition to three field pieces for each battalion, amounting in all to one hundred pieces of cannon. The army was plentifully supplied with artillery, but on account of the advantage which the elevated situation of the enemies' guns afforded them, it would have been the height of imprudence to have trusted the event of the day to artillery alone. In the afternoon several partial skirmishes took place between the contending armies, and general Harville was enabled with 600 men, to take possession of the heights of Framery, while Dumouriez occupied a position with his right towards Framery and his left extending towards Horine, having the enemy immediately in front. On the morning of the 6th, he ordered twelve sixteen-pounders, the same number of twelve-pounders, and of six-pounders, to be advanced and disposed in the front of his lines, by which disposition Harville obtained the advantage of flanking his enemy's left. Dumouriez in person commanded the attack on the right, that of the centre was led by other generals. At seven in the morning a very heavy fire of artillery commenced on both sides, which continued without intermission and without any decided effect, till ten o'clock. The troops of France had displayed the greatest eagerness to engage the enemy with fixed bayonets. This mode of attack was recommended by general Egalité, the eldest son of the duke of Orleans, and by general Bournonville. But it was previously necessary to approach certain batteries of the enemy, and to occupy the village of Carignon, then in possession of the Austrians, of which the capture was indispensible to the attack of the lines of Jemappe. The direction of this attack was entrusted to colonel Thevenot, an officer of merit and experience. His efforts were to be directed against the village, and, as soon as he should obtain his object against Jemappe, and the right of the Austrian entrenchments. To the left, Harville was ordered to carry his batteries nearer to the enemy, by which means he could produce a more considerable

impression, and was supported by Bournonville, who received instructions at noon to attack the left, to keep them in check towards that quarter. This was the time appointed for the general assault, when the centre of the French army moved on in columns, in regular order, to carry the lower tier of the Austrian batteries, a service which was readily effected, but not without considerable confusion and disorder in the enemy's line. Of this disorder the Austrian general wished to take advantage, and for that purpose detached the cavalry to charge the French. This movement was soon discovered by Dumouriez, who instantly gave orders for the hussars and chasseurs to cover the infantry, and to charge and repel the enemy. He was, himself, of considerable service in forming and directing the manœuvre. While the French cavalry were thus successfully employed, the infantry under the command of Egalité, pushed on to gain the second tier of redoubts. After this was performed with great bravery, there was still another effort to be made, in order to gain the summit of the heights where the Austrians had been posted to make their last and greatest stand. The intrepidity of the French, and their coolness in surmounting the complicated difficulties which occurred in the course of a long engagement, had very considerably deranged the order of the Austrians. At five in the afternoon they gave way on all sides, nor did they attempt to occupy or dispute any of the posts which remained to be defended, between the heights of Mons and Jemappe. They entered the latter town with a precipitation more resembling a positive flight than the retreat of a regular army. The Austrians, according to the account of Dumouriez himself, lost in this action 4000 in killed and wounded, and the same number missing and disbanded. The loss of the French is stated by the general at 300 killed, and double the number wounded. It was well understood, however, that Dumouriez was in the habit of estimating his loss, not by the actual number of the unfortunate boys whose lives were so freely expended, (the old troops of the line being reserved for particular occasions,) but by the difference between the number of those he led into battle in the morning, and that of his army on the following day.

The troops now insisted on being led to the attack of Mons, which they were fully determined to carry by storm. M. Dumouriez was under the necessity of promising them that satisfaction, and was delighted to perceive that neither hunger nor fatigue could repress their ardor and intrepidity. It was his intention to draw a line of circumvallation round the city, and attack it at once in different quarters. But his preparations were found to be unnecessary, and the Austrians, having rapidly retired, he entered the town without opposition, Tournay, Ostend, Antwerp, and Ghent, shared the same fate: the French commander entering Brussels, in triumph, on the 14th of November. The Austrian archduchess Christiana, in order to avert the impending danger, vainly offered, previous to her flight, the restoration to the people of Brabant of their antient charter of liberty, which the tyranny and injustice of the court of Vienna, had hitherto withheld. When Dumouriez promised that he would celebrate the festivity of Christmas at this city, he was viewed in the light of a vain self-confident man, by those superficial observers who were unacquainted with the positions and the numbers of the enemy, but his promise was fulfilled within five weeks of the stipulated period.

M. Labourdonnage was equally victorious with the army under his command, having reduced Tournay, Malines, Ghent, and Antwerp. General Valence took possession of Louvain and Namur: a French fleet entered the port of Ostend, and thus, with the single exception of Luxemburgh, the republicans had become masters of the Austrian Netherlands, before the termination of the year 1792. At this time the commander-in-chief received proposals for an armistice from the prince of Saxe Teschen, commissioned by general Clairfait, a measure to which Dumouriez himself would probably have acceded, but; on which he thought it expedient to obtain the opinion of the convention. He therefore transmitted Clairfait's letter to the executive council, and returning a verbal message

that he should, in the mean time, continue the campaign, proceeded in his victorious career. He then followed up his late marches and successes by pursuing the retreating army into the territory of Liege. Having obtained possession of Tirlemont, and then advanced towards Liege, he came up with the rear guard of the Imperial troops, amounting to 12,000 men, under the command of general Stardy. A desperate and sanguinary contest ensued, in which the Austrians were defeated with considerable loss. The rapidity of Dumouriez's movements, during the whole of the campaign, considering the smallness of his force, and the imperfection of its discipline, was unrivalled indeed in military tactics; but the distresses of the army were great, and its situation precarious. While immense sums were voted in the convention for the avowed purpose of supplying the soldiers of Dumouriez with provisions and necessaries, their arms were nearly useless for want of covering from the rain; they were destitute at this inclement season of the year, of shoes, coats, and beds; and many of them to avoid sleeping on the wet ground, tied themselves to the trunks of trees, and passed the night in a standing attitude. To retard the present exertions of the general, and counteract the result of his previous efforts, the minister, Paché, supported by a criminal faction, suffered the victorious army to be disbanded by famine and nakedness. Fifteen thousand men were in the hospitals, 20,000 deserted through misery and disgust, and more than 10,000 horses died of hunger. These misfortunes were the more to be lamented on the part of the general, as every possible means of defensive and offensive warfare was preparing by the Austrians, and their armies were as remarkable for the superiority of their numbers as for the skill of their commanders, the superiority of their discipline, and the extent and certainty of their resources.

While Dumouriez was thus achieving an enterprise which Lewis XVI. in the zenith of his glory, and with all the resources of his empire was unable to accomplish, by extending the French frontier to the Rhine. General Biron guarded Alsace from invasion; Kellermen, though he was removed on a charge of culpable inactivity, entered the electorate of Treves; and Custine, with more enterprise than prudence, after reducing Spires and Worms, (October 23rd) passed the Rhine, made himself master of Mentz and Frankfort, and levied upon them heavy contributions for having afforded protection to the emigrants. The movements of this adventurous general brought the king of Prussia again into the field. That monarch, who was no longer to be considered as the protector of the emigrant princes, or the ally of Austria, was, notwithstanding, deeply interested in the welfare and independence of the empire. When informed therefore of Custine's invasion, he ordered his forces to rejoin the coalition, and recovered Frankfort before the close of the campaign.

The king of Sardinia had long been regarded as hostile to the revolution, and general Montesquieu was commanded to enter the territories of Savoy. He was welcomed with enthusiastic joy. At Chamberry he received the homage of the magistrates and citizens, and the whole country submitted without resistence. After the reduction of Savoy, the general presented himself before Geneva, but agreed on condition of the Swiss troops in the garrison retiring on parole, to withdraw from the vicinity of the Genevan territories. This was a resolution by no means conformable with the ambitious views of the convention, and a commission was dispatched to inquire into Montesquieu's behaviour, but the latter thought it prudent to retire from the French dominions to avoid the result of an investigation by his irritated adversaries.

HISTORY OF THE WAR.

CHAP. V.

AFTER admiring for a moment the heroism of the French armies, their patriotic spirit, and, until they had been deserted by the convention, their determined intrepidity, it will be necessary to dwell with a minuteness, as painful as necessary, on the melancholy scenes which were transacting in the capital of the empire. A decree having been published prescribing a plan for the election of representatives to the proposed convention, the republicans employed themselves with assiduity in prepossessing the nation in favour of their cause. The National Assembly had been intimidated and rendered subservient to the republican faction, and they now endeavoured, by various expedients, to render the body of the people their partizans. The needy and the distressed were allured to support their power, by dispersing among them the popular idea of an equal division of property, and they were encouraged to hope for the realization of this chimerical project by the rigid execution of the decrees respecting the forfeiture of the estates of the nobles and ecclesiastics. Men of property, on the contrary, were intimidated into acquiescence by menaces and proscriptions issued against the aristocrats. Circular letters countersigned by Danton, as minister of justice, were sent to all the municipalities, justifying the late massacres, as acts

necessary to keep in awe the traitors who were still within the kingdom, an expression which implied all who were adverse to the Jacobins. Emissaries were sent to influence the electors, and procure the return of persons well affected to the reigning faction.

The elections were conducted under the auspices of pike and bludgeon men, who beset the electors, and compelled them to vote according to their dictates. The effects of such assemblages, and of the practices I have described, may be calculated by the return which was made for Paris, among whom was the duke of Orleans. This worthless traitor, to render himself a fit object of popular election in such times and for such a city, belibelled his mother, declared himself the son of a coachman, renounced his family appellation, and took by appointment of the commune he represented, what they were pleased to denominate, "the *beautiful* name of *Egalité*." The second legislative assembly 1792, was thus succeeded by or rather engaged, in the national convention, on the 20th of September, after having bequeathed to the nation a war with all Europe and in La Vendee : colonies in flames and revolutionized ; millions of assignats or fictitious paper, and a revolutionary tribunal, which was afterwards the instrument of indiscriminate massacres. This assembly passed 1227 laws, and during its reign 8047 persons were murdered ; many of them by an instrument introduced at that period, called the *Guillotine*, from the name of its supposed inventor, though it had been used in Scotland some centuries before, under the appellation of the *Maiden*. The members of the second legislative assembly were much inferior to their enlightened predecessors, but unfortunately the individuals who occupied the seats of the national convention, were inferior to both. The worst portion of the late legislature were alone returned ; and Robespierre, Petion, Sieyes, and the profligate Egalité, were worthily associated with Brissot, Condorcet, and Chabot, while the ranks were filled up with foreign criminals and adventurers, with the assassins of September, the authors of atrocious libels, and the lowest refuse of the populace. In this list of vice and baseness, the names of Marat, Anacharsis Cl otz, Thomas Paine, Legendre, Drouet, and Collet D'Herbois, stood conspicuously prominent. It would indeed be too much to affirm that even in this degraded assembly no men of talent or virtue were to be found, but their exertions were overpowered by the irregular and splendid eloquence of Danton, the studied periods and pointed sarcasms of Robespierre, or the plausible sophistry of Barrere.

In this as in the former legislatures, two parties prevailed, but their hostility was more acrimonious and deadly, because each knew the nature of his opponent, each knew that the ascendancy of the other was his own destruction. The Brissotines were indignant at beholding Robespierre, whom they had hitherto regarded in the light of a political mendicant, elevated far above their level in the public favour, pointed out by Marat and other writers of a similar class, as the only pre-eminently honest man in France, and as a fit person to govern the country with the rank of dictator. Danton was known to be attached to Robespierre, and, in conjunction with Marat and other Jacobins, formed what was denominated the *Mountain party*. Robespierre was gradually rising into

reputation for the display of talents, matured by repeated contention with his political opponents, and the genius of Danton far eclipsed that of any of the *Girondists*, the other great party, in the state of which Roland was the head. On the side of Robespierre were Danton, Couthon, St. Just, Camille Desmoulins, Chabot, Clootz, Collet D'Herbois, and Marat ; and on the side of Roland, or the *Coté droit*, were Brissot, Condorcet, Petion, Manuel, Vergniaud, Guadet, Gensonne, Barbaroux, Kersaint, and Louvet. A large body not inconsiderable in talent or influence, kept for a time cautiously aloof from the clash of the two parties, yet apparently flattering the prejudices of both, hoping, by accurate observation, to preserve themselves from danger and rise with the victors. Barrere and Sieyes were among the chiefs of this division. The party of the Girondists was denominated *Le coté droit*, from its occupying the right side of the hall, and that of Robespierre denominated the Mountain, because it took possession of the highest seats.

To record the debates that ensued on every important resolution, would be to embody the ravings of madness, and to circulate the effusions of ostentatious and sometimes deliberate blasphemy. As the foundation of all their proceedings, they declared that " there can be no constitution but that which is accepted by the people ;" and on the 21st of September they unanimously decreed that " royalty is abolished in France, that all public acts shall be dated the first year of the French republic, and that the great seal shall have the words " *French republic*" for its legend.

When Dumouriez had driven the allied invaders from the territory of the republic, he hastened to Paris for the purpose of concerting the winter campaign in Flanders, and in the not unreasonable hope of receiving from the grateful inhabitants of the capital the applauses deserved by his skill, his valour, and his success. Having attached himself, however, to the more moderate party of the Girondists, and endeavoured to effect a reconciliation between the contending parties, he excited the jealousy of both, and was accused by Marat of urging the conquest of Flanders with the view of making himself duke of Brabant. Ambition, it must be admitted, was the greater error of Dumouriez's character, nor is it improbable that he may have entertained designs similar to those imputed by his enemies. On my referring to this imputation of Marat, in an interview with the general during his visit to London, he exclaimed, " Duke of Brabant ! sir, at that period it was much more probable that I should have fought for the empire of Austria ! Had the convention done every thing we might have accomplished all ; as it was, I thought, that even the duchy of Brabant would be ultimately as far from our reach as the city of Vienna."

Immediately previous to the return of Dumouriez, it was decreed " That the French republic no longer acknowledges princes, and therefore their *apanages* have ceased. In every oath to be administred it was resolved that the term *republic* should be substituted for nation, and that the pension of one thousand livres, formerly granted to the nonjuring clergy, should be no longer paid to any under fifty years of age ; and this abolition was followed by a motion from M. Manuel, that the abolition of the order of priests and of every religious establishment, should accompany the abolition of royalty. The national convention, however, on this occasion, acted inconsistently with its usual character, and the proposition was rejected with every indication of abhorrence.

Having lately conquered Savoy, the legislators of France, notwithstanding their protestations against the infamy of unprovoked conquest and national aggrandizement, resolved to incorporate that territory with the republic, and it became therefore the eighty-fourth department. So open and important a violation of those principles by which they professed to be actuated, diminished the confidence of the friends of France, and exasperated the jealousy or resentment of her enemies. These sentiments were powerfully confirmed by the fatuity and inhumanity of the convention in its conduct towards its most fortunate

VOL. I.

generals. La Fayette was denounced as a traitor ; Luckner incurred the same disgrace, if disgrace it could be called, and was dismissed the service ; and general Dillon, when he obtained a fortunate and judicious armistice, instead, as the convention expected, of a decisive victory, was doomed to hear a decree of accusation issued against him, but had the influence to obtain its repeal.

The factious coincided in nothing but in cruelty and injustice. By the exertions of Danton, Roland was excluded from the legislature ; Robespierre and Marat were repeatedly accused and severely attacked, but escaped by the exercise of their accustomed self-confidence and dexterity. Many of the unfortunate emigrants returned to their native country, cherishing the idea that they should be able to procure the forgiveness and protection of their fellow citizens ; but the convention, with a policy and humanity worthy of itself, issued a decree by which they were ordered to quit the kingdom or be instantly put to death, should they refuse to comply. This decree was succeeded by another, in the promulgation of which, the convention discovered their ignorance of the law of nature and their defiance of the law of nations. A rupture having taken place between the bailiwick of Darmstadt and the duke of Deux Ponts, in whose territories it was situated, the people of that district, with their magistrates at their head, intreated the protection and support of the French republic, against the alleged tyranny and oppression of a man whom they were determined no longer to consider as entitled to their loyalty or their obedience. The national convention in compliance with their representations, issued a decree on the 19th of November, 1792, in the name of the French nation, declaring that they will grant fraternity and assistance to all those people who wish to procure liberty, and charging the executive power to send orders to the generals to aid such people as have suffered, or are now suffering, in the cause of liberty. The circulation of this extraordinary document has never been advanced by any of the belligerent powers

M

as a prominent ground of justification for the commencement of hostilities ; yet in my opinion, this declaration alone would have decided the *right* of England to de- mand from the government of France the most satisfactory explanations, whatever may have been the future expedience of engaging in actual warfare. The armies of the continental powers had indeed invaded the territories of France previous to this decree, and they can derive no other ad- vantage in point of argument from its sub- sequent enforcement, than as it tended to confirm their avowed suspicions, and to justify the continuance if not the commence- ment of the contest.

The Brissotines now endeavoured to recover the advantages they had lost in the convention by a paper war, but Robes- pierre possessed superior talents as a writer, and by a witty and sarcastic epistle, rendered Petion, who had entered the list against him, the object of general ridicule. The mountain party was not content, how- ever, with the honour acquired, or the se- curity afforded by literary triumph. They foresaw that it would be necessary to in- timidate their opponents by decisive mea- sures, and to divert the attention of the public from accusations against themselves, to charges and enquiries of more universal importance. They were afraid that the moderate party might extend its influence and its numbers, and at length effect a counter-revolution in favour of the king. Actuated therefore by motives of self- interest and self-preservation, as well as by the malignant spirit of faction, they drew up a series of charges, which, after long and violent debates, were laid on the table of the hall ; and it was commanded that the individuals entrusted with the person of the king, should perform their duty with redoubled vigilence.

The royal family were confined in the tower of an antient building belonging originally to the grand prior of the Knights Templars, situated at the north-east ex- tremity of Paris, in a division which formed a refuge for debtors, crowded with build- ings of the meanest description, and par- ticularly dirty, melancholy, and unwhole-

some. They were treated with every in- jury and insult which malice, meanness, and brutality, could devise. They were deprived of all their attendants, but clergy ; the valet de chambre of the dauphin, whose zeal and perseverance in the service of this illustrious family, which he has narrated in a modest and artless manner, will im- mortalize his name, and render his memory dear to all who can appreciate fidelity dis- played in times so critical and disadvan- tageous. The delineation which he has given, exhibits a picture of fortitude be- neath the pressure of adversity, at once delightful and improving, but coloured with all the prejudice of humble and fervent attachment. The royal family were com- pelled to endure numerous delays before they obtained the most common necessaries : the king was obliged to borrow changes of raiment from his valet de chambre, and the queen and the dauphin from the countess of Sutherland and other ladies : but these acts of kindness were almost immediately prevented. Even in the smallest articles the persecutors of the king displayed an anxious desire to increase his distress. He wore a repeating watch marked with the maker's name, and the addition " watch- maker *to the king*." The last three words were concealed by the commissioners with a wafer. Such examples of insolence were borne with religious calmness, and even the declaration of one of the com- missioners, Turlot, that " should the execu- tioner refuse to guillotine that d—d family, he would perform the office of executioner himself," was heard with patient and humble resignation.

When the sentinals caught a glimpse of any of the royal family, they ostentatiously performed a different manœuvre from that which testified respect. The porter, when he opened the various gates for the family to take the air, amused the national guard by blowing from his pipe volumes of smoke in the faces of each as they passed, par- ticularly the females, while the delighted soldiers obstructed the passages, indulging in obscene remarks, or singing indecent and revolutionary songs. The walls of the prison were covered with the most brutal effusions of vulgar malignity in the form of inscriptions and caricatures, and the superscriptions of the letters addressed to his majesty previous to the decree of the national convention, were erazed to make room for the ironical address of " Mons. Veto."

On the 28th of October the charges against Lewis were referred in the convention to a national committee, with the intention of preparing the public mind by a short delay for the intended catastrophe. The harangues of the mountain party were in favour of immediate condemnation, and Robespierre demanded that " sentence should be pronounced against Lewis, as a tyrant condemned by the insurrection of the people ; instead of which proceedings were instituted against him as in the case of an accused citizen, whose criminality was doubtful. The revolution ought to have been cemented by his death, instead of which the revolution itself was rendered a subject of litigation." The violence of this proposition was opposed by the Brissotines, but in a tone enfeebled by the consciousness that they had expressed similar sentiments, and condemned the king on the same grounds with Robespierre in the last assembly. At length the incendiary Marat assumed the merit of proposing that the king should not be accused of any facts which had taken place previous to his acceptance of the constitution.

In a short time the success of the armies, the sanguinary petitions lately presented, the violence of the pamphlets circulated in the metropolis, and the passiveness of the well-disposed body of the people, emboldened the regicides to retract their former measures of delay, and it was decreed on the motion of Legendre, that all the speeches intended to be delivered, should be laid on the table and printed, but the question on the king's trial should be decided on the 4th of December. These resolutions were reinforced by a sanguinary petition of the revolutionary municipality of the 10th of August, which had been annulled by the convention, and who delivered this atrocious scroll as their last corporate act.

This was the instant for those who wished to save the king's life to have exerted themselves. The inviolability which the constitution had conferred on the person of the king, the responsibility which it imposed upon his ministers, and the incompetency of the tribunal, afforded them firm ground on which to make their stand. But they suffered themselves to be carried along by the stream rather than expose themselves to the vengeance of his inveterate enemies.

The inviolability of the king's person being done away by an *ex post facto* law, and the convention being declared a competent tribunal, France, which had been so long the theatre of the most tragic scenes, at last presented to the world the awful spectacle of a sovereign, distinguished by his virtues and his integrity, above all the monarchs who had filled the throne of France, brought to trial as an enemy to the welfare of his realms, by men who afterwards proved, the most cruel tyrants that ever afflicted their country, or mankind.

The charges being prepared and the mode of trial arranged, the mayor was sent to conduct the king to the hall of the assembly. Lewis was informed that the mayor could not speak with him in the presence of his son, and the child was therefore sent into his mother's apartment. His majesty protested against the appellation of Lewis Capet by which he was distinguished, and informed the mayor he would accompany him, not in compliance with the authority of the convention, but in submission to its force. After enduring every variety of insult, he at length arrived at the hall of the assembly. He entered not only without perturbation, but with majestic dignity. He cast his eye around the hall with a look equally remote from fear and from contempt of the assembly before which he had been illegally cited. He had been totally deprived of all social intercourse since his confinement in the temple, that he was quite uninformed of the previous proceedings of the convention. It was evidently the design of his enemies that he should be taken by surprise, and it was expected that the awfulness of the occasion and the nature of the tribunal

M 2

would have discomposed his temper and
embarrassed his replies.   But under all
these disadvantages, he exhibited a readiness
of intelligence, a dignified courtesy of
demeanour, and an aptitude of remark,
which produced an evident effect on every
member of the convention who was not
previously determined to pronounce him
guilty

His majesty, approaching the bar, the
president Barrere, addressed him in these
words, "Lewis, the French nation accuses
you! the national convention resolved, on
the 3rd of December, that you shall be
judged by itself. On the 6th, it was decreed
that you should be brought to the bar.
They are about to read the act which
announces the crimes imputed to you.
You are permitted to seat yourself while
the charges are read." The king, tacitly
submitting, the several charges were read,
and he made his reply to each.   The most
important of these related to his attempts
to prevent the establishment of a free
government : his escape to Varennes after
he had accepted the constitution : the plan
concerted with de la Fayette and Mirabeau
for setting aside the existing constitution
and framing a new one : his remissness
in giving information of the treaty of Pilnitz :
his correspondence with the emigrant
princes, who had formed anti-revolutionary
designs, and his pecuniary remittances to
them : the pay remitted by him to the life
guards, at Coblentz : his neglect to provide
for the national safety, and his encouragement of anti-revolutionary projects.   The
evidence in support of these charges was
derived chiefly from letters addressed to
his majesty, and other papers with marginal
notes in his own hand writing, amounting
merely to presumptive proof of intentions
inimical to the established constitution,
and of which, had they been fully substantiated, the criminality would have been
extenuated by the ungenerous treatment
which he had received.   When the charges
and the papers on which they were grounded
had been read, Lewis was reconducted to
the Temple, where the cup of his affliction
was embittered in his last days by his
brutal persecutors: He was refused the

comfort of association with his family, and
even his son, who was only seven years
old, was not permitted to approach him to
alleviate his sufferings.

On the 26th of December he was 1792.
again brought up, attended by the
three council who were allowed him,—
Malesherbes, Tronchet, and Desezé. His
cause was ably and eloquently opened by
the last of these. After descanting on
the several charges, he thus closed his
address to the assembly. "In this hall
men have contended for the glory of the
10th of August. I come not to dispute
that glory ; but, since it has been proved
that that day was premeditated, how can
it be made a crime to Lewis. And you
accuse him ! and you would give judgment
against him ! against him who has never
given a sanguinary order ! against him
who at Varennes, preferred returning a
captive, to exposing the life of a single
man ! against him, who on the 20th, refused
every kind of aid, and preferred remaining
alone in the midst of his people. Hear
history speak. Lewis mounted the throne
at the age of twenty ; he exhibited upon
it an example of morals, of justice, of
economy : he abolished servitude in his
domains ! the people desired liberty, he
gave it. We cannot deny to Lewis the
glory of having always anticipated the
wishes of his people. I do not draw con-
clusions ! I appeal to history ! recollect
that history will *judge* your *judgment.*"

Before Desezé ventured upon the performance of his task, he had made every
preparation necessary for his own death ;
so sure was the fate, which seemed to
await all those who openly adhered to
the interests of the throne. His discourse,
written in the course of four nights,
embraced and triumphantly refuted, all
the topics of accusation preferred against
his royal client. It contains some most
pathetic appeals, and many bold strokes
of eloquence. His enunciation was uncommonly fine, and was in every respect
adapted to the importance of the subject.
The journal of Malesherbes, states that
the peroration, as it originally stood, was
of irresistible pathos. "When Desezé

read it to us," says his illustrious associate, " we could not refrain from shedding tears, but the king remarked, that it must be suppressed, as he did not wish to make an appeal to the passions." The monarch, after his condemnation, asked Malesherbes with visible emotion, what he could do to reward his advocate. This was reported to Desezé, who asked no other recompence than the honour of kissing his master's hand. The request was immediately granted ; and, as he approached to bend the knee, Lewis pressed forward, threw his arms about his neck, rested his head upon his shoulder, and sobbed bitterly for some time, exclaiming, "My poor Desezé." It will gratify the feeling reader to be told that he was one of the few survivors of revolutionary fury. Soon after the execution of his sovereign, he was thrown into an obscure prison, where he remained for a long period, apparently forgotten by those who had ordered his arrest. His wife, a woman of a most accomplished and vigorous mind, applied for his release to Barrere, on whom her husband had conferred some important benefits at his outset in life. Barrere shed tears when he was informed of the miseries of his benefactor, but commanded the wife to abstain from all further application in favour of her husband, lest the attention of the revolutionary government should be drawn towards him ; and after the lapse of a few months had him secretly removed to a house for the reception of invalids and lunatics. No other favourable trait is recorded of that furious and wily demagogue ; who, after governing the legislative assemblies of France, and occupying so much of the attention of mankind, dwindled into absolute insignificance, and now drags out a solitary and sordid existence in Paris, contemned as much by the present government as by the past, and shunned by all orders of men. In the hospital to which he was consigned, Desezé remained during the whole period of terror, secluded from public notice, and occupied in the education of his children. He ventured forth when the fury of the tempest was past ; and

lately, (September, 1814,) lived in a retired part of the capital, enjoying in tranquillity the society of individuals, adorned by equal talents and congenial virtues.

The pathetic address of Desezé had little apparent effect on the audience, whatever might be the amount of its secret influence. It cannot be doubted that the deliberations of the assembly were considerably influenced by the clamours of the rabble who surrounded the hall, and afterwards accompanied the king on his return to the temple, loading him with the most brutal insults.

Preparations, such as might have been expected, were made for the day of trial. All the resources of art and violence were employed to obtain a sentence of death and execution, and to influence the populace against the king ; sanguinary petitions demanded his head, and a procession was made of all the diseased and wounded people in the hospitals, who were exhibited as patriots wounded on the 10th of August, and came to the bar of the convention, claiming vengeance on the tyrant.

The form and arrangement of the questions to be decided, occupied a whole day. They were in substance, 1st, Is Lewis guilty or not ? 2nd, Shall the judgment to be pronounced, be submitted to the people in the primary assemblies ? 3rd, What punishment has he incurred ? It is evident that the last of these questions embraced every other, and ought to have been taken into consideration in voting on the other two. But it was easy to perceive that a verdict of guilty by the convention, would lead to the desired and expected sentence. On the first question there was a general affirmative of guilty ; on the second a majority of fourteen against an appeal to the people : the third question or appeal nominal, lasted two days, because almost every member accompanied his vote with some reason or reflection. The number of suffrages was reduced by death, absence, and refusals to vote, to seven hundred and twenty-one. Thirty-four gave their opinions for death, with various restrictions ; two for imprisonment in chains, and three hundred and nineteen for confinement or banishment: total, three hundred and fifty-five. The number of votes for death absolutely was three hundred and sixty-six. The president Vergnidud, sometimes called Verniduz, after enumerating the suffrages, said, "The punishment pronounced against Lewis, is DEATH."

In the whole course of this sanguinary transaction, nothing excited greater horror and surprise than the conduct of Egalité. He deliberately pronounced these words from the tribune. "Influenced by no consideration but that of performing my duty : convinced that all who have conspired or shall hereafter conspire against the sovereignty of the people deserve death ; I VOTE FOR DEATH." Even many of the wretches who surrounded him, heard his vote with an exclamation of abhorrence. "I know not," said the king, "what I have done to my cousin to make him behave to me in the manner he has ; but he is to be pitied. He is still more unfortunate than I am. I would not change conditions with him."

We are now arrived at the last scene of the unhappy monarch's life. The final interview between him and his family was not arranged without difficulty. The commissioners of the commune, whose brutality seemed to increase as the life of their victim drew to a close, insisted on a literal execution of their orders, not to lose sight of Lewis for a moment, while Garat declared it to be the intention of the assembly that he should see his family in private : a compromise was at length effected by assigning the dining room as the place of meeting : it had a glass door, which being shut, the commissioners could see through it without hearing. At half past eight o'clock, the queen, dauphin, madame royal, and madame Elizabeth, rushed into his arms. Their conversation which lasted an hour and three quarters, was not heard, but it was observed, that after each sentence pronounced by the king, the sobs of the princesses were renewed, from whence it is inferred, that he himself informed them of the sentence. Lewis rose first to end the interview. He promised another meeting at seven the next morning, but madame royal fainted at his feet, and he tore himself with difficulty from their ardent embraces.

During his passage to the place of execution, a profound silence prevailed among the people. The escort amounted to 1200 men ; the streets were crowded with national guards ; the doors of the houses were shut, and the police had strictly forbidden any one to appear at the windows. The king continued reading his breviary with great devotion during the slow and silent progress of the procession, till he arrived at the foot of the guillotine erected between the pedestal which had supported the statue of Lewis XV. and the Champs Elysées or Elysian Fields. JAN. 21, 1792.

The king, having recommended his confessor to the care of the national guard, threw off his coat, and was preparing to ascend the scaffold, when they seized his hands to tie them behind his back : his first movement was to repel the insult, but Edgworth, his confessor, said, "Sire, this new humiliation is another circumstance in which your majesty's sufferings resemble those of our Saviour, who will soon be your reward." The king's repugnance was instantly subdued, and with a dignified air of resignation, he presented his hands. The executioners drawing the cords with all their force, he mildly said, "There is no need to pull so hard." While he was ascending the steps, his confessor exclaimed, "Lewis, son of Saint Lewis, ascend to heaven." As soon as the king came upon the scaffold, he surveyed for a few moments the immense multitude. He then pronounced loud enough to be heard at the garden of the Thuilleries, "Francois ! Je meurs innocent. Je pardonne a tous mes ennemis, et je souhaite que la France"—"Frenchmen ! I die innocent. I pardon all my enemies, and I wish that France"—Here Santerre, fearing the effect of his address on the people, interrupted him by giving a signal for the drums to beat and the executioners to perform their office. They seized their victim, and placed him under the axe of the guillotine. The stroke was then given, and one of the executioners, · holding up the head to be seen by the people, a few persons more cruel or more mercenary than the rest, cried, Vive la nation ! Vive la republique ! A troop of young men placed there for the purpose, commenced a dance round the scaffold. Several persons dipped the points of pikes, pieces of paper, and pocket-handkerchiefs, in the blood. The king's hair had been cut off before he mounted the scaffold, and sold in small parcels for considerable sums. The theatres were shut in the evening, and the whole city appeared the residence of confusion and dismay, which was augmented by the assassination of Lapelletier de St. Fargeau, a member of the convention, who had voted for the king's death, and who was stabbed at an eating house.

M. Le Duc, an old servant of the king's father, prayed for leave to inter him at Sens with the rest of his family ; while Legendre required permission to divide the corpse into eighty-four pieces, of which one should be sent to each of the departments, and the heart to the convention. At length it was determined to bury him in the cemetary of that section of Paris in which he had been imprisoned ; and the body was thrown, without any funeral ceremony, into a space in the church-yard of St. Mary Magdalen, which was filled with quicklime, carefully guarded, till the body was supposed to be entirely consumed, and then levelled with the circumjacent ground, that every trace of the spot where the monarch was deposited might be effectually obliterated.

We may learn from the example of this unfortunate monarch, that it is not moral virtue, it is not philanthropy, it is not the most exemplary conduct in domestic life, that will ensure prosperity to the most upright sovereigns, without a firm, energetic, enlarged, and well-instructed mind. It was the . great and fundamental error of Lewis, as a king, that he neglected to take advantage of favourable circumstances, when fortune presented them for his benefit. He was frequently resolute and determined, till he found himself powerfully

opposed, and then his compliance was so easy, and his concessions so liberal, that his enemies ascribed them to fear or hypocrisy. When he had accepted the new constitution, a want of firmness exposed him to the seductive counsels of his courtiers, and led him to pursue an equivocal line of conduct, that presented to his enemies the opportunities they had so long desired for the abolition of royalty, and his own persecution and death. The humane and the indulgent, however, will be more disposed to pity than to condemn a monarch whose greatest faults were the benevolence of his affections, and the amiable graces which adorned his character. Had he possessed the malignity or the ferocity of his enemies, independently of higher attributes, he might have revenged his wrongs, and extended the triumph and the duration of the most oppressive and unprincipled despotism.

In forming our judgment respecting the causes and origin of the most important contest which ever involved the interests of mankind, we must, in justice to Great Britain, carefully distinguish between the *war of invasion*, to which all the future calamities of Europe may be attributed, and in which we remained perfectly neutral, and the 'war of *general defence*, in which we became the most prominent and active ally. Before the indication of hostile feelings and principles on the part of France, towards the legitimate governments of Europe, and towards ourselves in particular, had become too frequent and too offensive to be mistaken, we studiously abstained from all participation in the measures of either party, and received the accredited agent of France, even after we could no longer regard him in the light of an official character, with every testimony of confidence and respect. The duplicity. of Chauvelin himself, first excited and justified the distrust of the English cabinet. A note was presented to him by lord· Grenville, as secretary of state, which was intended to explain away the real meaning of the offensive decree of the 19th of November ; but was calculated with the

1793.

most exquisite artifice to sow dissention between the government and the nation. In the conclusion it admonishes the English minister of the responsibility which he must have in case of a declaration of war; "the consequences of which must be fatal to other countries, and to all mankind, and in which a *generous and free people* could not consent to betray their interests, by serving to assist a tyrannical coalition." Lord Grenville adverted to the general tenor of the conduct of the French government, in promoting sedition throughout the kingdom, and charged them with violating the neutrality of the Dutch republic, and insulting the ally of Great Britain, by sending a vessel up the Scheldt to attack Antwerp. "If France," he observed, "be really desirous of maintaining friendship and peace with England, she must shew herself disposed to renounce her views of aggression and aggrandizement, and confine herself within her own territories, without insulting other governments, disturbing their tranquillity, or violating their rights." The convention, in return, endeavoured to justify their conduct respecting the Scheldt, on the grounds of the gross injustice committed towards the Belgians, by the treaties which deprived them of the navigation of a river flowing through their provinces: and they again endeavoured, in the course of their explanation, to conciliate the favour of the English people, and to imbue them with a feeling of hostility against the government. "If warlike preparations are continued in the ports of England, we shall combat with regret the English, whom we esteem; but we shall combat them without fear." A member of the executive council, sanctioned by his colleagues, transmitted to the secretary of one of the conventional societies in London, a declaration to this effect. "The king and his parliament mean to make war against us. Will the English republicans suffer it? Already these free men shew their discontent, and their repugnance to bear arms against their brothers, the French. Well! we will fly to their succour,—we will make

a descent on the island; we will lodge there 50,000 caps of liberty; we will plant there the sacred tree, and we will stretch out our arms to our republican brethren; the tyranny of their government shall soon be destroyed." The final reply of lord Grenville again denied the sufficiency of the explanation presented by M. Chauvelin, and maintained the necessity of certain naval preparations, which had been objected to by the convention. "All those measures," he said, "will be continued which may be judged necessary to place us in a state to protect the safety, tranquillity, and rights of this country, as well as to guarantee those of our allies, and to set up a barrier to those views of ambition and of aggrandizement, dangerous at all times to the rest of Europe; but which became still more so, supported as they are by the propagation of principles destructive of all social order."

From an apprehension of the intrigues of the French and of other turbulent foreigners, who were already in this country, or might be inclined to repair to it, a bill was introduced into the house of peers for the control of aliens. The marquis of Lansdowne and the earl of Lauderdale opposed it with warmth, as tending to involve the nation in a war, and they advised that an ambassador should be sent to France, to assist in composing the troubles of the continent, and avert, by personal expostulation, the danger which seemed to impend over the unfortunate king. Mr. Fox ridiculed the alarm of those who dreaded the influence of French opinions; but Mr. Pitt declared that the arts, machinations, and violence of the French, afforded grounds for the most serious apprehensions, and called for the strictest vigilence. The bill soon received the royal assent; M. Chauvelin complained of the arbitrary principles of a bill which encroached on the lawful freedom of the French in Great Britain, and rendered them liable to expulsion or exclusion. Lord Grenville replied, that it only authorised such precautions as already existed in France, and when the envoy desired to obtain an exemption from its effect, no hope of indulgence was given, as his credentials from the convention were not allowed to be the credentials of legitimate authority ; though he was regarded and confided in as the only apparent medium of communication between the executive powers of the two countries. The ministers indeed were reduced to a dilemma, as unpleasing as it was singular. They refused to acknowledge M. Chauvelin in his official capacity, yet reasoned on his memorials as those of the French government, and replied to them with all the formality of official precision. So unavoidable an inconsistency does not change the general merits of the question, which must always be decided in favour of the illustrious individual, (lord Grenville) to whom its discussion was committed.

It is of importance in this place, to notice a decided and material distinction between the views and sentiments of Mr. Burke, and of Mr. Pitt and his friends. *The latter were uniformly consistent in maintaining* that the *internal changes of France did not preclude amity with England.* Mr. Pitt declared to M. Chauvelin, that it was his desire to avoid a war, and to receive a proof of the same sentiments from the French ministry, and a long conversation which he held with M. Marat, during that person's residence in this country, sufficiently demonstrates the sincerity of his attachment to peace, and his willingness to conclude it with any executive power firmly established by the French nation.

When the death of the unfortunate monarch of France was known in England, a general mourning was announced. M. Chauvelin was informed, that the king could no longer, after such an event, permit his residence in England, and that his majesty had thought fit to order that he should retire from the kingdom within eight days. Two days after Chauvelin's dismission, and before he had left London, Marat was again sent to England, but his commission proved fruitless for want of instructions. About the same time de Meulde was sent to the Hague, to assist general Dumouriez in his proposed

negotiations with lord Auckland, but before the conferences could be opened, war was proclaimed by the French convention against England and Holland.

That portion of the British public which felt an interest in political questions, and particularly on the subject of the French revolution, may be divided into two classes: those who wished the establishment in England of a system resembling the French republic, to the entire subversion of the British constitution ; and those who, varying in their plans and measures, desired the preservation of the existing establishment. The democrats and Jacobins were generally averse to a war with France, because it would interrupt their communication by which they expected to establish their favourite system. The friends of the British constitution, both within and without the houses of parliament, whether for or against the war, in a great measure adopted the tone and opinions advanced, and maintained by three of the highest parliamentary characters ; Edmund Burke, Charles James Fox, and William Pitt. Burke continued to regard the French revolutionists, " of every opinion, kind, and succession," as the " determined and inveterate enemies of religion, virtue, rank, and property, throughout the world ;" as eagerly and resolutely bent on disseminating disorder, vice, and misery. Mr. Fox replied, that, criminal as the French republicans were in their disorders and massacres, and in the murder of their king their acts were no crimes against England : if the French nation chose to abolish existing orders and to annihilate the monarchy, they were not invading the rights of England : such a pretext of going to war was totally unjust ; our efforts would spill the blood of our brave countrymen, and would overwhelm us with additional debts. We ought to receive an ambassador from the ruling powers of France, because they were the ruling powers. With all foreign nations we considered neither the history of the establishment, nor the justice of the tenure. France, Spain, and other monarchies negotiated with Cromwell ; England ought now to pursue the same course : we ought to treat with those who possessed the power of doing what we wanted, for the same reasons which justified our negotiations with Algiers, Turkey, and Morocco. Mr. Pitt, though he urged the necessity of a war on the ground of extreme provocation, and from an acute and comprehensive survey of the affairs of Europe, was far from coinciding with Mr. Burke, in proposing to carry on a war for the restoration of the monarchical government. The source of war was not our refusal to treat, as many believed or pretended to believe, but the refusal of the French leaders, to make satisfaction for injuries and insults. On the one side, party zeal represented Messrs. Burke and Pitt as the abettors of tyranny, regardless or ignorant of their difference in opinion ; on the other, Mr. Fox and his adherents appeared as the abettors of Jacobinism and anarchy. Notwithstanding the numbers who were averse to war, on the constitutional grounds of Mr. Fox, and on the unconstitutional grounds of the democrats and the Jacobins, public opinion was on the whole favourable to hostilities. And in declaring war against France in 1793, whether influenced by intemperance or just resentment, by wisdom or by folly, it cannot be doubted that the minister spoke the voice of the British nation.

When the king intimated to both houses his dismission of the French agent, he expressed his reliance on their support, in ulterior measures of caution and defence. In the discussion of this message, lord Grenville inveighed against the atrocious act which then engrossed the attention of Europe, remarked that the promise of neutrality given by our court, was conditional, depending on the humane and honourable treatment of the royal family of France ; and urged the necessity of taking arms for the assistance of our allies, and the prevention of the dangerous aggrandizement of the common enemy. In the house of commons Mr. Pitt deplored the death of the French king, and expatiated on the enormity of those principles which actuated the rulers of the republic ; principles which tended to destroy all religion, morality, and social order, and reduce mankind to a state of the most dreadful anarchy. With such men a continuance of peace could not be expected. They had formed schemes of arbitrary encroachment on the rights of neutral powers, aimed at a total change in the government of those countries in which their arms should happen to prevail, proposed a subversion of the long established law of nations, and attempted the propagation of a general spirit of revolutionary insurrection. After unsatisfactory explanations of an obnoxious decree, and palliations of offensive proceedings, their agent in England had persisted in what was equivalent to an avowal of every thing dangerous to Great Britain, and had thrown out menaces of hostility in the event of our inacquiescence. Mr. Fox admitted that it was our duty to assist the Dutch if they should demand our aid ; but he did not think that we ought to force them into a war by which they might be endangered, as this constraint would be an abuse of treaty. He allowed that the decree of fraternity was an insult to the world, but it was not a just ground of war. He blamed the ministry for insisting on security in terms not sufficiently precise, as equivocal language afforded no promise of obtaining satisfaction. The object of contest ought to be clearly stated. If the court imagined that all Europe was exposed to danger from the progress of the French arms, the peril would not be increased by proposing terms before we should engage in war. The real cause of the war might be referred to the desire of restoring despotism in France ; a motive of which he highly disapproved, though he was by no means pleased with the existing government of that country. After other speeches on both sides of the question, an address corresponding with his majesty's message passed without a division.

The next communication from the king announced the French declaration of war against Great Britain and the United Provinces. It was alleged by the convention, that his Britannic majesty had persisted more particularly since the revolution of August 10th, 1792, in giving proofs of his attachment to the coalition of princes, had refused to acknowledge the new government of France, had violated, in various instances, the treaty of 1786, had equipped an armament against the republic, and had seduced the stadtholder into similar measures of hostility. The royal message censured this "wanton and unprovoked aggression," and called for the ".zealous exertions of a brave and loyal people," in the prosecution of a "just and necessary war." Mr. Fox, on this occasion, repeated his former sentiments, and expatiated with his usual eloquence, on the necessity of moderation, and on the obvious advantages which would accrue from a rigid adherence to a pacific and forbearing line of policy. After several debates, similar in their tendency and result to those at the commencement of the session, a bill was introduced by Sir John Scott, now lord Eldon, for the prevention of traitorous correspondence in trade or other respects, with the king's enemies. Its opponents affirmed, that it involved an arbitrary extension of the act of the 25th of Edward III. that it would lead to perjury, and put any man in the power of a malignant adversary; and that it was, at the same time, a bill by which we should gain less and our enemies lose less, than if it were not enacted. But the attorney-general and Mr. Burke, said that it was framed in the spirit, if not according to the letter, of the former acts, and that its rigor was not greater than the urgency of the crisis required. After an animated debate on the necessity of reform, and on the abolition of the slave trade—subjects which have been more ably and warmly discussed within the last ten years, than at the period when they first became the incidental topics of parliamentary investigation and popular curiosity: the trade to India was productive of fresh discussions. It was the wish of many that it might be opened; but when the company petitioned for a renewal of its charter, the continuance of the monopoly was deemed advisable on the ground of experience, though it was rendered less strict than it had been under the former regulations. The system of government established in 1784, was considered as worthy of retention. Mr. Dundas pronounced an elaborate speech in favour of those objects; and the bill which he framed met with the concurrence of the two houses. When a prorogation was expected, Mr. Fox took an opportunity of recommending a speedy negotiation, as the French had been so successfully opposed that no ground of alarm for our own security or that of the Dutch, could be truly alleged. But Mr. Burke and Mr. Pitt contended that no government with which we could safely treat existed in France, and a majority of one hundred and forty voted for the continuance of the war. A convention was signed in the spring between our court and that of St. Petersburgh, stipulating for the prosecution of hostilities till the French should relinquish all their conquests. A treaty was soon after concluded with the landgrave of Hesse Cassel, for a subsidiary body of 8000 men; a number, which by a subsequent agreement, was extended to 12,000 The king of Sardinia, for a subsidy of £200,000 per annum, engaged to keep up an army of 50,000 men, to be employed in the particular defence of his own dominions, and in general service against the enemy. Comparing the power of this monarch with the amount of the stipulation, it is impossible not to admit that in this instance the ministers were guilty of the most inexcusable profusion. Compacts of alliance were adjusted with Spain, Naples, Prussia, Austria, and Portugal. Besides the stipulations of vigorous hostility, it was agreed that the conduct of other powers should be watched with extraordinary circumspection, lest at an epoch so momentous, they should abuse their professed neutrality, by protecting the commerce or property of the French.

HISTORY OF THE WAR.

CHAP. VI.

Invasion of Holland by Dumouriez—Battle of Nerwinden—Origin of the War of La Vendée—Treachery of Dumouriez—His Escape to the Austrian Army—Contention between the Mountain Party and the Brissotines—Trial and Acquittal of Marat—His Assassination by Charlotte Corday—Revolution of the 31st of May—Triumph of the Mountain Party—Progress of the Campaign—Successes of the Allies—Their subsequent Disasters—The Levy en Masse—Failure of the Siege of Dunkirk—War in La Vendée—Siege of Lyons.

WE left the French armies in tranquil possession of their extensive conquests. Custine at the head of a very large force occupied Worms, Spires, Mentz, and and the whole of the country on the French side of the Rhine. Bournonville was in possession of the electorate of Treves. Valence commanded a respectable force stationed at Liege and its environs; while Dumouriez, with a numerous army, occupied Belgium. But however formidable, numbers, valor, and the recollection of former successes, rendered these forces, their future operations were likely to be much impeded by the want of military stores and ammunition, which they experienced in consequence of the unpardonable negligence of Paché, the war minister. Dumouriez, who appears to have been entrusted by the executive council, with a considerable degree of discretionary power, conceived the bold resolution of invading Holland, and of penetrating to Amsterdam, before the inhabitants, long unaccustomed to warlike operations, and from their characteristic lethargy, little disposed to vigorous exertion, should have time to provide adequate means of defence. Such at least was the *projet* of invasion transmitted to the convention, which looked to the conquest of Holland with an anxiety not disproportionate to its importance. After war had been declared and hostilities actually commenced, Holland had become the chief object of attention to the French republic, as the conquest would give them the decided superiority over the belligerent powers. It has been supposed that Great Britain and Holland, from some concealed reason, had calculated on the defection of Dumouriez, or they would not have commenced hostilities in so precipitate a manner. His steadiness to the cause of France, would speedily have decided the contest, but the allies were deceived as well as himself, respecting the aid he probably designed to give them, for the greater part of his army were so strongly attached to the interest of the republic, as to be incapable of defection. Such dependence had the combined powers on the treachery of Dumouriez, that they considered that event as intimately connected with the subjugation of France. He had long meditated his escape into some foreign country, as he could not reconcile his private sentiments with his duty to the public. His ostensible plan appears to have been to advance, with a body of men posted at Mordyck, and covering that place, and Gertruydenburgh on the right, and Bergen-op-Zoom, Steinburg, Klundert, and Williamstadt, on the left, to penetrate into the interior of Holland by the sea of Dort. He gave orders to general Miranda to proceed against Maestricht with a detachment of his army, to annoy it as much as possible with red hot balls and bombs, but to attempt no regular siege on account of the lateness and severity of the season : he was ordered, as soon as he should receive information that the general had advanced beyond Mordyck, to leave the siege to the management of general Valence, who was expected from Paris, and lose not a moment in pushing on to Nimeguen. Having thus far succeeded, he (Miranda) was to march by the duchy of Cleves to stop the progress of the Prussian army, should they take that route. These commands of Dumouriez were afterwards regarded as decided evidence of his treachery. It was asserted that Maestricht, being at some distance to the left of his line of march, it was not probable that, uninfluenced by sinister views, he would have weakened his army, and retarded his progress by detaching so considerable a force to attempt a difficult and useless siege. On the 1st of February Maestricht, commanded by the prince of Hesse, was summoned by Miranda to surrender ; a requisition with which he positively refused to comply ; and the French immediately opened a tremendous battery, which set the town on fire in several quarters. While the siege was vigorously prosecuted, Dumouriez collected his army in the neighbourhood of Antwerp, and before his attempt to penetrate into Holland, published a manifesto addressed to the inhabitants of that country whom he denominated Batavians, and warmly entreated to emancipate themselves from the tyrannical yoke of their oppressors and the government of the stadtholder. His force consisted of twenty-one battalions, only two of them troops of the line, and amounting, by his own computation, to 13,700 men, including his cavalry and light troops. His army entered the territories of Holland on the 17th of February, though he did not leave Antwerp to join it in person till the 23rd. The rapidity of his march, and the skill by which

his manœuvres were distinguished, rendered Brêda an easy conquest ; and notwithstanding the ramparts were lined with two hundred and nine pieces of artillery, it surrendered in four days. Klundert and Gertruydenburg followed, and it was not till he arrived at Williamstadt, that Dumouriez experienced any effectual resistance. At one and the same time, Williamstadt, Bergen-op-Zoom, and Bois-le-Duc, were invested, and each [of these enterprises, as might have been expected from the manifest inadequacy of the force employed, completely failed of success. It has been asserted that the gallant defence made by the first of these places ensured the safety of Holland ; but it now appears extremely probable, that had Dumouriez obtained possession of the fortress, he would have pushed on so far into the country, that his retreat, which other circumstances rendered necessary, would have been completely cut off, and the victor of Jemappe would have been inextricably entangled in the marches of Holland. The circumstances which rendered a retreat from Holland indispensibly necessary to the salvation of the French army, are the success of the allies in forcing the passage of the Roer, and the necessity to which Miranda was subjected, of raising the siege of Maestricht. Dumouriez had entrusted the defence of the Roer to his friend Valence, and the trust was of the most important kind ; for the whole success of his expedition to Holland depended on this army being able to maintain its position, and prevent the allies from crossing the river. Valence ill requited the confidence placed in him, and it was to his treachery or unpardonable negligence, that the disasters which the French experienced in such rapid succession were chiefly to be attributed. I mean not, however, to detract from the praise which is justly due to the allies for their skill with which they planned the attack of an extensive line of posts, and the vigor and celerity with which the plan was executed.

The advanced guard of the French army consisting of 8000 men, was encamped at the distance of six leagues from Aix-la-

Chapelle. Notwithstanding their vicinity to the enemy, notwithstanding it was well known that a serious attack was meditated, this advanced guard, instead of presenting a firm and complete line of defence, was dispersed over an extensive plain, was almost destitute of cavalry, and in cantonments with intervals of four, five, and nine leagues ; so that the enemy might have penetrated without firing a single shot. But this was not all ; when the formidable attack of the enemy, which might have been long before anticipated, was made, not a single general officer was found at his post. · ·

On the 3rd of March, the prince of Saxe-Cobourg, an officer who had acquired great reputation in the Turkish war, and who was now commander-in-chief of the Austrian forces, attacked this part of the French army in their cantonments, and, after a slight resistance, obtained a signal victory. Two thousand of the French were killed, 16,000 remained prisoners of war, and the remainder fled with precipitation, and without rallying, till they joined Valence himself, whose head quarters were at Liege.

While such was the success which attended the first operations of Cobourg, Clairfait, the second in command, was no less fortunate. Having crossed the Roer at Aldenhoven, this general attacked the French posts which were extended along this part of the river, and compelled these brave men, who, through the treachery or neglect of their commanders, were completely surprised to retreat with precipitation, and fall back on Liege. In the meanwhile, a body of 30,000 Prussians, under the command of prince Frederic of Brunswick, forced the passage of the Roer at Ruremonde, and took possession of that town, in which the French had collected an immense magazine of provisions, artillery, and ammunition. The several divisions of the French army were now driven from post to post, with a very considerable loss of men, artillery, and military stores ; and the shattered remains of this once formidable force, with great difficulty, assembled at Liege. The covering army being thus entirely routed, Miranda was

compelled to abandon the bombardment of Maestricht and Venlo. Fortunately he was enabled to make good his retreat with very little loss, and effected a junction with Valence at Tongres, whence they retreated to St. Tron, and from this last place to Louvain, where they entrenched themselves and determined to make a stand. In consequence of these disasters, it became necessary for the French to change their whole plan of operations. Dumouriez could no longer persist in his operations against Holland without the utmost hazard of having his retreat cut off. He was therefore compelled to quit his prey, and joined the concentrated French army at Louvain, on the 10th of March. He somewhat unaccountably left his own army still engaged in the sieges of Williamstadt, Bergen-op-Zoom, and Bois-le-Duc, which were soon raised while Breda, Klundert, and Gertruydenburg, were evacuated.

The French army having united at Louvain, and having been joined by all the detached bodies which their precipitate retreat from Aldenhoven and Aix-la-Chapelle, had separated ; and having received considerable reinforcements, Dumouriez, who had resumed the command of the whole, took a position before Louvain towards Tirlemont, which, by covering Austrian Brabant, and particularly Brussels, might also serve to keep up the communication towards Dutch Brabant. The French soldiers felt all their ardor rekindled by the presence of their favourite general, and loudly demanded to be led against the enemy. The Austrians, who had advanced from Tongres to Tirlemont by St. Tron, flushed with their recent success, panted with equal ardor for an opportunity of acquiring fresh laurels. Animated by such a disposition, it cannot be supposed that two powerful armies would remain many days within a few miles of each other, without coming to action. The eyes of all Europe were upon them : two celebrated and victorious generals were immediately opposed to each other ; and on the event of the contest depended the fate of many provinces, and possibly of the empires to which they belonged. The hard fought battle of Nerwinden terminated the suspense of Europe. The Austrians began the attack. On the 15th of March they succeeded in making themselves masters of Tirlemont, which was defended by a corps of 400 French soldiers. On the 16th Dumouriez, advancing with part of his army, compelled the enemy to abandon Tirlemont with considerable loss, and to retire, with precipitation, to St. Tron. This check served only to inspire the Austrians with fresh courage, for on the 18th they returned to the charge, and a bloody engagement ensued, which lasted from seven in the morning till eight in the evening. The battle was fought exactly on the confines of Austrian Brabant and those of Liege. The left wing of the French army being covered by Dormael, and the right by Landen. After an obstinate contest, the left wing of the Austrians was compelled to yield to the impetuous valor of their antagonists, and retreated in considerable confusion. Flushed with this success the French pursued their advantage, but, advancing with too much precipitation, they were, in their turn, thrown into disorder, and compelled to retreat with great loss. Valence pierced the enemy's line at the head of the cavalry, but, being ill supported, he was surrounded by a corps of Austrians ; accompanied only by his aids-de-camp and a few troopers, with whom he cut his way through, but received three wounds in the head, a contusion on the arm, and had three of his aids-de-camp killed by his side. In the mean time, the other wing and the centre of the Austrian army were more successful, and made a more prudent use of their advantage than the French had done. Night put an end to the contest, and both sides returned to their former positions, the Austrians having lost 3000 men, and the French 4000, besides thirty pieces of cannon. Although upon the whole the Austrians may be said to have remained masters of the field on this memorable day, the advantage was so dearly purchased, that it led to no decisive consequences ; and, had the French retained the impregnable position which they occupied on the Tron Mountain, they might

have preserved their conquests, at least till reinforcements could have been received from France, when they might have been once more enabled to act offensively with a reasonable prospect of success. But the impetuous Dumouriez could brook no delay. He determined to try once more the fortune of the field, and another battle, less bloody but more decisive in its consequences, was fought on the 22nd of March. In this engagement the loss of the French amounted to 4000 men, while that of the Austrians did not exceed 1000. In consequence of this defeat, Dumouriez was obliged to retreat to Halle, fourteen miles beyond Brussels, where he might yet have made an effectual stand, and at least retarded the progress of the enemy, had he been faithful to the trust reposed in him by his country.

While such were the disasters which tarnished the lustre of the French arms in Belgium, their operations in other quarters were not attended with better success. In the beginning of April the Prussian army, headed by the king in person, defeated a division of the French army of the Rhine, near Bingen, and was enabled in consequence to form the blockade of Mentz, while the French were compelled to abandon Oppenheim and Worms. A naval expedition which the French undertook in the beginning of the year against Cagliari, in Sardinia, completely failed of success. The troops under the command of general Casa-Bianca, made a good landing, but in consequence of some unaccountable mistake, fired on each other, and were compelled precipitately to re-embark. At this unpropitious moment, a formidable insurrection broke out in La Vendeé and the other departments ; the standard of royalty was unfurled ; the peasantry, awakened to a sense of native loyalty, were encouraged, by the promise of foreign aid, to rally round the ruins of the throne, and impressed the existing government with a terror occasioned by the justice of their principles, rather than by the number of their effective force, or the perfection of their discipline.

The conduct of Dumouriez had long

been extremely equivocal, and his attachment to the republic extremely doubtful. The Jacobin party suspected him : he was denounced by Marat while in the splendid career of victory, and it is not improbable that this suspicion and denunciation tended to produce the very treachery against which the convention guarded. On the 29th of March, the committee of general defence having announced to the convention that there was reason to apprehend the existance of a plot in the northern army to overturn the republic, it was decreed almost unanimously, that Dumouriez should be ordered to the bar ; that the minister at war should immediately set out to examine the state of the army in the north ; and that four members of the convention should be sent thither as commissioners, with power to suspend, arrest, and send to the bar of the convention, all generals and military officers who should become objects of their distrust and suspicion. Dumouriez, however, had thrown off the mask before these commissioners could reach his camp. He had already entered into a treaty with Cobourg, to attempt the restoration of monarchy, and to evacuate, without delay, the whole of Belgium. When the commissioners arrived at Lisle, they found that Dumouriez was encamped at St. Amand, whither they dispatched a summons to appear before them ; and, on refusing to comply, they proceeded to the camp, with the intention of arresting him at the head of the army. At first Dumouriez endeavoured to persuade them to join in his attempt, but when they refused their concurrence, he gave them in charge to a guard of soldiers, who were in waiting, with orders to carry them instantly to Tournay, the head quarters of general Clairfait. The names of the persons whom Dumouriez thus treacherously delivered into the hands of the enemy, were Camus, Lamarque, Quinette, and Henri Baneal, members of the convention ; Faucard, their secretary ; Bournonville, minister at war ; Memoire, his aid-de-camp; and Willeneuve, secretary to the war office. Having concerted with the prince of Cobourg a manifesto, in which Austria renounced all idea of conquest, and declared that her sole intention was to assist in restoring the constitution established in 1791, Dumouriez addressed his army in the camp at Maulde, and, after causing the manifesto to be read, earnestly exhorted them to join him in so glorious an achievement. But he immediately perceived that the officers were disaffected to his cause, and the murmurs which were heard along the line sufficiently discovered the disposition of his troops. Sensible of the danger by which he was threatened, he lost not a moment in providing for his own security. Decamping suddenly with about 700 men, accompanied by the duke of Chartres, colonel Thouvenot, and some other officers, he escaped to the Austrian army, and was escorted by colonel Mack, to Mons. Thus terminated the adventurous career of this enterprising and ambitious man. He was appointed to a commission in the imperial army, but the reproach which attaches itself to treachery, even under the most favourable circumstances, still adhered to him. He was regarded with suspicion, and soon sunk into insignificance.

The French were now compelled not only to relinquish its conquests, but to witness once more the invasion of their own country by the confederated powers. There can be little doubt but that the sudden evacuation of Belgium is to be attributed to the treachery of Dumouriez ; for, notwithstanding the severe defeats they had experienced, the French army might have maintained their strong position on the Tron Mountain, till the troops, which were advancing to their relief from all parts of France, had arrived. At all events, the garrisoned towns might have resisted the progress of the enemy, but it suited the views of Dumouriez to enter into a treaty with the enemies of his country, and the evacuation of Belgium became the preliminary article of the armistice.

The month of March was indeed a month of carnage. In the course of three weeks, at least, 50,000 of our fellow men were swept by violence from the face of the earth, and fell by the hands of their brethren. Yet after twelve months of almost uninterrupted fighting, after millions had been spent and the lives of thousands sacrificed, the hostile powers found themselves nearly in the same situation as at the beginning of the contest.

The flight of Dumouriez soon occasioned the ruin of the infamous Egalité, whose son being a partner in the general's flight, the father could not hope to escape suspicion. After being frequently denounced, and frequently escaping, he was at length condemned with his family to imprisonment at Marseilles.

At this period the affairs of France presented an appearance as alarming to herself, as exhilirating to her enemies. Russia and Spain had joined in declared hostilities ; Austria and Prussia were making united efforts to invade the frontiers : a considerable land force under the duke of York was preparing to embark from England ; a well appointed and victorious navy was employing every effort in the Mediterranean to intercept supplies, and increase the distresses of the country, while an irresistible naval force intercepted the trade, and seized the colonies of the republic. The principles and conduct of France excited universal horror abroad, while jealousy, treachery, and cabal, distracted her at home. But before any effectual measures could be adopted for resisting this formidable combination or for restoring the military power of the country, it was found necessary to terminate the disputes which raged between the two factions in the convention, and which were now enflamed to a degree of rancor, which disdained all control, and which nothing could appease but the sacrifice of one of the contending parties. The Girondists, who had been long declining in authority, and who were more than ever abhorred by the *mountain*, since their endeavours to save the king, had constantly supported Dumouriez against the invectives of Marat and the Jacobins. As soon as Dumouriez was driven into exile, the mountain raised an outcry against his late protectors, the Girondists. They were represented to the furious multitude as a band

of traitors and counter-revolutionists. The municipality of Paris and the Jacobin clubs resounded with complaints, threats, and imprecations, against a party which retained some sentiments of humanity, some love of order, and some regard for justice. The Girond party still possessed considerable influence in the convention, but the mountain continuing to gratify the avarice and inhumanity of the Parisian rabble, by regarding every outrage with complacency, exercised the supreme command in the city. In the month of March the revolutionary tribunal was established for trying offences against the state. This celebrated and dreadful court was wholly without appeal. The crimes on which it was to pronounce were vague and undefined ; extending not merely to actions but to the most secret thoughts. On the 1st of 1793. April a decree was passed abolishing the inviolability of members of the convention when accused of crimes against the state. The chiefs of the Brissotines (or Girondists) appeared to be astonished and confounded at these daring and desperate measures of their adversaries, and made only a feeble and desultory opposition, to decrees which were evidently intended to prepare the way for their destruction. A petition was presented by the commons of forty-eight sections of Paris, demanding that Brissot, Gaudet, Vergniaux, Gensonne, and some other deputies should be impeached and expelled the convention. This was followed by a deputation from the turbulent Fauxbourg of St. Antoine, attended by 8000 persons, charging the convention with misconduct, demanding a redress of grievances, and declaring that Fauxbourg to be in a state of insurrection. On the other hand the Girondists denounced Marat as an incendiary, and took advantage of their majority to procure an accusation against him.

This victory, gained after a long and arduous contest, shewed that the Girondists, when united and active, were in formidable force, but they seem to have lost the judgment and sagacity requisite for pursuing and completing their success. The trial of Marat was a triumph. No attempt was made to gain a verdict against him; and the moment the jury pronounced him not guilty, he was carried in victorious procession to the convention, reinstated amidst universal plaudits, and complimented by Danton, who pronounced this to be one of the *beaux jours*, one of the *beautiful days* of the revolution. It was now too obvious that the Girondists were inferior to their antagonists in vigor and decision; and, notwithstanding the intellectual and literary accomplishments of the leaders of the party, grossly deficient in that practical skill which can alone secure pre-eminence in political contention.. The mountain had secured the favour of the Jacobin club, and of the lower classes of the community. While their opponents were reasoning, deliberating, and denouncing, the party of Robespierre conspired, acted with decision, and obtained an easy triumph. On the 31st of May, early in the morning, the tocsin was sounded; the barriers were shut; Brissot, Roland, and many others of the most distinguished Girondists, were seized and committed to prison; and the republic became subject to a detestable and inhuman tyranny. Robespierre, Danton, Marat, Collot D'Herbois, Billaud, and Couthon, became the rulers of France. They selected as their associates, a certain number of ferocious individuals, whose talents were necessary to the administration, and who consented to be retained in their service from fear, policy, or ambition. They hastily drew up the celebrated constitution of 1793, and no policy ever existed more absurd or more favourable to anarchy. Legislation was confined to a single council, of which the members were elected without any regard to property: the executive power was divided among twenty-four ministers, appointed by the convention, and dismissed at their pleasure. They were composed of two sections, each consisting of twelve deputies. The one was called *the committee of public safety*, the other *the committee of general safety*. They were to be renewed every month; but this retention of power on the part of the convention, was more than counteracted by the clause which empow-

ered the committees of public safety to imprison the members of that assembly. In the mean time a few of the Girondist party, who escaped proscription, excited insurrection. Several departments indicated a disposition to revenge the wrongs they had sustained, and to resist oppression. Lyons, where the royalists had always possessed considerable influence, was instantly in a state of revolt, and a resolution was passed by a congress of the department, to send a force for the reduction of Paris. Its example was followed by Marseilles, Bourdeaux, and the department of the Gironde. In the midst of these scenes of civil disorder and national tumult, the unprincipled and blood-thirsty Marat, who, at an early period of the revolution, declared that three hundred thousand heads must be struck off before liberty could be established, fell by the hands of Charlotte Corday. While many of the Brissotines were resident at Caen, this young lady had obtained an interview with Barbaroux, whom she had long known. Inflamed by conversation with the fugitive deputies, she came forward as the avenger of that injured party, and of the cause of liberty. Having repaired to Paris, and after many ineffectual efforts, obtained admission to the dwelling of Marat, who had been for some time confined with a leprous complaint, she found him in the act of coming from the bath. After a short conference, in which he declared that all the Brissotines should suffer death, she plunged a knife which she had bought for the purpose, into his heart. He fell; and, after uttering a short exclamation, expired. The murderer was conveyed to prison, and as she made no attempt to deny the fact, the revolutionary tribunal passed sentence of death, which was immediately executed. The death of Marat was deplored by the *mountain* party as a national calamity: deputations, and individuals, vied with each other in fulsome adulation; his body was laid in state; the convention and constituted authorities attended his funeral; fetes were given in honour of his memory; and it was decreed that the bust of Mirabeau should be removed from the Pantheon, to make room for that of a deliberate but capricious murderer; cruel in his temper, disgusting in his habits, decrepid in his person, and hideous in his countenance, beyond the usual limits of human deformity.

Immediately previous to the death of Marat, the misery which had hitherto affected the Bourbons individually, was extended to the whole race by a decree, that its members, and all Austrian officers and other members of the Germanic body, taken prisoners, should be detained as hostages for the safety of the arrested deputies, and that all the Bourbons should be removed to Versailles, except those who were confined in the temple. The ci-devant duke of Orleans, Egalité, notwithstanding his quality as a member of the convention, was involved in the ignominy and misfortunes brought on his family by this decree: and to efface as far as possible, the remembrance of their former grandeur, the hall of the Thuilleries, once the seat of their splendor and magnificence, was now occupied by the convention, and became the scene of intestine tumult.

When posterity shall contemplate the history of this eventful year, it will become the theme of astonishment, that a nation so agitated by faction, should have been able to confront with success, the numerous foreign armies which were threatening to invade it, and to unite their arms with those of the revolters, who sprung up at this period in every quarter: that the most desperate and unprincipled faction that ever disgraced the history of any people should have maintained its usurpation, in defiance of the intrigues, the influence, and the violence of its adversaries. Yet the apparent anomaly may be easily and satisfactorily accounted for on the principle of *fear.* By the terror of its proscriptions and executions, the government suppressed revolt; when milliards of assignats were issued to provide supplies, they were circulated because resistance would have been useless and dangerous. When the property of the rich was to be seized and appropriated to the same use, they were accused of disaffection to the republic. For, while

tyranny retained its spies and agents of oppression in every part of the country, injured virtue, unless it courted protection by servile submission, was every where abandoned to its rigor, and dared not even to utter its grief in lamentation. The want of other motives of action was also compensated for the moment by the energy which distinguished the movements of this eccentric government; an energy excited by that enthusiastic fondness for their ideal liberty, which the Jacobin leaders, with admirable knowledge of the human character, were able to inspire in the breasts of their votaries. To this it was owing, that when Barrere (August 15th) proposed that the people should rise in a mass in defence of their country and in support of the constitution, his proposal was received with shouts of applause, and a decree for that purpose was immediately carried into execution. Twelve hundred thousand men were prepared for the field, and their payment provided for by the unjust but necessary expedient of an extorted loan. Had the allied powers consented to act merely on the defensive, or had the tenor of their proceedings coincided with the declaration of the prince of Cobourg, it is not improbable that the first efforts of the undisciplined masses forming the French armies, might have exhausted their first enthusiasm in fruitless and irregular efforts; discouraging and destructive to themselves, while they gave confidence and system to the operations of the confederates. Proposals of peace might then have been offered with sincerity and received with gratitude. But success produced upon the allies its usual effect. The Prussians had been successful against Custine upon the Rhine; they had foiled the efforts of that general to regain his ground; and were now besieging Mentz. The French government, they were well aware, was rent and weakened by faction, and distressed by revolts, in different parts of the kingdom. The allies believed it impossible that the French should withstand the forces of so powerful a confederacy as that which had now been formed; they determined to avail themselves of the advantages they apparently possessed, and, pursuing their successes to compel the Parisians to establish such a form of government as they might deem essential to the general welfare of Europe. Every prudential consideration having thus been sacrificed to the dictates of vanity and ambition, a congress was held at Antwerp, by the prince of Orange, the duke of York, the prince of Saxe Cobourg, and the ministers of the emperor. Great Britain, Prussia, Spain, Naples, and Holland. It was there determined that the allied forces should invest the fortresses on the frontiers, while Great Britain should send out her fleets to distress their trade and annoy their coasts, and the royalists should make a diversion in their favour by an insurrection in the department of the Vendée and the Loire. In pursuance of this plan, the allies proposed to besiege Condé and Valenciennes. To guard these fortresses, general Dampierre, who had succeeded Dumouriez in his command, possessed himself of a strong position at Famars. After the allies had made several unsuccessful attempts to dislodge him, Dampierre, as soon as he had reinforced his army and restored discipline among his troops, made an effort to drive the Austrians from some villages, of which they had taken possession in order to cut off the communication between the two fortresses, but was repulsed in his turn. A few days after, he renewed his attempt in greater force, and was again repulsed with the loss of 4000 men, an event which was rendered more disastrous by the death of their commander, who expired of his wounds. On this occasion the Coldstream regiment of guards, part of the force with which the duke of York had reinforced the confederate army, distinguished themselves by the intrepidity of their attack on the batteries which the enemy had constructed in the wood of St. Amand. The dislodgment of the French army from this position being essentially necessary to the prosecution of their proposed plan of operations, the allies determined to make another vigorous effort for that purpose. Their forces were formed into four columns, and

every precaution was adopted to give them success, by ordering diversions to be made in their favor. When the sun had dispelled the fog which covered their movements, early in the day, they were seen advancing in such admirable order, that the beauty and splendor of their appearance appeared to soften the terrific aspect of war. The attacks were made by the several commanders with exemplary bravery, amidst a tremendous roar of artillery from the enemy's batteries. After a severe engagement, the French were compelled to leave the allies in possession of the ground. In consequence of this victory, the sieges of Valenciennes and Condé were prosecuted with vigor. The French army, however, retired in perfect order, took possession of the camp of Famars, where they entrenched themselves; and, while they were able to maintain this position, not only covered Valenciennes, but in some degree kept up the communication with Condé. General Lamorliere was provisionally appointed to the chief command. In order to facilitate the siege of Valenciennes, it became necessary to dislodge the French from Famars; and the English and Austrians, having effected a junction, it was resolved to make the attack. On the 23rd of May, the outposts of the French were attacked by a considerable detachment under the command of the duke of York; and, after an obstinate resistance, obliged to fall back. The duke, however, did not consider it advisable to pursue his advantage immediately, by attacking the main entrenchments of the French army. He advanced with part of the troops, to a hollow way within a small distance of the enemy's entrenchments, but, observing from the disposition of the French, that they could not be carried at that time without considerable loss, he thought it better to defer the attack till next morning, and in the meanwhile approach and turn the works during the night. It is to be observed that this is the account published by the allies, after it was found that the French, during the night, had very unaccountably retired from works which there was every reason to believe might have been defended. Had they remained firm at their posts, it is doubtful whether the allies, after experiencing a reception so severe in carrying the outposts, would have ventured to attack the French, entrenched as they were, or rather buried in their formidable works. The latter had taken so much advantage of the natural situation of the ground, heights, and water, and had, by incessant labour, so covered themselves with abattis, and earthen works of unusual depth and size, that there was every reason to suppose their entrenchments impregnable.

The French army in their retreat, carried off the whole of their artillery and stores, and, after throwing a considerable reinforcement into Valenciennes, fell back on Bouchain. The next morning the combined armies took possession of the camp at Famars, and the advantage which in this instance they obtained, without meeting with any resistance, was the most considerable they had met with since their first appearance on the French frontier. It enabled them to pursue their most important designs without interruption, and to prosecute, with still greater effect, the sieges of Condé and Valenciennes, which were now left to their own strength, and to the valor and fidelity of their garrisons.

About this time the French generals formed a plan for making a diversion by an attack on West Flanders. On the 24th of May a division of the republican army advanced from Lisle, and attacked the Dutch posted near Menin, in three different points. The attack succeeded. The Dutch abandoned all their posts, with the loss of three pieces of cannon, seven waggons of ammunition and provisions, 500 men killed and 300 taken prisoners. Their military chest also was taken, and such was the rapidity of their flight, that twenty-two waggon loads of wounded were left to the mercy of the French, who conducted them to Lisle. On the 30th of May 7000 French troops marched from Dunkirk, and attacked 1200 Austrians and Dutch posted at Furnes, the whole of whom were cut to pieces or taken prisoners. After this advantage the French were advancing

rapidly to Ostend, and would have destroyed the depot of military stores in that town, on which the grand armies entirely depended, had it not been for the unexpected arrival of a large body of troops from England, of which the numbers and strength were considerably magnified on the first report. Notwithstanding, therefore, the success which attended their first movements, the French were obliged to relinquish, for the present, the invasion of West Flanders.

The war was carried on in other quarters with varied success. The French army of the Rhine, commanded by Custine, and seconded by the army of the Moselle, under Houchard, was opposed to the Austrian and Prussian armies, commanded by Wurmser and Hohenloe, and met with alternate success and defeat. In the beginning of May, Custine formed the design of cutting off a body of 7000 or 8000 of the enemy, who were posted at Rheinzabern. Before he could execute this plan, the national convention ordered him to give up the command of the army of the Rhine, and to assume that of the army of the North. Anxious to execute his projected enterprise before quitting the army, and unwilling that his successor, Alexander Beauharnois, should have the merit of executing his plan, the success of which he deemed to be infallible, Custine hastened the attack, which failed of success in consequence of the precipitance with which it was made, though he imputed its failure to the disobedience of the inferior generals.

On the side of Spain, the French were almost totally unprovided with the means of defence. A few raw recruits without discipline, without an able leader, and without military stores and ammunition, were opposed to the formidable force which the Spanish monarch had ordered to invade France. As might be expected, the French made but little resistance: a battle was fought in the neighbourhood of Perpignan, in which the Spaniards were victorious, and in consequence of their success were enabled to form the siege of that important fortress, which seemed the only bulwark of France in that quarter. While such was the progress of the external enemies of France, the success of her internal foes was scarcely less formidable. The insurrection in La Vendée acquired every day more and more consistence. Between the enthusiasm of loyalty and the ardor of republican zeal, the conflict, as might be expected, was obstinate and terrible. The success was various, but, although the republican armies were able to keep the field, though the principal towns were preserved from the contagion, the insurgents occupied the greater portion of the department, peopled the small towns and villages, and were continually recruited by proselytes from the neighbouring provinces.

In the course of July, Condé, Mentz, and Valenciennes, were compelled to surrender to the allies. The garrisons of the two latter places were not made prisoners of war, and were only restrained from bearing arms against the allies for one year. They were immediately ordered by the convention to march into La Vendée, a measure which the allies, through presumption or inadvertence, had not regarded or foreseen, and were of considerable service in restraining the progress of the insurgents.

Hitherto the most brilliant success had attended the operations of the allied powers, and, if there ever was a moment at which the object of their enterprise did not appear utterly visionary and romantic, it was most assuredly the present. As the confederate kings were engaged in a cause of infinite importance to themselves, and in which they had a common interest, it was not probable that discord should impede their operations. A conjecture so reasonable was however falsified by the event. After the surrender of Valenciennes, the British ministry ordered that part of the allied army, which was in the pay of Great Britain, to attack the west side of French Flanders; in order to take the towns of Berg, Dunkirk, Gravelline, and Calais, in the name of the king of Great Britain. The conquests which the British troops had hitherto contributed to achieve, had been taken in the name of the emperor.

The Dutch troops were ordered to co operate with the British in the attack on French Flanders. This project of separating the armies, was stated in some of the foreign prints to have been highly disapproved by the Austrian commanders; who strongly recommended a continuation of military operations upon the present plan, with the whole allied army.

A short time after the capture of Valenciennes, a council of war was held upon the future operations of the war; and more particularly on the project proposed by the British cabinet of separating the armies, The Austrian commanders offered two plans against it: viz.

The first was, to penetrate to Paris by the assistance of the rivers which fall into the Seine. These rivers, they said, would save an immense fatigue and expense of land carriage for their heavy artillery, baggage, and stores. They would have but twenty miles of land carriage in conducting their stores from the Scheldt to the Oise. The objection to it was, that this plan supposed a second campaign; and for its prosecution a number of floats must be provided; and therefore it was rejected. The convulsed state of Europe, the indisposition of every thinking man (out of the privileged orders) to the principle of the war, and the alarming consequences to every government in Europe, with which a dilatory and expensive war, for such an object, is pregnant, made it expedient rather to adopt any other course that gave the prospect of terminating the struggle in one year.

However, notwithstanding these objections, urged probably more from motives of design to mislead and deceive, than from any impulse of sincerity; it is shrewdly suspected, that the dread of another campaign made no part of the true cause for rejecting the proposal.

The next plan was that of the prince of Cobourg and general Clairfait, and this had the concurrence of all the Austrian and Prussian generals. It was, that they should take instant advantage of the consternation, into which the unexpected surrender of Valenciennes had thrown the people of

France, and the disorder of all their armies by the denunciation of their generals. That 40,000 or 50,000 light troops should instantly penetrate to Paris, while a debarkation should be made on the coast of Brittany and force a junction there with the mal-conteats. General Clairfait pledged himself on the success of this project.

Upon a moment's view of this plan, it will be perceptible to every one, that the debarkation spoken of, must have consisted of British troops from British vessels. The British ministry unquestionably did not approve of it :—their plan was, to divide the armies—to take as many of the frontier garrisons as possible—that those on the coast should be taken in the name and retained by the arms of his Britannic majesty ; and that in this position they should wait to take advantage of the disorders, which, in the course of the winter, were expected to arise in a country, so hemmed in from without and so convulsed within.

This plan, therefore, *as the general paymaster*, Britain succeeded in imposing on the allies.

In consequence of this plan, the duke of York with the British, the Hanoverians, the Dutch, some Hessians, and a body of the Austrians, separated from the main army, and began their march for Dunkirk. But the vigilance of the French government rendered ineffectual the courage and the rapidity of the British troops. No sooner did the committee of public safety receive intimation of the separation of the grand army and the march of the duke of York against Dunkirk, than the most effectual measures were taken for its defence. General Souham, who had risen from the ranks, was ordered to march with a chosen body of troops, to the assistance of the garrison. They soon afterwards entered the town under the command of Hoche, now an adjutant-general, and formerly a private in the national guards. Houchard, having now arrived with an immense body of troops, it was determined to relieve the place by general and repeated attacks. The French accordingly marched out from

the camp of Cassel; as well as from the towns of Bergues and Dunkirk, for the purpose of assaulting the whole of marshal Freytag's posts ; and, though the troops of the latter displayed great bravery; the enemy obtained possession of Bambecke, Rousebrugge, and Popperinghe, and obliged part of the army to retreat to Hondschoote. On the next day the marshal was again attacked ; on the succeeding morning the centre of the line was forced, and general Walmoden driven behind a canal with the loss of three pieces of cannon, and 800 men.

This action proved decisive of the fate of Dunkirk, and of the campaign. The duke of York was obliged to abandon his position, and leave 32 heavy cannon, much baggage, and many of the military stores behind him. The retreat, however, was conducted with equal ability and success by sir William Erskine.

About this time general Custine was deprived of the command of the French northern army, sent to Paris, and sentenced to be guillotined on a charge of treachery. Whether this charge was well or ill founded is yet uncertain : it appears extraordinary that this general should not have attempted to relieve Valenciennes, during the many weeks that the siege of this place lasted. Houchard, who had succeeded Custine in the command of the army of the Rhine, was again appointed his successor, and proceeded with the army to oppose the duke of York.

The taking of Quesnoy was the last instance of success on the part of the allied armies. The tide of affairs was now completely turned, and, during the remainder of the campaign, the French arms were attended by the most astonishing good fortune. This change is in a great measure to be attributed to the new and extraordinary measure of the *levy en masse*, to which the convention had so lately had recourse, and of which the execution was enforced by the subjoined decree.

Art. I. From this moment till all our enemies shall have been driven from the territory of the republic, all Frenchmen shall be in permanent readiness for the service of the armies. The young men shall march to the combat; the married men shall forge arms and transport provisions; the women shall make tents and clothes, and assist in the hospitals; the children shall make lint of old linen; the old men shall cause themselves to be carried to the public squares, to excite the courage of the warriors, to preach hatred against kings and the unity of the republic.

II. The national edifices shall be converted into storehouses; the ground of the cellars shall be washed with ley to extract the saltpetre.

III. The musquets and arms of calibre shall be immediately delivered to those who are to march against the enemy; the internal service of the republic shall be performed with fowling pieces.

IV. All saddle horses shall be given up to complete the cavalry; the draught horses and others, except those employed for the purposes of agriculture, shall convey the artillery and provisions.

V. The committee of public safety is charged to take all necessary measures to establish, without delay, an extraordinary manufactory of arms of all kinds, suitable to the efforts of the French nation. It is authorized, in consequence, to form all the establishments, manufactories, and working-places, which shall be deemed necessary for the execution of those works, and to summon, throughout the republic, all the artists and workmen, who can contribute to their success. The sum of 30,000,000 livres shall be at the disposal of the minister at war, to be taken out of the 428,000,000 of livres in assignats, which are in reserve in the chest with three keys. The central establishment of this extraordinary manufacture shall be at Paris.

VI. The representatives of the people sent into the departments to execute the present law, shall have the same authority, and shall concert measures with the committee of the public safety; they are invested with the unlimited powers attributed to the representatives of the people with the armies.

VII. No Frenchman summoned to serve, shall send a substitute. The public functionaries shall remain at their post.

VIII. The rising or movement shall be general. The unmarried or widowed citizens, from the age of eighteen to twenty-five, shall march first; they shall form, without delay, in the chief place of their district; they shall daily be exercised till the day of their departure.

IX. The representatives of the people shall regulate the calls and the marches, so that the armed citizens may not reach the place of rendezvous before the supplies and ammunition, and all the mechanical part of the army, shall have been brought together in a competent proportion.

X. The general point of rendezvous shall be determined by the circumstances and pointed out by the representatives of the people, sent out to enforce the execution of the present law, by advice of the generals in concert with the committee of public safety and the executive council.

XI. The battalion which shall be organized in every district, shall be ranged under a banner with this inscription, "The French nation risen against tyrants."

XII. The battalion shall be organized according to the established laws, and their pay shall be the same as that of the battalions now on their frontiers.

XIII. In order to collect a sufficient quantity of provisions, the farmers and stewards of the national lands, shall pour into the principal revenues of every district, a sufficient quantity of corn, the produce of the said lands.

XIV. The proprietors, farmers, and holders of corn, shall be obliged to pay their arrears of taxes in the produce of the fields, and also two thirds of the taxes for the present year. 1793.

XV. The national convention appoints citizens Chabot, Tallien, Carpentier, Reynaud, Dartygoyne, Laplauche of Nievre, Mallarme, Legendre, Lanot, Roux-Fusillac, Paganel, Boisset, Tallifer, Baille, Pinet,

Fayau, Lacroix, and Ingrand, as adjuncts to the representatives of the people, who are actually in the armies and in the departments, in order to execute in concert with them the present decree.

XVI. The commissioners of the primary assemblies are invited to repair, without delay, into the departments, to fulfil the commission entrusted to them, by the decree of the 14th of August, and to receive the commissions which shall be assigned to them by the representatives of the people.

XVII. The minister at war is charged to take all the measures necessary for the execution of the present decree. The sum of 50,000,000 shall be put at his disposal, to be taken out of the 458,000,000 of assignats in the chest with three keys.

XVIII. The present decree shall be sent into the departments by extraordinary couriers.

The immense resources of which this decree was immediately productive, enabled the government to strengthen and new model the army of the north, extending from Dunkirk to Maubeuge; that of the Ardennes, reaching from Maubeuge to Longwy; that of the Moselle, from Longwy to Bitche; that of the Rhine, from Bitche to Porentrui; that of the Alps, from the Aisne to the borders of the Var; that of Italy, from the maratime Alps to the mouth of the Rhone: the army of the oriental Pyrenees, from the mouth of the Rhone to the Garonne; the army of the western Pyrenees, from the department of the upper Pyrenees, to the mouth of the Gironde; the army of the coasts of Rochelle, from the mouth of the Gironde to that of the Loire; the army of the coasts of Brest, from the mouth of the Loire to St. Maloes; and lastly, that of the coasts of Cherbourg, from St. Maloes to the northern department.

The remaining armies of the republic were employed in opposing the insurrections in various parts of the country. Aisnes and Marseilles had, as we have already seen, presented strenuous complaints against the proceedings of the

government: the people of Lyons, irritated by the Jacobin missionaries, who plundered and insulted them without remorse, had risen in arms, and rescued themselves from the persecution and the cruelty of their oppressors; Nantes and Amiens had made energetic appeals in favour of the Brissotines, and several neighbouring departments followed the example of Bourdeaux.

These efforts, however, were of small importance when compared to the war of La Vendée; though its seat was not confined to the department properly called by that name, but extended over those of Les deux Levres, La Loire inferieure, Mayenne, and Maine et Loire. It exhibited the unusual and interesting sight of peaceable religious people, animated by their love for the altar and the throne, braving every danger and encountering every difficulty to retain to themselves the rights of worship, and the privileges of devoted royalty. At the period of the king's flight they prepared to tender their assistance, but his arrest frustrated their zealous intentions. Their discontents were inflamed by the persecution of the nonjuring clergy, to whom they constantly afforded shelter and assistance, refusing to admit or communicate with those who took the oaths. The murder of Lewis XVI. and successive provocations, at length impelled the quiet and industrious inhabitants of these departments, to commence one of the most bloody and obstinate civil wars which history has recorded. Armed only at first with pitchforks, staves, and implements of husbandry, they attacked the municipality, recovered the arms of which they had been deprived, and, displaying the white flag, declared themselves a loyal and catholic army. Their first successes surpassed all expectation: with incredible rapidity they made themselves masters of Machecoul, Legé, Clisson, Montaigu, Beaupred, Chalonnes, Chatillon, and many other towns. Having divided their force into several bodies of 10,000 and 12,000 men, they made successful attacks in various points, and were joined by great

reinforcements of priests, nobles, malcontents of every class, French and foreign
deserters, game-keepers, smugglers; by all,
indeed, whom principle, necessity, disappointment, or ambition, rendered dissatisfied with the revolution. The convention,
deceived by false reports, treated them
at first as a handful of robbers, but repeated intelligence of their successes
changed their opinion, especially when
after a long series of victories, Fontenay,
the capital of La Vendée, fell into their
hands. Having captured Thonars, they
evacuated Fontenay, and pressed towards
Saumur : at Doné they defeated general
Liganier, who was then displaced, and
general Menou appointed his successor.
He was equally unsuccessful in his defence of Saumur, and the insurgents having
captured that town, crossed the Loire, and
took Angers, threatened Tours and Mans,
and laid siege to Nantes. The convention, alarmed at these rapid conquests,
used every exertion to reinforce their
armies, and the Vendéans were disappointed in not being joined by many recruits on this side the Loire. General
Biron, called from the army of Italy to
conduct the war in La Vendée, surprised
the chateau of Lescure, one of the royalist
leaders at Parthenay. Westerman, the
second in command, made similar ravages
at Bressuire, and burnt the chateau of
Laroche Jaquelin, another chief of the
insurgents ; promising to capture the
towns of Chatillon and Chollet, and finally
to exterminate the rebels. He succeeded
indeed in taking Chatillon, but was surrounded by the insurgents ; his infantry
was cut to pieces, his artillery taken, and
he himself escaped with great difficulty,
attended by his cavalry. The republican
generals now meditated a general attack
on the insurgents, entered La Vendée by
the bridges of Cé, and encamped at Mar-
tigné Briand. Here they were attacked
by 40,000 men, whom they repulsed, but
immediately began a retreat towards
Montaigu. In their march they were
constantly harassed by large parties, and
when fatigued with three days' progress,
they were attacked by 50,000 men, who
routed them, and drove them in disorder
across the country in every direction.
So great was the panic, that even arms,
knapsacks, and accoutrements, were thrown
away as impediments to flight, and such
was the extent of their dispersion, that
their generals, attempting three days
after, to make a muster at Chinon, could
collect only 4000 men. The whole country
which separates Nantes from the Sables,
was now occupied by Charette ; notwithstanding all the exertions of the government, the people of Lyons established a
committee of public safety, raised an army
of 30,000 men, and issued a paper currency for their own department. The
people of Marseilles renounced the authority of the convention, forcibly confined the Jacobin club, and raised a military
force. Several neighbouring towns espoused their cause. The co-operation
of many others was expected, and plans
were agitated for the organization of a
force to march to Paris. The insurrection
at Marseilles, however, was soon subdued
by general Carteaux, who, by intrigue
rather than by force, gained admittance
into the city, superseded every authority
but that of the convention, and gratified
his revenge by every species of brutal and
inhuman atrocity.
Previous to the capture of Marseilles,
a plan had been projected by the British
government, to aid the royalists in Brittany
and the places adjacent. The numbers
and confidence of the insurgents had been
increased and confirmed by their recent
successes, but the progress of events did
not justify their reasonable expectations.
The royal and catholic army was divided
by factions, originating in jealousy of
D'Elbée, Bouchamp, and the president of
their council. Charette led a separate
army, formed entirely in the department of La Vendée, interfering with
none of the other parties, but jealous of
them all. The convention employed the
garrisons of Valenciennes, Mentz, and
Condé, in recruiting the army of La Vendée;
thus obtaining the advantage of employing
veterans in that important service. The
committee of public safety by their orator

Barrere, obtained a decree uniting the armies acting in La Vendée under one commander, nominating Lachelle to that situation, and declaring the confidence of the legislature that this execrable war would be terminated before the 20th of the month (October.) A variety of successes had almost rendered the decree prophetic, and before the end of the year Charette was reduced to the bare possession of the isle of Noirmoutier. The prince de Talmont, having passed the Loire, took possession of Laval with so much ease, as excited suspicion of treachery. He was twice attacked by the republicans under Lachelle, who, failing in both attempts, and being ordered to Paris, anticipated his impending fate by swallowing poison.

Notwithstanding the disasters and divisions of the royal army, the troops under the command of the subordinate generals and of the count de Talmont, amounted to 90,000 men. They were destitute, however, of provisions, ammunition, and clothing, and the prince was compelled to push forward to gain a position on the coast, where he might receive succours from England. In prosecution of this plan, he captured Mayenne and Dol, from the last of which places he could easily proceed to St. Malo. While they awaited the expected supplies, the royalists made an unsuccessful attack on Grandville; but, threatened on all sides by the republicans, in danger of being surrounded, and receiving no intelligence of the expected aids, they returned with precipitation to the interior. Their impatience was as culpable as the exertions of the British government were strenuous and expeditious. The earl of Moira, with ample supplies, arrived off the coast in eight days after their departure. He repeated his signals and renewed his efforts in vain, and was compelled, after a month's expectation, to return to the shores of Great Britain.

At Angers, the royalists, pressed by want, consumed their force in attacking the principal towns. After sustaining a repulse at Augers, they took La Fleche by surprise. At Mans, however, their approach was anticipated; they were defeated and put to hopeless and irreparable rout; they obtained no quarter, and the massacre was computed at 18,000 men. A remnant of the army endeavoured to regain the friendly territory of La Vendée, but were pursued by the republicans, and, after a conflict of two days, again defeated with similar slaughter at Savenay. Nothing now remained for the victors but to secure the conquered departments against future insurrections, which they endeavoured to accomplish by the commission of every barbarity. Carrier was stationed on a mission at Nantes, and exhibited in his proceedings all the depravity of his character. The prisons were filled by false denunciations; military tribunals were erected, which condemned without the appearance of trial, and the guillotine, being found too slow for the savage purpose, of rapid execution, the shooting of whole detachments, and the drowning of hundreds at a time, by means of a barge with a false bottom, were put in practice, and known by the name of Noyades and Fusilades.

In the south, Lyons presented an aspect of formidable resistance and desperate energy. General Kellerman, who commanded the army of the Alps, was ordered to besiege that city; but his movements, not corresponding with the impatience of the convention, he was removed, and general Doppet appointed to succeed him. The inhabitants were not only unused to arms, but ill provided with the means of defence, and with the necessaries of life. Doppet was preparing to make a last attack, when the people opened their gates and surrendered at discretion. General Précy, at the head of 2500 men, and escorting many women and children, made his escape; but the explosion of an ammunition waggon occasioned great destruction among his helpless followers; and the fugitives, being pursued by a part of the victorious enemy, the whole detachment was put to the sword. A great part of the city had been reduced to ashes by the continual bombardment; the victors were filled with furious resentment, and gratified their revenge by the most savage and ingenious cruelty. The wretched victims, too numerous for the operation of the guillotine, were driven in large bodies with the most brutal and blasphemous ceremonies, into the Rhone, or hurried to the squares in order to be massacred by musketry and artillery. A decree was passed in the convention for razing all the buildings of Lyons, except the abodes of the poor, of murdered patriots, and houses of industry and instruction. On the site of the town a column was to be raised with the inscription, "LYONS WARRED AGAINST LIBERTY—LYONS IS NO MORE, and the name of the city was changed to *Ville Affranchie*." No time was lost in prosecuting the work of destruction : the agents of the convention boasted of their responsibility, and a petition from the inhabitants of this large, beautiful, and wealthy city, imploring mercy, was coolly referred to the committee of public safety, which had ordered its destruction.

HISTORY OF THE WAR.

CHAP. VII.

Extraordinary Exertions of the French Government—Continuance of the Campaign—Lord Hood takes Possession of Toulon—Events during the Possession of that Port—Its Evacuation—Atrocities of Robespierre—Execution of General Custine—Trial and Death of the Queen of France—Reformation of the French Calendar—State of Parties and Opinions in Great Britain—Jealousy excited in Foreign Courts by the Prosperity of England.

THE pressure of the confederates and their supposed designs, cherished the ferocious tyranny of Robespierre. In one momentous object, this relentless tyrant promoted the first wish of the French nation, not to be controlled by foreign invaders. In opposing the confederacy of princes, the revolutionary government displayed an energy that triumphed over all obstacles. In the prosecution of their ambitious views they endeavoured to emancipate mankind from the restraints of religious belief, and practical morality. Their predecessors had progressively promoted infidelity, confiscation, and the destruction of rank and order; but there still remained a considerable degree of religion, a sense of propriety and decorum, honesty of principle, and an involuntary feeling of political subordination. Robespierre and his band, (as we shall see) abolished Christianity; publicly and nationally abjured the Supreme Being; accelerated the ruin of commerce, that the multitude might be stimulated to plunder, and seized all property belonging to owners incapable of resistance, or destitute of influence. Totally free from every principle of religion and virtue, without humanity, pity, or remorse, they proscribed, they murdered, and they plundered; the war facilitated the extension of their power,

because it enabled them to accuse all persons obnoxious to themselves, as traitorous agents of foreign enemies. Pressed on all sides by invaders, who were supposed to entertain the design of dictating their form of government, an ardent zeal to maintain their national independence, diverted the attention of the people from internal despotism; and the spirit of patriotism was yet more ardently inflamed by the belief that was generally circulated of an intention on the part of the allied powers to dismember the kingdom.

After raising the siege of Dunkirk, the French army took a strong position in the neighbourhood of Maubeuge, where they were immediately blockaded by the united force of the allies, collected under the prince of Cobourg. Elated, however, by their recent successes, the French were impatient of being restrained within their entrenchments. On the 15th and 16th of October, general Jourdon attacked the combined army, and compelled them to abandon the field with considerable loss, and recross the Sambre. The French army pursued and attacked the allies in several places at once. They invaded West Flanders, took possession of Werwick, Menin, and Furnes, and formed the siege of Nieuport. The allied leaders trembled for the fate of Ostend, which would probably have fallen into the hands of the victorious republicans, had not a considerable English armament under sir Charles Grey, which had been destined for the West Indies, unexpectedly arrived before that port. Early in September Landau was invested by the allied Austrian and Prussian armies ; but, while the French maintained the strong lines at Weissenburg, and on the Lauter, there was little prospect of the siege terminating successfully. On the 13th of October the Austrian general Wurmser, made a grand attack upon the lines of Lauter, and if the account published by the convention be authentic, the French generals permitted the Austrians, almost without resistance, to force the lines ; the whole of which, together with the town of Lauterburg, were carried with so much rapidity, that the French were unable to remove their artillery. The town of Weissenburg made a more formidable resistance, and was not carried without the loss of nearly 1000 men on the part of the assailants. The French retreated towards Hagenau, from which, on the 18th, they were dislodged. The Austrian general lost no time in proceeding towards Strasburgh, one of the strongest fortresses in Europe. A plot had been formed by some of the magistrates, and by the principal citizens, to surrender this important place to the enemy ; but the completion of their design was prevented by the arrival of two commissioners from the convention, at the head of a considerable force. These commissioners were sent for the express purpose of reorganizing the armies, and of infusing fresh spirit into the minds of the soldiers. Complete success attended their measures. They ordered immense reinforcements from the neighbouring departments ; the individuals concerned in the plot to deliver up the city were imprisoned, and general Irimbert, who was convicted, but on uncertain evidence of treachery, in giving up the lines of Weissenburg, was shot at the head of the army on the 9th of November. These spirited proceedings, however, were not sufficient to save Fort Vaubau, formerly called Fort Lewis, situated on an island in the middle of the Rhine, from falling

through the treachery of its commander into the hands of general Wurmser. At this place terminated the successes of the Austrian general. On the 21st of November he was compelled to retreat, and the republican army penetrated almost to the gates of Hagenau. In the meanwhile the French army of the Moselle advanced to co-operate with the grand army of the Rhine, and the united armies were entrusted to the command of general Pichegru. Immediately after their junction they defeated the Prussians in the neighbourhood of Saarbruck, thirty-six miles east of Metz ; on the subsequent day they forced the camp of the enemy at Bliescastle, and, without giving them any time to recover from their consternation, they proceeded towards Deux Ponts. By the skill and bravery of general Hoche, the heights of Millback and Hornback were speedily subdued, and the Prussians discovered that Deux Ponts was no longer tenable. On the 29th and 30th, the republicans, under Hoche, suffered severely by making a desperate attack on the posts of the duke of Brunswick, in the neighbourhood of Lautern ; but they soon experienced an ample compensation in the victories of the commander-in-chief, who, on the 8th of December, obtained all the redoubts of the enemy which defended Hagenau, at the point of the bayonet. The 22nd was equally glorious to the French, who made a prodigious slaughter of the allies, in dislodging them from Bischoilers. Two days afterwards the republicans pursued the fugitives as far as the heights of Wrotte, where the enemy were reported to be as strongly fortified as at Jemappe, but nothing could now resist the impetuosity of the French. Pichegru began to attack the allies with his artillery in the usual form, but finding that the cannonading proved ineffectual, and that the ardor of his troops was no longer to be restrained, he marched up to the very foot of the entrenchments, which he carried after a desperate resistance of three hours, obtaining possession of all the posts which the allies had abandoned. He made a triumphant entry into Weissenburg on the 27th of the same month, general Wurmser effected his retreat to the Rhine, and the duke of Brunswick obtained, with difficulty, a temporary refuge under the walls of Mentz.

On the 10th of August lord Hood, who had been dispatched with a powerful fleet from England, appeared off Marseilles, but too late to prevent its surrender. He then repaired to Toulon, where he was reinforced by a Spanish squadron under rear-admiral Gravina. Langara, the commander-in-chief of the Spanish fleet, afterwards joined him. Immediately on appearing before the port, he transmitted the first of the following documents to the constituted authorities of the town, and adopted the usual means of promoting the circulation of the second.

PRELIMINARY DECLARATION.

" If a capital and explicit declaration in favour of monarchy is made at Toulon and Marseilles, and the standard of royalty hoisted, the ships in the harbour dismantled, and the port and forts provisionally at my disposition, so as to allow of the egress and regress with safety, the people of Provence shall have all the assistance and support his Britannic majesty's fleet under my command can give ; and not an atom of private property of any individual shall be touched, but protected ; having no other view than that of restoring peace to a great nation upon just, liberal, and honourable terms : this must be the groundwork of the treaty.

" And whenever peace takes place, which I hope and trust will be soon, the port, with all the ships in the harbour, and forts of Toulon, shall be restored to France, with the stores of every kind, agreeable to the schedule that may be delivered.

" Given on board his Britannic majesty's ship Victory, off Toulon, this 23rd of August, 1793.

(Signed)   " HOOD."

PROCLAMATION,

By the right hon. Samuel, lord Hood, vice-admiral of the red, and commander-in-chief of his Britannic majesty's squadron in the Mediterranean, &c.

" *To the inhabitants in the towns and provinces in the south of France.*

" During four years you have been involved in a revolution, which has plunged you in anarchy, and rendered you a prey to factious leaders. After having destroyed your government, trampled under foot the laws, assassinated the virtuous, and authorized the commission of crimes, they have endeavoured to propagate throughout Europe their destructive system of every social order. They have constantly held forth to you the idea of liberty, while they have been robbing you of it. Every where they have preached respect to persons and property, and every where in their name it has been violated ; they have amused you with the sovereignty of the people, which they have constantly usurped ; they have declaimed against the abuses of royalty, in order to establish their tyranny upon the fragments of a throne still reeking with the blood of your legitimate sovereign. Frenchmen ! you groan under the pressure of want, and the privation of all specie ; your commerce and your industry are annihilated, your agriculture is checked, and the want of provisions threatens you with a horrible famine. Behold, then, the faithful picture of your wretched condition ; a situation so dreadful sensibly afflicts the coalesced powers ; they see no other remedy but the re-establishment of the French monarchy. It is for this, and the acts of aggression committed by the executive power of France, that we have armed in conjunction with the other coalesced powers. After mature reflection upon these leading objects, I come to offer you the force with which I am entrusted by my sovereign, in order to spare the further effusion of human blood, to crush with promptitude the factions, to re-establish a regular government in France, and thereby maintain peace and tranquillity in Europe. Decide, therefore, definitively, and with precision. Trust your hopes to the generosity of a loyal and free nation. In its name I have just given an unequivocal testimony to the well-disposed inhabitants of Marseilles, by granting to the commissioners sent on board the fleet under my command a passport for procuring a quantity of grain, of which this great town now stands so much in need. Be explicit, and I fly to your succour, in order to break the chain which surrounds you, and to be the instrument of making many years of happiness succeed to four years of misery and anarchy, in which your deluded country has been involved.

" Given on board his Britannic majesty's ship Victory, off Toulon, the 23rd of August, 1793.

        . (Signed)   " HOOD.
" By command of the admiral,
     . (Signed) " JOHN M'ARTHUR."

Declaration made to admiral lord Hood.

The general committee of the sections of Toulon having read the proclamation of admiral lord Hood, commander-in-chief of his Britannic majesty's squadron, together with his preliminary declaration; and, after having communicated these two papers to all the citizens of the town of Toulon, united in sections;

Considering that France is torn by anarchy, and that it is impossible to exist longer a prey to the factions with which the country is agitated, without its total destruction;

Considering that the southern departments, after having made long efforts to resist the oppression of a party of factious men, who have conspired to ruin them, find themselves drained and deprived of all resources to annihilate this coalition of the evil-disposed;

Considering, in short, that, determined not to submit to the tyranny of a convention that has sworn to ruin the nation, the people of Toulon, and those of Marseilles, would rather have recourse to the generosity of a loyal people, who have manifested the desire of protecting the true Frenchmen against the anarchists who wish to ruin them,

Declare to admiral Hood,

I. That the unanimous wish of the inhabitants of Toulon is to reject a constitution which does not promote their happiness, to adopt a monarchic government, such as it was originally by the constituent assembly of 1789; and, in consequence, they have proclaimed Lewis XVII. son of Lewis XVI. KING, and have sworn to acknowledge him, and no longer suffer the despotism of the tyrants which at this time govern France.

II. That the White Flag shall be hoisted the instant the English squadron anchors in the road of Toulon, and it will there meet the most friendly reception.

III. That the ships of war now in the road will be disarmed according to admiral Hood's wishes.

IV. That the citadel and the forts of the coast shall be provisionally at the disposal of the said admiral; but, for the better establishing the union which ought to exist between the two people, it is requested that the garrison shall be composed of an equal number of French and English, and that nevertheless the command shall devolve to the English.

V. The people of Toulon trust that the English nation will furnish speedily a force sufficient to assist in repelling the attacks with which they are at this moment threatened by the army of Italy, which marches towards Toulon, and by that of general Carteaux, who directs his forces against Marseilles.

VI. That the people of Toulon, full of confidence in the generous offers of admiral Hood, trust that all those who hold civil and military employments shall be continued in their places, and shall not be annoyed in their respective occupations.

VII. That the subsistence and succours of every kind, of which Toulon stands so much in need, will be assured to the inhabitants by the combined fleet of the powers coalesced.

VIII. That when peace will have been re-established in France, the ships and forts which will be put into the hands of the English shall be restored to the French nation, in the same state they were in when the inventory was delivered.

It is according to this declaration, if approved by admiral Hood, that the Toulonese will regard themselves, with good heart and will, as belonging to the English and the other powers coalesced, [and by whose succour will be brought about that peace after which they have panted so long.

(Signed)

Beaudeal, *president*. Reboul, *vice-president*. Reynaud, *secretary*. La Poype Vertrieux. Deydier Cadel. Andraw. Vialis. Barthelemy, *commissary of the department*. Possel. Fournier. Grival. Bte. Devant. Antoine Gabert. Porte. Joffre, and L. Cadiere, *commissaries of the municipality*. C. Garribow. Boullement. Ferrand. Chaussegros, *commandant of arms*. Burgues. Richaud, *commissary of the municipality*. Metfrund, *president of the municipality*. Bertrand. Sicard.

Though it appears from these documents that the central committee composed of the chief inhabitants of Toulon, had agreed to surrender the port, arsenals, and forts, in trust to admiral Hood, and had proclaimed Lewis XVII. yet a great proportion of the people and even the galley slaves were averse to these measures. But the most formidable opposition originated on the part of the sailors on board the fleet. Rear-admiral Trogoff had entered into all the views of the British commander, but he found a powerful adversary in his colleague, superintendant of the naval force at Toulon, Mons. St. Julien. This officer had been warped by two of the deputies on mission at Marseilles, to cause himself to be recognized as admiral-in-chief, and to adopt proper measures for the safety of the navy. He accordingly assembled the crews of the men of war, and was instantly elected their chief. On this, Trogoff retired to the city, and took possession of the forts on the left of the harbour. After a variety of unsuccessful measures had been adopted, with the view of gaining over the captains, the revolutionary committee declared that it would only allow them the space of half an hour to consent to the

VOL. I.

introduction of the combined fleet, at the expiration of which period, the forts should fire with red hot shot on their ships. These menaces, instead of intimidating the squadron, seemed to render it more determined, and it was declared by the council of officers, that they would rather destroy the city and perish themselves, than consent to the entrance of the enemy's squadron into the port of Toulon. Both parties were now preparing to have recourse to extremities, when some of the townsmen, knowing that the commanders of several of the ships were not unfriendly to their views, determined to enter into a negotiation, and effect their object by conciliatory measures. Means were accordingly recurred to, which proved successful. Trogoff, having hoisted his flag on board a corvette, under protection of the ramparts, immediately sailed for and anchored in the roads. On his arrival within sight of the fleet, he fired a gun, and threw out a signal for the ships to join him. On this, nearly all of them saluted their former admiral, and placed themselves under his command. St. Julien, who is described in lord Hood's dispatches, as a turbulent, hot-headed democrat, and to whom the crews of seven vessels still remained faithful, was desirous of opposing the entrance of the English fleet ; but, seeing himself abandoned by the officers, he found himself under the necessity of withdrawing, and made his escape in a boat. All opposition being terminated, 1500 men were landed from the English fleet, and immediately took possession of Fort Malgue. The French ships were warped into the inner road, according to agreement, and on the next day the combined squadrons anchored in the outer road ; after which, 1000 Spaniards were sent on shore to strengthen the English garrison. Rear-admiral Goodall was declared governor, and rear-admiral Gravina *commandant* of the troops.

Immediately after the surrender of Marseilles, Carteaux directed his march to Toulon, his army being augmented by a *levy en masse* of the southern provinces. In his progress a portion of his force was defeated at Ollioules, by a part of the garrison under sir George Keith Elphinstone. Lord Mulgrave arriving at Toulon, and being invested provisionally with the command of the troops, proposed evacuating that post, but before he could execute his intention, it was attacked by 5000 French, who drove out the allies in number only 400, who escaped without any considerable loss. The garrison was far too small for the defence of the place, though reinforced by 3000 Spaniards from the army of Roussillon, and bodies of Sardinians and Neapolitans. The protection of Toulon depended on the power of retaining a great number of posts, which could only be accomplished by an ample provision of force, which it was found impossible to collect. The duty, therefore, was excessively fatiguing, and the affairs of posts were frequent and bloody. Lord Mulgrave, with great intrepidity, gained the heights of La Grasse, where a fort was established, called, in honour of that commander, by his name. The enemy, in hopes of annoying the shipping in the harbour, occupied the heights of Pharon, from which they were dislodged after a severe action which lasted the whole day, by a body of British, Spanish, and Sardinian troops.

By this time Lyons had surrendered, and considerable draughts from the troops employed in its attack, and from the army of Italy, augmenting the force of the besiegers to 30,000 men; their spirit of enterprise became more vigorous in proportion, and affairs of posts became more and more frequent. Terror and treachery began to operate among the inhabitants of Toulon, and jealousies prevailed among the allied troops forming the garrison. In the beginning of November, the command of the army of Italy devolved upon general Carteaux, while that which laid siege to Toulon was conferred upon Dagobert. Reinforcements for the British troops having arrived from Gibraltar, under the command of general O'Hard, who had been previously appointed governor and commander-in-chief, the garrison on the 30th, made a sortie, with a view to demolish the works of the enemy, which they were erecting within cannon shot of the town. The troops sent to accomplish this object performed it with secrecy and success. The republicans being unexpectedly attacked, were seized with a panic, and precipitately fled. Animated by the facility with which they obtained the first advantage, the allied forces incautiously pursued the fugitives, and were unexpectedly attacked by a strong body of troops which was destined to cover the retreat of the forces, in case they should be discomfited. While general O'Hard was using every effort to bring off his troops in as regular a manner as possible, he was wounded in the arm and made prisoner by the French. The loss of the allies in this engagement, did not amount to less than 1000 men in killed, wounded, and prisoners.

The French having concentrated their forces, proceeded to attack Fort Mulgrave, situated on the west side of the great or outer road, which commands the entrance into the inner, and which here contracts to about 3900 feet. The assault and the defence of the besieged, were equally desperate. The fort was defended by twenty pieces of cannon, several mortars, and more than 3000 men; but it was impossible to resist the vigor and intrepidity by which it was assailed. It was attacked at five in the morning of the 15th of November, and the republican flag was displayed on its summit by six. The loss sustained by the French on this occasion, amounted to 200 men killed, and 500 wounded; of the allies, 800 were killed, and 500 taken prisoners, in the latter of whom were eight officers, and a Neapolitan prince, whose name has not been recorded. The loss of this fort gave the republicans the command of entrance to the inner harbour, and such was the terror of the allies at their unexpected success, that they abandoned all the other forts of which they had previously obtained possession, and found it necessary to remove their shipping beyond the reach of the shot and shells with which they were assailed by the enemy. On the 19th of December, the town, and part of the shipping, were set on fire in different places by the allies, after which they began a precipitate retreat, and the positions they evacuated were occupied by the republicans on the ensuing morning. The surrender of the naval arsenal must be in a great measure attributed to the skilful direction of the French artillery, which was committed to the superintendence of NAPOLEAN BUONAPARTE, a Corsican, who had lately been distinguished by the patronage of Barras. He was the reputed son of Charles Buonaparte, an attorney of Ajaccio, and of his wife Letitia Raniolini, afterwards mistress of count Marbœuf, through whose interest she obtained for her husband the office of solicitor-general for the island of Corsica. Marbœuf, whose claims to regard him with paternal affection were by no means equivocal, obtained the young Napolean admission to a provincial school in France, and afterwards removed him to the military school at Paris. He entered the service as lieutenant of artillery, and soon after returned to Corsica, where general Paoli appointed him successively captain and colonel of the national guards. On the English taking possession of Corsica, Buonaparte offered his services to Mr. Elliot, then viceroy of Corsica, which were refused. In consequence of this disappointment, he removed to France with his mother and the rest of his family, and resided for some time in obscurity near Toulon. On the capture of that port by the English, Salicetti recommended him to Barras, the acting commissary, and to the opportunity which the evacuation of the fort presented him, of testifying his skill, his intrepidity, and his inhumanity, the last of which qualities was always a recommendation to the French government, must be attributed the origin of his future greatness. After having contributed to the expulsion of the confederates, he was entrusted with the punishment of the inhabitants who had abjured the authority of the convention, and favoured the enemies of France; and exhibited in the execution of his sanguinary office, the same ferocity of temper, the same insensibility to all the sympathies of human nature, and the same determined and ingenious malignity, which marked his conduct on more important occasions,

and in situations more open to public scrutiny.

The haste with which the allies abandoned the city, enabled the conquerors to detain much valuable property, and to take possession of a number of vessels belonging to the allied powers. The deplorable situation in which the inhabitants were left by the desertion and flight of the allies, afforded a decisive and melancholy proof of the cruelty and impolicy of this expedition; and I shall have too many opportunities, as the narration proceeds to condemn that system, (if system it can be called) of narrow and unenlightened policy which projected the conquest of possessions which could not be retained, and to the vain ambition of momentary triumph, sacrificed the most sacred feelings of humanity, and the most obvious considerations of justice and policy. When the inhabitants perceived that the allies had determined to leave them to their fate, they repaired in multitudes to the shores, and appealed to that protection which they had expected to receive from the generosity and honour of the British commanders, and which had been promised under the most solemn and deliberate sanctions. It must indeed be acknowledged that several efforts were made to convey thousands of them to the ships, yet it was found impossible not to leave multitudes behind, to suffer the persecution and the tortures which would be inflicted upon them by their countrymen. Numbers of them were beheld as they stood on the beach to perpetrate the crime of deliberate suicide, deeming that a more lenient mode of terminating existence, than the revengeful cruelty of their countrymen; others threw themselves into the water, vainly endeavouring to reach the British vessels. The flames continued to spread with astonishing rapidity, and the ships, previously set on fire, were every moment expected to blow up, and to bury the persons, the buildings, and the property that surrounded them, in irretrievable destruction.

But if the land exhibited a scene of unexampled horror, the spectacle on board

Q 2

the fleet, was, if possible, still more dreadful. The ships were filled with a motley group of all descriptions, men, women, and children, old and young, and of various nations. The groans of wounded and dying patients from the various hospitals, the mournful exclamations and despairing cries of multitudes, for their parents, wives, husbands, and children, who had been unavoidably left on shore, and the frantic gestures and melancholy countenances of those who had been reduced by the late events, from the highest affluence to the most deplorable poverty, presented in their combination a picture of misery, anguish, and distress, disgraceful to the government, which, in the pursuit of a minor object of policy, had thus endangered the happiness of thousands, and multiplied the sources of guilt, misfortune, and despair. I have already expressed my candid but decided approbation of the general policy of William Pitt, but it was unfortunately the great and repeated error of him and his coadjutors, that in their prosecution of extensive schemes, and in their views of general benevolence, they utterly disregarded the nature and the immediate consequences of the incidental measures by which their plans were to be accomplished. At the moment when they were seriously and enthusiastically employed in arranging the defence or projecting the deliverance of Europe, their subordinate measures were fatal to ourselves, destructive to our allies, and injurious to the objects of our compassion. It was the duty of a British minister to be well assured that his designs on the coast or the possessions of the enemy, should not conduce by their possible failure, to the punishment, disgrace, and discouragement, of the friends of England; that if any conquest were gained, it should be so permanent as to prevent the possibility of our partizans becoming the victims of Gallic revenge, or so tenable as to permit the most secure and extensive stipulations in their favour. In the expedition to Toulon we acted as if we had proceeded on a regular plan to expose the friends of loyalty and of England, to the exemplary vengeance of the republican

government. We neither provided a force sufficiently numerous to secure our conquest after it was made, nor withdrew from a position no longer to be retained, at a moment when negotiation in favour of the inhabitants, or the flight of individuals most obnoxious to the convention, might have been possible. We attempted the enterprise at any risk, and without any regard to the welfare of the inhabitants; we occupied the town as long as we could without foresight, without reflection, and without any feeling of humanity. We retired as soon as we found the place untenable, leaving the inhabitants to evade the fury or endure the persecutions of the government they had offended; dispirited by misfortune, exasperated by disappointment, and loud in their expressions of resentment, against English injustice and ingratitude.

The British found thirty-one ships of the line at Toulon, of which thirteen were left behind, nine burnt in the harbour, and one at Leghorn, besides four more which lord Hood had sent to Rochfort and Brest with 500 seamen belonging to France, as he laboured under considerable apprehension that it would be dangerous to confide in them. Great Britain, therefore, acquired by this sanguinary and expensive expedition to Toulon, no more than three ships of the line and five frigates; lord Hood finding it impossible to bring off a greater number. The French took from the allies 100 pieces of cannon, 400 oxen, sheep, and hogs, vast quantities of forage, and every other species of provision. When the news arrived in Paris of the recapture of Toulon, a grand festival was ordered to be celebrated in that city on the 30th of December. It was attended by all the members of the convention, who went in procession from the gardens of the *Palais National* to the *Champs de Mars*.

Rear-admiral Trogoff, on board the commerce de Marseilles, with the Puissant and Pompée, two other ships of the line, and the Pearl, Arethusa, and Topaze frigates, with several corvettes, formed part of the English fleet, which, under the command of lord Hood, proceeded to Hieres bay, and soon after landed the men, women, and children, with which his decks were encumbered.

Thus after a siege of three months and an incessant assault of five successive days and nights, Toulon was restored to France: the besieging army, which had provided four thousand ladders for an assault, having entered it at seven o'clock in the morning subsequent to the evacuation. Of the inhabitants who had borne arms against their country, or favoured the cause of the allies, some still remained, and these either put an end to their existence by a voluntary death, or perished by the guillotine and the musket. The most cruel punishments were inflicted on the royalists, and the conquerors sullied their victory, and disgraced themselves by a terrible and indiscriminate carnage. Workmen were invited from all the neighbouring departments to destroy the principal houses ; the population was visibly decreased by daily butchery ; the name of Port de la Montague was substituted, by a decree, for that of Toulon ; and the citizens were declared to be no longer within the protection of the law.

The fleets of the contending nations had no engagement in this year, but some maritime expeditions were undertaken. An armament sailed to Tobago, and the island was easily reduced : but when a squadron had appeared with a similar view before Martinique, the debarkation of a small force proved fruitless, and the invaders quickly retired. In the northern part of the western hemisphere, the islands of St. Pierre and Miquelon were added to the British possessions. In India the ships and factories of the enemy were taken as soon as intelligence of the war arrived, and Pondicherry was surrendered by a spiritless garrison. In the Mediterranean, our naval commanders endeavoured to intimidate the grand duke of Tuscany and the republic of Genoa, into a union with the allied powers, but these efforts were counteracted by the desire of peace, and the influence of French intrigue. On the 20th of October, a declaration was published on the part of Great Britain, vindicating the employment of external force for the establishment of order in France, as such interference was essential to the security and repose of other powers ; recommending an hereditary monarchy, yet not insisting on the exclusion of any other form of government which might prove compatible with the safety and peace of Europe.

It is now time to return to the proceedings of the successful party in France after the destruction of the Girondists. The faction of Robespierre was indisputably triumphant, the system of terror was completely established, and the government of France was become a government of blood, to be sustained by the terrors of the guillotine. The execution [of Custine was succeeded by that of the unfortunate queen. After the murder of her ill-fated husband, she had been separated from her family in the Temple, and on the 1st of August she was suddenly conveyed to the Conciergerie, a prison destined for the reception of the vilest malefactors. In this situation she was treated with every variety of vulgar insult, and subjected to every torture, short of personal violence, which inhumanity could invent. The cell in which she was immured was only eight feet square, her bed was a mattrass of straw, and her food of the meanest kind. She was denied the privilege of being alone, two soldiers being appointed to watch her night and day. On the 15th of October she was brought before the revolutionary tribunal. A committee of the Jacobin club was selected to prepare the act of accusation, and Hebert, one of the agents, accused her of having formed an incestuous intercourse with her own son, a prince not more than eight years old. The act of accusation was a repetition of the libels which had been repeatedly pronounced | in the convention, and circulated with so much malignity and industry. Some allusions to the irregularities of her life were made in the interrogatory to which she was subjected ; but she answered with magnanimous defiance, that no one could rejoice more than herself, that every act of her life should be closely investigated. During the progress of her trial, her deportment was firm, dignified, and composed; her acquittal was not expected; the pronunciation of the sentence being resolved before the commencement of the trial, she was found guilty (October 15th) of all the charges, and sentenced to die on the following day. Before she was conducted to her dungeon it was four in the morning, and twelve was the hour appointed for the infliction of the sentence. She was not allowed a clergyman of her own choice, but provided with a constitutional priest. At half past eleven the queen was brought out of prison, and conducted in a common cart to the place of execution. Her hair was entirely cut off from the back of her head, which was covered with a small white cap: she wore a white undress, her hands were tied behind her, and she sat with her back to the horses. The royal victim met her fate with courage, and, during her progress to the place of execution, betrayed neither weakness, nor affectation of superior heroism. She submitted to her fate with calm resignation, on the same spot where her husband had formerly suffered. The body was thrown into a grave in the church yard of La Madelaine, which was filled up with quicklime.

The death of the queen was succeeded by the massacre or execution of every individual whose talents or opinions rendered him the object of suspicion or alarm to the faction of Robespierre. In the catalogue of victims were found the names of Manuel, president of the commune of Paris, the learned and philosophic Bailly, and the virtuous Rabaut de St. Etienne. La Brun the minister, made his escape from Paris, but was seized in a cock-loft and put to death. Claviere, on receiving his act of accusation, stabbed himself, and his wife swallowed poison. Roland was twice arrested during the contest of the two factions, and had both times the good fortune to be liberated. On the last occasion he made his escape from Paris, and his wife was taken into custody as a hostage for him. She was afterwards liberated, and again more formally imprisoned in St. Pelagie, where she awaited her fate with firmness, and passed a great portion of her time in writing. After the execution of the Brissotines, she was interrogated before the revolutionary tribunal, and, after a short abode in the Conciergerie, sentenced to death. Roland, when he heard of his wife's execution, quitted his assylum at Rouen, and stabbed himself on the high road to Paris.

To secure the triumph of murder, injustice, and rapacity, Robespierre was well aware that it would be necessary to efface from the mind of the people every impression of religion. Every endeavour was made to degrade the character and aggravate the distresses of the priesthood. Fouché being sent on a mission to Nevers, issued a decree, that all religious signs in streets, squares, and public places, should be *annihilated*. Every citizen deceased, was, within forty-eight hours, to be buried without ceremony, in a burying-place common to all persuasions, planted with trees, under the shade of which was to be an image resembling sleep; and on the door of the enclosure an inscription, "DEATH IS AN ETERNAL SLEEP." Several members of the clerical body attended at the bar of the convention, declaring their intention to divest themselves of the character with which they had been clothed by superstition; and the triumph of impiety was completed by the celebration of a splendid fête, in which *Reason* was represented as a goddess, personated by a superanuated courtezan. A number of allegorical deities, liberty, equality, indivisibility, and many others, were consecrated as objects of worship. To promote this system of paganism, agents were dispatched to all the departments to complete the change. The populace, who, in consequence of these proceedings, considered themselves as authorised to plunder every place of worship, public or private, divided, with the convention, large heaps of shrines, figures, and vessels, hitherto employed in the offices of religion. As the recurrence of Sunday had a natural tendency to recal the minds of the people to the remembrance of their former faith, and to indulgence in sober and virtuous habits, it became one of the first objects of Robespierre to abolish the sabbath. A new calendar therefore was introduced, which destroyed all reference to Christian history and precepts, and which acknowledged no distinction of holy-days and sacramental periods. Instead of the seventh day, the tenth was appointed as an interval of civil respite, to the total exclusion of all religious exercises. They divided the year into twelve months, consisting each of thirty days, and distinguished by names expressive of their usual produce, temperature, or appearance; while to complete the year, five supplementary days are added, and denominated, Sans culloïdes. As an acquaintance with the dates of the foreign journals and the chronology of French affairs during a period of many years, considerably depends on a knowledge of this calendar, I shall here insert it.

NEW FRENCH CALENDAR

FOR THE YEAR 1793, COMMENCING SEPTEMBER 22nd.

New French Names of the Months.	English.	Term.	Duration days.
AUTUMN.			
Vindemiaire	Vintage Month from	September 22 to October 21 includes	30
Brumaire	Fog Month —	October 22 to November 20	30
Frimaire	Sleet Month —	November 21 to December 20	30
WINTER.			
Nivose	Snow Month —	December 21 to January 19	30
Pluviose	Rain Month —	January 20 to February 18	30
Ventose	Wind Month —	February 19 to March 20	30
SPRING.			
Germinal	Sprouts Month —	March 21 to April 19	30
Floreal	Flowers Month —	April 20 to May 19	30
Priaireal	Pasture Month —	May 20 to June 18	30
SUMMER.			
Messidor	Harvest Month —	June 19 to July 18	30
Fervidor	Hot Month —	July 19 to August 17	30
Fructidor	Fruit Month —	August 18 to September 16	30

SANS CULLOTIDES, as Feasts dedicated to

Les Virtus	The Virtues	September 17	1
Le Genie	Genius	September 18	1
Le Travil	Labour	September 19	1
L'Opinion,	Opinion	September 20	1
Les Recompenses	Rewards	September 21	1

365

The intercalary day of every fourth year is to be called

LA SANS CULLOTIDE,

On which there is to be a national renovation of the oath, *To Live Free or Die.*

The month is divided into three DECADES, the days of which are called, from the Latin numerals,

1. Primidi   4. Quartidi   7. Septidi
2. Duodi   5. Quintidi   8. Octodi
3. Tridi   6. Sextidi   9. Nonodi, and
10. Decadi, which is to be the day of rest.

The agitated state of the metropolis of France, the distresses of the provinces, and the succession of cruelties which attended the government of Robespierre, might have been expected to repress the efforts of genius, and to discourage every species of literary and philosophical research; but the ingenuity and mental activity of the French people, even on subjects of abstract speculation, was conspicuous under a concurrence of the most unpropitious : circumstances. A portion of the convention formed a committee exclusively devoted to useful projects, and under the title of the committee of public instruction, became the medium through which many extensive reforms and useful regulations were recommended. A decree was passed for dividing money, weights, and measures, into decimal parts ; the erection of telegraphs, according to the plan of Chappe, an engineer, who does not seem to have been aware that this instrument of communication had been described by an English author a century before, was facilitated by the measures of the committee of public safety ; and a stipend of 2400 livres each, (£100, valuing the livre at ten pence,) was allowed to twelve students in the arts, who should reside in Italy and Flanders.

The measures relative to religion, afford us an opportunity of observing another feature in the character of Robespierre. On the publication of a decree for shutting up the churches, he saw that the people were shocked at the impiety of the measure ; and therefore with an hypocrisy well adapted to the temper of a villain, he made a timely sacrifice to popularity by recommending a repeal of the decree. His influence over the multitude was at this period unbounded ; and, by securing the popular favour, he was enabled to acquire undisputed ascendency over his associates. Of these one of the ablest was Danton. This revolutionist, though much superior to Robespierre in the talents and accomplishments which would have commanded attention in the Roman or British senate, did not equal him in the arts which conciliate an ignorant rabble. The Parisian populace loved and revered Robespierre, because in manners, appearance, and temper, he was one of themselves. His ruling passions were fear and envy ; a jealousy of superior talent, which rendered him the cruel and inveterate persecutor of his ablest coadjutors and opponents ; and a dread of their political ascendency, rendered doubly intense by the consciousness of the fate to which he would be justly consigned, on his removal from the arbitrary government of the republic. He hated and feared the aristocracy of genius, as superior to his own pretensions, and as the means of effecting his downfall. But his tyranny, dreadful as it was, produced by its very terrors the most gigantic efforts against the enemies of France.

The success of the French revolutionists was regarded with unfeigned satisfaction by the democrats, and disaffected subjects in other countries. Several proofs were adduced of the perfect understanding between the French convention and many societies established in Great Britain, professedly with the intention of promoting a reform in the system of representation and of government. Even when the acts of the 10th of August, 1792, had deposed and imprisoned the king and murdered his friends ; when, during the month of September, the nobility, gentry, and clergy, were devoted to destruction ; the English societies eagerly testified their joy and congratulations on the success of those with whose principles they declared their own to coincide, and with whose feelings they avowed the most cordial sympathy. The chief democratical clubs of England were at this period the *revolution club*, the society for constitutional information, and the London Corresponding Society, connected with numerous bodies of the same description throughout the kingdom. The addresses transmitted by these clubs intimated their approval of the doctrines of the revolutionists, and that of the society for constitutional information, was accompanied by a present of shoes. The address of the London Corresponding Society was subscribed by Thomas Hardy, a shoe-maker, and Maurice Margarat, a knife-grinder. The convention received the addresses with great satisfaction; and expressed in their reply the most confident hopes that they would shortly obtain the opportunity of establishing a national convention in England. The convention conferred the honour of citizenship on several of their correspondents, and some of the departments chose for their representatives such Englishmen as they supposed to be best adapted to the expression of their doctrines and sentiments. Of these the most conspicuous were Dr. Joseph Priestley and Thomas Paine. The latter was contented with a plain acknowledgment of thanks, but the reciprocations of civility between Priestley and the convention were unworthy of a man so justly and proudly distinguished by his scholastic attainments and his philosophical discoveries.

Though the arm of the law was sufficiently strong to restrain the open invader of the constitution, it was not able to oppose, with immediate energy, the secret arts of its enemies. To remedy the imperfection of the law, by the adoption of means of counteraction to which the government could not have recourse, an association was formed by Mr. Reeves, a lawyer, for the avowed purpose of protecting liberty and property against republicans and levellers. It would be useless to descant on the evident folly, injustice, and oppression of such associations; and the measures of this in particular, were distinguished by hypocrisy, bigotry, and insolence. If any

thing can excite the warm indignation of the historian, and justify the unpremeditated expression of his resentment, it is the spectacle of a just and noble cause injured and debased by the interference of injudicious partisans. The pamphlets of Mr. Reeves and his coadjutors, might be read with some degree of pleasure by those who enthusiastically espoused the opinions which he supported, but they were well calculated by their violence, intolerance, and bigotry, to decide the wavering, provoke the temperate, and exasperate the discontented.

The spirit of innovation and reform extended from England to her sister kingdom, and to Scotland. In Ireland a society was established for the emancipation of the Roman catholics. This club, constructed on the model of the Jacobins, assumed the name of United Irishmen, an appellation afterwards rendered so worthy of remembrance. The United Irishmen, as a party, were not connected particularly with the catholics, but consisted of the votaries of innovation in general. In Scotland the prevalence of seditious practices was so notorious, that it was deemed necessary for the public safety to proceed with the utmost severity against offences of that description. Messrs. Muir and Palmer were sentenced to transportation by the circuit court of justiciary; the former for exciting sedition, the latter for circulating a seditious hand-bill. Muir pleaded in his vindication, that he only advised the people to pursue constitutional measures to obtain a reform. Both these gentlemen possessed fair and unimpeached moral characters; and it was easily perceived that the judges, if they had not acted contrary to the express letter of the law, had extended its severity to the utmost limit. To obviate the effects of this severity, several bills were introduced to emancipate the people of Scotland from the evils of which they most bitterly complained. The lenity of the government, however, tended rather to aggravate than to correct the evil: a club of persons entertaining similar sentiments to those of Muir and Palmer, met at Edinburgh, and under the title of the Scotch Convention of Delegates, imitated and supported all the proceedings of the

London Corresponding Society. Their proceedings were as intemperate as destructive to the welfare of society, and before they had brought their deliberations to a conclusion, they were interrupted by the civil power and dispersed. Skirving, Margarot, and Gerald, three of their most active members, were tried for sedition, and received sentence of transportation. The conduct of the judges who passed the sentence, was severely reprehended even by the friends of government, and became the subject of future discussion in the English parliament.

Notwithstanding the decisive evidence which Great Britain had adduced of her determination to support the dearest interests of the continental powers, she became at this period the object of selfish and malignant jealousy. Her commercial prosperity excited the envy and the hatred of many of the continental powers, and was regarded by Prussia in particular, as injurious to the interest of the other states of Europe. Though it was notorious that by her excellent constitution, and by the spirit of industry which it protected, exerting itself in agriculture, manufactures, and commerce, Great Britain was enabled to maintain her station among the principal states of Europe ; and was enabled, at this moment, to preserve the balance of power against the overwhelming influence of France : though it had been repeatedly proved, that what is invidiously termed a monopoly of commerce, is highly beneficial to other nations, when considered in their individual capacity ; that it facilitates to other nations the supply of many useful articles of life, and that, where a competition

is permitted among the numerous merchants of the same nation, monopoly is impracticable ; yet the English have been accused by nations less free, less industrious, and consequently less flourishing, than herself, of monopolizing trade, engrossing the sources of wealth, and counteracting the industry of others. These impressions created that jealousy which the indolent always feel towards the active and the prosperous, and which the contemplation of our abundant resources excited in states, whose supplies were less copious or attended with greater difficulty. They were ignorant that the only respect in which it is at all important to the consumers, whether they be provided with colonial produce by this or that European people, is the degree of industry and wealth in the nation with which they deal. Among nations equal in other respects, the richest and most industrious will always sell at the lowest price. The greater the capital, the more active the industry, the more perfect the art and ability employed in any business, so much more productive does it prove, so much less is the equivalent required from the consumer. The productions of the East and West Indies in the markets of Europe, are fruits of the navigation, the capital, the labour, and ingenuity of the British nation. As far as others possess not the same advantages and resources to enable them to sell at the same prices, and as long as they continue incapable of so doing, so far and so long must the commercial predominance of the English, or what is improperly called commercial monopoly, remain a decided and evident advantage to the consumer in every part of Europe.

HISTORY OF THE WAR.

CHAP. VIII.

THE disasters sustained by the confederates in the latter part of the campaign, did not change their opinion, or enfeeble the resolution of the British cabinet. The minister appeared to be stimulated by misfortune to still more vigorous exertions, and he looked forward with confidence to the decline of that national spirit, which appeared to him to have been chiefly supported by a system of paper currency, and by the influence of a despotic government acting on the momentary frenzy of the people.

In opening the session, the king observed that he and his subjects were engaged in a momentous contest, on the issue of which depended the maintenance of the national constitution, laws, and religion, and the security of all civil society. Having mentioned the advantages obtained by the arms of the confederate powers, he added that the circumstances by which their further progress had been impeded, not only proved the necessity of vigorous perseverance, but confirmed the expectation of ultimate success. Their enemies had " derived the means of temporary exertion from a system which had enabled them to dispose arbitrarily of the lives and property of a numerous people; but these efforts, productive as they had been of internal discontent and confusion, tended rapidly to exhaust the national and real strength

1794.

of the country." He regretted the necessity of continuing the war; but he thought he should ill consult the essential interests of his people, if he desired peace on any grounds exclusive of a due provision for their permanent safety, and for the independence and security of Europe. Again referring to the " true grounds of the war," he begged his hearers to recollect, that an attack had been made on his allies, founded on principles tending to the destruction of of all property, to the subversion of the laws and religion of every civilized nation, and to the general introduction of a horrible system of rapine, anarchy, and impiety.

An address was warmly supported by lord Auckland, who inveighed in strong terms against the French government, and execrated that spirit of impiety, despotism, inhumanity, and rapine, which defied the laws both of God and man. He allowed that the republican leaders had shown considerable abilities, and had called into action a most formidable force; but he trusted that Great Britain and her allies would be able to stem the torrent, and rescue the civilized world from the danger of anarchy and ruin. The earl of Guildford wished for a speedy negotiation, as we had rushed into the war without necessity; and he proposed an amendment for that salutary purpose. The duke of Portland justified the war as strictly defensive, and

R 2

as necessary for the preservation of the Christian religion, political and civil liberty, law, and order. Earl Spencer traced the same line of argument; and the earl of Coventry, with equal zeal, supported the cause of hostility. This nobleman did not prove himself a true prophet, or repose sufficient confidence in the "wooden walls" of our island, when he said that the consequence of the subjection of the United Provinces to the power of France would be ruinous to Great Britain, whose "proud navy" would no longer be able to protect her. The duke of Norfolk asserted, that he had as strong a zeal for the support of our constitution as any of the peers could have; but he was not impelled by that zeal to an encouragement of the war, as he did not conceive that our happy establishment was endangered by the proceedings of the French. The earl of Derby wished that the object of the war might be defined; but the earl of Mansfield said, that it was sufficiently marked out in the speech from the throne. It was not, as it had been called by many, a war of kings. It was of a much more important nature, being directed to the preservation of general order, religion, and morality. As the French had not abandoned those alarming principles which had roused us to arms, and as their government was that of a faction, instead of the permanent power of legitimate rulers, it would be impolitic and unsafe to negotiate with such an enemy. Lord Grenville also animadverted on the declarations, the opinions, and the conduct, of the different parties in France, and endeavoured to show, from the convulsed state of that country, the fallacy of all hopes of a successful negotiation. On a division, the supporters of the address were 97, while only 12 peers voted for its modification.

In the house of commons, when an address had been offered, abounding with strong expressions of zeal for the Anti-Gallican cause, lord Wycombe proposed an amendment in recommendation of pacific overtures, as the war, even if it should be much more ably conducted than it had hitherto been, did not promise the desired success. Colonel Tarleton denied the justice of the war, and was unwilling to concur in thanking the minister for losses and disgraces. The earl of Mornington vindicated the war, as founded in justice, policy, and necessity; referring to the authority of Brissot for a proof of the aggression of France, and her wish to revolutionize every regular government. He was so pleased with the general result of the campaign, that he entertained confident hopes of decisive success. He considered the foundations of the French power as so unsound, and the new government as so weak, that the effect of the confederate arms would soon be triumphantly striking. He acknowledged that the enemy had displayed extraordinary vigor and energy; but he was convinced that power obtained by a system of terror would not be permanent. He opposed a negotiation as unlikely to be effectual in the present circumstances, and advised a continuance of the most resolute exertions of hostility.—Mr. Sheridan did not pretend to know what were the real grounds of the war; but he knew the means by which we had been led into it. Whatever had been said or written by weak enthusiasts or violent demagogues in France, calculated to rouse the indignation or excite the fears of our countrymen, had been brought forward with studious aggravation, to aid the views of those who had determined to plunge us into hostilities. It could not be denied that horrible enormities had been committed in that distracted country; but the chief guilt of those excesses rested on the officious zealots who had treated the French as beasts and monsters, and had driven them into a state of desperation and frenzy. It had never been proved, to the conviction of any reflecting mind, that the French were desirous of a war with Great Britain. It appeared to be, on our part, a war of choice rather than of necessity; we were the aggressors rather than the French. But, notwithstanding the rage with which we had inspired them, there was reason to believe that they would conclude peace on terms not dishonourable or disadvantageous to us, if we would engage to leave them to the exercise of their own will within their own territories. It had been asked, "With whom shall we treat?" The answer was obvious;—"with those men (whatever may be their denomination) who administer the French government, and direct both the civil and military affairs of the nation." With these rulers a peace might be as secure as if the monarchy of France still subsisted.—Mr. Windham, considering the French as the enemies of every regular government, represented the war as just and necessary, and protested against the idea of negotiating with a set of factious revolutionists. Mr. Dundas extolled the success of our arms, and gloried in his participation of the honour which the ministry might derive from so auspicious a commencement of hostilities. Mr. Fox, on the other hand, spoke very contemptuously of the management of the war, and prognosticated disgrace from the continuance of Mr. Pitt and his friends in power, unqualified as they were for the direction of naval and military concerns. He earnestly wished that the war had been avoided; and, that we were not obliged to rush into it, he was fully convinced. But, as we had entered into it, it ought either to be conducted with ability and vigor, or to be closed by a prudent negotiation. It had been said, that no treaty with any modification of Jacobin government would be secure. The security, indeed, would not be as secure as if the monarchy of France still subsisted, would not be as secure as a true friend to the permanent interest of this country might be inclined to wish; but he had no doubt that an eventual peace with the republicans would be as secure as any peace which had been concluded with monarchical France. If, however, a negotiation should fail, we should at least have the advantage of proving the continued war to be on our part strictly defensive, and should thus render it more popular; and, in France, the enthusiasm which had been so signally evinced would be considerably diminished, as the people would then find that they were not contending against unjust aggression.—Mr. Pitt combated the proposal of negotiation as unseasonable and humiliating. The grounds of contest, he

said, still existed in their full force. The French continued to act upon principles subversive of all regular government, and destructive of social order. They had been guilty of territorial usurpation, had formed hostile intentions against Holland, and disclosed views of the most unbounded ambition and rapacity. They had disgraced themselves by the most outrageous cruelties and the most execrable enormities; and their conduct was so dreadfully dangerous to the independence and security of other nations, that, unless they should follow a new course of action, peace would be less desirable than even the most disastrous war. If the war had been ill conducted, a change of ministers might be expedient; but nothing which had recently occurred could justify a change of our system.—An amendment moved by Mr. Fox, in favour of peace, was now rejected by a majority of 218; and the address was voted in the form prescribed by the minister.

When the late treaties had been communicated to the two houses, Mr. Fox objected to that which had been adjusted with the king of Sardinia. By this agreement, he said, we were to receive nothing, in return for a considerable subsidy and for a complete guaranty of dominion. We were to pay a prince for defending his own territories. This was a curious instance of modern diplomatic skill—an act of unnecessary liberality, a strange prodigality of service. Mr. Powys vindicated the treaty, and observed that the subsidy was not granted for the mere defence of the territories of his Sardinian majesty, but for the general purposes of the war. Mr. Canning approved the particular terms of the treaty, and justified its grand object; and it received, without a division, the sanction of the house.

The detention of a body of Hessians in the Isle of Wight, without the previous consent of parliament, furnished a topic of debate. Mr. Grey moved that the commons should declare it to be contrary to law; and the earl of Albemarle contended for the propriety of enacting a bill of indemnity on account of this invasion of the constitution: but neither house would allow that the ministers deserved the least blame.

No opposition was made to a demand of 85,000 men for the maritime service; but the increase of the army to 60,000 men did not appear to every member to be necessary, though the majority allowed that number. The whole supply of the year exceeded 20,228,000 pounds. As a loan was negotiated for eleven millions, spirituous liquors, glass, bricks, paper, and other articles, were subjected to new duties; and an additional revenue was drawn from attorneys.

To guard against an invasion with which the French menaced this country, a bill was enacted for the augmentation of the militia; and the court encouraged the formation of volunteer companies both of cavalry and infantry, not only with that view, but also for the suppression of riots. Subscriptions were solicited for defraying the expense of these associations; and thus considerable sums were levied by ministerial requisition, before the consent of the parliament was obtained; an irregular proceeding which was justly censured in both houses.

Amidst this rage for arming, it was proposed that French emigrants should be enlisted in the king's service, chiefly to act on the continent. The danger of intrusting the crown with an army of this description, and also the cruelty of sending these men to almost certain destruction, were noticed by Mr. Sheridan and the duke of Bedford; but Mr. Burke and Mr. Dundas, and various speakers in each house, recommended the bill of enlistment as a just and politic measure, which would furnish the refugees with a desired opportunity of honourable exertion.

An address was proposed by Mr. Grey against the treaties of alliance which had been concluded with foreign powers to the prejudice of British interests; and a similar application to the throne was moved by the earl of Guildford. These motions, however, were as unsuccessful as that of the marquis of Lansdown for a negotiation with the French, or those of earl Stanhope for the acknowledgment of the republic, and

the forbearance of all encroachment on the independent rights of that nation.

The folly of reposing great confidence in our allies, and the weakness and credulity of the minister, became topics of spirited animadversion when a treaty was announced by which the king had bound himself, in concert with the Dutch, to the payment of £50,000 per month for a Prussian army of 62,400 men, of £300,000 for putting that force in a state of action, and of a large sum for bread and forage. It was observed, that the king of Prussia was more interested in opposing the French than we could be; that he had been one of the chief instigators of the war; that former engagements required him to continue hostilities without being subsidised by Great Britain; that the terms were extravagantly high; and that the men who thus lavished the treasures of their country had no reason to expect good faith from a venal and fickle prince, who would probably employ our subsidies for the subversion of the Polish state. It was said in reply, that the terms were moderate, that it was our interest to secure the continuance of Prussia in the confederacy, and that it was illiberal to doubt the honour of that court.

A message from the king, more essentially connected with the interests of this country, was soon after delivered. It referred to the seditious practices of democratic societies, and intimated the necessity of taking measures for baffling their dangerous designs. The papers belonging to these clubs were examined by a committee; and a report was soon presented by Mr. Pitt. It was affirmed, as the result of the inquiry, that the "society for constitutional information" and the "London Corresponding Society," under the pretence of reform, aimed at the subversion of the government; that other associations, in different parts of the kingdom, pursued the same object; that they had endeavoured to promote a general convention of the people; that they had provided arms for the more effectual prosecution of their nefarious purposes; that meetings of popular delegates took place at Edinburgh in 1792 and the following year; that their proceedings were regulated on the French model ; and that, after the dispersion of this convention, the two leading societies exerted their efforts to procure a similar meeting in England, which should supersede the authority of parliament.

Having expatiated on the flagitious schemes of the societies, the minister proposed that the *habeas corpus* act should be suspended in cases of treason and sedition. Mr. Fox was of opinion, that this stretch of power was not justified by the evidence which had been adduced against the associations ; and Mr. Sheridan deprecated, as unconstitutional and dangerous, the grant of an arbitrary power of imprisonment : but Mr. Burke was convinced that the power in question would not be abused, and that it would be attended with salutary effects ; and Mr. Windham eagerly advised the strongest measures of coertion. The bill of suspension was rapidly enacted ; and, after spirited debates, an address was voted, promising the strenuous co-operation of the two houses with the executive power for the suppression of all seditious attempts and treasonable conspiracies.

The conduct of the war was the subject of strong censure in various debates ; and the improbability of its final success was repeatedly noticed. Mr. Jenkinson exposed himself to misplaced ridicule in one of those discussions, by asserting the practicability of marching to Paris, and overturning the obnoxious government.—After a review of the French revolution and the progress of the war, the duke of Bedford proposed, as preliminaries to a peace, a candid and explicit declaration of the object of the war, and a renunciation of all concern with the internal affairs of France ; and Mr. Fox ably harangued the commons on the same ground ; but both houses exploded all propositions of this nature.

On the day of prorogation, the king rewarded, with posts of honour and emolument, the zeal of some of those supporters of the war who had formerly gloried in the appellation of Whigs. Earl Fitz- william was appointed president of the council ; the duke of Portland became one of the secretaries of state ; earl Spencer was declared keeper of the privy seal, and Mr. Windham secretary at war.

At the beginning of this year the French royalists in the island of Noirmoutier, had considerably strengthened their fortifications. Convinced, however, that their cause was desperate, they made a voluntary surrender of the town on the 3rd of January, before the republican army arrived within reach of their batteries. It was natural to expect that the sanguinary disposition of the republicans would impel them to treat these unhappy men with merciless severity. Five hundred of them were shot at Nantz on the 15th of February, the guillotine being laid aside as not sufficiently expeditious. Multitudes were dispatched by grape-shot from the mouths of cannon, or sunk in barges according to the humor of their conquerors ; and more than 4000 were smothered in a single pit.

The extirpation of the royalists enabled the convention to prosecute the war with renovated vigor, and their designs were materially assisted by the serious misunderstanding which now distracted the councils of the allies. The duke of Brunswick was disgusted with the conduct of general Wurmser, in abandoning the lines of Weissenburg without risking a battle, a measure which had compelled his serene highness to raise the siege of Landau. He had written a letter to the king of Prussia complaining of the want of concert, and extending his animadversion to the two campaigns. The emperor, on the contrary, though he was far from blaming the duke of Brunswick individually, openly expressed his dissatisfaction at the conduct of the Prussian king. The jealousy which had long subsisted between the houses of Brandenburg and Austria, and which at the commencement of the war seemed absorbed in enmity to the French revolutionists, was now revived in all its violence. Frederick William did not regard the operations on the French frontiers as necessary to the security of his own dominions. If such were his feelings, he was justified in receding from the confederacy, but he ought to have done so with promptitude and allow that the ministers deserved the least blame.

No opposition was made to a demand of 85,000 men for the maritime service; but the increase of the army to 60,000 men did not appear to every member to be necessary, though the majority allowed that number. The whole supply of the year exceeded 20,228,000 pounds. As a loan was negotiated for eleven millions, spirituous liquors, glass, bricks, paper, and other articles, were subjected to new duties; and an additional revenue was drawn from attorneys.

To guard against an invasion with which the French menaced this country, a bill was enacted for the augmentation of the militia; and the court encouraged the formation of volunteer companies both of cavalry and infantry, not only with that view, but also for the suppression of riots. Subscriptions were solicited for defraying the expense of these associations; and thus considerable sums were levied by ministerial requisition, before the consent of the parliament was obtained; an irregular proceeding which was justly censured in both houses.

Amidst this rage for arming, it was proposed that French emigrants should be enlisted in the king's service, chiefly to act on the continent. The danger of intrusting the crown with an army of this description, and also the cruelty of sending these men to almost certain destruction, were noticed by Mr. Sheridan and the duke of Bedford; but Mr. Burke and Mr. Dundas, and various speakers in each house, recommended the bill of enlistment as a just and politic measure, which would furnish the refugees with a desired opportunity of honourable exertion.

An address was proposed by Mr. Grey against the treaties of alliance which had been concluded with foreign powers to the prejudice of British interests; and a similar application to the throne was moved by the earl of Guildford. These motions, however, were as unsuccessful as that of the marquis of Lansdown for a negotiation with the French, or those of earl Stanhope for the acknowledgment of the republic, and

the forbearance of all encroachment on the independent rights of that nation.

The folly of reposing great confidence in our allies, and the weakness and credulity of the minister, became topics of spirited animadversion when a treaty was announced by which the king had bound himself, in concert with the Dutch, to the payment of £50,000 per month for a Prussian army of 62,400 men, of £300,000 for putting that force in a state of action, and of a large sum for bread and forage. It was observed, that the king of Prussia was more interested in opposing the French than we could be; that he had been one of the chief instigators of the war; that former engagements required him to continue hostilities without being subsidised by Great Britain; that the terms were extravagantly high; and that the men who thus lavished the treasures of their country had no reason to expect good faith from a venal and fickle prince, who would probably employ our subsidies for the subversion of the Polish state. It was said in reply, that the terms were moderate, that it was our interest to secure the continuance of Prussia in the confederacy, and that it was illiberal to doubt the honour of that court.

A message from the king, more essentially connected with the interests of this country, was soon after delivered. It referred to the seditious practices of democratic societies, and intimated the necessity of taking measures for baffling their dangerous designs. The papers belonging to these clubs were examined by a committee; and a report was soon presented by Mr. Pitt. It was affirmed, as the result of the inquiry, that the "society for constitutional information" and the "London Corresponding Society," under the pretence of reform, aimed at the subversion of the government; that other associations, in different parts of the kingdom, pursued the same object; that they had endeavoured to promote a general convention of the people; that they had provided arms for the more effectual prosecution of their nefarious purposes; that meetings of popular delegates took place at Edinburgh in 1792 and the following year; that their proceedings were regulated on the French model ; and that, after the dispersion of this convention, the two leading societies exerted their efforts to procure a similar meeting in England, which should supersede the authority of parliament.

Having expatiated on the flagitious schemes of the societies, the minister proposed that the *habeas corpus* act should be suspended in cases of treason and sedition. Mr. Fox was of opinion, that this stretch of power was not justified by the evidence which had been adduced against the associations ; and Mr. Sheridan deprecated, as unconstitutional and dangerous, the grant of an arbitrary power of imprisonment : but Mr. Burke was convinced that the power in question would not be abused, and that it would be attended with salutary effects ; and Mr. Windham eagerly advised the strongest measures of coertion. The bill of suspension was rapidly enacted ; and, after spirited debates, an address was voted, promising the strenuous co-operation of the two houses with the executive power for the suppression of all seditious attempts and treasonable conspiracies.

The conduct of the war was the subject of strong censure in various debates ; and the improbability of its final success was repeatedly noticed. Mr. Jenkinson exposed himself to misplaced ridicule in one of these discussions, by asserting the practicability of marching to Paris, and overturning the obnoxious government.—After a review of the French revolution and the progress of the war, the duke of Bedford proposed, as preliminaries to a peace, a candid and explicit declaration of the object of the war, and a renunciation of all concern with the internal affairs of France ; and Mr. Fox ably harangued the commons on the same ground ; but both houses exploded all propositions of this nature.

On the day of prorogation, the king rewarded, with posts of honour and emolument, the zeal of some of those supporters of the war who had formerly gloried in the appellation of Whigs. Earl Fitz-william was appointed president of the council ; the duke of Portland became one

of the secretaries of state ; earl Spencer was declared keeper of the privy seal, and Mr. Windham secretary at war.

At the beginning of this year the French royalists in the island of Noirmoutier, had considerably strengthened their fortifications. Convinced, however, that their cause was desperate, they made a voluntary surrender of the town on the 3rd of January, before the republican army arrived within reach of their batteries. It was natural to expect that the sanguinary disposition of the republicans would impel them to treat these unhappy men with merciless severity. Five hundred of them were shot at Nantz on the 15th of February, the guillotine being laid aside as not sufficiently expeditious. Multitudes were dispatched by grape-shot from the mouths of cannon, or sunk in barges according to the humor of their conquerors ; and more than 4000 were smothered in a single pit.

The extirpation of the royalists enabled the convention to prosecute the war with renovated vigor, and their designs were materially assisted by the serious misunderstanding which now distracted the councils of the allies. The duke of Brunswick was disgusted with the conduct of general Wurmser, in abandoning the lines of Weissenburg without risking a battle, a measure which had compelled his serene highness to raise the siege of Landau. He had written a letter to the king of Prussia complaining of the want of concert, and extending his animadversion to the two campaigns. The emperor, on the contrary, though he was far from blaming the duke of Brunswick individually, openly expressed his dissatisfaction at the conduct of the Prussian king. The jealousy which had long subsisted between the houses of Brandenburg and Austria, and which at the commencement of the war seemed absorbed in enmity to the French revolutionists, was now revived in all its violence. Frederick William did not regard the operations on the French frontiers as necessary to the security of his own dominions. If such were his feelings, he was justified in receding from the confederacy, but he ought to have done so with promptitude and openness. He continued, on the contrary, to exhibit all the external indications of attachment to the general cause, while he was secretly determined to abandon it on the first opportunity. The projects and plans of the campaign were formed on the supposition of his active and effective co-operation. Such a spirit of selfishness prevails among princes and states, that the associations of many powers, unless united by the most imminent and portentous danger, are rarely effective or successful. They are not merely intent on the ruin or the humiliation of the object of their attack, but each is desirous of deriving more considerable advantages than the rest of the confederates. The contest for pre-eminence terminates in jealousies, murmurs, and complaints ; a want of concert soon appears ; the conditions of the league are not faithfully observed ; and a secession from the alliance of some principal power, relieves the menaced nation from the impending danger.

The resignation of the duke of Brunswick, was soon followed by a complaint from the Prussian monarch of the great expense of the war, and a proposal that the states of the empire should provide for the subsistance of his troops ; a request to which they did not accede. When the emperor desired that the diet would order the people on the frontier circles to rise in a mass, the court of Berlin strongly opposed the measure as fruitless and dangerous. The general levy did not take place, and the contingents of the German princes were imperfectly and tardily provided.

The following was the distribution of the armies of the French republic, at the commencement of the campaign.

	Men
Army of the North	220,000
United armies of the Rhine and Moselle.	280,000
Army of the Alps	60,000
Army of the Eastern Pyrenees	80,000
Army of the South	60,000
Army of the West	80,000
Total	780,000

The force which the allies stipulated to bring into the field to oppose the French army of the north, amounting to 230,000 men, was 200,000 ; and only three-fourths of the number were actually equipped. To these are to be added, a force left for the defence of the province of Luxemburg, under general Beaulieu, and the army of Clairfait, which was to keep in check the numerous garrison of Lisle, and to cover West Flanders.

Several weeks were passed in making the necessary preparations, and though, in the mean time, some trifling skirmishes occurred, it was not till the middle of April that the hostile armies seriously began to put themselves in motion. Great dependance was placed on a new plan of operations projected by the Austrian colonel Mack, which was so much admired by the court of Vienna, that the emperor determined to take the field in person, and superintend its execution. A grand council of war, to which it was submitted, and at which all the principal officers assisted, assembled at Brussels. If any conclusion may be drawn respecting the nature of this plan from the preparations which ensued, it was this : the siege of Lisle was not to be attempted, and no other towns were to be besieged except those which were in the direct road to Paris, of which the principal were Landrecies, Avesnes, and Guise. Should these towns surrender, the chief part of the army, with the emperor at their head, were to march to Paris, and execute what the duke of Brunswick had only threatened, while the remainder of the allied forces distributed as garrisons in the conquered towns, was supposed to be amply sufficient to keep in check any force which the French could spare from the defence of the metropolis. One part, however, of colonel Mack's plan was not agreed to by the council. Conceiving from the events of the last campaign an opinion unfavourable to the military pretensions of the duke of York, the Austrian court proposed that general Clairfait should assume the command of the English army, his royal highness serving under that experienced general. This was positively refused, and a quarrel ensued between the prince of Cobourg and the duke of York. In what manner the dispute terminated, has not been recorded in any authentic history, but the result renders it probable that the English cabinet coincided in opinion with the duke, for he still retained the chief command. The court of Vienna having in view the subsidy under the name of loan which would soon be wanted from England, thought it prudent to concede, and the two armies commenced operations in concert. Several days, however, were wasted in this idle dispute, and if the success of colonel Mack's plan depended on celerity, this delay must have been considerably injurious.

On the 9th of April his imperial majesty arrived at Brussels, and was inaugurated duke of Brabant. The pomp and splendor of this ceremony, the enthusiasm with which he was greeted by the people, and the acclamations that attended his departure for Valenciennes, formed a singular prelude to that series of disappointment, disaster, and disgrace, which succeeded the first demonstrations of offensive hostility, and attended the continuance of the war.

At length the combined armies, consisting of Austrians, British, Dutch, Hanoverians, and Hessians, and amounting to 187,000 men, assembled on the heights above Cateau, and were reviewed by the emperor. In pursuance of the plan previously concerted, they advanced during the preceding day in eight columns, three of which were intended as corps of observation. The first composed of Austrian and Dutch troops, under the command of prince Christian of Hesse Darmstadt, seized on the village of Catillon, where they obtained four pieces of cannon, and, having crossed the Sambre, immediately occupied a position between that river and the little Helpe, so as to invest Landrecies on that side. The second, led by lieutenant-general Alvinzee, took post in the forest of Nouvion. The third, headed by the emperor and the prince de Cobourg, after forcing the enemy's entrenchments, advanced to the heights known by the name

of the Great and Little Blocus. The fourth and fifth columns were formed from the army of the duke of York: the column of which his royal highness took the direction being intended to attack the village of Vaux. Major-general Abercrombie commenced the assault with the van, supported by the two grenadier companies of the first regiment of guards, under the command of colonel Stanhope, and stormed and took the star redoubt, while three battalions of 'Austrian greaadiers,' commanded by major Petrask, attacked the wood, and made themselves masters of the works which the French had constructed for its defence. Sir William Erskine was equally successful with the other column, for, finding the enemy posted at Premont, the brigade of British infantry, with four squadrons of light dragoons, was detached under lieutenant-general Harcourt, to turn their position, while he himself attacked in front, aided by the regiment of Kaunitz, supported by a well-directed fire of Austrian artillery, under the orders of lieutenant-colonel Congreve, and not only obtained possession of the redoubts, but of two pieces of cannon and a pair of colours.

The success of this extensive and complicated attack, in consequence of which the French lost thirty pieces of artillery, enabled the allies to commence the siege of Landrecies. The direction of this important enterprize was committed to the prince of Orange; while his imperial majesty, with the grand army estimated at 60,000 men, covered the operations on the side of Guise, and the troops under the duke of York, amounting to near 30,000, were employed in a similar service towards Cambray. A body of Hessians and Austrians, to the number of 12,000, under general Worms, were at the same time stationed near Douay and Bouchain; count Kaunitz, with 15,000 men, defended the passage of the Sambre, and general Clairfait, with 40,000 more, protected Flanders from Douay to the sea. Such was the strength and position of the allies, even without the assistance of the Prussians, who made no movement in their favour, that all the generals of the old school imagined success to be inevitable. Appearances for a time confirmed these conjectures. The hereditary prince of Orange made a general attack on the posts still occupied by the enemy in front of Landrecies; he took their entrenched camp by storm, and obtained possession of a strong redoubt within six hundred yards of the body of the place. The French were also driven from Cæsar's camp near Cambray, and a few days after repulsed with great slaughter in an attack on the heights of Cateau, where the duke of York was posted; on which occasion, lieutenant-general Chapuy, with 330 officers and privates were taken prisoners, while thirty-five pieces of cannon fell into the hands of the English.

Though the enemy was not only worsted in this quarter, but in an attack conducted by their commander in person, they were successful in another point of this general assault, which took place along the whole extent of the frontiers. Pichegru having advanced on the same day from Lisle, defeated general Clairfait at Moucron, and in a short time obtained possession of Werwick, Courtray and Menin. These successes were in some measure counterbalanced by the fall of Landrecies, and the defeat of a body of 30,000 troops, who had attacked the army of the duke of York at Tournay. A few days afterwards, general Clairfait, having effected the passage of the Heule, had an engagement with the French, of which the result was doubtful. It is certain, however, that he commenced a precipitate retreat, that he was compelled to continue that retreat to Thielt, and confined his views to the protection of Ghent, Bruges, and Ostend.

The northern republican army passed the Sambre and made themselves masters of Binche, a movement which subjected general Kaunitz to the necessity of retreating and occupying a station between that place and Rouveray, for the purpose of defending Mons against any attack from that quarter. From this place the French were determined to dislodge him, and they accordingly attacked him on the 14th of May, with their accustomed impetuosity; but they were defeated with the loss of 5000 men, and compelled to repass the Sambre. Elated by this victory, the emperor resolved to march to the assistance of the duke of York at Tournay, from which place the enemy had not been able to dislodge him. It was intended that the forces of the emperor, the duke, and general Clairfait, should form a junction and act in concert against the line of the republicans, in which attack they expected that they should be able to drive the invaders from the whole of Flanders. The attempt, however, proved unsuccessful, for two of the five columns employed upon this occasion, were unable, from fatigue, to perform the requisite duty; and a third column found the enemy in such force at Moucron, that it retreated to Tourcoing. In the mean time, seven battalions of British, five of Austrians, and two of Hessians, with six squadrons of light dragoons, and four of hussars, led by the duke of York, compelled the French to evacuate Lannoy and Roubaix, and advanced against Mouveaux. General Abercrombie, seconded by lieutenant-general Churchill, then attacked, with four battalions of guards, and the 14th and 15th light dragoons, and compelled the enemy to retire.

Tourcoing was attacked by the French on the morning of the 18th. The duke of York, on receiving this intelligence, dispatched to the relief of that place, two battalions of Austrians; but an opening being left in their right, the enemy took advantage of this unfortunate incident, and his royal highness was so briskly assailed both in front and rear, that his troops gave way, and he himself found it impossible to join the brigade of guards, on the division commanded by general Fox. At length, however, he was enabled to escape to a body of Austrians commanded by general Otto, accompanied only by a few dragoons of the 16th regiment, while major-general Abercrombie, with some difficulty, accomplished his retreat to Templeuve, and major-general Fox, fortunately succeeded in gaining the village of Leers. It is difficult to say to whom the blame of this unfortunate affair attaches. The allies are accused of want'ng firmness and vigor, while the Austrians attribute the disaster to the conduct of the Hanoverian troops. It is asserted that they were the first to retreat; and that, in their confusion, their cavalry not only destroyed [the foot, but threw the whole army into such disorder, that they became a helpless prey to the pursuing enemy.

His imperial majesty, who had been taught to believe that his appearance in the Low Countries was alone sufficient for the deliverance of the antient dominions of the house of Austria, and the overthrow of its enemies, was convinced by personal experiment, and by the disasters of his army, that the Belgians were averse to his government, and the French too formidable for his vengeance. Dissatisfied with the past and uncertain of the future, he abandoned the field in the middle of the campaign, and returned to his capital.

Four days after this calamitous defeat, the French again attacked the combined armies with a force of more than 100,000 men. The attack began at five o'clock in the morning, but scarcely became serious till nine; when the whole force of the enemy fell upon the right wing of the combined army, in order, if possible, to force the passage of the Scheldt, and invest Tournay. The allies firmly retained their post till nine o'clock at night, when, being strongly reinforced, they compelled the enemy to retreat, with the loss of 12,000 men. The spirit and conduct of general Fox, who commanded the British brigade, were particularly conspicuous. The calamitous failure of the late grand attack on the French lines, and the subsequent misfortunes, were in some measure counterbalanced by the repulse of so numerous a force, and by the successes in Bouillon, of general Beaulieu, who had defeated the enemy, killed 1200, and taken 300 prisoners, with six pieces of cannon. General Kaunitz also had obtained a fresh victory over the enemy, on the banks of the Sambre, where he had killed 2000 and taken 3000 prisoners. Important as these advantages appeared to the allies, the numbers, the ardor, and the perseverance

of the French, were insurmountable. At this very time, they marched an army of 40,000 men, under Jourdan, into the duchy of Luxemburg, which obliged Beaulieu, immediately after his success at Bouillon, to evacuate Arlon, and fall back upon Marche, in order to cover Namur.

No sooner was Jourdan enabled to intercept the communication between Charleroi and Brussels, than he prepared to lay siege to the former of these places. But the prince of Orange attacked him on the 3rd of June, and compelled him to raise the siege, and to repass the Sambre with considerable loss. So great, however, was their superiority of numbers, that general Jourdan crossed the Sambre for the third time, stormed the Austrian camp at Betignies, and prepared to commence once more, the siege of the city of Charleroi, which had so long eluded his attacks. After a resistance of three weeks, the garrison, amounting to 3000 men, surrendered at discretion. The prince de Cobourg, assisted by the prince of Orange and general Beaulieu, not being acquainted with this event, marched in the course of that evening, with the combined army, divided into five columns, and early on the succeeding morning, (June 26th,) made preparations to relieve the place. Having attacked the enemy's entrenchments in the direction of Lambrisart, Espinies, and Gosselies, he obliged a few detached bodies to retreat, notwithstanding the protection of several strong redoubts: but such was the opposition experienced by the allies, that it was evening before the left wing had arrived at the principal heights, which were fortified by an extensive range of field-works, lined with an immense number of heavy artillery. Though a variety of unforeseen obstacles had interposed, an attempt was made to force this strong position with the bayonet, while Jourdan, being reinforced by the besieging army, in consequence of the surrender of Charleroi, determined to decide the fate of Flanders in a pitched battle. He accordingly advanced, and, by the most judicious disposition, enabled the greater part of his numerous forces to contend with the left wing only of the allies

s 2

Notwithstanding the assailants repeatedly penetrated the French lines, and formed several times under the fire of their cannon ; the advantages obtained by Jourdan towards the close of day, were decisive, and victory, which had been hovering by turns over each of the contending armies, finally declared in favour of the republicans. The combined troops taking advantage of the night, immediately fell back first on Marbois, and afterwards on Nivelles, with the intention, if possible, to cover Namur.

Though the battle of Fleurus was more distinguished for the obstinacy with which it was contested, than interesting for the skill or the variety of its evolutions, it is rendered memorable by the only instance in which the recent discovery of ærostation had been converted to any purpose of real or apparent utility. A balloon was constructed and frequently elevated during the action, for the purpose of observing the movements and positions of the Austrians. " I was attacked," says general Etienne, " with hisses as well as grenades, but none of them reached me. I corresponded with the generals during the action, and informed them of every new position assumed by the enemy." The intelligence was conveyed in a note fastened to an arrow, while the balloon itself was attached to a cord. Whatever other merit might be ascribed to this contrivance, it served the purpose at least of gratifying the love of novelty, and the enthusiasm on trivial subjects so conspicuous in the temper and deportment of the French soldier.

The real loss of the allies on this day was never precisely ascertained. The numbers returned by the French general in his report to the convention at Paris, was upwards of 10,000, while the prince of Cobourg reduces that number to 1500. Its ultimate effect, however, was the entire expulsion of the confederates from the Netherlands.

The French under Pichegru, in Maritime Flanders having defeated Clairfait, who had marched to the relief of Ypres, which contained a garrison of 7000 men, com-

menced the siege of that place, which was soon obliged to surrender to MOREAU, who had but lately exchanged the lawyer's robe for the truncheon of a general. He was the son of an advocate at Morlaix in Brittany : at the age of eighteen he entered into the army as a common soldier, but was persuaded by his father, who purchased his discharge, to return to his family and resume his studies. At the commencement of the revolution he was elected provost of Rennes, and was deputed, with three others, to confer with the assembly of the states. On the formation of the national guards in 1789, he was appointed commander of a battalion, and abandoned the profession of the law. At the beginning of the present year he was deputed to command a division of Pichegru's army, with the rank of general ; and the talents which he displayed at the opening of the campaign and during the siege of Ypres, prepared the way for his elevation to the chief command.

The body of English and allies, under the duke of York, participated in the disasters of the campaign. His royal highness, after vainly endeavouring to form a junction with general Clairfait, was obliged to retreat from Tournay to Trenaix, and general Walmoden, having been compelled to abandon Bruges, all communication with Ostend was cut off. The ministry, greatly alarmed by this event, requested the earl of Moira, who had been nominated to the command of a separate body of troops, now encamped in the vicinity of Southampton, and destined in conjunction with several regiments of emigrants, for a secret expedition against France, to repair to the Low Countries. Notwithstanding, this nobleman had before intimated that any orders for serving in that quarter must occasion his immediate resignation, he determined to wave his former resolution at so critical a period. After landing a body of troops in Maritime Flanders, he proposed a junction with generals Clairfait and Walmoden, so as to enable them to act from Bruges to Ghent, on the left wing of the French, with the intention of covering Ostend, and producing a diversion in favor of the duke of York. The situation of the prince of Cobourg rendered this plan impracticable ; but at the pressing invitation of the duke, and by a rapid and judicious movement, he formed a junction with the English and allied army. After his lordship had defeated the French in their attacks on Alost and Malines, the duke retreated across the Meuse, and retired into Holland. In the mean time the prince of Cobourg, having assembled his army at Halle, advanced, and assumed a formidable position, from which he was compelled to retreat by the superior numbers of the enemy, and to occupy a yet stronger position. But nothing could withstand the fury of the assailants, who rushed in with fixed bayonets, and obtained a decisive victory. The flying Austrians retreated through Brussels amidst the insults and the violence of the inhabitants ; who, on the approach of the French, opened their gates, received them with the most lively demonstrations of joy, and signed the articles of submission to the *armies* and to the *sovereignty of the republic.*

Here let me suspend the narrative of military incidents, that I may notice the political contests and sanguinary scenes which occurred in the metropolis of the French empire. When the republican party had effected the subversion of the constitution of 1792, they were divided into two parties, bearing towards each other the most inveterate enmity. After the Girondists had fallen victims to the machinations of the Jacobins, the parties were next divided into the Jacobins and Cordeliers. The former of these were again triumphant, and the contest finally lay between Danton and Robespierre. The latter obtained the victory by his superior activity and address. Suspecting Hebert and other chiefs of the Cordelier club, of aiming at political pre-eminence, he accused them of being traitors to the republic, and subjected them to the blade of the guillotine. He coolly ordered the arrest of many of his former associates, and sacrificed them without remorse to his fears, and his ambition   The Cordeliers had

rendered themselves, even in this distracted and profligate metropolis, generally hateful by their infidelity and atheism. Their principal leaders were Hebert, Vincent, Ronsin, Fabre d'Eglantine, and Camille Desmoulins, the chief promoters of the decree by which the Christian religion was abolished. As Robespierre had been formerly attached to this party, and as he found it conducive to the increase of his popularity, to appear the enemy of atheism, he relinquished all connection with their leaders, and determined to subject them to the guillotine. He therefore obtained immediately subsequent to the death of Hebert, a decree of accusation against Danton, Camille Desmoulins, La Croix, and other members of the convention, as accomplices in plots against the sovereignty of the people and the safety of the republic. The greater number of the condemned individuals were guilty of suicide, or displayed the most unmanly terror of the fate which awaited them. Danton, a giant among the pigmies of the revolution, maintained the superiority of his character even in his fall. He was collected in his demeanour, and seemed only anxious to leave behind him favourable impressions of his character. His conversation, composed, as usual, of oaths and obscenities, was intermingled with vindications of his past conduct, expressions of regret at the state of the republic, and praises of nature and of rural life. He refused to answer interrogatories, unless confronted by Barrere and Robespierre, his accusers, and amused himself, during the examination, by shooting paper bullets in the face of the chief judge. Though he entertained no hope of saving his life, he made a defence that it might be transmitted to the public. The attempts of the president to silence him were vain ; his stentorian voice drowned the tinkling of the bell, by which the president imposed silence and demanded attention ; but he was at length persuaded to retire under pretence of taking some refreshment, and in his absence sentenced to the guillotine. He submitted to his fate with fortitude, and quibbled on his progress to the place of punishment on the word *vers*, which signifies *worms* as well as *verses*. He was accompanied by Camille Desmoulins, who had excited the antipathy of Robespierre by anticipating his plan of a committee of clemency, authorized to pardon crimes which did not arise from evil intentions. But the destruction of the enemies of Robespierre tended only to render his own situation more critical, and to hasten the just reward of his inhumanity. As he advanced in his sanguinary schemes of ambition, his danger still increased; stronger measures were still required to secure him against the conspiracies of the Cordeliers, who were actuated by hatred to his person and revenge, for the death of their partizans. Every new attempt against the prevailing faction produced new objects of vengeance ; the prisons throughout the kingdom were crowded with persons imprisoned for state offences, and the guillotine could scarcely perform its work with sufficient dispatch. Domiciliary visits were made in search of the accused, and spies were dispersed into every quarter, to watch the motions of men, and to report every expression which implied disapprobation of the existing government. Unsatiated by revenge, and dissatisfied with the power already vested in himself through the medium of the committee of public safety, he procured the passing of a law which deprived the accused of any defender, and dispensing with legal evidence, required only moral proofs to justify their condemnation.

But tyranny is generally seen to defeat its own purpose. While some were intimidated by the cruelty of his proceedings, others were emboldened by despair. An attempt was made on the life of Collot, D'Herbois, and another on that of Robespierre. Led by curiosity, or impelled by fanaticism, a young woman named Aimée Cecile Regnault, the daughter of a stationer in Paris, called at Robespierre's lodging, requiring to see him ; on receiving an answer that he was not to be spoken to, she pertly replied, that a public functionary ought to be accessible at all times. These words were sufficient to occasion her arrest. L'Amiral, the assassin of Collot, D'Herbois, and Cecile Regnault, were declared, without trial, guilty of a conspiracy against the republic ; and sixty persons, obnoxious to Robespierre, but unconnected with the designs or the acts of these individuals, were associated with their fate. Accustomed as were the Parisians to witness, with unconcern, the most unexampled scenes of injustice and inhumanity, this last atrocity excited in the pubic mind a sensation highly favourable to the cause of the tyrant's enemies. Alarmed and astonished by the expression of public opinion, he made an effort to regain his popularity, by procuring decrees for the punishment of petty peculation, for the better and more speedy execution of justice in the civil courts, and for enforcing the residence of ecclesiastics in the departments to which they belonged. Having failed in all his endeavours, to eradicate religion, he now adopted a different line of policy, and, coming forward as its friend and protector, he obtained a decree by which France acknowledged the existence of a Deity. When the celebration of a festival in honour of the Supreme Being was ordained, he appeared at the head of the convention, of which the members were dressed in their robes, and bore a conspicuous part in the pompous ceremonies of the day. This ostentatious parade might impose on the spectators, but the time was now arriving when neither his policy, his perfidy, nor his hypocrisy, were to avail him. Abhorrence of his crimes overcame the terror of his authority, and the power of inflicting immediate vengeance on his enemies, was destroyed by the courage and good sense of an hostile party. He had obtained a repeal of that article of the constitution which gave inviolability to the persons of the members of the convention, and was by this means enabled to take revenge on his adversaries, by denouncing them before the revolutionary tribunal, which was ever ready to obey his mandates. The first object therefore of that band of conspirators, now leagued against him under the auspices of Tallien, Bourdon D'Oise, and other powerful members of the convention, was to accomplish the restitution of this privilege. Having thus deprived him of the power of denouncing his adversaries, they became more daring, and concerted a regular plan for his destruction. In vain did he endeavour to regain his ascendency by his influence with the Jacobin club, and the support of Henriot, commander of the national guards. He was accused of aspiring to the rank of dictator, and one of his prosecutors concluded his speech by observing, " we must either fall on him with our bodies, or suffer tyrants to triumph. He would have mutilated the convention and murdered its representatives." When Robespierre would have possessed himself of the tribune, with an intention to harangue the audience, he was forcibly prevented, and his voice was overpowered by cries of " Down with the tyrant! Down with the tyrant!" Tallien displayed, with vehement eloquence, all the crimes which disgraced his character, comparing his proscriptions to those of Sylla ; and, drawing forth a dagger from his girdle, while he turned to the bust of Brutus, whose genius he invoked, he swore " that he would plunge it into the heart of Robespierre, if the representatives of the people had not courage to order his arrest and to break their chains." A decree was immediately passed for the arrest of the two Robespierres, St. Just, Couthon, Henriot, and La Valette. Robespierre was seized, but released by a party of Jacobins, who conducted him to the hotel de Ville, where the commune of Paris was assembled. The Jacobins and the municipality of Paris were decidedly in favour of Robespierre, and Henriot, who had made his escape from the guards, brought a strong body of troops to his support. But the Parisians declared for the convention, and many of Henriot's troops, when they heard that their leader was outlawed, followed their example. The resolute aspect assumed by the convention, and the want of promptitude on the part of their antagonists, in availing themselves of the military force under their command, decided the fortune of the day. When Paris was a scene of uproar and

confusion, Bourdon d'Oise, rushing with a band of soldiers into the hall of the commune, ordered the outlawed members to be arrested. The younger Robespierre leaped out of a window, but was taken up miserably bruised and wounded. St. Just, too pusillanimous to effect his own destruction, implored Lebas to shoot him. " Coward," answered Lebas, " I have something else to do," and immediately blew out his own brains. Goffinhal, in a rage, threw Henriot out of the window ; he crept into a common sewer, and was drawn forth covered with blood and filth by some soldiers who beat out one of his eyes : the remaining adherents of Robespierre were captured without difficulty, and he himself was found in one of the apartments of the hotel de Ville, sitting squat against the wall, with a knife in his hand, apparently intended for the purpose of destruction, but which he durst not use. A soldier who discovered him, apprehending some resistance, fired two pistols at him, one of which wounded him on the head, and the other broke his under jaw : he was taken and conducted before the committee of general security in an arm chair ; his broken jaw bound up with a cloth. As he was carried along in this condition, he rested his chin on a handkerchief which he held in his right hand, while the elbow was supported by his left. A message was sent to the convention to know if he should be brought to the bar, but the members unanimously exclaimed, that they would no longer suffer their hall to be polluted by the presence of such a monster. He lay for some hours in an anti-chamber of the committee of general security, stretched on a table, motionless, apparently insensible of corporeal anguish, though the blood flowed from his eyes, mouth, and nostrils ; but, torn by distracting recollections, and abandoned to remorse, he pinched his thighs with convulsive agony, and scowled gloomily around the room when he fancied himself unobserved. After enduring, in this situation, the taunts of all who beheld him, he was replaced in the arm chair, and carried to the hospital named the *hotel dieu*, where his wounds were dressed merely to prolong his existence, and from thence was sent to the prison of the Conciergerie. He was brought, on the same day, before the revolutionary tribunal, where sentence of death was demanded against him and twenty-one others, by their former friend and creature Touquier Tinville, the public accuser. At five o'clock in the evening they were conducted to the place of execution, amidst the acclamations of the numerous spectators. Even the guards who escorted them, partook of the general transport, and joined the cry of *Vive le convention !* A group of women stopped the carts and danced round them to testify their joy. Robespierre, pale and disfigured, held down his head on his breast, and never looked up except once, when a woman decently dressed approached the cart, and uttered such heart-piercing exclamations and deep-drawn maledictions, as proved to the observers that she was a mother whom his cruelty had deprived of her son, or a widow from whom he had snatched her husband. At hearing her horrible denunciations, Robespierre turned his eyes languidly towards her, and shrugged up his shoulders. He suffered the last but one. When he was about to be tied to the fatal plank, the executioner snatched the dressing from his broken jaw, which immediately fell, and a profusion of blood gushed out ; the horrible chasm occasioned by this accident, rendered 1794. his head, when severed from his body, and held up to the public view, a hideous and disgusting spectacle.

On the ensuing day (July 29th,) the tyrant was followed to the scaffold by sixty-two other members of the convention, who also had been outlawed. Barrere, in the name of his associates, proposed the further proscription of those who had been most deeply interested in the late system of policy ; but this proposition was overruled, and *strict justice, tempered with moderation,* declared to be the *order of the day.* Many thousands of those who had been imprisoned on the bare suspicion of disaffection to the ruling faction, were liberated in defiance of the opposition of the remaining terrorists. The principal agents of that dreadful oppression and odious tyranny which had been practised in the provinces to the generals who commanded the troops and to the inhabitants themselves, were brought to punishment ; the Jacobin club was suppressed. The powers of the two committees of general and public safety, were circumscribed by a regulation that they should be renewed monthly, and the scheme of a temporary government, intended to correct the abuses practised by the late administration, was proposed by Barrere, and adopted. Intelligence of these changes was dispersed through the different departments, and the French nation indulged a hope of again enjoying the blessing of domestic tranquillity. The alteration in the tone and temper of the government was also displayed in the repeal of a murderous edict, which had prohibited the armies from granting quarter to the English. The outrageous inhumanity of Robespierre had extorted this decree, but the troops were not so base as to comply with its stipulations. They resolved to treat their enemies according to the general rules of war, not merely from the dread of retaliation, but from a sense of honor which the turbulence of the revolution had not extinguished.

The same good fortune which distinguished the operations of France on the side of the Netherlands, attended her armies in Italy. They reduced Oneglia, forced the Col de Tende, and subdued several districts in the southern parts of Piedmont. The defensive strength of mount Cenis served only to inflame their ardor : they stormed the well-fortified posts of that difficult pass, and, having defeated their opponents in other parts of the country, looked forward to more important successes.

The English in the Mediterranean, were employed, while their Sardinian ally was thus harassed, in the reduction of Corsica. An armament under lord Hood attacked the town and forts of Bastia, after the acquisition of San Fiorenza ; the soldiers and sailors co-operated with emulous zeal,

LORD HOWE.

and the place was taken with inconsiderable loss. General Paoli, having exerted his influence over his countrymen, they voted in a regular assembly on the 24th of June, that the sovereignty of the island should be transferred to the king of Great Britain. Sir Gilbert Elliot, in the name of his majesty, accepted the offer, but from the fickle temper of the natives, it did not promise to remain a permanent appendage to his dominions.

Though fortune had not been propitious to the arms of the confederates, the success of England on her appropriate theatre, unincumbered by her allies, was uniform and triumphant. The channel fleet, which, during the last summer had performed nothing worthy of the reputation of its veteran commander, put to sea in the spring in search of an enemy who had hitherto eluded pursuit. Lord Howe was particularly solicitous on the present occasion to vindicate the honour of his country, and to rescue his own character from unmerited reproach, and the powerful armament now under his command, left no doubt relative to the result of the contest.

The anxiety of the French government for the fate of a convoy expected from America, with the produce of the West India islands, induced the convention to equip a fleet of 26 sail of the line for its protection ; of which the command was given to admiral Villaret. On the 28th of May the rival fleets descried each other at the same time, in latitude 47° 33′ N. and longitude 14° 10′ W. the wind blew strongly from the South-West, accompanied by a boisterous sea, and the French possessed the weathergage. Villaret, however, endeavoured as much as possible to form a regular order of battle on the starboard tack, a circumstance that greatly facilitated the approach of the English. As the conduct of the enemy indicated an intention to avoid an action, the British commander displayed the signal for a general chace, and to prevent their escape, detached admiral Pasley to make an impression on their rear. That officer on the close of day, came up with the Revolution-
Vol. i.

aire, a three decked ship of 110 guns, but his topmast being disabled during the action, lord Hugh Seymour Conway, in the Leviathan, gallantly advanced, and received her fire ; and, as soon as it was dark, captain Parker, of the Audacious, having arrived close to the rear ship, which was supposed to be the Revolutionaire, before engaged, fought her within the distance of half a cable. The Revolutionaire now attempted to board her assailant, and, having failed, made sail before the wind, after having been supposed to strike her colours. The Audacious, herself, was so severely crippled, that the captain, pursued by two of the French ships menaced by nine sail of the enemy's line, stationed to windward, and, fired upon occasionally by a frigate and two corvettes, returned to Plymouth-Sound.

In this manner terminated the first day's action, which, considering the frail condition of many of the French ships, rendered almost unserviceable by age or long-continued service, was regarded by the people of England as highly derogatory to the naval reputation of England.

The rival fleets, of which the English was now reduced to 25 ships, remained within sight of each other during the whole night, on the starboard tack, and in a parallel direction with the French, who were still to windward ; but on the next morning the English tacked by signal and with some degree of irregularity, with the view of making an impression on the enemy's rear. After many intricate manœuvres, in which the English obtained the weathergage, the action terminated without any decisive advantage to either side, and a fog that interfered during this night and the greater part of the ensuing day, prevented the renewal of the engagement. In the mean time rear-admiral Neilly joined the commander-in-chief of the French fleet with three sail of the line, which enabled him to detach his crippled ships, and to form an efficient force of 26 ships of the line, 12 frigates, and eight corvettes. The force of the English on the 1st of June, amounted to 25 ships of the line, five frigates, and eight sloops or cutters. The dawn

T

exhibited the French line to leeward drawn up in order of battle, and prepared to renew the contest. The British admiral perceiving that there was time sufficient for the various companies to take refreshment, made a signal for breakfast, a measure which by procrastinating the commencement of the action, induced the enemy to believe that the British were disposed to decline the engagement. But their hopes were fallacious. In about half an hour lord Howe, relaxing the usual sternness of his countenance into a smile, gave orders for steering the Royal Charlotte along side of the French admiral. His command was obeyed. and, by an extraordinary display of seamanship on the part of his master, he was enabled to assume a most excellent position, and to contend with advantage against a vessel of far superior strength and size. While some of the English commanders penetrated the line of battle and engaged to leeward, others occupied such stations as enabled them to combat with their antagonists to windward.

So close and severe was the contest, that the fate of this day depended but little on the exertion of nautical skill. Yet upon this occasion, when the drapery of the three-coloured flag not unfrequently intermingled with that of the British cross, the superiority of the English seamen was eminently conspicuous. Disciplined into war, the steady arm, the undaunted eye, the animated countenance, denoted that they were familiar with the element on which they fought. And while the shot of the enemy occasioned but little bloodshed on decks which were not crowded by useless men, every broadside spread death and despair through the crowded ranks of their antagonists.

In about fifty minutes after the action had commenced in the centre, admiral Villerat determined to relinquish the contest. Several of his ships were already dismasted, one of them was about to sink, and six were captured. He crowded off with all the canvass he could spread, and was followed by nearly all the ships in his van that were not completely crippled.

The enemy had, as usual, chiefly aimed at the rigging, and the victors were thus disabled from pursuing the vanquished. The British endeavour to destroy the effective force of the enemy's ships; the French to secure the means of safe and easy flight. The Queen Charlotte was prevented from capturing her antagonist, La Montagne, by an unlucky broadside from Le Jacobin, which rendered her nearly unmanageable. The slaughter of the English was comparatively trivial. Captain Montagu, of the Montagu, was the only commander who fell in the engagement. Vice-admiral Graves, the honourable G. Berkley, and captain J. Harvey, were wounded, and the rear-admirals Pasley and Bowyer, with captain Hutt of the Queen, lost their legs. Hutt and Harvey died on their return to port. Pasley and Bowyer were created baronets, and each received a pension of £1000 per annum. Admirals Graves and Hood were honoured with the peerage. Too much praise indeed cannot be given to the skill of the officers or the courage of the men ; and had not the bravery of the French seamen and the firmness of their commanders far surpassed every former display of these qualities in naval conflict, the prowess, coolness, and tactical expertness of the British navy, would have obtained a more immediate and still more decisive result.

The loss of the French, in consequence of the mode of action to which I have alluded, was nearly four times that of the English, who had 272 killed, and 787 wounded. That of the enemy has been estimated at 1300 killed, and 2380 wounded. On board the six captured ships there were 690 killed, and 580 wounded ; while on board the six English ships that suffered most, there were only 125 killed, and 335 wounded. Notwithstanding the disastrous result of this engagement, the French obtained the object for which the fleet had been equipped, but the splendor of the victory elevated the maritime renown of our countrymen, and swelled the hearts of the people with exultation. The skill and energy of the officers, the courage and activity of the men under their command, were loudly applauded ; and confident hopes were entertained, by the sanguine public, of the total ruin of the French navy.

An expedition to the West Indies also proved, in a great degree, successful, Sir Charles Grey landed, with a respectable but not numerous force, on the island of Martinique, while sir John Jervis superintended the naval operations. Several strong posts were quickly seized ; and the reduction of Pigeon isle opened the bay and harbour of Fort-Royal to the shipping. Of the works near St. Pierre the invaders gained possession with small loss ; and that town was then evacuated by the enemy. To complete the investment of Fort-Bourbon, it was necessary that the heights of Sourier should be gained. Bellegarde, a bold leader of the mulattoes and negroes, might have defended this post for a considerable time, if he had not been prompted by the impetuosity of his spirit to rush from the heights with a part of his force, and attack the left division of the British army. Pleased at the opportunity, the general sent three battalions from his right to storm the weakened camp, which was soon forced by the valor of this detachment, while Bellegarde was repelled by the defensive firmness of the corps which he engaged.

Preparations were now made for assaulting Fort-Royal ; and a detachment of grenadiers and light infantry, under the conduct of colonel Symes, marched to the back of it, while commodore Thompson directed the exertions of a select naval force. Captain Faulknor particularly distinguished himself on this occasion. He pushed forward at the head of the crew of the sloop which he commanded, and scaled the walls in defiance of volleys of grape-shot. This daring act concurred with the approach of the flat boats, and the appearance of the soldiery, to intimidate the garrison into a surrender. The commandant of Fort-Bourbon, no longer inclined to resist, proposed a capitulation ; and the acquisition of this fortress completed the reduction of the island.

Major-general Dundas and prince

Edward afterwards landed in St. Lucia without loss of men, and proceeded to the investment of la Morne Fortunée. Lieutenant-colonel Coote stormed a redoubt and two batteries ; and the dread of an assault of the fort produced its speedy surrender. The isles called the Saints were then reduced ; and a disembarkation was effected at Gosier-bay in Guadaloupe. Fort Fleur d'Epée was quickly stormed ; and the ferocity of the assailants' spared only a small part of the garrison. Fort Louis, and other posts of Grande-Terre, were abandoned with great precipitation ; and the English proceeded to the conquest of Basse-Terre. Palmiste, the strongest post of this division, was soon taken ; and, after other exploits, they became masters of the whole island and its dependencies.

They did not long retain the last of these conquests. The yellow fever began to diffuse its ravages, to diminish the number of the armed occupants of the island, and weaken the survivors. Expecting to find the works inadequately manned, a French force approached the coast, attacked Fleur d'Epée and other posts, and recovered them with little difficulty. The English soon regained the post of St. Anne, where they (not very humanely) put to death about 400 of the enemy, without losing an individual of their own party. After various actions, brigadier Symes and colonel Fisher, with a body of soldiers and seamen, endeavoured to surprise the enemy in the night on the heights near Point-à-Petre ; but they were saluted in their march with so severe a cannonade, that great confusion arose ; and, instead of attempting to gain the heights, the major part of the corps entered the town, where many were mowed down by grape-shot from the batteries, and musketry from the houses. A retreat was now ordered ; and, for some time, from the prevalence of disease, the troops were almost inactive. When the camp at Berville was at length attacked by the French, it was so bravely defended that they suffered considerable loss ; but their repeated exertions constrained the English to capitulate.

After farther hostilities, Fort Matilda was the only place of strength which the English retained in Guadaloupe. Here they were besieged by Victor Hugues for eight weeks; and, as the fort was no longer tenable, they found it expedient to retire in the night. The embarkation was well conducted; and the garrison lived to serve the king on other occasions. Not long after the total loss of the island, the brave Faulknor, who had so eminently contributed to the reduction of Martinique, lost his life in an engagement with a frigate near Marie-galante. More than 70 men are said to have been killed in the French vessel, and above 100 wounded; while only 29 suffered in the victorious ship.

In the island of St. Domingo, the English had so far profited by intestine commotions as to acquire some territorial possessions. That island, in a remarkable degree, had suffered the mischievous effects of the French revolution. When the people in the mother country asserted their right to freedom, the claims of the colonial subjects of France were also recognised; and a society called *les Amis des Noirs* (or friends of the negroes) warmly supported the pretensions of the slaves to emancipation, and of the mulattoes to all the privileges enjoyed by the white inhabitants. The declaration of rights promulgated by the National Assembly increased the ferment which the first intelligence of the revolution had produced in the islands; and sanguinary disturbances or acrimonious contests were apprehended. Deputies from the different districts of the French part of St. Domingo met by the king's order, to prevent tumults and reform abuses by seasonable regulations: but their endeavours were thwarted by the partisans of the old *régime*; and the governor dissolved the assembly. Many of the representatives sailed to France to justify their conduct; and, during their absence, Ogé, an enterprising mulatto, returned to the island from Europe for the execution of a scheme which had been suggested to him by Brissot and Grégoire, who wished that the people of color (as the mulattoes were styled) might be stimulated to rise in arms, and redress their own grievances. He found means to excite an insurrection; but it was quickly suppressed, and his life was sacrificed to the demands of public justice. The claims of his brethren, however, were confirmed by a decree of the ruling assembly of the parent state, which admitted them to all the privileges of French citizens. Before the death of Ogé, the negroes had been instigated to join the mulattoes in a general rebellion; and the recent decree gave vigor to their intentions.

While a new colonial assembly deliberated on the conduct which prudence required at this crisis, the slaves in the neighbourhood of Cape François attacked the whites, murdered a great number of them, and destroyed the plantations. The insurrection soon spread to other districts; and, though many hundreds of the negroes and their confederates were slain in battle, or perished by famine, they seemed to multiply like the heads of the Hydra. In the vicinity of Port-au-Prince, however, the insurgents agreed to an accommodation, on condition of the observance of the late decree; but, about the same time, the French legislature thought proper to annul it. When the intelligence of this repeal reached the island, the mulattoes accused the planters and their adherents of insidious duplicity, and again had recourse to arms. They destroyed a third part of Port-au-Prince by fire, and committed barbarous outrages, which exposed them, when taken, to severe retaliation. Commissioners were sent from France to heal the disorders of the colony; but they did not succeed in their endeavours. A new decree respecting equality of privilege was enacted; and new delegates were sent to enforce it. These men behaved in an absurd and arbitrary manner, and disgusted the colonists by their rapacity and violence. Having produced by their misconduct a civil war among the whites, they invited to their aid a body of rebel negroes, who, thus encouraged, perpetrated a horrible series of massacres at Cape François, and burned the greater part of the town.

The convulsions of the colony induced

many of the planters to solicit succour from the British government; and, as they asserted the probability of a speedy acquisition of the whole French division of the island, major-general Williamson was ordered to detach an armament from Jamaica, to take possession of those settlements which the people might be disposed to surrender. Lieutenant-colonel Whitelocke now sailed to Jeremie, and was gratified with the submission of the inhabitants: the town and harbour of St. Nicolas were also given up to the English; and to these possessions Leogane and other towns and districts were soon added. An expedition was undertaken for the reduction of Cape Tiburon; and a bribe was offered to general Lavaux for the surrender of Le Port de Paix. The enterprise was successful; but the bribe was rejected with disdain. The fort of Acul was stormed by the English and the colonists; but, at Bompard, they were repelled with loss. They defended Cape Tiburon against an army of blacks and mulattoes, who were routed with considerable slaughter.

The arrival of a reinforcement from Great Britain, under brigadier Whyte, elevated the hopes of the English; and preparations were made for the conquest of Port-au-Prince. Fort Bizotton was attacked by sea with little effect; but, when it was assaulted on the land side by a small party under captain Daniel, amidst a violent thunder-storm and torrents of rain, it was taken at the point of the bayonet; and the town was soon after evacuated. The French commissioners intended to have set fire to the buildings, and the vessels that were in the harbour; but this havoc was prevented by the vigilance of the English. The unhealthiness of the climate now occasioned a great mortality among the troops, and checked the extension of their conquests. They lost Leogane, were severely harassed in the town of St. Marc and at Fort Bizotton, and were deprived of Tiburon by the mulatto general Rigaud.

While the French were fully employed in various parts of the world, they had no opportunity of interfering in the affairs of Poland, which they would gladly have rescued from the grasp of the Russians and their associates. After that dismemberment which was effected in 1772 by the injustice of three potent neighbours, those powers dictated some alterations in the government of that part of Poland which they did not seize: but their regulations tended to promote their own views of arbitrary influence, rather than correct the errors and absurdities of the old constitution. The Russian empress, in particular, long enjoyed a domineering control over the king and the state; but, in 1788, when that princess and her Austrian ally were engaged in a war with the Turks, the chief nobility listened to the persuasions of the British and Prussian courts, and procured from the diet the annulment of that constitution which Catharine wished to maintain. A new code was deliberately prepared, and at length adopted by the assembly; and the friends of their country hoped, that a constitution which declared the throne hereditary, and provided for the reform of notorious abuses, might be effective and durable.

The king of Prussia, who had agreed to a treaty of alliance with Poland, expressed his satisfaction at the recent display of national independence; but he was by no means sincere in his professions. The empress, being assured of his readiness to concur in the most iniquitous schemes of ambition, made preparations for crushing that spirit of liberty which a just and magnanimous princess would have encouraged; and she did not scruple to send an army to establish, by rapine and murder, her sway over the country. Her troops prevailed over the feeble opposition of the Polanders: Stanislaus, and many of the nobles, renounced the late constitution; and new encroachments were concerted with the court of Berlin. On pretence of securing Poland from the dangerous effects of French principles, and of extinguishing the flames of democracy in that part of Europe, Frederic William took possession of Dantzic and Thorn, while Catharine seized various towns and districts which bordered on her dominions; and the diet was compelled to give its sanction to these usurpations.

The daring rapacity of the czarina, and the perfidy of her royal accomplice, roused the indignation of the oppressed Polanders, many of whom took the field under the command of the gallant Kosciuszko. The Russian invaders were defeated in several conflicts by the impetuosity of the natives, and were driven from the capital with great loss. The Prussians were attacked by Kosciuszko, and found difficulty in repelling his small force. Their monarch and his son assaulted the entrenchments near Warsaw; but the defence was so obstinate, that a confused retreat ensued. In a battle with the Russians, however, the patriotic general was vanquished and made prisoner; and, when Souvarof had forced his way to Praga, and had stormed that suburb, he recalled to the recollection of the world the atrocious massacre which he had ordered or suffered his soldiers to perpetrate at Ismael (in the late war with the Turks,) by conniving at the exercise of similar barbarities over the unfortunate Polanders. Warsaw was now yielded to the ferocious enemy: the whole country was reduced; and the two despots shared the spoils, with the exception of a part which they allowed to the emperor. Stanislaus, supported by a pension from Catharine, passed the remainder of his life in obscurity. The divided provinces were governed by new regulations; and Poland ceased to exist as a separate state.

To express indignation at the conduct of these arbitrary violators of the rights of an unoffending nation, would be merely to re-echo the voice of the honest and independent portion of every community. Some zealots have asserted, that the interference was very expedient and useful, as Jacobinism had taken deep root in Poland; but this was rather a pretence than an ascertained fact; and, if the Jacobins of Warsaw or of Cracow had been much more numerous and turbulent than they appear to have been, the proceedings of the oppressors of the nation could not

have been justified. What would these writers have thought or said, if the empress of Russia, because 80,000 incorrigible Jacobins existed, as Mr. Burke affirmed, sent a horde of Barbarians to seize a great part of the kingdom, and erase the name of Great Britain from the list of independent governments?

The defence of Namur was seriously intended by the combined powers, but the rapidity of the enemy's progress rendered the execution of their design impossible. The town was therefore evacuated by general Beaulieu, and on the 20th of July the keys were presented at the bar of the convention. On the 24th, the republicans obtained possession of Antwerp, where they found immense magazines of hay, and 30 pieces of cannon. The retreat of the Austrians from Louvain, left the whole territory of Liege exposed to the incursions of general Jourdan. He pressed the enemy closely to Maestrict, from which place his advanced guard proceeded towards the river Jaar, at which time the combined army was stationed before Liege, where it for some time resisted the cannonade of the French, but was at length obliged to retreat with loss. The republicans entered Liege, while the allies entrenched themselves on the heights of Chartreux.

During these transactions, the allies were compelled to abandon Fort Lillo on the Scheldt, while general Moreau obtained possession of the island of Codsand, in which were found 70 pieces of cannon and a quantity of military stores and ammunition. General Almain summoned the garrison of Sluys to surrender, but Vanderdugan replied, "The honour of defending a place like Sluys, that of commanding a brave garrison, and the confidence they repose in me, are my answer." This brave officer sustained the incessant assaults of the besiegers till the 25th of August, when the garrison surrendered themselves prisoners of war. The armies of the Rhine and the Moselle continued their rapid and irresistible advance. General Michaud gave battle to the Austrians and Prussians at Spires, and, after a desperate conflict of two days, obtained possession of the important posts which the Prussians had fortified on the summit of Platoburg, the loftiest mountain in the territory of Deux Ponts. The remainder of the Prussian troops, commanded by the prince of Hohenlohe, retreated to Edickhossen. At Tripstadt, after a severe and sanguinary contest, the French were completely victorious, and took possession of two howitzers, with six pieces of cannon. On the afternoon of the 15th, the French attacked every post belonging to the enemy from Newstadt to the Rhine, a distance of 17 miles along the river Rebach. A heavy cannonade was commenced at two o clock, and continued till eight in the evening, at which time the troops of the emperor retreated with the utmost precipitation and disorder, and effected the passage of the Rhine, while the Prussians under Hohenlohe, retired towards Guntersblum, and another detachment towards Mentz. Kieserslautern surrendered to the French without opposition.

The army of the Moselle having marched in three separate columns, engaged to meet together at Treves. In their route they attacked and carried many posts belonging to the allies, fulfilling their engagement by meeting on a spacious plain, and immediately surrounding Treves. The imperial troops having deserted the city, one of the columns entered in the afternoon, the magistrates, robed in the insignia of their office, presenting them at the gates with the keys.

Jourdan, having routed the enemy on the banks of the Sambre, while Pichegru extended his conquests on the borders of the Scheldt, it was now determined to regain those fortresses which had fallen into the hands of the allies. Landrecies was besieged by general Scherer. The governor at first declined to capitulate, yet he did not permit any of the fortifications to be injured, and on the completion of the besiegers preparations for assault, the garrison, consisting of 2000 men, surrendered at discretion. Previous to the death of Robespierre, a decree had been passed by the convention, declaring that the garrison of every town which should presume to continue its defence beyond the period of twenty-four hours after the summons to surrender, should be put to the sword. In this, however, and similar instances, the decree was disobeyed, and the officers were treated with the utmost humanity. Quesnoy, defended by 12,000 men, followed the example of Landrecies, and in a few days Valenciennes submitted to its antient masters. The surrender of Condé immediately succeeded to that of Valenciennes; and, in these different captures of the frontier towns, the French were so fortunate as to obtain 500 cannon, and a proportionate quantity of ammunition and provisions.

The British army, in number 25,000 men, on retreating from Antwerp, proceeded to Breda, which it was determined to defend. The right column of the English marched through Breda on the 4th of August, while the left took a sweep round the town. They then occupied a position which had been previously surveyed, about four miles distant. They retreated in the end of August to Bois-le-duc, where a Dutch garrison was posted of 7000 men. In the beginning of September general Pichegru advanced with an army of 80,000 men, and a division of his troops attacked and stormed the posts on the Dommel and the village of Boxtel, which, notwithstanding the obstinacy of their resistance, found it impossible to withstand the numbers of the enemy. The duke therefore, with a force so inferior, perceiving his situation to be totally untenable, crossed the Meuse on the 16th of September, and occupied a position which had been previously reconnoitred about three miles from Grave. So vigorous had been the resistance of the British, that, with 25,000 men, they withstood the republican army of 60,000, and afterwards of 80,000, from the beginning of July to the middle of September. On the Rhine, the decided success which attended the efforts of the republicans, was promoted and confirmed by the conduct of the king of Prussia, to which I have already alluded, and by the dissatisfaction expressed at the court of Vienna with the conduct of the Austrian generals. The prince of Cobourg was dismissed from his command under the pretext of treachery, a measure by which Europe was astonished, and the emperor disgraced. The disasters of the army under his command, arose from the superior ability of the French generals, directing a much more numerous force, and inspired with the most ardent enthusiasm. So disastrous was the aspect of the allied cause at this period, that a general conviction prevailed of the hopelessness of the contest. After evacuating the Netherlands, general Clairfait, leaving general Latour to cover Maestricht, posted himself at Juliers. Jourdan, in the beginning of September, proceeded to march against Latour, but it was the middle of the month before he was ready for the assault. On the 18th, the French, in four columns, attacked the whole line, from the Aywaille to Emeux. All the passages were carried at the point of the bayonet, and the camps taken at full charge. The Austrians left 2000 men on the field of battle, and several of their battalions were reduced to one hundred and fifty men. Seven hundred prisoners, twenty-six pieces of large cannon, three pair of colours, one hundred horses, and forty ammunition waggons, were taken, as well as the general's carriage, secretary, and papers. The remnant of Latour's army was completely routed and dispersed. General Clairfait, having in vain endeavoured to resist Latour, fortified himself with great skill and ability at Juliers. Against that place the allies directed their efforts. On the 29th the French advanced from Aix-la-Chapelle, crossed the Roer, and attacked all the Austrian general's extensive posts from Ruremonde to Juliers and Duren. The conflict lasted during the whole of the 29th and 30th of September, and was renewed on the 1st and 2nd of October.

The battle was severely contested, but Clairfait, having lost 10,000 men, found it necessary to retreat with as much rapidity as possible. He retired across the Rhine, and Juliers was left to the French, who reduced Cologne, Worms, Bonn, and all the fortresses on the left bank of the river. Pichegru, in the mean time, was advancing towards Holland. He informed the national convention, that with 200,000 men, he would subjugate the United Provinces; and, though the whole force which he required was not immediately sent, yet so numerous an addition was dispatched to his army, that he deemed himself able to proceed with his operations. In the beginning of October he invested Bois-le-duc, which in a few days surrendered. On the 20th of October a conflict occurred between the republicans and the English, in which, though the event was not decisive, the loss was considerable. The duke of York, now crossing the Waal, fell back to Nimeguen, and was pursued by the innumerable forces of the enemy, who, after forcing the British outposts in front of the place, immediately attacked Fort St. André. Lieutenant-general Abercrombie, and lieutenant-colonel Clarke, were slightly wounded in the skirmish that ensued, and captain Picton, in a sally from the place, sustained the same misfortune. The troops employed in the sally were 3000 British, Hanoverians, and Dutch, and their object was to destroy the batteries which had been constructed to annoy the city. The French were informed of this design, and were prepared to obstruct its execution. The conflict was extremely obstinate, but our troops were victorious without considerable loss. It now appeared evident that the place could not be taken until all intercourse with the English army was cut off: two strong batteries were immediately erected on the right and left of the line of defence, and these were so effectually served, that they at length destroyed one of the boats which supported the bridge of communication. The damage sustained was immediately repaired by the exertions of lieutenant, now sir Home Popham, but the duke of York being aware of the superiority of the enemy's fire, abandoned the town to the protection of 2500 men. Dispirited by this desertion, the Dutch garrison determined also to evacuate the place, but an unfortunate shot having carried away the top of the mast of the flying bridge, it swung round, and about 400 of the garrison were immediately taken prisoners, a circumstance which induced those who remained to open the gates to the besiegers.

Phillippine on the Scheldt also surrendered. The French army on the right was rapidly advancing, and, after the victories over the Austrians, laid siege to Maestricht. The city was regularly invested in the month of October. The republicans repeatedly summoned the town to surrender, and, receiving no reply, they began to pour a dreadful shower of shot and shells from all their works, with which they had surrounded the place. The public buildings and private houses were demolished, and great numbers of the inhabitants were killed and wounded. During three days this destructive fire continued, and at length the governor, moved by the entreaties of the magistrates and the people, entered into a negotiation with general Kleber, and the city capitulated on the 4th of November. After the capture of Nimeguen and Maestricht, the troops on both sides were inactive during the remainder of the month. But, even when not engaged in battle, they were exposed to the severest hardships. Though the republicans did not advance with their accustomed rapidity, the combined powers found it extremely difficult to act on the defensive. The winter began with extreme severity, the soldiers were in want of clothing and other necessaries for encountering a winter campaign, and in a country so much more cold and damp than Great Britain, that season far exceeded its usual rigor. and the sickness and mortality among the soldiers were augmented by the want of medical as-

Vol. 1

sistance and medicine. Like the victims of Walcheren, they were sacrificed to courtly pride and official negligence. The arrival of numerous reinforcements enabled the French, in December, to proceed in their operations. On the 7th of that month they made a fruitless attempt to cross the Waal, in four rafts from Nimeguen ; two of the rafts were sunk by the English forces who were stationed on the opposite side near the village of Lant. One floated to the side occupied by the Dutch, and only one of the four regained that which was in possession of the republicans. On the 11th the attempt was renewed, and with better success : they crossed the river above Nimeguen, and near the canal, in boats, and on rafts, to the number of 5000 men. Another detachment, however, attempting the passage, was repulsed with considerable loss. About the middle of December, the frost became extremely intense, and in a few days the Maese and the Waal were frozen over. Pichegru determined to take the opportunity presented by this circumstance, to complete his projects. On the 27th of December, two brigades under generals Daeudels and Osten, received orders to march across the ice to the isle of Bommel, while a detachment at the same time proceeded against Fort St. André, and the reduction of these places, which, but for the frost, would have been attended with the utmost difficulty, and with the copious effusion of human blood, was now accomplished with facility. Sixteen hundred prisoners, and an immense number of cannon rewarded the toils of the invading army, while the allies retired to the entrenchments between Gorcum and Cuylenburg. A successful attack was made at the same time on the lines of Breda, Oudebosch, and Sevenbergen, and the town of Grave, considered as a masterpiece of fortification which had already resisted a blockade of full two months, being destitute of provision and ammunition, was now forced to surrender, the garrison becoming prisoners of war. In consequence of these disasters, the duke of York, in conjunction with the prince of Orange, endeavoured to excite the Dutch to prompt and vigorous exertion: but the circumstances of the times and the dispositions of the people, were equally changed, and his royal highness, finding every appeal to their patriotism, their justice, and their gratitude, ineffectual, abandoned the hope, and possibly the inclination, of defending Holland, and returned to England.

HISTORY OF THE WAR.

CHAP. IX.

Proceedings of the Revolutionary Societies—Policy of the English Administration—Debates in Parliament, on several interesting Subjects—Conquest of Holland by the French, and Disastrous Retreat of the British Army—Desertion of the Confederacy by Prussia—Invasion of Spain—Naval Exploits of Hotham and Cornwallis—War in 'La Vendée—Unfortunate Expedition to Quiberon—Distresses of the Loyalists and Emigrants.

THE punishment of the Scotch revolutionists did not alarm the fears or retard the machinations of the English associations. Of the three societies which had congratulated the French convention on the downfall of monarchy, the revolutionary club had been dissolved, and the constitutional and corresponding societies formed the bond of connection among the friends of Jacobinism and the advocates of disaffection. The secretaries of these institutions were Danièl Adams, a clerk, and Thomas Hardy, a shoe-maker. In the course of their proceedings, the two societies had called several meetings, especially at Chalk Farm near Hampstead. At this place several intemperate speeches were delivered, and many inflammatory toasts proposed. Some of the most active members of the meeting manifested themselves inimical to the British constitution, as far as their enmity could operate; hostile to every description of kingly government, and desirous of establishing a Jacobinical democracy. One of the number, Mr. John Thelwall, an individual who has lived to atone for his early errors, by the moderation of his opinions and the utility of his pursuits, was separately and personally instrumental to the purposes of sedition, by the delivery of periodical lectures; declamations abounding with the most violent invectives against every existing establishment, and vehement exhortations to resume the rights of nature. The administration observed the open proceedings of these societies and individuals, and suspected the secret machinations of the ring-leaders: to discover the truth, they adopted the policy of every antient and modern government, whether limited or arbitrary, and employed those despicable instruments of power, which are to be found in all great cities as spies, commissioned to attend the conventicles of sedition, and to become members of the societies in order to betray the secrets with which they might be entrusted. In consequence of the information they received, the ministers ordered Hardy and Adams to be arrested and their papers to be seized, and, immediately after, Thelwall, Loveit, a hairdresser, Martin, an attorney, and a few others, to be apprehended. In a few days these measures were extended to men of higher rank and reputation. Mr. Joyce a respectable clergyman, chaplain to lord Stanhope, Mr. Kydd, a barrister of talents and of rising character, and the eminent and celebrated Mr. Horne Tooke were among the numbers of the imprisoned. The papers being examined, it was found that the two societies had concerted a project for as-

U 2

sembling by their joint influence, a. national convention. This design, in combination with many other proceedings,
was construed by ministers into a conspiracy against the constitution, and consequently a conspiracy against the king,
amounting to high treason. The suspected
persons were therefore committed to the
Tower, there to be confined till evidence
should be prepared for their trials. On
the 5th of November the commission was
opened, and Mr. Hardy was first tried,
but, though the proceedings were continued to the 8th day, no evidence of
treasonable criminality could be substantiated against him by all the efforts of the
council for the king : he was therefore
pronounced not guilty, after being ably
defended by Messrs. Erskine and Gibbs.
The next trial was that of Mr. Tooke, who
endeavoured to prove that he had merely
followed the example of Mr. Pitt in recommending a plan of parliamentary reform. The minister was examined on
the occasion, chiefly with regard to the
proceedings of the popular party, previous
to the close of the American war, for the attainment of that object, but he evaded the
most important questions by alleging a
want of recollection. The acquittal of
Mr. Tooke being followed by that of Mr.
Thelwall, a despair of convicting any one
of the supposed traitors, produced the
immediate termination of the proceedings.
Had the prisoners been indicted for sedition, it is probable that they might have
been convicted, but to condemn them as
traitors, would have been a flagrant per-
version of the forms and principles of.
justice.

The appointment of commissioners to
decide with respect to disputed captures
between England and America, and the
equipment of the embassy to China, under
lord Macartney, scarcely attracted the
notice of the public amidst the turbulence
of political contention. Complaints of
territorial aggrandizement and illegal
seizure of merchandise and shipping, had
been repeatedly urged by the Americans ;
and they also requested a perfect understanding of the terms on which they were

to trade with British subjects. After
frequent discussions between lord Grenville and Mr. Jay, the boundaries of dominion were more precisely marked, and
a general but not unrestricted trade was
permitted from America to the East and
West Indies.

The successes which had attended the arms
of France, the defection of one of our most
powerful allies, and the mutinous disposition
which had been displayed by the various
associations throughout the kingdom, were
considered by many men of dispassionate
minds, as reasons sufficient to counterbalance the various objections to a negotiation with the enemy. But the con-
clusions deduced from these very considerations by the administration, by a considerable majority in both houses of parliament, and by a great portion of the individuals throughout the kingdom, who
entertained a zealous attachment to the
existing government, were directly the
reverse. The successes of France, were,
in their opinion, at once the motive and
the justification of determined resistence,
to power so formidable and encroachments
so extensive, and the turbulence and activity of the revolutionary societies the
most powerful inducements to avert, by
the adoption of vigorous measures, the
danger to be apprehended from their designs. Actuated by these sentiments, and
stimulated by the hope that the experience
of democratic tyranny and the pressure
of taxes in France, would favour the efforts
of the royalists in accomplishing a counter-
revolution, the English government persevered in warlike councils, even after the
Prussian monarch, who had basely deserted
his allies, was now applying the subsidies
of Great Britain to the prosecution of his
views on Poland ; and, when it was evident that nothing but the pecuniary support
of England would retain the house of
Austria in its attachment to the confederacy.

At the commencement of a new parliamentary session on December 30th,
the speech from the throne, after an
allusion to the disappointments and   1794.
reverses of the late campaign, signified his

majesty's conviction of the necessity of persisting in the war, as perseverence alone could produce a secure and honourable peace; and repeated the remark of the progress and rapid decay of the French resources, and the probable instability of the violent and unnatural system pursued by the French leaders. The reflections excited by a comparison of this speech with the actual appearance of circumstances and events, were of so gloomy a nature, as put the firmness of the British minister and the national loyalty and fortitude to a severe trial, but they were not seen to shrink from the burden, nor to be intimidated by the dangers and difficulties to which they were subjected.

The address was defended and attacked by arguments nearly similar to those which had been employed in preceding sessions. The proposal of a loan of £4,000,000 to the emperor was opposed by the leading members of the minority in both houses, but without success, and was acceded to by great majorities. The various propositions brought forward by the opposition, were almost uniformly rejected. A motion was made in the house of peers by lord Stanhope, that a declaration should be made that Great Britain neither would nor ought to interfere in the internal affairs of France. Successive motions were made in the two houses by Mr. Grey and the duke of Bedford, purporting that the nature of the French government ought not to be considered as precluding a negotiation for peace; and these were followed by others made by Mr. Fox and the earl of Guildford, importing that a committee of the whole house should take into consideration the state of the kingdom. All these endeavours to oppose and distract 1795. the policy of the minister, terminated only in the disappointment and gradual diminution of the minority.

A second motion from Mr. Grey recommendatory of a negotiation, gave an opportunity for an animated display of the eloquence of both parties. That gentleman, apprehending from some expressions of the minister, that the war was intended to be conducted beyond the limits of reason

or of justice, deprecated the general adoption of such alarming sentiments. His own opinion was, that it was the duty of the cabinet to treat for peace without delay. He wished the house to consider how far the object of the war on our part was attainable, and how far under the present circumstances it was politic to continue it. Much had been said of the exhaustion of the French finances, but no wise statesman would merely on that ground conclude that a people struggling for supposed freedom would soon relinquish the contest. While iron could be found in the bowels of the earth and grass upon its surface, there was no end to the resources of a nation inflamed with enthusiasm in such a cause. Even our resources, great as they were stated to be, would be inadequate to the task of forcing a government on such an enemy, and our allies were not in a condition to give us effectual assistance. There appeared not the smallest chance of an anti-republican revolution, and, though we might be aided by many traitors, the great body of the people appeared to be attached to the existing government. Mr. Pitt moved an amendment declarative of a resolution to concur with his majesty in the prosecution of the war, and expressive of a reliance on the desire which he had uniformly manifested, to effect a pacification on just and honourable terms with any government in France, under whatever form which should appear capable of maintaining the accustomed relations of peace and amity with other countries. It appears from the sentiments expressed in this motion, that at this period the restoration of the Bourbons was not the object of ministerial policy, nor regarded as an indispensable condition of the termination of hostilities with France. Mr. Pitt allowed that he sincerely wished for the re-establishment of monarchy in France, but observed, that security was the great object of our concern, and at present we had no chance of obtaining it. The instability of the power of the ruling party, that revolutionary spirit which had not yet subsided, the total absence of true moderation of sentiment, the decline of religious principles, and the virulence of animosity against our government, precluded the hope of a secure peace. Mr. Fox was pleased to find that the tone of the cabinet had become less imperious, and that the sentiments for which the members of opposition had been reviled as Jacobins and traitors, were now adopted by the ministers of the crown. Yet he did not think that all the members of the cabinet agreed with the premier in this change of sentiment, or ⬤ut it was sufficient to restore to him the confidence of the people. It would be more agreeable to them that a treaty should commence without delay, than that we should wait for what the minister might consider as a capability of maintaining the due relations of peace and amity. Two divisions followed; in one a majority of 183 opposed the motion; in the other the amendment was sanctioned by a plurality of 164 votes.

An attempt was made by Mr. Sheridan, to obtain a repeal of the bill which suspended in particular cases, the acts of Habeas Corpus. He was apprehensive that the operation of the bill might be continued in time of peace as an instrument of power, and that ministers would then allege the necessity of guarding against the dissemination of French principles. He denied the reality of the plot on which the suspension was professedly founded, and deprecated a recurrence to that bugbear of the minister, "a war of plots and conspiracies." He lamented the encouragement given to spies and informers, as disgraceful to any government. He reprehended Mr. Windham, the secretary at war, for the intemperance of his language and conduct, and severely blamed the other members of the cabinet for having directed the prosecution of men whose guilt merely consisted in following the path which their present adversaries had trodden. Mr. Windham replied with warmth to the strictures upon his character, and vindicated the suspension on the plea of serious danger. Mr. Erskine contended that the late verdicts had not merely by probable inference, but almost directly and technically disproved the conspiracy alleged in the charge; and therefore the pretence

for the suspension no longer existed. Serjeant Adair was convinced of the seditious views of the societies, and did not wish that the privelege of *habeas corpus* should be so soon restored. Mr. Fox asserted, that the pretended plots had no existence but in the imagination of the deluders and the fears of the deluded; and that from the obvious difference between the present state of Britain and that of France before the revolution, as well as from the different habits and feelings of the people, there was no real ground for supposing that any considerable number of persons or any respectable portion of the community would aim at the ruin of the constitution. The motion was then rejected by a great majority, and a bill for prolonging the suspension was soon after introduced and carried through both houses after warm debates.

The abolition of the slave trade was again recommended by Mr. Wilberforce, who affirmed that recent information tended to establish his conviction of the impolicy of this traffic. Mr. Barham and Mr. East dreaded the ruin of our plantations from the adoption of this measure. But Mr. Pitt and Mr. Fox treated these apprehensions with ridicule, and again condemned the atrocity of the system. By a majority of 17, however, in a crowded house, the hopes of the friends of humanity were disappointed.

As it does not accord with the intention of this work to detail the domestic history of England, except as it is connected directly or indirectly with that of the rest of Europe, or on occasions of singular and general importance, I shall pass but slightly over many topics which in a history of England alone, would demand the most detailed and minute narration. Among these was the marriage of the prince of Wales to the princess Catherine of Brunswick Wolfenbuttel, which was celebrated on the 5th of April, in the royal chapel at St. James's. It is generally understood that his royal highness was induced to acquiesce in the wishes of his father, and the formation of a nuptial union by the promise of relief from his numerous embarrassments. His debts, amounting to £630,000, were paid, and his revenue augmented to £125,000, subject to an annual payment to his creditors of £65,000, besides the rents of the duchy of Cornwall, amounting to £13,000. The events which immediately succeeded to the consummation of this unfortunate alliance, the separation of the illustrious pair, and the distress and mortification to, which their dissentions subjected almost every member of the royal family, will become the subject of inquiry and historical record in a future chapter. While the people were indulging in misplaced rejoicing at this unfortunate union, the acquittal of Mr. Hastings, by a great majority of the peers, a defensive treaty with the empress of Russia, and the affairs of Ireland, chiefly attracted the attention of the political circles. The first indications of that rebellious spirit, which shortly afterwards rendered that country the seat of military law and sanguinary rebellion, were excited by the prevailing influence of revolutionary principles; and the lower classes took advantage of the discontent excited among the catholic gentry by the acts of government, to convert every instance of resistance on the part of their superiors, into the means of their own protection and encouragement.

The Irish catholics had conceived the hope of obtaining, from the liberality of their sovereign and the parliament, a grant of those rights or favours which had not been included among the concessions of 1793; and, when earl Fitzwilliam, whose zeal for the war had recommended him to the ministry, was appointed to the government of that realm, he encouraged the leaders of the sect with promises of support. He was, indeed, prohibited by the cabinet from bringing forward the bill of farther relief; but he was not instructed to oppose it, if it should be introduced by any member, uninvested with an official character. Yet, when the measure had been proposed to the commons, by whom it did not appear to be disapproved, he was suddenly recalled, at the instigation of that party which had long enjoyed a.

dangerous influence in Ireland, and had been suffered by the British ministry to thwart the views of every lord-lientenant who did not submit to its dictates. His recall excited great discontent in that kingdom, both in and out of parliament. Earl Camden (son of the celebrated chancellor) succeeded him in the lieutenancy; and the bill was then rejected by the influence of the intolerant faction. After the return of the former viceroy to England, the duke of Norfolk condemned in strong terms the dismission of that nobleman, and moved for an inquiry into the subject, not merely as it involved the honour and character of a very respectable peer, but as it was connected with the tranquillity of the country which he had been deputed to govern. The earl courted an investigation of his conduct, that his zeal for the public welfare might be manifested. He referred to the extraordinary concord which he had observed among the people of Ireland, and the unexampled zeal which had appeared for the support of the crown; and lamented that such a favourable prospect should be clouded by the continuance of a plan of government which derived its support from the corruption of one part of the community and the depression of the other. The earl of Caernarvon and other peers affected to think that the inquiry would be unconstitutional, and might be hazardous; but the earl of Guildford strenuously contended for its propriety. The earl of Moira said, that the recall of a viceroy at a critical period, in the midst of the most important business, and when his conduct and views were approved by the generality of the nation, was very different from a common dismissal, or the discharge of an ordinary placeman, and therefore required every explanation that could calm and satisfy the public mind. It was known, that a leading feature in the administration of the nobleman whom the premier had thus endeavoured to stigmatise, was a disposition to correct those flagrant abuses which had long disgraced the government of Ireland. By this part of his system he had exposed himself to the hostility of a corrupt faction; but, if the minister should pertinaciously oppose the redress of those grievances, alarming discontent might arise. Lord Grenville declined all mention of the grounds of the recall, and animadverted on the indecorous interference which the supporters of the motion recommended; and, by a majority of 75, the house voted against it.

The commons were urged to an inquiry by Mr. Jekyll, who censured the deception practised upon the Irish, the meanness of the attempt to degrade lord Fitzwilliám by making him a party to the delusion, and the obstinate adherence of the ministry to the interest of Mr. Beresford and his friends. Mr. Pitt replied, that the conduct of the cabinet would bear a strict scrutiny; that no promises had been violated, and no deception attempted; that a difference of opinion in an important case was a sufficient ground for the removal of an officer of state; and that a free discussion of the topics connected with the recall might be construed into an encroachment on the independence of the Irish parliament. Mr. Grey wished for an immediate agitation of the question respecting the catholics, who derived a full emancipation from all invidious restraints, and who, having been led to expect it, ought to be informed of the grounds of delaying or refusing the grant. But the majority did not adopt this opinion; for 188 opposed the motion, and only 49 assented to it.

When the king found that all the requisite parliamentary business was concluded, he acknowledged, in his speech on the 27th of June, the zealous and uniform regard which both houses had shown to the general interests of his people, and the prudent, firm, and spirited support, which they had continued to afford him in the prosecution of the war. "It is impossible (he added) to contemplate the internal situation of the enemy with whom we are contending, without indulging a hope, that the present circumstances of France may in their effects hasten the return of such a state of order and regular government, as may be capable of maintaining the relations of amity and peace with other powers. The issue, however, of these extraordinary transactions is out of the reach of human foresight."

While the war raged on the continent of Europe and in the narrow seas, the minister had recourse to every measure which might best promote his object, and displayed a power of eloquence, a promptitude of resource, and a firmness and composure of mind, which commanded the respect and admiration of his inveterate opponents.

The duke of York having quitted the British army, and the army itself having retired as the republicans advanced, the allies called a council of war on the 4th of January, at which it was determined to desert their positions on the river Waal. They hastily spiked all the heavy cannon which they could not remove, and destroyed vast quantities of ammunition. On the 8th, however, a skirmish took place between the troops of general Dundas and the enemy, and, during the course of the day, the British and the French were alternately repulsed. 1795.

On the 10th of January, general Pichegru crossed the Waal at different places, and attacked the position occupied by general Walmoden, between Nimeguen and Arnheim. The allies were every where defeated. Equally unprepared for effectual resistance and for flight, they were exposed to still more severe privations and distresses than those to which they had been subjected when commanded by the duke of York. Patriotic contributions had been raised in this country to supply the army with under vests and other necessaries; but, owing to neglect or mismanagement, they seldom reached the place of destination. The sickness of the army increased daily with the extreme severity of the weather, and the total inattention to their comforts and convenience rendered their situation pitiable in the extreme. Invalids were constantly sent to the general hospital at Rheuen, without any previous orders having been issued to prepare for their reception, and therefore no accommodations were provided. They were usually conveyed in by-landers, a small kind of vessel, down the Rhine from Arnheim, without even a sufficient supply of provisions ; and at one time above 500 miserable objects were embarked with only a single hospital mate to attend them, with scarcely any covering, and with a very scanty allowance of straw. A gentleman who was daily an eye-witness of these lamentable scenes, declared that he himself counted forty-two dead bodies on the banks of the river, of men who had perished on board the by-landers, where they had been left, because, as he was informed, there were no quarters remaining for them in the town. The French took possession of Utrecht without opposition, for the troops in the pay of Great Britain continued to retire by the way of Amersfort to Zutphen. Rotterdam surrendered on the 18th, and Dort followed the example on the succeeding day.

The rapid advance of the French, when announced at the Hague, excited consternation and dismay. The princess of Orange, with the younger female branches of the family, escaped on the 15th, with the plate, jewels, and every other article that could be conveniently removed. The stadtholder and the hereditary prince of Orange did not depart from Holland till the 19th, the day on which Dort surrendered to general Pichegru. His serene highness went into an open boat at Scheveling, having among the persons along with him only three who were acquainted with rowing, and had the good fortune to arrive at Harwich on the 21st. The French party having insisted that the stadtholder should be made responsible for all the calamities and troubles of the country, he was solely indebted to the invincible fidelity of his body guards of horse and to a regiment of Swiss, for his escape. They fired upon the populace, and his life was secured at the expense of the lives of some of the most forward patriots. Dr. Krayenhoff, who had been sent into banishment for his opposition to the measures of the stadtholder, arrived at Amsterdam on the 17th of January, with a letter from

the republican commander-in-chief, in order that the people might be prepared for the reception of the French army, and on the 19th that valuable city was taken possession of by no more than 30 hussars. In every spacious square belonging to the town the tree of liberty was immediately planted by the French, and the hats of the Dutch were decorated with tri-coloured cockades, The apathy and indifference of the common people excited the surprise of the invaders themselves. The inhabitants stood at the doors of their houses as the hussars were galloping through the city with the utmost unconcern, smoked their pipes with the most inflexible composure, and retired to rest with their customary tranquillity: The Dutch republicans established a revolutionary tribunal or committee, composed chiefly of those persons whom the old government had cast into prison ; and on the 20th of general Pichegru, at the head of 5000 men, made his triumphal entry. On the day before, a proclamation had been issued by the revolutionary committee, "declaring to all the world that the United Provinces were free and independent :" it recommended the choice of a new magistracy, consisting of several individuals whom it named; particularly M. Schimmelpinninc, and they were accordingly chosen provisional representatives of the different states.

Harlem and Leyden adopted the same measures taken at Amsterdam, and declared themselves for France in the most solemn manner. In the province of Zealand, lay, at this time, a considerable number of ships of war ; and the admiral who commanded it was warmly attached to the interest of the French. On the 30th of January he hoisted the French flag, and took possession of Flushing and Middleburgh, the two chief towns in the island, every part of which acceded, on the 4th of February, to the terms arranged with general Michaud, who commanded the French troops in the neighbourhood. Exclusively of liberty of conscience, and of religious worship, which the French introduced every where, it was stipulated that no place in Zealand should be garrisoned by the French, nor their assignats be forced into circulation. The fortresses on the frontiers of Brabant, particularly Bergen-op-Zoom, were in an excellent state of defence; but the revolutionary tribunal, having issued proclamations enjoining all the garrison towns to give admittance to the French troops, that strong and almost impregnable fortress opened its gates to the enemy. It was garrisoned by 4000 men, among whom were included the 37th regiment belonging to Great Britain. The governor requested that the British troops might be permitted to return home, but the French general refused to comply, and they were detained as prisoners of war.

The provinces of Guelderland, Utrecht, Holland, and Zealand, were now completely in possession of the French, who were fully sensible of the value of their acquisitions, and their wants prompted them to apply to their new allies for immediate assistance. The constitution intended to supersede the present not being yet completed, the states-general were directed to publish a proclamation in their own name, demanding a supply of clothes and provisions for the French army, and the French republic pledged itself for the faithful repayment of the value.

On the 27th of February, when this proclamation was issued, an assembly was held of the provisional representatives of the people of Holland, of which Peter Paulus, a man of moderation and abilities, was elected president. They began by deposing the stadtholder from all his offices, and abolishing the offices themselves. They next proceeded to an abrogation of all the other forms of the lately established constitution, and to the institution of others in their stead. They commenced an inquiry into the circumstances of the bank of Amsterdam, by which it appeared, though destitute of specie, to be perfectly solvent in bonds and unexceptionable securities. In consequence of the further deliberation of this assembly, a solemn declaration of the rights of men and of citizens was published at the Hague, accompanied by a proclamation annulling

the sentences passed against the democratic party in 1787, and recalling home to their country all who had been banished for their opposition to the stadtholder.

Much, undoubtedly, of the facility with which this revolution was accomplished, must be attributed to the judgment, the moderation, and the humanity of Pichegru; but still more must be ascribed to the cautious and prudent habits of the Dutch themselves. They had made every preparation for their approaching subjugation. The magistrates who had acted under the old government were neither impeached nor punished: the municipality of almost every city and town had undergone a radical change of its internal government and police before the arrival of the republicans; and messengers had been dispatched to the French in every direction, to procure the most favourable conditions or terms of surrender. The people of property volunteered their services to prevent tumult or insurrection, but the phlegmatic disposition of the people rendered their interference unnecessary.

The conquest of so rich and powerful a state as Holland, was a subject of great alarm to the princes who formed the coalition against France. This country was the centre of all pecuniary loans and negotiations, and its ready assistance on all such occasions, rendered its independence an object of general interest, but more particularly to the northern powers. It was now foreseen that France would engross all the resources which had formerly aided the exertions of her enemies, and that the power and wealth of Holland would be at the mercy of the republic. These were mortifying reflections to the enemies of this formidable nation, now become more dangerous by the accession of so many countries to its dominions, and by the partiality of the majority of the people in its new acquisitions to revolutionary principles.

The situation of France at this period, was such as to inflame the ambition and gratify the pride of a nation already too confident in its own superiority. A list of recent conquests and victories was printed and affixed to a tablet which was hung up in the hall of the convention, and copies of it were sent to the armies. The recent acquisitions consisted of ten provinces of the Austrian Netherlands; the Seven United Provinces; the bishoprics of Liege, Worms, and Spires; the electorates of Treves, Cologne, and Mentz; the duchies of Deux Ponts, Juliers, and Cleves, and the Palatinate. It was asserted, that in the last seventeen months, there had been 120 actions of inferior consequence to those particularly named, and that the following were the results of the late successes.

Killed of the enemy,	80,000
Prisoners,	91,000
Strong places and cities taken,	116
By siege or blockade,	36
Forts and redoubts,	230
Cannon,	3800
Muskets,	70,000
Powder,	1,900,000lbs.
Pairs of colours	90

These advantages were regarded by the admirers of military heroism, and by all who affected to believe that the glory of a great nation is promoted by extensive conquest, however destructive and unjust, as the more extraordinary from the peculiar circumstances under which they were accomplished. The successes of the French had been obtained over the best disciplined armies of Europe, elated with their past triumphs over warlike enemies, and commanded by generals of consummate experience and exalted reputation. Their own armies, at the commencement of the contest, consisted of officers and soldiers unaccustomed to military service, and their commanders were far from eminent in their profession. Yet so general was the impression produced by their successive victories, that several of the allies had for some time meditated a retreat from the field of action, and a total secession from that confederacy which had exposed them to so many losses and disappointments.

In the mean time the British army was closely pursued by that of the republicans, consisting of 30,000 men. On reaching Deventer, the 27th of January, after one of the most distressing and fatiguing marches that was ever experienced by a retreating army, the British troops expected the respite of a few days from their almost insupportable sufferings. With unexampled courage and perseverance, they had conveyed to this place all the ammunition and military store, and implements of war belonging to the army, but they could carry them no further. The diminution of their strength, through the numbers that fell ill or died in this disastrous retreat, compelled them to destroy vast quantities of these articles, to prevent them from falling into the possession of the enemy, who pursued them so eagerly, that they were obliged to quit Deventer two days after their arrival. But, notwithstanding the immense superiority of the French, and the celerity of their motions, they were not able to interrupt the British troops, whose movements were so firm and steady as to surmount the numerous and increasing obstacles which impeded their retreat. It was not, however, without heavy losses that they overcame the difficulties and discouragements opposed to their progress by the enemy or the elements. Their marches were generally performed through ice or snow, mud or water, often up to their middle. On the 10th of February they crossed the 1795. Vecht, which divides into two parts the province of Overyssel, and on the 12th they passed the Ems at Rheine. On the 24th a body of French came up with them, and an engagement ensued, in which the British acted with such firmness, that they were enabled to retire with inconsiderable loss. Resuming their march with little interruption, they at length arrived in the county of Bremen about the close of March. Here they were joined by other divisions of the army. That which was under the command of lord Cathcart had to encounter even more than a common share of distress. The French, hung upon its rear during the whole retreat; and scarcely a day elapsed without a skirmish. The country was hostile : the town of Groningen shut its gates against them, and they were equally harassed by want and by fatigue, with the troops commanded by Abercrombie.

The undesponding perseverance with which the British troops met, and surmounted every hardship and obstacle arising from the various incidents of war, was the more remarkable since they contended against an enemy in the full possession of every advantage accruing from victory, and whom they could only hope to impress with a sense of their valor. Assailed in every direction, they manfully fought their way through the provinces of Utrecht, Guelderland, Overyssel, and Groningen, almost destitute of necessaries, and encumbered with a heavy train of artillery, baggage, and waggons, loaded with the sick and wounded. This dreadful trial of courage, patience, and military skill, lasted upwards of two months, and deservedly excited the admiration of Europe.

The savage barbarity of the Dutch boors to our suffering soldiers, was strongly and fortunately contrasted by the kind and cordial reception which they received from the inhabitants of Bremen. "It is something like a dream," observes a witness, and partaker of those pains and pleasures, "or fairy vision, and we could hardly give credit to our own senses : We who had been so lately buffeted about by fortune, driven like vagabonds through frost and snow over all the wilds of Holland, and who, in our greatest extremities, when we asked for sustenance with money in our hands, were answered only with a shrug of the shoulders, 'Nothing for an Englishman.'—Now to be seated in the most elegant apartments, servants attending ready to anticipate every wish, beds of the softest down to repose upon, without being disturbed in the morning with the thundering of cannon or the usual alarms of war,—it seemed like some enchantment, but it was real. The elegant and gener-

ous entertainment we met with far exceeded any thing we ever experienced before, and I may venture to say, ever will again."

The British troops began to embark in the transports on the 14th of April, at the mouth of a creek near Bremen lake. The whole fleet, with the convoy, consisted of more than 200 sail. On the 24th it cleared the mouth of the Weser. The ships were tossed about and driven by tempestuous weather far to the northward of their usual course. The Greeks, whose admirable retreat is recorded by their commander Xenophon, were not more transported at the sight of the Ionian sea, than the British soldiers, when on the 27th, being off the coast of Northumberland, they espied the Cheviot Hills. The weather becoming favourable, the fleet steered southward towards the Nore, when it parted into different divisions. One bound for Harwich, another for Portsmouth, and a third for Greenwich. They all arrived safely at their places of destination.

During the progress of these events in the Low Countries, the republican troops on the Rhine remained in a state of torpor and inactivity. At length, however, they collected in the neighbourhood of Mentz a prodigious quantity of heavy artillery with the view of besieging that city, the only place of importance remaining to Austria on that side of the river. In order to facilitate this object, they laid siege to Manheim, the reduction of which would open an entrance to the interior parts of the empire, divert the attention of their enemies, and prevent them from attempting the relief of Mentz. Manheim surrendered to the French on the 24th of December, 1794. Impatient to obtain possession of Mentz, they made three assaults on the fort of Zahlback, in its neighbourhood, but were repulsed with considerable loss. This check completely retarded their operations until the spring of 1795, as it was found impossible, while the frost lasted, to undertake the regular siege of so strong a fortress

After the French had made themselves uncontrolled masters of the Netherlands, and driven the last remains of the allied armies from their lately acquired territories, they next resolved to pursue them into the countries where they had taken shelter. They first made themselves masters of Bantam, a dependence of the Dutch republic, and then carried their arms into Westphalia, where they defeated a body of imperial forces. The expectation, however, of concluding a peace with Prussia, suspended their operations. It did not appear difficult to detach that power from the confederacy, by sowing the seeds of jealousy between the courts of Berlin and Vienna. The jarring interests of Austria and Prussia had been reconciled by the occurrence of the revolution, which impelled them to unite by a feeling of common danger. But the first panic had subsided. It was not imagined that the French, after being relieved from the apprehension of internal invasion, would persevere in hostilities from the love of conquest, or that, having abolished monarchy in their own country, they would continue the war for the purpose of destroying it in others. An intimate connection had subsisted between France and Prussia before the subversion of the monarchy: the motives for that connection remained in their full force, and were rendered still more powerful by the connection between Prussia and its antient rival the court of Vienna, of which the politics were incessantly occupied with plans for the recovery of the rich and extensive province of Silesia. This was the first acquisition that had placed the house of Brandenburg on an equality with its neighbours; and so fortunate an event created the more deep and lasting rancour, because it was wholly at the expense of the house of Austria. Prussia was aware of the bitterness with which these sentiments were entertained, and foresaw the danger to which her dominions would be subjected, should her neighbour and rival be entirely relieved from all solicitude with respect to France. She perceived too clearly that the discomfiture of the latter would enable Austria to resume her pretensions, to demand the restitution of Silesia, and to enforce her demands with the undivided devotion of her resources.

The ambitious disposition of the house of Brandenburg, was proverbial; but the Prussian monarch, unable to extend his territory on the side of France, was anxious to conclude a pacification which might enable him to share, without interruption, in the dismemberment of Poland. This object could not have been accomplished had Prussia continued with the coalition; its associate, Russia, in the partition, might have availed itself of the absence of its confederate to have seized a larger share than was its due; and, as possession is usually the right of the strongest, might not have been persuaded by amicable means to resign the possessions it had clandestinely obtained.

A confidential agent was immediately dispatched by the king of Prussia, to open a formal negotiation, and he was shortly followed by an ambassador, openly commissioned to treat with the French minister at Basle, M. Barthelemy. The Prussian ambassador was baron Goltz, who had formerly filled that situation at Paris, where his abilities and moderation had procured him much esteem. The respect with which he was regarded by the French, contributed materially to forward the treaty; when, to the surprise and regret of the public, he fell ill, and was carried off, not without suspicions of poison, which were unhappily not discountenanced on opening his body. As it was suspected that this act of treachery was perpetrated by the enemies of peace and of France, who regarded with dissatisfaction the rapid progress of the negotiation, it was some time before any person would undertake an office apparently accompanied by so much danger. Another individual was at length appointed. Mr. Hartenburg, a gentleman less exceptionable to the friends of the coalition. The articles of the treaty were highly favourable to France. The Prussian territories on the left bank of the Rhine were ceded to France, and those on the right alone restored to Prussia. The regulations for the internal settlement of the countries thus ceded, were referred for final discussion to the period of a general peace between France and Germany. A cessation of hostilities was agreed to, and it was stipulated, that those princes whose dominions lay on the right side of the Rhine should be entitled to make proposals to France, and to be favourably treated.

The conclusion of this treaty, which was presented to the convention on the 10th of April, for its approval and ratification, filled the members of the assembly and the friends of the republic with the highest exultation. It was the first acknowledgment of the republic, formally made by any of the great powers of Europe ; and this power was precisely the one which had been most forward in the coalition. It was not without violent debates that the rigid republicans consented to admit the insertion of secret articles in this or any other treaty. They pleaded the precedent of the Romans, whose treaties with their enemies had always been exposed to the scrutiny of the world. It was asserted with a singular forgetfulness of themselves, that the dignity of the republic, and its respect for moral truth, were inconsistent with concealment. These objections, however, vanished before the more important considerations of ambitious policy, and a pacification with Prussia enabled the convention to pursue, with renovated ardor, their schemes of conquest.

The military force of the republicans was not less successful in Spain than their intrigues in Germany. The only obstacles which impeded their advance into the interior of the country, were the badness of the roads and the steepness of the mountains. The French regarded the pass of Rosas in Catalonia, as an object of the utmost importance, but, prior to the reduction of this port, it was absolutely necessary to become masters of Fort Bouton, by which the bay and the naval force were commanded. The fort was compelled to surrender, but, on laying siege to the town, the inundations from rain and melted snows, obliged them to desist. Finding it impossible to open the second parallel,

they erected a strong battery, and, on the 3rd of January, commenced their attack on the city. The garrison, apprehending their design, evacuated the town on the 5th of January, and did not attempt to recover it during an interval of five months. Five hundred and forty men, who had been left in the city, surrendered at discretion. On the 5th of May, 3000 Spaniards, having made their appearance on the side of Sistellia, and discovered an intention to surround the republicans, were defeated with great slaughter. The French were so much elated by this success, that their commander, general Moncey, in whose camp some spies had been detected, sent them to the Spanish quarters with a letter, informing the enemy of his strength, position, and designs. So confident were the French, and so depressed the Spaniards, that his arrival at Madrid was no longer regarded as beyond the limits of probability. No army or fortified city remained to obstruct his march. The peasantry were a wretched and heartless race, worn down by poverty and oppression, and the inhabitants of the towns were an indolent generation, debased by superstition, and apparently incapable of masculine exertion.

In this extremity, the court of Madrid saw no other expedient to extricate itself from unavoidable ruin than the conclusion of peace with the French republic. Every resource had been exhausted ; the nobility, the gentry, the clergy, and the monastic orders, had all contributed to the support of the war ; the orders of knighthood, which have large possessions in Spain, had lately granted liberal donations to the government, and submitted to a tax of eight per cent on their estates ; but their patriotic exertions were counteracted by the discontent or sluggishness of the nation. The views of France coinciding with those of Spain, a treaty of peace was concluded between them at Basle, by M. Barthelemy, on the part of France, and Don Domingo Dyriante, on the part of Spain. In this treaty two articles were highly inimical to Great Britain. The Spanish port of Hispaniola was ceded to France, and the court of Spain engaged to employ every means in its power to detach Portugal from its present alliance with Great Britain against the French republic. The secession of three powerful allies from the confederacy, at first appeared to be decisive of the fate of Europe, but the mutual understanding between England and Austria more than counterbalanced the superior numbers and resources of a jealous and uncertain confederacy.

If France was victorious by land in every quarter to which her arms extended, she was not capable of contending at sea, with Britain alone. It would be uncandid to assert that the French were destitute of courage, but they were unquestionably inferior in point of skill, and contrary to what might be expected from their versatility of character ; they were by no means so active as the British tars. The destruction of their shipping at Toulon was an irreparable loss, not on account of the vessels, but of the mariners, whom it was impossible to replace ; and the tyranny of Robespierre had a decided tendency to weaken the naval force of the republic. In reinforcing the armies on the frontiers, both seamen and landsmen were blended together, and while these men were taken from their proper element, France was gradually unfitted for a contest on the ocean.

The effects of this wretched policy were soon apparent, for in the preceding and the present year their efforts were ineffectual, notwithstanding the naval commanders of the republic acted with unusual skill and caution. Several frigates during this year were captured by the British ; and, though a few displayed the most desperate courage, the greater number surrendered after a slight resistance. On the 4th of January an engagement took place off Martinique, between the British frigate Blanch of 32 guns, and La Pique of 34, which lasted, without intermission, for the space of five hours. The masts of the French frigate were carried overboard during the action, on which 30 men perished, 76 were killed, and 110 wounded. The loss on the part of the British frigate was eight men killed, including captain Faulkner and twelve wounded.

On the 14th of March an action was fought in the Mediterranean between a British fleet of 14 sail of the line and three frigates, under the command of admiral Hotham, and a republican fleet of 15 sail of the line and an equal number of frigates with the British. The British commander received on the 8th, information that this fleet had been seen off the island of St. Marguerite, a report which exactly accorded with a signal received from his majesty's ship Mozelle, then in the offing. He unmoored his fleet, and immediately put to sea. Understanding that the enemy's fleet was directing its course to the southward, he steered towards Corsica; and dispatched the Tarleton with orders to the commander of the Berwick to join him off Cape Corfe, but that ship had been unfortunately captured two days before. On the 12th the hostile fleets came in sight of each other, and admiral Hotham, on the 13th, gave the signal for a general chace. One of the line of battle belonging to the enemy had lost her topmast, a circumstance of which the Inconstant attempted to take advantage. She began to rake and harass her in a dreadful manner, till she was joined by the Agamemnon, when the united force of both ships materially damaged and disabled the enemy. Perceiving, however, that many French vessels were hastening to her assistance, they were obliged to leave her. Admiral Hotham on the morning of the 14th, discovered the disabled ship towed by another, to be so far to leeward of their own fleet, as to afford a strong probability that they might both be cut off. For the accomplishment of this object, nothing was left unattempted, and the French were reduced to the necessity of giving them up for lost, or of coming to a general engagement. The latter did not appear to be their wish, although they made a feeble attempt to support them, but they were at last cut off by the Bedford and the Captain, and immediately deserted by the main body of the fleet. The captured ships were the la Ira of 80 guns, and the Centaur of 74. Admiral Hotham had 75 men killed, and 280 wounded ; but no accounts have been recorded of the loss of the French, though it must have been considerably greater than that of the English from the number of seamen and marines with which all their vessels are crowded. The Illustrious separated from the British fleet during a heavy gale of wind, was cast on shore near Avenza, and lost. Two ships of the line were captured on each side, and the French prizes were discovered to be constructed from the hulks of ships destroyed at Toulon.

Admiral Cornwallis, while cruizing off Belle Isle with five ships of the line and two frigates, fell in, on the 7th of June, with a fleet of merchantmen, under convoy of three ships of the line and six frigates. The ships of the line effected their escape, but he had the good fortune to capture eight of the merchantmen, all richly laden with wine and military stores. On the 16th, cruizing near Penmarks, he received a signal from the Phæton, that an enemy's fleet was in sight, which was found to consist of 13 sail of the line and two brigs, besides a cutter and several frigates, a force to which all resistance would have been fruitless. At this critical period the wind shifted in favor of the enemy, so that in the morning the ships in front of their line began to fire upon the Mars, which, as well as the rest of the fleet, kept up a running fire during the whole day. Admiral Cornwallis effected his éscape from this perilous situation by a singular manœuvre. He exhibited signals indicating the approach of a British fleet, and the French admiral, acquainted with their purport, relinquished the pursuit.

The fleet from which admiral Cornwallis thus unexpectedly effected his escape, was destined on the 23rd of the same month to be attacked by lord Bridport, (late admiral Hood,) who commanded a fleet of 14 sail of the line and eight frigates. On the morning of the 22nd of June, a signal was given that an enemy's fleet was in sight, and the British admiral, perceiving that they had no inclination to bring him to action, hoisted a signal for chasing the enemy with four of the swiftest vessels under his command. They came up with the republican fleet on the morning of the 23rd, when an action commenced, and continued, without intermission, till three in the afternoon. The British admiral obtained possession of the Alexander, formerly belonging to the English navy, the Formidable, and the Tigre. The enemy being protected by the batteries on shore, his lordship was not only unable to complete his victory, but found it difficult to retain possession of the ships he had already captured. The remaining part of the enemy's fleet escaped into L'Orient, 70 miles south east of Brest. The loss sustained by the British during the action, amounted to 31 men killed, and 115 wounded, but the loss of the French has not been recorded.

The month of February produced an event of the greatest importance to the interest of France, and no less fatal to that of the combined powers. It was announced to the convention, that the committee of public safety had concluded a treaty of peace with the grand duke of Tuscany, who had deemed it necessary to abandon the cause of the allies. After several intemperate debates, the treaty was ratified amidst the loud acclamations of the members and spectators ; and a declaration was issued, importing that the grand duke of Tuscany, having revoked all acts of adhesion, consent, and accession, to the armed coalition against the French republic, there would ensue peace, friendship, and a good understanding between the two powers.

An event of greater importance than any treaty of peace with a foreign enemy, had in the meantime occurred in the interior of France. The proclamation of an amnesty to all those of the royalists in La Vendée who would lay down their arms, had gradually induced the majority of the insurgents to confide in the promises of the government. Numbers, however, still adhered to their chiefs. Accustomed to predatory war, and consequently habituated to habits of lawless depredation, they became a dreadful nuisance to the inoffensive and peaceable inhabitants. It was at last resolved, as the surest and most effectual' experiment, to induce the chiefs themselves, by the proposal of honourable and advantageous terms, to lay down their arms. Charette, who. commanded the remainder of the Vendeans, and Cromartin, the principal leader of the Chouans, consented to a meeting, accompanied by all the other chiefs, with the deputies of the convention. The terms arranged at this meeting were highly favourable to the insurgents, who received the most complete amnesty and ample compensation for the damage sustained by their lands and property. In the declaration which was signed at Nantes, the place of meeting by Charette and the other chiefs, they apologized for their insurrection by ascribing it to the tyranny of the late rulers, and bound themselves in the strongest terms to be faithful to the French republic. Beneath their sanction an address was published to the people of La Vendée, advising them to submit to the convention, and laying before them the danger and imprudence of resisting the established government of their country. In this general submission, Stoflet, one of the chiefs of the insurgents, at first refused to consent, and the sincerity of the Chouan leaders, was strongly suspected. The mass of the insurgents were subject to independent leaders, who only acted in concert when it accorded with their peculiar views of interest, duty, or ambition ; and these in their turn were under the influence of the intrigues of the French princes, and the pecuniary aids and promises of the English ministry. A constant correspondence was supported between the royalists in La Vendée and Mr. Windham. The money with which they were supplied, consisted, at first, of false assignats, afterwards in Louis d'Ors and guineas, and lastly, of English bank notes. Charette, although he was induced to conclude a peace with the republicans, does not appear any more than the other chiefs,

to have been averse to the continuation of the war ; but they were probably induced to acquiesce in the proposals of the government, by the clamors of their wearied and exhausted partizans.

The Vendean chiefs were afterwards accused of having violated many of the articles of capitulation : they retorted on the republicans by asserting, that many of the insurgent officers were still detained in close confinement. It is probable that both these accusations were just, but the real or supposed injuries sustained by the Vendeans might not have stimulated their chiefs to the demonstration of resistance, had not many of the loyalists, the most attached to the royal family, and the princes of the house of Bourbon themselves, severely reprehended their consent to any accommodation with the regicides. No sincere and cordial understanding, however, existed between Lewis XVIII. and the princes of the coalition or the court of London. It was the evident design of that prince to render himself independent of the coalition, and to effect his restoration independently of any assistance but that of England. With singular indiscretion he at once provoked the resentment of the British ministry, and awakened the suspicion of the French by hastening to Toulon immediately after its possession by the allies : the count d'Artois committed an act of similar indiscretion by visiting this country. Had Lewis condescended to participate in the views of the allied powers, or to confide his hopes and his plans to the British ministry, such arrangements might have been formed as would have deserved, even if they had not secured, success. But ignorance of the internal state of France, and probably some portion of distrust with respect to the designs of Lewis, were the apparent causes that one of their most decisive measures in favor of the royalists was conducted with apathy, and supported by a force wholly inadequate to the intended purpose. While the disaffected Vendeans, and more particularly the discontented Chouans, were endeavouring to evade the scrutiny and avert the resentment of the convention by every variety of artifice, an armament was preparing in England to second their intended insurrection. In the beginning of June, it sailed to the southern coast of Brittany, under the command of sir John Borlase Warren. The insurgents were assembled in great force in La Vendée, but as they were not masters of any sea-port at which the troops could be landed, the squadron proceeded to the bay of Quiberon. Here a body of about 3000 men landed on the 27th, and dispersed a small number of republicans, who had endeavoured to oppose them. They besieged and captured a fort garrisoned by 600 men, and prepared to advance farther into the country. Multitudes flocked in from all parts, to whom vast quantities of arms were distributed, and it was expected that an army might be formed capable of facing the republican troops in the neighbourhood.

Count D'Hervilly, who had acted a generous and heroic part on the 10th of August, placed himself at the head of 3000 Chouans and endeavoured to penetrate into the country, but, on the approach of a few hundreds of the republicans, they threw aside their arms and fled. This disaster obliged him to retire within the intrench ments that had been thrown up on the peninsula of Quiberon.

The republican commanders, to improve this advantage, raised three redoubts to guard the passage of the main land. The chiefs of the royalists, alarmed at these preparations, immediately perceived the necessity of raising the blockade in order to secure their communication with the disaffected in the interior parts of the country, and therefore determined to assault the republican lines by break of day. But intelligence of this important operation was communicated on the preceding evening by four different deserters, and preparations were made to render the design abortive. On the approach of their columns general Humbert fell back, and the assailants were not only exposed to a severe fire of grape-shot from two masked batteries in front, but to a charge of infantry and cavalry on both their flanks. So unexpected a

reception entirely disconcerted the emigrants, of whom 300, with the count de Talmont and a number of nobles, were left dead on the field. General D'Hervilly, who commanded on this occasion also, was desperately wounded, and three pieces of cannon fell to the lot of the victors, who were alone prevented by five English gunboats, from entering Fort Penthieve along with the fugitives.

General Hoche had by this time collected a considerable force, consisting of the national guards of Brest and on all the adjoining towns on the coast, in addition to a powerful reinforcement of regular troops. He therefore determined to leave the lines hitherto occupied by his forces, and attack the invaders who were now imprisoned, as it were, in the peninsula. But, as it was first necessary to render himself master of Fort Penthieve, he resolved to attack it, and though the engineers in his army were of opinion that it could be reduced by regular approaches alone, he declared his intention to carry it by assault. He was undoubtedly influenced by the number and the zeal of the deserters from the royal standard, who not only made him acquainted from time to time with all the movements in the enemy's camp, but undertook to conduct the troops and obtain the surrender of the fort.

Accordingly 3000 of the republicans led by Humbert and Valle, left the camp of St. Barbe about midnight, (July 21st,) notwithstanding their march was impeded by a storm, that circumstance serving to conceal their operations from the enemy. The forces being divided into three columns, two of them moved along the shore, and were occasionally obliged to wade breast high : they were perceived by the English gunboats, which immediately commenced a heavy fire of grape, and they would actually have returned had not some person about two o'clock in the morning exclaimed that the tri-coloured flag was flying on the ramparts. This proved to be actually the case, for while one of the detachments had proceeded to assault the fort in front, the adjutant-general Menage, at the head of about 300 chosen soldiers and deserters, braving the violence of the waves and the fire of the enemy, scaled the rocks on the west side, and, being favoured by part of the garrison, obtained possession of one of the advanced works.

On receiving intelligence of this event, the remainder of the French army was immediately put in motion, and the commander-in-chief, assisted by two representatives, Tallien and Blad, penetrated into the peninsula in three columns, one of which marched straight forward, while the other two followed the direction of the coast, with an intention to cut off the enemy's retreat. It was now five o'clock in the morning, and, though the French had been in possession of Penthieve upwards of two hours, this event seems still to have been unknown to the ill-fated emigrants in the camp at Kousten ; but a number of Chouans, perceiving the danger with which they were menaced, found means to escape in boats to the continent.

Notwithstanding they were surprised, and left destitute of a leader by the flight of M. de Puisaye, who, on the first alarm, fled to one of the British men of war : the royalists rallied under the gallant Sombreuil, who, unmindful of his own preservation, was only anxious to hold out till the women, who precipitated themselves into the sea with their children, had obtained an assylum on board the English fleet.

The entrenched camp was ultimately forced, and, while nearly one half of the invaders joined the army of Hoche and protested their inviolable attachment to the cause of the republic, the remainder retired to a rock where they had posted a piece of cannon, and defended themselves with the greatest intrepidity. But it being found impossible to resist the numbers and the artillery of the assailants, the vanquished demanded leave to capitulate, and a parley was accordingly concluded. At this moment some of the chiefs took advantage of the opportunity to escape on board the boats sent to their succour : the fire of the republicans recommenced ; and, being now reduced to the deplorable alternative of perishing by

the swords of the victors or the waves of the sea, these wretched and unhappy men surrendered at discretion. In Fort Penthieve and the peninsula were found 70,000 muskets, 150,000 pairs of shoes, and all the artillery landed from the fleet. 1795. The beach of Quiberon was covered with stores, wines, and provisions; and a regiment of infantry, taking advantage of the general consternation, obtained possession of several vessels laden with flour, rice, and other articles of necessity. Six hundred emigrants perished at the foot of the rock de Portignes, beneath which they had taken shelter ; 2000 were saved by the boats of the fleet. The bishop of Del and fourteen of his clergy, received death with the most exemplary resignation : M. de Broglie and several men of birth, to the amount of 300, suffered upon this occasion ; and the execution of Charles de Sambreuil, who had embarked in the expedition from sentiments of honour, and conducted himself with skill, generosity, and courage, excited, in a peculiar degree, the sympathy of Europe.

Notwithstanding this heavy disappointment, the hopes of being enabled by perseverence to make some impression on the enemy, induced the British government to continue the squadron on the coast of France. It made a fruitless attempt on the island of Noirmoustier, lying on the coast of Poitou, and defended by 20,000 men, who possessed an easy communication with the land, and could receive hourly supplies. It was more successful in the attack on the island, Isle Dieu, which, after being reduced, was put in a posture of defence. Small as this acquisition might appear, it tended to keep the contiguous coast in a state of suspense respecting the intentions of the British ministry, and occasioned the republican government to station very considerable forces in all the adjoining parts. This was the more requisite, since a communication had been opened between the British squadron and the royalists on shore; the supply of money and of military stores which they had most in view, would alone have enabled them to maintain an obstinate resistance, by the encouragement it would have presented to those numbers who would readily have joined them had they been sure of a comfortable subsistence.

Unaided by the resources of Great Britain, it was now too evident that little could be expected from the spontaneous efforts of the insurgents, and, had the communication between them and the English fleet been preserved, their successes would have been more brilliant than lasting or important. Unity of purpose and devotion to a single chieftain, the indispensible requisites of success, were now no more.

The auspicious moment had been suffered to elapse in empty promises and fruitless preparations, when a d'Elbee, a Stoflet, a Bonchamp, and a Charette, united for the first time under a prince of the blood. Supported by a body of the British soldiery, under the beloved and gallant lord Moira, they might have imitated the followers of Henry IV. and even at that time encircled the head of the present monarch of France, then the count de Provence, with the crown of his illustrious progenitor

HISTORY OF THE WAR.

CHAP. X.

Banishment of the Jacobin Members—Death of Lewis XVII.—Contentions of the Different Parties—Massacre of the 5th of October Conducted by Napoleon Buonaparte — Formation of the Directory, and the Character of its Members—The Issue of the Campaign Unfavourable to France—War is Declared by England against the Dutch, and many of their Colonies are Surrendered—Treaties with Russia and Austria—Affairs in the West Indies—Insurrection of the Maroons, and their Banishment from Jamaica—Two Bills of Coercion are Introduced into the British Parliament— State of the Nation.

THE internal proceedings of the French republic were at this time more determined and energetic than the operations of the armies. In the month of May, M. Fouqniere Tenville, the president of the late revolutionary tribunal, with three of the judges, the public accuser, and eleven of the jurors of that dreadful engine of human butchery, were found guilty of the most gross injustice and cruelty during the exercise of their functions, and were executed in the place de Greve. These individuals were followed to the grave by the most obnoxious of the terrorists. The moderate party could not regard their own or the public peace as founded on a durable basis, while the associates of Robespierre retained their influence in the government. Conscious of their present strength, and that the sense of the nation was in their favour, they resolved to take' advantage of the general sentiment to free themselves from their adversaries who were endeavouring to justify their sanguinary measures by representing the moderate principles of their opponents as arising from a counter-revolutionary design. Such temperate and rational measures were adopted as might conciliate the good opinion and esteem of the nation, and the deputists whom the terrorists had driven from the convention, were recalled to reinforce their party. Barrere, Billaud Varennes, Collot D'Herbois, and Vaudier, were denounced; a decree for their examination before a commission, appointed for that purpose, was passed, and it was declared that they had been accessary to the tyranny exercised over the people and the convention. The nation still remained, n anxious suspense respecting the fate of these demagogues, when the Jacobin leaders, reflecting on the popularity which they had once enjoyed in the city, determined to make one effort in their support, which, if successful, might lead to the re-establishment of their own influence. Availing themselves of the extreme dearth of bread, they contrived to exasperate the populace against the administration, by persuading them that the public misery originated in the measures of the convention; and, artfully blending the cause of the imprisoned terrorists with the national welfare, they endeavoured to persuade the people that their interests would be more attentively regarded were these individuals restored to power.

Availing themselves of the lenity professed by government, the Jacobins assembled in various places, and endeavoured, by artful discourses, to exasperate the populace to insurrection. Whether this complaint of scarcity was real or affected, through their machinations, an immense croud assembled on the 1st of April, and proceeded to the hall of the convention, demanding bread, and the constitution of 1793. The Jacobin members of the convention explicitly abetted their demands. Emboldened by this support, the spokesman of the insurgents told the convention that those in whose name he addressed them, were the men of the 14th of July, the 10th of August, and the 31st of May; that they would not suffer the accused members to be sacrificed to their enemies, and expected the convention would change its measures. When the populace broke into the hall, the convention was employed in a discussion on the measures best calculated to remedy the scarcity of which the nation complained, but this sudden interruption compelled them to take immediate means of preservation from the fury of the mob. They directed the alarm bells to be rung, and the citizens to be called to the aid of the convention. They readily obeyed the summons, and assembled to the number of 20,000. Delivered from their perilous situation by the firmness of Pichegru at the head of the Parisian military, combined with the courage and patriotism of the citizens, the convention passed a decree for the punishment of the authors of the riot. As it had been evidently excited to prevent the trial of the denounced members, it was moved that they should be sentenced to immediate punishment. In order to mitigate the rigor of a condemnation that might appear precipitate, their lives were spared, but they were banished to Guiana, and ordered to be transported thither without delay. In this manner terminated the career of Barrere, Collot D'Herbois, and Billaud Varennes, after having made so conspicuous a figure during the two first years of the republic. Vaudier, their associate, had found means to make his escape.

The tumult being suppressed, the convention proceeded to such measures as they deemed essential to the public welfare. Among these the most important was the appointment of a committee of eleven, to frame a new constitution and system of government, which might remedy the evils of that established under the Jacobin administration in 1793, and might correct the abuses of which it was productive.

Had the Jacobins been less confident in their own strength, the severity of the proceedings against them, might have had the intended effect of deterring them from further attempts against the public peace; but, conscious as they were of their influence over the lower orders of the community, and sensible of the danger which they should incur from the triumph of the moderatists, they produced a contrary effect. Actuated by motives of revenge and of self-preservation, they determined to have recourse once more to that engine which they had so often employed with success. Incendiary papers were dispersed, calling upon the *starving people* to avenge their own wrongs, and to repair to the convention, there to demand bread, and the consititution of 1793, the dissolution of the convention, the arrest of all its members, and the immediate convocation of the primary assemblies for the election of another.

In compliance with these exhortations, the multitude a second time assembled tumultuously round the door of the convention. And when they learned that, instead of compliance with their wishes, a decree had been passed to outlaw the leaders of the insurrection, they burst into the hall of the assembly. Ferrand, one of the members, fell a victim to their fury, and the Jacobins in the convention, were, for a short time, victorious. But the multitude having dispersed, on learning that general Hoche was approaching with an armed force, they were at last obliged to give way, and the moderatists, on the same day, resuming their seats, proceeded to cancel the acts which the Jacobins had passed. On the ensuing day, the populace being provided with some pieces of artillery, took the convention by surprise, and, directing their cannon against the hall of the assembly in the Thuilleries, they obliged them to consent to the renewal of the constitution of 1793, and to several other stipulations in favor of the degraded terrorists. The triumph of the anarchists, however, was of short continuance. Their confidence was not less remarkable than the negligence of the convention had been culpable. As the officers of justice were conducting the assassins of Ferrand to the place of execution, they were attacked by the multitude, who rescued their prisoners.

It now became evident that the public peace could not be restored till more effectual means should be adopted for subduing the Jacobin demagogues and their tumultuous adherents. The peaceful citizens rallied round the standard of the convention; and the convention, finding that they were supported by all the friends to the public welfare, adopted the most vigorous measures of resistance to popular anarchy. General Menon, the commandant of Paris, appearing at the entrance of the rebellious fauxbourg, St. Antoine, at the head of a body of troops, with several pieces of artillery, issued a proclamation denouncing vengeance to the insurgents if they did not immediately lay down their arms and deliver the assassins of Ferrand into his hands. Audacity giving way to force, his commands were obeyed, and an unconditional capitulation put an end to the reign of terror in the metropolis. Six members of the convention and fifteen others, distinguished for their atrocious violations of the public peace, were attended to the guillotine with the acclamations of a fickle populace.

Amidst these scenes of disorder, the Bourbon dynasty *in France*, which had been for ages so illustrious, but was now celebrated only for its misfortunes, was terminated by the death of the dauphin Lewis Charles, the only surviving son of Lewis XVI. in his 12th year. This unfortunate prince, who had, from his infancy, been doomed to imprisonment without the possibility of a crime, appears to have fallen a victim to confinement. But those who wished to vilify the present administration, alarmed the friends of humanity, and endeavoured to excite the feelings of the populace by unproved, and probably unfounded, insinuations of poison. As soon as these aspersions had subsided, the convention liberated Sophia, the sister of the dauphin, who, by the Salique law, could not succeed to the inheritance of the throne, and sent her to Vienna in exchange for those persons whom Dumouriez had delivered into the hands of the Austrians.

The unsettled state of France, the disturbances by which Paris had been lately convulsed, and the factions and divisions which were apparent even in the bosom of the convention, seemed imperiously to demand a regular system of government, of which the executive power might be so efficient as to triumph over all opposition, and stifle insurrection in the bud. The convention was incessantly employed in the formation of a new constitution; and, after two months discussion, investigation, and amendment, they declared, on the 23rd of August, that the object of their labours was completed, and transmitted it to the primary assemblies for their acceptance and confirmation.

This constitution consisted of fourteen chapters, with an exordium or introduction respecting the rights of man, differing in no material point from that which was prefixed to the first constitution. The first chapter contained an account of the territorial possessions of the republic, and its division into departments, cantons, and communes. The second chapter defined the political state of citizens, and declared every man born, and residing in France, whose name had been inscribed in the civic register, or who had lived one year in the territory of the republic and paid à direct contribution, to be a French citizen. The third chapter contained a definition of the power of the primary assemblies, who were to nominate members of the elective assemblies. The power of the elective assemblies was defined by the fourth chapter, by which they were empowered to elect the members of the legislative body of the tribunal of annulment, the high jurors, the administrators of the department, the president, public accuser, and registrar, of the criminal tribunals, and the judges of the civil tribunals. The fifth article made the legislative body consist of a *council of antients*, and a council of five hundred, who were both to reside in the same commune. The council of antients consisted of 250 members, of whom one-third were to be annually renewed, and consequently each member retained his seat for the period of three years. The power of proposing laws belonged exclusively to the council of 500, but the antients might adopt or reject them as they pleased. It was enacted by the sixth chapter, that the executive power should be delegated to a directory of five members chosen by the legislative body, of forty years old at least, and formerly members of the legislature, or general agents of the government. One member annually was to retire and be succeeded by another formally elected. The directory was to provide for the internal and external security of the republic, to dispose of the armed force, choose generals, and superintend the execution of laws and the coining of money. The council of 500 was to draw up a list of 50 members by secret scrutiny, from among which the council of antients were to elect five members to compose the directory.

While the 48 sections of Paris appeared cordial and unanimous in accepting the new constitution, 46 of them vehemently rejected the decree, connected with its promulgation that two-thirds of the members composing the present convention, should be re-elected for the new legislature, and which declared that if the departments would not re-elect two thirds, the convention would become an elective body, and supply the deficiency by its own nomination. No language can do justice to the scene of horror and tumult which prevailed in Paris. The protests against a law by which the elections were rendered compulsory, gave rise to the most animated debates, and the independent spirit of the Parisians was imitated by many of the departments. The primary assemblies

were distracted by vehement and fruitless contention, and the language in which the sentiments of the nation were expressed became at length so violent, and their menaces so decided, that the convention determined to claim the protection of a military force from the different committees of government. On the 3rd of October it was decreed that the primary assemblies of Paris should be commanded to separate, and that the electors should not assemble before the period fixed by the decree. The convention declared itself in a state of permanence. At seven o'clock in the evening Etienne Dupin, secretary of the department of the Sein, appeared with six dragoons and two trumpeters, on the place de Theatre Francois, to proclaim the decree, and while he was reading it a numerous party rushing from the theatre, and increasing the crowd without, were discovered to consist of members of one of the primary assemblies, which had met in the theatre contrary to the decree. The armed force was ordered by the convention to secure them, but did not arrive till the multitude had dispersed.

The convention continued to order troops into the metropolis ; and, as an expedient for providing themselves with an immediate reinforcement, they gave the numerous terrorists imprisoned in Paris, their liberty. Incensed by this proof of incousistency and of a disposition to terrorism, the citizens appeared openly in arms. Menou was ordered to advance against them with the troops then in Paris, but that general, incurring their displeasure by entering into a negotiation with the insurgents, was dismissed in disgrace.

The deputy Barras, who had been charged with the direction of the armed force, was appointed in his stead, and determined to confide the most arduous and unpopular part of his duty to his protegé, Napoleon Buonaparte. After the siege of Toulon, in which his achievments were so conspicuous as to obtain for him the rank of general, Buonaparte had been sent to Nice under arrest, by the deputy Beffroi, who had previously displaced him from his command, on charges of being attached

Pub.d by T Kinnersley London Oct 7 1817

NAPOLEON BOUNAPARTE.

to the terrorists, and of having treated the inhabitants with relentless and unnecessary cruelty. He was soon released, and still retained the rank, though he did not perform the duties or enjoy the emoluments, of a general. He remained for some time at Nice, and, on a visit to Paris to lay before the committee of public safety a statement of his services and his wrongs, he was offered the command of a regiment of infantry, which he declined, demanding his discharge and permission to retire to Constantinople, both of which requests were refused. He accepted, in 1794, the command of the expedition fitted out against Ajaccio in his native island, a situation in which he had the mortification to. be repulsed by one of his own relatives, named Masteria, who was at that time in the British service, and had served under general Elliot at the siege of Gibraltar. The object of the expedition was defeated, and he returned to France. During the interval between his return and his nomination to the second command of the conventional troops, he appears to have lived in indigence and obscurity, notwithstanding the friendship of Barras, who evidently entertained a sincere and ardent interest in his behalf, long before the union of Napoleon with madame Beauhernois.

The sections beat to arms, and appeared every successive moment more serious and formidable in their military preparations. The inhabitants were awakened at midnight by the sound of drums and a knocking at almost every door, accompanied by the incessant cry of "To arms, to arms, citizens! every one to his section,—liberty or .death." This intimation did not produce any material effect, but about noon the next day, (October 5th, the 13th of Vendemiaire) the people were again in motion, with a view to march their forces against the Thuilleries.

The convention had deceived the people during the morning, in sending messages to the sections, and in receiving propositions of peace, an artifice by which they gained time for reinforcing their positions and encouraging the troops to perform their duty. While the people were de-

liberating instead of fighting, the post of the citizens at St. Roch, opposite the Thuilleries, was suddenly exposed to a tremendous fire, and a dreadful scene of carnage ensued.

During the time that the citizens on the northern side of the river were engaged in close and sanguinary combat, those on the opposite side were attempting to reach the scene of action by the quay of Voltaire, though the cannon of the convention which defended each end of the bridge, presented to their view a most menacing appearance. The conflict on the one side of the river was not of long duration, for the commander of the column of citizens having endeavoured to force the passage even without artillery, and but ill provided with ammunition, a charge of musketry was made which instantly dispersed his followers. The artillery in this conflict was commanded by Buonaparte. The battle near the Thuilleries, where the convention was sitting, raged with great obstinacy, the cannon having been frequently seized by the insurgents, and as often retaken by the national troops. Though the sectionaries were destitute of artillery, they made a gallant opposition, after many severe repulses, still returned to the charge, and did not retreat till after a bloody conflict, which lasted four hours. After an interval of two hours the firing of the cannon was heard again, and did not terminate till midnight, when the troops of the convention became masters of the field of battle, and routed the citizens at every post. The church of St. Roch and the palais d'Egalité were forced ; the gates were burst open by the cannon, and the people who had taken refuge within the walls were slaughtered. During the conflict, the few deputies who were in the convention remained in their places with their president at their head. Many of the other deputies mixed with the troops. The number of the people slain on this memorable day has been estimated at 8000, but the calculation is probably inaccurate.

Buonaparte, on this occasion, having had the chief command, received all the honors and all the credit that the convention attached to the services of the day, and duty which had performed was little calculated to endear him to the people; but the firmness and ability he had displayed, contributed to elevate him in the opinion of a nation, which, in its admiration of talents, is always regardless of virtue, and ensured the respect of his patron, as much as he had before commanded his esteem.

The severity with which the Parisian insurgents were punished by the convention, excited the apprehension of the more moderate republicans that they were about to revive the system of terror. The Jacobins began to regain their ascendency in an assembly, whose chief object, like that of Robespierre, appeared to be the possession of uncontrolled dominion. This party procured a commission to be appointed consisting of five persons, who were empowered to consult together what measures were proper to be adopted in order to save the country. Such an arbitrary assumption of power alarmed the nation, and it was apprehended that the days of Robespierre were about to be revived, but the circumstances were changed; the dread of foreign enemies being removed, the moderate republicans and constitutionalists were too numerous and too powerful to submit to this new project of despotism. In the convention itself, the ablest men were among the moderates, though in a temporary minority, they soon found means to prevail over a considerable number of the others, and at length to overbalance the opposite violence of the Jacobins and of their too zealous opponents. By the exertions of Thibandau, the designs of Foeron, Legendre, and Tallien, were counteracted; the commission of five was annulled, the constitution was finally agreed to, and the convention dissolved itself.

The nation awaited with the utmost impatience the assembling of the new legislature, and looked forward with sanguine hopes, to a period when they should experience the happy effects of their new constitution. On the day appointed the two councils nominated by the new constitution took their seats and entered upon the execution of their respective offices. The important business which first engaged their attention and exercised their talents for intrigue, was the election of persons to the directory; and on this occasion the preponderance of those who had declared for measures of coercion in opposition to the moderatists was too evident. Of five directors, four, viz. Reubel, Letourneur Delamanche, Barras, and Sieyes, were advocates for that system of conduct; and Reveillere Lepaux alone was of the opposite party. Sieyes, declining the honour conferred upon him, Carnot, a man of distinguished talents but obdurate disposition, was chosen in his place.

The members of the directory were not entirely unknown during the vicissitudes of the revolution. Reubel was a native of Colmar, formerly an advocate of some eminence in the sovereign court of Alsace, and a deputy to the states-general. He was appointed commissary to the army of the Rhine, and subsequently to that of La Vendée. He became a member of the convention and of the committee of public safety. He was indebted for his nomination partly to his republican principles and partly to the friendship of Sieyes. BARRAS descended from one of the most noble and antient families of France, was born in 1755, at Foxemphoux, in the department of Var. He entered the dragoons very early in life, and was sent to the Isle of France. From thence he went to Pondicherry, where he was made prisoner by the English, but was liberated and engaged in the service of France at the Cape of Good Hope. On his return to his native country, he was reduced by licentious and expensive indulgencies to the most extreme distress, and was only relieved from the most deplorable state of obscurity and indigence, by a revolution, which confounded the distinctions of rank and character, and subjected the private fortunes of private individuals to the vicissitudes which formerly attended states and nations. Reveillere Lepaux had been by turns, a professor of botany and a member of the convention; but his original rank in life was far more humble, for he rose from the station of a journeyman apothecary to participate in the honors of the Gallic purple. Letourneur and Carnot were bred to the profession of arms, and served as engineers: the first, however, had only been distinguished by the direction of a battery or the construction of a camp; while the second presided over the evolutions of armies, and obtained, by the boldness, decision, and sagacity of his plans, the most important accessions to the glory and advantage of the republic.

Such were the men designed by fortune to preside over and direct the fate of France. That they did not fulfil the just expectations of the people, or impress the powers of Europe with that decided conviction of their political energy which might have prepared the way to a durable and honourable peace, was owing to their utter destitution of principle, rather than to deficiency of talent. The ministers of Great Britain were precluded from proposing directly or indirectly, a negotiation with men whom they suspected, but did not fear; and, while our distrust was awakened and justified by their obvious policy, our confidence in the successful termination of the war was increased by the languor and inefficiency of their preliminary measures.

The directory, immediately on their assumption of office, were guided by the policy rather than inclination, in selecting for their associates and dependents many of the most active terrorists. They dissipated, however, the suspicions which this conduct naturally excited, by commanding that the pantheon where the Jacobins assembled, to lament the fall of Robespierre, should be shut; and, notwithstanding the endeavours of their opponents to stigmatize the pomp and ceremony of the installation of the directors, as partaking of monarchical splendor, and inconsistent with the simplicity and humility of a republican government; their exertions in favor of a free press, which had become subservient to the moderate party, and their enactment

of several laws for the extension of religious liberty tended to sooth the feelings and conciliate the good opinion of the people.

When the speculators upon political and military events reflected on the successes of the French both at home and abroad in the course of the two last campaigns, when they compared the present situation of the French government respecting foreign powers with its prospects at the commencement of the war, when they perceived the disunion and jealousy that prevailed among the powers which had been leagued for its destruction, and when they witnessed the convention crumbling into atoms, and supported only by the determined councils of one state, they expected to have seen the French armies proceed in the same prosperous career, and that the German empire, in the space of a few months, would have become an easy conquest to the invader. But the vicissitudes of war are peculiarly calculated to repress the confidence of the disputant, and to baffle the sagacity of the most judicious inquirer. The extraordinary exertions of the preceding year had exhausted the resources of a nation too cruelly distracted by domestic convulsions, and too intently occupied by the revolutions which successively occurred, to œconomize, arrange, and augment, the means of offensive warfare. During the latter part of the present year, the campaign, while it languished on both sides, was decidedly in favour of the allies. Hostilities in Flanders were commenced by the siege of Luxemburg, which surrendered to the republicans on the 3rd of June. The greatest part of the army of the Sambre and Meuse crossed the Rhine near Dusseldorf: they obtained possession of that town, and invested Mentz. The army of the Moselle and the Rhine, under general Pichegru, accomplished the passage of the former river opposite to Manheim, and immediately obtained possession of the city. He then occupied a position on the right bank, which intercepted the Austrian armies on the north and south of the Maine, respectively commanded by

z 2

generals Clairfait and Wurmser. A division of Pichegru's army having attacked the Austrians with the usual impetuosity, put them to the route. But the spirit of plunder was so predominant among the French, that as soon as they had defeated this part of Wurmser's army, they dispersed on all sides in quest of pillage. The Austrian cavalry, informed of their disorder, returning, completely surprised and defeated the plunderers, compelling them to make a precipitate retreat. Pichegru, in consequence of this disaster, being no longer able to second the efforts of Jourdan, the latter was under the necessity of raising the siege of Mentz and retreating before the victorious Austrians to Dusseldorf, where he repassed the Rhine; while the former fell back upon Manheim, and was happy to follow the example of his colleague by crossing the river. Marshal Clairfait appearing before Mentz, carried the entrenched camp of the French, constructed as it was, at a great expense of time, labour, and money. General Schaal, who occupied this strong position, on the retreat of Jourdan, was obliged to retire, and leave 106 pieces of cannon, 200 ammunition waggons, and about 2000 prisoners, among whom were two generals, in the hands of the assailants. Notwithstanding the disasters sustained by the French army, the garrison of Manheim, consisting of about 9000 men, persevered in their defence, and were not compelled to surrender but after a long resistance, and the junction of numerous reinforcements with the besieging army. Wurmser and Clairfait, taking advantage of their first successes, had crossed the Rhine, and, having formed a junction, reconquered many of the acquisitions of the French, and even threatened to recapture Luxemburg. Pichegru and Jourdan marched to oppose the triumphant enemy, but were repulsed in their separate attacks on Kreusnach and Kayserslautern. The severity of the season and an unexpected armistice of three months, terminated a campaign, which disappointed the hopes of the partizans of France, exhibited the most exemplary skill and the most laudable enthusiasm on the part of the Austrians, and excited the mutual distrust, while it clouded the reputation of Pichegru and Jourdan.

As the Dutch, though nominally independent allies of the French, were easily induced to become the enemies of their former confederates, letters of marque and reprisal were issued against them by Great Britain; and directions were given for the seizure of their colonial territories, which, however, the king professed an intention of restoring whenever the stadtholderian government should be re-established. Vice-admiral Elphinstone appeared with a fleet in Simon's-Bay, near the Cape of Good Hope, and took all the vessels which he there found; and, as it was suspected that the governor intended to set fire to Simon's-Town, from which he had ordered all the inhabitants to retire, major-general Craig landed, and took possession of the place, but prohibited his men from committing any other act of hostility. When the militia, however, fired from the neighbouring hills, it was thought proper to retaliate; and an attack was meditated upon the pass of Muysenberg. While a select body advanced with that view, the well-directed fire of some vessels occasioned an evacuation of the post; and a spirited assault soon dislodged the foe from a rocky eminence which might have been long defended. After some weeks of inaction, an attempt to surprise the most considerable of the out-posts failed; and, though the English repelled a fierce attack, their efforts did not deter their adversaries from preparing for a general engagement. At this crisis, the appearance of a British reinforcement at sea checked the eagerness of the enemy. This force was commanded by major-general Clarke, who, as soon as he had made proper arrangements, marched toward Cape-Town. At Wynberg, the Dutch made a show of resistance; but they were soon driven from the post; and, when the vice-admiral had detached four vessels to raise an alarm on the side of the town, the governor proposed a cessation of hostilities, that terms of capitulation might be adjusted. It was agreed that terms of capitulation might be adjusted. It was agreed that the troops should be prisoners of war, and that the property of the Dutch East-India company should be delivered up to the captors of the settlement; but private possessions and civil rights were left inviolate.

Some of the Asiatic settlements of the Hollanders were also seized by the English. Trincomalè, in the island of Ceylon, was taken by a small armament; and the fort of Oostenborg was soon after reduced, with Jaffnapatam and other towns. To these acquisitions were added the colonial districts of the Malay peninsula; and, on the coast of Malabar, Cochin was seized by a detachment from Bombay.

On the conquest of Jamaica by the English, a description of persons in that island called Maroons, who had been slaves to the Spaniards, neither choosing to submit to the English nor to share the fortune of their former masters, made their escape, and took refuge among the mountains. Increasing in numbers they had frequently issued from their fastnesses, and, after making their predatory incursions and maintaining a contest with the troops sent against them by their irregular mode of fighting, returned with their plunder. In process of time they were formed into regular communities, erected buildings chiefly on lands granted by the state, and were governed by one of its superintendents. They subsisted on the prey obtained in hunting, the remuneration obtained for their services to the planters, and the product of their ill cultivated lands.

The causes of the present insurrection, as formally represented to the council, were an infringement of their treaty by the magistrates of Montego bay, in causing the punishment of whipping to be inflicted on some of their people by the hand of a slave; that the land originally granted them was become sterile from repeated cultivation, and that the reappointment of their late superintendant, captain James, instead of captain Croskel, whom they accused of incompetence, would be one indispensable condition of their tranquillity.

The justice of these complaints was not admitted, and suspicions were entertained that some people of colour and certain Frenchmen, were conspiring with the Maroons, and endeavouring to extend revolutionary principles from St. Domingo to Jamaica. Martial law was therefore proclaimed, and the most active measures adopted to suppress the insurrection. The desperate expedients were then adopted of offering a reward of 300 dollars for taking or killing a trelawny Maroon, and of sending to Cuba for a number of Spanish chasseurs, with their dogs, to assist in chasing the Maroons, in discovering their places of ambush, and aiding in their destruction. These dogs are perfectly broken in, and will not kill the object they pursue unless resisted. On coming up with a fugitive, they bark at him till he stops, and then crouch near him, terrifying him with a ferocious growling if he stirs. In this position they continue barking, to give notice to the chasseurs, who come up and secure their prisoner. Each chasseur, though he can hunt only with two dogs, is obliged to have three, which he maintains at considerable expense and at his own cost. The chasseurs live with their dogs, from which they are inseparable. At home the dogs are kept chained, and when walking with their masters are never unmuzzled or let out of ropes, but for attack. Fortunately for the interests of humanity, the terror occasioned by the arrival of forty chasseurs with their dogs, precluded the necessity of employing them. The Maroons made their submission, and a treaty was concluded by general Walpole who had been employed to suppress them, which was ratified by lord Balcarres. Some difference of opinion afterwards arose respecting their future destination: the council and assembly of the island not approving of a secret article by which it was agreed that they should be suffered to remain on the island under certain restrictions. It was the general wish of the white inhabitants that they should be transported to some other country, and the neglect of a great number to surrender before the day appointed afforded a plea for refusing to conform to this article. An act of the assembly was consequently passed, banishing the Maroons from Jamaica, and making it felony to return. They were transported to Nova Scotia, but it being afterwards discovered that they were troublesome to the province, they were, in 1800, again removed by an agreement with the company, to the settlement of Sierra Leone.

In Grenada, an insurrection was excited by the arts of the enemy. Many of the French inhabitants and negroes were encouraged to revolt by promises of aid; and, on the arrival of a small body of soldiers from Guadaloupe, they perpetrated many acts of violence. Their camp was assaulted without effect; but they were not so successful on other occasions as to be induced to prolong offensive hostilities. In Dominique, likewise, an insurrection took place, and a party of French landed; but the rebels were reduced to submission, and the invaders were either killed or made prisoners. In the island of St. Vincent the Caribs rose in arms, and committed brutal ravages; and, being joined by the majority of the French colonists, they boldly withstood the efforts of the English. In St. Lucia similar disturbances arose; and the new possessors, after having fiercely contended for different posts, were constrained to relinquish the island to the French.

Compared with these violations of the tranquillity of social life, the riots which occurred in some parts of Great Britain were of no moment. The difficulty of procuring ordinary sustenance, and the shameful practice of *kidnapping*, gave rise to these temporary infractions of the peace of the country.

Among the negotiations of the year were an agreement with Spain and treaties with Russia and Austria. His catholic majesty, before he concluded peace with France, ordered the surrender of the lands which (in repugnance to the former convention) he had retained at Nootka. With the court of Petersburg the king entered into new stipulations of alliance; but the only result was the appearance of a Russian

fleet in the channel. The emperor was more earnest than the czarina in the cause of the confederacy; and on his engagements our court more confidently relied.

The Germanic body, wishing for the termination of a calamitous war, desired the emperor to treat with France, under the mediation of the king of Prussia. He promised to forward the object of this requisition; but, in reality, he rather checked than promoted it; and the French executive directory refused to agree to an armistice which was proposed by the mediator, as a preliminary step to a congress.

His Britannic majesty affirmed in his speech to the two houses of parliament on the 26th of October, that the prospect resulting from the general state of affairs, had in some important respects been materially improved in the course of the year. He was of opinion, that the success of the French on particular occasions, and the advantages which they had derived from the conclusion of separate treaties with some of the belligerent powers, were far from compensating the evils which they experienced from the continuance of the war. He spoke of " the destruction of their commerce, the diminution of their maritime power, and the unparalleled embarrassment and distress of their internal situation;" yet he did not think that their rulers were so humbled by the increasing pressure of difficulties, as to be disposed to " negotiate for a general peace on just and suitable terms:" it therefore seemed necessary to prosecute the war with the utmost energy and vigor.

As the king, in his way to and from the house of peers, was insulted by the people, some of whom even threw stones at his person, both houses expressed their indignation at this disloyal behaviour, which was imputed to the intrigues of the seditious members of the London Corresponding Society, who, at a numerous meeting in a field near London, three days before, had harangued the rabble in favour of peace.

In the speeches for and against the usual

addresses, there was little novelty of remark. The necessity of a continued war was urged on one hand ; and, on the other, a negotiation was recommended. The king's speech was censured by Mr. Fox as not giving a just view of the situation of affairs ; but the minister would not allow that it exhibited a delusive picture.

The freedom of debate was exercised with great warmth in the discussion of two bills which the court deemed necessary for the safety of the constitution. One was brought forward by lord Grenville, who, referring to the late unjustifiable treatment of his majesty, the reviving spirit of turbulence, and the increase of seditious publications, proposed the enactment of a new law for the repression of such alarming practices. He did not mean that the bill should render any offences punishable but such as were already acknowledged to be deserving of legal chastisement ; and its provisions, he said, were conformable to the principles of several acts of the reigns of Elizabeth and Charles II. The duke of Bedford and the earl of Lauderdale contended, that the existing laws were sufficiently strong and severe for the discouragement of treason and sedition ; that the new bill would infringe those rights which every Briton claimed from the constitution framed by his progenitors ; that it was a libel on the loyalty of the people, and on that patience which they had shown amidst the evils of unnecessary war ; and that it would create and nourish, not stifle, disaffection. On the second reading, those two noblemen opposed it with redoubled energy ; and the earl hinted that oppressive laws might justly be resisted ; an innuendo which inflamed the wrath of lord Grenville, who observed that such language, if it had been used out of parliament, would have rendered his lordship amenable to the law. The earl of Mansfield vindicated the bill, and dreaded serious mischief if it should not be enacted. The earl of Abingdon wished it to be rejected, as he disapproved all innovations upon the laws, whether planned by arbitrary tories or mad republicans. When the house divided, the votes were ten to one in favour of the measure, the numbers being eighty and eight.

At the commitment of the bill, lord Thurlow reprobated the severity of some of its clauses. The lord-chancellor replied, that the punishment would not be too rigorous for the offence. The bishop of Rochester (Dr. Horsley) wished that all licentious freedom of remark or complaint might be strictly and vigilantly repressed ; adding, that the " people had nothing to do with the laws but to obey them." When he was reproved for this imperious declaration, he qualified it by allowing that individuals had a right to remonstrate against those laws by which they were particularly effected.

Messieurs Fox, Sheridan, and Erskine, were the principal opposers of this bill when it reached the house of commons. They affirmed that it was unjust in principle and oppressive in detail ; that it was palpably repugnant to the constitutional rights of the people ; and that nothing which had recently happened called for such a violation of their freedom.

After frequent divisions, the third reading was voted by a majority of 181. It passed under the title of " an act for the safety and preservation of his majesty's person and government against treasonable and seditious practices and attempts." One clause ordained the capital punishment of every one who should express, utter, or declare, by the publication of writings, or by any overt act, such imaginations, devices, or intentions, as were calculated to injure the king, impair his authority or that of the parliament, or promote an invasion of his dominions. Another provision was, that all declarations tending to excite hatred or contempt of the king, or the government and constitution, should be considered as high misdemeanors ; and it was decreed that a second offence of this kind might be punished either in the ordinary mode, or by banishment from the realm for a term not exceeding seven years.

The other bill of coercion was introduced by Mr. Pitt, whose aim was to restrain popular meetings. If the daring licentiousness of the democratic faction should not be checked, the constitution, he apprehended, would not long subsist. When he had stated the outlines of his scheme, he was accused by Mr. Fox, on fair grounds of presumption, of an intention of stifling that freedom of discussion which every one might claim, of superseding the bill of rights, and subjecting the people to the yoke of despotism. Mr. Halhed, not being convinced that the late outrage was the result of the meeting near Copenhagen-house, or that it arose from a general or formidable combination, was unwilling to agree to the proposed bill. Mr. Curwen thought, that no member who had the feelings of an Englishman would support this impudent attempt to rob the people of their dearest liberties. Mr. Wilberforce was highly pleased with the bill, as it tended, without the exercise of despotic measures, to prevent the success of schemes of unconstitutional reform. Mr. Sheridan opposed it with animation, and hoped that the house would not be so spiritless as to submit on this momentous occasion to the dictates of the minister. Mr. Windham said, that it was the duty of the house to support the constitution against the attacks of Jacobins and traitors; but Mr. Grey replied that it was more endangered by arbitrary schemes of this kind than by the intrigues of supposed malcontents. On a division, the numbers were 214 and 42, affording a superiority of 172 for the introduction of the bill.

A regular inquiry into the true nature and extent of the dreaded danger was recommended by Mr. Sheridan; but Mr. Powys said, that general notoriety was a sufficient ground for the present proceedings. Mr. Fox warmly promoted an inquiry, and conjured the minister to relinquish the odious system of terror; but the proposal of investigation was rejected by a great majority.

The bill was defended by the solicitor-general (sir John Mitford) as strictly constitutional. It would not, he said, prevent public meetings, but would subject them to proper regulations; and it would

not suppress debating societies, though it would debar them from that free discussion of political subjects which might lead to sedition and tumult. Mr. Erskine disputed its expediency, and denied that it was compatible with the spirit of the constitution. Mr. Anstruther and the earl of Mornington exercised their eloquence, not merely in vindicating, but in panegyrising the measure. Mr. Sheridan indulged himself in sarcastic animadversions on the arguments of some of the advocates of the bill, and on the violent conduct of the ministry. Mr. Dundas allowed that the new regulations would in some degree encroach on popular rights; but he was convinced that they would secure the general frame of the constitution. Mr. Fox said, that the bill tended to destroy, or alarmingly to diminish, the benefits of the revolution: but Mr. Pitt maintained that it would contribute to secure those benefits.

During these discussions a general alarm prevailed throughout the country, and many petitions were presented for and against the two bills. The signatures to the former were 30,000, those to the latter exceeding 130,000. The ministerial addresses were very strenuously supported by Mr. Reeves, who, for a pamphlet in which he had elevated the monarchical branch of the government beyond all due bounds, was stigmatized by an address of the commons for his prosecution; but he was acquitted of criminal intention, though the jury pronounced the work to be a very improper publication.

On a resumption of the subject, Mr. Grant distinguished himself as a supporter of the bill. Lenient measures, he said, would not have the effect of conciliating the good-will or allaying the discontent of men who wished to overturn the constitution. There was no security, but in coercive acts, against the machinations of those who thought more of their supposed rights than of their political and social duties. In another debate, Mr. Hardinge spoke on the same side of the question, alleging that Jacobin clubs, affiliated societies, *imperium in imperio*, would in all probability prevail, if this bill, or one of a similar kind, should not pass. Mr. Sheridan said, that no patriotic magistrates would act under such a law, and that to attempt the enforcement of it would be an unpardonable insult to a free nation. Mr. Abbot severely censured Mr. Fox for having stimulated the people to rebellion ; but the orator replied, that he had addressed his speech to the governors, not to the governed, and had merely uttered the sentiments of every manly advocate of freedom, in declaring that resistance would become a question of prudence, not of morality, if the parliament should enact a bill against the sense of the majority of the public.

If Mr. Fox roused the indignation of the courtly phalanx by these bold expressions, Mr. Windham excited equal resentment among the opposite ranks by recommending, with views of counteraction, the exercise of a vigor beyond the law : but Mr. Sheridan trusted that no minister would ever be suffered to act the part of Robespierre in England. On another occasion, the language of the secretary at war was highly offensive ; for, with an air of inhuman indifference, he mentioned the fall of his brave countrymen in the field of war as if it had been the destruction of contemptible insects or vermin, by saying that they had been *killed off*.

The peers who most warmly attacked Mr. Pitt's bill, were the earls of Derby, Moira, and Lauderdale, the marquis of Lansdown, and the duke of Bedford : lord Thurlow and the duke of Leeds also condemned its unjustifiable rigor. But all opposition to it was fruitless ; and it received the royal assent with the equally obnoxious bill of lord Grenville.

It imported that no meeting of any description of persons, exceeding the number of fifty (except such as might be called by sheriffs or other officers or magistrates,) should be holden for political purposes, unless public notice should have been given by seven housekeepers ; that,

if such a body should assemble without notice, and twelve or more individuals should continue together (even quietly) for one hour after a legal order for their departure, they should be punished as felons without benefit of clergy ; and that the same rigor might be exercised, if any person, after due notice of the meeting, should use seditious language, or propose the irregular alteration of any thing by law established. With regard to the delivery of lectures or discourses, or the exercise of debate on topics connected with the laws and government of the country, a licence was declared to be necessary for such meetings.

It was not without surprise, that each house received, during the discussion of the two bills, a message from the king, holding out a prospect of peace. Alluding to the new constitution and the directorial government of France, he said that such an order of things had arisen, as would induce him to meet any desire of negotiation on the part of the enemy, with a full readiness to give it the speediest effect. When an address of thanks for this communication was moved, Mr. Sheridan suggested an amendment, tending to produce an immediate negotiation, and to remove, by a renunciation of the principles on which the war had been conducted, all obstacles to the attainment of peace. Mr. Fox also wished that the first offer should proceed from our court ; but Mr. Pitt and Mr. Dundas thought it adviseable to wait till the enemy should manifest a disposition to negotiate. Similar observations were made in the house of peers.

At the beginning of 1796, the debates in parliament became still more animated and important than at the close of the preceding year. It was moved by Mr. Grey, that an address should be presented to his majesty, entreating him to assure the government of France of his readiness to enter into a negotiation for the establishment of peace on reasonable terms. He was sorry to observe that the court appeared to be more intent on warlike preparation than eager to promote peace. Overtures from this country, he thought, could not be degrading; and he flattered himself with the hope that they would be successful. Mr. Pitt wished that this affair might be left to the discretion of the ministry. It was proper, he said, that the allies of Great Britain should be consulted, as a close concert with them would give greater dignity and effect to a negotiation. Steps had been already taken to ascertain the disposition of the enemy; and, if there should be a prospect of an honourable peace, the opportunity would be embraced with pleasure. Mr. Fox said, that a better season for treating than the present might not occur for a long period; and he hoped that, as the French had renounced the decree of fraternity, every idea of interference in their interior concerns would on our part be disclaimed. This would be a good preparative to negotiation; and a subsequent offer of moderate terms would expedite the accomplishment of the desirable object. Only 50 members supported the motion, while 189 voted against it.

The active spirit of Mr. Grey soon brought him forward on another subject. He accused Mr. Pitt of having encroached on the right of the commons to control and direct the application of the public money, by the demand of a vote of credit for two millions and a half, at a time when there was no reasonable ground for withholding the estimate, or declining to state the particular services for which that sum was intended. The charge was answered by a declaration that ministers were accountable for the proper expenditure of the money in question. The bill which sanctioned the vote was opposed by the earl of Lauderdale and other peers; and, in a protest which followed the assent of the majority to the measure, it was pronounced to be "a part of a system that acted in contempt and in defiance of those wholesome forms and regulations, which the wisdom of our ancestors devised for the protection of the public purse against the encroachments of corrupt ministers."

A supposed deviation from strict honor, and an instance of partiality in the negotiation for a loan, formed new grounds of censure. Mr William Smith repeatedly urged a complaint of the minister's neglect of the principles of fair and open competition in bargains of this kind; and Mr. Jekyll charged him with gross fraud, and collusion, in a pecuniary transaction with Mr. Boyd. But the majority of the house justified the management of the loan, and refused to stigmatize the alleged fraud.

An inquiry into the state of the nation was moved by Mr. Grey, who declaimed against the war with eloquence and energy, combated the pretences on which it had been undertaken, and censured the misconduct which its directors had so glaringly evinced. He particularly noticed the prodigality of the minister and the disorder of the finances. He affirmed, that above seventy-seven millions of debt, incurred by this war, had been funded; that twenty-two millions of floating debt remained; that the burden which had thus accumulated in three years exceeded the whole amount of the national debt contracted before the year 1756; that enormous sums had been lavished without the sanction of parliament; and that all the success which had attended our arms might have been obtained with an expenditure comparatively small. He calculated the peace establishment (if the war should immediately cease) at twenty-two millions, and estimated the applicable revenue at nineteen millions and a half—a deficiency which would require additional taxes to the annual amount of two millions and a half. He animadverted on the dangerous augmentation of the number of barracks, and treated of other points of serious import. Mr. Jenkinson, in answer to these remarks, contended that the expenses of the war were not unnecessarily multiplied; that the managers of the treasury were as attentive to economy as the nature and circumstances of the contest would allow; that the war had exhibited some splendid instances of success; and that the commerce of the nation was in a more flourishing state than had ever been known even in time of peace. By a majority of 162, the proposal of inquiry was rejected.

The increase of barracks became a topic of subsequent debate. General

Smith inferred, from this unconstitutional system, that the minister cherished despotic intentions. Mr. Fox said, that the freedom of the constitution greatly depended on the amicable intercourse between soldiers and citizens, and that the habitual separation of the two classes would render the former too subservient to the crown. Mr. Pitt replied, that soldiers were more conveniently and usefully, as well as more cheaply, quartered in barracks, than in public houses; and Mr. Windham hinted, that the system might be advantageous in another point of view, by preventing the troops from being infected with the seditious humors of the populace.

Amidst these and other debates, the failure of an application for peace excited animadversion. Mr. Wickham, the British minister in Switzerland, had proposed a general negotiation to M. Barthelemy, the French ambassador to the cantons; but the executive directory, understanding that one of the demands at an eventual congress would relate to the restoration of the Netherlands, evaded the proposal, and furnished Mr. Pitt with a pretence for declaring, that, as the enemy had refused to listen to any requisition for the surrender of what was considered as the inalienable territory of the republic, "nothing was left for the king but to prosecute a war equally just and necessary."

A new loan was now negotiated, for the invigoration of those hostilities, which, it was alleged, the arrogance and obstinacy of the French compelled our government to continue. Above twenty-seven millions and a half had been previously voted; and a loan of eighteen millions had formed a part of the ways and means. The supply was at length augmented to 37,588,000 pounds: and, to make up the greater part of the new demand, seven millions and a half were borrowed. The guards and garrisons were reduced to 49,000 men; the forces in the colonies were increased to 77,000 men; the sailors and marines were 110,000. Taxes were imposed on legacies to collateral relatives; wine, tobacco, salt, and sugar, were rendered additionally contributive to the public exigencies; hats

furnished a small sum; the proprietors of horses and dogs were also burdened; and all who were liable to the assessed taxes were required to pay ten per cent. extra. These burdens were not voted without remonstrance or opposition; but all objections were overruled.

A neglect of the due means of rendering the West-Indian expedition of sir Charles Grey completely successful, and a gross inattention to the health and accommodations of the soldiers employed under that officer, were imputed to the ministry by Mr. Sheridan. Mr. Dundas replied to the charge, but did not wholly refute it.

The slave trade for the supply of the islands occasioned various debates. A bill had been introduced for its abolition; but, though it was ably supported, it was unsuccessful; and the house would not even receive a bill proposed by Mr. Francis for improving the condition of the slaves.

A long speech from the marquis of Lansdown, calling the attention of the peers to the danger which menaced the constitution from the enormous increase of ministerial patronage and influence, and to the necessity of a retrenchment of expenditure, produced a feeble reply from lord Grenville, and a boast from lord Auckland of the great extent of the revenue. The endeavours of the earl of Guildford to promote peace and a change of system were also abortive.

Mr. Grey proposed a series of resolutions, adducing such charges as he thought would justify an impeachment of some of the ministers. He affirmed, that the provisions of the act of appropriation had been frequently violated; that the statute for the regulation of the office of paymaster to the army had also been infringed; that false accounts had been presented to the house; and that other mal-practices had marked the ministerial proceedings. The premier acknowledged that some irregularities had occurred; but declared that nothing criminal had been wilfully committed, and that an attention to duty, and a regard for the public service, had formed the chief features of official management.

Mr. Steele moving the previous question, 209 votes, against 38, appeared for the ministry.

An address for a change of measures, was moved by Mr. Fox, after an harangue of extraordinary length. He satirised the rashness which had plunged the nation into the war, and the incapacity which appeared in the conduct of it. He condemned the connections of the court with despotic allies, who had no wish to promote the general good, but aimed only at the gratifications of self-interest. He lamented the great injury to which the people were exposed by the war, and deprecated the increase of burdens already oppressive. He censured the answer given to the note of Barthelemy, and said that peace might be obtained by a less arrogant demeanor. Mr. Pitt reasserted the justice of the war, vindicated the spirit and judgment with which it was prosecuted, and attributed the delay of peace to the restless disposition of the enemy. The motion was rejected by a majority of 174. This was the last debate of importance during the session, which terminated on the 20th of May. The distant prospect of a negotiation with France was highly gratifying to every class of society, but more particularly to the middle and lower orders. The war had begun with the approbation and applause of a great majority of the British people; but the disasters of our army in Holland, the pressure of taxes, and the occurrence of an unusual scarcity, all contributed to excite the murmurs of the nation at the continuance of hostilities. Every domestic evil, whether occasioned by private imprudence or by the dispensation of providence, was attributed to the war; and the general discontent was cherished and exasperated by the inflammatory proceedings of the innovating societies. The more able advocates of sedition imitated the example of Thelwal, and gratified the populace by the delivery of lectures, in which they represented all wars, and this war in particular, as contrived by courts and ministers for plundering the people. The Corresponding Society resumed their proceedings at Chalk Farm, and a meeting held at Copenhagen-house, near Islington, was frequently attended by 50,000 persons. The statutes enacted, and the sentiments expressed, during the present session of parliament, had a visible and immediate effect in restoring the tranquillity of the nation, and silencing the expression of public discontent. Some means of coercion had indeed become absolutely necessary; and, while the vigorous measures suggested by Mr. Pitt and adopted by the parliament, contributed to repress the turbulence of the advocates of disaffection, the conciliatory tone adopted by his majesty and by the minister, was productive of the most salutary influence on the virtuous but mistaken zealots of sedition.

CHAP. XI.

1796. WHEN the French directory had established themselves in their station by the destruction of their political opponents, it became their next object to confirm the ascendency which they had acquired by the adoption of measures which might attach the nation to their persons and interests. During the last campaign, the efforts of the republicans had been much less successful than might have been expected from the victories obtained, and the experience acquired, during the former year. They were anxious to recover their military superiority, and the most vigorous preparations were made for the equipment and reinforcement of the armies. It was proposed to the legislature, and solemnly decreed, to annex their acquisitions in the Low Countries and on the left side of the Rhine to the dominions of the republic. In the relative circumstances of the belligerent powers, a resolution of this nature precluded all expectation of peace. The British ministers were stedfastly determined to restore the Austrian Netherlands, if possible, to their former owner; and Austria, exaggerating the advantages of the late campaign, preserved the hope of recovering her antient possessions. It was the secret intention, therefore, of the allied powers, to continue the war, unless certain terms should be obtained, to which the directory, still more partial to hostilities,

would not in all probability accede. To gratify the people, however, the belligerents found it expedient to assume the appearance of a pacific disposition, and Mr. Wickham, ambassador to the Swiss cantons, was instructed to apply to M. Barthelemy, then resident at Basle, who had concluded the treaty with Prussia, to ascertain the sentiments of the directory on the subjects of peace and war. The answer received from M. Barthelemy, intimated, in the name of the directory, that it felt the most sincere desire to terminate the war on such conditions as France could reasonably accept, and which were specified in the answer, but positively insisted on the retention of the Austrian dominions in the Low Countries; and assigned, as a reason, their formal annexation to the republic, by a constitutional decree that could not be revoked. An answer so decided, which explained to their full extent the ambitious views of the government, and rendered the decrees of the legislative body the criterion of the rights and interests of foreign states, suspended the negotiation, and both parties proceeded to open the campaign.

The Imperial and French armies were situated in the following manner. From the frontiers of Switzerland to the environs of the town of Spires, where it ceased to be their common barrier, they were separated by the Rhine. Beyond that city the cantonments which they respectively occupied at the distance of some leagues from each other, extended across the Upper Palatinate, the duchy of Deux Ponts, and the Hundsruck. The line occupied by the imperial army, passed through the towns of Spires, Neustadt, Kayserslautern, Kussel, and from thence crossing the Nabe, terminated at the Rhine, in the neighbourhood of Bauharoch, where that river became again the point of separation to both armies, and continued so beyond Cologne, between the river Sieg and the town of Dusseldorf. The Austrians and French occupied an equal share of the space between the river and the last mentioned fortress, before which the republican army had an entrenched camp. The imperialists possessed on the Rhine the strong fortresses of Philipsburg, Manheim, Mentz, and Ehrenbreitstein. The French, on their part, possessed on the Upper Rhine, the fortresses of Alsace, and on the Lower Rhine, that of Dusseldorf.

With respect to the strength of the opposed armies, it is obvious that no one could be able to appreciate them with correctness, but the commander-in-chief or the officers of the staff. From the information, however, of individuals, whose local position and military situation, enabled them to form a probable estimate, the numbers of the French and imperial armies, at the opening of the campaign, may be nearly determined. They authorise the supposition, that at this time the two French armies, commanded by Moreau and Jourdan, amounted to more than 160,000 men; and that the imperial forces, commanded by his royal highness the archduke Charles, including the Saxons and other contingents of the empire, amounted to 150,000 men.

Every motive which determined the French government to continue the war, imposed upon them the necessity of carrying it beyond the Rhine and into the heart of Germany. Their numerous soldiery were destitute of clothes, money, and subsistence. The Netherlands, Holland, and the countries situated between the Meuse and the Rhine, and sustained, during two years, the whole burden of maintaining the French armies. These countries, a short time before so rich and so abundant, were exhausted; their specie was absorbed by contributions, their manufactures were suspended, and their produce consumed. An immense quantity of paper money of no intrinsic value, had operated to paralyze their commerce and their industry. Two years had been sufficient to place the countries subdued by France on a level with herself, and to subject them to one common equality of dearth and misery. It was become, therefore, absolutely necessary that the French should march forward into other countries in search of subsistence, of horses, of clothes, and above all, of money. These views were openly expressed by the directory, in the order given to their generals, that they should *maintain their troops by victory.*

To the urgent call of necessity were added, the motives of ambition. The directory was persuaded, that by an invasion of Germany it would accomplish the disunion of the Germanic body; that the inferior princes, in their alarm, would hasten by turns to purchase a separate peace; that the emperor, reduced to dependance on his own resources, would at length subscribe to such conditions as it should please his conquerors to impose; and that, at the conclusion of the war, its final result would place all the countries on the right side of the Rhine in possession of the French, and the fate of Germany at their disposal, leaving them enriched with the spoils of the empire, and dictating laws to Europe.

Every consideration, on the other hand, seemed to prescribe to the court of Vienna a line of conduct directly the reverse. A concurrence of military and political considerations should have induced it to persevere in the defensive system, which it had adopted and pursued with advantage in the preceding year. The situation of the French and imperial armies, offered to the latter no prospect of success in an offensive war. The result, of several campaigns had borne evidence to the difficulty of penetrating into Alsace. France was nearly invulnerable by the route of the Sarre and the Moselle, which were defended by a great number of strong places. They could have entertained no prospect of retaking the Netherlands, and of advancing between the Moselle and the Meuse : the French being masters of Dusseldorf, of all the fortified towns on the Meuse, and the strong places of Holland.

If in a military point of view the interest of the emperor prescribed to him a defensive war, it was still more consonant with prudence in its political aspect. The loss of the Netherlands and Holland, and the defection of Prussia and Spain, deprived the rest of the coalition of every possibility of making conquests upon France. The combined plan of England and Austria was less directed against the armies of the republic than against her finances and military resources. To pursue this system with advantage, it became the object of the campaign to exhaust the enemy and to gain time rather than to win battles. The first and most important purpose, which, if steadily pursued, would have averted the long and unexampled series of calamities which ensued, was to confine the French to their own resources for the payment and maintenance of their numerous armies, and to prevent them, from penetrating into Germany. The most natural and most easy method of accomplishing this object would have been to take the course of the Rhine as the line of defence, and to give to the different corps of the imperial army the same disposition which marshal Clairfait had established in 1795, a disposition of which that general's success had proved the advantage. It appeared advisable after his example, to abandon to the French the Hundsruck, and the duchy of Deux Ponts, countries of little importance in themselves, already exhausted by the war, and which always belong, except in the case of great superiority of force, to the possessor of Landau, Bitche, Sar Louis, Traerbatch, and Coblentz. By abandoning these, countries and carrying the greater part of their forces to the right bank of the Rhine, the Austrians would have been enabled to strengthen their positions on that river with a sufficient number of men, to defend the passage from Basle to Manheim, and to place between the latter fortress and that of Mentz a large body of troops, which could readily advance to the succour of either of those places, and support their garrisons. By adopting this disposition, the imperialists would have been enabled to place on the Lahn and the Sieg more than a third of their army, to reinforce their right wing, the point at which they were most endangered ; to oppose a powerful resistance to any enterprise of the French on the lower Rhine, to confine them in the camp before Dusseldorf, and to profit of any favourable opportunity of attacking them with advantage.

The first movements of the Austrian generals seemed to indicate the adoption of a different plan. The army of the Upper Rhine, under the command of general Wurmser, was strongly reinforced, a circumstance which gave reason to suppose that it was intended he should cross the Rhine to penetrate into Upper Alsace. At the same time the greater part of the army of the Lower Rhine, under the immediate orders of the archduke Charles, took post in the Hundsruck and the duchy of Deux Ponts, and appeared to menace, at the same time, Lower Alsace and the fortresses on the Sallee and the Moselle. The misfortunes which rapidly followed these indications soon obliged the Austrians to renounce their first dispositions, and to adopt, in part, those which have been already mentioned.

The armistice, concluded at the end of the year 1795, between the French and Austrian generals, was broken by the latter on the 21st of May ; and an interval of ten days being required between its rupture and the renewal of hostilities, the respective armies became at liberty to recommence their movements on the 31st of the same month.

On that day the French army of the

Sambre and the Meuse, commanded by general Jourdan, made a movement forwards on the two banks of the lower Rhine. It was on the right bank, however, that the French employed the greater part of their force against the very inferior numbers of the enemy under the prince of Wurtemburg, who had taken a position in front of the Sieg. On the 1st of June he was driven from his position by general Kleber, after an engagement of several hours; and, abandoning the Sieg, occupied the strong position of Uckerath. The French being unable to attack it in front without the certainty of considerable loss, availed themselves in the morning of their superiority of number, to outflank and turn it. The Prince of Wurtemburg was therefore compelled to retire to Altenkirchen, from which he was again dislodged by superiority of numbers. The capture of the Austrian magazines enabled the French to subsist in a country exhausted by the consumption of the armies, and compelled the former to retire behind the Lahn, leaving uncovered the fortress of Ehrenbreitstein, which the French invested.

The apprehension that after forcing the passage of the Rhine the republicans would direct their march to the Lahn, and entirely outflank his right, induced the archduke to abandon his auxiliary operations in the Palatinate and the Hundsruck, and hasten to Mentz with the view of reinforcing the prince of Wurtemburg. He passed the Rhine on the 9th, and, not doubting that general Jourdan would hasten to cross the same river and join general Kleber, determined to engage the French on the Lahn, amounting to 50,000 men, before their junction.

1796. On the 15th of June, the archduke made the right wing of his army pass the Lahn and the Dille at Wetzlar. General Werwick, who commanded it, attacked the French, but was repulsed, and could not succeed in dislodging them from the advantageous position which they occupied. A brisk cannonade continued on both sides for the rest of the day; but towards seven o'clock in the evening a reinforcement of Saxon cavalry having arrived, the archduke immediately attacked the enemy. The Austrian cuirassiers of Karacksay and Nassau, in defiance of the obstacles arising from the nature of the ground, and a tremendous fire of grape-shot, made their way up the heights which were defended by the French infantry; and, charging them several times with the greatest intrepidity, at length entirely dispersed them, and took from them several pieces of cannon. At the same moment a body of Austrian grenadiers attacked the enemy's centre, and dislodged them from the woods which they occupied.

The French, driven from their position, took up another in their retreat, equally good with the former. They were very soon attacked again. Four squadrons of Austrians and Saxons gained the steep heights on which some of the enemy's battalions were posted, charged them with impetuosity, and completed the victory. It cost the imperialists about 500 men, the loss of the French was more considerable. Four of their battalions were cut to pieces by the Saxon and Austrian cavalry, which took fourteen pieces of cannon and made many prisoners.

The French troops which defended the Lower Lahn not having met with better success, were obliged to quit the banks of that river and fall back on the Sieg. The archduke pursued them without allowing them any respite, and obtained possession of a large quantity of provisions, cannon, artillery, waggons, and baggage, which the difficulty of the country, the animosity of its inhabitants against the French, and the disorder of their retreat, rendered it impossible to save.

The archduke, observing their confusion, pursued his advantage with vigor and celerity. He manœuvred in such a manner, as to oblige general Jourdan, who had passed the Rhine at Niewied on the 12th of June, to repass it on the 18th, with the right wing of the French army. At the same time he sent forward his advanced guard, amounting to 11,000 men, under the orders of general Kray, in pursuit of Kleber, who slowly retired towards the Sieg with 28,000 men. General Kray, on the 20th of June, came up with Kleber, who, finding himself superior in numbers, attacked the Austrians with all his forces, and carried the most important points of their position. They were deprived of the victory anticipated from this first success, by the bravery of three Austrian battalions, who, unshaken by the numerous artillery of the French, suffered nine battalions to advance within a hundred yards and, charging them with fixed bayonets, put them completely to the rout. This advantage gave time to the Saxon and Austrian cavalry to rally, to return victoriously to the charge, and finally to stop the progress of the enemy. The loss of the imperialists, whose numbers were only half of those of the French, amounted to nearly 600 men, that of the enemy to 2200, even according to the authority of Frenchmen engaged in the conflict. General Kleber defeated, in the same position, from which a fortnight before he had dislodged the Austrians, was obliged to continue his precipitate retreat, as far as the lines of Dusseldorf. To this place he was driven by the pursuit of the archduke Charles, who had thus marched from the banks of the Upper Nahe, to those of the Upper Lahn, gained two battles, and driven the French from the walls of Wetzlar, to their present position. The bravery of the young prince, the rapidity of his movements and the ability of his manœuvres, gave promise of a brilliant career of military glory.

During the occurrence of these events on the Lower Rhine, the imperial army, commanded by field-marshal Wurmser, and the French under the orders of general Moreau, had also opened the campaign on the Upper Rhine. When the archduke quitted the Hundsruck to march to the right bank of the Rhine, marshal Wurmser at the same time withdrew his troops from the lines of Spire back, and made them take an excellent position before the fort of the Rhine, opposite to Manheim. His right extended to the town of Frankenthel, and was covered, as well as his front, by an inundation, and canals adjoining to the

little river of Rehach, which bounded and defended his left.

General Moreau made two attacks on this position on the 14th and 20th of June, which produced no effect but the loss of many hundred men on both sides, and the circumscription of the imperialists within their entrenched camp on the fort of the Rhine. These attacks were undertaken by Moreau with no other intention than to deceive general Wurmser with respect to his real designs. After leaving a small corps of observation before the Austrian camp, he turned suddenly back, and marched with the greatest part of the army towards Strasburg, where preparations were making for a more important enterprise.

The loss of the Milanese, which I shall soon have occasion to record, determined the court of Vienna to send marshal Wurmser into Italy, with 30,000 men, selected from the army, which he commanded in Germany. Their departure diminished the army imperial on the Upper Rhine by nearly one-half, and, by increasing proportionately the superiority of the French, opened to them the gates of Germany. They were informed of these movements by the traitors in the Austrian cabinet, even before they had occurred, and determined to take advantage of the intelligence. A few days before the resumption of hostilities, an Austrian having been sent to hold a parley with Moreau, that general did not affect to conceal his acquaintance with the projected removal of 30,000 men from Germany to Italy. The officer carried this intelligence to the Austrian headquarters, where the order for the departure of these troops did not arrive till two days after: a singular proof of the success of the bribes and intrigues of the republicans in the courts and camps of their enemies.

By the departure of so large a force, an opening was left in the line of defence on the Upper Rhine; an opening which the expedition of the archduke to the Lower Rhine would not permit him to defend. The French prepared to carry their designs into execution with no less promptitude than secresy, and disguised them under the pretext of some other expedition.

Before the break of day, on the 24th of June, general Moreau embarked in boats 3000 men, who landed in several small islands that lie between Strasburg and the fort of Kehl. They dislodged from thence the imperial picquets, who had not time or address to destroy the bridges which communicate with the right bank of the Rhine; and the progress of the French remaining unimpeded, they crossed the river and suddenly attacked the redoubts of Kehl, which were occupied by a small body of troops from the circle of Suabia. Equally destitute of experience and of discipline, these troops were incapable of the slightest resistance; and, though they were attacked only by infantry, without any cannon, they suffered this important post to be taken by the enemy, who found within it 500 men, and 15 pieces of cannon. They immediately placed it in a state of effectual defence, and laboured incessantly during the course of the day, to establish a bridge of boats between Kehl and Strasburg.

General Latour, who commanded the imperial army on the Upper Rhine [in the place of general Wurmser, had no suspicion that the French would attempt the passage of the river opposite to Kehl, but a small number of light troops were stationed near the fort. The nearest corps was composed of some thousands of Suabians, who were encamped at Marle and Wildstedt, about three leagues from Kehl. The slightest exertion would have enabled them to defend the fort, or to retake it before the French could have been able to transport cannon and cavalry across the river. But they remained in a state of inexcusable inaction; and their military behaviour during the remainder of the campaign, exposed their generals to the suspicion of holding correspondence with the enemy. The French took advantage of their misconduct to complete their bridge of boats, and to pass over with their cavalry and artillery. They spread themselves over the plain, to prevent the approach of any force

that might be sent against them from Offenburg or Rastadt. On the 25th they attacked the camp at Wildstedt, and drove from thence the Suabian troops. The only resistance they experienced was from the Austrian regiments of Auspach cuirassiers, who, arriving at that instant, furiously charged a corps of French infantry, broke through them, and cut to pieces a considerable number.

No sooner was M. Latour informed of the French having passed the Rhine, and invaded the territory of Baden, than he gave orders to the advanced regiments to march, and moved forward with the greater part of his forces, to meet the enemy and interrupt his progress. The corps of the prince of Condé moved rapidly towards Offenburg, hoping to arrive there before it should be surrendered to the republicans. The prince effected this object, and joined on the 27th at Biel before Offenburg, some Austrian detachments, and troops of the circles which had been driven from the camp at Wildstedt. On the 28th, however, this corps of imperialists was obliged to abandon its position, as well as the town of Offenburg, the French having brought against them several strong columns. They made this movement to prevent the junction of the prince of Condé with several Austrian corps which were marching to his assistance, and thus to divide the imperial army of the Upper Rhine. This latter object was of the utmost importance, and on its accomplishment, the success of the invasion in a great measure depended. Towards this point, therefore, general Moreau directed all his movements, and devoted all his resources. He divided his army, amounting to 80,000 men, into three columns. That on the right was under the orders of general Ferino, an officer who had formerly served in the Austrian service, but had visited France during the revolution in search of employment. He was made a lieutenant, and afterwards a general, and was appointed to his present command from his personal acquaintance with the scene of action. He was directed to drive back into the Brisgau, the corps of the prince of Condé and of general

Frolich. He met with some success, and obtained possession of the town of Bibrach in the valley of Kintzig.

General St. Cyr, with the centre, forced the passes which lead along the vallies of Renchen and Kintzig, to the mountains of Suabia. Continuing to advance, he made himself master, on the 4th of July, of the mountain of Kniebis, and of the town of Freydenstadt, posts of the utmost importance, which the Suabians resigned to the French almost without resistance.

The left and strongest column was under the orders of general Desaix ; it was opposed to general Latour, and was intended to act against the Austrian force which was marching in great haste from the Lower Rhine. General Desaix pressed forward to attack Latour before its arrival. On the 29th of June, he gained over him a decisive victory at Renchen, where the Austrians lost ten pieces of cannon and 500 prisoners. On the 4th of July he pushed still further forward to the river Murg and the city of Rastadt.

General Latour, who had taken an excellent position in front of the Murg, was attacked on the 5th along his whole line by general Moreau, who had just arrived with a reinforcement to general Desaix. The action lasted the whole day, and was very bloody on both sides. It terminated to the disadvantage of the imperialists, who retreated to Etlingen.

The archduke Charles having driven the army of the Sambre and Meuse across the Rhine and the Sieg, immediately returned. He arrived on the banks of the Murg at the very moment when general Latour was yielding to the efforts and the numbers of the French. His royal highness assumed the command of the army which formed a junction with his own at Etlingen.

The possession of the town and pass of Freydenstadt by the enemy, opened to them an entrance into the duchy of Wurtemburg, cut off the communication between the armies of the Prince of Condé, general Frolich, and the archduke, and threatened the left of his royal highness's position. This latter circumstance obliged him to send a considerable corps into the mountains to secure his left flank, and to endeavour to re-establish his communication with the corps above-mentioned. Notwithstanding the disadvantages of his position, and the inferiority of his numbers, the archduke determined to risque a battle. It presented the only means of expelling the French from Suabia, and of maintaining himself on the banks of the Rhine. The commanders of the army of the Sambre and Meuse when they received information of his movements, resumed their offensive operations, and on the 28th and 29th of June, marched from Dusseldorf and Cologne towards the river Sieg, from whence they compelled to retire the few light troops which defended it. On the 2nd of July the commander-in-chief, general Jourdan, also passed the Rhine opposite to Nieuwield, where the Austrian general Funck suffered himself to be surprised, and did nothing to oppose the progress of the French. The divisions of Jourdan, Grenier, Kleber, and Lefebvre, then effected a junction, and advanced with more than 65,000 men against general De Wartensleben, who had scarcely 50,000 to oppose them. Notwithstanding this inferiority, he gained over them a considerable advantage on the 3rd of July, near Montebauer, where general Werneck took several hundred men and three pieces of cannon. But, having sustained a repulse on his right, and finding that he was in danger of being surrounded by the various corps of the enemy, general Wartensleben retired behind the Lahn, which the whole French army passed on the 9th of July, in three columns. The advanced guard of the same column was attacked on the same day by the Austrians and defeated ; but the main body coming up to its support, a warm action ensued, of which the success was various, but in which the Austrians had finally the advantage. On the 10th, however, the latter were attacked on all the points which they occupied between the Mein and the Lahn, and, after an obstinate engagement, which they maintained near Friedberg, in which they suffered some loss, general Wartensleben was again obliged to retreat in order to secure the position of Bergen before Frankfort, which was soon evacuated. He then continued his retreat up the Mein, directing his course towards Aschaffenburg and Wurtzburg, in order that he might approach the army of the archduke, and establish with his royal highness a regular communication.

While general Wartensleben experienced the most mortifying disasters on the Lower Rhine, the archduke Charles had been still less fortunate on the Upper. After the retreat to Etlingen, the prince was informed that general Jourdan had again crossed the Rhine, and compelled general Wartensleben to abandon the defence of the approaches to the Lahn. It was easy to perceive that the latter, with a force so inferior, would be obliged to abandon Frankfort, and would find himself equally menaced by the armies of Jourdan and of Moreau. Determined, therefore, to incur the hazard of a battle, and circumstances not admitting of delay, he was only restrained from immediately executing his design by awaiting the arrival of troops from the Lower Rhine. He employed the 7th and 8th in making the necessary preparations, and in fortifying his position. His right extended to the Rhine as far as the village of Durmersheim; his centre was in front of Etlingen, and his left rested on the town and mountain of Frauenalli.

General Moreau having obtained intimation that the archduke had not received all the reinforcements he expected, resolved to prevent the impending attack. He reinforced himself on the 8th with the whole of the centre column, commanded by general St. Cyr. In the morning of the 9th, while the archduke was completing his dispositions and arranging the different corps which were to be engaged on the following day, he found himself attacked in every point of his position by the whole French army. They directed their principal efforts against the left of the imperialists, and endeavoured to turn it by passing round the mountains. Though all the troops intended to form the left of the Austrian line were not yet arrived,

general Keim, by whom it was conducted, made a firm resistance. He repulsed four successive attacks; but the French, having made a fifth with fresh troops, and the Saxons who were ordered to support general Keim not having yet come up, he was obliged to abandon his position which the French had outflanked, and to fall back to Pfortzheim, where he was joined by the Saxons.

The archduke had been more fortunate on his right and in front, where he had completely repulsed all the attacks of the French. But the retrograde movement of general Keim having entirely uncovered the left of the army, and enabled the enemy to take possession of the mountains which commanded it, the prince was himself subjected to the necessity of quitting the field of battle, and of retreating towards Pfortzheim, where he arrived on the following day.

The imperialists lost in this action 2000 men, of whom 1000 were made prisoners. The loss of the French was equally great, but the victory enabled them to detach the Austrians from the banks of the Rhine, and from the fortified towns of Philipsburg and Manheim. Both of these places had been supplied with sufficient garrisons before they were invested by the French.

The archduke was of opinion that the enemy would be obliged to leave behind them a portion of the army to blockade the captured fortresses, and thus the garrisons of Philipsburg and Manheim might almost entirely interrupt the communication between the armies of Moreau and Jourdan. In conformity with his views, the garrisons of Manheim and Philipsburg made many useful excursions, interrupted and prevented the formation of the enemy's magazines, and captured some French couriers and detachments in the very heart of Franconia.

The armies of the Sambre and Meuse, and of the Rhine and Moselle, being now enabled to co-operate with each other, Moreau seized upon Stutgard, and obliged the duke of Wurtemburg, the margrave of Baden, and all the princes of Suabia, to sue for peace. After this, he resumed his march, and experienced, on the 18th of July, the first attack of the enemy at Dunselchingeu, where two French demi-brigades were defeated, and nearly cut in pieces, but a combat of two days duration at Neresheim, terminated once more in favor of the assailants.

The invading armies now advanced to the centre of Germany, along both sides of the Danube ; one traversing Franconia, a province abundantly provided with all the necessaries of life, the other taking the rout of Upper Suabia, a country entirely destitute of resources. While general Ferino penetrated beyond the lake of Constance, Moreau compelled the elector of Bavaria to sue for peace, and Jourdan, seizing on Nuremburg, Ingoldstadt, and Amberg, and making incursions as far as Ratisbon, menaced the house of Austria with inevitable ruin.

At this critical period, notwithstanding its armies had been repeatedly discomfited in Italy, and all its possessions in that quarter, with the exception of Mantua, were in possession of the enemy, the cabinet of Vienna displayed the most heroic firmness, relying implicitly on the gallantry of the troops, and the fortitude of their commander, who had hitherto retired step by step, baffling the superior numbers and rapid movements of the enemy.

The archduke having received considerable supplies of men and artillery, determined at length to arrest the progress of the victorious armies ; for, by overcoming one, he knew that he should arrest the career of both, and liberate Germany from the invaders, who had rendered themselves detestable to the inhabitants. He concluded that by leaving a part of his forces to keep general Moreau in check, he might gain some marches over him, and fall unexpectedly with the rest of his army on general Jourdan. The archduke was perfectly aware of the danger to which this plan exposed him. He was conscious that he left Moreau with little opposition or impediment ; but he flattered himself that the general would hear of his march too late to afford the least assist-

ance to his colleague, and that even when he heard of it, he would be tempted to postpone his retreat, and to attack the insignificant force opposed to him, by the hope of creating a diversion in favor of Jourdan. The event bore testimony to the justice of the archduke's conjectures, and fully corresponded with his expectations.

On the 14th of August, prince Charles made at Donawert every preparation for the execution of the plan which he had formed. He left one half of his army with general Latour, with orders to defend Bavaria and the river Lech. On the 15th, having recalled all the corps on the other side of the Danube, he ordered the bridge of Donawert to be burnt, and left that town with 20,000 of his best troops. The next day he continued to march rapidly along the right bank of the Danube, and crossed that river on the 17th at Neuburg and Ingoldstadt. He halted on the 17th and 18th before these two towns. His first resolution was to attack a column of Jourdan's army which had taken possession of Nuremburg, and threatened Ratisbon ; but he was informed on the night of the 18th, that general Wartensleben had been driven from the town of Amberg, and had retreated to Schwartenfeldt, behind the river Naab.

In consequence of this change in the position of the armies of Jourdan and Wartensleben, the intended movement of the archduke became extremely dangerous, as it rendered his communication with that general very precarious, and, should he be obliged to retire, would render that intention extremely difficult.

The prince, on this occasion, altered his line of march, advanced in a direction more to the right, and arrived on the 20th at Hemmau. His vanguard, led by major-general Nauendort, proceeded on the same day to take possession of the heights of Taswang, while a column under the orders of lieutenant-general Hotze, marched towards Bellugriess, at the same time, to secure the left of the archduke and the road from Ratisbon to Nuremburg.

A column of the French had marched

from Nuremburg and Neumarkt, as far as the village of Teining, under the com-command of Bernadotte. They were attacked on the 22nd by general Nauendorf, and dislodged and driven back to Neumarkt. It was again attacked at that place by the united columns of the arch-duke and general Hotze, and pursued to the neighbourhood of Altdorf, to which place it retired.

These preliminary successes having placed the archduke on the right flank and even in the rear of general Jourdan's army, who was still upon the Naab, he hastened to profit by the advantages of his situation. The whole army set forward on the 24th, divided into seven columns, of which three marched against the French army while the others were designed to turn it on the right and left.

As soon as Jourdan was informed of Bernadotte's defeat, and of the movements directed against himself, he abandoned, with precipitation, all the posts which he occupied, and retired to Amberg on the night of the 23rd of August. The Austrians, without giving him leisure for recollection, attacked him on the 24th, and compelled him to fall back to Sultzbach, leaving 900 men in the hands of the Austrians, who cut in pieces two battalions of his rear-guard. During eight days of continued retreat, at the end of which he halted near Lauringen and Schwienfurt, Jourdan was pursued and incessantly harassed by the imperial light troops, who frequently intercepted his couriers, and obtained possession of a part of his baggage. The celerity of his retreat prevented the archduke from coming up with the main body of his army and forcing him to engage. The prince, however, directed the march of the different columns with so much ability, that one of them reached Nuremburg before the French, and prevented them from passing through that town and along the great road to Franconia. This skilful manœuvre compelled Jourdan's army to retire by a worse and a longer rout, obliged that general to repass the Mein with his whole army, and deprived him of the prospect of a junction

with Moreau, or of receiving from him the most trivial assistance. The retreat at its commencement was conducted with the utmost regularity, and without the slightest loss ; but no sooner had the fugitives reached the neighbourhood of Wurtsburg, than they were once more overtaken and defeated, and, being seized with terror, immediately disbanded. Deserted by the greater part of his army, Jourdan fled with his few remaining followers towards Dusseldorf, while the gallant general Marceau made a useless sacrifice of his life in attempting to effect a diversion in favor of his commander. It has been sometimes advanced as an apology for war, that it developes those talents, and displays those virtues, which would not have been called forth in the tranquil scenes of common life, and it is pleasing to have our attention diverted from its horrors and calamities by examples of this kind. The archduke sent his own surgeon to the aid of the unfortunate general, and, on his death, ordered his own troops to join with those of the enemy in performing the military honors.

The disorderly conduct of the army of the Sambre and Meuse, placed that of the Rhine and Moselle in the most critical position, for all the conquests of Moreau were now become useless in consequence of the retreat of Jourdan. The former, after conducting his victorious troops from the banks of the Rhine to those of the Danube and the Iser, and proving successful in five pitched battles, and a multitude of skirmishes, was now obliged to commence his retreat, which may be compared, without injury to the reputation of the French general, with that of the Ten Thousand ; more especially as Xenophon conducted the Greeks through the territories of a cowardly and effeminate people, and exposed only to occasional and desultory attacks, while Moreau traversed a country inhabited by one of the most warlike nations of the universe, and sustained the regular and formidable attacks of a disciplined, numerous, and persevering enemy.

On the 18th of September Moreau drew

together the different corps of his army, and, repulsing the Austrians, extended his line to Landsberg, Fridberg, and Rain.

General Petrarch having marched into the margraviate of Baden, had successively driven from Bruschsal, Durlaseh, Carluhe, and Rastadt, several small bodies of the enemy, who occupied the valley of the Rhine. These detachments, after their defeat, having thrown themselves into the fort of Kehl, general Petrarch was ordered to follow them, and to attempt a *coup de main* on that important post, the capture of which would have cut off Moreau's principal communication with France, and have multiplied the difficulties of his retreat. On the 17th of September he caused an attack to be made on the fort of Kehl by two battalions, who carried it by storm, killed 1200 men, took 800 prisoners, and forced the remainder to retreat beyond the Rhine. But one of the two staff officers who conducted the attack having been killed in the action and the other taken prisoner; the inferior officers, deprived of their leaders, supplied their place with but little intelligence and activity. With a degree of negligence scarcely credible, they omitted the obvious precaution of immediately breaking down the bridge of Kehl, and permitted the soldiers to ramble in disorder about the town and fort. Meanwhile a reinforcement of 3000 men, who at the beginning of the action had marched from Strasburg, passed over the bridge, and attacked and easily routed the Austrians, who, supposing the engagement at an end, were entirely off their guard. They were driven from the fort of Kehl and from all the entrenchments, with the loss of 400 men. Thus were they deprived by a few moments of improvidence and disorder, of an invaluable post which afterwards cost them so enormous an expense of blood and treasure. Few examples can be adduced which have more strikingly proved the absolute necessity in war of unremitting vigilance, or more clearly shown the fatal consequences which may result from a single mistake or from a moment of

forgetfulness. The inadvertence of the officer on whom the command at Kehl devolved by the loss of his superiors, cost the emperor, in the sequel, many thousands of his best soldiers, and occasioned the most enormous demands upon his treasury.

Pressed on his rear by general Petrarch, who was repulsed in an attempt to recover fort Kehl, and turned on both flanks by generals Nauendorf and Frolich, Moreau was obliged to recommence his retreat. On the 20th he repassed the Lech at Augsburg and Rain, marched up the Danube in close columns, and arrived on the 22nd at Weissenhausen. His plan was to retire across the duchy of Wurtemberg and the county of Baden, through Ulm, Stutgard, Canstadt, and Kehl. For this purpose he had sent forward the commissaries of provisions, the army bakers, and a part of the baggage. The whole of the escort was captured on the 23nd, on the road from Ulm to Stutgard, by an Austrian detachment from the latter town.

Having passed the Danube, with the apparent intention of assisting his defeated colleague, the archduke ordered a proclamation to be read at the head of every battalion, in which it was stated, that the commander-in chief expected every thing from his soldiers, and was conscious that the momentary success of the enemy in another quarter, and the measures he was obliged to pursue in consequence of that event, would not diminish any of the energy and valor so frequently displayed by his own army. He added, that the moment would soon arrive when they should have an opportunity of obtaining new laurels, and in the mean time he hoped that the signal for combat would be also the signal for victory.

After having crossed the Lech, Moreau ascended along the banks of the Danube, and stationed his head quarters at Ulm. During the whole of his movements, he was harassed and distressed by the violence of the peasantry, who denied his troops the most urgent necessaries, and treated their leaders with every variety of insult. The excessive contributions raised by the French, and their depredations and outrages on the inhabitants of Suabia, had irritated the latter to the highest degree. They supported with impatience the presence and the yoke of these greedy and tyrannical conquerors. The peasants every where flew to arms, massacred or took prisoners the smaller detachments of the French, seized their sick and wounded, pillaged their magazines, and retook a part of those spoils of which they themselves had been plundered. The Austrian generals taking advantage of the disposition of the natives, pointed out to them the most eligible places for assembling, placed at their head officers of experience, and posted their new auxiliaries in the woods, in the defiles, and on the mountains, through which they had to pass.

Menaced at the same time in every point by the imperialists and the armed peasants, and opposed by the difficulties of the surrounding country, Moreau was placed in the most critical situation. To escape from Suabia called for more determined courage and for greater efforts than had been required to enable him to penetrate into it. It was incumbent on him to fight that he might retire; his safety could result only from a victory.

Surrounded by a multitude of small corps scattered over a great number of points, he was sensible that instead of facing them all at the same time, his situation demanded the adoption of a contrary disposition, and that he ought to march in a mass and in very close order. By thus concentrating his army, he would be enabled to attack with superior force, and to break through some one point of the circle which was forming around him. In order to relieve his army from the burden of the sick, the wounded, and the train of equipage, so properly denominated by the Romans, *Impedimenta*, he sent into Switzerland by the way of Schaffhausen, a great part of his heavy baggage, accompanied by a considerable number of soldiers. On their entrance into the territory of Switzerland, they were disarmed by the troops which the cantons had assembled on their frontiers, and sent into France. Moreau

by this means disengaged himself from every incumbrance that might impede his retreat, and retained only those troops which were best calculated for action.

After the engagement of the 30th, M. de Latour advanced as far as Grouth and Steinhausen, presenting his front to Moreau, who was posted between Schnssenreid and a small lake called the Feder See. The situation of the latter general became every day more and more precarious, and his retreat more difficult. The corps of general Petrarch posted between the sources of the Necker and of the Danube, incessantly harassed his rear. He retained no longer any communication with France; and, reduced to absolute dependence on his own forces, he could only rely for safety on the courage, of his troops, on the skill of his manœuvres, and the inadvertence of his enemies.

The corps of M. Latour being the most numerous, the nearest, and consequently the most to be feared, Moreau resolved to make a new effort against it. He judged that general Nauendorf, having separated himself from De Latour, the right of the latter would be unprotected, and might be attacked with advantage. He made his dispositions with great ability, and they were executed with secresy, promptitude, and success.

In the night of the 1st of October, he made the left wing of his army cross the Danube at Reidlingen. It recrossed that river at Munderkringen, and at day-break fell upon the right of the Austrian army, posted between the Danube and the Feder See. Major-general Kospoth, who commanded this right wing, having been deficient in vigilance, was surprised and completely beaten. Nearly two battalions were cut off, and the rest sought for safety in flight. As soon as Moreau was informed of the success of his left wing, he attacked the whole front of M. de Latour's line, of which the right was under general Kospoth, the centre under prince Furstenburg, and the left under prince Coudé and general Mercantin. Informed of their success against the right of the imperialists, he made a faint and distant attack on the centre, which occupied an excellent position on the heights of Grouth. The left was attacked at the same time, but so feebly, that it could easily have advanced and flanked the enemy's corps, which was making the attack of Grouth. De Latour, informed of the defeat of general Kospoth, urged by prince Furstenburg, and distrusting the firmness of his infantry, among which there were a great number of recruits and of new battalions, ordered at the same time the retreat of the centre and the left, enjoining that any one of the two columns which should arrive first, at a place where there was only one road for both, should continue its march, and that the other should halt and cover its retreat. An admirable expedient which accelerated the speed of every rival corps, and subjected the most sluggish and tardy of the two to the necessity of a disadvantageous conflict with the enemy.

The different regiments of Austrian infantry which composed the centre, were probably informed of this disposition, for they retired with a precipitation which approached nearly to flight. The corps of Condé therefore, which followed behind more slowly, found itself charged with covering the retreat, general Mercantin having, in obedience to the orders which he received, fallen back towards Mulhausen. In the mean time, the fugitives of the right wing and the baggage, sought for safety by retreating from Biberach to Uhmedorf, where the infantry had to pass a deep and marshy ford, which retarded its progress. On the other side of the ford, the road of Ochsenausen passes over a very high and long mountain, which was covered with more than 600 waggons, laden with baggage and ammunition, and with all the artillery. Such was the position of the Austrian army when the enemy came up with the prince Condé, who formed the rear-guard.

In this situation, at once dangerous and honourable, the prince of Condé displayed the talents of an able general, and his army the most determined intrepidity.

Having sustained all the weight of the French army, he attacked it with success, and was indebted to the prowess of the duke D'Enghien for the favourable result of three successive charges of cavalry. Had not the skill and firmness of Condé's army accorded with the importance of the emergency, the centre of the Austrian army, its equipage and artillery would have fallen into the hands of the enemy, and the successes of the archduke would have placed him between the army of Moreau and that of Jourdan, reinforced by the succours which it had received on its return to the Rhine.

After these and subsequent dispositions, the centre of the French, to which the artillery and all the baggage had been entrusted, was covered on the right by the corps which was marching to the forest towns, and on its left by the two divisions which had passed the Danube. Thus did the army retreat in three parts in parallel lines, the right and the left opening the march, and protecting the centre. It was in this regular and well-arranged order of retreat that Moreau directed his course towards the mountains of Suabia, and prepared to force their defiles.

On the 1st of October, general Desaix having formed a junction with the two divisions which had passed the Danube, made an attack on general Petrarch, defeated him, and drove him from Schweyningen and from the towns of Rothwiel and Vellingen, two very important posts, without which the French would have been unable to penetrate the defiles of the Black Forest.

Whatever advantage might be derived from possessing the post of Rothwiel, it by no means decided the certainty or safety of their retreat : they had only surmounted a part of the difficulties by which it was attended, and the most formidable impediment still remained. It was absolutely necessary that the French should force their way through the valley of Kintzig to Kehl, or through the *valley of Hell* to Freyburg.

The last of these routs was adopted, and the centre of the French army, which its two wings had hitherto preceded, and which had marched in a parallel line behind them, advanced in its turn to force the passage of the valley of Hell. Having forced a close column, it attacked, on the 10th, colonel D'Apre, who defended the entrance of the valley. The 'inferiority of his forces did not admit of a successful defence. He was driven from post to post and severely wounded. The French at length succeeded in passing this terrible defile, situated between the towns of Neustadt and Freyburg. It is six miles long, and in many places not more than ten paces wide. A proverb of the country says, that in this place we meet with *Paradise* and *Hell.* There is an inn on the right bank called the *Kingdom of Heaven.* Having passed the defile, Moreau arrived on the 13th at Freyburg, from whence he drove the Austrians, and afterwards advanced beyond this city, the possession of which secured and completed his retreat.

Moreau having thus escaped all the dangers attending his enterprise, having conducted his army without any considerable loss over the mountains of Suabia, having obtained by the possession of the whole valley of the Rhine, and of the two bridges of Huningen and Brisach, a safe and perfect communication with France, might have been expected to rest content with the laurels he had gained, and to have retired with the army so miraculously preserved, across the Rhine. Accustomed, however, from the beginning of the campaign, to successes, for which he was indebted to the errors of the Austrian generals, he determined, if possible, to crown his retreat with a victory. He was anxious to defeat the archduke, and to relieve the fort of Kehl from its blockade. With these intentions he entered, on the 18th of October, the valley of Kintzig, and marched to meet prince Charles, who had arrived, on the 16th, at Molburg, where he took the command of M. de Latour's army, which had been joined by the corps of Nauendorf and Petrarch.

Before we enter into the detail of the

battles which took place between the 17th and 27th of October, and which decided the issue of this campaign, it is material to state the positions respectively occupied by the two armies at the first of those periods. The line formed by the Austrian army had its right against the Rhine, extended itself along the river Eltz, crossed the mountains of Simonswald, and terminated on the left at the entrance of the valleys of St. Peters and St. Megers, where prince Condé and general Frolich were posted. The right of the French army occupied the mouth of the valleys just mentioned, from whence their line passed by Simonswald, Waldkirch, Emendingen, in front of the Eltz and Kintzingen, near the Rhine, to which river their left extended.

It was in these positions that the imperial and republican armies disputed the possession of the Brisgau. On the 18th, the duke D'Enghein, who commanded prince Condé's advanced guard, defeated the right of the French, from whom he captured the formidable posts of Hohlgraben, St. Megers, and St. Peters. On the same day general Frolich made himself master of some important points in the valley of Hell.

These actions were only the preludes to a general engagement, for which the archduke had made the following dispositions. The right of his army, commanded by Latour, was to attack the small village of Kintzingen ; general Wartensleben, with the centre, was ordered to carry the heights behind the village of Malmertingen ; general Petrarch, at the head of the left wing, was directed to advance on the road from Kiembach to Emindingen, while general Meerfield, with one brigade, was to penetrate the woods on the left, and prince Frederic of Orange, with another brigade, to gain the commanding parts of the mountains in order to turn the right of the French, who were to be attacked at the same time at Waldkirch, by general Nauendorf, and in the valleys of St. Peters and of Hell, by general Frolich and prince Condé.

On the 19th, in the morning, all these

corps put themselves in motion towards the points of their destination, but the badness of the roads, and the nature of the ground, retarded their progress. At length, however, their exertions were successful ; after repeated struggles, Moreau was obliged to take a new position behind the Eltz ; and the archduke, continuing to move forward, the advanced guards of the two armies were, on the night of the 20th, within half cannon-shot of each other. The French general retreated during the night, after having sent a considerable detachment across the Rhine at New Brisach, and destroyed the bridge.

Such was the result of Moreau's efforts to maintain himself in the Brisgau. The archduke entered Freyburg on the 21st, and Moreau having halted at Schlieuberg, twelve miles from Huningen, in a very strong position, the two armies prepared for battle. The right wing of Moreau was placed on the neighbouring heights of the villages of Kandern and Sutzenkurchen. Beginning at these two points, his line extended along that chain of hills which terminates the valley of the Rhine, fifteen miles from Basle, and passed by Ober and Neider Eckenheim, Liel, Schliengen, and Steinstadt. His left was posted above the latter village, beneath which ran the Rhine. The centre occupied the high grounds of the villages of Liel and Schliengen. The whole front of the line was protected by a small river, which takes its course in the mountains near Kandern, and runs by Ober and Neider Eckenheim, Liel, and Schliengen, to Steinstadt, where it falls into the Rhine. A large body of infantry in front of their centre, was stationed on a lofty point between the villages of Schliengen and Feldberg. To this detail of the position taken by Moreau, it must be added, that the high grounds on the left bank of this river completely command those on the right. This circumstance gave the French a great advantage in defending the approach of their line.

The attack of a series of positions so formidable and so admirably connected, required all the skill of the archduke and all the enthusiasm with which he had inspired his soldiers. The prince did not think it expedient to endeavour to turn round the heights occupied by the right wing of the French. The season and the bad condition of the roads rendered this measure extremely tedious and doubtful in its event. An attack by open force in defiance of danger, was more suitable to circumstances, and to the enterprising character of the archduke. He resolved, whatever it might cost, to dislodge the enemy from the heights of Kandern, Fuerbach, Sutzenkurchen, Ober, and Neider Eckenheim. The imperial army began its movement on the 23rd, in four columns : the two commanded by Condé and the prince of Furstenburg, received instructions to manœuvre in such a manner as to prevent the republicans from detaching any troops from their left. The third and fourth columns under Latour and Nauendorf, were instructed to attack the left wing, and, by marching in the direction of the Rhine, to endeavour to turn their flank. After an obstinate conflict, which continued till night, the republicans were compelled to retire, and the archduke prepared to attack them on the next day on the heights of Tannenkirchen, whither the right wing of the enemy had retired, and had occupied a position no less formidable than that from which he had been just driven. Moreau perceiving that if he was compelled to abandon this last post the Austrians might place themselves between him and the bridge of Huningen or drive him back upon the Rhine, determined to recommence his retreat, and to continue it till he reached the other bank of the river. He began his march during the night, and encamped on the 25th, at Etlingen. The day after his army passed the Rhine at Huningen, almost in the presence of the Austrians, who did not attempt to disturb the last moments of its retreat. The French army was protected by a strong rear-guard, under the orders of general Abbatucci and La Boissiere.

The successes of Moreau, from the 24th of June, the day on which he passed the Rhine at Kehl, till his entrance into

Bavaria, resulting chiefly from the great superiority of his forces, were not decisive of his military talents ; but his retreat was a satisfactory evidence of his claim to the highest military talents, and ranks him amongst the most distinguished generals. He conducted the army with infinite skill in the midst of the Austrian corps which surrounded him, and selected, with consummate judgment, the opportunities of attacking and defeating them in succession. His movement against Latour was well combined, and it was to the success of that manœuvre that he owed the safety of his retreat, which was judicious and methodical. He saved his sick and wounded, his artillery and his baggage. The gallantry, abilities, and good fortune, of the archduke Charles, were not less conspicuous. He had liberated Germany from the yoke of France, and an excellent opportunity was thus afforded of conveying succours to Italy. But that intention was prevented by the severity of winter, and as he durst not leave the Brisgau, exposed to the incursions of Moreau, the conquest of Kehl, and other offensive measures were of the utmost importance to the security of his troops while in winter quarters.

The operations of the army of the Sambre and Meuse were not of equal importance with those which have been just recorded. A severe indisposition having obliged general Jourdan to resign the command, it was conferred on general Bournonville, then commander-in-chief of the northern army. The posts of the Austrians and the French between the Lahn and the Sieg in the vicinity of Mentz, and along the Rhine as far south as Landau, were engaged in continual skirmishes, which, though accompanied by a copious effusion of human blood, produced no beneficial consequences to either of the contending parties. The bridges across the Moselle had been totally swept away by the impetuosity of the waters, which a rain of twelve days without intermission, had swelled to a prodigious height, and the wrecks of these destroyed the bridges between the right bank of the Rhine and

the isle of Nieuwied. The Austrians appear to have conjectured that general Bournonville had been subjected to the necessity of dispatching a number of his troops to defend the places which were threatened, and by this means had weakened his force upon the Lower Rhine Acting under this persuasion, they attempted to turn the division of general Grenier, which they concluded to be surrounded with water, and on the 20th of October made six debarkations between Andernach and Baccarach, that Grenier might be induced to weaken his force by sending detachments to oppose them. But their troops were attacked by Kleber and Championette, when the whole of them were taken prisoners or perished in the water. The imperialists, in the mean time, threatened the bridge, and attempted to carry it or destroy it by a terrible discharge of bomb-shells and balls ; but the tremendous fire of the French batteries compelled them to retreat without accomplishing their purpose.

The Austrians who had proceeded from Mentz to the Lower Nahe, were posted with their left wing on the heights in the vicinity of Kreutznatch, and their right on the hill of Rochusberg, for the purpose of defending the passage of Bingen. On the 26th, the right wing of general Bournonville's army, engaged the Austrian line between Kreutznatch and Kayserslautern, obliged them to abandon their position, and retreat behind the Seltz. As soon as the army of Moreau had effected the passage of the Rhine, two divisions of it were sent to Landau, and a division from the forces of Bournonville to the vicinity of Kayserslautern. These divisions dispersed the Austrians in the Hundsruck and Palatinate ; and general Hotze was obliged to fall back to his entrenched camp of Manheim, where he experienced many severe attacks from the republican troops.

This event was regarded by the directory as an important victory, but it was succeeded by no decisive movement on either side. It was believed that this reciprocal inaction would soon be followed by a suspension of hostilities on the Lower

Rhine, and this belief was confirmed by the repeated conferences of the Austrian and French generals at Nieuwied. Generals Kray and Kleber concluded on the 6th of December, a suspension of hostilities, which stipulated that the Austrians should retire behind the Seig, and the French behind the Wapper: that upon the left bank of the Rhine the river Nahe should be the line of separation between the two armies; and that upon giving ten days previous warning, they should mutually be at liberty to commence hostilities and to reoccupy the posts which they held before the suspension. The conclusion of this armistice excited much displeasure on the part of the archduke, and was disavowed by the higher powers on both sides. Whether the suspension, however, was in reality welcome or unwelcome to France or Austria, its conditions were scrupulously observed; a result to which the opposing armies were compelled by the rigor of the season, and the nature of the country which they occupied. The country on the right of the Rhine from Mentz to Dusseldorf is exceedingly mountainous, much covered with forests, and intersected by a great number of little rivers or rather torrents, which overflow the valleys during winter. There are very few roads, and those are almost impassable during the winter. When that season arrives, it is scarcely possible for an army to act; and it was therefore extremely natural for the generals on both sides to save their soldiers from unnecessary fatigues, and to agree on a state of inaction to which they were compelled by irresistable circumstances.

During the latter part of the campaign, the respective armies of Moreau and the archduke were separated by the Rhine, about the whole length of its course from Basle to Cologne; but immediately previous to the suspension of arms, great battles and decisive movements were even in this quarter no longer to be expected, and military curiosity was diverted from the combined movements of the hostile forces to the sieges carried on against the fortress of Kehl and the bridge of Huningen, events of so much importance, from the circumstances attending them, and in their influence on the next campaign, as to demand a more than casual notice. The celebrated fort of Kehl, so often taken and retaken in different wars between France and the empire, is situated on the right bank of the Rhine, opposite to the town and citadel of Strasburg. Before the war it communicated with that fortress by a bridge, built upon piles, and divided into two parts by an island. This bridge formed the principal communication between France and Germany, and had been broken down on both sides of the Rhine at the commencement of hostilities. At this period the fortifications of Kehl, once the bulwark of Germany, were almost entirely destroyed. I have already recorded the capture of this fort by the republicans, at the beginning of the campaign. From the time of its capture they hastened to make it, if possible, impregnable; and, to render it more difficult of approach and of attack, they covered it by an entrenched camp, the right of which was flanked by an island in the river, and by an elbow of the river itself. Its left extended to the fort. The front, which was more advanced than the wings, was covered by a strong dyke, armed with redoubts and protected by a good ditch. It concealed the entrenched camp, and thus secured it from the fire of the cannon. They increased the difficulties of the approach by cuts made in the Kintzig and the Schutter, small rivers which fall into the Rhine near Kehl.

The retrograde march of Moreau, and the capture of Kehl by general Petrarch, who, as we have already seen, lost it again on the same day, made the French redouble their labour and exertions to complete the defensive strength of the fort and of the entrenched camp. They supplied it with a numerous artillery, and, to render the communication with Strasburg more ready and more certain, they constructed a flying bridge, and another of boats.

The fort of Kehl was in this formidable state of defence when the archduke determined to make himself master of it.

This enterprise presented great difficulties, while it required the most severe labour and immense preparations. The task imposed on the assailants was less to take a fort than a formidable camp ; and the operations were of a magnitude resembling the siege of one army by another. The time that was necessary to bring together the troops, the workmen, the artillery, and the magazines, retarded the opening of the siege. More than half the month of November was employed in making lines of circumvallation, and other works preparatory to opening the trenches The archduke, that he might be nearer to superintend and to animate the labours of the siege, stationed his quarters at Affenburg, about ten miles from Kehl. In the night of the 21st of the same month, the trenches were opened on the right bank of the Kintzig. It was not there, however, that the Austrians endeavoured to make their principal efforts. Their works on this point had no other object but to establish a cross fire against the fort and the entrenched camp, in order to favor the approach from the village of Kehl, and to cover the right flank of the real attack. In the same night general Moreau caused the garrison to be reinforced with a strong corps of infantry, drawn from Strasburg. On the 22nd, at break of day, these troops, commanded by general Desaix, made a vigorous sortie, attacked with fixed bayonets the left of the line of contravallation, and obtained immediate possession of the village of Sandheim, and of three redoubts, of which they spiked the cannon.

Encouraged by their successes, the French attacked the other redoubts of the first line, and advanced at the same time against the second. They were less fortunate in this last enterprise. Prince Frederic of Orange, who was posted with a body of troops behind the dyke which joined the redoubts on the left of the first and second lines, resisted in this position all the efforts of the enemy. After an engagement, as bloody as it was obstinate, in which this young prince exhibited the strongest indications of bravery and talents,

he prevented the further advance of the French. They experienced no less resistance in their attack upon the other redoubts of the first line. Though surrounded, and for some time reduced to dependance on themselves, their defenders baffled all the efforts of the assailants. In vain did the French grenadiers leap out of the ditch, and endeavour, by scaling the palisadoes, to mount the parapet. They were constantly repulsed, and filled the ditches with their dead.

The long defence made by these redoubts and the firmness of the prince of Orange, gave time to general Latour to collect the corps of reserve, and bring them into action. He retook the village of Sandheim, and maintained himself there, notwithstanding a fresh attempt made on him by the French. The latter were soon after attacked at the same time by the prince of Orange, and the generals Latour and Stader, who dislodged them from the redoubts which they had taken, and forced them to retire within their own lines. The successful resistance of the prince of Orange was highly creditable to his talents and courage, and the vigor and intrepidity of the sortie made by the French, indicated the importance which they attached or feigned to attach to Fort Kehl, for it must not be concealed that the Austrians afterwards attributed, however unjustly, the protracted defence of that fortress to the desire of preventing them from joining their own armies in Italy. If such was the object of the French, it better became them to boast of their stratagem than their enemies to complain of it.

The unfortunate issue of several attacks, induced the archduke Charles to renounce, for the present, all attempts to carry the positions of the enemy by force, and to confine himself to the operations of art. The approaches were therefore continued, and a second parallel was constructed, but with incredible labour, the thaw which occurred at this time having filled the trenches with water, and rendered the removal of the artillery from one parallel to the other almost impossible. These obstacles produced new delays in the formation of the siege which had been successively retarded by cold, by snow, by rains, and by the overflow of the Kintzig and the Schutter. The enemy defended with obstinacy every inch of ground. The besieged and the troops which guarded the trenches were frequently engaged in desultory skirmishes, which, joined to an almost incessant cannonade and bombardment, destroyed the lives of a great number of men. A still greater number perished from disease, occasioned by the nature of the soil and the inclemency of the season. The sufferings of the besieged, severe as they, were, far surpassed those of the besiegers. The former, as well as the latter, were confined within their works, without any protection from the severities of the weather. The French possessed also the decisive advantage of being assisted and relieved at pleasure, by the troops stationed at Strasburg, where 30,000 men might be easily quartered.

But neither the dangers nor the fatigues attending these operations, enfeebled the confidence of the Austrian troops or the energy of Charles. He animated the men by his exhortations, and encouraged them by his example. He never ceased during the whole course of this memorable siege, to animate the men by his exhortations, to encourage them by his example, and to support them by the confidence with which he had inspired them. The soldiers endured with patience the sufferings shared by their commander ; and his recent triumphs were to them the most certain pledges of success. On the night of the 19th, the Austrians made a successful attack on one of the advanced works of the fort. They carried an entrenchment thrown up near the post-house of Kehl, made 200 prisoners, and took four pieces of cannon, with two howitzers.

The fort and the entrenched camp of Kehl deriving their principal means of resistance from their communication with Strasburg, the length of their defence necessarily depended on the preservation of the bridges, which they had neglected nothing to strengthen and secure. Their entrenched camp was so situated, that the Austrians could not fire directly on the bridges which were also protected by batteries raised in many islands which the French had occupied in consequence of their treaty with the margrave of Baden.

With a view of destroying the bridges, the archduke caused several strong fire-ships to be built in the river Kintzig, which, being launched in the Rhine and sent down the current, might break the bridges by their weight or their explosion. On the 22nd, at night, the Austrians launched one of these fire-ships. To divert the attention of the enemy, they redoubled the fire from their cannon and mortars, and at the same time attacked the advanced picquets. But the French, who had anticipated their design, constructed an *estacade* above the bridge, which stopped the machine. It was immediately seized by the French pontoniers, who had the good fortune to prevent the explosion by removing the match. Other machines of a similar nature launched a few days afterwards, shared the same fate. The Austrians were equally unsuccessful in their attempts on the enemy's entrenchments, but their repeated defeats did not abate the ardor of their exertions or their confidence of success. On the 1st of January, the prince of Orange advanced with his usual intrepidity, carried the enemy's works at the point of the bayonet, and pursued them to their camp. The darkness of the night, however, enabled the French to rally, and rendered the movements of the prince so insecure, that he retired to a position in front of the works, where he maintained himself, notwithstanding all the efforts of the enemy, and covered the workmen, who were forming behind him an advanced parallel. The formation of this parallel, the capture of a redoubt flanking the left of the dyke, and the junction of all the points of the offensive lines, was not effected without very considerable loss. But the French were by this time deprived of a free communication between the right and left wings of their entrenched camp ; and the Austrians now prepared to erect some batteries which might silence the artillery of the fort, whose fire afforded a powerful protection to the camp. These batteries were completed on the morning of the 6th of January, and the archduke gave orders for the assault, but the enemy, perceiving that if they were now defeated, they should have no means of safety but in crossing the line on a flying bridge, did not think it prudent to remain any longer in so perilous a situation, and evacuated therefore all the works of the right wing, on the night of the 5th.

This retreat having considerably diminished the enemy's front, the operations became more direct and more concentrated. The besiegers were enabled to play on the bridges and constructed batteries to destroy them. The archduke, impatient to terminate a siege so tedious, so expensive and so fatiguing, ordered the remaining wing of the entrenched camp to be stormed. The Austrians were completely successful, and drove the French from their camp into the fort, at a moment when the French were relieving their troops on service. The guards that were relieved and relieving, united on the glacis of the fort, and returned to the charge against the Austrians. The combat was obstinate ; but, notwithstanding the favorable circumstances which had doubled their forces, the French were unable to recover their entrenched camp, and retreated into the covered way of the fort. After this event, further resistance on the part of the besieged would have been worse than useless, and they were on the point of losing their communication with Strasburg, except by boats, as their bridges would be shortly destroyed by the batteries raised against them.

General Desaix obtained a conference with the archduke, in consequence of which the French abandoned the fort of Kehl on the following day, and withdrew entirely beyond the river, taking with them their arms, their baggage, and artillery.

Thus, after the trenches had been open for seven weeks, the imperialists recovered the possession of an important post which had been taken from them in a few hours.

History will record the siege of Kehl as one of the most remarkable events of the revolutionary war. If the Austrians did not display the same talents for attack which their enemies did for defence, it is but just to remember the obstacles of every description by which they were opposed and discouraged, the immense works which they were obliged to erect, notwithstanding the frost, the snow, the rains and the thaws. The constancy and the determination with which they supported the dangers, the fatigues, and the tediousness of the siege, were above all praise. The archduke discovered throughout, a firmness, resolution, and perseverance, not unworthy of a Frederic or a Wellington, and which are generally rewarded by ultimate success.

The loss of the Austrians in the siege of Kehl amounted to more than 10,000 men, and consisted of the flower of their infantry. The loss of the French was equally severe, and chiefly affected also their best troops. Whatever importance the latter attached to the possession of Fort Kehl, their chief motive for continuing its defence, was the hope of preventing the archduke from undertaking any other enterprise beyond the Rhine, or from retiring to seek new triumphs in Italy.

After Moreau had repassed the Rhine at the end of October, the archduke left a body of troops to blockade the *tête de pont* (the head of the bridge) of Huningen. As it was neither so well fortified, nor so advantageously situated as that of Kehl, it was not supposed that it would make so long resistance. But the perseverance of its defenders was not easily intimidated or subdued. Notwithstanding the commanding situation of the Austrian batteries, and the judicious direction of their fire, had broken the bridge which joined the two banks of the river, the French, by the most unwearied exertions, succeeded in repairing the misfortune, and in re-establishing the communication between the island, the town and the *tête de pont* of Huningen.

The month of December passed away unmarked by any important event: the Austrians refraining from hostile attack, and proceeding by silent but regular approach. Immediately after the reduction of Kehl, the archduke sent to prince Furstenburgh the heavy artillery which he had used in the siege of that place. Its arrival enabled the prince to attack, with sufficient vigour, the *tete de pont*, and the works which defended it. The French, unable to withstand the number and force of his assaults, determined to abandon the right bank of the Rhine; and, having agreed to a capitulation, recrossed the river with their arms and baggage. On the same day the Austrians took possession of the *tete de pont*. It was specified in the

capitulation, that the imperialists should not fire *on* the town of Huningen, that the French should not fire *from* the town on the Austrian posts, and that the right bank of the Rhine should be left in the same condition as before the passage of that river by the French. So indecisive was the issue of a campaign in which extensive provinces were laid waste, the principal towns over a large expanse of country destroyed, the inhabitants subjected to the brutality of a licentious soldiery, and 120,000 men became the unlamented sacrifice of revolutionary ambition.

HISTORY OF THE WAR.

CHAP. XII.

Marriage of Buonaparte—His Appointment to the Command of the Army of Italy—Operations of the Campaign—Battle of Lodi—Disastrous Retreat of the Austrians—Blockade of Mantua—Invasion of the Territories of the Pope—Conclusion of Peace between the Pontiff and the French Republic.

THE operations in Germany were regarded by the government of France as of minor importance when compared with the rapid and splendid triumphs of the army of Italy, which had been entrusted to general Buonaparte, in consequence of the intercession of Barras. For this important favor he was indebted to his marriage with madame Beauharnois, the widow of the viscount Alexander de Beauharnois, and for many years mistress of Buonaparte's patron. Her maiden name was Josephine la Pagerie, and her husband was a major in a regiment of artillery. Both were descended from noble families, both were natives of Martinique, and educated in France. The fortune of the beautiful Josephine was an acceptable addition to the slender income of the youthful viscount : their expenditure was liberal, and, having been introduced at court, their rank, their manners, and their hospitality, rendered them the most favoured and conspicuous members of the polished circles of Parisian society.

At the beginning of the revolution, M. de Beauharnois was chosen by the nobility of the bailiwick of Blois, a deputy to the states-general, and in June, 1791, was elected their president. He served under general Biron in 1792, in the capacity of adjutant-general, and afterwards succeeded Custine in the command of the army of the Rhine ; but he was suspended by the deputies in August, 1793, and soon after arrested with his wife. On the 23rd of July, 1794, he was consigned to the guillotine, and, had not Robespierre shared his fate after the lapse of a few days, madame Beauharnois, also, would have perished on the scaffold. On the 12th of August she was released ; Barras commanded the national seals to be taken off her house, and honoured her by sojourning in her mansion, until October, 1795, when his election to the directory demanded his residence at the palace of the Luxemburg.

Barras, thus unexpectedly elevated to the station of a chief magistrate, found it inconvenient to continue his connection with madame Beauharnois, and the lady agreed to an arrangement, which shewed her obedience to the wishes of her friend, or the indifference with which she regarded him. She consented to give her hand to Napoleon Buonaparte, if the general could be induced to acquiesce in the arrangement. The plan was formed, and Barras proceeded to provide his mistress with a husband and his friend with a wife.

The army of Italy was destitute of a leader, Carnot having displaced general Scherer for habitual intoxication. Barras offered to Buonaparte madame Beauharnois, 500,000 livres, and (by the influence of Carnot,) the command of the army. Barras reminded him that the lady and the army were equally necessary to a youthful and aspiring general, and as the terms of the offer intimated that his ambition could only be gratified by compliance, he became the husband of madame Beauharnois, and commander-in-chief of the army of Italy.

Buonaparte arrived at head-quarters in 1796. the spring. He lived familiarly with the soldiers, marched on foot at their head, suffered their hardships, redressed their grievances, and acquired, by attention to their desires, their esteem and admiration. His army, *according to the statement of the French*, was inferior to that of the enemy in point of numbers. On receiving this information, he replied, "If we are conquered, my forces will be too numerous, if victorious, it is numerous enough."

Many political and military considerations concurred to determine the French government to prosecute the war in Italy with unusual vigor. The example of the court of Spain, which had been induced to conclude a hasty and dishonourable peace by the invasion of its territory, impressed the directory with a belief that the same plan might be adopted with success against the king of Sardinia; and it was not improbable that they might be enabled to carry the war into the Italian states of the emperor himself, to destroy his preponderance in Italy, to exclude the English from its ports, and above all, to find in a rich and fertile country, money, subsistence, and resources.

To carry these designs into execution with the better chance of success, it was necessary to elude the vigilance of their enemies. Well assured that the falls of snow and the nature of the country would prevent the Austrians and the Piedmontese from attempting offensive operations during the winter, they abstained from reinforcing the army of Italy, and from repairing the losses it sustained in the campaign of 1795. The arrears of pay, and the scantiness of subsistence, having occasioned considerable discontents among the national volunteers, the French generals, finding that they could neither restore

subordination nor satisfy their demands, gave permission of departure to all who were inclined to return to their own country, regarded without jealousy or displeasure, the absence of those who quitted their colours without leave, and thus permitted many of their worst soldiers to return into France. The French government were extremely tardy in restoring order and discipline to the army of Italy. Its weakness and state of disorganization were known to the allies, and they were therefore led to conclude, that it would not be necessary to oppose them by any considerable force in the course of the next campaign.

During the months, however, of January and February, the directory, under the pretence of preventing disturbances in the south of France, assembled 4000 of their best troops in the provinces of Languedoc, Roussillon, and Provence. The greater part of them having been engaged in the campaigns of Spain, and having become accustomed to a hot climate, were therefore enabled to resist that of Italy. During the month of April, almost the whole of these troops arrived, by forced marches, in the territories of Genoa. Soon after the opening of the campaign, Buonaparte found himself at the head of an army of more than 60,000 men, of which 45,000 were under his immediate orders, in the position of Savona; the rest were posted on the Col de Tende, and in the other passages which lead from the Riviera de Ponente, to Piedmont. The exertions of the court of Vienna were by no means adequate to the importance of the emergency, and the promises it had made to the king of Sardinia, who had long resisted the bribes and the solicitations of the French, were no longer remembered after the occasion which gave them birth. The same promises had been made to general Beaulieu, to whom the command of the army was entrusted. He left Vienna with the hope of finding or receiving the promised reinforcements. His chagrin and astonishment were great, when he discovered that of the 60,000 men whom he had expected to precede him, only 30,000, even including

2 D 2

a corps of Neapolitans, had reached their places of destination, and that general D'Argenteau, the commander of the right of the army, retained his station, notwithstanding the express intimation of the court that he should be immediately recalled.

The forces of the king of Sardinia amounted to 60,000 men, including his militia : 20,000 commanded by general Colli, defended the Col de Tende, and the other approaches of Piedmont on the side of Nice and of Genoa ; 10,000 guarded the different valleys which separated Piedmont from France; 15,000, commanded by the duke D'Aoust, were in Savoy ; opposed to the French army of the Alps, amounting to 25,000 men, commanded by general Kellerman ; and the rest were divided among the places of the interior.

On reviewing the different statements of the opposing parties, it will appear that the effective and moveable force of the opposing armies at the commencement of the campaign exclusive of the troops employed in the occupation of garrisons, in the defence of insulated positions, and in the prosecution of minor objects, was on the side of the French 85,000, and on that of the allies 75,000. This estimate is the more worthy of confidence, as it is computed and attested by the generals of the enemy.

The allies were in possession of all the passes in that chain of mountains which divides the *Riviere* or coast of Genoa, from Lombardy and Piedmont. The French army commanded under Buonaparte by Massena, Berthier, and Angereau, was posted near the sea, having Savona on its right, the village of Montenotte on its left, and an advanced guard under general Cervonif, between Savona and Genoa. They were entrenched in these positions when Beaulieu, after waiting in vain for the expected reinforcements, advanced by the way of Novi, and the pass of the *Bochetta*, a name by which the Italians distinguished a chain of mountains forming many windings, through which passes the great road from Lombardy to Genoa. On the top of the highest of these mountains the road contracts itself so

much, that only three soldiers can march abreast. Having attacked Cervoni on the 9th of April, and forced him to retreat to the main army, he afterwards attacked in succession, the post which guarded his enemy's centre, and drove them from their ground till the division under D'Argenteau presented themselves before the redoubt of Montenotte, the last of the entrenchments, where they were destined to be arrested in their progress. Rampon, the gallant officer to whom its defence was entrusted, sensible of the importance of his charge, sustained the vigorous assaults of the Austrians, and held them at bay till the dawn of the ensuing day ; when the French generals who had made their preparatory movements during the night attacked his forces, fatigued by preceding actions with so much impetuosity, that they were routed after a desperate engagement, and were driven from the field with the loss of 1000 killed, and 2500 prisoners.

In the mean time Buonaparte having reinforced his right, and ordered general Laharpe to advance between generals Beaulieu and D'Argenteau, and, to turn the left of the latter, had marched forward in two columns, the one by the valley of Tanaro, and the other by the heights of Savona, in order to turn the right of the same general, and separate him from general Colli. The latter fearing to be cut off, and wishing to preserve his communication with the imperialists, fell back after an obstinate defence. Buonaparte having thus deprived M. D'Argenteau of the co-operation of the Piedmontese general, rapidly advanced upon his right flank, which he turned, while general Laharpe executed the same movement upon his left. The advantage remained at all points with the French, but their victory was dearly purchased. The loss of the Austrians was estimated at 3500, of whom 2500 were made prisoners. After this victory, the French advanced in the mountains, took possession of Careare, and proceeded to establish themselves on the heights surrounding Cairo, which the Austrians had abandoned. M. de Beaulieu, perceiving that the French had carried their principal forces against the centre and right of his line, fell back obliquely by his right, in order to effect his junction with general D'Argenteau, and to draw nearer to the Piedmontese.

Buonaparte determining to take immediate advantage of his first successes, rapidly advanced along the bank of the Tanaro, at every opportunity placed his forces between the Piedmontese and the Austrians, and outflanked the right of the latter. The centre and the right continued to advance on the 13th, and on the 14th of April forced the Austrians to risk a general engagement at Montelesino. Buonaparte executed the same manœuvres as had been attended with success at Montenotte. He directed the greater part of his forces against the right wing of the Austrians, so as to intercept its communication with the Piedmontese. By this arrangement, the left of the Piedmontese and the right of the Austrians, still commanded by D'Argenteau, were forced and put to flight. The centre of the Austrians was now placed in such a situation as to sustain the attack of the whole French army. It defended itself against the superior numbers of the enemy with the greatest bravery, attempted several times to pass through the centre of the French line, and for a long time rendered the conflict doubtful. The dispositions of Buonaparte corresponded with the urgency of the moment. He reinforced the right of his army, and ordered it to advance in three strong columns against the left wing of the Austrians, which was sustained by some entrenchments thrown up near Dego.

The left wing opposed a formidable resistance to the French, and the fire from the batteries was unusually destructive. But one of the columns, under Massena, succeeded in outflanking the left wing of the Austrians, and the latter, pressed on all sides by superior numbers, were at length overpowered and dispersed.

In the evening colonel Wuckassowich, who arrived near the scene of action a day too late, met the body of the army of D'Argenteau, which was flying in confusion, and which was vigorously pursued by the French, whom continual fighting, the heat of the climate, and the difficulties of the ground, had thrown into disorder. The Austrian colonel, defiling in good order by a lateral valley, charged them with vigor, put them to the rout, pursued them in his turn for several hours, and retook Dego. The event of the action might have been favourable to the imperialists had D'Argenteau advanced to the aid of this division; but, instead of supporting the movements of Wuckassowich, he continued his retreat, and the brave and able colonel, attacked in his turn by superior numbers, was, notwithstanding an obstinate resistance, obliged to retire with very considerable loss. He rejoined at Acqui, the remainder of the Austrian troops, which M. de Beaulieu re-united under his command.

The sudden irruption of Buonaparte having separated the detached corps of lieutenant-general Provera from general Colli, he attempted in the night of the 13th and 14th, to effect his retreat towards the Austrian army, from which he was separated by the Bormida; but this river having suddenly swelled, it became impassable; no other resource was left him than that of retiring to the summit of the mountain, which was commanded by an old castle, where he defended himself for two days, though his troops were destitute of water and provisions. Surrounded on all sides, he was summoned but in vain to surrender at discretion. The French assaulted him three times, and were repulsed with dreadful carnage. Generals Panel and Quenin were killed, and general Joubert severely wounded. It was not till the 14th in the evening, that the brave Provera and his gallant troops, exhausted by hunger and fatigue, surrendered themselves prisoners of war.

Buonaparte, in obedience to the orders received by the French generals, never to make public the number of their killed, wounded, and prisoners, observed a cautious silence on the amount of his losses in the conflict of Montelesino. It cannot be doubted, however, that it was fully equal to that of the Austrians, which is stated by the French general himself at 4000 killed, and 7600 wounded : an estimate far exceeding the bounds of probability, and corresponding in the extravagance of its falsehood, with too many of his subsequent statements during the continuance of the campaign.

The victory of Montelesino was the more important, as the supply of provisions and ammunition thus obtained, furnished the republicans with the means of marching, to new successes, and facilitated the necessary succours which they could not without extreme difficulty transport across the mountains. It also promised a speedy junction with the division of Serrurier, who guarded the banks of the Tanaro and the village of Oneglia. By effecting this object, the French general would augment his force, while according to his own statement he had diminished that of the Austrio-Sardinians by 10,000 men, 40 pieces of cannon, and all their magazines. The natural difficulties of the country must have rendered this loss still more sensible to the allies, to whom no alternative remained but that of attempting some unexpected enterprise, in order to arrest the rapid progress of the French.

The army, fatigued with the battle so lately fought, had resigned itself to the exultation and the security of victory, when on the 15th, at day-break, Beaulieu, with 7000 Austrians, the flower of his army, attacked and carried the village of Dego. General Massena, as soon as he had formed part of his troops, advanced to oppose him, but was repulsed in three different attempts. General Causse was not more fortunate. Having rallied the 99th demi-brigade, he attacked the enemy, and was on the point of charging with the bayonet when he fell, mortally wounded. In this condition he perceived Buonaparte, and, collecting his remaining strength, asked him if Dego was retaken. "The posts are ours," replied the general. "Then" said Causse, " *Vive la republique*, I die content." The affair, however, was not yet decided. Buonaparte ordered the 89th demi-brigade to form in column under the command of general Victor, while

adjutant-general Lanus, rallying the 8th demi-brigade of light infantry, precipitated himself at their head on the enemy's left. His troops hesitated a moment, but were decided by his intrepidity, and these combined movements carried Dego. The cavalry completed the rout of the enemy, who left 600 dead, and 1400 prisoners. During these operations, general Rusca obtained possession of the post of San Giovanni, which commands the valley of the Bormida. Angereau having dislodged the enemy from the redoubts of Montezemo, opened a communication with the valley of the Tanaro, where Serrurier's division had already occupied on the left of that river, and almost under Ceva, the posts of Batisola, Bagnasco, and Nocetto. The recapture of Dego secured Buonaparte's right from any further inquietude with respect to Beaulieu, thus separated from the Austrio-Sardinian army, and allowed him time to concert measures against that army, which occupied a strong entrenched camp under Ceva. He pushed forward to that place a strong reconnoitring party, which carried some of the enemy's posts, and rendered more certain and less dangerous the attack upon their camp.

The activity with which these measures were concerted, commanded the approbation of the directory, who in their letter to Buonaparte, expressed their satisfaction in finding that he had justified their choice by the laurels he had gained. " To-day," general, said they, " receive the tribute of national gratitude. Merit it more and more, and prove to Europe that Beaulieu, by changing the field of battle, has not changed his opponents : that beaten in the North he shall be constantly defeated by the brave army of Italy ; and that with such defenders, liberty shall triumph over the impotent efforts of the enemies of the republic."

Angereau left Montezemo on the 16th, and attacked the redoubts which defended the approach to the entrenched camp of Ceva, and which were occupied by 8000 Piedmontese. The columns commanded by generals Bayrand and Joubert, fought the whole day, and made themselves masters of most of the redoubts, when the enemy, who were on the point of being turned by Castellino, perceiving their danger, evacuated the entrenched camp during the night. Serrurier entered the town of Ceva on the 17th, and invested the citadel, in which was a garrison of 700 men ; but the heavy artillery not being able to keep pace with the rapid march of the troops in the mountains, had not yet arrived. The Piedmontese army took a position at the confluence of the Cursaglia and the Tanaro, with its right supported by Notre Dame de Vico, and its centre by the Bicoque. On the 20th, Serrurier attacked their right near the village of St. Michel, and, passing the bridge under the enemy's fire, compelled them, after three hour's fighting, to evacuate the village ; but the Tanaro not being fordable, the division intended to attack their left, could harass them only by its riflemen. The hostile army being reinforced on its right, Serrurier was obliged to retreat, and at night both armies resumed their former stations. The enemy's position was formidable. Surrounded by two deep and impetuous rivers, they had cut down all the bridges, and strengthened the banks with strong batteries.

The whole of the 21st of April was occupied by both sides in making preparations, and in seeking by false manœuvres to conceal their real intentions. At two in the morning Massena crossed the Tanaro near Ceva, and occupied the village of Lesegno, while Guieux and Fiorella, generals of brigade, obtained possession of the Torra bridge. Buonaparte's object was to bear down on Mondovi, and compel the enemy to change the field of battle. But general Colli, fearing the issue of an engagement, which must have been decisive on so extended a line, set out at two o'clock in the morning in full retreat, abandoning all his artillery, and taking the road to Mondovi. At day-break the two armies came in sight of each other, 1796. and the engagement began in the hamlet of Vico. Guieux advanced on

the left of Mondovi, while generals Fiorella and Dammartin attacked and carried the redoubt which covered the Sardinian centre. On this the army abandoned the field of battle, and the French entered Mondovi. The loss of the allies was estimated by the French at 1800 men, in killed and prisoners. One general was killed and three taken, besides four colonels, eleven standards, and eight pieces of artillery.

After the battle of Mondovi, the Piedmontese crossed the Stura, and occupied a position between Coni and Cherasco, a town not only strong by its position at the confluence of the Stura and Tanaro, but rendered additionally formidable by a chain of bastions strongly friezed and palisadoed. The 23rd was passed in crossing the Elero, and in throwing new bridges across the Pesio. On the day following, after some skirmishes of cavalry, the troops entered the town of Bend. General Serrurier marched with his division to La Trinite, and cannonaded the town of Fossano, the head-quarters of general Colli, while Massena advanced against Cherasco. Buonaparte sent general Dugard and his own aid-de-camp, Marmont, to reconnoitre the place, and plant howitzer batteries to beat down the palisadoes ; but the enemy, after some discharges of their artillery, evacuated the town, and repassed the Stura. This victory was of the most important consequences, for it supported their right wing, and furnished ample resources of subsistence. On the next day the weather became very unfavourable, and it rained in torrents, yet the troops were actively engaged in throwing bridges of boats across the Stura. Colli retired to Carignan, in order to cover Turin, from which the republican army was only nine leagues distant. Fossano surrendered, and was taken possession of by Serrurier. General Angereau marched against Alba, which surrendered. He was then directed to throw several bridges of boats across the Tanaro, at that town, to enable the army to pass the river, which is of considerable breadth and rapidity.

The Piedmontese army was from this

time, entirely separated from the Austrians, and obliged to depend only on itself in its defensive position behind the Stura. This position was the best that general Colli could have occupied ; it covered the strongest places of Piedmont, and defended the only routs by which the French could penetrate into that country, since the latter had not yet obtained possession of the Milanese. The safety of Piedmont and of Turin, depended upon this line of defence being perfectly preserved. Should the French succeed in breaking through it, they would be enabled to penetrate into the flat country, and, leaving it behind them, might advance to the very gates of Turin. The superiority of their numbers would have enabled them to mask those fortresses which might have given them inquietude, and to spread themselves over the plains of Piedmont, in defiance of the feeble and exhausted remains of general Colli's army.

The reverses which the allies had sustained at Montenotte, Montelesino, and Vico, and the rapid progress of the French, filled the court of Turin with just and serious alarms. The king of Sardinia, impressed with a due sense of the dangers by which he was menaced, was unwilling to expose his possessions and his crown to the risk of a single battle, and he hastened to conclude a suspension of arms, by which it was stipulated that the French should be put in possession of the strong places of Coni, Ceva, and Tortona ; that till the latter could be surrendered, the town of Alessandria should be given up to them ; that they should remain masters of all the country on the right bank of the Tanaro, from the source of that river to its junction with the Po ; that they should be permitted to cross the latter river below the town of Valenza, and that the French troops should be allowed to have a free passage through all the territories of the king of Sardinia. This armistice was soon after followed by a treaty of peace between the king and the French republic.

The unfortunate result of the late operations must be partly attributed to the remissness of the Austrian government, in its transmission of supplies and reinforcements, to the acknowledged intrigues and briberies of the French, to the unacquaintance of general Beaulieu with the country, in which he assumed the chief command, and to his deficiency in that address, and those conciliating manners which were necessary to secure the concurrence and the favourable opinion of the Piedmontese generals. Much, indeed, must be attributed to the skill and courage of Buonaparte, whose plans were wisely conceived and ably executed. He displayed great ability and promptitude in taking advantage of the superiority of his forces, and of the errors of his adversaries. There was but one object to which he directed all his movements and applied all his means ; and this object was to break the line of the allies. He succeeded in his efforts by bringing the greater part of his force to bear on the weakest part of their line, a simple manœuvre, and which can scarcely fail of success, when executed with foresight, celerity, and vigor.

The armistice concluded between the Piedmontese and French armies, was productive of the most important advantages to the latter. It delivered the republicans from one-half of their enemies, provided them abundantly with military stores and provisions, and secured their position in Italy. It gave them the means of acquiring new successes, and provided certain points of retreat in case of a reverse of fortune. Elated by so many victories obtained in so short a time, and strengthened by all the new resources he had procured, Buonaparte lost not a moment in pursuing the career of success. The possession of Tortona, with the liberty of passing the Po near Valenza, facilitated his access to the Milanese, which presented an easy conquest to an army already victorious and double in number to the forces by which it was opposed.

Since the 29th of April, the day on which the armistice was signed, the French army had continued its advance towards the Po. Massena reached Alessandria in time to seize the magazines, which the Austrians, unable to remove from the rapidity of their retreat, had sold to the citizens. On the

6th of May, the army of Italy took possession of Tortona, of which the new fortifications had cost the king of Sardinia 15,000,000 livres. They found in this town more than 100 pieces of brass cannon, immense stores, and casemates for 3000 men. By advancing towards the Lower Po, Buonaparte gained the advantage of alarming the petty states of levying contributions in the duchies of Parma, Placenza, and Modena, and of procuring money, provisions, and horses. After having made a feint of passing at Valenza, he proceeded on the 8th of May, by a forced march, to the neighbourhood of Placenza, and, perceiving but a small number of the enemy on the other side of the Po, he hastended to transport his vanguard to the opposite bank, on the rafts and flying bridges. M. de Beaulieu, having received information of the march of the French towards Placenza and the Lower Po, dispatched a force of 6000 men to defend the passage of the river, but they arrived too late for the performance of that duty, and being repulsed at Fombio, were compelled to retire upon the Adda. M. de Beaulieu had ordered another body of 4000 men from Casale to succour that which was attacked at Fombio. The corps arrived at Codogno on the road from Placenza to Cremona, which road it found occupied by the French. The encounter between the two parties produced a fire of musketry, in which general Laharpe received a ball, which killed him on the spot, and the detachment retired towards Lodi, where general Beaulieu had assumed a position with the rest of his army.

Every day was rendered remarkable by engagements or negotiations. On the 9th of May, in the same town of Placenza, which had witnessed the rapid passage of the river that washes its walls, the infant duke of Parma, its sovereign, signed an armistice, of which the conditions were dictated by Buonaparte. In his dispatches relative to this transaction, he intimated to the directory his intention of sending to Paris, as soon as possible, the finest pictures of Correggio, and among others;

the portrait of St. Jerome. " I confess," he observed, " that this saint has chosen an unlucky moment for his arrival at Paris, but I hope you will allow him the honours of the Museum." He concluded with requesting the directory to send some eminent artists who might charge themselves with selecting the most valuable productions of art, and superintending their conveyance.

Every step which Buonaparte advanced into Italy augmented his military resources, and each success prepared the way for others still more splendid and advantageous. He was now certain of being able to pay, equip, and subsist his army at the joint expense of his enemies and of the neutral powers. From the duke of Parma alone he had received as the conditions of the armistice, 2,000,000 French livres, or more than £80,000, 1700 horses, and 2000 oxen, and his passage of the Po secured an easy access to the fertile duchy of Milan.

He left the banks of the Po on the 9th of May, and found himself on the 10th, with his advanced guard in the presence of general Beaulieu's rear-guard, which was posted in front of Lodi and of the river Adda. A brisk cannonade was commenced on both sides, in consequence of which the Austrians evacuated the town of Lodi, and retired to the other side of the river. Major Malcamp, son-in-law to general Beaulieu, who commanded the Austrian corps, caused several pieces of cannon to be placed at the end of the bridge, so as to command the front, while some other pieces placed on the right and left, took it by a cross fire. He would not allow the bridge to be broken down, conceiving it impossible that the French would attempt to pass it. After he had been joined by the major part of his army, Buonaparte assembled his general officers, and communicated to them his determination to storm the bridge. They unanimously disapproved of the intention, as desperate in itself, and promising no advantage adequate to the inevitable expense of lives. Buonaparte, however, persisted in his design, and having assembled a council of grenadiers, addressed them in a spirited harangue, in which he did not dissemble, the dangers of the enterprise. The grenadiers replied, "give us some brandy, and we will see what is to be done." It was given them in abundance, and produced a greater effect than the speech of Buonaparte. Four thousand grenadiers and carabiniers formed themselves into a solid column, and marched towards the bridge. When they arrived at its extremity, they were received by a terrible discharge of grapeshot, which it was impossible to withstand. They fell back with great loss, returned twice to the charge, and were again forced back by the fire of the Austrian cannon, which enfilading the bridge, were all discharged at once, as they approached. The French had already suffered enormously, and it might have been expected that they would abandon the undertaking. But Buonaparte, persevering in his resolution, ordered fresh troops to reinforce the column engaged in the attack. Six generals placing themselves at its head, animated them by their example, inflamed them by their harangues, and led them back to the charge. Taking advantage of a moment when the thickness of the smoke occasioned by the incessant fire, prevented the Austrians from perceiving their movements or making a general charge, they rushed upon the bridge, crossed it with rapidity, and, falling impetuously on the troops and cannon which defended its extremity, overthrew the one, and obtained possession of the other. The bridge being forced, all the other columns instantly passed it to support the former. This action, equally brilliant and unexpected, disconcerted the Austrians, who abandoned their ground and began their retreat. It was protected by the Neapolitan cavalry, which, during the conflict, had charged the enemy several times, always with courage and sometimes with success, and displayed in their retreat a coolness, skill, and intrepidity, not unworthy of the most distinguished veterans.

Buonaparte wrote to the directory that the allies had lost in this action 2500 men, of which 500 were made prisoners, while he pretended that his own loss amounted only to 400 men. Had he mentioned ten times that number, it would have approached the truth. The very nature of the engagement rendered it more bloody than any of the preceding actions, and the cross-fire of the Austrians was peculiarly destructive. The assailants were exposed, without intermission, to a tremendous discharge of musketry and artillery; and, if they were three times compelled to fall back, it was in consequence of the destructive fire to which they were exposed, and of the havoc which it occasioned in their ranks. The enterprise exhibited a striking proof of the indifference with which the French generals regarded the waste of their soldiers' lives. By making other dispositions and by the delay of a few days, Buonaparte might have crossed the Adda with as little loss as he sustained at the passage of the Po. He would indeed have acquired less glory, but he would have deserved the more valuable praise that is due to patriotism and humanity.

After the engagement of Fombio, the Austrians were pursued by the French Pizzighitone, but the Adda, which covered that place, retarded its capture, as the troops were destitute of the necessary means for crossing the river. Beaulieu, who after the battle of Lodi fled towards Mantua, was unable to protect either Pizzighitone or Cremona. The French invested the first of those places on the 11th, and, entering it on the 12th, after a brisk cannonade, took about 400 prisoners. Cremona surrendered to the victors without attempting a useless resistance. The vanguard entered Milan on the 15th, having received on their march the submission of Pavia, where they found nearly all the magazines of the imperial army. Lombardy might now be regarded as completely conquered; for although the castle of Milan still held out, the tri-coloured flag floated from the extremity of the lake of Como, and the frontiers of the country of the Grisons as far as the gates of Parma

The succession of so many engagements and victories in so short a space of time, rendered some days of repose necessary to an army fatigued by a series of repeated triumphs.

During the short interval of repose, Buonaparte gave the Italian states a foretaste of that liberty which he had promised to confer, by levying the sum of £80,000 as a contribution on Lombardy.

To encourage the perseverance and fortify the courage of the troops, the most flattering testimonies of national gratitude and applause were given to them and their commanders by a splendid festival celebrated in honour of their victories, in the Champs de Mars at Paris. Inspired with the most lively ambition of military fame, by the plaudits of their countrymen, and the commendation of the directory, they returned with fresh ardor to that rugged path of glory which they had trod with so much success; and appeared to regard the most imminent dangers, and the most intolerable fatigues, with contempt and indifference, when placed in competition with the acquisition of military glory.

An insurrection was in the mean time threatened by the partisans of the old governments, but early information having been given to the commander-in-chief, it was easily suppressed. Buonaparte having inflicted exemplary punishment on the leaders of this conspiracy, did not suffer himself to be detained by the siege of the citadel of Milan. After obliging the duke of Modena to conclude a treaty of neutrality, he declared his intention to pursue the fugitive Austrians into the Venetian territories, where they had taken refuge by the connivance of the senate, who were acting a deceitful and timid part. Previous to the investment of Mantua, it was necessary to vanquish Beaulieu, who had taken a position behind the Mincio, between the lakes of Garda and Como, on the last of which Mantua is situated. When the French army was advanced to the bridge of Borghetto, some difficulties arising from the destruction of one of the arches by the Austrians, fifty grenadiers,

with general Gardanne at their head, threw themselves into the river, and crossed it with their firelocks in their hands in the face of the enemy. This act of daring courage had the desired effect. The French army having crossed the Mincio, a battle ensued, in which the Austrians were again defeated, and were obliged in consequence, to retire behind the Adige, into the Tyrolese, leaving their enemy in possession of all their conquests. Buonaparte then invested Mantua, but, not being provided with sufficient artillery for carrying on a regular siege, he converted it into a blockade.

A conqueror is generally provided with some plea by which he endeavours to satisfy his own conscience, and to evade the reproaches of the world. The powers engaged in the partition of Poland, were influenced according to their own declaration by a virtuous determination to remedy the evils of anarchy, and secure their own countries from the contagion of those principles which had been diffused among every class of Polish society. The wretchedness of the government under which the Italians had lived for so many ages, presented to Buonaparte a specious pretext for the gratification of his ruling passion. "He came not to subdue, but to liberate the nations of Italy, and put them in possession of their rights." These protestations received with credulity, and dictated by no intention of performance, were in a short time succeeded by the spoliation of the Italian cities of their most valuable remains of antiquity, by the sacrilegious robbery of the treasures collected in the churches, by the most rapacious and oppressive confiscations, and by the adoption of a barbarous and inexorable system of terrorism towards all who were suspected, or whom it was convenient to suspect of disaffection to the French. The professions of Buonaparte were those of a lover of liberty; his actions were those of a sanguinary and rapacious despot.

While the Austrian partisans in the imperial fiefs bordering on Piedmont, Genoa, and Tuscany, were endeavouring to distress him by attacking his convoys, he denounced vengeance against those who should repeat the offence. The wavering line of policy adopted by the pope supplying him with a plea for hostilities, he seized on the states of Bologna and Ferrara, and the citadel of Ancona. His holiness, on this occasion, experienced the fate which generally attends on timidity and irresolution in political affairs : being compelled to sue for an armistice by the intervention of Azara, the Spanish ambassador, and at last to purchase it by the cession of the conquered territories, by a contribution of 15,000,000 livres, and what to him was still more afflicting, by giving up one hundred master-pieces of painting and sculpture, and five hundred manuscripts from the Vatican library. This requisition and a similar contribution which Buonaparte had levied on the duke of Modena, might have presented him to the world as a depradator on the fine arts, and an enemy to the cause of art and learning. He therefore obviated this reproach by a kind and respectful letter to the astronomer, Oriani, and another to the municipalities of Pavia and Milan, requesting them to invite the students of Pavia to return to that university, and to inform him by what means he could add to the utility and the reputation of that seminary.

The situation of the grand duke of Tuscany, at this period, was particularly critical. We have seen that he had sacrificed his attachments to the interests of his family by declaring neutrality. But some indications of disaffection to the French cause having been discovered in the conduct of the governor of Leghorn, were deemed of sufficient importance to justify the most unjust and oppressive proceedings. A body of troops was sent to take possession of Leghorn, and seals were put on the magazines of goods belonging to the subjects of the English, and other enemies of the republic. This proceeding being very distressing to the British merchants and alarming to the government of his Britannic majesty in Corsica, sir Gilbert Elliot, viceroy of Corsica, sailed with a body of troops, and obtained possession

of Porto-Ferrajo, in the island of Elba, a spot which will be distinguished in the annals of history, as the circumscribed and precarious empire of a man, who, guided by common prudence, might have continued to sway the sceptre of continental Europe.

About the same time the French experienced once more the just consequences of that rapine and cruelty which they exercised upon the conquered countries. The inhabitants of a part of Romagna, driven to despair, armed themselves to the number of many thousands, and massacred the detachments employed in laying waste their country. Buonaparte sent an additional number of troops into the province, who killed several hundreds of the unfortunate peasants, and burnt the town of Lugo with the neighbouring villages. These sanguinary and uncalled for atrocities excited the hatred and the vengeance of the inhabitants. Numbers of the French became the unpitied victims of these sentiments, and the Italian stiletto, seconded by the climate, and the intemperance of the invaders, concurred as powerfully as the Austrian sword to the diminution of their forces.

During Buonaparte's transactions with the grand duke of Tuscany, he received intelligence that the citadel of Milan had surrendered. He was enabled by this event to devote his chief force to the siege of Mantua, the reduction of which city was to complete the paramount ascendancy of the French republic in Italy. Their power was already carried to a height destructive of the independence of the neighbouring states. While Buonaparte was violating the rights and laws of nations by possessing himself of Leghorn, and by placing a French garrison in Verona against the consent of the Venetian senate, that august assembly condescended to court his favor by sending the claimant of the French crown out of their dominions. Buonaparte declaimed with animation on the peace and tranquillity secured to every nation by the protection of the republic. The power of protecting in sovereign states is generally attended with the power of oppressing, and history presents too many afflicting proofs, that the latter of these prerogatives is the most frequently exercised. In the course of this history the reader will be enabled to judge whether this observation apply with justice to the conduct of the government of France.

Mantua has so much occupied the attention of Europe, has been the object of so many efforts, and the occasion of so many sanguinary contests, that some description of so celebrated a fortress, and of its military and topographical situation, may gratify the inquiries of the curious, and render the narration of warlike operations more interesting and distinct.

Mantua boasts of having been founded by the Etrurians before the Trojan war. It is situated upon a lake formed by the Mincio, twenty Italian miles in circumference, and two miles broad. It is large, well built, and contains a number of churches, of which some are very richly decorated. At the time when it still belonged to the dukes of Mantua, who resided there, its inhabitants amounted to 50,000, but they do not amount at present, (1814) to one-half that number. It has been considered for many centuries, and during every war, as the most important fortress in Italy. It has sustained several sieges, and, whenever it has surrendered, that event has been chiefly occasioned by a severe blockade, and by the utmost extremity of famine, rather than by open force, or the regular operations of art. Its chief means of defence consist less in its fortifications, and in the difficulties opposed to the approaches and attacks of an enemy. The town being entirely surrounded by water and marshes, is only to be entered by three bridges or principal causeways, covered by fortifications raised at each of their extremities, which must be carried by an enemy before he can approach the place. There is also a fourth communication, defended by the entrenched suburb Il Thé. If once the besiegers obtain possession of the exterior works, they may easily form and prosecute the blockade of Mantua, but they are scarcely more advanced towards the

formation of a regular siege, as they can only open the trenches upon the front of the narrow causeways which lead into the town. The waters of the lake stagnate in summer; the place at that time becomes very unwholesome, and those of the inhabitants who are in easy circumstances, generally leave it This unwholesomeness is not the least of its means of defence, for it is impossible to besiege it without risking the total destruction of an army by sickness. In almost every siege which this place has sustained, pestilential fevers have made deplorable ravages among the defenders and assailants.

These considerations did not intimidate general Buonaparte, who had been taught by recent triumphs, to be confident of future victories.

After having carried several out-posts of the town, he opened the trenches before it on the 18th of July. But the difficulties attending the siege, the fevers which broke out in his army, and the successful sorties of the garrison, rendered the progress of the French extremely slow, and enabled count Canta D'Irles, who commanded in the town, to defend it until relieved.

The Austrian general Beaulieu having been uniformly unsuccessful, he was superseded by Wurmser, a general of distinguished talents. Reinforcements were sent to the imperialists in Italy, and it was expected that the Austrian army would now out-number the forces of the enemy, which had been weakened by the detachments employed in the defence of the captured fortresses. Wurmser having strengthened the wreck of Beaulieu's army which he found in Tyrol, with the troops he brought with him, moved southward, and occupied the lines which his predecessor had formed between the lake of Garda and the Adige. But these positions were immediately forced by Massena and Joubert.

Wurmser was convinced that the fortune of the campaign would be determined by the fate of Mantua. After receiving a reinforcement of 20,000 men from Germany, he availed himself of this accession of force, to proceed to its relief. One division of his army taking its rout by the east of the Garda, forced the enemy's post at La Carona, and obliged him to evacuate Verona ; while the other, advancing by its western banks, dislodged him from Brescia and Salo.

The garrison of Mantua, commanded by a brave and upright governor, had sustained the vigorous assaults of the besiegers with exemplary firmness. They began to be in want of provisions, and their struggles for deliverance were rendered by this circumstance still more frequent and desperate. At length, on the night of the 31st of July, Buonaparte precipitately abandoned the siege. The garrison, attentive to all the movements of the besiegers, made a vigorous sortie while they were retiring, fell upon their rear-guard, took 600 men, and made themselves masters of all their artillery and ammunition, 134 cannons and mortars, and 140,000 shells or balls. It employed itself immediately in destroying the works which had been raised, either for the purposes of the siege or for those of the blockade. Placed between the two columns of Wurmser and Quosdanovich, Buonaparte was fully aware of the danger of his situation, and was sensible that if he gave these two generals time to form a junction, and to combine their attacks, it would be almost impossible to make head against both of them at once. He therefore adopted the only plan that could save his army and preserve the Milanese. He concluded that by concentrating his forces, and advancing rapidly against the corps of M. de Quosdanovich, he might defeat him before he could be succoured by M. de Wurmser.

His plan was no less rapidly conceived than ably executed. After having defeated general Quosdanovich, Buonaparte leaving only a small body of troops, who were directed to drive that general back into the Tyrol, hastened in search of marshal Wurmser. On the 3rd of August he met with the enemy's advanced guard, which he instantly attacked with his whole force. General Lyptay, the Austrian commander, disputed the ground, inch by inch, to give time for the arrival of Wurmser to his assistance. The latter, however, not arriving so soon as was expected, the general found it impossible to continue his resistance any longer, and came forward with his officers to surrender themselves to the French. But at this moment, the latter, perceiving at a distance the Austrian cavalry coming up at full gallop, retreated precipitately to take a fresh position against the new troops which were coming to attack them, and fell back before general Lyptay, who was advancing towards them to lay down his arms. The main body of Wurmser's army arrived in the interval, but, before it could form in order of battle, Buonaparte attacked it with the utmost impetuosity. The Austrians did not give way, but, fatigued by a long march, made during extreme heat, engaging in an irregular manner, and without any determinate object, against an enemy which possessed the advantages of ground, and whose dispositions had been arranged, their utmost exertions could only enable them to retain the positions which they occupied. The loss of the Austrians estimated by Buonaparte at 7000 men, did not exceed 700 ; the loss of the French was at least as great.

The two armies passed the night within musket-shot of each other, but they were too much overcome by fatigue to resume the contest. Had either of the armies possessed sufficient physical strength to attack the other, it would have obtained an easy victory. The 4th of August was employed by the French in preparing for future action, and in occupying and defending the most eligible positions, while the Austrians remained inactive in their disadvantageous situation. On the morning of the 15th, Buonaparte attacked with vigor the whole line of the Austrians, whose left he had turned, and whose rear was threatened by general Serrurier. The Austrians fought with their usual valor ; but every advantage was so entirely on the side of the French, that victory could not escape them. Had they succeeded in penetrating into the plain, the destruction of the Austrian army would have been inevitable. The officers of marshal

Wurmser's staff, perceiving the danger to which they were exposed, implored him to commence an immediate retreat. This brave, but aged commander, appeared uncertain and irresolute, but at length was prevailed upon by the friendly importunities of the English, under general Graham, to adopt the only step that could save the army from ruin and disgrace. But the French had already gained so many advantages, and the ground was so favorable to their movements, that the retreat could not be effected without considerable loss, or without the utmost disorder. It cost them near 3000 men in killed, wounded, and prisoners, besides 30 pieces of cannon and a great number of ammunition waggons. The Austrians repassed the Mincio and Valeggio, and encamped near that town. On the next and the following days they continued their retreat, and did not stop till they reached the entrance into the Tyrol, to which general Wurmser brought back not much more than one-half of his army. Notwithstanding the disasters which the general experienced, he attained his principal object, the relief of Mantua. During the five or six days that he retained an open communication with that city, he had thrown into it considerable supplies of provisions and ammunition, recruited the garrison, and again enabled the place to resist a long blockade.

Buonaparte, with no less expedition than judgment, took advantage of the faults of the opposing generals, and of the separation of Wurmser and Quosdanovich, gained two marches on the former, and fell unexpectedly on the corps of the latter, which being too much extended, was easily defeated and dispersed. His operations were considerably facilitated by the preservation of the fort of Peschiera, which defends the point of the lake of Garda, at the spot from whence the Mincio issues; a fort of which the Austrians could not obtain possession, and which much embarrassed their movements. From a particular account of the losses of the Austrians, furnished by each regiment to general Wurmser, it appears that they lost in the last eight days of conflict, in killed and prisoners, 17,000 men, of whom, 341 were officers. The loss of the French amounted to 10,000, of whom 4080 were made prisoners. Their army suffered severely from the heat, and from the fatigue of its rapid and frequent marches, and was in little less disorder than that of their enemies.

Buonaparte, in the course of this expedition, was twice in danger of being taken. The officer who commanded the Austrian flotilla on the lake of Garda, having, on the 31st of July defeated that of the French, disembarked his troops in the peninsula of Cermione, and placed them in ambuscade on the road from Brescia to Peschiera. His soldiers had orders not to fire, and to stop none who might seem to be of consequence. In the evening Buonaparte and Berthier, with their staff, returning from Brescia, passed along that road, preceded by three hussars. The croats who were in ambuscade hearing some cavalry rapidly approaching, sprung upon the high road and fired upon the three hussars. Two of them were killed, but the third having escaped their fire, turned his horse and gallopped off, crying, General, save yourself! The whole party turned about, fled with precipitation, and had the good fortune to escape all the shots which were fired at them. They returned to Brescia and took another road, which obliged them to make a tour of several leagues. On another occasion Buonaparte narrowly escaped being taken by the Austrian hussars at Goito, of which circumstance he sent a marvellous account, bearing internal evidence of its falsehood, to the directory. He informed them, that, being at Lonado with 1200 men, at the moment when 4000 Austrians were surrounding that town, he sent them an order to lay down their arms, which they instantly obeyed. The improbability of this circumstance is not decisive of the falsehood of Buonaparte's statement, but the silence of the other generals of the army, the omission of so important a circumstance in the most authentic military narrations, and the future employments of the Austrian officers, to whom the attack of Lonado was entrusted, afford the most decisive evidence of its absurdity.

The remainder of the month of August passed away without the occurrence of any important event. Marshal Wurmser was entirely occupied in recruiting the great diminution sustained in his army, which by the end of August amounted to 50,000 men. Buonaparte also received new reinforcements from the army of Kellerman. He reconstructed the works necessary for the blockade of Mantua, and devoted all his talents to the formation and the arrangement of new designs.

Encouraged by the continual triumphs of their armies, and convinced that they would be able to maintain them at the expense of Europe alone, the directory conceived the projects of uniting on the banks of the Danube, the three armies of Jourdan, Moreau, and Buonaparte, with an intention to invade the dominions of the house of Austria, to annihilate its supremacy over Germany, and to divide the riches, and decide the destiny of that extensive country. To realize this project as rash as it was gigantic, it was necessary that Buonaparte should destroy the remainder of Wurmser's army, should force the passes of the Tyrol, and march into Bavaria to form a junction with Moreau. More confident, more able, and above all, more fortunate, than the other republican generals, he hastened to concur in the plan of the directory. On the 20th of September, he forced the whole line of the Austrians, and by this success became master of the city and duchy of Trent. Marshal Wurmser having been made acquainted with the designs of Buonaparte, endeavoured to disconcert them by a diversion, and by an attempt for the deliverance of Mantua. He presumed that by advancing with a part of his army along the Brenta, and turning the right flank of the French, the latter would not dare to advance into the Tyrol, lest they should be separated from the troops besieging Mantua. He had flattered himself also that by this manœuvre, he should raise the blockade of that city and retain Buonaparte

in Italy. This expedition depended for success on the promptitude and precision with which it should be executed; and, being likely to be attended with great fatigue and danger, the Austrian general took with him the choicest men of his infantry and cavalry.

The two generals commenced their operations on the same day, and the departure of general Wurmser greatly facilitated the success of Buonaparte in the battle of Roveredo. The latter learnt with astonishment the march of the field-marshal, and was prevented by his movement from pushing forward into the Tyrol; but, instead of falling back along the Adige towards Verona, as the Austrian general expected, he marched by his right towards the valley of the Brenta, and pursued the field-marshal upon the road from Trent to Bassano. By this movement he separated him entirely from the rest of his troops, which remained in the Tyrol, and left him no other alternative than that of retreating upon the Upper Piava, and into the mountains, or making his way across the Vicentino and the Veronese, to Mantua. As the revictualling and relief of that place were the principal object of marshal Wurmser, he adopted the latter of these movements. He therefore prosecuted his march with the utmost rapidity, gained the advance upon Buonaparte, traversed the country of Vicenza, passed the Adige, defeated at Ceria the enemy's division, which guarded that river, and arrived at last, with about 10,000 men, under the walls of Mantua.

The vicissitudes of the war could not but have a material influence on the councils of the Italian princes and states. The transient successes of Wurmser opened a flattering prospect to the adversaries of France. The warm and precipitate temper of his holiness the pope, led him instantly to avail himself of the diversion of the French forces, by the operations in the Trentine, to break the armistice with France by retaking Ferrara; a proceeding which afterwards enabled the enemy to justify his persecutions and his cruelties by the charge of duplicity. The duke of Parma with more prudence, converted his armistice with the French general into a treaty of friendship with the republic, through the intervention of the Spanish ambassador. The popular partisans of Genoa testified their approbation of revolutionary principles, by celebrating the anniversary of the French republic. The leading persons in the government and university of Milan, dreading the re-establishment of the Austrian dominion, which must prove fatal to their own power, and to the cause of liberty which they had zealously embraced, not contented with displaying their attachment to the French interest by pompous celebrations and expensive festivities, laboured with much assiduity and success to impress the people with sentiments favorable to the revolution. Their unwearied labours co-operating with other causes, produced throughout Italy a general change on political subjects ; republican principles became daily more prevalent, and in several cities and states, particularly those of Modena, Reggio, and Bologna, the old governments were succeeded by others constructed on the French model. The sovereign princes at the same time found it advisable to accommodate themselves to the circumstances of the times, and the king of Naples followed the example of the catholic king and of the duke of Parma.

While the Italian princes were endeavouring to avert the vengeance, and conciliate the friendship of France, and the garrison of Mantua withstood all the efforts of the besiegers for its reduction, the court of Vienna, supported by British subsidies, renewed its struggle for the recovery of its dominions, by sending reinforcements under their ablest generals, into Italy. So active was the Austrian government in recruiting the forces, that before the close of the campaign, which had already proved destructive to two imperial armies, Alvinzi, who was invested with the chief command, entered the Trentine, at the head of a force which enabled him to recover Trent, the capital of that principality. He then left general Davidovitch to maintain the Austrian cause in this quarter, forced the

enemy to abandon several corps on the Piava and the Adige, and pressed forward to the neighbourhood of Vicenza. When Buonaparte was apprized of his enemy's movements, he first dispatched generals Massena and Augereau to oppose their operations in the Trentine and on the Brenta. On receiving information of Alvinzi's approach, he drew together his forces, and, passing the Adige, determined to bring that general to an engagement befo e he should have received his expected reinforcements from the Tyrol and the Trentine countries. This determination brought on the memorable battle of Arcola.

A less enterprising or less confident general than Buonaparte would have been discouraged and embarrassed by the remonstrances of the subordinate generals. During the last expedition against Wurmser, he had displayed all the qualifications of an accomplished warrior. The skill of his manœuvres, the briskness of his attacks, and the bravery of his troops, secured his success, and beneath his command, a battle and a victory were synonimous. His talent for intrigue was not less conspicuous than his military prowess, and while the Austrians were unable to conjecture his most important movements, he was himself acquainted with the most trivial plans and most secret intentions of his adversaries.

But in the opinion of Berthier, formerly an aid-de-camp to marshal de Broglio, and son of a first clerk in the war office, the crimes and follies of Buonaparte more than counterbalanced his merits as a general and a soldier. He was detained at Milan till the middle of December, by a sore in his leg, and, during this delay, the number of his requisitions and extortions had completed the ruin of the once fertile and flourishing province of Lombardy. He, and his uncle Salicetti, acquired immense fortunes by lawless and inhuman pillage. His behaviour was imperious, and with all their admiration of his talents, the officers of the army could not contemplate without horror, the indifference with which he had lavished during the whole campaign; the blood of his generals and his soldiers. The rumour of their dissatisfaction having reached France, the directory, alarmed at these dissentions, commanded Buonaparte and Berthier to write two letters, in which they disavowed all the motives of division which were said to exist between them. The injunction of the directors, the supreme authority of Buonaparte, and the military events which followed, restrained the spirit of jealousy and hatred, which animated the chiefs of the French army.

Alvinzi had in the mean time taken his position with great judgment, at Caldero, near the banks of the Adige, which could only be approached by two causeways, guarded by strong posts. Several of these were forced by the division of Massena. The other division under Angereau had borne down all resistance, till it came to the bridge of Arcola, a village situated in a morass, on the maintenance of which Alvinzi chiefly rested for his defence. Angereau and his subordinate generals, observing that their troops began to recoil at the firm resistance of the brigade which guarded the bridge, led them on to the attack, but they were repulsed and many of them disabled. Buonaparte now perceived that he must relinquish his enterprise, or carry the post by that signal display of valor united with address, which had led him to repeated victories. While general Guieux was making a circuit with his brigade to cross the Adige and fall on the rear of the Austrians in Arcola, Buonaparte presented himself in front of Angereau's forces, seized a standard, and, placing himself at the head of the grenadiers, boldly advanced to the bridge, exclaiming, *Follow your general.* His troops obeyed, but the assault was unsuccessful. Buonaparte was dismounted in the morass, and, though he was with some difficulty extricated from extreme danger, and rallied his men, the enemy immoveably maintained their ground. His failure was indeed in some measure compensated by the success of Guieux, who obtained possession of Arcola, with some artillery and prisoners. That village, however,

being recovered by the Austrians, became again the scene of contest on the ensuing day, when several severe but indecisive contests took place in its environs. The battle was renewed with equal warmth on the third day, November the 16th. The French army came to the attack in three columns. General Robert, with the centre division, found it necessary to retire; but Gardanne, whom Buonaparte had placed in a wood, assailing the victorious Austrians from his ambuscade, defeated them with great slaughter. Buonaparte observing that while other divisions had been engaged, the Austrian left wing, protected by marshes, was still unbroken, called artifice to his aid. By his orders, Hercules, an officer of distinguished intrepidity, came upon their rear at full gallop with a small brigade of horse; the trumpets at the same time sounding a charge. This stratagem proved decisive. The Austrians believing that they were attacked by a larger force, gave way, and were completely routed. Their overthrow reduced the third Austrian army which had been raised for this ruinous war, to a mere wreck; and the French, on the other hand, while they triumphed in a victory which decided the fate of Italy, had reason to lament the loss of a great number of their ablest veterans.

"Never," said Buonaparte in a letter to Carnot, " was field of battle so valorously disputed as that of Arcola: scarcely have I any generals left; their courage and devotion to their country were without example." The general of brigade, Lasnes, appeared in the field, though the wound he had received at Governolo, was not yet cured. He was twice wounded on the first day of the engagement, but hearing that Buonaparte in person was at the head of the column, he threw himself out of bed, mounted his horse, and hastened to find the general. As he could not walk, he was obliged to remain on horseback; but at the head of the bridge of Arcole he received a blow, which laid him senseless on the ground.

W.M.Craig del.   Pub.by . Brewer by Marsh....

Buonaparte attempting to force the Bridge of Arcola.

After these repeated disasters, it might have been expected that the court of Vienna would have abandoned the contest in despair. But the event was different. Such was the constitution of the Austrian states, and the character of the people, that, with the assistance of British subsidies, the government was always able to recruit its armies; and on the present occasion it was inclined to attribute its defeat to accidental causes, and to renew the combat, in hopes that the merit of its generals and soldiers might eventually produce a change in the fortune war. Its exertions were favored by the enthusiastic loyalty of many of its subjects. The Tyrolese, in particular, warmly resented Buonaparte's proclamation, in which, while he exhorted them to revolt, he threatened vengeance against the followers attached to the Austrian standard, and, in defiance of his menace, they pressed with zeal to reinforce the army under Davidovitch. As soon as the victory of Arcola had relieved Buonaparte from his apprehensions that Alvinzi might force him to raise the siege of Mantua, Massena was dispatched to the support of Vaubois, whose posts had been assailed by the Austrians, and was so successful in his enterprise, conducted with the usual celerity of the French armies, that the rear-guard of the imperialists, consisting of 12,000 men, were surrounded and taken prisoners on the heights of Campara, and in their attempt to escape, 300 were drowned in the Adige.

Every circumstance, and among others, the weak and ineffectual efforts of those Italian states which were friendly to the house of Austria, concurred with the military talents of the French general, to promote his success. The Venetians having discovered a strong predilection for the Austrian cause, by the service they had rendered the imperial armies, he availed himself of that partiality as a pretence for seizing on the castle of Bergamo, on the Milanese frontier, as a defensive measure, which might prevent his enemy from obstructing the communication of his forces on the Adige with those of the country beyond the Adda.

When we reflect on the occurrences of this campaign, and on the character of the French people, we cannot be surprised at the exultation with which the government and nation received the captured standards presented in the hall of the convention; nor can we regard, without feelings of respect, the eulogies bestowed by the president of the directory on the heroes of Italy. The conclusion of his speech, however, in which he asserted that the first object of the French government was *universal peace*, was strikingly and unfortunately refuted by the evidence of facts, and by the diplomatic history of the following year.

As the season was now too far advanced for the continuance of warfare among the mountains of the Tyrol, Buonaparte directed his attention to the settlement of Italy, and to the punishment of revolt. The power of the French over Italy, was become so extensive and irresistible, as to render opposition, however just, wholly inexpedient. The secular princes had faithfully adhered to the treaties concluded with the French republic. The court of Rome alone was guilty of the most unwise violation of its engagements. In order more effectually to inflame the minds of the people against the republicans, the pope, and his priests, had recourse to the convenient artifices known by the name of pious frauds. The streets were filled with processions of saints and images; the zeal of all classes and conditions was enflamed, and the general enthusiasm corresponded with the violence of the government. Buonaparte, desirous of conciliating the affections of the Italians, was anxious to remain on terms of friendship with the head of the Roman church, conscious that a respectful treatment of the pontiff would be gratifying to the Italian states and people. Determined, therefore, to refrain from coercive measures, he addressed a letter to cardinal Mattœi, prime minister to his holiness, representing to him the inutility of arming his subjects against men who had overcome so many formidable enemies. To this letter no answer was returned till after the triumph of the French at the battle of Arcola, when the pope instructed the minister in his reply to assure the general of his anxiety to remedy the disorders which had so long distracted France, and to restore the relations of amity between France and the Roman see. He appealed to the protection of the Almighty, and trusted to the justice of a conflict with infidels and pretended philosophers. A letter of this description addressed to a victorious general, at the head of a resistless army, was little adapted to interrupt his career, or change his resolution. His holiness in the mean time persisted in preparing for war, and endeavoured to awaken the interest of those powers who were chiefly interested in the preservation of the papal dominion. But circumstances and sentiments had changed since the period when the commands of a pontiff were sacred and imperative; and Spain herself, hitherto the chief support of papal domination, sent an answer, recommending the abandonment of all temporal power, and the devotion of the pontiff's leisure to the exercise of the heavenly virtues.

Buonaparte, perceiving that measures of conciliation were unavailing, resolved to recommence actual hostilities. He published a manifesto, charging the pope with a breach of the convention, and, having entered the Roman territories, issued a proclamation, assuring the inhabitants that he would protect religion as well as property, and warning them to abstain from any acts of enmity that might render them the victims of military vengeance. Every town and village that sounded the tocsin or the approach of the French, was threatened with instant destruction; and it was proclaimed that every district in which a Frenchman was assassinated, should be declared hostile, and subjected to heavy contributions. After taking Ancona and Loretto, the French continued to advance into the territories of the church, directing their march to Macerata and Foligno. Their progress was contemplated by the court and people of Rome with the most unfeigned alarm. In the person of

Buonaparte they recognized a second Attila, arriving in the capital of the Christian world and of the arts, obtaining possession of its riches, destroying its monuments, and overturning the pontifical throne. All the rich and considerable persons of Rome prepared to quit that city, and his holiness himself determined to retire to a place of safety. The riches of Loretto and of Rome were packed up and sent to Terracina. The object of Buonaparte, however, was less to advance to Rome, than to excite the apprehensions of the pope, and determine him to agree to such conditions as he should prescribe. He was conscious that, without imprudence, he could not penetrate further into the papal territories. It was possible that the Austrians might endeavour to take advantage of his absence, and the distance of a part of his army. He would have been obliged for the purpose of securing the obedience of a vast country and of a city so populous as Rome, to weaken his army by numerous detachments; and the ensuing campaign would be commenced before the expiration of a month. These considerations induced him to take advantage of the first pacific overtures made by his holiness. Having received from cardinal Mattœi a letter as affecting as it was dexterous, he returned an answer on the 13th of February, 1797, and announced to him that he granted his holiness five days for the purpose of sending a negotiator invested with full powers to treat for peace. To this letter he received a courteous reply; and, four plenipotentiaries arriving at his head-quarters, invested with full powers by the pope, their presence was immediately followed by the conclusion of peace. On this occasion Buonaparte returned to the pope the following answer.

" Most holy father,

I ought to thank your holiness for the obliging things contained in the letter which you have given yourself the trouble to write to me. The peace between the French republic and your holiness has just been concluded

I congratulate myself on having been able to contribute to your individual repose. I conjure your holiness to distrust those persons who at Rome are sold to the courts inimical to France, or who allow themselves to be exclusively guided by those malicious passions which always accelerate the ruin of states and empires. All Europe is acquainted with the pacific and conciliating virtues of your holiness. The French republic will, I hope, be always one of the truest friends of Rome. I send my aid-de-camp, chief of brigade, to express to your holiness the esteem and perfect veneration which I have for your person, and I beseech you to believe my desire to prove, on every occasion, the sincerity of that respect and reverence with which I have the honour to be your very obedient servant,

BUONAPARTE, general-in-chief.

From the head-quarters at Tolentino."

The articles of peace were nearly the same with those of the armistice concluded in the preceding June. The principal conditions were, that the pope should transfer irrevocably to France, Avignon, the comtat Venaissin, the duchies of Bologna and Ferrara, and the legation of Romagna, that he should pay in two months, 15,000,000 livres, over and above the 21,000,000 stipulated in the armistice concluded in the month of June, of which only 5,000,000 had been paid. It was stipulated that the French should remain in the possession of the citadel of Ancona, till peace should be estab-

lished on the continent, and of the provinces of Macerata, Umbria, Perugio, and Camerino, till the 36,000,000 livres due from the pope should be entirely paid. The articles were confirmed, by which the gift of the statues, pictures, and precious manuscripts, was enjoined, and leave was given to convey to Paris the most valuable antiquities of Romagna, the duchy of Urbino, and the march of Ancona. Such was the price at which the pope, who had never declared war against the French, and who had only assumed the attitude of justifiable self-defence, was obliged to purchase the preservation of the throne of St. Peter. It cost him nearly the third part of the dominions of the church, and more than one year's revenues to satisfy the ambitious views and the rapacity of the French government.

After having acquired by this treaty new pecuniary means for the subsistence of his army, from the chests, out of which a treasurer, named Flachat, had stolen 6,000,000 of livres, (£250,000) Buonaparte proceeded to levy contributions on the grand duke of Tuscany and the republic of Venice. In this manner did the French accomplish their purpose of making the campaign at the expense of the neutral powers; while the latter, for the sake of a neutrality, which was constantly violated, made greater sacrifices than it would have required to defend the entrance of Italy against the French, or to drive them from its territory after they had invaded it.

HISTORY OF THE WAR.

CHAP. XIII.

Naval Operations—Descent of the French at Bantry Bay—Abandonment of Corsica—Birth of the Princess Charlotte—Internal State of France—Affairs of Russia and Sweden—Visit of Gustavus of Sweden to St. Petersburg—Death of the Empress Catharine—Her Character—Debates in the English Parliament—Stoppage of the Bank.

DURING the campaigns of 1796, the attention of the French was so much occupied by military operations, that Britain encountered but little opposition to her maratime exertions, or to those military enterprizes which depended chiefly on naval co-operation. A considerable armament had been fitted out under general Abercrombie, to prosecute our successes in the West Indies. In April, leaving Barbadoes, he sailed to the valuable settlement of Demerary, belonging to the Dutch, which speedily surrendered to the British arms. In the month of May he recovered the island of St. Lucia, and soon after quelled an insurrection excited by Victor Hughes. The British still maintained their conquests in St. Domingo. The French had entirely abandoned the settlement, and the people of colour and the negroes possessed the interior country, while the English occupied various parts of the coast. But here they were doomed to encounter an enemy much more dreadful than the French forces; in a pestilence so fatally known by the name of the yellow fever, which, having raged with destructive violence in all the tropical latitudes of the west, and extended to the northern climate of Philadelphia and New York, was still more malignant and dangerous in St. Domingo.

In Saldahna bay, a Dutch fleet of seven sail of the line, which had sailed in hopes of retaking the Cape of Good Hope, was captured by admiral Elphinston. The Dutch settlements in the east were reduced, and among the rest the island of Ceylon, one of the most important possessions in European India. In the Mediterranean, the Corsicans, openly declaring their attachment to the French republic, the British ministers judged it expedient to relinquish a settlement of which the expense and inconvenience counterbalanced the advantages. At the close of the year, the French, encouraged by reports of disaffection in Ireland, attempted, with thirteen ships of the line and a large body of troops, to make a descent at Bantry bay; but the stormy season dispersing the armament, the commander-in-chief, who had arrived at his place of destination, returned to Brest, with the loss of one ship of the line and two frigates. In this manner terminated a campaign as glorious to Britain as disastrous to her ally, and propitious to her enemy.

Among the domestic events of this year, the most remarkable were the birth of the princess Charlotte of Wales, and the general election, in which the influence of the ministers universally prevailed.

The internal state of France little corresponded at this period, with foreign triumphs, and the successes of her armies.

Every expedient for providing a revenue adequate to the demands of the state had failed. The assignats being depreciated to a very trifling value, another description of paper currency was issued under the name of rescriptions. This expedient having in some degree shared the same fate with the former, they made a further issue to the amount of 240,000,000 of livres, (£10,000,000) under the name of *mandates*, upon the security of the lands forfeited to the state, and taken from the church and monasteries, or on the money accruing from their sale. That the measure might be rendered more beneficial, the government of the Austrian Netherlands was at this time required to pass a decree for the sale of the monastic estates in those provinces. By this expedient and by new taxes, they supplied the vast deficiency in the revenue of the current year, which had increased to the sum of £25,000,000, while the expenditure was not less than double that amount.

The execution of Stofflet and Charette, and the consequent termination of the war in La Vendée, had excited the most reasonable expectations in the allies of France, that, having subdued her domestic enemies, and thus obtained the means of directing her exclusive attention to foreign objects, she would be enabled to perform her liberal promises, and promote the general benefit of her political friends. But her efforts were enfeebled by the pressure of pecuniary embarrassment. The protection of the Dutch trade and settlements, if not an express stipulation, was an implied condition on which the states so willingly submitted to France. How bitter then must have been their mortification and resentment, when they saw their most valuable interests sacrificed to the spirit of military enterprise! They were first deprived of their independence, and then stripped of those sources of wealth on which their political importance had been founded. But these were only a part of the disasters with which the government was reduced to struggle. While Europe resounded with the achievements of the French arms, the kingdom was a scene of

intestine ferment, and the government was distressed by the enemies of the present system, or by the individuals who aspired to the power enjoyed by the existing administration. The zealous friends of the Romish faith and the antient monarchy, were of the former description : the constitutionalists, though not so rancorous in their enmity to the republicans, would gladly have assisted in the restoration of a moderate, well-constituted monarchy ; and they were daily augmented in number by the most respectable of the middle classes, who were ardently desirous of that tranquillity and good order which they despaired of enjoying in the present fluctuating state of domestic affairs.

But the most numerous and dangerous body of opponents were the Jacobins. These advocates of terrorism who were incensed at observing the preference given to the moderatists, in every state appointment, revenged themselves by exciting a spirit of disaffection, and exerting all their influence to render the prevailing party in the directory and the convention, odious to the nation, by representing them as apostates from those democratic principles on which the republic was founded. The Jacobins were now become so formidable, that the government found it necessary to adopt the strong measure of suppressing their assemblies, and enacted a law making it a capital crime to hold seditious meetings or to attempt the re-establishment of the constitution under which Robespierre had exercised his tyranny. They dismissed some of the faction from their offices, and ordered others to leave the capital. As a further precaution, they sent the troops then at Paris, who were ardently attached to the Jacobins, to the several regiments from which they had been drafted for the defence of the convention.

These proceedings still further exasperated the animosity of the Jacobins. Enraged at their exclusion from power, they formed a conspiracy the most horrible in its nature and extent, that ever entered the mind of man. The chief conspirators were a person named Bebeuf, who assumed the name of Gracchus, Drouet, the postmaster, who stopped the king's carriage at Varennes, Rossignol, for some time commander of the republican army in La Vendée, and three others who had enjoyed the confidence of Robespierre. Their design, which was to have been executed on the 11th of May, was to have massacred the directory, the councils, the field-officers of the Parisian militia, and the magistracy of the capital. This conspiracy, though conducted with the utmost secresy, was happily discovered by Cochon, the minister of police. Bebeuf was in consequence sentenced to death and executed : the other conspirators escaped from prison.

The terrorist faction was thus once more defeated in its views, and almost annihilated. But the influence of their indefatigable exertions in cherishing sedition, soon appeared in the tumults which happened at Marseilles. The Jacobins made an attempt to establish their ascendancy in that city at the election of magistrates. When the citizens on the 19th of July were convened for that purpose, their partizans appeared among the populace armed with a variety of weapons. Some of them, with all the ferocity which had marked the frantic agents of the revolution, ran through the city, exclaiming, " Live the Mountain, and the constitution of 1793 :" others rushed into the hall of election, drove the citizens thence, and murdered all who opposed them. This tumult appears to have been raised without any digested plan, and was easily suppressed ; nor would it have been noticed but as an additional proof of national character, concurring with a multitude of similar events, to demonstrate the expedience in such a nation and so extensive a country, of a government invested with all the authority and power, not entirely incompatible with freedom.

The affairs of Russia during the present year, demand from their future connection with the most important events, the peculiar attention of the historian. Since the partition of Poland, every acquisition of territory seemed only to increase the empress Catharine's insatiable passion for dominion. The situation of Courland,

and the wretched state of the country under the sovereignty of its dependent dukes, afforded a plausible excuse for annexing it to her empire ; and, having accomplished this favorite and important object, she directed all her efforts to the acquisition of the Persian provinces on the Caspian sea. She discovered a pretext for her intended conquest, in advocating the cause of Lolf-Ali-Khan, a descendant of the race of Sophis, against Aga Mahmed, the present possessor. After endeavouring in vain to engage the grand seignior in the war, the empress dispatched Valerian Zubof with an army into Daghestan. That general made an easy conquest of Derbent ; but, when Aga Mahmed was informed of his invasion, he marched to oppose him, and gained a victory, which obliged the Russians to take refuge in the conquered fortress.

While Catharine was preparing to send a stronger force for the prosecution of her design in this quarter, her attention was engaged by an affair of a different nature, the success of which she had much at heart. Since the success of Gustavus, king of Sweden, it had been one of the chief objects of her intrigues to supplant the regent duke of Sudermania, and to avail herself of the young king's minority to render Sweden again subject to her ascendancy. Every artifice was tried that might effect her purpose. The consummate address and engaging manners of count Stockleburg, who had been so successfully employed as her agent in Poland, were exerted in the capacity of her ambassador at Stockholm, to gain the affections of the king as the foundation of the plot, and a negotiation was commenced for a marriage between Gustavus and the grand duchess Alexandra, grand-daughter to the empress.

Insurmountable obstructions appeared at first to oppose the accomplishment of her wishes. The regent was known to entertain an aversion to Catharine from his experience of her enmity ; and the king, then in his 18th year, had been formally betrothed to a princess of Mecklenburg. But, to the astonishment of all who were acquainted with the state of the Swedish court, the regent's aversion to Catharine was overcome or repressed, the proposed marriage with the princess of Mecklenburg was set aside, and the regent and Gustavus accepted the invitation of the empress to visit her court. On their arrival at St. Petersburg, they were received with every demonstration of respect, and with all the pleasing attentions which Catharine was accustomed to pay to those whose favor she was anxious to conciliate. Gustavus was introduced to the princess, and was charmed with her manners, her person, and her accomplishments. The court of St. Petersburg, during several weeks, became the scene of splendid festivity. The affair was apparently in a prosperous train, when Catharine defeated her own purpose by a stroke of refinement, of which the consequences were directly opposite to those intended. The Swedish ambassador having demanded the princess in marriage for his sovereign, a day was appointed on which they were to be solemnly betrothed at a public audience.

On the day appointed, the empress and her court were assembled in the state apartment, and the archduchess made her appearance decorated as a bride, in the full assurance of her approaching nuptials. But neither the prince nor the regent appeared, and the air of joyful expectation which every countenance had worn, was exchanged for that of chagrin and disappointment. The occasion of this circumstance was of a nature so trivial, that in this instance at least, Catharine must have lost her usual sagacity. In the marriage articles drawn up by the Russian ministers, Zubof and Markof, Catharine, perceiving that the king was captivated by the princess, and calculating on the impression which she had already made on his heart, ordered it to be inserted, without previous information, that the princess, who was of the Greek church, should have her private chapel and her clergy in the royal palace. These stipulations being brought to Gustavus about an hour before the solemnization, he refused his consent to

them; observing that he would lay no restraint on the conscience of the princess, but that he could not allow her either a chapel or priests in the palace. He was urged and entreated to consent, and the courtiers, who entered his presence with repeated messages from Catharine, represented the insult which he offered to the princess by his refusal, and the rupture which must inevitably ensue between the two courts. But Gustavus withstood their importunities. And when he at last discovered that he could not evade the obnoxious condition, he gave his final answer, " I cannot, I will not sign them," and retired to his own apartment.

The king remained some days longer at St. Petersburg, and conferences were held with him and the regent by the Russian minister, in hopes of obtaining his consent. But he continued immoveable, declaring at the same time, " that as he could not grant what the empress desired, according to the laws of Sweden, he would refer the matter to the different estates that would be assembled on his arrival at the age of manhood, and, if they consented to have a queen of the Greek religion, he would send for the princess." Such was the result of an affair in which every one sympathized with the grief of the princess, which she was too ingenuous to conceal, and all agreed in blaming the empress and her ministers, for sacrificing to a trivial and absurd demand, the happiness of a favored and amiable relative.

Catharine was extremely mortified by the unpleasant result of a negotiation to which all her wishes and exertions had been devoted. She did not long survive the disappointment. Her health had been for some time declining, and the fatigue of attending the entertainments given in honour of the Swedish monarch, was supposed to have hastened her death, which occurred about six weeks after his departure. In the evening of the 4th of November, she was at a private party, and appeared with her usual cheerfulness. The next morning she transacted business of state with her secretaries, after which she was left alone

in her apartment. And when an attendant
who was ordered to wait in the anti-chamber,
growing uneasy at not being called for,
returned to her apartment, he found her
prostrate on the floor. Her physician
caused her to be bled. By that and other
medical means life was protracted, but
without sense or speech, and thirty-seven
hours after her seizure, she expired in her
sixty-eighth year.

There appears to be little difference of
opinion respecting the character of this
illustrious princess. In familiar life no one
approached her without being charmed
by her courteous manners, and the cheerful
gaiety of her conversation ; and, when she
assumed the empress, the graceful dignity
and the decorous stateliness of her deportment commanded involuntary respect.
She combined the amiable graces of the
female character with a vigor of understanding that were adequate to the exigencies of her high station. In her public
conduct there was much to admire and
much to condemn. Magnanimity was
one of the most striking features of her
character, but it was accompanied with
an excessive love of fame and thirst of
dominion. She frequently aspired to
some object which was beyond her reach,
or which she could not obtain without
sacrificing the feelings of humanity or
violating the laws of justice and of nations.
We cannot but admire the splendor which
distinguished her reign, the magnificence
of her public works and institutions, and
her patronage of the sciences and letters :
but we must condemn the profusion with
which she lavished the public money on
her favorites, and the unmerited confidence
placed in her ministers, and the inattention
to civil affairs, which gave rise to enormous
abuses in every branch of government,
particularly that of finance. In the course
of her reign she expended £50,000,000
upon the pandars to her licentious pleasures. Her constancy in adversity and the
fortitude with which she confronted danger,
demand our admiration ; and we are
pleased with the liberality and beneficence
which she discovered towards those who
came within the sphere of her personal

notice But the remembrance of all her
amiable qualities has been obliterated by
the contemplation of her injustice to
Poland, and her atrocities in the Crimea,
which will long survive the recollection
of her virtues, and expose her name to the
abhorrence and execration of posterity.

In England the new parliament met
on the 6th of October ; and his majesty
informed the houses that he had omitted
no endeavours for setting on foot negotiations to restore peace to Europe, and to
secure for the future the general tranquillity.
But nothing (he observed) could contribute
so effectually to this end, as to manifest that
we possessed both the determination and
resources to oppose, with increased activity
and energy, the farther efforts with which
we might have to contend. On the general
propriety of a negotiation, there was a
division of opinion between those who had
promoted the war and supported its
continuance. I have already stated, that
Mr. Burke, in inculcating hostility against
revolutionary France, chose different
grounds from ministers. In the progress
of the war he had adhered to his original
opinion, that the restoration of monarchy
and the antient orders, under certain
modifications, ought to be the sole and
avowed purpose of the war ; and that no
peace could be secure until that object
was effected. Under that impression, he
wrote his "Thoughts on a Regicide Peace,"
intended to prove, that the system of
France was impious, enormously wicked,
and destructive to all who were within
its sphere : we must either conquer the
revolution, or be destroyed ourselves :
peace would enable it to operate rapidly
to our ruin : let us, therefore, avoid peace.
Earl Fitzwilliam, the intimate friend of
Mr. Burke, in a considerable degree
adopted these opinions, and reprobated
negotiation. To restore order (he said ;)
to defend the civilized states of Europe
against the danger that threatened them ;
to protect persons and property from a
fatal devastation, and suppress the tendency
of innovating and pernicious doctrines ;
were the ostensible objects of the war,
and upon these principles they had

supported its continuance. If it were wise to negotiate now, the same wisdom ought to have been manifested four years ago ; for the causes of war, which then existed, still operated with equal force, and proved the necessity of perseverance in hostility to the French system. Ministers declared they had never stated, that the existence of a republic in France was an insurmountable bar to peace : they had expressed what they still believed, that the best issue to the contest would be, the re-establishment of monarchy in France; yet they had never pledged themselves, much less the parliament, to an opinion so extravagant, as that without the attainment of this object there was no hope or possibility of peace. They were always resolved to seek peace with France, whenever it was attainable with SECURITY. The French government now appeared to have some tendency to moderation ; our own country was very much improved in point of tranquillity, which might be chiefly imputed to the wise laws against sedition and treason that had been enacted in the last session. Those who had always reprobated the war, expressed their hearty approbation of the declared intention to negotiate. Judging, however, (they said) from the conduct, and not from the profession of ministers, they did not give them full credit for sincerity. Mr. Pitt strongly represented, that the surest way of obtaining favorable conditions of peace, was to be prepared for war ; and exhibited a very flattering account of the flourishing condition of the country, and the extent of her resources, which were increased beyond all former calculations or hopes.

A clause in his majesty's speech had declared the king's apprehension that the enemy were preparing an invasion upon this island. Mr. Pitt very early in the session recommended adoption of measures for repelling the designed, as well as future attempts. For this purpose he formed a plan for levying 15,000 men from the different parishes for the sea service, and another for recruiting the regular regiments. In the projected levies for the land service, he considered two objects ; first, the means of

calling together a land force sufficient of itself to repel an invasion, even independently of our naval armaments ; and, secondly, [to adopt such measures in the levies as should not materially interfere with the agriculture, commerce, and general industry of this kingdom. The primary object was to raise, and gradually train, such a force as might in a short time be fit for service. For this purpose he proposed a supplementary levy of militia, to be grafted on the old establishment, of the number of 60,000 men ; not to be immediately called out, but to be enrolled, officered, and completely trained, so as to be fit for service at a moment of danger. He also proposed to provide a considerable force of irregular cavalry, to be levied in the following manner : every person who kept ten horses, should be obliged to provide one horse, and one horseman, to serve in a corps of militia ; and those who kept more than ten, should provide in the same proportion ; and that those that kept fewer than ten, were to form themselves into classes, in which it should be decided by ballot, who, at the common expense, should provide the horse and the horseman : these troops were to be furnished with uniform and accoutrements, arranged into corps, and put under proper officers. The whole number of cavalry proposed to be raised by this mode was 20,000 : the other supplemental troops amounted to 75,000 men. Among the means proposed for internal defence, a bill was introduced by Mr. Dundas, for raising and embodying a militia in Scotland, and an act for that purpose was passed without opposition. The whole land forces of the country, intended for the year 1797, were to consist of 195,694 ; and the navy was to amount to 120,000 men. The pecuniary supplies of the year were 31,000,000 borrowed, besides the annual income.

Mr. Pitt still continued to display great financial skill in exempting the very lower class from the severest pressure of the new taxes, though the principal part bore very heavily on the comforts and accomodations of the middling ranks'; the fresh imposts were upon tea, coffee, spirits, sugars, and various other articles of daily and general consumption; upon assessed taxes, postage, stage-coaches, and canal navigation; and in the minister's plans of finance, it began to be complained that the very high and opulent did not contribute so much more than the lower classes, as the proportion of their property would have admitted.

While preparations were making for carrying on the war, lord Malmsbury was at Paris conveying from his court professions of a desire to negotiate a peace. The French government, elated with the brilliant successes of the campaign, were far from relinquishing their determination to retain in their possession the whole of the left bank of the Rhine; this resolution they had intimated to Britain, and to it they were resolved to adhere. Lord Malmsbury arrived at Paris on the 22nd of October. His first reception by the French government manifested a distrust of the sincerity of his employers; the negotiation was, however, opened by a proposition from lord Malmsbury for reciprocal restitution. Great Britain had made very valuable acquisitions, and had incurred no losses herself; seeking from war, not the possessions of her adversary, but the general security, she was willing to restore her own conquests in lieu of the acquisitions which France had won from her allies, as a basis for a treaty: therefore Britain proposed a general principle of reciprocal restitution. The directory replied, that receiving the British ambassador as the agent of Britain only, and not understanding him to have a commission to act for the allies of Britain, they could not now enter into the concerns of those powers: the mode which he proposed of an intermixture of other discussions with a treaty, they represented to be circuitous and dilatory; but to show their sincere and ardent desire of peace, if he procured credentials from the other belligerent states, they would take into consideration such specific proposals as he might then make. To these observations they added an opinion, that the British court was insincere in its overture; that its purposes were to prevent other powers from ne-

gotiating a separate peace; and to facilitate the attainment of the supplies from the people of England, through a persuasion that the French refused all accomodation. To this assignation of motives which, whether true or fanciful, was irrelevant to the discussion, the British minister, with becoming dignity, forbore to reply: confining himself to the answer, he stated, that he had not been commissioned to enter upon a separate treaty; that Great Britain proposed to make in this transaction a common cause with her allies. The directory rejoined, that in a question of reciprocal restitution, the chief object of consideration was the relative condition of the respective parties. Of the original confederates, some were become the friends of France, and others observed a strict neutrality. The remaining allies of Britain were now weakened by their losses, and the desertion of their associates. France, it was insinuated, would not in a negotiation of terms forget the circumstances in which she was placed. Besides the assertions and replications contained in official notes, conferences were carried on between lord Malmsbury and De la Croix, the French minister. In these they respectively unfolded in more detailed statements, the objects and resolutions of their employers.

The Netherlands constituted one of the principal topics of discourse. The British ambassador stated the restitution of Belgium as an indispensable article from which his Britannic majesty would not recede. From the outset indeed of the discussions, we find in his own letter, that he told the French minister that he must entertain no hopes that his majesty would ever consent to see the Netherlands a part of the French dominions. From the same official documents it appears, that the French minister proposed several schemes of equivalent for Belgium, but that lord Malmsbury considered himself as bound by his instructions to admit no proposition by which Belgium should continue annexed to France. On the other hand, the French minister declared, that the republic was resolved not to relinquish Belgium. In the course of their conferences, lord

Malmsbury delivered his opinions freely on certain effects of the revolutionary system, which, extending to the West Indies, influenced the conduct of some of the British islands, and produced confusion and disorder; at length the directory agreed to the general principle of compensation,. but required a specific description of the reciprocal restitutions proposed by Britain. The British ambassador stated the terms in contemplation to be, the restitution by France of her conquests from the emperor, the inclusion of Russia and Portugal in the treaty, and the restoration of the stadtholderian government in Holland. To these outlines, containing propositions so very contrary to the declared views of the French government, De la Croix answered by requiring the whole of his final demands, or, according to diplomatic language, his *ultimatum*, to be delivered in twenty-four hours. To this peremptory requisition lord Malmsbury replied, that it precluded at once all farther negotiation; that if they disapproved of his propositions, or refused to take them into consideration, they ought to bring forward their own, that he might lay them before his sovereign. But he received no other answer than, that they could listen to no terms inconsistent with the constitution, and the engagements that were formed by the republic. They farther signified to him, that since he was obliged to consult the British ministry previously to all replies and communications, it evidently appeared that his powers were inadequate to the conduct of a treaty; and if the British ministry were inclined to pacific measures, and determined to treat on their present plan, farther communications might be as well forwarded by an epistolary correspondence: his residence, therefore, in Paris being totally unnecessary, they ordered him to depart in forty-eight hours. This injunction was notified to him on the 20th of December; and thus terminated the first negotiation for peace between Great Britain and the French republic.

. The . British ministers professed to consider the abrupt conclusion of these overtures as arising totally from France, and published a manifesto on the 27th of December, setting forth the pacific dispositions of the British government, and the malignant hostility of France. " The repeated endeavours of the French government (this document states) to defeat this mission in its outset, and to break off the intercourse thus opened, even before the first steps towards negotiation could be taken; the indecent and injurious language, employed with a view to irritate; the captious and frivolous objections raised for the purpose of obstructing the progress of the discussion; all these have sufficiently appeared from the official papers which passed on both sides, and which are known to all Europe: the failure of the present negotiation arises exclusively from the obstinate adherence of France to a claim which never can be admitted; a claim that the construction which that government affects to put on the internal constitution of its own country, shall be received by all other nations as paramount to every known principle of public law in Europe, as superior to the obligations of treaties, to the ties of common interest, to the most pressing and urgent considerations of general security." On these allegations ministers justified the continuance of the war as indispensably necessary: they endeavoured to prove that the rupture of the negotiation was to be attributed to a systematical aversion to peace in the governing party in the French republic. The manifesto being laid before the houses of parliament, ministers assumed this declaration as a text, expatiated upon it in eloquent and impressive comments and suitable exhortations, and animated the indignant resentment of the parliament and country against the government of France. Mr. Pitt addressed the house in that style of splendid amplification which his oratory so happily assumed when his object was to strike the fancy, or rouse the passions. The question (he said) is not how much you will give for peace; but, how much disgrace you will suffer at the outset, how much degradation you will submit to as a preliminary? In these circumstances, then, are we to persevere in the war, with a spirit and energy worthy of the British name, and of the British character? or are we, by sending couriers to Paris, to prostrate ourselves at the feet of a stubborn and supercilious government, to yield to what they require, and to submit to whatever they may impose? I hope there is not a hand in his majesty's councils which would sign the proposal; that there is not a heart in this house which would sanction the measure; and, that there is not an individual in the British dominions who would act as the courier. In answering the speech of Mr. Pitt, Mr. Erskine took a general view of the causes and consequences of the war with France, and endeavoured to prove that the ostensible was not the real grounds of the rupture; but that we were actually to be at war for Belgium. Mr. Fox argued, that the whole amount of the minister's splendid oration that night, was to admit that we had been four years engaged in a war unprecedented in expense and force, and had done nothing: after all the efforts so honourable to Britons; after an addition of no less than 200,000,000 to the national debt, and of 9,000,000 to the permanent taxes of the country; after an enormous effusion of human blood, and an incalculable addition to human wretchedness; so far were we from having gained any object for which we had set out in the war, that the minister had this night come forward, in a long and elaborate speech, to shew that the only effect of all our efforts had been, that the enemy had, from success, become more unreasonable in their pretensions, and that all hopes of peace were removed to a greater distance than ever. To persevere in an undertaking productive of such prodigious expense and loss, without the least probability of advantage, or even indemnification, was altogether inconsistent, not only with wisdom but with common prudence and common sense. In private life, a person who should persevere in a ruinous undertaking, which wasted large property, and incurred overwhelming debts, without receiving any returns, would be, by all men in their senses, deemed an infatuated projector. The nature and character of such public conduct was the same; the only difference was, that the madness of the former involved a few individuals; the madness of the latter, a great, populous, and powerful nation, in its destructive effects. Persisting in a hostile spirit against the French republic, fondly wishing to restore their beloved arbitrary monarchy, ministers, in the face of the clearest and most decisive experience, still cherished their delusive hopes, embraced the most futile and often-exploded theories, and still conceived that France, exhausted by her efforts, would yield to our dictates. With these ideas and views, they had resolved to prosecute this war, surpassing in its miseries our pernicious project of subjugating and enslaving America. So obstinate in madness, they had pretended to negotiate, merely to induce the people to acquiesce in the expenses which they so severely felt. The negotiation, as it appeared from its circumstances and propositions, was never intended to be conciliatory. The British minister had categorically declared, that he could not recede from demanding the cession of Belgium; the French government as peremptorily declared, they would not recede from their refusal. The French, whether wisely or not, had merely availed themselves of the advantages which they had acquired in war. In denying to our demands the restitution of Belgium, they knew they could, by their power, support that denial; whereas we insisted on a concession which we had no means to enforce. As a question of expedience, it was extremely absurd to continue, on account of Belgium, so dreadful a war, when we were morally certain that all our exertions to regain it would be unavailing. Our offers of compensation were totally inadequate to this valuable acquisition of the French, and we could not therefore reasonably hope that they would have been accepted. We already saw in the unexampled depreciation of the national funds on lord Malmsbury's return, the dreadful shock which public credit received, and we might reasonably expect, that, as the pressure of the new incumbrances came to be felt, the shock would be much greater : dejection and despondency were spread through the country ; the nation was never before in so deplorable and dreadful a situation. On these and similar grounds, Mr. Fox in the house of commons, and lord Oxford in the house of peers, proposed addresses to the king, representing the conduct of ministry, in the whole of the war, as tending to national ruin, and describing the country as hastening to destruction through their infatuated councils. These addresses, however, were negatived, and opposite addresses, approving of the general system of ministers as well as of the principles and conduct of the negotiation, and throwing the whole blame of the rupture on the French, were carried by great majorities.

The pecuniary remittances to foreign princes, and the recall of cash from banking-houses for the purpose of securing it, had alarmingly diminished the circulation of coin ; and, after frequent consultations with the directors of the Bank, the embarrassed ministers discussed the affair in council. From these deliberations resulted an order against the issue of cash from the Bank ; an act of policy which, though it did not demonstrate insolvency, filled the minds of the timid with the dread of national bankruptcy.

When this order was taken into parliamentary consideration, Mr. Pitt recommended the appointment of a secret committee, for an inquiry into the amount of outstanding engagements, and the means of answering them. Mr. Fox deplored the unparalleled embarrassment in which the country was involved by ministerial misconduct ; censured the order of council as unconstitutional ; and advised a public and minute investigation of the concerns of the Bank. Mr. Sheridan moved, that the committee should inquire into the causes which had produced the

order ; but Mr. Dundas opposed this suggestion as tending to delay ; and it was exploded by a majority of 158.

Lord Grenville having also moved for a committee, the dukes of Grafton and Norfolk wished that it might be open rather than secret ; but most of the peers preferred secresy in an affair so delicate and critical. The marquis of Lansdown expatiated on the importance of public credit, but acknowledged his inability of defining its nature with precision. He affirmed that it existed in this country in a peculiar manner and degree, and was indeed the vital spirit of the nation. The shock which it had felt did not, in his opinion, arise from the alarms of invasion, but proceeded from the shameful prodigality of the government, the enormous increase of establishments, the want of that vigilant inspection, which might prevent the abuses of office, the sending of money out of the kingdom, and the delusions which had been practised with regard to the annual deficiencies of revenue. He hoped that every thing connected with this credit might be managed with the most scrupulous caution ; and the danger, perhaps, might then vanish or subside. He hinted that one ill consequence of the use of a multiplicity of notes in lieu of cash would be the prevalence of forgery, and that, as *assignats* had been counterfeited in this country with a view of increasing the distractions of the French, they would gladly embrace the opportunity of retaliation. He said (without predicting truly) that articles of trade would bear a greater price in paper currency than in money, and that great inconvenience, loss, and confusion, would arise from this source. He added, that the mischievous tendency of the measure would also appear in a course of boundless expenditure, and the improvident adoption of frantic schemes of warfare.

Each committee made a favorable report, stating, that the funds applicable to the discharge of the engagements of the bank exceeded those demands by £3,926,890, without including a debt of £11,686,800 from government ; yet each recom-

mended a continuance of the late prohibition, as the repeated applications of
individuals for money might otherwise
deprive the Bank of the means of supplying the cash requisite for the public service.
A bill was therefore introduced for confirming the restriction; and, to render it
less inconvenient, notes for small sums
(even for £1) were put into circulation.
Bank-notes, however, were not actually
obtruded on the people, who were still
allowed to refuse them, when offered
instead of cash for the payment of a
debt.

It was proposed by sir William Pulteney,
that a new bank should be instituted for
the revival of public credit. He did not
mean that the old establishment should
be suppressed, but that both should
concur in promoting the accommodation
of the public. He represented the Bank
monopoly as dangerous, from the opportunity which it might afford to an ambitious minister for the perpetuation of
his power; and there was also, he said,
a risk of its being employed by aspiring
directors to control and over-awe the
cabinet. The former ground of apprehension was less improbable than the latter; but the house did not attend to either
point.

The duke of Bedford and Mr. Grey
respectively moved a series of resolutions,
relative to the minister's intercourse and
concerns with the Bank, attributing the
embarrassments of that company to his
negligence and prodigality: but neither
house would agree to a vote of censure.

That profusion which excited frequent
and just complaint, occasioned a demand
of supplies to an enormous excess. Early
in the session, £27,647,000 had been
stated to be requisite for the exigencies
of the year; but, that sum being afterwards deemed insufficient, as redoubled
vigor was said to be necessary for humbling
an enemy who had rejected reasonable
terms of peace, above 15,000,000 were
voted in addition. The emperor was
indulged with a fresh loan, even at a time
when he was negotiating a separate peace:
and, as Portugal was menaced with an

invasion, pecuniary aid was afforded to
that realm, to which a body of British
soldiers and a corps of French emigrants
were also sent. The number of seamen
rose to 120,000; the guards and garrisons
consisted of 60,765 men; and above
64,000 soldiers were voted for the dependencies of Great Britain. A large
supplemental body of militia was levied;
and a respectable supply of cavalry was
provided for the defence of the kingdom
One loan (called the loyalty loan, from
the spontaneous and eager subscription
of the nobility and gentry) was for 18,000,-
000; and another for 16,000,000 and a half.
The new taxes were consequently numerous. Houses, stage-coaches, horses, auc-
tions, agreements, newspapers, ornamental
plate, spirits, tea, coffee, &c. contributed
to furnish interest for the two loans.

The earl of Oxford moved, that the
king should be desired to give unequivocal
indications of pacific views, and, after the
conclusion of peace, to promote a constitutional reform: but the peers were
adverse to the proposal. The earl of
Suffolk, with the same ill success, moved
for the dismission of the first lord of the
treasury from office. Alderman Combe
proposed, that this disgrace should be
extended to all the ministers; a motion
which the commons decidedly disapproved. Mr. Grey was convinced, that
the most effectual remedy for the national
evils would be found in a reform of that
assembly; but his scheme for the introduction of a more popular system of
representation was baffled by a great majority. Mr. Pollen having moved for an
immediate negotiation with the French,
the minister intimated his hope of a speedy
opportunity of renewing pacific overtures,
and condemned the motion as premature
and useless. When Mr. Fox strenuously
contended for a repeal of the two acts
which had been so warmly contested in
the preceding cession, they were defended
with zeal, and their continuance was
declared to be necessary. The duke of
Bedford recommended the removal of
the ministers on the grounds of public
expediency; but the votes of the house

sanctioned the prolongation of their power.

The people now began to manifest a spirit more resolutely hostile to the ruling party than they had before displayed. This zeal appeared in the presentation of a great number of addresses to the king from the counties and corporations of Great Britain and Ireland, advising a dismission of his ministers. Some addresses, of an opposite nature, were also voted in different meetings.

In many of the anti-ministeral applications to his majesty, indignant mention was made of the disordered state of Ireland; and the same subject was investigated in both houses. After fruitless efforts to stigmatise the late neglect of the naval defence of that kingdom, motions for such an interference from the sovereign as might allay the discontent of the people were brought forward by the earl of Moira and Mr. Fox. The benevolent peer recommended the substitution of lenient measures for the coercive rigor which the ministers were so fond of exercising; but the lords were unwilling to admit that the proceedings of the government were too severe, or that the advice of the British parliament was necessary or justifiable on this occasion. Mr. Fox and other speakers imputed the disturbances of Ireland to the misconduct of the cabinet; but the majority refused to agree to an address which suggested the propriety of moderation.

In July, the last month of this session, the country was deprived, by death, of the political exertions of one of the greatest men of the age—Mr. Edmund Burke. He had for some time retired from parliament, having resigned his seat to his son, whose decease in the flower of his age was a great shock to his declining parent. That Mr. Burke possessed great abilities, and a genius superior to that which is usually observed among mankind, will not, we think, be denied by any one. He had a great compass of mind, a considerable share of learning, and a never-failing stream of eloquence. He adorned every subject which he handled, and animated every speech with the excursions of fancy and the charms of imagery. His allusions, however, were sometimes of the coarsest kind, drawn from the lowest objects of nature and of art. He was too digressive, frequently deficient in argument, and so absurdly hyperbolical, that he would magnify a speck to an immense body, or, if it equally suited the temporary purpose of his oratory, would diminish a mountain to a mole-hill. His invectives, both in speaking and writing, were so bitter and severe, that they seemed to argue a malignity of disposition, though they rather proceeded from an irritability of temper. His political principles were more favorable to aristocratical claims than to popular freedom; and he was in his heart a Tory even when he affected (during the American war) to be a zealous Whig. In private life he was generally benevolent and friendly; a kind husband, father, and master. He was a pleasing and instructive companion; and no one could long be a witness to his conversation without being convinced of the extent of his knowledge and the vigor of his mind.

HISTORY OF THE WAR.

CHAP. XIV.

Reflections on the Successes of the French—Enumeration of their Conquests—Conduct and Policy of Buonaparte—Remarks on the late Campaign in Germany—Affairs of Russia—Accession of the Emperor Paul, and its Results—Commencement of the Second Campaign in Italy—Singular Skill and Splendid Triumphs of Buonaparte—The Effects of his Good Fortune on the Minds of the French.

IT would be useless to enlarge on the astonishing succession of events which distinguished the campaign of 1796, in Italy. Piedmont invaded, and the king of Sardinia reduced to the necessity of concluding an ignominious peace,—Lombardy subdued ; both banks of the Po republicanized,—the king of Naples detached from the coalition ; the pope deprived of one-third of. his dominions ; the north of Italy a prey to the miseries of war, and to political convulsions ; a country, notwithstanding the prevalence of indolence, superstition, and immorality, the most rich and fertile of continental Europe, robbed of its most valuable treasures, and its most admirable productions of antient and modern genius.— Such is the picture presented to the observer by this memorable campaign, which will equally excite the regret and the admiration of posterity, and be commemorated in the annals of modern warfare, as only equalled in the importance and rapidity of its events by that of 1706. In that year the French were masters of Lombardy, and of the city and duchy of Mantua. One of their armies occupied these territories, while another besieged Turin. After the battle of Cagliano, gained by the duke de Vendome over general Reventlaw, prince Eugene was obliged to retreat as far as Roveredo and Gavardo, but he speedily resumed the offensive, and advanced early in May as far as Verona. Two months afterwards he passed the Adige, notwithstanding all the efforts of the duke of Orleans, upon whom he had stolen several marches. He entered Piedmont, and endeavoured to raise the siege of Turin, after having gained a decisive victory over the French army. Returning, he re-entered the Milanese. successively drove the French from all their posts, and obliged them to evacuate Lombardy.

No one had contributed so much to the issue of the late campaign as the commander-in-chief : none of the generals of the republic had performed services so important and so difficult. He was the only individual entrusted with command. Active, enterprizing, able, and, above all, fortunate, he had committed few military faults, had not suffered his adversaries to commit any with impunity, and had not in person experienced one defeat. He made the war of Italy, which till 1796 had been an episode only of the general war, his principal and leading object, and, where the emperor appeared to entertain the slightest apprehension of disaster, occasioned him to experience the most afflicting losses and the most serious alarms.

If Buonaparte, as a general, deserved

the admiration of mankind, his conduct as a conquerer and a man, was not less impolitic than atrocious. The cruelty with which he treated the towns of Milan, Pavia, Lugo, and Arquata, the burning of Binasio and several other villages, the outrages and pillages perpetrated beneath his sanction, have tarnished the splendor of his victories, and left him no other claims to the admiration of posterity. The despotism which he exercised over the countries conquered by his arms, the excessive contributions which he imposed on the inhabitants, and the extreme and vindictive rigor with which he enforced the most sanguinary or rapacious measures of the French government, had fortunately contributed to weaken the admiration and enthusiasm which his triumphs might have produced among the Italian people. That nation must have been destitute of the common feelings of human nature, which could have remained unmoved by resentment and abhorrence at the declaration of Buonaparte, that all the expenses of the army of Italy, during eleven months, had been paid by the conquered countries, and that he had sent 30,000,000 of livres (£1,250,000) to France.

If Buonaparte, by his political conduct, placed himself below the height to which he had been elevated by his military triumphs, he was still less successful in supporting his reputation as a soldier, by the display of his personal qualities. The bombast, the boasting, and the love of the marvellous, which characterise all his letters to the directory, the constant exaggeration of the losses of the enemy, the absurdly diminished estimate of his own, the perpetual representation of the destruction of the Austrian armies, when they had only been repulsed, the annunciations of the expected capture of Mantua so many months before that event occurred, the assertion that 4000 men laid down their arms at Lonado, in submission to his command, gave to his narrative the appearance of a military romance, and have left behind them reasonable doubts, not of the reality of his victories, but of the extent of their results.

At the end of the campaign, immediately subsequent to the conclusion of peace with the Roman pontiff, the loss of Buonaparte had amounted to within 15,000 men of that sustained by the Austrians. That the loss of the victors should so nearly approximate to that of the conquered can only be attributed to the indifference with which Buonaparte always lavished the blood of his soldiers, an indifference to which he was indebted for much of his success, in the affairs of Lodi, Fonteniva, and Arcola. The mortality was rendered still more destructive by the diseases arising from the climate, the blockade of Mantua, and the intemperance of the soldiers.

After having sustained so many losses and expenses, the cabinet of Vienna formed, during this campaign, six powerful armies in Italy, and made greater efforts and displayed greater resources towards its close than at its commencement. Though its exertions might have been more successful had they been carried to their full extent at an earlier period, its conduct may be attributed to the obvious policy of reserving its means in a war of which it was easy to foresee the long duration. Even the means of warfare actually supplied, would have commanded success, had they been directed with ability. But the Austrian generals in Italy persisted in their antient plan of tactics, while the archduke was advantageously adopting new ones in Germany. Their mode of carrying on the war was methodical and slow, while those of Buonaparte were rapid and adventurous. They were occupied in making combinations while he was fighting battles ; they were making demonstrations on all points, while he considered it as indispensible to concentrate his forces so as to present a single aspect ; they extended themselves and endeavoured to circumvent him by their manœuvres, while he contracted his lines and positions, and, advancing rapidly en masse, broke in a moment the lines and the combination they had formed against him. It was to this system combined with other changes in the conduct of military operations, to which it will be necessary, as soon as I have closed the history of the next campaign, to devote a separate chapter, that he owed the victories of Melesimo, Montechiaro, Castiglione, Roveredo, and Rivoli : it was by the rapid transpositions and the unremitted employment of his troops that he gained the most brilliant successes in the months of August, November, and January ; and that at each of these periods, in less than six days, he concerted plans and dispersed armies which had occupied two months in their formation and arrangement. Several secondary causes contributed to the issue of the campaign. The council of war at Vienna, chose, as it had done in former years, not only to prepare the general plan of the campaign, but to direct its execution, and the local application of particular manœuvres. The Austrian generals, afraid to undertake any enterprise contrary to their positive instructions, and less responsible for events than for their obedience to the orders received, were frequently obliged to sacrifice the most favorable opportunities of success, and were less desirous to obtain applause than to escape censure. The first dispositions of the Austrians being made with care, exactness, and often with ability ; and the general executing them with scrupulous fidelity, were almost always crowned with temporary success. But when the talents of the enemy or the vicissitudes of war produced any unforeseen event, and reduced the Austrian generals to the necessity of deviating from the plan dictated at Vienna, and to reliance on their own discretion, their failure was nearly inevitable. Unaccustomed to obey the dictates of their own judgment, and fearing to commit themselves, they were incompetent and unwilling to act independently, and did not hazard those decisive movements which on many occasions would have secured an easy victory.

Buonaparte had very ably employed a means of securing success very different from military skill or personal bravery. Imitating the prince Eugene, he spared no exertion or expense, in procuring faithful spies, and obtaining the secrets of his enemies, while the Austrian generals, having little money to devote to the same object, were entirely unacquainted with the designs and intrigues of their adversary.

The theatre of war was, during the campaign of 1796, very disadvantageous to the Austrians. The mountains of Piedmont and the Tyrol, are extremely difficult of access. The valleys which separate them are covered with mulberry-trees and vines, planted in hedge-rows or in arbors, forming narrow covered ways, which must be forced by the soldier one after the other. The roads are defiles lined with walls, and are nevertheless the only places where the cavalry can act. The ground in Lombardy is not more favorable for war. It is not mountainous, but is equally divided by vine and mulberry-hedges, and the culture of rice requires a vast number of ditches full of water, which are no less embarrassing. A general must not hope to direct the movements of his troops on the ground ; he can only manœuvre on maps, and, according to the whole of his position taken together. In a country like this, where every footstep is difficult and dangerous, he is obliged to fight with a musket weighing eighteen pounds, to carry sixty cartridges, a very heavy knapsack, and a cloak around his breast, which almost stifles him. In this condition he is obliged to contend with the French soldier, whose musket weighs no more than a fowling-piece, who has nothing but a wretched coat upon his back, and whose natural agility and courage peculiarly qualify him for the species of warfare prosecuted by Buonaparte.

Every new system of military manœuvre and disposition have succeeded in war from the Macedonian phalanx to the tactics of Frederic. The French are indebted for a great part of their successes to the new mode of fighting which they have adopted. They precipitate themselves like a swarm of wasps on all the points which they desire to force. Fifty drums, attached to every army of 10,000 men, beat the charge without ceasing. At this noise, which animates the assailants and intimidates those who are to await their attack, the bravest advance, shouting and mutually encouraging each other. The youngest generals placed themselves at their head and shared their dangers. The timid mass followed at a distance and filled up the ground. Artillery contributed but little to the successes of the French in Italy. They generally charged with the bayonet. The Austrian army, had it been well managed, would have been the first in Europe. But nothing was done to animate and invigorate the spirit and loyalty of the soldier. He was left to all the horrors of his profession : the idea of killing or being killed was constantly presented to his mind, naked and unqualified. It was never forgotten in the enthusiasm of honor, by the sound of military music and the rolling of the drum. At the moment of action they sent into the rear the music and the colours, the most effectual stimulus to enterprize, and so often the pledge of victory and of the devotion of the soldiers. It was thus that an army perfectly organized and supplied with all the necessaries and all the requisites to successful war, was so often beaten by forces very inferior in their discipline, arrangement, and composition. Positions and entrenchments were always the chief dependence of the Austrians, though they were always carried. In the late contest, the obstacles presented by inanimate nature and by the usual means of artificial defence, were despised and overcome by the living and active energy of an able general and an enthusiastic soldiery.

We have seen that the most vigorous efforts made in the late campaign 1797. to bring the trial of strength and resources to an issue proved ineffectual. The pride of France had been flattered by the prudent but pusillanimous conduct of the king of Spain and other powers, which, after confederating to prevent the French republic from tyrannizing over Europe, had, like the Dutch states, tamely submitted to become subservient to its ambitious views. But France had still a confederacy to contend with ; of which the positive strength was still great, and the misfortunes were counterbalanced by the exhaustion of its rival. The Austrians had yielded to the enthusiastic ardor with which Buonaparte and his subordinate generals had inspired their troops in Italy ; but they had repulsed the armies of Jourdan and Moreau in Germany, and had foiled those generals in their grand design of prescribing terms of peace to the emperor at the gates of Vienna. The French continued to find in Great Britain a foe, who was determined to maintain the independence of Europe, and to assert her own pre-eminence on the seas or perish in the attempt. The late negotiation had failed of success, not only from the want of a cordial disposition towards peace, but from the wide difference of sentiment respecting the terms on which it was to be concluded. It had now become evident, that, before France could accomplish its purpose of making the Rhine its boundary, Austria must experience further humiliation ; and that before Great Britain could be brought to follow the example of other confederates in crouching under the arm of France, her naval force must be overpowered, and her government distressed by an invasion of her dominions. These were the objects of the present campaign, in the attainment of which the directory, while they were favored by the perilous situation of their adversaries, were themselves exposed to many difficulties and discouragements. To the extreme embarrassment of their financial system, to the molestation which they continually dreaded from the Jacobins on the one hand and the royalists on the other, and to the discontent which pervaded the whole body of the people, was now added the alarm excited by the intelligence of a formidable revolt of the negroes in St. Domingo, a further account of which event will be given in the history of the ensuing year.

These circumstances presented difficulties to the French directory, of the most discouraging kind ; but they knew that the existence of their own power depended in surmounting them, and their hopes were elevated by the remembrance of their past successes, and the promises of Spain and the Dutch states to assist the naval force of France with strong reinforcements. Their confidence was still further augmented by the death of the empress Catharine of Russia, an event which was expected to have a material influence on the affairs of Europe. That politic princess, though hostile to the French republic from political principles and rivalship in power, had availed herself of the remoteness of her dominions from the seat of war, and the ardor with which the southern potentates had confederated against France, and had suffered and encouraged them to exhaust their strength in the contest, while she steadily applied to the extension and organization of her own resources. But when she was informed of the triumphs of the French army in Italy, and perceived that every campaign gave some new accession to the territory of the republic, she became apprehensive lest the balance of power should be entirely destroyed, and the foundations of her own empire be ultimately shaken by political convulsions. Her people, she feared, might be awakened from their lethargy by the successes of the republicans, and, with the assistance of a powerful state which had proffered its services to all who were disposed to claim their freedom, might make a vigorous and dangerous effort to throw off the yoke of absolute power. To guard against these evils she had prepared an army of 150,000 men, to co-operate with the German emperor, when death, as we have seen, put a termination to her enterprizes, at the close of the last year. She was succeeded upon the throne, by her son, the emperor Paul, who was then in his thirty-sixth year. Unfortunately for this monarch, and for the Russian nation, personal dislike or jealousy had induced his mother to keep him at a distance from the seat of government : and he came to the throne not only deficient in understanding, but unacquainted with the world, unconversant in business of

state, and unqualified to discharge the duties of his station. Hence arose the ignorance, self-conceit, eccentricity, and perverseness which he so frequently displayed ; qualities peculiarly ruinous in an absolute monarchy. In free countries much depends on the genius of the age, the national taste, and the character and disposition of the people ; but, under a despotism, every thing is subjected to the personal influence of the sovereign. On the death of Catharine, the gaiety and the elegant amusements of the court gave way to military parade : the fine arts, which are the constant attendants on polished manners, were checked in the progress they had made during the two last reigns ; and, while the people at large were indifferent to the change, all who had been honoured by the personal notice of the empress, lamented the loss of a sovereign who had made her court the scene of cheerfulness and urbanity. The change of policy on the accession of her son, was not less remarkable or less to be regretted than the contrast of manners. Stimulated by mistaken policy, or by a determination to oppose the councils of his mother, he adopted a line of policy more favorable to the interests of France, and ordered the march of the troops to be countermanded. Sensible that he should be compelled to comply with most exorbitant demands of France, should the result of the next campaign prove unfavorable to his arms, the emperor of Austria spared no exertion that might contribute to augment the strength and the numbers of his armies. Within a few weeks after the battle of Arcola, Alvinzi was again at the head of an army with which he dared to confront the enemy. His forces amounted to nearly 50,000 men, among whom were a great number of young gentlemen of fortune, who repaired as volunteers to the imperial standard.

Buonaparte perceiving that it was the intention of his enemy to force his posts on the Adige, and advancing to the walls of Mantua to oblige him to raise the siege by co-operating with the garrison under Wurmser, was constrained once more to interrupt his operations before that fortress, and march to the support of Massena and Joubert, who were already engaged with the Austrians. On receiving intelligence that Joubert had been forced to retire before a superior army to Rivoli, he hastened, after strengthening Augereau's division on the Adige, with a strong reinforcement to the support of Joubert, of whose division he took the command in person. Unfortunately for the Austrian general he was totally unapprized of the arrival of Buonaparte, and of the reinforcements that accompanied him. He adhered to the plan of attack which he had previously projected, nor did he discover the real strength of the French till they had commenced their attack upon the Austrians, whom they drove from a post which had been occupied on the preceding day. This first success was obtained early in the morning of the 14th. It enabled general Joubert to occupy the high grounds on the right bank of the Adige, and to make an impression on the left of the Austrians. But their right assailed the left wing of the French so vigorously, that it gave way, and the centre of the Austrian army bore down in compact order on the centre of the French. Massena's division arrived at this instant, as the commander-in-chief had expected, on the field of battle. Buonaparte, who had succeeded in rallying his left wing, put himself at the head of this division. It fell with so much fury on the imperial centre, that the latter was instantly broken and thrown into disorder ; and the left of the French having been rallied, recovered the posts it had lost. But the Austrian centre also rallied, seconded by part of their right, returned to the charge, and surrounded general Berthier's division in the centre, which stood its ground with great firmness. He was attacked at the same time by a strong division from their left. The conflict at this point was extremely obstinate. But, while the Austrians were attempting to turn the centre and right of the French, who had concentrated both to resist the weight of the enemy's charge. Buonaparte directed a

large body of infantry and cavalry to take them in flank, and Joubert at the same instant fell upon them from the heights he had occupied with such impetuosity, that they were entirely routed and put to flight. Their centre, however, still maintained the contest, and, afforded time for a large column to turn the left of the French, and to cover the ground on their rear, by which their communication was cut off with Verona, and their posts on the lake of Garda. The republican forces were thus entirely surrounded. Wherever they cast their eyes they beheld the enemy. Buonaparte, who had fought in person during the whole day, was now driven to the centre. He called his field-officers around him, and coolly pointed out to each what he judged to be the least perilous means of extricating themselves from their imminent danger.

The Austrians, after a general discharge, rushed on to scale the entrenchments at Rivoli, of which they were three times in possession, but were successively repulsed. In the mean time a small battery of four field-pieces, had been brought to cannonade the right wing of the Austrians, through which Buonaparte at first meditated his escape, though he now resumed his expectations of victory. Two brigades, in three columns, under generals Brune and Monnier, were ordered to attack this wing and dislodge it from the commanding position which it occupied on the heights. This desperate service the soldiers effected, advancing at first in regular order, singing one of their war hymns. But they no sooner approached within gun-shot of the enemy than they rushed upon them with impetuosity. The Austrians, confounded and overwhelmed by the violence of the assailants, fled panic-struck towards the lake of Garda, and, meeting with a straggling party of light infantry, who were endeavouring to join the surrounded French army, whom they supposed to be a more considerable body, laid down their arms, to the number of 3000 men

The French army was now disengaged, and the main strength of the Austrians broken, but there still remained considerable divisions, without the dispersion or the capture of which, the victory obtained over them would not be complete, as they would either throw themselves into Mantua, join the papal forces, or retreat into the imperial territories, where they would contribute to the formation of a new army.

Not a moment therefore was to be lost in preventing the vanquished Austrians from effecting their retreat. On the night of the 14th, as soon as the battle had terminated in favor of the French, divisions were immediately dispatched to pursue the flying bodies of Austrians. They had not quitted a strong position at Corona, near Rivoli, where they remained in expectation of being able to collect and arrange their retreating troops: but, before this object could be accomplished, a large division of the French, after marching with the utmost expedition during the night of the 14th, fell upon their rear next morning while they were attacked in front by general Joubert. They resisted vigorously at first, but were afterwards thrown into disorder. Those who were able to effect a retreat, directed their flight towards the Tyrol; but 6000 of their troops were completely surrounded, and obliged to lay down their arms.

Buonaparte himself, with a strong division, having left the necessary orders with general Joubert, proceeded, immediately after the battle, in quest of Provera, who, at the head of 10,000 men, had crossed the Adige, compelled the French who guarded the passages to retire, and was proceeding with rapidity towards Mantua. But he was overtaken early in the morning of the 15th, by general Angereau, who cut off the whole of his rear. He made his way by a running fight to the French lines of circumvallation at Mantua, where he arrived at noon, after losing 2000 men, and 14 pieces of cannon. He was now reduced, by the various encounters on his march, to no more than 6000 men. With this diminished force he did not, however, hesitate to assault the entrenchments of the besiegers at the suburb of St. George, by carrying which, he would have secured his entrance into the city; but they were

so strong and well defended, that he was repulsed. His situation was now so critical, that, unless he could enter Mantua, he must yield to the enemy. To avoid this disaster, Provera made a resolute attack on the French post of La Favorita, another suburb, while a detachment from the garrison supported him. But this attempt, which was made on the night of the 15th, in the hope of surprising the enemy, failed in every point. The Austrians who had sallied out of the city, were beaten in all directions by general Victor, and general Serrurier proceeded to occupy a position between La Favorita and St. George, which secured this latter station, and enabled the corps by which it had been defended to join Serrurier. Thus reinforced, he fell upon Provera's rear, while his front was occupied in the attack of La Favorita, and other troops advanced upon him at the same time. Thus surrounded on every side, all hope of assistance from the garrison was abandoned, and he was compelled to surrender with his whole remaining force, consisting of nearly 6000 horse and foot, and 22 pieces of cannon. The disaster was rendered still more lamentable and unfortunate by the fate of young gentlemen of Vienna, who were all either slain or taken prisoners.

The issue of this day decided the fate of Mantua. Though it continued to make a courageous defence, it was evident that, being now deprived of all reasonable hope of relief, further resistance would only add to the numbers of those who had fallen in this destructive siege. Every day brought fresh tidings of the losses and defeats of the Austrians. The battle of Arcola had destroyed the fourth, and the battle of Rivoli the fifth, of the armies opposed to Buonaparte. He had, since the commencement of the year, been 1797. victorious in eight engagements, in which the loss of the Austrians amounted to 25,000 prisoners, exclusive of the slain, who were calculated at 6000. The various bodies of Austrians were now retreating to their strong holds on the Brenta, which Alvinzi was employed in rendering tenable against the pursuing enemy. But the expeditious movements of the French afforded him no respite. General Angereau crossed the Lower Brenta, and advanced to Citadella, a place of strength, from whence he dislodged the enemy, while Massena, passing it in front of Bassano, compelled the Austrians to evacuate it with precipitation, though they had prepared to defend it. They withdrew to Carpanodolo, higher up the river, but were pursued and defeated by the French, who forced their passage over the bridge at that place, after an obstinate conflict, in which they slew and captured 1000 of the fugitives. The heavy rains alone prevented their entire destruction, and enabled them to hasten to the narrow passes of the entrance into the Tyrol. A division of the French under Joubert overtook them at Avis, and a part of their rearguard was taken. They retired to Tortona, a place advantageously situated between the lake of Garda and the Adige, where they made preparations for disputing the march of the French to Trent, but they were driven from this post, and fled to Roveredo, which also they were compelled to abandon by Joubert, who, pursuing his success, made himself master of Trent, where 2000 sick and wounded fell into his hands, in addition to the same number, which had been made prisoners in the various encounters previous to the taking of the city.

The Austrians had now posted themselves at Lavis in considerable force, intending to stop the progress of the French by occupying the other side of the river Lavisio; but this intention was frustrated by the rapid advance of Joubert, who forced them from this important position, after sustaining a great loss of their best troops, and in particular of a select corps of Hungarians. At this place the division of Joubert was reinforced by that of Massena, who had been equally successful; and in his pursuit of the Austrians after the battle of Carpanodolo, had taken several places of strength, and driven them to the other side of the Pradas, after seizing a large part of their baggage.

The imperial armies were now totally expelled from Italy, and nothing remained to the emperor but the city of Mantua, which was so closely blockaded and so vigorously pressed, that no supplies of provisions or of men could enter. The garrison, despairing of relief, and weakened by the slaughter sustained in so many sallies, as well as by a contagious distemper, clamoured for surrender; and, on the 2nd day of February, Wurmser agreed to a capitulation. The terms were as honourable as the defence had been brave. The French general was anxious to pay due regard to the merit of his rival. He granted him an escort of 200 horse and 700 foot, whom he was permitted to select; the generals and principal officers were allowed to accompany him on parole; but the rest of the garrison remained prisoners of war.

The joy excited in France by this event, was proportioned to its importance. When the executive directory informed the legislative body of the occurrence, Villetard, mounting the tribune of the council of Five Hundred, exclaimed, " The proud Mantua has at last fallen into the power of the republic! Thanks to that army of heroes, whose successes have astonished Italy herself, formerly the theatre of the most glorious feats of arms. Thus, all the sinister projects of the enemies of the liberty of the people are crushed. Vile partisans of tyranny, pain yourselves in fabricating obscure conspiracies; contrive against the people imposture and perfidy; and devote to assassination their most intrepid defenders. These means are worthy of you and of your cause. Republicans triumph in the fields of honour. It is there, I predict, that your projects will be confounded, and your outrages expiated. How long shall these cowardly Sybarites pretend to give fetters to the valiant? Pigmies, who fashion in darkness the yoke of tyranny, with *aides, gabelles, corvees*, feudal rights, tenths, and other oppressions, do you flatter yourselves with replunging into slavery, misery, and debasement, the generous children of victory? No: I call eternal reason to witness, which wishes not that victorious France be hereafter so degraded. Perfidious men! they have lured our credulity by the words of humanity and justice; but this illusion of the most infamous hypocrisy is dissipated; the veil has dropt, and their plan of oppression been manifested to every eye. Every thing the most abominable, which the ingenious cruelty of butchers has invented,—such was the first gift which these men, so just and humane, prepared for the French nation on the advent of their regal domination.

"You feel indignant, magnanimous heroes, whom devotion to liberty has assembled in our camps, and whose toils the universe contemplates with admiration. Yes, such was the price which royalism reserved for your constancy, for the numerous evils you have suffered, for the blood you have shed for your fathers, for your wives, and for your children, slavery, ignominy, and punishments. But repose in your representatives; they view, with stoical firmness, the poignards directed by royalism against their breasts. Calm in the midst of dangers and the clamours of royalism, they will render impotent its efforts. They remain unshaken in the determination of confirming the present government, the lasting monument of your liberty, reared by the national convention, and consecrated by the French people;— by that convention, whose inflexible justice was directed against the last of your tyrants, and whose firmness has dissipated the league of kings, disconcerted all the plots formed in the interior against the people, and overcome obstacles regarded as insurmountable;—that convention, whose members have so often conducted you to victory, and who are still honoured with the hatred of bad citizens, which they have drawn on themselves by their efforts and their successes against tyranny. Yes, brave soldiers, the representatives of the French people, whom you immortalize by your victories, are united with you in heart, in object, and in will, for maintaining that government which has freed you from slavery, and restores you to your proper dignity. It is not to be again subjugated and oppressed by the cowardly slaves of a tyrant, that you have proved yourselves invincible; glory, liberty, and equality, the honourable purpose of your toils, shall be their reward. And you, brave Lombard legion, whose first steps in the career of liberty are signalized by victories,—you also have acquired claims to the gratitude of the republic and of the friends of liberty. Receive, as the guarantee of this, the new civic crown, with which the legislative body, the organ of the national gratitude, hastens to encircle your victorious brows."

The language of the members of the council of antients was no less remarkable for its energy and declamatory eloquence. In particular, the representative Lacombe-St-Michel delivered an impressive speech: "The clouds," said he, "which obscured the morning of the fair days, that liberty seemed some months ago to promise Italy, are at length dissipated, and Mantua is taken. Yes, successors of Camillus and the Catos, you shall be free. Engrave for ever, in the calendar of your *fasti*, the eternal gratitude you owe to the brave army of Italy,—to that army, and to the bold and intrepid genius of its chief, every step of whose progress beyond the Alps was itself a wonder. Those, who for eight years have fought for the establishment and confirmation of their own liberty, are doubtless well entitled to experience a lively transport, on beholding the triumph that secures the liberty of a sister republic. Far be from us the idea, that the war we maintain in Italy against the house of Austria, whose insulting pride, humiliated by so many victories, still presumes to question the existence of a French republic; far be from us, I say, the idea, that this war has for its object only a diplomatic project, to obtain from the emperor the countries conquered by the French armies, or to subjugate a people whom the love of liberty has already united to us! No, descendants of the Romans, think not that the French government, after having engaged you to march under the tri-coloured standard, entertains a design of enchaining you again, by restoring you to your former masters. No;—you would be unjust, should you be suspicious of our honour ; you have fought by the side of our phalanxes for the cause of liberty ; let liberty be your reward. It is one of the invariable principles of the French nation, to respect the government of every country, whatever may be its form ; but it is also dear to the hearts of the friends of liberty, to regard with complaisance the efforts of nations who wish to be free. To anticipate the future happiness of your destiny, and applaud that dignified sentiment, which recalls the picture of the fair days the French enjoyed with unanimity in 1789, is a moment of pleasure, which the austere wisdom of the council of antients will not disapprove. Let us pity the Frenchmen, who are base enough to proclaim the disasters of their country, while they diminish the importance of events favourable to liberty. May you, Cispadane republic, never know such unnatural children ! May the conquest of the happy land, where Virgil was born, be the certain omen of your brilliant destiny ! May you never experience the dreadful and numerous shocks, of which the French republic was so long the theatre ! Profit by our faults,—guard against our divisions ; and if ever discord attempts to brandish her torch between the two republics, let gratitude remind you what we have effected for your good ; and let prudence advertise you, that the common enemy will be ever on the watch to profit of our errors.—And you, brave army of Italy, it is no longer our province to appoint festivals in honour of your victories ; this care was reserved for the government. But it is permitted each of us to manifest, in this tribune, his impatience to approve the resolution, which, without doubt, will be adopted, that the army of Italy ceases not to deserve well of its country."

The intelligence of the capitulation of Mantua was published at Paris by sound of trumpet, and with a solemnity suiting an event, the consequences of which were so important to the operations of the campaign. Numerous detachments of troops of the line accompanied the public officer, who proclaimed the glory of the French arms in the midst of an immense multitude,

that seemed to share in it in the most sensible manner, and proceeded through the streets with the same enthusiasm which produced the wonders they celebrated. From the gaiety of their countenances it might be said, on learning they were French soldiers, that they were marching to battle. The sedentary national guard, wishing also to render homage to the conquerors of Mantua, hastened to send deputations to assist at the proclamation, and bore, with pride, the arms which they knew how to employ with the same readiness in succouring the victors.

The enthusiasm, excited by the triumphs of this army, was real and sincere with the greater part of Frenchmen ; but a numerous party already regarded them as the ruin of their hopes. An appropriate idea may be formed of the spirit, which began to display itself even in the councils, when it is learned, that the following motion could not find a proper support among men, who enjoyed there the greatest credit. Not but that many would have desired its success ; the fear, however, of not obtaining it, and the disagreement it might have occasioned respecting a general whom they venerated, hindered them from hazarding the motion. The purport of it was, that unlooked-for success called for extraordinary rewards : Hannibal performed not, in Italy, what Buonaparte had effected there ; Scipio, in Africa, did not surpass him ; and grateful Rome honoured her general with the name of Africanus. Spain ennobles her chiefs with the like glorious surnames ; thus, she has bestowed that of *Prince of Peace* on the minister, who signed the treaty granted her by France. Russia neglects not this mode of recompense, and the conqueror of the Crimea acquired the surname of *Tauricus*. This species of reward is truly republican, for Rome employed it in her best days, and it will make all the scarfs and batons of monarchy be forgotten.." The Frenchman, who, in a campaign of eight months, has forced the king of the Alps to put their keys for ever in our possession, the sovereign of the two Sicilies to a necessary peace, and the dukes of Parma and Modena, the one to pay us a tribute, and the other to fly from his states ; the Frenchman, who has shut up from the English all the ports of Italy, paralised their fleet in the Mediterranean, and re-conquered Corsica, without even allowing them to fight ; the Frenchman, who, by the most memorable victories, has torn from the hands of arrogant Austria, all the countries of Italy submissive to her yoke, and made five imperial armies and Mantua, fall before the tri-coloured ensign ; the Frenchman, who has recovered at papal Rome, the trophies which adorned the Roman republic, and given to France, now alone worthy of possessing them, those master-pieces of art, the happy fruits of the genius of Greece when free ; this Frenchman, who will destroy (let us at least hope so) in sacerdotal Rome, the focus from whence all our civil discords emanated, and whose uninterrupted triumphs promise us peace at home and abroad, assuredly merits the surname of ITALICUS, and the legislative body owes this honourable de-cree to his worth."

After humbling or rather annihilating the power and importance annexed to the see of Rome, the political views of the re-public were directed to the means of pre-venting their recovery by any future pontiff. They therefore planned and encouraged the confederation of a republic composed of the states of Reggio, Modena, Bologna, Ferrara, and Romagna, and assented to the petition of the people of the Milanese and the other districts of Lombardy who were willing to follow the last mentioned example, by framing a republican compact on a similar plan.

In addition to these measures, others were taken not less conducive to remove the charge of inhumanity against the French government than to gratify the Italians. As the laws enacted in France against the refractory clergy, though condemning them to banishment, did not forbid their resi-dence in the countries conquered by the French, Buonaparte availed himself of the powers with which he was invested, to issue a proclamation in favor of these exiles. He granted them a formal permission to reside in those parts of the pope's dominions

which had been subdued by the armies of the republic. The French troops were strictly forbidden to maltreat or insult them, and the inhabitants of the country were laid under the same restrictions. These refugees were to be provided with all the necessaries of life at the expense of the convents appointed for their residence ; and were, in return, enjoined to take an oath of fidelity to the French government. This permission extended not only to all those who had already taken refuge in the papal territories occupied by the republic, but also to those remaining in France who were desirous of availing themselves of the same indulgence. While Buonaparte was thus endeavouring to secure the attachment and respect of a numerous body of men, whose influence, even after their emigration, was powerful and extensive, the directory were endeavouring to degrade the Roman catholic religion and its clergy, by the public exhibition of the relics taken at Loretto.

In order to conciliate the minds of the Italian people to the republic, Buonaparte was particularly solicitous since his appoint-ment to the chief command, to distinguish himself by a punctual observance of all those maxims on which the zealous and sincere republicans chiefly prided them-selves. He cautiously avoided all ostenta-tion, and, in his personal demeanour, readily put himself on a footing of equality with every individual of respectable station in society. By the adoption of this mode of conduct he had obtained a number of friends, not only among the French, but among the Italians, who had hitherto ex-perienced little of that condescension from the Germans, who seldom studied to render their authority acceptable to the natives. The influence, on the contrary, which Buonaparte had acquired by his address, was not inferior to that which he had ob-tained by his exploits. His courtesy to the little republic of St. Marino, situated in the duchy of Urbino, confirmed the favorable prepossessions of the Italian people. He deputed thither citizen Monge, one of the commissioners of arts and a member of the National Institute, a man of genius and knowledge. The commissioner made a speech to the people of St. Marino, in which he observde, that liberty which had transformed the antient Greeks into heroes, and in latter ages had advanced the arts and sciences in the republics of Italy, had, while nearly banished from the face of Europe, still existed in St. Marino, where, by the wisdom of the government and the virtue of the people, it had been preserved for many centuries. "The French," he observed, "after a whole age of knowledge, had at length perceived their own slavery, and asserted their freedom. But the powers of Europe, shutting their eyes to the interests of mankind, had confederated against the interests of France, and had arranged among themselves the partition of the country. The French had been assailed on all their frontiers, and their calamities had been aggravated by the junction of many of their country-men with the enemy. They stood firm, however, notwithstanding the dangers which surrounded them, and gradually overcame all their enemies." The address concluded with a triumphant recapitulation of past successes, an enumeration of the disasters of the Austrians, and a promise to the people of St. Marino of the good offices of the French republic in defending their possessions, or adding to their dominion any adjacent territory that might appear necessary to their prosperity.

The answer to this address was respectful and temperate. The citizens of St. Marino declined those offers of addition to their small territory which had been made by the French commissioner, observing, that simplicity of manners, and the enjoyment of liberty, were the best inheritance transmitted by their ancestors ; and that, contented with mediocrity, they dreaded aggrandizement as dangerous to their freedom, and only solicited the protection of France.

Buonaparte had not merely distinguished himself by feats of arms : he had succeeded in another object equally requisite to the establishment of French influence. He strenuously endeavoured to revolutionize the minds of the Italians ; and, while he inflamed their imaginations by declamatory harangues on liberty, equality, and the

natural rights of mankind, he awakened and flattered their ambition by promising the restoration of Italy to its antient splendor. The remembrance of those celebrated names which every civilized people had regarded with veneration, was recalled with enthusiasm. Peculiar honors were paid to the birth-place of Virgil. A monument was erected to his memory, and similar memorials were intended to perpetuate the fame of other illustrious men who had adorned their country in antient or modern times.

At Faenza, the inhabitants erected a triumphal arch to Buonaparte and his army, specifying their victory over the papal army, and thereby securing the liberty of the city. The fact was, that the governments of Italy in the ecclesiastical state especially, were fallen so low in the estimation of the public, that a large proportion of the inhabitants were heartily desirous of a change. The clergy in the pope's dominions engrossed all the authority, and the other countries were in the hands of foreigners. Hence the national spirit of the natives was extinct, and they felt no interest in the transactions of their rulers; looking upon themselves as wholly unconcerned in the good or the ill success of their measures.

Notwithstanding the humiliating conditions to which the pope had been compelled to accede, he was destined to exhibit the mournful example of a state beset by a powerful enemy, who seemed to suffer its existence only to prolong its misery, and, languishing at the same time under all the internal disorders arising from temporal and spiritual tyranny. Destitute of the resources arising from agriculture, manufactures, and commerce, he was obliged to have recourse to the most unpopular expedients, to enable him to perform his pecuniary engagements with France. His subjects were required to bring the remainder of their plate to the treasury, and the ecclesiastics were called upon for the loan of a sixth part of their property at an interest of three per cent. These measures, however expedient, could not be adopted without exciting general dissatisfaction ; for the expedience of enormous taxes is not often admitted by those whom they distress. While therefore the unhappy pontiff was overwhelmed with grief and chagrin by the recent triumph of his enemies, and was meditating an escape from his dominions to liberate himself from a foreign oppressor, his cup of affliction was embittered by domestic discontent. The eyes of his subjects were now opened to the defects of his government, and they were prepared to "*fly to ills which they knew not of*," rather than endure the evils which they had so long sustained. Censures of his government were freely uttered ; songs and pasquinades were employed to render it odious, and the coercive means adopted to repress the spirit of disloyalty, only contributed to exasperate the national resentment.

THE ARCHDUKE CHARLES OF AUSTRIA.

HISTORY OF THE WAR.

Renewed Exertions of the Austrians—Appointment of the Archduke Charles to the Command of the Troops in Italy—Events of the Campaign to the Conclusion of the Armistice of Leoben—Internal State of Italy—Organization of the Cisalpine Republic—Invasion of the Venetian Territories by the French—Fall of Venice—Ratification of the Memorable Treaty of Campo Formio.

BUONAPARTE's combats with the Austrians resembled those of Hercules with the hydra of Lerna ; their armies were reproduced as soon as destroyed. The young archduke Charles had been successful in Germany, but had not acquired so much glory in forcing the French to evacuate it, as general Moreau had merited by one of the most skilful and difficult retreats, of which history has preserved the remembrance. Full of confidence in this prince, the court of Vienna thought, that, by calling him to the command of their forces in Italy, he would restore to them the superiority, which they had so long and so vainly disputed there. The greatest efforts were made to furnish him with a powerful army, and hostilities had commenced before Buonaparte granted peace to the pope.

Some skirmishes between the hostile armies were a prelude to more serious contests. General Guieux retook the post of Treviso on the 22nd of February ; and the advanced guard under general Walther, having encountered the imperialists in front of Lovadina, drove them back, and pursued them to their intrenchments on the Piava. Since the battle of Rivoli, the French occupied the banks of the Piava and the Lavisio, while prince Charles held the opposite bank of the Piava, having his centre posted behind the Cordevole, and his right supported by the Adige on the side of Salurn. On the 10th, the division of general Massena proceeded to Feltri, and the Austrians, evacuating the line of Cordevole, marched to Bellurn. General Serrurier's division advanced to Asolo during very stormy weather ; but wind and rain, on the eve of a battle, have always proved an omen of success to the army of Italy. This division crossed the Piava opposite the village of Vidor, on the 12th, and, having worsted an Austrian corps that attempted to oppose their passage, advanced rapidly to St. Salvador. But the enemy, having received intelligence of this, and afraid of being surrounded, abandoned their camp of La Campana. General Guieux passed the Piava at Ospedaletto, and arriving with his division at Sacile on the 13th, defeated their rearguard. Meanwhile, Massena's division having reached Bellurn, pursued the imperialists who had retreated towards Cadore, and surrounding their rearguard, took 700 prisoners, and, among them, general Lusignan, who commanded the centre of the army. This general having disgraced himself by his conduct towards the French sick at Brescia, Buonaparte gave orders to conduct him to France, without the liberty of being exchanged.

Early on the 16th, Guieux's division set out from Pordenone, that of Bernadotte left Sacile, and that of Serrurier proceeded from Pasiano, all directing their march to Valvasone. Guieux's division passed beyond it, and arrived on the banks of the Tagliamento at eleven o'clock of the day. The Austrian army was intrenched on the opposite side of the river, the passage of which it seemed determined to dispute. Bernadotte's division having arrived at noon, Buonaparte immediately ordered Guieux to proceed to the left, in order to cross the river, on the right of the enemy's entrenchments, under the protection of twelve pieces of artillery, general Bernadotte being directed to pass it at the same time on the right. Both divisions, having formed their battalions of grenadiers, ranged themselves in order of battle, each with a demi-brigade of light infantry in their front, supported by two battalions of grenadiers, and flanked by the cavalry ; the light infantry manœuvring as riflemen. After a brisk cannonade, Buonaparte gave orders for every demi-brigade to file off in close column, on the wings of their second, first, and third battalions. General Duphat, at the head of the twenty-seventh light infantry, threw himself into the river, and presently gained the opposite bank, being supported by general Bon, with the grenadiers of Guieux's division. General Murat made the same movement on the right, and was, in like manner, supported by the grenadiers of Bernadotte's division ; the whole French line putting itself in motion, each demi-brigade en echelons, with squadrons of cavalry placed at intervals in the rear. The imperial cavalry attempted several times to charge the French infantry, but without success ; the river was crossed, and the enemy routed in every direction. As they attempted to outline the right of the French with their cavalry, and the left with their infantry, general Dugua, and adjutant-general Kellerman were detached at the head of the cavalry of reserve, supported by a body of infantry under adjutant-general Mireur ; and having worsted the Austrian cavalry, took prisoner the general

who commanded them. Guieux ordered the village of Gradisca to be attacked, and, notwithstanding the darkness of the night, made himself master of it, after having completely defeated the enemy : prince Charles had just time enough to escape. Serrurier's division, as it arrived, passed the river, and ranged in order of battle to serve as a corps of reserve. In this affair, the French took six pieces of cannon, one general, several superior officers, and 400 or 500 prisoners. The quickness with which they formed and manœuvred, and the superiority of their artillery, so intimidated the hostile army, that the latter could not be brought to make a stand, and profited of the night to save themselves by flight.

The foresight of the directory had seconded every measure calculated to render certain the success of Buonaparte, and procure a glorious peace to the republic. Entire divisions had been drawn from the armies on the Rhine, and sent to Italy. Proceeding from the banks of that river, they traversed part of the republic, and surmounted, in the most rigorous season, the barrier of the Alps, till then deemed impervious. But general Kellerman, by dint of labour and vigilance, and struggling against climate, the elements, and the seasons, had succeeded in maintaining the free passage of the mountains. This march, the longest and the most difficult ever effected, on the continent, by an armed corps, during the winter season, enabled them, without experiencing any delay, and without being suspected, or perhaps believed, by the enemy, to contend in Carinthia with the men they had so often defeated on the other side of the Rhine. When these reinforcements formed a junction with the army of Italy, Buonaparte, who was supposed to be still before Rome, crossed the Trajamento, and shewed his troops, from the summit of the Noric Alps, (a barrier which no modern nation had hitherto passed,) the basons of the Adriatic and of the Danube, in the midst of which last, Vienna seemed to point out to them the termination or the object of their exploits. Thus Hannibal had formerly, from the crest of the Alps, shewn to his Carthaginians, the plains of that Italy, which he knew how to vanquish, but not to conquer. Scarcely had the campaign commenced, and scarcely, in climes more favorable, would they have thought of opening it, when Buonaparte already menaced the heart of the states of Austria. Nature was still dormant in these bleak regions, now become the theatre of war, when the mountains of the Tyrol and of Carinthia were scaled. Prince Charles was compelled to a continued and precipitate retreat, very different from that which had immortalized General Moreau, who led back his army, pursued indeed, but always victorious, from the banks of the Danube to the borders of the Rhine.

On the 18th, the division of general Bernadotte defiled by Palma-nova, and took a position on the Torre. General Serrurier took post on the right, and Guieux on the left, the citizen Lasalle being dispatched with the 24th regiment of chasseurs to Udina. The imperialists, on the approach of the French, evacuated Palma-nova, where the latter captured 30,000 rations of bread, and 1000 quintals of flour. It was only ten days since prince Charles had seized on this place, which belonged to the Venetians. His intention was to occupy it as a military post; but he had not time to establish himself in it. General Massena, proceeding by St. Daniel, Osopo, and Gemona, pushed his advanced guard into the defiles On the 19th, Bernadotte blockaded the fort of Gradisca, while Serrurier advanced opposite San Pietro for the purpose of passing the Lisonzo, on the other side of which the imperialists had several pieces of cannon and some battalions for defending the passage. Buonaparte ordered various manœuvres to be made with an intent to alarm the enemy; after which the passage was effected without opposition.

General Serrurier next proceeded to Gradisca, filing along the highest peaks that command the fort. To make a diversion, and prevent the Austrians from discovering this manœuvre, general

Bernadotte made the riflemen attack their entrenchments. But the French soldiers, impelled by their natural ardor, advanced with fixed bayonets to the walls of the town, where they were received by a very heavy discharge of musketry and grape-shot. In the mean time, Serrurier having gained the heights, rendered every means of retreat impossible to the garrison, who were equally convinced of the impracticability of defence. The governor accordingly agreed to a capitulation, his troops becoming prisoners of war. Three thousand prisoners, the flower of the army of prince Charles, ten pieces of cannon, and eight standards, were the fruits of this operation.

General Massena's division, having carried the fort of La Chiusa, encountered a body of imperialists, who attempted to dispute the passage of the bridge of Casasola. His grenadiers, in close column, forced the bridge, and, having beaten the enemy, notwithstanding their intrenchments and chevaux-de-frise, pursued them as far as Ponteba. Six hundred men of the regiments lately brought from the Rhine were taken prisoners; and all the magazines, which the Austrians had on this side of the river, fell into the hands of the French.

The capture of the fortress of Gradisca procured advantages, of which the French general hastened to profit. He addressed a proclamation to the inhabitants of the province of Goritia, with an intent to prepare their minds for the expedition he meditated across their territory. The French entered the town of Goritia on the 21st, the Austrian army having retreated with so much precipitation, that they abandoned four hospitals containing 1500 sick, and all their magazines of provisions and military stores. In these were 680 casks of flour, each weighing three quintals, making in all 2040 quintals, besides what was furnished to the divisions of Bernadotte. General Guieux proceeded with his division from Cividale to Caporetto, where he fell in with the imperialists, who had thrown up intrenchments at Pulero. These he attacked and carried, and afterwards pursued the enemy into the defiles of Caporetto, as far as Austrian La Chinse. Mean time, Massena approached Tarvis with his division. Buonaparte had therefore reason to hope, that the 2000 men, whom Guieux pushed before him, would fall into the hands of that general. Dugua entered Trieste on the night of the 23rd ; and, on taking possession of the celebrated mines of Ydria, the French found in them substance prepared for 2,000,000, which they carried off in waggons.

Massena, on his arrival at Tarvis, was attacked by an Austrian division from Clagenfurth, which had come to the assistance of the corps hemmed in by him on the one side, and driven by Guieux into the defiles. But after a conflict extremely obstinate, he routed them, with the loss of a great number of prisoners, among whom were three generals. The emperor's cuirassiers, who had arrived from the Rhine, suffered most severely. Meanwhile, Guieux, after a very warm engagement, carried Austrian La Chinse, a post extremely well intrenched. General Kables in person defended it with 500 grenadiers. By the laws of war these men ought to have been put to the sword ; but this barbarous right has always been disclaimed, and never exercised, by the French army. The hostile column, on finding La Chinse taken, hastened its march, and fell into the middle of the division of Massena, who made the whole of them prisoners. Thirty pieces of cannon, 400 waggons, 5000 men, and four generals, were taken by the French.

The chain of the Alps, which separates France and Switzerland from Italy, also separates the Italian part of the Tyrol from the German part, the Venetian states from the dominions of the emperor, and Carinthia from the counties of Goritz and Gradisca. Massena's division had crossed the Italian Alps, and now occupied the defiles of the Noric Alps, where the imperialists had been so imprudent as to entangle all their baggage and part of their army, which were of course taken. The battle of Tarvis was fought above the clouds, on a height commanding an extensive view of Germany and Dalmatia. In several places to which the French line extended, the snow lay three feet deep, and the cavalry charged on the ice. A continuity of such brilliant success abashed still less than it exasperated the internal enemies of the republic. One of the first cares of the directory, when they beheld the public spirit sinking, as it were, in proportion to their victories, was to support it at least in the armies, which so ably defended France against the efforts of external foes, who were perhaps less dangerous. To this motive, independently of the justice of the measure, may be ascribed their letters to different officers of the army of Italy ; and, in particular, to generals Berthier, Bernadotte, Massena, Guieux, Mireur, and Kellerman; Andreossi, chief-of-brigade of artillery ; Miquet, chief of the 88th demi-brigade ; and the commandant of the 10th regiment of chasseurs, in name of his corps. These eulogies the army answered, by meriting still more in their subsequent operations.

A French column, dispatched by Buonaparte to compel the submission of the Tyrol, and afterwards join him on the Drave, fulfilled their mission, and traversed, as conquerors, a country which Austria had always regarded as one of the strongest bulwarks of her empire. The divisions of generals Joubert, Baraguey d'Hilliers, and Delmas, put themselves in motion on the 20th, and surrounded an Austrian corps stationed on the Lavis. After a severe engagement, the French took 4000 prisoners, and killed nearly 2000, the greater part of whom were Tyrolean chasseurs.

Meanwhile, the enemy fell back along the right bank of the Adige, and manifested a disposition to maintain themselves in this situation. On the 22nd, general Joubert, with three divisions under his command, proceeded to Salurn. General Vial made himself master of the bridge of Neumarkt, and passed the river to prevent the imperialists from retreating to Botzen. The firing commenced with great warmth, and the issue seemed doubtful, when the general of division Dumas, who commanded the cavalry, pushed into the village of Tramin, and took 600 prisoners. In consequence of this, the wrecks of the Austrian column, under general Laudon, were prevented from reaching Botzen, and obliged to wander in the mountains. Joubert entered the town, and, having detached a sufficient force to follow Laudon, marched directly to Clausen. The imperialists, availing themselves of the means of defence which the country afforded, had made the best dispositions; but their centre was penetrated, they were obliged to give way, and the rout became general; in this action the French took 1500 prisoners. At Brixen, Botzen, and different other places, the French found magazines of every kind, and, among other articles, 30,000 quintals of flour. Through the whole of the Tyrol, Carinthia, and Carniola, the imperialists left behind them their hospitals.

On penetrating into Carinthia, Buonaparte published a proclamation to the inhabitants of the province, purporting that his army had not entered their country for the purpose of conquering it, or to effect any change in their religion, manners, or customs. They were the friends of all nations, and particularly of the brave people of Germany. The executive directory, he said, spared no pains to bring to a termination the calamities, which desolated the continent. Anxious to promote the accomplishment of this plan, they had sent general Clarke as plenipotentiary to Vienna, to commence negotiations for peace. The imperial court, however, refused to hear him, and even declared at Vicenza through the medium of M. de St. Vincent, that it did not acknowledge the French republic. General Clarke demanded a passport to go and speak to the emperor himself; but his ministers dreaded with reason, that the moderation of the propositions, which the general was charged to make, would influence his majesty to conclude a peace. If the war had been protracted for, six years by the ministers of the imperial court,

purchased by the gold of England, it was contrary to the wishes of the brave Hungarians, of the enlightened citizens of Vienna, and of the simple but honest natives of Carinthia. He proffered them the friendship of the French republic, which, although entitled to claim the right of conquest, was willing to renounce it. He invited them not to join in a contest repugnant to their sentiments, and to furnish what provisions the army might require; declaring that, on his part, he would protect their religion, customs, and property, and not exact any contribution. War itself was sufficiently disastrous, and they had already suffered too much, as the innocent victims of the folly of others.

On the 28th, three divisions of the army had cleared the passages leading from the Venetian territory into Germany, and encamped at Villach on the banks of the Drave. Next day general Massena fell in with the imperial army at the distance of a league from Clagenfurth, when an engagement ensued, in which the Austrians lost two pieces of cannon and 200 prisoners. The same evening the French entered the town, while prince Charles, and the wrecks of his army extremely disheartened, were flying before them. On the 1st of April, the French advanced guard was at a place between St. Veit and Freisach, and the division of general Bernadotte reached Laubach, the capital of Carniola. Buonaparte detached the Polish general Zajouzeck, at the head of a body of cavalry, with directions to folow the valley of the Drave, and, after gaining Lieuz; effect his junction with general Joubert at Brixen.

Since the commencement of this campaign, prince Charles had lost nearly 20,000 men taken prisoners. The imperialists were now entirely driven from the Venetian territories; and the Higher and Lower Carniola, Carinthia, the district of Trieste, and the whole of the Tyrolese, subjected to the arms of the republic. Near Villach the French found a magazine of cast iron, cartridges, and powder, and mines of lead, steel, iron, and copper; and near Clagenfurth they found magazines.

of arms and cloth. General Joubert, on the 28th of March, attacked the defile of Inspruck, which was defended by the Austrian battalions newly arrived from the Rhine. After a short cannonade he decided the affair by advancing at the head of the 85th demi-brigade in close column by battalion. The imperialists were driven back, leaving 100 killed, 600 prisoners, two pieces of cannon, and all their baggage.

The French army continuing to advance, Massena's division, forming the van-guard, encountered the enemy in the defiles between Freisach and Neumarkt. Their rearguard was driven from all the positions it endeavoured to dispute, and pursued with so much rapidity, that the archduke was obliged to bring back from his principal line of battle eight battalions of grenadiers, the same who had taken Kehl, and who now formed the hope of the Austrian army. The 2nd light infantry, who had particularly distinguished themselves since their arrival, without relaxing their movement a single instant, threw themselves on the flanks both of right and left, at the same moment. General Massena, in order to penetrate the defile, formed in column the grenadiers of the 18th and 32nd. The combat raged with fury; it was the flower of the imperial army, who had come to contend with the veteran troops of the army of Italy. The enemy occupied a grand position, bristling with cannon; but it only protracted, for a short time, the defeat of their rearguard. Their grenadiers were completely routed, leaving the field of battle covered with their dead, and from 500 to 600 prisoners. At day-break the French entered Neumarkt, their head-quarters being advanced the same day to Freisach, at both which places they found considerable magazines.

On the 3rd, the head-quarters were removed to Scheifling, while the advanced guard encountered the rear of the imperialists in the vicinity of Hundsmark, where the latter wished to dispute its quarters for the night. The 2nd light infantry still formed the van of the French. After an hour's fighting, the Austrian rearguard,

composed of four regiments from the Rhine, was again put to the rout, leaving 600 prisoners, and at least 300 men dead on the field of battle. That evening, our soldiers eat the bread, and drank the brandy, prepared for the Austrian army. The loss of the French in these two engagements was very trifling; the only officer killed was the chief-of-brigade, Carrere, a soldier of steady valor, and indefatigable activity. After these operations, the troops occupied Kintenfield, Murau, and Judenburg, the imperialists appearing decided on a precipitate retreat, and resolved not to hazard any more partial actions. Buonaparte ordered the division of Guieux to pursue the Austrian general Spork, who endeavoured to effect a junction by the valley of the Muhr, and whose advanced guard had already arrived at Murau; but the prompt arrival of the French at Schiefling rendered this junction impossible. The Austrians could now make no stand, except in the mountains in the neighbourhood of Vienna.

From his head quarters, at Clagenfurth, Buonaparte wrote a letter to prince Charles on the 31st of March. After remarking that the brave make war but desire peace, he reminded his royal highness that the struggle had already lasted six years; and asked, if they had not hitherto slaughtered men, and committed evils enough against suffering humanity. Europe, that had taken up arms against the French republic, had now laid them down; the Austrian nation alone remained;—and still blood was about to flow more than ever. The sixth campaign was now announced under the most portentous auspices; and, whatever might be the result, many thousands of gallant soldiers must still be sacrificed in the prosecution of hostilities. At some period, both must come to an understanding,—for time brings all things to a conclusion, and extinguishes the most inveterate resentments. The executive directory of the French republic, had expressed, to his imperial majesty, their desire to terminate a contest, which desolated the two countries; but their pacific overtures were defeated by the intervention of the British cabinet. Was there then no hope of accommodation? Must they continue to murder each other in order to promote the interests, or gratify the passions, of a nation far removed from the theatre of war? Was his royal highness, so nearly allied by birth to the throne, and raised above all the despicable passions which too often influence ministers and governments,—was he ambitious to merit the appellation of the benefactor of the human race, and the saviour of Germany? He begged the prince not to imagine he meant to insinuate, that his royal highness could not possibly save his country by force of arms. But even on the supposition, that the chances of war were to become favorable, Germany would not, on that account, suffer the less devastation. With respect to himself, if the overture, he had the honour to make to his royal highness, could be the means of sparing the life of a single individual, he would be prouder of the civic crown to which his interference might entitle him, than of the melancholy glory resulting from the most brilliant military exploits.

The archduke observed in answer, that in making war, and following the call of honour and duty, he himself, as well as the French general, desired peace for the good of the two countries, and from a regard to humanity. But as it did not belong to him, in the post intrusted to his care, to scrutinize or determine the quarrel of the belligerent nations, and as he was not invested, on the part of his majesty the emperor, with any powers for treating, general Buonaparte would perceive, that he could not enter into any negotiation, and that he must wait for superior orders on an object of such high importance, and not within the sphere of his present functions.

Two hours after receipt of this answer, and while the French troops were on their march to Freisach, the archduke, by one of his aides-de-camp, requested a suspension of arms for four hours; a proposition entirely inadmissible. It was obvious that

he wished, by gaining four hours, to gain the whole day, and thereby have time to effect a junction with general Spork. But this was the very reason which had made general Buonaparte hasten his march both night and day.

In Vienna, the consternation was extreme, and the most violent orders succeeded each other with a rapidity tending to increase the alarm. Many hastened to withdraw themselves from the horrors of a siege, by leaving the city; and although a numerous class appeared ready to rally round the monarch, and unite for the defence of the country, he could not be much encouraged by an attachment, which had cost so dearly to all those noble volunteers of Vienna, who had faced the army of Italy, only to meet with death, or to surrender prisoners. In vain had prince Charles appeared at the head of the imperial armies; he had been, perhaps, still more unfortunate than the generals his predecessors; and every effect expected from the influence of his talents, or the illusion of his dignity, had deceived their ultimate hopes.

During these transactions, Buonaparte transferred his head quarters to Judenburg, and prepared for decisive measures, unless the activity of the negotiation should supercede the necessity of carrying them into effect. On the 7th of April, lieutenant-general the count de Bellegarde, and major-general Meerveldt, wrote a letter to the French commander, in which they stated, that his imperial majesty had nothing more at heart than to concur in re-establishing the repose of Europe, and terminating a war that desolated the two nations. In consequence of the overture made by the French general to prince Charles, the emperor had now deputed them to learn his proposals on a subject of such great importance. Persuaded of the earnest desire, as well as the intentions of the two powers to terminate, as soon as possible, this disastrous war, his royal highness desired a suspension of arms for ten days, in order to facilitate the attainment of so desirable an object, and in order that all delay and obstacles, which the continuance of hostilities would occasion to the negotiation, might be removed, and every thing concur to the re-establishment of peace between the two nations.

Buonaparte observed in answer to this application, that, considering the military position of the two armies, a suspension of arms was in every respect disadvantageous to the French. But if it tended to open a road to peace, so much desired, and so beneficial to the two nations, he would consent without hesitation to their request. France had frequently manifested to his majesty her desire to put an end to this sanguinary contest. She still entertained the same sentiments; and he had no doubt, from the conference he had with them, that in a few days peace would be at length concluded between the republic and his majesty.

A convention was accordingly entered into, stipulating that hostilities should cease between the French and imperial armies, calculating from the evening of the 7th to that of the 13th. By the second article, the French were to retain the following line :—The advanced posts of the right wing to keep possession of the position they then occupied between Fiume and Trieste ; and their line to be extended by taking possession of Treffen, Littai, Windiscleistritz, Marburg, Chienhaussen, the right bank of the Muhr, Gratz, Bruck, Leoben, Trasayak, Mantern, the road from Mantern to Rottenmann, Rottenmann, Irdinng, the valley of Lems as far as Rastadt, St. Michael, Spital, the valley of the Drave, and Lientz. It was also arranged by the third and last article, that the suspension of arms should extend to the Tyrol ; and that the generals, commanding the French and imperial troops in that quarter, should. regulate together the posts they were severally to occupy. Hostilities were not to commence there until twenty-four hours after the generals-in-chief should have resolved on it ; and, in any case, not until twenty-four hours after the generals, commanding the French and imperial troops in the Tyrol, should be reciprocally informed of the circumstance.

This armistice enabled the French general to give to his army two or three days of repose, which the activity of their operations had rendered indispensably necessary. Accordingly, the division of general Serrurier occupied Gratz, one of the most considerable towns in the Austrian dominions, and containing 40,000 inhabitants. Prior to the conclusion of the convention, generals Joubert, Delmas, and Baraguey d'Hilliers, had several engagements at Botzen and Milbach, in which they constantly proved victorious ; and after traversing, as conquerors, the whole country of the Tyrol, and taking about 8000 prisoners, joined the grand army by the valley of the Drave. The whole French forces, being now united, took possession of the line of demarkation prescribed by the armistice. Buonaparte transmitted to the directory, by adjutant-general Leclerc, several plans of arrangement, which had been sent to Vienna, and upon which the plenipotentiaries waited for instructions. In the mean time, M. de Vincent, the emperor's aid-de-camp, having arrived, the plenipotentiaries resumed the negotiation ; and at the expiration of two days, the preliminaries of the treaty of peace were agreed upon and signed.

In the invasion of Germany, Buonaparte had descended, like a whirlwind, from the summits of the Noric and the Rhœtian Alps, sweeping before him the battalions of Austria, and advancing, with irresistible impetuosity, into the centre of the imperial states. When his army cleared the narrow track lying between the Helvetic territory and the Adriatic, the main body advanced with rapidity in the direction of Vienna, while the division of Bernadotte took the rout of Laubach, in order to cover the right wing and clear the country of the Austrian troops acting in that quarter. At the same time three divisions occupied the Tyrolese, and secured the left flank. Goritia, the district of Trieste, the Higher and Lower Carniola, the Upper and Lower Carinthia, and most of the Tyrol, were now in possession of the French, and their head quarters had been transferred to.

Judenburg in Upper Stiria. Their advanced posts reached within less than twenty miles of Vienna, and the general informed the directory in his dispatches, that he hoped at the head of 20,000 grenadiers, to plant in a few days, the standard of the republic in the capital of his imperial majesty.

While the Austrian armies fled in terror from the victorious bayonets of the French, the alarm of the cabinet of Vienna every moment increased. Immediate orders were issued to raise all the inhabitants of the hereditary states in a mass ; the nobility of Hungary and their vassals were summoned to the protection of the sovereign, while commands and entreaties were alternately employed to incite the zeal of the rest of his subjects. But these measures, now dictated by despair, ought to have been already completed, for many months must necessarily have elapsed before this undisciplined multitude could be brought into the field ; and even when in action, their irregular valor must have proved a feeble barrier against the veteran skill and courage of the army of Italy. In the capital, the consternation exceeded description. It was abandoned by many of the noble and wealthy inhabitants, and, to complete the general embarrassment, the bank stopped payment

To attempt the defence of Vienna could only oblige the enemy to level it to the ground, yet this measure was prosecuted with that infatuated earnestness which extreme alarm usually produces. The archives and royal treasures were packed up, the foreign ministers made preparations to quit the city, and, at length, the emperor himself intimated to the inhabitants his intention of retiring. Part of his court was destined for Prague, while the empress prepared to bid adieu to the seat of empire and take up her residence at Breda in Hungary. In the mean time, the greatest exertions were used to complete the entrenched camps in front of Vienna. The six companies of volunteers who had already suffered so severely in Italy, were recruited, and the number enrolled amounted to about 2000 Considerable parties of the neigh-bouring peasants repaired to their assistance, each body having in its standard the portrait of the tutelary saint of the place from which it had come ; thus blending a generous loyalty with that contemptible fanaticism which degrades the natives of the south of Germany.

It is unnecessary to recapitulate the correspondence of the hostile generals at the time of concluding the armistice of Leoben ; and I shall therefore confine myself to a detail of the subsequent diplomatic transactions. When the centre of the French army, under the immediate command of general Buonaparte, proceeded in a direct line towards Vienna, the divisions in the Tyrol and Western Carinthia filed off to the right, in order to keep pace with his rapid progress. The Austrian general, count Spork, occupied a position at Mukroe, on the Muhr, to the right of the archduke, in order to secure Saltzburg, and maintain the communication with the imperial troops in the Tyrol. When the left wing of the French abandoned Botzen and followed the main army towards Stiria, the Austrian detachments in the Northern Tyrol occupied the evacuated places ; and, as trifles become estimable by their rarity, these trivial successes were emblazoned by the imperial cabinet with all the parade of victory, and circulated through Europe with an appearance of triumph.

A work attributed to general Dumouriez, in which he labours to detract from the merit of Buonaparte, insinuates that he might have been enclosed in and captured in the mountains of Carinthia. It was not, however, suggested by whom this enterprize was to be effected. The archduke Charles was confessedly unable to withstand him, and the new levies were, by their want of discipline, incapable of service, while the vicinity of the enemy rendered nugatory and ineffectual every effort of the Austrian ministry. The French army on the Rhine were on the eve of commencing hostilities, and, from the paucity of imperial troops in Franconia and Suabia, no doubt could be entertained of their success. The corps therefore in Saltzburg and the Tyrol, even supposing them able to obtain possession of the posts in Buonaparte's rear, could produce only a very inconsequential and momentary effect.

The Venetian senate had displayed the most insulting conduct towards the French nation in the commencement of the war. Their provocations indeed were great, but their folly and their treachery were more than commensurate with their wrongs. They availed themselves of Buonaparte's irruption into Germany, to endeavor to cut off his communication with Italy, and co-operate with the imperialists in the Tyrol. In the Terra Firma, the governors circulated proclamations, inciting the populace to massacre the French. The people, animated by these exhortations, committed the most savage excesses, and several hundred soldiers fell victims to their rage. But the French brigades were not to be maltreated with impunity, and their commander lost not a moment in demanding and exacting satisfaction. He intimated to the doge, that it was in vain the senate affected to disavow commotions provoked by themselves. The blood of our brethren in arms (he proclaimed) shall be revenged, and there is not a French battalion charged with this mission which does not feel three times the courage and strength necessary to punish you. He concluded with informing his serenity, the doge, that if he did not immediately adopt the necessary measures for dispersing the banditti and arrest and deliver up the authors of these atrocities, *war was declared.*

The senate now thought proper to publish a proclamation respecting the disturbances in their territories. Their conduct, they asserted, during all the commotions of Europe, had always been, and still was, so perfectly neutral and friendly towards the belligerent powers, that they did not think it necessary to pay the least attention to the evil-disposed persons, who pretended to question their sincerity. But, as these malignant enemies of the Venetian republic had disseminated the vilest slanders against the sincerity of

its peaceable disposition, and had fabricated a proclamation bearing date from Verona, in which expressions injurious to the French nation were ascribed to the proveditor Battaglia, they were under the necessity of declaring that proclamation to be a forgery, and warned their subjects not to be deceived by the falsehoods and aspersions of malignant conspirators. These assurances neither interrupted the progress nor deceived the sagacity of Buonaparte. No satisfaction was offered by the senate, and the guilty were not only permitted to escape with impunity, but received the avowed patronage of those in authority. On the 3rd of May, the French general issued a manifesto from his head-quarters at Palma Nova, purporting that while the French were engaged in the defiles of Stiria and far advanced from Italy, and from the principal establishments of the army, the Venetian government had profited of a religious festival to arm 40,000 peasants. This body being afterwards joined by ten regiments of Sclavonians, was organized into battalions and sent to different points for the purpose of intercepting all communication between the army and Lombardy. Military stores of every description were sent from the capital to render these forces efficient. Several Frenchmen, after being grossly insulted, were driven from the city, and offices were bestowed on those who had shared in the massacre of others. The people of Padua, Vicenza, and Verona, had been ordered to take up arms, to second the regular troops, while the officers, it was asserted, carried their audacity so far as to proclaim that it belonged to the Lion of St. Mark to verify the proverb, that "Italy is the Frenchman's grave." The priests every where preached a crusade; and those who officiated in the state of Venice itself, uttered only the will of government. Pamphlets, perfidious proclamations, and anonymous letters were circulated with profusion through all their territories. The general then proceeded to a minute detail of the assassinations which had been committed. In this mournful list the most prominent atrocity was the massacre of the sick in the hospitals of Verona, where 400 Frenchmen, pierced with a thousand wounds from stilettoes, were thrown into the Adige. Buonaparte therefore required the French minister to leave Venice, and directed the generals of division to treat her troops as enemies, and to trample in every town on the Lion of St. Mark, the arms of the Venetian republic. In consequence of this manifesto, the French troops over-ran, and subjugated, in a few days, all the Venetian dominions. The Veronese, whose conduct towards the French had been remarkably atrocious, were condemned to an exemplary punishment. Some thousands of the peasants, who attempted to oppose the French, were put to the sword, and obliged to consult their safety in flight. The Sclavonians, who had come to their assistance, were routed, and fled to a fort filled with their powder and ammunition; but it was blown up by the cannon of the French, and they were all destroyed. Another engagement took place before the walls of Verona, and the Venetians fought with fury, but they were defeated with great slaughter, and the place was compelled to surrender.

Exhausted by her exertions, and yielding to the pressure of despair, Venice became as humble and abject in adversity, as she had been cruel and arrogant, during a moment of imaginary triumph. The doge having assembled the senate, it was resolved that the magistracy should suspend its functions, and that the republic, throwing itself on the mercy of France, should accept a provisional government. It was also decreed, that the proveditori, and other magistrates, of whose conduct the French had reason to complain, should be delivered up to punishment. On the 16th of May, a body of French troops occupied the city: a municipality was formed, and every thing modelled according to the democratic regime. The most perfect liberty of the press was established, the catholic religion remained unaltered, and persons and property continued unmolested; but the ships of war, and the

stores in the arsenals, were taken possession of in the name of the French republic.

Thus fell, after a splendid existence of fourteen centuries, the celebrated republic of Venice. No modern state had arisen from small beginnings to a situation of equal prosperity. Its fall was the subject of alarm and regret throughout all the countries of Europe, while it became a subject of exultation to the government and the armies of France, that a state which had resisted, during so many ages, the utmost efforts of its enemies, and had sustained, to the last extremity, its civil rights and its political pretension, even when surrounded by the most alarming dangers, should at length be compelled to yield to the good fortune of the republic.

It was impossible that Genoa, considering its vicinity to France, and the presence of the republican army, could escape the influence of the spirit of innovation. The nobility, however, exercised the supreme sway, and opposed the influence of the French by every impediment they could throw in their way; but the torrent of that irresistible fortune which attended the armies of France, overwhelmed them in common with all the rest of Italy. A desperate affray had taken place between the aristocratic and democratic parties shortly after the signature of preliminaries between the emperor and the French. Elated by this event, the republicans raised a violent commotion in the city, and proceeded to open force in support of their pretensions; but numbers of them were killed, and the insurrection was suppressed. As their principal leaders had fallen, their projects were considered as at an end, and they were treated with excessive severity. Determined, however, not to yield, they applied to Buonaparte for his protection against their antagonists. This request was readily granted; and the French, having taken possession of the city, the enemies of aristocracy could no longer, with safety, be opposed. It was intimated to the Genoese nobles, that, after the expulsion of the Austrians from

Italy, and the submission of all the principal powers in that country to the dictation of France, it would be the height of temerity to resist the general will of their fellow-citizens. They yielded prudently in time, and agreed to the establishment of a commonwealth on the principle of perfect equality of rank and privileges among all classes of society. The French system of legislation was enforced, and the territory of Genoa was distributed into communes and municipalities in imitation of France. A committee of legislation was appointed to frame a constitution, and a fundamental system of laws, with the reserve of doing nothing contrary to the catholic religion. As the people were now restored to the enjoyment of their rights, every kind of exclusive privilege was necessarily annulled. The subsequent articles of this convention regulated the establishment of a provisional government, over which the reigning doge was to preside. The security of all persons and parties was provided for by an act of amnesty, in favor of those against whom the French or the Venetians had ground of complaint, either on account of the late excesses, or of the events that had occurred in the imperial fiefs.

During these transactions, the negotiations between the French and Austrians did not proceed with the activity usually characterizing Buonaparte's measures; but he himself was busily occupied in consolidating the new republics which he had founded in Italy. Having accomplished these objects, he resumed his personal correspondence with Austria; and, during the remainder of the negotiation, both parties appeared to have forgotten their animosity, and to concur in the means of settling their contest at the expense of others. Exchanges of territory were proposed and acceded to, with that remorseless indifference which characterizes despotic princes; transferring to each other their subjects like cattle, without consulting any other title to their injustice than the incapacity of the helpless people thus treated, to vindicate their rights. In

conformity with those principles, a cession of part of the Venetian territories was mentioned at the very outset of the treaty, for which Venice was to be indemnified out of the pope's dominions, lately republicanized. In this act there was a total dereliction of those principles on which the French chiefly founded their claims to the respect and gratitude of nations; a scrupulous regard for the dignity of man, and a reference to his will and consent in every act of policy. The partition alluded to did not indeed take place; for Venice was doomed to sustain still more flagrant and extensive injustice, but the principle was strongly and clearly admitted.

In the mean time the confederations formed in the cities of Bologna, Ferrara, Modena, Reggio, and other provinces, comprised under the name of Lombardy, having consented to be converted into a single republic, and Buonaparte issued a summary proclamation to that effect from his camp at Monte Bello. The different arrangements that were made to render the incorporation of these states firm and durable, were due to his sagacity and exertions. He spared no pains to afford every reason to the people of these countries to prefer their present to their late condition. During these arrangements, events were taking place that fully demonstrated the connivance of the French at the endeavors of the court of Vienna, to seek an indemnification for its own loss of territories in those of the Venetians. The range of coast along the province of Dalmatia, had, since the downfall of Venice, excited a new species of ambition in the councils of Austria, that of increasing its naval strength, and succeeding to Venice in the dominion of the Adriatic. The idea of sharing in the spoils of an unfortunate friend, whose calamities in a great measure arose from the unsuccessful exercise of its good will, did not repress the usual propensity of the house of Austria to aggrandize itself, when opportunity offers, at the expense of justice, prudence, and humanity. In the month of June, the Austrian forces made an irruption into the province of Istria, a dependence of Venice, and reduced it to its own subjection. The excuses advanced for this act of unprovoked aggression, were of the most trivial nature, and the inhabitants of the province, perceiving too plainly the mutual understanding between the French and Austrians, submitted with silent reluctance, to an injury which they durst not openly resent.

On the return of Buonaparte to Udina, he signified to the imperial plenipotentiaries, that a speedy termination of the negotiations was necessary, and would no longer be deferred. They knew the impetuosity of his temper, and complied with his requisition. The treaty of peace between France and Austria was accordingly signed on the 17th of October, 1797, at Campo Formio, a village in the vicinity of Udina, by Buonaparte for the French republic, and by the marquis de Gallo, count Cobentzel, count Demeerfredt, and baron Dagelman, the imperial plenipotentaries. They were men of abilities, and had certainly exerted them in the course of these negotiations, as appeared by the advantages obtained for Austria, notwithstanding the state of depression to which she had been reduced.

The first article here, that there should be a solid, perpetual, and inviolable peace between his majesty and the French republic; and that the contracting parties should earnestly endeavour to maintain the most perfect harmony between their respective dominions, and carefully avoid, for the future, every thing which might infringe the union thus happily established. They farther pledged themselves, not to grant succour or protection to those, who should attempt any thing injurious or prejudicial to either of them. Immediately after the exchange of the ratifications of the treaty, the parties were to liberate from sequestration, the effects, rights, and properties, of individuals, or public communities, in their respective territories; and became bound to pay and reimburse all debts contracted for pecuniary advances, made to them, by such individuals and communities. All these stipulations were, by a special article of the treaty, declared to extend to the Cisalpine republic.

His majesty renounced the late Austrian Netherlands in favor of France, and consented, that the republic should enter on the perpetual possession of these countries and their territorial dependencies in full right and sovereignty; but she was to discharge all debts, mortgaged on them before the present war. The imperial plenipotentiaries were to transmit a statement of these debts to the French plenipotentiary, as soon as possible, and previous to the exchange of the ratifications, to the end that they might then come to an agreement on all the explanatory and additional articles of the treaty. The emperor consented, that the French republic should possess in full sovereignty, the former Venetian islands in the Levant, viz. Corfu, Zante, Cephalonia, St. Maura, Cerigo, and other islands dependent thereon, and, in general, all the Venetian establishments in Albany, situated lower down than the gulf of Lodriso. The French republic on her part, consented, that his majesty should possess, in full sovereignty, Istria, Dalmatia, the Venetian islands in the Adriatic, the mouths of the Cataro, the city of Venice, the Venetian canals, and the countries lying between his hereditary states, the Adriatic sea, and a military line specified in the treaty. The emperor renounced for ever, in favor of the Cisalpine republic, all title he might formerly pretend to over the countries now forming part of that republic, which should possess them and their territorial dependencies in full right and sovereignty. He acknowledged the Cisalpine republic as an independent power; and it was stipulated, that it should comprise Austrian Lombardy, the city and fortress of Mantua, all that part of the Venetian territories lying to the east and south of the frontier line; the Modenese, the principality of Massa and Carrara, and the three legations of Bologna, Ferrara, and Romagna.

By the tenth article, the countries ceded, acquired, or exchanged in virtue of the treaty, were to continue burdened with the debts mortgaged on their territories, which debts were to be discharged by the party, under whose dominion such territory might fall. The navigation of the rivers and canals, marking the boundaries of the possessions of his majesty and the French republic, were to be free, without either power being permitted to establish any toll or custom on them, or keep thereon any armed vessel; but it was agreed, that this stipulation should not preclude any precaution necessary for the protection and safety of the fortress of Porto-Legnago. All sales or alienations of property, and all engagements entered into by the cities, government, or civil and administrative authorities, of the former Venetian republic, for the maintenance of the German and French armies, up to the date of the signature of the treaty, were confirmed, and acknowledged as valid. The parties, being alike animated with the desire of removing every cause of interruption to the good understanding happily established between them, mutually bound themselves, in the most solemn manner, to contribute to the utmost of their power to the maintenance of internal tranquillity in their respective states. It was also agreed, that a treaty of commerce should immediately be concluded, founded upon an equitable basis, and such as should secure to both, advantages equal to those enjoyed by the most favored nations. Meanwhile, all commercial relations were to be re-established, as they existed anterior to the war; and no inhabitant of the countries occupied by the Austrian and French armies was to be prosecuted, or questioned, on account of his political opinions, or civil and military conduct, during the continuance of hostilities between the two powers.

His majesty, agreeably to the principles of his future neutrality, consented not to admit into his ports, during the course of the present war, more than six armed vessels belonging to any of the belligerent powers. He pledged himself to cede to the duke of Modena, as an indemnification for the territory that prince and his heirs possessed in Italy, the country of the Brisgaw, to be held by him in the manner he formerly possessed the Modenese. It was stipulated, that the value of the unalienated landed and personal property, belonging to the archduke Charles and the archduchess Christiana, and situated in the countries ceded to France, should be paid within three years; and that the same condition should take place as to the property of the archduke Ferdinand, in the territory of the Cisalpine republic. By the twentieth article, it was arranged, that there should be held at Rastadt, a congress solely composed of the plenipotentiaries of the Germanic empire and the French republic, for a pacification between these two powers; and, that this congress should be opened a month after the signing of the treaty, or as soon as possible. All prisoners of war, made on either side, and the hostages given or carried away during the war, were to be restored in forty days, calculating from the signing of the treaty; and the military contributions, imposed in their respective states, were to cease from the day on which the ratifications should be exchanged. The contracting parties agreed mutually to preserve towards each other the same ceremonial, with regard to rank and other etiquette, as was constantly observed before the war; and, it was farther stipulated, that the emperor and the Cisalpine republic should observe, with regard to each other, the same ceremonial and etiquette, as was formerly in use between his majesty and the republic of Venice. The present treaty was declared common to the Batavian republic; and the two powers obliged themselves to ratify it within thirty days from the date of signing, or sooner if possible; instruments of the ratification to be exchanged in due form at Rastadt.

Besides the preceding treaty, which was published, an additional convention, containing several secret articles, was signed by the plenipotentiaries on the same day at Campo Formio. But, although it was known that a secret treaty had been entered into by France and Austria, the particular terms did not transpire until a few months after, and a short time anterior to the re-commencement of the war. No unprejudiced person can peruse these secret articles, and combine them with late events, without being satisfied of the emperor's insincerity, and the same and procrastinating conduct, or rather pusillanimity, of the executive directory. By the first article, his majesty consented, that the boundaries of the French republic should extend to the Rhine ; and engaged to use his influence, that, by the peace to be concluded with the German empire, she should retain that line as her boundary. But if, notwithstanding his mediation, the Germanic body should refuse to consent to the boundary line of the republic, as regulated by this convention, he formally engaged to furnish to the empire no more than his contingent, which should not be employed in any fortified place, or otherwise it should be considered as a rupture of the peace and friendship re-established between Austria and France.

It was stipulated by the second article, that the emperor should employ his good offices, in the ensuing negotiation, to obtain, —1. That the navigation of the Rhine, from Huningen to the territory of Holland, should be free both to the French republic, and the states of the the empire, on the right bank ; 2. That the possessors of territory, near the mouth of the Moselle, should at no time, and on no pretence, attempt to interrupt the free navigation and passage of vessels from the Moselle into the Rhine ; and, 3. That the republic should have the free navigation of the Meuse; and the tolls, and other imposts from Venloo to Holland be abolished. His majesty renounced the sovereignty and possession of the country of Falkenstein and its dependencies ; and, it was agreed, that the countries taken possession of by Austria, in consequence of the sixth article of the public definitive treaty, should be considered as an indemnification for the territory given up, by the seventh article of that treaty, and by this clause. This stipulation, however, was only to be in force, when the imperial troops should occupy the countries ceded by these articles. The republic pledged herself to employ her influence, that the emperor should receive the archbishopric of Saltzburg, and that part of the circle of Bavaria, lying between the archbishopric, the rivers Inn and Saltz, and the Tyrol, including the town of Wasserburg on the right bank of the Inn. His majesty consented to give up to France, at the conclusion of the peace with the empire, the sovereignty and possession of the Frickthal, and all the territory belonging to the house of Austria, on the left bank of the Rhine, between Zurzach and Basle, provided his majesty received a proportionate indemnification. It was, moreover, stipulated, that in consequence of particular arrangements to be afterwards made, this territory should be united with the Helvetic republic, without farther interference on the part of his majesty or the empire.

The seventh article purported, that if France should make an acquisition in Germany by the ensuing peace with the empire, his imperial majesty should receive an equivalent ; and if his majesty should make an acquisition, the republic should, in like manner, receive an equivalent. The prince of Nassau-Dietz, late stadtholder of Holland, was to receive a territorial indemnification, but not in the vicinity of the Austrian possessions, nor in that of the Batavian republic. Although France made no difficulty in restoring to the king of Prussia his possessions on the left bank of the Rhine, it was agreed that no new acquisition should be proposed for his Prussian majesty, and this stipulation the two contracting powers mutually guaranteed ;—but in case he should consent to cede, to the French and Batavian republics, some small parts of his territory on the left bank of the Meuse, the emperor was to use his influence, that such cessions should be accepted and rendered valid by the Germanic body. His imperial majesty, by the eleventh article, pledged himself not to object to the manner in which the imperial fiefs had been disposed of by France in favor of the Ligurian republic, and to use his influence, that the diet of the empire should renounce all feudal sovereignty over the countries making part of the Cisalpine and Ligurian republics, as also over the imperial fiefs lying between Tuscany, the states of Parma, the Ligurian and Lucchese republics, and the adjacent points of the Modenese territory, which fiefs now make part of the Cisalpine republic. The two contracting powers were to employ, in concert, their influence in the course of the negotiation with the empire, that the electors of Mentz, Treves, and Cologne, the elector Palatine of Bavaria, the duke of Wurtemburg and Teck, the margrave of Baden, the duke of Deux Ponts, the landgraves of Hesse Cassel and Darmstadt, and the other princes and states of the empire, who should suffer any loss of territory or rights, in consequence of the stipulations in this convention, or in consequence of the treaty to be concluded with the empire, should receive proportionable indemnifications in Germany, to be settled by mutual agreement. It was stipulated, that the imperial troops should evacuate the towns and fortresses of Mentz, Ehrenbreitstein, Philipsburg, Manheim, Koenigstein, Ulm, Ingolstadt, and, in general, the whole territory of the empire to the boundaries of the hereditary states, within twenty days after the exchange of the ratifications. And lastly, it was agreed that these secret articles should have the same force as if inserted in the public treaty of peace, and be ratified at the same time by the two contracting powers,—the ratifications to be exchanged at Rastadt.

It was not without surprise, that the world beheld the antient state of Venice obliterated from the register of independent nations by the concert of two irreconcileable foes. A numerous party of the Venetian people were known to be dissatisfied with the abolition of aristocracy; but as the provisional government had now existed for several months, it was never suspected, that the executive directory, in their eagerness to terminate a continental war, would consent to the extinction of a new-born republic, and sacrifice it as the boon of peace. Buonaparte, however, beloved to follow his instructions; and perhaps the directory felt, that the repugnance of the Venetians to the reception of democratic freedom would require too great a number of troops to enforce obedience. France had done enough for glory; she

had secured her own independence, and established the Ligurian and Cisalpine republics; and, perhaps, the extension of her limits required a proportionate enlargement of the Austrian territories, in order to preserve the real or imaginary balance of power in Europe.

Thus terminated the Herculean labours of general Buonaparte in Italy; and the first deduction, arising from a review of the complicated and multitudinous transactions of the campaign, and the boldness and activity of his measures, is, that Italy was conquered, and Austria vanquished, chiefly by the power of his genius, and the novelty of his tactics. Feebly supported by his country, whose necessities did not allow her to send the necessary reinforcements to his army, he supplied every deficiency by his talents. The struggle was honourable even to the enemy; the Austrian soldiers fought with desperate valor; and the exertions of his imperial majesty, in pouring five successive armies into Italy, exceeded the most sanguine expectations of his friends. After rivalling Hannibal in Europe, the French general, even at this early period, was actuated by the ambition of emulating Alexander, by an oriental expedition. But brilliant as the exploits of Buonaparte were, in his Italian campaign, he must yield the palm of glory to the Carthagenian. Hannibal, after a tedious and circuitous march, scaled the Alps, and defeated the mountain nations; then descending into the plains of Italy, he destroyed four Roman armies, but neglected to advance to the capital, and sued for ever the destruction of the republic. Though far distant from his native land, abandoned by the jealous and ignominious government of Carthage, and obliged to incorporate bodies of undisciplined barbarians with his regular troops, he continued great and formidable even in his reverses. On the other hand, the vicinity of France facilitated supplies to the army of Italy; and Buonaparte, in case of a serious disaster, could easily have evacuated his conquests and fallen back to the frontiers of the republic. Such is the vicissitude of human events, that in less than two years, the exploits of this campaign had no other record than the page of history ; for the negligence of the directory, and the brilliant though ephemeral success of the imperial army, left no other monument of Buonaparte's labours than the literary productions, in which

"THEY POINT A MORAL, AND ADORN A TALE."

HISTORY OF THE WAR.

CHAP. XVI.

THE friends of liberty beheld, with marked satisfaction, the abolition of the Venetian senate, and especially of the council of Ten, and of the inquisition of state. The election of fifty individuals by the suffrage of the community, with six commissaries nominated by Buonaparte, had been received with applause as one of the most equitable modes of government. It was, therefore, with great regret and indignation that the inhabitants of Venice contemplated their return beneath the dominion of Austria : a power of which they well knew the despotic maxims, and which they regarded with tenfold abhorrence, since the introduction of French principles.

In France, however, the exultation of the people at the conclusion of the treaty of Campo Formio, was general and boundless. In imitation of the precedent of former times and of the last year, calculations of the number of victories won by the French armies were pompously distributed to all the members and departments of government, and published with much splendor and solemnity in all parts of the republic. In these it was stated, that the French had been victorious in 260 engagements, thirty of them pitched battles. Upwards of 150,000 of their enemies had

been slain, and near 200,000 made prisoners. About 8000 pieces of cannon had been taken, and 180,000 muskets. These achievements had occurred within the space of three years and a half, commencing with September 1793, and ending with February 1797 ; since which period 25,000 of the Austrians had been killed and taken, previous to the conclusion of a definitive treaty.

While the armies of France were thus triumphant abroad, the internal peace of that country was continually disturbed by the zeal and the perverseness of the enemies to the existing government. Inflamed by resentment at the many disappointments they had experienced in their efforts to overturn it, they determined to persevere, even should they fall in the attempt, rather than desist from the execution of their design. Such still continued to be the character of that resolute party which opposed the directory and was determined to obtain, if possible, the restoration of the monarchy. The blood which had been so profusely shed for the accomplishment of these objects, was considered only as a just and necessary tribute to the cause of loyalty. They were undeterred by the persecution and the sufferings to which they were subjected, and acted together with a boldness that exposed them to perpetual detection. But so exemplary was their courage and firmness, that they took no care to conceal their principles ; and their conduct at once provoked and gratified the enmity of their oppressors.

Among men of all classes it was not difficult to find agents and adherents to the cause of royalty. The republicans, dreading the effects of their combination, contracted on their side a rancour against the royalists, and a thirst for revenge that induced them to pry into all their actions. Those of the republican party who favored moderate measures, and who were disposed to treat their antagonists with lenity, incurred on many occasions the imputations of unsteadiness or treachery ; and the nation was deeply involved in this conflict of repugnant ideas and interests, when new jealousies and apprehensions arose to add fresh fuel to the flames of reciprocal animosity. On the 12th of Pluviose, (January 31st, 1797,) the directory informed the council of Five Hundred, that a conspiracy had been formed against the republic by the brother of the late king, styling himself king of France, and that four of the principal conspirators had been arrested. According to a report of the minister of police there had been for some time individuals in Paris commissioned by that prince to correspond with his partisans in all the departments, and to organize the plan of an insurrection. After preparing their own adherents, they ventured to make application to several officers in the republican army, and tampered with Ramel, commander of the guards, and Malo, the commanding officer of a regiment of dragoons. They both pretended to acquiesce in the proposals made to them, but in formed the minister of police of the business in agitation. A place was appointed where he might hear the discourse between the officers and the commissioners. Thither he repaired, and they disclosed in his hearing the whole plan of the conspiracy, producing at the same time their papers and credentials. Duverne, Duprale, *alias* Dunant, Laville Harnois Brothier, and Baron Poli,
VOL. I.

were immediately seized, and separately examined. The account of their proceedings and designs communicated to the public under the name of Dunant, is so absurd, incoherent, and contradictory, that it is impossible not to suspect either him or the directory of the most extravagant forgeries. It was asserted, that, had the conspiracy succeeded, deeds of the most atrocious nature would have ensued. Lewis XVIII. was, on his accession to have issued an act of oblivion, but this was to be declared null and void by the parliament, after his possession of the throne had been firmly established. The leading members of the present legislature were to have been taken into favor, and soon as their services should be no longer necessary, were to be condemned to exemplary punishment. Other frauds and barbarities were mentioned, such as exposing La Fayette in an iron cage, and sentencing the inferior actors in the revolution, to the galleys. Dunant asserted, that, notwithstanding the assistance which the royalists expected to receive from England, Lewis XVIII. and his council had always been of opinion that her services were perfidious, and would tend to no other purpose than the ruin of France. While the conspirators were under examination before a military tribunal, the most resolute exertions were made throughout France by the emissaries of the king, who circulated an address, in which he expressly acknowledged that he had numerous agents in France who were commissioned by him to urge the people to renounce the authority of the existing government. Encouraged by this declaration, the royalists proceeded to accomplish their avowed objects by the assiduous and skilful employment of the press. They circulated appeals to the antient loyalty of the nation, addressed exhortations and promises of reward to the military and to persons in office, and represented the republic itself as in a state of fluctuation and about to be destroyed. Their efforts were not entirely without reward. A considerable number of the public functionaries refused to renew their oath of hatred to monarchy ; the two parties charged each other with bribery and corruption, and their passions were daily more incensed by the violence and malevolence of their reciprocal aspersions. The directory, however, obtained a decree, that " every elector, previously to his entrance upon his functions, should formally declare his attachment to the constitution of the third year, and pledge himself to defend it and the republic to the utmost of his abilities."

This decree evinced the superiority of the strenuous republicans in the legislature, but it was not decisive of the contest. Both parties exerted themselves with the utmost energy. The opponents of the ruling party endeavoured to distress them by calling for a strict investigation of their proceedings relative to the war, and by recommending pacific councils as essential to the national welfare. They accomplished the repeal of certain severe laws against the royalists, enacted during the tyranny of Robespierre, and procured a degree to prevent the increase of the republican clubs, by formally prohibiting all meetings for political discussion, under heavy penalties.

These circumstances afforded matter of triumph to the royalists and the advocates of moderation, but added nothing to their strength. On the contrary, they enabled the democrats to render them odious in the eyes of the nation, by representing them as enemies to liberty. It also interested the army in the cause of government, and gave it the vigorous support of the generals who were leading the republican forces to victory, and, by their achievements were confirming the ascendancy which the French republic had acquired on the continent of Europe. Buonaparte embraced the opportunity presented by the anniversary of the revolution to declare his resolution to maintain the republican cause, and admonished his troops to beware of the counter-revolutionary designs now in agitation. Joubert, Massena, Angereau, Bernadotte, Vignolle, and Hoche, all manifested the same zeal to support the existing system of govern-

ment and the present administration : they declared their abhorrence of their adversaries, and especially of the priests, whom they accused of " heating the heads, and sharpening the daggers, of the enemies of the republic."

While the nation was distracted by the inflammatory harangues and publications of the several parties, the directory itself was divided. Barras, Reubel, and Larevillere, were strenuous advocates for republican government. Carnot and Barthelemy were thought to entertain sentiments more favorable to the opposition ; and these last derived confidence in themselves from the countenance of Pichegru and others, whose service in civil and military capacities had given them considerable influence in the nation.

The violent feuds which this difference of principles and opposition of interests occasioned, were carried to a greater height by an order from the directory for the approach of a strong body of troops within seven leagues of Paris. When questioned by their opponents, they justified the measure by insisting on the danger which threatened the commonwealth from the machinations of the royalists, and declared " that they should think themselves guilty of treason were they to conceal from their fellow-citizens, or from their troops, the attempts which were carried on to effect a counter-revolution." Confident in the support of the army, they now determined to bring the contest to an issue by still more decisive measures. Affecting to apprehend that the conspiracy which they had before announced was on the point of execution, they ordered Angereau, whom Buonaparte had sent to Paris under pretence of business, to arrest certain of the national representatives and conduct them to the Temple prison. A proclamation was then issued, that whoever should propose the restoration of royalty, the re-establishment of the constitution of 1793, or the elevation of any one of the Orleans family to the throne, should be shot. To secure the confidence of the nation at large, an address was published, importing that " the citizens would shudder with horror, when they should be apprised by the evidence about to be laid before them of the plots entered into against their persons, and their dearest rights and possessions." This address was preparatory to the final measures about to be adopted. Under the plausible pretence of preventing a renewal of the horrors of the civil war, a number of resolutions were adopted in the council of Five Hundred, and one among others by which the transactions of the primary, communal, and electoral assemblies, in fifty departments, were declared illegal : the persons elected by them to public offices and to seats in the legislature were compelled to resign them, and the directory were empowered to nominate to the situations vacated by the first of these classes. By another resolution, Carnot and Barthelemy, members of the executive directory, eleven members of the council of Elders, forty-two members of the council of Five Hundred, and ten other persons, were sentenced to transportation to any place appointed by the directory. Besides the two members of the directory, already mentioned, there were among the proscribed names, those of Pichegru, Boissy d'Anglas, Dumolard, Desmolieres, Villaret, Joyense, a naval officer of high repute, Pastoret, general Miranda, Cochon, late minister of police, and others who had distinguished themselves in various departments of the state.

The prevailing faction, though they were persuaded that this violent proceeding was necessary to the security of their power, were sensible of the impression which such an outrage against the constitution would produce on the minds of the people. The council of Five Hundred therefore published an address to the nation, vindicating their resolutions on the principle of state necessity, and as the only expedient by which they could hope to frustrate the horrid designs of the proscribed persons, for the ruin of. the republic. It was justly alleged, however, by those who condemned the measure, that the accused persons positively denied the charge, that even the existence of the conspiracy had not been proved, and that to pass sentence without bringing them to an open trial, implied a conviction that they would not be found guilty before an impartial jury.

Whatever weight these representations might have with the public mind, it was a subject of just regret to every man of reflection free from the influence of party spirit, that, after nine years of civil dissension, after repeated changes of constitution, and after the most mature deliberations of the wisest men in the, French dominions, France was only delivered from the yoke of a mild and enfeebled despotism, to be subjected to the iron pressure of a tyrannical oligarchy. Nor did the philanthropist, the philosopher, and the man of virtue, survey the general aspect of the other countries of Europe without regret for the past, and the most melancholy anticipations of the future. The misfortunes of our own country at this period would have overwhelmed the most ardent patriots of the soil with dismay and despondency, had not the valor of our naval heroes, and the consciousness of our most eminent statesmen, that we were hazarding our safety and existence in a just cause, confirmed the energy of the government, and supported the spirits of the people. Distressing as were the evils which must always arise to a commercial country from the depression of public credit, and the establishment of a paper currency, the English nation was at this moment threatened by a still greater calamity. In the midst of our pecuniary embarrassments, the government was alarmed by a mutinous disposition which made its appearance in the navy. No event could have been more alarming to Englishmen than the defection of its sailors at an instant when we were struggling with all the difficulties and dangers of foreign war. Had our naval bulwarks been destroyed, our only fortress would have been at once dismantled, and we should have remained at the mercy of an enemy who considered his own safety as involved in the subversion of the British power.

The spirit of the mutiny was first discovered in the fleet lying at Portsmouth by anonymous letters addressed to lord Howe, first lord of the admiralty. When the great body of the people or a numerous class of men are to be made the instruments of the indirect designs of disaffected persons against the state, their first object is the selection or invention of a pretext by which to justify their machinations. The smallness of their pay was the first resorted to by the sailors on this occasion, and its justice could not be denied by any one who compared the prices of all the necessaries of life, with those which they bore in the reign of Charles II. when the wages of seamen were last considered.

Little regard being paid to these letters, an unanimous agreement was entered into, that no ship should heave her anchor till redress of grievances should be obtained. On the 13th of April, lord Bridport ordered the signal for weighing anchor, but, instead of obeying, the sailors in the queen Charlotte, lord Howe's own ship, set up three cheers as the signal for commencing mutiny, and every other ship followed the example. The officers used their utmost exertions to recall the sailors to obedience, but their attempts were ineffectual. Delegates were appointed by the crews, who held their conferences in lord Howe's cabin, where the most solemn engagements were made to support the common cause. An oath was administered to every man in the fleet; ropes were then reefed to the yard-arms of the ships as the signal of the punishment that awaited those who might betray the cause, and several officers, particularly obnoxious to their respective crews, were sent ashore. In the mean time, though the admiral could not lead his fleet to sea, both he and the officers were treated with the greatest attention and respect, and the routine of naval duty was regularly performed. On the 19th, two petitions, one to the admiralty and the other to the house of commons, were drawn up, and signed by the delegates. The petition to the commons stated in very correct and respectful language the inadequacy of their pay, and their inferiority in various respects to the soldiers. Their petition to the admiralty

stated the low rate of their pay, and the insufficiency of their allowance of provisions; demanding, at the same time, the liberty of going ashore while in harbor, and the continuance of pay to wounded seamen till they should be cured and discharged.

The government was so greatly alarmed by these proceedings, that the lords of the admiralty went down to Portsmouth, to inspect, in person, the transactions of the fleet. Convinced of the firm determination of the sailors to persist in their demands, and aware of the dreadful consequences that must arise if the defenders of the country should continue refractory, they authorised lord Bridport to inform the insurgents, that an augmentation of pay, and a redress of their other complaints, should be, if their influence with the king extended so far, proposed to parliament. The delegates answered, that it was the determination of the crew to agree to nothing that should not be sanctioned by parliament and guaranteed by the king's proclamation. This declaration being made in a conference with several commanders, admiral Gardiner was so violently irritated, that he seized one of the delegates by the collar, and swore that he would have them all hanged with every fifth man throughout the fleet. The sailors were so much exasperated by his conduct, that this brave officer, with difficulty escaped alive: the ships loaded their guns and prepared for defence. On the next day, however, they wrote a letter to the lords of the admiralty, stating the motives of their conduct on the preceding day; and another to lord Bridport, expressing for him personally, the highest respect and attachment. On the 23rd of May, his lordship, pathetically addressing his crew, informed them that he had brought along with him a redress of all their grievances, and the pardon of the king for past indiscretions and delinquencies. These assurances being communicated to the other crews, were accepted after some deliberation, and every sailor returned to his duty. For a fortnight the fleet remained tranquil, expecting from parliament a confirmation of their demands; but, perceiving or imagining that no steps were taken for that purpose, they renewed their former menaces. Alarmed at this intelligence, the government dispatched, as the most proper person to quell the tumult, lord Howe, who was beloved throughout the fleet. This illustrious commander, having pledged his honor to the seamen that government would faithfully perform its promises, they declared their unlimited confidence in lord Howe's assurance, and returned to their duty. A mutinous disposition which had also appeared at Plymouth subsided on hearing of these transactions at Portsmouth.

Parliament immediately proceeded to take into consideration the demands of the seamen. On the motion of Mr. Pitt, an augmentation of pay was unanimously agreed to as necessary, both in justice and in policy; and it was hoped that these compliances of government, sanctioned by the legislature, would have prevented any further tumults. But this reasonable expectation was in a short time wholly disappointed by a fresh mutiny which broke out in the fleet at the Nore, on the 22nd of May. On that day the crews took possession of their respective ships, and elected delegates to preside over them, who drew up a statement of their demands and transmitted them to the lords of the admiralty. These demands were much more extensive than those of the seamen at Portsmouth or Plymouth, and from their exhorbitance did not appear entitled to the same indulgence. On the 6th of June, in the morning, the fleet at the Nore was joined by the Agamemnon, Ardent, Leopard, and Iris, men of war, and the Ranger sloop, all of which ships had deserted from admiral Duncan. When the admiral found himself deserted by part of his fleet, he called together the crew of his own ship and addressed them in the following speech.

"My lads,

I once more call you together with a sorrowful heart, from what I have lately seen: the disaffection of the fleets. I call it disaffection, for the crews have no grievances. To be deserted by my fleet in the face of an enemy, is a disgrace, I believe, which never before happened to a British admiral; nor could I have supposed it possible. My greatest comfort under God is, that I have been supported by the officers, seamen, and marines, of this ship; for which, with a heart overflowing with gratitude, I request you to receive my most sincere thanks. I flatter myself much good may result from such an example, by bringing those deluded people to a sense of their duty, which they owe not only to their king and country, but to themselves.

"The British navy has ever been the support of that liberty which was handed down by our ancestors, and which, I trust, we shall maintain to the latest posterity; and that can only be done by unanimity and obedience. This ship's company, and others who have distinguished themselves by their loyalty and good order, are, and ought, and doubtless will deserve to be, the favorites of a grateful country. They will also have from their inward feelings, a comfort which will be lasting, and not like the floating and false confidence of those who have swerved from their duty.

"It has often been my pride. with you to look into the Texel, and see a foe which dreaded coming out to meet us. My pride is now humbled indeed; my feelings are not easy to be expressed; our cup has overflowed and made us wanton. The all-wise Providence has given us this check as a warning, and I hope we shall improve by it. On him then let us trust, where our only security can be found. I find there are many good men among us; for my own part I have had full confidence of all in this ship, and once more beg to express my approbation of your conduct.

"May God, who has thus far conducted you, continue to do so, and may the British navy, the glory and support of our country, be restored to its wonted splendor, and be not only the bulwark of Britain, but the terror of the world.

"But this can only be effected by a

strict adherence to our duty and obedience, and let us pray that the Almighty God may keep us in the right way of thinking. God bless you all."

An address so unassuming, modest, and pious, was in full accordance with the character of the venerable speaker, whose services, even at this period, deserved the gratitude and admiration of his country. Adam Duncan was the second son of Mr. Duncan of Lundie, by a daughter of Mr. Haldane, of Gleneagles, in the county of Perth. He was born in the year 1731, and at a proper age was sent to the school of Dundee, where, as I am informed by a surviving contemporary, he remained till he had arrived at his fourteenth year, and gave early proofs of a clear and strong understanding. Soon after quitting school, he was sent to sea, and having served during the latter part of the war that was concluded by the peace of Aix-la-Chapelle, he was appointed, at the re-commencement of hostilities, to the rank of lieutenant. He had, by this time, reached his twentieth year, and was so remarkably distinguished by strength and beauty, that the passengers in the streets stood still to gaze with admiration. In the seven years' war, though the public is not acquainted with the particular services of Mr. Duncan, yet we may judge them to have been highly meritorious from their effect; as without any influence but that of his personal character, he was early in the war appointed post-captain. The first ship which he commanded in that capacity was the Valiant. During the war he gained the favor and esteem of rear-admiral Keppel, who hoisted his flag on board captain Duncan's ship, when about to set sail as second in command, on the expedition against the Havannah. Captain Duncan added greatly to his naval reputation during this expedition, and in the course of it acquired a considerable share of prize-money, which rendered his circumstances easy and independent. From the peace of Paris to the American war nothing occurred to call his abilities into action. In 1777, he married the daughter of Mr.

Dundas, the president of the Edinburgh court of justiciary, and in the following year the rupture with France requiring an augmentation of the navy, captain Duncan was appointed to command a ship of the line. In 1779, he formed one of the court-martial which sat on admiral Keppel, and soon afterwards sailed with admiral Rodney, and distinguished himself in the engagement off Cape Finisterre. From thence he proceeded to Gibraltar, and in the subsequent year ranged the West Indian seas. On the conclusion of a peace, he continued for some time in actual service, but his ship being at length put out of commission, he retired to Edinburgh. In 1789, when preparations were making for supporting the Orange interest in Holland, he was made a rear-admiral; but the dispute connected with that object having been for the time abandoned, he was not called to fulfil the duties of his station. In 1793, he was promoted to the rank of vice-admiral, and not long after this event, his brother, colonel Duncan of Lundie, dying, he became representative of his father's house, and heir to the estate. In 1795, he became admiral of the blue, and was soon after appointed to the command of the North sea fleet. In 1795, he filled that station, and prevented the Dutch fleet from leaving their ports, or co-operating with the designs of the republicans; an important service which he effectually performed during the severe and boisterous winter, immediately preceding the mutiny of the fleet.

His harangue to the sailors at this critical period was well calculated from its simplicity and truth, to touch the human heart, and the whole ship's crew were deeply affected. They declared their resolution to abide by the admiral in life or death; their example was followed by all the remaining ships; and the admiral, notwithstanding the defection of so considerable a part of his squadron, repaired to his station off the coast of Holland; resolved, notwithstanding the late unpropitious event, to provoke, if possible, the enemy to battle.

The principal person at the head of the

mutiny, was Richard Parker, a man of respectable abilities, decent education, and resolute disposition. Admiral Buckner, the commanding officer at the Nore, was directed by the lords of the admiralty, to inform the seamen that their demands were totally inconsistent with the good order and regulations necessary to be observed in the navy, and could not for that reason be acceded to; but that, on returning to their duty, they would receive the king's pardon for their breach of obedience. To this offer Parker replied by a declaration, that the seamen had unanimously determined to keep possession of the fleet until the lords of the admiralty had repaired to the Nore, and redressed the grievances which had been laid before them.

In order to put an end with all possible expedition to a mutiny that appeared so dangerous, lord Spencer, lord Arden, and admiral Young, hastened immediately to Sheerness, and held a board, at which Parker and the other delegates attended; but their behaviour was so audacious, that the lords of the admiralty returned to town without the least success. The principal subject of complaint on the part of the mutineers was the unequal distribution of prize money, for the omission of which they loudly blamed their fellow-seamen at Portsmouth. On the return of the lords of the admiralty from Sheerness, a proclamation was issued, offering his majesty's pardon to all mutineers who should immediately return to their duty; indicating at the same time that admiral Buckner was the proper person to be applied to on such an occasion. All the buoys were removed from the mouth of the Thames and from the neighbouring coast, a precaution by which any vessels attempting to escape, would be rendered incapable of directing their course in safety. Preparations were made at Sheerness for an attack from the mutinous ships, which had manifested indications of an intention to bombard that place, and furnaces and red-hot balls were kept in readiness.

Emboldened by the strength of men and shipping in their hands, and resolved to perseverance in their demands till they had extorted a compliance, the mutineers proceeded to secure a supply of provisions for that purpose, by seizing two vessels laden with stores, and sent notice ashore that they intended to block up the Thames and cut off all communication between London and the sea. They began the execution of this menace by mooring four of their vessels across the mouth of the river, and intercepting several ships that were coming from the metropolis.

They now changed their system of delegation, and, to prevent the acquisition of too much power by any individual, the office of president was entrusted to no one longer than a day. Their design in this alteration was to secure themselves from the treachery which might possibly arise, were the authority conferred for a length of time. They dreaded the effects which might accrue from the secret negotiations, or the open liberality of government. In addition to this precaution, they compelled those ships of which they suspected the crews to be wavering in their cause, to take their station in the midst of the others. But, notwithstanding these precautions, two vessels eluded their vigilance, and effected their escape. While these transactions excited in the nation the utmost alarm, they were violently reprobated by the seamen belonging to the two divisions of the fleet lying at Portsmouth and Plymouth. They addressed an admonition to their fellow-seamen at the Nore, warmly condemning their proceedings as a scandal to the name of British sailors, exhorting them to be content with the indulgence already granted by government, and to return to their duty without insisting on greater concessions than had been demanded by the rest of the navy. These warnings proved ineffectual: the delegates commissioned lord Northesk, whom they had kept confined in the Montague, which he commanded, to repair to the king in the name of the fleet, and to acquaint him with the conditions on which they were ready to deliver up the ships. The petition which he was charged to lay before his majesty was highly respectful and loyal, but abounded with the most bitter invectives against his ministers. It required a full and unconditional compliance with all their demands, and threatened, on refusal, to put immediately to sea. Lord Northesk undertook to convey their petition, but told them that, from the unreasonable character of its contents, he could not flatter them with the hope of success. No answer being returned to the message, and information being brought to the fleet that the nation at large disapproved of their conduct and proceedings, divisions took place among the delegates, and several of the ships, after much bloodshed, and many severe conflicts, deserted the others. The mutineers, now despairing of accomplishing their designs, struck their flag of mutiny : every ship was left at its own command, and they all gradually returned to their obedience. Parker was seized and imprisoned ; and, after a solemn trial on board the Neptune, sentenced to death. He suffered with coolness and intrepidity, acknowledging the justice of his sentence. With him the other chief ringleaders, after full proof of their guilt, were condemned and executed ; but mercy immediately, or at a more distant period, was extended to the rest. This mutiny, so much more dangerous than that in the other fleet, attracted the most serious attention of parliament, to which it was communicated by a message from the king : measures were adopted for preventing communication between the well affected and the present mutineers ; and precautions were adopted to prevent and punish future attempts to seduce soldiers and sailors from their allegiance. Mr. Pitt proposed a bill purporting that persons who should endeavor to seduce soldiers or sailors from their duty, or instigate them to mutinous practices, or commit any act of mutiny, or form any mutinous assemblies, should, on conviction, be deemed guilty of felony and suffer death. Having suppressed the insurrection of the sailors, government turned its attention to the army, which complained of the smallness of its pay, which had been increased about

two years before, and a further augmentation was established, by which the stipend of the soldier was fixed at one shilling per day. It is not often that government anticipates the just complaints of the people by unconstrained acts of justice ; and the measures pursued in favor of the army were the unwelcome and involuntary consequence of the spirit displayed, however wickedly and injudiciously, by their rivals on the watery element.

During the present year, the war between Great Britain and France was chiefly confined to naval operations, in which the former was uniformly victorious. The executive directory had frequently threatened this country with invasion ; but their first experiment of the kind was a mere burlesque unworthy of a great nation, and calculated only to excite the derision of the English. That part of the coast of Devonshire which is situated at the mouth of the British channel, was, on the 22nd of February, thrown into consternation by the appearance of three frigates, which entered the small harbor of Ilfracombe, scuttled some merchant ships, and endeavored to destroy every vessel in the port. From this place they soon departed, standing across the channel towards the side of Pembroke. They were discovered from the heights above St. Bride's bay, as they were steering round St. David's head. They afterwards directed their course towards Fishguard, and came to anchor in a small bay not far from Lanonda church, at which place they hoisted French colours, and put out their boats. They completed their debarkation on the morning of the 23rd, when numbers of them traversed the country in search of provisions, plundering such houses as they found abandoned, but offering little molestation to those inhabitants who remained in their dwellings. The alarm which they had first created, soon subsided, as their numbers did not exceed 1400 men, wholly destitute of artillery, though possessed of 70 cart-loads of powder and ball, together with a number of hand grenades. Though they committed no acts of wanton cruelty, two of the natives became the victims of their own temerity. In one of these instances, a Frenchman, having surrendered and delivered up his musket, the Englishman aimed a blow at him with the but end of it, when self-preservation induced the Frenchman to run him through the body with his bayonet which he had not delivered up. Immediately afterwards the invaders surrendered themselves prisoners of war to lord Cawdor, at the head of 650 men, consisting of volunteers, fencibles, and yeomen cavalry, reinforced by a multitude of colliers, who augmented his numbers without increasing his strength.

As soon as the frigates had completed the debarkation, they set sail for the coast of France, but were captured on the night of the ensuing month, while *standing in* for the harbor of Brest, by the St. Fiorenzo and Nymphe frigates. They proved to be La Resistance of 48 guns, and La Constance of 24. They were conjectured by many individuals to be insurgents from La Vendée, who had entered into the service of the republic, but whose principles rendered them unworthy of confidence. Others imagined them to be galley slaves and criminals of various descriptions, collected from the prisons of Brest, and sent to this country in a moment of arrogant caprice. The officer, however, commanding the expedition, declared that there were incorporated with his whole force 600 veteran soldiers. It has been alleged, in favor of the French government, that this expedition was only an experiment; but, if that apology be admitted, it will not justify the inhumanity of sacrificing so many individuals to the mere suggestions of official caprice.

While the principal fleets of France were confined within their own ports, their Dutch and Spanish allies were dreadful sufferers. On the 14th of February, a memorable action took place off St. Vincent, between a Spanish fleet of 27 sail of the line, commanded by Don Joseph de Cordova, and a squadron of British ships of war, under sir John Jervis, now lord St. Vincent. This illustrious nobleman was born in the year 1734, and is descended from a very antient and repect-

able family in the county of Stafford. He was the youngest son of Swynfen Jervis, esquire, a barrister of considerable reputation, who filled the offices of counsel to the admiralty, and auditor of Greenwich hospital. Lord St. Vincent's mother was the sister of lord chief-baron Parker. He entered into the royal navy in his eleventh year, and, having passed with distinguished honor through the different gradations of command, was raised, in 1759, to the rank of post-captain. Under the command of lord Hawke, he acquired the rudiments of that superior practical knowledge, the effects of which have been so repeatedly and so severely felt by the enemies of his country.

The distinguished skill with which admiral Jervis manœuvred the Foudroyant on the 27th, and 28th of July, 1778, and the gallant manner in which he fought the same vessel in the memorable action with the French ship, the Pegase, in the bay of Biscay, 1782, have been the subject of general panygeric. He afforded, in the engagement, a remarkable instance of skill and discipline; for, though it lasted nearly an hour, not a man on board the Foudroyant was mortally wounded; while the enemy's loss consisted of no fewer than eighty men, the greater part of whom were killed. For his gallant exertions on this occasion, his lordship was rewarded with the order of the Bath. In 1787, he was elevated to the rank of rear-admiral of the Blue, and in 1790, promoted to that of rear-admiral of the White. At this period he was a declared supporter of the measures of opposition, and uniformly acted and voted with Mr. Fox and his friends. Upon the commencement of the war, he thought it due to his country, to lay aside all political prejudices, and all attachment to party views. He therefore made an offer of his services to his majesty's ministers. The tender was accepted by government, and he was appointed, as we have already seen, to the command of the squadron which co-operated with sir Charles Gray, in the reduction of the French West India islands, particularly the valuable settlement of Martinique. In less than six months he returned from the West Indies, and, though he performed very important services in the bombardment of Cadiz, and the vigilence with which he guarded the Spanish ports, yet they were all eclipsed by the victory off St. Vincent. The ambition of the French was highly inflamed by the magnitude of the preparations against England, in the ports of Holland and of Spain. Conformably to the plans of the French and Spanish ministers, the most considerable part of the Spanish navy was to have effected a junction with the French fleet at Brest, and, after being joined by a numerous squadron of Dutch ships of war, they were intended to form collectively, a fleet of 70 sail, which might, by its preponderance, dispute with success the naval superiority of England.

In the list of the Spanish fleet intended for Brest, were six vessels of 110 guns, and one of 136. Of the other ships composing this formidable armament, two were of 84, and eighteen of 74 guns, but they were manned by an inconsiderable number of seamen. The Spanish ministry imagined that this deficiency might be supplied by the substitution of expert artillery-men ; but the number even of these was too inconsiderable to enable them to contend with the skill and courage of British seamen.

The squadron destined to oppose this armada amounted to 15 ships of the line and some frigates. On the 14th of February, Jervis descried the hostile fleet. He formed his line with wonderful celerity, passed through the Spanish line, separated one-third of their vessels from the main body, and, by a vigorous cannonade, compelled it to move to leeward. After having thus broken through the enemy's line and diminished his force from 27 ships to 18, he perceived that the Spanish admiral, in order to recover his superiority, was endeavoring to join the separated ships, by wearing round the rear of the British lines. But commodore Nelson, who was in the rearmost ship, directly veered, and, by standing towards him, prevented his design. His ship, the Captain, of 74 guns, no sooner passed the rear of

the enemy, than he gave orders to wear, and stand towards the Spaniards, on the other tack, in the execution of which undertaking, he came along-side of the admiral's own ship, the Santissima Trinidada. Notwithstanding the superior force of this enormous vessel, and the arrival of two three-deckers to her assistance, commodore Nelson continued the conflict till the appearance of the Culloden, and the Blenheim determined Cordova to retire. It was now evident that victory would declare in favor of the British ; for, while the advanced division was closely engaged with the centre and rear of the enemy's fleet, the admiral intended to join in the manœuvres of the detachment under his own immediate command, and to capture them one by one as they retreated from the rest of his fleet. The execution of this plan, however, was prevented by unforeseen circumstances, and a signal was consequently made to captain Collingwood of the Excellent, to bear up, while he himself, in the Victory, went to leeward of the rearmost ships of the enemy. In executing his orders, captain Collingwood passed between the two last ships of the Spaniards, and gave the San Isidro so dreadful a broadside, that she was under the necessity of striking. Collingwood then proceeded to the relief of the CAPTAIN, which was closely engaged with the San Nicholas, but, before his arrival, the latter vessel had surrendered. The San Joseph shared the same fate. The Victory, at the same time, was placed on the lee quarter of the Salvador del Mundo, the rear ship of the enemy, and poured into her so terrible a broadside, that she struck her colours. In the mean time, that part of the Spanish fleet which had been separated from its main body, had nearly rejoined it, with four additional ships, two of which had arrived since the commencement of the action. This was a strength more than equal to that which remained of the British squadron, after so severe an engagement. Had the conflict been renewed, there remained to the Spaniards 13 ships unhurt, while every one of the 15 originally composing the British squadron, had already suffered in the unequal encounter. It drew up in compact order, expecting the most vigorous efforts on the part of the enemy, to retake his lost vessels ; but such were the countenance and position of the British squadron, that the Spaniards, though so powerfully reinforced, did not dare to come into close action. Their fire was distant and ineffectual, and they left the British to move leisurely off with the four captured vessels : the slain and wounded on board of these alone, amounted to 600 ; and, on board the whole of the British squadron, to only half that number. The amount of the killed and wounded in the other Spanish ships was computed equal to that in the vessels that were taken. So singular a display of courage, skill, and good fortune, in which an armada of 27 sail was defeated by a fleet of 15 sail, deserved and obtained the gratitude of the community. To the just applauses of the public on admiral Jervis, government added the honors of the peer age, by creating him earl of St. Vincent, in order to perpetuate together with his name, the memory of this splendid and important achievement.

The vanquished fleet withdrew to Cadiz, whither it was immediately followed by the victors, who blockaded it so closely, that not one of the numerous ships of force belonging to Spain in that capacious harbor, durst venture out beyond the reach of the powerful batteries erected for its defence. The British squadron remained for some time within sight of the place, and in command of all the neighbouring seas, capturing numbers of the enemy's vessels, and performing many gallant actions. Various attempts were made by commodore Nelson to bombard the city ; of which many were disastrous, and only one partially succeeded.

The Batavian republic, which had been erected on the ruins of the antient government in Holland, had fitted out an armament in the course of the summer, consisting of four ships of 74 guns, five of 68, two of 64, and four of 56. They were in the best condition, completely manned, and provided with every requisite. The command was given to admiral de Winter, an officer of acknowledged merit in his profession, and of remarkable intrepidity. His principles were decidedly republican ; and he had therefore been appointed by the French to superintend the re-establishment of the Dutch marine, and afterwards to the command of the fleet.

A violent storm having reduced admiral Duncan to the necessity of returning to Yarmouth from the coast of Holland, the Batavian government ordered de Winter to sail with all possible expedition. They were influenced by the hope that he would be able, before the return of the English admiral, to effect his passage to Brest, and afterwards proceed to the coast of Ireland. In this expectation they were disappointed. Apprized by the signals of his advanced cruizers that the Dutch fleet had left the Texel, Duncan, on the 10th of October, sailed from Yarmouth roads, and, reaching the coast of Holland late in the evening, stationed his squadron in such a position as to prevent the enemy from regaining the Texel. Early in the morning of the 11th of October, he descried the Dutch fleet formed in line of battle about nine miles to leeward, between Egmont and Camperdown. To prevent them from approaching nearer the shore, Duncan resolved to break their line. This movement was accordingly executed, and admiral Duncan attacked the van of the Dutch, and admiral Onslow the rear. The ship commanded by Duncan lay nearly three hours along side of the Dutch admiral de Winter, and the conflict between these two brave commanders was remarkably obstinate and destructive. The latter did not strike his flag till all his masts were overboard, half of his crew were slain or wounded, and further resistance was impossible. The Dutch vice-admiral yielded to admiral Onslow, after he had been reduced to the same condition. About four in the afternoon the battle terminated in a decisive victory on the part of the British. Our fleet by this time was within five miles of the shore, and in no more than five fathoms water, so that the chief care of the admiral was to prevent his victorious fleet from being entangled in the shallows. This necessary precaution and the approach of night, compelled him to discontinue the pursuit, and saved from destruction a remnant of the enemy's fleet. No fewer, however, were captured, than eight ships of the line, two vessels of 56 guns, and two frigates. The loss of men on both sides in this bloody and well-fought battle, was considerable. In the British squadron it amounted to 700, and in the Dutch to twice that number; the choicest of their seamen. Such was the result of that skill, determination, and intrepidity, which distinguished the admiral from the beginning to the conclusion of the conflict. The victory was not less owing to the promptitude and judgment which carried the British fleet between the enemy and the shore, than to the valor of the subordinate officers and seamen.

Commodore Nelson having been promoted to the rank of admiral, was appointed to the command of an expedition against the isle of Teneriffe: He arrived at the place of destination on the 4th of July, and immediately prepared to carry his orders into execution. No individual could have been selected to undertake the enterprise, more worthy by his past exploits of the confidence of his country. To trace the progress of this illustrious character through the various vicissitudes of his eventful life is the province of the biographer rather than of the historian; and I shall therefore confine myself to the record of those events which more immediately tended to contribute to his future eminence, and to the elucidation of British history.

On the 11th of May, in the year 1749, the reverend Edmund Nelson, son of the then venerable rector of Hillborough, and himself rector of Burnham Thorpe, was married to Catharine, daughter of sir Maurice Suckling, rector of Barsham, in Suffolk, and of Woodton, in Norfolk, and prebendary of Westminster.

By this union the Nelson family gained the honor of being related to the noble families of Walpole, Cholmondeley, and Townsend : Miss Suckling being the grand-daughter of sir Charles Turner, Bart. of Warham, in the county of Norfolk, by Mary, daughter of Robert Walpole esquire, of Houghton, and sister to sir Robert Walpole of Woolterton, whose next sister was married to Charles, second son of viscount Townsend.

Of these virtuous and respectable parents, Horatio Nelson the fifth son, and the sixth child, was born at the parsonage house of the rectory of Burnham Thorpe, on Michaelmas-day 1758. He was educated at the high school of Norwich, and was afterwards placed at North Walsham, under the care of the reverend Mr. Jones. Here he continued till in the autumn of 1770, captain Suckling having obtained the command of the Raisonable, of 64 guns, one of the ships connected with the intended expedition to Falkland islands, immediately ordered his nephew from school, and entered him as a midshipman. After being properly equipped for this situation, he was sent to join the ship at Sheerness. His uncle being absent from the vessel, he paced the deck during the whole afternoon of his arrival, without being distinguished by the smallest notice; till at length, on the second day of his being on board, some one regarded him with compassion, and discovered, for the first time, that he was the captain's nephew. His hopes, however, of distinction, experience, or preferment, were nipped in the bud by the recal of the expedition with which he was connected, before the close of the year.

Two years afterwards, captain Suckling was appointed to the command of the Triumph, on board of which he placed his nephew, whose progress as a seaman he superintended with singular vigilance and assiduity, notwithstanding the obstacles opposed to his wishes by the detention of the ship at Chatham. In 1773, he accompanied captain Lutwidge as cockswain, in the voyage of discovery, under commodore Phipps, to the north pole. In the subsequent year he obtained a birth in the ship of the gallant and unfortunate captain Farmer, who, in the year 1779 perished in the flames of the Quebec,

NELSON

which accidentally took fire during its engagement with La Surveillante, a ship of superior force. Refusing to quit his vessel, though severely wounded, he was blown up with his colours flying. Under this brave and excellent commander, Nelson sailed to the East Indies, in the Sea-horse of 20 guns. He was at first stationed to watch at the fore-top; but captain Farmer soon discovered his abilities, placed him on the quarter-deck, and treated him with exemplary kindness. The climate proved, however, too powerful for the delicacy of his frame; and, by the advice of his friend, he returned home in the Dolphin, of 20 guns, commanded by captain, afterwards admiral Pigot. His uncle, captain Suckling, having now been appointed to the situation of comptroller of the navy, received him with his accustomed benignity, and obtained him the temporary rank of lieutenant in the Worcester, of 64 guns, under captain Mark Robinson. In this station he remained at sea with various convoys, till the 2nd of April, 1777; and, on his return, received a regular commission as second lieutenant of the Lowestoffe of 32 guns, commanded by captain William Locker. The Lowestoffe was ordered for Jamaica; and, during Nelson's absence, in 1778, his uncle bequeathed him, at his death, a handsome legacy. On the arrival of sir Peter Parker, to succeed admiral Gayton as commander-in-chief on the Jamaica station, the former of these officers successively promoted him first, second, and third lieutenant of his flag ship, the Bristol; and, on the 8th of December, appointed him to the command of the Badger brig, in which he was ordered to protect the Musquito shore, and the bay of Hunduras, from the depredations of American privateers. So ably did he acquit himself in the discharge of this duty, and so greatly had he endeared himself to the settlers during the short time he was among them, that they unanimously voted him their thanks for his services, and sensibly expressed their regret at his quitting the station, to accompany an expedition to the bay of Dulce. While these transactions were

taking place, he received the commission of post-captain, on the 11th of June, 1779. He had neither reason nor occasion to complain of the slowness of his promotion, for he had not yet completed his twenty-first year. In the bloom and vigor of youth, with an age of experience in the service, acquired in nine years, he was well qualified for the situation to which he was thus liberally promoted. The first ship to which he was appointed, after his advancement to the rank of post-captain, was the Hinchinbroke; and, in the month of January, 1780, he took a conspicuous part in the well-conducted but unfortunate expedition, fitted out in Jamaica under general Dalling the governor, against the Spanish territories in South America. In this unfortunate attempt he excited the warm admiration of his friends by his promptitude, intelligence, and activity. While he was thus bravely and arduously engaged, he was seized with the contagion, that ultimately rendered the expedition ineffectual. While he lay afflicted at the island of St. Juan with the plague, with scarcely a hope or a wish to survive the brave fellows who were every day falling around him, the reinforcement of troops which had been sent from Jamaica, brought intelligence that captain Glover, the commander of the Janus, of 44 guns, died on the 21st of March, and that sir Peter Parker had appointed captain Nelson to succeed him. His exultation at this testimony of respect and kindness, revived his spirits and saved his life. He immediately sailed to Jamaica on board the Victor sloop, to assume his command. His recovery, however, was not yet complete; and he returned home with an intention of trying the Bath waters. After the restoration of his health, he was appointed, in 1781, to the command of the Albemarle, of 28 guns; and, notwithstanding the smallness and craziness of the vessel, was employed, during the winter, in convoying and cruizing in the north seas. In 1782, he was ordered to join the Dœdelus in a convoy to Newfoundland, where he arrived with four sail of the convoy; and afterwards proceeded to Quebec, and from thence conducted a fleet of transports to New York. He soon afterwards joined lord Hood in the West Indies, and was sent to the Havannah, on a cruize of observation. He continued actively employed in the West Indies till the peace of 1783 ; and, on the occurrence of that event, he returned to England, where he arrived in July. Having taken a trip to France, from whence he was recalled to undertake the command of the Boreas, of 28 guns, which was fitted out as a cruizer ; and, being appointed to cruize on the leeward station, carried out lady Hughes and her family, to sir Richard Hughes, who commanded off Madeira. Having proceeded from that island to St. Kitts, he had the misfortune to incur the enmity of sir Richard Hughes, and of the inhabitants, in consequence of a misunderstanding with the latter. The quarrel, however, which proceeded to a legal contest, terminated in his favor, and several American vessels were condemned. Having appealed, while under the terrors of the law, to the gracious consideration of the king, his majesty had the goodness to order him to be defended at his own expense. In August admiral Hughes quitted the command, and shortly after captain Nelson received orders to take the Pegasus and Solebay frigates under his direction. The former of these ships was commanded by prince William Henry, the duke of Clarence, and the utmost cordiality subsisted between the commodore and his royal highness. At the island of Nevis, in March, 1787, he was united in marriage to the widow of Dr. Nesbit, daughter of Mr. Herbert, the senior judge. The marriage was celebrated with considerable splendor, and prince William Henry did them the honor to attend as the father of the bride. Of this lady he speaks in the first months of her marriage, with respect and indulgence ; nor would it have detracted from his estimation with posterity, had he displayed the same good sense and the same discretion at a future period. A few days after his nuptials, he proceeded to Tortola, and from thence to England, where he arrived at Portsmouth in the beginning of

July, with Mrs. Nelson and her son by a former marriage.

The Boreas was paid off in November, 1787, and the next five years of Nelson's life were spent in retirement and inactivity, chiefly at the parsonage house of Burnham Thorpe. In the year 1790, when the cruelties exercised by the Spaniards at Nootka Sound, seemed to have awakened the national vengeance, and an armament was ordered to be prepared, he immediately offered his services at the admiralty ; but, precluded by the claims of some, and the importunities of others, his efforts were ineffectual.

After two years more passed in retirement, the revolutionary war, having extended its baneful influence to this country, it became necessary to put forth all the resources of our naval power. His commission was immediately signed for the Agamemnon, then in January, under orders of equipment for the Mediterranean, as a part of lord Hood's squadron ; which soon after proceeded to the attack of Toulon. Lord Nelson, however, was not present at the final operations, as he was charged with dispatches from lord Hood to sir William Hamilton, minister plenipotentiary of the court of Naples ; a mission which almost equally contributed, by his introduction to the court and to lady Hamilton, to the glory and to the infelicity of his future life. He accomplished, however, the object of his voyage, and, after accompanying commodore Linzee to Tunis, was ordered to take the command of a cruizing squadron of frigates off the coast of Corsica. I have already noticed as far as they were worthy of detail, the cruizes and operations in which he was engaged during the two subsequent years. On the 11th of August, 1796, he obtained the permanent rank of commodore in his new ship, the Captain, to which he was appointed by sir John Jervis. Having convoyed in safety all the British troops from Corsica to Porto Ferrajo, he joined that admiral in St. Fiorenza bay, and proceeded with him to Gibraltar, where he remained but a short time, being ordered by the commander-in-chief to remove his broad peudant on board.

of La Minerve frigate : after several casual encounters with the enemy, and expending nearly a month in refitting ships and embarking stores and troops from Elba, he proceeded with sir Gilbert Elliot, late governor of Corsica, afterwards lord Minto, and other distinguished individuals, to Gibraltar. His junction with the fleet of admiral Jervis, and the exemplary skill, courage, and activity which he displayed on that occasion, have just been detailed in the account of the victory off St. Vincent. After that memorable conflict, the fleet sailed from Lagos bay, and proceeded to Lisbon, where they arrived on the 27th of February, 1797. While lying at anchor in the Tagus, his majesty's ships, the Orion, Minerve, Romulus, Southampton, Andromache, Bonne, Citoyenne, Leander, and Raven, received orders to place themselves under the command of commodore Nelson. The object of the secret expedition was a cruize in search of the viceroy of Mexico, who eluded his vigilence; and, having been appointed rear-admiral of the Blue, he was again ordered to Porto Ferrajo, to bring off the garrison; a service which he performed with his usual address. He then proceeded on his present expedition to the isle of Teneriffe. His force consisted of four ships of the line and three frigates. As he intended to surprise the enemy, the attack was deferred till night. At eleven, a thousand chosen men were embarked in the boats belonging to the squadron; they proceeded without being discovered, till they were within gun-shot of the Mole, which stretches from the town into the sea. Their approach being perceived, the alarm bells were rung, and a tremendous fire opened upon them from all the batteries extending along the platforms in front of the town. The night was so dark that only five of the boats could find the mole, which was defended by a body of 500 men. These the soldiers and sailors landing from the boats attacked and dispersed at the first onset; but so dreadful a fire of musketry and grape-shot was kept up from the citadel and the houses at the head of the mole, that they could not advance, and nearly all of them were killed or

wounded. This first division was commanded by admiral Nelson in person, having under him captains Bowen, Thompson, and Freemantle. The boat which conveyed captain Bowen never reached the shore; it was sunk by a cannon-shot, and he and his crew perished. The Fox cutter was lost in the same manner, with nearly 100 men. The other divisions under the commands of captains Troubridge, Hood, Millar, and Waller, landed at the south of the citadel, making their way through a raging surf that stove all their boats and wetted their ammunition. Notwithstanding these difficulties, they passed over the walls and batteries, and penetrated to the great square of the town, where, having formed to the number of 400 men, they marched towards the citadel, but found it too strong to be attacked with any hope of success. At this moment captain Troubridge was informed by his prisoners that 8000 Spaniards, assisted by 100 French, were preparing to attack them. Perceiving the impossibility of receiving aid from the ships, he sent captain Hood with a message to the Spanish governor, intimating, that if he would allow him freely and without molestation to re-embark his people, and would furnish him with boats for that purpose, instead of those which had been stove, the town should be no longer molested by the squadron before it. On the governor's replying to this message that the English should surrender prisoners of war, captain Hood answered that he was directed to tell him, that if the terms he had offered were not instantly accepted, the town would be fired, and an assault made by the English at the point of the bayonet. On this resolute declaration, the governor thought it prudent to comply with the terms offered. And captain Troubridge marched with his men, their colours flying, to the head of the mole, where they re-embarked in their remaining boats and in others furnished by the Spaniards.

In this manner terminated an unfortunate expedition, which cost the lives of numbers of our ablest seamen. Among the wounded was Nelson himself, who lost his right arm. The event might have been yet more disastrous, had not the forbearance and humanity of the Spanish admiral tended in conjunction almost every other circumstance of the war with Spain, to demonstrate that the court of Madrid had been reluctantly compelled to engage in hostilities. Early in the year, a British army appeared before Trinidad, a considerable island to the south of Tobago. Four Spanish ships of the line and a frigate, being observed in a bay nearly ready for sailing, dispositions were made to obstruct their escape. In the night, one vessel was seen to be on fire; three others were soon after involved in flames and destroyed, while one of 74 guns was taken by the English. The troops under sir Ralph Abercrombie landed without opposition : the chief town was not defended, and the governor tamely resigned the whole island. The same success, however, did not attend an expedition against the island of Porto Rico ; the troops being unable to force a passage to the islet, on which the capital is situated. They therefore retired after an ineffective bombardment of the town.

At the moment when the moderate party had regained their influence in the two councils of Paris, the English court, in conformity with the wishes of the people, again offered to negotiate. An official note dated the 1st of June, was sent to the French minister for foreign affairs, intimating the willingness of his majesty to open a negotiation for the re-establishment of peace, and for the regulation of preliminaries, to be definitively arranged at a future congress. The answer of the directory expressed an equal disposition to terminate the calamities of war ; but signified at the same time, a desire that negotiations should be set on foot for a definitive treaty. As they had determined not to enter into any arrangement which might give to England the advantage of consulting her allies, in transmitting the passports for the expected minister, they specified that he was to be entrusted with full power to negotiate a definitive and separate treaty. Lord Malmsbury was again appointed plenipotentiary, and arrived at Lisle early in July. He exchanged his powers with the French plenipotentiaries, Letourneur, Pleville, Pellay, and Maret, and had his first conference of business on the 8th of that month, when he delivered in the basis of negotiation proposed by the English court. The *uti possidetis*, or state of things as they stood before the war, was laid down as the fundamental principel of the treaty ; and it was offered on the part of the British, that every conquest they had made should be delivered up, except the islands of Trinidad, Ceylon, and the Cape of Good Hope. But it was expected in return, that the effects of the stadtholder should be restored as some compensation for the recent loss of his hereditary dignities. Some particulars were contained in the project of lord Malmsbury, on which the French ambassadors were unable to decide ; for which reason they transmitted them to the directory, and proposed to his lordship to discuss in the mean time, some other points within the sphere of their instructions. They strongly objected to the title of king of France, borne by his Britannic majesty, and declared that he could never be considered as acknowledging the republic, till its title should be abolished. They inquired whether France was to receive an adequate compensation for the ships taken or destroyed in the port of Toulon ; observing that they could only be held by Britain as a deposit till the republic was acknowledged, and that, this being done, it was necessary to restore them or grant an indemnification. On the 16th of July, lord Malmsbury received an additional intimation, acquainting him that the directory could not break their treaties with allies, and that consequently the restitution of all the conquests of his Britannic majesty would be an indispensible preliminary.

The British plenipotentiary replied, that a demand so unqualified and imperious, must immediately conclude the negotiation, as it proposed cession on the one side, and without compensation on the other. If this were the resolution of the directory, his functions were no more ; and it only remained for Great Britain to persevere in maintaining, with an energy and spirit proportioned to the emergency, a war that could not be ended but by terms so disgraceful. The instructions, however, of the plenipotentiaries were positive and precise ; and they therefore waited, or pretended to wait, during the whole of the month of August for further instructions from the directory. On the 28th, his lordship was informed that the answer respecting the stadtholder returned by Holland, was so unsatisfactory, that it was sent to the Dutch ministers at Paris, who durst not presume to alter it, in conformity with the wishes of the directory, without first applying to their own government for additional instructions.

While the negotiation was thus prolonged, the revolution of the 4th of September intervened, and the ambassadors were recalled from Lisle, Trielhard and Bonnier being substituted in their place. The new ambassadors informed lord Malmsbury that their powers were extensive, and hoped that the business before them would be terminated in a short time, if *his* powers were equally ample. As they were ready to proceed to treat with his lordship on the general principle of restitution, they wished to be informed if he was prepared to meet them on that ground, when he answered in the negative, and could not help remarking, that the demand of the directory justified him in doubting their sincerity. On the 15th, he was peremptorily asked whether he was possessed of powers which might enable him to proceed to the restitution of every possession taken from France or her allies. On his again replying in the negative, he was ordered to leave Lisle in twenty-four hours, and not to return without every necessary qualification from his court. Wearied by unnecessary delays, and baffled in his pacific overtures by the most mean and irritating finesse, his lordship hastened to comply with this command, and to lay before his sovereign the results of his unfortunate attempt. In the speech from the throne, November 2nd, the final rupture of the negotiation was justly attributed to the evasive conduct, the unwarrantable pretensions, and the inordinate ambition of the French ; and in particular to their inveterate animosity

against these kingdoms. Being thus compelled to persevere in hostilities, his majesty had the satisfaction of knowing that the country possessed means and resources proportionate to the nature and demands of the contest. He thought that the state of the war would admit some reduction of charges, but a heavy expense was still unavoidable, and the true value of any temporary sacrifices could only be estimated by comparing them with the importance of effectually supporting public credit, and convincing the foe of the continued spirit and the undiminished power of the nation.

When the papers relative to the conference of Lisle had been examined by both houses, lord Grenville requested the peers to vote an address, approving the conduct of the sovereign, and reprobating that of the enemy. In this address the commons readily concurred, no attempt being made to divide the house, though sir John Sinclair proposed an amendment for a speedy renewal of negotiation.

In mentioning temporary sacrifices for the support of public credit, the king alluded to a scheme for obtaining an extraordinary supply by a new and general tax, so as to diminish considerably the amount of that loan which would otherwise be required. Mr. Pitt expatiated on the supposed advantages of the plan, and then detailed its particular provisions. He mentioned such sums as would defray £6,450,000, desired a loan of 12,000,000, and proposed that 7,000,000 should be paid within the year, as a fresh tax. This impost was to be regulated by the assessed taxes of the current year ; but, if that criterion should raise it beyond a tenth part of the income of the most opulent individual, it would be reduced to that standard. All who were charged for male servants, horses, and carriages, besides houses and windows, would be subjected to treble assessment, in addition to what they already paid, where the old duty did not exceed £25, and where this rose to a higher amount, they would pay from three times and one half to five times the amount, *extra*. Those who lived in a less expensive style, would be less burdened; shopkeepers would be particularly favored, and some of the contributors would not pay more than the one hundred and twentieth part of their income. The plan was vehemently opposed in the house of commons, but was adopted by a large majority, notwithstanding the clamors of the people. In the house of lords it passed almost without opposition.

During the former session, Mr. Fox had absented himself from parliament, together with several gentlemen of opposition, declaring their attendance in support of the interests of the nation and of their constituents, totally unavailing. On the discussion of the assessed taxes, however, both he and Mr. Sheridan resumed their posts, and combated, with activity, all the financial regulations of the minister. To a bill for the commutation of the land-tax, Mr. Addington proposed an additional clause that voluntary contributions should be allowed; and the scheme of finance, after being farther combated in the house of peers with this annexation, was passed into a law. Voluntary contributions immediately commenced from the most opulent classes and individuals. Corporate bodies united with private persons, bankers, merchants, tradesmen, and mechanics, vied with each other in the extent and rapidity of their subscriptions, and the fair sex partook in the general enthusiasm. The amount of this contribution, calculated at £1,500,000, was of less consequence as a fund of supply, than as a testimonial of the public spirit. The discontents of the preceding years, and the influence of Jacobinism, had, in some degree, subsided. The signal victories of our naval commanders gratified the national pride, and removed the immediate apprehension of invasion. The re-appearance of gold and silver proved the responsibility of the Bank, and dispelled the alarm excited by the apparent uncertainty of public credit, and the abrupt termination of the embassy at Lisle being universally attributed to the French, awakened the general resentment. Even those who had most warmly disapproved of the commencement of the war, perceived the necessity of its continuance, and while they lamented the precipitance by which we had been involved in the miseries and distress of hostile contention, regarded it as their duty to their country and themselves, to co-operate with the minister in every possible means of defence and extrication.

HISTORY OF THE WAR.

Origin, Progress, and Termination of the Rebellion in Ireland—Subjugation of Switzerland by the French—Downfall of the Papal Power, and Misfortunes of Pius VI.—Affairs of the Smaller States of Italy—Humiliation of his Sardinian Majesty—The French take Possession of Turin.

GREAT Britain had defeated the fleets of her combined enemies, and foiled them in their plan of invasion; but it yet remained to frustrate their secret machinations. Disappointed in their design of seducing our seamen from their allegiance, the emissaries of France directed their attention to Ireland. That kingdom now became the field on which they practised their intrigues against the English government, and it must be acknowledged that their efforts were attended by too much success: but the turbulent scenes to which they gave occasion, will not be reviewed with unmixed regret by those who consider them as the immediate cause of the subsequent union between the sister kingdoms.

The Irish catholics had been gratified by the repeal of those penal statutes which had been enacted against them in ages of persecution, and had been admitted to a community of commercial privileges with the English. But while they acknowledged the supremacy of the pope, whose power and influence might interfere with the allegiance they owed to their natural sovereign, it was deemed unsafe to admit them to state appointments or to a seat in the Irish legislature, because the great majority which they formed would have endowed them with the whole power of the state, and the protestants who did not constitute above a third part of the in-

habitants, and whom, from the time of the reformation, they had regarded as intruders on their rights and property, would have been completely at their mercy. Valid as these reasons were considered by men of dispassionate minds, they were the very circumstances which augmented among the majority of the Roman catholics, their desire of emancipation.

The genius of the present times was favorable to their views. A spirit of innovation had gone forth under the mask of reform, which threatened the subversion of all antient governments, and the rejection of the principles by which they had been guided. Experience had not sufficiently convinced mankind that excessive tyranny might be practised under the cloak of freedom; and the mistaken zeal of the catholics was confirmed and inflamed by the disastrous state of the public affairs, which might possibly induce the government to conciliate the attachment of so powerful a description of its subjects, by compliance with their demands.

It may be doubted, however, whether the demands or expectations of the catholics at large, would ever have been supported and enforced by the most distant indication of rebellion. The majority of those who took a conspicuous part in the subsequent atrocities, were the outcasts of protestant society, imbued with revolutionary principles, and rendering the demand of catholic emancipation a stalking-horse to their own ambitious and revolutionary views. The great majority of the catholics kept aloof from the unfortunate contest, and the numbers of the lower orders of that persuasion, who followed the standard of rebellion, was by no means in proportion to the diffusion of the Roman catholic religion.

To promote the changes which they affected to desire, a number of turbulent individuals formed a society, in which they assumed the name of United Irishmen. This institution projected and organized by Wolf Tone, proposed to connect the whole Irish nation together, with the professed purpose of effecting a reform in parliament, and an equalization of catholic with protestant privileges. The plan of union combined secresy of proceeding with efficacy of council and of conduct. No meeting was to consist of more than twelve persons; five of these meetings were represented by five members in a committee, vested with the management of all their affairs. From each of these committees which were styled *Baronial*, a deputy attended in a superior committee that presided over all those of the barony or district. One or two deputies from each of these superior committees composed a committee of the whole county, and two or three from every county committee composed a provincial committee. The provincial committees, chose in their turn, five persons to superintend the whole business of the union: they were elected by ballot, and known only to the secretaries of the provincial committees, who were, in virtue of their office, the only scrutineers. Though their power therefore was great, their agency was invisible, and they were obeyed without being seen or known. Many misguided protestants accustomed to regard the Roman catholics as the cause of every evil by which the country was afflicted, and alarmed by the formidable numbers of the United Irishmen, formed counter-associations, and assumed the name of *Orange-men*, in honor of king William, the vindicator of protestant security, and the establisher of protestant

property and power in Ireland. The Orange-men proposed to disarm the catholics. Bodies of the latter associated to resist the attempt, and assumed the name of Defenders. Various quarrels occurred between the Orange-men and the Defenders, accompanied by many scenes of murder and depredation. Neither the prevailing disorder nor the several machinations were unknown to the French rulers; they dispatched one Jackson, a native of Ireland, and a protestant clergyman, but now an emissary of France, as a spy to Great Britain and to Ireland. In the latter country he formed a connection with Wolf Tone, Hamilton Rowan, and some of their associates, and proposed a plan of insurrection, which might facilitate an invasion from France. In England, Jackson had confided his treasonable plans to Cockayne, an attorney, who communicated his projects to Mr. Pitt, and undertook to accompany Jackson to Ireland, with an intention to discover his further views and intrigues, a service for which he was to receive £300, should his discoveries lead to the traitor's conviction. Cockayne being thus engaged to accompany his friend to Ireland, and pretending to participate in the plot, was introduced to Rowan and other conspirators. A plan was formed for the invasion of Ireland, and Jackson wrote several letters to correspondents abroad, explaining the state of that country, and the outlines of the project. The letters being sent to the post-office, Cockayne, who had perused them all, gave information to government; the letters were seized; and Jackson was tried. Cockayne was the sole oral evidence, but the papers, coinciding with his testimony rendered the case so clear, that the jury, without hesitation, found the defendant guilty. The prisoner was condemned to die, but escaped execution by the perpetration of suicide. By this discovery the correspondence with France was suspended; Tone and Rowan made their escape. Lord Fitzwilliam was by this time arrived in Ireland, commissioned to comply with the demands of the catholics, and thus, as it was imagined, to terminate the progress of disaffection. His efforts, however, were ineffectual, and upon his return to England, the discontent became still more deep and general. From this time the United Irishmen proceeded in their arrangements with greater vigor and dispatch: a military organization took place in the several provinces; arms were procured, pikes fabricated, and every preparation made for the immediate prosecution of their schemes. The activity of the leaders was unwearied, and extensively successful. They established a correspondence with the French government in France, through the medium of their Irish associates who had escaped after the apprehension of Cockayne; and the directory agreed to assist the Irish with a considerable body of forces, to enable them to throw off their connection with England, and form themselves into a republic. The offer was accepted, and lord Edward Fitzgerald and Mr. Arthur O'Connor, were appointed to arrange the terms of a treaty. For this purpose they went to France, met general Hoche in the summer of 1796, and arranged the business of the projected invasion, which was designed to be executed in the following November. In the latter end of autumn, however, intelligence arrived from France, that the expedition was deferred till the following spring. In the mean time the conspiracy proceeded with so much secrecy, that though the penetration of the Irish government discovered that there were strong grounds of suspicion, no precise information was obtained. On the 14th of April, however, 1797, they learned that a number of seditious people were to meet at a house in Belfast. On this information, the place of meeting was entered by a party of the military, and two of the associating committees were found actually sitting: their papers were seized, and documents were obtained which contained the most ample evidence of the nature and extent of the plot in agitation. Government immediately employed the most vigorous precautions against the impending danger, enforced the act against illegal conventions, and

seized great quantities of arms. In operations requiring military force and summary execution, bloodshed is unavoidable; and the malcontents set the example of atrocious violence by plundering houses and murdering the innocent inhabitants The soldiers were exasperated to revengeful and indiscreet retaliation, and the acts of both parties bore the character of infuriated passion and unrestrained licentiousness.

Whoever can conceive the image of a country rent by faction, threatened with a rebellion of its own people, and an invasion from a foreign enemy, ravaged by a desperate banditti, who committed every kind of enormity in the prosecution of their revolutionary plans, and, distressed by the dreadful consequences of martial law, will have some idea of the state of Ireland at this period. As an expedient for its relief, an attempt was made by the Whig party in the English parliament, for the removal of the most important pleas, by which the malcontents justified their proceedings by moving for a parliamentary reform. But the motion was rejected by a great majority on the ground of the danger which would attend the measure at so critical a period.

In July, the malcontents received information, that two armaments, one from Holland and the other from Brest, were ready to sail for Ireland as soon as they should be able to elude the British fleets. They therefore postponed their intended rise, and waited with impatience for the arrival of their expected auxiliaries. The defeat of the Dutch fleet in October, was a fatal blow to their hopes; and they now began to entertain a just suspicion of the designs of the French government against their independence. When they reflected upon the manner in which the Dutch provinces were oppressed, and how subservient the crown of Spain had been rendered to their dictates, they conceived suspicions that, under the pretence of establishing a republic in Ireland, the directory intended to subject them to their dominion or to their absolute control. These suspicions were confirmed when, instead of 10,000 auxiliaries which they requested, the French government insisted on the necessity of sending to their assistance an army of 50,000 men. Men of reflection were convinced, that conquest was the object of that tyrannizing power, and that the confederates were intended to be the instruments of its ambitious schemes, which were to lead the conquest of Great Britain, or its reduction to the same reproachful state of humiliation to which other powers had suffered themselves to be degraded. On ascertaining that the Irish were averse to their plan of invasion, the French directors turned their attention to objects which they deemed more advantageous and more practicable. They received the propositions of the conspirators with coolness; and the Irish, despairing of any effectual resistence from the French republic, prepared for an insurrection without waiting for co-operation from the continent. In the spring of 1798, they employed themselves in dispositions for war, and were guilty in the mean time, of the most savage atrocities. Conciliatory measures were at this moment brought forward in the house of peers by an Irish nobleman, after deploring the outrages committed on his countrymen by the infliction of martial law, recommended a parliamentary reform as the most rational and effectual means of restoring the national tranquillity. He was answered by the lord chancellor and lord Glentworth, who opposed to his arguments and his advice, that conciliatory expedients had been already tried, and gave it as their opinion, that nothing but force could subdue the glaring spirit of revolt which had manifested itself among the confederates. The motion was rejected, and this result was unexpectedly justified by a resolution of the confederates to pay no attention to any offer from either house of parliament, and that nothing should be deemed satisfactory but a total emancipation of their country.

Such was the secrecy of the chief conspirators, that though the plot was discovered, the plotters were unknown. At last one Reynolds, who had become an United Irishman, was struck with remorse, and prevailed upon by a friend, to disclose the names and proceedings of the secret committees, to the government. On this discovery fourteen of the delegates were seized in the house of Mr. Oliver Bond. Lord Edward Fitzgerald effected his escape; but, being afterwards discovered, resisted the officers sent to apprehend him, was mortally wounded in the scuffle, and died a few days afterwards. The remaining conspirators, now grown desperate, proposed a general insurrection; but captain Armstrong, a militia officer, who had insinuated himself into their confidence, apprized the government of their designs. The two Sheares of Dublin, Neilson of Belfast, and several other chiefs, were arrested on the 23rd of May. A plot laid by the conspirators for taking by surprise the camp, the artillery, and the castle of Dublin, was frustrated by a timely discovery; and their plans were disconcerted by the arrest of those chiefs on whose conduct they relied. But they persevered in their designs, though deprived of their leaders and ill provided for hostilities. They rose in arms in different parts of the kingdom, and, though they were defeated in several encounters, yet their behaviour proved them to be no contemptible adversary. They laid siege to Wexford, and, after defeating the garrison in an engagement near its walls, made themselves masters of the place.

The formidable aspect which they assumed, and the courage which they displayed in several subsequent actions with royalists, convinced the government that the most speedy and vigorous operations were necessary to suppress them. Alarmed at the progress which they were making in the province of Munster, the lord-lieutenant dispatched general Lake with a strong body of forces to check their advance. That officer, attacking them in their principal station near Enniscorthy, gained a complete victory after a desperate conflict. They fled on all sides: the insurgents in Wexford surrendered, and all the rebels, except those banditti who chose to live by plunder, availed themselves of the general pardon offered to those who should return to their allegiance, and retired quietly to their own homes. A similar result attended the revolt which took place in the counties of Down and Antrim, the insurgents being defeated in a hard-fought* battle at Ballinahinch. Immediately subsequent to these successes, lord Cornwallis was appointed to the station of lord-lieutenant; and that he might carry the olive-branch in one hand while he bore the sword in the other, he was commissioned to offer a general pardon to all who submitted, with the exception of very few of the most notorious rebels. The expedience of this measure was soon evinced. Before the minds of men were recovered from the agitation into which they were thrown by the rebellion in Munster and Ulster, their attention was called to another quarter by a very alarming affair in the province of Connaught. The agents of the Irish rebels in France, self-deluded by their own passions, and deceived by the representations of their correspondents, had persuaded the directory that the Irish nation was ripe for revolt, and that, if a French force should appear off the coast, the flames of rebellion would instantly burst forth. In this persuasion expeditions had been repeatedly planned, which had been frustrated by the vigilance and good conduct of our naval commanders. The French government could not spare so large a force as would be required to accomplish their design of reducing Ireland under the dominion of their republic, while they were prosecuting war in so many different quarters: yet it was thought advisable to cherish in this country a spirit of rebellion, and to cause a diversion of the British forces, in favor of the French armies elsewhere employed, by sending a body of troops to the aid of the insurgents. In the prosecution of this plan, general Humbert was sent with about 1500 men and three frigates, to make a descent in the north of Ireland. That officer,

appearing in the bay of Killala under English colours, easily effected a landing, having repulsed a small body of men who were hastily assembled to oppose him. So completely were the inhabitants deceived by the artifice of the French, that Edwin and Arthur Stock, the bishop's sons, and Mr. J. Rutledy, the port surveyor, were tempted to visit them, and were not undeceived till they were made prisoners. The British palace, to which the feucibles and yeomen retired after their repulse, being incapable of defence against the enemy's force, it was taken possession of by Humbert, who assured the bishop, on his appearing in the court yard, "that he came to give the inhabitants liberty, and to free them from the English yoke." Then hoisting a green flag with the Irish words, "*Ering go bragh*," *Ireland for ever*, in the front of the palace, he invited the people to join his standard, as the means of acquiring freedom and happiness. He assured them that the object of his expedition was to secure them from tyranny, to give them a free constitution under the protection of France, and to save from persecution the objects of religious intolerance. By the last assurance, the protestants, jealous of the catholics, and the catholics burning with resentment towards the protestants, were equally dissatisfied, and Humbert, by endeavoring to gratify the wishes and support the interests of each party, lost the favor of both. Surprised and disappointed by this result, he left colonel Charost to guard the palace of Killala, and advanced with all possible dispatch, to Castlebar, where, being reinforced by above 3000 rebels, he repulsed a body of forces brought against him by general Lake. His triumph, however, was of short duration. On the approach of an army under lord Cornwallis, Humbert, finding himself greatly outnumbered, embarked precipitately for France. The restoration of tranquillity was almost immediate. Holt, a daring and noted adventurer, surrendered himself to government: the recal of lord Camden and the appointment of lord Cornwallis, was highly acceptable to the Irish people; and the discomfiture of the malcontents was completed by the valor and good fortune of admiral sir John Borlase Warren. He fell in with a French squadron, consisting of one ship of the line, (the Hoche) and eight frigates, freighted with troops and stores for Ireland; the whole of which, with the exception of two frigates, fell (October 1st,) into the hands of the English. Among the prisoners taken in the Hoche was Wolfe Tone, who, being tried and condemned, avoided the infliction of an ignominious punishment by a voluntary death. Such was the termination of an invasion which evidently originated in the erroneous representations made to the French government respecting the general disposition of the Irish nation. The rebellious sentiments of a part of the people was misrepresented as a proof of general disaffection, and the French government was flattered with the sanguine but fallacious hope, that the majority of the Irish nation would, at a moment of partial discontent, submit themselves to a foreign yoke.

The apparent inattention of France to the affairs of Ireland, was occasioned by the multiplicity of her ambitious designs, and the number of her recent conquests. Holland, Spain, and Italy, might now be regarded as appendages of the French empire. Austria was prostrate at its feet; and the mountains and fastnesses of Switzerland had become the prey of revolutionary rapacity. The last of these events was well calculated to excite the astonishment of Europe; and it is even at this period impossible to conjecture the real causes by which a people of martial character, admired for their love of freedom, their industry, and their simplicity of manners, should have become so easy a prey to the French marauders. Much must be attributed, however, to the intrigues of the emissaries of France; the relaxation of moral principle among the people, and the corruption of their superior orders, many of whom were stipendiaries of the directory. In former ages the Swiss, who were not actually engaged in the military service of the neighbouring powers, devoted their time and labor to the cultivation of their fields and vineyards, and enjoyed the fruits of their industry in peace. But they had now become a nation of politicians. The literary societies, which had been established in every part of Switzerland, were the rendezvous of political disputants. Captivated with visionary projects of freedom, they joined in the popular cry of liberty and equality; assumed the appellation of the *friends* of *Rousseau*, or the *society of William Tell*; and became the ready instruments of the French agents, who were employed to promote dissention and revolt. So early as the year 1791, the democrats in the *Pays de Vaud*, testified their warm approbation of the French revolution, by a public celebration of the anniversary of its accomplishment. The beautiful country on the Leman Lake, once the blissful seat of every domestic and social enjoyment, now became the scene of faction and cabal. The Swiss, in their zeal for democracy, forgot the many instances of ill treatment which their countrymen, the Swiss guards and other troops, had received in return for their fidelity, in the progress of the revolution. Several individuals of distinguished character, carried on a correspondence with Clavieres, an intriguing Genevese, who was for a short time in the French ministry, and concerted with his associates, the means of effecting a change in their constitution.

When a government uniformly administers justice with impartiality, and in the general tenor of its actions demonstrates that the national welfare is the standard of its conduct, no man of sense who is well affected to the state, will complain of the necessary strictness of its discipline. Where unaccustomed severity, on the contrary, appears to proceed from party-spirit, it frequently betrays the weakness of the government, and irritates those whom it is intended to restrain. This remark is applicable to the state of Switzerland. The supreme council of Berne, which, by its want of energy, unanimity, and decision, had permitted and encouraged the progress of sedition, at length began to act with vigor, when the impending danger could be neither concealed nor averted. On receiving information of the intrigues which were carrying on in the *Pays de Vaud*, the favorite resort of the French emigrants, who were anxious to separate that district from the government of Berne, the council dispatched a special commissioner, accompanied by 2000 troops, to inflict punishment on the delinquents, and overawe the disaffected. When they opened their commission at Rolle, on the lake of Geneva, it appeared that the people were not disposed to give information against offenders. Two citizens of the society of *amis de Rosseau*, and three ecclesiastics who had disgraced themselves and their profession, by becoming incendiaries, were committed to prison: and Amadeus La Harpe, who afterwards signalized himself in the French army of Italy, having made his escape, was sentenced to die, should he return to Switzerland. Sensible, moreover, of the danger which threatened the public peace from the political clubs, the governments of Berne, Friburg, Soleure, Lucerne, and other cantons, issued orders for the suppression of all societies unauthorised by the state.

These governments, however, were destined to be convinced, by dear bought experience, of the extreme difficulty of remedying evils which originate in public opinion. The minds of the people were inflamed by the mania of innovation, and by the Utopian schemes which prevailed at this period of liberty and equality. Their dissatisfaction with the established governments was increased by the means employed to repress discussion. The advocates of reform being forbidden to appear in public places of resort, assembled in private houses, and at Basle, where a society of professed revolutionists had been established, a regular correspondence was opened with the national assembly of France.

Such was the disunited and agitated state of Switzerland at the commencement of the war between France and the two

great German powers. Had the cantons been united among themselves, and had they warmly and unanimously espoused the cause of the coalition, such an accession of strength might have turned the scale in favor of the confederates, and have averted the ruin and disgrace which awaited this once prosperous country. On the contrary, the want of harmony, which was the baneful origin of all their own evils, deprived the coalition of a useful ally.

Had not the Swiss been obstinately blind or enfeebled by distraction, the fate of Geneva would have operated as an admonition to their future conduct. Agreeably with the general maxim of the French government of disuniting in order to subjugate, they had insinuated themselves into the favor of the leading men in the Genevese councils, and by means of their faction procured the admission of a body of troops into the city, and rendered the state completely subservient to France. But neither the approach of danger nor the opportunity afforded by this event of observing the fatal consequences attending tame submission, had any influence on the policy of the Swiss. The Helvetic diet assembled at Arau, in 1792, declared that they would adhere to a strict neutrality between the contending parties. In the ensuing year their alliance was earnestly solicited by the confederates: but, being threatened with fire and sword, by the prevailing faction in the French government, they vainly endeavored to merit the friendship of that domineering state, by submissively repeating their assurance of neutrality. In the mean time the French government, being interested in preserving the neutrality of Switzerland during its hostilities with a powerful confederacy, and the insurrection of the royalists in La Vendée and the southern provinces, condescended to treat the Swiss as friends; and the cantons merited its friendship by acts of courtesy and by a strict adherence to their engagements. When the apostate Frederic William of Prussia was prevailed upon to desert his allies, Basle, as I have before related, was the place chosen for the conferences of the Prussian and French ambassadors. In the campaign of 1796, when Moreau was making his celebrated retreat, a part of his forces were suffered to pass through his Swiss territories, and were supplied with necessaries on their rout. During the subsequent sieges of Kehl and of the *tête de pont*, the Swiss drew a cordon along their frontier; and when, notwithstanding this precaution, the Austrian troops made irruptions on the Swiss territories, the cantons, on complaint from Barthelemi, the French ambassador, punished the Austrian officers who were charged with corruption. In 1797, they suffered Buonaparte arbitrarily to annex the Valteline, a territory belonging to their Grison allies, to the Cisalpine republic, without opposition or remonstrance. When that general passed through Switzerland on his return from Italy, he was received at Berne with the highest honors, which he repaid with disdainful neglect. He was justified by reasons of state in indulging his natural coldness and reserve. The French arms had been triumphant in every quarter, but it was with extreme difficulty that the government could find pecuniary resources. The directory therefore, instigated by a faction in Switzerland, who were violently inimical to the established government, determined on a breach with the cantons as an expedient for obtaining supplies, and for establishing a government subservient to their views. Preparatory to the accomplishment of this object, Mengaud, a warm republican, was sent to fill the station of French minister at Berne; and that ambassador, in the spirit of his masters, invited the Swiss to revolt, by promising the support of the *Great Nation*, to all who might "think themselves injured by their government."

To justify the meditated revolt of the Vaudois, a work was published entitled, *Essai sur la Constitution du Pays de Vaud*, of which the materials were provided by La Harpe, in which he stated that "this country had, while in the hands of the dukes of Savoy, possessed among other privileges, that of an annual assembly of the states, consisting of the dignified clergy, the nobles, and the chief magistrates of fourteen towns." He called upon his countrymen to assert their rights, to demand a convocation of the states, and, if refused, to claim the guarantee of the French republic; which might espouse their cause on the specious pretext of their late conquest of Savoy. As a further and more plausible ground of hostilities, the directory proclaimed to the world the injuries which France had sustained from the Swiss, which they could no longer suffer to pass unrevenged. They asserted that the Swiss had, during the war, made most usurious profits of their commercial intercourse with France: that not only their illicit traffic with assignats, but their fabrication of these securities, had greatly contributed to depreciate their value; they complained of the protection given to the emigrant priests and royalists, of the indulgence granted to a contraband trade, chiefly in British goods, and the suffering to reside in the country, an English minister, who, it was pretended by underhand practices, fomented sedition, and encouraged levies against the French republic; of persecuting the friends of liberty, and at all times displaying an aversion to revolutionary principles, and of having suffered the Austrians to pass the *cordon* at Huningen. Such were the most material charges suggested by the presumption which prosperous fortune inspired. In vain did Haller, a statesman of eminent talents, vindicate the conduct of his countrymen; the directory were deaf to his representations; and that the Vaudois might proceed with confidence in their revolt, they ordered Massena to advance with a division of the army of Italy, to the confines of the *Pays de Vaud*.

The governing powers in the cantons at length became sensible of their danger. But even now the same want of concord which had before created a diffidence in themselves, continued to have the most pernicious effects on their affairs. When the enemy was at their gates, and nothing but an united and vigorous resistance could save the country from subjection or dependence, the supreme council of Berne dispatched another special commission into the *Pays de Vaud*, to investigate the causes of discontent, and to suggest expedients for restoring tranquillity. The event of this measure proved its futility. While the commissioners were engaged in useless investigations, the malcontents, deriving confidence from the approach of the French troops, rose in arms on the 7th of January, 1798, and possessed themselves of the castle of Chillon, in which some of their associates were imprisoned. This proceeding was followed by the institution of committees of safety and other revolutionary acts.

In the mean time a general diet was announced at Arau, where, notwithstanding the assembly was awed by the presence of Mengaud, the French minister, all the deputies except those of Basle, renewed their confederacy by a solemn oath.

The city of Basle having been the place of congress for the treaties of peace, and Mengaud had made it his residence. That artful minister had, by his intrigues with Vischer, le Grand, Erlacher Huber, and other democratic chiefs, but above all with the grand tribune Peter Ochs, accomplished the defection of the canton from the Helvetic confederacy. They had instigated the peasantry to resist the present established authorities, and induced them to declare that the following were the only conditions on which they would adhere to the confederacy. I. An unqualified admission of liberty and equality, and the inalienable rights of man, and the consequent introduction of a representative government. II. An intimate union between the citizens and peasantry founded on the principle of perfect equality. III. A speedy convocation of a national assembly. This declaration of rights being accepted by the magistrates, who consented to the modelling of a constitution on democratic principles, the deputies were recalled from Arau, and the democrats celebrated their triumph by planting the tree of liberty. The example of Basle was followed by the prevailing democratic

parties in Zurich, Lucern, Schaffhausen, and Soleure; but in Friburg, and in some of the small cantons, the friends of the established order of things, had sufficient influence to prevent a revolution.

The government of Berne, in the mean time, where the aristocrats still preserved their ascendancy, prepared for resistance; but not with that energy and unanimity which alone could be expected to give them success. General Weiss was dispatched into the *Pays de Vaud*, to suppress the insurgents, to awe the seditious, and to retake the castle of Chillon. But he was not provided with a force adequate to these purposes, and acted with little spirit in the execution of his commission.

At the request of the Vaudois insurgents, general Menard, who commanded on the frontier towards Italy, prepared to afford them support. Preparatory to future measures, he dispatched Autier, his adjutant, to an interview with Weiss. Unfortunately for the honor and interests of the adherents of the established governments, Autier, and two hussars who escorted him, were assailed and killed on their rout. This outrage furnished the directory with a plausible ground of hostilities, and war was now to be waged, not merely in the capacity of allies to the Vaudois, but to revenge an insult committed against the French government itself.

This event was the more to be regretted on account of the state of affairs in the cantons. The council of Berne, in order to conciliate the affections of the people, had at this period called together delegates from the German districts of that canton, and was employed with their assistance in digesting a plan for remodelling the constitution. To inspire the people with confidence, they issued a proclamation, in which, while they acknowledged that there were defects in the constitution, they engaged that every defect should be remedied, and every error corrected. They then addressed letters to the French directory, stating the measures which they had adopted to remove the cause of its interposition, and dispatched deputies to

2 P 2

general Brune, who commanded the French troops in the *Pays de Vaud*, to solicit the privilege of reforming their constitution without the interference of a foreign power.

All these measures of prudence and precaution were found to be ineffectual, and they were reduced to the alternative of yielding to oppression, or, with a spirit worthy of their brave ancestors, of preparing for the resolute defence of their liberties. To preclude the possibility of effecting a settlement by conciliatory measures, Mengaud at once dictated the terms by a compliance with which they might merit the friendship of his government: that they should dismiss their antient magistrates and suppress their secret council and council of war, and that, until a new government should be formed, a provisional one, founded on democratic principles, and in which none of the antient governments were to be admitted, should be established. The rejection of these proposals was to be the signal of hostilities on the part of France; and that he might hold out the most inviting lure to the partisans of democarcy. Mengaud dispersed abroad copies of the plan of a new constitution, which, like those of France and Lombardy, was to be indivisible, democratic, and representative.

Nothing could have tended more effectually to rouse the spirit of the Swiss, than this dictatorial manner of imposing a system of government. " Notwithstanding some absurdities arising from ignorance of our situation," said the virtuous Lavater, in a letter written at this period, " I admire the constitution which you force upon us as a masterpiece of human genius, as a noble monument of great policy; I verily believe that nothing more sublime can be conceived for a polished nation, but I detest the means by which you require, command, and compel its acceptance." This sentiment, which prevailed in the minds of all who had any sense of the national honor, might have operated as their guardian genius, had not that ruin been brought on them by intestine distraction,

which no external force could have accomplished. The canton of Basle was already lost to the confederacy: that of Zurich was under the influence of the democrats. Those of Lucern, Friburg, and Soleure, jealous of the ascendancy of Berne, and desirous to see it humbled, not only neglected to send their proper contingent of troops to reinforce the Bernois army, but persuaded the smaller cantons to follow their example. Even the Bernois themselves were divided into three parties: the aristocrats were headed by the advoyer Steiguer, and general D'Erlach; the moderate party by general Weiss; and the democrats, countenanced and directed by Mengaud, Peter Ochs, and other warm advocates of revolutionary principles.

Under these unpropitious circumstances did general D'Erlach take the field with 22,000 Bernois troops, to oppose the conquerors of the Netherlands, of Batavia, and of Italy. Posting the several divisions of his forces between Soleure and Friburg, he prepared instantly to avail himself of the full powers with which he was invested, and of the indignation which the insolence of France had excited in the breasts of his countrymen, to bring his enemy to action. But at that instant, unfortunately, the prevalence of his opponents in the council enabled them to procure a repeal of his powers. The French general was no sooner aware that the council was rent by faction, and that D'Erlach was embarrassed in his intended operations by the repeal of his powers, than he rose higher in his demands, insisting on the immediate dismissal of the Swiss army. Having protracted the negotiation, and renewed the armistice which had been agreed to between him and the council, till general Schawenburg was arrived in the bishopric of Basle with a strong reinforcement, he then entered upon active hostilities.

While Brune prepared to attack the centre wing of the Swiss army, commanded by D'Erlach himself, near Morat, Schawenburg advanced from Basle, and, after some obstructions from the resolute stand made by the forces posted at the castle of Dornach and the village of Lengnau, he obliged the garrison of Soleure to capitulate. General Pigeon, with another division, made himself master of Friburg; and, with the concurrence of the magistrates, who were favorable to a revolution, he established in that canton a provisional government: On information of these disasters, D'Erlach retired towards Berne, before the united armies of Brune and Schawenburg, amounting to 50,000 men, and well provided with artillery. Though the movement was judicious, his present position being better calculated for defence, and for the protection of the capital, yet a retreat was deemed disgraceful; and a sense of the reproach attached to it, afforded the discontented an occasion of clamor against their general. A mutiny ensued, and great numbers deserted his standard. The whole country presented a scene of confusion; and the magistrates of Berne, whose wavering conduct had been throughout, instrumental to the revolution, forwarded its establishment by surrendering their authority to a number of persons hastily chosen by the people, under the denomination of *a provisional regency.*

This act soon brought the contest to an issue. The new administration would instantly have capitulated to that army by whose influence they had been vested with power, had they not been restrained by the moderatists and the people. To save their credit with the public, they gave orders for a general attack; and the memorable battle of Frauenbrunen ensued. While their forces were preparing for action, they were attacked themselves in different quarters, and behaved with a bravery sufficient to evince that the Swiss might have bidden defiance to the arms of the republicans, had they been united among themselves. The French artillery made among them prodigious havoc; yet they not only maintained their ground for a long time, but in one quarter repulsed a division of the enemy, with the loss of 2000 men, and seized all their artillery.

Unfortunately, this success was balanced by the issue of an attack in another quarter. So impetuous was the charge of the French cavalry, supported by the horse artillery, that the Swiss, who had only infantry to oppose them, were obliged to give way. They rallied, however, and, possessing themselves of a narrow pass, four miles from Berne, fought with a firmness and valor worthy of their illustrious ancestors. The women shared in every danger with the men; some of them joining the ranks, and [others rushing among the enemy and endeavoring to obstruct the artillery by clinging to the wheels of the carriages. Driven four times from their ground by dint of superior force, they rallied again, and made their fifth stand near the city gates: nor did they desist from the desperate conflict till more than a third part of their troops were slain. The remainder retiring to the mountains near Thun, left the enemy a victory purchased with the loss of 7000 men. General D'Erlach escaped from the field of battle, but was assassinated by his own troops, who suspected him of treason.

The provisional regency demanding a capitulation, the city was surrendered in the evening of this fatal day, (March 5th,) with no other terms than a mere gratuitous protection for the property and persons of the inhabitants. The French troops having entered the city, the tree of liberty was formally planted, amidst a concourse of people mourning the loss of their independence, and anticipating all the evils that might be expected to arise from the infatuation or wickedness of their rulers. Their apprehensions were realized in the conduct of their conquerors. The soldiers, regardless of their general's promise, pillaged the shops and rifled the persons of the citizens. The surrounding villages were delivered up to be plundered, and all who had property were reduced from affluence to extreme distress. Brune immediately proceeded to seize those public treasures which had been the great object of the expedition, and were to serve as supplies for the prosecution of other enterprises: and it was computed that, beside the contents of the storehouses, granaries, and arsenal, in the latter of which were found 300 cannon, the treasures and forfeited property of the patrician families would amount to 20,000,000 livres, (£858,333.)

Such were the first-fruits of the friendship of a state which had proffered its services to relieve the Swiss from oppression. But the inconsistency of the French government did not thus terminate. They, who had filled all Europe with complaints against the powers which had interfered in the domestic government of France, who had invited the Swiss to take refuge in their protection, by assuming the specious character of deliverers ; as if in derision of truth, honesty, and sincerity, having plundered them of their property, now proceeded to impose upon them a constitution.

This constitution, consisting of twelve articles, divided the whole country, including Rhœtia, or the Grison country, into twenty-two departments, each of which was to send four senators and eight counsellors, to the legislative assembly at Arau, by which a periodical choice was to be made of five directors, to whom the executive power was to be committed. Provision was to be made for a standing army, and for the organization of a national militia ; to be called together as occasion might require,

How must the bosoms of this once free nation have burned with indignation, how must they have regretted their lost freedom and independence, when they saw 1200 French grenadiers attending the diet at Arau, before which this constitution was to be laid under the pretence of affording it protection ? The representatives of ten departments accepted it : the other twelve departments either hesitated or positively rejected the summons. And yet we are informed that it was represented to the French directory, that the nation had celebrated this happy revolution with great exultation. The general sense of the people will be best collected from the occurrences which ensued.

It was from the small cantons where refinement and corruption had not found their way ; among the simple shepherds that the French experienced the firmest resistance to their power. Actuated by the love of indepedence, transmitted from their ancestors, the people of Schwitz, Uri, Underwalden, Zug, and Glaris, resolved to resist every attempt to introduce innovation ; and their deputies, assembling at Brunen, entered into a solemn engagement of mutual support. When it was known that they were adopting measures for the maintenance of their rights, the French general Carlion, dispatched Nouvion and Jordy with a strong body of forces to reduce them. Several conflicts ensued, in which the French fought with their customed bravery. But they were soon soon overpowered by numbers, and reluctantly constrained to accept the new constitution.

Even this result did not terminate the resistance of the small cantons, nor the sufferings of the Swiss. The people of Uri and Underwalden refused individually to take the civic oath, binding the whole nation to the constitution. They intreated the French general in the moving language of nature, to receive from a people ever true to their engagements, who among their craggy mountains had no other comforts but their religion and their liberty, whose only riches are their cattle, the sincere assurance that they will ever give to the French republic all the proofs of their devotedness, compatible with their liberty and independence. " Accept," said they, " citizen general, our solemn promise never to take up arms against the great republic, and never to join its enemies. Our liberty is our only blessing ; nor will any inducement excite us to fly to arms, except our duty to defend that blessing."

This artless and pathetic address wrought no effect on the French general. It was thought necessary to exterminate this band of shepherds, and so important was the achievement considered, that the general indirectly apologized for the abundance of blood which it had cost, by asserting that they were rebels whom it was necessary to subdue.

Thus was the subjugation of the Swiss completed; for though they were still flattered with existence as an independent people, yet an absolute dependence on France was evidently a part of the design of the French government. Domestic dissention was the cause of all the evils which befel them: yet we cannot reflect upon their history without commiserating a people, who, after liberating themselves from the oppression of the house of Austria, and struggling with a thousand difficulties, were rifled of their property and independence.

From these scenes of oppression we must carry our attention to the court of Rome, which was another source of those supplies which were necessary to the successful prosecution of revolutionary warfare. The Roman pontiff and his court were hastening to the last state of degradation. The abuse of the public money and of the sovereign authority to the purpose of *nepotism*, or enrichment of his nephews at the public expense, moved the indignation of the people: the requisitions made by France in consequence of the late treaty, together with the loss of territory, aggravated the national evils by rendering additional taxes necessary; and there subsisted a strong faction in the bosom of the state, which was hostile to the papal power, and desirous of seeing a form of government established more agreeable with the prevailing sentiments of liberty. A government under these circumstances, having no principle of stability in itself, deriving tranquillity from indolence, and the habit of oppression, though it might have continued in a state of torpor for some time, was rapidly approaching towards the verge of a revolution, which was only retarded by the superstition of the pope's Italian subjects. The burden of state affairs was sustained by cardinal Doria, a man of character and understanding, but not conversant in business of state; and the pontiff celebrated with the utmost regularity, the routine of court ceremonies and religious observances, apparently insensible of danger, while the storm was gathering which was to

prove fatal to the papal power. A contest had taken place between his holiness and the Cisalpine republic, respecting the pope's right to the fort of Santo Leone, on the frontier of the duchy of Urbino, which terminated in the reduction of the fortress by the republican troops. Pius deemed it advisable to acquiesce in the loss, and framed a memorial, to which Joseph Buonaparte, ambassador at the court of Rome, acceded; by which his holiness formally acknowledged that republic. The pope continued to appear in his accustomed state, yet held his power and his very existence at the mercy of France, when an incident occurred which proved the occasion of all the subsequent disorders. A tumult ensued in the city; and the populace, braving the papal government, boldly manifested the designs of their chiefs by exclaiming, "Huzza! for the republic, huzza! for the Roman people." Incensed at this insolence, the soldiers employed to repress the insurgents pursued them within the precincts of the French ambassador's palace, and fired upon them in his court yard, in defiance of his exhortations to withdraw. General Duphot, expostulating still more earnestly with the soldiery, and attempting to wrest a musket out of the hands of one of them, was shot through the body, and expired on the spot.

If the want of police in the capital or of discipline among the papal troops gave occasion to these rash and unjustifiable proceedings, it might have been expected that the pontiff or his secretary, conscious of their weakness, would have hastened to convince the offended party, that they were not implicated in the transactions, and that they were not unwilling to make atonement.

Buonaparte addressed a letter to cardinal Doria, acquainting him with what had passed; and, when the cardinal minister did not interpose, he wrote him a second, informing him of his determination to leave a city where he had been thus insulted. His inactivity was now converted into abject terror; and in a letter addressed to the marquis Massini, the pope's minister at Paris, after endeavoring to exculpate his holiness and himself from any participation in the offence, he added, "You are to request of the directory that they will demand whatever satisfaction they think proper, to ask and to obtain will be the same thing; for neither his holiness nor I, nor the court of Rome, will ever be content till the directory itself is satisfied." The consequences of a conduct so timid and humiliating, were such as might be expected. General Berthier, embarking with a body of French and Cisalpine troops at Ancona, advanced towards Rome. Approaching the walls of the city, he declared, by proclamation, that it was the intent of his mission, to bring to justice the authors of the assassination of general Duphot, and to take the citizens of Rome under his protection. This proclamation was the signal for the execution of the revolutionary design. Its advocates, invited by the friendly offers of France, assembled in the Campo Vaccino, and proclaimed the resumption of their antient sovereignty. They proceeded to constitute themselves a free and independent state, resembling that of France; placing at the head of the executive government five consuls, in whom was vested the authority formerly exercised by the pope and his council of state. A deputation was then dispatched to lay this revolutionary act before the French general, and implore his approbation.

He entered the city in military pomp, and, advancing to the capital, addressed the people in a harangue, on the magnanimity and benevolence of the French government. After admonishing the Italians to reflect on their ancestry, and to "resume their pristine greatness and the virtues of their progenitors," he acknowledged the independence of the Roman republic, which should consist of the provinces that remained under the papal dominion after the treaty of Campo Formio. To remove the apprehensions which the old government was endeavoring to impress on the minds of the people, that they would be despoiled of their effects, he declared that the severest discipline would be maintained, and that the persons,

properties, and lately-acquired liberties of the inhabitants, should remain inviolable. To prevent disturbance to the new government, he enjoined, by proclamation, the French emigrants to retire from the territory of the Roman republic within twenty-four hours. And that the world might not remain in uncertainty with regard to the grand object of his enterprise, after disarming the papal troops, confining the pope in the vatican under a guard of 500 men, and putting seals on his apartments, he demanded a contribution of 400,000,000 of livres in specie, 2,000,000 in provisions, and 3000 horses. In the mean time the cardinals, thinking it advisable to yield to a stream which they had not strength to resist, made a formal resignation of the temporal government of the state.

It being feared that the residence of the pope in a city where his pontifical dignity entitled him to reverence, and where his accustomed benevolence gave him influence, might be prejudicial to the revolutionary cause, he was commanded to leave Rome. His first place of retirement was a convent in the environs of Sienna. Being soon dislodged from this retreat by the shock of an earthquake, he was removed to a Carthusian monastery near Florence. The aged priest, divested by order of the French government, of the trappings of royalty, appeared more respectable than the stately pontiff had done, because he was more in character; and the resignation and humility with which he bore his degradation, were better calculated to excite reverential regard, than his former ostentatious performance of religious ceremonies.

Although the pontiff's fortunes were thus broken, yet the all-powerful republic of France did not think it advisable to suffer this shadow of ecclesiastical power to remain so near the seat of his former greatness. The grand duke was urged to send him out of his dominions; and, on his expressing an unwillingness to be the agent in doing what was so repugnant to his feelings, as that of denying the common rights of hospitality to the revered father of the catholic church, a sterner mandate was sent him by the directory. "Send him out of Tuscany; or we will hold you responsible for the disturbances which his proximity excites and may yet further excite in Rome." The grand duke, not daring to disobey the commands of France, it now became a matter of deliberation, where the successor of those spiritual potentates who had received homage from emperors, and had made all Europe tremble at the thunders of the vatican, should repose himself during the last mournful period of his life. When objections were made to his retiring to the territories of the emperor, or the king of Spain, Sardinia was at last chosen as his place of retirement. His removal, however, did not take place. Being seized with an illness during the negotiation respecting this affair, which rendered it impracticable without endangering his life, he was suffered to continue some time in his present residence.

The former subjects of his holiness, in the mean time, received daily testimonies of the high price at which they were destined to purchase the assistance of these descendants of the Gauls, in subverting their antient government, and " re-edifying the altars of liberty." Every state arrangement was made, every public measure was adopted, in conformity with the will of the French general; and multiplied exactions from every descriptions of persons possessing property, were made subservient to the pecuniary exigencies of the French republic. Had the duke of Braschi, the pope's nephew, who had amassed great wealth by his extortions and abuse of power, been the only victim of republican tyranny, his sufferings would have been unpitied. But when the whole sacred college, without regard to merit, were subjected to confiscation and exile, it excited commiseration towards them. When the world were informed that, in the course of a few weeks the requisitions in kind, the produce of pillage, the spoils of churches, and the contributions levied on persons of property, amounted to 8,000,000 sterling, their eyes were opened

to the farcical nature of those professions by which the French government had imposed on mankind, as the patrons of liberty and the protectors of natural rights; and men of reflection were convinced, that, should the European powers continue supinely to suffer their depredations, they would, under pretence of " re-edifying the altars of liberty," erect a system of tyranny far more tremendous than that spiritual tyranny which they were at this time endeavoring to subvert.

These grievances consequent on the revolution, would not, perhaps, have occasioned disturbance to the new government, had they not been accompanied with others which were more generally felt. The Roman populace, actuated by the love of novelty, and the harangues of those who had persuaded them of the advantages which they would derive from a revolution, had gladly assisted in the destruction of the old government, without considering by what means these benefits were to be attained, or what would be the immediate consequences of such an event. But when the pope and the rich ecclesiastics were driven from Rome, and the Roman princes, despoiled of their vast wealth, could no longer feed them at their gates; when the indignant populace found that the pittance which they had formerly obtained as the wages of servility or as the alms of the charitable, was withdrawn without any substitute, and that they were threatened with labour, to which they had an utter aversion, as the only means of supplying their wants; when all ranks felt the oppression of the military government, which was, in effect, established in Rome, they then began to look back, with regret, to the times when they had indulged their disposition to laziness under the drowsy lenient government of the pope, which was continually making an atonement for the effects of a wretched system of civil policy, by an ostensible attention to their wants, and the perpetual round of religious ceremonies and public shews with which they were amused.

The characters of the French generals

2 Q

who commanded in Rome aggravated these grievances. Berthier gave great occasion of complaint by his connivance at the outrages committed by his troops, particularly in the plunder of churches. These were so notorious, that the subordinate officers, to clear themselves from the suspicion of being implicated in them, signed an address to him, calling on the Almighty to witness their detestation of the extortions exercised in the city of Rome, and insisting, at the same time, on the payment of their arrears. When Berthier, now commander-in-chief in Italy, had been called on to quell a mutiny among the troops at Mantua, on account of the non-payment of their arrears, he was succeeded by Massena, whose rapacity was rendered more odious by brutal manners. Luxurious as well as ferocious, he disgusted his officers and the citizens by the sumptuous style in which he lived, amidst a scene of distress. General Brune, who was appointed his successor, on the earnest entreaty of the officers for his removal, restored tranquillity by the strict regulations which he made; and the government, to appease the people, punished some of the most notorious depredators severely for their crimes; endeavouring, at the same time, to throw the blame of the tumults, which these outrages of their troops and agents had occasioned, on the prisons of the pope.

In fact, all orders of men became dissatisfied and disgusted with the authors of the revolution, when they witnessed the abuses and outrages committed under the specious show of conferring liberty, and when they saw their new governors reduced to the capacity of instruments in the hands of the French republic, to extort enormous contributions with the forms of law. So odious and despicable was such an employment, that men of honor and humanity either resigned their appointments in the state, or were dismissed for their opposition to the measures which they were required to execute; and their places were filled with men who were well pleased to enrich themselves at the expense of their fame. These discontents afforded the counter-revolutionists an opportunity of forwarding their views, which they readily embraced. The oppression, the depredations, the exactions, practised by men who professed themselves the deliverers of nations, descendants of the Gauls, come, with the olive-branch of peace in their hands, to "re-edify the altar of liberty," were displayed by them in the most odious light. Nor did they fail of success. The populace, disappointed of the blessings which they had been taught to expect from the revolution, deprived of the bread which they had been accustomed to receive from the opulent, and of the spectacles and processions with which they had formerly been amused, readily became agents in destroying that system which they had assisted in erecting, and so edifying what they contributed to demolish. An insurrection took place at Fiorentino, in the Campagna di Roma, in which the clergy, dropping their pacific character, bore a distinguished part. General Macdonald, then commander of the French forces at Rome, dispatched a body of troops against them. A severe conflict ensued; and the insurgents were at last defeated, but not without much slaughter on both sides. A similar issue attended an insurrection at Terracium.

The consequence of these efforts to redress themselves was an increase of misery to the inhabitants of the ecclesiastical states. All the towns which had countenanced the insurrection, were given up to be plundered. And Macdonald, the fit agent of a tyrannical state, caused two laws to be published; by one of which, all who were implicated in these insurrections, were made liable to a capital punishment; by the other, the association, denominated, The company of the faith of Jesus, were rendered liable to be tried by a military court. He availed himself of the occasion which these disturbances afforded, to exact a forced loan, by which the possessors of from three to 6000 crowns a year were called upon for one-third of their income; those who had from six to 10,000, two-thirds; and those of 10,000, the whole.

The same dictatorial power was exercised in all the other countries which France had subjugated, under pretence of rendering them independent states. The Cisalpine republic was honored with the peculiar regard of Buonaparte: it was, indeed, the result of his successful enterprises; the formation of it carried him to the summit of his glory. When he bade adieu to the Cisalpines to revisit France, and digest with the directory the plan of his intended Egyptian expedition, he reminded them of their happiness in having recovered their liberty, and admonished them that it was their duty to preserve it.

However desirous those republicans might be to conform to his exhortations, they soon found the difficulty of doing it under the protection of France: they were informed, by experience, that, however dear their rights might be held by their patron, they were not deemed inviolable by the directory. That constitution which Buonaparte had framed, was destined immediately to give place to another, wherein the ascendancy of the French government might be better provided for. The new constitution proposed to the councils by Trouvé, the French ambassador, was vigorously opposed, but without effect. It was carried into execution by that minister, in conjunction with general Brune, who was sent into Italy for that purpose; and was followed by reinforcements of troops to the garrisons in Lombardy, to aid them in their proceedings, should occasion require their assistance.

The Cisalpines, about the same time, were constrained, contrary to their inclinations, to enter into an alliance with the French republic; by which they were bound to become a party in all the wars in which that state should engage, and to assist it with all its means and resources, when so required. This was accompanied with a commercial treaty between the two republics.

But they were soon to have fuller and more humiliating conviction of their subserviency to France. When it was seen that these changes occasioned dissatisfaction in the councils, lest the Austrian partisans should gain a majority, a considerable number of the members of those bodies, together with three directors and several of the ministry, were dismissed. These proceedings were protested against by the Cisalpines, as a violation of their independence. On their appealing to the French directory, the general and the ambassador were summoned to Paris, to give an account of the transaction; but no redress was given. That they might completely establish their power in Italy, and provide every possible security against the Austrian partisans, who began boldly to declare that they regretted a change of system which had laid heavier burdens on them, and destroyed their tranquillity without giving them independence; the directory ordered a correspondent change to be made in the Ligurian republic, which had been formed under their direction.

The same tyranny was practised by the French government towards the Swiss. Seventeen towns, and above a hundred villages had been sacked or committed to the flames; and the districts inhabited by those who had dared to disobey their commands, were laid waste. The advocates for more perfect liberty, hoped by these sacrifices to have attained their object. They were, however, destined, like others who had expected to obtain liberty by the assistance of France, to experience disappointment. Their new constitution was scarcely formed, when the French directory began to interpose in the administration of their government; and they sufficiently evinced how incompatible was the real enjoyment of freedom with their principles, by causing a law to be passed prohibiting citizens from presenting petitions in a corporate capacity. When this was opposed by the people, as inconsistent with their liberties, three officers waited on the senate and great council, by orders from general Schawenburg and Rapinat, the French commissioner, to inform them, "that the commissioner considered the country as conquered by the arms of France, and himself as entitled to direct all civil, military, and financial operations; therefore, whoever should endeavor to obstruct the measure taken by the French, for the arrangement of affairs in Switzerland would be viewed as an enemy, and as an agent of England."

These measures, though submitted to by the Helvetic government, were so warmly resented by the whole nation, that the directory, apprehensive of the ill-consequences of them, thought it advisable to rescind them; and assured the Helvetic body that they should remain in full possession of their independency. But so evident was it in every transaction, that they were expected to obey the mandates of France, even in their domestic affairs, and especially those of finance, that the advocates of liberty, who were in the French interests, exclaimed against such subservience, as a dereliction of their principles and a violation of that independency and freedom which they had pretended to confer. These persons were confirmed in their opinions and their apprehensions by an edict dictated by the partisans of France, of a most arbitrary and unreasonable nature, enjoining all the Swiss in foreign parts, to repair to their native country within the space of a month, in order to take the civil oath. So inauspicious was this interference of France, in the affairs of the Helvetic republic, deemed to the revival of liberty, that great repugnance was expressed by many to the alliance, offensive and defensive, concluded at this time between the two states; and it was already presaged, that jealousy would soon disunite them.

The transactions of this period in the Dutch provinces, were no less calculated than any of the preceding, to manifest to the world the determination of the French

republic to render every state which had accepted its proffered assistance in new-modelling their governments, subservient to its power. The Dutch nation were divided, with respect to political opinions, into two classes: the partisans of the nobles and other men of great landed property, who, with their estates, received from their ancestors an attachment to that government, under which, with all its imperfections, they had prospered during so many ages; and those of the merchants and other commercial men, who aspired to the importance to which they thought themselves entitled by their wealth, who were desirous of a revolution which should supplant the aristocrats in their power, and of a constitution better adapted to their views. The latter had been the partisans of France in the late revolt in 1786, when the stadtholder was driven from the Hague and deprived of his offices; and they had, from the time of the invasion in 1795, been endeavouring to accomplish the abolition of their antient federal union and distinct provisional constitutions, and to accomplish the formation of a constitution resembling that of France, by which they should be formed into one indivisible state.

The revolutionary partisans having at length overcome their opponents, accomplished their design. Thinking it proper to have the national sanction to a measure of such importance, the majority in the acting legislature, first collected the signatures of those who approved the fundamental articles of the proposed constitution. The president then convoked an assembly of the legislature, by the authority of which, six commissioners of foreign relations, and twenty-one members of their own body, who had been most active in opposing their measures, were put under an arrest. After these preparatory steps, having constituted themselves the sole governing and legislative power of the Batavian nation, they proceeded to abrogate all provincial governments and jurisdictions; and they constituted an executive government of directory, consisting of five members, who were to receive their nomination and general instructions from the legislature.

However conducive this measure might have been to the national prosperity, could the provinces have been independent of France, it was expected that the execution of it in so arbitrary a manner, by a party supported by that power, strictly forbade the nation to make remonstrances or present petitions in their corporal capacity, either to the legislature or the directory.

Thus was the Dutch nation told, at the very instant of their pretended regeneration, that they were no longer to enjoy that privilege which has ever been deemed essential to freedom, of making known their sentiments on national affairs, and petitioning for redress of their grievances. The subsequent measures of the government were correspondent with the same spirit of oppression, and pointed out the evil genius which was destined to preside over the councils of the Dutch states. The French partisans, not content with the establishment of a constitution, which, by bringing the national representatives together in one body, might render the state more liable to be influenced by France, prepared to engross every branch of power, by dismissing all who were suspected of disaffection to them from appointments, and replacing them with persons devoted to their interests. Under the specious pretext of attending to the public welfare and tranquillity, they excluded from the primary assemblies as dangerous to the national peace, all who presumed to condemn their measures ; and that they might establish their power, when the people had accepted the constitutional act, the sitting assembly passed a decree, declaring itself the legislative assembly of the Batavian republic.

His Sardinian majesty, to avoid a repetition of the evils which he suffered in the late war, had adhered with strictness to the treaty of neutrality with France, concluded in 1796. But his good faith was rewarded by the violation of every just engagement and every honorable feeling. An insurrection having occurred at Carosio, a town belonging to Piedmont, but inclosed by the dominions of Genoa, and the directory, having disclosed a disposition to protect the insurgents, a dispute ensued respecting the right of the king of Sardinia to march his troops, intended to suppress them through the intermediate territory. Guinguené, the French ambassador at Turin, unreservedly declaring himself their protector, insisted on their being pardoned, and was supported by general Brune. The Ligurian republic gave his majesty to understand that they would espouse the cause of the insurgents. The French minister, openly interposing in their behalf, demanded, in the name of the French directory, an absolute oblivion of the past, on condition of their laying down their arms. The king did not refuse compliance ; he only hesitated ; and the repugnance with which he complied, was deemed a sufficient apology for requiring the immediate cession of the city of Turin, as a security for the performance of his engagement to pardon the delinquents. Willing to avoid at any expense, however grievous, the renewal of war, the king agreed to the consignment, by admitting French troops into his fortress. He soon had reason to repent of his tameness, and learned, by fatal experience, that a prince ought to hazard existence itself, rather than submit to degradation in the eyes of his people. The encroachments of the French on the territories of this injured prince, accelerated the preparations of the emperor, who drew his forces to the Swiss frontier, apparently with the intention of protecting the Grisons, which the French government were preparing to seize, in order to complete their line of communication with the north of Italy. He at the same time opened negotiations with the court of Naples, and descanted on the necessity of vigorous opposition to a power which threatened destruction to all existing establishments. These sentiments perfectly corresponded with those of his Neapolitan majesty. The alarm which that monarch had conceived from the proceedings of the French in the ecclesiastical state, and in Piedmont, was heightened by the arrogance which he had repeatedly experienced, the augmentation of their forces at Rome, and the report of an intended enterprise under the command of Buonaparte in the Mediterranean. The necessity of a close alliance with the house of Austria, whose situation was similar to his own, became daily more evident; and arrangements were made with the imperial court, while recourse was had to the most eligible modes of raising the supplies. The French government observing these appearances of an hostile intention, endea-vored to divert Don Ferdinand from his warlike councils, by reminding him of the tenor of the late treaty; and to intimidate him, the French ambassador admonished him of the great number of malcontents in his dominions, who were ready to join the French army in case of an invasion. But these menaces had no longer their desired effect; and Don Ferdinand, as the best preservative of domestic peace, caused the malcontents who had been liberated, to be placed once more in durance.

HISTORY OF THE WAR.

CHAP. XVIII.

CONVINCED of the hopelessness of any direct attempt upon England, the French government, at the suggestion of Buonaparte, formed a bold and extensive plan of conquest which would ultimately menace the oriental possessions of Great Britain. The project was to subdue Malta, invade Egypt, and extend their sway to the shores of the Ganges. The pretended invasion of England was apparently prosecuted for a considerable time after the design had been abandoned, that their real purpose might be the more effectually concealed and accomplished. While bodies of troops and stores were drawn towards the coasts of Normandy and Brittany, other forces and supplies were collected at Toulon. This port was the rendezvous of the expedition which sailed under the orders of Buonaparte, on the 20th of May, 1798. It consisted of 13 ships of the line, seven frigates of 40 guns, and several smaller vessels, making together 44 sail. The transports amounted to nearly 200, carrying about 40 000 regular troops, with a proportionable number of horses and artillery, and immense quantities of provisions and military stores. Buonaparte, in all his expeditions and designs, included the advancement of knowledge. His fleet was crowded by artists and men of science; astronomers, mathematicians, chemists, mineralogists, botanists, physicians, and many other classes of ingenious and learned men: certainly a much more rational assortment of attendants than the buffoons, parasites, and prostitutes, who formed the usual retinue of the former monarchs of France. A variety of conjectures were formed respecting the destination of this formidable armament. Malta and Egypt were generally conjectured, however, as the event confirmed to be its principal objects. The riches of the former were a sufficient temptation to the rapacity of France; the latter appeared to be an acquisition of the highest importance, as presenting the means of access to our possessions in India, and affording the most evident facilities to the interruption of our Indian trade. On the 9th of June, the fleet arrived off Malta. The admiral first solicited permission to water the fleet; and the grand master, refusing to comply with the request, Buonaparte determined to attack the place. At day-break, on the 11th, a languid fire was maintained: a bark came out from the port, and was conducted to the L'Orient; at eleven, a second, under a flag of truce, conveyed on board the fleet those knights who chose to abandon Malta. It appeared that the garrison was almost totally unprovided with stores and provisions, and at four in the afternoon there were fewer men than guns on the walls of the fort. It was evident that the citizens and knights had disagreed; the gates of the forts being shut, and all intercourse between them and the town being at an end. The general sent his aid-de-camp Junot, with his ultimatum; soon after ten Maltese commissioners came on board the L'Orient, and on the 12th, at half past eleven, Malta was in the power of the French. The French troops took possession of the forts under a salute of 500 guns from the fleet, thus completing the conquest of the strongest post in the Mediterranean.

Within eight days Buonaparte organized a provisional government in the island of Malta, victualled the fleet, obtained a supply of water, and arranged all the dispositions. He quitted it on the 19th of June, leaving the command to general Vanbois.

On the 26th, the captain of the Juno received orders to make all sail for Alexandria, now sixty leagues distant, and there to learn from the French consul, whether the expedition had been heard of, and the disposition of the inhabitants with regard to the enterprise. He then issued general orders from on board the L'Orient, and shortly afterwards received a visit from the consul, to whom the Juno had been dispatched. That gentleman informed him that the appearance of the French frigate caused the immediate adoption of oppressive measures against the Christian inhabitants of the city, and that he had great difficulty in effecting his escape. He added, that fourteen English vessels appeared off Alexandria on the 28th of June, and that it was determined to defend the city and forts against any troops that should attempt to land.

The general-in-chief made on the same evening arrangements for landing, and fixed on the point at Marabou as the spot. He ordered the fleet to anchor as near the point as possible; but two ships of war, in preparing to execute his orders, ran foul of the enemy's ship, which caused the attempt to be abortive, and the armament remained at its then situation. They were at a distance of about three leagues from the shore. the wind was northerly, and

blew with violence, and the debarkation was equally perilous and difficult; but nothing could retard the impetuosity of the French, who were eager to anticipate the hostile disposition of the inhabitants. The sea was covered with boats, which stemmed the impetuosity of the waves. The galley which conveyed Buonaparte approached the nearest breakers, from which the entrance to the creek of Marabou was discovered. He waited for those boats that were destined to join him, but they did not arrive till after sun-set, and he could not, during the night, penetrate the ledge of breakers. Early in the morning, however, he was enabled to land on the scene of new achievements, at the head of the foremost troops, who formed in the desert about three leagues from Alexandria.

It would be a waste of time to enter into a detail of all the military arrangements, described by Denon and other French writers as preparatory to the attack on Alexandria. No such preparations were necessary. The fortresses were in ruins, and the people, unconscious of the enemy's approach, wholly unprepared for defence. As the narrative of Louis Buonaparte, afterwards king of Holland, exhibits at once the talents and character of the writer, and does not abound in extravagant assertion so much as the statements of his French comrades, I shall here insert it.

"At break of day on the 2nd, we invested Alexandria, after driving into the town several small detachments of cavalry: the enemy defended themselves like men; the artillery which they planted on the walls was wretchedly served, but their musketry was excellent. These people have no idea of children's play; they either kill, or are killed. The first inclosure, however, that is to say, that of the city of the Arabs, was carried; and, soon after, the second, in spite of the fire from the houses. The forts, which are on the coast on the other side of the city, were then invested; and in the evening capitulated.

"Since the 2nd of July we have been engaged in disembarking the troops, the

artillery, and the baggage. General Desaix is at Demanhur, on the Nile; the rest
of the army is to follow him.

"The place where we disembarked is
about two leagues from hence, at the
tower of Marabou, or the *Isles des Arabes*.
The two first days we had a number of
stragglers cut off by the Arab and Mameluke cavalry. I imagine that we have lost
about 100 killed, and as many wounded.
The generals Kleber, Menou, and Lascalle,
are wounded.

"I send you the proclamation to the
inhabitants of the country, which has produced an effect altogether 'astonishing.
The Bedouins, enemies of the Mamelukes,
and who, properly speaking, are neither
more nor less than intrepid robbers, sent us
back, as soon as they had read it, thirty
of our people, whom they had made
prisoners, with an offer of their services
against the Mamelukes. We have treated
them kindly: they are an invincible people,
inhabiting a burning desart, mounted on
the fleetest horses in the world, and full
of courage: they live with their wives and
children in flying camps, which are never
pitched two nights together in the same
place. They are horrible savages, and
yet they have some notion of gold and
silver; a small quantity of it serves to
excite their admiration. Yes, my dear
brother, they love gold; they pass their
lives in extorting it from such Europeans
as fall into their hands; and for what
purpose:—for continuing the course of
life which I have described, and for teaching it to their children. O Jean Jacques!
why was it not thy fate to see those men,
whom thou callest ' the men of nature?'
thou wouldest sink with shame, thou
wouldest startle with horror at the thought
of having once admired them!

"Adieu, my dear brother, let me hear
from you soon. I suffered a great deal
on our passage; this climate kills me;
we shall be so altered that you will discover the change at a league's distance.

"The remarkable objects here are,
Pompey's column, the obelisks of Cleo-
patra, the spot where her baths once stood,
VOL. I.

a number of ruins, a subterraneous temple,
some catacombs, mosques, and a few
churches. But what is still more remarkable, is the character and manners of the
inhabitants: they are of a *sang-froid* absolutely astonishing: nothing agitates
them; and death itself is to them, what a
voyage to America is to the English.

"Their exterior is imposing: the most
marked physiognomies amongst us are
mere children's countenances compared to
theirs. The women wrap themselves up
in a piece of cloth, which passes over their
heads, and descends in front to the eye-
brows: the poorer sort cover the whole
of their face with linen, leaving only two
small apertures for the eyes; so that, if
this strange veil happens to be a little
shrivelled, or stained, they look like so
many hobgoblins.

"Their forts and their artillery are the
most ridiculous things in nature: they
have not even a lock, nor a window
to their houses; in a word, they are still
involved in all the blindness of the earliest
ages.

"Oh! how many misantropes would
be converted, if chance should conduct
them into the midst of the desarts of
Arabia!"

Buonaparte, on establishing his head
quarters at Alexandria, issued the following

PROCLAMATION.

IN THE ARABIC LANGUAGE.

"In the name of God, gracious and
merciful.—There is no God but God;
he has no son or associate in his kingdom.

"The present moment, which is destined
for the punishment of the Beys, has been
long anxiously expected. The Beys,
coming from the mountains of Georgia and
Bajars, have desolated this beautiful
country, long insulted and treated with
contempt the French nation, and oppressed
her merchants in various ways. Buonaparte, the general of the French republic,

according to the principles of liberty, is now arrived ; and the Almighty, the Lord of both worlds, has sealed the destruction of the Beys.

"Inhabitants of Egypt! When the Beys tell you the French are come to destroy your religion, believe them not: it is an absolute falsehood. Answer those deceivers, that they are only come to rescue the rights of the poor from the hands of their tyrants, and that the French adore the Supreme Being, and honor the prophet and his holy Koran.

"All men are equal in the eyes of God : understanding, ingenuity, and science, alone make a difference between them : as the Beys, therefore, do not possess any of these qualities, they cannot be worthy to govern the country.

"Yet are they the only possessors of extensive tracts of lands, beautiful female slaves, excellent horses, magnificent palaces ! Have they then received an exclusive privilege from the Almighty ? if so, let them produce it. But the Supreme Being, who is just and merciful towards all mankind, wills, that in future, none of the inhabitants of Egypt shall be prevented from attaining to the first employments, and the highest honors.—The administration, which shall be conducted by persons of intelligence, talents, and foresight, will be productive of happiness and security. The tyranny and avarice of the Beys have laid waste Egypt, which was formerly so populous and well cultivated.

"The French are true Mussulmen ! Not long since they marched to Rome, and overthrew the throne of the pope, who excited the Christians against the professors of Islamism (the Mahometan religion.) Afterwards they directed their course to Malta, and drove out the unbelievers, who imagined they were appointed by God to make war on the Mussulmen. The French have at all times been the true and sincere friends of the Ottoman emperors, and the enemies of their enemies. May the empire of the sultan, therefore, be eternal ; but may the Beys of Egypt, our opposers, whose insatiable avarice has continually excited

disobedience and insubordination, be trodden in the dust and annihilated !

"Our friendship shall be extended to those of the inhabitants of Egypt who shall join us, as also to those who shall remain in their dwellings, and observe a strict neutrality ; and, when they have seen our conduct with their own eyes, hasten to submit to us ; but the dreadful punishment of death awaits those who shall take up arms for the Beys, and against us : for them there shall be no deliverance, nor shall any trace of them remain.

Article I. All places which shall be three leagues distant from the rout of the French army shall send one of their principal inhabitants to the French general, to declare that they submit, and will hoist the French flag, which is blue, white, and red.

II. Every village which shall oppose the French army shall be burned to the ground.

III. Every village which shall submit to the French, shall hoist the French flag, and that of the Sublime Porte, their ally, whose duration be eternal.

IV. The Cheiks and principal persons of each town and village, shall seal up the houses and effects of the Beys, and take care that not the smallest article shall be lost.

V. The Cheiks, Cadis, and Imans, shall continue to exercise their respective functions ; and put up their prayers, and perform the exercise of religious worship in the mosques and houses of prayer. All the inhabitants of Egypt shall offer up thanks to the Supreme Being, and put up public prayers for the destruction of the Beys.

"May the Supreme God make the glory of the sultan of the Ottomans eternal ! pour forth his wrath on the Mamelukes, and render glorious the destiny of the Egyptian nation."

It should seem, on first comparing this proclamation with the letter to the bishop of Malta, that the dissimulation was too gress to have been read without disgust, even by those Frenchmen who were interested in its consequences: but such is the effect of power, that the crimes of men in authority not only pass unobserved, but even find apologists. The Bedouins alluded to by Louis received some presents from this general at their departure; and the cheriff Cornim, when he saw himself surrounded by 30,000 Frenchmen and a formidable train of artillery, professed himself disinclined to make any resistance: yet, when the Bedouins got away, they robbed every Frenchman they met with; and, after the cheriff had been *honored by Buonaparte with a tri-colored scarf*, he was traitor enough to keep up a correspondence with some of his old friends, the Mamelukes in the country, (although they had received no scarves) merely because they had been the companions of his childhood and he had no quarrel with them. Denon can trace no other motive for this conduct than the habitual dissimulation of a savage mind; and Berthier affects to regard it with so much astonishment, that he concludes this tale with an apostrophe: " Such are the Arabians!" Yet a very slight acquaintance with the principles of justice, and a single moment's reflection, would have convinced both Denon and Berthier, that if dissimulation was an evidence of a savage mind, or if barbarity proved the existence of dissimulation, the cheriffs, the Arabians, the Beys, and the Mamelukes, had seen enough of both in the invasion of their country, without any cause of quarrel, to have given them the most utter-contempt of Buonaparte and his followers, and to have left them no other exclamation than, " Such are Frenchmen!"

By the combined operation of fraud and force, Buonaparte established himself at Alexandria, as he had done before at Malta; and it will appear, by the following orders of the day, that the delicacy of his justice was precisely that of an insolent conqueror and an arrogant tyrant.

ORDERS.

BUONAPARTE, *Member of the National Institute, Commander-in-chief.*

Head-quarters, Alexandria, July 3rd.

Article I. All the people of Alexandria, of what nation soever they may be, shall be obliged, twenty-four hours after the publication of the present order, to deposit, in a place marked out by the commander of the town, all their fire-arms. The Muftis, the Imans, and the Cheiks, alone shall be permitted to keep their arms, and to bear them.

II. All the inhabitants of Alexandria, of what nation soever they may be, shall be obliged to wear the tri-coloured cockade. The Muftis alone shall have the privilege of wearing a tri-colored shawl. The commander-in chief, however, reserves to himself the right of granting the same favor to such of the Cheiks as shall distinguish themselves by their knowledge, their prudence, and their virtue.

III. The troops shall pay military honor to every one who, in consequence of the preceding article, shall wear a tri-colored shawl; and whenever such persons shall visit the superior officer, or any of the constituted authorities, they shall be received with all the respect which is due to them.

IV. Foreign agents, to what power soever they may belong, are expressly prohibited from displaying their flags on their terraces. The consuls alone shall have the privilege of writing over their doors the nature of their employ: " Consul of——"

V. The present order shall be translated, without delay, into Arabic, and communicated to the most distinguished inhabitants. The cheriff shall have it proclaimed through the town, that every one may be obliged to conform to it.

(Signed) BUONAPARTE.

Having taken up the idea of the inhabitants and people being only barbarians,

2 R 2

and savages, Buonaparte took care to treat them as persons too ignorant to exercise any of the reasoning faculties : the next proclamation calls upon them for the most implicit reliance on his honor and friendship, in the very paper which acknowledges him the ally of the grand seignior, whose territories he had thus wrested from him !

Buonaparte, *Member of the National Institute, Commander-in-chief.*

Alxandria, July the 6th Year of the Republic One and Indivisible, the   of the Month of Muharrem, the Year of the Hegira 1213.

" For a long time the Beys, who govern Egypt, have insulted the French nation, and covered her merchants with injuries : the hour of their chastisement is come.

"For too long a time this rabble of slaves, purchased in Caucasus and in Georgia, has tyrannised over the fairest part of the world : but God, on whom every thing depends, has decreed that their empire shall be no more.

" People of Egypt ! you will be told that I am come to destroy your religion ; do not believe it : reply, That I am come to restore your rights, to punish usurpers ; and that I reverence, more than the Mamelukes themselves, God, his prophet Mahomet, and the Koran :

" Tell them, that all men are equal before God ; wisdom, talents, and virtue, are the only things which make a difference between them :

" Now, what wisdom, what talents, what virtues, have the Mamelukes, that they should boast the exclusive possession of every thing that can render life agreeable ?

" If Egypt is their farm, let them shew the lease which God has given them of it : but God is just and merciful to the people.

" All the Egyptians shall be appointed to all the public situations : the most wise, the most intelligent, and the most virtuous, shall govern ; and the people shall be happy.

" There were formerly among you great cities, great canals, and a great commerce : what has destroyed them all ? what, but the avarice, the injustice, and the tyranny of the Mamelukes ?

" Cadis ! Cheiks ! Imans ! Tchorbadgis ! tell the people that we are the friends of the true Mussulmen : is it not us who have destroyed the pope ; who said that it was necessary to make war on Mussulmen ! Is it not us who have destroyed the knights of Malta, because these madmen believed that it was the good pleasure of God that they should make war on Mussulmen ? Is it not us who have been, in all ages, the friends of the grand seignior, (on whose desires be the blessing of God !) and the enemy of his enemies ? and, on the contrary, have not the Mamelukes always revolted against the authority of the grand seignior ? which they refuse to recognise at this moment.

" Thrice happy those who shall be with us ! they shall prosper in their fortune and their rank : happy those who shall be neutral ! they shall have time to know us thoroughly, and they will range themselves on our side :

" But woe ! woe ! woe ! to those who shall take up arms in favor of the Mamelukes, and combat against us ! there shall be no hope for them : they shall all perish !".

(Signed) Buonaparte.
A true copy.   (Signed) Berthier.

To secure every possible advantage it was necessary to profit by that terror which the French arms had inspired, and to march immediately against the Mamelukes, before they should have time to arrange a system of attack or defence : with this view the general ordered Desaix, who had arrived with his division, to take with him two field-pieces that were landed, and to proceed, without delay, through the desert, on the rout to Cairo ; that general, accordingly, on the 6th, arrived at Demenhur, after being harassed by the Arabs, who skirmished with the advanced guards ; no one could stir from their columns : Desaix was nearly taken prisoner not more than fifty paces in the rear; and Le Meriar, having wandered from his place through absence of mind, fell' a sacrifice within one hundred paces of the advanced guard. Within a few yards of the troops, by passing a ravin, Delenau, an adjutant, was made prisoner; and the Arabs settled a quarrel, that had arisen amongst themselves about sharing the ransom, by blowing out his brains! Here the Mamelukes, who had been seen on a reconnoitring party at Demenhur, presented themselves in front of the army: these horsemen, always looking on infantry with contempt, retired, and, certain of victory, ceased to harass a march, which in itself, and under a burning sun, yielded nothing but hunger and thirst, which the delusive appearance of the soil much heightened: the soldiers cried for bread, while the dazzling sun-beams, playing on a sandy soil, displayed a resemblance to water so exact as to deceive, not only the stranger, but those who had before witnessed the same phenomenon.

Buonaparte having established a divan, and appointed general Kleber commandant at Alexandria, gave orders that the transport vessels should come into the port of that city, and immediately proceed to land the horses, provisions, and every thing with which they were laden, for the use of the expedition: the utmost diligence was used on this occasion by night and by day. The port not being capable of admitting the ships of war, they remained at anchor in the road, at some distance, which circumstance rendered the landing of the battering cannon a work of great difficulty.

Buonaparte arranged ' with admiral Brueys, that the fleet should anchor at Aboukir, where the road is good, and the landing easy; and whence a communication might be kept open with Rosetta, as well as with Alexandria; at the same time he ordered the admiral to cause the channel of the old port of Alexandria to be carefully sounded and examined, his intention being that the squadron should afterwards, if possible, enter it; or, in case it was found impracticable, that it should proceed to Corfu. Every consideration required that the debarkation should be as speedily completed as possible; the English might suddenly present themselves; the squadron, therefore, could not be too soon freed from the incumbrances of the expedition: it was also essential to march against Cairo to prevent the Mamelukes destroying or removing the magazines, and for this purpose also, it was necessary, as expeditiously as possible, to land the troops requisite for such an operation. During these proceedings, Buonaparte inspected the town and fortifications; he gave orders for the erection of new works, and took every measure that tended in a civil, as well as a military point of view, to ensure the tranquillity and defence of the city: and, finally, made such arrangements, that the troops intended for the purpose were soon enabled to march.

Two routs lead from Alexandria to Cairo, the first is through the desert, by Damanhour; to proceed by the second, it is necessary to arrive at Rosetta, by the sea-side, and by crossing at the distance of a league from Aboukir, a strait of about two hundred toises wide, which joins the lake Madie to the sea; but to go by this rout, for which they were entirely unprepared, would necessarily retard the progress of the army. Nevertheless, Buonaparte caused a small flotilla to be prepared, which he intended should proceed up the Nile. This flotilla was commanded by citizen Perree, chief-of-division, and consisted of seven small sloops, three gun-boats, and a xebeck, which would have been a considerable assistance to the army, had the rout of Rosetta been taken, in carrying the baggage and provisions of the troops, and co-operating with them on all occasions: but the French had not yet taken possession of Rosetta, and in proceeding by that rout Buonaparte would have retarded the progress of the army to Cairo, at least eight or ten days: he, therefore, determined to advance through the desert, by Damanhour, and by this rout general Desaix had been ordered to proceed.

The division of Kleber, commanded by general Dugua, received orders to proceed, together with the dismounted cavalry, to the mouth of the Nile, in order to cover the entrance of the French flotilla into that river ; the general was also instructed to take possession of Rosetta, to establish there a provisional divan, to leave a garrison in the place, to erect a battery at Lisbé, and to embark a quantity of rice in the flotilla : after which he was ordered to proceed towards Cairo, on the left bank of the Nile, in order to join the army near Rahmaniech, and the flotilla was to proceed up the river with all possible expedition.

The main army left Alexandria on the 6th and 7th of July : during their march they were greatly harassed by the Arabs, who had filled up all the wells at Beda and at Birkit ; so that the soldiers, scorched by the heat of the sun, felt all the torments of a parching thirst, which they had no means of assuaging. The wells, which generally yield a little brackish water, were explored, but a little muddy water could alone be obtained, and, at the moment, a glass of the pure element would have sold for its weight in gold ! The Arabs never appeared in great numbers, although many skirmishes took place, in one of which the general-de-brigade, Mireur, was mortally wounded.

On the 10th, when the army was proceeding on its march for Rahmaniech, the paucity of the wells obliged the divisions of generals Menou, Reguier, and Bon, to halt. The soldiers soon discovered the Nile : accoutred as they were, they plunged in, and drank plentifully of a water, comparatively delicious. But, speedily, the drums recalled them to their colours : a corps of about 800 Mamelukes were perceived approaching, in order of battle, the soldiers ran to their arms, the enemy retired, and took the rout to Damanhour, where they encountered the division of general Desaix, who had not advanced the discharge of cannon announced an action. Buonaparte instantly marched against the Mamelukes, but the artillery of general Desaix, had already compelled

them to retreat ; they were soon put to flight, leaving 40 men killed or wounded. Parmentier, of the 16th demi-brigade, was killed in this affair, as was one of the guides attached to the cavalry ; ten of the infantry were slightly wounded. The troops, exhausted by fatigue and privations, were greatly in want of repose ; and the horses, unavoidably harassed and enfeebled by the voyage, required it still more. These considerations induced Buonaparte to halt at Rahmaniech, the 11th and 12th, when he expected the flotilla, and the division under the command of general Dugua.

This general had taken possession of Rosetta without any obstacle, and, by forced marches, joined the army at the expected period. With respect to the flotilla, he announced, that it ascended the river with great difficulty, in consequence of the lowness of the water ; however, it arrived on the night of the 24th, and, during the same night, the army set out for Miniet-el-Sayd, where it rested ; and the 13th, before day-break, it proceeded again on its march.

In the course of that day, the Mamelukes, to the number of about 4000, were discovered at the distance of a league : their right was covered by the village of Chebreisse, in which they placed some pieces of cannon, and also by the Nile, on which they had a flotilla, consisting of gun-boats and armed dgerms. Buonaparte rdered the French flotilla to continue its course, disposing itself so as to cooperate with the left of the army, and to engage the enemy's vessels, at the moment the former should attack the Mamelukes, and the village of Chebreisse. The violence of the wind deranged this plan : the flotilla passed the left of the army, and was driven nearly a league higher up, where it was compelled to engage at a great disadvantage, inasmuch as it had, at the same time, to sustain the fire of the Mamelukes, the Fellahs, (peasants or husbandmen) and the Arabs, and to defend itself against the enemy's flotilla.

A number of the Fellahs, led on by a party of Mamelukes, advanced into the river, and getting on board some dgerms, they possessed themselves of one galley, and a gun-boat. The commander Perree, disposed his force so as to make a successful attack in his turn, and speedily retook the galley and the gun-boat. His xebeck, which on all sides dealt fire and death, prevented the recapture of those vessels, and destroyed several of the enemy's gun-boats : he was powerfully supported in this unequal contest by the coolness and intrepidity of general Andreossy, and by the citizens Mouge, Berthollet, Junot, Payeur, and Bourienne, secretary to Buonaparte, who were on board the xebeck.

In the mean time, the noise of the artillery made known to Buonaparte that the flotilla was engaged ; he marched the army au pas de charge, and, approaching Chebreisse, he perceived the Mamelukes ranged in order of battle in front of the village. The general-in-chief reconnoitred the position, and immediately formed the army ; it was composed of five divisions, each division formed a square, presenting at each side a front of six deep, the artillery was placed at the angles, and in the centre the cavalry and baggage. The grenadiers of each square formed platoons which flanked the divisions, and were intended to reinforce the points of attack. The miners, and those charged with the depot of artillery, posted and barricaded themselves in two villages in the rear, to secure places of retreat in case of that event. The Mamelukes, at this time, were not more than half a league from the army. Suddenly they advanced in crowds, without order or form, and wheeled about on the flanks and on the rear ; other masses fell with impetuosity on the right and front of the army ; they were suffered to approach until the grape-shot could effectually play upon them, when the artillery opened, and they were soon put to flight. Some of the bravest rushed, sabre in hand, upon the platoons on the flanks ; the onset was received with firmness, and nearly the whole were killed by the fire of the small arms, or by the bayonet.

Emboldened by this success, the army advanced rapidly against the village of Chebreisse, which the right wing was ordered to attack. This post was carried after a feeble resistance : the defeat of the Mamelukes was complete, they fled in disorder towards Cairo ; their flotilla retreated up the Nile with all possible expedition. The loss of the Mamelukes exceeded 600 men, of whom more were killed than wounded ; that of the French was about 70, besides the loss on board the flotilla.

The commandant Perree, in his account of the affair says, " I had 20 of my men wounded and several killed. A ball struck my sword out of my hand, and carried away a piece of my left arm. I do not think, however, that it will be attended with any bad consequences ; indeed, it is already nearly well.

" I cannot describe to you what we suffered in this expedition : we were reduced for several days to subsist entirely on water-melons, during which we were constantly exposed to the fire of the Arabs, although, with the exception of a few killed and wounded, we always came off victorious. The Nile is very far from answering the description I had received of it : it winds incessantly, and is withal very shallow."

There is, however, one circumstance that attended this skirmish, which none of the French writers have the candor to mention ; namely, that the Mamelukes accomplished their end by getting a temporary possession of the flotilla ; for each carried off as much of the baggage as he could, and, when the gallant Frenchmen recovered their squadron, they found that they " had nothing left but what was on their backs !"

After the action was over Buonaparte ordered the general-of-brigade, Zayoncheck, to proceed, with about 500 dismounted cavalry, along the right bank of the Nile, in a rout parallel to the march of the army, which advanced on the left bank. The 26th, the army halted at Shabour, and on the 27th, at Comscherif ; it was incessantly harassed during the march, by the Arabs ; it could not advance farther than the distance of a cannon shot without falling into an ambuscade. The assistant to the adjutant-generals, Gallois, was killed while carrying an order from Buonaparte ; the adjutant Deñano fell into the hands of the Arabs, and was killed. All communication, beyond three hundred toises from the rear of the army was cut off : no intelligence, therefore, could be forwarded to or received from Alexandria.

All the villages at which the army arrived were abandoned ; neither. men nor cattle were to be seen ; the soldiers lay upon heaps of corn, though they had no bread to eat ; they were equally destitute of animal food, and subsisted only upon some lentils, and a kind of thin cakes, which the soldiers made themselves, by bruising the corn. The army continued its march towards Cairo, and on the 19th of July general Zayoncheck united with the main army, where the Nile divides itself into two branches, those of Rosetta, and Damietta.

It is hardly possible to trace the march of the French in Egypt without examining the truth of a frequently repeated observation, " that its progress was marked with blood." So many : acrimonious remarks have been made by the different belligerent powers against each other, that the censures passed on either side should be received with great caution, and it would be even better that *harsh truths* should be altogether rejected, than that one statement should be admitted, originating only in passion. The same caution is to be observed in admitting the panegyrics that have been passed upon the different parties by their several admirers : if that arose out of passion, these arise out of flattery, and neither are entitled to credit. In examining the question before us, the testimony of an Englishman may be doubted, if he takes the affirmative side ; nor can that of a Frenchman be believed if he answers in the negative : it would be an extremely different thing if an Englishman were to appear on the negative side, for then he would adopt an argument against himself, and the candor he would display would demand confidence in return. Such

being the fate that must attend the question, were the fact contradicted by an Englishman, it is entitled to one directly opposite, if it be supported by an affirmative statement of a Frenchman. Thus posterity will doubtless judge ; and as a very few ages will add all the inconveniences arising out of distance of time, to those which we in this age feel to arise out of distance of place, it will only be by a comparison of isolated facts, that our successors will be able to form any opinion of those events. Having premised thus much, no apology can be required for introducing a single fact, as stated by M. Denon, without any comment: that traveller was deeply interested in the expedition ; he was witness of the desolation which he relates : he was a Frenchman, and, in many instances, he is known to have put the most favorable construction upon the conduct of his countrymen ; so much so, that he could not think that they had been guilty of any crime in invading and pillaging these feeble tribes, without any previous cause of quarrel ! The statement of M. Denon is, " That the people on the banks of the Nile, supposing that the French could not long maintain a footing in Egypt, against their all-powerful masters, allowed the army to proceed without molestation ; but to ensure a peace with the Beys, when they should again be conquerors, and from habits of depredation, they often attacked and fired at boats going up the river with supplies for the soldiers. A boat with a few troops was sent up, and received assurances of fidelity, and hostages for their behaviour. A vessel, which set off for Cairo, was missing ; and from the inhabitants themselves, it was, after some difficulty, discovered, that, being attacked a little above Fueh, or Fouah, the crew, all wounded, threw themselves into the river, and, having been forced on shore by the current, were made prisoners, and all of them shot at Salmia. An example was now necessary : 200 men were landed within a mile and a half of the village ; one party proceeded to turn it, a second marched by the edge of the river, while the third, stationed six miles below, completely surrounded it. A charge was made by the enemy's cavalry in front of the village, and repulsed by the bayonet : their leading men fell by the first volley of the French, when the others got into confusion. The Cheik, and the few that survived, escaped, from the third detachment's having arrived too late to prevent their flight. Salmia was plundered the whole of the day ; and at night the flames, with the firing of cannon without intermission, gave to the surrounding country assurance of the certain destruction which such conduct would bring upon the inhabitants."

Previous to reaching Cairo, Buonaparte learned that the two powerful chiefs, Murad Bey and Ibrahim Bey, were likely to annoy his army greatly, and many severities were inflicted upon those Fellahs who were friendly to the Arabs, in order to deter them from strengthening the ranks of the Beys. On the 19th, Murad Bey, at the head of 6000 Mamelukes, and a host of Arabs and Fellahs, was entrenched at the village of Embaba, waiting for the French ; and on the 22nd, Desaix, whose corps formed the advanced guard, arrived within two miles of the spot. The heat was intense, and the soldiers excessively fatigued, which induced Buonaparte to halt. But the Mamelukes no sooner perceived the army than they formed upon the plain, in front of his right : an appearance so imposing never yet presented itself to the French ; the cavalry of the Mamelukes were covered with resplendent armour. Beyond their left were beheld the celebrated Pyramids, of which the imperishable mass has survived so many empires, and braved for more than thirty centuries the outrages of time ! Behind their right was the Nile, the city of Cairo, the hills of Mokattam, and the fields of the antient Memphis.

When Buonaparte had given his last orders, "Go," said he, pointing to the Pyramids, "and think, that, from the heights of those monuments, forty ages survey our conduct." The army, impatient to come to action, was soon ranged in order of battle.; the disposition of the

forces was similar to that at the battle of Chebreisse. Buonaparte ordered the line to advance, but the Mamelukes, who, till then, appeared irresolute, prevented the execution of this movement ; they made a feint against the centre, but rushed with impetuosity on the divisions of Desaix and Regnier, which formed the right : they intrepidly charged these columns, which, firm and immoveable, reserved their fire until the enemy advanced within half musket-shot ; the ill-directed valor of the Mamelukes in vain endeavored to break through those walls of fire and ramparts of bayonets ; their ranks were thinned, a great number of killed and wounded remained on the field, and they soon retired in disorder, without venturing to return the charge.

While the divisions of generals Desaix and Regnier so successfully repulsed the Mameluke cavalry, the divisions of Bon and Menou, supported by that of Kleber, then under the command of general Dugua, advanced rapidly against the entrenched village of Embaba. Two battalions of the divisions of Bon and Menou were detached, with orders to turn the village, and, in the mean time, to take advantage of a deep ditch, that lay in the way, the better to defend themselves from the enemy's cavalry, and to conceal their movements towards the Nile. The divisions, preceded by their flank companies, rapidly advanced. The Mamelukes unsuccessfully attacked the platoons ;· they unmasked 40 pieces of bad artillery, which they discharged upon them, but the divisions rushed forward with such impetuosity that the Mamelukes had not time to re-load their guns. The entrenchments were carried by the bayonet, and the camp, as well as the village of Embaba, were soon in the possession of the French. Fifteen hundred Mameluke cavalry, and an equal number of Fellahs, whose retreat was cut off by generals Marmont and Rampon, occupied an entrenched position in the rear of a ditch that communicated with the Nile, and in vain performed prodigies of valor in their defence.; they were unwilling to surrender, and none of them escaped the sanguinary fury of the French soldiers ; they were all either put to the sword or drowned in the Nile. Forty pieces of cannon, 400 camels, the baggage, and the stores, fell into the hands of the victors.

Murad Bey, seeing the village of Embaba carried, attended only to his retreat : the divisions of generals Desaix and Regnier had already compelled his cavalry to fall back : the army pursued the Mamelukes as far as Gaza, beyond which they continued their flight ; and the French, after fighting, or marching and fighting nineteen hours, occupied a position at Gaza. Never was the superiority of modern European tactics over those of the orientals, or disciplined courage over ill-directed valor more conspicuous, or more sensibly felt, than on that day. The Mamelukes were mounted on superb Arabian horses, richly caparisoned, their armour was magnificent, and their purses well stocked with gold ; these spoils, in some degree, recompensed the soldiers for the excessive fatigues they had undergone. During an interval of fifteen days, their only nourishment consisted of a few vegetables, without bread ; the provisions found in the camp, therefore, afforded them a delicious repast.

The division of general Desaix was ordered to take a position in front of Gaza, and on the rout of Faium. The division of Menou passed, during the night, a branch of the Nile, and took possession of the isle of Roda. The enemy in their flight, burned those vessels which could not speedily reascend the Nile. The following morning, on the 23rd of July, the principal inhabitants of Cairo, presented themselves on the banks of the Nile, and offered to deliver up the city to the French : they were accompanied by the Kiaja of the Pacha, Ibrahim Bey, who had abandoned Cairo during the night, having carried off the Pacha with him. Buonaparte received them at Gaza : they required protection for the city, and engaged for its submission ; he answered, that the wish of the French was to remain in amity with the Egyptian people and the Ottoman Porte, and assured them that the manners, the

customs, and the religion of the country, should be scrupulously respected : they returned to Cairo, accompanied by a detachment under the command of a French officer. The populace took an advantage of the discomfiture and flight of the Mamelukes, and committed some excesses. The mansion of Murad Bey was pillaged and burned ; but it was contrary to the principles of Buonaparte to suffer other persons to plunder, and order was restored in consequence of the proclamations that he issued, and the appearance of an armed force.

On the 26th of July Buonaparte removed his head-quarters to Cairo : the divisions of generals Regnier and Menou were stationed at Old Cairo, the divisions of Bon and Kleber at Boulau ; a corps of observation was placed on the rout to Syria, and the division of Desaix was ordered to occupy an entrenched position about three leagues in front of Embaba, on the rout to Upper Egypt.

Established in the apparently quiet possession of Cairo, his first official act was one of the most unblushing and inhuman despotism. It was a favorite object of the general to transport the rarities of Egypt to the Museum at Paris ; and he ordered the Mamelukes, whom he had taken prisoners, to be transported along with his first collection of curiosities, to France.

During these operations of Buonaparte, the gallant Nelson was scouring the seas in search of the fleet which had so fortunately arrived on the shores of Egypt. His force consisted of thirteen 74, and one 50-gunships. Having repaired to the neighbourhood of Naples for information, he directed his course from thence towards Sicily. He there learned the surrender of Malta, immediately took on board expert pilots, and was the first commander who ever passed the straits of Messina with a fleet of men of war. He was now informed that the French had left Malta ; he instantly steered for Candia, and, being there assured that the enemy were actually destined for Egypt, he sailed thither, and arrived at the mouth of the Nile three days *before*

Buonaparte. After consulting the English consul, he supposed his former information to be false, repaired to Rhodes, and actually passed the French fleet in a fog. He then returned to Sicily, and in the bay of Syracuse, procured various supplies and assistance, of which his squadron stood in need.

In a few days the English admiral again sailed in search of the French expedition, and, being positively informed that it had arrived in Egypt some time before, he once more steered for Alexandria. On the 1st of August, at noon, he had the happiness to descry the port of Alexandria, with an aspect, however, far different from what it had before presented to their disappointed view. They perceived, with delight, that it now appeared filled with ships, and had soon the undescribable transport to behold the French flag flying on board several of them. A tumult of joy animated every bosom in the British squadron at the sight of the enemy. The humblest individual felt himself a hero, and had a great right so to feel, since every individual was eagerly prepared to risque his life for the safety and glory of his king and country. The brave admiral was calm, but no mortal can convey to another the sense of ineffable delight, which glowed in every fibre of his frame. The bliss of his bosom, (to use his own words) at this impressive moment, was that of extatic perfection; for it admitted not the smallest doubt of success. In a narrative formed from the minutes of an officer of rank, (the present sir Edward Berry, then captain of the Vanguard) it is observed, that the pleasure which the admiral himself felt, was perhaps more heightened than that of any other man, as he had now a certainty by which he could regulate his future operations. "The admiral had," continues this narrative, "and, as it, subsequently appeared, most justly the highest opinion of, and placed the firmest reliance on, the valor and conduct of every captain in his squadron. It had been his practice, during the whole of his cruise, whenever the weather and circumstances would permit, to have his captains on

board the Vanguard; where he would fully develope to them his own ideas of the different and best modes of attack; and such plans as he proposed to execute, on falling in with the enemy; whatever their position or situation might be, by night or by day. There was no possible position in which they could be found, that he did not take into his calculation, and for the most advantageous attack, of which he had not digested and arranged the best possible disposition of the force which he commanded." With the masterly ideas of their admiral, therefore, on the subject of naval tactics, every one of the captains of his squadron was most thoroughly acquainted; and, on surveying the situation of the enemy, they could precisely ascertain what were the ideas and intentions of their commander, without the aid of further instructions. Thus signals became almost unnecessary, much time was saved, and the attention of every captain could almost undistractedly be paid to the condition of his own particular ship: a circumstance from which, on this occasion, the advantages to the general service were almost incalculable. It cannot here be thought irrelevant to give some idea of the plans which admiral Nelson had formed, and which he explained to his captains with such perspicuity as to render his ideas completely their own. To the naval service, at least, they must not only prove interesting, but useful. Had he fallen in with the French fleet at sea, that he might make the best impression on any part of it that should appear the most vulnerable or the most eligible for attack, he divided his forces into three sub-squadrons, viz.

Vanguard,	Orion,	Culloden,
Minotaur,	Goliah,	Theseus,
Leander,	Majestic,	Alexander,
Audacious,	Bellerophon,	Swiftsure,
Defence,		
Zealous,		

Two of these sub-squadrons were to attack the ships of war, while the third was to pursue the transports, and to sink and destroy as many as it could. The destination of the French armament was involved in doubt and uncertainty; but it forcibly struck the admiral that, as it was commanded by the man whom the French had dignified with the title of The Conqueror of Italy, and as he had with him a very large body of troops, an expedition had been planned which the land force might execute without the aid of their fleet, should the transports be permitted to make their escape, and reach in safety their place of rendezvous: it therefore became a material consideration with the admiral, so to arrange his force as at once to engage the whole attention of their ships of war, at the same time materially to annoy and injure their convoy. It will be fully admitted, from the subsequent information which has been received on the subject, that the ideas of the admiral on this occasion were perfectly just, and that the plan which he had arranged was the most likely to frustrate the designs of the enemy. It is almost unnecessary to explain his projected mode of attack at anchor, as that was minutely and precisely executed in the action about to be described. These plans, however, were formed two months before an opportunity presented itself of executing any of them, and the advantage now was, that they were familiar to the understanding of every captain in the fleet.

It has been already mentioned, that the Pharos of Alexandria was seen at noon on the 1st of August. The Alexander and Swiftsure had been detached a-head on the preceding evening, to reconnoitre the port of Alexandria, while the main body of the squadron kept in the offing. The enemy's fleet was first discovered by the Zealous, captain Hood, who communicated, by signal, the number of ships, sixteen, lying at anchor in line of battle, in a bay on the larboard bow, which was afterwards found to be Abonkir bay. The admiral hauled his wind at that instant, a movement which was immediately observed and followed by the whole squadron; and, at the same time, he recalled the Alexander and Swiftsure. The wind was at this time N N. W. and blew what

seamen call a top-gallant breeze. It was necessary to take in the royals to haul up on a wind. The admiral made the signal to prepare for battle, and that it was his intention to attack the enemy's van and centre as they lay at anchor, according to the plan previously developed. His idea in this disposition of his force, was first to secure the victory, and then to make the most of it, as circumstances might permit. A bower cable of each ship was immediately got out abaft and bent forward. They continued carrying sail, and standing in for the enemy's fleet in close line of battle. As all the officers of the squadron were totally unacquainted with Aboukir bay, each ship kept sounding as they stood in.

The enemy appeared to be moored in a strong and compact line of battle, close in with the shore; their line describing an obtuse angle in its form, flanked by numerous gun-boats, four frigates, and a battery of guns and mortars on an island in their van. This situation of the enemy seemed to secure to them the most decided advantages, as they had nothing to attend to but their artillery, in their superior skill in the use of which the French so much pride themselves, and to which, indeed, their splendid series of land victories are in general chiefly to be imputed.

The position of the enemy presented the most formidable obstacles; but the admiral viewed them all with the eye of a seaman determined on attack, and it instantly struck his eager and penetrating mind, that "where there was no room for an enemy's ship to swing, there was room for one of ours to anchor." No farther signals were necessary than those which had already been made. The admiral's designs were fully known to his whole squadron, as it was his determination to conquer or perish in the attempt. The Goliah and Zealous had the honor to lead inside, and to receive the first fire from the van ships of the enemy, as well as from the batteries and gun-boats with which their van was strengthened. These two ships, with the Orion, Audacious, and Theseus, took their stations inside the enemy's line, and were immediately in close action. The Vanguard anchored the first on the outer side of the enemy, and was opposed, within half pistol-shot, to Le Spartiate, the third in the enemy's line.

The shores of the bay of Aboukir were soon lined with spectators, who beheld the approach of the English, and the awful conflict of the hostile fleets, in silent astonishment.

Sir Horatio Nelson, as rear-admiral of the blue, carried the blue flag at the mizen; but, from a standing order of the earl of St. Vincent, the squadron wore the white, or St. George's ensign, in the action. This being white with a red cross, the first quarter bearing the union, it occasioned the display of the cross on the renowned and antient coast of Egypt.

So entirely was the admiral resolved to conquer or to perish in the attempt, that he led into action with six ensigns or flags, viz. red, white, and blue, flying in different parts of the rigging. He could not bear to reflect on the possibility of his colours being carried away even by a random shot from the enemy.

In standing in, the leading ships were unavoidably obliged to receive into their bows the whole fire of the broadsides of the French line, till they could take their respective stations; and it is but justice to observe, that the enemy received their opponents with great firmness and deliberation; no colours having been hoisted on either side, nor a gun fired, till our van ships were within half gun-shot. At this time the necessary number of our men were engaged aloft in furling sails, and on deck in hauling the braces, and other requisite employments preparatory to casting anchor. As soon as this took place, a most animated fire opened from the Vanguard, which ship covered the approach of those in the rear, who were following in a close line. The Minotaur, Defence, Bellerophon, Majestic, Swiftsure, and Alexander, came up in succession; and, passing within hail of the Vanguard, took their respective stations opposed to the enemy's line. All our ships anchored by the stern; by which means the British line became inverted from van to rear. Captain Thompson, of the Leander of 50 guns, with a degree of judgment highly honorable to his professional character, advanced towards the enemy's line on the outside, and most judiciously dropped his anchor athwart hause of Le Franklin, raking her with great success; the shot from the Leander's broadside, which passed that ship, all striking L'Orient, the flag ship of the French commander-in-chief.

The action commenced at sun-set, which was at thirty-one minutes past six, with an ardor and vigor which it is impossible to describe. In a few minutes, every man stationed at the first six guns in the fore part of the Vanguard's deck was killed or wounded, and one gun in particular was repeatedly cleared: one of the midshipmen was just remarking the escapes he had experienced when a shot came and cut him in two. At about seven o'clock total darkness had come on; but the whole hemisphere was, at intervals, illuminated by the fire of the hostile fleets. Our ships, as darkness came on, had all hoisted their distinguishing lights by a signal from the admiral.

The van ship of the enemy, Le Guerrier, was dismasted in less than twelve minutes; and, in ten minutes after, the second ship, Le Conquerant, and the third, Le Spartiate, very nearly at the same moment, experienced a similar fate. L'Aquilon, and Le Souverain Peuple, the fourth and fifth ships of the enemy's line, were taken possession of by the British at half past eight in the evening. Captain Berry, at that hour, sent lieutenant Galway, of the Vanguard, with a party of marines, to take possession of Le Spartiate; and that officer returned by the boat the French captain's sword, which captain Berry immediately delivered to the admiral, who was then below, in consequence of the severe wound which he received in the head during the heat of the attack.

This wound seems to have been inflicted by langridge shot, or a piece of iron, which, cutting his forehead at right angles, the skin hung over his face; captain Berry fortunately happening to be sufficiently near, caught the admiral in his arms, and prevented him from falling. It was, at first, the universal opinion that their beloved commander had been shot through the head ; and, indeed, the appearance was rendered dreadfully alarming by the hanging skin and the copious effusion of blood. Not a man on board was now solicitous for his own life ; every brave fellow was alone anxious for that of the admiral This, however, far from repressing their ardor, served only to animate their fury, and prompt them, if possible, to still greater exertions. On being carried into the cock-pit, where several of his gallant crew were stretched with their shattered limbs and lacerated wounds, the surgeon, with the most respectful anxiety, quitted the poor fellows then under his hands that he might instantly attend on the admiral. "No," replied the commander, with the utmost composure, though he had then no hope of surviving, "I will take my turn with my brave fellows." The agony of his wound, in the mean time, greatly increasing, he became satisfied that the idea which he had long indulged of dying in battle was now about to be accomplished. He desired to see his chaplain, the reverend Mr. Comyn, and begged he would bear his remembrance to lady Nelson ; and, as the last beneficial office that he conceived he should be able to perform, he appointed captain Hardy, of La Mutine, to be captain of the Vanguard. Having expressed a wish to see captain Louis, of the Minotaur, captain Berry had hailed that ship, and the commander came on board. The admiral was desirous of personally thanking him for the assistance which he had, in the height of danger, been enabled to render the Vanguard. "My dear Louis," said the admiral, "farewell ! I shall never, should I survive, forget the obligation I am under to you. Whatever may become of me, my mind is at peace." He then, with the most exemplary composure, resigning himself to apparent death. As soon as the surgeon had, according to the express injunctions of the admiral, paid all necessary attention to every person previously wounded; he came forward to examine the wound of their commander. An awful silence prevailed ; but it was of short duration ; for the surgeon almost immediately pronounced it to be superficial, and of no dangerous consequence. The pleasing intelligence speedily circulated through the ship, and the excess of sorrow was instantaneously converted into the excess of joy : nor did the hero feel less delighted at hearing the grateful expressions of gladness from his generous crew, than at the unexpected announcement of his life being out of danger. This circumstance, indeed, greatly tended to alleviate his sufferings during the painful operation of dressing his wounded forehead.

At this time it appeared that victory had already declared itself in our favor ; for, though L'Orient, L'Heureux, and Le Tonnant, were not taken possession of, they were considered as completely in our power, which pleasing intelligence captain Berry had the satisfaction of communicating in person to the admiral.

At ten minutes after nine, a fire was observed on board L'Orient, the French admiral's ship, which seemed to proceed from the after-part of the cabin, and which increased with great rapidity, presently involving the whole of the after-part of the ship in flames. This circumstance captain Berry immediately communicated to the admiral ; who, though suffering severely from his wound, came immediately upon deck, where the first consideration that struck his benevolent mind, was, concern for so many lives. To save as many as possible, he ordered captain Berry to make every practicable exertion. A boat, the only one that could swim, was instantly dispatched from the Vanguard ; other ships that were in a condition to do so, immediately followed the example, and by their united exertions the lives of about 70 Frenchmen were saved. The light thrown by the fire of L'Orient on the surrounding objects enabled the commanders to perceive with more certainty; the situation of the two fleets, the colours of both being clearly distinguishable. The cannonade was partially kept up to leeward of the centre till about ten o'clock, when L'Orient blew up with a most tremendous explosion.

An awful pause and death-like silence for a few minutes ensued; when the wreck of the masts, yards, &c. which had been carried to a vast height, fell into the water and on board the surrounding ships. A port fire from L'Orient fell into the main royal of the Alexander; but the fire occasioned by this circumstance was extinguished in two minutes by the active exertions of captain Ball.

After this awful scene, the firing re-commenced with the ships to leeward of the centre, till twenty minutes past ten, when there was a total cessation of firing for about ten minutes; after which it was revived till about three in the morning, when it again ceased.

After the victory had been secured in the van, the British ships which were able to move had borne down on the fresh ships of the enemy. Le Guillaume Tell, and Le Genereur, were the only French ships of the line that had their colours flying. At fifty-four minutes past five, a French frigate, L'Ortemise, fired a broadside and struck her colours; but such was the unwarrantable and infamous conduct of the French captain, that, after having thus surrendered, he set fire to his ship, and, with part of his crew, made his escape on shore. Another of the French frigates, La Serieuse, had been sunk by the fire from some of our ships; but as her poop remained above water, her men were saved on it, and were taken off in the morning by the English boats. The Bellerophon, whose masts and cables had been entirely shot away, could not retain her situation abreast of L'Orient, but had fortunately drifted out of the line to the lee side of the bay, a little before that ship blew up. The Audacious was detached in the morning to her assistance. At eleven o'clock Le Genereur and Guillaume Tell, with the two frigates, La Justice and La Diane, cut their cables and stood out to sea, pursued by captain Hood in the Zealous, who handsomely endeavored to prevent their escape. But, as there was no other ship

in a condition to support the Zealous, she was recalled.

The whole day of the 2nd of August was employed in securing the French ships that had struck, and which were completely in our possession, except Le Tonnant and Le Timoleon. As these were both dismasted, and consequently could not escape, they were naturally the last of which it was thought necessary to take possession. On the morning of the 3rd, the Timoleon was set fire to, and Le Tonnant cut her cable and drifted on shore; but that active officer, captain Miller, of the Theseus, soon got her off again, and secured her in the British line.

The British force engaged, consisted of only twelve ships of 74 guns, and the Leander of 50, for, from the over anxiety and zeal of captain Troubridge to get into action, his ship, the Culloden, in standing in for the van of the enemy's line, had unfortunately grounded on the edge of a shoal, running off from the island on which were the mortar and gun-batteries of the enemy; and, notwithstanding all the exertions of that able officer, she could not be got off. This unfortunate circumstance was severely felt at the moment by the admiral and all the officers of the squadron; but their feelings were nothing compared with the anxiety and even agony of mind which the captain of the Culloden himself experienced during so many eventful hours. There was but one consolation amidst the distresses of his situation,—that his ship served as a beacon for three other ships, the Alexander, Theseus, and Leander, which were advancing with all possible celerity close in his rear. It was not till the morning of the 2nd, that the Culloden could be got off. It was then found that she had suffered considerable damage in her bottom, that the rudder was broken off, and that the crew could scarcely keep her afloat with all pumps going. The resources of captain Troubridge's mind availed him much, and were admirably exerted on this trying occasion. In four hours he had a new rudder made on his own deck, which was immediately shipped.

and the Culloden was again in a state for actual service, though still very leaky.

The admiral perceiving that the wounded of his own ships had been well taken care of, bent his next attention to those of the enemy. He established a truce with the commandant of Aboukir, and through him made a communication to the commandant of Alexandria, that it was his intention to allow all the wounded Frenchmen to be taken ashore to proper hospitals, with their own surgeons to attend them : a proposal which was accepted by the French, and carried into execution the following day.

On the 2nd the Arabs and Mamelukes, who had, during the battle, lined the shores of the bay, saw with transport that the victory was decisively on the part of the British fleet ; an event in which they participated with an exultation almost equal to that of the conquerors. On that and the following nights the whole coast and country were illuminated as far as the eye could penetrate in celebration of our success : a circumstance which had a great effect on the minds of the prisoners, as they conceived the rejoicings to be the consequence, not merely of the defeat of their fleet, but of some signal success obtained by the Arabs and Mamelukes over Buonaparte.

On the morning of the 2nd of August, admiral Nelson issued the following memorandum to the different captains of his squadron.

MEMORANDUM.

Vanguard, off the mouth of the Nile, 2nd August, 1798

Almighty God having blessed his majesty's arms with victory ; the admiral intends returning public thanksgiving for the same at two o'clock this day : and he recommends every ship doing the same as soon as convenient.

On the same day, after divine service had been performed, the admiral issued another

MEMORANDUM.

Vanguard, off the mouth of the Nile
August 2nd, 1798.

The admiral most heartily congratulates the captains, officers, seamen, and marines of the squadron, he has had the honor to command in the event of the late action ; and he desires they will accept his sincere and cordial thanks for their very gallant behaviour in this glorious battle. It must strike forcibly every British seaman, how superior their conduct is, when in discipline and good order, to the riotous behaviour of lawless Frenchmen. The squadron may be assured the admiral will not fail with his dispatches to represent their truly meritorious conduct in the strongest terms to the commander-in-chief.

Such were the circumstances attending the most decisive and splendid victory that adorns the naval annals of Great Britain. From the beginning to the termination of the conflict, 16 English officers, 156 seamen, and 46 marines, lost their lives ; and 37 officers, 562 seamen, and 78 marines, were wounded. Of the vanquished, the loss was incalculable. On a moderate estimate, it amounted to 3000 men, killed and wounded. The bay of Aboukir for many days after the battle, was so covered with the floating bodies of the slain, as to exhibit a horrid and painful spectacle : and, though all possible endeavors were exerted to keep them sinking wherever they appeared, the shot used for this intention, so frequently slipped off, that many of the bodies perpetually rose again to the surface. The shore, to the extent of four leagues, was covered by wrecks ; and, to procure a few nails or a few iron hoops, the wandering Arabs were employed in burning on the beach, the masts, gun-carriages, and boats, which had been constructed in the French ports at so enormous an expense.

The officers of the fleet vied with each other in causing numberless articles to be manufactured from parts of the floating wreck of L'Orient, as commemorations of the victory, which they affectionately presented to their commander. Captain Hallowelle in particular, with singular but eccentric zeal, procured a coffin to be made from the wreck by a carpenter on board the Swiftsure, constructed in as elegant a manner as the workman could effect with such materials, and so little skill in that particular branch of business. The present of this worthy and brave officer was received with the most affectionate regard. The hero immediately placed it upright in his cabin; and, though he was at length prevailed on by the entreaties of an old and favorite servant to have the coffin carried below, nothing could possibly prevent his resolution to have it finally devoted to its original purpose.

The honors and rewards obtained by admiral Nelson in testimony of his skill and prowess in the battle of the Nile, were commensurate with his services. His majesty conferred the dignity of a baron of Great Britain, with a pension of £3000 per annum, and he was accordingly called up to the house of peers by the style of baron Nelson of the Nile. The grand seignior transmitted a superb diamond Chelengk, or plume of triumph, taken from one of the imperial turbans; and the king of Naples, at a later period granted the title of duke of Bronte, with an estate in Sicily. Captains Berry and Thompson received the honor of knighthood. The Turkish sultan sent a purse of 2000 sequins to be distributed among the wounded, and a much larger sum was raised in England by subscription, for the widows and children of those who fell in the action.

The subsequent naval operations of the year were of little interest or importance. An expedition was undertaken at an early period of the year, for the infliction of exemplary chastisement on the possessors of the Netherlands. Major-general Coote landed with a small force near Ostend, and prepared to destroy the sluices of the Bruges canal. This service was executed with trivial loss; but, as the wind and surf prevented the re-embarkation of the troops, it became necessary to form a defensive post on the sand-hills. An attack

was made upon the invaders by a body which far outnumbered them; and, though they fought with distinguished courage, their front was broken, and their flanks were completely turned. In this perilous state their commander, who was wounded, called major-general Burrard to a consultation, and it was resolved that a general surrender should take place. About 50 men were killed in the conflict, and above 1100 submitted to captivity.

The grand seignior, though he had only a nominal sway over Egypt, was provoked by the French invasion of that country, to declare war. More important benefits were expected from the arms of the Russian emperor Paul, who now leagued himself with the Porte, and seemed to be impressed with the persuasion that his troops were destined to rescue Europe from the progress of disorder and the perils of anarchy. His magnanimity was panegyrised by the king of Great Britain, in a speech to his parliamentary subjects. But, before we proceed to the incidents of a new session, it will be proper to take notice of an expedition which, in the autumn of this year, added a Spanish island to the British possessions.

An armament sailed toward the island of Minorca; and a descent was made near the creek of Addaya. A body of Spaniards threatened to surround the first division of the invading army; but they were soon repelled; and our troops gained a position from which they might have attacked the enemy with advantage, if the latter had not retired n the evening. The army seized the post of Mercadal, and a detachment took the town of Mahon and fort Charles. The chief defence was expected at Ciudadella, where new works were added to the old fortifications. The approach of the English drove the Spaniards within the walls of that town; and general Stuart summoned the governor to surrender it without delay. To enforce compliance, two batteries were erected; but, as the invaders had few of the requisites of a siege, their adversaries might, with a small share of spirit, have made a considerable resistance. Intimidated, however, by the movements of the troops and the appearance of the squadron, the garrison capitulated ; and thus the whole island was reduced without the loss of a single man.

But, while the English gained one island, they lost the territories which they had for some time retained in another. In St. Domingo, they were unable, from the resistance of the French, the mulattoes, and the negroes, to extend their acquisitions in any great degree ; and the fury of disease made alarming havoc among them. At length, they resolved to surrender Port-au-prince and St. Marc, to Toussaint, a negro commander, who had nearly annihilated the dominion of the French in the island ; and, in the course of the year, they evacuated every other post. From the great loss of men and money, without a return of benefit, the government had reason to lament that any troops had been sent to St. Domingo.

Such were the chequered scenes of the war. But, in the opinion of the court, the good seemed to predominate over ill success. His majesty spoke with confidence of the expected deliverance of Europe. The ministerial speakers in both houses were equally animated, and loudly condemned the meanness of negotiation.

The produce of the augmented assessment having been inadequate to the expectations of the proposer of the tax, he resolved to enforce the payment of large sums, not by the criterion of expenditure, but by that of income. By the former impost, very few individuals paid so much as a tenth part of their income ; but, by the new scheme, all who were rich, and even many who might be termed poor, were required to resign at least a tithe of revenue.

It was now proposed, that no one whose income was less than £60 *per annum* should be obliged to contribute more than the taxes which he already paid ; but that every one who had an income of or beyond that amount should be additionally burdened, some in the proportion of ten *per cent.* others at a lower rate. All who had £200 a year would be required to sign a declaration of willingness to pay a certain sum, not less than a tenth part of their in-

come, without particularising the modes in which it accrued ; and a scale of easy contribution would be adjusted for the rest. If doubts of the fairness of the statement should arise, the commissioners might summon any individual before them, and demand, upon oath, a minute specification of income ; and, if, on a continuance of suspicion, full proof of accuracy should not be adduced, they might fix the amount of contribution. If they should require more than a tenth, no relief would be allowed, unless the books of the tradesman, or the ordinary accounts kept by others, should be submitted to inspection.

Having stated the outlines of his plan, Mr. Pitt mentioned the *data* upon which he formed an estimate of its produce. He was of opinion, that the annual rent of all the land in England and Wales amounted to £25,000,000 sterling ; a sum which, by the allowance of a fifth part for the exceptions under £60, and the modifications under £200 a year, would be reduced to 20,000,000. Six millions, he thought, might be assumed as the clear income of the land to tenants ; the tithes might be valued at 4,000,000 ; the produce of mines, canals, &c. at 3,000,000 ; the rent of houses at 5,000,000 ; and the profits of the liberal professions at 2,000,000. On all these heads, it might be sufficient to allow an eighth part for Scotland, which would be 5,000,000. Income drawn from possessions beyond seas might be stated at 5,000,000 ; annuities from the public funds at 12,000,000 ; the profits of foreign commerce also at 12,000,000 ; those of internal trade, mechanical skill and industry, at 28,000,000. These calculations formed an aggregate of 102,000,000 ; and from this source about 10,000,000 of supply were expected to arise.

Mr. Tierney, who had thought the increased assessment a mischievous tax, pronounced the new scheme to be a much more violent invasion of property, and more in the style of the French revolutionists. It was very unjust, he said, because it would be attended with great inequality. The rich, though they might not be pleased with such rapine, would be seriously injured by it ; but it would severely oppress the middle classes of the nation.

In another debate, sir John Sinclair made various objections to the measure. It was improper, he thought, to subject income to taxation without taxing capital: if both should be included in the new plan, those who depended on income only would be (as they ought to be) considerably relieved; and there would be no greater difficulty in estimating one than the other. The persons who would be affected by the tax on income might be divided into three classes—those who were accustomed to save some portion of their income—those who might save, but did not—and such as were unable to reserve any part. The first and second classes would soon be reduced to the condition of the third; and, by the consequent decrease of the consumption of taxed articles, the ordinary imposts would be much less productive than they had been. The baronet added, that the extension of the impost to property in Ireland and in the West Indies, the inquisitorial power which would be given to the commissioners, and the taxation of the funds (for that would be the effect of a part of the scheme,) would be impolitic and unjust. Mr. Simeon defended the scheme as the most seasonable that could be devised; and the solicitor-general thought it the best

mode of calling forth the resources of the people. Sir Francis Baring disapproved it, as it would harass commercial men, and yet might be easily evaded. Mr. Smith affirmed that it was unjust, cruel, and oppressive; but all objections were overborne, though not fully obviated, by the commanding eloquence of the minister, who exaggerated the benefits and extenuated the inconveniences of the measure, with his usual talent and animation.

Sir William Pulteny was a warm opposer of this bill of requisition, particularly of that part which involved the alternative of paying too much, or of submitting to the disclosure of private concerns. But being supported by a great majority, it triumphantly passed through the ordeal of debate, and became an operative law. It fell with great weight upon the middle orders of society, as it deprived them of many of those comforts which they could before command, while the higher ranks suffered no other inconvenience than the diminution of luxurious indulgences or unnecessary enjoyments. The vigilance of the commissioners did not prevent the frequent evasion of the act; for it cannot be expected that the most rigorous provisions will secure a full obedience to statutes of this complexion.

HISTORY OF THE WAR.

―――――――――

CHAP. XIX.

THE rebellion in Ireland seemed to point out the necessity of adopting a great political measure which had occasionally been recommended to the ministry, by writers as well as by parliamentary speakers, without making at the time any other than a transient impression. The risque of a revival of commotion, and the apprehensions of the formidable efforts of an ambitious enemy for the separation of that realm from the British empire, prompted the leaders of the cabinet to undertake the task of effecting that close union between the kingdoms which would give additional strength to both, and so improve and concentrate their resources and their power, as to enable them to defeat all hostile attempts. Strenuous opposition to the scheme was expected from the pride and prejudices of a considerable part of the Irish nation ; but it was hoped that the good sense of a great portion of the community would see it in its true light, and promote its happy accomplishment ; or, if it should be disapproved by the majority of the people, little doubt was entertained of the efficacy of various means of influence and persuasion, in securing a plurality of parliamentary votes for its adoption.

When a legislative union was recommended by implication to the parliament of Ireland, the peers approved the idea ;

but, in the lower house, after a very long discussion which ended in the appearance of a majority of only two votes for the scheme, a renewed debate produced a division which favored its opposers. The latter, however, were defeated in another trial of strength.

A preliminary debate, in the British house of commons, was distinguished by an animated speech from Mr. Sheridan against the measure. When it was again investigated, Mr. Pitt eloquently supported its propriety. That a permanent connection between Britain and Ireland was essential to the true interests of both countries, and that, unless the existing connection should be improved, there was great risque of a separation, he had strong reason to believe. The settlement of the year 1782, he said, was so imperfect, that it substituted nothing for that system which it demolished ; and it was not considered as final even by the ministers of the time. It left the two realms with independent legislatures, connected only by the identity of the executive power—a very insufficient tie either in time of peace or of war, inadequate to the consolidation of strength or the mutual participation of political and commercial benefits. The case of the regency exhibited a striking instance of the weakness of the connection ; and, if the two parliaments had differed on the subject of the war, the danger of a disjunction would have been seriously alarming The entire dissociation of the kingdoms was one of the great aims of our enemies ; and, as their eventual success in Ireland would expose Britain to extreme peril, the establishment of an incorporative union, by which their views might be effectually baffled, was a necessary act of policy. Great Britain had always felt a common interest in the safety of Ireland : but that interest was never so obvious and urgent as when the enemy attacked the former realm through the medium of the latter. The French had shown by their conduct, that they deemed Ireland the most vulnerable part of the empire ; and this consideration alone ought to enforce the adoption of a measure which would tend to strengthen and secure that country. It ought to be noticed, that the hostile divisions of its sects, the animosities existing between the posterity of the original inhabitants and the descendants of the colonists, the rudeness and ignorance of the people, and the prevalence of jacobinical principles among them, had produced a state of distress for which " there was no cure but in the formation of a general imperial legislature, free alike from terror and from resentment, removed from the danger and agitation, uninfluenced by the prejudices and uninflamed by the passions of that distracted country."

Among the advantages which would accrue to Ireland from an incorporation with Britain, he mentioned " the protection which she would secure to herself in the hour of danger, the most effectual means of increasing her commerce and improving her agriculture, the command of English capital, the infusion of English manners and English industry, necessarily tending to meliorate her condition ;" adding, that " she would see the avenue to honors, to distinctions, and exalted situations in the general seat of empire, opened to all those whose abilities and talents enable them to indulge an honorable and laudable am bition." He farther remarked, that the question was not what Ireland would gain, but what she would preserve ; not merely how she might " best improve her situation, but how she might avert a pressing and immediate danger." In this point of view, her gain would be the preservation of all the blessings arising from the British constitution.

After some commercial statements, tending to show the benefits derivable to Ireland from an union, he asserted the competency of the legislature, not by argument or demonstration, but by allegations of the danger of controverting such right. A denial of parliamentary competence, he said, would amount to a denial of the validity of the Scottish union, and of the authority under which the existing parliament now deliberated ; and it would even shake every principle of legislation. That a competency for any new or very important measure could only arise from the express directions or consent of the electors or the great body of the nation, was a jacobinical idea, connected with the dangerous doctrine of the sovereignty of the people.

As the supposed loss of national independence formed, in the minds of many, a strong objection to the scheme, he argued, that the dreaded loss would be a real benefit ; that the Irish would rather gain than lose in point of political freedom and civil happiness ; and that, though a nation possessing all the means of defence, dignity, and prosperity, might justly object to an association with a more numerous people, Ireland, being deficient in the means of protection and inferior in the requisites of political and civil welfare, could not be injured or degraded by such an union with a neighbouring and kindred state, as would connect both realms by an equality of law and an identity of interest. Her people would not less be members of an independent state, or, to any valuable or useful purpose, less free in the enjoyment of the benefits of society and civilization.

Mr. Sheridan opposed an union as particularly unseasonable amidst the irritation which prevailed in Ireland, and deprecated the exercise of force or intimidation, or the practices of artifice and corruption, for the accomplishment of an unpopular measure.

If the court wished to improve the state of
Ireland, there were, he said, means of attaining that object without destroying her
independence or involving her in servitude.
Lord Hawkesbury, however, was of opinion,
that nothing but an union would remove
the radical evils of the existing government
of Ireland.

Mr. Pitt's plan being submitted to the
house in eight propositions, a majority of
125 voted for their being referred to a
general committee. In the next debate on
this subject, Mr. Sheridan compared the
views of the minister with those of the
United Irishmen, who wished, as he did,
for the ruin of the constitution of Ireland.
Two motions from that speaker, condemning
all corruption and intimidation, and protesting against every measure which had
not for its basis the fair and free consent
of the parliaments of both kingdoms, were
rejected ; and the efforts of Mr Grey and
other gentlemen, who conjured the house
to explode the scheme, served only to
encourage the minister to the prosecution
of it. It was defended by Mr. Dundas,
who dwelt on the advantages of the Scottish
union, and alleged that the confidence
which ought to subsist between the governors and the governed could only be established under the auspices of an imperial
legislature, which would be free from the apprehensions and animosities interwoven
with the frame of the Irish parliament,
arising from the opposition between the
power and the population of the country.
Mr. Windham, though he abhorred innovation, was friendly to a measure which
promised a melioration of the state of
Ireland, by an infusion of British capital
and British manners ; and Mr. Grant
supported the general competency of
parliament, and the propriety of proceeding to a specification of the terms of union.

A substitute recommended by Mr.
Sheridan—namely, the abolition of all
incapacities incurred in civil affairs by
religious distinctions—did not satisfy the
majority ; nor did the remonstrances of
lieutenant-general Fitzpatrick, who deprecated the enforcement of a scheme which
would subvert the settlement of 1782, or

the arguments of Dr. Laurence, who reprobated a legislative union as unnecessary
and injurious, effectually impress the house.
In another debate, Mr. Bankes affirmed
that the disordered state of Ireland rendered it inexpedient and even unsafe to
coalesce with her ; but Mr. Addington
combated that assertion, and maintained
that an incorporation was calculated to avert
much probable evil from both countries,
and to produce positive and substantial
benefits to each. The propositions were
then adopted by the committee.

When the report was offered to the house,
Mr. Hobhouse and Mr. Jones opposed
the measure with plausibility rather than
with force : Mr. Peel defended it with
some hesitation and reserve : the lords
Temple, Morpeth, and Belgrave, strenuously recommended it. The solicitor-
general compared the political establishment of an empire which had two independent parliaments to a monster with
two bodies and one head influenced by
each, and gave it as his opinion that an
union would be the best mode of supplying the deficiency of a sovereign power
for the direction of imperial concerns. By
a majority of 104, the report was received ;
and the resolutions were soon communicated
to the peers.

The subject was discussed by lord Grenville in a long speech, which met with the
general approbation of the assembly. He
endeavored to show, that the pretended
bond of connection between Ireland and
this kingdom was not merely imperfect,
but was absolutely null. He illustrated
this point by referring to the chief branches
of the prerogative, in which the identity
of the sovereign of the two realms could
not enforce a desirable unity of action.
Under such a system, he said, there was
no security for the connection. The general
interest of the empire, therefore, required
new arrangements ; and the evils of Ireland, in particular, called for the application of a speedy remedy. He traced the
origin of those divisions and animosities
which had retarded in that country the
progress of civilization ; attributed the
late rebellion to the influence of jacobinical

principles; and contended, that nothing but a legislative union would furnish an effectual antidote to the poison of such doctrines, or correct the radical vices of the government. Earl Fitzwilliam wished that some attempts might be made to cure the disorders of Ireland without the hazard of an unpopular union : but the marquis of Lansdown recommended the ministerial scheme as the best of all experiments. Earl Camden decidedly favored the measure ; the marquis Townshend less strongly supported it. The earl of Moira and lord Holland advised the ministry to relinquish it, because it was odious to the Irish. Lord Mulgrave, and the earls of Carlisle and Westmoreland, professed contrary sentiments ; and the resolutions were adopted by the house.

When an address to the king was proposed, lord Auckland appeared as an advocate for the scheme, corrective as it would be of an anomalous, incompetent, and unsettled government ; the bishop of Llandaff gave it the weight of his approbation ; and lord Minto (formerly sir Gilbert Elliot,) with a mixture of declamation and argument, forcibly urged its expediency. The commons, being desired to join in the address, complied with the request after a renewal of debate ; and the resolutions were presented to his majesty.

Before this address was voted, the scheme was assailed by the vigorous hostility of Mr. Foster, speaker of the house of commons in Ireland, who, after endeavoring to show the finality of the settlement of 1782, entered into a detail of the ill consequences of what he termed the " rash quackery" of the minister ; and the eloquence of Mr. G. Ponsonby was also exercised in an attempt to prove that an union would be highly injurious to the freedom and prosperity of Ireland.

The spirit with which the idea of an union was opposed in Ireland, though it did not so far discourage the court as to produce a dereliction of the object, operated in recommendation of delay ; and it was deemed more prudent to wait the effect of a farther exertion of ministerial arts, than

to enforce the immediate accomplishment of an obnoxious scheme.

During the deliberations upon the union, the views of the mal-contents in both countries were examined by a committee of the British commons. The result was an act for the suppression of the London Corresponding Society and other clubs which were considered as inimical to the constitution, and for the more effectual restraint of sedition.

A bill which did not please the moderate part of the nation was sanctioned by both houses. It tended to perpetuate forfeiture of property and corruption of blood in cases of high treason, thus repealing the clauses of limitation contained in an act of the year 1709, and in one of 1744. The arguments by which it was opposed did not materially differ from those which were stated in our account of the last-mentioned statute.

The regulation of internal affairs, and the discussion of various bills, were interrupted by the annunciation of pecuniary and friendly engagements with the king's " good brother and ally" the emperor of Russia. That potentate had promised to employ 45,000 men against the French, in consideration of a subsidy from Great Britain ; and, after some objections to the waste of the public money, and strictures on the impolicy of continuing and extending the war, the commons voted £825,000 to supply the wants of the Russians, and assist the Portuguese and Swiss.

By the twentieth article of the treaty of Campo Formio, the contracting parties had agreed that there should be held at Rastadt, a congress solely composed of the plenipotentiaries of the German empire and the French republic, and that this congress should be opened a month after the signature of the treaty, or as soon as possible. Accordingly, in the beginning of 1797, the respective plenipotentiaries assembled at Rastadt, and continued sitting till the 28th of April, 1799, when the mysterious and horrid catastrophe occurred which I shall shortly have occasion to relate. The French legation at Rastadt was at first composed of the citizens Treilhard and Bonnier, who had acted as plenipotentiaries in the conferrences with lord Malmsbury at Lisle. To follow the meeting through the various details which occupied its attention, would trespass on my limits and exhaust the patience of my readers. The narration shall be confined to such proceedings as produced the recommencement of hostilities, and the renewal of a general confederacy with England.

By the treaty of Campo Formio, it was agreed that the Rhine should form the boundary between the French and German empires; and that a system of indemnities should compensate to the German princes for the losses which they should incur by this extension of the French empire. The proposed remedy was the seculariza- tion of the ecclesiastical states. The de- putation of the empire, after a protracted discussion, consented to this plan, though with extreme and natural reluctance. The arrangement of the boundary line next engrossed the attention of the congress. The directory proposed to take under their own special protection, the cities of Frank- fort, Bremen, and Hamburg, which they alleged to be coveted by German poten- tates; and that it therefore behoved the French republic to interpose its powerful mediation in their behalf. For these and other purposes, it was asserted, that France ought to possess a weighty influence be- yond the Rhine. I have already recorded the cession of the left bank of that river to the republic; but she extended her de- mands by proposing the free navigation of the river to the opposite bank, the re- establishment of commercial bridges, and a division of the islands on the Rhine, by which France would have possessed those positions which best suited her policy and convenience. The fortress of Ehrenbreit- stein, situated upon the right bank of the Rhine, commands the entrance into Ger- many on the side of Westphalia, the Upper Rhine, and Hesse. This post the French desired to be destroyed. The evident object of this demand was to secure an entrance into Germany. Elated also with success, the French added to their bound- less ambition an overweening and dictatorial insolence. The Austrians were now re- covering from their disasters: incensed by the arrogance of France, which was openly and ostentatiously exemplified by the elevation of the tri-coloured flag, before the residence of Bernadotte, the French am- bassador at Vienna, and inspirited by proffers of military aid from the emperor of Russia, they prepared to resist the ex- horbitant demands of France by the renewal of hostilities. The directory easily discovered the sentiments and designs so naturally resulting from their own insolence and ambition; having received information that a formidable army of Russian troops were on their march to the south, they no longer doubted that they were destined to co-operate with the imperial army of Italy. Having three great armies ready for motion, they threatened to cross the Rhine, unless the Russians should retreat from the con- fines of Germany; and, finding that the Austrians would not yield to their demands, they ordered their ambassadors to leave Rastadt, and immediately prepared for the commencement of hostilities.

The French, as we have seen, had totally changed their plan of warfare. Their utmost efforts were directed to the unremitted pursuit of the enemy. For- tresses, which in former wars had arrested the progress of an invading army, were passed with unconcern, as certain to share the fate of the capital or of the empire. It was in the superiority, therefore, of their military tactics, and not the mul- tiplicity of their resources or the extent of their numbers, that they confided for the successful result of the campaign. At the moment of the recommencement of hos- tilities, the directory had not more than 320,000 French soldiers in Europe, and with this number of men supported by about 80,000 auxiliaries, it hoped to be able to defend its frontiers from Amsterdam to Naples, a space of 2000 miles; to protect its coasts or those of its allies from the Texel to Bayonne; to command the

1799. obedience of 40,000,000 of men anxious to throw off the yoke, and to invade the dominions, and destroy or possess the capital of Austria.

The republican army had been reduced to this number by the losses it had sustained in the two last campaigns against the Austrians, in the war against Switzerland, in that which still continued in the kingdom of Naples, and by the return of a number of requisitionary soldiers to their homes. Of the 320,000 men who composed the French army, 45,000 under the orders of Massena occupied Switzerland, and the left bank of the Rhine, almost from its source to the western extremity of the lake of Constance, and from that point, the two banks of the river, as far as Basle. Between this town and Dusseldorf were stationed about 65,000 men, commanded by general Jourdan, and forming the army of Mentz. They occupied the fort of Kehl, on the right bank of the Rhine, lined the left bank from the frontier of Switzerland to Mentz, and from the latter town to Dusseldorf possessed all the country upon the two banks. The corps in the latter position amounting to about 20,000 men, was called the army of observation, and was under the command of general Bernadotte. It was therefore with only 110,000 men that the French had to carry the war into Germany; to hold themselves in readiness to repulse the neutral army in case it should march against them, and to keep in subjection Switzerland, and all the countries situated between the Sarre, the Moselle, the Roër, and the Rhine.

The situation and the views of the Austrians were as follow: more than 60,000 were concentrated under the archduke upon the Lech. Twenty thousand were collected in the Palatinate, in the environs of Auberg or at Wurtzburg, under the orders of general Stzarry; the same number was headed by general Hotze, in the Voralberg and the country of the Grisons. Nearly 25,000, commanded by general Bellegarde, were on the frontiers of the Grisons and the Tyrol. The forces in

Carinthia and in Friuli, were estimated at more than 60,000.

The Austrians being determined not to commence hostilities, acted at first on the defensive. Jourdan through Suabia, and Massena through Switzerland, advanced towards the Tyrol Between them, during a part of the march, was the Rhine and the lake of Constance; and on the eastern side of that great body of water they intended to form a junction; but the natural obstacles which Jourdan was obliged to encounter, had hitherto obstructed his design. A successful battle would, however, effectually accomplish that object and decide the fate of the campaign. On the 27th of April, therefore, he hazarded a pitched battle in the vicinity of Stockach, advancing in three columns, to attack the archduke. The battle was obstinately contested, and the French had almost proved victorious, when the archduke dismounting, led his infantry to the charge, and, by his presence and example, excited his soldiers to unwonted exertion. The French were yet unbroken; but the archduke charged them in flank, and throwing the enemy into confusion, completed the victory. On the next day the French general endeavored to renew the combat; but, finding his army to be so much reduced as to be incapable of making head against the enemy, he retreated and recrossed the Rhine. The archduke, in his report, calculated the French loss at 5000 men, of whom 2000 were made prisoners; and his own at 3000, killed, wounded, and missing. General Jourdan stated the loss of the imperialists at 4000 prisoners, but does not mention his own. Prince Maurice of Lechtenstein was killed, and general Meerfeldt wounded. In consequence of this disaster Jourdan was dismissed from the command of the army, and Massena appointed generalissimo of the French forces, from the Alpine frontiers of Italy to Mentz.

Prince Charles had it now in his power to advance in pursuit of Jourdan towards Strasburg, or, by turning to Switzerland, cross the Rhine, and fall on the left wing

of general Masséna. To provide against
either of these operations, Jourdan, immediately previous to his dismissal, had
directed his right at Ferino, to pass the
river at Schaffhausen, break down the
bridges, and occupy the left bank. By
this manœuvre Ferino was enabled to
harass his royal highness in flank and
rear, in case he should imprudently advance to the Brisgau, or to cover Masséna,
and retard the progress of the imperialists,
until new measures of defence should be
adopted.

The proclamation which the archduke
Charles addressed to the Grisons, was
similar to that issued by Jourdan on entering Germany with such modifications as
local circumstances rendered necessary.
On the 6th of April he attacked in several
points, the Austrian troops posted in that
country, and, after an obstinate action,
his main body obtained possession of
Luciensteig. This fort, situated at the
extremity of a pass formed out of a rock
along the channel of the Rhine, is the only
communication through the Rhœtian Alps,
between the Voralberg and the Grisons.
Massena, following up his success with
intrepidity, entirely routed the imperialists,
took prisoner their commander-in-chief,
general Auffenburg, with upwards of 3000
of his men, and entered Coire. On the
right of the centre, general Demont made
himself master of Reichenau, and the bridges
over the Rhine, while general Oudinot, on
the left, defeated the enemy, capturing
several pieces of cannon, and 1500 prisoners. During these operations, a French
corps amused general Hotze in the Voralberg with a feigned attack, which, however,
was conducted with so much vigor, that
Hotze was only able to preserve his main
position at Feldkirch, in consequence of
a powerful reinforcement from the archduke. The imperialists complained of the
ineffectual aid they received from the
Grisons, and we are informed that,
although the tocsin had sounded for several
hours, only sixty men from the levy of
peasants appeared in arms. The French
now entered the valley of Engaddin, where

3600 Austrians were taken prisoners, and
general Laudohn, their commander, with
difficulty effected his escape. The nature
of the country fortunately presently innumerable points of defence; and Laudohn,
though defeated, was still able to occupy
the defiles leading into the Tyrol. General
Lecourbe's division penetrated as far as
St. Martinsbruck, and Finstermuntz, in
the Lower Engaddin, after leaving a small
corps at Zernetz, to communicate with a
French detachment from the Valteline,
who were expected at St. Marie. On the
15th, general Laudohn made a spirited
attack in three points, at Zernetz, Schultz,
and Martinsbruck. In that at Schultz,
he surprised and captured the French
general Maimoni, with his detachment:
but in the other two attacks he did not
experience the same success. His first
good fortune appears to have rendered the
imperialists inconsiderately daring, for in
a subsequent engagement they were completely routed. General Lecourbe prosecuted his advantage by attacking St.
Martinsbruck, and Finstermuntz, while
a division of the army of Italy, under
general Desolles, advanced against Glurentz. Both operations succeeded; and
the Austrians, on the 25th, sustained
another defeat, with the loss of 27 pieces
of cannon, 1100 men, killed and wounded,
and 7000 prisoners.

An Austrian corps under general Stzarry
destined to watch the operations of Bernadotte, had slowly approached in the
direction of Heilbron. They now ventured
to push forward their advanced posts, in
order to create an alarm on the flank of
general St. Cyr, who was retiring by
Dornstadt, and followed by a detachment
from the archduke's main army. But
neither party retained in this quarter sufficient strength to undertake any important
operation; and it is unnecessary to record
a variety of incidental skirmishes, attended
with alternate success, and productive only
of bloodshed.

It is not easy to assign a reason for the subsequent inactivity of prince Charles. His delay in prosecuting the success which he had obtained, enabled Massena to dissipate the alarm occasioned by the rout of the French army, and to concert measures of defence. After arranging his positions along the line to the south of the lake of Constance, he hastened to the Rhine. Having been invested by the French government with the additional command of the army of the Danube, he directed a considerable reinforcement to advance to Basle, in order to strengthen his left wing, now converted into a front. His assiduity and perseverance were incessant, and formed a striking contrast to the tardy movements of his opponent, whose inactivity has been excused on the plea of indisposition. It was not till the 22nd of May that the archduke attempted to cross the Rhine into Switzerland, where his first slight and temporary successes were only the preludes to future disaster. The subsequent operations, however, were so much affected by the vicissitudes of the campaign in Italy, that it will be necessary to proceed to the narrative of Cisalpine operations.

In the autumn of the last year, the king of Naples, willing to avail himself of the weakness of the French army in Italy, took the field at the head of an army commanded by the Austrian general Mack, and penetrated into the territories of the Roman republic ; while a division of the British fleet made a diversion in his favor by taking possession of Leghorn. This movement was fatal to the interests of his Sardinian majesty. Warm disputes had occurred between the French garrison in the citadel of Turin and the Piedmontese, who felt with indignation the pusilanimity of their sovereign. The weak and disarmed monarch himself, had given no just cause of offence to the great nation. But the directory, impressed with a with a persuasion of his enmity, from a consciousness of the injuries which they had done him, and sensible of the danger which threatened their newly established power in Italy, should he join the Austrians and Neapolitans, resolved to prevent so sinistrous an event, by making themselves masters of Piedmont. Unrestrained by the antiquated principle of public faith, they compelled the king to renounce the exercise of his sovereign power, and to repair to the island of Sardinia.

The events of the subsequent hostilities proved highly disgraceful to the Neapolitans. Mack had obtained possession of a considerable extent of country. But no sooner had the French generals collected their forces, than they advanced to the encounter, in defiance of their enemy's great superiority in number ; confident that their own superior prowess would more than compensate the disparity. After defeating his detachments in several actions, generals Macdonald and Matthieu, attacked Mack himself in his entrenchments near Civita Castellana, gained a complete victory, and, having taken 5000 of his men, forced him to retire to Naples, and put himself on the defensive for the protection of that capital.

The operations, however, of the French, were neither so active nor so formidable, as might have been expected. The republican armies were comparatively feeble, and their inactivity was countenanced by the emperor, who was anxious that the Russians destined to reinforce his troops under general Kray in Italy, should have reached, as nearly as possible, the scene of action previous to the commencement of hostilities. The imperial army stretched along the left bank of the Adige, and occupied in force, the tract of country between that river and the lake of Garda. As the movements of the enemy intimated an approaching attack, general Kray strengthened the post of Legnago from his camp at Bevilaqua. General Kaim, who commanded the right wing, was strongly reinforced ; intelligence having been received that the French were concentrating their troops near Villa Franca, and Castel Nuovo. Similar precautions were adopted at Verona, and, where the ground admitted, particularly on the right, the position was further strengthened by entrenchments. In order to facilitate the retreat of the right, and also to preserve a communication with the left bank of the Adige, two bridges of boats were thrown over that river, each

2 u 2

having a double *tête de pont* defended by artillery.

At day-break, on the 26th of May, general Scherer, in three divisions, attacked the imperialists posted between the lake of Garda and the Adige, while two other divisions advanced against Verona, and a sixth attracted the attention of the Austrian troops posted at Legnago. The two divisions under generals Victor and Grenier, destined to act against Verona, attacked with impetuosity the posts of St. Lucia and St. Massimo, the central points of this part of the Austrian position. General Liptay, who commanded at St. Lucia, was wounded : soon afterwards the general next in command sustained the same misfortune, and the post was carried. The republican troops made seven successive attacks on the post of St. Massimo, and carried it seven times, but were obliged to abandon it on the approach of night. The divisions on the left carried the Austrian redoubts in front, while general Serrurier's detachment, seconded by the flotilla on the lake, cleared the adjacent heights. At Legnago, both sides fought with fury ; and it required every exertion of general Kray in person, to arrest the progress of the enemy. The country being intersected by canals, was happily favorable to defensive operations. After a sanguinary contest of eighteen hours, night terminated the struggle, and the hostile armies resumed their former positions. Not intimidated by the disastrous result of this attack, Scherer made another attempt on the 30th. He directed the division of Serrurier, and part of that of Victor, to, endeavor to gain possession of the heights behind Verona, and, after passing the Adige at Ronco, and turning the enemy's right wing, oblige him to retreat by Vicenza, and entirely separate him from Verona and Legnago. This detachment succeeded in forcing all the Austrian advanced posts ; but the farther they proceeded, the greater were the difficulties it became necessary to surmount. Sensible that it would be impossible to effect his object with so small a force, the French general prepared to retire. The imperialists, how-

ever, having collected all their troops, intercepted by a rapid manœuvre, the retreat of part of the French detachment, and took about 1000 prisoners. General Scherer made no effort to second this operation of Serrurier by a powerful diversion ; but with the most criminal indifference sacrificed the lives of men who sunk beneath the incumbent pressure of superior numbers.

After this disaster, the French ascended the Adige, and took a position between that river and the Tartaro, as if with an intention to cross the former. On the 2nd of April general Kray passed with his main army, and occupied a camp in front of Verona, his left being supported by the post of Tomba, and his right by that of St. Lucia. To create a diversion and distract the attention of the French, general Klenau made several movements on the Lower Po, as far as Ostiglia, where he encountered little opposition from the scattered parties of the enemy. General Kray, on the 5th of April, marched with his army in three columns, supported by a fourth, against the French camp at Magnan, opposite to that occupied by his main body under Verona ; and, as his antagonist had determined to make a similar attack on the imperialists, both sides were prepared for action.

Resolved to make a third attempt to pass the Adige, Scherer had concentrated his forces between that river and the Tartaro. He had evacuated the whole country near the lake of Garda, so that the communication with the Tyrol by the valley of the Adige was open to the Austrians, who had pushed their patroles as far as Paschiera, and thrown several bombs into the place. Instead of advancing to the Upper Adige, where the passage was easy, driving general Kray to the left side of the river, and re-opening a communication with the army of Helvetia (Switzerland) Scherer selected a place intersected by numerous canals and streams. Every step must have entangled his troops ; while the imperial general, who had crossed the Adige in great force, was in a condition to act against the flank and rear of the French, and threaten the annihilation of their army by a single blow.

Thus ensnared by his imprudence, Scherer had no other alternative than to endeavor to impede the progress of Kray on the right bank of the Adige, by hazarding a battle. He accordingly directed generals Victor and Grenier to proceed along the banks of the river below Verona, and take possession of the village of St. James ; while Delmas, with the advanced guard covered their attack. General Moreau, with the divisions of Hatry and Moutrichard, was charged with the task of engaging every hostile corps he might find between Villa Franca and Verona ; and Serrurier, who was entrusted with the attack on the former of these places, was instructed to carry it, and follow the imperialists to the Adige. Serrurier, although at first repulsed, succeeded in a second attempt ; and general Moreau, having forced the enemy in the plain to fall back, advanced towards Verona. But Victor and Grenier, notwithstanding some advantages gained at first by the impetuosity of their troops, were compelled in the evening to yield to the valor and numbers of the imperialists. The retreat of these two divisions uncovered the flank of the French army ; and, had this incident occurred at an earlier hour, the success of the Austrians must have been decisive. The two other columns maintained their ground until the approach of darkness, after which they retired ; and, during the night, the whole French army abandoned the field of battle and their camp. Pressed in every direction, Scherer abandoned all his positions, and fell back behind the Mincio, whither he was closely followed by the imperialists, who had been joined by several Austrian corps, and a powerful body of Russian auxiliaries.

Scarcely had the new sovereign of Russia succeeded amidst the acclamations of the people to the throne so splendidly filled by his mother, than he displayed an enthusiasm in the cause of European independence against French aggression, that good men were willing to attribute to the wisdom of his policy and the rectitude of his feelings. Whatever motives had induced him to observe a neutrality at his accession to the throne, they were now superseded by those which recommended warlike measures. The terror of the French arms had reached the remotest parts of Europe ; and Paul, whose disposition was at once obstinate and romantic, regarded the very successes of the republicans as the most powerful inducement to hostilities. His prepossessions were confirmed when he experienced the insolence of the French government, and was informed of Buonaparte's expedition to Egypt. On receiving information that the executive directory had in the pride of prosperous fortune declared " that if any ship shall be suffered to pass the Sound with English commodities on board, such permission shall be considered as a formal declaration of war against the French nation :" he ordered 22 ships of the line, and 250 galleys to proceed to the Sound, to protect the trade against the oppression of the directory,

In conformity with the same principles, when the knights of Malta, indignant at a late capitulation in favor of the French, consented to by Hompesch, their grand master, solicited his protection, he courteously received their overtures, and accepted the office of grand master. This proceeding was followed by measures still more resolute. Towards the year 1798, a treaty of alliance, as we have seen, was concluded by the emperor with his Britannic majesty, by which Paul engaged to send 45,000 men, with proper artillery into the field, on receiving £225,000 to defray the first expenses, and £75,000 per month, after his troops should pass the Russian frontiers. When the Turkish court was overwhelmed with consternation by the rapid progress of the French in Egypt, the Russian emperor entered into a defensive alliance with the Porte, in which they reciprocally guaranteed each others possessions.

By the misconduct of Scherer, and the consequent successes of the Austrians, the French army had already been reduced to the most perilous situation. It continued its retreat by its right beyond the Oglio ; and by its left beyond the Chiusa General Kray, who had already marched his vanguard to Gorito, passed the Mincio with his main army, and pushed his advanced guards as far as these two rivers. Having been joined by general Melas, who was to have taken the command of the army, but who left it in the hands of Kray till the arrival of Suwarrow, that general reached Verona with the vanguard of the Russians, and, pressing the march of his columns, joined the Austrian army, of which the command was immediately assigned to him.

The French, on the 24th, had abandoned the Oglio, which the imperial army soon after passed, and advanced in three columns, to the Adda. General Moreau, who now commanded the French troops in the place of Scherer, fortified Cassano, and erected formidable batteries along the right of the river, with a strong *tête de pont* on the left. He fixed his head-quarters at Inzaego, where two divisions of his army were posted. General Serrurier defended the Upper Adda; one half of his division occupying a position behind Lecco, a port near Porto Imberzago, and the rest near Trezzio. On the Lower Adda towards Lodi, general Delmas was stationed with a detachment, having his flank covered by Pizzighitone. The Russians under general Vukassowich forming the right of the imperial army, attacked, on the 26th of April, all the French corps posted in front of Lecco, and, after an obstinate contest, drove them back to the *tête de pont*.

After this action, the situation of the French general became daily more distressful. With the disadvantage of being opposed to superior armies, commanded by two of the first generals of the age, he had to contend with the Brescian malcontents, and with the discontented in the other parts of the Cisalpine republic; a great number of whom, disappointed of the benefits which they expected from the revolution, had joined the enemies of France as soon as they dared to confide in their protection. They had received freedom as a boon at the hands of Buonaparte; they had hailed him as their deliverer; they had planted the tree of liberty with great parade; but they were now to learn

that liberty is not to be received as a boon, but asserted as a right; that those alone deserve this inestimable blessing who have spirit to maintain it, not by the protection of others, but by their own native force; and that it is vain to plant the tree of liberty unless it be guarded by good morals, by the pride of personal independence, and by that union among the members of the state which arises from their common attachment to the constitution under which they live. After the dispersion of the French at Trezzio, Suwarrow compelled his enemy to retire before him through the Milanese, gained possession of the capital, and caused the citadel to be invested.

Having reached the centre of Lombardy more rapidly than he had conceived it possible, and after taking possession of Milan, he divided a great part of his forces in pursuit of four different objects. On the west, and in front, he had to follow up his operations against the army of Moreau in order to hasten his retreat and force him to abandon Piedmont and Genoa, before he received reinforcements: on the north and on his right he designed to penetrate into the valleys above the lakes, and to facilitate the movements of the left of the archduke's army beyond St. Gothard: on the east and behind him, Kray besieged Mantua with a body of 25,000 men, while general Klenau invested Ferrara, and blockaded Bologna; the vigorous defence of which places caused a favorable diversion to that division of the French army which was retreating from Naples and Rome towards Tuscany, under the command of Macdonald. Towards the south and on his left, Suwarrow had detached general Ott with a strong division to support general Klenau, to stop the progress of Macdonald's army, to seize the passage of the Apennines in Upper Tuscany, and intercept the communications with that country and with the Ligurian republic. In this manner the whole of Italy was occupied by the French and imperial armies; the different divisions and posts of both being intermingled. From the centre of Lombardy to the two seas, there was not a place or a post, whether supported by the French armies or insulated, which was not attacked or defended with vigor. There was not, within the vast circle of the Alps, or in the long chain of the Apennines, a single pass which had not at this moment a relative importance to the immediate operations, and which was not seized upon or disputed either by detached troops, or by the inhabitants of the country.

We shall look in vain into the history of the former wars of Italy for any parallel to the last and the present campaign. The world had never seen a conquest so rapid, or more solid than that of Buonaparte; if it be true that a total change in the form of government, the disposal of the public resources, and the command of the public forces, confirms the dominion of conquerors. Yet never were so many advantages lost, so many means of preservation destroyed, within so short an interval of time, and almost at a single blow.

Suwarrow having thus disseminated his forces, Moreau, after the passage of the Adda and the evacuation of Milan, made his retreat in good order, in three columns; that of the right marching from Lodi upon Piacenza; that of the centre by the road of Milan to Genoa, upon Pavia and Voghera; that of the left by Vigevano and Novarra. While the main army thus retreated upon the Ligurian republic, Moreau paid a visit to Turin, where he repressed many disorders which had taken place, made preparations for the evacuation of the city and the arsenal, and provided for the defence of the citadel, which he confided to general Fiorella. He also reestablished the communications, which, if not altogether cut off, were at least interrupted by parties of the insurgents, of which the preservation was highly important, on account of the succours which he expected from Switzerland by the Lower Vallais, mount St. Bernard, and the valley of Aust; from the southern departments by mount Cenis and the valley of Sussa, and from Biançon by the valley of Exiles. Unable, with an army reduced to about 25,000 men, to defend with any prospect of success the plains of Piedmont, to cover the

country of Genoa, and to secure the communications necessary for the junction of his army with that of Naples, and for the arrival of succours by way of Nice, Moreau left Turin on the 7th of May, and transferred his head-quarters to Alessandria. He had previously taken a position under Tortona, extending his advanced posts on his right towards the Apennines, in order to narrow that interval as much as possible, and favor the retreat of Macdonald by retaining Suwarrow on the left bank of the Po. Suwarrow in the mean time had advanced as far as Pavia, and detached from his right a strong vanguard, under Vukassovich, to take possession of Novarra, and other places evacuated by the French. He had orders likewise to ascend the Po as far as Turin, and divert Moreau's attention to his rear, by attacking or flanking his left wing. At the same time general Hohenzollern marched upon Piacenza with part of the left of the allied army, and, ascending the right side of the Po, had forced back the vanguard of the French beyond Voghera, near Tortona. In aid of this movement, and with a view of seizing at a later period the passages into the country of Genoa by the Apennines, Suwarrow took post at Bobbio, on the road from Piacenza to Genoa.

General Kray, after taking Peschiera, had marched upon Borgoforte, and assembled all his forces round Mantua. The garrison made frequent sallies, some of which became serious engagements. The siege of the castle of Milan was begun on the 6th of May, by general Letterman, and on the same day general Kaim opened the trenches before Pizzighitone, of which he gained possession in four days from the explosion of a powder magazine. Ferrara, Bologna, Ravenna, Fort Urbin, and Ancona, still held out. Suwarrow's main army was much diminished by these different operations and diverging movements, which, considering the weakness and situation of the French, were not only inexpedient and useless, but lost him the opportunity of exterminating the whole of the French armies in Italy, and of opening a passage into the southern departments of

France. Suwarrow's ignorance of his advantages, and the skilful tactics of Moreau, preserved both. The Russian general nevertheless, kept close on Moreau, and attempted to dislodge him from the strong position he had taken in a kind of entrenched camp, where he had fortified himself behind the Po and the Tanaro, between Valenza and Alessandria. Tortona was attacked on the 9th of May, by general Chasteler, who blew up the gates under the fire of the castle, into which the French garrison withdrew. On the 10th, the greater part of the allied army, strongly reinforced after the capture of Pizzighitone, passed the Scrivia, and encamped at Torre Garrafolo. General Karacksay was detached with a corps to take possession of Novi, Serravalle, and Gavi. This movement of Suwarrow by his left flank, and the excursions of his light troops into the country between the course of the Tanaro and the Apennines did not shake the French general's determination. Moreau had flanked his right by Alessandria, and his left by Valenza, and had thrown strong detachments into Casal and Verica ; nor was he deceived with respect to the projects of Suwarrow, who menaced the right of the French army and its communications with Genoa, only to surprise a passage over the Po on his left, and to surround and engage that division in a general and decisive action. This intention was seconded by the attacks of the inhabitants of Mondovi, Cherasco, Seva, and Oneglia, who suddenly took arms, and who dispersed a battalion sent to join the French army. Moreau's position was such, that, had he lost a battle, his retreat on either side of the Apennines, would have become almost impossible.

The attack against the left of Moreau was attempted on the 11th of May, by a vanguard of imperial troops, who, having passed, the Po above Valenza, had been rudely treated and driven back. But, on the following day, the affair became more serious : a Russian division of 7000 men, under the command of general Schubarf, passed the river below Valenza, near the confluence of the Po and the Tanaro, and marched towards Pechetto, between Alessandria and Tortona, in order to cut the line of the French. The first shock of the Russians was met by the division under general Grenier ; when Moreau, attacking them in flank with the division under Victor, the Russians were driven back, and a great number killed or wounded in the Po, among whom was the Russian commander. After this second attempt, Suwarrow determined to march his main body along the left side of the Po to Turin, in order to dislodge Moreau from his camp, and make him fall back on the frontiers of France, or retreat into the Ligurian republic. With this view general Vukassovich made attacks at Verus, Ponte Stura, and Casal, while a part of the troops under general Melas, on the right side of the Po, received orders to pass over on the night following, to the left side, and march upon Candia. Whether Moreau had received information of this design, or perceived certain movements in the Russian camp at Torre di Garafolo, where there ought to have remained but an inconsiderable body, he threw a bridge, in the night, over the Bormida, near Alessandria, and passed it in the morning with a column of 7000 men, leading the cavalry in person. He attacked and broke the chain of advanced posts at Marenzo, and pursued them to Santo Giuliano. He then detached a body of troops by his left, to drive in the advanced posts of general Melas, and march upon the camp of Torre di Garafolo, then under the command of general Lusignan, whom he forced to abandon his position, and whom he separated for some time from a body of seven Russian battalions under prince Pankration. At length, however, these two imperial divisions, after considerable loss, rallied against the French, who retreated across their bridges to Alessandria.

This was the last effort of Moreau to preserve the position. Suwarrow, whose head-quarters were at Lumello, hastened the attack on the French posts on the right side of the Po, above Valenza : general

Vuckassowich also attacked and carried Casal. The French entrenched camp being no longer tenable, Moreau, compelled to evacuate Valenza and Alessandria, made good his retreat, after having provided for the defence of the citadel of the latter place, and marched his army, (May 22nd,) by Asti and Chierasco, upon Coni. He detached also a body of troops upon his right, to occupy Ceva and Mondovi, and to open the communications with Genoa and that part of the coast which had been interrupted by the insurrections of the peasants. This position was the best which he could have taken, to receive the reinforcements which he expected from the southern departments of France, and by Oneglia, Finale, and the other small seaports.

By manœuvres thus skilfully combined, Moreau not only saved the wrecks of Scherer's army, but gave time to general Macdonald to reach the frontiers of the Ligurian republic, and enabled general Perignon to occupy the passages on the side of the mountains, to strengthen his means of defence, and to secure such advanced positions as might best favor the junction of the two armies.

Suwarrow, who, from inadvertence or ignorance of the country, had taken disadvantageous positions on both sides the Po, below the double confluence of the Bormida, and the Tanaro had been unable to execute his plan of surrounding the French army in the camp of Alessandria. After the evacuation of that place which he now occupied, he formed the blockade of the citadel with the division of general Schweikosky : a corps under general Seckendorf had advanced on the side of the Acqui, and the centre of the allied armies, under the orders of Melas, had marched upon Candia. Considerable falls of rain retarded, for some days, these marches directed against Turin, on both sides the Po. On the 26th of May, general Melas, having crossed the Sesia, continued his march to the Stura. The Russian divisions under general Karacksay, passed this river and the Doria, and took an advantageous position in face of the Char-

treuse. The corps under general Vuckassowich, advanced by the right side of the Po, and took post on the heights of the Capuchins. The city of Turin was thus invested, and summoned to surrender ; the French commander, Fiorella, made no reply, and returned the fire of the besiegers : but a bomb, having set fire to a house under the gate of the Po, the armed inhabitants took advantage of the disorder, and, having seized on the gate, opened it to the allies. The garrison, consisting of about 3000 men, retired to the citadel : the division of general Kaim occupied the town, and that of prince Pankration, the environs ; while the generals Frolich and Zoph formed a camp of observation on the road of Pignerol. Ten weeks only had elapsed from the beginning of hostilities on the Adige, before Suwarrow encamped within sight of the frontiers of France.

But, though the Russian general had made this progress in front, he had yet behind him an army against which it was necessary to assemble no inconsiderable force. General Macdonald, on receiving intelligence of the retreat from before Mantua, had evacuated the kingdom of Naples. He had ordered camps to be formed at Caserta and Madaloni, and created at Naples a numerous national guard. Fort St. Elmo, Capua, and Gaeta, were provisioned as if destined to sustain a siege ; the government was organized, and the Neapolitans were well disposed to defend themselves. Several English vessels were cruizing at the entrance of the road, and intercepted every kind of communication by sea. As soon as Macdonald had received positive orders from Scherer to join the army of Italy, he recalled the division which was in the Pouille, and that on the frontiers of Calabria, and leaving the camp of Caserta, marched by Rome upon Florence, leaving a strong garrison at Fort St. Elmo, Capua, and Gaeta. The first division, commanded by general Olivier, which traversed St. Germano, and Isola, found the country in insurrection. Two villages were taken by storm, and almost the whole of the inhabitants perished in the attack. The patriots of Naples had perceived with consternation, the retreat of the French. The same sensation prevailed at Rome; and a garrison was left in that city, which, in case of attack by superior forces, was directed to retire into the fort of St. Angelo.

Generals Gauthier and Miolis, who commanded the corps of French troops in Tuscany, had made preparations to receive the army of Naples, and had formed a camp of observation between Florence and Bologna, closing up all the passes of the Apennines. Suwarrow had not a moment to lose in preventing a junction which might disconcert his designs and change the whole face of affairs. The celerity of Macdonald's march with so considerable a force, the manœuvres of general Moreau, and the firmness of the corps of observation in Tuscany and the Bolognese, had rendered possible the most difficult retreat that had ever been attempted by military enterprise.

It was this consideration which induced Suwarrow to prosecute his sieges with redoubled vigor. This description of offensive warfare prevented him, however, from disposing of all his forces in the field, retarded his operations against Tuscany, and interrupted his manœuvres against the intermediate positions occupied by the French. The siege of the castle of Milan was interrupted by the necessity of transmitting succours to the prince of Rohan, who had to contend against superior forces, between the lakes of Como and Lugano, at the entrance of the Italian bailiwicks, where, notwithstanding the insurrection of the inhabitants in his favor, he had not been able to maintain himself against Lecourbe. The French were at length obliged to retreat from Lugano across mount Cenere to Bellinzone, and regain Switzerland by the Levantine valley; after which the imperial troops were recalled, and the trenches opened against the citadel of Milan, the commander of which capitulated, and obtained for his garrison, consisting of 2200 men, a free passage and the honors of war, with the condition only of not serving for a year against the imperial armies. The citadel

of Ferrara having a garrison of 1500 men, surrendered to general Klenau on the same conditions. Ravenna was taken a few days after, the peasants aiding the attack: a few other posts of very secondary importance in the Roman republic successively surrendered, and Ancona was bombarded by a combined squadron of seven Russian and Turkish ships, and six frigates, under the orders of vice-admiral Pastokin. The siege of Mantua was still continued, under general Kray, who, having repulsed a brisk sally of the garrison, received orders to draw off his troops, leaving a number sufficient to continue the blockade, which were afterwards reinforced by other divisions, and, to form with those troops and with the divisions of Ott and Hohenzollern, a new army, of which he afterwards took the command. His first object was to force the French to evacuate Bologna, which they vigorously defended, headed by the brave Bolognese. Of all the places beyond the Apennines Bologna was of the most importance. By its situation it retarded the march of the allies towards Tuscany, and yielded the most favorable protection to the retreat of the army of Naples. It was only by dislodging the French from the city that Kray could rally his forces and march to meet general Macdonald, who had already reached the Tuscan territory. His vanguard was at Florence; and Leghorn and Lucca had been put in a state of defence, in order to provide a last retreat towards the sea, should it be found impossible to effect the junction of the two armies by the Ligurian territory.

It appears that the principal part of the plan concerted between the archduke and Suwarrow, was to cut off successively, the communications of the two French armies of Switzerland and Italy; and to open, in the speediest manner possible, the communication between the two imperial armies, by the conquest of the north of Italy, the Milanese, and Piedmont. It has been remarked with how much ardor and constancy those two generals alternately detached their troops, the one from his right in Italy, and the other from his ieft in Switzerland, to support the continual attacks of general Bellegarde, whose aim it was to dislodge the French from the whole chain of the Rhœtian Alps, to St. Gothard, an operation which became more difficult from the stubborn resistance and the active and skilful manœuvres of the French generals, Lecourbe, De Solles, and Loison. Moreau, too weak to occupy a line of defence from St. Gothard to the sea, had been forced to abandon his communications with Massena, and to fall back with his right on the Ligurian republic. His great objects were to preserve, untouched, the barriers of the Apennines, and to afford Macdonald an opportunity of effecting his retreat. Suwarrow, by taking possession with his main army, of the interval which Moreau abandoned, by keeping up a war of posts in the passes of Switzerland; and, by determining to prosecute the siege of Turin, assisted the views of the French general without perceiving his error, to their full extent. Suwarrow had so unskilfully manœuvred his army, that he could neither surround Moreau, dislodge him from the Apennines, nor collect a sufficient force in Upper Tuscany to take up an offensive attitude against the recruited divisions of the French. Every retrograde march by which Moreau had retired to the frontiers of France, would have doubled the space which his colleague Macdonald had to measure. Even in his present situation, Moreau's camp at Coni was nearly fifty leagues from Macdonald's advanced post on the frontiers of Tuscany: yet he drew as near as he could towards the French frontiers, in order to favor the arrival of the feeble reinforcements which joined him by way of the Col de Tende. From the latter place he detached a division under general Victor to cross the Ligurian republic, to join the army of Naples, to enable Macdonald to act on the offensive, and to open the frontier passes, so as to reach Genoa. The French had retaken Mondovi, and blockaded Ceva; but general Vuckassowich, who had possession of Carmagnole, Alba, and Cherasco, disengaged those two places. By these manœuvres at Coni, Moreau diverted as much

as possible the attention and principal forces of the allied army.

Suwarrow, after the capture of Turin, had sent the principal divisions of his army into the valleys of Susa, Morienne, Aust, and Lucerne, where the Vaudois had taken up arms in favor of the French, exciting alarm on the old frontier of France, and threatening to open an immediate passage across the Alps, turning by the departments of Mont Blanc, the last line of defence in Switzerland. The menace and the alarm were equally vain. Moreau's position on the flanks of the Russian general, and a French army in his rear, rendered all further progress impracticable. Suwarrow had hoped to keep Moreau continually in his front, and thus prevent his junction with Macdonald more certainly and effectually than if he had relinquished his pursuit and taken positions on the heights of Genoa.

After thus disposing of part of his forces, Suwarrow marched in person against Moreau, who, straitened in his positions after leaving a strong garrison in Coni, withdrew, on the 7th of June, to the Col de Tende. The other principal passes of the Alps, Mount Cenis, the pass of Susa, and Little St. Bernard, were put in a respectable state of defence; but neither at Briancon nor in any other part of the frontier, were there any bodies of French troops of strength sufficient to effect those diversions which might at this moment have considerably harassed and weakened the pursuers. General Xantrailles, whose division had been destined by Massena to reinforce Moreau's left, after reducing the insurgents, had limited his operations to the occupation of a position in the Upper Vallais, not daring to hazard a descent towards Italy. The sieges of Tortona, Alessandria, and Turin, were in the mean time prosecuted with indefatigable vigor. Macdonald, who had been joined on the 17th of June, by general Victor, marched forward from Placenza upon St. Giovanni, a village at six miles distance, on the left of the little river Tidone, behind which general Ott had retreated; his advanced posts on the Trebbia having also fallen

2 x 2

back. General Melas came up to his assistance at the beginning of the action, with
his vanguard. Macdonald, who had dispatched a column on the road to the castle
of St. Giovanni, endeavored with his right
wing to detach the left of the imperialists,
and take possession of the road to Pavia,
on the Po, in order to surround the centre
of the position of general Melas, who had
assumed the command, and cut off the
communication with the forces which followed him. This first attack was repulsed
by the Austrians. Ott's division and a
part of that of general Frolich, maintained
their position till the arrival of Suwarrow
with a strong advanced guard of Russian
troops. The engagement then became
general, and lasted till night, when the
French withdrew to their positions between
the Tidone and the Trebbia.

On the next day (the 18th,) Suwarrow,
having assembled all his troops, took measures for a decisive engagement. Macdonald also prepared for the conflict,
ranging his army in line of battle, on the
left side of the Trebbia. The allies formed
in four columns; the first, or that of the
left, on the side of the Po, was to march
by Calendano, on Ponte di Mora; the
second followed the road on the right of
Piacenza; and the third marched upon
Vaccari. These three columns were composed of Russian troops. The fourth
column marched on Rippalta and San
Giorgio, and was formed by the divisions
of Ott and Frolich. These dispositions,
and the necessity of giving respite to the
troops, retarded the attack till five in the
evening. As soon as the columns came
up, notwithstanding the difficulty of the
ground in front of the French line, no
manœuvres were adopted, but a furious
shock took place on the whole front of the
two armies. The French were beaten, and
lost this second battle, after an obstinate
and sanguinary resistance.

Macdonald, nevertheless, did not retreat
to Piacenza, but withdrew behind the
right side of the Trebbia, meditating
another effort against the troops of Suwarrow, whose infantry, in particular,
was exhausted by fatigue. The next day

therefore, while they thought him in full
retreat, Macdonald in his turn, attacked
the allied army with the greatest impetuosity. He repulsed at first all the advanced posts upon the Trebbia, and sent
across the Po one of his columns, at the
same time that another passed the Trebbia, to turn the right flank of Suwarrow,
whose troops were nearly surprised.
General Melas sustained the first attacks
with the Austrian cavalry; the carnage
was horrible, and all the country from St.
Giovanni to Piacenza, between the Tidone
and the Trebbia, was strewed with dead.
The latter river was choked up with
corpses. The Polish legion, under Dom-
brouski, surrounded by Russians, formed
themselves into a square battalion, defended themselves with desperation, and
were almost entirely destroyed. Notwithstanding all his efforts, Macdonald's army
was forced to repass the Trebbia. Suwarrow, complimented on his victory,
replied in the words of a general of antiquity, " *Victory ! another such, and we
are ruined.*"

During the night which followed this
third day of dreadful and desperate conflict, Macdonald re-entered Piacenza, which
he evacuated on the next day, abandoning
3000 of his wounded, among whom were
the four generals, Rusca, Salm, Olivier,
and Chambran. Macdonald, who had
himself received several wounds, made his
retreat in good order, in two columns, of
which one followed the great road of
Parma, and the other the foot of the mountains. He pretended to be directing his
march upon Modena, and to be returning
to his camp at Pistoia ; but he took the
posts at Fornovo, ascending the valley o
Tanaro, and advanced along the road
of Sestri to enter the Ligurian republic, and
effect his junction with Moreau. Generals
Ott, Klenau, and Hohenzollern, whose
corps he had dispersed in his march upon
Piacenza, united at Parma, and went in
pursuit of him.

Suwarrow had repaired by the quickness
of his march, and by gaining the battle ot
St. Giovanni, the fault of having divided
his forces by insulated operations; which

had given time to Macdonald to finish the most difficult of retreats, and to reach, without obstacle, places, positions, and reinforcements, which had doubled his means of defence. If it was a premeditated design on the part of Suwarrow thus to succeed by the celerity of his marches rather than by the concentration of his troops, fortune justified his temerity. Had he displayed less activity in the prosecution of his extraordinary march, the combinations of the two French generals would not have left him the chance of victory. He would have found them with their forces united at Voghera, where he could not have attacked them without hazarding the fate of his army. In fact, while he was attacking with the whole of his force, Macdonald's army in Trebbia, Moreau, after having marched a strong detachment on Bobbio, commanded by general Lapoype, sallied forth from Genoa as from an entrenched camp, with an army fresh, and reinforced of about 25,000 men, and marched by Bocchetta, Gavi, and Novi, upon Tortona. The Austrian divisions under general Bellegarde were attacked and driven from their positions at St. Giuliand, Cassinio, Grando, and Spinetta, and forced to retreat precipitately across the Bormida. Among the advantages of this victory, was the raising the blockade of Tortona. Suwarrow, following up his success at St. Giovanni, had continued the pursuit of Macdonald beyond Piacenza, in expectation of overtaking him on the Tara, and by rallying the corps of of Klenau and Hohenzollern, surround him before he crossed the mountains. But, on receiving intelligence of the victory of Moreau over general Bellegarde, he abandoned the pursuit of the army of Macdonald, which he confided to general Ott, and departed with the strongest part of his army to meet Moreau, and to oppose his progress. This countermarch was not less happy than the preceding. While on his return, Suwarrow received intelligence of the surrender of the citadel of Turin, against which batteries of 300 pieces of artillery had been erected, and plied so briskly, that in two days the fire of the besiegers was extinguished, and a great number of officers of artillery and cannoneers killed, and magazines destroyed. The commander, Fiorella, demanded a capitulation, and obtained terms similar to those which had been granted at Ferrara and Milan. This unexpected occurrence was at this moment of so much greater importance to the allies, as the corps of general Kaim was already on foot to join the grand army. The efforts and activity of the French generals, who had not yet received from France the reinforcements which they expected, induced Suwarrow to press the rallying of his troops in every quarter. General Vuckassowich had orders to bring nearer the main body the column of Russian auxiliary troops, lately arrived on the Adige. The army which was slowly forming at Naples, and which was only confronted by a few insulated posts occupied by Macdonald's rearguard, was summoned to hasten with all possible speed to the north of Italy. Suwarrow's army, reinforced by the corps under general Haddick, amounted to 60,000 men. Moreau, after another engagement on the 26th of June, with Kaim and Bellegarde, having an army amounting only to one-third of that of the allies, was obliged to fall back on Genoa. At the end of June, the allies were masters of almost the whole of Italy, and of nearly half of the Helvetic republic, when a kind of involuntary truce or suspension of carnage took place on both sides of the Alps, while the opposing armies waited for reinforcements, that they might resume the labors of death.

We left Macdonald accelerating his retreat into Tuscany after the bloody battle near Piacenza, in which 20,000 men had been killed and wounded. This retreat would have been extremely difficult had Suwarrow continued to press upon his rearguard with all his forces, and had turned them on the side of the mountains; while generals Klenau and Hohenzollern had rallied between Reggio and Modena, and attacked them on the flank, and retarded its march. But the success of the diversion effected by Moreau, had recalled Suwarrow and the main body of his army towards Alessandria. Macdonald retreated into Tuscany, marching in two columns, one by the road of Modena, which he surprised, and the other by Tornovio. The right column threw reinforcements into Bologna, which, garrisoned chiefly by Cisalpines, continued to make a most spirited defence, and into fort Urbino ; and, while Moreau supported at Bobbio the division of general Lapoype in order to protect the left of the army of Naples, Macdonald resumed his former positions at Lucca and Pistoia.

General Victor's division, after ascending the valley of the Taro, occupied along with that of Lapoype, the passes of the Apennines. From that moment the communication by the rout called La Corniche, by Sarzana, La Spezza, and Sestra di Levante, were covered, and Macdonald was relieved from his fear that this last outlet would be shut against him.

The Austrian generals Ott, Klenau, and Hohenzollern, soon perceived that the rearguards which Macdonald had left behind him were very weak. Under this impression they pursued them, and forced them to evacuate Modena and Bologna. Fort Urbino surrendered to general Ott, at the end of a fortnight. Macdonald was unable to make any longer resistance to the imperial forces beyond the Apennines. The desertion of the Cisalpine, general La Hotze having weakened his right, and the progress of the insurgents of Strezzo, animating the people of Florence to active enmity, he determined to finish his retreat, and to evacuate Tuscany altogether. Though it was more than uncertain whether the artillery and baggage could be transported by sea, from Leghorn to Genoa, on account of the English squadron cruising before these ports, Macdonald did not hesitate in attempting this desperate measure ; and from the 1st day of July he continued to send off his columns of artillery with strong escorts, which were destined to reinforce the garrison of Leghorn. He left Florence on the 8th of July, broke up his camp at Pistoia, marched upon Lucca with the rest of his army, reduced to 14,000 men, and began to file

off to Sarzana. The march was slow and painful ; and it was only towards the end of the month that the head of the column reached the environs of Genoa.

The forces in Tuscany were immediately reinforced by the troops of the allies, united to the insurgents of Arezzo, the mass of which was increased so as to form a corps of 30,000 men, under the orders of general Ingerauni. The advanced guard of general Klenau entered Florence on the 8th of July, when the people rose, and, destroying every mark of the domination of the republic, re-established the ensigns of the antient government.

The garrisons of Leghorn and of Porto Ferrajo in the island of Elba, formed the last rearguard, and retreated also by Sarzana. General D'Argubet, who had made preparations for a vigorous defence, and reinforced the garrison of Fort D'Artigano, received orders to evacuate (July 16th,) Leghorn. He concluded a capitulation with the old governor, the Tuscan general La Villette, by which he secured the retreat of the garrison of Porto Ferrajo, and the free return of the sick. The evacuation was executed with order and fidelity, and the old administration was re-established on the same day. The last French troops evacuated Pisa and Lucca, and general Macdonald, forced to leave behind him, or to destroy, his heavy artillery, his camp-equipage, and the remains of the spoils of Italy, finished his retreat. This army, which, after its union with auxiliary divisions, amounted to more than 30,000 men, was now reduced to 18,000 ; but not a single corps of this trivial force, surrounded as it was by superior numbers, and menaced with apparently inevitable ruin, had laid down its arms in the field, or submitted to be captured, but in a few detached and insignificant forts, in which resistance would have been as culpable as useless.

Suwarrow, who had joined general Bellegarde between Tortona and Alessandria, called in the corps of generals Kaim and Vuckassowich, and marched upon Moreau, who, having fallen back upon Novi, soon evacuated that post, and retreated by the Bochetta into the Ligurian territory.

Thus terminated, as much, in all probability to the pleasure of the reader as of the combatants themselves, that series of marches, manœuvres, and engagements, which for the last six weeks had kept the troops on both sides in continued action. Moreau now employed himself in reinforcing his posts at the outlets of the valleys. He had taken a position at Sarena to secure his rear and his communication with Nice, waiting the arrival of the wrecks of Macdonald's army. The entrenched camp in which he took refuge, was too large for his army as far as regarded their numbers, but still more circumscribed by its situation than extensive in its circumference.

The main body of the allied army encamped on the river at the entrance of the valley of Orbe, which position covered the attacks on Tortona and Alessandria, General Bellegarde, who, after the irruption of Moreau, had been unable to carry on the blockade of both places, and had limited himself to covering that of Alessandria, was charged with the regular siege of this last place, of which the capture was necessary to Suwarrow's future operations. The first parallel being finished on the 14th of July, and 21 batteries being ready to open, the French commander, Gardanne, was summoned, and refused to surrender. The works were continued with unremitting ardor, and the fortress was heated by the constant play of 210 pieces of cannon. Six days afterwards the second parallel was finished, the covered way taken, lodgments made, saps carried to the foot of the ramparts, and batteries erected to open a breach. General Gardanne, finding it impossible to sustain an assault, proposed a capitulation, and the garrison, consisting of 2600 men, remained prisoners of war. Suwarrow fixed his head-quarters in Alessandria, the conquest of which had cost him dear in the loss of general de Chasteler, the chief of his staff, whose activity and talents had been eminently useful in the siege of Alessandria. Moreau, whose forces were insufficient for the relief of the place, extended his line to the frontier of France,

without abandoning either Genoa, the Bochetta, or the other passes of the Apennines. He fixed his head-quarters at Cornegliano, and occupied positions and posts at Ultri, Savona, Vado, and Loano, which had been possessed by the French army in 1796. General Colli had been detached with a small corps, and occupied an entrenched position between the Bochetta and Terra Valle; after having made those dispositions which could alone secure the integrity of the Ligurian territory, and the successive arrival of reinforcements, Moreau resigned the command of the army to general Joubert.

The successes of the allies inspired the Tuscans with the hope of recovering their independence, and their antient establishments. A counter-revolution commenced in Tuscany, on the anniversary of the day from which its invaders dated the origin of the French republic. On the 14th of July, many inhabitants of Florence assembled in the Place of PITTI, and cut down the tree of liberty, which had produced to them such bitter fruits. A division of French dragoons hastened to the spot and dispersed the people. Meanwhile the tumult increased: the people every where destroyed the symbols of liberty and equality, hoisted some old standards of the Medici, decorated the portraits of Francis II. and Paul I. with laurels, placed them by the side of the grand duke and the pope, and illuminated the city at night with such tumultuous rejoicings, that the French garrison found it expedient to leave the town. On the next day the senate of Florence took upon them the government in the name of the grand duke, and dispatched couriers to the chief of the insurgents at Arezzo, and to several other cities, to apprise them of the counter-revolution which had been so suddenly effected. Four deputies were sent to general Klenau at Bologna, and a deputation was also sent to the grand duke at Vienna, inviting him to return to his dominions. When Macdonald had advanced to assist the northern army, he had left small garrisons in the Tuscan, as well as in the Neapolitan and Roman territories. These were every where attacked by the inhabitants; taken prisoners, and the forts garrisoned by the natives. At Leghorn the inhabitants proceeded in the same manner as in Florence and other parts of Tuscany. On the 17th of July, the French marched out of that place, completely evacuating Tuscany; and soon afterwards Lucca, in their march to the territories of the Genoese, with the view of forming a junction with Moreau. Similar counter-revolutions took place at the same moment at Naples, where the bulk of the inhabitants were no sooner acquainted with the disasters of the French, than they declared for the restoration of monarchy, and placed themselves under the command of cardinal Ruffo, who attacked and defeated the republican army. This loyal and enterprising character pursued his advantages with so much vigor and effect, that he entered Naples, and took possession of that capital in the name of its lawful sovereign. Proceeding northwards, he occupied the different forts and towns. In the course of these exertions, the Lazzaroni, who had so eminently distinguished themselves during the last struggle for Neapolitan independence, flew with earnestness and rapidity to the standard of their king and country. By this concurrence of propitious circumstances the kingdom of Naples and the duchy of Tuscany, were restored to the civil and ecclesiastical establishments which had descended from their ancestors.

Suwarrow, after the capture of Alessandria, had marched a part of his army, for the second time, into Piedmont; had invested Coni, attacked Fenestrelles, and sent general Haddick with a corps of 12,000 men, up the valley of Aust, to penetrate into the Vallais. The column detached under the orders of the prince of Rohan had not discontinued its skirmishes in the upper valleys, or ceased to harass the principal posts of the French. This column being reinforced, undertook at length more serious and extensive enterprises, and threatened the frontiers of Dauphiny, with the design of compelling the French to pass the Var.

The great and inestimable advantage accruing to the allies from the battle of Piacenza, was the tranquillity in which general Kray's army was left to continue the siege of Mantua. The capture of that city was expected by Suwarrow, to justify his projects, rectify his errors, and permit him to send effective succours to the archduke. Nothing was spared that might hasten the surrender of Mantua: the quantity of artillery was augmented: 600 pieces and mortars were destined for the siege, and artillery of a bore, which had been long regarded as useless, was transported to the batteries. Two Austrian regiments, and the corps of Russian artillery, reinforced the besieging army. All the country people forty miles round, were obliged to labor at the works.

The garrison of Mantua consisted of 10,000 men, under the orders of general Latour Foissac, an engineer of the old regime. General Kray attacked the place on the southern side, and carried first the outward posts, such as the Cerese, the head of the bridge which covered the sluice, and the communications with the works of the fauxbourg de Thé, separated from the main land by an arm of the Mincio. The trenches were opened opposite to this fauxbourg on the night of the 14th of July, under favor of a truce, during which the commander of the place celebrated the anniversary of the French revolution. The fire from the town, which was very brisk, when the opening of the trench was perceived, did not prevent the first and second parallels from being connected and completed. The batteries were, with unexampled labor, finished and mounted in less than a week.

This principal attack was seconded by those directed on the other forts detached from the body of the place on the same side of the lake: the horn-work of the gate Pradella, and fort St. George, against which approaches were made at the same time. The principal sluice having been broken, and the draining of the water having facilitated the erection of works and the establishment of new batteries, which were to protect the passage of Bajuolo general Kray attacked the entrenchments

In the dykes between Cerese and the faux-bourg, which were carried sword in hand. The next day, (July 26th,) the French attacked fort St. George. The horn-work of the gate Pradella, which, from the opening of the third parallel at the fort of the glacis, they apprehended might be carried by storm, was also abandoned after spiking the pieces. The allies obtained a lodgment in this work, whence they bombarded the body of the place: the garrison was so much weakened as to be wholly ineffective, the greater part of the officers were in the hospitals, the batteries of the Isle de Thé were dismounted, and the quantity of bombs which fell in this part of the works rendered every manœuvre of the artillery, every description of defence, useless and impossible.

Thus situated, the commander accepted, on the 28th of July, the capitulation offered him, and gave him up the keys of Mantua, which had remained in the hands of the French since February, 1797. Two days after, the garrison marched out with the honors of war, and grounded their arms on the glacis. Conformably to the terms of the capitulation, the garrison was to be escorted to the frontier of France, on condition that they should not serve till exchanged. General Latour Foissac and all his staff were detained prisoners, and conducted to Gratz, where they remained three months, after which period they were permitted to return into France upon their parole.

That Mantua had been treacherously surrendered, admitted of no doubt in the opinion of the directory, and, in proportion to the value of the place, was the indignation against its commander, and against the late government, which had entrusted to a man, of unsuspected character, a fortress so eminently important. The directory ordered a court martial to be formed for the trial of Latour Foissac, and of the commander of the citadel of Turin, who was likewise suspected of treason.

Of the importance of the surrender of Mantua to the ulterior operations of the allies, it is not difficult to form an estimate.

Italy being almost entirely reconquered, and all the magazines and forces of the allies being collected together, at the moment of the arrival of their reinforcements, the balance in favor of the confederates was so decisive, that nothing could compensate to the republic for the surrender of Mantua, which had acted as a diversion in favor of their armies, more powerfully than the united operations of two great armies. So long as general Kray with his forces was occupied before it, Suwarrow could not act with vigor against Switzerland or Nice. The new plan by which the frontier of France was to be defended, was established during this state of suspense and consternation, to the advantage of the party inferior in number; and every day during which the siege was prolonged, was actively employed in repairing losses, and preparing new obstacles to the progress of the allies. By the fall of Mantua, Suwarrow regained the full liberty of his movements, and reverted to the simple combination of mutual and alternate succour between the archduke's army and his own. The French themselves, confessed by the loudness of their clamors, and the bitterness of their declamation, that the capture of Mantua was the most sensible loss which the republic could have experienced.

Macdonald, in the mean time, had joined the grand army with the remains of the forces which he had brought from Naples, which, with the reinforcements under Joubert, the successor of Moreau, placed that general at the head of 40,000 men. Reflecting on the critical situation to which the French armies were reduced, and particularly that the reduction of Mantua would enable general Kray to reinforce Suwarrow with the besieging army, Joubert determined, as his only chance of ultimate success, to attack the allies before they should have effected this junction. The memorable battle of Novi ensued, on the 16th of August. Joubert took up his head-quarters at Campo Marino, between Savona and Montenotte. He implored Moreau to delay his departure, that he might aid him with his counsels. Moreau generously accepted the invitation, and took a command under his orders. After having detached, on the 13th of August, strong advanced guards, and taken advantageous positions in the valleys of the Orba and the Bormida, Joubert formed on that side three columns of attack. The first followed the valley of the Bormida, directing itself on Acqui by the road of Dego; the second descending by the valley of Erra, marched against Castel-Ferzo; the third moving from Campo-Froddo, following the little valley of Lemer, and afterwards that of Orba, was to enter the plain by Ovado. A fourth column, stronger than the rest, and in reality destined to raise the blockade of Tortona, descended by the defiles of the Bochetta. This column was commanded by general St. Cyr, to whom Moreau and general Desolles had united themselves, for the purpose of conducting an operation similar to that which they had already executed at the battle of St. Giovanni.

On the same day the corps of general Bellegarde, which occupied before Acqui the positions of Trezzio and Bistanga, was vigorously attacked. Joubert, who headed the left at Basaluzzo, was to follow the mountains which extend along the right bank of the Scrivia, and march upon Tortona. This movement, which Suwarrow could not prevent but by dislodging the French army from its strong position, decided him to attack it. The assault began by the right of the allies under general Kray, against the left of the French, where Joubert commanded in person. The action was scarcely begun when the general, to whose talents and character the French of all parties, render equal justice; wishing to animate, by his presence, a charge of infantry, crying out, "Forward! Forward!" was struck by a ball which pierced his heart. His ruling passion was strong in death, for he fell repeating till he expired, "Forward! Forward!"

While general Kray endeavored to turn Novi, the Russian general Pankration attacked in front, but both were repulsed. The Russian division under general Derfelden at the centre, and the left wing of

general Melas, then received orders to attack: the first by the road of Novi, and Melas by ascending the left bank of the Scrivia. But this double attack had no better success than that of the other two generals. Derfelden tried in vain to gain the heights on the left of Novi, and the two armies were now engaged along the whole of their line, and the carnage was horrible. At three in the afternoon, the corps of general Kray having been twice repulsed with great loss, Suwarrow 1799 projected a second attack against the heights of Novi, with the Russian divisions under generals Derfelden, Pankration, and Miloradovitch. But the resistance of the French was so firm, that they retained their position, notwithstanding reiterated charges of the columns. The centre of the allied army was almost destroyed in the charges which Suwarrow sustained, and renewed three times with unshaken constancy. Moreau, who had taken the command after the death of Joubert, fought in person, and performed, as well as the generals St. Cyr and Desolles, prodigies of valor.

In the mean time general Melas, with eight battalions of grenadiers and six of Austrian infantry, which formed the left wing of the army, having reached the first heights of Novi on the side of Pietallo, and dispatched general Nobili's corps along the bank of the Scrivia, attempted to turn entirely the right of the French army. He reached Sarravalla, took possession of Arquata, and marched by the road of Sarravalla upon Novi. He attacked with general Frolich's division, the right flank of the French. The front of this attack was formed by the first battalion of Furstenburg, and by the brigade of general Lusignan, who in the first charge was vigorously repulsed, desperately wounded, and made prisoner. General Melas supported this column, which formed the right, and the chief strength of his attack by a second, under the orders of general Laudohn: a third, commanded by the prince of Lichtenstein, had orders to pass the line of the French to the rear of their right, seizing, at the same time, on all the advantageous points which could be found in the intervals of the columns. Melas strengthened this movement by batteries, corresponding with the movements of the troops, and that precaution decided the victory.

Towards five in the evening, general Melas attacked in flank with the grenadiers of Paar, the post of Novi, which had cost so much blood from the beginning of the action, and which Moreau had just reinforced with the intention of covering his retreat, on which he had now determined. The French being almost surrounded, were obliged to abandon the post. The column of the prince of Lichtenstein having cut off their communication with Gavi, they could retreat only by their left flank upon Ovada. This retreat was executed at first in good order; but the artillery, having choked up the road in passing through the village of Pasturano, the division which formed the rearguard found the village so encumbered, that, forced to halt, it was thrown into disorder, and overtaken by the corps of general Karacksay. The French generals, Periguon, Grouchy, and Parthenau, made the last exertions to rally this rearguard, but without success. All three were wounded and made prisoners at the same time, with the Piedmontese general Colli. Night alone put an end to the combat. The French had defended with the courage of despair, against the multiplied attacks of very superior numbers, a position unusually strong by nature, and covered by trees and bushes, which rendered the access difficult on every side. This position was rendered still more formidable by a numerous artillery, advantageously placed, and skilfully directed. But in the same degree that their confidence had been supported throughout the day by these advantages of ground, by the result of general Kray's attacks, and by the repulse of the Russian divisions on the left and in the centre, was the greatness of their loss and the precipitation of the retreat, when general Melas, by the skill and ingenuity of his manoeuvres, had succeeded in dislodging their right. If we except the battle of Malplaquet, gained by the duke of Marlborough and prince Eugene, against

marshal Villars, in 1709, in which 30,000 men were destroyed; and that of Frankfort on the Oder, in 1759, between the Prussians and the Russians, when Frederic left nearly 20,000 men on the field of battle, and did not abandon it till he had made as horrible a carnage of the Russian infantry: no military conflict in the last century was so bloody as that of Novi. The loss on both sides amounted to 25,000 men. As at Malplaquet the two armies, engaged on points of their line, did not cease destroying each other till the close of day, and the conflict so far resembled that of Frankfort, that they were both decided after a long and doubtful struggle, by a single and critical manoeuvre.

One of the principal causes of the carnage in this engagement, was the heroic ardor with which the generals on both sides led on their troops, exposed themselves to the hottest fire, and excited by their intrepidity the enthusiasm of their soldiers. Joubert became the victim of his thirst of glory, and this barren honor deprived his army of the soul which animated its movements. His plans, indeed, were well supported by Moreau, but, during an important action, the loss of him who commands is never *sufficiently* supplied, even by the genius and bravery of the most able successor.

The French army retreated during the night to the Apennines, pursued by general Karacksay, who had taken possession at Pasturano of a part of the field artillery. Moreau covered his retreat by occupying the Red mountain, where general St. Cyr posted himself with his division, within the reach of defending towards the road of Gair, the approaches towards the Bochetta. The rest of the French army rallied by degrees, and reoccupied its former positions. Moreau hastened to Geneva, and pressed general Championette to accept the command, to which he was afterwards named by the directory.

The victory of Novi, of which Suwarrow generously attributed the whole honor to Melas, was so bravely disputed, that the only immediate advantage which it yielded to the allies, was the certainty of capturing the citadel of Tortona. The siege of that fortress had hitherto been slowly conducted on account of the rockiness of the soil ; but the attacks were now more incessantly and more vigorously directed. Suwarrow, after detaching his right wing under general Kray towards the valleys of Novera, to support the left of the Austrian army, or, if that were impossible, to close on that side the entrance into Italy, marched with his centre towards Asti, to prevent the junction of Championette with the army of Joubert, or at least to oblige him to form it beyond the Alps, and to evacuate the Ligurian republic. The allies also covered by this movement the siege of Coni, to the prosecution of which the fineness of the season was peculiarly favorable.

The city of Tortona had capitulated, on condition that ten days should elapse before its surrender to the allies ; and provided that in the interval, it should receive no succour. The situation of Genoa became every day more critical : general Klenau, who had taken possession of fort St. Maria, and of Sistri di Levante, advanced on that side, and admiral Nelson blocked up the port with a squadron. The French, however, did not abandon this city, so important and unfortunate in the wars of Italy, the prey of the conquerors, and the last refuge of the discomfited and despairing fugitives.

HISTORY OF THE WAR.

CHAP. XX.

WHILE Austria exulted in the gradual recovery of her Italian possessions, the country of the Grisons was the scene of active warfare and diversified success. Massena remaining inactive in his head-quarters at Chur, committed the invasion of the Tyrol, to his subordinate generals Desolles and Lecourbe. Their first exertions were propitious to the republic cause ; but general Bellegarde, assisted by the Tyrolesian peasants, soon forced them to retire from a country which they had ravaged with remorseless cruelty. Bellegarde then entered the country of the Grisons, intending to favor the movements of the archduke on the northern borders of Switzerland. But a division of his army acting with more ardor than discretion in an attack on the French posts, suffered a defeat, and the greater part of them were made prisoners.

The congress at Rastadt, for the settlement of the affairs of Germany, had made but little progress in the ostensible object of discussion. The commencement of hostilities had created a schism among the members of the Germanic body, and several of the northern states, evinced a determination to enter into a separate negotiation with France. To counteract this intention so far as his absence from congress might produce that effect, the imperial plenipotentiary, count Metternich, left Rastadt on the 12th of April, having 1799. previously refused to receive a note

transmitted by the French ministers. At the same time the Austrian general pushed forward a detachment to that place ; in the vicinity of which their troops committed some irregularities against the French legation, and insulted the Prussian and Danish envoys. Several of the deputies withdrew ; and, as the safety of those who remained was considered as in danger, the French minister at Mentz was requested to make a representation on the subject of colonel Barbacsy, the Austrian commander at Gernsbach. His answer being unsatisfactory, the deputation expressed their intention of quitting Rastadt. The French minister intimated to baron de Albini the directorial envoy, their resolution of leaving the place within three days. But, wishing, as they declared, to give to Germany a last and signal proof of the moderation of their government, they added they would repair to Strasburg, and there await the renewal of the negotiations, as soon as military violence should have been repressed. They prepared to leave Rastadt on the morning of the 28th of April, and every thing was in a state of readiness for their departure. But, remembering that patroles of huzzars were continually traversing the road to Seltz, and, yielding to the importunities of their friends, they determined to await the result of a second letter to Barbacsy, the commander of the Austrian forces, in which they demanded an explicit answer to the question " Are we likely to meet with any interruption." Their alarm had been excited, and their suspicion justified by the arrest of a French courier, on his mission to Strasburg, and the seizure of his papers. No written answer was returned to their application; but, between seven and eight in the evening, an officer, with a squadron of hussars, followed by the greater part of the regiment, arrived at Rastadt, and occupied the town and its vicinity. The officer immediately declared in the name of his colonel, that the French legation might travel in perfect safety, and that the period of twenty-four hours was fixed for their departure. From the impulse of the same spirit which determined lord Malmsbury to quit Paris and Lisle, the French ministers resolved to set out immediately. The carriages had been in readiness during the whole day; and, about half an hour after the order for their leaving the town, they departed with their suite.

The Zekler hussars, after taking possession of all the gates of Rastadt, intimated that they had received orders not to allow any person belonging to the congress to enter or leave the town. When reminded that the French ministers were commanded to depart, he replied, that he was not directed to prevent them; and, when application was made for an escort, he answered, that he had no orders to that effect, but that the legation would find no interruption in their rout. At length, between nine and ten o'clock, the plenipotentiaries began their journey; and, as the night was dark, torches were carried before their carriages. But scarcely had a quarter of an hour elapsed, before intelligence arrived that the carriages had been attacked by the Austrian hussars, and the ministers murdered. About a quarter of a mile from the town, the foremost carriage, in which was Jean de Brie and his family, was suddenly attacked by a party in the dress of hussars, who rushed from an adjoining wood, and that ambassador narrowly escaped with his wife. The minister Bonnier, was dragged out of his carriage and cut in pieces. Robert was slaughtered in the presence of his wife, with

circumstances of peculiar atrocity. Rosenthiel, the secretary of legation, being in the last carriage, had the good fortune to effect his escape through the adjacent gardens, at the commencement of the attack, and reached the house of the minister of Baden, where he remained for some time in a state of delirium. The hussars pillaged the carriages, and stript the ministers and their retinue of their jewels and valuables; but no person was murdered except the two ministers. The papers were carried off, and conveyed to the Austrian commandant.

The report of this outrage excited the astonishment of Europe; and the directory denounced it, in the name of the French nation to all good men, and to the governments of every country, as an atrocity commanded by the cabinet of Vienna, and executed by its troops. The emperor, that he might clear himself and his court from these vile aspersions, instituted a legal inquiry, and charged the diet of the empire to appoint deputies who might assist in the scrutiny. But, after long and patient investigation, no evidence could be produced sufficient to convict any individual, nor has the history of this singular transaction ever been explained. It is probable, however, that the assassins were influenced by no other motives than resentment for the insults and privations which the Austrians had sustained, and that the simple result of private and individual revenge, has been mistaken for the consequence of political intrigue.

All prospect of peace from this time disappeared. The directory, with the view of exposing the emperor to reproach in the eyes of his confederates, and of weakening the coalition, published a state paper, purporting to be a secret article in the treaty of Campo Formio, from which it appeared that he had consented to sacrifice the interests of the German empire to his own personal views by the cession of Mentz, Manheim, and other places, to France, on condition of being gratified, among many valuable possessions, with the bishopric of Saltzburgh.

Active operations, after a short inter-

ᅠ

uption, were renewed with great spirit: The Austrian generals were determined to improve their past successes. A plan was concerted by generals Hotze and Bellegarde for gaining complete possession of the Grison country, where the inhabitants were well affected to the Austrian cause. Hotze was foiled in his attempt on the fort of Luciensteig, by the activity of general Menard, and the slow advance of one of the columns destined to the attack. By this misfortune his partisans were exposed to the revenge of the French general, and several thousands cut off. Being favored, however, by the excellent position which Bellegarde had taken to cover his movement, he returned with his whole force, and, having obtained possession of the fort of Steig, forced his enemy to abandon the Grisons and the adjacent cantons of Switzerland. General Bellegarde then devoted his attention to active operations near the sources of the Adda and the Rhine; and, with the assistance of a body of forces under general Haddick, he constrained general Lecourbe to leave the Austrians in possession of that vast range of mountainous country, called St. Gothard.

After the recal of Jourdan, who was succeeded by Massena, and the disasters of Scherer, the archduke approached with his army, the frontiers of Switzerland, which soon became the chief theatre of Transalpine war. He who knew in what manner to conquer at Stockack, knew also what is perhaps more difficult and more honorable, when to repress the desire of profiting by his victories. He did not immediately endeavor to drive the French army to the other side of the Rhine, but remained with the greater part of his force near the lake of Constance, rightly judging, that if he abandoned that point, and advanced into the Brisgau, his left and rear would be exposed to the incursions of Massena. He sacrificed the trivial glory of driving a vanquished enemy beyond his frontiers, to considerations of higher moment, and more worthy of his character. All his thoughts were devoted to the invasion of Switzerland. The French had

converted that country into a kind of strong hold, from which they intended to fall upon Germany. Switzerland was a two-edged sword, which could be employed either against France or the empire. It became necessary to deprive the republicans of so important a possession, to be able in return to menace their own country. Prince Charles resolved to accomplish that object, and began his preparations for the enterprise.

The French general had, for six weeks, endeavored to retard the invasion of Switzerland by hostile movements before Kehl, and on the Mein, and the Necker. He had also carefully entrenched all the weak points of the left bank of the Rhine, from Schaffhausen to Basle, and had fortified the suburb opposite to that town on the other side of the river. The hostile demonstrations in Suabia had induced the archduke to change the concentrated position which he had occupied between Stockack and Schaffhausen; nor did the entrenchments made along the river deter him from passing it. He had determined not to enter Switzerland till the south and the east of that country should have been invaded. That event having now occurred, he lost not a moment in executing an enterprise so long delayed, and which had been expected with the utmost anxiety by every friend of freedom and humanity.

When the Austrians successfully commenced their operations in the country of the Grisons, in the beginning of the month of May, Massena, having reason to fear that they would soon invade Switzerland on all sides, and foreseeing that, after that event, it would be impossible for him to preserve the semicircle formed by the Rhine, from the source of the Linth to the mouth of the Glat, wished at least to defend its diameter, and more particularly the middle of that diameter. He therefore caused that chain of mountains to be fortified, which lies in front of Zurich, between the Limmat and the Glat, the position which first presents itself at the east of Switzerland. His right, entirely composed of infantry, was posted upon the zurichberg, the most elevated part of the chain of mountains. Access to it was rendered almost impossible, by a thick wood, by several ranks of abatis and redoubts, and by a formidable artillery, which crowned the circumference of the heights. Between his right and the lake of Zurich, there was no point through which it was possible to penetrate. The town of Zurich also was covered by the position. The left was placed upon the same chain of mountains, and the approaches to it had the same means of defence as the approaches to the right. Between these two wings, the ground sloping gradually, was open and intersected by the roads, from Schaffhausen and Constance, to Zurich. Here Massena placed his cavalry; but, as it might be beaten, and as the two wings would then be separated and irretrievably lost, he linked them together by a chain of strong redoubts, which defended the centre in front, while it was protected by the fire of the two wings. Fearing that the imperialists might endeavor to gain the left flank of his position, and that, after having passed the Glat, they would also pass the Limmat, and thus fall upon his rear, Massena placed a small flanking corps between Regensberg and the Glat, with the design of covering the lower part of the Limmat.

This position was so well selected, that the archduke could make no effectual progress until he had dislodged the French, and this could only be done by attacking them in front, or by turning their flank upon the left bank of the Limmat, an attempt which would have been arduous, tedious, and dangerous. The prince therefore adopted the first expedient, and resolved to attack the zurichberg, which, when once forced, must cause the loss of the position. After having marched his right to Bulach, his centre to Kloten, and his left to Basserstorf, he reconnoitred the French position, and caused their right to be attacked upon the 3rd of June, by his vanguard, which drove them from the villages of Vitikon, Zulicon, and Riespach. These villages were taken and retaken several times during the course of the day. This engagement was but the prelude to

a general attack. On the next day, (June 4th,) the Austrians advanced in several columns against the zurichberg, and attacked it upon several points at the same time; chiefly, however, upon those of Seebach and Schwammendingen. The approaches to the zurichberg were so formidably entrenched, and the fire of the batteries so commanding, that generals Hotze and Rosemberg, who conducted the attacks, were unable for some time to make any progress, though two columns acting upon their flank, had already penetrated to the foot of the abatis. The Austrians even sustained a slight repulse on the side of Seebach. To that point prince Charles sent successive reinforcements, drawn from his centre, and, anxious to terminate the doubtful and sanguinary conflict, ordered four battalions, conducted by general Wallis, to advance by Schwammendingen, and to assault the zurichberg with fixed bayonets. The Austrian grenadiers marched forward under a dreadful fire, and attacked with so much valor, that they made their way through the abatis, and carried the first line of the entrenchments. But they could advance no further; the redoubts and abatis still before them being rendered impenetrable by the number and fire of the battalions and batteries which lined them. The Austrians, however, did not retire, but kept the French within their entrenchments, and gave time to the other attacking columns, to arrive to their support. Night put an end to a contest which had raged with destructive obstinacy during the whole day. Each party lost, at a moderate computation, in killed alone, 2500 men. The armies passed the night in presence of each other.

On the 5th, the archduke again reconnoitred the position of the enemy, and resolved to assault it, but delayed the enterprise till the 6th, in consequence of the fatigues his army had sustained. It did not, however, take place; for whether the boldness with which the Austrians passed the day at the foot of the zurichberg, had shaken the courage of Massena, or that he did not believe his position to be tenable, he abandoned it with precipitation on the night of the 5th of June, and retired to the other side of the Limmat. The Austrians took possession of the French entrenchments, in which more than 20 pieces of cannon had been left, and found themselves masters of the town of Zurich, which had been purchased with so much bloodshed, and which might have produced much more had not Massena retreated.

; After having evacuated Zurich with a precipitation strikingly contrasted by the vigor, the promptitude, and the enthusiasm of the archduke, Massena assumed a position on the chain of mountains named Albis, which lies between the lake, the Limmat, and the Reuss. Its left reached to the Rhine near Zurzach, and extended to Baden and the Limmat. Its centre was upon the Albis, in front of Zurich, and the right extended to the lake of Zug. The head-quarters were at Bremgarten. This central position was the nearest which Massena could possibly have taken: it was safe and strong, and was the second of the three great defensive positions which Switzerland presents: those of the Limmat, the Reuss, and the Aar.

After the victory of the 4th of June, the archduke was determined to relinquish all active operations in Switzerland. To this determination he was induced by the strength of the French position; the trivial nature of the assistance which he received from the inhabitants; the weak state in which his army had been left by the departure of general Bellegarde for Italy; the expected arrival of 35,000 Russian auxiliaries; and, above all, the secret orders of the cabinet of Vienna. He contented himself, therefore, with passing the interval between the beginning of June and the middle of July, in recruiting his army. At that period the line of the Austrians, setting out from St. Gothard, proceeded along the valley of the Reuss and the lake of Lucerne, crossed the canton of Schwitz, and joined near Rapperschwile, the body of the army which occupied the left bank of the Limmat and the Aar, as far as the Rhine. The head-quarters were still at Kloten. The line of the French army,

beginning at Brieg in the Vallais, crossed the mountains of the Oberland and the Underwald, passed by Stanz, Lucerne, Bremgarten, Mellingen, and Baden, and extended from thence as far as the mouth of the Aar. The head-quarters were established at Lenzburg, to which place they had been removed from Bremgarten.

There was not, at the beginning July, any considerable disparity of force between the opposing generals; and the slight superiority of Massena was more than counterbalanced by the insurrection of the people, occasioned by the severities which the French had exercised. The month of July was distinguished by no action of importance; but the whole of that month and part of August, were devoted by the contending parties to the augmentation of their political and military resources. The French accelerated the levy of the conscripts, composed them into battalions, and formed two new armies. One was destined to act upon the Rhine, and invade Franconia and Suabia: the other, under the name of the army of the Alps, was to cover France on the side of Dauphiny and Provence, to act offensively if occasion should require, in Piedmont, and to cooperate with the army which occupied the Genoese. They marked out a camp near Geneva, to defend the entrance of France by the way of the Vallais and Savoy. They were equally active in concerting defensive measures and offensive plans; and the assiduous and sanguine Bernadotte, then minister at war, did not despair of seeing, before the end of the campaign, the return of victory to the banners of the republican armies.

On the opposite side they had experienced unlooked for success; and the extravagance of their hopes and wishes was proportionate. With a force originally designed to act on the defensive, they had made the most brilliant of all campaigns: but, after so many destructive victories, their numbers were insufficient to secure the continuance of splendid success, and it became a question of policy whether to keep all that had been acquired, or to pursue at every risk the career of conquest.

The court of Vienna inclined to the first of these alternatives; but those of London and St. Petersburgh more courageous, more enlightened, and more liberally attached to the general interests of Europe, were anxious to seize this great opportunity of rescuing it from the arms and principles of France, and to push the fortune of the campaign as far as it would go. To accomplish this object, money and troops were necessary. London offered the one, and St. Petersburgh the other. But, when so generous a line of conduct was pursued by two powers, to whom the seat of war offered nothing to conquer or to save, it was natural and necessary that the states of the German empire should come forward with their efforts and sacrifices in a cause which was more immediately their own. The emperor therefore addressed, on the 12th of July, an aulic decree to the diet of Ratisbon, requesting the different states to furnish their proper contingents. The characteristic slowness, however, of that body, not permitting the expectation of an immediate reply, the allies negotiated for auxiliaries with those continental princes who were not unwilling to barter troops for money.

The king of Prussia, persisting in remaining neutral, and having won over to his opinion all the northern princes of Germany, except the king of Sweden, the allied courts addressed themselves with more success to the elector of Bavaria and the duke of Wurtemberg. The former, who, before his accession to the electoral dignity, had shewn himself the invariable partisan of France, and dependent on Prussia, suddenly changed his apparent system, and engaged not only to march his contingent of troops, but to furnish many thousand men whom England proposed to take into her pay. The duke of Wurtemberg engaged to furnish 6000 men, including his contingent of 3000 men, on condition of a subsidy from England. These subordinate aids, however, would have proved of little avail, had not they been anticipated and surpassed by the exertions of the emperor of Russia. By a subsidizing treaty concluded between that monarch and the king of England, a treaty advantageous to both parties, but still more advantageous to the emperor of Germany, who reaped the benefit of its conclusion, without incurring the expense, the former engaged to send to the banks of the Rhine a new army of 45,000 men. More than 10,000 of this number had already been sent to reinforce the Russians already in Italy. The remaining 35,000 had been upon their march many months, and were expected to join the archduke in Switzerland about the middle of August. It was intended, therefore, that, during the month of September, the operations of the campaign should assume the extensive scope, contemplated by the courts of London and St. Petersburgh. It was expected that, before the middle of that month, the allies would have reduced the fortresses which were necessary to consolidate the conquest of the north of Italy, and that the Austrian corps stationed in that country would be sufficient to ensure their quiet possession. Marshal Suwarrow, with his Russians, covered on both their flanks by Austrian corps, would, it was imagined, turn Switzerland on the south side, where the French would be attacked in front by the new Austro-Russian army, leaving time to the archduke, at the head of his own troops, of those of the empire, and of the peasants, to attack the left flank of Massena, or attempt some other important enterprise. It was in this manner that the allies expected to obtain possession of Switzerland, which they justly regarded as the most formidable barrier of France; while Holland was to be conquered by 30,000 English and 18,000 Russian troops. The embarrassments of the French republic were to be completed by a renewed insurrection of the royalists of Brittany, Normandy, and the south of France. The cabinets of London and St. Petersburgh spared neither exertion or expense in the furtherance of their object; and, had the future wisdom or unanimity of their counsels equalled the vigor of their present efforts, the independence of Europe might have been re-established on a just and durable basis.

In the beginning of August the archduke and Massena found themselves in the same positions which they occupied in the month of June. In the midst of all the embarrassments of the French government, political, military, and financial, and at a moment when it seemed incapable of defending its own frontier, it entertained the bold design of resuming the offensive, and combined a plan of general attack along the whole line of the theatre of war, across the Alps, through Switzerland, Piedmont, and the states of Genoa, from the Mein to the Mediterranean. Though it did not possess sufficient means to ensure the success of this great design, circumstances were in some measure favorable to its execution. All the armies, and particularly that of Switzerland, had been reinforced by conscripts, while the Russian army was still at some distance from its destination; and, while the allies in Italy were obliged to divide their force to cover the siege of Tortona and to guard the outlets of the Alps.

On the 14th of August, the whole French army put itself in motion, and marched on all sides against the enemy. Massena, who in the preceding days had made some movements on his left, directed himself against the position of the Austrians in front of Zurich, on the points of Wallishofen, Altstettin, and Wiedikon, and caused a strong detachment to pass to the other side of the Limmat. This attack almost exactly resembled that of the 1st of June, and had the same issue. Lecourbe in the mean time prepared the way for the movements of the grand army by driving the Austrians from the cantons of Schweitz and Uri. Had that object been more early accomplished, the situation of the archduke would have become in the highest degree difficult and precarious. Being very inferior to the enemy in number, he would have been probably obliged to evacuate the whole of Switzerland. But, on the very day in which Massena began his general attack, the first division of the Russian army, under Korzakow, followed by five others, arrived, by forced marches, at Schaffhausen, from whence it marched,

two days afterwards, towards Zurich; thus rendering the situation of the archduke as tenable as it had been insecure.

The loss of the battle of Novi in Italy, had entirely deranged the offensive plans of the republicans. The part assigned to Massena in a great measure depended on the success of the two other armies, in Italy and Germany, which might be considered as two wings of that which he commanded. It was necessary that one, at least, of these should advance, in order that the centre might do so without danger. It wanted a point of support; and, not being able, since the battle of Novi, to obtain it on its right, it was necessary to look for it on its left. The army which the directory had lately formed on the Rhine, received orders therefore to advance on the Mein and on the Necker. The great object of this movement was not so much to enable Massena to resume offensive operations as to prevent the archduke, by a powerful diversion, from turning against him the mass of force which the arrival of the Russians had placed at his disposal. To preserve Switzerland by threatening Germany; to procure in the latter country money and provisions; to employ, for the benefit of the republic, the rich granaries of the Palatinate, which the harvest had just filled; to derange the plan of general attack with which it was supposed that marshal Suwarrow and the archduke would crown the campaign; and to take advantage of the faults which either of these generals might commit, were the great objects which now attracted the attention of the directory, and demanded all the skill, the fortitude, and activity, of the French generals.

Nothing important had passed upon the right bank of the Rhine, since the engagement of the 29th of July; but the plan of combined operations having been at length adjusted, the republicans, on the 25th of August, to the number of 10,000, passed the Rhine at Manheim, and in the vicinity of that town, whither they had just removed their head-quarters. After sustaining a trifling and irregular opposition, they entered Heilbron on the 29th, but too late to obtain possession of the Austrian magazines, of which it was the depot. Another division of the army of the Rhine, under general Baraguay D'Hilliers, set out from Mentz, levied contributions on the town of Frankfort, notwithstanding its neutrality, pushed an advanced-guard towards Aschaffenburg, and then marching towards the Lower Necker, joined, on the 2nd of September, the centre of the army of the Rhine. By this manœuvre general Muller was enabled to advance, and to bombard the city of Philipsburg.

No sooner had the news of this inroad reached Donaneschiugen, where general Stzarry commanded a corps of reserve, than some thousands of men, followed by that general, set forwards on their march towards the Necker and the Ens, some of them directing their course to Lauffen, and others to Pfortzheim. At their approach, the French, who had pushed so far as into the neighbourhood of Pfortzheim, but whom the light imperial corps which they had driven before them still kept in check, evacuated the country of Baden Durlach, and concentrated themselves in the bishopric of Spire and the Palatinate. A number of men from the troops of Wurtemberg, joined the Austrians at Lauffen, on the right bank of the Necker. They dispatched couriers to Munich, to solicit the assistance of the Bavarian troops cantoned upon the Lech. With the arming of the peasants of the Odenwald and Bergstrass, that of the inhabitants of the Spessart was connected, thus guarding the Mein and the approaches of Aschaffenburg.

It would have been fortunate for the interests of the coalition, if the views of the court of Vienna had permitted the archduke to render these extensive and rapid preparations effectual. It was generally expected, that, after the conquest of Italy had been secured, Suwarrow, at the head of his victorious army, would invade the southern part of Switzerland, while prince Charles would take it in flank by the north, and the army of Massena should be attacked or kept in check on

the eastern side by a body of troops composed of Austrians, Russians, and Swiss. This plan had been formed by the courts of London and St. Petersburgh; but its execution was rendered impossible by the selfish and mistaken policy of the cabinet of Vienna. The archduke was severely censured for having prosecuted offensive measures to so great an extent, and having drawn Austria into a situation which would demand the most explicit declaration of her future designs. The differences between the allies in council, was naturally attended with divisions in the camp. The almost unavoidable jealousy between the troops of the two emperors, between soldiers of acknowledged bravery, and their rivals, who had never witnessed defeat, was too soon converted into open enmity, and was not, as in Italy, restrained by a vigorous authority, and diverted by active operations and uniform success.

The incursion of the French upon the Mein, and their march towards Suabia, furnished the archduke with a pretext for avoiding a co-operation with the Russian general. Affecting to be alarmed at the danger which threatened Germany, and that part of his army stationed on the right bank of the Rhine, he ordered his troops to hold themselves in readiness to quit Switzerland, and sent off several divisions to Schaffhausen. He entrusted general Hotze with the defence of the small cantons, and sent him some reinforcements, which made the force of the latter amount to 26,000 men. His head-quarters were placed at Kaltsbrun. During the last days of August, the Russians replaced the Austrians along the banks of the Limmat and the Aar, and in front of Zurich, where general Korsakow, the chief in command, fixed his head-quarters. General Nauendorf was left with about 10,000 men on the right bank of the Rhine, to form a body of observation and reserve. His head-quarters were Tengen ; and he overlooked, at the same time, the defile of the Val de Enfer, and that of the frontier towns. Such were the arrangements which prince Charles had made before his departure, for the defence of the conquered part of Switzerland. He left behind him 55,000 men, of whom more than 40,000 were opposed to Massena, from the Grison country, as far as the mouth of the Aar. One part of the Austrian troops which quitted Switzerland, marched towards the duchy of Wurtemburg, and the other part towards the Brisgau. The archduke in person followed this last column, and transferred his head-quarters, on the 31st of August, to Schaffhausen. A few days afterwards, he moved forward to St. Blaise, in the Black forest. On the 11th of September, he reached Vahingen, where he formed a junction with general Stzarry.

The French, after evacuating Heilborn, had concentrated themselves in the neighbourhood of Baden Durlach, and the bishopric of Spire, in order to cover the siege of Philipsburg. The march of the archduke's army towards the Necker, induced the French to anticipate his attack on general Muller, by attacking the Austrian posts in the valley of Kintzig. They fought near Kork, Marlen, and Bischoffsheim, and, being discomfited, returned into the fort of Kehl. The arrival of general Baraguay D'Hilliers at the gates of Frankfort, had, as I have already recorded, occasioned the subjects of the elector of Mentz, and the inhabitants of the Spessart, to take up arms. Almost all the population of the country on both sides of the Mein, had been organized in a military manner, by baron Albini, who had borne an active part at the congress of Rastadt; and general Faber, distinguished for his gallant defence of the fortress of Ehrenbreitstein. These men, being regularly divided into companies, instructed in the use of arms and military service by the mentzer and imperial officers, serving by rotation only, receiving from the elector of Mentz provision, and a trifling pay, and assisted by the regular troops of that ecclesiastical prince, formed a useful and efficacious support to the right wing of the imperial army. Having established an immediate communication with the inhabitants of the Odenwald, and forming a total of 15,000 men constantly

under arms, they marched with some artillery, against a column of the French, which had advanced along the banks of the Mein, and compelled it to retreat. Baraguay D'Hilliers himself, apprehensive for his communication with Mentz, as the landsturm or levy-in-mass had already established posts between that place and Frankfort, returned to the city.

The approach of this powerful body, formed by the united troops of the archduke and general Stzarry, induced the French before Philipsburg to raise the siege of that place, and retire with precipitation, after having in vain endeavored to carry some of its works, and having bombarded it with uninterrupted fury. Neither the works nor the garrison, which was sheltered under casemates, were materially injured by the violence of the besiegers' fire; but its result was highly disastrous to the inhabitants. Many perished under the ruins of their dwellings; not a single house was preserved from destruction; and the streets presented the appearance of heaps of ashes. No other town, except that of Landrecies, had, during the course of the war, so much reason to regret, the substitution of battering by mortars, for battering in breach.

After raising the siege, the French crossed the Rhine, and proceeded towards Worms. General Muller, who had removed his head-quarters to Manheim, caused his artillery and baggage to be carried over on the 10th of September, to the other side of the river. Two days after, he withdrew his troops from Heidelberg, which the Austrians entered as soon as they departed. He stationed his army along the Rhine, from Spirebach to Mentz, the only part of the line unprotected by any fortress, and where, consequently, the presence of the troops was necessary. A division, under the orders of general Laroche, was left in Manheim, and in the works which the French had raised during the summer. Being desirous that this town should be a post of strength to themselves, without affording the same advantage to the Austrians, they had with one hand destroyed that part of the fortifications which fronted the Rhine, and with the other re-edified those which faced the plain. Not contented with these exertions, they had linked the works of the place to an island, which, though formed by the Rhine, is called Neckerau, the Isle of the Necker, and which they had likewise fortified with care. This chain of works defended the approaches of Manheim, and covered the bridge of boats upon the Rhine; without which, the possession of the town would have been of greater danger than utility.

The archduke, on the 18th, at break of day, attacked the village of Neckerau, which was accessible only by two bridges, defended by pallisadoed redoubts and abatis. The Austrians experienced an obstinate resistance, and were exposed to a destructive fire. But their own fire becoming superior, and the soldiers being animated by the presence of the archduke, in a second attack, carried the village and island. All the French which it contained were killed or taken. The success of this brilliant attack enabled the Austrians to take in flank a fortified post, named Holtzof, situated upon the Rhine, between Manheim and Neckerau. It was still more briskly attacked and defended than the latter place, was taken and retaken twice, and remained at last in the hands of the imperialists. The French, having no means of retreat, were cut to pieces or made prisoners. The Austrians having thus become masters of all the works which flanked Manheim, along the Rhine erected batteries upon the Holtzof, to cannonade and bombard the bridge, and at the same time assaulted the chain of works raised in front of Manheim on the land-side. These were carried with such impetuosity, that the imperial troops intermingled with the French, and all the latter, who had not passed the bridge, fell into the hands of the Austrians. The number of prisoners taken during the day, amounted to 1500, including two generals: the number of the killed and wounded was not less. Eighteen pieces of cannon fell into the hands of the victors, who purchased the honor and advantage of the day with the loss of 400 men. Few

affairs of posts have been more spirited or more worthy of remark. It was in the face of the French army ranged on the opposite side of the river, that the Austrians carried a fortified town with its formidable entrenchments.

After having left a garrison at Manheim, the outward entrenchments of which he ordered to be destroyed, the archduke stationed his head-quarters at Schwetzingen, and assembled the main body of his army in the extensive plain which surrounds the town. Having no more enemies on the right bank of the Rhine from Kehl to the Mein, he dispatched upon the latter river a corps of light troops with flying artillery. This assistance enabled the landsturm of Mentz to recover from the French the two banks of the Mein, to drive them back into Mentz, and to send out skirmishing parties in all directions. These excursions gained the landsturm prisoners and booty, inspired them with confidence, and inured them to the fatigues of war.

The position of the imperial troops in the countries which France had possessed at the commencement of the campaign; the magazines which the archduke was employed in forming at Schwetzingen; the presence of more than 40,000 Austrians on the right bank of the Rhine; the grand attack which 45,000 English and Russians were at that time making on the north of Holland; and the expected march of Suwarrow into Switzerland, all tended to impress the political observer with a conviction, that the war already so extended, would take a still wider range; that the Lower Rhine would present a new theatre of hostilities; and that, before the end of the campaign, the flames of war would burn from the Zuyder-Zee to the banks of the Tiber. Such was the public expectation towards the end of September. The French shut up in Mentz and Ehrenbreitstein, dared not to keep the field at those points; and general Muller, whom the war in Holland had deprived of his expected reinforcements, remained at Turckheim, where he waited with anxiety till the views and designs of prince Charles should be developed

His conjectures and uncertainty did not last long. On the 27th of September, the archduke received, at Schwetzingen, intelligence of the passage of the Limmat, and of other events in Switzerland, which compelled him to abandon his offensive projects, and to return to Schaffhausen with greater expedition than that with which he had left it in the preceding month.

HISTORY OF THE WAR.

CHAP. XXI.

IN conformity with the extensive plan of operations adopted by the cabinets of London and St. Petersburgh, the preparations for an expedition to the north of Holland were rapid, energetic, and effectual. Early in August, 20 000 men were assembled on the coast of Kent, and 15,000 men were preparing to reach the same rendezvous. It was imagined that, independently of the utility of the enterprise as a powerful diversion in favor of our allies, it might enable the secret friends of the stadtholder to assert their rights and regain their independence. It was presumed, that even the numerous individuals, who had been seduced for a moment into subservience to the interests of France, would combine with their deliverers as soon as they could act with safety, according to their secret sentiments and wishes. Instead of the benefits expected from their nominal alliance with France, they had sustained the most enormous exaction, and experienced the most insulting demeanor, from their pretended friends. Their eyes it was imagined, were now opened to their true interests, and their sufferings would induce them to unite in delivering themselves from their miserable thraldom. With a view to the attainment of these objects, admiral Mitchel sailed, on the 13th of August, with a squadron from Deal, on board of which was the first division of the British forces,

1799.

consisting of 12,000 men. He was directed to join admiral Duncan in the north seas, and thence to proceed to the mouth of the Zuyder-Zee. The disembarkation was entrusted to the command of the gallant and veteran sir Ralph Abercrombie.

This distinguished officer was the descendant of a very antient and respectable family. Of his father's numerous issue, three sons distinguished themselves in the defence of their country. James, a lieutenant-colonel in the 22nd regiment of foot, fell at the memorable battle of Buuker's Hill, near Boston, in America: another son, Robert, was for some time colonel of the 75th, or Highland regiment, stationed at Bombay, and was entitled to a considerable share of military fame for his vigorous exertions in forming a junction with lord Cornwallis, at the siege of Seringapatam, in 1792. Sir Ralph Abercrombie entered the army in 1758, with a cornet's commission in the 3rd dragoon guards. On the 12th of February, 1760, he obtained a lieutenancy in the same regiment, in which he continued till the 24th of April, 1762, when he obtained a company in the 3rd regiment of horse. In this regiment he rose to the rank of major on the 6th of June, 1770, and, on the 19th of May, 1773, he was promoted to that of lieutenant-colonel. In November, 1780, he was a brevet colonel, and, on the 3rd of November, 1781, was made colonel of the 103rd, or Irish infantry, a newly raised regiment. At the peace of 1783 this regiment was reduced, and the colonel placed on half pay. On the 28th of September, 1787, he was promoted to the rank of major-general; and on the 17th of September, 1790, obtained the command of the sixty-ninth regiment of foot, from which he was removed in April 1792 to the 6th regiment; and on the 5th of November again removed to the 7th regiment of dragoon guards. On the 25th of April 1793, he was promoted to the rank of lieutenant-general, in which station he served under his royal highness the duke of York on the continent. By his military skill and exertions, he acquired the esteem and confidence of that general, who, in his dispatches relative to the action on the heights of Cateau, April 16th, 1794, where sir Ralph commanded the advanced guard, remarks, " I have obligations to lieutenant-general sir William Erskine, as well as to lieutenant-general Abercrombie." In his dispatches of the 19th of May, his royal highness further says: " The ability and coolness with which lieutenant-general Abercrombie and major-general Fox conducted their different corps under these trying circumstances require that I should particularly notice them." On the 27th of October following, he was wounded at Nimeguen. In the succeeding winter, when the British army retreated into Holland, the care of the sick and wounded was confided to sir Ralph; and, in the execution of his difficult and important duty, his sensibility and humanity were conspicuous. Early in 1795, the success of the French in the West Indies claimed the attention of the English government; and a military force was sent out, of which the charge was given to sir Ralph Abercrombie, who was also appointed commander of the forces in the West Indies. I have already had occasion to record the various enterprises in which he was engaged in the two years during which he remained on that station. On the 2nd of November, 1796, sir Ralph, who had lately received the honour of knighthood, was presented, notwithstanding his absence, to the second, or North

British dragoons, commonly called the Scotch Greys; in the same year was made lieutenant-governor of the Isle of Wight, and was afterwards further rewarded with the lucrative governments of forts George and Augustus. Upon his return from the West Indies he was, selected as a proper person to allay the discontents which prevailed in Ireland. In this, as in every other cause in which he was engaged, he exerted his utmost efforts. Destined to take the chief command of the forces in that kingdom, he paid the strictest attention to the discipline of his army, and was anxious to restore to the soldiers that reputation which they had lost by, repeated acts of licentiousness. It was his frequent declaration, that their irregularity and insubordination had rendered them more formidable to their friends than to their enemies. Shortly after his arrival in Ireland, it was found expedient to unite the civil and military power of that kingdom in one person. Sir Ralph was, therefore, recalled and succeeded by marquis Cornwallis. On leaving Ireland he was appointed to the command of his majesty's forces in Great Britain, and soon afterwards nominated by his sovereign to the command of the troops employed on the present expedition.

The weather proving unusually stormy considering the season of the year, the fleet encountered great difficulties and danger in its voyage. It was not till Wednesday, the 21st of August, that they came in sight of the Dutch coast: on the 22nd they made preparations to land, but were forced out to sea by a heavy gale of wind. On Saturday the 24th, they were again within sight of the Texel; but the weather was too boisterous and the sea too high to favour a landing, and it did not abate till the morning of Monday the 26th. On that day they came to anchor near the shore of Helder, a strong point in the northern extremity of the main land of Holland, commanding the Mars Diep, a narrow channel which joins the Zuyder Zee with the German ocean, between the continent and the island of the Texel; and which is the principal passage to Amsterdam. Here they made preparations for effecting a landing the next morning. At day-light on the 27th they began to disembark. The enemy had assembled a numerous body of infantry, cavalry, and artillery, and were posted at Callanstog, to the right of the Helder, but did not oppose the landing of the first division, waiting in hopes of attacking them before they could be supported by the rest of the troops. Admiral Mitchell, with very great skill and ability, covered the landing of the troops, which sir Ralph superintended with equal intrepidity and vigor. Both the army and navy acted with the most perfect unanimity, inspired by mutual confidence, and the most perfect reliance on the courage, professional knowledge, and wisdom of their respective leaders. In the nervous language of admiral Mitchell, they *pulled heartily* together. When the first division was landed, the enemy attacked the right flank; the position of the troops was on a ridge of sand-hills that stretch along the coast from north to south. The British had no where sufficient ground on the right to form more than a battalion in line; yet, as sir Ralph observes, " the position, though singular, was not, in our situation, disadvantageous, having neither cavalry nor artillery." The contest was arduous, and the loss was considerable; but the courage and perseverance of the British troops at length compelled the enemy to retire to a position six miles distant. Our loss amounted to about five hundred. As the enemy still held the Helder, with a garrison of near two thousand men, the troops being now all landed, it was determined to attack it the next morning. The Dutch fleet in the Mars Diep got under weigh; the garrison was withdrawn, and two regiments, commanded by major-general Moore and the marquis of Huntley, on the 28th took possession of the Helder.

Having thus effected one part of their first object, to land their troops, and take possession of a post of security, they soon after succeeded in the second part. On the 30th of August admiral Mitchell summoned the Dutch fleet to surrender to the squadron under his command, and· to

hoist the flag of the prince of Orange, in the following letter to admiral Story :—

Isis, under sail in line of battle, Aug. 30, 1799.
" Sir,
I desire you will instantly hoist the flag of his serene highness the prince of Orange. If you do, you will be immediately considered as friends of the king of Great Britain, my most gracious sovereign; otherwise take the consequences. Painful it will be to me for the loss of blood it may occasion, but the guilt will be on your own head. I have the honour to be, &c.

ANDREW MITCHELL,
Vice-admiral and commander-in-chief of his majesty's ships employed on the present expedition.

To rear-admiral Story, or the
commander-in-chief of the
Dutch squadron.".

This letter was succeeded by the subjoined declaration :—

Isis, Aug. 30, 1799.
" Sir,
The undersigned vice-admiral in the service of his majesty the king of Great Britain, charged with the execution of the naval part of the expedition to restore the stadtholder and the old and lawful constitution of the Seven United Provinces guaranteed by his majesty, having agreed that in consequence of the summons to rear-admiral Story, the ships, after hoisting the antient colours, will be considered as in the service of the allies of the British crown, and under the orders of his serene highness the hereditary stadtholder, captain and admiral-general of the Seven United Provinces, has thought it proper to give an account of this agreement to the brave crews of the different ships, and to summon them by the same to behave in a peaceable and orderly manner, so that no complaints may be represented by the officer; the undersigned will send on board each of the ships to keep proper order, until the intentions of his majesty

and his serene highness the prince of Orange, as admiral-general, shall be known, for the farther destination of these ships, on account of which dispatches will be immediately sent off. And to make them aware, that in case their conduct should not be such as may be expected from the known loyalty and attachment of the Dutch navy to the illustrious house of Orange on this occasion, any excess or irregularity will be punished with the severity which the disorders that may have been committed merit.

, ANDREW MITCHELL."

To this manifesto the following answer was returned :—

On board the Washington, anchored under the Vleiter, Aug. 30, 1799.

" Admiral,

Neither your superiority, nor the threat that the spilling of human blood should be laid to my account, could prevent my shewing you to the last moment what I could do for my sovereign, whom I acknowledge to be no other than the Batavian people and its representatives, when your prince's and the Orange flags have obtained their end. The traitors whom I commanded refused to fight; and nothing remains to me and my brave officers but vain rage and the dreadful reflection of our present situation: I therefore deliver over to you the fleet which I commanded. From this moment it is your obligation to provide for the safety of my officers and the few brave men who are on board the Batavian ships, as I declare myself and my officers prisoners of war, and remain to be considered as such.

I am, with respect,

S. STORY.

To admiral Mitchell, commanding his majesty's squadron in the Texel."

The following is a list of the ships taken possession of by vice-admiral Mitchell :—

Washington, rear-admiral Story, 74

guns; Guelderland, admiral de Ruyter, Utrecht, Cerberus, Leyden, 68; Urwachten, 66; Beschermer, Batavier, Broederschep, 54; Hector, Unie, Bell Antoinette, Diuffee, Expedition, Constitutie, Amphitrite, Mars, 44; Ambuscade, Helder, 32; Follock, Minerva, Venus, Alarm, 24; Galathea, 16; Dreighlerlahn, Howda, Vreedelust, Iudiamen, and a sheer hulk.

The proclamation of sir Ralph Abercrombie, expressing the same sentiments and objects with the letters of admiral Mitchell, and likewise that of the prince of Orange, which, temperate, dignified, and persuasive, tended so powerfully to impress his countrymen with a sense of their duty and real interest, are worthy of insertion :—

" Lieutenant-general sir Ralph Abercrombie being intrusted by his majesty the king of Great Britain, the antient and good ally of the United Provinces, with the command of a body of British troops to be employed in delivering these provinces from the degrading tyranny of the French republic, has received his majesty's commands to make this public and explicit declaration of the intentions of his majesty, and of the august sovereigns who are united with him in this great work.

" It is not as enemies, but as friends and deliverers that the British troops enter into the territory of the United Provinces. It is to rescue the inhabitants of this once free and happy country from the oppression under which they now groan; to protect their religion from the intolerant and persecuting spirit of infidelity and atheism; to deliver their civil government from the despotism of a rapacious anarchy, and to re-establish their antient liberty and independence, by restoring to them the benefits of that constitution for which, under the auspices of the illustrious house of Orange, their ancestors fought and conquered, and in the enjoyment of which they so long flourished in friendship and alliance with Great Britain.

" For this object, and under the same auspices, his majesty doubts not that the antient valour and energy of the Dutch nation will be now exerted with the same spirit and success. The hand of Providence has already shewn itself in the deliverance of a great part of Europe from those miseries in which the arms and principles of French republicanism have for a time been permitted to involve it. The forces which his majesty has confided to lieutenant-general Abercrombie, and those which his majesty's allies have destined to the same object, are abundantly sufficient for the protection of those who shall stand forth in the cause of their country. It is principally by the efforts of the Dutch nation that these sovereigns wish the deliverance of the republic to be accomplished. In the steps which are to lead to this salutary end, his majesty earnestly recommends to all the inhabitants of these provinces union and concord, forgiveness of the past, and a determined resolution to protect, against every tumultuous or vindictive excess, the lives and properties of their fellow-citizens, even of those whose errors or misconduct have contributed to the calamities of their country, but whom the irresistible conviction of experience shall now unite in this great cause.

"On these principles, and in this spirit, the British army will conduct itself amongst a people whom Englishmen have long been accustomed to regard as their friends and allies : but if from henceforth there shall be found any Dutchmen, who, by their adherence to the oppressors of their country, at the moment when, by the blessings of God, its deliverance is at hand, shall shew themselves unworthy of the blessings of tranquillity, of lawful government, and of religious and civil liberty, those, and those alone, his majesty's troops will consider and treat as decided and irreconcileable enemies ; not only to his majesty and to his allies, but to the prosperity of their own country, and to the general interests and safety of Europe.

RALPH ABERCROMBIE,
Lieut.-General.

FRED. MAITLAND, Sec.
to the Commander-
in-chief."

TRANSLATION OF THE PRINCE OF ORANGE'S PROCLAMATION.

" We William, by the grace of God prince of Orange and Nassau, hereditary stadtholder, &c. &c. To all those to whom these presents shall come, greeting :—

" DEAR COUNTRYMEN,

" The long-wished-for moment when you are at last to be delivered from so many calamities, under which you have suffered for more than four years past, is, we hope, arrived, and we now enjoy the satisfaction again to address you under that pleasing prospect. It would be superfluous to enumerate the different hardships under which you have groaned, ever since the violence you have suffered in consequence of the French invasion, and the events which have followed it. If cruel experience has made you feel them but too severely, and if our ardent wishes could have been sooner fulfilled, you would have been relieved long ago from that intolerable burden. We have been but too long obliged to confine ourselves to the deploring your fate in silence, without having it in our power to alter it. At last that time is come. His majesty, the king of Great Britain, moved by his affection and friendship towards the republic of the United Provinces, and pitying your misfortunes, has taken the generous resolution, as soon as the general circumstances of Europe have allowed it, to employ, in concert with his allies, vigorous measures for your deliverance. The military force which is now sent for that purpose, is to be followed by still more numerous troops.

" The object of this expedition is made known to you in the name of his Britannic majesty, by the commander-in-chief of the first body of troops which is to open this glorious career. Those troops do not come to you as enemies, but as friends and deliverers, in order to rescue you from the odious oppression under which you are held by the French government, and by the French troops, and to restore you to the enjoyment of your religion and liberty, those invaluable blessings for which, with the Divine assistance, your and our own ancestors fought and conquered. Hesitate not, therefore, brave inhabitants of the United Provinces, to meet and to assist your deliverers. Receive them among you as friends and protectors of the happiness and welfare of your country. Let every difference of political sentiments and opinions vanish before this great object. Do not allow the spirit of party, nor even the sense of the wrongs you may have suffered, to induce you to commit any acts of revenge or persecution. Let your hands and your hearts be united in order to repel the common enemy, and to re-establish the liberty and independence of our common country. Let your deliverance be as much as possible your own work. You see already, and you will experience it still more in future, that you may depend upon being vigorously and powerfully assisted. As soon as the first efforts which are making towards your delivery shall have acquired some consistency, our dearly beloved son, the hereditary prince of Orange, who is in possession of our entire confidence, and is deserving of yours, and who is perfectly well acquainted with our intentions, will join you, put himself at your head, and, following the steps of our illustrious ancestors, spare neither his property nor his life, in order to assist with you, and for your sake, in bringing this great undertaking to a successful issue. We ourselves also will then, as soon as circumstances shall allow it, proceed to join you. And as we have always considered our own happiness and welfare as inseparably connected with that of our dear country, we will then, after having seen your laws and privileges restored, and yourselves re-established in the possession of those benefits which belong to a free people under a lawful government, make our greatest and most heart-felt satisfaction consist (under the Divine blessing) in the advancement of the public good, and of that prosperity and welfare which formerly made our once happy country an object of admiration to the surrounding nations.

Done in the palace of Hampton Court, the 28th of July, 1799.
W. Prince of Orange."

Lord Duncan, naval commander-in-chief in the North Sea, was off the Texel during an engagement in which both his public and private affections were strongly interested; his eldest son, a lieutenant in the guards, a youth of nineteen, of the highest promise, and worthy of such a father, being in the heat of the battle. By this time a reinforcement of five thousand men had arrived. Our armaments prepared to proceed in a southerly direction, to co-operate in assisting the real patriots of Holland and reducing the enemy, having however taken the precaution to fortify the Helder more strongly.

Meanwhile ten thousand more forces sailed for Holland; and on the 9th of September, his royal highness the duke of York set off to take the chief command of the army. Expecting the arrival both of the additional British and Russian troops, sir Ralph continued at the Helder, while in the mean time the island of the Texel was taken possession of by our fleets. The French and Batavian forces making a powerful army, occupied a strong position between the Helder and Alcmaer. Their numbers, and the strength of their position, determined sir Ralph to continue on the defensive until the arrival of the powerful reinforcements, which he with certainty expected. The enemy, under general Brune, confident in their numbers, September 10th, ventured an attack, and a very obstinate engagement ensued, in which they were repulsed with the loss of a thousand men, killed, wounded, or taken prisoners, while our loss amounted to two hundred. The enemy retired to Alcmaer. His royal highness landed in Holland on the 13th of September, and soon after the Russians, and the third embarkation, consisting of 10,000 British troops, joined the army. The army now consisted of 41,000 men, and being deemed sufficiently strong for offensive operations, a general attack was resolved on by his highness; and on the 19th every arrangement was made. The army advanced in four columns, extending from the right to the left coast. The column to the extremity of the right consisted chiefly of the Russians in twelve battalions, assisted by the 7th light dragoons, and general Manners's brigade, and was commanded by the Russian lieutenant-general D'Hermann, and extended to the sand-hills on the coast near the famous Camperdown, on which heights a column of the enemy were placed at a very great advantage. The second, commanded by lieutenant-general Dundas, consisted of two squadrons of the 11th light dragoons, two brigades of foot guards, and major-general his highness prince William's brigade. Its object was to force the enemy's position at Walmenhuysen and Schoreldam, and to co-operate with the column under lieutenant-general D'Hermann. The third column, commanded by lieutenant-general sir James Pulteney consisted of two squadrons of the 11th light dragoons, major-general Don's brigade, and major-general Coote's brigade. This column was intended to take possession of Ouds Carspel at the head of the Lange Dyke, a great road leading to Alcmaer. The fourth and left column, under the command of lieutenant-general sir Ralph Abercrombie, consisted of two squadrons of the 18th light dragoons, major-general the earl of Chatham's brigade, major-general Moore's brigade, major-general the earl of Cavan's brigade, first battalion of British grenadiers of the line, first battalion of light infantry of the line, and the 23rd and 55th regiments, under colonel Macdonald, was destined to turn the enemy's right on the Zuyder-Zee. To the attainment of these many and important objects the most formidable obstacles presented themselves. To the right, where the Russians were to advance, the country was almost covered with woods, especially near the village of Berghen, where the principal force of the enemy was placed. The Russians, advancing with an intrepidity that overlooked

the powerful resistance they were to meet, were, by their impetuous courage, transported beyond the bounds of that order which would have ensured safety and success; and, after a most valiant contest, obliged to retire with considerable loss. Both the second and third columns had also great difficulties to encounter in the deep ditches and canals by which the scene of their operations was intersected; the second under general Dundas, after renewing the battle with considerable success, was at length obliged to retire. Lieutenant-general sir James Pulteney, with the third, effected his object in carrying by storm the post of Ouds Carspel at the head of the Lange Dyke; but the disappointment of the right prevented our army from profiting by this advantage; it became expedient to withdraw the third column. The same circumstances led to the necessity of recalling the corps under lieutenant-general sir Ralph Abercrombie, who had proceeded without interruption to Hoorn, of which city he had taken possession, together with its garrison. The whole of the army returned to its former position. The soldiers and officers, both of Britain and Russia, displayed a valour and enterprise most honourable to themselves and their respective countries, though not crowned with the success that, from the comprehensive and able plan of attack, was naturally and reasonably expected. As the French and Batavians also fought very gallantly, the loss on both sides was considerable; and several officers of distinction were among the wounded and prisoners.

The duke of York was not intimidated, by the adverse events of the 19th of September, from a design of renewing the attack on the enemy with all possible expedition. Animated at once by all the hereditary courage of his family and the generosity of the cause in which he was embarked, and trained up in the elements of war under a prince who rose with an elastic force under misfortune, he determined not to relax in the most vigorous efforts for bringing the British enterprise in favor of the United Provinces, and the great commonwealth of European states and nations, to a happy conclusion. Nor were several important considerations wanting to fortify the inclinations of the will by the authority of the understanding. The expedition, in a military point of view, was wisely planned. The co-operation of the fleet had been attended, and was in a fair way of being still farther attended with the most prosperous success; succours might be expected with certainty from the two greatest powers of Europe; and the just resentment and indignation of the Dutch nation, it was not extravagant to suppose, would be roused at last by the prospect of deliverance from their oppressive invaders.

If the territory of the United Provinces affords many advantages for defensive war to the possessors, it offers some also to powerful maritime invaders. The contiguous districts of North Holland and West Friesland are deeply peninsulated by the Haerlemeer, the Zuyder-Zee, and the German Ocean: and by these means a road is opened to an irresistible naval force a great way into South Holland, where the land is almost every where lower than the sea, and crossed by the mouths of the Rhine and the Meuse, by several small rivers and a great number of canals. The harbour and arsenal of the Helder were already reduced. The possession of one other point of land, together with the dominion of the adjacent and nearly surrounding waters, would give the command of the peninsula just described, and present many advantages and opportunities for concerting measures, and co-operating with the friends of the stadtholder, in Amsterdam, Haerlem, Leyden, and other cities. That point is the narrow isthmus at Beverwick; the importance of which does not escape a military eye, as will appear in the course of this narrative.

The nature of the country, intersected by navigable rivers, lakes, and arms of the sea, occasioned a resemblance between the mode in which Great Britain made war on the coast of Holland and that which takes place in the Baltic, the Archipelago, and other narrow seas, where the Russian, Swedish, Turkish, and other flotillas attack their adversaries, sometimes at sea, sometimes at land. The fleet under admiral Mitchell, consisting of the lighter ships of war, and having on board a proper military force and apparatus, proceeded to make captures at sea, and descents on the shore. On the 12th of September, captain Portlock, of the sloop Arrow, and captain Bolton of the Wolverene, near the Fly Island, or Vlie Island, situated at the mouth of the Zuyder-Zee, a few miles from the Texel, took a Dutch ship and brig of superior force. They had to turn to windward, towards the enemy, against a strong lee tide, during which time they were exposed to the raking fire of the ship, which they afterwards found to be the Batavian republican guardship, de Draak, mounting 29 guns. They anchored at the Fly Island on the 15th, when captain Portlock, the first in command, sent captain Bolton to take possession of the Batavian republican ship, the Dolphin, riding at anchor close to the town of the Fly. The ship, on the approach of the English, hoisted the Orange colours; and the same step was taken in the island. A person came from the municipality, with a request to captain Bolton to surrender the place to the government of the prince of Orange; which request, by the authority of admiral Mitchell, was without hesitation complied with.

On the 21st, admiral Mitchell, with a squadron of frigates, and other armed ships and bomb vessels, came to anchor off Enchuysen; when a boat came off from that town wearing Orange cockades; in consequence of which the admiral went on shore, attended by the captains. They were received by all the inhabitants with every testimony of joy at their deliverance from their tyrannical government, and the highest expressions of loyalty and attachment to the house of Orange. The admiral proceeded to the stadthouse, and summoning all the old and faithful burgomasters, who had not taken the oath to the Batavian republic, reinstated them in the magistracy, until instructions should be received from the prince of Orange. At the dissolution of the municipality, and the reinstatement of the old magistrates, the inhabitants surrounding the stadthouse expressed their joy by loud acclamations. A party of them at the same time cut down the tree of liberty, which they instantly burned. All this was done in the most quiet and regular manner. Meidenblick, Lemmer, and other towns observed the same conduct, and expressed the same dispositions with those of Enchuysen.

The British cause was further strengthened and encouraged by a reinforcement of Russians, consisting of upwards of four thousand men, which landed at the Helder on the morning of the 26th of September, and immediately marched forward to join the main army.

The inclemency of the weather, the sole cause of suspended operation, having in some measure subsided, the British army was again put in motion, and on the morning of the 2nd of October an attack commenced on the whole of the enemy's line. A severe and obstinate action ensued, which lasted from six in the morning until the same hour at night. The right wing of the British army was commanded by sir Ralph Abercrombie the centre division by general Dundas, and the left wing by major-general Burrard: all of whom greatly distinguished themselves on this day by their cool courage and excellent conduct. The first impression was made on the adverse line by the right wing of our army; the next by the centre, and lastly, the left wing also overcame all resistance. The enemy being entirely defeated, retired in the night from the positions which they had occupied on the Lange Dyke, the Koe Dyke at Bergen, and on the extensive range of sand-hills between this last place and Egmont-op-Zee. According to some accounts, they not only destroyed the bridges, but burned all the villages in their retreat. They attempted to get into Alcmaer, but the inhabitants refused them entrance, and fired upon them, which obliged them to continue their retreat farther to the southward. On the night after the battle the British troops lay on their arms: and on the 3rd of Octo-

ber, moved forward and occupied the positions of the Lange Dyke, Alcmaer, Bergen, Egmont-op-Hoof and Egmont-op-Zee. The enemy's force was computed to be about twenty-five thousand men, of which by far the greater part were French. The duke of York, in the account he gives of the action of the 2nd of October, bestows warm and liberal praise on the whole army under his command. " Under the Divine Providence," says his royal highness, " this signal victory obtained over the enemy is to be ascribed to the animated and persevering exertions which have been, at all times, the characteristics of the British soldier, and which, on no occasion, were ever more eminently displayed : nor has it often fallen to the lot of any general to have such just cause of acknowledgment for distinguished support. I cannot, in sufficient terms, express the obligations I owe to general sir Ralph Abercrombie and lieutenant-general Dundas, for the able manner in which they conducted their respective columns ; whose success is, in no small degree, to be attributed to their personal exertions and example : the former had two horses shot under him." Very distinguished praise is also bestowed by his highness on colonel Macdonald, lord Paget, major-general Coote, general sir James Pulteney, and many other officers.

The loss sustained by the enemy exceeded 4000 men killed, about three hundred prisoners, seven pieces of cannon, and a great many tumbrils. But the victory obtained by the British army was dearly purchased by the loss of about 2300 men.

The exhausted state of the troops, from the difficulties and fatigues they had to encounter, prevented the British commander from taking that advantage of the enemy's retreat, which in any other country, and under any other circumstances, would have been the consequences of the operations of the 2nd of October.

The French general having with great prudence taken post at the narrow isthmus, above mentioned, between Beverwick and the Zuyder-Zee, the duke of York determined, if possible, to force him from thence, before he should have an opportunity of strengthening by works the short and very defensible line which he occupied, and to oblige him still farther to retire before he could be joined by the reinforcements, which, he was informed, were upon their march. Preparatively, therefore, to a general and forward movement, he ordered the advanced posts which the army had taken up on the 3rd in front of Alcmaer, and the other places already mentioned, to be pushed forward, which was done, accordingly, on the 4th. At first little opposition was shewn, and the British succeeded in taking possession of the villages of Schermerhoorn, Archer, Sloot, Limmen, Baccum, and of a position on the sand-hills, near Wyck-op-Zee. The column, consisting of the Russian troops, under the command of major-general D'Essen, in endeavouring to gain a height in front of their intended advanced post at Baccum (which was material to the security of that point) was vigorously opposed by a strong body of the enemy, which obliged sir Ralph Abercrombie to move up for the support of that column with the reserve of his corps.

The enemy, on their part, advanced their whole force. The action became general along the whole line from Limmen to the sea, and was maintained on both sides until night, when the Batavian and French army retired, leaving the British in the field of battle. This conflict was as severe as any of those that had been fought since the arrival of our troops in Holland, and, in proportion to the numbers engaged, attended with as great a loss. Of the British 900 were killed or wounded, of the Russians not less than 1200. The loss of the enemy was also very great in the killed, wounded, and prisoners which fell into our hands to the number of 500. The post to which the British army directed its march was Haerlem. But intelligence was received from the prisoners taken in this action, that the enemy, who had been just reinforced by 6000 infantry, had strengthened the position of Beverwick, and thrown up very strong works in its rear: and, that they had stationed a large force at Parmirind, in an almost inaccessible position, covered by an inundated country; the debouchés

from which were strongly fortified, and in the hands of the enemy; and farther still, that, as our army advanced this corps was placed in our rear.

Intelligence being received of all these circumstances, the British commander naturally paused. The obstacles enumerated might have been overcome by the persevering courage of the troops under his command, had not the state of the weather, the ruined condition of the roads, and the total want of the necessary supplies, arising from the above causes, presented additional difficulties, which demanded the most serious consideration. The duke of York, therefore, having maturely weighed the circumstances in which the army under his command was placed, thought it adviseable, with the concurrence of general Abercrombie, and the lieutenant-generals of the army, to withdraw the troops from this advanced position to their former station at Schagenbrug: from whence, on the 9th of October, his royal highness dispatched his secretary, colonel Brownrig, to London, in order to give a circumstantial account of the state of affairs in Holland, and to receive his majesty's farther instructions.

The colonel soon returned to the army, with orders for its immediate evacuation from Holland. Transports were sent for this purpose, and works were thrown up on the commanding heights of Keck-down, to cover the re-embarkation of our troops.

In the mean time the enemy harassed our line of defence at Schagenbrug, by daily though partial attacks; the most serious of which was that which was made by general Daendels in person. That general, on the 10th of October, attacked the right wing of the British forces upon an advanced post near Winckle, under the command of prince William of Gloucester, with 6000 men and six pieces of cannon, endeavouring to force this post by every exertion. To resist this formidable attack the prince had only 1200 men, and two pieces of cannon; yet he obliged the Dutch General to retreat, with the loss of 200 men killed, and one French general. But general Daendels being almost immediately reinforced by 4000 Dutch troops, the prince of Gloucester was under the necessity of falling back to Cohorn. The loss of the English in this action did not exceed three killed and about twelve wounded. The prince, during the action, had his horse shot under him; but he received no injury himself, though exposed to the greatest personal danger, under a heavy fire, being frequently in the front of the line, animating the exertions of his troops by his example.

The efforts of our naval force in the Zuyder-Zee, and on other parts of the Dutch coast were continued during these transactions on land with unabated activity. Many gun-boats, and several light ships of war, were taken from the enemy; and an attack on the 11th of October, on the town of Lemmer, was gallantly repulsed by the British sailors and marines under the command of captain Boorder, of the Wolverene bomb-ship. On the 17th of October, a suspension of arms was concluded between the captain-general of the Anglo-Russian army, and the generals Brune and Daendels. It was agreed that all prisoners should be given up on both sides, and that as the price of permission to the British troops to re-embark on board their transports without molestation, 8000 of the seamen, prisoners in England, whether French or Batavians, should obtain their liberty. The combined English and Russian army was to evacuate Holland before the end of November. No time was lost in the embarkation of the British and Russian troops, who were accompanied on their voyage to England by 2000 Dutch loyalists. The Russians were landed and quartered in Jersey and Guernsey.

The retreat of the army of the duke of York was followed by the evacuation of the Zuyder-Zee, by the fleet of admiral Mitchell and by the abandonment of the islets and of the port of Lemmer.

It would be impossible to recapitulate within the limits of a compendious narrative, the causes which retarded the union of the four English and Russian divisions, which had hindered the duke of York from profiting by the success of the first debarkation, so skilfully executed under the command of general Abercrombie.

It cannot be asserted that unforeseen misfortunes, or the inadvertencies of the allies were the only, or even the principal causes of general Brune's success. His plan of defence was judicious and able; and he had no occasion in the course of the campaign to change his first disposition, a circumstance which in defensive war, is the best proof of military skill. The excellence of his arrangements was evinced by the trivial nature of the advantages which the duke of York obtained from the battle of Bergen and Egmont-op-Zee. The dispositions before and after the action, the correspondence in the attacks, and the skilful manœuvres of generals Abercombie and Dundas, succeeded indeed against the most obstinate resistance recorded in history, and against the most serious and almost insurmountable obstacles, presented by the positions of the enemy and the nature of the ground.

Yet at the trivial distance of two leagues from the field of battle, a position parallel to the first and nearly impregnable, checked the progress of the victorious army. The French general already prepared to support the defences of his third line, attacked upon an extended front still more favorable to his manœuvres, obtained in his turn a decided advantage over an enemy reduced to the necessity of fighting, or of perishing for want of sustenance.

In this manner terminated a maritime expedition, the most considerable which had been attempted by any modern nation; and which was designed to be productive of the most important influence on the general aspect of the war, and the situation of Europe. The circumstance which above all others occasioned the misfortunes attending the expedition, was the apathy and the total indifference of the Dutch nation. The capture of the Russian general D'Hermann, whose abilities had obtained him the entire confidence of his troops, and the subsequent misunderstandings among the commanders were extremely unpropitious to the allied cause. As it too frequently happens in unsuccessful enterprises, the different parties interested expressed their chagrin by reciprocal charges of misconduct;

but the impartial inquirer will find, in the plan of the campaign, and the execution of the manœuvres, but little to condemn, while the skill and gallantry of the officers and the discipline and bravery of the troops, deserve the warmest approbation, and put to shame the vulgar and malignant calumnies which avarice, envy, and malice have so actively and so successfully endeavoured to circulate.

HISTORY OF THE WAR.

CHAP. XXII.

Proceedings of Buonaparte in Egypt—Insurrection at Cairo—The French General proceeds on his Expedition to Syria—Siege and Massacre of Jaffa—Assault of Acre and its Gallant Defence by sir Sidney Smith—Discomfiture and Retreat of Buonaparte —Deplorable situation of the French Army—Clandestine Flight of Buonaparte from the Shores of Egypt.

FROM a scene of warfare adjacent to the shores of England, and almost within the immediate observation of the parents, the wives and the orphans whom it reduced to penury and despair, our attention is called to a distant theatre of hostility, still more destructive of the human race, and equally important in its results. The details of the second campaign in Egypt derive additional and peculiar interest from the character of him to whom its direction was committed: an individual whom even his dispassionate adversaries will acknowledge to have been endowed with splendid talents, and who was actuated by passions which animated him to their full exertion and display. Active, restless, and adventurous, his mind was always employed in the formation of some enterprise which might conduce to his own triumph, or the glory of the state. Thoughtful, penetrating, and inventive, he possessed an unrivalled power of rapid and decisive observation: he displayed an intuitive knowledge of human nature; and was equally distinguished by the fertility of his expedients, and the boldness of his designs. The atrocity of his character was not less remarkable than the vigor of his mind ; nor was he restrained in the gratification of his rapacity or ambition, by any principles of religion or any feelings of humanity.

He was now at the head of an army, which, with the marines and volunteers by whom it had been augmented, amounted to 50,000 men composed of the best troops of Europe, accustomed to victory ; confident in their own prowess, and in the military skill and good conduct of their generals. To turn the fortune of war, to convince such men, that though their enthusiasm had led them to exhibit prodigies of valor, on the Po, the Adda, and the Adige, there were troops prepared to dispute with them the palm of victory, and capable of setting bounds to the enterprises of their leader, was reserved for the generals and the soldiers of England. If Buonaparte animated his men, by telling them that they would be distinguished among their countrymen, as having served in the army of Italy, higher honours must be awarded to their conquerors.

The situation of Buonaparte in Egypt after taking possession of Cairo, was such as required and displayed all the resources of his genius and address. He was surrounded with enemies, and being, by the late destruction of the French fleet, deprived of the protection and the succours on which he had relied, it was of the utmost importance that he should remain on terms of amity with the inhabitants of the country. He not only therefore issued proclamations similar to those which he had circulated on his first arrival in Egypt, and conformed to the customs and manners of the people, but enjoined his troops to follow his example, and denounced the punishment of death on every act of depredation or extortion. "The Roman legions," said he, "protected all religions. You will find here usages different from those of Europe. You will reconcile them to yourselves by custom." To secure the kind offices of the natives he repeated his declarations that he came as their deliverer from every kind of oppression. To ingratiate himself in the friendly opinion of the bashaw of Egypt, he represented himself as united in policy and interest with the porte, for the purpose of chastising the insolence and extortion of the beys. "You know," said he, to the bashaw, "that the French nation is the only ally which the sultan has in Europe. Come then, and meet me, and curse along with me the impious race of beys." He observed the same accommodating maxims as far as was compatible with his general design in the organization of the Egyptian government. Conformably with the French model, a general assembly was to be held at Cairo of the chief men of the fourteen provinces into which Egypt was divided. There were also provincial assemblies; and the French generals who commanded in the provinces, were ordered to make choice of such members as had most influence with the people, and were most distinguished for their talents and their kindness to the French. Deputations were appointed from each province consisting of three lawyers, three merchants, and three cheiks or chiefs of the Arabs, to form a divan or national council.

The conduct of Buonaparte was admirably calculated to deceive the natives; but that common sense which nature has dispensed to the whole human race, came to their assistance. They were led to suspect that, amidst his professions of friendship and of tenderness for their feelings, his grand and ultimate object was the establishment of the absolute ascendancy of France. Their conjectures were confirmed by the publication of an order, "that the whole of the inhabitants of Egypt should wear the tri-coloured cockade, and that all the Egyptian vessels navigating the Nile, should hoist the tri-coloured flag." The enunciation of this order was not attended by any immediate indications of discontent. The country wore an appearance of tranquillity and of submission to the conquerors: the people were supposed to be accustomed by little and little to the new forms of government. The *notables* deputed by the different provinces assembled at Cairo; the cheik Abdallah Kaskaoni, assuming the rank of president, and Monge and Berthollet exercising the functions of commissaries of the French government. They deliberated with the affectation of temper and dignity on the establishment and division of taxes, on the final organization of the legislative bodies, and on various subjects of general police and administration. In the midst, however, of their futile and ludicrous proceedings, they were alarmed by the clamor and the violence of a dangerous insurrection. A combined revolt was attempted in various quarters of the city and in its immediate environs. General Dupuis, who was sent with a regiment of dragoons to suppress the insurgents, fell a victim to their rage, and 4500 of the malcontents were slain before tranquillity was restored. They seized upon and stabbed or strangled every Frenchman whom they found in the streets; the house of Caffarelli, the commandant general was surrounded, and its defenders massacred. The *generale* was beat; the French flew to arms: Buonaparte collected in the city several battalions, and directed all his efforts against the mosques in which the Turks had fled for refuge. These were attacked with all the ardor of vengeance, and defended with the obstinacy of despair. The general of artillery, Dommartin, commenced a heavy bombardment on the mosques and edifices, from which the Turkish fire was directed, and from which showers of stones were cast forth to a considerable distance and in all directions. The citadel opened upon the town, and chiefly upon the grand mosque, where the explosion of the bombs called forth one general cry of affright and horror. The gates were forced, and the French made an horrible carnage of all who fell into their hands. The general summoned these unfortunate persons to deliver up their keys, but they returned no answer, continued to fight with blind and desperate fury, and were nearly all put to the sword. The whole of the next day was past in the repetition of the same sanguinary scenes ; and, several of the French having been deliberately shot, every Turk who could be found fell a victim to the revengeful fury of the soldiers. The loss of the French was estimated in these two days at 400 men ; that of the Turks at more than 5000. On the third day order and tranquillity were re-established in the city of Cairo. Several armed bodies of insurgents hoping to escape, sallied out from the city, but were pursued by the cavalry ; and those whom the French were unable to destroy or detain, were captured and plundered by the Arabs.

These testimonies of general disaffection were highly unpropitious to the views of Buonaparte, and could not be contemplated without serious apprehension of danger. He had also reason to be chagrined at the failure of his endeavors to impose upon the Turkish government, when he was informed of a treaty which the sultan had concluded with Russia, and of the correspondent movements of the bashaws. In conformity with the hostile views of the porte, Djezzar Oglou, bashaw (or pacha) of St. John D'Acre, in Syria, had offered refuge to Ibrahim Bey, when he fled before the French general, and had since assembled a numerous force, of which the destination was unknown. That he might oblige the bashaw to act decisively, Buonaparte demanded that he should dismiss Ibrahim Bey and his mamelukes. To this requisition Djezzar made no reply, and expressed the resentment of his sovereign and himself, by putting the French who were at Acre in irons.

The French general was convinced that so formidable an enemy must be subdued, or that his enterprise must finally fail of success. But, before he could leave Egypt, without extreme danger, it was necessary that he should provide for its defence against the disaffected Arabs, and against those foreign enemies from whom he expected an attack. In adopting this precaution, he was neither aided by places of strength already built, nor by those large rivers and those narrow defiles which are calculated for the defence of mountainous countries. Having no other dependence than his military force, he adopted the plan of erecting fortified posts in different parts, to awe the inhabitants and protect his troops. Grand Cairo was the intended centre of his military operations and the seat of government, and to its defence and security his attention was peculiarly directed. He constructed magazines on the Nile, and formed on that river a marine force for the protection of them and of his convoys. Alexandria being the chief emporium of Egyptian commerce, he endeavored to strengthen and restore its communications, and to preserve a communication between its port and Ramanich on the western branch of the Delta ; a town which he selected as the centre of his operations on the Lower Nile and on the coast. He provided so far as his force would permit for the defence of Rosetta and Damietta, at the mouths of the Nile and of Suez, which he designed for his port of shelter and communication on the Red sea. As soon as he had finally determined on the expedition against Djezzar Pacha, he erected posts and established magazines at convenient places near the Syrian frontier.

Having made these preparations for the maintenance of his establishment in Egypt; and aware that promptitude at the present crisis was absolutely necessary to his safety, he began his march towards St. John D'Acre, at the opening of the year, with an army of 12,000 men, commanded under himself, by generals Kleber, Regnier, Bon, and Lasnes. The rapidity of his measures was still further accelerated by the prospect of a definitive treaty between Turkey, England, and Russia. His plan of operations was in the same spirit with his bold and masterly conduct, during the siege and blockade of Mantua in 1796. At that period a formidable Austrian army was advancing from the Tyrol to raise the siege. Had the French army which covered the siege awaited their approach, and given them battle near Mantua, a sortie from the garrison might have decided the action in favor of the Austrians. Influenced by this consideration Buonaparte with his covering army advanced to a considerable distance, northward from Mantua, beat the Austrian army, and returned to, and carried the siege of that city.

After his departure from Cairo about eight days were expended in crossing the desert, and in this march, he lost a great number of men and horses from the unwholesomeness of the provisions, the scantiness of water, and the hostility of the Arabs. He took possession of Larissa, commonly called El-Arisch, a town of considerable trade pleasantly situated on the river Peneus, the seat of a Greek archbishop, and adorned by several mosques, for the use of the votaries of the Mahometan religion, into which place Djezzar Pacha had thrown for its defence 2000 men. On the 9th of February, a detachment under general Le Grange, which had preceded the commander-in-chief with the main army, advanced with rapidity across the mountains of sand which command El-Arisch, where he took his position and placed his artillery. The village of El-Arisch being carried by the bayonet, the enemy took refuge in the fortress, but with so much precipitation and confusion, that in barricadoing the gates, they shut out 200 men who were put to the sword or made prisoners. On the 18th of February, the main army occupied a position before El-Arisch. Buonaparte ordered one of the towers of the castle to be cannonaded, and a breach being effected summoned the place to surrender. The garrison was composed of Arnautes, and Maugrabins, rude barbarians destitute of leaders, and uninformed in any of the principles of war. They returned for answer, that it was their wish to evacuate the fort with their arms and baggage, and to

take refuge in Acre. Influenced by their entreaties, Buonaparte delayed the assault: but at length on the 20th of February the garrison surrendered on condition of being permitted to retire to Baydel by the desert. A few of the Maugrabins entered into the French service.

The artillery requisite for the siege of Acre could only be conveyed by sea, and Buonaparte directed admiral Perrée, to convey it from Alexandria to Jaffa, and to cruise before the latter place till he should receive further instructions.

The secresy and promptitude of the first preparations for the incursion into Syria, excited the astonishment of the Turkish officers. Unaccustomed to rapidity of execution or promptitude of design, they were confounded by the celerity of the invaders' movements; and the measures by which they had endeavoured to avert the impending triumph of their enemies were tardily and feebly prosecuted.

Sir Sidney Smith having been entrusted with the command of a squadron in the Archipelago, was afterwards instructed to hasten to Alexandria, which he bombarded on the 3rd of February. From thence he proceeded to the assistance of the pacha of Syria, who, previous to his arrival, had determined to abandon the defence of St. John D'Acre, and had prepared for the transportation of his women and his treasure. He immediately sought refuge in the road of Caiffa, his household and himself being received on board the Tiger, the Theseus, and the Concord frigate.

The French army continued its painful journey through the desert, and proceeded in divisions, succeeding each other at the distance of one and two days' march, lest the wells should be exhausted. It is impossible to describe the privations which they endured; or the difficulties opposed to the regular march of the infantry and horse. General Kleber with his division was bewildered by his guides; the two divisions which he preceded were deceived by the traces of the first; and it was not till 48 hours had elapsed that the army after sustaining a devouring thirst, arrived at Kaa Jounesse, the nearest village of

Palestine, left the desert, and beheld before them the cultivated plain of Gaza. Having defeated a corps of cavalry commanded by Abdallah Pacha, they obtained possession of the village, of several prisoners, and of all the magazines.

It was at Jaffa, the ancient Joppa, that Buonaparte experienced the first serious and formidable resistance. This town is a sea-port on the coast of Palestine, between which and Damietta the whole extent of surface is wild and barren. The city is surrounded by a wall without a ditch, and defended by strong towers provided with cannon. Trenches were opened, batteries erected, and a practicable breach made in the wall. Notwithstanding two desperate sorties, and every exertion on the part of the garrison which amounted to 4000 men, the assault succeeded. According to the testimony of sir Robert Wilson, who served in the ensuing campaign, the greater part of the garrison flying into the mosques, and imploring mercy from their pursuers, were granted their lives. "Let it be well remembered," he proceeds, " that an exasperated army in the moment of revenge, when the laws of war justified their rage, yet heard the voice of pity, received its impression, and proudly refused to be any longer the executioners of an unresisting enemy." Three days afterwards if we may confide in the narrative of sir Robert, Buonaparte who had expressed much resentment at the compassion manifested by his troops, and determined to relieve himself from the maintenance and care of 3800 prisoners, ordered them to be marched to a rising ground near Jaffa, where a division of French infantry formed against them. When the Turks had entered within the fatal line, and the mournful preparations were completed, the signal gun fired. Volleys of musquetry and grape instantly played against them, and Buonaparte, who had been regarding the scene through a telescope, when he saw the smoke ascending could not restrain his joy, but broke out into exclamations of approval. Kleber had remonstrated against this outrage in the most strenuous manner, and the officer of the etat-major who commanded, the general to whom the division belonged,

being absent, refused to execute the order without a written instruction; but Buonaparte was too cautious, and sent Berthier to enforce obedience.

When the Turks had all fallen, the French troops humanely endeavoured to put an end to the sufferings of the wounded, but some time elapsed before the bayonet could finish what the fire had not destroyed, and many of the sufferers probably languished for many days. Several French officers by whom these details were partly furnished, declared that this was a scene of which the remembrance haunted their imagination, accustomed as they had been to sights of cruelty.

The prisoners thus destroyed were those, whom Assalini in his able work on the plague, alludes to when he says, "that for three days the Turks showed no symptoms of that disease, and that it was their putrifying remains which contributed to produce the pestilential malady, which afterwards made such deplorable ravages in the French army."

Their bones still lie in heaps, and are shewn to every traveller who arrives, nor can they be mistaken for the bones of those who perished in the assault, since this field of butchery lies a mile from the town.

"Such a fact," observes sir Robert " should not be alledged without some proof or leading circumstances stronger than assertion : but there would be a want of generosity in naming individuals, and branding them to the latest posterity with infamy for obeying a command, when their submission became an act of necessity, since the whole army did not mutiny against the execution. Therefore to establish further the authenticity of the relation, this only can be mentioned, that it was Bon's division which fired, and thus every one is afforded the opportunity of satisfying themselves respecting the truth, by inquiring of officers serving in the different brigades composing this division."

The narrative of sir Robert is corroborated by the indirect testimony of Dr. Wittman, and by the language of a French writer who in a work entitled *Memoires sur L'Egypte*, published during the consulate of Buonaparte, admits, that the garrison was *passée au fil de L'Epee*, an expression which implies that they were not slain in action with their arms in their hands, but slaughtered in revenge of their courageous and protracted defence. This manner of waging war so inconsistant with that humanity which is essential to heroism, perfectly corresponded with Buonaparte's denunciations of vengeance on his entering the Syrian frontier. In a letter to the cheiks, ulemahs, and commandants of Jerusalem, he charges them to make it known to the inhabitants, that he is terrible as the lightning towards his enemies, but compassionate and merciful towards the people and those who are willing to be his friends.

The silence of the officers attached to Bon's division, the inconsistency on the part of Buonaparte himself of condescending to notice the accusation in his subsequent complaints to the English government, without attempting to refute it, and the actual accumulation of human bones on the surface of the plains of Jaffa, all conspire to corroborate the testimony of sir Robert Wilson, and to render probable the commission of one of the most atrocious acts of deliberate inhumanity that ever disgraced the military character. Dr. Clarke indeed, in his travels through Egypt, supposes that the skeletons extended along the plain, may have been conveyed thither, and lightly covered with sand by the relatives of individuals afflicted with the plague; but this is only a conjecture and cannot be received, as a satisfactory refutation of the distinct and deliberate accusation of an English officer of distinguished honour, and exemplary veracity.

Having entered the town of Jaffa, Buonaparte formed a divan composed of the principal Turks remaining in the town, and gave orders for adopting every necessary measure, for defending the place. Jaffa proved a situation of the highest importance to the army. It became the port and the entropôt of every description of supply from Alexandria and Damietta. From Jaffa Buonaparte wrote the following letter to Djezzar Pacha, dated on the 9th of March:

- " Since my arrival in Egypt I several times informed you, that I had no design to make war against you, and that my only object was to expel the Mamelukes. You returned no answer to the overtures which I made. I announced that I desired you would drive Ibrahim Bey from the frontiers of Egypt; I was obliged then to depart from Cairo to direct in person the war which you seemed to invite. I have conquered the districts of Gaza, Ramley, and Jaffa, I have treated with generosity such of your troops as surrendered at discretion, but I have been severe towards those who violated the rights of war. In a few days I shall march against Acre, but why should I deprive an old man, with whom I am not acquainted, of the few remaining years of his life. What are a few miles, more of territory in comparison with those which I have already conquered? If God grants me victory, I will, like him, be clement and merciful, not only towards the people but towards the great. You have no solid reason for being my enemy, since you were also the enemy of the Mamelukes. Your government is separated from that of Egypt, by the districts of Gaza, and Ramley, and by impassable marshes. Become my friend: Be the enemy of the Mamelukes, and the English, and I will do you as much good as I have done you hurt, and can still do you more. Send me a short answer by some person invested with full powers that I may know your views. He need only present himself to my advanced guard with a white flag, and I have given orders to my staff to send you a pass of safety. On the 21st of March I shall proceed against Acre; I must therefore have an answer before that day. BUONAPARTE."

To this insulting and confident epistle Djezzar returned a verbal answer in terms similar to the following:

" I have not written, because I am resolved to hold no communication with you. You may march against Acre when you please. I shall be prepared for you, and shall bury myself in the ruins of the place rather than let it fall into your hands."

The army marched to Zetta, under the tower of which it passed the night of the 15th of March. On the 16th, they encamped at Sabarien, after extricating themselves from the narrow passes of mount Carmel, on the plain of Acre. A division of the army under general Kleber marched against Caiffa, which the enemy abandoned at their approach. On the 17th, late in the evening, they arrived at the mouth of the little river of Acre, which is situated at the distance of about 1500 fathoms from the fortress. The night was employed in constructing a bridge, over which the whole army passed on the morning of the 18th.

The maritime fortress of Acre, called Accho by the Hebrews and Phenicians, by the Greeks Ptolemais, and by the French *St. Jean D'Acre*, on account of its being the antient residence of the knights of St. John of Jerusalem, is the last and most southern city on the Phenician coast. It was a considerable place so early as the time of the Israelite judges, for it is related that the tribe of Ashur could not drive out its inhabitants. After being in possession of the emperor Claudius, it fell into the hands of the Turks and Arabs, who retained it till the holy war, when it was retaken by the Christians in 1104. The Turks took it a second time, under Saladin, and it was again wrested from them in 1193, by Guy, king of Jerusalem, Richard I. king of England, and Philip, king of France. It was then given to the knights of St. John, who defended it for about one hundred years with great bravery. But a dispute concerning its possession among the Christians themselves, gave an opportunity to sultan Melech Seraff, with an army of 100,000 men, to reduce it once more under the Ottoman yoke, in the year 1291. The greater part of the inhabitants fled for refuge to the island of Cyprus. Acre was immediately entered and plundered by the Turks, who made a horrible slaughter of those who remained in the city, razed its fortifications to the ground, and destroyed its magnificent edifices. It was in this city that Edward I. of England, then prince Edward, received a wound from a poisoned arrow, which was cared by the affection of his wife Eleanor, who sucked the poison from his arm.

Acre, by the excellence of its situation, enjoys all the advantages to be derived from sea and land. It is encompassed on the north by a spacious and fertile plain, on the west by the Mediterranean, and on the south by a large bay extending from the city to mount Carmel. These advantages led to its adoption as a fit *entrepôt* for commerce, to Faccerdino, not improperly called the Great, the chief of the Druses, who, towards the end of the 15th century, threw off the Turkish yoke, fortified Acre with additional towers, and, in order that it might be inaccessible to the Turkish gallies, deposited large masses of stones in the deepest parts of the entrance to the harbor. Without the harbor in the bay, there were roads, in which vessels lay at anchor, and to and from which the commerce of Acre was carried on in lighters or boats. Faccerdino carried on a correspondence and commerce with India, the Grecian islands, and Italy. At that period, the most opulent and commercial, and indeed the most accomplished and princely family 'in Europe, were the Medici, who gradually rose through the usual gradations of democracy to the sovereignty of Florence and of the dependent districts, under the title of the grand dukes of Tuscany. Faccerdino paid a visit to Cosmo de Medici, at Florence. He was received with the most elegant hospitality, and returned to Syria and to St. John D'Acre, accompanied by a number of artists from Italy. Bridges, highways, palaces begun, but unfinished, improvements in navigation, fortification, and agriculture, and some approached to science and literature in Syria, were the result of the visit paid by Faccerdino the Great to Cosmo de Medici.

While Buonaparte was preparing for the siege of Acre, general Desaix marched to Upper Egypt to attack Murad Bey, who had encamped on the left bank of Joseph's canal, on the borders of the desert. Murad, on the approach of the enemy, retreated to Siout, and afterwards beyond Dirge, whither he was followed by Desaix. A body of Mameluke horsemen, aided by some armed bodies of peasantry on foot, who had assembled at the village of Souagui, were defeated by general Davoust on the 3rd of January, and dispersed with the loss of 800 killed. Scarcely, however, was this multitude put to the rout before a 'more formidable insurrection occurred near Siout, in the rear of the French. The intrigues of the Mamelukes had not only incited the peasants to resistance, but prevailed on great numbers in the different provinces to join their standard. It became necessary, therefore, to make such an impression as might intimidate the insurgents from taking similar steps in future. General Davoust returned with the cavalry to Thata, where he encountered the enemy on the 8th of March, and killed about 1000. On the 18th, the French flotilla on the Nile arrived at Girge, and dissipated the alarm excited by its tardy navigation. In the mean time a body of Scherifs from Yambo and Jedda, crossed the Red sea, and disembarked at Cosseir. They afterwards advanced to Kene, and joined Murad Bey, who was also reinforced by a corps of Mamelukes, several bodies of Nubians and Maugrabins, and 2000 or 3000 Arabs, while the whole country as far as the cataracts was in arms. On the 22nd, the two armies met near Samanhout. The French infantry were divided into two squares; that on the right, commanded by general Friant, and that on the left by general Belliard. General Davoust, with the cavalry, which was also formed in a square battalion, stationed in the interval between these two divisions, was protected and flanked by their fire. Murad instantly advanced his horse, and endeavored to surround the enemy, while a column of his infantry occupied a large canal on their left flank, and began to annoy them with the fire of musquetry. Having detached a corps to clear the canal, Desaix made himself master of the village, which, however, was attacked with great fury by the Arabs of Yambo, while several corps of infantry

and the Mameluke horse, assailed generals Friant and Belliard. In a few moments, however, the army of Murad was totally defeated.

After this engagement, the beys, exhausted by fatigue, and having lost great part of their baggage, horses, and men, retired beyond the cataracts into the sterile country of Brida. Desaix advanced to Sienna and afterwards to Hesso, or Hesne, whence he sent out parties in pursuit of the enemy, One of his corps made an incursion into Ethiopia ; another fell in with and routed Osman Bey Hassan, on the road towards Cosseir ; and detachments scoured both banks of the Nile, where many partial actions ensued and proved extremely fatal to the peasants. Numerous encounters occurred, particularly at the antient Caphtos, and in the neighbourhood of Kene, which is the debouché from the desart, and the point where the road from Cosseir meets the Nile. At Aboumana an engagement took place between general Friant and the Arabs of Yambo, who were joined by a vast assemblage of the warlike inhabitants of the right bank of the river. French discipline and valor prevailed as usual. The hostile cavalry and the natives took to flight ; but the Arabs, throwing themselves into a village, fought with great firmness, till, being attacked by a body of grenadiers, they were all cut to pieces. In the battles of Birambra, Bardis, Girge, and Gehemi, the French were equally victorious ; and at Benedi the combined army of Arabs, Maugrabins, and Mamelukes, were defeated with the loss of 2000 men. The village itself was reduced to ashes ; and an immense booty, consisting among other articles, of several boxes full of gold, rewarded the toils and peril of the soldiers. The hostile inhabitants of Abon Girge were put to the sword, their village burnt, and the province of Benesouef subjected to obedience. It would be superfluous to enumerate the frequent but unimportant actions fought on the frontiers of Nubia, and in the once celebrated Thebais. The movements of Desaix, though skilful and brilliant, were more productive of momentary glory than per-

3 c 2

manent advantage : he defeated his enemies without subduing them ; and the
excesses of which the French were guilty,
continually increased the number of their
foes. By his constancy in misfortune, and
the fertility of his resources, Murad Bey
shewed himself an adversary worthy of
Desaix ; nor can it be decided whether
the ingenious and reiterated attacks of the
one, or the circumspect resistance of the
other, was most to be admired.

The French, in their narrative of the
contest in Upper Egypt, are loud in their
expressions of abhorrence at the inhumanity and hostility of the Arabs. Yet
one of the literary favorites of Buonaparte,
and an enthusiastic eulogist of the virtues
of his countrymen, records a series of
atrocities which might well have provoked
to retaliation the most timid and gentle
people. "We," says Denon, "who
boasted that we were more just than the
Mamelukes, committed daily and almost
necessarily, a number of iniquitous acts.
The difficulty of distinguishing our enemies by their exterior form and colour,
was the cause of our continually putting
to death innocent persons. The soldiers
who were sent out on scouting parties,
frequently mistook for pilgrims from and
to Mecca, the poor merchants belonging
to private caravans ; and, before justice
could be done them, which in some cases
the time and circumstances would not allow,
two or three of them had been shot, a part
of their merchandise plundered or pilfered,
and their camels exchanged for ours, which
had been wounded. The gains which
resulted from these outrages fell invariably
to the blood-suckers of the army, the civil
commissioners, copts, and interpreters :
the soldiers, who sought every opportunity
to enrich themselves, being constantly
obliged to abandon or forget their projects
by the drum beating to arms or the trumpet
sounding to horse. The situation of the
inhabitants, for whose happiness and prosperity doubtless, we had come to Egypt,
was no better. If through terror they had
been obliged to quit their homes on our
approach, on their return, after we had
withdrawn, they could find nothing but

the mud of which the walls were formed.
Utensils, ploughs, roofs, doors, every thing
in short of a combustible nature, had been
burnt for cooking. The earthen pots were
broken, the corn consumed, and the fowls
and pigeons roasted and devoured.
Nothing was to be found except the bodies
of their dogs, killed in endeavoring to
defend the property of their masters. If
the French made any stay in a village,
the unfortunate inhabitants, who had fled
on their approach, were summoned to
return, under pain of being treated as
rebels who had joined the enemy, and of
being compelled to pay double contributions."

If this expedition had no material effect
on the final issue of Buonaparte's enterprise, it will always be memorable to the
lovers of the belles-lettres, for the labors
of Vivant Denon, who held a commission
in the army of Desaix. Amidst scenes of
war and devastation, that ingenious artist
investigated the ruins of Thebes and other
celebrated places of antiquity, and, by the
accuracy of his drawings, rescued from
oblivion the curious specimens of sculpture
and architecture, and the monuments of
opulence and devotion, enabling the
learned to trace the progress of the fine
arts from the remotest ages of the world.

The means adopted by Buonaparte for
the advancement of arts, sciences, and
letters, though they can only be considered
as accessaries to his principal objects,
the conquest of Egypt and the ruin of the
English trade to the east, were yet the
most meritorious part of the expedition.
He appears to have been convinced that
the splendor of military atchievements
would soon fade, unaccompanied by the
more lasting fame arising from the patronage of every liberal pursuit. In the interval of active hostilities, he devoted his
leisure to the encouragement and cultivation of art, learning, and science, and
adopted many judicious measures which
may be regarded as some atonement
for the bloodshed and misery occasioned
by his selfish and boundless ambition.
Without adverting to his motives it is a debt
which candor owes even to the merit of

Buonaparte to commemorate such actions. While the artists, philosophers, and literati who attended him on this expedition were employed in their several departments, as astronomers, naturalists, chemists, mechanics, and antiquarians, he provided for their establishment by founding a national institute at Cairo on the model of that of Paris. He established a public library, and a commercial company in that city. He visited Suez, an antient decayed mart, situated on the southern side of the isthmus, which divides the Mediterranean from the Red sea. He encouraged its trade by lowering the duties formerly paid to the bashaws, and establishing a caravan for the conveyance of merchandise to and from Cairo. He also inspected the traces of the canal by which an attempt had been made to connect the two seas, and ordered it to be accurately surveyed by an able engineer.

On the 18th of March the French army under Buonaparte having crossed the little river of Acre encamped upon an insulated eminence near to, and parallel with the sea. On the 20th, the trenches were opened at about 150 fathoms from the fortress. In the mean time Djezzar Pacha having sent timely notice of the approach of Buonaparte to sir Sidney Smith, on whom the command of the British naval force in the Archipelago had devolved, after the departure of commodore Trowbridge. Sir Sidney hastened to the anchorage in the bay of Acre, where he arrived in time to place it in a state of comparatively tolerable defence. On the 7th of March he proceeded to the coast of Syria, and on the 11th arrived before Caiffa. On the 15th he steered for St. John D'Acre, to concert measures with Djezzar Pacha, having arrived at the place of destination two days earlier than the enemy. On the 16th, about eight in the evening, after a chace of three hours sir Sidney captured the flotilla which conveyed the greater part of the enemy's ammunition and artillery. As the vessels of which it was composed were doubling mount Carmel, they were descried by the Tiger, pursued, and shattered by the English fire. Seven of the number lowered their flags; a corvette, and two shallops effected their escape.

The artillery consisting of 44 pieces was immediately mounted on the ramparts of Acre against the lines and batteries of the enemy, or planted on gun vessels. To this unexpected and important capture the fortress of Acre was chiefly indebted for its safety.

The nature of the ground permitted the French to carry their trenches within half a musket-shot of the ditch. On the 30th of March, having effected a breach on the north-east part of the town, they endeavoured to take it by assault but were vigorously repulsed by the garrison with considerable loss. The troops of Djezzar Pacha afterwards effected three successful sorties; of which the last was intended to destroy a mine which the enemy had constructed under a covered way, to the northward of the town. The English took charge of this enterprise, and, while 2000 Turks were engaged in the sortie, jumped into the mine, tore down the supports, and destroyed the whole construction. After this event an uninterrupted fire was kept up from the fortress of Acre; the artillery being served by English and Turkish artillery men, who had arrived from Constantinople. These men were placed under the immediate command of colonel Phellipeaux the chief engineer in the place, to whose counsels, plans, and unwearied exertions, the safety of Acre, the important consequences which followed, were by the most intelligent part of the Anglo Turkish garrison, principally attributed. As the town of Acre stands upon a rectangular point of land in the form of a square, of which two sides are washed by the sea, the British ships in the bay of Acre were enabled by their fire to contribute to the protection of the garrison, and of the working parties employed in throwing up two ravelins or half moons, which taking the enemy's nearest approaches in flank, considerably impeded his operations. "It would be endless" says sir Sidney Smith, whose accounts I have compared with those of Berthier and others, 'to enter into the detail of the events of this most singular siege. Suffice it to say that we have been within a stone's throw of each other for nearly two months. The enemy having nearly made a lodgment on the crown of the glacis and mined the tower forming the inward angle of the town wall, which is composed of curtains and square towers after the manner of the 12th century. Buonaparte who had transported the cannon he found at Jaffa, and effected a breach on the 14th day of the siege attempted to storm, but was repulsed; since which time he has made no less than eleven desperate attempts to carry the place by assault, in each of which he has been unsuccessful, and was obliged on the 20th of May to retreat."

It was not however till after a long and sanguinary contest that Buonaparte abandoned an enterprise of which the success was equally necessary to his safety and his reputation. On the 7th of May, being the fifty-first of the siege, a fleet of corvettes and transports under the command of Hassan Bey, made its appearance in the bay of Acre. The approach of this additional strength was the signal to Buonaparte for a most vigorous and persevering assault, in the hopes of obtaining possession of the town, before the reinforcements to the garrison could disembark. The gun-boats being within the distance of grape-shot from the attacking column, added to the Turkish musketry, did great execution. Still however the enemy gained ground, and made a lodgment in the north-east tower, the upper part being entirely battered down, and the ruins of the ditch forming the ascent by which they mounted. Daylight on the morning of the 8th of May discovered the French standard on the outer angle of the tower. The fire of the besieged was much slackened in comparison with that of the besiegers, and the flanking fire of the former from the ravelins, was become of less effect, so that the enemy was able to cover himself in the lodgment just mentioned, and to secure the approaches by two traverses across the ditch, which they had constructed even under the fire of the Turkish batteries. These traverses were now seen, composed of sand-bags, intermingled and built in with the bodies of the dead, their bayonets only being visible above the surface. The troops of

Hassan Bey were at this moment in the boats, but only half way on shore. This was a most critical moment of the contest, and an effort was necessary to preserve the place for a short time till their arrival. Sir Sidney therefore landed the boats at the mole, and took the crews armed with pikes up to the breach. The enthusiastic gratitude of the Turks, men, women, and children, at the sight of this reinforcement at such a time, is not to be described. Many troops who had deserted their posts returned with the crews to the breach, which was defended by a few brave Turks, whose most destructive missile weapons, were heavy stones, which striking the assailants on the head, overthrew the foremost down the slope, and impeded the progress of the rest. Successive numbers however ascended to the assault, the heap of ruins between the two parties serving as a breast-work to both. The muzzles of their muskets touched each other, and the spear-heads of the standards were locked together. Djezzar Pacha hearing that the English were in the breach, quitted his station, where, according to the Turkish custom he was sitting to reward such as should bring him the heads of the enemy, and distributing musket cartridges with his own hand. The energetic old man coming behind the English officers in the breach, forcibly pulled them down, observing, " If any thing happens to our English friends, all is lost." This amicable contest for the honor of defending the breach, occasioned a rush of Turks to the spot, and time was thus gained for the arrival of the first body of Hassan's troops. It became necessary to combat the Pacha's repugnance, to the admission of any forces but his Albanians into the garden of his seraglio, now became a very important post, as occupying the level behind the rampart, and there were not above 200 of the thousand Albanians left alive. This was not a moment for debate. His objections were overruled. A regiment called the Chifflick was introduced, consisting of 1000 men, armed with bayonets, disciplined after the European method, under sultan Selim's own eye, and placed under the immediate command of sir Sidney Smith.

Sir SYDNEY SMITH.

SIR SYDNEY SMITH,
Who with 300 British Sailors, defended the Breach of Acre

The garrison, animated by the appearance of such a reinforcement, crowded to the breach in numbers sufficient for its defence. Sir Sidney now proposed to the pacha to relieve him from the Chifflick regiment, the objects of his jealousy, by opening his gates, and commanding them to make a sortie and take the assailants in flank. With this request Djezzar readily complied. The gates of the seraglio garden were thrown open, and the Turks rushed out, but were driven back to the town with loss. The sortie, however, had this good effect, that it obliged the enemy to expose themselves above their parapet, so that numbers were destroyed by the flanking fire of the besieged: the assailants at the breach no longer supported, withdrew from the conflict, and the small number remaining in the lodgment, were killed or taken prisoners.

The group of generals and aids-de-camp which the shells from 68 pounders had frequently dispersed, was now re-assembled on the mount of Richard Cœur de Lion. Buonaparte was distinguishable in the centre of a semicircle. His gesticulations indicated an intention to renew the attack, and his dispatching a staff officer to the camp, shewed that he waited only for a reinforcement. A little before sunset a massive column appeared, advancing to the breach with a solemn step. The plan of Djezzar was not on this occasion to defend the breach, but to admit a certain number of the enemy, and then close with them, according to the Turkish mode of warfare. The French column, therefore, mounted the breach unmolested, and descended from the rampart into the pacha's garden, where, in a few minutes, the bravest and most advanced among them lay headless corpses; the sabre, with the addition of a dagger in the other hand, proving more than a match for the bayonet. The rest precipitately retreated, and the officer, (general Lasne) commanding the column, in the act of encouraging his men to mount the breach, was severely wounded. General Rambaud was killed. During this contest, immense numbers of spectators on the surrounding hills, awaited the result of the contest determining, after the manner of Asia, to join the victors.

Sir Sidney Smith, taking advantage of the impression produced by the repeated disasters of the French, wrote a circular letter to the princes and chiefs of the Christians of mount Lebanon, recalling them to a sense of their duty, and engaging them to cut off the supplies from the French camp. He sent them at the same time a copy of Buonaparte's impious proclamation, accompanied with a suitable exhortation, calling upon them to choose between the friendship of a "Christian knight," and that of an "unprincipled renegado." This letter had all the effect that he could desire. They immediately sent him two ambassadors, professing not only friendship, but obedience; assuring him that, as a proof of their sincerity, they had sent out parties to arrest such of the mountaineers as should be found carrying wine and gun-powder to the French army. Buonaparte's career northward, was thus effectually cut off by a warlike people, inhabiting an impenetrable country.

The division of the French army under general Kleber, had been sent eastward, towards the fords of the Jordan, to oppose the army of Damascus, but it was recalled to take its turn in the daily efforts to mount the breach of Acre, which every other division had attempted, with the loss of their bravest men and above three-fourths of their officers. Much was expected from the bravery of this division, as it had, by its firmness, and the steady front it opposed in the form of a hollow square, kept upwards of 25,000 men in check for a whole day, in the plain between Nazareth and mount Tabor, till Buonaparte came up with his horse artillery and extricated these troops, dispersing the multitude of irregular cavalry, by which they were completely surrounded.

The Chifflik regiment made a fresh sally on the ensuing night, the lieutenant-colonel Soliman Aga, being determined to retrieve the honor of the regiment by the punctual execution of the orders he had received, to make himself master of the enemy's third parallel, a service which he performed most effectually; but the impetuosity of a few carried them on to the second trench; where though they spiked 4 guns they lost some of their standards. The division of Kleber, however, contrary to Buonaparte's intention, instead of mounting the breach, was obliged to waste its time and strength in recovering its third parallel, an object in which it at length succeeded. But the French grenadiers refused to mount the breach any more over the putrid bodies of their unburied companions. A flag of truce was therefore sent into the town by the hand of an Arab dervise, with a letter to the pacha proposing a cessation of arms for the purpose of burying on both sides the dead bodies of which the stench had become intollerable, and equally threatened the existence of the garrison and the besiegers, many soldiers having died delirious a few hours after being seized with the first symptoms of infection. It was natural that the besieged should gladly listen to this proposition, and that they should be *off their guard* during the conference. While the answer was under consideration, a volley of shot and shells unexpectedly announced an assault, which however, the garrison was ready to receive, and the assailants only increased the number of the dead bodies. Sir Sidney saved the life of the Arabian dervise from the fury of the Turks, by conveying him on board the Tigre, and afterwards sent him back to the French general with an indignant message. Such is the statement of sir Sidney, but it appears from the testimony of general Berthier, that the flag of truce proposed not only the burial of the dead but an exchange of prisoners, and that being fired at by the garrison it returned. On the 13th its efforts were successful, and it obtained access to the town, though the cannonade of the besieged continued without interruption, and about six in the evening of that day they made a sortie.

Subordination was now at an end, and all hopes of success having vanished, there remained to the enemy no alternative but a precipitate retreat, which was put in execution the night of the 20th of May, after a siege of 60 days. It has been already mentioned that the enemy's battering train of artillery fell into the hands of the English cruisers. Their howitzers, and 12 pounders, originally conveyed by land with much difficulty, and successfully employed to make the first breach at Acre, were embarked in *germs* at Jaffa, along with several of the severely wounded, that they might be conveyed coast-wise. This operation was expected by sir Sidney, and he hastened with an adequate force to a station between Jaffa and Damietta before the French could arrive at the former place. The vessels being hurried to sea without seamen to navigate them, and the wounded being destitute of every necessary, even water and provisions, they steered straight to his majesty's ships, in full confidence of receiving the succours of humanity. They were sent on to Damietta to receive such further aid as their situation required. Their expressions of gratitude to the English sailors, were mingled with execrations of their general, who had, as they asserted, exposed them to destruction rather than fairly and honourably renew the intercourse with the English, which he had broken off by a false and malicious assertion that the British commander had intentionally exposed his former prisoners to the infection of the plague.

The utmost disorder prevailed in the retreat, and the whole track between Acre and Gaza, was covered with the dead bodies of those who had sunk under fatigue, or from the effect of trivial wounds. They were able however to destroy an aqueduct of several leagues in length, which supplied Acre with fresh water, and to burn all the magazines and harvest in its vicinity. The rowing gun-boats annoyed the van column of the retreating army in its march along the beach; and its rear when it turned inland to avoid their fire, was harassed by the Arabs. Ismael Pacha entered Jaffa by land, at the same time that the English squadron approached the town. The plunder and massacre of the helpless inhabitants began by our Nablusian allies, was stopped by the united efforts of Ismael Pacha and the English commodore. The British flag, rehoisted on the consul's house, served as an assylum for all religions, and for every description of the surviving inhabitants. Two thousand cavalry were dispatched to harass the rear of the French, who, previous to the evacuation of Jaffa, had levied a contribution of £7500, blown up the fortifications, and thrown the artillery into the sea. But the enemy's army, after all the losses it had suffered, and the disadvantages under which it laboured, returned from this unfortunate and disastrous expedition to Grand Cairo, where the genius and activity of Buonaparte found early occasions of retrieving his disgrace. Notwithstanding his discomfiture at Acre, he boasted that he had accomplished the most important purposes of the expedition. He had destroyed or dispersed the greater part of Djezzar's forces; he had prevented the reunion of the troops formerly under the command of the grand vizir, and the organization of an army which would have threatened his positions in Lower Egypt; and had impressed the people of the country, notwithstanding his retreat, with a deep conviction of the skill, the fortitude, and perseverance, of their invaders. It cannot be denied, at the same time, that his advance into Syria, was productive in addition to the shame of defeat, of many disadvantages. After the first indications of obstinate resistance on the part of the garrison of Acre, he should have reflected on the imprudence of dissipating his strength, and wasting his time in a siege which ought not to have extended beyond a week's bombardment. The purpose of his invasion was to make an impression, an object which could only be accomplished by rapid movements.

The army engaged in the Syrian expedition, amounted, according to the French accounts, to 12,943 men, of which, in four months, 700 perished by the plague, 500 died in battle, and 1000 were wounded. The same statements estimate the loss of the allies at 7000 men, killed, wounded, and prisoners, besides 40 pieces of cannon, and 60 standards, taken in the course of the expedition. On the absurdity of this

computation, it would be superfluous to dilate, after the copious narrative which we have given of the circumstances attending the siege of Acre. The best informed and most impartial of those who speak from the result of their personal inquiry, estimate the loss of the French at 4300 men, in killed and prisoners; that of the Turks and English, at 3500. The loss of the invaders, during their retreat, was considerably augmented by the revengeful hostility of the natives. The general order given to the French columns was to burn the villages as they proceeded, and waste the adjacent country. The cavalry proceeded along the right parallel with the coast, scoured the downs, and secured all the cattle that had been there collected. The division of general Kleber formed the rear-guard, and, when it arrived as far as Kan Jounesse, the surrounding plains presented a continued blaze of fire. Berthier, in his elaborate narrative of the expedition, endeavors to justify these atrocities, by adducing the inhumanity and active enmity of the inhabitants of the country to their invaders; yet he shortly afterwards affirms, that many of the Egyptians esteemed the French as brothers, and that the army looked upon Cairo as a second country.

While the greater part of the French army was employed in Syria, the enemy were not idle in Egypt. The Mamelukes in Saia, although much enfeebled, still possessed a powerful influence in the country and among the nomade Arabs. They had divided their forces into two bodies, one of which directed its course by Lake Sheib, towards the vicinity of Gaza, whither Ibrahim Bey had proceeded, while another under Murad Bey, descended by Feium, to the lakes of Natron, as if with an intent to favor the attack on the castle of Aboukir, the bulwark of Alexandria, which was besieged by a Turkish army, supported by an Anglo-Russian fleet, which had just arrived off the coast of Egypt. He therefore adopted the necessary measures for checking this combined movement, and dispatched general Lagrange on the 10th of July, against the corps advancing on the eastern side. The Mameluke encampment was taken by surprise, and all their baggage captured, with 700 camels. General Murat, with another moveable column, marched to the lakes of Natron, to disperse the Arabs and cut off the retreat of Murad Bey, who fell back with precipitation, on learning the approach of the French. Murad afterwards encamped near the pyramids of Gizeh, on the side of the desert; but, being closely pressed, fled once more to Upper Egypt. Unruffled amidst all his misfortunes, this Egyptian Fabius, combining the exercise of patient courage, with all the resources of active policy, had calculated his means, and justly appreciated their effects amidst the various occurrences of a disastrous war. Though he had to oppose at the same time, a foreign enemy, and the rival pretensions of his jealous equals, he continued to preserve a firm authority over his party, by sharing in their privations. He was become their rallying point, the leader of their destiny, and of all their movements, and commanded them as absolutely as in the time of his greatest prosperity.

Buonaparte, having repaired to Gizeh in person, was there informed that a Turkish flotilla of 100 sail, had anchored on the 11th, at Aboukir, of which they had taken the castle and fortified the peninsula. Sensible of the necessity of bringing the enemy to immediate action, he took a position at the village of Birket, near one of the angles of lake Maidi, a point from which he could march with equal facility to Etko, Rosetta, Alexandria, and Aboukir. This disposition had likewise the advantage of confining the enemy to the peninsula, intercepting their reinforcements, and cutting off their communication with the country. On the 24th, the head-quarters were removed to Alexandria, and in the afternoon removed to the wells between that place and Aboukir; while Kleber occupied Fena, on the opposite side of the Nile, in his rout to join the main army. At day-break, on the 25th of July,

the French troops began to advance. The vanguard, commanded by Murat, was composed of 400 horse, and three battalions of infantry, under the immediate direction of general Destaing. It was followed by the division of Lasnes, forming a kind of right wing, while the division of Lanusse and that of Kleber, whose arrival was expected in the course of the day, formed the reserve. A detachment was ordered to take a position between Alexandria and the army, to preserve a communication with that city, and to oppose Murad Bey and the Arabs, who threatened to effect a junction with the Turkish army. On the opposite side of lake Maidi, or Maadie, and near Rosetta, general Menon was posted with directions to harass the enemy's left, and cannonade such vessels as might appear on the lake.

The first line of the Ottoman army was ranged about half a league in front of the fort of Aboukir. On its right, 1000 men occupied a mount of sand, defended towards the sea by entrenchments, and supported by a village, into which 1200 troops had been thrown, with four pieces of cannon. The left was stationed on a detached sand-hill, about 600 toises in front of the line and to the left of the peninsula. Their second position was nearly 300 toises in the rear of the village, and 600 behind the right of the first line. The centre occupied a French redoubt, which had been stormed on their landing; the right of the centre was behind an entrenchment, and the left posted on some low sand-hills, between the battery and the sea, and under the protection of the battery and the gun-boats. These two lines were defended by 8500 men. In the interval between them, 2000 men were placed with six pieces of cannon, aided by some gun-boats, and in the rear of the second, and about 100 toises behind the redoubt, lay the village and fort of Aboukir, occupied by 1500 troops. The collective force of Mustapha Pacha, the commander, amounted to 15,000 men. His first line was badly fortified, but was rendered of consequence by covering the important wells of Aboukir. In these sultry regions, a spring of water often forms the subject of dispute between contending tribes, and is generally the central point of attack and defence. The second line was his main position, and was defended by 12 pieces of cannon.

When the foremost of the advanced guard touched the Arabian van, Buonaparte ordered the columns to halt and made dispositions for the attack. General Destaign with three battalions was to carry the eminence on the Turkish right, while a picquet of cavalry was to prevent its defenders from retiring to the village. Lasnes was directed to advance against their left, and in like manner send part of his cavalry to intercept their retreat while the rest proceeded against the Turkish centre. In a few moments the Turkish right gave way, but fell back on the village, and their left consisting of 2000 men, being also discomfited, were killed or driven into the sea. The troops in the village reinforced by a detachment from the left of the second line, made a spirited resistance, but were compelled to abandon their post and retire to the redoubt in the centre of their next position. This point being flanked by a ditch of communication extending to the sea on the right and bending to the left, was of considerable strength, and now defended by 9000 men.

After a short cannonade Destaign's battalions were ordered to advance against the redoubt, while a column marched along the shore to charge with the bayonet the Turkish right. The French cavalry attacked their left, but rushing inconsiderately between the redoubt and the gun-boats they were driven back, and notwithstanding repeated charges, experienced each time a similar repulse. The French column on the left was also checked by the flanking fire of the redoubt and the batteries, the Turks occasionally advancing with great bravery armed with sabres and pistols, and having their muskets slung behind them. Several of them, undismayed by the heavy fire of the French artillery, even darted from their entrenchments to cut off the heads of the wounded and the dead,

that they might receive the reward which their government bestows on these acts of barbarity. So firm an opposition disconcerted the French army and obliged it to fall back a few paces that it might form and rally. Buonaparte ordered two battalions under general Lasnes, to march against the Turkish left. This officer availing himself of the enemy's imprudence in issuing from their entrenchments, vigorously attacked the fort on its left and on the breast-work. His troops rushing forward leaped into the ditch, mounted the parapet, and entered into the redoubt. The whole French line, animated by one impulse now rushed forward with impetuous fury, swept the enemy's entrenchments, and traversed their positions as far as the ditch of the fort. By this fortunate and unexpected movement, the retreat to Aboukir was cut off. One half of the Ottoman army was driven into the sea; and either shot, cut in pieces, or drowned. Two thousand lay dead on the field of battle, and the rest with Mustapha were taken prisoners, or surrendered in the fort with all their tents, baggage, and artillery. The loss of the French amounted to 5000 killed and wounded: but of the unfortunate Moslems, whose ships were moored in the road of Aboukir, two leagues distant from the shore, not a man escaped to communicate the destruction of his countrymen. Sir Sidney Smith, who arrived at Aboukir to join the Anglo-Russian fleet, was a witness to the defeat of his allies without the power of rendering them the most trivial assistance. His squadron united with that of the Russians and of Allah-Fetah Bey, could only collect the wrecks of an expedition destined to effect the recovery of Egypt, and the extermination of "the remains of the French army" as the forces of Buonaparte were termed, in the language of the seraglio.

On the day after the battle of Aboukir, Buonaparte returned to Alexandria. He had been informed by some communications with the pilots of the English vessels, of the first reverses that had occurred to the French armies in Italy and upon the Rhine, and acquainted with the disorders which prevailed in the administration of the government, the struggles of contending factions, and the impatience of the people. Exulting in the victory of Aboukir, which, in his opinion, more than counterbalanced his defeat at Acre, he was not unwilling to abandon Egypt at a moment so propitious to his military reputation; confident in the superiority of his genius and the fertility of resources he looked forward with enthusiastic ardor to the opportunity of retrieving the conquests and the glory of his country. He contemplated with his usual sagacity the exaltation that might possibly await the exertion of his talents for intrigue, amidst contending parties, and the exercise of his military skill. With an ambition that stimulated him to the most arduous enterprises he possessed that secrecy which is frequently of eminent advantage in their execution. Absorbed in his own reflections, he silently meditated his ambitious schemes, without subjecting them to be defeated by the indiscretion of a confident. His prudence and reserve were particularly observable at the present important crisis, when his departure from Egypt might have been justly regarded as a desertion of troops which had served him so faithfully, which had devoted their lives to the accomplishment of his favourite enterprise, and which, apprised of his intention, might in their first emotions of surprise and disgust, have made him a victim to their resentment. For these reasons he practised the most profound secrecy in the execution of his design. Admiral Gantheaume whom he instructed to prepare the frigates which were to convey him to France, was not informed of their destination; nor was general Kleber, his successor in the command, apprised of the honor which awaited him. Generals Berthier, Lasnes, Murat, Andreossi, Marmont, and Bessieres, with Berthier, Monget, and Arnaud, three men of science, all of whom were to accompany him to

France, came to the place of embarkation on the 22nd of August, in conformity with a letter addressed to them: but even then, Berthier alone was made acquainted with his intention. In conformity with his orders Kleber opened a letter, which the general left for him, twenty-four hours after he had sailed, expressing the regret with which he abandoned the army, and the expedience of returning to France, and appointing Kleber to succeed him as commander-in-chief. He fortunately escaped the hostile fleets which were cruising in the Mediterranean, and, having touched at his native town Ajaccio in Corsica, proceeded on his voyage, and on the 7th of October landed at the port of Frejus. A prodigious concourse of people attended his journey to the capital, he was perpetually hailed with joyful acclamations, and the cities and towns through which he passed vied with each other in the extravagance of their homage and adulation. But all these demonstrations of attachment were exceeded by the plaudits and caresses of the Parisians, when he made his appearance at the theatre. The simplicity of his dress, so decorous in those who derive distinction from their atchievements, gave additional effect, to the studied courtesy, and artful condescension which he displayed to all classes, and particularly to the soldiers who had shared his triumphs in former campaigns. A few days after his arrival a festival was celebrated in his honour, strikingly characteristic of the French people and of the object of their adoration. That he might not be disappointed in his views by that envy which an excess of good fortune is apt to excite, he requested that Moreau might be joined with himself in the honors intended by the celebration and treated that general with the respect and, affability due to his merit. The church of St. Sulpice was formed into the temple of victory: the walls were decorated with the utmost magnificence and with the richest tapestry; and the standards captured from the enemies of France were exhibited as trophies to the generals by whose valour and conduct they had been won. Buonaparte courteous, unassuming, and simple in his address and manners, lulled by the frankness and modesty of his demeanor, the suspicions of his enemies, and secured the affection of a people whom he probably despised, and over whom he had secretly resolved to usurp the sovereign dominion.

HISTORY OF THE WAR.

CHAP. XXIII.

Policy of Tippoo Sultan—His Intrigues with the French—Arrival of Lord Morning-ton at Calcutta—His Negotiations with the Sultan—Commencement of Hostilities—Biographical Sketches of General Harris, and the DUKE OF WELLINGTON, then Colonel Wellesley—Siege of Seringapatam—Capture of the Place, and its Results—Death of Tippoo—Division of his Dominions.

THE last war between the East India Company and Tippoo Saib, was terminated in 1792, by a pacification, which deprived the sultan of one-half of his dominions, and exhausted his finances by the exaction of an enormous tribute. Conditions so humiliating planted in his breast the seeds of resentment and revenge, and he continued to keep a watchful eye on every circumstance in the politics of Europe and Asia that might be improved into the means of destroying the ascendency of the English in India. Of his determination to recover his hereditary possessions, and to inflict the most signal vengeance on his enemies, his posthumous journal presents a singular example. "The means" (he observes) "which I have taken to keep in remembrance the misfortunes I experienced six years ago, from the malice of my enemies, are, to discontinue sleeping in a cottou bed, and to make use of a cloth one ; when I am victorious, I shall resume the bed of cotton." The first indications of his ambitious and revengeful designs, were exhibited in his intrigues with Madajee Scindia, and afterwards with his successor Dowlet Ron Scindia, a powerful Mahratta chief at the court of Poonah, for the purpose of undermining the authority of the Paishwa, Ron Pundit Purdham, under whose administration the treaty of alliance had been formed

with the English company. The dissensions of the court of Hyderabad, where the aged Nizam was sinking to the grave, were equally favorable to the intrigues of his emissaries. Agreeably with the general practise of the Indian princes at this period, a corps of 14,000 men had been formed and disciplined according to the European manner, under the direction of Monsieur Raymond, a French officer ; and, influenced by the party, by whose advice this measure had been adopted, the Nizam dismissed a British detachment, which had served him as a body-guard since the conclusion of the late war. The purpose of that prince's evil counsellors was evinced by an event which immediately ensued. Before the troops had reached the company's territories, he was obliged to solicit their return, to subdue a rebellion raised by Ali Jah, one of his sons. The intrigues at Poonah and Hyderabad, may be considered as accessaries only to the general system of policy pursued by Tippoo. He determined not only to overthrow the British power, but to accomplish an entire revolution in all the governments of India : a design in which he was encouraged and assisted by Zemaun Shah, a descendant from Ahmed Kaun Abdalla, an Asghan chief, who followed, in 1739, the standard of Nadir Shah, and who possessed dominions so extensive and populous, that his forces amounted to 150,000, chiefly cavalry. While he was endeavoring to impress lord Mornington, now governor of Madras, with his intention to adhere firmly to the treaty of Seringapatam, Tippoo's ambassadors were negotiating with the utmost privacy at Kabul, the residence of Zemaun Shah, to stimulate the Asghan chief to the invasion of Hindostan, and the prosecution of his various projects of ambition. The Mysorean ambassador was commissioned to propose for his selection several plans, and obtain a written engagement for the execution of that which should receive his approbation. In the mean time he transmitted letters to general Malartic, governor of the French islands, and to general Mengalon, imploring their assistance, professing the utmost reverence for the "sublimity of the French constitution;" and descanting at considerable length on the affairs of India. With the purpose of diffusing the principles of equality, and of complimenting the republicans, he established a Jacobin club at Seringapatam, and sacrificed his evident interests, as an absolute monarch, to his ruling passion, hatred of the English. General Malartic immediately complied with the wishes of the sultan, and injudiciously disclosed in a proclamation to his troops, and to the inhabitants of the isles, the plans, the views, and the sentiments, of his august correspondent. The affairs of the English were in this critical situation when lord Mornington, afterwards created marquis of Wellesley, arrived at Calcutta, (May 18th, 1798,) to take upon him the chief government: a nobleman, whose experience in all the civil and political departments of public business, qualified him for a station which had been so ably filled by lord Cornwallis.

The proclamation of Malartic, and the movements of Zemaun Shah, were in themselves sufficient to awaken the alarm, and demand the vigilant attention of the governor; and his embarrassment was redoubled by the intelligence that a formidable fleet was preparing at Toulon, of which the probable destination was to the countries of the East; and his distress

was heightened by intelligence from Madras, that the dispersion of the forces on that establishment was so great, that it would require several months to assemble and equip them.

Debarred from the execution of those prompt and decisive measures which often determine the fate of military enterprises, he endeavored to embarrass the measures of his enemies, and, if possible, to deprive them of a part of the resources on which they relied. He knew that they depended on effecting a revolution in the Nizam's council's, and making that state subservient to their views, with the concurrence of the body of troops commanded by Monsieur Perou. While the Madras government, therefore, was expediting his orders for assembling an army at Vellore, he dispatched 4000 men to Hyderabad, which executed his orders with so much address, that the French corps was completely surrounded and disarmed without bloodshed or tumult, and its place supplied by 6000 British troops. Thus auspiciously were our movements on the scene of action commenced, with an exploit that deprived Tippoo of a body of forces from which he expected to derive essential service in his meditated invasion of the Carnatic. That he might avert, however, the evils of war, if it could be done consistently with the company's safety and the dignity of the crown, lord Mornington proposed by letter to the sultan, to send an ambassador to Seringapatam, to attempt the restoration of mutual amity; intimating, at the same time, that he had received intelligence of the sultan's hostile correspondence with France. To this communication, Tippoo, after a long delay, returned an evasive answer, indirectly declining a compliance with the governor's proposals, and evidently intended to protract the correspondence till he should strike some decisive blow in conjunction with his confederates.

The sultan's intentions were notorious, but that he might afford him every opportunity of amicable accommodation, consistent with his plan for the ensuing campaign, lord Mornington soon after his arrival at Madras on the last day of December, 1798, dispatched another letter, in which he indirectly charged him with the basest perfidy by contrasting his professions of satisfaction at the naval victory of the Nile, with his secret intrigues against the power and interest of England. About five weeks after the transmission of this letter, Tippoo returned an answer, in which after a bombastic exordium he observed with an air of indifference, that " being frequently accustomed to hunt and make excursions, he was proceeding on a hunting excursion," and he added " you will be pleased to dispatch major Doveton, about whose coming your friendly pen has repeatedly written, slightly attended," an expression by which he meant to insinuate that he expected him to arrive at the head of an hostile army. The governor-general having thus thrown upon his adversary the blame of aggression with the accumulated guilt of the grossest perfidy, settled his plan of operations with his allies, and prepared for the vigorous prosecution of warlike councils, as the only means to avert the impending storm. The troops on the Madras establishment assembled at 1799. Vellore, were reinforced with 4000 men from Bengal, with the 6000 subsidiary troops which were with the Nizam, and with 6000 of that prince's best cavalry and as many sepoys. The command of these forces which formed collectively the finest army that had ever been seen in India, attended by an excellent train of artillery and well provided with all kinds of military stores, was vested in general Harris, an officer of distinguished merit. He was the son of a respectable clergyman of the established church, who dying in early life left a family of two sons and three daughters, in that kind of moderate circumstances which would naturally result from a small living, and the necessary expenses of decently educating a large family.

A friend of Mr. Harris took the youth under his patronage, and educated him for the army, into which he entered at the commencement of the American war, and upon all occasions was distinguished as a brave and intelligent officer. During the greater part of the war he acted under the immediate command of lord Rawdon (now earl Moira,) and performed the various services committed to his care, more especially in the adjutant-general's department, in a manner, which obtained the repeated approbation of that gallant and amiable nobleman. Having returned from the American continent towards the close of the war, with the rank of major, he soon after went on service to the West Indies, where he acquired additional rank and an increase of honour. He afterwards accompanied general sir William Meadows to England, having then arrived at the rank of colonel, and recommended himself so strongly to the marquis of Cornwallis by his active and spirited behaviour, and by the extent and correctness of his military attainments, that his lordship left him in India with the rank of lieutenant-general, and of commander-in-chief of the British army. His conduct in the present important enterprise and on many subsequent occasions, proved in every respect a full justification of the hopes and the predictions of his friends.

In order to give the Nizam's force the utmost respectability the commander-in-chief not only strengthened it with some of the company's battalions, but appointed the 33rd regiment to join it, giving the general command of the British forces thus serving,. to colonel Arthur Wellesley, an officer who even at this early period of his military career displayed a promptitude of expedient, a union of bravery with prudence, and a masculine energy of understanding which commanded the admiration of his superiors, and the enthusiastic devotion of his troops. This eminent soldier and statesman, is descended from the respectable and antient Irish family of Colley, of whom Richard Colley was the first who adopted the name of Wellesley or Wesley, in 1728, as heir to his first cousin Garret Wesley of Dangan, who left him all his estates, on condition of his taking the name and arms of that family. He held several offices under

London Pub.d by J Kinnersley Jan.y 1.1816

HIS GRACE the DUKE of WELLINGTON.

the crown; was auditor and registrer of the royal hospital of Kilmainham second chamberlain of the court of exchequer, sheriff of the county of Meath in 1734, and member of parliament for the borough of Trim. He married Elizabeth daughter of John Sale, LL. D. registrer of the diocese of Dublin, and representative in parliament for the borough of Carysfort. His eldest son Garret having succeeded him in his barony was in 1760 created viscount Wellesley and earl of Mornington, having before that event held the office of custos rotulorum, of the county of Meath. He married Anne, eldest daughter of the right honourable Arthur Hill, viscount Dungannon, and had issue the present marquis of Wellesley, William, now William Wellesley Pole, in consequence of inheriting the estates of William Pole of Ballifin, Esq. Arthur, the subject of the present narrative, and several other children. Arthur was born on the 1st of May, 1769. At an early age he was sent to Eton that he might receive the benefit of a public education, and as he had chosen the army for his profession, he afterwards went at the close of the American war to Angiers in France, in order that he might acquire the first principles of military science under the celebrated *Pignerol*, who had long been considered as the Vauban of modern fortification and engineering. After acquiring a fund of useful information, he returned to his native country, and, at the early age of twenty-three, obtained the rank of captain in the 18th regiment of light dragoons, from which corps on the 30th of April 1793, he was appointed to the majority of the 33rd regiment, on the resignation of major Gore. In this junior rank he did not long remain, but availed himself of his seniority to purchase in succession from lieutenant-colonel Yorke, who resigned his commission in the regiment, and his appointment took place on the 30th of September, 1793.

Lieutenant-colonel Wellesley, now scarcely four and twenty, engaged in active service under his gallant countryman the earl of Moira, and early in 1794, embark-

ed with that force which was intended to erect the standard of loyalty in Brittanny; but the fate of the Netherlands and of Flanders, was no sooner decided by the misfortunes of the campaign under the duke of York, than his lordship was ordered to proceed with his little army to Ostend, from whence after a precipitate re-embarkation, he hastened to join the army of general Clairfait. On the march and during the conflict in the vicinity of Alost, colonel Wellesley, commanded a covering party in the rear, and was highly instrumental in the repulse of the French army. On the 8th of July 1794, general Clairfait having retreated to Ghent, lord Moira effected a junction with the duke of York. The movements of the subsequent disastrous retreat to Bremen were covered by colonel Wellesley at the head of three battalions, and in the midst of the most serious and distressing obstacles he acted in a manner equally beneficial to the army and honourable to himself. On the arrival of the troops in England, every exertion was made to prepare them for foreign service, and the 33rd regiment being under orders for the West Indies, lieutenant-colonel Wellesley, embarked in the fleet which, under the command of admiral Christian, was intended to proceed to that station. But the heavy equinoctial gales in the autumn of 1795 having repeatedly driven them back, the destination of a great part of the forces was altered. The 33rd regiment was ordered to Ireland to recruit, and colonel Wellesley remained inactive till the nomination of his brother to the vice-royalty of India, and the commencement of the war with Tippoo, opened a new and splendid field for the exertion of his military talents.

Undaunted by the formidable demonstrations of the English government, and determined to retrieve his fortunes or to perish, Tippoo continued his negotiations with France; each power intending to make the other an instrument of its own political designs: the former aspiring to the destruction of the British ascendency, and the recovery of his dominions; the latter determined to supplant the English in their East India trade, and their territorial possessions. For the final adjustment of their treaty of alliance, Tippoo had dispatched general Dubuc, lately arrived from Mauritius, as his ambassador to the French executive directory, to solicit the support of 10,000 or 15,000 troops, and a large naval force, to drive the English out of Hindostan. To induce them to conclude an immediate alliance, he proposed that all the conquests which should be made from the enemy, excepting the provinces which had been ceded to the English, should be equally divided between the two nations, and according to their respective convenience. He had been gratified at the same moment by the reception of a friendly communication from the agents of France in the isles of India, and by a letter from the commander of the troops in Egypt, couched in the following terms :

" Buonaparte, to the most magnificent sultan, our greatest friend. You have learned my arrival on the shores of the Red sea with a numerous and invincible army, wishing to deliver you from the yoke of England. I take this opportunity to testify my desire for some news relating to your political situation by the way of Muscatti and the Morea. I wish you would send to Suez or to Cairo, an intelligent and confidential person with whom I might confer. The Most High increase your power, and destroy your enemies."

Confident, therefore, in the active friendship of the French directory, and the ultimate arrival of Buonaparte on the plains of India, the sultan opened the campaign.

The progress of the English was encumbered by the ponderous baggage and numerous attendants attached to the Nizam force, the immense quantity of public stores and provisions, and the long train of ordnance, with 40,000 Benjarries, formed altogether such an host as not to admit of being covered by the effective force. Had Tippoo displayed his usual talent and discretion, he might, without hazarding an engagement, and by means of desultory

skirmishes, distant cannonades, and other hostile movements, have so effectually harassed the infantry and weakened the cavalry, that a great part of the baggage, stores, and ammunition, would have fallen into his hands.

The march commenced at day-break, on the 10th of March. The cavalry were in advance, the baggage on the right, and the detachment under colonel Wellesley, which had marched by the left, moved parallel at some distance on the right flank of the army. Even on the first day's advance, the enemy began to annoy them. Parties of Tippoo's horse were detached in all directions, and were not only active in burning the forage and destroying the villages, but had even the audacity to attack colonel Wellesley's rear-guard, consisting of a company of sepoys. Of these, 20 were killed upon the spot, and lieutenant Reynolds and 36, wounded. The enemy, however, was immediately repulsed.

1799.

While the commander-in-chief was moving with the grand army from the east, by the rout of Talgautporam and Cankanelli, general Stuart had advanced to the opening of the Poodicherrum Ghaut, in the range of mountains which surround the Mysore country. These mountains rise to a surprising height, and oppose to the eastern borders of the Carnatic a mural front of *ghauts* or *passes*. From the word ghaut, the whole chain derives its name : they give an entrance into the lofty, fertile, and populous plains of boundless view, which they support, as buttresses do a magnificent and extensive terrace. The Mysore country being at least 2000 feet higher than the level of the Carnatic, is thence called the Table-land, and the ascent is not to be accomplished by a single traveller without the fatiguing labor of many hours. The path-ways up the Ghauts are worked by the hand of man, along the deep-worn channel of some rapid torrent, or skirting the hollow ravines and winding excavations which have formed themselves on the face of this mountain, into precipices. In many of these passes the obstructions of art, in conjunction with those of nature, are opposed to the progress of an invading army. General Stuart, surrounded by these difficulties, had taken a position in the territories of the Coorga Rajah, a friendly power. His army was posted in brigades, on account of the nature of the country, which precluded the possibility of a more compact encampment, when the advanced division, under Montressor, was suddenly attacked by Tippoo, with a strong body of cavalry, in flank and rear. The brigade did not exceed 1400 men, and it was separated from the other divisions by extensive jungles or thickets ; but it maintained its ground with impenetrable firmness against the superior numbers of the enemy, who surrounded them, till general Stuart brought them relief. The Mysoreans were defeated after a severe conflict, and driven from the field with great slaughter; and Tippoo, after halting a few days near Periapatam, retired to the defence of his capital. General Harris, in the mean time, was slowly moving in the direction of Seringapatam. On the 19th, after a fatiguing march through a country full of jungles and defiles, intelligence was received, that the army of Tippoo had advanced to Allagoor, a village adjacent to Sultanpettah ; and, on the 10th of March, the left wing and the cavalry having encamped close to a pass about seven miles from Cankanelli, the right advanced to Arravelly, and colonel Wellesley's division took up its ground at some distance in the rear.

On the 23rd, after securing several posts and passes of importance, the right wing of the cavalry marched from Achil, and encamped at Sultanpettah, the left wing and the battering train advancing to Achil, while colonel Wellesley, with his detachment, marched from Cankanelli, and encamped in front of the army, at Allagoor, from which place Tippoo's forces had retired. Early on the morning of the day, as the colonel and his advanced corps approached Sultanpettah, a cloud of dust to the westward, denoted that the army of Tippoo was in motion, and it afterwards appeared that it had just quitted its

position on the western bank of the Maddoor river, and encamped at Mallavelly. Pursuing their march, the right wing, the cavalry, and the detachment under colonel Wellesley, halted on the 25th of March, and were joined by the left wing and the battering train. On the 26th, the whole moved forward in compact order, and encamped five miles to the east of Mallavelly. It was the intention of Tippoo to attack the English as soon as they emerged from the jungles, and the openness of the ground now occupied, favored his intentions. On the morning of the 26th, the enemy's advanced parties, among which were some elephants, were seen from a distant ridge. After reconnoitring the British encampment for a considerable time, they retired, and in the evening 14 or 15 guns were seen in motion. On the 27th, therefore, at day-break, colonel Wellesley's division was ordered to move parallel to the left, but at some distance, so as to cover the baggage and be in readiness to act as circumstances should require : while the main body of the army marched from its left flank, on the great road leading to Mallavelly. Major-general Floyd commanded the whole advance, having under him all the picquets and five regiments of cavalry. He approached within a mile of Mallavelly, but was there obliged to halt, in consequence of discovering on the right flank a numerous body of the enemy's cavalry, while their infantry remained on the heights beyond the town.

Convinced that this was the grand army of Tippoo, and observing several guns moving on the right of the enemy's line, towards a ridge which enfiladed the low ground on the eastern flank of the village, he determined to make an instant attack, and directed colonel Wellesley with his division, to proceed against the sultan's right flank. The picquets under colonel Sherbrooke, supported by the right wing of the main body under major-general Brydges, were to penetrate through the village of Mallavelly, to the centre of the enemy's line. Major-general Popham, with the left wing and the rear-guard, was to remain near the fort of Mallavelly, for the protection of the battering train and the baggage : the five regiments of cavalry being formed on the left of the road, with orders to support colonel Wellesley's attack.

The colonel no sooner put his force in motion, and his manœuvre was perceived by the sultan, than the guns were drawn off to a ridge beyond that which they first occupied. General Harris regarding this movement as an indication of the enemy's unwillingness to advance, gave orders to mark out the ground for a new encampment. His orders however had scarcely been obeyed, when twelve or fourteen guns were opened from different parts of the enemy's line, at a distance of 2000 yards, Even at this distance their fire was severely felt, and the discharge of a species of rocket peculiar to Hindostan, was singularly annoying to the troops. This weapon combines the missile power of a javelin with the impulse of gun-powder. From the force and irregularity of their motion these flying plagues are difficult to avoid, and often make considerable havoc. The rocket consists of a tube of iron about eight inches long, and an inch and a half in diameter closed at one end. It is filled in the same manner as an ordinary sky rocket, and fixed to a piece of stout bamboo from three to five feet long, the head of which is armed with a heavy iron spike. At that extremity of the tube which points to the shaft of the weapon, is the match, and the man who uses it placing the butt end of the bamboo upon his foot, points the spiked end in the direction of the object to which he means to throw it, and setting fire to the fusee, pitches it from him. It flies forth with great velocity, and on striking the ground by a bounding horizontal motion, acts with an almost certain effect in fracturing and breaking the legs of the enemy. To disperse the cavalry and more particularly the rocket men, colonel Sherbrooke hastened immediately to a village in front of the left of the hostile army, where he was dreadfully harassed by the enemy's cannonade, though he succeeded in his object. At this juncture colonel Welles-

ley supported by major-general Floyd with the three remaining regiments of cavalry advanced in battalions, and the whole line moving slowly and steadily, time was given for every part to act together, the enemy's cannonade being answered by as many field-pieces as could be brought up, the action thus becoming general along the whole front. At this moment a desperate - attempt was made on the part of Tippoo, by moving forward a column of 2000 men in excellent order towards the 33rd regiment, but this gallant corps reserving its fire with the utmost steadiness received that of the enemy at the distance of 60 yards, and continuing to advance, the column gave way and was thrown into disorder. At this critical moment general Floyd making a rapid charge completed the rout with great slaughter. The enemy's first line with the whole of its guns, was now forced by the advance of the British line to retire to the next height, where their second line was formed. They were at this time almost beyond the reach of our guns, and the cannonade which had lasted three hours having ceased on both sides, on account of the distance, the enemy retreated. The loss of the English and their allies consisted only of 10 killed, and 50 wounded chiefly by the rockets. That of the enemy amounted to 1000 men.

On the 1st of April, 1799, the whole army arrived within 13 miles of Seringapatam, and on the 5th of that month took up its ground opposite the west face of the capital of Mysore, at the distance of 3500 yards, the left being stationed towards the river Cauvery while the division of colonel Wellesley was placed on the right. The preparatory movements were all equally successful. While the commander-in-chief was on his march colonels Read and Brown were employed in reducing the forts in the Baramaul country, and collecting provisions for the grand army. And when general Harris had reached his destined point colonel Floyd with his cavalry marched to meet the Bombay army, and escorted it safe to Seringapatam, Cummer el Dieu who was sent against the latter force, not daring to give them battle, when united.

The sultan who reflected on the event of the last siege, desirous to protract his enemy's operations, and trusting that the want of provisions might compel the confederates to retire, or that the elements might come to his aid at the approaching monsoon, now endeavoured to retard the besiegers' operations, by opening a correspondence with the general. In a short letter to the commander-in-chief he declared that he adhered to treaties, and demanded the meaning of the approach of the English army, and of the prosecution of hostilities. To this remonstrance the general replied by referring him to lord Mornington's letters.

Not a moment was lost by the confederate general. In front of the British camp were several ruined villages, and rocky eminences, besides an aqueduct which, passing from the left of the camp, takes an easterly direction till it approaches within 1700 yards of the fort, where it winds off to the right among an extensive grove of cocoa-trees, called the Sultanpettah Tope. These positions afforded a cover for the enemy's infantry and rocket men so near to the camp that many of the rockets fell into the tents. In order to dislodge them from these positions colonel Wellesley received orders, on the evening of the 5th of April, to have the 33rd regiment and the 2nd Bengal regiment in readiness at sun-set, while general Shaw with the 12th, and two battalions of sepoys with their guns received similar orders, the former being destined to scale the Sultanpettah Tope, while the latter was to attack the posts at the aqueduct.

It was a little after sun-set before these battalions advanced, though the obscurity of the night proved unfavourable to their operations. Colonel Wellesley immediately on entering the Tope, was assailed on every side by a hot fire of musketry and rockets, a circumstance which, added to the darkness of the night, the uncertainty of the enemy's force and position, and the badness of the ground obliged him to confine his operations to the mere object of making a diversion, and to postpone the attack of the post till a future opportunity. General Shaw was enabled to seize on a ruined village within 40 yards of the aqueduct, and to secure his troops from the musketry of the enemy. On the next day the attack on the Sultanpettah Tope was again attempted, by colonel Wellesley. General Shaw was instructed at the same time to advance from the ruined village which he occupied, and to dislodge the party posted in the aqueduct, while colonel Wallace was ordered to attack a village on the enemy's right flank, with the grenadiers of the 74th, and two companies of sepoys. At nine o'clock in the morning of the 7th, colonel Wellesley advanced to the attack of the Tope, with the Scotch brigade, two battalions of sepoys, and four guns. The enemy commenced a galling fire under cover of the bank of the aqueduct, which was returned by discharges from the English field-pieces, and the whole corps rushed forwards with enthusiastic gallantry. The colonel having judiciously detached parties, to take the post in flank, the enemy were thrown into confusion, and precipitately fled. At this moment colonel Wallace, took possession of the village on the right flank which commanded a considerable part of the aqueduct, and general Shaw having quitted the ruined village, rushed upon the enemy and drove them from that part of the aqueduct from which he had been annoyed during the preceding conflict. The whole of the advanced line of posts was immediately occupied by our troops, who thus rapidly and brilliantly secured a strong connected line of posts, extending from the river to the Tope, a distance of about two miles, and forming by means of the aqueduct a complete line of contravallation, at a proper distance from the camp and from the line of attack.

The bravery and fortitude of the confederate troops during these preparatory operations, were not less worthy of admiration than the patience with which they endured the hazard and distresses of the siege. The climate of India and the nature of the country, render the most casual move-ments of the troops, dangerous, fatiguing, and destructive. If any European recruits happen to do duty in the line, the march scarcely commences before they are fatigued and overcome by the intolerable heat. They soon exhaust all their allowance of Arrack, which is too frequently replenished by stagnant water, sometimes so muddy, rotten, and green, that it cannot possibly be drunk without adding at least one-half of spirits, and then sucking or strain-ing the mixture through a handker-chief. The veteran Europeans, after a little while, begin to flag upon the march, being miserably scorched by the acute rays of the sun, which first dart upon the sand, and then revert with accumulated heat upon their faces. Each soldier carries a small branch in his hand, to fan off the miriads of flies, by which he is constantly tormented; yet all his exertions yield him but little relief, for the battalion is so much covered with these insects, par-ticularly if the weather be sultry and dry, that at the distance of 200 yards, a spec-tator would suppose that they were ac-tually clothed in black. It is distressing to witness the severe struggles which the sufferers often have, with the oppression of the weather, and the numerous diseases to which they are hourly subject. Some, from a redundancy of bile, drop down in a state of insensibility, and are seized with violent *cholera morbus*; others fall down suddenly in contortions, with the cramp, which runs acutely through every limb, centres in the stomach, and kills the per-son afflicted upon the spot. But the coup de soleil, is, of all others, the most fatal attack. It first affects the crown of the head; the victim complains that his brain begins to boil, a convulsive fit is the imme-diate consequence, of which he dies in a very few minutes; and the body becomes completely putrid before a hole can be dug into which it may be thrown.

Many of these dreadful inflictions ac-companied the army from the field to the camp; and, as the besiegers were making their approaches, they were incessantly galled by the discharge of musketry and rockets from the numerous works thrown up for the defence of the city. Their ranks were also thinned by the fire from the artillery of the fortress. To the dangers of open hostility, were superadded the privation of wholesome water, that of the tanks and reservoirs being poisoned by the flying detachment of Tippoo. But thirst, fatigue, and all the painful incidents of war, were patiently endured, and inces-sant labor in the trenches borne with cheer-fulness.

The siege proceeded with great gallantry and perseverance on both sides until the 26th, when the enemy, still retaining pos-session of parts of an entrenchment at the distance of 240 yards from the approaches, it was found necessary, in order to facilitate the future operations of the siege, that they should be dislodged. The direction of the attack was given to colonel Wellesley, who on that day commanded in the trenches. He stormed the entrenchment with great spirit, and, succeeding in es-tablishing his posts, which were imme-diately secured as effectually as possible from the annoyance of the enemy's fire.

The siege had been carried on eleven days, the enemy were dislodged from all their advanced posts, and the allies had erected their first breaching batteries, when Tippoo made overtures for a treaty. In reply to these, general Harris sent him the preliminaries of peace, of which the conditions were, that he should cede half his territories in perpetuity to the allies, that he should pay two crore of rupees to indemnify the English for the expenses of the war, and should renounce the alliance of France for ever. Perilous as the sultan's situation might be regarded, he was de-termined to continue his defence, depending on the strength of his fortress and the bravery of his troops, rather than accede to terms of peace so ruinous and disgraceful, and a dread of scarcity stimulating the besiegers, their operations were pressed with increasing ardor. The breaching batteries having been erected, the roar of artillery on both sides was tremendous, and the situation of the sultan became every day more critical. On the 20th day of the siege, he made his last effort to avert his total ruin by negotiation, and in reply was referred to the propositions before sent him, with a small variation in the number of the hostages required by the allies.

When it was seen that even despair did not induce him to yield, the batteries were opened on the last day of April. In three days a practicable breach was made, and about half past one in the afternoon of the 4th of May, general Baird, having completed his arrangements, stept out of the trench, drew his sword, and in the most animating and heroic manner, said to his men, "Come, my brave fellows, follow me! and prove yourselves worthy the name of British soldiers." Both columns instantly rushed from the trenches, and entered the bed of the river under cover of the fire of the batteries, but, being immediately discovered by the enemy, were assailed by rockets and musketry. In six minutes, the forlorn hope, closely followed by the rest of the troops, had reached the summit of the breach, led by serjeant Graham of the light company of the Bombay European regiment. He ran forward to the summit of the breach, mounting it, pulled off his hat, and, with three cheers, called out, "Success to lieutenant Graham," (alluding to the reward of a commission if he survived,) on which he rejoined his party, and remounted along with them, the colours in his hand. On reaching the rampart, he struck the colour staff in it, exclaiming, "I'll shew them the British flag!" and was at that moment shot through the head.

Lieutenant-colonel Dunlop, who greatly distinguished himself, received his wound from one of Tippoo's sirdars, who assailed him with his scymeter, about half way up the breach, making a desperate cut at the colonel, which the latter was so fortunate as to parry, and instantly returned by a stroke that laid his adversary's breast open. The sirdar, though mortally wounded, made another blow at colonel Dunlop, which struck him across the wrist of the right hand, and nearly cut it through. The sirdar instantly reeled back, and fell

on the level of the breach, where he was pierced by the bayonet as the soldiers passed. Colonel Dunlop continued to advance at the head of his men until he ascended to the top of the breach, where he fell from the loss of blood, and was conveyed to the rear by his soldiers. The passage of the counterscarp presented a gratifying and animating sight to the rest of the army, whose anxiety was immediately relieved, for, until our troops had crossed the ditch, though every precaution was taken for filling it, if necessary, even the most sanguine minds could not be utterly devoid of doubt. In a few minutes more, the breach, 100 feet wide, was crowded with men, who, having collected in sufficient force to enter upon the rampart, filed off to the right and left, according to general Baird's instructions.

The conduct of Tippoo, was, on this occasion, highly creditable to his personal character. According to his usual custom, he went out early in the morning, to one of the cavaliers of the outer rampart, whence he could observe the operations on both sides. He remained there until noon, when he took his usual repast. At this time he seems to have been unconscious of the approaching attack, though his lines were crowded with Europeans, and merely sent orders to Meer Goffer, a favorite officer, to keep a strict guard. He was informed a few minutes afterwards, that Meer Goffer was killed by a cannon-shot. "Well," said he, "Meer Goffer was never afraid of death." Yet he was evidently agitated, ordered the troops nearest his person to resume their arms, and desired his servants to load his carbines. Hastening along the rampart towards the breach, he met a number of his troops flying before the van of his assailants. He exerted himself to rally the fugitives, encouraging them by his voice and his example. He repeatedly fired on our troops himself, and brought down several Europeans who were mounting the breach.

At this critical moment the front of the European flank companies approached the spot where he stood. He now found himself almost deserted, and retired to the traverses of the northern ramparts. These he defended one after the other with the bravest of his officers and men, and, several times assisted by the enfilading fire from the inner walls, obliged the English troops to halt in their advance, until the 12th regiment, crossing the inner ditch, took him in flank. Yet even then, while any of his troops remained with him, he disputed every inch of ground, until he approached the passage across the ditch to the gate of the inner fort. Here he complained of pain and weakness in one of his legs, in which he had been severely wounded at an early period of life, and mounted his horse: but, seeing the Europeans still advancing on both the ramparts, hastened to the gate, followed by his palanquin, and by a number of officers, troops, and servants. As he was crossing to the gate, he received a musket-ball on his right side, nearly as high as his breast; but he continued to press forward, until he was stopped about half way through the arch of the gate-way, by the fire of the 12th light infantry, from within, when he received a second ball, close to the other. His horse being wounded, sunk under him, and his turban fell to the ground. Many of his people fell at the same time, by musketry, within and without the gate. The fallen sultan was immediately raised by some of his adherents, and placed on his palanquin, under the arch and on one side of the gate-way, where he lay or sat some minutes, faint and exhausted, till the entrance of many Europeans. One of the soldiers seized his sword-belt, which was very rich, and attempted to pull it off: the sultan, who still held his sword in his hand, made a cut at the soldier with all his remaining strength, and wounded him about the knee; on which he put his piece to his shoulder, and shot the sultan through the temple, when he instantly expired. Three hundred men were killed under the gate-way, and considerable numbers wounded, so that it soon became impaseable, except over the bodies of the dead and dying. Search was made in the evening for the body of Tippoo, which

was at last found under a heap of the slaughtered, and retaining in his countenance an expression of stern composure. He had been stript of his turban, which was adorned with a jewel of great value, his rich pearl rosary, his ruby ring, and all his apparel. Being recognised by his people, he was delivered to the survivors, and interred in the mausoleum of his father. In the mean time the troops spread themselves into the town. The houses of the chief sirdars, as well as of the merchants and shroffs, were completely pillaged; while the affrighted females hastened to purchase an uncertain protection, by emptying their coffers, and bringing forth whatever jewels they possessed. The city was exposed during the night to the brutal licentiousness of the soldiery, amounting to nearly 40,000 men, and composed of so many nations. Female innocence became the prey of the midnight ravisher; and the acquisition of a princely fortune was the labour of a moment.

By the precautions of the general, the palace was saved, and all its contents reserved as captured property for the army at large. The sultan had appropriated for the reception of the wealth of the reigning dynasty of Mysore, several extensive buildings, consisting of a succession of quadrangles with ranges of storehouses, of which the galleries were filled with articles least susceptible of injury. The jewelry set in gold in the form of bracelets, rings, necklaces, aigrettes, plumes, and other decorations, and all the royal gems, were deposited in coffers, and kept in large dark rooms, properly secured. A vast apartment contained the silver plate of all ashions and dimensions, several massive pieces, richly inlaid with gold, and two elephant mangers of silver. Extensive warehouses were filled with the richest furniture, the most costly carpets, telescopes of every size, and beautiful porcelain. The collection of military stores was immense, and the quantity of grain deposited in the magazines surpassed credibility. Among the most valuable curiosities of the place, was the library of Tippoo, consisting of many thousand volumes contained in chests, each with a separate wrapper and in excellent condition. Great numbers of these volumes were richly adorned and beautifully illuminated in the style of the Roman missals. This most valuable portion of the sultan's treasures was afterwards presented by the army to the court of directors, and now enriches the oriental repository in Leadenhall street.

Tippoo Sultan, at the time of his death, was about fifty-two years of age. His constitution was much impaired, and a complication of disorders rendered necessary a constant course of medicine. In person he was between five feet eight and five feet nine inches high, and rather inclined to corpulence, though formerly very thin: his face was round, with large full eyes; and there were much animation and intelligence in his countenance. He wore whiskers, but no beard. He had eleven children; but only two of these, a boy and a girl, were born in marriage. His disposition was naturally cruel, his temper passionate and revengeful, and he was prone to abuse, when dissimulation was not required, to the execution of his purposes. He professed himself to be a Naib, or forerunner to one of the twelve prophets, who, the Mahometans believe, are yet to come; and under this pretence he persecuted all other casts, compelling great numbers to become Mussulmans. In the war of 1790, in particular, when he had ravaged the country of the Nairs, on the Malabar coast, it was computed that about 20,000 persons had suffered by his persecutions, in the short space of four months. The men who refused to submit to circumcision, were hanged on the trees surrounding the villages; and the women of the cast, the noblest in India, on refusing to adopt the Mahometan custom of covering their bosoms, which they considered as a mark of degradation and slavery, had their breasts cut off, and suffered many other insults and indignities.

Shortly after his expedition to Malabar, he had nearly lost his life in an attack on

the lines of Travancore, where he was forced to leave his palanquin behind him, together with his pistols, and a signet or seal ring, so very small, that the finger on which it was worn, must have been delicate in the extreme. His wealth, after the conclusion of his first war with England, was very great, and his total revenue enormous: but his financial talents were inconsiderable; and he was not less frequently meanly avaricious than ostentatiously extravagant. During the last seven years of his life, his conduct had been a tissue of folly, caprice, and weakness. All his actions seemed to proceed from the impulse of the moment, and it is impossible to trace any one fixed principle by which his conduct was directed. It is difficult to suppose that he wished to introduce the principle of equality among his subjects; yet he disgusted every man of rank, and his father's servants, by an indiscriminate and capricious mixture of men of the lowest origin with those of family and of long services. Upon the whole, he was more remarkable for ferocity of temper, than comprehension of mind. Selfish, cunning, and rapacious, he acted on narrow principles, and was deficient in that vigor of intellect, and that expansion of view, which are essential ingredients in the composition of all true greatness; though it must be confessed that he possessed a considerable degree of prudence, and was not deficient in promptitude or judgment.

The obstinacy of his defence, and his refusal to escape when flight was in his power, must be chiefly attributed to his confidence in the strength of his capital. To any other officers indeed than those who commanded on this occasion, the difficulties opposed to a regular siege would have proved insurmountable. The act of storming displayed a most animating and unrivalled picture of British gallantry, for we have seen that the columns of grenadiers, dashed across the river at noon day, despising the difficulties of the passage, to mount the breach, which could have been practicable alone to their irresistible force and bravery. The impetuous spirit which led them on in the face of a very heavy and continued fire, the rapidity with which they ascended the ladder, and the resistless courage with which they drove the affrighted enemy from the walls, combined to throw the works into their possession. The hour of attack was fortunate and judiciously chosen; it being one at noon when numbers of the besieged had retired to take refreshment.

Nor was the humanity of the besiegers less conspicuous than their bravery. The slaughter of the natives was immediately restrained, and the republican officers having shut themselves up with the defenders of the palace till the first burst of violence was past, partook of the mercy by which they were preserved.

By the death of the sultan and the reduction of his capital, the allies obtained possession of the whole Mysorean territory, the minor fortresses presenting little resistance to the forces sent against them, and the conquerors were enabled to devote their undivided attention to the disposition of Tippoo's sovereignty and dominions. Fortunately for the company and for the British government, the mode of settlement most conducive to their safety was sanctioned by equity. Hyder Alli, the father of Tippoo, had dispossessed the rightful rajah, Kistna Raije Warrier, in whose army he had served in the exercise of the sovereign power, but that his usurpation might not excite a revolt, he affected to govern with the concurrence of the monarch, who was in fact his state prisoner. On the death of Kistna in 1796, Tippoo laid aside the veil and openly assumed the sovereign power. The widow of the deposed prince was suffered to live in poverty with her son, the heir to the Mysorean kingdom. By a singular revolution of fortune this prince was now brought from obscurity to be placed on the throne of Mysore. The policy and justice of this proceeding were generally acknowledged. By elevating to the sovereignty the rightful heir, the company se-

cured an ally who was bound to them by all the ties of gratitude and interest, and the act was recommended to the neighbouring powers by the prospect which it presented of permanent tranquillity.

The surviving branches of Tippoo's family were removed to the fortress of Vellore, which was appropriated to their future residence, and garrisoned by an English detachment. The remains of Tippoo's army were immediately disbanded, and sent to their respective homes, and the territories of the late sultan were partitioned among the company, the Nizam and the rajah. To merit the friendship of the Mahrattahs, who had been prevented by their domestic broils from engaging in the war, a valuable share of territory was allotted to the Peishwa.

From the conclusion of the first war with Hyder Alli, the tranquillity of the company's possessions had been continually menaced by the chiefs of Mysore, even in the intervals of peace which succeeded the various contests with Hyder and Tippoo, and the baneful effects of the uncertainty and solicitude in which the company were involved had been felt by the natives themselves in the decline of agriculture, and the interruption of peaceful industry. To the other consequences of this state of affairs were added, a rebellious spirit in certain descriptions of the company's native subjects, a diminution of British influence and consideration at the native courts, the rising hopes of the turbulent and disaffected, the decline of public and private credit and the constant necessity of guarding against surprise from the sudden aggression of an enemy whom no pledge could bind, no clemency or moderation could conciliate. The conquest of Mysore repressed the designs of the factious and secured the undisputed ascendency of the British power, while the wisdom and moderation which characterised the restoration of the legitimate prince, contributed to the extension of our moral influence, over the people subservient to our sway. May the English government be always distinguished by the same moderation which directed the distribution of the conquered territories! and may the descendants of the native Indians have reason to congratulate their forefathers and themselves, on the ascendency of a state which, with the balance of power in one hand, holds the balance of justice in the other!

HISTORY OF THE WAR.

CHAP. XXIV.

TO the circumstance of the imperial troops which had quitted Switzerland, having been succeeded by an inferior number of Russians, was added the loss of unity of views, of action, and of authority. Nor was this the only unfavourable effect produced by the change. However great and well merited was the reputation of the Russian troops it was apprehended that they might not experience their usual success in a country of mountains, where the operations of warfare are of a nature uncongenial to the habits and military discipline of the Russians. The Austrian army on the contrary contained but few officers, or non-commissioned officers, who had not served in the Tyrol, Carinthia, or the Black Forest, and it possessed many corps consisting of mountaineers, Tyrolians, and Styrians, or of active and intelligent Walloons, and Hungarians. It was a still more important advantage that the Austrians were well acquainted with that part of Switzerland which they had conquered, and which for three months they had leisure and interest to study. They likewise spoke the language, and therefore possessed the advantage of familiar communication with the inhabitants. This inequality however was at first imperceptible, and the impressions of the French were the reverse of

the truth. The reputation of superiority which the Russians had acquired and maintained in Italy imposed on the republicans. They did not even attempt any enterprise of importance from the 29th of August, the day on which the Russians relieved the Austrian advanced posts before Zurich, till the 8th of September. On that day they renewed the attack which they had so often made on the post of Wallishoffen. It had the same issue as those which preceded it, and they returned to their position with some loss. Massena on this occasion repeated what Frederic had formerly said of the Russians, " You may kill them, but you cannot make them retreat or surrender."

Three days after this affair, which had no other object on the part of the French than to bring the Russians to the test, and to familiarize themselves with their manner of fighting, the right of the republican army had gained some ground, and obtained possession of the important post of Kerenz, the point of communication between the valleys of Maderan and the Rhine, a post which the Austrians retook in the following day. After the departure of the archduke Charles for Suabia, Massena had been superior to his enemy by 20,000 men. Notwithstanding the disorder produced by replacing the troops of that prince by those of general Korzakow, and the total ignorance of the Russians respecting the geography of the country, the republican general had continued in a state of inactivity as extraordinary as beneficial to the allies. After many ineffectual exhortations on the part of the directory to offensive measures, they determined to deprive Massena of the command, leaving it at the same time in his power to avoid this disgrace by an immediate and general attack: He determined, therefore, to gratify their wishes, and prepared to make it along his whole line.

The Russians meditated at the same moment a movement no less decisive. The views of the court of Vienna, the obstacles which the middle of the campaign had presented, and the motives which caused the archduke's departure from Switzerland had rendered it necessary to substitute for the original plan of turning Switzerland on the north and the south, an arrangement of less magnitude, which required a less considerable force, and was purely military. The object proposed was to recover immediate possession of the small cantons, and to turn the position so long held by Massena on the lakes of Lucerne and Zug, and on the Albis, which would have obliged him to retire on the Aar, without the possibility of preserving its whole line. General Korzakow was to attack the French on the chain of the Albis, while generals Hoche and Jellachich should endeavor to drive them from the cantons of Schweitz and Glarus, and from the Grey League, an attempt in which they would be powerfully assisted by general Suwarrow, who designed to force the St. Gothard, to descend the valley of the Reuss, to turn the lakes of Lucerne and Zug, and thus to take post on the flank of the enemy's centre and on the rear of its right, which would have been placed between two fires. The three allied corps were to unite in the canton of Lucerne, under the command of general Suwarrow, and thus to form an army of 60,000 men, with which he expected that

he should terminate the campaign in Switzerland as brilliantly and as usefully as he had begun it in Italy.

Massena was acquainted with these projects, and, having learned that generals Korzakow and Hotze had resolved to begin their execution on the 26th, he determined to anticipate their design. There remained to him no other means of success, and even the plan which he adopted ought rather to have failed than succeeded. In the night of the 24th, 50,000 French put themselves in motion on the line from the Linth to the Aar. At break of day, the division of general Soult, reinforced by part of Lecourbe's, assembled between the lakes of Wallenstadt and Zurich. It threw a bridge over the Linth near Wesen, a point protected by a single battalion of the regiment of Bender, which resolutely sustained the assault of five French battalions, and was cut to pieces. A Hungarian battalion, which came to its support, was not able to restore the engagement, and was obliged to retire towards Utznach. At the sound of musketry, general Hotze, along with his staff, hastened from his head-quarters at Kaltbrum. Too well informed of the localities of the country, not to conclude that this was a serious attack, he wished to reconnoitre closely, the force and the positions of the enemy. A party of French rangers made a discharge upon him and his suite, which struck him from his horse, and killed or wounded the greater part of the officers who surrounded him. This brave and able general fell into the hands of the enemy and died after languishing a few hours. His death, which would at any time have been a serious loss to the Austrian army, was at this time a misfortune to Europe. He alone could have repaired or prevented the subsequent disasters of the day. Deprived of their commander, the regiments which defended the right bank of the Linth, and covered the entrance of the valley of the Toss, bravely stood their ground, notwithstanding so discouraging an event, and for a long time maintained the action.

While these events were passing on the

left of the allies, the French had established
a bridge at the extremity of the lake of
Zurich, and advanced in force towards
Schmerickens, but were attacked by the
Russians who marched from Rapperschwell,
and repulsed as far as their bridge, which,
being broken down, all who remained on
the right bank were taken, killed, or
drowned. This circumstance might have
resolved affairs on the Linth, if general
Petrarch, to whom rank and seniority gave
the command on general Hotze's death,
had also stood firm on his side ; but,
fearing to be turned by his right, he precipitated his retreat by the Toggemburgh,
nor discontinued it till he reached the
Rhinthal, thus abandoning the whole of
eastern Switzerland, uncovering the left
flank of the Russians ; leaving without
remedy, any check which they might
experience, and rendering of no avail,
the success which might attend their re-
resistance.

At break of day Massena had marched
a division near to Bruck, which feigned on
that point a serious attack. While this
feint attracted the attention of the Russians,
another division threw a bridge over the
Limmat, near Dietikon, and two others
attacked Wallishoffen, as well as all
the other points which the enemy had in
front of Zurich, between that town and
the Albis. Here the Russians on their
guard, and in sufficient force, vigorously
repulsed the French, and pursued them
closely as far as the summit of the Albis.

In conformity with the general plan of
attack adopted by the allies, a corps of
5000 Russians was destined to act on the
right of general Hotze. Three Russian
battalions had been stationed for some
days at Rapperschwell for this purpose,
and five others were sent in the night of
the 25th, of which three were drawn from
the camp of Seebach, behind Zurich, and
two from before that town. The departure
of this strong detachment very much
weakened the defence of the right bank of
the Limmat, and there remained to defend
it only 12,000 men, from Zurich to the
Rhine. This number would have been
sufficient to punish the temerity of the

enemy had it been promptly and skilfully
employed. But general Durazzow, completely duped by the false attack which
the French had made on the side of Bruck,
instead of reconnoitring the actual situation
of the left, and closing up the centre, which
was really attacked, remained stationary
on his own ground. The enemy's column,
which had thrown a bridge over the river
at Dietikon, was enabled to complete it
without interruption, and to advance
rapidly on the right bank of the Limmat :
general Markoof, who commanded in that
position, being too weak to oppose the
movement, and receiving no reinforcement
from the left, in consequence of the departure of the five battalions, nor from the
right paralyzed as it was by the misconduct of general Durazzow. The latter
perceiving that he was separated from the
rest of the army by the division of general
Lorge, which had crossed the river instead
of marching against it, and thus placing
it between two fires, turned about and
directed his course towards the Rhine.

General Lorge who had been followed
across the Limmat by reinforcements,
and by Massena himself, experiencing little
opposition, left a part of his division to
observe general Durazzow, and marched
with the remainder to Zurich. He found
on his way no enemy to encounter, but a
division of cossacks, one battalion of the
regiment of Sacken, and four squadrons of
dragoons. Consulting only their bravery,
this handful of men attacked the French,
and twice succeeded in repulsing them ;
but, after keeping the enemy in check for
four hours, was obliged to fall back to
Zurich. About one o'clock, the French
were masters of part of the zurichberg,
and of the northern approaches to the town.
In order to extricate himself from the
critical situation in which general Korzakow was now placed, much greater presence of mind, boldness, and ability, was
requisite, than he displayed. He made
no prompt and vigorous dispositions, nor
did he attempt to take any advantage of
local circumstances to defend, with regularity, the heights commanding Zurich.
Having, however, been reinforced in the,

afternoon by a part of the five battalions which had been sent to Rapperschwell, and by a part of the other corps which defended the left bank of the Limmat, he made many unsuccessful attacks on the division of general Lorge. The French, scattered in the vineyards, poured upon the Russians a destructive fire ; and, whenever the latter rushed upon them with fixed bayonets, retired under the protection of their cannon, which, raking the Russians in front and rear, made great havoc in their line. The French ultimately remained masters of the zurichberg. About six o'clock, they threatened to turn the Russian corps in the plain of Zurich. General Korzakow therefore caused his camp to be burnt, and withdrew his troops into the town, of which all the gates were shut except that of Rapperschwell. Towards the evening, the French completed the investment of the town on the north and east, and shortly after on the west ; for the Russian corps, on the left bank of the Limmat, after an obstinate resistance, weakened by the reinforcements which it had sent to the town, and incessantly attacked by superior numbers, was compelled to fall back under the walls of Zurich. General Korzakow, dispirited and embarrassed by the occurrences on the Linth, passed the night in preparing for battle, or for retreat, as occasion might demand.

Massena, concluding that the Russian general, surrounded as he was on all sides, would not endeavor to maintain possession of the town ; but, knowing what he had to fear from the bravery of Russian soldiers, if he reduced them to the necessity of cutting their way with the bayonet, and being himself too weak to occupy at the same time the roads of Winterthur and of Eglisau, withdrew his troops in the night from the former, and contented himself with guarding in force the heights which command the latter. He sent, at the same time, an officer with a flag of truce to the Russian general, offering conditions for the quiet evacuation of the town, and for his retreat to the Rhine ; but the cossacks robbed this officer of his dispatches, and

he was detained in the town till the following day.

On that day, while it was expected that the Russians would make a capitulation with the French general Oudinot, general Korzakow, taking with him all the troops that he could collect, began his retreat, having his baggage and artillery disposed in the intervals of his columns : but, instead of taking the road to Winterthur, which the enemy had left open for his retreat, he sent in that direction only a small part of his troops and of his baggage, and pursued his march with the body of his army towards Eglisau. The French had no desire or expectation of being called into action ; but, seeing the Russian army approach, concluded that it was coming to attack them. Advantageously posted on the heights which command the road, they suffered the Russians to approach, and then opened upon them a terrible and commanding fire of artillery and musketry. Thus the battle began but partially, and without regularity. The Russian regiments, which were rather in order of retreat than of battle, fought individually without concert or object. Overwhelmed along the whole of their column by the grape-shot of the French, whose flying artillery, manœuvred with great effect, they rushed repeatedly with fixed bayonets upon the enemy, and forced them for some moments to give way ; but, as the prodigies of valor performed by the Russian infantry, could not be turned to account by the superior officers, they only served to render the defeat more bloody and more complete. Their little army was broken on all points, and a considerable number of men were captured, with part of the artillery, baggage, and treasure. General Korzakow, with all that escaped from the enemy, forced his way to Eglisau, at which place he hastened to pass the Rhine. The Russians having thus placed the Rhine between themselves and the French, and the Austrians retiring towards the Rinthal, all eastern Switzerland was open to the inroads of the republicans, who lost no time in overrunning it. The event will shew how much it was to be lamented that this extent of country was not disputed some time longer.

Conformably to the plan which has been already stated marshal Suwarrow was to have left Asti on the 8th of September, out the French, having shewn a disposition to relieve Tortona, which had engaged to surrender on the 11th of that month, unless it should be relieved in the mean time, he deferred his departure till that day. Anxious, however, to regain the time thus lost, and pursuing his favorite method of warfare to which he had owed so much success, he marched his army, composed of 17,000 effective men, the remains of the 30,000 which had been sent into Italy, with so much rapidity, that in five days it advanced 116 miles, and reached Taverna, near Bellinzona, on the very same day (the 15th,) on which he had proposed to arrive before the delay took place. Here he experienced another interruption, which was highly fatal to the cause of the allies. Instead of finding ready at Taverna, as had been promised him, the necessary beasts of burden, he was obliged to lose three days in endeavoring to obtain them ; and, being unable to procure a sufficient number, was obliged to dismount his cossacks, and to employ their horses in transporting the baggage. The impossibility of using carriages in the road of the great Alps, had obliged him to send his artillery by the lake of Como, and the rout of Chiavenna, from whence it afterwards rejoined him in the country of the Grisons.

Every preparation being made for the passage of the Alps, general Rosenberg, with the Russian advanced-guard, 12 battalions strong, began his march on the 19th, and arrived on the same day at Bellinzona. This corps was directed by the source and the valley of the Middle Rhine, to turn the St. Gothard, which it was probable the French would endeavor to defend, and it was necessary therefore that he should be a day in advance before the rest of the army. On the 21st, this general marched to Donjio, and, on the same day, marshal Suwarrow, whose advanced-guard was now composed of some Austrian light troops who had joined him, under the command of colonel Strauch, advanced to Bellinzona. On the 22nd, general Rosenberg arrived at St. Marie, and Suwarrow at Giurnico. On the 23rd, the former advanced to Tavetseh, and the latter to Polmengo ; his advanced-guard being at Piolta, and his head-quarters at Faido. On the 24th, the army arrived at the foot of the St. Gothard, and encountered the first posts of the enemy, about a mile from Airolo. Colonel Strauch attacked and defeated them. The Russian army cleared the St. Gothard, and carried the last post at four in the afternoon. About an hour before general Rosenberg had arrived at Urseren, where he rejoined general Suwarrow. The French general Gudin, who commanded in that quarter, caused his troops to fall back, partly by the Devil's bridge, and partly by Hospital, towards the Furca. On the 25th, the Russian army followed the course of the valley of the Reuss, and arrived in the evening beyond Wesen.

Marshal Suwarrow had so concerted his plan of attack, as to be supported on his right and left. While the latter was protected by the manœuvres which general Haddick and prince Victor de Rohan were making on the frontiers of the Valais, the Austrian corps which occupied the country of the Grisons, and which had not been attacked, put themselves in motion to cooperate with the Russians. General Auffenburg, with the advanced-guard, four battalions strong, set off from Dissentis on the 24th, and following the course of the Madernerthal, arrived on the same evening at Amsteig. General Lecourbe, who had begun his march on the same day, and arrived at Wesen, found himself placed between this Austrian column and the Russians. Falling back before the latter, he threw himself, on the 25th, upon the former, and forced it to retreat towards the Maderanthal. It was not, however, without leaving some hundreds of his men on the field of battle, or in the hands of the enemy, that he succeeded in cutting his way. He retired to Altorf, evacuated that town, and passed to the other side of the Reuss, in order to cover the country of Underwald and the Engelberg. Had the Russians been able on the 24th or 25th to advance a few miles further, this French corps would have been entirely taken or destroyed. On the 26th the allied army 1799. arrived without meeting any obstacles at Altorf, having conquered in less than a month, the whole canton of Uri, which is about 70 miles long.

On the 27th Suwarrow, pursuing the execution of his designs pushed his advanced guard across the Culmerberg as far as Mutten, where he captured a French picquet, from whom he learned that the republicans were still masters of Glarus. On the 28th the remainder of the army arrived at Mutten, and it was there that marshal Suwarrow learned by a dispatch, from general Lincken the events which had occurred on the Linth and the Limmat. The bitterness of his regret on receiving this unwelcome information may well be conceived. It could be no trivial disappointment for this old and active warrior to lose in one day and through the misconduct of others, an opportunity of crowning his labours, and of completing the glory of his campaign, and it was excusable that he should sustain this stroke of fortune with some impatience. Too tenacious however of his purpose to measure back his steps, too evidently threatened to permit his farther advance or his sojourn in the canton of Uri, and too adventurous to shrink even from the most arduous enterprise, under circumstances so critical, instead of falling back towards St. Gothard, or retiring into the country of the Grisons he resolved to pass by the valleys of Mutten and Clonthel, into the canton of Glarus, there to join general Lincken, flattering himself that on the news of his arrival and of the departure of Massena, to engage him, generals Korzakow and Petrarch, relieved from the pressure of a very superior force might be able to resume offensive measures, and retrieve their late disasters. It was in this hope, so glorious for Suwarrow, that he still retained, that he wrote to the Russian gene. rals in Korzakow's army, " You will answer

with your heads, for every further step that you retreat: I am coming to repair your faults.".

Whatever astonishment had been felt by marshal Suwarrow on learning the disasters of the allies, no less surprise was experienced by Massena when informed of the rapid and victorious march of the Russian general. Suspending for a moment all his designs against generals Korzakow and Petrarch, he sent off on the 26th one division to Schweitz, and another to Wesen, marching himself with a third upon Altorf by way of Lucerne. It may be seen from the direction of these columns, that Massena wished to prevent marshal Suwarrow from approaching further on his rear, and at the same time to shut against him the pass between the lakes of Wallenstadt and Zurich ; a pass which would have brought him most easily to generals Lincken and Petrarch. He placed only 300 men at the double debouché of Ensilden, persuaded that Suwarrow would be tempted to take it, and thus present him an opportunity of fighting the Russians in the plain, with superior numbers and on three different sides. The French considered their little army entangled among the defiles of the small cantons, without artillery, and almost without cavalry, (the cossacks having dismounted that their horses might carry their bread and baggage,) as a prey which could not escape them: and had already deluded themselves with the expectation of treating this second Russian army like the first, and burying under the mountains of Switzerland the glory of the conqueror of Italy.

On the 30th of September marshal Suwarrow proceeded by the Muttenthal, prince Bagration commanding his advanced guard and general Rosenberg remaining with the rear-guard at Mutten. On the same day the French division which had been sent upon the Linth, and which had taken an advantageous position on the Clon thalersee, on perceiving the arrival at that place of the small column of general Aufenberg, attacked and having almost surrounded it summoned their general to surrender. Far from acceding to this proposition he defended himself with obstinate bravery and gave time to prince Bagration, to arrive with the Russian advanced guard to his assistance. The allies then attacked the French in their turn, with fixed bayonets, broke their ranks and put them to the rout. Near 400 of them fell into the hands of the allies, and a much greater number were killed. Two pieces of cannon were taken by the conquerors, whose loss was not inconsiderable. Prince Bagration himself was wounded. The Russian army arrived on the Clonthalersee at the close of day, both sides passed the night under arms, and in presence of each other, the French occupying the mountains, and their enemies the road through the valley, and on the banks of the lake. It would have been difficult for the latter to continue their march with safety the following day, had they left the French masters of a position which entirely commanded their flank. It was turned by prince Bagration during the night, and pursued by marshal Suwarrow, who afterwards proceeded to Naefels, which he reached on the same day, the 1st of October.

Massena who, on the 30th of September, had joined Lecourbe at Altorf had also begun the pursuit of the Russians in the valley of Mutten. His advanced guard amounting to 4000 men, came up on the same day with general Rosenberg and on the next day general Massena in person arrived with 7000 men, and attacked the enemy in three columns, but was severely repulsed, with the loss of 2000 men in killed, wounded and prisoners.

His progress impeded by the natural difficulties peculiar to the country, and menaced on every side by superior numbers, Suwarrow reluctantly and indignantly determined to abandon his positions. He began his march on the 5th towards the Grison country, and arrived with some interruption at Elm. On the 6th he marched towards the valley of Fleim, and after losing a great portion of his baggage, and many soldiers, reached on the 8th of October the valley of the Rhine, where his army amounting to 14.000, reunited in

the environs of Chur. His loss in this short but destructive campaign was 3000 in killed, wounded, and missing; that of the French was considerably greater.

Pursuing his success, Massena attacked suddenly the entrenched posts before the city of Constance, which were occupied by the prince of Condé's army, and succeeded in entering the town. But the corps of noble infantry, the huzzars of Baur, and other corps, continued to defend the entrenched camp, animated by a supposition that in the event of surrendering they would be treated as emigrants. They fought with desperate fury, retook the city, and repulsed the enemy. In the morning of the 8th of October the prince of Condé quitted the city of Constance, the strength of the enemy being more than double his own, and on the 9th fixed his head-quarters at Stahringen, near Stockach, on the other side of the lake. The republicans were still less successful on other points; they were repulsed in all their attempts on the bridge of Dissenhoffen, and general Korzakow having passed the Rhine on the morning of the 7th, with about 8000 men, attacked with fixed bayonets the advanced guard of the enemy, strongly posted near the village of Schlatten, and drove it from its position. It took a second which it lost in the same manner; and was attacked a third time with so much vigor that two of its battalions had already laid down their arms, near the village of Trublickon, when Massena himself at the head of the main body of the French army, arrived at Andelfingen for their support. At the sight of this reinforcement and at the approach of the enemy's cavalry, the Russians desisted from all their attacks, and retired; the enemy followed and attempted but in vain, to obtain possession of the tete de pont of Busingen, which general Korzakow quitted for no apparent reason, in the night. This affair, and those of Dissenhoffen and Constance, cost the allies 2000 men, killed, wounded, and made prisoners. The loss of the French was at least as great, notwithstanding the concealments and exaggerations of the

directory's reports. It would be a waste
of time indeed, to refute the extravagant
estimates transmitted by the French generals, of the losses of the enemy throughout
the whole of the campaign. The statement sent by Massena on the 9th of October, in which he asserted the total loss
of the allies, from the 25th of September,
to have amounted to 30,000 men, nearly
doubled its actual amount. The loss of
the French did not exceed 9000; they
suffered but little in their engagements with
Petrarch and Korzakow; and their principal loss was in their combats with generals
Lincken, Bagration, and Rosenberg. In
every estimate of this kind, the evidence
of gazettes and official reports is uncertain
and fallacious. The testimony of impartial
observers, afterwards removed from the
scene of political influence, can alone be
consulted with advantage for the detection
of error and the exposure of credulity;
and the historian, who regards the communication of truth as the first object of
his writings, will too often find, on calm
investigation, that battles and exploits,
which rumor has clothed with every marvellous and sanguinary attribute, have
been accomplished by simple means,
with trifling loss, and under ordinary circumstances.

The termination of the battle of Zurich,
and the series of conflicts by which it was
preceded and followed, was singularly
propitious to the views of the French general, notwithstanding the accumulation and
concentration of the allied forces. On
one side of the lake of Constance, the troops
which had returned with the archduke
joined to those which remained on the
right shore, to the wrecks of Korzakow's
army, to the forces of the prince of Condé
and to the Bavarian contingent, amounted
to more than 45,000 men. On the other
side of the lake, the junction of marshal
Suwarrow with the Austrians, supported
by about 5000 armed inhabitants, formed
no less than 30,000 men. But, though
their army was much more numerous than
the French, and its resources in money
and provisions were more certain and
extensive, yet it had suffered so much,

and especially the Russians, by marches and
engagements, and the late events had made
such an impression on the minds of the
troops, that it was neither physically nor
morally adapted to undertake a second
time the conquest of Switzerland. After
resting his army for a few days in the environs of Chur, marshal Suwarrow recommenced his march, to proceed and operate
with the other Russian army upon the
banks of the lake of Constance. On the
13th, he arrived at Feldkirch, and was
joined at Lindau on the 18th, by the corps
of general Korzakow, which had reascended the Rhine, and had been succeeded
upon the river by the army of the archduke. The two Russian armies united,
independent of the allies, formed a body
of 25,000 effective men, the remains of
50,000 who had been sent during the campaign into Italy and Switzerland. After
removing his head-quarters to Lindau,
Suwarrow departed from that place, quitted
the banks of the lake of Constance with
his whole army, and that of the prince de
Condé, and marched to Augsburg, where
he arrived with all his staff, and fixed his
head-quarters. Chagrined by disappointment, and burning with indignation at the
conduct of the Austrians, to whose negligence in supplying him with mules for
conveying his stores and baggage, he
openly ascribed the delay which prevented
him from reaching the theatre of hostilities
before the defeat of Korzakow, and the
consequent occurrence of his own disasters. At Augsburg, he prepared for
his return to Russia in pursuance of the
command of the emperor Paul, whose
change of policy I shall have immediate
occasion to record; and, after recruiting
his troops by a short repose, marched
through Bohemia and Moravia into Poland.

It is impossible to contemplate the vicissitudes of the campaign in Switzerland
without sentiments of admiration for the
fortitude, the gallantry, and the skill, of
the Russian soldiers and their commander.
After having marched from the interior
of Russia, and after a bloody and active
campaign of five months' duration, this

army, reduced to one half its original number, penetrated into the middle of the Alps, opened a second campaign, fought new battles, and engaged against superior forces in a description of warfare to which it was totally unaccustomed. Generals Bagration and Rosenberg, already so distinguished in Italy, acquired new glory in Switzerland. Marshal Suwarrow confirmed the reputation he had already obtained, and gave fresh proofs of his resolution and heroism ; and the only fault of which he has been accused during his final operations, his long sojourn in the canton of Schweitz, arose from a noble reluctance to retire before a victorious enemy.

At the period of Suwarrow's departure, the archduke Charles continued to command all the Austrian troops within the Alps. Massena, on the contrary, quitted his army, and hastened to Paris, to cultivate the good graces of Buonaparte, who, suddenly returning from Egypt, had no less suddenly overthrown the revolutionary labors of ten years, and usurped the sovereign power under the title of Chief Consul. The assent of Massena and Moreau to this new order of things, secured to them a continuance of the chief command ; but they changed armies. The first proceeded in the room of the second, to place himself at the head of the army of Italy ; the other assumed the command of the army of Switzerland, to which was united that of the army of the Rhine, and which he went to exercise at the end of December.

In consequence of the departure of Suwarrow, prince Charles was obliged to send part of his troops to Bregentz, Feldkirch, and Meyenfield, and gave orders to raise the inhabitants in a mass, to assist as they had done in 1796, in defending those important posts which cover the Voralberg and Tyrolean frontier. Similar measures were taken to arm those residing in the duchy of Wurtemburg and the neighbouring states on the Rhine. His royal highness, as field-marshal of the empire, also addressed a proclamation to all the people of Germany which is remarkable for concluding with a proposal, that betrays

the severe necessities under which he labored. After giving a concise account of the conduct of the French before the recommencement of hostilities, he observed, that the empire, and Suabia in particular, was never so near utter ruin, as in the moment of that invasion, when they were lulled into security by perfidious professions of peace. It was, he said, only by the aid of the imperial army, which immediately marched to repel this aggression, that Suabia was saved ; and his majesty shewed his paternal care, in the most effectual manner, by securing the empire from the ravages of the enemy. How much the courage and gallantry of the troops contributed, in that critical conjuncture, to the safety of the provinces threatened, and those already invaded, and with what precipitation the republican forces were compelled to retreat, must still be in the grateful recollection of the natives. The danger was not yet altogether removed ; and as the enemy drew continual reinforcements from France, the greatest exertions were requisite to render permanent the security and tranquillity of the country, and deprive them of the power of renewing their former incursions.

The extraordinary efforts, made by his imperial majesty for the common defence of Germany, had, for these many years past been attended with very heavy expences, which were daily increasing. Yet neither former calamities, nor the present urgency, had induced the states to give the assistance which was so necessary for the preservation of their possessions. " Under all these circumstances," continued the archduke, " I feel myself compelled, in quality of commander-in-chief, to demand instant succors for the security of the provinces protected by the imperial arms, and menaced by the enemy ; and request the states to furnish, each in proportion to its means, such aids as are requisite for the operations of war, and the subsistence of the troops. I entertain no doubt, that, deeply convinced of the necessity of the case, in which they are so immediately implicated, the states of the empire, and the inhabitants of the different provinces, will cheerfully comply with a demand so clearly founded in justice, and connected with their own interest; more especially when they consider the severe hardships' inflicted on countries occupied by the enemy, whose plan is not only to exhaust them by plunder and devastation, but to destroy their happiness and tranquillity by the introduction of anarchy.

" As such is the situation of all countries unfortunately invaded by the French, the demands, which I now make for the security of the empire, can bear no comparison with the miseries they must experience from their oppressions and unbounded extortions. I therefore trust with confidence, that the states and inhabitants will comply with the proposal now made to them, and also voluntarily come forward with free gifts, conformable to their means and resources. These donations may be as various as the wants of the troops; and may be furnished in ready money, obligations, corn, forage, serviceable horses, linen cloth, leather, or any other commodities useful to an army. Many, whose dispositions lead them to make patriotic gifts, may not have the immediate power of carrying their intentions into effect; because, though not in possession of specie or commodities necessary to the support of troops, they may have articles in gold or silver, either ornamental, or of real use. In order, therefore, to enable such persons to be of utility to their country, and make their property of permanent value to themselves, I hereby," concluded his royal highness, " declare, that such gifts in gold and silver will be accepted at full value,—the mark of gold at 380 florins, and that of silver at 24 florins 30 kreutz; and I also declare, that such persons shall receive in return obligations at four per cent.; the gold and silver so furnished to be delivered at the royal mint at Guntzburg."

It would be superfluous to extend this narrative by an useless relation of the numerous, but trivial, engagements, which happened in Suabia and Franconia, where victory inclined sometimes to the one party, and sometimes to the other. On the 15th, general Lecourbe, now invested with the command of the army of the Rhine, attacked, in four divisions, the whole Austrian line between Phillipsburg and the Neckar. After a warm contest, the imperialists were constrained to retreat, with the loss, according to Lecourbe, of 1200 prisoners. Prince Schwartzenberg took post at Heilbron, Ludwigsburg, and the Enz. Phillipsburg was once more blockaded; but the French general was too weak, and the season too far advanced, to hazard any distant expedition from the frontiers of the republic, especially when not seconded by a movement of the army of Helvetia.

General Stzarry marched, with a strong body of forces, to the assistance of the Austrian corps which opposed Lecourbe: and, on the 11th of December, attacked and carried the French post at Weiler, on the left bank of the Elsenz. Prosecuting this success, he obtained possession of Munzingen, and of Wisloch, after a severe action, in which the French, according to his dispatches, had 4000 killed and wounded, with 800 prisoners; while his own loss amounted only to 325 killed and wounded. The blockade of Phillipsburg was raised, which was the object of his operation, and occurred very opportunely, as the garrison, being reduced to great distress, were on the point of surrendering. The French also abandoned Manheim and the intrenchments of Neckerau on the 19th, and withdrew behind the Rhine, leaving only a competent force to protect Kehl.

During these transactions in Helvetia and Germany, the armies were daily fighting in Italy, with alternate and inconclusive success. General Championnet, having taken the command as the successor of Joubert, used every endeavor to remedy the disorders occasioned among his troops by the want of pay, clothing, and subsistence; and was equally assiduous in enforcing a rigorous observance of discipline. Their miserable condition, and scattered posts, prevented him from undertaking any important - enterprise, and confined his operations to alarming the enemy's quarters, or opposing their attacks. Corps were stationed at Cornigliano, Novi, Fossano, Coni, Pignerol, Rivoli, Susa, Aosta, and along the lakes, thus forming a semicircle round the imperialists. If we trace this line through the Grisons, along the banks of the Rhine, the military masses, opposed to each other, held a position, which resembled the letter S reversed, general Massena occupied the interior of one of segment, and general Melas the other.

These detachments were not of sufficient strength to ottempt a junction at one common point, and still less te meet the enemy in the plain, where they were exposed to the attacks of the Austrian cavalry, whose number was very great, and to oppose whom they could not, even at the opening of the campaign, muster 3000 horse. It would seem from this distribution of their forces, that the French government wished to act solely on the defensive, and perplex the enemy by continual attempts in different points. By these means they prevented Melas from concentrating his troops in order to invade the republic; while they gained time to collect reinforcements, and maintain a footing in Italy, until their numbers, or the approach of winter, should give them greater security.

To circumscribe their incursions, the imperial commander was under the necessity of weakening his principal army, by detaching corps of observation. Klenau watched Genoa and the gulph of Spezzia, Kray the Genoese and Montferrat, and the general-in-chief the frontiers of France. General Haddick acted in the duchy of Aosta, and prince Rohan towards the Valais. We cannot devote time or space to relate the useless waste of blood in the numberless actions, which happened along this widely extended line. Prince Rohan was driven from Domo D'Ossola, but recovered his ground: Haddick was obliged to fall back; and Saluzzo was taken and retaken. The French lost Pignerol, and were repulsed at Rivoli; but as Melas was unable to besiege or blockade Coni in form, detachments from the garrison were continually beating up his quarters in the neighbourhood.

On the 14th of October, the divisions of Victor and Muller forced the Austrians to evacuate the village of Bezinette, the point supporting their chain of advanced posts; but a very powerful reinforcement arriving, the French retired. Having brought up more troops, they again advanced the same day, and fell on the Austrian left flank, and the village in front The engagement continued till night with great loss on both sides, and was successively renewed during several days. General Melas was finally constrained to abandon the projected siege of Coni, until the arrival of the promised succours from Germany. In the mean time many severe combats took place along the rest of the line at Villa-Neva, Novi, and particularly towards the Riviere du Levanti. On the 12th, a body of 4000 French from Torriglia drove general Klenau to Sarzano, and carried the defiles of the mountains of Pontremoli, Borgo, Val-di-Tarro, Varese, and as far as Bobbio. But after retaining these for eight days, they withdrew towards Sestri, and their former concentrated position.

The Austrian general Karackzay, who commanded a corps of 6000 men near Novi to observe the principal debouché from Genoa, was obliged, after a stubborn engagement, to retreat on Alessandria, and take a position behind the Bormida. Lemoine's division was attacked on the 27th near Mondovi by general Melas, and, on the day following, the imperial commander was attacked in his turn. very sanguinary, but still undecisive, battles took place upon the 29th and 31st on both banks of the Stura. In the course of these the French not only raised the siege of Coni which had been begun, but pushed to the vicinity of Fossano.

An obstiuate action occurred on the 1st of November near Pignerol between general Dubesme and an Austrian detachment intrenched at that place. On the 2nd, the French advanced towards Mondovi, which they carried: they even sent parties beyond the Pesio, repulsed the Austrian posts, and occupied Carru. Next day general Victor passed the Stura, and took a position at Murazzo near the reserve and Grenier's division. These combined movements forced the imperialists to quit their intrenched position at St. Marguerite and Murazzo, in consequence of which, Grenier entered Savigliano, Victor reached the walls of Fossano, and Duhesme took possession of Saluzzo. As their movements seemed to indicate an intention to surround the right of the imperial army, and cut off the communication with Turin, General Melas resolved to throw his whole force on his right, in order to return the French left, and make a feint of retreating and taking a position between Fossano and Marenne. He accordingly evacuated, in the night of the 2nd, the whole right bank of the Stura, after throwing the garrison of Mondovi into Cherasco.

At day-break on the 4th, General Melas, having assembled all his forces, marched against Victor and Grenier, who were advancing with a design to give battle. Both armies were divided into three columns. One part of Grenier's division proceeded by Savigliano and Marenne, and the rest by Genola, while Victor bore down on Fossano. Lieutenant-general Ott led the right column of the imperialists by Marenne towards Savigliano, and field-marshal-lieutenant Mittrowsky the centre to the same point by Lorenzo. Lieutenant-general Elsnitz marched with the left by Fossano towards Genola, while the brigade of major-general Gottesheim, reinforced by the garrison of Fossano, were to make two false attacks on Murazzo and Madalena, in order that Ott and Mittrowsky might gain time to take Savigliano, and thereafter advance on the enemy's left flank.

As general Ott was on his rout from Marenne to Savigliano, he encountered Grenier's left. After a warm contest the French fell back, but in complete order towards Savigliano. The unperceived approach of general Mittrowsky, however, obliged them to continue their retreat to Genola with the loss of three

hundred prisoners. Generals Elsnitz and Gottesheim, who proceeded in the direction of Genola, the main point of the enemy's line, were three times repulsed. At last, general Ott having gained the French rear by Valdegnasco, and Mittrowsky advancing from Savigliano to Genola which the enemy abandoned, they united their forces, and marched against Valdiggio; upon which the French, afraid of being surrounded, retired to Centalo. From this place part of them withdrew to Coni, but Victor's division took post at Murazzo and Ronchi.

Gottesheim durst not venture to attack Murazzo, until he was reinforced by general Elsnitz's column. Meanwhile general Ott, still supported by field-marshal Mittrowsky, made an attempt on Ronchi; when the enemy, after a spirited engagement, left their camp, and withdrew to Coni in their immediate neighbourhood. These advantages enabling Ott to penetrate between that fortress and Murazzo, the French, to prevent their retreat being cut off, abandoned the latter place in disorder. In this battle, the imperialists succeeded chiefly by the number of their cavalry. The French do not mention their own loss, but state that of the Austrians at about four thousand prisoners, and sixteen pieces of cannon : and these again calculate the loss, sustained by their opponents, at three, four, or five thousand troops, with four pieces of artillery ; and their own, at nearly sixteen hundred men.

The French had been so successful on the side of Novi, as to threaten Alessandria ; and it was not until the 5th, that general Kray was in sufficient strength to force them from Bosco to Rivalto, and approach their position at Novi. On the 6th, an engagement ensued on the heights of that place, and was attended with much bloodshed but no material advantage. After the battle at Genola, general Grenier's division composing one column of the French army encamped near Borgo Santo Dalmazzo behind Coni And the other consisting of the divisions of Victor and Lemoine took post round

Mondovi. In the night of the 10th, the small garrison of Mondovi being too weak for effectual resistance evacuated the town, the army at the same time retiring towards the Col-de-Tenda; Garesio, and Lezegno while detachments occupied the Col-de-Tornada, the bridge of Nava, St. Jacques, Montenotte, and the heights of Gavi, so as to protect Genoa, and the whole length of the Ponent as far as Nice. By these movements the imperial general was at liberty to form the blockade of Coni, which being already exhausted of stores and provisions surrendered on the 4th of December, its garrison of 2500 men becoming prisoners of war.

The circumstances attending the flight and return of the king of Naples were so singular and so various as to demand a more particular notice than the less important events by which they were immediately attended. For several days preceding the meditated departure of the king, sir William, and lady Hamilton, took in charge the jewels and treasures of the palace, and arranged the means of secret escape before the suspicion and resentment of the people should be awakened. Neither sir William Hamilton nor lord Nelson, judged it safe to appear publicly at the palace, yet notwithstanding every precaution, a conviction of the king's design prevailed among the inhabitants of Naples. No time therefore was to be lost. The king and queen accompanied by the junior members of the royal family, proceeded at night through subterraneous passages, and were conveyed in barges amidst a most tremendous sea, on board the Vanguard. They sailed on the 23rd of December 1798, and were exposed in the course of the night to the rage of a furious tempest. At ten o'clock they entered the bay of Palermo, and at midnight the viceroy and nobility arrived on board, with assurances of their attachment and obedience. While the royal family resided at Palermo, cardinal Ruffo with his army of 20,000 Calabrians, aided by some hundred Russian troops, had defeated the Neapolitan republicans, and proceeding

to Naples, which had been evacuated by Macdonald, took possession of the whole capital except the castles of St. Elmo, Ovo, and Nuovo. For the purpose of co-operating in the movements of the cardinal, lord Nelson immediately put to sea, attended by a few Sicilian regiments, under the gallant hereditary prince. On their passage from Palermo to Naples, a dispatch overtook them from lord Keith with the news of the French squadron having again put to sea: and our fleet was therefore obliged to return to Palermo to disembark the troops. In consequence of this return the republicans began to resume their courage, and Ruffo apprehensive that English assistance might not arrive, offered indulgent terms to the adherents of France. Lord Nelson afterwards learning that lord Keith had been reinforced, set sail a second time from Palermo and arrived in the bay of Naples. In the mean time cardinal Ruffo had concluded the proposed convention with the French, and the Neapolitan rebels; an act which excited the warm indignation of the British admiral. His lordship declared in a note more remarkable for energy than justice that not having been ratified by his majesty's ministers the treaty was null and void. One of the first articles of the convention, was the free pardon of prince Caraccioli the chief of the revolutionary party. Lord Nelson ordered the prince to be immediately arrested, and carried on board the Mercury, a Neapolitan frigate, where he was tried by a court martial and hanged in twenty-four hours after the sentence was pronounced. It would be a task equally invidious and afflicting to record the various indiscretions of lord Nelson, during his anchorage in the bay of Naples, the inhumanity with which he suffered the body of Caraccioli to float before his ship in the presence of his visitors and himself, or his public levities with lady Hamilton. The naval service is seldom the nursery of virtuous habits, or humane propensities and it is my duty to record lord Nelson's services, rather than to scrutinise his faults.

Cardinal Ruffo had granted permission to the French to carry several valuables out of the city, which were not their lawful property, and to the rebels he had given the option of quitting or remaining in the Neapolitan dominions. These conditions were set aside by lord Nelson, and many rebels were apprehended. Nothing was now wanting to the re-establishment of the king and the tranquillity of the city, but the expulsion of the enemy from St. Elmo. Its situation precluded its capture by storm; batteries were therefore erected by the English and Russians, and a severe and constant fire kept up for ten days. The parapets were knocked down, and a great many guns dismounted, while the fire of the enemy produced little or no effect on the besiegers. Six thirty-two pounders, under the direction of capt. 'n Hallowell, were opened within one hundred and fifty yards of the castle. After two hours' battering, a flag of truce was hoisted, and the garrison surrendered, on condition of being sent to France, but not to serve till exchanged. On the 10th of July, his Sicilian majesty arrived in the bay of Naples, and shortly afterwards retook possession of his capital.

After the reconquest of Naples, the royal army advanced into the Roman state. They were preceded by a proclamation, declaring that his majesty sent his victorious troops, " not composed of his *former* warriors, but of his faithful Calabrians, to deliver the people from the degrading yoke to which they had been subjected under the false denomination of liberty and equality,—to restore religion to its former splendor—to put an end to oppression, disorder, and massacre,—and to re-establish, on the ruins of anarchy, the throne of truth and justice. What satisfaction, Romans, must you not feel," continued the proclamation, " at the arrival of this auspicious moment? Those now coming amongst you are the adorers of the cross, of that sacred ensign which victory attends, and at the appearance of which the enemies of God, of the throne, and of

humanity, are terrified and dispersed. It is that cross whose greatest triumphs were performed in the midst of you,—that cross which is the assylum of the just, and the scourge of the wicked. On the appearance of that triumphant standard borne by the soldiers, all the males shall exhibit its sign on the right side of their hats, and all the women on their right breasts : on the left side they shall wear the Neapolitan cockade. Hasten, Romans, to tear up that infamous tree, which, to your disgrace, is suffered still to remain within your territories. In place of that fatal sign of irreligion, dissolution, and all the most abominable vices, plant the sacred sign of the cross, the purest source of all the virtues. Receive amongst you our courageous soldiers; it is a duty which religion imposes upon you. They come to defend your honor, your families, and your existence."——These evangelical arguments, however, had less influence with the Romans, than the terror of the enemy's swords.

After providing Bologna, Florence, and Leghorn, with the necessary garrisons, field-marshal Frolich entered the papal territory, and in his march occupied Civita-Castellana, from whence he proceeded towards Rome. On the 21st of September, the French troops in that city, seconded by a body of patriots under the ex-princes Borghese, Santa-Croce, Marescotte, and Bonelli, attacked and routed the Neapolitans posted at Monte-Rotondo on the left bank of the Tyber. Next day they defeated Frolich at Cornetto and Civita-Vecchia: but the commandant general Garnier, convinced of his inability to resist long such superior forces as pressed him on every side, concluded a capitulation on the 24th, with commodore Trowbridge of the Culloden man of war. By this convention the French at Rome and Civita-Vecchia, and the Italian and Polonese troops serving with them, were at liberty to quit the Roman state and return to France, without being considered as prisoners of war. Such Romans as chose, were allowed to embark with the garrison, and carry their property along with them.

General Bouchard, wno commanded fhe Neapolitan troops, was a party to the capitulation; but when Garnier intimated the terms to marshal Frolich, and proposed a line of demarcation, he refused to acquiesce, and threatened to continue hostilities. Accordingly an engagement took place on the 28th, between Cornetto and Civita-Vecchia, in which the imperialists were so warmly received, that the marshal at last acceded to the convention, and marched with his troops towards Ancona No inference, honorable to the views' of the Austrian cabinet on the dominions of the church, can be deduced from this unseasonable hesitation and forced compliance.

Soon after the recommencement of the war, in which the court of Rome had originally engaged with so much zeal, it was deemed expedient to remove the aged pontiff to a considerable distance from the seat of hostilities. He was therefore conveyed to Valence, in Dauphiny, and was greeted on his rout and at the place of his final destination, with the respect due to his character and venerable age. This was the last, and, at present, the most acceptable tribute that could be paid him. Before he had been many days at Valence, he breathed his last, on the 19th of August, after a short illness, in his eighty-second year.

When the Neapolitan army entered Rome on the 30th, the tree of liberty, placed in front of the Vatican, was solemnly burned, the head of Brutus carried by the populace in derision through the city, and the houses of the patriots destroyed. About the 16th of October, general Frolich arrived at Ancona, which had been besieged ever since the beginning of the campaign, by a body of Austrians, aided by some Russian and Turkish corps, while a Turco-Russian squadron blockaded it by sea. The parallels being completed on the 2nd of November, the Austrian and Russian artillery began to batter the fortress, while the infantry advanced to the walls with a design to scale them, and storm the place.

General Mounier, the commandant, did not return this fire until day-break; when, perceiving the enemy's intention, he opened such a dreadful cannonade from the three main forts, and the whole front of the principal ramparts, that the besiegers recoiled instantly in confusion. Not content with this, the intrepid Mounier made two successive sallies and attacks, particularly against the heights in the neighbourhood, as the possession of them enabled the besiegers to bombard the town. He could not, however, spare troops to maintain his acquisition; and on his retiring, the heights were re-occupied by the enemy. The place was bombarded for some days, and the fire as vigorously answered by the garrison; but their stores failing, and their number being much reduced by active service during so long a blockade, they surrendered prisoners of war. About 2000 men were taken; and in the harbour were found three old ships of war, of 70 and 64 guns, besides several small vessels.

Marshal Frolich, after this conquest, marched with 12,000 troops to join general Melas in Piedmont.

Daily and bloody actions ensued towards Susa, Aosta, and the lakes on one side, and the Genoese frontiers on the other. Championnet has been blamed for scattering his army, by occupying a circular line of about four hundred and twenty-nine English miles in extent, along uninhabited mountains, and in a sterile country. As this ridge had twenty-five debouchés, to defend each of which we may calculate that 3000 men were necessary, his whole position required a force of 90,000 troops, at least, for defensive war, and 40,000 additional for offensive operations. But the French force in Italy, comprising both Joubert's army and that of the Alps, never exceeded 60,000 men, of whom only 2000 were cavalry.

The more concentrated position of general Melas enabled him to act with superior effect, either by a rapid junction, or combined movement of his troops. This, however, was not the only advantage which he enjoyed. He was continually receiving reinforcements, while his antagonist had to struggle against wants of every kind. Destitute of bread, of clothes, and of shoes; disheartened by defeat, chagrined by want of pay, and the shameless neglect of their government; worn out with fatigue, and lying exposed in the fields to the inclemency of the weather, the French soldiers were engaged in continual battles. Their hospitals were unable to accommodate the sick and wounded. In vain the general represented his peril and distress, in vain he implored assistance: the minister promised ample supplies; but neither stores nor reinforcements were sent to the unfortunate army of Italy.

3 H 2

HISTORY OF THE WAR.

CHAP. XXV.

AMIDST the scenes of festivity which lulled the suspicion, and gratified the vanity of the Parisians, the plan of another revolution in the government was secretly arranged. In this enterprise, Buonaparte was chiefly assisted by the Abbé Sieyes, who had succeeded Rewbell in the directory ; a man of deep thought, endowed with much sagacity ; dark, sullen, and intriguing, yet possessed of every persuasive art, and fertile in expedients. His ambition was not accompanied by Buonaparte's adventurous spirit. He valued himself on guarding the actions of others and directing the machine of state, without taking so active a part in the public councils as might endanger his own safety. They first admitted to their confidence a monsieur Rœderer, a man of business, and a strenuous republican, who had been solicitor to the municipality of Paris in 1792, and had taken an active part in the progress of the revolution ; and, when they had digested their plan, they communicated it to a few others, whom they deemed most capable of promoting its execution.

It might have been difficult to impress the body of the people with a conviction, that the present constitution was defective, or that its subversion would contribute to the happiness of the nation, had they not labored under some personal grievance. Not all the taxes which had been imposed since the commencement of the war, nor the naval and military conscriptions, contributed so much to the unpopularity of the existing government, as the law of hostages passed in the present year, 1799. by which it was decreed, among other articles, that, " when a commune or department was notoriously in a state of civil disorder, the relations of emigrants or nobles, comprehended in the revolutionary law of the third year of the republic, their fathers and mothers, grandfathers and grandmothers, and individuals who, without being relations or ex-nobles, were known to form part of the assemblies or bands of assassins, should be personally or civilly responsible for whatever assassinations or robberies should be committed in their communes. If a murder was committed on any public functionary, defender of the country, or purchaser of national domains, or any person of this character were carried off, four hostages were to be banished for each person so murdered or carried off, besides paying a fine of 6000 livres. Every hostage was made responsible for the payment of 4000 livres in case of any murder in his commune, to be paid into the public treasury, of 6000 more to the widow, and of 3000 to the children of the person assassinated. The same indemnification was allowed to every person mutilated ; and the same responsibility extended to all damage or waste of property. The law was to remain in full force till the conclusion of a general peace. This law of which it was the tendency to place a great part of the nation at the mercy of the directory and their agents by rendering them liable to fines and imprisonment, was the signal of revolt in many provinces, and was the cause of discontent in all. Those of Mayenne and Normandy and an extensive district on the Loire, were in a state of actual insurrection, and the malecontents were headed by persons of influence from their property and character.

The Abbé Sieyes though a strenuous revolutionist was at this time one of the chiefs of the moderate party. He was convinced of the expedience of strengthening the executive power, and was an advocate for vesting it in a chief magistrate, assisted by a senate, while the republican form of government was in some degree preserved. Reserved and cautious, he had revolved these plans in silence, during the predominance of the democratic parties, and had lived on terms of friendship with many of their leading men. But he now perceived a favourable opportunity of executing his designs, presented by the public opinion of the existing government, and the dissatisfaction occasioned by the law of hostages, and he found in Buonaparte a proper instrument for effecting his purposes.

The next step taken by the partizans of the intended revolution, after securing a majority in the council of elders, was to avail themselves of a law, passed in 1795, enabling that body to change the seat of the legislative assembly, to remove it to St. Cloud under the pretence that the Jacobins were conspiring against the constitution, and that the removal was necessary to the independence of the legislature. " Due protection," said the advocates of this measure, " was now about to be afforded to liberty and property, the constitution would now be restored, the reign of terror and factious intrigue overthrown, and a basis established on which foreign powers would treat with confidence for peace, which was in fact, the grand object of the present measure."

They had made their previous arrangements with so much privacy, that of the five directors two only, Sieyes and Ducos, were apprised of their design before the 9th of November, when it was to be carried into execution. On the night preceding, Buonaparte, who had been invested by the council of elders with the command of the troops at Paris, posted several military bodies at the different avenues leading to the hall of assembly in the Thuilleries. In the morning he was seen at their head surrounded by his staff-officers, and by the facility with which he accomplished this preparatory measure, demonstrated that the constitution was about to be changed, into an absolute and military government " The army" said he in an harangue to his troops " has cordially united with me, as I act cordially with the legislative body." Nothing is more easy than for an artful leader to impose on the minds of an unthinking audience, and to conceal his real intention by specious language. The troops became willing instruments in effecting a revolution which by gratifying the ambition of their favourite general, would promote their own interests ; and the people readily acquiesced in any means of deliverance from the existing tyranny.

The three directors to whom the plan of a counter-revolution had not been communicated, attempted to oppose its execution. They ordered general Lefebre who commanded their guards, to surround the house of Buonaparte with his troops, but that officer answered, " that he was then under the orders of Buonaparte, as commandant of the troops at Paris." Perceiving that they were left without resource the opposing directors now thought only of escaping the vengeance of their adversaries. Barras, formerly the patron and friend of Buonaparte, made his peace by the resignation of his office. Moulins disappeared ; and Gohier gave the measure his sanction as president of the directory, by affixing his seal to the decree for translating the assembly to St. Cloud. Conformably with this decree the two councils of elders and of Five Hundred, met on the ensuing day (November 10) at the palace of St. Cloud, and the warmth of their debates was expressive of a conviction that the proceedings of the day would finally determine the state of the two parties. The partisans of the director would willingly however have arrested their proceedings by calling in question the legality of their removal, and their objections were still agitated when Buonaparte entering the hall, addressed the assembly in an harangue, intended to convince them of the danger which threatened the nation from the machinations of active and designing men. " Your solicitude" he exclaimed " for the salvation of your country has called me to come before you. I will not dissemble for I will always speak with the frankness of a soldier. You stand on a volcano ; but you may depend on our devoted attachment. Let us not be divided. Associate your *wisdom to the force which surrounds us ;* I will be nothing but the devoted arm of *the republic.*" To this one of the members, desirous that the general should be forced to declare his whole scheme of policy which he knew would disgust the friends of liberty, and even a great number of Buonaparte's admirers, added in a loud voice "and of *the constitution.*" " The constitution! " answered Buonaparte in a tone of indignation, " does it become you to talk of the constitution, have you not trodden it under your feet, in various instances." He then proceeded to accuse his enemies of treason and misconduct, and, asserted that Barras and Moulins had proposed to him that he should seize the government. Cornudet one of the elders confirming his charge of treason and conspiracy, the assembly was instantly in a flame. Buonaparte perceiving that his harangue had not produced its full effect, and conscious that he must depend for the success of his ambitious projects on the army and the people, retired from the assembly and harangued the soldiers and the multitude, in the same

specious language " Turn your bayonets against me" said he, " whenever you find me an enemy to liberty." Then returning to the hall and addressing himself to the assembly, he said, " It is time to speak out, and I have no designs which I wish to keep a secret. I am not the instrument of any faction. I am the servant of the French nation. The constitution too often violated is utterly inadequate to the salvation of the people. It is indispensibly necessary that we should have recourse to the most effectual means of carrying into execution the sacred principles of the sovereignty of the people, civil liberty, freedom of speech, as of thought, and in a word the realization of ideas hitherto only chimerical." A warm altercation ensued between the members on the expedience of a change in the constitution, which ended in the assembly resolving itself into a committee and adjourning till nine o'clock in the evening of the same day. In the council of Five Hundred, Gaudin, a member of that assembly, after representing the dangerous situation of the commonwealth, moved that a committee of seven persons should be chosen, who should make a report on the actual state of the nation, and who should propose such measures as they should think necessary for the public interest. The constitutionalists aware that they must resist the question with all their strength, or give up the contest, set up a cry of " The constitution! the constitution, or death ! No directorship !" Lucien Buonaparte the president, that he might appease the uproar, exclaimed, " I am too sensible of the dignity of my office to suffer any longer the insolent menaces of some speakers : I call them to order." The debates however were continued with much violence : and Grand Maison after severely descanting on the present measures, moved that a message be sent to the council of elders, requesting them to transmit a detailed account of the extensive conspiracy which was attempting to overthrow the republic, and that all the members should be compelled to renew their oath to the constitution.

Both these motions were received with cries of *Vive la republique! Vive la constitution!* The assembly had gone through the ceremony of taking the oath, and its attention was engaged in business of less importance, when the door of the hall opened, and Buonaparte advanced, followed by four grenadiers of the guard, belonging to the national representation, while a number of officers and soldiers remained at the door. A violent uproar ensued on his entrance, and the hall resounded with the words Outlaw! and Dictator! and with exclamations against the interference of the troops. Some of the members attempted to thrust him out of the hall by force; and his usual presence of mind had totally deserted him, when Lefebre, hearing the fray, suddenly entered the hall at the head of a party of grenadiers, and rescued the general.

When the agitation into which the assembly had been thrown, was sufficiently subsided, Lucien Buonaparte, addressing himself to the assembly, vindicated his brother with spirit and composure. He admitted that the commotion which had taken place was natural, and that the feelings of the house on the proceedings which had just occurred, were in unison with his own. But, after all, it was reasonable to suppose that the general, in the step he had taken, had no other object in view than to give an account of the state of affairs, or to communicate information interesting to the public; at any rate he did not think such suspicions ought to be entertained of him. From this sentiment the constitutionalists loudly expressed their dissent, exclaiming, "Buonaparte has this day sullied his glory. He has this day conducted himself like a king," and demanding that he be brought to their bar to give an account of his conduct. The debates on the merits of the present measure being continued with increasing violence, Lucien Buonaparte cast aside his robes, declaring that he thus laid down the office of their president. A fray ensued, and some of the members advancing towards him with pistols, as if they meant to constrain him to resume his office, the

general sent a party of grenadiers to rescue his brother. He had been haranguing the troops on the insolence and violence offered him in the council, when Lucien arrived, and, mounting on horseback, rode to the different regiments, and addressed them in animated language on the proceedings of the council. "I confide in the warriors to whom I speak the deliverance of the majority of their representatives from the oppression they endure, in order that they may deliberate in peace. General and soldiers, you will not, I am persuaded, acknowledge as legislators of France, any but those who will rally round me." He concluded his harangue with the popular cry of *Vive la republique,* which was re-echoed by the soldiers and the multitude.

The general, observing that the troops were ready to support him, commanded a body of grenadiers to advance, the drums beating the *pas de charge,* the signal for an attack with fixed bayonets. The troops gradually entering the hall, according to this order, an officer said aloud, "Citizens, representatives! There is no longer any safety in this place! I exhort you to withdraw! It is the order of the general!" This was answered by the cry of *Vive la republique.* The officer then mounting the tribune, exclaimed, "Representatives! withdraw! it is the order of the general." The order not being obeyed, and its annunciation being succeeded by a violent tumult, another officer called out, "Grenadiers! Forward!" The drums beating the charge, and the troops advancing to the middle of the hall, the deputies at last retired, exclaiming as they departed, *Vive la republique.*

The contest in the council of Five Hundred being thus ended, a committee of five elders brought forward their report of the measures proper to be adopted at the present moment. In this it was stated, that the council of elders had become the organ of the nation, and after what had passed the whole of the national representation: that it was their duty, as it was in their power, to provide for the safety of the country, and for liberty: that the executive power existed no longer, since military power was no more than the instrument of the executive. In consequence of these positions, together with the further circumstance that four of the five directors had given in their resignation, and the other was under arrest, the five elders proposed that an, executive provisionary commission, composed of three members, Buonaparte, Sieyes, and Duclos, should be appointed under the name of *Consuls*; that the legislative body should be adjourned till the 21st of December; that an intermediary commission should be formed for preserving the right of the national representatives, and that the assembly be adjourned till nine in the evening, when the present measures should be taken into consideration. The report was in reality a mere apology for Buonaparte's usurpation of the whole power of the state, by the interposition of military force, and on the ground of necessity. The leaders of the counter-revolution, that they might obtain every sanction from the old system which was compatible with their views, caused such of the council of Five Hundred as were devoted to their interests, to be summoned to an assembly of the elders at St. Cloud, under pretence of deliberating on the measures to be pursued. Barringer, one of the deputies, having opened the council by moving that the officers and troops had deserved well of their country, who had formed a shield for Buonaparte, and had saved a majority of the legislative body and the republic, attacked by a minority consisting of assassins; Chasal proposed the plan of an intermediary government, which was submitted to the consideration of a commission of five members. During their deliberations, Lucien Buonaparte, passing from the president's chair to the tribune, addressed the assembly in a florid harangue, enforcing the absolute necessity of the measures which were now adopting for saving the republic and the country from impending ruin, and was followed by Cabarris and Bonlay de la Meurthe. Having endeavored by the force of eloquence to prepossess their hearers, and

the nation in favor of their measures, the plan of an intermediary government, which was to be the outline of their intended constitution, having been arranged according to order, was laid before the assembled antients, and received their approbation. After another speech from Lucien Buonaparte, descanting on the glorious prospects which accompanied the election of consuls, the latter issued a proclamation in justification of the present counter-revolution. Buonaparte himself, in a proclamation as commander-in-chief, after adverting to the transactions at St. Cloud, congratulated the nation in the result of his exertions for its welfare.— "Frenchmen! You will doubtless recognise in this conduct, the zeal of a soldier of liberty, and of a citizen devoted to the republic. The ideas of preservation, protection, and freedom, immediately resumed their places on the dispersion of the faction who wished to oppress the councils, and who, in making themselves the most odious of men, never ceased to be the most contemptible."

When the conductors of the counter-revolution had advanced thus far in the prosecution of their designs, letters were dispatched to the foreign ministers, instructing them to announce to the respective courts at which they resided, that the government had been confided to a consulate of three; while the legislative committees of twenty-five members, divided into committees of five members each, entered on their functions, which consisted in preparing laws of police, legislation, and finance; a civil code, and a new constitution.

The first measure of the consular government was well calculated to impress the nation with a conviction of its regard for freedom. A repeal was immediately promoted of the forced loan, and of the law of hostages, which had brought universal odium on the late government. This was followed by a repeal of the severe decree against priests, who refused to abjure their loyalty, substituting a simple oath of fidelity to the present constitution. By a decree passed at the same time, the churches were restored to the Roman catholics, without restricting them as before, to the decade or tenth day, and freedom of religious worship was granted to its full extent. To supply the place of the revenue which was to have arisen from the forced loan of 100,000,000 livres, a fourth part was added to all contributions or imposts on property, territorial, personal, and sumptuary. The principal bankers of Paris consented to a loan of 500,000 livres, for the present exigencies of the state, secured by promissory notes from government. These supplies enabled the administration to carry on the war without any relaxation of energy, while the committee of finance were devising expedients, for providing further resources, and reviving the public credit. Among other measures calculated to conciliate the affections of a great majority of the people, it was decreed, that the remains of the pope, which had remained unburied at Valence since his death, should be interred with the usual honors of his rank and office.

During these proceedings, the committee appointed to digest a new constitution, had completed their labors. Being submitted to the commissions of Five Hundred and of elders, in which Lucien Buonaparte and Le Brune presided, it was approved, after some debate, by a great majority, and received their collective sanction. As the outlines of this celebrated constitution were adopted as far as regards the rights of private individuals, and with some modification in the *Code de Napoleon*, which shall hereafter be inserted, it will only be necessary in this place to state that the government was declared to consist of three consuls, or rather one chief consul and two assessors, who had votes only in matters of secondary importance ; *a conservative senate*, and *a legislative body*, divided into two parts, *tribunes* and *senators* : the tribunes to reason or plead on any proposition, but not to vote ; the senators to vote and decide in silence, but neither to argue, nor declare the grounds on which they gave their opinion. It was arranged by

a special article, that Sieyes and Duclos, who exchanged the consular robes for those of the senator, and the second and the third consuls elected in their stead ; Cambaceres and Le Brune, should, for the first time, nominate the majority of the members of the senate, who were then to complete their own number. The translation of Duclos from a siuation of trust and dignity to the legislative body, did not excite surprise or interest ;' but the retirement of Sieyes, whom Buonaparte, aware of his talents and his ambition, and anxious for his removal, induced to vacate the consulship by the grant of a national domain of £600 a year, was the source of equal disappointment to his own friends, and to the enemies of the first consul.

It cannot be doubted that the willing and joyful acquiescence of the people of France, in the establishment of an executive power so despotic and extensive as that assumed by Buonaparte, was occasioned by their weariness of the changes incidental to popular governments, and by an indignation against the conduct of the directory, partly merited and partly unjust. To load with criminations the directorial constitution itself, furthered indeed the purpose of Buonaparte and his confederates, though the grievances to which the people were subjected during its existence, arose not from the defects of that constitution, but from the misconduct of those to whom its exercise was committed. That the constitution had been repeatedly violated, was a satisfactory motive for the punishment of the culpable, but presented no substantial argument for its farther violation. The consular government was not less subject to abuse than that of the directory ; but the former presented to the view of the people a desirable relief from the turbulence and uncertainty of faction, and the majority were not reluctant to sacrifice the appearance of freedom to the attainment of permanent tranquillity.

The inhumanity and the weakness of Buonaparte's personal character ; the irritability of his feelings, the selfish malignity of his views, and the violence of his passions had hitherto been repressed and concealed with a vigilance, commensurate to the importance of his secret designs and the ardor of his ambition. The massacre at Jaffa, which I have already recorded, and the administration of poison to his sick, were yet unknown, and unsuspected. The atrocities perpetrated in Italy were forgiven as the inevitable contingencies of war; his flight from Egypt was regarded as the most decisive testimony of his attachment to the military glory of his country, and if some few individuals more observing and more sceptical than the rest, reflected with doubt and alarm on his exploits before the Thuilleries, and his open appeal to the power and the suffrage of the army, their murmurs were overpowered by the enthusiastic plaudits of a vain and warlike people, exulting in the return and elevation of the CONQUEROR OF ITALY.

HISTORY OF THE WAR.

CHAP. XXVI.

State of the Public Mind at the Opening of Parliament—Proceedings in the Second Session of 1799—Overtures of Peace from Buonaparte in a Letter to the King—Debates in the First Session of 1800—Proceedings of the English and Irish Parliaments on the subject of an Union—The Plan is carried into Complete Effect.

IN Great Britain the energy of 1798 had continued through a considerable part of 1799. The battle of the Nile had re-animated the hopes of Europe, had encouraged the imperial powers to a renewal of hostilities, and the retreat of Buonaparte from the siege of a fortress, defended chiefly by Englishmen, added to the national exultation. The formidable armament prepared against Holland augmented the confidence of the multitude, and was regarded with no unjustifiable expectation of success by the most calm and intelligent observers. Those who considered the restoration of the Bourbons to the throne of France, as indispensible to the happiness of that country, and the interests of the world, looked forward to the coalition between Russia and the rest of the allies as decisive of the issue of the present contest. Even the moderate supporters of the war expected that the campaign of 1799 would be decidedly successful. Such was the state of the public mind, as influenced by the aspect of European affairs, when parliament was called so early as the 24th of September. The objects of this extraordinary convocation were to pass a law for extending the voluntary service of the militia, and while the regular forces were employed on the expedition, and the vote of certain pecuniary supplies on account of the unforeseen expences. The bill respecting the militia being accompanied with numerous regulations respecting the mode of its execution underwent considerable opposition as tending to diminish by donative the constitutional and patriotic force of the militia and to increase the standing army dependent on the crown: and as proving that the only real reason for alluring the militia to become soldiers was to increase the standing army and ministerial patronage. These objections were strongly urged, but the bill was passed into a law, and the other objects of the minister being soon and easily accomplished, an end was put to the session which lasted only from the 27th of September, till the 12th of October.

Before the opening of another session a series of disappointments and disasters on the part of the allies, had effected a considerable revolution in the state of public opinion. The failure of the expedition to Holland was a source of general disappointment, and the people unjustly but not unnaturally concluded that the destination of so powerful, and gallant an army was unwise, or its conduct unskilful.

The efforts of the British nation in the contests with the Batavian republic, were, as usual in the history of Britain, more successful at sea than on land; and not only in the northern sea, but beyond the Atlantic. The rich colony of Surinam, in which there is so striking an assemblage of luxuriancy of soil accumulation of riches, and luxury of manners, was added to our colonial possessions. This Dutch settlement voluntarily surrendered, August 20th, to lord Hugh Seymour, commander-in-chief of his majesty's land and sea forces in the leeward and windward Caribbee islands, who conducted against it a small squadron of ships, with troops collected from Grenada and St. Lucie. The principal articles of the capitulation were nearly the same that, in an earlier period of the war, had been granted to French islands. The inhabitants were to enjoy full security to their persons, and the free exercise of their religion, with the immediate and entire possession of their private property, whether on shore or afloat. All ships of war, artillery, provisions and stores in the public magazines and warehouses, as well as the effects of every description, belonging to the public, were to be given up to his Britannic majesty, in the state they then were; regular lists being taken by officers appointed for this purpose, by each of the contracting parties. In case the colony of Surinam should remain in the possession of his Britannic majesty, at the conclusion of a general peace, it should enjoy every right and every commercial privilege enjoyed by the British colonies in the West Indies. The troops then in Surinam, as well as the officers belonging to the different corps serving under its present government, should have it in their option to enter into his Britannic majesty's service, on the same footing, with respect to appointments and pay, as the rest of his army, provided that they took the oath of fidelity and allegiance to his majesty.

The parliament met on the 7th of February 1810. The first consul of France had at this time indicated to his majesty a desire of peace, with the design in the event of a rejection of his overtures to throw the odium on the English government. In a letter addressed to the king of England, he asked, "Is the war, which has for nearly eight years ravaged the four quarters of the world to be eternal? How can the two most enlightened nations of Europe, whose strength and resources are more than sufficient to answer the purposes of safety

and independence, sacrifice commercial prosperity, public welfare, and private happiness, to fallacious ideas of greatness. Why are they so insensible to the attractions of peace, an object of the first necessity and the highest glory. These sentiments he added could not but inspire the heart of a prince who was at the head of a free state, and whose sole view in the exercise of royalty was to make his people happy. France and Great Britain might long continue hostilities, without exhausting the strength which they abused, but he would venture to affirm that the fate of all civilized nations depended on the termination of the war.

His majesty commanded lord Grenville, to reply, that a negotiation could only be acceded to by the British court, at a period when France might be deemed more fully capable of maintaining the relations of peace and amity. The secretary after referring to the mischievous effects of French ambition and rapacity, observed that while the same system continued to prevail no defence but that of open and steady hostility promised to be effectual; that his majesty would feel the greatest joy whenever the danger, to which his dominions and those of his allies had been so long exposed, should really cease, and principles of justice and equity should operate among the rulers of France: but that the conviction of such a change could result only from experience and the evidence of facts; that the most natural pledge of its reality and permanence would be the restoration of the monarchy to the house of Bourbon; but, as the king had no right to dictate a form of government to France, he would content himself with such a state of affairs in that country as might hold out a prospect of security to the nations now endangered.

The minister Talleyrand was ordered to reply to some parts of lord Grenville's note, and to renew the offer of a negotiation. He denied that the French had been the aggressors, and retorted the charge upon the English court. A reply, justifying this and other imputations, was immediately sent to Paris.

When these papers were communicated

to the parliament, the secretary enlarged on the multiplied acts of injustice of which the French had been guilty, and on the danger of trusting to the professions of a government which paid no regard to the most solemn stipulations. He took a survey of the treaties concluded in the course of the war, not one of which, he said, had been kept inviolate. He examined the supposed grounds of better expectation from the new government, and pronounced them to be weak and unsatisfactory. Even if the first consul should be really disposed to peace, there was no security for the continuance of his power; and his acts might be annulled by another usurper. But there was no reason to think that he was sincere, or to repose any confidence in him; and, to prove this point, his lordship reviewed the chief traits of Buonaparte's conduct. He also argued at great length the disputed point of aggression, and concluded with moving an address, promising to support the king in the continuance of the war. The duke of Bedford thought the present moment favorable to negotiation, and proposed such an alteration of the address as suited his pacific ideas. He drew a gloomy picture of the state of the nation and of the miseries which the war had produced; and appealed to the humanity of the peers for the rescue of their countrymen from an increase of calamity. Lord Boringdon would not admit the probability of success in a negotiation with the present rulers of France; and the earl of Carlisle thought, that the only chance of security depended on the prosecution of hostilities. Lord Holland said, that there was a sufficient change in the principles of the French government to render a treaty more secure than it would have been some years ago; and that, if an ambitious spirit characterised the first consul, this was not a circumstance which ought to preclude negotiation, thought it might claim attention in the adjustment of terms. The earl of Caernarvon wished that the address might only thank his majesty for his gracious communication; yet he would not vote against it, as it

seemed proper to pause before we should treat of peace with an unsettled government. The earl of Liverpool spoke chiefly of the danger of a rash and premature negotiation, by which, when our commerce was prosperous beyond all example, and that of France was nearly annihilated, we should furnish our enemies with opportunities of reviving their trade and manufactures. The earl of Carlisle observed, that such an argument might operate to the prejudice of peace at any time, and was tantamount to a declaration of eternal war; and added that it indicated either a want of judgment or a want of feeling; but perhaps his lordship only referred to the case of an unsuccessful negotiation, in which we might by an armistice afford the enemy advantages that might quickly be turned against us, so that we should renew the war under circumstances less favorable than the predicament in which we stood when the conferences were opened. On a division, the address was voted according to the wish of the court, by a majority of 86.

An address to the same purport was offered for the approbation of the commons by Mr. Dundas, who animadverted with great freedom on the character of Buonaparte, and on the yet unchastened and dangerous spirit of the French government. Mr. Whitbread had a good opinion of the sincerity of the first consul in his late offer, and therefore advised that we should negotiate with him; but Mr. Canning said, that a more unfit season for treating would probably never occur. Mr. Pitt reviewed the origin of the war, and imputed it solely to French aggression; but, he was more general than particular in his references. He maintained that our court had no concern in the promotion of a confederacy before the year 1792 had nearly elapsed, and that, even then, we only proposed a general concert for the establishment of peace, not for the propagation of war. We had, he thought, been too cautious, rather than too forward or eager to interfere. We did not then know the true character of the mischief which threatened Europe, of those revolutionary principles which we had since found so destructive of the peace and happiness of society. It was the Jacobin system which produced the war, not the jealousy or the hostile disposition of the European powers. The French were the aggressors in every instance; and other nations were obliged to take arms in their own defence. The successive rulers of the republic had acted upon one general principle of arbitrary encroachment; and the late change of governors presented no hope of a cessation of the mischief, nor offered any security for negotiation. Mr. Fox was still of opinion that Great Britain was the aggressor in the contest; and he had not the least doubt of the aggressive conduct of Austria and Prussia. These powers had made preparations for interfering in the internal affairs of France; and our court, instead of fairly stating the grounds of its displeasure, or the terms which it required to secure its neutrality, declared war in effect by the abrupt dismission of M. Chauvelin. To call this a war of religion was an insult to God and man. To speak of the atrocities of the French, and not reprobate the iniquitous acts of the pretended advocates of social order, argued a gross inconsistency and a criminal partiality. To refuse to negotiate because Buonaparte was a military despot, whose character was not of the purest or most upright description, showed a wanton disregard to the happiness of nations and the lives of mankind.—The ministerial address was then sanctioned by a majority of 201 votes, the numbers being 265 and 64.

A debate of a similar complexion arose when the naval estimates were brought forward; and repetitions of stricture and invective occurred when Mr. Sheridan moved for an inquiry into the origin and conduct of the expedition to Holland. He wished to know precisely on what grounds and from what information it was undertaken, and to whose ignorance, misconception, or mismanagement, its failure was imputable. He did not believe that its main object was the acquisition of the

Dutch fleet, as that would be deemed a trifling point when compared with the restoration of the stadtholder and the promotion of social order and good government. He admitted the policy of endeavoring to rescue Holland from the dominion of France; but, before so many valuable lives were risqued, proper knowledge ought to have been obtained of the dispositions of the people and of the defensible state of the country, and the probability of success ought to have been maturely weighed. He did not dispute the courage of the army, or the abilities of the chief commanders; but he wished that the expedition had been more wisely planned. Mr Dundas spoke highly of the importance of the capture of the Dutch ships, which the French intended or wished to employ in the invasion of Britain or of Ireland; and he maintained that our contest with the French in Holland had, by a diversion of force, considerably weakened their exertions in Germany and Italy. He did not think it necessary or prudent to state the sources of intelligence on which the ministry had acted, or the instructions which had been given for the management of the expedition; but he contended that it was justifiable in every point of view, though it had failed in one of its three objects; and an inquiry was disapproved by a majority of 171. In the upper house, the same subject was brought forward by lord Holland, who moved for an immediate investigation: but the earl of Moira opposed it, as it might lead to dangerous disclosures. Lord Mulgrave said, that it would be merely an inquiry into the conduct of the winds and the discretion of the clouds; lord Grenville affirmed that no real grounds of blame existed; and only six peers voted for the motion, while 51 appeared against it.

In adjusting the accounts of the year, Mr. Pitt estimated the supplies at 39,000,000 and a half. He lamented that the tax upon income had not been so productive as it ought to have been; but he hoped that it might be so enforced as to become more effective. Though he had bargained for a loan of 18,000,000 and a half, he said that he should only have occasion to propose new taxes for the interest of 5,000,000, as a part of the income tax would serve for the remainder. Thus the people were threatened with the permanence of a burden which was at first imposed merely as a war-tax.

A considerable number of bills varied the business of this session. The bills for improving the income-tax tended to exact more from farmers, and to diminish the facility of evasion. The suspension of the *habeas corpus* act was continued by a new bill, though Mr. Sheridan and sir Francis Burdett indignantly opposed it. The time for the redemption of the land-tax was extended, as the pretended advantage was not eagerly embraced. Several bills were enacted for lessening the restrictions upon the trade of neutrals, and other commercial purposes. Various regulations, tending to remedy the inconveniences arising from the high price of corn, were enforced, without producing great benefit or relief.

With the necessaries of life, public morals occupied the attention of the legislature. The crime of adultery being extremely prevalent, was by many supposed to exceed in frequency the dissolution of former times. It was conceived by various political moralists, that the permission granted to the offending parties, after a divorce, to intermarry, was one powerful cause of the seduction of married women. To remove this incentive, lord Auckland proposed a bill, making it unlawful for any person, on account of whose adultery a bill of divorce should be applied for in that house, to intermarry with the woman from whom the complaining party might be divorced. This restriction, his lordship observed, always prevailed, and still did prevail in Scotland, where the parties, after being divorced, were never permitted to marry. The diversity of the case here, in his opinion, in a great measure accounted for the prevalence of the crime. This bill was strongly contested in the house; both the supporters and opponents admitted and

lamented the frequency of a crime, cutting asunder the most important ties of social life; both shewed themselves friends of religion and morality, pursuing the same object through different means. Lord Auckland reasoned, that the certain preclusion from subsequent marriage, would in many cases operate as a preventative of the crime; the force of their reasoning obviously depended upon the admission of a general fact, that the hopes, or at least the probality, of a future permanent relation, facilitated the temporary success of a seducer. The opponents of the bill, the most active of whom was the duke of Clarence, took a different view of the tendency of circumstances and situation, in determining female affections and conduct: the prohibition would not act as a discouragement of the vice; the obstacle might inflame the passion, and furnish new materials to the dexterity of an accomplished seducer. Inadequate to the prevention of the crime, it would produce the most pernicious consequences to the weaker of the parties concerned in the commission. Heinous and hurtful as this vice was, still it was possible that the seduced person might not be entirely profligate and abandoned. To the preservation of virtue, next in moral wisdom was recovery from vice, before it became habitual and inveterate: the present bill, if passed into a law, would drive the females to desperation and unrestrained licentiousness. Lord Carlisle also very strenuously opposed the bill in question: the law lords, and the bishops in general, supported lord Auckland's proposition; but it was rejected by a considerable majority. This bill attracted the public attention much more than any measure which was introduced into parliament, in the course of the whole session. It was supported by the highest political, legal, and ecclesiastical authority; was evidently devised from the best intentions, and framed with great ability: it may, however, be doubted, whether the prospect of the restriction, would in many instances prevent the crime; and it was morally certain that after it was committed, · the restriction itself must powerfully tend to drive a female to infamous profligacy.

An incident that happened near the close of this session warmly interested the feelings, not only of both houses of parliament, but of the whole nation. On the 15th of May, his majesty went to the theatre-royal Drury-lane : as he was entering the box, a man ·in the pit near the orchestra, on the right hand side, suddenly stood up and discharged a pistol at the royal person. The king had advanced about four steps from the door : on the report of the pistol, his majesty stopped, and stood firmly. The house was immediately in an uproar, and the cry of " seize him !" resounded from every part of the theatre : the king, not the least disconcerted, came nearly to the front of the box. The man who had fired it was immediately dragged into the orchestra, and carried behind the scenes : his name was found to be Hadfield. Being examined by a magistrate, he exhibited symptoms of insanity ; though some of his answers were rational. The veneration and love that the nation bore to his majesty's person, was by this accident awakened into an enthusiastic joy at his escape ; even the spirit of faction was lost in a general stream of loyalty and exultation. Addresses of congratulation on the king's escape were presented by both houses of parliament, the universities, the corporation of London, and by all the other corporations as well as the counties. Hadfield was tried in the court of king's bench for high treason ; and it was proved that he had been for some years insane, chiefly in consequence of wounds received in his head, when he acted as a serjeant in the army, in 1794, in Holland : he was therefore acquitted, but not discharged. In consequence of Hadfield's act, and repeated instances of insanity, being directed against a personage whose safety was so dear and important to the state, two additional clauses, by way of amendments, were added to the insanity bill. The first was to hinder individuals confined for alleged lunacy, from

being bailed, in any circumstances, without the concurrence of one of the magistrates who committed him ; except by the judges, or at the quarter-sessions of the peace. The second clause proceeded on a principle similar to the first, and provided more especially for the personal safety of the sovereign, repeatedly endangered by insane persons.

The most important deliberations of this period were those which related to an union of the parliaments of Great Britain and Ireland. When the ministry conceived that the influence of government had been sufficiently exercised in favor of the scheme, the marquis Cornwallis prepared to submit it to the peers and commons of the kingdom which he governed.

Whatever may have been the wishes of England and Ireland to form together an incorporative union, and in the language of royalty itself, to " settle such a complete and final adjustment as might best tend to improve and perpetuate a connection essential for their common security, and to consolidate the strength, power, and resources of the British empire ;" it is not a little singular that they should be indebted for that important event, to a measure which aimed a deadly blow at the constitution and happiness of the latter, and imminently endangered the safety of the former. Had not the society of United Irishmen existed, the legislation of both countries would, in all probability, have continued distinct. The establishment of the independence of the Irish parliament, the enjoyment of a free trade, and the concessions made to the catholics, must have rendered not only the majority of the commons of Ireland; but a vast majority of the people, at large, decidedly inimical to the plan of legislative union. But an event which could not be expected in the common course of affairs, was at length produced by the machinations of its most resolute opponents ; and the intrigues of those who wished not merely for an absolute separation from Great Britain, but were anxious to destroy at home, every legal institution. Of all the conspiracies formed for the overthrow of modern governments, that of the United Irishmen was the most dangerous. The ends which it proposed to achieve, the number of its partizans, the abilities and boldness of the leaders, the extraordinary secrecy with which its operations were conducted, the encouragement held out to perseverance by the promised assistance of the French republic; and the ignorance of the people whose passions were inflamed by the agents of anarchy and faction, combined to confer on this combination a criminal pre-eminence unprecedented in the history of rebellion.

After surmounting the various and formidable perils which threatened the life, property, and dearest interests of society, it would have been unnatural, and impolitic for the ministers of Britain, to remain tranquil, and indifferent to the future. It was equally natural for the members of both houses, the principal inhabitants and the more enlightened classes of the community in Ireland to be dissatisfied with what had yet been done. The rebellion indeed was extinguished but there existed no positive pledge, no certain security for the preservation of their civil and religious institutions, their property, and the relations of social life. The threats of the common enemy did not expire with the death of the conspiracy; Ireland was in the opinion of France, a vulnerable point which might still be successfully attacked, and few denied that some fundamental regulations were necessary to guard against the threatened danger.

A measure of so much moment could not be expected to pass, without strong and tumultuous opposition. It was opposed by many from motives of interest, or from the spirit of anti-ministerial opposition, and by a few from conscientious and patriotic motives. Aware of the intended revival, sir Laurence Parsons in the Irish commons moved for the continuance of a separate parliament, after a speech in which he strongly censured the arbitrary spirit evinced by Great Britain in her desire of trampling on the independence of Ireland, and urged his countrymen to repel

Vol. I.

1800. such attempts with indignant zeal. A long debate followed; and the thunders of eloquence attacked, but did not blast, the unpleasing scheme.

When lord Castlereagh and Mr. Latouche had defended the views of the court, lord Cole inveighed against the measure, and the means by which it was promoted; and Mr. Ogle protested against the surrender of the Irish constitution Mr. Fitzgerald conjured the house not to extinguish the light of the realm, as it would not be easy to find, in the event of a change of sentiment, "the Promethian heat which could that light relumine;" and he hinted, that the people would not be disposed to respect, as sacred, a compact adjusted under the influence of martial law. Mr. G. Ponsonby was disgusted at that want of patriotism which sought the destruction of a parliament whose exertions had benefited the country; and he could not persuade himself to believe that the people or the majority of their representatives would consent to such an ignominious sacrifice. Mr. Bushe, after the infliction of oratorical chastisement on the attorney-general for his invectives against the anti-unionists, called on every man of spirit in the house to resist a measure which would subject Ireland to a degrading and oppressive yoke. Mr. Arthur Moore affirmed, that it would entail slavery on both nations; and Mr. Grattan condemned it with great acrimony. He maintained the finality of the settlement of 1782, from the nature of the agreement, and the sense in which it was understood at the time by the contracting parties. He reproached the English minister for having deferred his scheme till he had reduced Ireland to the condition of a conquest, and for reviving that doctrine of the incompatibility of two independent legislatures in one empire, which had deprived Britain of her American colonies. He had no fear of the prevalence of such discord between the parliaments as might injure imperial connection; and he arraigned, as weak and mischievous, the conduct of that statesman, who, affecting to foresee an improbable event, exaggerated

3 K

its danger, and offered a remedy which would render that peril not only imminent but deadly. To the fabric intended as a substitute for the pile that would be overthrown, there were, he said, two striking objections. It would not be an identification of people; for it would exclude the catholics. It would merge the Irish parliament in another assembly, and would thus extinguish the constitution. There was not in the plan any one profound or exalted conception. What would be the elements of the imperial legislature? Irish deserters of their country, and a British parliament which had destroyed the constitution. From such an assembly what favor, what protection, could Ireland expect?—Having expatiated on other points, he declared that, if he were expiring on the floor, he would utter his last breath against a project so unconstitutional and ruinous.—Mr. Corry allowed that the adjustment of 1782 was conclusive with regard to its particular object, viz. the ascertainment of the independence of Ireland; but he could by no means admit, what was palpably absurd, that the parliament was precluded by such a settlement from entering into an agreement with any other legislature, or from applying to the future advantage of the country the circumstances arising from new situations. He also controverted, as equally absurd, the idea that the Hibernian parliament would be annihilated by an union. The three estates—the king, lords, and commons of Ireland—would continue, he said, to legislate for that country. He argued, that, without an incorporation, there would be a constant risque of dissension, as experience had proved the insufficiency of the existing bond of connection; that the inferiority of the constitution of Ireland to that of Great Britain appeared in the minister's non-responsibility to the parliament of the former kingdom; and that an union would most effectually secure to his countrymen a due participation of the blessings enjoyed by the British community.—After a debate of extraordinary length, the baronet's motion was rejected by a majority of 42.

The resolutions of the British parliament being at length communicated to the Irish peers and commons by the lord-lieutenant, a full developement of the scheme was given by lord Castlereagh in an elaborate speech. The first article provided, that the two realms should be incorporated, under the appellation of the United Kingdom of Great Britain and Ireland. The succession to the monarchy was continued, not altered, by the second; the third ordained an union of the parliaments of the two countries; the fourth assigned the representation of Ireland in the united legislature to four spiritual and twenty-eight temporal peers and one hundred commoners; the fifth related to the union of the churches; the sixth tended to the adjustment of commercial concerns on a general basis of equality; the seventh fixed the amount of financial contribution at the rate at fifteen parts for Great Britain to two for Ireland; and the eighth respected the continuance of the existing laws and courts of justice.

The three first provisions, he said, would establish the complete identity of the executive power in every possibility of circumstance and in every application of authority. Without such an identification, the connection was so imperfect, that a total separation might be apprehended. To avoid that danger, Ireland was obliged, in imperial questions, to acquiesce in the edicts of Britain, and to sacrifice every feeling of pride and independence; and this state of subordination, in the progress of her prosperity, might inflame her discontent, and augment the risque of separation. The irresponsibility of the minister to the Irish parliament formed another objection to the prevailing system; and nothing but an union, by which the jurisdiction of parliament would be rendered as comprehensive as the executive power, would secure a due and desirable responsibility.

He supported the fourth article by a reference to the proportional wealth and population of each country; proposed that the prelates should sit by rotation of sessions, and the temporal peers for life; recommended a continuance of the permission granted to Irish noblemen to represent a British county or town, on condition of a suspension of the privileges of the peerage; advised, that sixty-four of the commoners should be chosen for the counties—that the university, the metropolis, and Cork, should depute five members—and that thirty-one towns, selected according to the contributions of the inhabitants for hearths and windows, should send the remaining number.

On the subject of the church, he prognosticated the happy effects of the new plan. During a separation, the church of Ireland would be liable to be impeached on local grounds, and might be unable to withstand the argument or the attack of physical force; but an incorporation with that of England would remove all grounds of alarm, by giving the superiority of number to the members of the establishment. The protestants, thus strengthened, would be less jealous and distrustful of the catholics: the latter would submit with less repugnance to an imperial majority than they had to a national minority, and might expect a more impartial discussion of their claims; and hence would arise a pleasing prospect of concord and harmony.

The commercial regulations, he said, would establish a mutual freedom of intercourse, as far as the difference of internal taxes, and the necessity of securing particular manufactures by protecting duties, would allow. The British and Irish bounties on the exportation of Irish linen would be perpetuated, and a full participation in the article of sail-cloth would be afforded to his countrymen, who would also secure for ever many raw materials which they could procure from no other country than Britain.

Having illustrated the equity of the ratio proposed for the arrangements of finance, by comparative estimates of commerce and consumption, he observed, that the past public debts would be separately borne by each country; that the assigned proportion was destined for twenty years, at the expiration of which term it might be revised by the parliament; and that, by the union, Ireland would save above £950,000 sterling per annum in the future charges

of the war and about £450,000 in the expense of the peace establishment.

When he had concluded his details and his reasonings, he trusted that he had proved the proposal to be honorable for Britain to offer and for Ireland to accept; that he had demonstrated its tendency to remove from the executive power such anomalies as were the constant sources of jealousy and discontent, to extinguish the possibility of separation, to diminish considerably the financial expenses of Ireland, to encourage the produce of her soil, augment the resources of her commerce, and establish the representation of her people on a basis of just proportion, preclusive of all disputes respecting parliamentary reform.

Mr. Ponsonby renewed his attack upon the scheme, and ridiculed or reprobated its various articles. Mr. Dobbs argued, that it would be ruinous to Ireland, and render her the devoted slave of Britain. It was stigmatised by colonel Vereker as a most detestable measure; was less severely censured by Mr. Claudius Beresford; was vehemently opposed by Mr. Burrowes; and was again furiously assailed by Mr. Grattan: but it was defended by Mr. Smith and other intelligent speakers, and a majority of 43 voted for its prosecution.

It was soon after discussed by the peers. The earl of Clare, to demonstrate the necessity of its adoption, took a survey of the history of Ireland from the time of her first connection with this country. He imputed her turmoils and misfortunes principally to the impolicy of the English government, and traced the sinister progress of civil and religious dissensions. He spoke of the adjustment of 1782 as one which was not intended to be conclusive; and affirmed that, even if it had been deemed final at the time, a revision of it was strictly justifiable, when practice and experience had proved that it had sown the seeds of ceaseless contention. Such, he said, was the nature of the connection, that it could only depend on the admitted inferiority of Ireland; and the only security for the concurrence of the two countries in imperial acts, was the commanding influence of the English executive

2 k 2

parliament of Ireland regulated the representation of that country, according to the plan stated by lord Castlereagh. The second comprised the eight articles of union, with the few alterations which they had received from the British senate. A third bill provided for the grant of pecuniary compensation to the individuals who had a commanding influence in the boroughs intended to be disfranchised : but, as this was a species of property unauthorised by the constitution, the patriotism of these gentlemen ought to have prompted them to reject the offer

These bills did not pass without a renewal of spirited debate among the members of the expiring parliament. In England, the progress of the bill of union was not marked by the asperity of altercation : and, after its enactment, the king declared, that he should "ever consider this great measure as the happiest event of his reign." That it was one of the most judicious acts of this eventful period, few are disposed to deny ; and it is the sincere wish of the present writer, that its beneficial effects may be attested by uniform experience.

HISTORY OF THE WAR.

CHAP. XXVII.

Prudence and Address of Buonaparte on his Accession to the Consulate—Suppression of Internal Disturbances—Execution of the Count de Frotté—Foreign Policy of the first Consul—Siege of Genoa—Its Surrender.

AT no period of his career did Buonaparte discover more prudence and sagacity than in the general system of his policy, subsequent to the establishment of the new constitution. He was sensible of the importance of public opinion to the confirmation of his authority, and regulated his conduct by the wishes and expectations of the people. He knew that the nation was disgusted with the tyranny and oppressions of the directory, looked forward with sanguine hopes to a more just and liberal exercise of the supreme authority, and was ardently desirous of peace. He was aware, at the same time, that, though by the aid of a strong party and by his ascendency over the army, he had been enabled to possess himself of almost unlimited power, yet the people were flattered with the idea of liberty, and that it was necessary to encourage their delusion till his authority should be established beyond the possibility of successful opposition. Moderation therefore, a regard for freedom, and a love of peace, were the ostensible outlines of his policy. He demeaned himself with liberality towards the exiled princes and nobles; he empowered general Hedoville, who commanded what was called the army of England, now employed in suppressing the Chouans and other royalists, to conclude an armistice with several of their chiefs, and to invite their followers to return to their obedience to the existing government, by displaying the merits of the new constitution. "Frenchmen," said he, in a proclamation now issued, "the happy change which has taken place in the government, will bring to our country peace, both internal and external. The legislative committees and the consuls of the republic belong to no faction. Their object is the happiness and glory of the French nation. They have the firmest confidence in the victories of our armies, and every heart partakes with them in this confidence. There is already a suspension of arms in some of the western departments, and orders have been given for carrying it into execution. It is not to be doubted but the chiefs of insurgents and the inhabitants of districts occupied by the armies, will submit without delay to the laws of the republic. A solid peace in the interior is to be established only by the united efforts of all good citizens to conciliate a mutual affection." To bring the revolters back to their duty, he signified that he viewed them in the light of deluded persons, and that their crimes had originated in the late unjust and oppressive government. "It is," he assured them, "in order to remedy these acts of injustice and these errors, that a government founded on the sacred basis of liberty, equality, and a system of representation has been proclaimed to the nation, and joyfully received." While he adopted these prudential methods of attaching the people to the new constitution, he endeavored to conciliate their zealous support in his views of foreign policy. To persuade the nation that he was desirous of peace, to throw the odium of continued warfare on the hostile powers, and thus to reconcile the French people to the expenses and exertions which would be required to accomplish his ambitious enterprises, he addressed the pacific letter already quoted, to his Britannic majesty. The answer transmitted by lord Grenville, which received his assurances with expressions of disdain, and of diffidence in the person whom the French people had raised to the station of chief magistrate, enabled him to make the desired impression on the public mind, and to prepare the way for the vigorous prosecution of his warlike measures. His first care was to subdue the royalists, who had again assembled in considerable force in the western departments, and in Brittany were become so confident in their strength, that they affixed placards in the most public places of the city of Dinan, inviting the people to join the standard of Lewis XVIII. and threatening vengeance against those who should refuse. These unhappy partisans, however, with much indiscreet zeal, had neither union, resources, nor able chiefs, and their unsuccessful efforts tended only to prejudice the government against the moderate and prudent royalists. The chief consul perceiving that they were inattentive to his conciliatory overtures, adopted the most determined measures for suppressing them. General Brune, who was sent to take the command against them, easily dispersed the detached bodies of insurgents, and reduced them to submission. A pacification was at length concluded by which the royalists in the western departments, were required to surrender their arms. Count Louis de Frotté, the only chief of repute since the death of Charette, refusing to purchase his life at the expense of his principles, was taken prisoner in his place of refuge with six of his officers. Being condemned by a court-martial to be shot, they suffered the sentence with great magnanimity, falling

the last victims to the dynasty of Bourbon. When news of the final termination of the rebellion by the capture and death of count Louis de Frotté was received by Buonaparte, he communicated the intelligence to the legislative assembly. It was received with tumultuous applause. When the unfortunate and fugitive prince of the Bourbon family, the count D'Artois or *Monsieur*, was made acquainted with the death of M. de Frotté, he immediately paid a visit to the father of that young hero, in London, and mingled his tears of condolence with those of the unhappy parent. It was a younger brother of M. de Frotté who aided the escape of sir Sidney Smith from the tower of the temple, and afterwards served under him in the rank of major, at the siege of Acre.

At the same time that Buonaparte was employing every mode of conciliation for reclaiming the armed royalists, the constitutional bishops assembled at Paris, invited the non-spiring bishops to evangelical communion, and RELIGIOUS PEACE. If such pacification could indeed have been effected, it would have been far more wonderful than that which was gained by Buonaparte, partly by conciliatory and partly by compulsory measures with the warrior chiefs of the royalists.

The determination of the British ministry on the subject of peace or war with France, has been already recorded in the abstract of debates in parliament. They had no objection to treat with any form of government in France that should appear from experience or the evidence of facts, to be able and willing to negotiate on the principles established among European nations, and to preserve and support the usual relations of peace and amity; but a peace concluded with a precarious government must itself be precarious. The peace that did not promise to be permanent was good for nothing, and was pregnant with danger and dishonor. But no secure and lasting peace could co-exist with a system of aggression, aggrandisement, and universal destruction, from which it did not by any means appear that the new chief, the first consul, Buonaparte, had at all departed. In circumstances like these, the only means of obtaining an honorable, secure, and lasting peace, was to prosecute the war with vigor. Such also were the sentiments of the great ally of Britain, the emperor of Germany.

Of the political situation of Austria and of the Germanic body in relation to France, some idea may be formed from the following circular letter of the archduke Charles, dated at Donaueschingen, to the anterior circles of the empire.

"It is from the impulse of the most invincible necessity that I am induced to speak to you of an object, and of dispositions from whence there may arise the greatest detriment to the common cause of Germany. I perceive with regret that the late events in France, through which the supreme power has passed into new hands, have revived the hope already so often deceived, of an approaching pacification, and that on the strength of this premature supposition, an idea prevails, that it is not, for the present, necessary to call on the princes and states of the empire for their contingents, and the discharge of the other duties they owe to the constitution. A true German and patriotic heart, and an understanding enlightened by so much sad experience, can never be led into so great an error: an error, which would deprive us of the only means of concluding a speedy peace, on fair and proper terms, and such as might be solid and lasting. It would be wrong, for a moment, to lose sight of the maxim, that the most vigorous preparation for war is the surest way to obtain peace. This we shall acquire both the sooner, and on the better terms, if the enemy shall see that we are in a state for continuing the war, in case of his persisting in an imperious tone, and pretending yet once more to prescribe a peace, accompanied with disgrace and slavery, or that should put it into his power to involve us in disgrace and slavery hereafter. We have been too often deceived by a precipitate hope of

peace, on the part of France, to be lulled, by the late events, into a sleep of fallacious security. It has been invariably found, that every new faction in France has talked a great deal about peace. The word peace has been always in their mouths, never in their hearts. By the plausible assurances of peace they only aimed at drawing over public opinion to their side, and acquiring popularity. They have uniformly commenced new wars. They have never shewn a disposition to make peace on equal terms. By peace, they mean nothing more than the extermination of their enemies.

"The revolution of the 9th of November, when closely contemplated, cannot, all at once, inspire full confidence in the new government. A part of the persons, into whose hands the supreme power has fallen, are the members of former councils, who, both by their professed principles, and the whole of their public conduct, have sworn eternal enmity and mortal hatred to all states not constituted like their own; several of which they have overthrown, and others of which, in the midst of perfect peace, they have perfidiously brought under their subjection. Nor is the spirit that reigns in the publications of France of the most pacific nature. In these, it is often said, that the late revolution has no other end in view, than to raise the republic to the rank which she ought to hold in the scale of European nations. The old directory, in those writings, is censured, not for having made war on their neighbours, but for having made war unsuccessfully; for not having made new conquests, and for having lost provinces that had been before conquered. The French proclamations set out always with a discourse about victory, and speak of peace only in the last place: which shews that they do not yet consider circumstances as sufficiently favorable for pacification; and that they have a mind, before the conclusion of peace, to try the chances of war. The minister of war announces openly, that he is busily employed in recruiting the army, and providing all things necessary for its equipment and support. He adds, that he will join it himself, and share its dangers, as soon as the season will admit the opening of the campaign ; and that he is preparing new (pretended] triumphs.

" In the warlike preparations of France, there has been no remission, that can induce the Germans to admit of any relaxation in theirs ; on the contrary, a new military corps is to be formed in the four departments not united to the republic. But, even on the supposition, that there is no reason for mistrusting the views and the projects of the new rulers of France, the late revolution is not yet sufficiently confirmed and consolidated to afford any reasonable assurance that it will not be overthrown as the others have been. On the whole, the present question is not concerning such a peace, as a convention for a short time, or an armistice. The point in hand is, conditions of perfect security ; conditions demanded by honour, dignity, liberty, the integrity of the German empire, and the inviolability of the most sacred treaties. The object contended for, is a fit, just, and permanent peace, according to the sense of the decisions of the diet ; such as shall secure religion, property, civil order, and the constitution of the German empire.

" I invite you to take all these objections into your most serious consideration, according to the sentiments of patriotism with which you are inspired ; and, having done so, you will undoubtedly agree with me, that prudence imperiously demands that you do not suffer yourselves to be thrown into a state of inaction, by rumors of approaching peace, and more moderate principles ; but to keep your arms in your hands, and to preserve a military attitude until peace be actually signed. You will perceive, as I do, how fatally imprudent it would be to let any langor creep into measures of defence, and how necessary it is to redouble our efforts for a due augmentation of the troops, and to accomplish, with the greatest activity, and, in the most serious manner, the renewed decision of the diet, and the resolutions it entered into and confirmed, for the common defence ; in order that we may have it in our

power to oppose an energetic mass of efforts, to the views of the enemy, whatever they may be. It is only by an imposing military force that it is possible to hinder the enemy from new attacks and devastations ; to shorten or to terminate the evils of war ; to improve the terms of pacification ; and, in a word, to accelerate a peace worthy of the name, and to compensate the multiplied sacrifices by which, for so long a time, we have endeavored to procure it."

The court of Vienna fortified, as we have seen, by pecuniary supplies from England, and the accession of Bavarians, Wurtemburgers, and other German troops in British pay, and mindful of both the past and recent glory and conquests of the Austrian arms, was not to be shaken or diverted from its resolution of persevering in war, by the offer of a negotiation for peace, by Buonaparte, on the general ground of the treaty of Campo Formio. The imperial ministers replied to the overtures of the first consul, that the emperor would not negociate for peace, but in conjunction with his ally the king of Great Britain. Though the circles of the empire were not to be roused from that lethargic indifference to the common prosperity and safety, into which, from the prevailing luxury and selfishness of the age, and the hope of security and advantage they had fallen, the Austrians, seconded by the English, prepared for military operations with great alacrity and vigor, notwithstanding the defection of the Russians, and the opposition of a powerful party at court, headed by the archduke Charles. Nor were the military preparations of the French suspended or relaxed, during the short period of correspondence with the Austrian and English courts. The insurrections in the western departments, while they justified military movements and conscriptions, were the pretext for assembling and exercising a vast body of troops, to be employed as occasion might require and in any direction.

After the installation of the consuls, a ceremony which was performed with considerable pomp, at the Thuilleries on the 19th of February, and the final ; reduction of the rebellion in the west, the first consul gave official notice of the rejection of those overtures for peace, which he had tendered to different powers. He addressed a proclamation complaining of the obstinate determination of the English to continue the war, and inviting the French to furnish the subsidies and men, that might be necessary for the acquisition of peace by force of arms, since it could not be regained by conciliatory measures. It was at the same time decreed by the consuls that an army of reserve should be raised, to consist of 60,000 men, composed of conscripts, to be assembled at Dijon, where the first consul was to take the command in person. A part of the new consular guard amounting to 36,000 men, of the finest youth of France, received orders to hold themselves in readiness to march to Dijon to join the army of reserve. Berthier, minister at war, was to accompany the general-in-chief, and the ex-director Carnot, was to take charge of his department in his absence. Bernadotte was appointed to be one of the lieutenant-generals.

While the French army of reserve is drawing from the different parts of France to Dijon, it will be proper to look back to the situation of military affairs at the close of the preceding campaign. At the end of 1799 the French retained nothing in Italy but the city and republic of Venice, and all the passes of the mountains which divide that country from France were in the possession of the Austrians. On the other hand the French commanded and occupied the whole left bank of the Rhine from its source to where it falls by divided streams, into the ocean, or from Switzerland to Holland both inclusive.

General Macdonald having demolished the works constructed for the siege of Coni, and left a garrison there, proceeded to establish his advanced posts in cantonments, among the openings and passes of the Piedmontese and maritime Alps. He then distributed the rest of his army in winter quarters, throughout Piedmont and

Lombardy fixing his head quarters at Turin. Championnet retreating to his defensive posts in the maritime Alps stationed the principal part of his troops between Savona and Genoa, the ordinary asylum of the republicans after their defeat. In the beginning of December he quitted a command which he had held without reputation and without success. It would not however be just to appreciate his talents by the result of the three last months of the campaign which he conducted, for his army was left so totally destitute of money, provision, clothing and military equipage, that he was less occupied in fighting than in providing for the existence of his troops, in preventing and appeasing their discontent, in repressing their excesses occasioned by hunger and despair, and in protecting them from the vengeance of the inhabitants of the country.

The situation of the French army quartered in the territories of Genoa was still more disastrous. The vessels of the allies constantly cruizing on the coast of Genoa, prevented or intercepted the supplies of foreign grain, which are at all times necessary for the maintenance of that country and which were become much more requisite by the additional consumption of the troops. The scarcity of grain was at different times so excessive that a real famine was to be dreaded, and the price of bread was always exorbitant. The wants of the French, as may easily be supposed, were always the first supplied, and the people were left to the horrors of their fate. Several insurrections broke out, not only in the country, but even in Genoa ; and the French, incapable of remedying the evils which occasioned them, under the pretext of defending the town against the imperialists, declared it to be in a state of siege, that is to say, they suspended the authority of government, and subjected it to their own. The Ligurian republic, thus reduced under subjection to their ally, consoled themselves by imitating, both in June and November, the changes of government which took place, at those periods, in France. It was in this state of things, not unlike that in which he had left

Switzerland, that general Massena took the command of the army of Italy, in place of Championnet ; and, according to the custom of the French commanders, announced himself before-hand, by a proclamation, in which he promised plenty and victory.

These engagements he found it the more difficult to fulfil, as while his army was held in a state of blockade by an English fleet, under lord Keith at sea, the victorious Austrians were in possession of all the territories that environ those of the Genoese republic.

Though no armistice had been agreed on between the French and Austrians, the grand operations of the war, in other quarters, were suspended by the rigor of the seasons. Yet there were some parts, such as the banks of the Levante and the Scrivia, where there was still some fighting. In a course of actions between a part of the French army, on the 14th, 15th, and 16th of December, and the Austrian division, under the generals Klenau and Hohenzollern, in which several hundreds of men were killed on each side.

These skirmishes finally closed the campaign, and the corps of the generals Klenau and Hohenzollern on the one side as well as those of the French generals St. Cyr and Vatrin on the other, took up their winter quarters.

The positions of the opposite armies, in the beginning of January, 1800, were these :—The Austrian army of Switzerland ended at the upper valley of the Tesino, and was there met by the army of Italy, which had absorbed that of the Tyrol. General Davidovich occupied Bellinzona, and his advanced posts extended as far as Ariolo, thus observing the openings of the St. Gothard. That of the Simplon was guarded by a part of the corps which prince Victor de Rohan had commanded in the valley of Ossola, on the frontier of the Upper Valais. The troops left in the valley of Aosta by genera'. Haddick, when at the end of October, he went to reinforce general Kray, were stationed along the frontier of the Lower Valais, and occupied the foot of the Great and

Little St. Bernard. The passages of the Maurienne, the foot of mount Cenis, the valley of Suza, till beyond Exiles, and that of Cluzon till beyond Fenestrelles, which was held in blockade, were guarded by different detachments, all under the orders of general Kaim, who commanded at Turin, where the right of the army ended. The centre, under the orders of the generals Sommoriva, Ott, Gottesheim, and Bellegarde, extended in a waving line by the roots of the maritime Alps to Oneglia, Albinga, and Finale, and held several posts on the very borders of France. The left wing of the Austrian army, under the command of general Kray, occupied the valleys of the Bormida, Erno, the Orba, and the Scrivia. It was in possession of Sasello, Ovada, Novi, and Serravalle, and masked Gavi. A small body of troops, placed in the imperial fiefs, held the roads leading from Genoa to Pavia and Plantia. Another was posted in the upper valley of the Taro, where it communicated with another, under general Klenau, whose principal force was concentrated on the Magra ; his advanced posts reaching as far as Lestria and Varese. Such was the semicircular line occupied by the imperial troops opposite to the enemy. Some others were dispersed in Tuscany, the march of Ancona, the territories of Bologna and Ferrara, the Mantuan, and the Milanese. The reinforcements, which had arrived during the last three months of the campaign, raised the number of Austrians, spread over the face of Italy, to at least 60,000 : and they had about 10,000 Piedmontese auxiliaries. About 20,000 Tuscans and Neapolitans, too, embraced their cause : but they had no enemies to contend with, or rather to punish, but the disarmed soldiers of the Cisalpine, Roman, and Partheropian republics.

The positions which at the end of the campaign remained in possession of the French, on the side of Italy, were as follows : the right wing of the army of the Alps occupied the valley of the Rhone, and had its advanced posts in the different small passages of the Valais and the Great St. Bernard. The left of the united armies of the Alps and of Italy, possessed the Little St. Bernard, mount Cenis, and the extremities of the other passages of the Tarenfaise and of the Maurienne. It supported, with some detachments of infantry, the Vandois, who were armed in favor of the republic, and opposed the imperial posts placed near to Chenale and to Argentiere, in the valleys of the Vraita and of the Stura.—There the left of the united army of the Alps and Italy, under the command of Massena, ended. The centre guarded the two roads from Coni to Nice, and in spite of the rigor of the season, had posts on the Col de Fennestre, and the Col de Tende. It lined the Riviera di Ponente as far as Savona, and kept strong detachments in the middle of the Ligurian Alps, and on all the passages which lead to the valley of the Tanaro. The right of the French army garrisoned Savona and Genoa, as also the towns between them, and had cantonments on the four roads which lead to the valleys of the Bormida, the Erno, the Orba, and the Scrivia. On the 1st, their picquets went beyond Cairo : on the 2nd, beyond Sassolo ; on the 3rd, beyond Campo-Freddo ; and, on the 4th, beyond Voltaggio, having also, on the latter, a garrison in the fort of Gavi. They faced the imperialists in the two roads which go from Genoa to Voghera and Bobbio across the imperial fiefs, possessed a part of that chain of mountains which separates the valley of the Trebbia from the Riviera di Levante, and covered on that side, the approaches to Genoa.— Upon this long and irregular line from Genoa to the Great St. Bernard, there were not more than 40,000 men. From the Var to Genoa, there were scarcely 25,000, almost all infantry. A reinforcement of 15,000 men, from Switzerland, or from the interior, were on the march to join the army of Italy. Others were likewise promised ; but those which arrived, were few in number, and so great was the void in the ranks of the French army, produced by an epidemic fever, and by the desertion, that Massena, in the month of April following, had not more than 35,000 men in the whole of the extent of the county of Nice, and of the state of Genoa. The privations, distresses, and miseries, in which the soldiers were left, during the rigors of winter, were felt more sensibly, and suffered with more impatience, during the idleness of winter quarters, than they would have been amidst the toils of marches, and the tumults of action. Several insurrections broke out among the troops that occupied the territories of Genoa. Companies of infantry, and even whole battalions returned into France with arms and baggage. Buonaparte and Massena exhausted their oratorial exhortations in vain. Nothing but severe examples, and some hundreds of thousands of livres extorted from the wretched Genoa, could stop this contagious malady of insubordination and desertion, which, no less than the fever before mentioned, threatened to leave the mountains of Liguria, and the frontiers of France, without defenders.

On the Upper Rhine, general Moreau had, by the end of February, made the necessary dispositions for the immediate commencement of the campaign. The force under his command was estimated at 130,000 men : without taking into the account the army of reserve at Dijon, under the immediate orders of Buonaparte, which, it was universally believed, was destined to support and co-operate with that of Moreau. Neither the Austrians nor any of the politicians of Europe, penetrated the first consul's design of marching his army, by the almost impracticable rout, which he actually took, into Italy. The cavalry of general Moreau amounted to 20,000 ; and he had eight regiments of light artillery, with 32 field-pieces, and 16 arquebuziers to each regiment.—His head-quarters were at Strasburg. The right wing of his army extended to the Helvetic Rhine, and he had a considerable body of troops assembled in the environs of Rheineck. To this quarter he sent a numerous park of artillery, with a corps of pontonniers, so that there was every appearance that this wing of his army was to pass the Rhine at this point. The force and the position of this army announced it to be the *primum mobile*, of the campaign

His left wing, and his rear, were protected by the forts of the Rhine, Holland, and the neutrality of Prussia; and the direction of the whole army towards Vienna rendered it formidable to the emperor. An official note from Buonaparte, communicated to the Helvetic government, the rejection of peace by the enemies of France, and at the same time expressed a hope of his being able to force them to accept it.

Buonaparte, in his personal demeanor, began now to assume a military air, which indeed he had sustained pretty much ever since his elevation to the supreme authority. He reviewed, in the Champ de Mars, all the troops that were in Paris and its vicinity. The French as well as the imperialists, every where moved out of their cantonments. Skirmishes between parties of hussars, advanced-posts on both sides surprised, cannonading from one side of the Rhine to the other, and proclamations of the opposite generals, announced an approaching and terrible campaign.

The communication between the Austrian army of Italy and that of the archduke was still maintained by the corps commanded by general Davidovich, which occupied Chiavenna and Bellinzona, and stretched towards the country of the Grisons. Unfortunately it is not in the writer's power to embellish his narrative of the present campaign with the active services of that brave, wise, and virtuous prince, who was obliged to quit the army from ill health, and perhaps some other circumstances. A better choice of a commander, to supply, as far as possible, his place, could not have been made, than that of general Kray, who took the chief command of the army, on the 16th of March. But it was remarked, even at this early stage, as a bad omen, that there was not a good understanding between the general and the minister at war, count Lherbach; who were both of them quick in their tempers, and of dispositions equally obstinate and imperious.

General Kray received a reinforcement of 1000 Wurtemburghers, and as many Palatines, who were destined to support the Austrians posted between Rastadt and Kehl. The different corps of the Wartemburgh, Palatine, and Mayence, militia were stationed behind the Austrian army of the Rhine, at the entrance of the defiles of Suabia, between the river Enz, the Necker, and the Mayne, between Widbad and Psoutzheim, as far as Haideberg, and from thence by the Odenwald towards Eschaffenburg on the Mayne, and between Frankfort and Mayence, along the Nidda.

The Bavarian troops assembled at Donawert. The first column, under the orders of general baron de Deux Ponts, formerly in the service of France, was composed of

Six battalions of infantry, consisting each of 400 men - -	2400
Three squadrons of light cavalry, of 100 men each - - -	309
Two companies of arquebuziers, of 40 men each - - -	80
Three companies of artillery, of 40 men each - -	120
Total	2900

This first division was to be raised to 3500 men, by a levy of recruits. This corps was reviewed on the 4th of April, and, on the 5th, began their march to the camp of Ridlingen, on the Danube.

The second division of the Bavarian troops passed a review at Donawert, on the 27th of April, and had the same destination. The corps of the 1000 Wurtemburghers assembled at Ridlingen, and together with three regiments of emigrant Swiss, were joined to the Bavarians. The particular destination of the corps of Condé was not at that time known. They had been in the service of Russia, and had passed into that of England. They received orders to march to the coast of the Mediterranean. General Melas, who commanded the Austrian army in Italy, set out from Turin on the 27th of March, and, on the evening of the same day, arrived in Alessandria, where he established his head quarters, and immediately issued a proclamation to the army, announcing the opening of the campaign, and exhorting the troops to remember their former bravery, and to acquire fresh renown, by new achievements. The greater part of the Austrian troops that had passed the dead of winter, in Alessandria, were now sent to the frontier of the state of Genoa.

General Berthier, on the 20th of April, joined the army of reserve at Dijon, of which he took the chief command, until the arrival of Buonaparte. This army was at least 50,000 strong, well appointed, and in all respects in most excellent order. By this time, a detachment of 800 Austrians had taken possession of mount Cenis. General Berthier, informed of this circumstance, on his arrival at Dijon, reviewed the army, and went directly to Basle, where he had a conference with general Moreau. It was determined that military operations should be begun on the Rhine, on the week thereafter. Intelligence being received that the Austrians had taken possession of mount Cenis, general Thureau, set out from Briançon, proceeded to Exiles, from thence towards Suza, and coming up with the rear of the detachment, which the Austrians had pushed forward to mount Cenis, he obliged them to retreat, and took a part of this small garrison prisoners of war.

Massena, commander-in-chief of the French, in Italy, considering the miserable state of his troops, came to a determination to concentrate the whole of his forces on the river of Genoa.

The general system of war, adopted by the consul, was, to keep the whole of the troops together in a mass on some favorable points, whether for offence or defence.—The reader already perceives his secret design, in establishing what, for a blind to the enemy, he called the army of reserve, though it was destined to be the most active, at Dijon. From this central point he menaced at once Germany, Switzerland, and Italy; but those countries the most where his attack was not intended. The war in Germany he confided to the strong army under Moreau, while he, with the army under his command, should go to reconquer Italy, the theatre of his most splendid victories. But the first object, in

his present career, was to arrive in time to save Genoa, and the unfortunate army of Massena, which defended that place; the most important in Italy, to be preserved or to be conquered.

The principal object and aim of the Austrians, who, in the course of the last campaign, had recovered all that they had lost in Italy, was to keep the French armies in Switzerland and on the Rhine, in play, while they should push with all possible vigor the siege of Genoa: the possession of which was alone wanting to render them complete masters of all Italy. This object, which they considered as now within their grasp, and soon to be accomplished, would have enabled them to bear with their whole united force on Switzerland, by the possession of which, it would be in their power to force the French to keep on the defensive, on the side of the south as well of the east. Such then, being the opposite views of the two contending armies, it will be proper to begin the narrative of the campaign with the memorable siege of Genoa.

On leaving Paris Massena proceeded through Lyons to Toulon and Marseilles, in order to take measures for revictualling the army, and the city of Genoa. At Lyons he found the cavalry with the heavy artillery, which had been sent back about the middle of autumn, as forage was scarce, and the guns were of little service in the defence of a place environed by mountains. Massena was not a little surprised at the wretched condition of the battalions; and on his arrival at Toulon at the negligence and knavery of the army contractors. He had such regulations at the latter place as might remedy part of the evil. He made purchases of grain and shoes, which he sent off to his army by sea; and being informed that Championnet had died at Antibes, of the same epidemic distemper that raged in the army, he went immediately to Genoa, where he arrived on the 9th of February, and where he issued proclamations for re-establishing confidence among the troops and the inhabitants of the territories and of the city. The ravages of war had reduced the French army to one half of its original number, and its remains were exhausted by famine and disease. The military chests and magazines were empty, while the exertions of the chief officers of the army only evinced their incapacity to afford any material relief. No pay had been received for seven months, and the number of deserters who endeavored to escape the jaws of death by seeking relief in some more hospitable clime, threatened the entire dissolution of the army. Nearly 30,000 men perished in the territory of Genoa by disease and famine, unmolested by a single enemy. Nor was this disorder confined to the army of Genoa; for the troops in the southern parts of France, and in the countries contiguous to the Rhine, were nearly in the same condition. Even in the heart of the republic, the soldiers were reduced to subsist on arbitrary requisitions extorted from the people for want of clothing and pay. Massena endeavored to bring the deserted battalions back to their colours; and was finally successful by a judicious distribution of rewards and punishments, in obtaining their return to their respective standards. The miseries of famine, however, and the enmity of the Genoese were not easily surmounted. The higher classes of the community, who considered the French as the plunderers of their country, and as the destroyers of their rank and political importance, were inwardly delighted with their wretchedness, and secretly assisted in every measure which might possibly compel them to evacuate the country. The Austrians in the mean time enjoyed abundant communications with Genoa, by means of Italian refugees, by the treachery of the Genoese general, Assaretto, and also by the agency of the republican soldiers themselves, who were sometimes tempted to sell their *watch-word* for the purpose of procuring bread. No adequate reform could be effected, therefore, with means so inadequate as those of Massena; for he was promised 60,000 men, but had the mortification to find himself at the head of no more than 25,000, after the most indefatigable exertions,

and this number he was obliged to extend between mount Cenis and the frontiers or Tuscany, a distance of more than 230 miles.

Massena lost no time in intimating to the French government that it would be impossible to save the Ligurian republic should he be seriously attacked. He dismissed the whole of the generals, not from any feeling of personal animosity, or a conviction that they were not qualified to discharge their duty, but because the army would have associated with the idea of these men, the remembrance of the defeats which they had formerly experienced under their command.

A portion of their pay was given to the troops, and some clothing, particularly shoes, an article of which the army stood eminently in need. Having perceived these exertions to alleviate their situation, the soldiers became more submissive, obedient, and ready to engage the enemy whenever they should be required. But, formidable as the Austrians were in this quarter, Massena soon discovered that they were not the only enemy with which he had to contend. The people in the eastern territory of Genoa, had been in a state of insurrection for some months before this period; and the disorders among the troops were alleged as a pretext for this hostile deportment, though no pretext was necessary to the Italians, when they saw the French retreating in presence of a force so decidedly superior.

While the republicans found themselves unable to suppress the insurrection in the east, they were alarmed by the rapid advances of a similar disposition in the west. Massena, therefore, left the care of the city to the national guard, issued a number of manifestoes, which the rebels viewed with contempt, and sent the first division of his army to reduce them. They succeeded in checking the progress of the rebels, but found it impossible to subject them to obedience; and few of the plans which Massena judiciously devised, were successfully executed. Corn had been purchased at Marseilles, but only a part of it was sent to his army, a circumstance which rendered it necessary to reduce the troops to *short allowance*, each man having no more than two ounces of bread per day. Relief by sea had been precluded by contrary winds, and the harbor was at length blockaded by the British fleet under lord Keith, which appeared on the 5th of April in the gulf off Genoa, while the army of general Melas approached the city by land, and extended its front along the whole line of the French army. The French generals themselves admit that the opening of the campaign by general Melas, was entitled to the highest praise, on account of the address with which he concealed the immense force which he had in Italy. Being well acquainted with the weakness of the republican army, he contented himself, during the winter, with watching its movements by means of a simple and slight cordon; while he disposed his own throughout Piedmont, Lombardy, the Venetian state, the Bolognese, and the march of Ancona and Tuscany. Thus divided, the Austrian army had the appearance of weakness; but it possessed all the means of being easily recruited, and provided with every thing necessary for action. The reinforcements which it received from time to time, during its long repose, were, in like manner, dispersed over an immense extent of country, and were scarcely to be perceived. The French were deluded by this arrangement, into a conviction that it would be late in the season before the Austrians could take the field, and even flattered themselves that they should be beforehand with the enemy, at the very time when the different corps intended to form the Austrian armies were on their march to the general rendezvous. Cities, towns, and villages, all at once, as by a spontaneous movement, sent forth companies, regiments, and battalions, for the formation of an active army. In a few days general Melas was enabled to assemble 10,000 men before Bobbio, 10,000 before Tortona, 30,000 at Acqui and Alessandria, and to advance with this irresistible force against Massena; while he left behind him in the plains of Piedmont, the

whole of his cavalry, a fine park of artillery, and 20,000 infantry. The astonishment excited by all these circumstances was great and universal. Massena adopted the only measure that was prudent and practicable, in his situation. He contracted his lines; he formed masses, which, though disproportioned to the numerous bodies to which they were opposed, might yet make an impression, and divide the enemy by darting upon them at points favorable to an attack; thus obtaining different advantages, according to local circumstances, and the genius and combinations of the chief commander. The defence of Genoa was undertaken by Massena himself, at the head of one of his divisions; but the right wing of the army of Melas, which bore principally on Vado and Savona, took Vado on the second day of the siege, and by this means isolated the right wing of the army under Massena. A division under Suchet was cut off from the army on the second day of the siege, by the reduction of Vado. From that moment the French were cut off from all communication with France by sea as well as by land, and Suchet's division was unable to return to its own country, till after a long series of engagements and disasters.

Prior to these events, a large quantity of wheat had fortunately entered the port of Genoa, and prevented the necessity of immediate capitulation. On the 5th of April, therefore, the attack of the Austrians on the French army became general. On the morning of that day the French were driven as far back as Ruha, which they entered in the evening. At Bergo di Sornoni the Austrians made an attempt to break the French line, but were repulsed by general Panisot, of the second division. The same result attended their efforts against the heights of Cordibona where the French firmly maintained their ground.

The second day of the siege, the 6th of April, was more terrible. A general attack on the right of the French line was made by general Otto, who fell on the first division with 12,000 men in front of Bobbio. His object was to cut his way through the French line, and press on directly to Genoa. The principal attack was made at Monte Coruna ; the first division was compelled to give way and to fall back towards Novi and Monte Jaccio, as far as Quinto, where he rallied and made a successful stand for the defence of the city. The second division was also attacked but with less fury. General Gazau however who commanded, deemed it prudent to retire behind the Scrivia towards some mills upon that river. The third division commanded by general Gardanne sustained a dreadful conflict. Of the 30,000 men whom general Melas had assembled, in the province of Acqui, 20,000 marched under his command to Savona, where the third division, though but weak, withstood the shock, till the arrival of general Soult, who by the most extraordinary display of skill and valor succeeded in throwing 600 men and provisions into Savona, but could not save Vado, nor prevent the division of Suchet from being cut off. On the same day a frigate from lord Keith's fleet, with a view of encouraging the inhabitants to insurrection, came within cannon-shot of Genoa, and after firing forty rounds, again withdrew, the people paying no attention to the signal.

The result of these and similar actions was, that the French exhausted of money, men, and provisions, were obliged to reconcile their minds to the idea of retreating by little and little to Genoa, a plan which was carried into complete execution, after daily fighting, on the 20th of April. The kind of war carried on by an army necessarily depends on the force which it possesses, and the situation in which it is placed. It was natural therefore that generals Melas and Massena should pursue opposite systems of operation. The object of Massena, continually in action with an army superior in numbers, was to divide the enemy by marching his own troops in two columns. It was contrived that these columns should not be equal in strength. The one weaker than the other, made it its chief business to manœuvre as much as possible so as to occupy the enemy without attacking him or waiting to receive an attack, unless

it was unavoidable: the other and the stronger column, endeavored to keep up the tone of offensive operations, by bearing in favorable circumstances its whole and undivided force on the different divisions of the enemy, and beating their different corps in succession.

The Austrians on the contrary, being able to divide without too much weakening themselves studied on every occasion to surround the French, and never met them without attempting an attack. The consequences of these opposite plans were mortifying to the Austrians, repulsed and baffled by an inferior army, but were highly destructive to the French who could little spare the soldiers slain, disabled, and taken prisoners, in a series of arduous encounters. The republicans with difficulty fell back to Genoa, the Austrians being several times on the point of cutting off their retreat. During this succession of events the right of the army of Genoa under general Miolis had tried the same kind of warfare and received orders at last to fall back to Genoa.

In the course of the fifteen days that the defence was maintained, Massena having lost one third of his men, could not dissemble that he had nothing more to expect from the force of his arms. He therefore began to fortify himself in his positions, to explore farther resources of subsistence, and to exercise the most severe economy in the use of those which yet remained. By means of some small vessels, which the army had been able to retain, notwithstanding the vigilance of the English fleet, he sent letters to Corsica to general Suchet, and to Marseilles. Several officers whom he had sent to Suchet, and to the first consul, with an account of his situation, were taken by the enemy. In the mean time, Massena became acquainted with the march of the army of reserve, under Buonaparte. He was not less encouraged by the courage of his troops. There was not a day that passed without skirmishing between advanced posts, in forced reconnoitrings, and efforts to penetrate within the positions of the besieged army.

On the 30th of April, the Austrians,

who by this time had carried the post of Deux Freres and fort Quezzi, blockaded Fort Diamant, and commanded the works of Fort Eperon. In this posture of affairs, Massena, perceiving that they had in view to take the post of la Madona del Monte, from whence they might drive the French from Alboro, the only point from which they would be able to bombard Genoa, he formed a resolution to make a last effort with his corps of reserve, which had not yet been brought into serious action, and to force the enemy to abandon their most advanced positions. In this he succeeded, but it was at the expense of a series of bloody actions, desperate and obstinate, and loss on both sides ; insomuch, that the combatants being too near each other to make use of musketry, had recourse to their bayonets, the butt ends of their muskets, and even to stones. The loss in killed, on both sides, was great. The French made a great number of prisoners, even to the amount of several thousands, and took all the scaling-ladders destined for the escalade of Genoa, and the forts adjacent. The scaling-ladders were so formed as to admit of three men abreast. They were burned by the French in the night. General Soult carried the post of Deux Freres, and the rout of the Austrians was complete. The situation of the Austrian prisoners in Genoa was dreadful. The French suffered extreme privations themselves : their prisoners, after attempting to prolong life by eating their shoes and knapsacks, died of hunger.

This day, the most memorable in the siege, the victory, which was so decidedly on the side of the French, only served to hasten its conclusion. Such combats, so destructive to both parties, added to the miseries of the French and Genoese, by the increase of prisoners without an increase of provisions. The army of Buonaparte was yet at too great a distance to come to the relief of Massena before the last of his soldiers should have perished with hunger. In the sorties, which he made in the course of the month of May, he lost a great many of his officers, and among these some of the generals of his staff, in killed and severely wounded.

The city of Savona had surrendered to the Austrians on the 15th of May. The English fleet began now to bombard Genoa every night. The populace, particularly the women, running about the streets, set up frightful cries for peace. And a general insurrection of the people, of Genoa against the French, would have ensued, if the efforts of the French soldiers to restrain it, had not been seconded by a number of individuals among the inhabitants. The illusions of hope at last vanished. There was no longer the smallest expectation that the succours so long looked for would come in time. The provisions were entirely exhausted ; even the last horses and dogs were nearly consumed, when general Massena received a letter from general Melas, inviting him to an interview with lord Keith, and the generals Otto and St. Julian, who offered him a capitulation on the most honorable terms. To this first overture, he replied, that he would consider of it ; though he had, in truth, nothing farther to consider. The day after, he received another message with the same terms. He then sent the adjutant-general Andreaux, under pretence of some business relating to the prisoners, to Rivoli, to receive the proposals of the enemy, and to enter, without any farther delay, into a negotiation for peace.

The first article of capitulation proposed by the allies, was, that the army should return to France, but that the general should remain prisoner of war.—" You, sir," said lord Keith to Massena, " are worth 20,000 men." But Massena said, " that no negotiation would be gone into, if the word capitulation was to be made use of." On the 4th of June the allied generals, having departed from their first proposal, resumed the negotiations. In the mean time, while this was going on, the city of Genoa, containing a population of 160,000 souls, though a prey to all the horrors of famine, remained quiet. A great number of old people, women and children, reduced to the necessity of attempting to sustain nature by herbs, roots, and impure animals, died of disease or inanition. This melancholy picture was often exhibited to view by the rising sun. Mothers were often found dead with hunger, and children at the breast also dead, or dying.

On that day, the 4th of June, the principal articles for the evacuation of Genoa were agreed on between the French adjutant-general Andreaux on the one part, and major-general Best, a staff officer in the imperial service, with the English captain Rivera, on the other. And it was settled that the chiefs of the opposite armies should meet on the day after, being the 5th of June, for signing a definitive treaty. At nine o'clock in the morning of that day a conference was held by the opposite parties, in a small chapel, which is situated in the middle of the bridge of Cornegliano, and between the posts of the Austrians and the French. Here lord Keith, commander of the combined naval forces in the Mediterranean, general Otto, commander of the blockade of Genoa, with general St. Julian, who was charged with the political part of the negotiation, were met by general Massena, commander-in-chief of the French army in Italy. Each of these parties was accompanied by only two or three gentlemen.

In this conference Massena displayed much finesse, under the cloke of an apparent gaiety, which formed a complete contrast with the gravity of the other contracting party, and was attended with this advantage, that it did not look as if he were greatly alarmed for the situation of his army. And it is owing to that ease and gaiety of manner that he ultimately obtained all which he demanded. A degree of misunderstanding had taken place between the English as individuals and the Austrians, the former reproaching the latter with the great length to which the siege had been protracted. Massena endeavored to take advantage of this want of harmony by flattering the pride of one party at the expense of the other. Lord Keith disclaimed all hard conditions, observing to Massena; "General, the defence you have made has been so heroic, that it is impossible to refuse you any thing you ask:" and to the surprise of Europe, the right wing of the French army charged with the defence of Genoa, and the commander-in-chief with his staff, were permitted, by the articles of capitulation, to leave Genoa with their arms and baggage and *to rejoin the centre of the French army by land.* The same liberty was granted to 8100 men, who obtained permission to enter France by Nice; the rest were transported by sea to Antibes and were plentifully supplied with provisions. Passports were granted to the Genoese patriots. The Austrians took possession of the gates of the city, and the English of the entrance into the harbor. French commissioners remained at Genoa, to witness the execution of the articles which related to the sick and the hospitals; and Massena was allowed to send a courier with a passport to Buonaparte, to announce the evacuation of the city.

HISTORY OF THE WAR.

CHAP. XXVIII.

Campaigns of 1800 on the Rhine and in Italy—Activity and Intelligence of Buonaparte—Dexterity and Enterprise of Moreau—Buonaparte hastens from Paris, Passes the Alps, and gains the Battle of Marengo—Its Influence on the Hopes and Opinions of the French People.

I HAVE already observed that general Moreau had been appointed to the command of the French troops composing the army of the Rhine, which had been formed by the junction of the armies of the Rhine and the Danube. That general arrived at the latter end of January at Basle, where he established his head-quarters. The army having been considerably reinforced since the close of the last campaign, was not less formidable from its numbers, than from the excellence of the troops of which it was composed. The most brilliant results were expected from the strenuous exertions of the government in providing for the comfort of the troops, abandoned as they had been to all the extremities of want; from the skill displayed in their military organization; and above all from the appointment of the " great and beloved" Moreau to the chief command.

On the other hand the departure of the Russians had reduced the Austrian army to its native strength, and restored the opposing numbers to some appearance of equality. The coalition it is true had supplied some part of the deficiency occasioned by the departure of its allies, by the march of 10,000 Bavarian troops and of the corps of Condé, both in the pay of England. The English party at Vienna having obtained by their intrigues the recal of the archduke Charles, the only general who was worthy to oppose Moreau, the command of the Austrian army was confided to general Kray who had been advantageously distinguished in the course of the preceding campaign in Italy. The main armies opposed were nearly equal in number, and the following was their respective situations at the recommencement of hostilities.

The right wing of the army of the Rhine under the command of Lecourbe composed of the remains of the late army of the Danube, was arranged in three divisions with a reserve. It amounted to 38,000 combatants independent of some battalions destined to form under the orders of general Moncey, the left wing of the army of reserve which was intended to penetrate into Italy by the St. Gothard. It occupied all the eastern and northern frontier of Switzerland, and bordered the course of the Rhine from its sources to its junction with the Aar. It was opposed to all the Austrian troops posted in the Grisons and the Voralberg under the orders of the prince de Reuss, besides a portion of Kray's left wing stationed along the Rhine between the lake of Constance and the Wutach, and which had strong reserves at Singen and at Stockach, under the orders of general Sporch.

General Moreau commanded in person the centre, or reserve, which, composed of three divisions, was assembled at Basle and in its vicinity, to the amount of 30,000 men.

It was opposed by the centre of general Kray, placed at Donaweschingen.

The third corps d'Armee, under the orders of St. Cyr, to the number of from 15,000 to 20,000 men, was stationed in the neighbourhood of New Brisach. It was opposed to that portion of the forces of Kray which occupied Fribourg, bordering the course of the Rhine, in the Brisgau.

The corps of general St. Susanne, forming the left wing, and the weakest in number, occupied Kehl, Strasburg, and the environs. He commanded a body of 5000 men placed at Offenburg, and all the troops collected in the valley of Kintzig, and on the chain of Knubis.

The total effective force therefore of the army of the Rhine could not amount to less than 95,000 men; and the forces of the enemy, without computing the corps of the lower Rhine now posted on the Mein, were equal in number: but possessing the central position of Donaweschingen, with the body of his troops, general Kray was enabled to act as he thought fit on the left or the right, along the chord of the great arch which is formed by the meanderings of the Rhine in its course to Basle. His position was such as enabled him from the chord of the arch, to command its circumference, and consequently his movements against the two extremities of the French line, became infinitely more rapid, than those which the enemy were able to execute on the Austrian wings.

The intention of Moreau to assume an offensive attitude notwithstanding the obstacles presented by his position to the union of his troops were successively developed by the movements of the army, and more particularly by the passage of the Rhine, on the part of the right wing.

The only points at which the republicans could hope to repass the Rhine, were the bridges of Basle, of Brisach, and of Kehl. It was the intention of Moreau by his manœuvres to the right, to collect his army before Schaffhausen, and to advance into Suabia by the shortest rout, supporting his left by the Danube. Aware that in effecting this object, his detached corps would be exposed to many painful marches

in their endeavors to avoid the doubtful conflicts, which the central position of the Austrians at Donaweschwingen would enable them to challenge; Moreau determined if possible to deceive the enemy by pretended demonstrations, and to seduce general Kray into the commission of an erroneous movement, which might enable the French to reassemble and concentrate their forces before the enemy should recover from his surprise.

With this design the right wing under Vandamme, made some movements towards the Reinthal, and dispatched some useless boats to Roschach, as if with an intention to pass the Rhine above the lake of Constance, but in reality with no other purpose than to retain the right wing of the Austrian army in the Voralberg and the Grisons. To the left the corps of St. Susanne was intended to take a position in front of Kehl, while the corps of St. Cyr passing the Rhine at Brisach advanced towards Waldkirch. The third division of the centre commanded by general Richepause was at the same time to bear upon St. Blaise, and to march to the left after passing the Rhine at Basle: and still further to deceive the enemy, the general's head quarters were removed from that city to Colmar, while Lecourbe established his own at St. Gall. 1800.

Such were the combinations by which Moreau endeavored to attract the attention of the enemy to the two wings of his position, presuming that by this artifice he might induce him to leave his centre unprotected between the lake of Constance and the Brisgau, and thus present an opportunity to the French divisions to surmount in separate bodies the numerous defiles, and reunite in safety. These and other subordinate dispositions were crowned with the most complete success. The French army on the 25th of April crossed the Rhine in four great divisions under the respective commands of general St. Susanne general St. Cyr, general Moreau, and general Lecourbe. The division under general St. Susanne advanced to Offenburg, while general St. Cyr who had crossed the Rhine at Old Brisach advanced at Fribourg.

The manœuvres of St. Cyr seemed to indicate an intention to form a junction with St. Susanne, and a determination on the part of Moreau, to penetrate through the Black mountains by the valley of Kintzig towards Donaweschingen. The movement of general Susanne, however, was only a feint, for he received orders on the 27th, to remove from Offenburgh to Kehl, and, proceeding upwards from thence, along the banks of the Rhine by forced marches, he arrived at Fribourg on the 30th of April. General St. Cyr, who had reached Fribourg without loosing a man, pursued in the mean time that course of march which was necessary to form the junction of the whole army between Schwetlingen and Schaffhausen, near the lake of Constance. The division under the immediate command of Moreau, crossed the Rhine at Basle, and proceeded without any considerable opposition, to the place of general rendezvous. General Lecourbe crossed the Rhine between Schaffhausen and Stein ; and, after, some fighting and the capture of many prisoners, the whole army, with the exception of the corps under general St. Susanne, was assembled at Schaffhausen, or in its vicinity. The magazines of the Austrians were at Kampten, a town in Upper Suabia. The French general, directing his march to that point with a view to cut off general Kray from his principal depot, drove all the Austrian advanced posts before him, and advanced to attack the imperialists at Stockach.

The consequences of Moreau's plan were immediate. General Kray, mistaking the feint of Susanne for the main attack, concentrated all his forces at Donaweschingen, at a moment when, under cover of that feint, Moreau was enabled to cross the Rhine and turn the position of the Austrian army. Abandoning the angle of Suabia, general Kray was now reduced to the necessity of leaving or destroying his stores and ammunition : the left wing of the French under Susanne, entered Donaweschingen on the 3rd of May, and continued to press forward on the Austrian rear. The fugitives endeavored to establish themselves in the lines of Stockach and Engen, of which, the latter were commanded by Kray in person. He was attacked, on the 4th, by Moreau, who, in repeated charges, lost a number of men. In the course of these conflicts, a body of the Austrian army under the archduke Ferdinand, were attacked in their rear by general Susanne's division, and nearly cut off. The archduke, on this occasion, displayed that personal bravery which distinguishes the princes of his house. By the most judicious and spirited resistence, he was enabled to join the main army. General Kray maintained his post, prevented the enemy from making any great impression, and kept the field during the night. But at day-break he thought it prudent to commence a retreat, which he had continued to the length of about fifteen miles, when he was again attacked on the 5th, at Moskirk, by the indefatigable Moreau ; of whom it was the leading maxim to hang on and harass the enemy at every turn, and in every fortune, and to give him no respite for the formation or execution of new designs. Being ably assisted by Lecourbe, he made some impression on the Austrian battalions, but, though superior in number, did not think it proper to renew the combat. Mr. Wickham, the British narrator of these engagements, affirms that no prisoners were made on either side : the statement of Moreau estimates the number taken from the enemy at more than 10,000.

The Austrians, in their retreat from Moskirk, were pursued by a division of the French under general Ney, who took 1500 prisoners.

The position now occupied by the French, enabled them to detach troops for the purpose of clearing the eastern bank of the lake of Constance. They could also intercept Kray's communications with the prince of Reuss at Lindau, and general Hiller in the Grisons. The marshal therefore perceived the necessity of changing the line of his retreat. By crossing the Danube at Sigmaringen, he had left it in

the enemy's power to reach. Ulm before
him, and to deprive him of his remaining
magazines, and of his entrenched camp
near that city.   By forced marches he
gained the line of the Riss, and occupied
the lines in front of it.   The French centre
and reserve advanced in this direction on
the 9th, and on their march fell in with the
imperialists.   Two of St. Cyr's divisions
having traversed the woods, drove them
into a deep ravine formed by the river,
and penetrated as far as Biberach.
General Richepause's division of the reserve was obliged to sustain a violent cannonade for four hours; but he succeeded
in obtaining possession of the fort which
commanded the town, while his cavalry
formed in the enemy's rear. 'In consequence of this unfortunate event, the
Austrians retired, leaving, according to the
French accounts, 2000 dead, and 3000
prisoners.

The right wing was now at liberty to
act against Bregentz and the Tyrolean
frontier.   Lecourbe, however, continued
to press forward to Memmingen, and on
the 11th, forced the imperialists to abandon it.   In the late obstinate and sanguinary actions, general Kray had contested every inch of ground with the utmost
resolution, so that the roads and fields of
battle were covered and choked with the
dying and the dead.   After the loss of
Memmingen, he retired to Mindelheim;
but, instead of crossing the Lech, which,
from the excessive drought, was at this
time too low to present any obstacle to
the French, he turned off to his entrenched
camp at Pfuel, half a league from Ulm.
In the mean time the left of the French
marched along the left bank of the Danube,
as far as Ehingen, in order to interrupt
the communication of generals Kray, and
Sztarry, and Moreau, drew closer his
blockade of Ulm, in accomplishing which
object he had several severe encounters
with the enemy.

On the side of Switzerland, the Austrians evacuated Lindau, Bregentz, Feldkirch, Coire, and all the Grisons. Lecourbe having now cleared his right as

far as the Lech, was in a condition to detach general Lorge with a strong corps
to reinforce general Moncey, who was to
penetrate by mount St. Gothard into Italy.
After so many rapid marches and engagements, both armies found it necessary to
take some repose; and Moreau employed
the interval in levying contributions for
the support of his troops.   His line extended from Erbach to Weissenhorn and
Krumbach, and that of general Kray from
Ulm to Guntzburg, while a corps of imperial cavalry stationed at Mildenheim,
maintained a circuitous and uncertain
intercourse with prince Reuss at Renti.

Moreau now environed Ulm in the hope
of carrying it by storm; but he soon renounced that design, as the city afforded
to the enemy one of the most advantageous
posts in Germany.   By occupying stations
on both sides the Danube, and in a line
at right angles to the river, he would expose both sections of his army to the attempts of marshal Kray, whose concentrated force could act with readiness against
either.   The imperialists indeed availed
themselves of this circumstance, to make
a vigorous sally from Ulm against Susanne's division, which formed the French
left wing.   This general was at first driven
from his ground; but, on the arrival of
general Collard with the reserve, the enemy were repulsed.   Soon afterwards,
Moreau withdrew his troops from the
Blauthal and the left bank of the Danube,
and destroyed all the bridges on the river.
He took a position with his left wing on
the Hiller, and his right leaning towards
Augsburg; thus preventing all communication between the imperial armies, while he
enabled Lecourbe to press on generals
Jellacrich and Auffenburg, in the Grison
country.   On the 28th, the left of the
French right entered Augsburg, from
whence they pushed on to obtain possession of the important post of Friedberg,
and the defiles leading to Landshut.   It
was the intention of Moreau, by diversions
on different points, to draw the Austrians,
if possible, from their intrenchments, to
a situation adapted for general action '

and his plans were regarded by the Austrian general as of so menacing a nature, that he resolved to hazard an engagement in order to arrest the incursions of his antagonists into the Bavarian states.

After several movements and manœuvres on both sides, marshal Kray collected about 40,000 men between Illerberg and Weissenhorn; and, on the 5th of June, attacked general Richepanse's division, posted on the left of the Hiller. Moreau, on receiving intelligence of this occurrence, gave orders to Grenier to advance with the division of St. Cyr, to the support of Richepanse, by the bridge of Kilmentz. General Lecourbe, who had fallen back towards the left on the Wertach, and occupied Augsburg and Landsberg only by detachments, took post between the Guntz and the Kamlach, on the road to Babenhausen, in such a manner as to cover the *débouchés* from Burgau and Augsburg, and occupy Mindelheim. The corps of reserve supported the left wing, and general Delmas passed the Guntz at Babenhausen to assist Grenier, while the division of Decaen filed towards that town.

The imperialists advanced in five columns, and attacked Richepanse with so much impetuosity, that his division was separated into three portions. This general had been directed not to expose his left, but to lean to the right, in order to defend the bridges, and not to hazard his force before he was certain of support. While his centre, under general Sahue, maintained a very unequal contest, general Neiz, with part of Grenier's division, approached by the bridge of Kilmentz to his aid, and, uniting his troops with those of Sahue, drove the enemy as far as Dietenheim. In the mean time an Austrian column, advancing with eight pieces of artillery on Kirberg, where a strong body of Ney's brigade was posted, continued their march to the bridge already mentioned. General Ney therefore was obliged to draw the whole of his troops towards Kirberg, which he attacked and carried on the 13th of June, at the point of the bayonet: the enemy losing 800 prisoners, and abandoning the whole of their artillery.

This success animated the division of Richepanse to attack, in its turn, with so much boldness and decision, as to repulse the imperialists with very considerable loss.

During the occurrence of these events, the plan of co-operation between Buonaparte and Moreau began to be clearly developed. While Moreau still made a shew of directing the main force of his army to the countries on the left bank of the Rhine, he began to detach part of his troops towards the lake of Constance, whither he afterwards withdrew with the main body, with an intention to remain on the defensive, and favor as much as possible the operations of the campaign in Italy.

The splendid successes of Moreau enabled Buonaparte to prosecute his original design, and to send the army of reserve into Italy.

On the morning of the 6th of May, the first consul set out from Paris to Dijon, where he arrived the next morning, being only twenty-five hours on his journey. His abode in the capital, after his intention of assuming the command had been announced, materially contributed to confirm the delusive security of the enemy. Several divisions of his army had already defiled by Geneva, Lausanne, and Villeneuve, on their rout to Italy. He himself reached Geneva, three hundred miles from Paris, on the 8th, and on the 13th, reviewed his advanced guard, which began its march on the same day by the Great St. Bernard, the same mountain, according to the hypothesis of Mr. Whitaker, from which Hannibal first beheld the plains of Italy. On the 16th, general Laanes arrived with the van at Aosta, having in three days travelled eighty miles across lofty mountains. After a few slight skirmishes, he proceeded by Chatillon against the fort of Bard. By the 20th, all the columns of the army had passed mount St. Bernard, their progress, and that of the artillery, being much impeded by the snow and the steepness of the ascent. The troops were compelled to march in this dangerous journey, one by one, in each other's foot-steps, like an army of Indians, as the smallest deviation might have precipitated the wanderer and his horse into some hideous abyss. Trees were hollowed for the reception of the cannon; and, while one half of a battalion carried their accoutrements and baggage, and those of their comrades, with provisions for five days, the other half were employed in dragging a single field-piece. The ammunition was put into boxes of fir and carried by mules. When the head of the file halted, the soldiers appeased their hunger and thirst with biscuits steeped in melted snow, and beguiled their labors with national songs. In descending, the whole army, but particularly the cavalry, experienced the most imminent peril from their slippery and uncertain footing, and the numberless crevices formed by the liquefaction of the snow. Buonaparte accompanied the infantry on foot, and at one time was obliged to slide on his breech down a height of two hundred feet, followed by his aides-de-camp, Duroc, Maroi, and Merlin. By the indefatigable labors of the troops, and the ingenious contrivances of general Marmont, commander of the artillery, and the several engineers, every difficulty was at length surmounted; and, on the 16th of May, the vanguard of the army reached Aosta. This place was garrisoned by a Hungarian battalion, which, after some loss, evacuated the place; and a deputation of the inhabitants waited on the consul to surrender it. The vanguard next proceeded to the attack of Chatillon, from the bridge of which fortress, built over a precipice, the Austrians were driven with considerable loss, and shut themselves up in the fort de Bard, which, situated amidst craggy rocks, stopped the progress of the whole army; and, if it could not have been reduced in four days, every soldier must have perished of hunger. Had general Melas foreseen this obstacle, he might have frustrated the success of Buonaparte's expedition. It was garrisoned by 500 men, with 14 cannon, and considered by the enemy as an insurmountable barrier, having been so constructed by art and formed by nature, as to com-

mand the entrance of Piedmont, at a point where the approach of two mountains narrows the breadth of the valley to one hundred and fifty feet. Between the two mountains runs the Doria, a deep, rapid, and dangerous river, touching the road at the foot of the mountain of Bard, and having its other bank covered with high rocks inaccessible to man. It was necessary, however, to carry the fort, or to endeavor to avoid it by finding another passage. Three companies of grenadiers having effected a lodgment in the suburbs, were joined at midnight by several additional troops; after which, the whole party, passing silently over the scattered pieces of rock, reached the palisadoes, and scaled them amidst a shower of balls. Continuing to advance with the same audacity, they forced the enemy from work to work, and compelled them to retire in disorder within the castle. The garrison kept up an incessant and dreadful discharge of canister and grape-shot, at the same time rolling down masses of stone from the top of the parapet. Many of the assailants were crushed to death, but a greater number were killed by the artillery. Intrepidity could do no more. To proceed was impracticable, and the grenadiers were obliged to abandon their enterprise.

This repulse determined the consul to attempt the discovery of another passage, and a way was found on the summit of the rock Albaredo. The soldiers, impatient of delay, notwithstanding the steepness of the ascent, carried on their shoulders a four pounder, to the peak of a rock commanding the enemy's battery, while the carriages at every risk, and notwithstanding the recent failure, were conveyed through the suburb. At night, the ordnance and ammunition tumbrils, each having its carriage-wheels twisted with hay-bands to deaden the sound, and, drawn by 30 men harnessed in a line, began to move through the streets of Bard, but with considerable loss. In the mean time a party of soldiers, having conveyed a cannon into the lofty belfry of a church in the suburbs, were enabled to destroy the tower of the principal gate. This incident so alarmed the garrison that fearful of an assault they surrendered prisoners of war, thus opening a passage to the republican army, who arrived without farther interruption at Ivrea, already in the possession of general Boudel. Two thousand imperialists, whom the French had driven before them, were posted at Romagna; and these had been joined by four thousand more, drawn from Turin and the neighbouring garrisons. They occupied an intrenched position covered by the river. On the 24th, Lasnes carried the redoubts and camp with the bayonet, and pursued the enemy towards Turin. To conceal his real design Buonaparte caused two divisions to menace this place, while Lasnes marched to the Chiusella and the Po. These movements led the enemy to suppose, that he wished to intercept the troops on their march from Nice to Turin. On arriving at the Chiusella, Lasnes found an Austrian corps upon the opposite bank, in great force, both in infantry and cavalry. But notwithstanding the resistance he encountered, he forced his passage, defeated the enemy with the loss of 500 of their cavalry, and penetrated to Chivasco. In this action, the French, according to the Vienna Gazette, had 2500 killed and wounded, and 300 taken prisoners.

From the apparent direction of general Lasnes' march, the imperial commander, who had arrived at Turin, was led to expect his immediate approach; but this movement was merely a feint. General Murat, with the cavalry, turned to Vercelli, where he was joined by Lasnes, and afterwards proceeded to Novarra, which he entered on the 30th, and pursued the enemy beyond the Tesino. Still more to distract the attention of Melas, General Thurreau's division made themselves masters of Susa and La Brunetta, and took 1500 prisoners. Another column, penetrating by the Simplon, reached Domo-d'Ossula, and turned the Austrian line in that point. General Moncey, having marched by Altorf with 25 000 men in three divisions, under generals

Lorge, Leclerc, and Lapoype, passed St. Gothard on the 25th and 26th, pushed his advanced-guard to Airolo, and drove the imperial general Dedovich to the Lago-Maggiore.

So many irruptions, and complicated movements, bewildered general Melas. He at first imagined, that the army of reserve intended to effect a junction with Thurreau near Susa, and advance against Turin; and he took his measures according to this opinion. When he learned that Murat had passed the Sesia and the Tesino, he was unable to divine the motive; but his uneasiness increased on receiving intelligence that general Lasnes, having recrossed the Dorea-Baltea, and defiled by Cressentino and Vercelli, had hastened to Pavia, and captured all the magazines of the imperial army. General Lechi, with the Cisalpine legion, marched to Cassano, and general Duhesme's division to Lodi, where it passed the Adda in pursuit of the enemy. After forcing the passage of the Tesino, Murat continued his rout to Milan, which he entered on the 2nd of June, and sent out parties to occupy all the neighbouring places in Lombardy, and seize the Austrian stores. The citadel, into which 4000 of the enemy had retired, was blockaded by the infantry of the advanced-guard. Three thousand sick were found in the hospitals; and the celebrated Fontana, whom the court of Vienna had imprisoned for having filled a high official station in the Cisalpine republic, was liberated from his fetters. Immediately on the arrival of the first consul, a provisional administration was established, and the republican form of government restored.

During these transactions, and while Berthier was clearing the Milanese between the Po and the Adda of all the enemy's troops, the imperial general kept his principal forces on the right bank of the former, in Piedmont, and towards the river of Genoa. He appears to have been hitherto shamefully ignorant of the strength of the French, and to have beheld their operations with a kind of supercilious indifference; but he now found it necessary to recal generals Elsnitz and Bellegarde from the banks of the Var. Suchet, who had been considerably reinforced, did not omit to profit by this retreat. He hung on the enemy with such incessant and strenuous exertions, that they lost nearly 5000 prisoners. As the French had seized on the Col-di-Tenda, Elsnitz could not effect a passage in that direction, but was forced to gain the sources of the Tanaro, and retire by Ormea, a rout which considerably impeded his march. In the hospitals in Lombardy, the consular army found 5000 or 6000 sick. At Pavia they took 300 or 400 pieces of cannon with their carriages, one part of which was for the field, and the other for sieges. They also captured 10,000 firelocks, besides immense magazines of provisions and military stores.

After occupying Lodi, general Loison passed the Oglio, and took possession of Orsinovi and Brescia. He then moved towards Cremona with an intent to seize on the imperial magazines at that place, cross the Po, and join general Murat, who had carried Placenza. In the mean time general Lasnes, after a cannonade in different points, pushed his troops over the river, made himself master of the important position of Stradella, and completely intercepted the enemy's communication with the Milanese. Here he was attacked by a hostile corps, which, after a sharp action, was obliged to retreat. Having now liberated his left and rear towards the Adda and Oglio, general Berthier endeavored to concentrate his principal strength at Stradella; an operation which was much retarded by the heavy rains and the swelling of the Po.

When the Austrians retreated from the maritime Alps, Suchet gained possession of the whole country as far east as Savona. The vicinity of Nice had been the theatre of several engagements; and, notwithstanding strong reinforcements were sent to check the progress of the Austrians in that direction, it was owing to the invasion of Piedmont that he accomplished his object with trivial loss. Such was the infatuated security of the imperial commander,

that he had equally neglected to establish the necessary means of epistolary communication, and to provision the strong holds in his rear. Buonaparte had actually arrived within a short distance of Marengo before Melas suspected that he had joined his army; and the delay occasioned by this unfortunate error was singularly favorable to his antagonist.

General O'Reilly had been detached to Placenza, and general Ott stationed on the Tesino, while 6000 men made a diversion on the left of the Po towards Chivasco. But O'Reilly was defeated by general Murat, and obliged to fall back on general Ott at Stradella and Montebello. During these operations, the commander-in-chief, Berthier, took a position on the right of the Po, at its junction with the Tesino, after clearing its banks of the hostile corps which endeavored to impede his passage. On the 8th of June, Ott arrived with thirty battalions at Voghera, for the purpose of opening the communication with Placenza. General Lasnes quitted his position at Broni to attack them on their approach; and general Victor prepared to support him. The imperialists, 16,000 in number, occupied Casteggio with their artillery. General Watrin fell in with their advanced posts at San-Diletto, and, driving them in, attacked the line in front. One of the French columns endeavored to turn them on the right, while another imitated its example on the left, and a third pierced their centre. The village of Casteggio was taken and retaken three several times, as well as the adjacent heights; but the imperialists, being thrown into confusion by a general charge of the enemy, retreated to Voghera.

The vast plain extending from the Suza to the Oglio, and from the Swiss Alps to the Po, was now in possession of the consular army. The left of Moncey's corps had turned the lake of Como, and the Italian legions took possession of Lecco, covering the passages from the Grisons and the entrance of the Valteline. Berthier's left leaned on the Adda and the Oglio, after driving general Vuckassowich into the Venetian territory. The centre had established itself on the right of the Po, defeated general Ott, and driven him towards the main imperial army, which was now assembled in the plains of Alessandria. Turin and other towns in its immediate neighbourhood were abandoned, and Massena and Suchet had advanced in one direction as far as Acqui, and in another to Sassello. Without a moment's intermission, Buonaparte, with the main body of his army, marched directly to Marengo, a spot which fate had destined to rival in celebrity the plains of Pharsalia and the promontory of Actium.

The French were at first astonished to see the enemy desert the plain between St. Juliano and Marengo, adapted as it was to facilitate the movements of their superior numbers, and attributed that circumstance to a secret intention of passing the Po on the north, or the Scrivia on the east, or of taking the rout to the territories of Genoa and Bobbio. While measures were adopted for defeating such attempts, the French guard was attacked, and the Austrians evinced their resolution to hazard a general engagement. The troops of Victor were ranged in order of battle; the centre occupied the village of Marengo, the left wing extended to the Bormida or Bormio, and the troops under Lasnes formed the right. The wings of the army were supported by a body of cavalry. The Austrians having collected their whole force, commenced the attack on every point. General Gardanne for two hours sustained the shock of the enemy's centre and right wing, still maintaining his ground, although the artillery of the Austrians was greatly superior to his own, and the left wing of Victor was supported by the cavalry under Kellerman. The republican centre was at length obliged to give way, and the Austrians advanced to Marengo, a movement in which the imperialists, after a dreadful slaughter, and having been strongly reinforced, ultimately succeeded. The right wing still maintained its ground with obstinate valor, but was itself too warmly engaged to afford any assistance to the centre division, thus defeated and obliged to retreat. As Victor perceived

that it was impossible to retain his ground any longer, he gave orders to retreat on the corps de reserve. The right wing was in the mean time attacked by two lines of Austrian infantry, with a strong body of artillery. When nearly outflanked, the republicans were defended for some time by a brigade of dragoons; but the centre, having been compelled to retreat, they were obliged to follow the example. The salvation of the army now depended on the exertions of the body of reserve, under general Desaix, who had followed the example of Buonaparte, by a hasty flight from Egypt, and was immediately appointed by the first-consul to a command in Italy. As the reserve was not yet ready to take the field, it was necessary to make every sacrifice that might prolong the contest; and Buonaparte therefore proceeded to the right wing, in order to delay its movements. The retreat was made under the fire of 80 pieces of cannon, and the slaughter was dreadful; but, as the places of those who fell were supplied with fresh troops, the French were enabled to keep their ranks. Victory at this moment appeared to have decided in favor of the Austrians, as their cavalry was numerous, and supported by different squadrons of light artillery, which threatened to turn the republican army. But the right wing of the French army was now reinforced by the grenadiers of the consular guard, who advanced, to use the phraseology of an eye-witness, like a wall of granite, and sustained three desperate charges from the Austrians. Mounier likewise came up with his division, which constituted a part of the corps de reserve, having received instructions to assault the battalions by which the Austrian cavalry were protected in the pursuit of the centre and left wing of the French army, which continued to retreat.

The troops under Desaix were drawn up on the plain of St. Juliano, in two lines, supported to the right and left by Marmont's artillery, and the cavalry under Kellerman, behind which were formed the fugitives from the centre and left wing. Their dying courage was rekindled by the presence of the commander-in-chief, who flew with rapidity from rank to rank ; and at four in the afternoon the battle was about to recommence, though it had already raged for the space of seven hours. The Austrians rested assured of victory, as they had already defeated more than two-thirds of the republican army, and almost surrounded the remainder : but, elated by momentary success, they had improvidently scattered their troops, which were yet dispersed in all the disorder and confusion of a hot pursuit, when Desaix at the head of his reserve, impetuously rushing among the victors charged them furiously at the point of the bayonet. The enthusiasm of the reserve was caught by the whole army and produced the most astonishing effects. The Austrians were confounded at this regeneration of vigor and activity, their artillery was drawn out of the field, and their infantry began to give way. At this moment Desaix was mortally wounded, a circumstance which redoubled the desperate enthusiasm of the troops who fought with a determination to avenge his death. It was still doubtful on which side victory would finally declare, for notwithstanding the first line of the Austrians had been driven back, the French were for some time unable to penetrate the second. A furious charge of cavalry decided the fortune of the day, and threw the imperialists into the utmost confusion. Six thousand men, and generals Zag and St. Julian with a majority of the officers of the staff were taken prisoners.

A third line of imperial infantry still remained as a corps de reserve, supported by the remaining part of artillery and the whole of the horse. The right wing of the French army and the grenadiers of the consular guard with a portion of the reserve commanded by Baudet, supported by Marmont's artillery advanced against this last division of the enemy. The republican cavalry under Murat defeated that of the Austrians, and the pursuit and slaughter were scarcely terminated by the approach of night. The French obtained a decisive and splendid victory ; but not without sustaining a loss still more considerable than that of the Austrians which amounted to 15,000 men in killed, wounded and prisoners.

The fate of Desaix was much and deservedly regretted. In his last moments he exclaimed to the young Lebrun " Go, tell the first consul that I die with regret at not having performed enough to live with posterity." "And why," replied Buonaparte, " is it not permitted me to weep?" A few months before this event Desaix had been recalled by general Kleber from Upper Egypt, and sent to El-Arish where he signed the capitulation with the grand vizier, under the guarantee of sir Sidney Smith. He afterwards embarked in a neutral ship on his return to France, carrying with him a passport from the Turkish and English commanders and accompanied by an English officer to secure respect to the treaty. On his arrival at Leghorn he was confined in the Lazaretto, as a prisoner of war by lord Keith who allowed him only twenty sous per diem, being the subsistence money given to the privates, his fellow-prisoners. The admiral Keith is reported to have added ironically " that French equality did not permit a general to be better treated than his soldiers." The acquiescence of England in the convention gave liberty to Desaix. When he arrived at Toulon, he was informed of Buonaparte's expedition to Italy. He posted to Milan, was immediately entrusted with the command of a division, and marched to Marengo. On the road a kind of languor seemed to oppress him, " Something will befal me," said he, " the bullets of Europe have forgot my person." His corpse was conveyed to the monastery of St. Bernard, where a mausoleum has been since erected to his memory. A marble tablet records his name and his exploits, and entwines the cypress with the laurels of Marengo.

In reviewing this momentous battle it is impossible not to perceive and to lament the errors which distinguished the operations of the Austrian general before and during its occurrence. Time was every thing to Melas, yet he did not display in his operations, celerity of movement, or boldness of execution. Two months were required to gain a hundred and fifty miles of country, and the mountain passes of Italy were left unfortified. Even supposing the consular army to have had no existence, a discreet commander would have guarded the defiles by strong corps of troops, and by entrenchments. Favored by the localities of the Piedmontese and Milanese Alps, 15,000 men commanded by able generals would have opposed an insurmountable barrier to the progress of Buonaparte. The Austrian general ought to have remembered that the French were in possession of Switzerland, and that Berthier was left at liberty to bend his course to Italy. The latter unable as he was to carry across the mountains the necessary supplies of artillery, military stores, and provisions, penetrated between Melas and his magazines of which he took possession, and deprived his enemy of those resources on which he depended. The plan of Moreau in Suabia was exactly similar, and both generals completely succeeded. The information of the imperial commanders was singularly defective. At the moment Genoa surrendered Melas was stationed at Turin, ignorant of Berthier's force and motions, and the other Austrian generals spoke of the consular army in their intercepted letters, as a weak and trifling corps sent to create alarm, or attempt some unavailing diversion.

The force of Berthier amounted to 40,000 men, of whom only 3000 were cavalry, with 30 pieces of cannon, and two companies of light artillery. The vast body of imperial infantry and cavalry, when they suddenly deployed in the open field with 100 pieces of artillery thundering in their front, threw the new levies into disorder, and obliged the foremost divisions to recoil: but the consummate skill of the French generals, and the peculiar excellence of their system of military tactics finally triumphed. The valor of the Austrian soldiers was unimpeachable, and so disastrous a defeat after the successes of the greater part of the day, could result only from the inefficiency of the Austrian military system, and the comparative incapacity of the general and subordinate officers. "There is room for glory," said the vanquished Melas, "though we may rank beneath general Buonaparte."

In this manner the court of Vienna by a want of promptitude, vigilance, and precaution allowed the enemy to recover those conquests, which Austria had so dearly purchased, yet so feebly and precariously maintained. On the day after the battle, the imperial commander sent general Skal to the enemy's head-quarters with proposals to conclude an armistice. When this officer intimated the object of his mission the first consul exclaimed in a peremptory tone " *Your army shall retire to*,"—and traced the line it was to occupy. By the subsequent convention the imperialists were to withdraw beyond the Mencio, and retain possession of the country between that river and the Lower Po: including Mantua, Peschiera, and Borgoforte the whole left side of the Po to the sea, and the town and citadel of Ferrara on the right bank. They were likewise to preserve Tuscany and Ancona, but the territory between the Chiusa and the Mincio was declared neutral. The French were to occupy the countries lying between the Chiusa, the Oglio and the Po. The citadels of Tortona, Alessandria, Milan, Turin, Pizzighitone, Arona, and Placenza, Coni, Ceva, Savona, Genoa, and fort Urbino, were to be delivered up. It was stipulated that no persons should be ill-treated on account of his political opinions, or his services to the Austrian army. Neither army was to send detachments to Germany during the armistice which was to continue until an answer should be received from the court of Vienna, and whatever that answer might be hostilities were not to commence until after a notice of ten days. While the discussions respecting an armistice continued, the citadel of Placenza surrendered, its garrison of 1200 men becoming prisoners of war. On the 26th of June general Massena was invested with the command of the army of reserve and of Italy now united into one. Genoa was evacuated on the 24th, by count de Hohenzollern, between whom and lord Keith a dispute had arisen in

consequence of an attempt on the part
of his lordship to carry off the stores,
artillery, and vessels in the harbor.
Buonaparte left Milan on the 25th of
June, ten days after the victory of Marengo,
and travelling by Turin, mount Cenis,
Lyons, and Dijon, arrived at Paris on the
2nd of July. He was received by the
unthinking people with the most enthusiastic demonstrations of applause. In their
congratulations on the military glory which
their country had acquired, they were blind
to the danger that threatened their domestic
liberty. They exulted in the occurrence
of an event which, while it decided the fate
of Italy, and apparently of Europe, tended,
by increasing the consul's power, to confirm the foundations of tyranny, and gild
with deceitful splendor, the chains of despotism.

CHAP. XXIX.

THE good fortune of Buonaparte in escaping from a scene of inglorious misery, at a moment so propitious to the gratification of his ambitious designs, was strikingly contrasted by the fate of Kleber, whom he had entrusted with the chief command of an army exhausted by fatigue, reduced in numbers by a series of sanguinary conflicts, afflicted by all the privations and diseases peculiar to the climate, and deprived by a concurrence of mortifying events of the last consolatory hope that they might yet return to their native country. The soldiers were destined to endure the torments of the Egyptian ophthalmia, and were exposed to the effects of the sultry and destructive *Siroc*, of which the following pathetic and impressive account is given by an intelligent eye-witness. " I had often heard speak of the Kamsin, which may be termed the hurricane of Egypt and the desert. It is equally terrible by the frightful spectacle which it exhibits when present, and by the consequences which follow its ravages. We had already passed in security one half of the season in which it appears, when, in the evening of the 18th of May, I felt myself entirely overcome by a suffocating heat : it seemed as if the fluctuation of the air was suddenly suspended. I went out to bathe, in order to overcome

1799.

so painful a sensation, when I was struck on my arrival at the bank of the Nile with a new appearance of nature around me. The sun without being concealed, had lost its rays ; it had even less lustre to the eye than the moon, and gave a pale light without shade : the water no longer reflected its rays, but appeared in agitation ; every thing had changed its usual aspect ; it was now the flat shore that seemed luminous, and the air dull and opaque ; the yellow horizon shewed the trees on its surface of a dirty blue ; flocks of birds were flying off before the cloud ; the affrighted animals ran loose in the country, followed by the shouting inhabitants, who vainly attempted to collect them together again ; the wind, which had raised this immense mass of vapor, and was urging it forward, had not yet reached us ; we thought that by plunging our bodies in the water, which was then calm, we could prevent the baneful effects of this mass of dust, which was advancing from the south-west ; but we had hardly entered the river when it began to swell all at once, as if it would overflow its channel ; the waves passed over our heads, and we felt the bottom heave up under our feet. Our clothes were conveyed away along with the shore itself, which seemed to be carried off by the whirlwind, which now reached us. We were compelled to leave the water and our wet and naked bodies being beat upon by a storm of sand were soon encrusted by a black mud, which prevented us from dressing ourselves. Enlightened only.by a red and gloomy sun, with our eyes smarting, our noses stuffed up, and our throats clogged with dust so that we could scarcely breathe, we lost each other on our way home, and arrived at our lodgings one by one, groping our way, and guided only by the walls which marked our track. The next day the same mass of dust, attended with similar appearances, travelled along the desert of Lybia ; it followed the chain of mountains and when we flattered ourselves that we were entirely 'rid of this pestilence, the west wind brought it back and entirely overwhelmed us with its scorching torrent ; the flashes of lightning appeared to pierce with difficulty through its dense vapor; all the elements were still in disorder; the rain was mixed with whirlwinds of fire, wind, and dust, and the trees and all the other productions of nature seemed to be plunged into all the horrors of chaos."

It was not long before the commencement of actual operations afforded Kleber an opportunity of appreciating the skill and spirit of his troops. The grand vizier had been already dispatched with a numerous army to Asia Minor, from whence he was to proceed through Syria towards Egypt. He spent six months in marching from Scutari to Damascus, and in his rout levied enormous contributions on the people of Anatolia. At Ervan he learned the issue of the battle of Aboukir. The intelligence produced so powerful a sensation among his troops that more than one half of them deserted : and on his arrival in Syria his army had dwindled to an inconsiderable number. His efforts to obtain the assistance of the janissaries were partially and reluctantly acceded to, and Djezzar Pacha influenced by jealousy, prudence, or caprice, refused him a passage through his dominions.

Informed of the vizier's movements, Kleber in the month of October, left El-Arisch with 2000 dragoons, and a regiment of 1000 men mounted on dromedaries

each with a foot soldier behind him : and making a circuit in the desert, arrived at day-break in the rear of the enemy's camp. At the same time a body of 10,000 of his infantry reached the wells of Sebabiah, at the distance of a league and a half from the Turkish army. The vizier alarmed at his own critical situation made little resistance, but precipitately abandoned his camp, the greater part of his baggage, and several thousand prisoners retreating with the wreck of his army towards Damascus. Kleber imposed upon the prisoners the task of completing, under the superintendence of able engineers, the fortifications of El-Arisch, where he left a garrison and returned with the rest of his forces to Egypt.

Previous to abandoning Egypt Buonahad opened a negotiation with the vizier, and with the view of gaining time directed Kleber to continue it. The dissatisfaction of the troops impressed Kleber with the necessity of entering with sincerity into negotiations, which had been at first intended to relax the vizier's preparations for war. General Desaix and citizen Poussielgue, on the proposal therefore of sir Sidney Smith, went on board the Tigre, and proceeded to the camp of his highness, who had again advanced from Gaza with a new army of 45,000 men and fifty pieces of cannon all directed by European officers. The fort of El-Arisch was given up to him by the cowardly and deluded garrison, who, as the reward of their treachery and fatuity, were beheaded by the Turks.

The forces of general Kleber did not amount to more than 15,000 men, and of these a considerable number were employed in the defence of Rosetta, Aboukir, and Alexandria, were stationed at Lesbe, to collect provisions and keep the country in subjection, or were scattered along a line of 150 leagues in Upper Egypt, to oppose the desultory attacks, and repress the insolence of the beys and partisans. Aware of his own inferiority of force, alarmed and distressed by the clamors, the privations, and the afflictions of his soldiers, he concluded on the 24th of January 1800, the memorable treaty of El-Arisch, of which the subjoined is an authentic copy.

Convention for the evacuation of Egypt, agreed upon by citizens Desaix, general of division, and Poussielgue, administrator-general of finances, plenipotentiaries of the commander-in-chief Kleber, and their excellencies Moustapha Raschid Effendi Tefterdar, and Moustapha Rassiche Effendi Riessul Knitar, ministers-plenipotentiaries of his highness the supreme -izier.

The French army in Egypt, wishing to give a proof of its desire to stop the effusion of blood, and to put an end to the unfortunate disagreements which have taken place between the French republic and the Sublime Porte, consents to evacuate Egypt on the stipulations of the present convention, hoping that this concession will pave the way for the general pacification of Europe.

I. The French army will retire with its arms, baggage, and effects, to Alexandria, Rosetta, and Aboukir, there to be embarked and transported to France, both in its own vessels and in those with which it will be necessary for the Sublime Porte to furnish it; and in order that the aforesaid vessels may be the more speedily prepared, it is agreed, that a month after the ratification of the present convention, there shall be sent to the fort of Alexandria a commissary, with fifty purses, on the part of the Sublime Porte.

II. There shall be an armistice of three months in Egypt, reckoning from the time of the signature of the present convention; and in case the truce shall expire, before the aforesaid vessels to be furnished by the Sublime Porte shall be ready, the said truce shall be prolonged till the embarkation can be completely effected, it being understood on both sides, that all possible means will be employed to secure the tranquillity of the armies and of the inhabitants, which is the object of the truce.

III. The transport of the French army shall take place, according to the regulations of commissaries appointed for this purpose by the Sublime Porte and general Kleber; and if any difference of opinion shall take place between the aforesaid commissaries respecting the embarkation, one

shall be appointed by commodore sir Sidney Smith, who shall decide the difference according to the maritime regulations of England.

IV. The forts of Catchich and Salachich shall be evacuated by the French troops on the eighth day, or, at the least, on the tenth day, after the ratification of this convention. The town of Mansoura shall be evacuated on the fifteenth day; Damietta and Belbeys on the twentieth day; and Suez shall be evacuated six days before Cairo. The other places on the east bank of the Nile shall be evacuated on the tenth day. The Delta shall be evacuated fifteen days after the evacuation of Cairo. The west banks of the Nile and its dependencies shall remain in the hands of the French till the evacuation of Cairo: and in the mean time, as they must be occupied by the French army till all the troops shall have descended from Upper Egypt, the said western bank and its dependencies will not be evacuated till the expiration of the truce, if it is impossible to evacuate them sooner. The places evacuated shall be given to the Sublime Porte in the situation in which they are at present.

V. The city of Cairo shall be evacuated after forty days, if that is possible, or at the latest after forty-five days, reckoning from the ratification of the treaty.

VI. It is expressly agreed, that the Sublime Porte shall use every effort that the French troops may fall back, through the different places on the left bank of the Nile, with their arms and baggage towards the head-quarters, without being disturbed or molested on their march in their persons, property, or honor, either by the inhabitants of Egypt or the troops of the imperial Ottoman army.

VII. In consequence of the former article, and in order to prevent all differences and hostilities, measures shall be taken to keep the Turkish always at a sufficient distance from the French army.

VIII. Immediately after the ratification of the present convention, all the Turks, and other nations without distinction, subjects of the Sublime Porte, imprisoned or retained in France, or in the power of the French in Egypt, shall be set at liberty;

3 o 2

and, on the other hand, all the French detained in the cities and sea-port towns of the Ottoman empire, as well as every person of whatever nation they may be, attached to French legations and consulates, shall also be set at liberty.

IX. The restitution of the goods and property of the inhabitants and subjects on both sides, or the payment of their value to the proprietors, shall commence immediately after the evacuation of Egypt, and shall be regulated at Constantinople by commissaries appointed respectively for the purpose.

X. No inhabitant of Egypt, of whatever religion he may be, shall be disturbed either in his person or his property, on account of any connections he may have had with the French, during their possession of Egypt.

XI. There shall be delivered to the French army, as well on the part of the Sublime Porte as of the courts of its allies, that is to say, of Russia and of Great Britain, passports, safe conducts, and convoys, necessary to secure its safe return to France.

XII. When the French army in Egypt shall be embarked, the Sublime Porte, as well as its allies, promise that till its return to the continent of France, it shall not be disturbed in any manner : and on his side, the general-in-chief Kleber, and the French army in Egypt, promise not to commit any act of hostility during the aforesaid time, either against the fleets or against the territories of the Sublime ¡Porte ; and that the vessels, which may transport the said army, shall not stop on any other coast than that of France, except from absolute necessity.

XIII. In consequence of the truce of three months, stipulated above with the French army for the evacuation of Egypt, the contracting parties agree, that if, in the interval of the said truce, some vessels from France, unknown to the commanders of the allied fleets, should enter the port of Alexandria, they shall depart from it after having taken in water and the necessary provisions, and return to France with passports from the allied courts ; and in

case any of the said vessels should require repairs, these alone may remain till the said repairs are finished, and shall depart immediately after, like the preceding, with the first favorable wind.

XIV. The general-in-chief Kleber may send advices immediately to France; and the vessel that conveys them shall have the safe conduct necessary for securing by the said advices, to the French government, the communication of the news of the evacuation of Egypt.

XV. There being no doubt that the French army will stand in need of daily supplies of provisions, during the three months in which it is to evacuate Egypt, and during other three months, reckoning from the day on which it is embarked ; it is agreed, that it shall be supplied with the necessary quantities of corn, meat, rice, barley, and straw, according to a statement to be immediately given in by the French plenipotentiaries, as well for the stay in the country as for the voyage. Whatever supplies the army may draw from its magazines, after the ratification of the present convention, shall be deducted from those furnished by the Sublime Porte.

XVI. Counting from the day of the ratification of the present treaty, the French army shall not raise any contribution in Egypt : on the contrary, it shall abandon to the Sublime Porte the ordinary leviable contributions which remain to it, to be levied after its departure, as well as the camels, dromedaries, ammunition, cannon, and other things, which it may not think necessary to carry away. The same shall be the case with the magazines of grain arising from the contributions already levied, and the magazines of provisions. These shall be examined and valued by commissaries sent to Egypt by the Sublime Porte, and by the commander of the British forces, conjointly with those of the general-in-chief Kleber ; and paid by the former, at the rate of the valuation so made, to the amount of 3000 purses, which will be necessary to the French army for accelerating its movements and its embarkation : and if the objects above-mentioned do not amount to this sum, the deficit shall be advanced by the Sublime Porte, in the form of a loan, which will be paid by the French government, upon the bills of the commissaries appointed by the general-in chief Kleber to receive the said sum.

XVII. The French army having expenses to incur in the evacuation of Egypt, it shall receive, after the ratification of the present convention, the sums stipulated in the following order, viz. the 15th day and the 20th day, 500 purses ; the 40th day, 50th, 60th, 70th and 80th day, 500 purses ; and finally, the 90th day, 500 purses. All the said purses, of 500 Turkish piastres each, shall be received in loan from the persons commissioned to this effect by the Sublime Porte : and in order to facilitate the execution of this article, the Sublime Porte, immediately after the ratification of the convention, shall send commissaries to the city of Cairo, and to the other cities occupied by the armies.

XVIII. The contributions, which the French may receive after the date of the ratification, and before the notification of the present convention in the different parts of Egypt, shall be deducted from the amount of the 3000 purses above stipulated.

XIX. In order to facilitate and accelerate the evacuation of the places, the navigation of the French transport vessels, which may be in the ports of Egypt, shall be free during the three months truce from Damietta and Rosetta to Alexandria, and from Alexandria to Damietta and Rosetta.

XX. The safety of Europe requiring the greatest precautions to prevent the contagion of the plague from being carried thither, no person either sick, or suspected of being infected with this malady, shall be embarked ; but all persons afflicted with the plague, or any other malady, which may not allow their removal in the time agreed upon for the evacuation, shall remain in the hospitals, where they are placed under the safeguard of his highness the vizier, and shall be attended by the French officers of health, who may remain with them until their health allows them to set off, which shall be as soon as possible. The 11th and 12th articles of this convention shall

be applicable to them, as well as to the rest of the army ; and the commander-in-chief of the French army engages to give the most strict orders, to the different officers commanding the troops embarked, not to allow them to disembark in any other ports than those which shall be pointed out by the officers of health, as affording the greatest facility for performing the necessary, accustomed, and proper quarantine.

XXI. All the difficulties which may arise, and which shall not be provided for by the present convention, shall be amicably settled by commissioners, appointed for that purpose by his highness the grand vizier and the general-in-chief Kleber, in such a manner as to facilitate the evacuation.

XXII. These presents shall not be effectual until after the respective ratifications, which are to be exchanged in eight days ; after which they shall be religiously observed on both sides.

Done, signed, and sealed, January 24th, 1800.

DESAIX, &c. &c.

In the completion of this convention, which afterwards gave rise to so much discussion, sir Sidney Smith acted as intermediary and mediating agent ; and his honorable and prudent conduct on the occasion merits the highest eulogium. Although, said he, in his correspondence with Kleber, measures had been taking for surrounding the French army on all sides ; yet, their bravery, courage, and fame, remaining still unconquered, gave them full right to believe, that they might be able to resist for some time. They were not, therefore, in a situation which obliged them to capitulate ; but were entitled to retain their arms and baggage, and to be provided with means to enable them to evacuate Egypt. Such were the motives, which led him to forward the treaty. He did every thing in his power for the protection and safety of the French plenipotentiaries, and placed his tent along with theirs, in order to run the same risks with them in the midst of the vizier's camp. At the conclusion of the transaction, he informed general Kleber, that the disorder and want of discipline of the Turks gave him some uneasiness respecting the perfect execution of the convention, but that he would take all possible care to guarantee it; and in a subsequent letter, he recommended it to the French commander to be constantly on his guard. It is probable, that sir Sidney was induced to hasten the business, not only from a wish to clear Egypt of the French by any means, and as soon as possible, but by the promise, on the part of the Russian envoy in the course of the conferences, of the speedy arrival of a Russian fleet and 10,000 men, a force which would have given too great an influence to the court of St. Petersburgh in the fate of Egypt.

In whatever view this convention may be regarded, it was a most favorable incident to Britain. By the evacuation of Egypt, the English establishments in the east were freed from danger, and the enemy deprived of a colonial establishment of incalculable importance; while the value of this success was enhanced by its peaceable accomplishment. One might be inclined to suppose, that the allies would have congratulated themselves on the facility of getting rid of a formidable enemy, and eagerly promoted the measure, rather than endeavored to retard it. But Europe heard with surprise, that the policy of the British ministry enjoined lord Keith to annul the convention, by opposing the embarkation and passage of the French troops.

By the articles of the treaty, the Porte had engaged the consent and good faith of its allies. It communicated the capitulation to the ministers of these powers, and collected a great number of vessels of all nations for the purpose of taking the French on board at Alexandria. The captain Pacha was also preparing to sail, with a respectable squadron, to superintend the embarkation, and escort them on their voyage. But the refusal of England to concur in an engagement, concluded under the auspices of its accredited agent, and by an ally independent and not tributary, disconcerted every thing. In this dilemma the grand vizier knew not how to act. He durst not advance from his camp at Belbeys: yet he adhered to the convention, as far as in his power, by paying 3,000,000 of the stipulated sum; and the French, in return, gave him possession of the forts they had agreed to surrender. Meanwhile lord Elgin, the English ambassador at Constantinople, signified to the Ottoman government, that his court could not subscribe to the capitulation, and that the English ships would not suffer the vessels to pass, which were destined to convey the enemy's army. Lord Keith, and sir Sidney Smith, in like manner intimated officially to general Kleber, that Great Britain refused to permit the execution of the treaty. His lordship's letter bore, that he had received positive orders from his majesty, not to consent to any capitulation with the French troops in Egypt and Syria; unless they agreed to lay down their arms, surrender themselves prisoners, and deliver up all the ships and stores in the port of Alexandria to the allies. Besides, in the event of such a capitulation, he could not allow any of the men to depart for France, until they were exchanged. All vessels, therefore, having French troops on board, and intending to sail from Egypt with passports given by others than those fully authorised to grant them, would be forced by the British fleet to remain in Alexandria: and those, met with on their return to Europe, and having passes granted in consequence of a particular capitulation with one of the confederated powers, would be retained as prizes, and the persons on board them considered as prisoners of war. "Soldiers!" exclaimed Kleber, in a laconic proclamation communicating this proceeding to his army, "behold the letter which I have received from the commander of the English fleet in the Mediterranean—We know how to reply to such insolence by victories:— prepare for battle."

During these transactions, the Aga of the janissaries advanced to Maturia within two leagues of Cairo; and the French general, thus pressed, was obliged to come to an immediate determination, on the line of conduct he was to follow. In the present unsettled state of affairs, he was unwilling to suffer his only remaining military post to be occupied by the enemy; and although inclined to execute fully the convention on his part, common prudence required that he should watch over the safety of his army. To give up the strong holds was placing himself at the mercy of lawless Turks, in whose good faith he could repose no confidence. Defeat itself could not be attended with more pernicious consequences: but the issue of a battle might be fortunate; and Kleber, with his characteristic boldness, resolved to have recourse to arms. He apprised the Turkish commander of his intention to resume hostilities, and soon afterwards marched towards Heliopolis. The janissary Aga, with part of the Ottoman army, lay in the vicinity of that town, and an immediate engagement took place in which the advantage of European discipline and the European system of war was immediately seen. The French army which did not amount to more than 15,000 men, steadily received an onset from the janissaries: and proceeding in their turn to the attack, put their enemy to immediate flight. After some vain attempts to rally they retreated precipitately to Jaffa, and lost half their numbers by hunger, fatigue, or desertion, while Kleber was consoled in his distress by a victory obtained with the loss of only ten men killed, and about forty wounded.

This victory would have been of signal benefit to the French interests in Egypt had not Kleber been prevented from taking advantage of his success by a revolt at Cairo. During the interval of his pursuit Nusuff Bashaw entered the city with a strong body of janissaries and Mamelukes. Having impressed the citizens with a belief that the Turks had been victorious in the late battle, they were welcomed with enthusiasm. Being supported by the adherents of the beys Osman Effendi, Ibrahim Kiaja, and Mahomet El-Elfi, they penetrated to the quarter inhabited by the French, and made great slaughter among them. So prevalent was the spirit of revolt, that in a short time the insurgents rein-

forced by those who poured in from the adjoining country: were supposed to amount to 50,000 men. The city now presented a dreadful scene of uproar, war, and bloodshed. The white flag was every where displayed, and the criers, from the tops of the mosques, proclaimed curses on the heads of the infidels. Amidst hideous yells of war, the acclamation of joy, called hoololoos, was heard every where among groups of women and children. Mustapha Aga superintendent of the police under the present government was seized and put to death. All who favored the French interests shared the same fate, and the houses and magazines were sacked by the insurgents. During this scene of confusion 250 French troops had guarded their head-quarters against the furious assaults of the insurgents, till Legrange, with his column, arrived to their relief and repelled the assailants.

In this situation Kleber found the city on his return from the pursuit of the Turks, March the 26th, five days after the victory of Heliopolis. He entered with promptitude on the means of recovering a city on which the existence of his army depended. He formed new entrenchments and constructed new batteries. While he looked with anxious expectation to the arrival of reinforcements under Regnier and Belliard, he undeceived the people respecting the issue of the battle of Heliopolis. Having concluded a treaty with Murad Bey, by which the provinces of Ginsee and Assuan were allotted to him, with the title of prince governor for the French republic, he caused the documents to be published, in order to intimidate others, by shewing that he was so powerfully supported; and he endeavoured by his intrigues to create divisions among the beys. After the troops under Regnier and Belliard had arrived he laid siege to the city. In the several assaults great slaughter was made on both sides. When he had made himself master of several important posts, the frantic efforts of the beys being overpowered by the steady attacks of the assailants, Murad Bey interposed with his entreaties to Osman and Ibrahim Beys, and Nusuff Bashaw, that they would capitulate; a proposal to which they at length consented, and the Turks evacuated the city. The French had lost since the return of Kleber, 500 men ; the Mamelukes, 500 killed and 1000 wounded ; and the Turks, 1200 killed and 1000 wounded.

After the battle of Heliopolis and the siege of Cairo, the army of the east obtained a momentary respite from many of the evils they had hitherto endured. The inhabitants of Egypt, astonished to see the vizier of the Porte, the greatest personage to whom their knowledge extended, defeated by the French, were now convinced that the efforts of the Turks to regain the country would be finally ineffectual ; and, considering Egypt as the property of their new masters, sullenly acquiesced in the dispensations of providence. They had experienced, on various occasions, the facility with which revolt had been suppressed by an inconsiderable number of the invader's forces : the expenses of the war levied on the rebels would deter them from similar attempts, and the treaty with Murad Bey had a powerful tendency to conciliate the peaceable and discourage the hostile inhabitants. The extraordinary contributions imposed upon Cairo as a punishment for its revolt, supplied resources for paying the arrears of the army, amounting to £500,000, including the soldiers' pay, and of tranquilly waiting till the ensuing season for the collection of the ordinary imposts.

The measures of Kleber for ameliorating the condition of his troops, for facilitating their movements, and confirming the tranquillity of the country, were decisive and judicious. The army had found it extremely difficult to procure the means of carriage in moments of urgency, because at such times the Arabs, who let out their camels to hire, disappeared. To secure this important service, the general established a park of 500 camels for the use of the army ; which were employed when the troops reposed from their military labors in various useful services. He established flying bridges over the branches of the Nile, and established posts of com-

munication between the different stations of the army. He laid down a plan of great simplicity for works to be constructed at Cairo, which might overawe the inhabitants of the city, and command the avenues to its entrance. He established a committee of works consisting of five members, with whom he deliberated on the improvement and amelioration of the country ; and put a stop to the dilapidations and peculations of the commisariat on the inferior officers and soldiers, whose condition he greatly improved by enforcing a regular delivery of rations, of forage, and provisions, and distributing the clothing of the different corps beneath his own inspection.

The Turkish fleet, commanded by the capitan Pacha, appeared off Alexandria in the latter end of May. Kleber instantly marched with part of the 1800. troops from Cairo, learned at Rahmanieh that the capitan Pacha appeared off Alexandria merely to open a friendly correspondence, prohibited the landing of any Turkish agent, and returned to Cairo, leaving in the Delta opposite to Rahmanieh a flying camp of two demi-brigades, and two regiments of cavalry, to march to any point that might be menaced, or to the frontier of Syria. It became his first object after his return, to avail himself of the rupture of the convention of El-Arisch, and to excite the jealousy of the Turks towards their English allies. It was his intention to decline all communication with the Turkish and English commanders-in-chief, while he endeavored to open a direct correspondence with Constantinople. By this policy he expected to be able to correspond with the French government, to receive its instructions, and to cajole the Turks into a neutrality, which would have diminished the number of his enemies, and have augmented his resources by reviving the commerce of Egypt.

The merit of Kleber did not screen him from the shafts of malice. A faction was formed against him, at the head of which was Menou, who had held a high place in the opinion of the first consul.

Assassination of General Kleber in Egypt.

He testified the utmost personal disaffection to the commander-in-chief, displayed the most studied inattention to his orders; and, to undermine him in the confidence of the troops, he circulated a report that Kleber had sold Egypt to the Turks by the treaty of El-Arisch. On the 18th of June, the general was walking on the terrace of his garden, when he received several stabs from a poignard. The assassin had followed Kleber from Gizeh, and having introduced himself into the house along with the workmen, seized, for the execution of his purpose, the moment when Kleber was deeply engaged in conversation. Menon was suspected of having employed or instigated the assassin, but no evidence transpired to justify the charge, nor before his execution by impalement did the criminal make any confession of the causes, or the advisers of the act.

After the interment of Kleber and the execution of the assassin, general Menon assumed the title of commander-in-chief. The army regarded his advancement with reluctance, but its murmurs were appeased by the persuasions of the generals. Menon received with attention the generals and the heads of the civil departments, paid them frequent visits, and seemed to anticipate their views and wishes, but having once secured the object of his ambition he laid aside the mask, and openly endeavored to enrich *himself*, at the same time that he provided by pecuniary exactions for the vast expenditure of the establishment, which increased from 13,000 to 18,000 francs per month, after the death of Kleber.

We have seen that lord Keith refused to sign the treaty of El-Arisch because it was contrary to the instructions received from his government. But it is necessary to observe that the ratifications of that treaty which were exchanged on the 28th of January 1800, could not have been known by the English government when the instructions were given, because the latter were despatched in the preceding month. Though unofficially concluded, ministers confirmed the treaty as soon as it was apprised of the transaction. On the 9th of June lieutenant Wright arrived at Cairo with a flag of

truce, bearing dispatches from the vizier and sir Sidney Smith; but Menon, who was well aware that the colonization of Egypt was Buonaparte's favorite object, and associated the most extensive views of personal ambition with the desire of gratifying the first consul, refused to renew the negotiation.

While the army of the east was thus successful on the plains of Egypt, the exploits of the army of the Rhine affected the court of Austria with feelings of disappointment and dismay. After the engagement on the Iller, already described general Lecourbe again advanced towards the Lech, and on the 10th of June took a position on the Wurtach; and after a great variety of unimportant, but difficult and complex manœuvres, was ordered to obtain possession of one of the bridges between Dillingen and Donawert. After a spirited assault he carried that in the vicinity of the former place, and thus enabled the commander-in-chief to make preparations for gaining, the next day, the bridges of Grensheim, Blenheim, and Hochstedt. Eighty men stript themselves naked and swam across the river dragging after them three boats loaded with their muskets and cartouche boxes. Without a moment's delay they siezed on the villages of Grensheim and Blenheim, and the artillery planted on the bank. At these villages the warriors, naked as they were, maintained themselves with extraordinary valor, while the pioneers and pontoneers labored to repair the bridges, and these being completed, succours crossed over, the cavalry passing one by one. Part of the reinforcements sent by the enemy were destroyed and the rest driven back. The Austrian main army soon after retreated from Ulm; general Moreau took possession of Munich, and levied heavy contributions on the territories of Bavaria. The elector was compelled to pay to the French a great part of the subsidy of £500,000 which he had received from Great Britain. After the retreat of the Austrian army from Suabia, the French took possession of the principal places in the duchy of Wurtemburg which, as well as Bavaria, was laid under severe contributions, and treated altogether as an enemy's country. The duke and duchess of Wurtemburg, with their family and suite, retired to Anspach, and the French, at the same time, by the occupation of El-Wangen, became masters of the electorate of Treves. To augment the disasters of the Austrians, an army of 30,000 men, French and Bavarians, was on its march to the Lower and the Upper Rhine, and ready to pass by Mentz and Dusseldorf into Franconia.

In these circumstances, the Austrians imitated the example of their friends in Italy, and solicited an armistice, which, at the desire of Buonaparte to Moreau, was granted on the 15th of July. The line of demarcation was chiefly traced by that of the advanced posts. The Austrians retained the places which they still occupied within the French line, comprehending Ulm and Ingoldstadt; and the renewal of hostilities was to be preceded by a notice of twelve days.

Previous to his return from Italy, Buonaparte had established a provisional government for Poland, and re-organised the republican constitution of Liguria. The army of Massena assumed its positions in conformity with the armistice. The surrendered fortresses were provided with garrisons, and provisioned out of the magazines captured from the Austrians. It was calculated that the artillery of the places given up by the convention, amounted to more than 2000 pieces, and the gunpowder to more than 2,000,000 pounds.

The advantages acquired by Buonaparte, were beyond the reach of calculation. Besides the important places of strength surrendered to his forces, he gained time to confirm himself in the possession of his conquests, to rear without interruption an auxiliary power in the Cisalpine republic, to concentrate in one body all his forces in Italy, and to procure with facility the necessary succours from France. The suspension of arms was no less beneficial to general Moreau. His forward position, which required him to bridle the country with detachments, materially diminished his advancing army. He had experienced

a trifling disquietude from wandering parties of the enemy in his rear; and as St. Susanne's corps was weak, and had only just begun its march, he was still exposed to have his intercourse with France interrupted. In planning the campaign, the French government committed a palpable mistake; for it is impossible not to condemn the impolicy of sending an army in the rout followed by Moreau, without having collected a strong military force in Franconia to engage the attention of any hostile corps posted on the left of the Danube. Buonaparte was so much convinced of this, that he had resolved to form an army under general Augereau on the Main; and, in fact, this officer was already on his way with part of the Batavian army, and some French troops from Holland, where he held the chief command.

General Moreau's army, on debouching between the Swiss Rhine and the sources of the Danube, had to take a very extensive line. Its left wing could not leave the right bank of this river with safety; and its right had not only to display a front towards the Voralberg and Tyrol, but also towards the Bavarian frontier, while it supported the centre and left in their engagements with the enemy. Kray's falling back by Ulm and Ingoldstadt, and clinging so tenaciously to the Danube, do not indicate an enterprising genius. Perhaps he wished to save his magazines by retrograding in that direction; and certainly an object of such magnitude was not to be lightly abandoned. Yet a very few days were sufficient for that purpose; and if it could not have been executed with dispatch, a cold and parsimonious disposition alone would have hesitated to destroy them.

Ulm presented the imperial general with an excellent position; but it could not save the rest of Suabia from being overrun by the enemy, nor prevent them from penetrating to the Lech, and threatening to cut off all further retreat. In fine, a failure of provisions, which in such a post he would soon have experienced, must have menaced him with speedy destruction, if not absolutely accomplished. His position obliged the enemy to push their left wing across the river, while the left of their centre rested on the right bank. At the same time, their right wing, stretching to a great distance, made an extensive sweep by Kempten and Augsburg; and then part of it uniting with the centre, and passing the Danube, perforated the line of the imperial army. In this situation it was only by a rapid and circuitous march that Kray could draw off his right to a new position at Ingoldstadt. By that manœuvre Moreau cleared the passage of the Lech, and, having traversed the Iser, was preparing to prosecute a similar plan, which must have driven Kray from the banks of the river, and compelled him to make a long detour by the left of the Danube. The imperial commander was sensible of his danger, and withdrew precipitately to Ingoldstadt. He had merely time to escape by the bridge of Moesburg on the Iser, and to reach the Inn, by forced marches, before the enemy.

In the late armistice, Buonaparte had prudently stipulated, that neither party should send troops into Germany. General Kray being by this stipulation deprived of all reinforcement from Italy, was obliged soon after to solicit the armistice which we have seen him concluding with Moreau.

The successes of the arms of France, and the broken state of the coalition, had rendered the Austrian cause almost desperate. But such was the humiliation which his imperial majesty must suffer, and the loss of territory to which he must submit by a treaty of peace, that, while there remained a glimpse of hope, he was determined not to be the author of his own disgrace and his enemy's aggrandisement. Encouraged by the offer of a loan of £2,000,000 from Great Britain, the emperor determined to persist in the arduous struggle, and a subsidiary convention was signed at Vienna on the 20th of June, by which the contracting parties engaged to act with the most intimate confidence and concert, and promised not to lay down their arms unless by common

consent, or without obtaining a peace on the basis of the *uti possidetis*, (or state of things before the commencement of the war.) Their British and imperial majesty's promised to carry on the war during the present campaign, with all possible vigor : the Bavarian, Wurtemburg, and Swiss troops, in the pay of England, were placed at the disposal of the emperor; the payment of a loan of £2,000,000 was guaranteed, and the duration of the convention was fixed for a period terminating on the last day of February, 1801. Two days before the convention was signed at Vienna, count St. Julien arrived with the official copy of the armistice of Alessandria. The knowledge of this circumstance, and of the fatal battle of Marengo, had no weight with baron Thugut ; and, notwithstanding the critical situation of affairs, he pledged the emperor to prosecute the war for another year. It was necessary, however, to conceal the transaction, and do something in order to gain time. The count was accordingly dispatched from Vienna to Paris with a letter intimating the nature of his mission. He arrived at the French capital on the 21st of July, having proceeded by the way of Italy in the expectation of finding Buonaparte in that country. The alleged object of his journey was to regulate the conditions of a regular armistice, and clear up some doubtful points connected with the convention of Alessandria.

After a few conferences, the count and the minister Talleyrand, on the 28th, signed at Paris the following " preliminaries of peace between France and Austria."

His majesty the emperor, king of Hungary, and Bohemia, &c. and the chief consul of the republic, in the name of the French people, equally animated with the desire of putting an end to the evils of war; by a speedy, just, and solid peace, have agreed upon the following preliminary articles ::

Art. I. There shall be peace, friendship, and good understanding between his majesty the emperor and king, and the French republic.

3 P 2

II. Until the conclusion of a definitive treaty, the armies both in Italy and Germany, shall respectively remain in the positions in which they are, without extending these more to the south of Italy. On his side, his imperial majesty engages to concentrate all the forces he may have in the states of the pope, in the fortress of Ancona, to put an end to the extraordinary levy which is making in Tuscany, and to prevent all disembarkation of the enemies of the French republic at Leghorn, or any other point of the coast.

III. The treaty of Campo-Formio shall be taken as the basis of the definitive pacification, excepting, however, the changes become necessary.

IV. His imperial majesty does not oppose the French republic keeping the limits of the Rhine such as they were agreed upon at Rastadt; i. e. the left bank of the Rhine, from the spot where it leaves the territory of Switzerland to the point where it enters the territory of the Batavian republic; and engages moreover to cede to the French republic the sovereignty and property of the Frickthal, and all that belongs to the house of Austria between Zurzach and Basle.

V. The French republic is not understood to keep Cassel, Kehl, Ehrenbreitstein, and Dusseldorf. These places will be razed, on condition that there shall not be raised on the right bank of the Rhine, and for the distance of three miles, any fortifications, either of stone work or earth.

VI. The indemnities, which his imperial majesty the emperor and king was to have in Germany, in virtue of the secret articles of the treaty of Campo-Formio, shall be taken in Italy: and therefore it shall be reserved until the definitive treaty, to agree on the position and the extent of the said indemnities. Nevertheless it shall be established as a basis, that his imperial majesty the emperor and king shall possess, besides the country which had been granted to him in Italy by the treaty of Campo Formio, an equivalent to the possession of the archbishoprick of Saltzburg, the river of the Inn and the Sabra, and the Tyrol, comprising the town of Wasserbourg on the left bank of the Inn with a circuit of three thousand toises, and the Frickthal which he cedes to the French republic.

VII. The ratification of the present preliminary articles shall be exchanged at Vienna before the 27th Thermidor (August 15.)

VIII. Immediately after the exchange of the ratifications, the negotiations for a definite peace shall continue; both sides shall agree upon a place for negotiation: the plenipotentiaries shall be there in twenty days at the latest, after the exchange.

IX. His majesty, the emperor and king, and first consul of the French republic, reciprocally engage on their word of honour, to keep the present articles secret till ratification.

X. The powers of M. St. Julian being contained in a letter from the emperor to the first consul, the full powers invested with the usual formalities shall be exchanged with the ratification of the present preliminaries, *which shall not bind* the respective governments, till after the ratification.

We the undersigned, have agreed upon, and signed the present preliminaries at Paris the 18th of July, 1800.

Signed Count de St. Julien.
C. Maurice Talleyrand.

St. Julien on his return from Vienna was accompanied by Duroc, the aid-de-camp of Buonaparte. They arrived on the 4th of August at Alt Oettingen the head-quarters of general Kray, but Duroc was not permitted to proceed further. The party of Thugut reinforced by the recent arrival of the queen of Naples, and her influence with her daughter the empress, succeeded in preventing a ratification of the treaty. The emperor alleged that St. Julien had exceeded his instructions, avowed the conclusion of a treaty with his Britannic majesty, and expressed his determination to abide by its conditions. It was the obvious policy however of Buonaparte to divide the members of the confederacy by proposals of separate peace, and we shall find on recurring to the affairs of England, that the consul lost no time in transmitting full powers to citizen Otto, the French commissary, for prisoners in England, authorising him to propose and sign, conformably to his instructions, a general armistice between the republic and his Britannic majesty. The French government, about the same time, informed the generals of its armies, that the emperor, having refused to subscribe to the conditions of the preliminaries, which had been signed by his plenipotentiary at Paris, the government was under the necessity of continuing the war. The armistice, therefore, must be considered as broken off, and would cease to have effect on the 7th of September, at one in the afternoon. The general officers, and chiefs of division, were instructed to profit by this interval, to pass the troops in review, and to make such arrangements as might enable them to march and fight, as soon as their orders should arrive.

The resolution of the emperor, to put himself at the head of his army, was taken, no doubt, with a view to rouse the antient courage of the Germans ; and to give efficacy to proclamations, which he issued at the same time, for calling forth the force of the country in volunteer associations. But the emperor had no sooner joined the army, which was under the immediate and sole command of the archduke John, than he made application to the French government for a prolongation of the armistice. The first consul, on conditions presently to be mentioned, agreed to this, declaring at the same time, that the renewal of hostilities, or the improvement of a suspension of arms into a permanent peace, would wholly depend on the rejection, or the ratification of the preliminaries concluded with M. de St. Julian. The consul, at the same time, declared that he thought it his duty, not to waste the remainder of the autumn in idle conferences, or to expose himself to endless diplomatic discussions, without securities for the sincerity of the enemy's intentions. The securities he demanded, were Philipsburg, Ulm, and Ingoldstadt, with their dependent forts. This condition, though it exposed the hereditary dominions of Austria, in a great

measure, at the mercy of the enemy, being agreed to at Hohenlinden, a suspension of arms was concluded for forty-five days, commencing from the 21st of September.

There was not, during this interval, any remission of military preparation on either side. Recruits were sent from the camp at Dijon to the French armies ; and the Austrians were reinforced by battalions raised in all parts of the hereditary states. The French army of the Rhine, seconded on its left by the army of Augereau, and on its right by that of the Grisons, formed, on the Mayne, as far as the entry into the Tyrol, a line ready to advance on the first signal. It was composed of 12 divisions, comprising at least 100,000 men, and was divided into four corps ; of which, that under general Lecombe, consisting of three divisions, occupied Upper Suabia, Upper Bavaria, and the entry to the Tyrol. That under the immediate orders of the commander-in-chief in person, consisting of three other divisions, occupied the two banks of the Iller, as far as Landshut. That of general Grenier consisting of three more divisions, held all the left banks of the Danube, nearly to Passau, and the right bank of that river as far as the mouth of it at Altmuck : and, lastly, that of general St. Susanne, composed of three other divisions, occupied the country between the Maine and the Danube, from Bamberg as far as Aix-la-Chapelle.—While the French were thus formidable in front, there was nothing to be apprehended on either of their flanks. Italy was reconquered, Switzerland was in their possession, and moulding its government just as the French pleased : and a Prussian army maintained the neutrality of the north of Germany.

The Austrian armies advanced to the frontiers, and occupied a chain of posts in front of the hostile army, bending their main force to strengthen their line, from the frontier of Austria to the gulf of Venice. An army of 30,009 men was stationed in Bohemia, under the command of the archduke Charles. The right banks of the Maine were occupied by the Austrians in great force. And an army, under the command of general Klenau, in the Upper Palatinate, was opposed to the French division under general St. Susanne, whose head-quarters were at Mayence

The positions and first movements of the invading army seemed to indicate an intention of carrying the great weight of the war into Bohemia. But the grand plan of Moreau's operations was not fully or certainly developed; this winter campaign being speedily cut short, by decisive advantages obtained over the Austrians. The French troops, under Augereau, drove those of Mayence from Aschaffenberg, on the 24th of November, and marched through Franconia towards Bohemia, to communicate with the left of the division, under general Moreau.

On the 29th, general Moreau recommenced hostilities, near the Inn, and carried the Austrian works at Wassenberg. He was less successful in a battle, on the 1st of December, near Haag, where he was vigorously attacked by the archduke John, at the head of three columns. The Austrians were repeatedly driven back, but at last prevailed. The French were forced to retreat, with great slaughter. On the same day, an attack was made by the French on an Austrian post at Rosenheim, but were repulsed, after a hot engagement. In this action, the prince of Condé's corps acquired great reputation, by their firmness and cool courage. The prince of Condé's son, and the duke of Angouleme, were particularly distinguished.

The archduke John, encouraged by these successes, on the 3rd of December, assaulted the French post at Hohenlinden, memorable for the last convention, and rendered still more memorable by the battle of this day. The archduke had no sooner begun his march than there fell a heavy shower of snow and sleet, by which his march was so much retarded, that only the central column had arrived at the place of destination, at a time when all the divisions ought to have been ready for action. A division of the French, conducted by Richepanse, pierced between the left wing of the Austrians and the centre, reached

the great road behind the centre, and assaulted the left flank and rear of that column, at a moment when it had formed in front, and commenced an attack. The Austrians, with their usual courage and bravery, sustained the conflict for several hours: but the centre being repelled by the impetuosity of the French, great disorder ensued. Their left wing was also defeated: and the battle seemed to be completely decided in favor of the French, when a vigorous attempt was made, by the right wing, to turn the tide of victory.

General Grenier sustained this unexpected charge with firmness; and, being well supported, threw his adversaries into the utmost confusion. The Austrians were forced to retire to the heights of Ramsan, with very great loss: and general Kinwayer, being attacked on his march, by a corps from Arding, likewise suffered severely in that retreat, to which he was driven by intelligence of the disaster that had befallen the main army.

According to the account of the battle of Hohenlinden, given by general Moreau, the French took 80 pieces of cannon, 200 caissons, 10,000 prisoners, and a great number of officers, among whom were three generals. The loss of the French did not exceed 3000 in killed, wounded, and missing. The victorious republicans, after a long and unremitted pursuit of the flying Austrians, took possession of the city of Saltzburgh.

In the mean time the Gallo-Batavian army and that of Italy were not idle. On the day distinguished by the battle of Hohenlinden, general Augereau gained an important advantage near Banburg. General Macdonald defying the inclemency of an Alpine winter, passed from the country of the Grisons into the Valteline, drove the enemy before him and opened a communication with the army of Italy. A division of his own army, after a series of actions with the Austrians, crossed the Mincio on the 26th of December. Vienna was struck with terror. The archduke repaired to the camp to re-animate the troops; but this prince, on a comparative review of his own and the enemy's strength, proposed an armistice which was readily agreed to and concluded at Steyer on the 25th of December, though the French, in violation of their faith, had dismantled the three towns which had been delivered to them as pledges. The emperor even consented to the surrender of many other posts relying on the promise of restitution; and was at length constrained to declare his readiness to detach himself from his allies, while the British court duly sensible of the alarming situation in which he was involved released him from his engagement; and the armistice was succeeded by the treaty of Luneville. In this manner terminated a campaign between Austria and France in which German courage, tactical skill, and military experience, when destined to contend with French valor, experience, and discipline, invigorated and guided by genius, were found unequal to the contest. Much must undoubtedly be attributed to the superior genius of Buonaparte and Moreau, and still more to the peculiar system of military tactics adopted by the French immediately subsequent to the opening of the first revolutionary campaign. The system of successive reserves which I shall shortly have occasion to elucidate was not less destructive to the armies of Austria, than the manœuvre of cutting the line to the navies of France, and when conducted by a Nelson, and a Moreau, both were equally resistless.

The treaty of peace and friendship was signed at Luneville, on the 9th of February, in the ensuing year. To avoid the delay of a tedious negotiation with the empire, his majesty undertook to stipulate, not only for himself, but in the name of the Germanic body. The peace of Campo Formio formed the basis of the present. The cession to France of the Belgic provinces, the country of Falkenstein, and the Frickthal, was renewed. Istria, Dalmatia, the islands of Venice, and the continental territories belonging to that republic, as far as the Adige, were to belong to Austria; and Mantua as part of the Cisalpine came into the possession of the French. The republic was to enjoy the countries on the left bank of the Rhine, the

Brisgau was to be given as an indemnity to the duke of Modena, and the fortresses on the right bank were to be restored by the French, on the express condition that they should afterwards remain in the state in which they might be found at the time of the evacuation. This last stipulation, so vaguely expressed, was held by the consul to imply a liberty of demolishing the fortifications which were accordingly laid in ruins. By these cessions in favor of France, several princes on the right bank of the Rhine were dispossessed of their territories in whole or in part: and the emperor bound himself to give these princes an indemnity within the empire. He ceded to the Cisalpine republic the countries forming that state, and the imperial fiefs to the Ligurian republic. Both the contracting parties guaranteed the independence of the Batavian, Helvetic, Cisalpine, and Ligurian republics. Contributions, requisitions, and orders for supplies to the French armies were to cease on the day of exchanging the ratifications at Luneville. The armies were to remain in their respective positions till that period; but, ten days after it, the imperial troops were to re-occupy the hereditary possessions of his majesty, and within thirty days the French were to evacuate the empire.

The only difference between this treaty and that of Campo Formio, was in the fifth article, by which it was stipulated, that the grand duke of Tuscany should renounce his duchy and portion of the isle of Elba, in favor of the duke of Parma: in return for which concession he was to receive an indemnification in Germany. The treaty was ratified in France, by the legislative body, and by the diet of the Germanic empire. The article, however, which stipulated the grant of indemnities to the princes whose territories had been ceded, or divided, was immediately productive of dissatisfaction, and debate. On the death of the electoral archbishop of Cologne and Munster, the emperor procured the election of his brother, the archduke Anthony, to the vacant see of Cologne. But the king of Prussia protested against the election, as inconsistent with the above article, and with the general sentiments of the empire. The emperor endeavored to remove his majesty's objections, but Frederic William, who acted in concert with the French government, not satisfied with this assurance, continued his opposition to a transaction which he was apprehensive might contribute to extend the power of his rival. The importance of the negotiation with the emperor, did not divert the attention of Buonaparte from subordinate objects. After the persecution which the unfortunate Pius VI. had undergone, it was expected that the arbitrator of the fate of Italy, would have demolished the ecclesiastical state, and the papal dignity But he was influenced by political motives, which the ensuing year more clearly developed, to suffer their existence. With his acquiescence cardinal de Chiaramonte was this year elected to the papal chair, and assumed the name of PIUS THE SEVENTH. The first consul in a letter of congratulation, on his accession to the pontificate, expressed his zeal for the support and security of religion, and his admiration of the pontiff's character, implored a blessing on his own political labors, and breathed a fervent hope, that his exertions would terminate in the tranquillity of the world

1800.

HISTORY OF THE WAR.

CHAP. XXX.

Riots in Cold Bath Fields—Disturbances arising from the Dearness of Bread—A Nego-
tiation is Opened with France—Reasons of its Failure—Naval Exploits—Unfortunate
Expedition to Ferrol—Arrival of the English Fleet off Cadiz—It Retires from that
Port—Proceedings in Parliament—Conclusion of the Union between Great Britain
and Ireland—Arrangements consequent upon that Event—Rise, Progress, and Ratifi-
cation, of the Northern Confederacy.

THE English parliament had scarcely been prorogued, before the inhabitants of London were alarmed by the indications of tumult and insubordination among the prisoners in Cold Bath Fields. They refused to submit in the evening to the usual shutting in of their cells, and uttered loud complaints of the miseries to which they were subjected. The multitude assembled round the walls of the prison, and threatened to force the gates. At this crisis the keeper Aris, a rigorous and hard-hearted man, sallied out and procured the aid of peace officers, while the volunteers of Clerkenwell, St. Sepulchre, and other adjoining districts, repaired from their shops to assist in quelling the disturbance; and peace and order were at length restored. The contagion of this example was the more to be dreaded, as the price of bread had risen to an height so exorbitant as to excite the murmurs of the people. This dreadful evil had progressively increased during the summer, but was borne with meritorious patience, in the belief that the growing crop, alleged to be generally promising, would remove the calamity. When harvest commenced the prices fell with considerable rapidity, but in September bread again rose, and convinced that so unexpected a circumstance could only arise from the monopoly of corn, the multitude determined to preserve themselves from famine by their own exertions, and take vengeance on monopolists, and forestallers. In the morning of the 15th of September, a mob, appearing in Mark-lane, insulted the corn-factors, and clamorously demanded the reduction of the price of bread. Mr. Combe, the lord mayor, justly and forcibly represented to the populace, that tumult and violence could only aggravate the evil of which they complained. Compelled by their perseverance to read the riot act, he at length succeeded in dispersing them without recourse to military aid. The riot was afterwards renewed, and though the mob was violent, the chief magistrate, now supported by the volunteers, still hoping to quell them without bloodshed did not order the troops to fire. For several days the tumults were repeated in various parts of the city, but the firmness and ready attendance of the volunteers intimidated the populace, and, without the actual use of arms repressed the commotions.

The negotiation between France and Austria drew from the British court expressions of a pacific tendency, and several communications passed between the two governments through the medium of M. Otto, a French agent, resident in England, for the exchange of prisoners. The French insisted on a naval armistice, and an abandonment of our blockade of their ports, as preliminaries to its further discussion. Lord Grenville, as secretary of foreign affairs, after objecting to the principle of the armistice, as affording unequivocal and important advantages to France, proposed a counter-project, which prohibited all means of defence from being conveyed to the island of Malta, or to any of the ports of Egypt, but allowed the necessaries of life to be introduced from time to time. It provided for the discontinuance of the blockade at Brest, Toulon, and other French ports, but tended to prevent all naval or military stores from being conveyed thither by sea, and the ships of war in those ports from being removed to any other station. The French government, dissatisfied with these propositions, offered this alternative. If Great Britain would agree to a separate negotiation, her scheme would be adopted; but if she should insist on a general negotiation, the proposals of France must be accepted. Lord Grenville insisted on the terms already offered by Great Britain. After a fruitless discussion, M. Otto intimated that the joint negotiation was at an end, but added that the first consul was disposed to receive any overtures towards a separate treaty with Great Britain; an intimation to which the government, true to its ally, returned a decided negative.

From scenes of internal commotion, and unavailing correspondence with an artful, and designing enemy, it is pleasing to retrace the exertions of national energy on its native element. A squadron under the command of sir Edward Pellew, on the 4th of June, attacked the south-west of the peninsula of Quiberon on the coast of Bretagne, silenced the forts, and cleared the shore of the enemy. A party of soldiers then landed and destroyed the forts. An attack was afterwards made on various posts, and six brigs, sloops, and gun-vessels, were taken, a corvette burned, and a fort dismantled. This event was immediately followed by an interception of supplies destined for the use of the French fleet at Brest. In this service, eight boats were employed under lieutenant Burke and other officers, who, amidst a severe fire of cannon and musketry, took three armed vessels, and eight ships laden with provisions, after driving several others upon the rocks of St. Croix. Some French ships having escaped to Quimper-river, boats were sent to attack them, but they removed to an inaccessible distance up the river. On the 8th of July, an attempt was made to take or destroy four frigates in the road of Dunkirk, and captain Campbell of the Dart, took the La Desirée; the other ships escaping with considerable damage. An exploit performed by lieutenant Jeremiah Coghlan, excited general admiration, and exhibited a signal instance of the prowess, courage, and intrepidity, which peculiarly characterise the British sailor. This young hero was commandant of the Viper cutter, under the orders of sir Edward Pellew. While watching Port Louis, near L'Orient, he conceived the design of cutting out some of the gun-boats stationed at the entrance of the harbor. With the permission of Pellew, he made the attempt in a ten-oared cutter, and, with a midshipman and 18 sailors, determined on boarding a gun-brig, mounting three 24 pounders, and four 6 pounders, having her full complement of men, and within pistol-shot of three batteries. On the night of the 29th of July, he and his valiant comrades undertook the enterprise. They boarded the brig, and, with the loss of one killed and eight wounded, including the commander himself, overpowered the *eighty-seven* men who formed the crew of the brig, and made her a prize. Sir Charles Hamilton, making his appearance with a small squadron near Goree, the governor surrendered without resistance, and a British garrison took possession of the forts, and of Joul, a dependant factory. In August, a fleet under the command of sir John Borlase Warren, with a military force under the orders of sir James Murray Pulteney, set sail on a secret expedition. Its first object was the conquest of Belleisle; but the strong works that had been provided for its defence, discouraged the attempt. The armament, therefore, proceeded to the coast of Spain; and, on the 25th of August, appeared before the harbor of Ferrol. The troops landed without opposition, and advanced towards the heights which overlook the port. A skirmish ensued with a body of Spaniards, which terminated in favor of the invaders. Lieutenant-colonel Stuart, who commanded the British, was wounded. The next morning another engagement succeeded, and was attended with the same result. A hundred of the Spaniards were killed or wounded, and the loss of the English amounted to half that number. The opportunity of survey presented by the heights, did not give the British commander any hope of success; particularly when he learned, from the report of the prisoners, that the place was furnished with the means of effectual defence. He therefore ordered the troops to re-embark, and they retired unmolested. Of the sensation excited by this unfortunate event, the parliamentary discussions of the subsequent year, will enable the reader to form an estimate. It was even asserted by a noble lord in the house of peers, that at the very moment when the British army received orders to disembark, measures were taken within the town for its immediate surrender, and for presenting general Pulteney with the keys. About this period, sir Ralph Abercrombie, with an army of about 20,000 men, and a fleet of 20 ships of the line, commanded by lord Keith, appeared off Cadiz, where an epidemic disease raged with pestilential violence. The governor Morla, sent a letter to the British admiral, stating to him the situation of the inhabitants, and the universal odium which must attend an attack on a city thus afflicted by the visitation of Heaven.

To this letter the admiral and general replied, that, as the ships in the harbor were destined to be employed in increasing the naval force of the French republic, they could only avert an attack by surrendering the vessels. This proposal was received by the governor with indignation, and the British general began to make arrangements for a descent. But, when

it was found that the precautions of the enemy, and the strength of the works, were adequate to the defence of the place, and that the health and existence of the besiegers would be endangered by the pestilence, the British armament withdrew from Cadiz.

To alleviate the severe pressure of dearth, and prevent the danger of its recurrence, his majesty, in his opening speech on the 11th of November, proposed to the parliament, that the earliest and the most ample encouragement should be given to the importation of every species of grain, and that steps should be taken for the permanent extension and improvement of agriculture. He also recommended an inquiry into the state of the laws respecting the commerce which took place in various articles of provision, that undue combinations and fraudulent practices might be checked, without encroaching on the rights of the dealers in these commodities, or obstructing that established course of trade which appeared to be requisite for the proper supply of the markets.—Adverting to the late communications with the enemy, he remarked that peace was at present " unattainable without the sacrifice of those essential considerations on the maintenance of which all its advantages must depend."

The debate upon the address, in the upper house, was not very long or remarkable. Lord Hobart said, that economy was the best (because it was the most certain) remedy for the great evil of which the public complained, but which, he thought, did not arise from the war. Lord Holland affirmed that war and scarcity were closely connected: and, having condemned the conduct of the king's advisers, moved an amendment, stating that a change of administration was necessary for the attainment of a safe and honorable peace. Lord Grenville wished for a peace of that description; but, as the inconciliatory disposition of the foe, prevented us from obtaining it, he was convinced of the policy of continuing the war. The amendment was rejected by a majority of 45 peers.

3 q 2

The chief speeches in the house of com-
mous were those of Mr. Pitt and Mr.
Grey. The minister contended that the
war was not the cause of the high price of
corn, as this article bore a moderate price
in several years of increased pressure from
the weight of taxes required for the prosecution of the great contest in which we
were engaged. The cause might more
obviously be found in the deficiency of the
last year's produce of grain ; and the late
harvest, though not so scanty as the preceding, had not been remarkably abundant.
The best expedients for reducing the price
seemed to be the encouragement of importation, the practice of economy, and
the use of various articles in lieu of bread.
On the subject of negotiation, Mr. Pitt
justified the king's repugnance to a separate
treaty, and censured the arrogance of an
enemy who insisted on the disjunction of
confederate powers before he would con-
descend to treat with them. Mr. Grey
called upon the house to inquire into the
causes which had impaired the prosperity
of the country, and produced a rapid accumulation of misfortune. He hoped that
a blind confidence would no longer be
reposed in men who were destitute of
political wisdom, and whose inability and
folly threatened the ruin of the state. He
had reason to think that peace might have
been obtained at the beginning of the year ;
but the prospect was blasted by the obstinacy of the cabinet. The supposed
strength and cordiality of our allies had
produced that elation of mind which rejected the offer of a negotiation ; and we
could not now expect such favorable
terms as we might then have commanded ;
yet, as the decline of our affairs and interests might be progressive, it would be
prudent to expedite rather than postpone
a treaty of pacification. The house,
however, thought otherwise, and voted an
address which re-echoed the royal speech.

A proclamation, recommending economy,
was issued by the king, who particularly
" exhorted and charged all masters of
families to reduce the consumption of
bread by at least one third of the quantity
consumed in ordinary times, and in no case

to suffer the same to exceed one quartern
loaf for each person in each week ; to
abstain from the use of flour in pastry ; and
restrict the consumption of oats and other
grain for the subsistence of horses." Many
families attended to this advice ; but it was
not strictly regarded by the generality of
the higher or middle classes.

Three bills were prepared without delay,
prohibiting the use of grain in distillation,
and the exportation of provisions in general.
Bills granting bounties on importation followed ; and other regulations were adopted,
which did not sufficiently check the rapacity or subdue the obstinacy of the great
dealers in corn. The idea of fixing the
highest price at which corn should be
sold, was suggested by the earl of Warwick ; but this proposal was rejected as
inconsistent with the just freedom of
property. These discussions also gave
occasion for a bill calculated to ascertain the extent of the demand for
which a supply was to be provided,
by ordering an account to be taken of
the population of the kingdom : from
which it appeared on full inquiry, that, in
England and Wales, the males amounted
to 4,245,113, and the females to 4,627,867 ;
and that, of these, 1,713,289 were employed in agriculture. The addition of
convicts, soldiers, and seamen, swelled the
number of males to 4,715,711.

After various debates, a motion from
Mr. Sheridan, recommending a separate
treaty with France, as far as good faith
would allow, and opposing all new engagements which might preclude such a
negotiation, subjected the proposer to the
animadversions of Mr. Windham, who
wished that vigorous support might still
be given to the house of Austria. Mr.
Grey did not think that the conduct of
our allies entitled them to so much respect
or deference, as could render it prudent
to sacrifice the hope of a speedy peace to
their supposed interests : but Mr. Dundas
remonstrated against what he regarded
as an illiberal and impolitic desertion of our
friends, and the house, by a majority of 121
votes, rejected the motion.

The last day of the eighteenth century

was likewise the last of the parliament of Great Britain. The next assembly of the peers and commons in the presence of his majesty, formed an imperial body, exercising the legislative, and executive power of the united realms. The 1st of January, 1801, was the day appointed for the consummation of that memorable union, which has so powerfully contributed to the peace, prosperity, and civilization of the Irish people, the stability of the empire, and the deliverance of Europe. Had this been the only splendid characteristic of Mr. Pitt's administration it would have deserved the gratitude and admiration of posterity; amidst the splendid and important services rendered to his country, it fades into insignificance. It is to his firmness, intelligence, and virtue alone, that we are indebted for the increase of personal industry, comfort, and happiness, and that notwithstanding the injudicious violence of the less able and respectable part of the Roman catholics, national prejudice and party spirit have given place to the more noble rivalship of patriotism and industrious exertion.

The subordinate regulations connected with the final adoption of this important measure were easily arranged. The title of king of France, of so little importance to the sovereign of England, yet so frequently productive of disputes, was wisely abandoned. His majesty assumed the style and title of *Georgius tertius, Dei gratia, Britannorum rex, fidei defensor.* The arms and flags of the united kingdom were subjected to appropriate alterations; and in addition to many subordinate changes, the house of lords was augmented by the introduction of an archbishop, and three bishops of Ireland, and of twenty-eight temporal peers elected by the body of the Irish peerage for life, and not removeable like those of Scotland at every dissolution of parliament. Into the house of commons, the union introduced 100 new members, of whom sixty-four were representatives of counties, nine of cities, twenty-six of boroughs and towns, and one of the university of Dublin.

Since the failure of his attempt to ne-

gotiate a peace with England, Buonaparte had continued with increased importunity to represent to the maritime nations of Europe, the haughtiness, injustice, and rapacity of the British government. By his ministers and other agents at the courts of Petersburgh, Stockholm, Copenhagen, and Berlin, he insinuated that the present posture of the affairs of Europe, was peculiarly favorable to the revival of the armed neutrality of 1780, founded on the principle that free bottoms make free goods, and that the present was the only opportunity of supporting and securing the liberty of the seas.

The desultory and frantic mind of the emperor Paul, had been irritated by various circumstances against the courts of London and Vienna. Disputes had arisen even to the height of action, between the Russians and Austrians, after the reduction of the Ex-Venetian isles, in 1799; the Austrians had not duly supported the Russians during their joint campaign in Switzerland; and it was asserted, not without apparent justice, that a neighbouring and rival monarch was not actuated by the principles which had drawn the Russian potentate into the confederation against France, but by views of individual aggrandisement. When the emperor of Germany therefore announced his intention of sending an extraordinary ambassador to St. Petersburgh, to offer excuses for the disturbance at Ancona, Paul refused to receive him, and gave orders that no answer should be returned to the notification from Francis. With respect to England, mutual accusations had taken place, between the Russian and the English generals, after the unsuccessful and disastrous expedition to Holland. The nascent resentment of Paul against the court of St. James's, was likewise inflamed by the failure of his plans in the Mediterranean.

The genius of the Russian government, amidst the caprices and singularities of individual character, preserves, on the whole, the impulse and determination that was communicated by Peter the Great, whose aim it was to obtain a firm footing in the Mediterranean, as well as on the northern ocean, and the Baltic. In pursuance of this general aim, Paul had been led by a concurrence of circumstances, which it is unnecessary to enumerate, to cast his eyes on Malta ; and though no absolute promise of fulfilling his wishes was made by the other allies, yet it would appear that his expectations had been tacitly encouraged, and that he was allowed, without any attempt to undeceive him, to entertain a sanguine expectation of becoming master of the island. A fleet with troops had sailed from the Black sea, in August, 1800, for the express purpose of taking possession of the place when it should surrender. No remonstrances were made when Paul assumed the title of grand master of Malta, and when he pretended to make captain Home Popham a knight of the order, his right to do so was recognized in the London Gazette. When the destination of the Russian fleet was frustrated by the surrender of Malta, and its occupation by the English, it remained long at anchor, in the canal of Constantinople waiting for orders how to act. The resentment of the emperor was in the first instance, and in conformity with his usual custom, wrecked on a weak party presenting itself as a ready object, for the gratification of his passion. He demanded from the grand seignior, the ally of England, a large sum, stipulated, as he alleged, to be paid by the Turks, for the maritime aid of the Russians. A sharp dispute arose on this subject. The Russian admiral refused to return to the Krimea till the money should be paid, and threatened the commencement of hostilities against Constantinople. The Porte was obliged to yield to the menaces of the enraged czar of Muscovy. Nor is it by any means unimportant, however ludicrous to mention, that Paul was highly offended by the caricatures of his person, and character, published in the streets of London ; which Buonaparte took especial care to transmit to Petersburgh. On the irritable and irritated temper of the emperor, disgusted with Austria, and much more with England, but as prone to sentiments of gratitude and generosity, as to those of resentment, Buonaparte operated with

consummate wisdom and with complete success.

The world was not a little surprised at the arrival of an embassy in Paris, from Paul I. not more than a year after his famous proclamation for restoring the throne of the Bourbons. The embassy consisted of the general baron de Springporten, prince Dolgorowki an old Swedish refugee at the court of Russia, the count de Tissenhaveen a captain in the Russian army, M. de Scheping son of the grand marshal of Courland, and other gentlemen. They were met by general Clarke at Brussels, and by him conducted to Paris, on the 18th of December, 1800. The ostensible object of the embassy was to treat for the release of the Russian prisoners, who had fallen into the hands of the French to the number of 7000. For this body of Russians, the British government had refused to exchange an equal number of French prisoners. The chief consul in compliment to Paul, gave orders that all the Russian prisoners should be newly clothed, and accoutred in the uniforms of their respective regiments, and freely restored without exchange or ransom. Each man was presented with a fusil of French manufacture.

The baron de Springporten bore the title of envoy. He was followed early in the year by an ambassador, attended by a splendid retinue. The envoy and his train had been treated with studious respect, but still greater marks of respect and reverence were in reserve for the ambassador count Kalitchef, a man of modest, elegant, and unassuming manners, who had before sustained the character of Russian ambassador at Berlin, and other courts. The count must doubtless have been astonished, to find himself received with a degree of magnificence, and of adulation, exceeding all the marks of honour and devotion, that he had ever known to be paid to his imperial master. On his entrance into Paris he was saluted by the fire of all the cannon. A magnificent palace was appropriated to his residence, and he was entertained at the expense of the republic. He was honored with a body guard

1801.

It was shrewdly contrived that petitions should be presented to him from persons under the prosecution of the sentence of the law, imploring his interference with the chief consul in their behalf. The protection of Kalitchef was never extended to any one without effect; his applications to the consuls were never made in vain. But the climax of compliment to Paul, was the affectation of granting, *only* through his intercession, peace and independence to the king of Naples; whose consort, justly appreciating the character of Paul, had visited St. Petersburgh in November, 1800, with the intention of persuading the emperor to continue the war, or at least to support the interests of the kingdom of Naples. A lady in distress could not solicit in vain the protection of a knight-errant, after so long a journey in pursuit of it, and the emperor's zeal in the cause of the Neapolitans was increased.

The French government expressed a disposition to yield to the intercession of Paul, a boon which would have been granted without it. General Murat, on the 24th of January, wrote from Florence 1801. to general De Damas, commander of the Neapolitan troops, to the following purport.

"It is almost a month, general, since the French ministry acquainted you, that the interest which his majesty, the emperor of Russia, takes in the king of Naples, had induced the first consul to bury in oblivion the innumerable injuries of all kinds of which your government has been guilty towards the French people. After this opening towards a good understanding, we entertained a hope that you would have remained a quiet spectator of a contest in which you can be of little consequence on one side or the other: Yet the king of Naples, forgetting for the tenth time, the dictates of sound policy, and what was due to the generous conduct of the French government, dispatched his troops into Tuscany, where they only arrived to be beaten by general Miolis. But war is attended with so many calamities, that the French government studies all possible

means of avoiding it. I. Evacuate all the ecclesiastical states and the castle of St. Angelo. II. Make no farther claims of any benefits from the armistice of Treviso, in which you are not mentioned, or on the influence of a power which must no longer protect you. The only prince in whom you can now confide, and for whom the first consul bears the highest personal regard, is the emperor of all the Russias. Let it be the study, sir, of your government, to merit a continuation of that prince's goodness, which cannot be done but by shutting all the ports of Sicily and Naples against the navigation of the English, and laying an embargo on all the ships of that nation, which it is now high time to expel from all the points of the continent."

But the most important object of Buonaparte's correspondence with Paul, was the possession of Malta; which he proffered as a gift to Russia, whenever it should be wrested by arms or negotiation from the English. It is almost superfluous to mention, that, amidst so many acts of studied complacence, orders were given by the French government, for the cessation of all hostilities against Russia. On the 19th of January, the consuls issued a decree by which all vessels of the republic and all cruizers bearing the French flag, were forbidden to interrupt the ships of war, or the commerce of the emperor of all the Russias, or of his subjects; but were enjoined, on the contrary, to afford succor and aid to the ships of that nation. Paul, whose animosity was augmented by the lapse of time, being informed of the capture and detention of a Danish brig and her convoy, suddenly appeared in the character of a champion for maritime rights, and laid an embargo on all the English ships in his harbors; which, however was taken off as soon as he understood that the dispute had been amicably adjusted. But his zealous endeavors to unite the other northern powers with himself, in confederacy against Great Britain, were continued. The same prince, who in 1798 applauded our detention of the Swedish convoy, and who threatened Denmark with war in 1799, for assisting the commerce of the French republic, took the most active part in a league with those very powers, in favor of that common enemy, whom he had engaged to Britain and to the world, to resist to the utmost extent of his power. He recruited his army and his navy; and established considerable armies on the side of the Baltic, and on the confines of Turkey; the former intended to defend every assailable point against the power of England, and the latter to prosecute the designs of Buonaparte against the Ottoman empire.

During these transactions, the emperor of Russia had exhibited the most evident indications of insanity. When dispatches were presented to him from the British government, containing proposals of reconciliation, he returned them unopened, after piercing them in many places with a penknife. At a review in front of his palace, an officer was thrown from his horse, and dislocated his arm. The brutal monarch, instead of displaying any indications of compassion, kicked the officer as he lay extended on the ground. Yet his madness, though somewhat tinctured with violence, was frequently diversified by a mixture of whimsicality, and of quaint but original humor. A few days before the young king of Sweden, who had visited the capital to concert the preliminaries of an armed neutrality, left St. Petersburgh, the emperor gave a tournament, a diversion to which he was enthusiastically attached, and in which he performed personally as a combatant. In the evening, while the convivial glass circulated with Russian briskness, a dispatch was received from Buonaparte, containing several caricatures drawn and engraved by English artists, in which Paul was represented as a lunatic. The conversation turned on the military successes of the French; the projects formed by the northern confederacy to humble the pride of England; and the invincible prowess which the emperor had displayed in the tournament. His majesty, fired by the spirit of chivalry, immediately resolved to send a defiance to all the potentates of Europe. The court Gazette of St. Petersburgh, December 30th, 1800, contained the following notification: "*It is said* that his majesty the emperor, seeing that the powers of Europe cannot agree, and wishing to terminate a war which has raged eleven years, intends to propose a place, whither he will invite all other sovereigns to fight with them in barriers closed up; for which purpose they are to bring with them their most enlightened ministers, and most skilful generals, as squires, umpires, and heralds; men for example, such as Thugut, Pitt, and Bernstorf. He himself intends to have with him count Vander Pahlin, and count Kutusof."

It is the usual policy of princes and statesmen to conceal their designs till the moment of execution. Paul was equally destitute of political prudence and common discretion. He gratified his resentments by an effusion of words before it was in his power to express them by actions. The annunciation of his intention to quarrel with England, was followed up in the end of October, with an official declaration that he had determined to revive the armed neutrality. He stated that, on mounting his throne, he found his empire involved in a war, provoked by a great nation which had fallen into anarchy and disorder; that, conceiving the coalition to be a measure of mere preservation, that motive alone had induced him to join it; that he did not *then* conceive it necessary to adopt the system of an armed neutrality at sea, for the protection of commerce, not doubting that the sincerity of his allies and their reciprocal interests, would be sufficient to secure from insult the flag of the northern powers. But being disappointed in his expectations by the perfidious enterprises of a great power, which had sought to enchain the liberty of the seas by capturing Danish convoys; and the independence of the maritime states of the north being thus openly menaced, he conceived it a measure of necessity to have recourse to an armed neutrality, of which the success and utility had been acknowledged in the time of the American war.

The rupture with England, which Paul

had predicted as not improbable, was announced by the publication in the Petersburgh Gazette, November 7th, 1800, of an official note sent to the foreign ministers at the Russian court.

" Whereas, his imperial majesty had learned that the island of Malta, lately in the possession of the French, had been surrendered to the English troops ; but it yet remained uncertain whether the agreement of December 30th, 1799, stipulating the restoration of the order of St. John of Jerusalem, under their grand master the emperor, would be fulfilled ; his imperial majesty determined to defend his rights, had been pleased to command, that *an embargo should be laid on all English ships in the ports of his empire till the abovementioned convention should be fulfilled.*"

In consequence of the emperor's orders, not only an embargo was laid on nearly 300 British ships in the ports of Petersburgh, Riga, Revel, and Cronstadt, but the crews, with their commanders, were taken out of the vessels, and imprisoned in the interior parts of the country, and in bodies of 12 men, at the distance of from 100 to 1000 miles. On shore, all British property was sequestered ; seals were placed on the warehouses containing English goods, and the owners were obliged to take inventories of their effects for the use of government. When the embargo on the English ships took place at Narva, on the 5th of November, the crews of two vessels, on the arrival of a military force to put them under arrest, made resistance with pistols and cutlasses, weighed anchor, and escaped.. The emperor, in his anger at the intelligence of this event, ordered the remainder of the ships in that harbor to be burnt. On the 21st of November, the Petersburgh Gazette, after recording the " mutiny" at Narva, repeated the determination of the emperor, that the embargo should not be revoked till his demands were satisfied by the surrender of Malta.

For the accomplishment of the emperor's purposes, Denmark had afforded an occasion, by her complaints respecting the

unfortunate occurrence to which I have incidentally alluded. Resistance, attended with violence, had been opposed to the British claim of right of search, in December, 1799. The English frigates, Emerald, and Flora, met near the straits of Gibraltar a Danish frigate, named the Hasenau, commanded by captain Van Dockum, escorting a convoy. To enquiries made by an English officer, sent on board respecting his destination, the Dane answered, *Gibraltar.* The English officer replied, that if he meant to stop at that port, he should not visit the convoy, but otherwise he must. Van Dockum said, that he must in that case make resistance ; and, when the boat of the Emerald approached the convoy, musketry was actually fired from the Danish frigate ; a British sailor was wounded, and the boat of the Flora, which the Dane had seized, was not released till the English captain threatened immediate hostilities. Van Dockum then joined his convoy in the bay of Gibraltar ; but, although required by lord Keith, refused to produce the instructions by which he had been guided, verbally declaring that, in firing into the king's boats, he had only fulfilled his orders. In a subsequent conference in presence of the governor of Gibraltar, he repeated the same assertion, and promised to surrender himself before a judge ; but, on his return to his ship, he thought proper to disavow the engagement he had made, and sailed away with his convoy. Merry, the chargé d'affaires at Copenhagen, presented a candid statement of the facts, insisted on the right of visiting and searching merchant vessels on the high seas, and demanded from the Danish government, disavowal, apology, and reparation. In answer to this letter, count Bernstorf, the Danish minister, asserted, that, as the right of search was merely conventional, its privileges could not be extended at the *fiat* of one particular power, without violence and injustice. But no maritime independent power had ever acknowledged the right of permitting neutral ships to be searched when escorted by ships of war, nor could they do so without exposing their flag to degradation, and forfeiting an essential portion of their own rights. This doctrine had been acknowledged in a number of treaties concluded between the most respectable courts of Europe. By escorting with its armed vessels the commercial ships of its subjects, a neutral state afforded to the belligerent powers the most authentic and positive pledge of the regularity of their cargoes, nor could it under such circumstances, without incurring dishonor and disgrace, admit of the least suspicion. Captain Van Dockum by resisting a violence, which he had no right to expect, had only fulfilled his duty to his sovereign; and it was on the part of the English frigates that the violation of the rights of a neutral monarch, had been committed. Instead therefore of guaranteeing the reparation, demanded by Mr. Merry, count Bernstorf demanded in the name of his sovereign, a compensation from his Britannic majesty, adequate to the extent and nature of the outrage.

In this state of affairs another Danish frigate named the Freya, commanded by captain Krabbe, was appointed to convoy some merchant vessels, and instructed to resist any attempts of the cruizers belonging to either of the belligerent powers, to search, or interrupt the vessels, under his protection. At the mouth of the channel he fell in with four English frigates, a brig, and a lugger. He awaited their coming along side, and a British officer desiring to search the convoy, answered by a direct refusal, but offered to lay all the papers before the British commander. An English frigate then approached one of convoy and fired a ball for the purpose of bringing her to, a compliment which was immediately returned. A parley ensued, but Krabbe persisted in refusing a search, and in pursuance of his threats gave orders to fire on a boat which attempted it, though the gun only flashed without taking effect. The English frigates immediately attacked him, and after a short engagement in which several men were killed and wounded on both sides, brought the Freya and her convoy into the Downs.

Considerable delicacy was observed in the circumstances of their detention. Two English officers, and thirteen men unarmed, were put on board the frigate, and Krabbe was allowed free intercourse with the shore, though the ships of the convoy did not experience the same indulgence.

Lord Whitworth was now dispatched to Elsineur to demand satisfaction from the Danish government, and admiral Dickson, with a respectable squadron of men of war, and gun-vessels, was desired to attend for the purpose of giving effect to his remonstrances. The admiral after remaining for a short period before Copenhagen, removed to the road of Elsineur, leaving a chain of communication between himself and Copenhagen, composed of bomb and gun-vessels, which served as a telegraph of correspondence, and threatened the capital of Denmark with bombardment.

Lord Whitworth in his representations to the Danish government, descanted on the absurdity of Bernstorf's reasoning, and observed, if the principle be once admitted that a Danish frigate may legally guarantee from all search six merchant ships, it naturally follows that the same power or any other power, may, by means of the smallest ship of war, extend the same protection to all the commerce of the enemy. Count Bernstorf endeavored to invalidate this argument, by alleging that the disgrace which any state would bring on itself by lending its flag to such a fraud, and the evils which would ensue from its committal were sufficient to prevent it: and that the Danish government had made the officers who commanded convoys responsible that the cargoes of ships under their protection, do not contain articles prohibited by the laws of nations, or by the treaties subsisting between Denmark and the belligerent powers. Notwithstanding this reply the unprovided state of the national resources, and the presence of the English squadron induced the Danish government to agree to a convention, by which it was stipulated, that the question with regard to the rights of searching neutral ships, sailed under convoy, should be referred to a future discussion: that the Danish frigate and the vessels under her convoy should be instantly released and the frigate be repaired in the English port; and that to prevent the recurrence of disputes of a similar nature, his Danish majesty should suspend his convoys, till ulterior explanations should prepare the way to a definitive treaty.

Scarcely had this accommodation been effected, before a dispute of a similar nature between England and Sweden, renewed the danger of northern hostility. On the 4th of September, the Swedish ketch, Hoffnung, fell in with the British ship Minotaur and a frigate, which were blockading the ports of Barcelona. The Swede was boarded, and his papers were examined, but, although they were acknowledged to be perfectly correct and satisfactory, he was commanded to follow the British vessels, who continued to approach the shore. At the close of day several English officers and men came on board, compelled the Swedes to preserve silence, and towed them into the road. A gun was fired by a Spanish frigate, but the English being within the batteries, manned their boats, and captured the Spanish and another frigate, which they carried off in safety. A man on board the Hoffnung was mortally wounded by the firing from the Spanish frigate.

The chevalier d'Urgijo, the Spanish minister for foreign affairs, immediately addressed a letter to the Swedish minister, containing a partial narrative of the facts, and exhorting the Swedish government to prompt and vigorous retribution. The final answer of baron Erenheim to this requisition did credit to the forbearance of his court, and attributed the occurrence of several unfortunate events similar to the last, to the injustice and insolence of the Spaniards themselves. A remonstrance on the part of the Dutch government, to the same effect, was received with the same reluctance, and was answered by an evasive reply, in which it was insinuated, that the court of London, " for its own safety," would prevent similar irregularities in future.

The interference of the court of Madrid was accompanied by the most injudicious indications of hostility on the part of Prussia. A vessel, called the Triton, laden with contraband articles, was captured at the mouth of the Texel by a British cruizer, and carried into the port of Cuxhaven. The king of Prussia immediately ordered a division of his army to enter the bailiwick of Ritzebuttel, and the village of Cuxhaven. Alarmed by so unexpected an aggression, the senate of Hamburgh gave a sum of money to the British captors, and restored the Triton. In reply to the representations of lord Carysfort, the British plenipotentiary at Berlin, it was asserted that the measure had been adopted with the consent of the inhabitants of Hamburgh, that Cuxhaven was necessary to their navigation on the Elbe; that the surrender of the Triton by the Hamburghers was contrary to their duty, and to the usages of war; and that the measure having been once projected could not be revoked. The pertenacity of Prussia revived the expiring confidence of the Danes; the menaces, and importunities of the emperor of Russia diverted the court of Sweden from its usual line of policy, and a treaty hostile to the interests of Great Britain, was concluded by Sweden, Denmark, and Russia, and afterwards received the assent of his Prussian majesty. The principles established by this compact were the following.

I. Every ship may navigate from one harbor to another, and on the coasts of the belligerent nations.

II. The effects which belong to the subjects of belligerent powers, in neutral ships with the exception of contraband goods shall be free.

III. In order to determine what shall be considered as a blockaded harbor, such shall only be admitted to apply where the disposition and number of the ships, of the power by which it is invested shall be such as to render it apparently hazardous to enter; and that every ship which shall go into a blockaded harbour, (*evidently* so blockaded,) violates the present convention as much as if the commander was informed of the state of the harbor, and had nevertheless endeavored by force and artifice to obtain admission.

IV. With regard to neutral ships, except those which for just reasons, and on evident grounds shall be detained, sentence shall be pronounced without delay. The proceedings against them shall be uniform, prompt, and lawful. Over and above the remedy to which they may be entitled for the damage which they have sustained, complete satisfaction shall be given for the insult, committed against the flag of their majesties.

V. The declaration of the officers who shall command the ship, or ships of war, of the king or emperor, which shall be convoying one or more merchant ships, that the convoy has no contraband goods on board shall be sufficient, and no search of his ship or of the other ships of his convoy shall be permitted. The better to insure respect to these principles, and the stipulations founded upon them, which their disinterested wishes to preserve the imprescriptable rights of the neutral nations have suggested, the high contracting parties to prove their sincerity and justice, will give the strictest order to their captains, as well of their ships of war as of their merchant ships, to load no part of their vessels with articles of contraband. For the more completely carrying into execution this command, they will respectively give directions to their courts of admiralty, to publish it wherever they shall think it necessary: and to this end the regulation which shall contain this prohibition, under several penalties, shall be printed at the end of the present act, that no one may plead ignorance.

On the 14th of January the British privy-council directed an embargo to be laid on all Russian, Danish, and Swedish vessels in the ports of Great Britain; and on the 15th, lord Grenville informed the Danish and Swedish envoys of the occurrence. He stated the concern, with which his majesty had heard of the conclusion of a treaty with Russia, for maintaining a naval and armed confederacy in the north of Europe, at the moment when that court had adopted the most hostile measures against the persons and property of British subjects. Any doubt, which could be entertained as to its object, was now removed by the declarations of Russia, and still farther by those of Denmark. Then alluding to the attempt in 1780, to introduce a new code of public law, and support by force a system of innovation inimical to the dearest rights of Great Britain, his lordship added, that his majesty had hitherto the satisfaction to see these arbitrary measures completely abandoned. The court of St. Petersburgh, which had taken so active a part in promoting that alliance, had, at the beginning of the present war, entered into a treaty with his majesty, the articles of which were not merely incompatible with the convention of 1780, but directly in the face of it. The king was entitled, upon every principle of good faith, to demand the reciprocal execution of these engagements, during the continuance of the war: and his conduct towards the other powers of the Baltic, and the decisions of his courts of justice in regard to prizes, were uniformly and openly founded on principles, which, prior to the year of 1780, had guided all the courts of admiralty in Europe.

The purpose, continued his lordship, of the preparations of the confederated states, was to place themselves in a situation to maintain pretensions, which were so obviously inconsistent with justice, that the powers, which, when neutral, brought them forward, were, when belligerent, the first to oppose them. As the establishment of these pretensions must tend to overthrow the strength and security of the British empire, his majesty would be acting contrary to the interest of his people, the dignity of his crown, and the honour of his flag, were he to delay adopting the most effectual means to oppose and repel the attacks of those arming against him. But in thus announcing the embargo, his lordship declared, that no violent or severe proceedings would be exercised, on the part of Great Britain, towards innocent individuals; and that his majesty was still animated with the most anxious desire, that he might be enabled, by the removal of circumstances which rendered these steps necessary, to return to his former relations of amity and concord with the courts of Stockholm and Copenhagen.

Although the British ministry were certain of the accession of the king of Prussia to the northern league, they durst not venture on so bold a step against him as against the other states. England, indeed, had it in her power to interrupt or annihilate the foreign commerce of his subjects; but, on the other hand, he possessed a ready indemnification in the electoral states of the house of Hanover. This acquisition he was suspected of having long regarded with avidity, and he could now accomplish his purpose without experiencing any opposition, in the present temper of the northern courts, during the humiliation of Austria, and while the friendly disposition of France countenanced him in an enterprise injurious to her enemy. Policy, therefore, required a studied precaution on the part of the court of London. Lord Carysfort, its ambassador at Berlin, was directed to communicate to the Prussian government a copy of the note, which had been presented to the ministers of Denmark and Sweden. At the same time, his lordship stated to count Haugwitz, that he could not discharge this commission without expressing his satisfaction at being authorised to declare, how thoroughly his majesty was convinced, that Prussia could never have sanctioned the measures, which had given rise to that note. He recapitulated the circumstances of the transaction, and observed, that the proceedings of those powers indicated an intention to prescribe rules to Great Britain on a subject of the greatest importance. Without the smallest intimation, they had entered into a league, the object of which was to force them on her, and renew pretensions she had deemed hostile to her rights, and so declared when an opportunity occurred; pretensions which Russia had not only abandoned, but which, by a treaty still in force, she was bound to oppose. When a Danish ship of war resisted the execution of a right, which his Britannic majesty had demanded by virtue of the

clearest stipulations in his treaties with that state, he confined himself to what steps the occasion required. A conventional arrangement put an end to the dispute; and he flattered himself, not only that all misunderstanding was removed, but that the former amity between the two courts was strengthened and confirmed.

In this situation of affairs, said his lordship, his majesty learned, that the Danish court was employed in negotiations to renew the hostile confederacy which took place in 1780, and that great preparations were going on in its ports. He was informed, that a convention was actually signed at St. Petersburgh; and on his demanding explanations from the Danish government, the answer of its minister left no doubt, respecting the nature and object of the league. The contracting parties engaged to maintain, by force, principles of maritime law which had never been recognised by the tribunals of Europe, and to compel other nations to adopt them; and these principles were still more repugnant to the stipulations of treaties which subsisted between Sweden and Denmark, and the British empire. This convention also was negotiated at a time, when the court of St. Petersburgh had adopted violent measures against several of his Britannic majesty's subjects, and when his extraordinary moderation alone could have authorised other powers not to consider him as at open war with that government. Nothing certainly could be more incongruous with the idea of neutrality, and nothing could more distinctly indicate a hostile disposition, than that engagements, of the nature alluded to, were not postponed, until it should have been ascertained, whether Russia was to be considered as a belligerent power. Such forbearance was the more to be expected, and especially from the court of Copenhagen, as its ports and havens in Norway, by an express article of the league in 1780, were placed at the disposal of Russia, for the purpose of facilitating the prosecution of hostilities out of the Baltic. When, therefore, the king was informed of the conclusion of a convention, by which the former confederacy was revived, to press upon him a new code of laws to which he had already refused to assent; when he ascertained, that the powers, engaged in this transaction, were forwarding warlike preparations with the utmost activity; and when one of these powers had placed itself in a state of actual hostilities with Britain, no other alternative remained, but to submit, or to put an effectual stop to the operation of a league, which, by the declaration of the Danish court itself, was openly directed against his majesty.

His lordship next proceeded to remark, that the conduct of Great Britain towards neutral states had been conformable to the acknowledged principles of laws, whose basis and sanction were to be found, not in partial interests and momentary convenience, but in common justice; of laws which had been received and observed by the admiralty courts of all the maritime powers of Europe. Firmly convinced of this, his majesty did not yet forego the hope, that the courts of Stockholm and Copenhagen would not take upon them the responsibility, attaching to the authors of a war for the introduction of innovations, which were adverse to existing treaties, and resisted by those powers who first broached them. After observing that the steps adopted by the British government must have been long foreseen, and that it had disavowed the offensive dogmas introduced into the league of 1780, his lordship reminded count Haugwitz of his expressly declaring, at the first conference on his arrival at Berlin, that his majesty would oppose the attempt to renew the principles agitated at that time, and never submit to pretensions, which were irreconcileable with the sound maxims of public law, and struck at the foundation of the maritime power of his kingdoms. Still later, in the beginning of November, and since that time, he had represented to his excellency the disagreeable consequences which must follow from the attempt of the northern powers to urge such pretensions. He had likewise communicated his majesty's resolution to tolerate no measures, the object of which was to innovate the maritime law now in force; but to defend that system, and maintain its entire execution, as it subsisted prior to the year 1780, in all the courts of Europe.

If, added his lordship, the Danish cabinet had announced, in a manner unequivocal, the real purpose and terms of the engagements it had contracted, its declaration, that Prussia was a party to the negotiation, would have been sufficient to satisfy the king, that it could have no hostile views against his government; and even still he was convinced, that he might implicitly rely on the friendship of his Prussian majesty. It was true, that, in relation to Great Britain, there could be no similitude between the northern powers and Prussia, as these powers were connected with Britain by treaties, less favorable to their present claims, and modifying the rigor of the general law; while no treaty of commerce existed between her and Prussia, and their intercourse was regulated by established usages, and the principles of the law of nations. If his majesty, however, were to consider his own sentiments, and his constant wish to preserve the friendship of a monarch with whom he was connected by so many ties, he could not anticipate the possibility of a difference, which might not be easily and speedily terminated by an amicable discussion. The repeated assurances of similar sentiments, on the part of Prussia did not countenance the supposition, that it had entered, or could enter, into a confederacy with states, whose hostile views against England were apparent. His Britannic majesty was convinced, that the Prussian government would approve of his steady resolution to defend his rights. But whatever opinion it might entertain in regard to the novel principles agitated by the allied powers, it was too just, and knew too well what sovereigns owed to their people, and to one another, to favor for a moment any design to employ force in order to induce his majesty to acknowledge a code, which he deemed inconsistent with the honor and security of his crown.

The Danish ambassador, count Jarlsberg, having communicated lord Grenville's note to his court, was ordered to renew his remonstrances against the embargo. He remarked, he said, with surprise, that the British government should confound the cause of the measures taken in Russia against their interests, with the object of conventions relative to neutral navigation ; and mix two affairs, which evidently had not the least connection with each other. It was a subject of perfect notoriety, that the incident of the occupation of Malta, by the troops of his Britannic majesty, had alone been the occasion of the embargo on the English ships in the Russian ports ; and that the ministers of the neutral states at St. Petersburgh acted according to the full powers and instructions, which they had received prior to that event. The dispute respecting it was wholly foreign to the Danish court, which knew but very imperfectly either its origin or its cause, but whose engagements with Russia had no relation whatever to that affair. The nature of the treaty was merely defensive ; and it was inconceivable, how general principles, conforming to the obligatory stipulations of treaties, could be justly considered as attacks on the rights or dignity of any state whatever. The minister invoked the serious attention of the British cabinet to these reflections and incontrovertible truths, which were analogous to the sentiments of a sovereign who was the antient and faithful ally of Britain, and not only incapable of offering any injuries real or voluntary, but had well-founded titles to a return of forbearance and justice. In the confidence of finding on the part of England, a prompt cessation of proceedings hostile to the interests of Denmark, he insisted on the removal of the embargo, as affecting Danish vessels. By a constant series of moderation on the part of the court of Copenhagen, the measures, to which the outrageous conduct of the British government authorised the former to have recourse, were suspended, his Danish majesty deeming it an act of glory to give this decisive proof of the falsehood of the suspicions advanced against him. But if, contrary to his expectations, England persisted in her violent resolutions, he would, with regret, be reduced to the urgent necessity of exerting the means, which his dignity, and the interests of his subjects, imperiously prescribed. To this requisition lord Hawkesbury, now minister for foreign affairs, replied, that the result of the opinions of the English court would be communicated by its charge d' affaires at Copenhagen ; and on count Jarlesberg's renewal of his demand, a similar answer was returned.

HISTORY OF THE WAR.

CHAP. XXXI.

Admiral Sir Hyde Parker and Lord Nelson proceed on the Expedition against the Danes—Position and Arrangements of the Naval Combatants—Enthusiasm of the Inhabitants of Copenhagen—Heroic Actions on both Sides—Ultimate Discomfiture of the Danes—Coolness and Humanity of Lord Nelson—Conclusion of a Convention with the King of Denmark—Death of Paul, Emperor of Russia—Dissolution of the Northern Confederacy—Accession of Alexander—Meeting of the United Parliament of Great Britain—Resignation of Mr. Pitt—Exploits of Saumarez, Cochrane, Nelson, &c.—Affairs of Portugal—Internal State of France—Conduct of the first Consul.

AGAINST the combination of the northern powers, the British ministry had not neglected to provide the means of vigorous resistance. An armament of 54 sail, of which 14 were ships of the line, was collected at Yarmouth. They were manned with the flower of the British army, supported by several regiments of marines and riflemen. Sir Hyde Parker was appointed to the chief command; and under him the victor of the Nile, the heroic Nelson. Admiral Graves also accompanied the expedition; and several corps of marines were placed beneath the orders of lieutenant-colonel Stuart.

1801. The equipment sailed for its destination on the 11th of March; the Invincible, of 74 guns, being left behind to convey cannon and ammunition for the gun-boats and floating batteries. This vessel commanded by captain Rennie, but having rear-admiral Totty on board, struck on a ridge of sand called the Hippisburg, situated sixteen miles from the town of Winterton, in Norfolk, and foundered in deep water with her captain, great part of her crew, and several passengers. About 400 persons miserably perished, and only 195 were saved. The loss was owing to the ignorance of a pilot, who became the victim of his own unskilfulness. The destruction of the Invincible did not retard the proceedings of the fleet. It approached the Cattegat, and, after some impediments arising from the weather, prepared to pass the Sound, but not before sir Hyde Parker had endeavored to ascertain the disposition of the Danes, by a letter to the governor of Cronberg castle, which defends that pass, enquiring whether he had received orders to fire upon the British fleet in its passage to the Sound, as the first shot must be deemed a declaration of war on the part of Denmark. M. Stricker, the governor of Cronberg, returned for answer, " As a soldier, I cannot meddle with politics, but I am not at liberty to suffer a fleet, whose intentions are not yet known, to approach the guns of the castle where I have the honor to command.". The British admiral stated in reply, that he considered this answer as a declaration of war; and, on the ensuing day, the wind blowing favorably, the whole fleet entered the Sound. In their passage, they kept as near as possible to the Swedish side, where little impediment was offered, answering the Cronberg cannon with equal spirit; but the shot of neither party was effectual on account of the distance, and in four hours the British fleet uninjured, came to anchor about six miles from the island of Huin.

At Copenhagen the intelligence that a British fleet, had appeared off the Sound, created great and general alarm. But the inhabitants did not suffer any vain hopes and unfounded expectations to impede their defensive exertions. They adopted every means of self-protection, which their population, their navy, and their batteries could afford. Even the students of the university formed themselves into a corps, amounting to twelve hundred, and the professors and tutors whose years did not allow of similar exertions, contributed by their purses to the reward and encouragement of those fellow-citizens who so gallantly stood forward in the hour of danger.

During the first two days after the British fleet had arrived off Copenhagen, the wind was unfavorable to its progress, but on the third, the Danes observed the English frigates and lighter-vessels, employed in taking soundings, while admiral Parker and lord Nelson divided their force, the latter taking the command of twelve men of war, four frigates, as many sloops and several fire-ships and bombs, while the residue continued with Sir Hyde Parker. The two admirals had ascertained the soundings and fixed buoys for their guidance and having accurately surveyed the defences of the enemy, formed the plan of an attack, to be conducted by lord Nelson, who shifted his flag on board the Elephant, and anchored off Draco Point. He was supported by admiral Graves, and accompanied by colonel Stewart and his marines.

The Danes entrusted their defence to the following force, as enumerated by one of themselves, and the more likely to be correct, as it exceeds the estimate of lord Nelson. Three ships of 74 guns, five of 64, one of 58, two of 50, one of 44, one of 26, a floating battery of 24, four prames and bombs of 20, seven brigs, sloops, and floating batteries of 18, eleven gun-boats, having each two guns, and the battery of

the three crowns which mounted eight 36 pounders, fifty-six 30 pounders, three mortars, and two carronades. Of the vessels many appear to have been without masts, but they were not less useful in their assigned position. The vessels in the best condition; two of the seventy-fours, three frigates of 44 guns, and two brigs of 18 guns each, were stationed in the inner roads, and therefore were rendered incapable of assisting in the action. The ships on which the Danes chiefly relied, were judiciously posted in such a manner as to prevent the British fleet from injuring Copenhagen; which was further protected by the citadel, and by batteries in the new dock yard, as well as on the isle of Amack, but none of these were brought into action. It was determined to assail the enemy from the southward; lord Nelson conducting the greater force, while admiral Parker should weigh to menace the crown batteries, and the ships at the entrance of the arsenal, and to cover his coadjutor's disabled ships as they came out of action.

On the ensuing morning, April 2nd, 1801. the wind blowing from the desired point, this plan was put in execution. The ships were under weigh before ten o'clock; admiral Parker bearing up against wind and current to assail the battery, while the hero of Aboukir bore down on the line. M. Fiscker, the Danish commodore, hoisted the flag of defiance on board the Danbrog of 64 guns, and all his ships being moored with four anchors, and numerously but indiscriminately manned, were placed with their broad-sides to the approaching foe.

The passage to be cleared by lord Nelson's ships, was, notwithstanding all his measures of precaution, extremely difficult and intricate. The Edgar led the van, her captain, George Murray, exhibiting a noble example of intrepidity, and succeeded in attaining her destined station. But the Bellona and Russel unfortunately grounded, and the Agamemnon unable to weather the shore of the middle ground, was obliged to anchor beyond cannon-shot. The Polyphemus remained at too great a distance, but this misfortune was amply compensated by the favorable position of La Desirée frigate, which raked the enemy's most southerly vessel from stem to stern, without her being able to return a shot, and after she had been previously saluted by the fleet in passing.

The British sailors behaved with their usual valor, the Danes animated by every patriotic feeling fought like men, who, with their own characters, were to establish the safety of their country. They were stimulated by the immediate presence of the heir apparent to the kingdom, called the crown prince, who, from the peep of dawn, had taken his station on a battery, and amidst showers of shells and balls encouraged the proceedings of the combatants. Soon after ten o'clock the Danbrog taking fire, the commodore was obliged to shift his flag to the Holstein another 64, but captain Braun of the Danbrog continued fighting till he lost his right hand, and Lemming, who succeeded him, persevered notwithstanding the flames which surrounded him, till the close of the engagement, immediately after which the vessel blew up. Early in the action captain Thura of the Indfoedfretten, a sixty-four, was slain and all his subalterns, except one lieutenant and one marine officer, were either killed or wounded. In the state of confusion attending this destruction, the colours were accidentally struck, but as the vessel was moored within reach of a Danish battery no attempt was made to take possession. A boat was dispatched from the ship with the tidings of the commander's death to the prince regent, who turning to those around him said, "Gentlemen; Thura is killed. Which of you will take the command?"—"I will," replied Mr. Schroedersee, in a feeble voice, and repaired instantly on board. This gentleman had been a captain in the navy, but on account of extreme indisposition had lately resigned. The hour of emergency seemed to invigorate his wasted form, and in the hope of serving his country, he forgot his personal infirmities. The crew perceiving a new commander coming along side, hoisted their colors, and fired a broadside When he came on deck he found great numbers killed and wounded, and therefore instantly called to those in the boat, to get quickly on board. It was his last effort, a ball struck him, and he fell lifeless on the deck. Nissen, a lieutenant of the navy, next assumed the command, and continued to fight the ship during the remainder of the day. The eleven gun-boats had retired from the moment the British fleet bore down.

It appears to have been the intention of lord Nelson, that when the ships of the Danish line, which were first attacked, should have been subdued, the British vessels which had opposed them should cut their cables, and sail to a station a-head of the line; but as part of this plan depended on the Agamemnon, which could not clear the middle ground, the Monarch and the Defiance sustained great loss from the fire of the batteries, and the two outer ships in the mouth of the harbor, and the same disaster attended six frigates and sloops, employed under captain Riou to support the attack on the battery and on those vessels. Riou himself was killed. The bomb-vessels took the station assigned to them, and threw some shells into the arsenal, but the gun-brigs notwithstanding the judicious and vigilant exertions of captain Rose, to whose command they were entrusted, could not, during the action, render the expected servi... owing to the current. The b... however, of the ships which were... employed in the attack, were powerfully effective.

When the engagement had continued nearly four hours, the fire on both sides was considerably abated; the Danish vessels were reduced to a miserable condition; the commodore had again shifted his flag from the Holstein to the crown battery, which kept up a destructive fire on the ships within its reach, and against which the vessels under sir Hyde Parker were prevented from acting by the current. The Danes overpowered on all sides except that of the battery, confined their efforts to the preservation of two or three of the crippled ships, esteeming them rather as trophies of their honorable perseverance, than as objects of intrinsic value, while the residue remained in the power of the victors

When the first resisting force opposed to him was subdued, the generous conqueror, reflecting on the extensive calamity which must attend his next operation, retired to his cabin, and in brief, but expressive terms, announced that his instructions were to spare Denmark when no longer resisting ; but, if the fire on her part was longer continued, he must be obliged to burn the floating batteries he had taken, without the possibility of saving the brave men who had defended them. This note, addressed " to the brother's of Englishmen, the Danes," was sent in an English boat with a flag of truce, along side the pricipal Danish vessel, whence it was forwarded by an officer of that country to the crown prince. The Danish battery kept up a heavy and incessant firing while this friendly message was unanswered, and lord Nelson patiently awaited the return which might be made to his humane proposition ; the white flag continuing to fly from his main-top. · Shortly afterwards, he had the satisfaction to find that the battery desisted, in consequence of orders from the crown prince, and two flags of truce were dispatched from shore to him and sir Hyde Parker, while unmolested possession was taken of the prizes.

To ascertain the exact motive of lord Nelson's letter, the Danish prince sent adjutant-general Lindholm on board the admiral's ship, and the result of their conference was a second despatch, in which his lordship declared, that, as he was actuated solely by humanity, he consented that hostilities should cease, and that the wounded should be taken on shore. He would take the prisoners out of the prizes and burn or carry off the vessels as he should think fit. The conqueror, at the same time, presented his humble duty to his royal highness, observing that he should consider this as the greatest victory which he had ever gained, if it might prove the cause of a happy reconciliation between his own most gracious sovereign and his majesty the king of Denmark.

A cessation of hostilities being now concluded, lord Nelson, anxious to secure the principal object of his enterprise, went on shore, and repaired amidst the acclamations of the people, to the royal palace, called the Octagon ; was introduced to Christian VII. and proposed the terms of a final arrangement. The king immediately agreed to the renunciation of the armed neutrality ; and in a few days a convention for the cessation of arms was ratified by sir Hyde Parker.

The scene presented to the eye after the termination of the battle, was awfully interesting. The carnage on board the Danish vessels, crowded as they were with zealous adventurers of every class, had been dreadful, and medical attendance not being provided, the wounded had been left till many had bled to death. The exertions of Nelson to relieve the afflictions of his unfortunate enemies, did the highest credit to his humanity. The English boats were despatched for the conveyance of the wounded on shore ; the hospitals were thronged with their numbers ; females of every class were employed in preparing lint for the surgeons ; and every mode of charitable relief adopted. Those who fell in battle were buried in the naval church-yard, and their funeral was attended by a solemn procession. Gold medals of honor, in commemoration of the event, were struck and delivered to the officers who deserved them ; and the pulpit, the press, and the theatre, were equally active in promoting the laudable efforts of national benevolence, and in maintaining and exerting the public spirit : nor was the following circumstance among those which produced the least effect upon the people. A prame, called Nyeborg, of 20 guns, had towed another out of the action, to a certain distance, when she went down, and the Nyeborg herself, as soon as she had reached the custom-house, sunk to her gunwale. The sight of the prame was dreadful in the extreme ; nothing was left standing but the stump of her foremast ; her shrouds were shattered ; all her guns, except one, dismounted ; her cabin stove in, and her decks covered with dead bodies and severed limbs. The spectators shuddered with horror or wept with anguish ; but curiosity

3 s 2.

and sympathy soon received a more noble direction from the publication of a paper in these words, " Countrymen ! repair to the custom-house ! view the Nyeborg, and be convinced how a Danish ship must be disabled before a Danish seaman can persuade himself to retire from action !"

Lord Nelson was particularly struck with the gallantry of a young lieutenant, a stripling of seventeen, named Villamoes, who commanded a floating *battery*, which was in fact, a wretched raft, formed of a number of beams nailed together, with a flooring to support the guns, and with a breastwork full of port-holes. His lordship also visited the naval academy, and endeared himself even to those whom he had conquered, by the frankness of his praises, and by the donation of medals to be distributed among the most deserving of the midshipmen.

The loss of the Danes in killed and wounded has not been recorded. Seventeen of their vessels were taken, sunk, or destroyed in the action ; but all those which had been captured, were burnt by the victor on the ensuing day, except the Holstein, which was then thirty years' old. The official return on the part of the British, was 254 killed, of whom 20 were officers, including captains Riou and Mosse. Nine hundred and forty-three were wounded, in which number were 48 officers. Of the merits of these brave men, the country was not unmindful. The merchants of London began, and all parts of the kingdom concurred in, a subscription, to alleviate the distress of the wounded, and to support the widows and families of the slain.

The subjoined were the stipulations of the armistice.

The Danish government on the one hand, and admiral sir Hyde Parker, commander-in-chief of his Britannic majesty's naval forces in the road of Copenhagen, on the other, being, from motives of humanity, equally anxious to put a stop to the effusion of blood, and to save the city of Copenhagen from the disastrous consequences which may attend a further prose-

cution of hostilities against that city, have mutually agreed upon a military armistice, or suspension of arms.

His Danish majesty having for that purpose appointed major-general Ernest Frederic Walterstorff, chamberlain to his Danish majesty, and adjutant-general Hans Lindholm, his commissioners for agreeing about the terms of the said armistice ; and admiral sir Hyde Parker, knight, having with the same view, duly authorised the right honorable Horatio lord Nelson, &c. and the honorable William Stewart, lieutenant-colonel in his Britannic majesty's service, &c. :—these said commissioners have met this day, and having exchanged their respective powers, have agreed upon the following terms :—

Art. I. From the moment of the signature of this armistice, all hostilities shall immediately cease between the fleet under the command of admiral sir Hyde Parker, and the city of Copenhagen; and all the armed ships and vessels of his Danish majesty in the road or harbor of that city, as likewise between the different islands and provinces of Denmark, Jutland included.

II. The armed ships and vessels belonging to his Danish majesty, shall remain in their present situation as to armament, equipment, and hostile position: and the treaty, commonly understood as the treaty of armed neutrality, shall, as far as relates to the co-operation of Denmark, be suspended while the armistice remains in force. On the other side, the armed ships and vessels under the command of admiral sir Hyde Parker, shall in no manner whatever molest the city of Copenhagen or his Danish majesty's armed ships and vessels on the coasts of the different islands and provinces of Denmark, Jutland included ; and in order to avoid every thing which might otherwise create uneasiness or jealousy, admiral sir Hyde Parker shall not suffer any of the ships or vessels under his command to approach within gun-shot of the armed ships or forts of his Danish majesty in the road of Copenhagen ; this restriction shall not, however, extend through the Gasper, or King's channel.

III. This armistice is to protect the city of Copenhagen, as also the coasts of Denmark, Jutland, and islands included, against the attack of any other naval force which his Britannic majesty may now or hereafter, during its remaining in force, have in these seas.

IV. The fleet of admiral sir Hyde Parker shall be permitted to provide itself at Copenhagen, and along the coasts of the different islands and provinces of Denmark and Jutland with every thing which it may require for the health and comfort of its crews.

V. Admiral sir Hyde Parker shall send on shore all such subjects of his Danish majesty as are now on board the British fleet under his command, the Danish government engaging to give an acknowledgment for them, as also for all such wounded as were permitted to be landed after the action of the 2nd instant, in order that they may be acounted for in favor of Great Britain, in the unfortunate event of the renewal of hostilities.

VI. The coasting trade carried on by Denmark, along all such parts of her coasts as are included in the operation of this armistice, shall be unmolested by any British ship or vessels whatever, and instructions given accordingly by admiral sir Hyde Parker.

VII. This armistice is to continue uninterrupted by the contracting parties for the space of fourteen weeks from the signature hereof, at the expiration of which time it shall be in the power of either of the said parties to declare a cessation of the same, and to recommence hostilities upon giving fourteen days previous notice.

The conditions of this armistice are upon all occasions to be explained in the most liberal and loyal manner, so as to remove all ground for future disputes, and facilitate the means of bringing about the restoration of harmony and good understanding between the two kingdoms.

In faith whereof we, the undersigned commissioners, in virtue of our full powers, affixed to it the seal of our arms.

Done on board his Britannic majesty's ship the London, in Copenhagen roads, 9th April 1801.

E. F. WALTERSTORFF.

HANS LINDHOLM.

NELSON and BRONTE.

WILLIAM STEWART.

After refitting his disabled ships, and sending home those which had sustained the greatest damage, the admiral proceeded over the grounds, into the Baltic, with a design to execute the remaining part of his instructions. The Swedish gallies consisting of about 50 sail, had put to sea on the 3rd of April, in order to form a junction with the Russian squadron, supposed to be under weigh from Revel, after which the combined fleet was to proceed to the Sound. But before this intention could be performed intelligence of the fatal issue of the battle of Copenhagen, and of the death of the emperor Paul, obliged the Swedes to return to Carlscrona. Parker proceeded directly towards that port, which nature has rendered much stronger than the Danish capital, and sent a letter to the governor informing him of the termination of the dispute with Denmark, and demanding in 48 hours, an explicit declaration of the sentiments and intentions of the court of Sweden. The answer purported that the determination of his majesty whose immediate arrival was expected, would be notified to him; and four days afterwards the governor sent information, that the king would not hesitate to fulfil with honourable fidelity his engagements with his allies. His majesty was resolved to act with sincerity without any reference to the intervention of another power, the effect of which could never be extended to the common interests of the neutral states. During this parley a messenger sent by the Russian ambassador at Copenhagen overtook the English commander at sea. He brought him information of the death of Paul, and offered such proposals as induced the admiral to returned to Kioge bay at the entrance of the Baltic.

About the middle of March Paul had given his minister a warrant for banishing or imprisoning his wife the empress, and two sons, Alexander and Constantine. The minister did not put this order into execution, but informed the sons of its purport, exclaiming, " Your father is ruining the country and himself: he will now destroy you. Is this to be endured?" He then suggested, that something must be done to stop him in his course. The sons replied that they could advise nothing and would take no part, but would leave it to the ministers to pursue such measures as were best calculated to promote the interests of the empire. Upon this the minister called a secret meeting of the court party; consisting of the ministers, military commanders, officers of state, and chief nobility, amounting in all to nearly forty persons. They dined together, that the bottle might give them courage, perhaps; and the minister proposed that the emperor Paul should be desired to abdicate the throne; that he should retire to a palace at a distance from St. Petersburgh, where he should be protected, and pass his life in private. This proposal, to which all parties had agreed individually before, was unanimously adopted; and the party proceeded in a body, late in the evening of the 24th, to the emperor's palace, to put their project into force.

The emperor Paul had heard of a plot to dethrone him, and for a considerable time lived in a state of the greatest alarm. He stationed the most faithful guards at the avenues of his palace, and took every precaution against surprise. The guards challenged the party when they approached; the party gave the watchword, but that would not satisfy the guards; at last their own commanders came forward from among the party, when of course the whole were allowed to pass. They did not go up a back stair-case, as it has been reported, but went up the grand entrance, to the emperor's bed-room, knowing that was the hour at which he would be retired. At the bed-room door, a trusty hussar was stationed, who refused the party permission to pass on any terms, and a violent struggle ensued, in which the hussar was overcome. They then entered the bedroom, and to their utter astonishment perceived that the emperor had left the bed. They saw nothing of him in the room, and now concluded their design had wholly failed, that it could not be concealed, and that their lives must pay for their attempt. But, in searching around, the emperor was discovered standing behind a screen, just as he had leaped out of bed, alarmed by the struggle made by the hussar, and apprehensive of some plot. The party now told him the object of their visit, stated to him the acts of injustice and tyranny of which he had been guilty, the ruin he was bringing upon the nation, and the general discontent at his conduct, concluding by recommending that he should abdicate the throne in favor of his son Alexander, and presenting for his signature an instrument to that effect. Paul trembled, confessed his misconduct, admitted the truth of all with which he had been reproached; but promised to act with the strictest propriety, and just do as they should direct in future, if he was permitted to reign. His abdication, however, was insisted upon, and he was consenting, when, among others, count Z——g, whom he had stripped of all the honors and emoluments bestowed upon him by the empress Catherine, began to reproach him in very severe terms for his personal illtreatment. Paul, who disliked this person much, replied with bitterness and rage, and a violent altercation ensued, when count Z——g, who is a very athletic man, lifted a chair, and striking Paul, with the corner point of the seat of it, a severe blow on the forehead, the emperor fell senseless to the ground.

This was a circumstance neither foreseen nor provided against; and the whole party were greatly at a loss how to proceed. After such a breach, it was thought it would be impossible to cajole the emperor into abdication; it was dreaded that nothing could blind his rage, if he recovered. Having gone so far, it was deemed necessary for their own safety to go farther; and it was agreed that the emperor should be put to death. This, however, it was necessary to do, leaving as little appearances of violence as possible. He was strangled, trampled upon, and bruised, for several hours, till it was quite certain he was dead. His body was then laid in the bed, and in the morning a physician was called in, to certify that he died of an apoplexy.

But the revolutionary party did not finish the business completely like masters. They left the hussar at the door, to overhear, and partly witness, all that passed, and they allowed him to escape. If he had been put to death also, the truth would not now be so well known; perhaps it might have been for ever concealed from the public. But the hussar went forth, and whispered what he knew; the story got abroad, and the empress, Paul's widow, hearing it, sent for the hussar, and took him under her protection.—Such is human ambition, or rather vanity, that the empress, who might have rejoiced at being freed from a husband who neglected her for the worst of favorites, and was even going to banish her far from his throne, no sooner found her greatness eclipsed by the loss of her lord, and that she was to sink into the antiquated, the neglected character of an empress dowager, than she pretended the most violent grief, threw herself in public over the corpse of Paul, caressed the hussar, published his tale in every quarter, and took all possible steps to stir up a party against the government to espouse her cause.

The young emperor Alexander was proclaimed on the day succeeding his father's death, and declared for the laws and customs of his august grandmother. It was among the first acts of his reign to give orders that the British sailors and masters who had been taken from the British ships, should be set at liberty, and carefully conducted to the several ports from whence they were taken. The prohibitions against the exportation of corn were revoked, and peace and friendship were re-established between the courts of London and St. Petersburgh. With respect to Malta, the principal occasion of Paul's hostility, Alexander merely took the knights under his protection, appointing count Soltikof lieutenant to the grand master during pleasure.

Lord Nelson succeeding to the command of the English fleet on the recal of sir Hyde Parker, remained in the Baltic for some time, with a force sufficient to maintain the cause of his country, had force been necessary; and, when the affairs of the north no longer required his presence, his lordship left the command to sir Charles Maurice Pole, and returned to England for the benefit of his health. Lord St. Helens was dispatched to Petersburgh as minister plenipotentiary. Before his arrival, Sweden had consented to become a party in the projected treaty: the emperor of Russia and the king of Prussia had dispatched a courier to Copenhagen, inviting the king of Denmark to evacuate the town and territory of Hamburgh, and the occupation of Hanover by Prussia, was avowed to be only temporary. All matters in dispute were finally arranged on the 16th of June, by a convention, of which the following are the most important articles. As this convention will, in all probability, become a prominent subject of discussion, even at the distance of many years, and of peculiar interest to posterity, I have adopted the precise language of the original.

III. His imperial majesty of all the Russias and his Britannic majesty, having resolved to place under a sufficient safeguard the freedom of commerce and navigation of their subjects, in case one of them shall be at war, whilst the other is neuter, have agreed:—

1. That the ships of the neutral power shall navigate freely to the ports, and upon the coasts of the nations at war.

2. That the effects embarked on board neutral ships shall be free, with the exception of contraband of war, and of enemy's property; and it is agreed not to

comprise in the number of the latter, the merchandise of the produce, growth, or manufacture of the countries at war, which may have been acquired by the subjects of the neutral power, and transported on their account, which merchandise cannot be excepted in any case from the freedom granted to the flag of the said power.

3. That in order to avoid all equivocation and misunderstanding of what ought to be considered as contraband of war, his imperial majesty of all the Russias and his Britannic majesty declare, conformably to the 11th article of the treaty of commerce concluded between the two crowns on the 10th-21st February, 1797, that they acknowledge as such only the following objects, viz.—cannons, mortars, fire-arms, pistols, bombs, grenades, balls, bullets, fire-locks, flints, matches, powder, saltpetre, sulphur, helmets, pikes, swords, sword-belts, saddles and bridles, excepting, however, the quantity of the said articles which may be necessary for the defence of the ship and of those who compose the crew; and all other articles not enumerated here, shall not be reputed warlike and naval ammunition, nor be subject to confiscation and of course shall pass freely without being subjected to the smallest difficulty, unless they be considered as enemy's property in the above settled sense. It is also agreed, that what is stipulated in the present article shall not be to the prejudice of the particular stipulations of one or the other crown with other powers, by which objects of a similar kind should be reserved, prohibited, or permitted.

4. That in order to determine what characterises a blockaded port, that determination is given only to one where there is, by the disposition of the powers which attack it with ships stationary, or sufficiently near, an evident danger in entering.

5. That the ships of the neutral powers shall not be stopped but upon just causes and evident facts: that they be tried without delay, and that the proceedings be always uniform, prompt, and legal.

In order the better to ensure the respect due to these stipulations, dictated by the sincere desire of conciliating all interests, and to give a new proof of their loyalty and love of justice, the high contracting parties enter here into the most formal engagement to renew the severest prohibitions to their captains, whether of ships of war or merchantmen, to take, keep, or conceal on board their ships any of the objects, which, in the terms of the present convention, may be reputed contraband, and respectively to take care of the execution of the orders, which they shall have published in their admiralties, and wherever it shall be necessary.

IV. The two high contracting parties, wishing to prevent all subject of dissension in future, by limiting the right of search of merchant-ships, going under convoy, to the sole cases in which the belligerent power may experience a real prejudice by the abuse of the neutral flag, have agreed:

1. That the right of searching merchant-ships belonging to the subjects of one of the contracting powers, and navigating under convoy of a ship of war of the said power, shall only be exercised by the ships of war of the belligerent party, and shall never extend to the fitters out of privateers, or other vessels, which do not belong to the imperial or royal fleets of their majesties, but which their subjects may have fitted out for war.

2. That the proprietors of all merchant-ships belonging to the subjects of one of the contracting sovereigns, which shall be destined to sail under convoy of a ship of war, shall be required, before they receive their sailing orders, to produce to the commander of the convoy their passports and certificates, or sea-letters, in the form annexed to the present treaty.

3. That when such ship of war, and every merchant-ship under convoy, shall be met with by a ship or ships of war of the other contracting party, who shall then be in a state of war, they shall, in order to avoid all disorder, keep out of cannon-shot, unless the state of the sea, or the place of meeting render a nearer approach necessary; and the commander of the ship of the belligerent power shall send a sloop on board

ciprocally to the verification of the papers and certificates which are to prove on one part, that the ship of war is authorised to take under its escort such or such merchant-ships of its nation, laden with such a cargo, and for such a port; and on the other part, that the ship of war of the belligerent party belongs to the imperial or royal fleet of their majesties.

4. This verification being made, there shall be no pretence for search, if the papers are found in due form, and if there exists no good motive for suspicion. In the contrary case, the captain of the neutral ship of war, (being duly required thereto by the captain of the ship of war or ships of war of the belligerent power,) is to bring to, and detain, his convoy during the time necessary for the search of the ships which compose it; and he shall have the right of naming and delegating one or more officers to assist at the search of the said ships, which shall be done in presence on board each merchant-ship conjointly with one or more officers selected by the captain of the ship of the belligerent party.

5. If it happen that the captain of the ship of war of the power at war, having examined the papers found on board, and having interrogated the master and crew of the ship, shall see just and sufficient reason to detain the merchant-ship in order to proceed to an ulterior search, he shall notify that intention to the captain of the convoy, who shall have the power to order an officer to remain on board the ship thus detained, and to assist at the examination of the cause of her detention. The merchant-ship shall be carried to the nearest and most convenient port belonging to the belligerent power, and the ulterior search shall be carried on with all possible diligence.

V. It is also agreed, that if any merchant-ship, thus convoyed, should be detained without just and sufficient cause, the commander of the ship or ships of war of the belligerent power shall not only be bound to make to the owners of the ship and of the cargo a full and perfect compensation for all the losses, expenses,

a detention, but shall further be liable to an ulterior punishment, for every act of violence or other fault which he may have committed, according as the nature of the case may require. On the other hand, no ship of war with a convoy shall be permitted, under any pretext whatever, to resist by force the detention of a merchant-ship or ships, by the ship or ships of war of the belligerent power; an obligation which the commander of a ship of war with convoy is not bound to observe towards privateers and their fitters out.

VI. The high contracting powers shall give precise and efficacious orders, that the sentences, upon prizes made at sea, shall be conformable with the rules of the most exact justice and equity; that they shall be given by judges above suspicion, who are not interested in the matter. The government of the respective states shall take care, that the said sentences be promptly and duly executed, according to the forms prescribed. In case of the unfounded detention, or other contravention of the regulations stipulated by the present treaty, the owners of such a ship and cargo shall be allowed damages proportioned to the loss occasioned by such detention. The rules to be observed for these damages, and for the case of unfounded detention, as also the principles to be followed for the purpose of accelerating the process, shall be the matter of additional articles, which the contracting parties agree to settle between them, and which shall have the same force and validity, as if they were inserted in the present act. For this effect, their imperial and Britannic majesties mutually engage to put their hand to the salutary work, which may serve for the completion of these stipulations, and to communicate to each other without delay the views, which may be suggested to them by their equal solicitude to prevent the least grounds for dispute in future.

VII. To obviate all the inconveniencies, which may arise from the bad faith of those, who avail themselves of the flag of a nation without belonging to it, it is agreed to establish an inviolable rule, that any vessel whatever, to be considered as the property of the country the flag of which it carries, must have on board the captain of the ship, and one half of the crew of the people of that country, and the papers and passports in due and perfect form; but every vessel which shall not observe this rule, but infringe the ordinances published on that head shall lose all right to the protection of the contracting powers.

VIII. The principles and measures adopted by the present act shall be alike applicable to all the maritime wars, in which one of the two powers may be engaged, whilst the other remains neutral. These stipulations shall, in consequence, be regarded as permanent, and serve for a constant rule to the contracting powers in matters of commerce and navigation.

IX. His majesty the king of Denmark, and his majesty the king of Sweden, shall be immediately invited by his imperial majesty, in the name of the two contracting parties, to accede to the present convention, and at the same time to renew and confirm their respective treaties of commerce with his Britannic majesty; and his said majesty engages, by acts which shall have established that agreement, to render and restore to each of these powers, all the prizes that have been taken from them, as well as the territories and countries under their dominion which have been conquered by the arms of his Britannic majesty since the rupture, in the state in which those possessions were found at the time the troops of his Britannic majesty entered them. The orders of his said majesty for the restitution of those prizes and conquests shall be immediately expedited after the exchange of the ratification of the acts, by which Sweden and Denmark accede to the present treaty.

The convention after a short delay was acceded to by Sweden and Denmark, and clearly established the principal positions contended for by Great Britain, while the restrictive regulations on the right of detention and search, were calculated to allay the jealousy, and secure the property of neutral nations. In the existing situation of Europe, its conclusion appeared to establish the naval pre-eminence of England, and the acquiescence of the northern powers in her just and moderate demands. Nor have the expectations of the world been falsified by the experience of the last thirteen years. The time however in all probability approaches, when it will become the duty of our common country, to engage in a still more arduous and unequal contest. The recent acquisition of power on the part of Russia, the obvious bias of her policy, and the evident determination of the united states of America to contest our naval rights, and dispute our naval superiority, and the facility of a maritime combination, which may gratify the ambition of the northern powers, while it aids the hostile enterprises of America in a future war, forcibly demand the reflection of the patriot, and are well calculated to impress upon the minds of the nation at large the most useful lessons of fortitude, resistance to injustice, and stedfast perseverance in the defence of Britain's only bulwark, her NAVAL EMPIRE.

The united parliament of Great Britain and Ireland assembled at Westminster on the 2nd of February. Addressing the two houses, the king observed that at a crisis so important to the interests of his people, he derived great satisfaction from being enabled for the first time to avail himself of the advice and assistance of the united parliament. " This memorable æra," he said, " distinguished by the accomplishment of a measure, calculated to augment and consolidate the strength and resources of the empire, and to cement more closely the interests and affections of my subjects, will I trust, be marked with that vigor, energy and firmness which the circumstances of our present situation peculiarly require." He referred to the unjust and violent proceedings of the court of St. Petersburgh, and censured the convention lately concluded as tending to establish by force a new code of maritime law, inconsistant with the rights, and hostile to the interests of this country. In the debates which ensued on moving the address, occasional reference was made to the case of Hibernian catholics, whose claims after the completion of the act of union, formed the most important subject of discussion in the cabinet. The premier and lord Grenville represented an acquiescence in the wishes of those sectaries as necessary for the perfect consolidation of the interests of the united kingdom, and affirmed that as no danger could arise from it, policy required the concession. Several of the royal counsellors expressed opinions opposite to these, and his majesty took a decided part in the dispute, alleging that the oath he had taken at his coronation, precluded his assent to a scheme which might in its consequences endanger the religious establishment. As this repugnance obstructed the recommendation of the measures to parliament and diminished the probability of its success, Mr. Pitt declared that he conceived himself bound by his duty, his conscience and his honor, to resign a situation in which he was not at full liberty to pursue his ideas of equity and public benefit. His resignation and that of lord Grenville were accepted: and earl Spencer, at the same time relinquished all concern in the affairs of the admiralty, which he had directed with credit to himself and advantage to his country. After some deliberation his majesty appointed Mr. Addington to the office of first minister. Lord Hawkesbury was selected for the vacancy occasioned by the resignation of lord Grenville, and the earl of St. Vincent was deemed a proper successor to earl Spencer. Mr. Pitt remained in office after the virtual appointment of his friend, that he might adjust the national accounts, and regulate the supplies of the year. While he was thus employed, the nation was alarmed, and the public business retarded by the *indisposition* of the sovereign, and it was apprehended that a regency would be necessary, but the return of health, after an illness of three weeks, enabled his majesty to renew his attention to affairs of state. He then gratified Mr. Addington with a formal appointment to the offices which Mr Pitt had so long enjoyed; substituted lord Hobart and Mr. Charles Yorke, for Mr. Dundas and Mr. Windham (who had followed the example of resigna-

tion,) and sent the earl of Hardwicke to Ireland as lord-lieutenant.

The vigilance of the ministry having procured some evidence of the renewal of those machinations which had been formerly checked by coercive laws, the *habeas corpus* act was again suspended, and a bill was re-enacted for the suppression of seditious meetings. It was provided by statute that martial law should be continued in Ireland, and a bill of indemnity was passed for the protection of all who had been concerned in the arrest and detention of supposed traitors and malcontents.

The nomination by lord Camelford of Mr. Horne Tooke to represent a borough was productive of warm discussion, and of a bill for the perpetual exclusion of clergymen from the house of commons. After some debates in which the *tirades* and sallies of Mr. Tooke highly amused the house, lord Temple observed that only the superior clergy were summoned to parliament before the twenty-third year of Edward I.; and that their parliamentary powers ceased under the sway of Henry VIII.: and with reference to Mr. Tooke's abandonment of the priesthood, he denied that a priest could divest himself of his clerical character. Mr. Tooke while he ridiculed the officious zeal of lord Temple and his parade of historic learning, protested against the practice of punishing an individual by an ex-post-facto law. He conceived the right of representation was a necessary accompaniment of the right of voting at elections. In conformity with the minister's proposal a declaratory bill excluding every priest was adopted by both houses, but was prevented by a clause from having a retro-active power to expel Mr. Tooke from the existing parliament, which was prorogued on the 2nd of July.

The orders which the late ministry had issued for vigorous operations 1801. against the Danes and Swedes in the West Indies were speedily carried into effect. Lieutenant-general Trigge and rear admiral Duckworth sailed from Antigua with a small fleet and about 1500 soldiers, and steered to the Swedish isle of St. Bartholomew. The governor having no means of

effectual defence acquiesced in the demand
of an immediate surrender. Leaving a
garrison in the chief town, the associated
commanders would have proceeded without
delay to the island of St. Thomas, but the
appearance of a reinforcement from England induced them to extend their views to
the reduction of St. Martin, though an attempt on that island was not included in
their instructions, instead of entering the
straits of Gibraltar. One brigade landed
in the Dutch quarter, and another in the
French territory. The former approaching the heights near fort Amsterdam met
with some resistance but prevailed in
every skirmish. The enemy having attacked (March 25th) one of the positions
occupied by the invaders, a spirited conflict ensued, which soon terminated in
the defeat of the assailants. This success discouraged further resistance, and
a capitulation was signed before the next
morning. The Danish islands were the
next objects of attack. The fleet sailing
to the westward, the isles of St. Thomas
and St. John were taken without opposition,
and Santa Cruz, or St. Croix was added to
the number of the British conquests.

In the beginning of February admiral
Gantheaume escaped from the port of
Brest, with a squadron having about 4000
troops on board. He was followed by sir
Robert Calder, who missing the track,
shaped his course for the West Indies. A
division under sir J. B. Warren, was next
despatched in pursuit of Gantheaume,
but with as little success. This commander also had the good fortune to elude
lord Keith's fleet, and cruizers, as well as
those of sir Richard Bickerton; and, after
various cruizes, during six months in the
Mediterranean, returned in safety to Toulon. On the 24th of June he fell in with
the Swiftsure of 74 guns, in the passage
between Candia and Egypt. She endeavoured to get before the wind, and escape
by maintaining a running fight athwart
the French squadron while much separated
in the chace. But two of their men of
war obtaining the start, brought her to
action, and after a brisk engagement, and
the loss of a great number of men, she was

compelled to strike. Rear admiral sir
James Saumarez was cruizing near Cadiz when it was reported to him that
three French ships of the line and a
frigate had been seen near Gibraltar. He
immediately directed his course to the entrance of the strait, and finding that the enemy had anchored in the bay of Algeziras, he
sent the Venerable to begin the attack. Rear
admiral Linois arranged his ships in a
closer line, and warping them near the
batteries which defended the bay, a brisk
fire was opened (July 6th) not only from
the ships but from the fortifications and
from a number of gun-boats so disposed as
to rake the English squadron. Captain
Stirling in the Pompée made a great impression on the flag-ship of Linois, till a
change of wind disabled him from acting.
As soon as the wind favored, the Hannibal,
captain Ferris, pushed forward in the hope
of passing between the French vessels and
the batteries. But his ship unfortunately
grounded, and as no efforts could extricate
her, she was abandoned after a considerable
loss of men and the destruction of a great
number of his adversaries. A breeze having enabled two other ships to approach
the enemy, they kept up for a time a heavy
fire, which, if the wind had not declined,
would have enforced the surrender of the
opposing vessels. The impracticability of
a closer conflict at length induced sir
James to withdraw his force after about
360 of his men had been killed or wounded.

This disappointment only stimulated
the eagerness of the English seamen for
another contest. The ships were prepared
with great expedition; and when the
French, joined by a Spanish squadron, were
sailing towards Cadiz, the rear of the united
fleet was attacked by the Superb. This
vessel having fired between the Spanish
admiral's ship and another of 112 guns, and
then retiring, a mutual error amidst the
darkness of the night, occasioned a conflict
between those ships. One of them took
fire, the flames rapidly extended to the
other, and both blew up with the loss
of 2000 men. This melancholy accident
discouraged Linois and his associates,
and tended to accelerate their flight.

The San Antonio could not escape seizure, but the Formidable baffled a severe attack from captain Hood, whose ship struck upon a rock, and was with difficulty towed off in a disabled state. The enemy reached Cadiz without further molestation, and Saumarez sailed with his prize to Gibraltar, boasting, with justifiable exultation, of that discipline and valor which had defeated a squadron more than treble the force of the English assailants. Of the detached actions performed by single vessels of either squadron, it is little necessary to speak; but the first personal exploit of lord Cochrane, the son of lord Dundonald, deserves to be recorded for its signal gallantry. His lordship being off Barcelona, (May 6th,) in command of the Speedy, mounting only 14 four-pounders, and navigated by only 54 persons, including officers and boys, engaged the Spanish ship El Gamo, having 22 long twelve-pounders, 8 nine-pounders, and two carronades, with 319 men. Notwithstanding this prodigious disparity of force, his lordship boarded the enemy, and, surprising him by the impetuosity of his attack, succeeded in making a prize of the Gamo. In this action, only three Englishmen were killed, and eight wounded; and on board the Spaniard, 15 were killed, and 51 wounded.

Notwithstanding the progress of a negotiation between the hostile governments, the menace of an invasion from France agitated the public mind, but did not depress the spirit of the people. Judicious schemes of defence were adopted; and lord Nelson was ordered to sail toward the French coast to obstruct the preparations of the enemy. Advancing to Boulogne, on the 18th of August, he made an attempt for the destruction of the armed vessels in that port. As only a few were then sent to the bottom or disabled, a more serious attack was risqued when he had reinforced his armament. The boats intended for boarding the flotilla were sent off in the night, in four divisions, under the respective conduct of the captains Somerville, Parker, Cotgrave, and Jones; and some boats furnished with howitzers

were detached under captain Conn, to join in the dangerous enterprise. Parker's division first approached the enemy, and commenced a fierce attack. He made strenuous efforts with undaunted courage, and with sanguine hopes of success; but an unforeseen obstacle baffled all his exertions. This was a very strong netting, traced up to the lower yards of the French vessels, which were also fastened by chains to the ground and to each other. So effectual was the resistance of the foe, thus guarded, that about two-thirds of the crew of the boat in which he acted, were repelled in their attempts to board a large brig, by a furious discharge of cannon and musketry. Many of these intrepid assailants lost their lives, many were wounded and maimed. The gallant captain received a shot which carried off his leg and part of his thigh; and his boat would have been seized by the enemy, had not a cutter seasonably towed her off. Somerville, in the mean time, silenced the fire of a brig near their pier-head; but, far from being enabled to bring her off, he found difficulty in securing the retreat of his own boats. Cotgrave, after a spirited attack, was deprived of the services of many of his men, by the fire from the flotilla and the shore. Jones felt so strongly the obstructions of the tide, that he could not approach before the break of day, when the other captains were returning: he therefore retired without making any hostile attempts.

The zeal and courage displayed in this enterprise were admired, while its ill success was lamented. The commander of the French flotilla affirmed, that about 450 of our men were killed or wounded; but lord Nelson, with greater regard to truth, estimated the number at 172. His able assistant, captain Parker, died of his wounds after the return of the fleet to the Downs.

The attention of the English government was now diverted to the affairs of Portugal. By an article of the treaty of Luneville, the throne of Tuscany was bestowed upon the young duke of Parma. The king of Spain could no longer withstand the importunities of France, which had bestowed a crown on his relative. Coinciding in the views of Buonaparte, he determined to act as a principal party in the projected campaign A convention was concluded between the two powers at Madrid, by which it was stipulated, that they should form a combined army, to oblige Portugal to detach herself from her alliance with England, and occupy a fourth of her territory until the conclusion of a definitive treaty of peace. A satisfactory arrangement was afterwards made between the two governments with respect to the establishment of the duke of Parma in Tuscany, in conformity with the treaty of Luneville. The new kingdom was declared to remain for ever united to Spain ; and an infant of that family was to be called to the throne of Tuscany in case the present monarch or his children should have no posterity. The contracting parties were to obtain for the duke of Parma an indemnity in possessions or revenue, proportionate to the loss he sustained by renouncing his principality. During these negotiations, an auxiliary French army was assembled at Bourdeaux, under general Le Clerc, to co-operate with the Spaniards in the invasion of the territories of the queen. On the 26th of April, the advanced-guard under general Monnet, consisting of about 10,000 men, arrived at Burgos. But its future progress was unaccountably tardy, and, before it approached the enemy's frontiers, some partial actions between the Spanish and Portuguese armies had occurred, which were soon followed by a treaty of peace.

In reply to a hostile manifesto, issued towards the end of February, by the king of Spain, the court of Lisbon addressed a proclamation to its subjects, which alluded to the assistance which Portugal afforded to Spain in 1793, and to the ungenerous return made by that power, for her friendly support. It dwelt on the infamy of the proposition that the Spanish troops should garrison the ports of Portugal, and descanted on the antient glory and bravery of the Portuguese nation.

In the beginning of March, the prince regent directed all the regular troops, and even the greater part of the garrison of Lisbon, with three emigrant regiments in British pay, to proceed to the frontiers. The province of Alentejo was invaded by the prince of Peace, a warm partisan of France. The events of the campaign were a burlesque on warfare, and scarcely fall within the province of the historian. The Spaniards easily obtained possession of the frontier fortresses ; and the court of Lisbon, totally unprepared for war, consented to a treaty of peace, concluded on the 6th of June, at Badajoz, by which it agreed to shut its ports against the ships of Great Britain, and ceded the fortress and territory of Olivenza, to the crown of Spain.

Portugal had evinced a sincere desire to preserve, during the present war, a strict neutrality ; but this advantage was denied, and she was at last destined to sustain a portion of its evils. While her frontier was invaded by a French army, as a chastisement for her attachment to Great Britain, her firmest ally, the English government, being anxious to obtain some possession of which it might avail itself, in the conclusion of a peace which was now foreseen, dispatched a squadron with a body of troops on board, " to take the island of Madeira into its protection and possession." The governor, convinced of the friendly intentions of Great Britain, or unprepared for resistance, resigned to colonel Clinton, who conducted the expedition, the possession of two forts which commanded the bay of Funchal, the capital of the island.

The French republic, eminent in military station, powerful in dominion, and formidable in its alliances, exhibited in its interior the weakness produced by a protracted struggle, carried on by means unknown in the history of civilized man, and attended by the subversion of every law, human and divine. As the government increased in strength, and became less dependent on public opinion, every appearance of that liberty and equality which had been so fatally abused, was suppressed, and every appeal to the principles of freedom punished or disregarded. Measures of severe regulation calculated to revive under another form, the system of terror were resorted to, in consequence of the attempt to destroy the first consul by means of the machine termed *infernale*, and of another plot said to have been formed in the month of October 1800 for his assassination with a poniard. The persons accused of this last offence were Dominic Demerville, Joseph Ceracchi, Joseph Areno, a Corsican, late member of the council of Five Hundred, John Francis Baptist, Topino Lebrun the celebrated historical painter, Joseph Diana, Magdalen Charlotte Claudine Fumey, Armen Deiteg, and Dennis Lavigne. The accused defended themselves with equal spirit and ability, and produced many witnesses to character, among whom was David the painter. The jury found Demerville, Ceracchi, Areno, and Topino Lebrun, guilty. Diana, Fumey, Deiteg, and Lavigne, were declared not guilty, and discharged. Those who were convicted appealed to the proper court, but the judgment against them was confirmed, and they were shot on the place de la Grève.

Before this process began, an attempt had been made to destroy Buonaparte by means of the *infernale*, a machine, which placed at the side of the street through which the consul proceeded to the theatre, exploded as he past, and but for the fidelity of his coachman, who, suspecting his danger, lashed his horses into a gallop, would have terminated the first consul's career. Under pretext of this conspiracy, a law was immediately enacted, by which 133 persons, without a charge, and without a hearing, were sentenced to be placed under a watchful inspection, in places out of the European territory of the republic. A tribunal of safety was appointed, which possessed the most inquisitorial power over the liberty of the subject, and the government was authorised to remove from any town or city, any person whose presence might become injurious. As a justification of these proceedings, the minister of police published (January 31st) a report, containing a long narrative of the origin of the attempt on Buonaparte, which was now ascribed to the Chouan Georges, who, it was stated, had returned from England with new projects of assassination, and with guineas to embolden and pay his accomplices. In addition to the individuals already sentenced to departation, sixteen persons, of whom ten were women, were tried at Paris, and two men named Carbon, and St. Regeut, were condemned and executed. The emigrants who had been allured by specious proclamations and delusive promises, to revisit their native land, were treated with great harshness and injustice. To remunerate the French people for these violations of humanity, and to divert their attention from the atrocities of his government, Buonaparte endeavoured to astonish and to amuse them by the splendor of his plans, and the number of his public processions, and entertainments. But the arts of himself and his dependents were only partially effectual. The poverty of the lower classes was so extreme, that even fear could not repress their outcries : the officers of the army of Germany loudly complained, that their services were slighted, while every favor was conferred on those who had acted in Italy and Egypt; and even Moreau himself was regarded with jealousy and suspicion. The consular guard was augmented to 16,000 men, and in the midst of triumph, flattery, and uncontrolled dominion, the chief was distrustful, and the nation dissatisfied.

HISTORY OF THE WAR.

CHAP. XXXII.

SOON after the surrender of Malta to the British forces, orders were received for the armies of sir Ralph Abercrombie, and sir James Pulteney, to separate, the larger force remaining under the former officer, and being destined for an expedition then undisclosed, but which the opinions and hopes of the army directed to Egypt. At the time of receiving their orders the British troops were at Gibraltar, indisposed by a long continuance at sea, and dejected in mind, by a series of disappointments and unexpected failures. While part of the force proceeded to Minorca, where they were to meet lord Keith; the residue with sir Ralph Abercrombie went directly to Malta, where they were soon rejoined by the party who had been at Minorca, and by the noble admiral. The combined force then proceeded to the coast of Asia Minor, and anchored in the beautiful and spacious bay of Marmorice. At this place the sick were landed and encamped; regiments were successively brought on shore, and practised the manœuvres requisite in their next attempt, the ships were cleared, and the officers employed themselves in purchasing horses, expecting from Constantinople, those on which the men were to be mounted. These animals at length arrived, and severe was the disappointment of the troops, when instead of those admirable breeds peculiar to Turkey, they received

some hundred horses of a feeble race, and in a deplorable condition. With difficulty and disgust 200 were selected for the cavalry, and fifty for the artillery. The rest were shot as unfit for service, and unsaleable. The assistance derived from the Turks was limited to a few gun-boats, and the reports from the camp of the grand vizier, and the non-arrival of the capitan pacha, rendered it more than doubtful whether any serious co-operation was intended. Notwithstanding these discouragements, sir Ralph Abercrombie assembled all the general officers on board the Kent, explained his intentions, and communicated his final instructions. The embarkation was performed with the greatest speed, the horses were placed on board of several vessels arrived from Smyrna; and the fleet and transports amounted to 175. The weather during the voyage was extremely boisterous; the Greek vessels on board of which the horses were stowed, badly manned, and unprepared for sea, separated from each other, and from the fleet, carrying with them the greatest part of the artillery, and of the cavalry horses.

After enduring these calamities a week, the ships came in sight of Alexandria, but the weather did not permit an attempt to land. The troops also received the discouraging intelligence of the disastrous fate of two brave officers, Majors Mackarris and Fletcher, of the engineers, had been sent in the Penelope before the fleet sailed from Marmorice, to reconnoitre the coast; but when off Alexandria, they left the Penelope and the Peterell, and in the boat of the latter ship proceeded (February 27th,) into Aboukir bay, in order to discover the proper point of landing. In vain was major Mackarris advised not to penetrate too far into the bay. He advanced, and landed; but, at the dawn of day, as he was returning, a French gun-boat, full of soldiers from lake Maadie, appeared to windward, and bore down, firing a volley of carronade and small arms. A shot disabled the English boat from continuing sail, and a musket-ball having killed major Mackarris, the master of the boat surrendered.

For another week continual tempests prevented every attempt to land the troops. Excellent general orders for their conduct on approaching the shore, had been issued by sir Ralph Abercrombie before he left Marmorice. The troops were instructed to enter the flat-bottomed boats with the utmost expedition, and in good order, to sit in profound silence while they were rowed to land, to reserve the loading of their pieces till they should have formed for landing, and to pay the most scrupulous respect to the manners, customs, and religious opinions of the people of Egypt.

While the British expedition was thus struggling with adverse circumstances, the divisions in the French army raged with unrestrained fury, and the turbulence of faction, as well as his own indiscretion, prevented Menou, from turning to the best account, the many advantages he possessed. By his harshness, insolence, and suspicious temper, he disgusted and offended many of the beys, whom he might have retained in bonds of friendship or of neutrality: a plague broke forth at Cairo, yet he refused to adopt the necessary precautions for securing his troops from its contagion: his extravagance was boundless; and th magazines were neglected, and inadequately supplied. Yet the French force was more than amply sufficient, had it been prudently directed, to resist every attempt which could be made against it;

and at the very moment when the English fleet appeared, Menou's army was cheered by the prosperous arrival of La Regenerée and the Lodi. La Regenerée, which had accidentally fallen into the midst of the British fleet before it reached the shores of Egypt, by the admirable dexterity of the commander, sailed with it undetected, till the moment arrived, when, without the fear of pursuit, he could gain the port of Alexandria.

The appearance of the English fleet was known at Cairo on the 4th of March, and the general officers importuned Menou to concentrate his troops. But the commander-in-chief, alarmed at dangers which his brother officers overlooked, and jealous of their interference, refused even to dispatch a vessel to watch the movements of the English, and assigned to the various generals scenes of service far distant from those which they judged most elligible. At the same time he addressed a proclamation to the inhabitants of Egypt, in which, after [a bombastic boast that the sword of the angel of God always shone before the French troops, he threatened that if the English set foot on shore, they should be thrown into the sea. The force on which he relied, to prevent the landing, amounted to upwards of 2000 men, under general Friant; they had 15 pieces of cannon, and, while the English were prevented from landing, were diligently employed in throwing up works on the sand-hills.

It was not till the 6th of March that the wind abated; but even then, the swell of the sea, and the fierceness of the surf, prevented all attempts to land: but sir Sidney Smith, always anxious to be actively employed, went on shore with two armed launches to attack a French gun-boat which had stationed itself at the entrance of lake Maadie, or Aboukir, and was soon abandoned after the first fire of the English.

On the 8th of March, the wind continuing favorable, the first division of the army, under major-general Coote, proceeded in their boats about three o'clock, to the rendezvous near the brig Mondovi, at the distance of gun-shot from the shore. Their right flank was protected by the Cruelle cutter, the Dangereuse and Janissary gun-vessels, and two launches ; the left by the Entreprenant cutter, the Malta schooner, the Negresse gun-vessel, and the other launches. The Tartarces and Fury bomb-vessels, were so stationed, as in some measure to cover their landing with their fire ; The Peterell, Camelion, and Minorca, were moored with their broadsides towards the shore. Sir Sidney Smith, with a detachment of 350 seamen, captains Bibeleau, Guion, Saville, Burn, and Hilliar, were directed to co-operate with the troops on shore, and 112 artillery-men had charge of the launches which carried their field-pieces and ammunition.

At nine o'clock, the signal was made for the boats to advance. They sprung forwards at the same instant, and the whole scene became one of animation. The French, to the number of 2000 men, posted on the top of the sand-hills, formed a concave arch of a circle, of about a mile on the front ; in the centre of which arch was a perpendicular elevation of sixty yards, apparently inaccessible. They had beheld with wonder the preparations of the English, and have since confessed that they did not believe the attempt would be persisted in. But when they observed the boats moving with rapidity towards the shore, and the armed vessels opening their guns, they could no longer doubt the seriousness of the intention, and directly poured all the fire which the artillery on the heights and the castle of Aboukir could discharge. The quantity of shot and shells, and, as the boats approached, the shower of grape and musketry, ploughed the surface of the water in such a manner, that nothing on it could live. For a moment, the fire even checked some of the boats, and compelled them to close upon the left ; but the impulse returned with increased ardor, and, pressing through the storm, the rowers forced to the beach. The reserve leaped out of the boats on shore ; the 23rd and 40th regiments rushed up the heights with almost preternatural vigor, never firing a shot, but charging with the bayonet the two battalions which crowned it, breaking

them, and pursuing till they carried the two nole-hills in the rear, which commanded the plain to the left, taking, at the same time, three pieces of cannon. The 42nd regiment had landed, and formed as on a parade, and then mounted the position, notwithstanding the fire from two pieces of cannon and a battalion of infantry. The moment they gained the height, 200 French dragoons attempted to charge them, but were as quickly repulsed.

The boats of the guards had scarcely felt the beach, and the men began to jump out, before the same body of cavalry which had rallied behind the sand-hills, charged suddenly upon them. This unexpected attack occasioned a momentary disorder ; but the 58th regiment checked the enemy by their fire, and gave time for the guards to present a front, when the cavalry again retreated with considerable loss. The 54th, and royals being in transport boats, did not reach the shore so soon as the others, but landed at the instant a column of 600 infantry was advancing with fixed bayonets through a hollow against the left flank of the guards. The French observed them for awhile, fired a volley, and leisurely retreated.

The enemy observing the English to be in possession of the heights, and general Coote advancing with the guards and his brigade, quitted every point of their position, but kept up for some time a scattered fire ; after which the greater portion retired to Alexandria, the rest taking refuge in Aboukir. The number of English soldiers engaged in the enterprise, amounted to 4800, of whom 102 were killed, 515 wounded, and 35 drowned by the oversetting of the boats.

The British army, at the commencement of the debarkation, amounted to 15,336 men, of whom 999 were invalids. A great portion of this force being landed, sir Ralph Abercrombie proceeded to a position nearly three miles distant, which he occupied with his right flank to the sea, and his left to the lake Aboukir, called by the French, Maadie, and Mahadie. He also left a party to reduce the fort of Aboukir, which, on being summoned, refused to surrender

The day after the landing, the position of the army was advanced a short way to an outpost of the enemy, which they abandoned, spiking and throwing over the work, a twelve pounder, and destroying a large quantity of biscuit and barley, which they had not time to carry away. During the whole day the wind prevented the landing of stores and provisions, but the troops carried with them three days' allowance, and the fear of wanting water was agreeably relieved. Sir Sidney Smith had asserted, and it was confirmed by experiment, that where date-trees grew, that necessary element could not be wanting; nor was the date-tree useful alone, as it indicated where water might be found, for the troops were tolerably sheltered in huts made from its branches. In the course of the 10th, the rest of the troops came on shore. The Greek vessels having rejoined the fleet, the horses were landed, and provisions, stores, and forage in abundance were brought up from the ships with the greatest facility by the lake of Aboukir, which likewise afforded a harbor to the gun-boats, and added great security to the left flank of the army. Several skirmishes occurred between the outposts of the British and French armies, but no regular engagement ensued till the 13th of March. Upon the preceding day the forces of sir Ralph Abercrombie marched forward beyond the redoubt of Mandara, and notwithstanding the opposition which they experienced from the augmented cavalry of the enemy, they continued to advance while the French retreated. The army of general Menou was at length discovered on a range of sand-hills. Their right was stretched towards the canal of Alexandria, and their left supported by a ruined palace. The British army halted during the night upon the plain, and formed in two lines, from the sea on the right, to the lake of Aboukir on the left.

The situation of the enemy was certainly strong, but in proportion to its importance it was necessary for the British to possess it. The army received orders to be in readiness, for marching at five o'clock in the morning, but owing to some unavoidable arrangements and delays, it was past six before they were ready to advance. The whole were required to form into columns, and they began their march in the following order. Major-general lord Cavan's brigade was on the left, supported by the brigades of brigadier-general Stuart, and general Doyle, and by the dismounted cavalry. The forces commanded by major-general Cradock were on the right, and were supported in the rear by general Coote's brigade. The reserve marched in two columns along the sea-shore, parallel with the forces of major-general Coote, and the guards in the rear of general Cradock were opposite to the dismounted guards, in the line of columns led forward by lord Cavan. The 90th regiment formed the advanced guard of major-general Cradock, and the 92nd had a similar appointment in the front of lord Cavan. Thus the whole army was placed in columns with the left companies of every regiment in front.

As the English troops approached within gun-shot of the enemy's lines, a tremendous fire was opened upon them, and they formed by dexterous movements into two lines, continuing the same advanced guards and having the same troops in rear, the dismounted cavalry and reserve remaining in columns throughout the action. The French advanced with rapidity, determined if possible, to attack the British army before it recovered its firmness, after having altered its form, and changed its position. Sir Ralph Abercrombie had given it as the leading order of the day that his men should endeavour to turn the right of the French army, for the left was so placed, that it could not be approached without enduring a destructive fire from the other parts of the line. But the army of Menou having advanced from the heights varied their position, and rendered it easy to attack them in a different manner.

The 90th regiment was rapidly advancing towards the heights, when the 22nd French chasseurs darted upon them with all the swiftness of the best mounted cavalry, but a well directed fire from the English ranks,

3 U 2

compelled them to skirt along the line, or become individually the victims of their own temerity.

The fourth light dragoons which general Lanusse had left in reserve, sprung forward to the assistance of the disordered chasseurs ; but, though a temporary impression was made on the lines of the 90th regiment, the French were ultimately obliged to retreat with considerable loss. The 18th regiment of the French, when they saw the disasters of their countrymen, pushed forward in order of battle, but were opposed, and thrown into disorder by the 8th regiment of the British. Upon the left of the French army, the brave 61st demi-brigade advanced with two fieldpieces, but the 92nd regiment received them with firmness, and put them to flight.

Thus beaten and repulsed at every point, the French army retreated, and were driven from station to station, till they took post near Alexandria on the heights of Nicopolis, the site of an antient city, built by Julius Cæsar, in honor of the complete victory which he finally obtained over the Egyptians. It was now in agitation that the British should follow up the advantage already obtained, and attempt to drive the French from their new position. Sir Ralph Abercrombie, advancing across the plain, ordering general Hutchinson, with the second line, to move forward and occupy a rising ground on the left, which projected into the plain ; and major-general Moore, with the body of the reserve, to advance to the right, in order that both flanks of the enemy might be assaulted at once. General Hutchinson detached the 44th regiment to dislodge a body of French infantry and cavalry, posted at a bridge across the canal of Alexandria, a service which they performed with great gallantry, but were soon obliged to retreat, being exposed to the fire of a number of pieces of cannon. This bridge lay in front of the rising ground occupied by general Hutchinson in the bottom between it and the right of the French position. The French had now begun a general and well-sustained fire ; the column under general Hutchinson

derived some shelter from its situation, and the reserve was protected by the uneven and broken surface of the soil ; but the centre of the army remained exposed to a most destructive fire during several hours of indecision and uncertainty, while sir Ralph Abercrombie was employed in reconnoitring. The work of death was never more quick, nor greater opportunity afforded for destruction. The French, no longer in danger, had only to load and fire ; aim was unnecessary ; the bullets plunged into the lines, and were sure to take effect. Finding that further perseverance would be equally unavailing and destructive, the general withdrew the troops to the position from which they had driven the enemy The loss of the British army was 156 killed, and 1081 wounded, of whom the greater part were incapable of further service, having received their injuries from cannon balls. The loss of the enemy was estimated at 700. The want of cavalry and the deficiency of artillery, were severely felt throughout the whole of the day, as they deprived the English of the advantage they might have derived from their superiority of numbers, which amounted to double those of the French, being 14,000 against 7000. Sir Ralph Abercrombie had his horse shot under him during the action.

The position of the British now extended from the sea on the right, to lake Mareotis on the left. From the lake, a flat ground extended for about a quarter of a mile, then a rising ground about three quarters of a mile, then a valley about 400 yards further, quite to the sea. This last mentioned high ground projected towards Alexandria, and the French lines on the heights of Nicopolis, about a quarter of a mile in front of the rest of the position, and on it were the ruins of a Roman edifice. On this projecting eminence were posted the 28th and 58th regiments, supported by the 23rd, the 40th, the 42nd, and the Corsican rangers. In the valley between this eminence and the high ground, in the centre of the position were the cavalry of reserve, but somewhat in the rear. On

Their left, and on the central hill, were, first, the guards, then the royals ; the 92nd, and the second and first battalion of the 54th. From this central hill, were placed *en echellon*, along with these, the 8th, 18th, 90th, and 13th, in succession, towards the canal of Alexandria and lake Mareotis. And at right angles to their left, and in the rear of the lake and the canal, the 27th, 79th, and 50th, were posted. The second line was formed from the right by the Minorca, De Rolle's, Dillon's, the queen's, the 44th, the 89th, the 30th, the dismounted cavalry of the 12th dragoons, the mounted part of the same regiment, and the 26th. On the right of the position, nearly opposite to the front of the projecting eminence, surmounted by the old ruins, were stationed some gun-boats and armed vessels, within 150 yards from the sea-shore, under the command of captain Maitland. Two batteries were ordered to be constructed on the canal, to defend the left of the position, of which the rear was protected by some armed launches, under captain Hillier, in lake Aboukir. In this situation, they severely felt the want of horses and camels, to assist in bringing up the heavy guns. Even the provisions were brought on men's shoulders from the magazine, a mile and a half distant, and the heavy casks of liquor required great labor to roll them through the sands. After some time, and by the unremitted exertions of Mr. Baldwin, the consul, a market was established, notwithstanding the denunciation by Menou, of exemplary punishment to all who should supply the English with necessaries and provisions. Till this time the army had no covering, except their great coats, but tents were now brought up which sheltered them from the night air, which is sometimes in the Egyptian climate intensely cold. After a blockade of five days, the castle of Aboukir surrendered to the British troops, and it was found to contain 12 French guns, a considerable quantity of ammunition, and 190 men. On the 19th, general Menou, having made some advances, the supply of provisions totally failed, in consequence of the destruction by the French of several

Arabs, carrying sheep to the market. On the 20th, a column of French infantry and cavalry were seen passing the ground near lake Mareotis, into Alexandria. An Arab chief also informed sir Sidney Smith by letter, of Menou's approach with a considerable force, and of his intention to attack the British camp the next morning. On this night the British army was strengthened by a battery, open in the rear, but closed in front, a little to the left, and near the ruins of Pompey's palace. The guards had likewise a redoubt in front of their right, and a battery on their left, called the citadel, having the signal staff hoisted upon it. On the left, also, of the whole line, there was a redoubt, which, in its whole extent, contained two 24 pounders, and 34 field-pieces.

On the 18th of March, a skirmish took place between 80 of the English cavalry under colonel Archdall, and a body of 150 French cavalry and infantry, which was observed reconnoitring on the canal of Alexandria, near the village of Beda, under general D'Estin. The ill-judged ardor of the troops occasioned a loss of 33 men killed, wounded, and taken, and 43 horses. Colonel Archdall himself, lost an arm. Sir Ralph Abercrombie immediately issued public orders, expressing his disapprobation of this excessive impetuosity which occasioned loss and danger without commensurate advantage.

On the memorable 21st of March, the army as usual was under arms at three o'clock in the morning : all was quiet till half-past three, when the report of a musket was heard at the extremity of the left, instantly afterwards a cannon fired, scattered musketry followed, and then two more guns. All were now convinced that a general attack was commencing, and general Moore, who was officer of the night, on the first alarm proceeded to the left, but was so impressed with the idea that it was too far distant, that he turned back to the right. A solemn stillness now succeeded, but it was only of a short duration, every ear was all attention, and every eye directed towards the eastern sky, when on a sudden, loud acclamations were heard on the right, to which a roar of musketry instantly succeeded, and the enemy's attack in that quarter was now no longer doubtful. The enemy advanced upon and continued to push in all the videts and picquets upon the main body, but colonel Housten of the 58th, faintly perceiving a French column advancing upon him, and dreading lest the English picquets should be between them and his men, suffered it to come so near him, that he could plainly see the enemy's glazed hats, before he ordered his grenadiers to fire. Their discharge was now followed by that of the whole regiment, and being rapidly repeated, soon made the French retire to a hollow some distance in their rear. Soon after they wheeled to the right, and attempted to pass a redoubt opposite to its left, in conjunction with another column, but the 28th regiment seeing them approach the battery, with a heavy fire checked those who attempted to storm the redoubt where they were stationed But now the main body of the two columns joined a third, and forced in behind the redoubt, while others were to attack it in front ; when colonel Crowdjye commanding the left of the 58th, wheeled back two companies, and, after firing two or three rounds, ordered a charge with the bayonet, and being at this instant joined by the 23rd, while the 42nd were also advancing, the French troops that had entered the rear of the redoubt, after sustaining a very severe loss, were obliged to surrender. Here both the 58th and 28th had been attacked in front, flank, and rear. It is allowed, that the 28th experienced a momentary relief from the advance of the 42nd, but, during the time they were engaged, the first line of the enemy's cavalry, passing the left of the redoubt, and charging in a mass, for awhile overwhelmed that gallant corps, but which, though broken, was not defeated. In fact, such was the dilemma in which they were placed during this contest, that colonel Spencer, with a part of the 40th, having taken a station in the avenues of the ruins, was, for some moments, afraid to fire, lest they should destroy the 42nd, then intermingled with the enemy. But even when he began

to fire, which in some 'measure, checked the progress of the French cavalry, he must certainly have been overpowered, if general Stuart had not advanced with the foreign brigade, pouring in such a heavy and well directed fire ; which, as nothing could withstand, the enemy, from destruction and flight, was no longer visible. In this furious charge of cavalry, general Abercrombie received his mortal wound. He was alone, near the redoubts just spoken of, when some French dragoons, penetrating to the spot, he was thrown from his horse. From the tassel of his sword, the man that rode at him, and endeavored to cut him down, must have been an officer. This sword, however, the veteran general seized and wrested from before he could effect his destruction ; and at the same instant, this daring assailant was bayoneted by a private of the 42nd. Sir Ralph only complained of a contusion in his breast, supposed to have been given, in the scuffle, by the hilt of the sword, but was entirely ignorant of the moment he received the wound in the thigh, which occasioned his death. After this wound, sir Sidney Smith was the first officer that came to the general, and from him received that sword which the latter had so gloriously acquired from the French officer. The cause of this present was the general's observation, that sir Sidney's sword had been broken. As soon as the French cavalry were driven out of the camp, sir Ralph walked to a redoubt, where he could take a view of the whole field of battle. Then to the right it appeared, the reserve of the French cavalry had attempted another charge against the foreign brigade, without success. After this, their infantry, one battalion excepted, no longer acting in a body, fired only in scattered parties. As the ammunition of the British was exhausted, several of the regiments of the reserve not only remained some time without firing a shot, but even the guns in the battery had but one cartridge left. But, while this was the state of affairs on the right, it was found the centre had been attacked. At day break, a body of French grenadiers had advanced upon it, supported

R.H.S.del.   Pub.^d by I.Kinnersley April 25.1818.   I.Wallis sculp.

Sir Ralph Abercrombie in the Battle of Alexandria.

by a heavy line of infantry. The guards were posted there, and at first threw out their flankers to oppose the enemy; but these being driven in, and, as the enemy's columns had approached very close. General Ludlow ordering the brigade to fire, they did so with the utmost precision; and after some local manœuvring, the advance of general Coote with his brigade, determined the enemy to retire, and separate themselves as sharp shooters; and thus, while the French cannon played without intermission, the former kept up a very destructive fire. And thus the left of the British was never engaged any farther than being exposed to a distant cannonade, and a partial discharge of musketry. During the interval the British were without ammunition; the French on the right, advancing close to the redoubt, were pelted with stones by the 28th; and returning the same measures of offence, they killed a serjeant of that regiment, by beating in his forehead. But as these troops as well as the British were without ammunition, they were very easily driven away by the grenadiers, who moved out after them; and, soon after, the whole of the enemy's force moved off the ground. Thus, unable to make the impression expected upon the British lines, general Menou made a retreat in very good order, but this was principally owning to the want of ammunition among the British; otherwise the batteries, as well as the cannon on the left and the king's cutters on the right must have done great execution. About ten in the forenoon the action had every where terminated, while sir Ralph Abercrombie never quitted the battery he retired to; but as he continued walking about, many officers had no suspicion of his being wounded, but from the blood trickling down his clothes. At length getting faint, he was put on a hammoc, and conveyed to a boat, which carried him on board lord Keith's ship, being accompanied by his friend sir Thomas Dwyer. The battle was fought by the right of the English army alone. The French army was 9700 strong, including 1,500 cavalry, with 46 pieces of cannon. The whole British army, reduced

by the actions on the 8th and 13th, by the men left in care of the wounded, the absence of the 92nd regiment, the marines and dismounted dragoons, did not yield an effective force of 10,000 men, including 300 cavalry; yet it must be remembered that it was only the half of this number that contested with the whole united force of the enemy. The field of battle in front of the British works being very contracted the killed and wounded presented a distressing spectacle. Near 1700 French and 400 horses were found on the field. On the part of the British there were 60 officers and 233 men killed; and 16 officers and 1,190 men wounded. Though this battle neither decided the fate of Egypt nor gained any ground, yet it answered many important purposes, principally that of securing the position to our army, and the impression it made on the Bedouin Arabs of the British valor; in consequence of which a communication was opened with the interior of the country, and the market supplied with every commodity. For thousands of these people came to be eye witnesses of the contest, and declared it to be such an one as their fathers never recorded. On the 28th of March this brave general breathed his last. His death was first made known to the army the next morning. For his cure he had undergone the most painful operations with great firmness; but as the ball could not be extracted, a mortification ensued. In his military character sir Ralph Abercrombie was strictly uniform and regular, and preserved the best order and discipline possible throughout all ranks of those under his command. In action he possessed that intrepidity, coolness, and presence of mind requisite; and characteristic of the British nation. In his private character he was modest, and unassuming; in all his transactions, disinterested and upright, and in his morals circumspect, and unstained by licentious vices. In company he was naturally reserved, and in promiscuous or mixed society extremely silent; yet perfectly easy of access, and free from haughtiness. In his domestic relations he was unimpeachable, and fulfilled the several duties of a son, brother, husband, father, and friend,

with that rectitude inseparable to a character of his magnanimity. The remains
of this brave general were deposited under
the castle of St. Elmo, in La Valetta, in the
island of Malta, facing the entrance of the
harbor, over which was erected a handsome, but plain black marble slab, with the
following inscription:

Memoriæ
RODOLPHI ABERCROMBIE,
Scoti,
equitis ordin. a Balneo dicti,
viri
probitate,
mentis magnitudine, animo
maximo,
et armis in bello Americano atque
Hollandico,
clarissimi;
quem
Georgius III. Magnæ Britanniæ
Rex,
populis plaudentibus,
Britannicæ terrestris exercitus
ad mare Mediterraneum
duce supremum dixit,
quo munere
expeditionem Ægyptiacum con-
ficiens,
oram Ægypti universam,
Gallorum copiis strenuis undique
adversantibus,
uno impetu occupavit, tennit,
idemque progrediens
earum conatus non semel fugit,
compressit
donicum signis cum Gallo conlatis
cruenti prælio ad Alexandriam
commisso,
anno 1801, die XXI m. Martii,
in prima acie, in ipsa victoriæ sinu,
lethale vulnus pectore excipiens,
magno suorum desiderio extinc-
tus est
die XXVIII ejusdem mens. anno
ætatis suæ
LXVIII.
dux, rei bellicæ peritia,

providentia in consulendo,
fortitudine in exequendo
ac fide integra in Regni et Regis
gloriam spectatissimus.
Hunc Rex, hunc Magna Britannia,
flevit.
Henricus Pigot,
præpositus gen. regia potestate,
præsidia militum,
in hanc insulam consistentium,
optimi ducis, cineribus eodem,
anno die XXIX Aprilis,
funere publico huuc inlatis,
bene merenti faciendam curavit
pietatis causa.

To the Memory of
RALPH ABERCROMBIE,
Of Scotland,
Knight of the Bath;
in a word,
A man of probity,
Great mind, and the most invincible courage,
and in the wars with America and
Holland
acquired great fame;
whom
George III. King of Great Britain,
to the satisfaction of his people
appointed commander-in-chief
of his army in the Mediterranean,
and intrusted
with the Expedition against
Egypt,
to dispossess the French of that
coast;
where he opposed that powerful foe,
firmly maintain'd his post,
and never desisted
his pursuit,
till at length
in a cruel and bloody battle
fought at Alexandria,
March 21, 1801,
in th beginning of the action,
and in the moment of victory,

received a mortal wound in his
breast,
and died,
universally beloved by all,
on the 28th of the same month,
and in the 68th year of his age :
a most skilful general,
prudent in his counsels,
brave in execution,
and of inviolable faith,
conspicuous
for preserving the glory of
his king and country.
His king and country regret his
loss :
Henry Pigot,
appointed by royal authority,
commander-in-chief of the armies
of this island,
caused the ashes of this best of
generals .
to be here publicly interred
the 29th day of April, in the same
year,
for the love of his country.

Sir Ralph died of a wound in the hip,
and not in the breast as is mentioned in
this epitaph.

In the detail of a battle like that which
marked the glory of this day, it will
naturally be expected some mention should
be made of that corps which had the honor
of taking the enemy's standard, till then
justly stiled the standard of the Invincibles.
This signal honor has been disputed and
claimed by several, but of the various
statements that have been made, the greatest
credit is undoubtedly due to the testimony
of sir Robert Wilson, who has reconciled
the seeming contradictions, and faithfully
detailed the capture, loss, and recapture
of the invincible standard.   Sir R. Wilson
declares it was first taken by serjeant
Sinclair, who being ordered forward by an
officer gave it to a private who was killed,
and the standard consequently fell into the
hands of the enemy : but the honour of retaking it justly belongs to Antoine Lutz, a
native of Rosheim in Alsace. The regiment of Stuart, or the Queen's German regiment, in which this gallant soldier served

as a private ; pursuing the enemy's infantry.
Lutz being one of the foremost, came within a few yards of the French officer who
bore this standard, and who was consequently in the rear of his regiment. Lutz
levelled his musket at this officer, and shot
him in the back. He immediately fell
forward on his face, and the colors dropped from his shoulder to the ground. Lutz
after taking the prudent precaution to re-
load his piece, seized the colors, and was
in the act of carrying them back to his
regiment as his lawful prize, when two
French dragoons galloped towards him.
On their near approach he threw down his
standard, and fired, when he killed one of
their horses, and the rider's foot being entangled in the stirrup, Lutz rushed upon
him, when the dragoon begged his life
and gave up his pistol as a token of submission. The other dragoon fled. Lutz
took up the colors again, and making the
dragoon march before him, conveyed them
back in safety to the regiment. The
colors he presented to colonel Moncrief, who
gave him all the money he happened to
have about him, and sent him off with them
to the head-quarters, where he received
from the adjutant-general, by order of the
commander-in-chief twenty dollars, as a
remuneration for his conduct.

The battle of Alexandria gave rise to
serious animosities among the French
generals, and the wounded Lanusse refused
to survive a day so inglorious to the republic.   Their discontent and insubordination were promoted by the inability of
Menou, whose talents were better adapted
to the station of a general of division, than
to that of a commander. The death of sir
Ralph Abercrombie revived their hopes,
and animated their enthusiasm, but the
skill, the heroism, and the activity of general Hutchinson who now succeeded to the
chief command, soon repressed their sanguine expectations.   This celebrated officer
was born in Dublin on the 15th of May, 1757.
His grandfather Mr. Hely, was an attorney
of some eminence. His father, the right
honorable John Hely Hutchinson, a man
of transcendent abilities and insatiable
ambition, changed the paternal name in

consequence of a marriage with a rich heiress, and occupied high situations in the country that gave him birth. He commenced his splendid career as an advocate, and realized £80,000 in his professional capacity. In 1774, this gentleman obtained the lucrative and honorable situation of provost of Trinity college, Dublin, and succeeded Philip Tisdale, esquire, as secretary of state. In return for the opulence acquired with his wife, he had now interest enough to ennoble that lady and her progeny, which consisted of no fewer than ten children, six sons and four daughters. Mr. Hutchinson was the second son, and it was therefore necessary that he should " push his fortune" in the world. He was sent to Eton, and afterwards returned to Trinity college, Dublin. Having discovered an early partiality to a military life, Mr. Hutchinson obtained a commission in the army. At the age of eighteen years, he was appointed to the 18th dragoons, as an officer of horse, and served successively in the 67th regiment of foot, and in the 77th Highlanders. Nor were any pains or expense wanting to qualify him for command, as he was sent to a military academy at Strasburgh, in order to obtain a knowledge of tactics under the best French masters. Having acquired considerable fluency in the language of our rival nation, Mr. Hutchinson frequently visited the continent. Considering the French camp as an instructive school of military knowledge, he was introduced to La Fayette, the commander of the revolutionary forces on the frontiers, immediately preceding the flight of that general from the army. At this period, however, he had obtained no higher rank than that of captain, in a regiment commanded by his relative, captain Crossby.

Mr. Hutchinson was scarcely of age, when he obtained a seat in the Irish parliament, having been returned a member for the city of Cork, so early as the year 1777, on the independent interest. In the prosecution of his parliamentary duty, he became a strenuous advocate of catholic emancipation, and of the union of the two kingdoms. The war that soon after ensued with

France, opened all the avenues to preferment. On this occasion, the family of the Hutchinsons was distinguished by its loyalty and zeal; for lord Donoughmore raised one regiment, and his brother, colonel Hutchinson, the subject of my narrative, was permitted to recruit and embody another.

At the commencement of the unhappy conflict in the sister kingdom, colonel Hutchinson took a manly and decided part in favor of the government; and, during the invasion under general Humbert, conducted himself like an active, able, and indefatigable officer He was second in command at the battle of Castlebar, and afterwards proceeded as a volunteer in the expedition to Holland, under sir Ralph Abercrombie, who appointed him to the situation of supernumerary *aid-de-camp*. In the second and last expedition to the same country, he served under the duke of York, with the rank of major-general, and was mentioned in the most honorable manner in the despatches of his royal highness. On the return of Abercrombie to England, and the equipment of an expedition to the shores of Egypt, general Hutchinson was recommended by his celebrated friend as an officer worthy of the confidence of government, and fully capable of seconding his efforts. He therefore embarked on the expedition as next in command.

The victory of the 21st of March, though productive of some immediate advantage, was far from securing the possession of Egypt to the conquerors. Confirmed success alone could give confidence to the timid natives, who feared the vengeful fury of the French, and remembered the horrors they had recently endured. Even 500 Turks, who had joined the British army, remained in the rear during the action; but, when the danger was over, they paraded on a small hill in front, with great ostentation. The battle of Alexandria had made but little alteration in the balance of force. The enemy continued to be greatly superior in numbers, and were in possession of the chief places of strength. When a proposal, therefore, of surrender, addressed by the naval and military com manders to the governor of Alexandria was disdainfully rejected, the British general entered methodically upon the requisite measures for wresting the country from the hands of the French. In this attempt he was materially favored by the impression which his late achievement had made on the mussulman powers. The terror of the French arms, which Buonaparte had endeavored to associate with a lively impression of the blessings to be derived from his friendship, was dissipated, when they were discovered not to be invincible. When that general told the sheiks and other inhabitants of the provinces of Gaza, Ramleh, and Jaffa, " it is proper you should know that all human efforts against me are vain, since all my enterprises must succeed. Those who declare themselves my enemies, perish :" when he kindly admonished them to profit by the examples of Jaffa and of Gaza, assuring them, that " if he was terrible to his enemies, he was kind towards his friends, and compassionate and merciful towards the poor people," they could not but feel the impressive influence of such declarations. But when the affairs of Acre and Alexandria had proved that the deliverer of Egypt was equally unfortunate as a general, and inhuman as a conqueror, the natives were easily excited to unite with the English in expelling their invaders. Some days after the victory of Alexandria, the capitan Pacha, who had a strong body of forces under his command, came, accompanied by lord Keith, to visit the English general in his camp. The grand vizier, who had remained motionless at Jaffa from the time of his disgraceful retreat from Cairo, advanced to Balbeis, to co-operate with the British forces in their movements ; and Osman Bey Tambourgi, in conformity with the dying injunctions of Murad Bey, whom he at this time succeeded in his principality, assured the commander-in-chief of his support.

When the general was concerting the means of accomplishing his grand purpose, contemplating the difficulties by which it must be attended, and anxious for the event, he was cheered with the intelligence

that a division of the forces which, with the assistance of the capitan Pacha, and the flotilla which sir Sidney Smith commanded in the Nile, had (May 1st,) reduced Rosetta, and this event was followed ten days after, by the reduction of fort Julien, which guards the entrance to the harbor. The possession of these places opened a free intercourse between the fleet and army, and the good disposition of the natives afforded the troops ample supplies of necessaries and provisions.

The reduction of Alexandria was one of the chief objects of the campaign. But as the siege of so strong a city was at present incompatible with the commander's general views, and as lord Keith had assured him that, after October, he could no longer remain off the coast with the shipping, he determined to reserve the capture of that city for his ultimate object, and in the mean time to proceed to the reduction of other places in the interior. Previous to his departure from his present position, a measure was adopted highly conducive to his final success. Alexandria is flanked on the south side by lake Mareotis, a great part of which, adjacent to the city, is a strand and generally passable on foot. This is parted from lake Aboukir, which has a communication with the sea only by a narrow neck or isthmus, along which passes the canal, from Alexandria to Ramanieh. The bed of lake Aboukir being several feet higher than that of Mareotis, by making a cut between them, the water from the former would be let into the latter : lake Mareotis would be brought to the walls of the city, and the duties of the besiegers would be diminished, by contracting the parts on which the garrison might be relieved. The practicability of this design was suggested in a letter from Menou, found in the pocket of general Roiz, who was killed in the late battle, expressing a fear that the measure would be adopted. The English general was prevailed upon with reluctance to execute an enterprise so injurious to the inhabitants of the city and its neighbourhood, but considerations of policy overpowered his scruples : the attempt was begun and executed in a short time, and the water rushing into lake Mareotis with a fall of six feet, soon inundated a large tract of cultivated land.

The commander-in-chief then proceeded with uninterrupted success in the prosecution of his military plans. In his subsequent operations, though his enemies were not inactive, yet their resistance was not to be compared with the difficulties and hardships which the troops endured from the excessive heat of the climate, the sultry siroc winds, and the torment of opthalmia, occasioned by the reflection of the burning soil, and by the light sand blown into their eyes. They had signalized themselves by their valor, and they were now to evince their patience of fatigue and misery by submitting to the severest sufferings without a possibility of relief, or the prospect of glory. But even in these struggles the British soldiers were not without some consolation from the admiration and gratitude expressed by the natives when they observed the strict order maintained among them, and their readiness to make a compensation for every kindness. "The British soldiers" says sir Robert Wilson "only required water; frequently even rewarding the trembling natives who brought it, and whose only hope had been to escape ill usage."

The general having completed his preparations, the fleet of lord Keith being strengthened with four ships from Warren's squadron, and the detachment which reduced Rosetta having with the assistance of sir Sidney Smith's flotilla captured the fortress of El Aft on the same branch of the Nile, the army advanced to the siege of Ramanieh, the situation of which, at the junction of the two arms of the Delta, rendered it a most desirable object; commanding the whole navigation of the Nile, and enabling him to cut off the communication by water between Cairo and Alexandria. The place was suffered to fall (May 9th) into the hands of the English general, after a defence by no means proportioned to its importance. It was indeed supposed, that the success of the British arms was much favored by the variance which had prevailed among the French generals since the appointment of Menou to the chief command. Such however was the effect of this acquisition that Menou and Belliard, the one of Alexandria and the other at Cairo, were entirely cut off from all intercourse with each other, and from the navigation of the Nile, while a free communication with the interior country was secured to the English army.

Grand Cairo was now the general's chief object. On their rout over the intervening sandy and trackless deserts, his troops were cheered by the intelligence that the grand vizier, assisted by a detachment under major Holloway, had gained a complete victory at El Hanca over a body of forces sent by Belliard to oppose his march from Balbeis, and had pursued the enemy to the plains of Heliopolis. This event and the capture of two valuable convoys on their progress, which afforded the army a supply of provisions and camels, with the intelligence of the surrender of fort Lesbé and of Damietta, animated the troops with sanguine hopes of the final success of the expedition. On the 23rd of May general Hutchinson had his first interview with the grand vizier at Menouf, about thirty miles north of Cairo. With that commander and the capitan Pacha, he concerted his plan for the reduction of the city, and being assured of the co-operation of the Mamelukes, by the arrival in his camp of several of the chief beys, among whom were Ibrahim, the rival of Murad, Osman Tambourgi, Mahomed Elfi, Hassan, and Osman Bardici, he lost not a moment in carrying it into execution. His designs were assisted by the landing of colonel Murray at Cossier, in the middle of May, with the first division of a corps from Bombay, commanded by general Baird. The inhabitants deserted in crowds, and even the nations of Asia, attracted by the prospect of plunder, entered Egypt in a hostile manner. All the resources of general Belliard, who had hastily returned to the city, were nearly exhausted, and he had formed a resolution to withdraw into Upper Egypt. In these perilous circumstances, general Belliard, as his last resource, sent a flag of truce to the English head-quarters. A conference immediately took place between generals Moran and Hope, and a capitulation was concluded, by which it was agreed that the French forces should be conveyed to the French ports in the Mediterranean, with their arms and effects, fifty days after the date of the ratification: men of letters, and naturalists, were permitted to retain their papers and collections, an exoneration was granted to such of the people as had adhered to the cause of France; and it was stipulated that Menou might avail himself of those conditions for the surrender of Alexandria, providing his acceptance of them was notified to the general commanding before Alexandria, ten days from the date of the communication being made to him.

When this capitulation was made known to Menou, he refused to accede to conditions which he regarded as disgraceful, because he did not believe them to be necessary; and in this opinion he was supported by generals Rampon and Friant, and the unanimous resolution of the council of war. His garrison consisted of 9000 men, including the sailors and members of the civil administration, who had all taken up arms. The intrenched camp was secure from a coup-de-main, and defended the approaches to the city, the fortifications of which were likewise increased and strengthened. As soon as general Hutchinson had expedited the march of Belliard's troops from Cairo; he moved towards Alexandria, where all his reinforcements from England, Minorca, and Malta, had already arrived. The army from Bombay, consisting of 4000 men, under the command of general Baird, was also on its rout to the same quarter. Menou's works towards the east side of the town, where the British were encamped, were very formidable, and scarcely to be approached on account of the narrowness of the space between the lake and the sea, and the nature of the ground: but they were less strong towards the west. The besieging army occupied lines from the sea to the lake Mareotis, upon which, on the southern-side, the town was closely blockaded, by more than 120 gun-boats,

besides the English fleet, and nearly all the men of war and shipping of the Turkish empire, lying off the port. Yet so unpromising was the operation, that general Hutchinson, in a despatch of the 19th of August, only eight days before the conference for a capitulation, says, " I cannot, on the whole, flatter myself that Alexandria will be in our possession in a short time, unless some event takes place, of which we are not at present aware."

Menou had calculated, but unwarrantably, that Cairo would have been able to hold out at least two months and a half longer, during which Alexandria might have been provisioned, and its defences completed, while topical diseases thinned the enemy's ranks. He hoped, that Egypt might, by these means, be still preserved to the republic: but the fall of the capital disappointed his expectations, and precipitated his fate. What he ought to have long ago anticipated and provided against, he now began to experience. He wanted forage for his horses, medicines for the sick, and subsistence for all: his fresh water was exhausted, without the possibility of a supply either for the garrison or the inhabitants: the inundations had rendered the place unhealthy: the number of his troops was inadequate to the defence of the intrenchments, forts, and town; and their extreme fatigue from continual duty promoted diseases, and discouraged their exertions. All the avenues, by which provisions and assistance could be received, were, to use the expression of the council of war, hermetically stopped up; while, in every action, the troops were attacked in front by the allied army towards the land, and on flank and rear by an immense number of gun-boats, bomb-vessels, and other craft, the fire of which carried from sea to sea.

On the 17th the operations of the besiegers became more active. Availing himself of the inundation, major-general Coote landed with a strong corps to the westward of Alexandria without any opposition, and immediately invested the strong castle of Marabout at the entrance of the western harbor. At the same time two corps were detached, on the east side of the town, to get possession of some heights in front of the enemy's intrenched position. The fort of Marabout, after sustaining for two days the attack of general Coote with open batteries, and an equally vigorous one from several Turkish corvettes and small vessels of the British fleet, was surrendered by its garrison, which consisted only of 180 men. After this success, general Coote endeavored to gain the approaches to the town; and on the morning of the 26th, four batteries were opened on each side of it against the French camp. Considerable advances were made by the besiegers, when Menou, finding all his efforts fruitless, sent an aid-de-camp to desire an armistice for three days, which was granted him. He would willingly have renewed it, but general Hutchinson declared that he would recommence hostilities if an answer to certain proposals now transmitted were not instantly given. A capitulation was then concluded; the garrison, consisting of 10,528 men, surrendered, and 312 pieces of artillery were found in the fortifications.

Articles of the capitulation proposed by Abdoullahy Jacques François Menou, general-in-chief of the French army now in Alexandria, to the generals commanding the land and sea forces of his Britannic majesty, and of the Sublime Porte, forming the blockade of Alexandria, dated the 12th Fructidor, 9th year of the French republic, (30th of August 1801.)

Article I. From the present date to the 30th Fructidor, (17th of September, 1801,) there shall be a continuation of the truce and suspension of arms between the French army and the combined armies of his Britannic majesty and the Sublime Porte, upon the same conditions with those which actually subsist, with the exception of a regulation, to be amicably settled between the respective generals of the two armies, for establishing a new line of advanced posts, in order to remove all pretext of hostility between the troops.

Answer.—Refused.

II. In case no adequate succours shall arrive to the French army before the day mentioned in the preceding article, that army shall evacuate the forts and intrenched camp of Alexandria upon the following conditions.

Answer.—Refused.

III. The French army shall retire, on the first complementary day of the French æra, into the city of Alexandria and forts adjacent, and shall deliver up to the allied powers the intrenched camp in front of the lines of the Arabs, the fort Le Turc, and the fort Du Vivier, together with their artillery and ammunition.

Answer.—In forty-eight hours after the signing of the capitulation, namely, on the 2nd of September at noon, the intrenched camps, the fort Turc, and that of Du Vivier, shall be delivered up to the allied powers. The ammunition and artillery of these forts shall be also delivered up. The French troops shall evacuate the city, forts, and dependencies of Alexandria, ten days after signing the capitulation, or at the time of their embarkation.

IV. All individuals, constituting a part of the French army, or attached to it by any relations, military or civil: the auxiliary troops of every nation, country, or religion; or of whatever powers they might have been subjects before the arrival of the French, shall preserve their property of every description, effects, papers, &c. which shall not be subject to any examination.

Answer.—Granted, provided that nothing be carried away belonging to the government of the French republic, but only the effects, baggage, and other articles belonging to the French, and auxiliary soldiers who have served during six months in the army of the republic: the same is to be understood of all the individuals attached to the French army, in civil or military capacities, of whatever nation, country, or religion they may be.

V. The French forces, the auxiliary troops, and all the individuals described in the preceding article, shall be embarked in the ports of Alexandria, between the 5th and the 10th of Vendemiaire, 10th year of the republic, at the latest, (27th of September and 3rd of October, 1801;)

together with their arms, stores, baggage, effects, and property of all kinds, official papers, and deposits, one field-piece to each battalion and squadron, with ammunition, &c.; the whole to be conveyed to one of the ports of the French republic in the Mediterranean, to be determined by the general-in-chief of the French army.

Answer.—The French forces, the auxiliary troops, and all the individuals described in the fourth article, shall be embarked in the ports of Alexandria, unless, after an amicable convention, it should be found more expeditious to embark a part of them at Aboukir, as soon as vessels can be prepared, the allied powers at the same time engaging that the embarkation shall take place, if possible, ten days after the capitulation shall be signed. They shall receive all the honors of war, shall carry away their arms and baggage, shall not be prisoners of war, and shall moreover, take with them ten pieces of cannon from four to eight-pounders, with ten rounds of shot to each gun; they shall be conveyed to a French port in the Mediterranean

VI. The French ships of war, with their full complement, and all merchant-ships, to whatever nation or individuals they may belong, even those of nations at war with the allied powers, or those which are the property of owners or merchants who were subject to the allied powers before the arrival of the French, shall depart with the French army, in order that the ships of war may be restored to the French government, and the merchant-vessels to the owners, or their assignees.

Answer.—Refused. All ships shall be delivered up as they are.

VII. Every single ship, which, after the present day to the 30th Fructidor, shall arrive from the French republic, or any of her allies, into the ports or road of Alexandria, shall be comprehended in this capitulation. Every ship of war or commerce, belonging to France, or the allies of the republic, shall arrive in the ports or road of Alexandria, within the twenty days immediately following the evacuation of the place, shall not be considered a lawful prize, but shall be set at liberty, with her

equipage and cargo, and furnished with a passport from the allied powers.

Answer.—Refused.

VIII. The French and auxiliary troops, the civil and military agents attached to the army, and all other individuals described in the preceding articles, shall be embarked on board such French and other vessels, presently in the port of Alexandria, as shall be in a condition to go to sea; or on board those of his Britannic majesty and of the Sublime Porte, within the time fixed by the fifth article.

IX. Commissaries shall be named by each party to regulate the number of vessels to be employed, the number of men to be embarked upon them, and generally to provide for all the difficulties that may arise in carrying into execution the present capitulation.

These commissaries shall agree upon the different positions which shall be taken by the ships now in the port of Alexandria, and those which shall be furnished by the allied powers, so that, by a well regulated arrangement, every occasion of difference between the crews of the several nations may be avoided.

Answer.—All these details will be regulated by the English admiral, and by an officer of the French navy named by the general-in-chief.

X. Merchants and owners of ships, of whatever nation or religion they may be, and also the inhabitants of Egypt, and of every other country, who may at the present time be in Alexandria, whether Syrians, Cophts, Greeks, Arabs, Jews, &c. and who shall be desirous of following the French army, shall be embarked, and enjoy the same advantages, with that army; they shall be at liberty to remove their property of all kinds, and to leave powers for the disposal of what they may not be able to take away. All arrangements, sales, and stipulations, whether of commerce, or of any other nature, made by them, shall be strictly carried into effect after their departure, and be maintained by the generals of his Britannic majesty and the Sublime Porte. Those who may prefer remaining in Egypt a certain time, on account of their private affairs, shall be at liberty to do so, and shall have full protection from the allied powers ; and those also who may be desirous of establishing themselves in Egypt, shall be entitled to all the privileges and rights, of which they were in possession before the arrival of the French.

Answer.—Every article of merchandise, whether in the town of Alexandria, or on board the vessels that are in the ports, shall be provisionally at the disposal of the allied powers, but subject to such definitive regulation as may be determined by established usage and the law of nations. Private merchants shall be at liberty to accompany the French army, or they may remain in the country in security.

XI. None of the inhabitants of Egypt, or of any other nation or religion, shall be called to account for their conduct during the time the French troops have been in the country, particularly for having taken up arms in their favor, or having been employed by them.

Answer.—Granted.

XII. The troops, and all others who may be embarked with them, shall be fed during their passage, and until their arrival in France, at the expense of the allied powers, and conformably to the rules of the French navy. The allied powers shall supply every thing that may be necessary for the embarkation.

Answer.—The troops, and all others who may be embarked with them, shall be fed during their passage, and until their arrival in France, at the expense of the allied powers, according to the usage established in the marine of England.

XIII. The consuls, and all other public agents of the several powers in alliance with the French republic, shall continue in the enjoyment of the privileges and rights which are granted by civilized nations to diplomatic agents. Their property, effects, and papers, shall be respected, and placed under the protection of the allied powers. They shall be at liberty to retire or to remain as they may think fit.

Answer.—The consuls, and all other public agents of the powers in alliance with the French republic, shall be at liberty to remain or retire as they may judge fit. Their property and effects of any kind, together with their papers, shall be preserved for them, provided they conduct themselves with loyalty, and conformably to the law of nations.

XIV. The sick, who may be judged by the medical staff of the army to be in a state for removal, shall be embarked at the same time with the army, upon hospital ships properly furnished with medicines, provisions, and every other store that may be necessary for their situation ; and they shall be attended by French surgeons. Those of them, who may not be in a condition to undertake the voyage, shall be delivered over to the care and humanity of the allied powers. French physicians and other medical assistance shall be left for their care, to be maintained at the expense of the allied powers, who shall send them to France as soon as their state of health may permit, together with every thing belonging to them, in the same manner as has been proposed for the army.

Answer.—Granted. The ships destined for hospitals shall be prepared for the reception of those, who may fall sick during the passage. The medical staff of the two armies shall concert together in what manner to dispose of those sick, who, having contagious disorders, ought not to have communication with the others.

XV. Horse-transports for conveying 60 horses, with every thing necessary for their subsistence during the passage, shall be furnished.

Answer.—Granted.

XVI. The individuals composing the Institute of Egypt, and the Commission of Arts, shall carry with them all the papers, plans, memoirs, collections of natural history, and monuments of art and antiquity, collected by them in Egypt.

Answer.—The members of the Institute may carry with them all the instruments of art and science, which they have brought from France; but the Arabian manuscripts, the statues, and other collections which have been made for the French republic, shall be considered as public property, and subject to the disposal of the generals of the combined armies.

General Hope having declared, in consequence of some observations of the commander-in-chief of the French army, that he could make no alteration in this article, it has been agreed that a reference thereupon shall be made to the commander-in-chief of the combined army.

XVII. The vessels which may be employed in conveying the French and auxiliary army, as well as the different persons who accompany it, shall be escorted by ships of war belonging to the allied powers, who formally engage that they shall not in any manner, be molested during their voyage. The safety of such vessels as may be separated by stress of weather, or other accidents, shall be guaranteed by the generals of the allied forces: the vessels conveying the French army shall not, under any pretence, touch at any other than the French coast, except in case of absolute necessity.

Answer.—Granted; the commander-in-chief of the French army entering into a reciprocal engagement that none of these vessels shall be molested during their stay in France, or on their return; and also engaging that they shall be furnished with every thing which may be necessary, according to the constant practice of European powers.

XVIII. At the time of giving up the camps and forts, according to the terms of the third article, the prisoners in Egypt shall be respectively given up on both sides.

Answer.—Granted.

XIX. Commissioners shall be named to receive the artillery of the place and of the forts, stores, magazines, plans, and other articles which the French leave to the allied powers; and lists, and inventories shall be made out, signed by the commissaries of the different powers, according as the forts and magazines shall be given up to the allied powers.

Answer.—Granted; provided that all the plans of the city and forts of Alexandria, as well as all maps of the country, shall be delivered up to the English commissary. The batteries, cisterns, and other public

buildings, shall also be given up in the condition in which they actually are.

XX. A passport shall be granted to a French armed vessel in order to convey to Toulon, immediately after the camps and forts before-mentioned shall be given up, officers charged by the commander-in-chief to carry to his government the present capitulation.

Answer.—Granted: but if it is a French vessel, it shall not be armed.

XXI. On giving up the camps and forts mentioned in the preceding articles, hostages shall be given on both sides, in order to guarantee the execution of the present treaty. They shall be chosen from among the officers of rank in the respective armies: namely, four from the French army, two from the British troops, and two from the troops of the Sublime Porte. The four French hostages shall be embarked on board the English ship commanding the hostages, and the four British and Turkish squadron, on board one of the vessels which shall carry the commander-in-chief or the lieutenant-generals. They shall all be reciprocally delivered up on their arrival in France.

Answer.—There shall be placed in the hands of the commander-in-chief of the French army, four officers of rank as hostages; namely one officer of the navy, one officer of the British army, and two officers of the Turkish army. The commander-in-chief shall, in like manner, place in the hands of the commander-in-chief of the British army four officers of rank. The hostages shall be restored on both sides at the period of the embarkation.

XXII. If any difficulties should arise during the execution of the present capitulation, they shall be amicably settled by the commissaries of the armies.

Answer.—Granted.

KEITH, Admiral.
J. HELY HUTCHINSON, Lieutenant-General, Commander-in-chief.
ABBDOULLAHY JACQUES FRANCOIS MENOU, General-in-chief of the French army.
HUSSEIN, Capitan Pacha.

Such was the termination of the campaign in Egypt, so glorious to the British arms, and so gratifying to the hopes and wishes of the nation. Honors were liberally bestowed on the army and navy collectively. A monument was voted to the memory of sir Ralph Abercrombie; a peerage to his widow, and a pension of £2000 per annum. Major-general Hutchinson was first invested with the order of the Bath, together with the rank of lieutenant-general in the Mediterranean, and subsequently created a British peer, with a pension of £2000 per annum. Proportionate rewards were conferred on the other individuals who had been distinguished for their skill, good fortune, or bravery. Under all the circumstances, it cannot be denied that the victors had fully merited these testimonies of national approbation. Though the employment of the British army was on some occasions injudicious from the unavoidable ignorance of the commander-in-chief, and impatience in the subordinate generals, yet in the field they uniformly discomfited the enemy whether in large parties or in small, notwithstanding the great superiority of the latter in local knowledge, in cavalry, in habituation to the climate, and frequently in numbers. Nor was their forbearance as men, less conspicuous than their bravery as soldiers. They alleviated the distresses inevitably attendant on warfare, by the exercise of the nobler but less splendid virtues, and while they commanded the respect and confidence of the natives by their prowess, they cultivated and secured their attachment by the humanity of their general deportment.

By the issue of the campaign in Egypt, Buonaparte was completely foiled in his intended colonization of that country, and in all the plans of eastern conquest to which his success might have led. The result of the battle of Copenhagen, and the change of councils which had taken place at the court of St. Petersburgh, in consequence of the death of the emperor Paul, had dissipated the sanguine hopes which he had founded on the success of the northern confederacy. The French nation, though it dared not resist the conscriptions and taxes levied for the prosecution of the war, which became annually more burdensome, as their external resources became scanty and precarious, were ardently desirous of peace. Buonaparte therefore who had made his way to the supreme power by his warlike achievements, whose reputation in the present situation of Europe, might be diminished by the continuance of hostilities, but could not be increased, whose prospect of ascending the throne depended on conciliating and securing the favorable opinion of the people, and *whose passions were yet in subservience to his reason*, was not less anxious for the return of peace, than the British ministry. Many personal obstacles to negotiation were removed by the appointment of a cabinet to which he could advance no real or apparent objection, which had borne no other part in the war than that of carrying it on with the same energy as had distinguished their predecessors; and who had readily acceded to the first propositions of M. Otto. The correspondence was conducted with the utmost secresy, and the despatches were forwarded by Mr. Merry, who was sent to Paris as envoy extraordinary for that purpose. Intelligence arrived in London on the 2nd of October, that the preliminaries of a treaty between his Britannic majesty and the French republic, had been signed at Paris on the preceding day by lord Hawkesbury on the part of the British, and M. Otto on the part of the French government. The treaty obliged Great Britain to restore to the republic and its allies, all possessions and colonies occupied or conquered during the war, except the island of Trinidad, and the Dutch possessions in Ceylon. The Cape of Good Hope was to be a free port, and Malta to be restored to the order: but for the purpose of securing its independence, it was to be placed under the guarantee and protection of a third power, to be agreed on in the definitive treaty. Egypt was to be restored to the Porte. The possessions of the queen of Portugal were to remain entire: the French to evacuate Naples and the Roman states, and the English to relinquish Porto Ferrajo, and all islands and ports which they occupied in the Mediterranean, or the Adriatic. The French were to acknowledge the republic of the seven isles, and all sequestrations laid in either country on the subjects of the other power, were to be removed.

Such were the principal articles of the treaty on which any observations would only anticipate the discussions of the ensuing year. After the preliminaries had been ratified at Paris, general Lauriston was employed to convey them to London. On his arrival, the most violent joy was manifested by the populace : his horses were taken from his carriage by the rabble ; and a general illumination took place with the usual demonstrations of resentment against those who refused to concur in the general expressions of satisfaction.

The marquis of Cornwallis was appointed minister plenipotentiary on behalf of Great Britain, to attend a congress, which it was understood would assemble at Amiens, for the purpose of arranging a definitive treaty with all the nations against which England had been engaged. Commerce, in the meantime resumed its rights, captures at sea were discontinued, and, before the end of the year, the intercourse of Great Britain with France, Holland, and Flanders, was restored to its usual channels.

3 Y 2

HISTORY OF THE WAR.

CHAP. XXXIII.

A Succinct and Connected History of the Island of St. Domingo, from the Year 1791 to the Middle of the Year 1802; intended as preparatory to a Narration of the Rise, Progress, and Establishment of the Empire of Hayti.

IN narrating the occurrences connected with the history of the West Indian islands, the author has been chiefly guided by a consideration of their relative importance to the affairs of Europe. The history of St. Domingo, however, demands the peculiar attention of the annalist, as tending to record and to develope the origin, progress, and establishment of a West Indian empire, which may hereafter obtain a decided influence over the interests and policy of its parent nations.

The affairs of St. Domingo began to claim the attention of the French government so early as the year 1791. The inhabitants of this island and other West India settlements, are of three descriptions, —1st, Pure whites.—2nd, People of colour, who are a mixture of the whites and blacks, and blacks of free condition.—3rd, Negroes in a state of slavery.—Of these the whites were estimated, in 1789, at 30,000. The people of colour at 24,000; and the negroes in a state of slavery, at 480,000.

There were causes of dissatisfaction in the condition and circumstances of all these descriptions. Of these they became more sensible, when the works of the French philosophers, which were industriously dispersed through the islands, had awakened the people to a sense of their grievances: and they became more restless when the revolution in the English provinces had afforded an example of colonists who had rendered themselves independent of the parent state. But it was the French revolution which had the greatest influence in exciting the insurrection of the country. When the inhabitants of St. Domingo were informed of the successful revolt of the advocates of freedom in the mother-country, they began immediately to be desirous of participating with them in their enjoyments: and, when the white people were informed that the French nation had assumed, in effect, almost the whole of that authority, which had been formerly exercised by the crown, they became impatient of a government in which the whole power, even that of enacting laws, was vested in the governer-general and the intendant. When the people of colour were told " that it had been declared by a solemn decree, that all men are born and continue free and equal as to rights," they no longer submitted patiently to a disparity of privileges, or to deprivations which reduced them to a condition little preferable to that of slaves. The negroes heard with avidity the sentiments and exhortations of those who told them that a difference of colour was not intended by nature to be accompanied with a difference of condition ; that no reason could possibly be adduced why liberty should be enjoyed by one person and slavery inflicted on another ; that they were an injured race, and that it concerned them to avail themselves of their superior numbers to obtain redress:

It could not be expected that tranquillity

would be long enjoyed in a country where the seeds of discontent and rebellion were sown in the minds of all the different classes of the inhabitants; where each class aspired to privileges which were incompatible with their condition and political circumstances. While St. Domingo existed in the subordinate state of a colony, it was impossible that even the white inhabitants could enjoy precisely the same privileges with the inhabitants of France; nor was it compatible with the relative circumstances of the other classes, that they should be admitted to the same privileges with the whites. But when the love of liberty was become a rage, when all men were declared to be born equal as to rights, and the French government was calling on all men to assert their claims to this equality, it was reasonable to expect that its own colonists, taking the expression abstractedly, would carry the meaning of it to its utmost extent, and would not rest satisfied with only a portion of those natural and social privileges, to the whole of which they were told, they had a well-founded and indisputable claim.

The demeanor of the St. Domingans appears to have been the natural result of these sentiments. In the year 1789, the provincial assemblies of the island, unanimously declared their opinion of the necessity of a full and speedy colonial representation. The ensuing year a *General Colonial Assembly* was held at St. Marks, where the pretensions of the St. Domingans were notified in a decree which manifested a spirit inconsistent with subordination to the French legislature.

The islanders were therefore instantly divided between the adherents of the Colonial Assembly, whose party comprised a great majority of the whites, and the mulattoes, or people of colour, countenanced by Peynier, the governor-general, and the chevalier Mauduit, commandant of the troops. A civil war was on the point of breaking out, when the members of the General Assembly adopted the resolution of embarking for France,
August 8th, 1790. there to justify their conduct to the king and the National Assembly.

§The state of affairs in France was very unfavorable to their design, which was that of conciliating the support of government to the establishment of the authority which they declared themselves to be invested with. A society had been formed at Paris, under the *denomination of amis de noirs*, or friends of the blacks, by those who were desirous to extend liberty equally to every description of the human race. The ruling faction, headed by Petion, Brissot, and Robespierre, professed these principles. And, by their influence, a decree was passed, May 15th, 1791. "that the people of colour resident in the French colonies, born of free parents, were entitled as of right, to all the privileges of French citizens, and, among others, to those of having votes in the choice of representatives, and of being eligible to seats both in the parochial and colonial assemblies."

The consequences of this measure were such as might have been expected to result from it. The mulattoes, headed by Oge, an enthusiastic advocate for the new opinions relative to an equality of rights, had rebelled in the preceding year. But they had been subdued; and their leader, who had fled to the Spaniards for refuge, had been delivered up by them and executed. They had before been notorious for their oppression of the negroes. But, when informed of their late decree, and of the general bent of the public opinion in favor of equalization of rights, they associated themselves with them, and, breathing vengeance against the whites, rose in arms, and murdered all who fell into their hands, committing such cruelties and devastations during two months, that it was computed that, "in that short space, 2000 white people had been massacred—that between 10,000 and 12,000 of the insurgents perished by the sword, by disease, or by famine—that 180 sugar plantations, and 900 of coffee, cotton, and indigo settlements, had been destroyed—and 1200 Christian families reduced from a state of opulence to depend altogether for their clothing and sustenance on public and private charity."

The evils brought on the community by popular fury at last provided a temporary remedy for themselves. When the rage of the mulattoes had spent itself, and they saw the horrid effects of that anarchy which they were introducing, they appear to have been shocked at the savage barbarities which they had themselves occasioned. They made overtures for a reconciliation with the white people; which being readily accepted by the planters, the general assembly agreed to the decree of the national convention of France, by which (September 20th) the people of colour were admitted to a free participation of privileges with themselves.

The friends of peace were now cheered with the prospect of enjoying that blessing. But the subsequent events proved how delusive were their hopes, how unpropitious the present circumstances of the French colonists, and the state of the mother country to their expectations. When it was represented to the French governments in the early petitions of those who were interested in the trade and plantations of St. Domingo, that their ruin was inevitable, unless means were immediately adopted for checking the progress of civil war, they opened their eyes to the ill tendency of their own measure. And, not being apprised of the compromise which had taken place between the planters and the mulattoes, they repealed the decree which had been represented as so obnoxious to the latter, at the instant when the confirmation of it by the colonial assembly was made the terms of reconciliation.

This hasty proceeding by a legislature that was soon to be dissolved, and wished to recommend themselves to the esteem of the nation, by an act which they thought would be received with gratitude, rekindled the flames of civil war. When intelligence of the repeal arrived in the West Indies, the mulattoes supposing that the planters had only deceived them with a false shew of amity, whilst they had been treacherously employed in procuring this act, instantly flew to arms, declaring that they were determined to avenge their wrongs by exterminating the white people, or to perish in the attempt. The consequences of this insurrection were dreadful in the extreme. A pitched battle was fought in a district called Cul de Sac, in which 2000 mulattoes and negroes were slain. But the slaughter in the field though more destructive, was not so horrible, or so repugnant to all the feelings of human nature, as the acts of atrocity which mutual abhorrence and a remorseless spirit of revenge suggested to the different parties.

Three commissioners from the French convention were despatched from St. Domingo, in the autumn to re-establish good order by conciliatory means. But the evils bade defiance to their endeavors: and the island continued a scene of civil hostilities, during the remainder of this year.

In this calamitous state were the French West India settlements when the faction headed by Danton, Robespierre, and Marat, had acquired a complete ascendency in the government. These tyrant-democrats founded their power on their professed love of liberty. Robespierre had declared in the national assembly that " He had rather that the colonies should perish than sacrifice one iota of his principles."

Consistently with these principles they now effected the abrogation of 1792 the act of repeal, and caused a decree to be passed, by which, among other things, " the national assembly acknowledged and declared that the people of colour and free negroes ought to enjoy an equality of political rights with the whites."

In pursuance of this measure of government, Messieurs Sauthonax, Polverel, and Ailhaud, three violent Jacobins, were sent as commissioners to St. Domingo, with 8000 men to unite with Monsieur Desparbes, as commander-in-chief, in carrying the decree into execution.

From the moment of their arrival in the island, turbulence and civil war gave place to oppression. It was feared by the planters that a general emancipation of slaves was meditated. But whatever were the intentions or powers of the commissioners, it was not thought adviseable to carry it into execution at this moment. And to remove the apprehensions of the planters, they declared that "Their views extended no further than to see the decree of the 4th of April, in favor of the free people of colour, properly enforced, to reduce the slaves in rebellion to obedience, and to settle the future government and tranquillity of the colony on a solid and permanent foundation."

It was soon evinced, however, that a system of tyranny was to be established worthy of the delegates of that hateful triumvirate under whom they acted. Having secured the troops by largesses and conciliated the attachment of the mulattoes, they proceeded to practise the rankest oppression, under colour of punishing an infringement of liberty. By their ascendency in what was denominated *une commission intermediaire*, which was substituted for the colonial assembly, they levied money on the inhabitants, and disposed of it as they thought proper. They arrested Desparbes and sent him prisoner to France, because he would not submit to be made the tool of their power. And four members out of six whites, who composed a moiety of the commission intermediaire, were doomed to the same punishment on a similar account. In the mean time, offenders of less note were punished for their opposition to their plans with the arbitrary confiscation of their effects.

When Monsieur Galbaud, a military man of respectable character, arrived at St. Domingo in 1793, to take the government in the room of Desparbes, some hopes were entertained by the white people that they might be relieved from the oppression of the commissioners, and they were confirmed in their expectations by the conduct of Galbaud, and his declaration that h should not consider himself as dependent on the commissioners, or bound to enforce their proclamations.—Such a declaration which portended embarrassment to the schemes of oppression and peculation, which the commissioners were carrying on, could not but be highly offensive to them.

A violent altercation ensued. The commissioners insisted that Galbaud was disqualified for his appointment, according to a decree of the national assembly, by his being possessed of a plantation in the island, and ordered him to return to France.

The governor being determined to maintain the validity of his commission, the contest was referred to the sword. After repeated contests between the partisans on each side, the negroes came to the support of the commissioners, and suddenly entering St. Domingo, they murdered, indiscriminately, men, women, and children, and set fire to the city, more than half of which was soon consumed. Fortunately for Galbaud, and his partisans, they had embarked on board their vessels in the harbor before the irruption of this savage army.

At this crisis the war assumed a different aspect. Many of the fugitive whites taking refuge in St. Domingo, offered to throw themselves under the protection of his Britannic majesty, and requested that an armament might be sent to take possession of the island, and receive the allegiance of the people. An agent was in consequence despatched from the English court with orders to general Williamson, the governor of Jamaica, to accept the proffered capitulation, and to send what troops he could spare to protect the British partisans.

It soon, however, appeared that the representations of the fugitives respecting the general disposition of the St. Domingan proprietors, as it too frequently happens on such occasions, were the result, not of well-founded information, but of their own sanguine wishes. The commissioners were at this time supported by 25,000 regulars, militia, and armed mulattoes. On intelligence of the projected invasion, they adopted the desperate expedient of reinforcing themselves by a general emancipation of the slaves. This measure decided the fate of St. Domingo. Many of the negroes thought it advisable to attach themselves to their masters and share their fortunes. A few only were seen to join the standard of the commissioners. The remainder computed to amount to above 100,000, escaping to their fastnesses among the woods and mountains subsisted like the wild Caribbees of St. Vincent's, on what they could get by hunting, and the plunder of the adjoining districts.

Such was the state of St. Domingo when colonel Whitlocke arrived with the first division of British troops, consisting only of 677 men, to receive the capitulation of the St. Domingans. He received the allegiance of the inhabitants of St. Jeremie; and the garrison at the mole of St. Nicholas surrendered to him. But this small success was followed by a series of unpropitious occurrences. When he undertook an expedition for the reduction of the neighbouring fort of Tiburon, Duval, his partisan, who promised to reinforce him with 500 men, did not make his appearance, and he was, in consequence, obliged to retreat with the loss of 20 men. The autumnal rains setting in, interrupted their operations; and the yellow fever made dreadful havoc among the troops. The destruction which surrounded the remainder, was sufficient to appal the bravest men. Yet general Williamson, as the only means to protect such of the inhabitants as had declared for Great Britain, despatched a second division, amounting to about 700 or 800 men, on this hopeless enterprise; and, on their arrival at the close of the year, the inhabitants of the small towns of Jean Rabell, St. Marc, Arcahaye, Boucassin, and Leogane, swore allegiance to his Britannic majesty.

The British general, strengthened with the troops which had arrived in the autumn, resumed the design of reducing Cape Tiburon, the possession of which was deemed essential to the conquest of the southern peninsula of St. Domingo, as Cape St. Nicholas was to that of the northern. This was happily accomplished, with the loss of only three men on the part of the assailants. L'Acul, a fortress near Leogane, was afterwards surrendered to the British troops; an acquisition of the greater importance, on account of its vicinity to Port au Prince, which was now the general's grand object. This was followed by an attempt on Fort Bompard, a strong post, fifteen miles from

1794.

Cape St. Nicholas. But here the British troops experienced a reverse of fortune. The same valor was displayed by them as in other enterprises; but they were overpowered by numbers, and forced to retreat.

A vigorous attempt made by the enemy, under general Rigaud, for the recovery of Cape Tiburon, was defeated by the firmness of the garrison, but with a loss of men which was severely felt at a time when there were not above 900 effective men in the island.

April 16th.

In the month of May, general Whyte arrived with three regiments, to take the command. The expedition against Port au Prince was then undertaken. The value of this fortress, on account of its local advantages, being situated at the bottom of the vast bay, enclosed between Capes Tiburon and St. Nicholas, was enhanced by the magazines which it contained. It was strongly garrisoned and well secured by artillery. But fort Bizottou, on which it chiefly depended for defence, was carried sword in hand, by the exemplary bravery of a detachment employed in its attack. After that, the town itself surrendered, and 22 top-sail vessels, laden with merchandise, valued at £400,000, together with other effects, became the reward of the victors.

June 4th.

With this achievement the good fortune of the British arms terminated. General Whyte being disabled by ill health, was succeeded in the command by general Horneck, and a small reinforcement was sent, some months after his arrival, to the remains of his army. But they came only to witness the terrible destruction made by disease among the troops which had demeaned themselves so gallantly, against the enemy, and at last to yield to the same dreadful scourge themselves. No further enterprise could now be undertaken: our partisans began to grow disaffected to a cause which wore so inauspicious an aspect: the planters, who had stood aloof, intending to be determined by events, now became hostile: the fortresses of Jean Rabell and St. Marc, were

September.

lost by defection; and the events of this year were closed with the reduction of Tiburon by the French forces under Rigaud.

1795. The war was still prosecuted in St. Domingo, though the British forces were constrained by necessity, to act chiefly on the defensive. Sir Adam Williamson, whom his majesty had appointed governor-general and 'commander-in-chief in the island, arriving in the month of May, prepared to make every exertion for the maintenance of the British interests. These were, however, at this time, in a state bordering on despair. The English troops in the month of January, amounted only to 1490 men. They were reinforced with 1400 men from England, in the month of April. But the whole of the force then in the island was not by competent judges deemed sufficient for the defence of the fortress of Port au Prince alone. In the mean time, every day afforded melancholy evidences of the baneful consequences of war carried on by Europeans in this climate, where its own calamities lose their terrors when compared with the sickness, and the devouring pestilence with which it is accompanied.

A most severe and unusual burden was imposed on the soldiers. They were compelled, with but little intermission, to dig the ground in the day, and to perform military duty in the night; exposed, in the one case, to the burning rays of the sun, in the other to the noxious dews and heavy rains of the climate. Such extraordinary and excessive labor imposed on men, most of whom had been actually confined six months on ship-board, without fresh provisions or exercise: the malignancy of the air co-operating, produced its natural consequences. They dropped like the leaves of autumn, until at length the garrison became so diminished and enfeebled, that the deficiencies of the guards were frequently made up from convalescents, who were scarcely able to stand under their arms. In 1797, the French forces under general Rigaud made a vigorous effort to recover those places which were

in possession of the planters, who had thrown themselves under the protection of Great Britain, and were guarded by English troops. He invested Trois, a strong place which had lately fallen into their hands, but was repulsed by the small garrison which defended it. Returning to a second and more furious assault, he was again repulsed by the garrison, aided by captain Ricketts, in the Magicienne frigate, and was, in the event, obliged to retire with the loss of 1000 men. But the successes of this description tended only to retard the ultimate evacuation of the island by the British army. The combined army of French and Indians was now confided to the command of Touissaint Louverture, a negro, and a native of St. Domingo. He was born a slave. His master, a rich planter, carried him to France when young, and, as he discovered a good understanding, more attention was paid to his education than usual. He returned to St. Domingo, where he still continued a slave, till the troubles commenced. Amidst the events of the revolution, Touissaint discovered his talents on many occasions. At last he was selected by his brethren to command a black army of 100,000 men, accustomed to the climate, and by this time inured to war. To the talents of a general and politician, Touissaint joined more valuable qualities, moderation, gratitude, and humanity. Although he was, in reality, absolute monarch of St. Domingo, he concluded, after repeated advantages over the British troops, a treaty with general Maitland, not as an independent chief, but, in the name of the French republic. The English general agreed to evacuate the island, and to leave the forts then in his possession, in perfect order, on condition that Touissaint should guarantee the lives and properties of all the inhabitants who might choose to remain. Elated by success, and sensible of the ascendancy which he enjoyed among the negroes, Touissaint now determined to relieve them from oppression. This object, however, he was desirous to accomplish without violence; anxious only to be considered as a citizen of,

France, and to be continued in the command by the appointment of the French government.

Early in the year 1800, he addressed a letter to the civil and military authorities, and the French citizens of the southern department, inviting those who had revolted against the government, to return to their obedience, by the most liberal offers of pardon. He communicated, at the same time, a letter which he had received from the French minister of the marine and colonies, informing him of the revolution which had occurred, and of the good disposition of the first consul towards him. He convoked a meeting of deputies from the departments, and, with their concurrence, drew up a constitution for the colony. The ambition of Touissaint, so long disguised, was first developed in an article, declaring that St. Domingo was subject to its own laws only : an article which rendered merely nominal its connexion with the parent state. Touissaint was declared governor for life, with liberty to name his successor, and invested with very extensive powers. But it would 1801. be superfluous to give a minute detail of this ephemeral plan. Its more important parts respecting the authority and nature of the executive power, varied but little from the consular constitution of France. His proclamation, announcing its acceptance by the colonists, was filled with humane professions, although strongly tinctured with an affectation of religious enthusiasm.

From the strict blockade of their ports, Touissaint probably inferred that the French government would not be able to detach any military force sufficiently strong to cope with him, and that he might prosecute his designs without interruption. He continued, however, to write letters to the first consul, replete with expressions of zeal and loyalty ; and, in his despatches, accompanying a copy of the constitution, intimated in respectful terms, the necessity he was under of putting it in immediate force, in order to terminate the anarchy which existed in the island. The

unexpected conclusion of the war between France and England disconcerted his plans. The republic was now at liberty to direct all her attention towards his proceedings, and the court of London was too much interested in the suppression of his power to oppose her.

On the 14th of December, the combined fleet, consisting of a very strong French squadron under admiral Villaret Joyeuse, and a Spanish one, commanded by admiral Gravina, sailed from Brest ; and, being joined by a third, from L'Orient, 1801. arrived, after a stormy passage, at Cape Samana, on the 29th of January, where it met with a fourth squadron, from Rochefort, under rear-admiral Latouche. The British government despatched a powerful fleet to the same quarter, in order to guard against accidents. Great indeed was the necessity of a military force from both countries. Disturbances had broken out at Guadaloupe, from which the governor and several other persons had fled : these commotions, however, originated chiefly from personal dislike, and betrayed no dangerous symptoms of disaffection. Tobago, Martinique, Grenada, and, in fine, all the Antilles were threatened with insurrectional movements ; but whether these were owing to the agency of Touissaint, or what other cause, is unknown. The declaration of the French government, as to the continuance of slavery in those islands which were to be restored by the peace of Amiens, likewise announced that it should remain abolished in Guadaloupe and St. Domingo : but the rebellious conduct of Touissaint induced the consulate to retract this beneficent concession. He had been employed for several months in making defensive preparations, collecting immense treasures, and drawing military stores from North America. His army consisted of ten demi-brigades, each composed of 1100 or 1200 men, with a body of 1200 or 1500 cavalry, making in all, about 14,000 troops ; but he was able to increase this force to a much greater number, by embodying the black cultivators.

As Touissaint's intentions were doubtful,

general Leclerc, the commander-in-chief of the French armament, had been directed to be equally prepared for war and peace; and from the troubled state of the islands he concluded, that no time was to be lost, in hastening military operations, and stifling the general conspiracy in its birth. The armament on reaching the heights of La Grange, separated into three divisions. The first under rear-admiral Latouche, was to disembark at Port au Prince a body of troops commanded by general Boudet, in order to occupy Fort Republican, and the southern quarter. The second division, having general Rochambeau on board, proceeded to Manceville and Fort Dauphin; while admiral Villaret's squadron, with the rest of the forces under the commander-in-chief sailed towards the Cape, the most important settlement in the colony. When Boudet's advanced guard landed, a crowd of blacks calling out *No whites, no whites!* poured down upon them, but were soon routed and dispersed. In the meantime Fort Liberty opened its fire on the vessels, but the soldiers throwing themselves into the canoes, entered the embrasures and put the enemy to flight. In this fort and its vicinity 150 pieces of cannon were taken. Among the papers of the commandant was found an order of Touissaint, commanding his forces to sink the French ships and to hold out to the last extremity.

On general Leclerc's approaching Fort Piccolet, the black general, Christophe, began to cannonade the squadron, and dispatched a messenger to inform him, that until the arrival of orders from Touissaint, he would oppose a landing, burn the town, and massacre the whites; and a similar answer was returned by an officer, whom admiral Villaret had sent with a proclamation of the French government. It was therefore resolved, to disembark at some leagues from the Cape, and march to the elevations behind it, while Rochambeau gained the heights of St. Suzanne, Dondon, and Grand Riviere. A land breeze prevented the ships from reaching the shore; and the rebels having set fire to the town, the French commanders were obliged to remain, during the night, melancholy spec-

tators of the flames, without having it in their power to render any assistance to the wretched inhabitants. As soon as the wind would permit, the troops disembarked, carried the batteries, and hastened to the place to terminate the work of destruction. Happily a part of it, and all the surrounding plantations, were rescued from the conflagration; and a few only of the natives were massacred by the blacks.

No doubt could now remain as to the designs of Touissaint. General Leclerc, however, sent him his children, who had resided for some years in France, but accompanied the expedition. This generosity had no influence on their father; he sent them back with a letter to Leclerc, to assure him that there was nothing he so much desired as the prosperity of the colony, and that he was ready to obey the orders that might be given him; at the same time he demanded restitution of that part of his treasure, which had been taken at Port au Prince. He was desired to repair to head-quarters, under a solemn promise from the commander-in-chief, that he would be employed as his lieutenant-general. But his equivocal replies were designed only to gain time, and as these artifices were likely to render the colony the theatre of a long and destructive civil war, it became necessary to have recourse to more effectual measures. The forts of St Joseph, Picolet, and all the country between the Cape and Fort Dauphin were now in possession of the French. Port de 1781. Paix was retaken by general Humbert, and most of the Spanish part of the island occupied, in consequence of the enemy's submission or defeat. In all their engagements, the black troops fought with considerable valor, though not with the requisite steadiness. They wanted commanders, sufficiently experienced to contend with French veterans, and differences, of opinion arising, many of their officers suspected of an intention to surrender, were barbarously murdered by their men. Touissaint's followers began to desert him, notwithstanding the unfavourable reports which he had circulated, and the refusal of his generals to suffer the proclamations of the

consuls to be read to their troops. Seven
hundred men who had been attached to
Rigaud, and who had taken refuge at Cuba,
sent a deputation to request permission
to fight under the banners of the republic,
and two frigates were accordingly despatched to convey them. About 20 sail of
the line French and Spanish, had already
entered the ports of St. Domingo, besides
several frigates armed *en flute* having on
board nearly 16,000 men. The Spaniards soon afterwards sailed for the Havannah. Several other squadrons were on
their way, or preparing to follow with reinforcements, and Touissaint though far from
being subdued was driven from the sea-coast
and forced to take shelter in the mountains,
where he sustained a desultory warfare.
His occasional successes against the French
detachments could not restore his affairs,
which became every day more desperate.
Numerous bodies of the cultivators delivered up their arms, and accepted the
amnesty granted by the victor. General
Clervaux and his men submitted, and a
series of unpropitious and unexpected
events, appeared to prepare the way for
the undeserved and melancholy fate, of
the brave, the patriotic, and benevolent
Touissaint.

The details of general Leclerc exhibit
an afflicting picture of the nature of the
contest. Every description of brutal and
savage violence, was perpetrated by the
negroes, in actual conflict, and upon their
unfortuate prisoners. The rebels in their
turn were beaten, and dispersed in every
direction. Terror filled their camp, destitute of powder, and of stores, and they
were compelled to eat bananas. In the
emergency of distress, Christophe, and
Dessalines, the most brave and powerful
of the native chiefs, were allured by the
promises of the French general Leclerc,
to repair respectively, on parole to the
Cape, and to the plantations of St. Mark.
The intelligence of this desertion, dispirited
the followers of Touissaint, and induced
him to confide in the assurances of the
French general, at whose request he consented to repair to a plantation near
Gonaives, with a promise never to

1802.

leave it without the general's permission.
This act of almost inexcusable weakness,
was succeeded by the arrest of Touissaint
and of his family, and their transportation in
a frigate to the coast of France. Christophe
and Dessalines alarmed, and irritated by
the intelligence of this unexpected outrage,
effected a precipitate escape; the negroes
complaining that they had been betrayed
and deceived, were once more exasperated
to revolt. The climate, to use the language
of Christophe, " came to the assistance of
these avengers of tyranny and falsehood."
Leclerc himself fell a victim to its inclemency, seven generals of division were
among the dead ; and in the month of September, one third of the original army had
perished by the sword and by disease, or
lingered in the hospitals.

The internal measures of Buonaparte
were designed to preserve domestic tranquillity, and to attach individuals of different persuasions to his government. The
anarchists as the only effectual means of
accomplishing their purposes, had endeavored to destroy all religious faith and
had failed in the attempt. Buonaparte, on
the contrary, perceiving the attachment of
the French nation to the religion of their
ancestors, determined to re-establish the
Roman church. A convention was entered into between the French republic and
Pius VII. in which among other articles
it was stipulated, that the nomination of
all vacant sees should be in the first consul,
and that of parish priests in the bishops.
That he might not however irritate the
protestants by this predilection to the
church of Rome, he gave them, under certain restrictions, a perfect toleration.

His popularity was confirmed and extended by the signature of the definitive treaty
of peace between France and England.
The plenipotentiaries of France, Spain, and
Holland, repaired towards the close of the
year 1801, to Amiens, for the final adjustment of the treaty. Some difficulty arose
on the subject of the articles, which related
to the retention of Trinidad and Ceylon
by Great Britain, and to the future disposal
of the island of Malta. These obstacles
being at length overcome, the following

definitive treaty was signed on the 25th of March, 1802, by lord Cornwallis, on the part of his Britannic majesty, by Joseph Buonaparte on that of France, by the chevalier Azara for the king of Spain, and by Mynheer Schimmelpennick for the Batavian republic.

DEFINITIVE TREATY OF PEACE

Between the French republic, his majesty the king of Spain, and the Indies, and the Batavian republic, on the one part; and his majesty, the king of the United Kingdom of Great Britain and Ireland, on the other part.

The first consul of the French republic, in the name of the French people, and his majesty the king of the United Kingdom of Great Britain and Ireland, being equally animated with a desire to put an end to the calamities of war, have laid the foundation of peace, by the preliminary articles which were signed in London the 9th Vendemiaire, tenth year (1st of October, 1801.)

And as by the 15th article of the preliminaries it has been agreed on, " That plenipotentiaries should be named on the part of each government, who should repair to Amiens, and there proceed to arrange a definitive treaty, in concert with the allies of the contracting powers :" The first consul of the French republic, in the name of the French people, has named as plenipotentiary, the citizen Joseph Buonaparte, counsellor of state. His majesty the king of the United Kingdom of Great Britain and Ireland, has named the marquis Cornwallis, knight of the most noble order of the garter, one of his majesty's privy-council, general in his majesty's army, &c. His majesty the king of Spain and the Indes and the government of the Batavian republic, have appointed the following plenipotentiaries, viz. his catholic majesty has named Don Joseph Nicolas d'Azara, his counsellor of state, grand-cross of the order of Charles III. ambassador extraordinary of his majesty to the French republic, &c. And the government of the Batavian republic has named Roger Jean Schimmelpennick

its ambassador extraordinary to the French republic, &c—Which said plenipotentiaries having duly communicated to each other their respective powers, which are transcribed at the conclusion of the present treaty, have agreed upon the following articles :

Article I. There shall be peace, friendship, and good understanding between the French republic, his majesty the king of Spain, his heirs and successors, and the Batavian republic on the one part, and his majesty the king of the United Kingdom of Great Britain and Ireland, his heirs and successors, on the other part. The contracting parties shall use their utmost efforts to preserve a perfect harmony between their respective countries, without permitting any act of hostility whatever, by sea or by land, for any cause, or under any pretext. They shall carefully avoid every thing which might for the future disturb the happy union now re-established between them, and shall not give any succour or protection, directly or indirectly, to those who would wish to injure any one of them.

II. All the prisoners made on one side and the other, as well by land as by sea, and the hostages carried off or delivered up during the war, and up to the present day, shall be restored without ransom, in six weeks at the latest, to be reckoned from the day when the ratifications of the present treaty are exchanged, and on paying the debts which they shall have contracted during their captivity. Each of the contracting parties shall respectively discharge the advances, which shall have been made by any of the contracting parties for the support and maintenance of prisoners in the countries, where they have been detained. There shall be appointed by mutual consent for this purpose a commission, specially empowered to ascertain and determine the compensation, which may be due to any one of the contracting parties. The time and the place shall likewise be fixed by mutual consent for the meeting of the commissioners, who shall be entrusted with the execution of this article, and who shall take into account, the expenses incurred on account of the prisoners of the respective nations, who before being taken were in the pay, and at the disposal of one of the contracting parties.

III. His Britannic majesty restores to the French republic and its allies, viz. his catholic majesty and the Batavian republic, all the possessions and colonies which respectively belonged to them, and which have been either occupied or conquered by the British forces during the course of the present war, with the exception of the island of Trinidad, and of the Dutch possessions in the island of Ceylon.

IV. His catholic majesty cedes and guarantees in full property and sovereignty the island of Trinidad to his Britannic majesty.

V. The Batavian republic cedes and guarantees in full property and sovereignty to his Britannic majesty all the possessions and establishments in the island of Ceylon, which previous to the war belonged to the republic of the United Provinces, or to the Dutch East India Company.

VI. The port of the Cape of Good Hope remains to the Batavian republic in full sovereignty, in the same manner as it did previous to the war. The ships of every kind, belonging to the other contracting parties, shall be allowed to enter the said port, and there to purchase what provisions they may stand in need of, as heretofore, without being liable to pay any other imposts than such as the Batavian republic compels the ships of its own nation to pay.

VII. The territories and possessions of her most faithful majesty are maintained in their integrity, such as they were antecedent to the war. However, the boundaries of French and Portuguese Guiana are fixed by the river Arawari, which empties itself into the ocean above Cape North, near the islands Nuovo and Penetentia, about a degree and a third of north latitude. These boundaries shall run along the river Arawari, from its mouth the most distant from Cape North to its source, and afterwards on a right line, drawn from that source, to the Rio-Branto towards the West. In consequence, the Northern bank of the river Arawari, from its distant mouth to its source, and the territories that lie to the north of the line of the boundaries laid down as above, shall belong in full sovereignty to the French republic. The southern bank of the said river, from the same mouth, and all the territories to the south of the said line, shall belong to her most faithful majesty. The navigation of the river Arawari, along the whole of its course, shall be common to both nations. The arrangements which have been agreed upon between the courts of Madrid and Lisbon, respecting the settlement of their boundaries in Europe, shall nevertheless be adhered to, conformably to the stipulations of the treaty of Badajos.

VIII. The territories, possessions, and rights of the Sublime Porte, are maintained in their integrity as they were before the war.

IX. The republic of the Seven Islands is recognised.

X. The islands of Malta, Gozo, and Comino, shall be restored to the order of St. John of Jerusalem, to be held on the same conditions on which it possessed them before the war, and under the following stipulations:

1. The knights of the order, whose tongues shall continue to subsist, after the exchange of the ratifications of the present treaty, are invited to return to Malta, as soon as the exchange shall have taken place. They will there form a general chapter, and proceed to the election of a grand-master, chosen from among the natives of the nations which preserve their tongues, unless that election has been already made since the exchange of the preliminaries. It is understood, that an election made subsequent to that epoch shall alone be considered valid, to the exclusion of any other that may have taken place at any period prior to that epoch.

2. The governments of the French republic and of Great Britain, desiring to place the order and island of Malta in a state of entire independence with respect to them, agree that there shall not be in future either a French or English tongue; and that

no individual belonging to either the one or other of these powers shall be admitted into the order.

3. There shall be established a Maltese tongue, which shall be supported by the territorial revenues, and commercial duties of the island. This tongue shall have its peculiar dignities, an establishment, and an hotel. Proofs of nobility shall not be necessary for the admission of knights of this tongue; and they shall, moreover, be admissible to all offices, and shall enjoy all privileges in the same manner as the knights of the other tongues. At least half of the municipal, administrative, civil, judicial, and other employments depending on the government, shall be filled by inhabitants of the isles of Malta, Gozo, and Comino.

4. The forces of his Britannic majesty shall evacuate the island and its dependencies, within three months from the exchange of the ratifications, or sooner if possible. At that epoch it shall be given up to the order in its present state, provided the grand-master, or commissaries, fully authorised according to the statutes of the order, shall be in the island to take possession, and that the force which is to be provided by his Sicilian majesty, as it is hereafter stipulated, shall have arrived there.

5. One half of the garrison, at least, shall be always composed of native Maltese; for the remainder, the order may levy recruits in those countries only, where tongues continue to be retained. The Maltese troops shall have Maltese officers. The nomination of the commander-in-chief of the garrison, as well as that of the officers, shall pertain to the grand-master, and this right he cannot resign even temporarily, except in favor of a knight and in concurrence with the advice of the council of the order.

6. The independence of the isles of Malta, Gozo, and Comino, as well as the present arrangement, shall be placed under the protection and guarantee of France, Great Britain, Austria, Spain, Russia, and Prussia.

7. The neutrality of the order, and of the island of Malta, with its dependencies, is proclaimed.

8. The ports of Malta shall be opened to the commerce and the navigation of all nations, who shall there pay equal and moderate duties : these duties shall be applied to the support of the Maltese tongue, as specified in paragraph 3, to that of the civil and military establishments of the island, as well as to that of a general *Lazaret*, open to all flags.

9. The states of Barbary are excepted from the conditions of the two preceding paragraphs, until by means of an arrangement to be procured by the contracting parties, the system of hostilities, which subsists between the states of Barbary, and the order of St. John, or the powers possessing tongues, or concurring in the composition of the order, shall have ceased.

10. The order shall be governed, both with respect to spiritual and temporal affairs, by the same statutes, which were in force when the knights left the isle, except in as far as they are abrogated by the present treaty.

11. The regulations contained in the paragraph, 3, 5, 7, 8, and 10, shall be converted into laws and perpetual statutes of the order, in the customary manner; and the grand-master, or, if he shall not be in the island at the time of its restoration to the order, his representative, as well as his successors, shall be bound to take an oath for the punctual observance of them.

12. His Sicilian majesty shall be invited to furnish 2000, men, natives of his states, to garrison the different fortresses of the said islands. That force shall remain one year, to bear date from their restitution to the knights; and if, at the expiration of this term the order should not have raised a force sufficient, in the judgment of the guaranteeing powers, to garrison the island and its dependencies, such as is specified in paragraph 5, the Neapolitan troops shall continue there until, they shall be replaced by another force deemed sufficient by the said powers.

13. The different powers designated in the 6th paragraph, viz. France, Great Britain, Austria, Spain, Russia, and Prussia, shall be invited to accede to the present stipulations.

XI The French troops shall evacuate

the kingdom of Naples and the Roman states. The English forces shall also evacuate Porto-Ferrajo, and generally all the ports and islands, which they occupy in the Mediterranean, or the Adriatic.

XII. The evacuations, cessions, and restitutions, stipulated by the present treaty, shall be executed in Europe within a month ; on the continent and seas of America and Africa in three months ; on the continent and seas of Asia within six months after the ratification of the present definitive treaty, except in case of special reservation.

XIII. In all cases of restitution agreed upon by the present treaty, the fortifications shall be restored in the condition they were in at the time of signing the preliminaries ;" and all the works, which shall have been constructed since their occupation, shall remain untouched.

It is agreed besides, that in all the stipulated cases of cessions, there shall be allowed to the inhabitants, of whatever rank 'or nation, a term of three years, reckoning from the notification of the present treaty, to dispose of all their property and effects, whether acquired or possessed by them before, or during the continuance of the present war ; during which term of three years they shall have free and entire liberty to exercise their religion, and to enjoy their fortunes. The same privileges are granted in the restored countries to all persons, whether inhabitants or not, who shall have formed any establishments there, during the time that these countries were in the possession of Great Britain.

As to the inhabitants of the countries restored or ceded, it is hereby agreed, that no person shall under any pretence be prosecuted, disturbed, or molested, either in person or property, on account of his political conduct or opinion, or for his attachment to any of the contracting parties, or on any account whatever, except for debts contracted with individuals, or for acts subsequent to the present treaty.

XIV. All the sequestrations laid on either side on funds, revenues, and credits, of what nature soever they may be, be-

longing to any of the contracting powers, or to their citizens and subjects, shall be taken off immediately after the signature of this definitive treaty. The decision of all claims among the individuals of the respective nations, for debts, property, effects, or claims, of any nature whatsoever, which should, according to received usage, and the law of nations, be preferred at the epoch of the peace, shall be referred to the competent tribunals, and in those cases speedy and complete justice shall be done in the countries, wherein those claims shall be respectively preferred.

XV. The fisheries on the coasts of Newfoundland, and of the adjacent islands, and in the Gulph of St. Laurence, are placed on the same footing as they were before the war.—The French fishermen of Newfoundland, and the inhabitants of the islands of St Pierre and Miquelon, shall have liberty to cut such wood as may be necessary for them in the bays of Fortune and Despair, during one year, reckoning from the ratification of the present treaty.

XVI. To prevent all ground of complaint and dispute, which might arise on account of captures, that may have been made at sea subsequent to the signing of the preliminaries, it is reciprocally agreed, that the ships and property, which may have been taken in the Channel, and in the North seas, after a space of twelve days, reckoning from the exchange of the ratifications of the preliminary articles, shall be restored on both sides ; that the term shall be one month from the Channel and the North sea, as far as the Canary islands inclusively, as well in the ocean as in the Mediterranean ; two months from the Canary islands to the equator ; and finally, five months in all the other parts of the world, without any further exception, or distinction of time or place.

XVII. The ambassadors, ministers, and agents of the contracting powers, shall enjoy respectively in the states of the said powers, the same rank, privileges, prerogatives, and immunities, which were enjoyed before the war by agents of the same class.

XVIII. The branch of the house of

Nassau which, was established in the *ci-de-vant* republic of the United Provinces, now the Batavian republic, having experienced some losses both in private property and in consequence of the change of constitution adopted in that country, there shall be obtained for them a suitable compensation for the said losses.

XIX. The present definitive treaty of peace is declared common to the Sublime Ottoman Porte, the ally of his Britannic majesty; and the Sublime Porte shall be invited to transmit its act of accession as soon as possible.

XX. It is agreed, that the contracting parties, upon requisitions made by them respectively, or by their ministers, or officers duly authorised for that purpose, shall be bound to deliver up to justice persons accused of murder, forgery, or fraudulent bankruptcy, committed within the jurisdiction of the requiring party, provided that this shall only be done in cases, in which the evidence of the crime shall be such, that the laws of the place in which the accused person shall be discovered, would have authorised the detaining and bringing him to trial, had the offence been committed there. The expenses of the arrest, and carrying him back for trial, shall be defrayed by the party making the requisition; but this article has no sort of reference to crimes of murder, forgery, or fraudulent bankruptcy committed before the conclusion of the definitive treaty.

XXI. The contracting parties promise to observe sincerely and faithfully all the articles contained in the present treaty, and will not suffer any sort of contravention direct or indirect to be made to it by their respective citizens, or subjects; and the contracting parties guarantee, generally and reciprocally all the stipulations of the present treaty.

XXII. The present treaty shall be ratified by the contracting parties within the space of thirty days, or sooner, if possible, and the ratifications shall be exchanged in due form at Paris.

In testimony whereof, we the undersigned plenipotentiaries, have signed with our hands, and in virtue of our respective full powers, the present definitive treaty, causing it to be sealed with our respective seals.

Done at Amiens, the 4th Germinal, in the year 10. March 24, 1802.

J. BUONAPARTE. CORNWALLIS.
AZARA. SCHIMMELPENNICK.

Such was the result of ten campaigns, the most destructive, the most eventful, and the most important in their consequences, of any that history had recorded. During their progress, so entire a revolution had taken place in France, that not a wreck was left of the old system as a memorial of its existence. Lewis XVI. and all the princes of the original stem of the house of Bourbon, were brought to the scaffold, or driven into exile; and the republic founded on the ruins of the antient monarchy, accomplished amidst scenes of turbulence, bloodshed, and distress, what Lewis XIV. had attempted in vain, the conquest of the Austrian Netherlands. It made the Rhine the boundary of its dominions towards Germany, and the Alps towards Italy. In the course of the war the house of Austria lost a considerable part of its territories, and still more of its weight in the scale of Europe; the Prussian monarch lost his reputation; the Dutch and Swiss republics, though indulged with the appellation of independent states, were rendered absolutely dependent upon France; the pontiff was suffered to slumber in the papal chair as long as he should be content with the mode of existence which was assigned him; the Italian states were entirely new modelled, and subjected to the power of the first consul; and the king of Sardinia and the remaining sove reigns of the house of Bourbon could only be regarded as captive monarchs, gracing the triumphal chariot of the conqueror.

Far different was the state of Great Britain at the close of the contest. In all that was essential to dignity of character, her conduct claimed a distinguished pre-eminence. She had it is true made a full trial of her resources, and had strained the sinews of public credit, but she had preserved the honor of the British crown unsullied. If she was disfigured with wounds and bruises in the combat, they were all in front: if her shield was battered it was yet resplendent: *Intaminatis fulget honoribus.* While other states were crouching before a foreign oppressor, she still maintained her proper station among the powers of Europe, and braved his utmost efforts to subdue her spirit. *Hoc illud est præcipue in cognitione rerum, salubre ac frugiferum, omnis te exempli documenta illustri posita monumento intueri; inde tibi, tuæque reipublicæ quod imitere capias; inde fædum incepta, fædum exitu quod vites.*

HISTORY OF THE WAR.

CHAP. XXXIV.

THE *definitive* treaty was only opposed by a very small part of either house. Mr. Windham endeavored to prove its weakness, fallacy, and insecurity, and to rouse the zeal of the country against the insatiate eagerness of Gallic ambition, and the restless spirit of Jacobinical machination. In discussing the terms to which we had agreed, he contended that we had placed Malta in the hands of the French, that the Cape of Good Hope was in fact at their disposal, that from this settlement and Cochin, they might make hostile preparations against British India, and that we had suffered them to trick us in that part of the negotiation which concerned Portugal. He blamed the ministers for the non-revival of former treaties, as the omission might affect our interests in the bay of Honduras, and even shake the foundation of our power in India. He also complained of their acquiescence in the cession of Louisiana, to the French, who, by this advantage might obtain the command of North America, while that of South America would be in a great measure secured to them by the medium of the river of Amazons. In treating of the war he lamented that it had been pursued merely as a common war, and that it had not been carried on with that extraordinary spirit,

which alone could prevent the mischievous extension of Jacobinical principles. Our exertions, he thought, had by no means been equal to our resources; and we certainly had not been successful in repelling the danger which we sought to avert. We had suffered the French to acquire as great a degree of power in ten years, as the Romans had obtained in several centuries. While we were menaced by their ambition, we ought to be extremely vigilant and alert; and he would therefore move for an address to his majesty, promising to keep inviolate the public faith, but hinting a disapprobation of some of the engagements into which he had entered, and requesting him to take measures, both by negotiation, and by ample establishments, naval, and military, for obviating the danger that might arise from such stipulations, or from other circumstances in the posture of affairs. Lord Hawkesbury was sensible of the enormous aggrandisement of the French republic, but did not deem that a sufficient reason for an indefinite continuance of the war. He was surprised at the apprehensions entertained by Mr. Windham of the influence of France in North and South America, as it appeared to him to be very inconsiderable. He maintained that the treaty amply provided by a strong

4 A 2

guarantee for the independence of Malta,
that while we had a powerful army we had
no cause to be alarmed at the sway which
the French might obtain at the Cape; that
although we had resigned many of our
conquests, we had insisted on retaining
two of the most important naval stations
in the East and West Indies; and that
the ministers had in all the proceedings,
consulted the honor and security of the
nation, as strenuously as any of the opponents of the peace could expect upon
an impartial review of the state of Europe
at the time of the negotiation. Mr. Dundas highly disapproved the cession of
Malta and the Cape, yet refused to concur
in a vote of censure. Mr. Addington allowed that the treaty was not such as the
people could receive with extravagant joy
or exultation, but he did not think it dishonorable. He had endeavored to procure
the best terms, and in agreeing to those
which were now concluded, he had yielded
to the dictates of prudence. Mr. Sheridan
imputed greater blame to those ministers
who had reduced the country to a state
which rendered such a peace necessary,
than to those who had concluded the treaty.

Only 20 members voted for the address
proposed by Mr. Windham, while 276
gave their suffrages against it. An amendment moved by lord Hawkesbury, expressing an approbation of the treaty, was
then adopted. A debate of the same kind
occurred in the house of peers, on the motion of lord Grenville, for an address of
dissatisfaction. The duke of York
1802. having suggested such an amendment as coincided with the views of the
ministry, a majority of 106 voted in favor of
the peace.

Some alarm was excited during the
session, by a mutiny which arose in the
bay of Bantry, from the reluctance among
many of the seamen of the Temeraire to
serve in the West Indies. Twenty of the
offenders were tried by a court-martial at
Portsmouth, and eleven were subjected to
capital punishment. About the same time,
the impartiality of our criminal law was
evinced in the condemnation of lieutenant-
colonel Wall, who, while he acted as

governor of Goree, had occasioned, by
cruel flagellation, the death of a serjeant.
Neither the station which he then filled,
nor the length of time, nineteen years and
a half, between the murder and the trial,
rescued him from the strict execution of
his sentence, which was accompanied by
the most violent and outrageous demonstrations of ferocious joy among a brutal
populace.

While the treaties concluded with various
powers consolidated the stability of the
French government abroad, the creation
of a legion of honor, and Buonaparte's
self-exaltation to the presidency of the
Italian republic added to his security at
home. During this year, Charles Emanuel,
of Sardinia, wearied by the nominal possession of the sovereign power, voluntarily
abdicated his throne in favor of his brother
Victor Emanuel; the duke of Aoust then
retired in voluntary banishment to the
island of Sardinia: Piedmont and the
duchy of Parma, were added as integral
departments of France. The once magnificent city of Genoa, and all its territory
under the name of the Ligurian republic,
became French provinces in every thing
but the name, though the government was
vested in a doge, whose functions were to
endure six years, and a senate of thirty
members, one-third of them to be changed
every three years. Even in this little
establishment a naval force was not overlooked: Genoa was bound to support
ten ships of 74 guns, two frigates, and four
corvettes. But, though Russia and Turkey
had been fortunate enough to obtain treaties
with the head of the French government,
with England he was too wary to be surprised into any measure of this nature: in
vain did the minister and the merchants
flatter themselves with the idea of a commercial treaty with France. To our
pressing solicitations on this subject, and
our anxiety for a commercial connection,
the cry on their part was, relative to England, "The treaty of Amiens! and nothing
but the treaty of Amiens!" About this
time also, a decree, prohibiting the importation of British manufactures on the
left bank of the Rhine, soon put the matter

beyond all doubt. This and several other measures, the first consul adopted, merely to employ and excite the industry of his own subjects; and the English newspapers, on this account, became so coarse and personal in their abuse, that, on the 20th of August, 1802, their circulation was prohibited in France. In the mean time Buonaparte, after obtaining an additional ten years to his consulship, proceeded to secure his election as first consul of France for life. The senates next enabled him to appoint his successor. It can scarcely be doubted that he then entertained the design of becoming an emperor, and that these steps were adopted as measures preparatory to that important end. When made consul for life, (with what propriety his subsequent actions will best declare,) he obscurely hinted at something like a divine right to that station, and observed, that "he was called by Him from whom all things emanate to restore upon earth justice, order, and equality."

The daily extension of Buonaparte's power, gave very serious uneasiness to the emperor of Germany, as well as to the English; so much so, that the imperial cabinet, though bound by the treaty of Luneville, to admit the German indemnities and the secularization of several of the ecclesiastical sovereignties, was extremely averse to the prosecution of this ungrateful business. The court of Vienna even remonstrated against the recent proceeding of the first consul, in annexing the duchies of Parma and Placenza to the French republic. It appeared, that by the treaty of Aix-la-Chapelle, 1748, the house of Austria claimed the succession to these sovereignties in case of the failure of issue in the present reigning branch. This, however, was no time to revive old claims, and the reluctance of the emperor to enter upon the German indemnities, probably urged Buonaparte to hasten them. The French treaty with Russia, it soon appeared, referred to the business that was to be opened at Ratisbon. The emperor of Russia was called in as one of its guarantees. It was in some degree an unhappy precedent, because it was upon the ground

of the emperor of Russia's guarantee, that he afterwards interfered, together with the king of Sweden, to preserve the Germanic constitution. In a matter where so many jarring interests were implicated, where states and principalities were to be again portioned out, where the lesser powers were to be sacrificed as remunerations to the greater, it was not strange that the proceedings should be rather tardy. Nothing was effectually done till the 17th of July; when the emperor of Germany transmitted a rescript to the diet of Ratisbon, stating that he had not ceased to occupy his attention with the means of terminating the important business of the peace; but that he found the principal parties had applied in the mean time to Russia and France, and solicited the mediation of these powers in order to obtain the indemnities they waited for; that Russia had consequently proposed to open negotiations at Paris, in February, 1802, that soon after a convention was concluded *without his participation*, between France and Russia, in which his imperial majesty was desired to direct the definitive arrangement of it according to the constitution. It was thus, that by the superior policy and influence of Buonaparte, the antient and stupendous fabric of the Germanic empire was loosened and destroyed. However, the emperor, seeing all his authority about to be taken from him, submitted for the time with the best grace he could, and by his persevering objections, obtained terms rather more advantageous than might have been expected, for his royal relative, the grand duke of Tuscany. The newly-modified scheme of indemnities was called a Supplement to the Plan; according to this, the elector of Mentz obtained the cities of Ratisbon and Wetzlar; the princes of Baden, Wurtemberg, and Hesse Cassel, were made electors; and the king of Great Britain accepted the cession of the bishopric of Osnaburgh, as a compensation for Hildesheim, Corvey, and Hoexter, provided Osnaburgh was given him in perpetuity, as formerly he had only the right of alternate nomination to that bishopric. He now abandoned, on behalf of the cities of Hamburgh and Bremen, the rights and property he exercised in and over them. But to raise the interest of France in the German empire, upon the ruins of the house of Austria, the first consul and the emperor of Russia agreed, that it was at once possible and suitable to preserve in the empire an ecclesiastical elector. They proposed in consequence, that the arch-chancellor should be transferred to Ratisbon, with the abbeys of St. Emeran, Ober, Munster, and Neider Munster, preserving his antient possession of the great bailiwick of Aschaffenburg, on the right of the Main. This new officer afterwards proved to be a person of great consequence in promoting the interest of the French empire.

In the mean while a dispute between the elector of Bavaria, and his neighbour, the bishop of Passau, had nearly proceeded to hostilities. The emperor of Germany supported the latter, and took possession of the bishopric to keep it out of the hands of the elector.

On the 22nd of August, the emperor could no longer refrain from causing his commissary, baron Hegel, to express his displeasure to the diet. He flattered the newly conquered Germans, by styling them a free, independent nation; and mentioned the emperor's surprise, that they should permit two foreign powers to prescribe to it in its internal concerns. On the 24th, the same complaints were renewed in an imperial rescript; which was answered on the 28th by the French minister Laforet, who simply enforced the declaration of the two mediating powers. The emperor again expressed his dissatisfaction as to indemnities granted to the grand duke of Tuscany; but on the 8th of September the influence of France rose predominant in the diet: the plan of indemnities, after much debate was accepted, and a *conclusum* voted accordingly. The court of Vienna still thinking its interests neglected, had instructed baron Hugel, the imperial plenipotentiary, to refuse to ratify the *conclusum*. At length in the thirtieth sitting of the deputation, on the 22nd of November, a final *conclusum* was voted, which was ultimately, though with great reluctance, ac-

cepted by the emperor, with very few alterations; and thus it was observed a total and violent alteration was made in the map of Germany; of which the constitution suffered a much greater infraction than that effected by the treaty of Westphalia, and by the thirty years' war, when the arrogance of the house of Austria had been humbled by the heroic Gustavus Adolphus, and prince Maurice of Saxony.

The designs of France, on the remaining independence of the Swiss, excited the jealousy and the ultimate resistance of the people. In the Valois, or Pays de Vaud, the symtoms of disaffection were first publicly manifested, though the presence of a French army soon quelled the malcontents. In the three cantons of Schweitz, Uri, and Underwalden, the opposition was most violent; they, with Appenzel, openly declared themselves in a state of insurrection. A considerable part of the summer of 1801 was passed in threats and recriminations between the French party in Switzerland, called the new government, and the refractory cantons. The latter, were called the patriots, though in reality the partisans of the old aristocracy; and, notwithstanding the inferiority of their force, appointed commanders, formed magazines, and prepared to take the field. General Andermatt, and the commissary-general Keller, were despatched against them: but without waiting for the attack, on the 27th of August, the insurgents advanced and carried the post of Rany, occupied by a company of carabineers, the captain of which and about thirty men were killed. On the 7th of September a suspension of arms was agreed upon, only to be broken after three days notice. In the mean time the cantons of Glasis, the two districts of Baden, and a part of the Grisons, openly joined the confederacy; that of Zug manifested the same spirit, and the French general Andermatt, was compelled to send several companies of troops of the line to take possession of Zurich, but the inhabitants refused to admit them. The unexpected arrival of this force produced great agitation among the citizens, they collected very tumultuously, and as the effervescence seemed to be carried to a very high degree, the municipality, not choosing to take upon themselves all the responsibility, thought proper to call to their assistance six persons of the greatest influence in the town. After due deliberation it was resolved to guard against all surprise by refusing admission to the troops. The municipality of Zurich wrote to the Helvetic commandant, that the citizens would guard their own walls, and wished to see no more foreign troops among them : that, notwithstanding, he would be permitted to enter, on condition that his soldiers should be lodged in barracks, guarded by the citizens. Immediately afterwards, citizens Veiss and Sehintz, left Zurich to have an explanation with the central government. An interview took place on the 7th of September. General Andermatt informed of these movements left Lucerne on the 12th with all the troops and artillery in the place. He arrived at night before Zurich ; and at half-past two in the morning caused the town to be summoned by the sound of trumpet to open its gates. The commandant of Zurich replied, that he would send his request to the municipality, and would wait their orders ; upon which general Andermatt began to bombard the town ; he fired 160 shells, besides some four and six pound balls : but his ammunition was soon expended and he had no more than 2000 men. He offered at nine o'clock to suspend hostilities, provided a part of the town was put into his hands, until he could receive ulterior orders from his government. In effect an armistice was agreed upon, till the 18th, at six o'clock in the evening ; but the citizens enraged at the attack made upon them, and encouraged by the bad success of the morning assault, refused all other arrangement. Their friends from the country were arriving every hour, to the succour of Zurich, particularly general Steiner, who entered the city at the head of 300 men well armed.

In the meanwhile the cantons of Baden and Argovia, rose in a mass and took Brugg and Lensbourg. Aloys Reding, who had taken part against the French, from the first invasion of the country was declared their chief ; and though Zurich was obliged to capitulate to general Andermatt, Fribourg reconstituted itself, and Berne was obliged to capitulate in its turn to the Swiss party, on the 18th of September, after an obstinate action under the walls. The Swiss insurgents were commanded by Messrs. Watteville, d'Erlach, and Effinguer, and consisted of the peasantry of Argovia, Soleure, and Oberland. The Swiss troops, on the French side, fired from the ramparts of Berne, upon these peasants, who threw some shot into the place, which only damaged the town house. At length after a severe combat the French party were obliged to capitulate ; a suspension of arms was also agreed upon, which included general Andermatt and the troops under him. M. de Watteville, the Swiss commandant was named commander-in-chief, and waited on the French minister Verninue, who gave him a most obliging reception.

About the same time the city of Aran, surrendered to the forces under d'Erlach ; Soleure, submitted to a party of Argovians, without firing a gun ; and Andermatt, who had been abruptly called from Zurich before the capitulation of Berne, and left that city in possession of his heavy artillery, being closely pursued by Aloys Reding, must have been taken or destroyed, had he not been included in the late capitulation.

The Swiss insurgents, on the other hand, were no sooner established at Berne, than they began to assume the reins of government. They issued a proclamation in which they gave each of the cantons leave to choose and regulate their local governments, and recommended a liberal and rational plan for regulating and insuring Helvetic independence.

But while this new Swiss government were settling themselves at Berne, it should be observed that the members of the old one, established by the partisans of France, were at Lusanne, to which place they had been followed by the Spanish and other ministers at peace with France. In the meanwhile, as neither of the parties were conquered, but both seemed to act as if they meant to gain time, when a proclamation appeared which terminated all the hopes the insurgents had indulged of a new modification in their favor.

On Sunday morning, the 3rd of October, hostilities were renewed between the Swiss and the French party, along the whole line ; and in every point the Swiss were successful. The main attack was made on the Helvetic troops covering Lusanne. The Helvetic government were preparing to fly from Lusanne to Geneva, when, on the 4th, citizen Rapp, the chief consul's aid-de-camp, arrived with the proclamation. This gave the Helvetic government courage to remain in Lusanne ; and citizen Rapp proceeded to lay his proclamation before the Swiss committee at Berne. They returned for answer, that they had referred it to the Swiss diet, sitting at Schweitz, which had the charge of all important state matters. On the 6th, the commander of the Swiss troops and another officer found it necessary to proceed to Lusanne with a flag of truce to propose an armistice between the Swiss and Helvetic troops, till the diet at Schweitz should come to some resolution with respect to Buonaparte's proclamation. The armistice was refused in an humble but determined expostulation.

This, it has been observed, was the expiring effort of Helvetic freedom ; as all resistance to the arms of France was now deemed unavailing, and the first consul's terms were found to be easier than they were expected to have been, the remaining troops of the Swiss insurgents were disbanded, and, on the 17th of October, the senate resumed the possession of Berne. In vain had the patriots, or, as they should have been termed, the old aristocrats of Switzerland, appealed to the powers of Europe. The court of Vienna dreaded Buonaparte so much, that they would not hold any correspondence with them. England, though at peace with France, sent an agent in the person of a Mr. Moore, to negotiate with the insurgents, but he arrived too late. On the 28th of October, the diet of the patriots held at Schweitz, thought proper to dissolve itself ; and, as a mode of prevention, the French government took care to have a force in and near Switzerland, sufficient to overawe any new movements. To finish the business, deputies from the cantons were ordered to proceed to Paris to decide upon the points at issue.

Aloys Reding, and general Aufder-Maur, together with the brother of the former, and several others of the Swiss patriots, were brought prisoners to Zurich, and conveyed before general Serras. They were sent to the castle of Challon, on the banks of the lake of Geneva, till farther orders. The senate of Berne, as might be expected, declared that Buonaparte would give them a constitution which should ensure tranquillity, and that they should gratefully accept it.

The decisive settlement of the new constitution of Switzerland was reserved till the deputies from the cantons should have arrived at Paris. In consequence of this determination, on the 10th of December, they were requested to assemble at the office of the minister of foreign affairs ; they met accordingly, and Barthelemy, one of the senators of the commission, with Roux and Roederer, its secretaries, there communicated to them a letter from the first consul, dated St. Cloud, December 10th, and addressed to the deputies from the eighteen cantons of Helvetia, the substance of which was as follows :

" The present critical situation of Helvetia demands from all parties an entire sacrifice of their factious and selfish passions. The first consul will fulfil his engagements and restore tranquillity to Switzerland. He expects the deputies to aid his intentions. Switzerland is a country distinguished from all others by the peculiarity of its local circumstances. It is formed for a federative republic, by the very hand of nature. Circumstances had there established a sovereign state among others that were dependent ; other circumstances have introduced a general equality of right. There are in Switzerland both pure democracies and oligarchies, or governments engrossed by particular families ; both cannot continue to subsist together. The three principles upon which alone tranquillity can be re-established, are these : a general equality of rights among all the eighteen cantons ; an entire renunciation of all aristocratic family rights ; a federative conformation in respect to each particular canton.

"The eighteen Swiss cantons are confederated by the articles of the new constitution framed by Buonaparte : they mutually guarantee their constitutions, their territory, their liberty, and their independence, both against foreign powers and the usurpation of an individual canton or faction. The quota of troops and money to be supplied by each canton here follows :

"The diet to meet alternately and from year to year, at Fribourg, Berne, Soleure, Basle, Zurich, and Lucerne.

"Citizen Louis d'Affry is landamman for Switzerland for the current year.

"He is to have the charge of all diplomatic negotiations ; he is to watch over all the laws and ordinances of the diet, and of those of the particular constitutions.

"The diet is to be composed of a deputy from each canton, who is to have full powers, with instructions by which he is strictly bound. The deputies from the cantons have thirty-five voices. The diet is to assemble every year on the 1st of June ; it is to continue its sittings but one month ; in that time it may conclude treaties of peace, of alliance, and of commerce, with foreign powers.

Given at Paris.
(Signed) Buonaparte, &c. &c."

The final result of the introduction of the new constitution was, that the Helvetic troops were passed into the service of France. On this occasion, the landamman issued a proclamation, informing them that they were received into the armies of the first consul, whose paternal care would make them forget all they had suffered. An address of thanks was also voted to Buonaparte by the diet, on the specific ground, that he had restored to them their antient constitution, the only one adapted to the wants, or consistent with the wishes

of the nation : and the people, exhausted as they were by internal tumult, and by a long series of calamities inflicted by the hostile armies of the opposing powers, beheld these arrangements with silent indifference.

The subjection of Switzerland to the paramount influence of France, was an object too easy of attainment, and comparatively too insignificant in its consequences to divert the attention of the first consul from his disputes and negotiations with the English ministry.

In the definitive articles of the treaty of Amiens, the maritime and commercial interests of the English nation had been sacrificed to the negligence or precipitance of the new administration. Our ships were excluded from the ports of France, or detained and condemned as presenting facilities to the introduction of articles of contraband., The readiness with which the first consul adopted any pretext that might justify his interruption of our commerce, and his confiscation of our property, were not less remarkable than the apathy and complacent acquiescence of our rulers in his unjust and arbitrary measures.

The negotiations immediately preceding the recommencement of the war, exhibited a melancholy but striking picture of finesse on the one hand, and of imbecility on the other. The editors of the London Newspapers, and more especially the literary partisans of the exiled family of Bourbon, had long been accustomed to insult the feelings of the rival nation, and debase the character of its first magistrate in every form of gross and exaggerated accusation. Had the ministers been influenced by any motive or feeling of regard for the liberty of the press, in repressing this abuse, they would have deserved the thanks and approbation of the community. But their conduct was equally inconsistent with the object of conciliating Buonaparte, and of protecting the freedom of the public journalists.

The *Courier de Londres*, conducted by French emigrants, was remarkable for the virulence and vulgarity of its declamation. The remonstrances of Buonaparte on the licentiousness of this and similar productions, were justly and nobly answered by a declaration of the ministry, that they could not, and would not endanger the palladium of national freedom, the liberty of the press. But these professions were disgracefully falsified by the event. In proportion as the first consul's vehemence on the subject increased, the patriotism, and confidence of the ministry subsided; and on the repeated remonstrances of the French court, a prosecution was instituted against the principal offenders.

Among other important subjects of expostulation on the part of the French government was the general circulation of the most infamous and unfounded calumnies, on the character of the first consul, by sir Robert Wilson in his narrative of the expedition to Egypt. These portions of sir Robert's history were read and quoted with avidity by that numerous portion of the anti-jacobin party, who mistook impertinence for wit, and ribaldry for argument. They first began by criticisms on the stature of Buonaparte, and seldom mentioned him but by the appellation of *little Boney.* They asserted that he was a puny, self-conceited bastard, and indulged in the most indelicate allusions to the barrenness of his wife. When he had proved however by his actions, that he was not deficient in courage or capacity they had recourse to more serious modes of aspersion. The narratives of sir Robert Wilson supplied them with the materials of copious and sanguine declamation. Nothing was heard but execrations of the poisoner and the murderer, and witless abuse supplied the place of reasoning and eloquence.

I have already recorded sir Robert Wilson's statement of the massacre at Jaffa; in his accusation that Buonaparte, with the aid of a mercenary physician deliberately poisoned 500 of his troops, then sick in the hospital of that town, he appeals to the members of the National Institute: and his assertion is supported by the testimony of Dr. Wittman; to whom an individual was pointed out as having been the executioner of his commands. Time, however, which

dissipates the allusions of prejudice, and folly, has gradually weakened the credibility of this last atrocious charge. It has been observed indeed that no officer of Bon's division, nor any individual connected with the hospital, came forward in vindication of a master who could repay sedulity so well. But even at that period Buonaparte was sufficiently versed in the policy of despotism, to be aware that to acknowledge the authority of public opinion is more dangerous than to labor under the most criminal imputations; the consul was too wise as well as too proud to descend to exculpation; and an officious and uncalled for defence was more likely to be visited with proofs of his displeasure, than to be received with gratitude. Many years have now elapsed since the alleged commission of these atrocities. Our intercourse with France and Egypt has been frequent and unrestrained; there has been no want of inclination or encouragement to display the crimes and errors of Napoleon, yet not a single evidence has come forward to relate *from his own knowledge,* the particulars of these extraordinary acts, nor has the story been sanctioned by the *name* of one individual present at their supposed perpetration.

Considerations of personal policy would alone have dissuaded the general of the French armies from the commission of a useless crime. To leave his sick behind him, or to remove them to a distance where they might perish by hunger would have been easier and more politic than to destroy them by poison. Their desertion might have been justified by the necessities of war: the destruction on the contrary of 500 men by poison could not be concealed, and its discovery would expose the general to the hatred and execration of his army. Even attributing to Buonaparte an intention to destroy his sick, no poison can be administered so as to act with equal rapidity and efficacy on a number of individuals. If the sick in the camp of Buonaparte were poisoned we must suppose that they all sat down to partake of their mess at the same moment, that the operation of the poison was instantaneous, and that in the same minute the pangs of death seized on every individual of the multitudes. That all these suppositions are impossible, is as obvious to the general reader as to the physician. Out of 500 men to whom poison is administered, some will fall sick before the rest, an alarm will be excited, antidotes will be employed by a few, others will abstain from a further use of the viands, or the beverage in which the poison is infused, strength of constitution will overcome in a considerable number the operation of the poison: those who recover will relate the history of their comrades; and instead of the intended crime being silently and securely accomplished,' a hundred witnesses would arise to proclaim the martyrdom of the brave and unfortunate victims.

The execution of the duke D'Enghien was an act of obvious policy, and its expedience might justify, in the opinion of Buonaparte, its injustice and inhumanity; but every accusation of malignant and superfluous cruelty is not to be credited on the testimony of suspected and prejudiced individuals. Captain Wright having been employed in promoting the naval operations on the coast of France, was taken prisoner, and committed to the Temple, from which he had formerly escaped with sir Sidney Smith, and soon afterwards the fact of his death was communicated on respectable authority to his friends in England. Mr. Lewis Goldsmith, after mentioning his confinement, asserts, without reserve, that red-hot irons were applied to his feet, and that he died in the utmost extremity of torture. But a statement like this refutes itself by its evident absurdity. Had Buonaparte been guilty of an act so unsusceptible of apology and so easily concealed, it is not probable that he would have hazarded its disclosure by suffering it to be known to Mr. Lewis Goldsmith; nor does it appear that captain Wright was personally more obnoxious to the emperor of France than any other native of England. Many of the individuals whom Napoleon accused of aiding the insurgents, and of clandestine correspondence, were then lingering in the prisons of France, but had no occasion to complain of the severity of their sufferings, or the extent of their privations.

Shortly after the publication of Sebastiani's report, the loyal and intrepid, but indiscreet and eccentric Peltier was tried in the King's Bench, on an indictment for a libel against Napoleon Buonaparte. After the libel had been read, the attorney-general began by observing to the jury, " You are now by the indictment that has been read, put distinctly, openly, and fully in possession of every information on the subject on which you have been brought here to decide. The case is simple, and the question, in my mind, by no means difficult to be tried. It will be for you to examine, whether or not the defendant be the author of these publications, and whether or not the prosecution be rightly brought forward before a British jury, and in a British court of justice. It is impossible not to know, that considerable interest and curiosity are attached to this trial; and when I cast my eye about the court, and observe an attendance so different from what usually graces trials in courts of justice, I feel that such motives must have operated in a more than ordinary degree. Many, no doubt, have been curious to hear the observations that may fall from me, in conducting the present prosecution. Yet, sorry as I should be to disappoint such an assembly, the course which duty and inclination point out to me will not be likely to gratify such expectation. This duty, and inclination confine me to the dry and dull trial of the intention; for the law will determine by what takes place in court, by reason, by justice, whether a publication of this kind can be defended as innocent, or tolerated as inoffensive. In discussing these questions, so notorious and so recent, there can neither be much instruction nor amusement; and if any one could suppose that on this, or any other occasion, I should derogate from the dignity of my public duty, or shrink from the faithful discharge of it, he will be disappointed. Though no person can entertain a higher opinion than I do of the abilities and acquirements of the learned gentleman who is to lead the defence; though no person be more unaffectedly convinced of his splendid talents, his brilliant imagination,

4 B 2

his cultivated mind, and his enlightened reason, yet I doubt if even he can satisfy much curiosity on this occasion. The points to be considered are, Whether the defendant be the author of the publication or not? What was the intention of publishing? What is the legal character of guilt or innocence belonging to it? These questions are the only points at issue between us; and these will afford no opportunity of displaying the powers of imagination and reasoning, to excite interest or gratify curiosity; for I cannot bring myself to suppose that the learned gentleman would so far adopt the spirit of the libel as to make his defence a republication of the slanderous matter that it contains; neither can I be persuaded, that he could have been instructed by his client to come into court for the purpose of making the proceedings here a vehicle for the wider dissemination of the libel. If such were his intentions, he would have a wide and abundant field to expatiate on. Of all the extraordinary and eventful facts that arose out of the late extraordinary revolution, that which originated the present government is most surprising. Yet if no other considerations than those of an ordinary discretion were to influence his management of the defence, he will abstain from that course which may exasperate justice, without serving the cause of his client. Discretion alone must guard against that. What is it brings me here in the discharge of a public duty? I prosecute this libel because it endangers the tranquillity of this country. When the question shall arise for consideration of the punishment, I appeal to my learned friends, if I should not ill discharge my duty to the public, to the honor and character of the law, if I should not earnestly press the consideration, that proceedings, which had been made the vehicle of defamation and slander, should not escape in a British court with impunity. The disappointment of curiosity is no part of the business. The present prosecution is to satisfy justice, and to see that the law be not disappointed. Without previously troubling you with stating what the prose-

cution is, I shall state to you what it is not. It is not a work containing an impartial account of the transactions of any given period;—it is not a historical narration of events in a neighbouring country, accompanied with philosophical reflections on their causes and consequences;—it is not a publication whose author, even approaching to licentiousness, had dealt in simple defamation in any particular instance. But the case which the present prosecution brings to notice was conceived originally in libel and in defamation. Defamation is its best object. Its further object is, to excite the subjects of the first magistrate of the French republic, at peace with this country, to deprive him of his authority, and to assassinate him. It was published with the intention of traducing and defaming Napoleon Buonaparte, first consul of France, and of exciting the hatred of the subjects of this country and of his own against him. It tended to excite assassins against his life, and to disturb the peace existing between the republic and this country. Such is the tendency by which it is characterised and was published. Gentlemen, I shall now say a few words on the subject of law: I do not feel myself called upon to define to what extent the subjects of one country may carry their observations or strictures on the administration of affairs in another. But I have no difficulty in asserting, that a publication like the present, tending to embroil the tranquillity of nations, and encouraging the assassination of one who is, de facto, first magistrate of France, is not more opposite to the feelings and sentiments of Englishmen, than it is libellous and illegal. The fair detail of history, the impartial recital of events, the unprejudiced account of transactions, not rendered the vehicle of defamation, is not the subject of information. Defamation constitutes the whole of this publication; and I am confident no lawyer will maintain that it is not an offence of the deepest die, and meriting the severest reprehension. It is not possible that there can be any difficulty in supporting the proposition, that such an offence against the laws of the country ought to be severely punished. The prosecution is not unprecedented. Instances of the same kind occur in the history of the country. I shall cite you two : Lord George Gordon was prosecuted for a libel against the queen of France. J. Vint was accused and convicted of a libel against the emperor of Russia, though defended by my honorable friend not now present ; yet the libel with which he was charged was not marked by any such foul and hideous features as the subject of the present prosecution. It stated only, " that the emperor was rendering himself obnoxious to his subjects, and ridiculous in the eyes of Europe ; that he had lately passed an edict, prohibiting the exportation of timber, &c. in consequence of which 100 vessels returned to this country without a freight." This had no tendency to excite rebellion, to provoke assassination, or to interrupt the relations of amity subsisting between the two countries : yet, being charged as traducing his imperial majesty, and creating danger, the publication was found libellous, and the author convicted. If you find, then, that upon that principle and this authority that crime was punished by a British court of justice, it will only be necessary for me to call your attention to the libel that is the subject of the present prosecution. It is not immaterial to observe, that two of those charged are in the first number of the " Ambigu." And here it may not be amiss to recommend to your notice the frontispiece of this work. It bears a Sphynx, as you may perceive, with a variety of enigmatical Egyptian figures, of which it would neither be easy nor of consequence to discover the meaning. There is one circumstance, however, which is decisive of the object of the publication. The face of the animal resembles that of the prints which are publicly known in this country to be intended as likenesses of Buonaparte. Having never seen the first consul, I cannot positively affirm that it is a *fac simile* of his countenance ; but, as it bears a striking resemblance to the prints that are said to be like him, this circumstance, coupled

with the matter of publication, can leave little room to doubt, that its object was to defame, and render him vile in the eyes of the world in general. Two numbers, the first and third of the " *Ambigu*," are subjects of prosecution. I shall direct your attention first to the matter of the third. The title of it is, An Harangue of Lepidus against Sylla, originally Latin, but translated and altered so as to render it applicable, in all the circumstances, to Buonaparte. It begins with stating, that, from the mild character of his countrymen, the writer would find much difficulty ; that he was fearful they would be more inclined to obey the sentiment that reconciled them to tranquillity, than that which would lead them to revenge. Here the learned attorney stated, that as he had, to save himself the pain of going through the whole libel, procured a learned friend to read it through, he would not follow him, but observe upon the material parts as he proceeded. This libel asserts, that they had in vain maintained a glorious contest against Austria, Russia, and the powers of Europe, if their liberties were to be sacrificed to the Corsican. It goes on—" and now the tiger dares to call himself the founder and regenerator of France, possessing himself of the fruit of their labors, as of a spoil taken in war. There have been lists of proscription, banishment without trial, by which, even children unborn are oppressed. It excites them to rise, to march, to regain their liberty, and seek revenge. Buonaparte has no longer any object of ambition, but security. His Mamelukes, having no contact with the army, nor speaking the language of France, are ready to act as mutes, cut-throats, and hangmen. Every thing—justice, the law, the finances, is in the possession of the despot. It then calls upon them to avenge their wrongs or perish with glory." After having read these passages, the learned attorney called the attention of the jury to the two libels contained in the first number of the "*Ambigu*." The libellous matter was there contained in an ode, or poetical composition. It sets out with representing all nature agitated by a dreadful tempest, and the elements themselves confounded. It then avows an expectation, that the heavens were at length determined to avenge the ambitious attempt of a soldier. Having made the exclamation, " O too vain hope of vengeance !" it represents the heavens as blind or cruel, declaring, that " whatever ravages the thunder may commit, it always spares tyrants ; which remark it illustrates, by the destruction of the merchants' vessels, while the Corsican's bark, bearing the fortune and designs of Cæsar, escapes." This appeared an evident allusion to the Roman republic, in which 'Cæsar had found Pompey, Cato, and the senate, against him. The libel then proceeds : " But oh ! eternal disgrace, after the victory of Pharsalia there still remained a poniard among the last of the Romans !" In this bombastic rhapsody the learned gentleman contended, that no other view could be discovered than that of holding out an example of assassination. The second part contains the wish or prayer of a good patriot. This wish describes the fortune of Buonaparte, from his leaving Corsica, follows him flying from victory to victory in Italy, in Egypt, then back to France, where he overthrows the five tyrants, is chosen consul, makes and unmakes kings, dictates peace, and has crowned heads at his feet. Far from envying his lot, it wishes him a successor, and· that he may have his apotheosis to-morrow. This is an allusion to the fate of Romulus, who was assassinated, and afterwards deified, to extinguish the infamy of his murderers. Upon what principle, I will ask, said the attorney-general, are those examples of assassination recalled, if not for the purpose of exciting the subjects of that chief magistrate to rebellion and assassination ? Let me not be told that I am an enemy to the English press, when I prosecute the abuse of it ; a licentiousness that would bring it into discredit, infamy, and disgrace. I will put to your breasts, whether such a publication would constitute a crime in this country ; a publication so base, so disgraceful, that even in a time of war I should

not hesitate to pronounce it unjustifiable. We were then, and are happily now, at peace ; and the conduct that a state of war cannot sanction, must be criminal, in a high degree, in peace.· Let me not be told of character. The first magistrate of a great nation, no matter whether descended from a long line of royal ancestors, or lately raised from the abyss of obscurity, is entitled to respect, and should be treated with decorum. We may be told, gentlemen, of abusive articles in the *Moniteur :* I am not here to vindicate the conduct or the publications of the French government, or its journalists. If there be any feelings in another country that can reconcile such vile calumnies, let them have the benefit, but let us not have the disgrace."

The evidence was then called in support of the prosecution ; which consisted merely of proving the publication of the two papers, at the desire, and by the request, of the defendant Mr. Peltier, by Mr. De Boffe, against whom an information was also filed ; but he suffered judgment to pass by default.

An interpreter read the whole of the original, and then verified an English translation ; and also, at the request of the defendant's counsel, read a number of extracts out of the " *Ambigu,*" that were not included in the information ; which they said was necessary, in order to give to the jury the whole context of the publication.

All the readings, both French and English, being concluded, the case for the prosecution closed.

Mr. Mackintosh then rose, and addressed the jury, on the part of the defendant; for nearly three hours ; but the substance of his speech was as follows :

" My lord, and gentlemen of the jury, the time is now come for me to address you ; but I must confess I feel myself unworthy of those high eulogiums which the kindness of my learned friend has been pleased to bestow upon me.; but he has done me but justice, when he supposed that I would not prostitute whatever small talents I may possess, so far as to lend myself out to answer the ends of a faction, or to defend my client on any principles that are inconsistent with the honor of the profession to which I belong : I do not mean to justify him from the example of the *Moniteur,* or any other foreign journal ; I do not mean to contend, that an indefinite liberty is to be allowed even with respect to political discussion, much less would I pretend to justify any expressions which could be fairly construed as tending to provoke *assassination.* In professing this, I cannot claim the least merit to myself ; my feelings are the same with those of all who hear me ; and I believe there is no one who wears the gown of our profession that would so disgrace it as to defend the principle of any libel provoking to assassination. If there are any libels in foreign journals which more than others call forth the indignation of every British reader, it is those libels which do not hesitate to charge the British nation with feelings that cannot enter into a British bosom. Such a libel, for instance, as in a very recent *Moniteur* charged a distinguished British officer (general Stuart) with provoking to assassination. Such libels as have been thrown out against our gracious sovereign, a prince who, through a long and tumultuous reign of forty-three years, has ever preserved a blameless and amiable career of private life; when against a prince so respected and so beloved, we read in the *Moniteur,* that if the assassination of Buonaparte had taken place in France, the assassin would have been rewarded with the *order of the garter,* what British bosom does not feel indignant at so foul a calumny, so atrocious a libel ? What ! can that illustrious order instituted by our first Edwards, in the days of the battles of Cressy and Poitiers, be polluted by an association with murderers ? Shall that unsullied garter, which has been hitherto the proud distinction of what is most noble and most valued in our nation, serve to adorn the person of an assassin ? And is it our amiable and virtuous sovereign that is to give the ribbon of this order to a cut-throat and an assassin, and affix the star of honor on the breast of infamy ?

Were I to pursue these observations, it might lead our minds somewhat from that even temper in which we should weigh the defence against the accusation ; I shall therefore proceed directly, and as shortly as the nature of the case will allow me, to state for my client that defence which seems to grow out of the circumstances of the case. The real prosecutor in this case is the master of the greatest empire the world ever saw. We cannot believe but it was from his suggestions that this prosecution originated. The defendant, John Peltier, is a poor, proscribed exile, a French royalist, one of those unfortunate men who have survived the shipwreck of their fortunes and of their country, but who still cannot be persuaded to give up all principles which they had learned in early life. It is true, that many of these unfortunate emigrants have been allowed to return to their native land, on the condition of paying an implicit allegiance to the first consul. There still remain a handful, which, whether rightly or foolishly, cannot bring themselves to pay this allegiance that their hearts disclaim. Among this number is John Peltier. He had cultivated literature much in his youth, and in his exile ; after the loss of his fortune he made it his profession, and his means of livelihood. He had set up a little obscure journal in London, which served to solace the miseries of his fellow-exiles, by affording a variety of miscellaneous reading, and, among other things, political miscellanies, which were peculiarly interesting to that ill-fated class; but in this avocation he had the misfortune to offend the master of the continent of Europe, and he is now under prosecution. Gentlemen of the jury, he stands now on the only spot in this earth where, by the justice of our laws, he can be on an equality with his powerful prosecutor ; he sees that sight which is the most pleasing to accused innocence, the honest countenance of a British jury. Here then, in this only asylum which remains for persecuted innocence, I do not fear to defend him ; and if I can succeed in convincing you that the publications were not written in the spirit in which they have been alleged to have been written, and that they have not that tendency, I am convinced you will, without considering the rank or power of the prosecutor, find my client not guilty. I shall now, gentlemen, submit to your attention some observations on the publications in question, which I trust will induce you to consider them in a light very different from what they might appear to you without the context. As to the *Prospectus*, I think the last part of it, which has been read as explaining the intentions of the author, is by no means so full and explicit as in the beginning of the *Prospectus*, which declares the object of this new work to be merely a collection of miscellanies of every sort : and the work itself seems to confirm the statement of this *Prospectus* ; for, excepting those three political pieces which are the subject of this prosecution, all the rest of the work was purely miscellaneous. And as to these works themselves, I mean to justify them on this principle, that they were not the compositions of Peltier, but merely the republications of what had circulation before, and ' of which he only made a selection for his readers. I am convinced that the attorney-general will see and confess the wide difference there is between an original publication and a republication of what was before in circulation. For instance, the English papers copied the grossest libels from the French papers ; but they were never prosecuted on that account, because there was no libellous intention in those who republished them ; but rather, on the contrary, it was their wish, by exposing the malignity of our then enemy, to unite the people of this country the closer, to resist any foreign aggression : if, therefore, he could prove that this was merely a republication, it would come within that principle. To prove this there was pretty strong internal evidence. Peltier was known to be a Royalist. Were those pieces of a royalist stamp ? Nothing like it. As to the ode which was introduced in his journal as the reputed work of Chenier, had it not every appearance of his Jacobin pen ? Was there a sentiment of a royalist from the beginning to the end of

it ? As to the second copy of verses, which was inserted as coming from the pen of a Dutchman, what was more likely than that a Dutchman should feel indignant at the oppression . of his country, and write verses against him whom he considered as the principal cause of it ? As to the construction on the word *apotheosis*, he thought it was overstrained when supposed to imply assassination ; for it was well known, that though the *apotheosis* of Romulus might have taken place after his death, yet that Augustus, Tiberius, and even Nero and Caligula, were worshipped as gods during their lives. On this subject he could remind them of the remarkable passage—

> Præsens divus Cæsar habebitur
> Adjunctis Britannis imperio.

He trusted, however, that no modern Cæsar would ever elevate himself to divine honors by adding *Britain* to his empire. The labors of Hercules would be light compared to such a task. As to the long paper given as the harangue of Lepidus to the Romans, he did not see that it was, in itself, so criminal as it had been represented. It is not every one who talks of Brutus with applause, that is, on that account, to be supposed to provoke assassination. But he must recal to the jury the manner in which this article was inserted in Peltier's journal : it was stated as the paper upon which *Camille Jourdan* (one of the most enlightened and best men in Europe) was arrested. This paper, it was mentioned, was thrown by one of Fouche's spies among *Camille's* papers, in order for a pretext to throw him into prison. Is that improbable ? Gentlemen of the jury, we are not now trying the character of Fouche ; but if we were, I should shew you that it was not improbable that he should so act. I have in my hand letters of citizen Fouche ; one of them is from Lyons, in which he laments that the destruction of that city went on so slowly. He said, " Kings punished slowly, because they were feeble ; but the anger of republicans should be as prompt as their will ; they should *annihilate* their enemies, and never spare the tears of repentance." He concluded by mentioning, "that he would spring a mine which should at once destroy that guilty city:" and yet this man had afterwards the effrontery to lay to the English the charge of having destroyed Lyons. Is it then improbable that such a person as Fouché should have practised this infamous trick, and got such a paper as this slipt among the papers of Camille Jourdan, for the purpose of having him arrested and thrown into prison? As to the internal evidence, gentlemen of the jury, I have already told you, that there is not a line in all these publications which contains a royalist sentiment; but, on the contrary, they are furiously Jacobinical. Does any body suspect Peltier of being a Jacobin? Certainly not. Whenever anger is expressed in these pieces against Buonaparte, it is for overturning the Directory. Is that like the rage of a royalist or a Jacobin? And is it not, then, more likely that these articles were really the productions of those they are attributed to, Chenier, Fouché, &c.? In that case, Peltier is not to be considered as the author, but as a person who, with innocent motives, reprinted them in a miscellaneous work, for the amusement of the small circle of his readers. The circulation of the "Ambigu" could not be intended to be among Englishmen, as it is written in French; nor in France, for Buonaparte knows effectually how to prohibit the entry of such articles into his dominions. Having now endeavored to prove to you, that it is not probable that Peltier was the author or original publisher of those works, or that he at all wished to inculcate the Jacobin principles they contain, I must warn you of the immense importance of the free discussion of political events. If at all times the liberty of the press was dear to Englishmen, it should be more peculiarly dear now that it is the only free press in the world. Gentlemen, I consider this as the first contest between the greatest power on earth and the British free press; the only one now remaining. That it is so is a

melancholy reflection to the friends of human nature. Till that great earthquake, occasioned by the French revolution, had swallowed up the presses of the continent, there had, by the indulgence of the larger powers, existed many states in which a free press had been tolerated. This was the case in Holland, Switzerland, and the free towns of Germany. Holland and Switzerland are no more, and fifty of the Germanic free states have been erased fourthe map by a dash of the pen. These states I consider as a very interesting part of the antient system. Great nations cannot exist without considering their military system, but small states are obliged to devote themselves to industry and the arts of peace; and they form a kind of control over the superior ones; for no depravity can so sink any man in his own esteem, as to render him regardless of the opinion of the world. The undisturbed repose which the states I have referred to were suffered to enjoy, enabled them to become models attesting the civilization to which Christian Europe had reached. Nothing so much proved the civilization of the continent at the period I refer to, as the freedom enjoyed by the little republic of Genoa. It was suffered to remain undisturbed and unthreatened, while surrounded by myriads of the armies of France. All this is now past and gone. What the new system is to be is not for me to conjecture; but I am perfectly convinced that the arbitrary violence of ambitious monarchs has been checked by the dread of the opinion of the impartial audience formed among the smaller states, and in which no sooner were any acts of oppression known than a thousand presses were set to work to communicate them to the world. At present there is not such a thing as a free press from Palermo to Hamburgh: not one asylum for the liberty of discussion remains—no public voice, the expression of which can control the despotic attempts of arbitrary tyrants. Happily, however, those presses are still secure which are protected by the British government, and by the valor of Englishmen. The antient fabric, raised by our ancestors, still endures; though surrounded with ruins, it stands solid and unshaken. Gentlemen of the jury, to shew you of what importance our ancestors always held this privilege, I shall trace a little the origin of it. Queen Elizabeth was the first who established a newspaper in England; she did so at the time of the Spanish armada, when it was necessary to preserve high the tone and spirit of the people. In Cromwell's usurpation, the freedom of the press was protected by British juries, and Cromwell's attorney-general was twice defeated in this court. In Charles II. days, though the times were corrupt and profligate, yet the press was safe; and in the days of the revolution, and ever since, it has been held one of the dearest privileges of Englishmen. In latter times we can speak more positively, from our own experience, on this very point. In that first grand breach of the social system of Europe, that national robbery, called the first partition of Poland, did not the English papers vent the strongest feelings of indignation? Catherine and Frederic were not treated according to their rank, but according to the crime in which they had partaken. We were then at peace and amity with Russia and Prussia; and yet the attorney-general of the day never thought of prosecuting the editors and publishers of those papers. In the second partition of Poland, too, the British press expressed the honest indignation of the country; and it is well, not only for this country, but for the social order of Europe in general, that it should be so. However formidable a sovereign's military establishment may be; however great his power and extensive his sway; still the feelings of human nature compel him to wish for the approbation of his fellow-men, and bring him to the bar of the tribunal of public opinion. Newspapers, I am aware, are not very popular in this place; nor is it very surprising, because they appear in this place only to be checked for their faults. With all their faults, however, their increased circulation is a proof of the increasing curiosity and desire of knowledge in this country, of which they are

at once the cause and effect. Perhaps it would be better to treat those engaged in this difficult employment with a little more indulgence, in order to teach them that self-respect which is the best way to lead men to cultivate that of others. Be this as it may, however, every thing that increases the number of those who take an interest, and exercise a judgment, in public affairs, is, in effect, to increase the real democracy of a country, much more than those forms to which some people are so much attached. If it be important that the public mind should be fortified against the design of foreign power, it is fit that the discussion most calculated to disseminate a public spirit should be encouraged. Upon every occasion in which the public opinion of this country could be displayed respecting foreign affairs, it has been uniformly given, and no attempt has been made to repress it. From the seizure of Corsica down to the different partitions of Poland, the public sentiment of England has most strongly been expressed against such unwarrantable robberies. Next followed an event, in comparison of which the atrocity of preceding spoliations become trivial. Switzerland, a country for three hundred years the abode of peace; a country, as it were, raised above the storms of political events; a country boasting of a gallant and disciplined army, without ever attacking its neighbours, rich without imposing taxes, till its riches tempt the spoiler, and become a cause of its ruin. Switzerland is doomed to fall under the imposing ravages of the French revolution. Had such an event taken place in times of peace, would it have been necessary for the public of this country to stifle the voice of sympathy and sorrow, for fear of giving offence to the ruthless tyrants? Had Alois Reding, a name worthy to compare with the first of names, for true simplicity of virtue and unaffected magnanimity of character; had Alois Reding, who, with a handful of peasants, defeated the conquerors of Europe on the soil where, three hundred years before, their ancestors fought the oppressors of their liberty, sought an assylum in England, attracted by the renown of this mighty empire, would my learned friend have told him, that he must conceal his tears, and breathe low his sighs, for the ruin of his country, lest his potent enemy should drive him from his asylum, or lead him into court, the victim of prosecution? I am sure that no Englishman could think with patience of such an ignominy; and sure I am that my learned friend has a heart too thoroughly English to brook such disgrace. Had we been at peace between 1792 and 1794, could an English court or an English jury have been called upon to protect the reputation of a Robespierre, president of the Committee of Safety; of his friend Marat; of a carrier, his agent, who drowned 2000 priests in the Loire, and caused 600 children, under fourteen, to be shot by the soldiery? Could the laws of England have been called upon to protect, because they were in place, those butchers who perpetrated, within that period of two years, atrocities which, contrary to the practise of mankind, are generally under-rated, not exaggerated? Atrocities so prodigious as to compel the mind to seek refuge in scepticism; and which, but half believed, are now but half remembered. But I cannot, with regard to my own feelings, or the respect I bear my learned friend, pursue this train of interrogation. Had such things taken place, the courage of our courts, and the integrity of our juries, had been our only resource. All would have been lost, but the unextinguishable spirit of an English jury. To conclude—I trust that on this, as on all former occasions, the unsubdued spirit of the country will appear. All I ask is, a favorable construction for what may appear ambiguous."

The speech of Mr. Mackintosh had a powerful influence on the feelings of the audience, but the *prepossessions* of a special jury are not easily counteracted, and but for the recurrence of hostilities, Mr. Peltier might have sustained a long imprisonment; and every species of privation, for the employment of the very phrases which had been echoed from one ministerial member to another, since Buonaparte

returned from Egypt and assumed the consulate.

Weak and wavering as they were, the English ministry could not remain entirely unconscious of the designs and machinations of their formidable enemy; and in October and November 1802, orders were sent out for the retention of the Cape of Good Hope and the West Indian islands, which had not yet been surrendered to the French. Had their precaution been justified by no other circumstance, the mission of colonel Sebastiani alone would have fully acquitted them of unjust suspicion. That celebrated emissary arrived at Corfu, harangued the constituted authorities, and inculcated the doctrines of liberty and equality. From that place he proceeded to Egypt, for the purpose of conciliating the good opinion of Djezzar Pacha, and counteracting the influence of the English. The distrust between the two nations was still further promoted by the representations of the French government, on the protection afforded to Georges and other royalists, and the marked respect so frequently, and, perhaps, injudiciously evinced, to the members and adherents of the Bourbon family.

But the retention of Malta formed the most prominent topic of remonstrance on the part of France. By the treaty of Amiens, it had been stipulated, "That a grand master should be elected in full chapter by the knights of St. John of Jerusalem; that a Maltese league should be established in the room of the French and English, which were for ever to be abolished; that the British troops were to evacuate the island, provided that there were a grand master, or commissioners fully empowered to receive the possession, and that a force of 2000 Neapolitan troops were to remain till the knights had raised a sufficient force to protect the island. These were to be furnished by his Sicilian majesty. Great Britain, France, Austria, Russia, and Spain, were to guarantee this arrangement, and the independence of the island."

It appears that Buonaparte, during the first part of the discussion respecting

4 c 2

Malta, trusting to the pacific wishes of the government of Britain, insisted only on the *positive* stipulation of the treaty, the surrender of Malta. The *condition* annexed to that article, the guarantee of the independence of the island by the powers of Europe was left unmentioned. Observing however that the British ministry regarded this guarantee as an indispensible preliminary, he employed his influence at St. Petersburgh with so much dexterity, that Alexander agreed to guarantee its independence. To this arrangement the British court objected as including only the guarantee of a *single* power, and the project of the emperor Alexander was returned for alteration. Lord Whitworth was informed by M. Talleyrand on the 25th of January, 1803, that the difficulties respecting the guarantee of the island by Alexander would be speedily removed, and that he was instructed to demand an explanation of the designs of the king of England, with regard to the tenth article of the treaty. The conduct of Buonaparte freed the British ambassador from the embarrassment to which he might otherwise have been subjected, as the publication of Sebastiani's report, enabled him to justify the conduct of the English government by the views of France on Egypt and the Ionian isles. It would be unnecessary to detail the minute particulars of the negotiation respecting this island, the proposal of England to retain it for the space of ten years; the offer to accept the island of Lampedosa in exchange, and the requisition of substantial security, for objects which might be materially endangered by the removal of the English troops. But the important document which follows, had so direct a bearing on the progress of subsequent events, and embraces so many objects of complaint, that it deserves to be inserted.

DECLARATION.

" His majesty's earnest endeavors for the preservation of peace having failed of success, he entertains the fullest confidence that he shall receive the same support from his parliament, and that the same zeal and spirit will be manifested by his people, which he has experienced on every occasion, when the honor of his crown has been attacked, or the essential interests of his dominions has been endangered.

" During the whole course of the negotiations, which led to the preliminary and definitive treaties of peace between his majesty and the French republic, it was his majesty's sincere desire, not only to put an end to the hostilities which subsisted between the two countries, but to adopt such measures, and to concur in such propositions, as might effectually contribute to consolidate the general tranquillity of Europe. The same motives by which his majesty was actuated, during the negotiations for peace, have since invariably governed his conduct. As soon as the treaty of Amiens was concluded his majesty's courts were open to the people of France for every purpose of legal redress; all sequestrations were taken off their property; all prohibitions on their trade, which had been imposed during the war, were removed, and they were placed, in every respect, on the same footing, with regard to commerce and intercourse, as the inhabitants of any other state in amity with his majesty with which there existed no treaty of commerce.

" To a system of conduct thus open, liberal, and friendly, the proceedings of the French government affords the most striking contrast. The prohibitions which had been placed on the commerce of his majesty's subjects during the war have been enforced with increased strictness and severity; violence has been offered, in several instances, to their vessels and their property, and in no case has justice been afforded to those who may have been aggrieved in consequence of such acts, nor has any satisfactory answer been given to the repeated representations made by his majesty's ministers or ambassador at Paris. Under such circumstances, when his majesty's subjects were not suffered to enjoy the common advantages of peace within the territories of the French republic, and the countries dependent upon it, the French government had recourse to the extraordinary, measure of sending over to this country a number of persons, for the professed purpose of residing in the most considerable seaport towns of Great Britain and Ireland, in the character of commercial agents or consuls. These persons could have no pretensions to be acknowledged in that character, as the right of being so acknowledged, as well as all the privileges attached to such a situation, could only be derived from a commercial treaty, and as no treaty, of that description, was in existence between his majesty and the French republic.

"There was, consequently, too much reason to suppose that the real object of their mission was by no means of a commercial nature; and this suspicion was confirmed, not only by the circumstance that some of them were military men, but by the actual discovery, that several of them were furnished with instructions to obtain the soundings of the harbors, and to procure military surveys of the places where it was intended they should reside. His majesty felt it to be his duty to prevent their departure to their respective places of destination, and presented to the French government the necessity of withdrawing them; and it cannot be denied, that the circumstances under which they were sent, and the instructions which were given to them, ought to be considered as decisive indications of the dispositions and intentions of the government by whom they were employed.

"The conduct of the French government, with respect to the commercial intercourse between the two countries, must, therefore, be considered as ill-suited to a state of peace, and their proceedings in their more general political relations, as well as in those which immediately concern his majesty's dominions, appears to have been altogether inconsistent with every principle of good faith, moderation, and justice. His majesty had entertained hopes, in consequence of the repeated assurances, and professions of the French government, that they might have been induced to adopt a system of policy, which, if it had not inspired other powers with confidence, might, at least, have allayed their jealousies. If the French government had really appeared to be actuated by a due attention to such a system; if their dispositions had proved to be essentially pacific, allowances would have been made for the situation in which a new government must be placed after so dreadful and extensive a convulsion as that which has been produced by the French revolution. But his majesty, has, unfortunately, had too much reason to observe and to lament that the system of violence, aggression, and aggrandisement, which characterised the proceedings of the different governments of France during the war, has been continued with as little disguise since its termination. They have continued to keep a French army in Holland against the will, and in defiance of the remonstrances of the Batavian government, and in repugnance of the letter of three solemn treaties. They have, in a period of peace, invaded the territory, and violated the independence of the Swiss nation, in defiance of the treaty of Luneville, which had stipulated the independence of their territory, and the right of the inhabitants to choose their own form of government. They have annexed to the dominions of France Piedmont, Parma, and Placentia, and the Island of Elba, without allotting any provision to the king of Sardinia, whom they have despoiled of the most valuable part of his territory, though they were bound, by a solemn engagement to the emperor of Russia, to attend to his interests, and to provide for his establishment. It may, indeed, with truth, be asserted, that the period which has elapsed since the conclusion of the definitive treaty has been marked with one continued series of aggression, violence, and insult, on the part of the French government.

"In the month of October last, his majesty was induced, in consequence of the earnest solicitation of the Swiss nation, to make an effort, by a representation to the French government, to avert the evils which were then impending over that country. This representation was couched in the most temperate terms ; and measures were taken by his majesty for ascertaining, under the circumstances which then existed, the real situation and wishes of the Swiss cantons, as well as the sentiments of the other cabinets of Europe. His majesty learned, however, with the utmost regret, that no disposition to counteract these repeated infractions of treaties and acts of violence was manifested by any of the powers most immediately interested in preventing them ; and his majesty, therefore, felt, that, with respect to these objects, his single efforts could not be expected to produce any considerable advantage to those in whose favor they might be exerted.

" It was about this time that the French government first distinctly advanced the principle, that his majesty had no right to complain of the conduct, or interfere with the proceedings of France, on any point which did not form a part of the stipulations of the treaty of Amiens. That treaty was unquestionably founded upon the same principle as every other antecedent treaty or convention, on the assumption of the state of possessions, and of engagements subsisting at the time of its conclusion ; and if that state of possession and of engagements is materially affected by the voluntary act of any of the parties, so as to prejudice the condition on which the other party has entered into the contract, the change so made may be considered as operating virtually as a breach of the treaty itself, and as giving the party aggrieved a right to demand satisfaction or compensation for any substantial difference which such acts may have effected in their relative situations ; but, whatever may be the principle on which the treaty is to be considered as founded, there is, indisputably, a general law of nations, which, though liable to be limited, explained, or restrained by conventional law, is antecedent to it, and is that law or rule of conduct to which all sovereigns and states have been accustomed to appeal, where conventional law is admitted to have been silent. The treaty of Amiens, and every other treaty, in providing for the objects to which it is particularly directed, does not, therefore, assume or imply an indifference to all other objects which are not specified in its stipulation, much less does it adjudge them to be of a nature to be left to the will and caprice of the violent and the powerful. . The justice of the cause is, alone, a sufficient ground to warrant the interposition of any of the powers of Europe in the differences which may arise between other states, and the application and extent of that just interposition is to be determined solely by considerations of prudence. These principles can admit of no dispute ; but if the new and extraordinary pretensions advanced by the French government, to exclude his majesty from any right to interfere with respect to the concerns of other powers, unless they made a specific part of the stipulations of the treaty of Amiens, was that which it was possible to maintain, those powers would have a right, at least, to claim the benefit of this principle in every case of difference between the two countries. The indignation of all Europe must surely then be excited by the declarations of the French government, that, in the event of hostilities, these very powers, who were no parties to the treaty of Amiens, and who were not allowed to derive any advantage from the remonstrances of his majesty in their behalf, are, nevertheless, to be made the victims of a war, which is alleged to arise out of the same treaty, and are to be sacrificed in the contest, which they not only have not occasioned, but which they have had no means whatever of preventing.

" His majesty judged it most expedient, under the circumstances which then affected Europe, to abstain from a recurrence to hostilities, on account of the views of ambition, and acts of aggression, manifested by France on the continent ; yet, an experience of the character and dispositions of the French government could not fail to impress his majesty with a sense of the necessity of increased vigilance in guarding the rights and dignity of his crown, and in protecting the interests of his people.

" Whilst his majesty was actuated by these sentiments, he was called upon by the French government to evacuate the island of Malta. His majesty had manifested, from the moment of the signature of the definitive treaty, an anxious disposition to carry into full effect the stipulations of the treaty of Amiens relative to that island. As soon as he was informed that the election of a grand master had taken place, under the auspices of the emperor of Russia, and that it had been agreed by the different priories assembled at St. Petersburgh, to acknowledge the person whom the court of Rome should select out of those who had been named by them, to be grand master of the order of St. John, his majesty proposed to the French government, for the purpose of avoiding any difficulties which might arise in the execution of the arrangement, to acknowledge that election to be valid ; and when, in the month of August, the French government applied to his majesty, to permit the Neapolitan troops to be sent to the island of Malta, as a preliminary measure for preventing any unnecessary delay, his majesty consented, without hesitation, to this proposal, and gave directions for the admission of the Neapolitan troops into the island. His majesty had thus shewn his disposition, not only to throw no obstacle in the way of the execution of the treaty, but, on the contrary, to facilitate the execution of it by every means in his power. His majesty, cannot, however, admit, that, at any period since the conclusion of the treaty of Amiens, the French government have had a right to call upon him, in conformity to the stipulations of that treaty, to withdraw his forces from the island of Malta. At the time when this demand was made by the French government, several of the most important stipulations of the arrangement respecting Malta remained unexecuted : the election of a grand master had not been carried into effect. The 10th article had stipulated, that the independence of the island should be placed under the guarantee

and protection of Great Britain, France, Austria, Russia, Spain, and Prussia. The emperor of Germany had acceded to the guarantee, but only on condition of a like accession on the part of the other powers specified in the article. The emperor of Russia had refused his accession, except on the condition that the Maltese *langue* should be abrogated ; and the king of Prussia had given no answer whatever, to the application which had been made to him to accede to the arrangement. But the fundamental principle, upon the existence of which depended the execution of the other parts of the article, had been defeated by the changes which had taken place in the constitution of the order, since the conclusion of the treaty of peace. It was to the order of St. John of Jerusalem, that his majesty was, by the first stipulation of the 10th article, bound to restore the island of Malta. The order is defined to consist of those *langues*, which were in existence at the time of the conclusion of the treaty ; the three French *langues* having been abolished, and a Maltese *langue* added to the institution. The order consisted, therefore; at that time, of the following *langues*, viz. the *langues* of Arragon, Castile, Germany, Bavaria, and Russia. Since the conclusion of the definitive treaty, the *langues* of Arragon and Castile, have been separated from the order, by Spain ; a part of the Italian *langue* has been abolished by the annexation of Piedmont and Parma to France. There is strong reason to believe that it has been in contemplation, to sequestrate the property of the Bavarian *langue*, and the intention has been avowed of keeping the Russian *langues* within the dominions of the emperor.

" Under these circumstances, the order of St. John cannot now be considered as that body, to which, according to the stipulation of the treaty, the island was to be restored ; and the funds indispensibly necessary for its support, and for the maintenance of the independence of the island, have been nearly, if not wholly sequestered. Even if this had arisen from circumstances which it was not in the power of any of the contracting parties to the treaty to control, his majesty would, nevertheless, have had a right to defer the evacuation of the island by his forces, until such time as an equivalent arrangement had been concluded for the preservation of the independence of the order and of the island. But if these changes have taken place in consequence of any acts of the other parties to the treaty; if the French government shall appear to have proceeded upon a system of rendering the order, whose independence they had stipulated, incapable of maintaining that independence, his majesty's right to continue in the occupation of the island, under such circumstances, will hardly be contested. It is indisputable, that the revenues of the two Spanish *langues* have been withdrawn from the order by his catholic majesty; a part of the Italian *langue* has, in fact, been abolished by France, through the unjust annexation of Piedmont, and Parma, and Placentia, to the French territory. The elector of Bavaria has been instigated by the French government, to sequestrate the property of the order within his territories; and it is certain, that they have not only sanctioned, but encouraged the idea of the propriety of separating the Russian *langues* from the remainder of the order.

" As the conduct of the governments of France and Spain have, therefore, in some instances directly, and in others indirectly, contributed to the changes which have taken place in the order, and thus destroyed its means of supporting its independence, it is to those governments, and not to his majesty, that the non-execution of the 10th article of the treaty of Amiens must be ascribed.

" Such would be the just conclusion if the 10th article of that treaty were considered as an arrangement by itself: it must be observed, however, that this article forms a part only of a treaty of peace, the whole of which is connected together, and the stipulations of which must, upon a principle common to all

treaties, be construed as having a reference to each other.

" His majesty was induced, by the treaty of peace, to consent to abandon, and to restore to the order of St. John, the island of Malta, on condition of its independence and neutrality. But a further condition (which must, necessarily, be supposed to have had considerable influence with his majesty, in inducing him to make so important a concession) was, the acquiescence of the French government in an arrangement for the security of the Levant, by the 8th and 9th articles in the treaty, stipulating the integrity of the Turkish empire and the independence of the Ionian islands. His majesty has, however, since learned, that the French government have entertained views hostile to both these objects, and that they have even suggested the idea of a partition of the Turkish empire. These views must now be manifest to all the world, from the official publication of the report of colonel Sebastiani; from the conduct of that officer, and of the other French agents, in Egypt, Syria, and the Ionian islands, and from the distinct admission of the first consul himself, in his communication with lord Whitworth. His majesty was, therefore, warranted in considering it to be the determination of the French government to violate those articles of the treaty of peace which stipulated for the integrity and independence of the Turkish empire and of the Ionian islands; and, consequently, he would not have been justified in evacuating the island of Malta without receiving some other security which might equally provide for these important objects: his majesty, accordingly, feels that he has an incontestible claim, in consequence of the conduct of France since the treaty of peace, and with reference to the objects which made part of the stipulations of that treaty, to refuse, under the present circumstances, to relinquish the possession of the island of Malta.

" Yet, notwithstanding this right, so clear and so unquestionable, the alternative presented by the French government to his majesty, in language the most peremptory and menacing, was the evacuation of Malta, or the renewal of war.

" If the views of ambition and aggrandisement, which have thus been manifested by the French government since the conclusion of the treaty of peace, have, in so very particular a manner attracted the attention of his majesty, it has been equally impossible for him not to feel, and not to notice, the repeated indignities which have been offered by that government to his crown and his people.

" The report of colonel Sebastiani contains the most unwarrantable insinuations and charges against his majesty's government, against the officer who commanded his forces in Egypt, and against the British army in that quarter. This paper cannot be considered as the publication of a private individual : it has been avowed, and, indeed, bears evidence upon the face of it, that it is the official report of an accredited agent, published by the authority of the government to which it was addressed, who, thereby, have given it their express sanction.

" This report had been published a very short time, when another indignity was offered to this country, in the communication of the first consul of France to the legislative body: in this communication he presumes to affirm, in the character of chief magistrate of that country, " That Great Britain cannot, singly, contend against the power of France ;" an assertion as unfounded as it is indecent, disproved by the events of many wars, and by none more than by those of the war which has been recently concluded. Such an assertion, advanced in the 'most solemn official act of a government, and thereby meant to be avowed to all the powers of Europe, can be considered in no other light than as a defiance publicly offered to his majesty and to a brave and powerfull people, who are both willing and able to defend his just rights, and those of their country, against every insult and aggression.

" The conduct of the first consul to his majesty's ambassador, at his audience, in presence of the ministers of most of

the sovereigns and states of Europe, furnishes another instance of provocation on the part of the French government, which it would be improper not to notice on the present occasion ; and the subsequent explanation of this transaction may be considered as having the effect of aggravating, instead of palliating, the affront.

" At the very time when his majesty was demanding satisfaction and explanation on some of the points above-mentioned, the French minister at Hamburgh endeavored to obtain the insertion, in a Hamburgh paper, of a most gross and opprobious libel against his majesty ; and, when difficulties were made respecting the insertion of it, he availed himself of his official character, of minister of the French republic, to require the publication of it, by order of his government, in the gazette of the senate of that town. With this requisition, so made, the senate of Hamburgh were induced to comply ; and thus has the independence of that town been violated, and a free state made the instrument, by the menace of the French government, of propagating throughout Europe, upon their authority, the most offensive and unfounded calumnies against his majesty and his government. His majesty might add to this list of indignities the requisition, which the French government have repeatedly urged, that the laws and constitution of his country should be changed, relative to the liberty of the press: his majesty might, likewise, add, the calls which the French government have, on several occasions, made upon him to violate the laws of hospitality, with respect to persons who had found an asylum within his dominions, and against whose conduct no charge whatever has, at any time, been substantiated. It is impossible to reflect on these different proceedings, and the course which the French government have thought proper to adopt respecting them, without the thorough conviction, that they are not the effect of accident ; but that they form a part of a system, which has been adopted for the purpose of degrading, vilifying, and insulting, his majesty and his government.

" Under all these insults and provocations, his majesty, not without a due sense of his dignity, has proceeded, with every degree of temper and moderation, to obtain satisfaction and redress, while he has neglected no means, consistent with his honor and the safety of his dominions, to induce the government of France to concede to him, what is in his judgment, absolutely necessary for the future tranquillity of Europe : his efforts, in this respect, have proved abortive ; and he has, therefore, judged it necessary to order his ambassador to leave Paris. In having recourse to this proceeding, it has been his majesty's object to put an end to the fruitless discussions which have too long subsisted between the two governments, and to close a period of suspense peculiarly injurious to the subjects of his majesty.

" But, though the provocations which his majesty has received might entitle him to larger claims than those which he has advanced ; yet, anxious to prevent calamities, which might thus be extended to every part of Europe, he is still willing, as far as is consistent with his own honor and the interests of his people, to afford every facility to any just and honorable arrangement, by which such evils may be averted : he has, therefore, no difficulty in declaring to all Europe, that, notwithstanding all the changes which have taken place since the treaty of peace ; notwithstanding the extension of the power of France, in repugnance to that treaty, and to the spirit of peace itself : his majesty will not avail himself of these circumstances to demand in compensation all that he is entitled to require, but will be ready to concur, even now in an arrangement, by which satisfaction shall be given to him for the indiguities which have been offered to his crown and to his people, and substantial security afforded against further encroachments on the part of France.

" His majesty has thus, distinctly and unreservedly, stated the reasons of those proceedings to which he has found himself compelled to resort. He is actuated by no disposition to interfere in the internal concerns of any other state, by no projects of conquest and aggrandisement ; but solely by a sense of what is due to the honor of his crown and the interests of his people, and by an anxious desire to obstruct the further progress of a system, which, if not resisted, may prove fatal to every part of the civilized world.

Westminster, March 8th, 1803.

The message was received with approbation by a large majority, and an address was voted, assuring his majesty of the loyalty and attachment of his faithful commons. From these discussions the public attention was for a time diverted by the discovery of a treasonable conspiracy, and the trial, and execution of the traitors, who acted beneath the influence and auspices of colonel Edward Marcus Despard. A society was established at the Oakley arms, in Westminster, " for extension of liberty," of which two men named Frances and Wood were the most active members. They frequently attempted to seduce soldiers into the association, and sometimes with success. In the summer of 1802, they removed from the Oakley arms, for the purpose of evading suspicion, and colonel Despard with a condescension unworthy of his rank, and fully indicative of his clandestine purposes, was introduced to two of the members, at an ale-house in Newington, where he conversed with coolness on the capture, and murder of the king. When the scheme was nearly completed, about thirty prisoners consisting of the lowest orders of the people, with the exception of colonel Despard, were arrested at the Oakley arms, and a sufficient body of evidence collected to prove them guilty. Several were discharged, and colonel Despard was ably defended, on the 7th of February, in the Southwark court of special commission, by Mr. serjeant Best, who put it to the good sense of the jury, how it was possible that fourteen or fifteen men, with no fire arms but their tobacco pipes, men of the lowest order of society, without mind or intelligence, were to seize the king, the bank, the tower, and the members of both houses of parliament? Lord Nelson, sir A. Clarke, and sir Evan Nepean, spoke highly in favor of the colonel's character, and on the strength of these recommendations the prisoner, being found guilty, was recommended to mercy, but was executed on the 21st of February, with seven of his associates, after declaring his innocence to the multitude, reprobating the injustice and tyranny of ministers, and prophesying the ultimate triumph of liberty, justice, and humanity, over falsehood, despotism, and delusion.

HISTORY OF THE WAR.

CHAP. XXXV.

DURING these indications of mutual hostility between the governments of France and England, the generals and soldiers were reaping in India an enviable harvest of wealth and glory. The 1803. predatory states composing the Mahratta empire had never been united under any regular form of alliance, or by any system of laws or of established treaties, which can be compared to the imperial constitutions or general confederations existing in Europe. A vague and indefinite sentiment, however, of common interest, founded principally upon their common origin and civil and religious usages, and upon kindred habits of conquest and depredation, established among them a certain system of union from the period of their first success, throughout every stage of the decline of the Mogul empire. The same indefinite, but acknowledged confederacy, subsisted between the Mahrattas after the final destruction of the mogul's authority, and enabled several of these adventurers to erect states of considerable military resources and political power. Among these, the descendants of Sevajee, who had established the capital of the empire at Satarrah, were distinguished by the title of rajahs, and became the nominal heads of the Mahratta empire. Beneath their sanction, a prime minister, or peishwah, was elected, to whom, while

the sovereign resigned himself to indolence and voluptuous enjoyment, was confided the exclusive right of concluding treaties and engagements with foreign powers in the name of the Mahratta empire, and the principal chieftains had always been considered ostensibly as the subjects and officers of the peishwah's government.

The authority of the peishwahs, and its real or supposed abuse in favor of the British government, excited the jealousy of the native chieftains, and rendered the Mahratta empire the scene of discord and discontent, which were eagerly promoted by Monsieur Perron, established with a considerable number of forces in the neighbourhood of Delhi. The endeavors of the governor-general had therefore been employed for some years past, to establish between the peishwah and the British government, such a connection as might secure the stability and efficiency of the peishwah's authority under the protection of the British power, without injury to the rights of the feudatory chieftains of the Mahratta empire.

The efforts of the governor-general for that purpose were renewed at those seasons of difficulty and danger, when the peishwah's independence was controlled, and when the existence of his government was exposed to hazard by the violence, rapacity, and ambition of his enemies. Had the peishwah then assented to the moderate and salutary propositions which were offered to his acceptance, he would not have been exposed to a disastrous event by which, on the 25th of October, 1802, he was expelled from Poonah, his authority subverted, his person endangered, and his capital and country abandoned to devastation and plunder.

Notwithstanding the frequent disappointments which occurred in the accomplishment of his salutary views the governor-general determined in the month of June, 1802, to renew his negotiations for the conclusion of an improved system of alliance with the court of Poonah. The increased distractions of the Mahratta state, and the successes of Jeswunt Rao Holkar, a subject of the peishwah's, against the forces of Scindiah, appeared to constitute a crisis of affairs favorable to the complete establishment of the interests of the British power, without the hazard of involving itself in a contest with either party. A treaty with the peishwah was therefore concluded at Bassein, which Scindiah admitted to be neither injurious to his own rights nor to those of the feudatory chieftains. Notwithstanding these professions of satisfaction, he secretly solicited the junction of the rajah of Berar, for the purpose of employing their united power and resources to invade the territories of the allies and of the company, and to subvert the arrangements concluded between the British government and the peishwah at Bassein.

Under these and other indications of hostility on the part of these chieftains, the British government merely required that they should retire with their armies to their usual stations in Berar, and the north of Hindostan, proposing that the British army in the Dekan should retire in a similar manner.

It would be equally useless and impossible to detail the various means by which the aggressors endeavored to intimidate the English presidency; the insults in which they wantonly indulged, or the intrigues by which they endeavored to induce Jeswunt Rao Holkar to form a junction with the confederate armies. The repeated and unexampled provocations offered to the English government, did not exasperate it to violate its resolution of forbearance, nor was it till the positive refusal of a proposal from major-general sir Arthur Wellesley to withdraw the troops under his command from the vicinity of Ahmednugger, on moderate conditions, that the government determined to resort to arms against Scindiah and the rajah of Berar.

The season pressed for decision. The actual prevalence of the rainy monsoon in the provinces of India, which must become the theatre of war, was highly favorable to the operations of the British, and equally unpropitious to any movements of the hostile powers. To have permitted the confederate chieftains to remain unmolested till the close of the rain, would have enabled them to prosecute with rapidity their operations against the territories of the nizam, of the peishwah, of the rajah of Mysore, and eventually of the company, at the commencement of the favorable season, while the British forces would have been weakened and dispirited by the very causes which gave confidence and facility to the movements of the confederates.

The arrangements adopted by the governor-general during this arduous crisis of affairs, were directed to provide for a combined attack on the united army of Scindiah and the rajah of Berar, under their personal command in the Dekan, and on all their most valuable and vulnerable possessions in every part of India. The plan of operations comprehended a tract of country extending from Delhi, and the presidencies of Fort William, Fort St. George, and Bombay, to Poonah, Hyderabad, Guzerat, and Orissa; and embraced together with the security and defence of the British dominions, the important objects of defeating the confederate chieftains in the field, of establishing our allies, the peishwah and the nizam, in their legitimate governments, of securing the final settlement of the government of the Dekan, of delivering the unfortunate and aged emperor Shah Allum, and the royal house of Timour from misery, degradation, and bondage ; of extirpating the last remnant of French influence in India, and of destroying the powerful artillery, and military resources belonging to the French under Monsieur Perron, who now occupied a state on the north-west frontier of Hindostan, founded on the ruins of the mogul's authority, under the auspices of Scindiah.

By the most accurate accounts which have been received on the subject of the forces of the enemy, it appears that towards the close of the month of July, 1803, the troops opposed to major-general Wellesley, under the immediate command of Scindiah and the rajah of Berar, amounted to about 38,500 cavalry, 10,500 regular infantry, 500 match-lock men, 500 rocket men, and 190 pieces of ordnance. Two brigades under Monsieur Dudernaige and major Brownrigg, amounting to 12 battalions, with a large train of artillery, had been ordered to Hindostan. Monsieur Pohlmau's brigade had been directed to return to Buhranpoor, leaving with Scindiah only eight battalions, consisting of about 4500 men. The rajah of Berar's infantry consisted of 6000 men. These forces were posted at Julgong in the Dekan. In addition to the troops already stated, Scindiah had an advanced party of a few thousand horse, dispersed through the Adjuntee hills.

The force under the immediate command of Monsieur Perron, Scindiah's general in the northern provinces of Hindostan, amounted to 16,000 regular and well-disciplined infantry, and a well-appointed and numerous train of artillery : together with a body of irregular troops, and from 15,000, to 20,000 horse. His head-quarters were established near Coel, in a commanding situation in front of the British possessions, and on the most vulnerable part of our extensive empire. The destruction of this force necessarily became a primary object of the war, without any reference to the existing relations between Great Britain and France, but in distinct grounds of complaint against Scindiah.

The total number of British troops including garrisons at Guzerat, and Surat, (3071 men) prepared at the commencement of the month of August, to support the arrangements concluded with the peishwah amounted to 54,918 men. 1803.

Major-general Wellesley received intelligence of the issue of the British resident's negotiation with Scindiah and the rajah of Berar, on the 6th of August, but was prevented from moving by a very heavy fall of rain, which lasted for three days and which had rendered the road from Walkee to Ahmednuggur totally impassable. The weather cleared up, however, on the 7th, and on the 8th. Major-general Wellesley commenced his march towards the fortress of Ahmednuggur, of which the fortified town was, on the morning of the same day attacked, and carried by escalade. On arriving within a short distance of the fortress three parties were immediately formed for the purpose of assaulting the fortified town. The party on the left was commanded by lieutenant-colonel Harness, the centre attack was composed of eight companies under the orders of lieutenant-colonel Wallace, and the party on the right was conducted by captain Vesey. The attack under captain Vesey succeeded without difficulty, but the scaling ladders of the party on the left, were placed against a part of the wall which had no rampart, and the troops were fired upon on the inside of the town, as soon as they had reached the top of the ladders, without the possibility of descending into the town to charge the enemy. Colonel Harness finding that he could not obtain a footing on the wall, drew off his party, and entered the town at another point. In the mean time the centre attack under lieutenant-colonel Wallace, had moved on and placed the ladders against a bastion, which they carried with great ease. The enemy made some resistance in the streets, and a party of Arabs, actually charged the grenadiers of the 78th. They were instantly repulsed and put to flight; and the town was soon afterwards evacuated by the enemy, who had suffered some loss. On the 10th of August, batteries were opened against the fort which surrendered on the 12th of the same month. 1803.

The possession of this fortress is of peculiar importance to the prosecution of our military operations, by securing the communication with Poonah, and by affording a depôt for supplies of provisions, and military stores. Major-general Wellesley immediately after the capture of the fort, proceeded to take possession of all the districts dependant on Ahmednuggur, yielding an estimated annual revenue of 634,000 rupees. These districts were placed under the temporary management and authority of a British officer.

A respectable garrison was also stationed in Ahmednuggur, and every other arrangement being completed, major-general Wellesley moved to the Godavery river, which he crossed with the whole of his army by the 24th of August.

On the 29th of August, major-general Wellesley arrived at Aurungabad. Dowlut Rao Scindiah and the rajah of Berar, had, on the 24th of August, entered the territories of the nizam, by the ghaut of Adjuntee, with a large body of horse. They passed between colonel Stephenson's corps (which had moved to the eastward towards the Badowly ghaut) and Aurungabad, and reached Jainapoor, a small fort, the capital of a district of the same name, about forty miles east from Aurungabad. As soon as the enemy heard of major-general Wellesley's arrival at Aurungabad, they moved to the southward and eastward, with an intention, as it was reported, to cross the Godavery, and march upon Hyderabad. Major-general Wellesley immediately marched to the banks of that river, and continued to move to the eastward along its left bank. The river at that period of time, was fordable in every part, which is a circumstance that was never before known to have happened at that season of the year.

This movement checked the enemy's operations to the southward, and they immediately returned to the northward of Jalnapoor. It also afforded complete protection to two important convoys of grain and treasure, which had been detached by lieutenant-general Stuart from Moodgul, and of which the last convoy under major-

general Hill joined major-general Wellesley's force on the 18th of September.

Colonel Stephenson returned from the eastward on the 1st of September, and on the 2nd attacked and carried the fort of Jalnapoor. While general Wellesley was engaged in covering the advance of his convoys, and in preventing the enemy from crossing the Godavery river, colonel Stephenson made several attempts to bring the confederates to action. He was successful in the night of the 9th of September in surprising their camp, but the nature of the attack makes it impossible to know the exact amount of the loss which the enemy sustained on that occasion.

During their incursion towards the Godavery river, the enemy's irregular horse occasioned little injury to the nizam's territories, and in many places they were defeated by the common peons stationed in the villages which they attacked. Finding that this mode of warfare was not attended with success, the confederate chieftains determined to change their plan of operations, and moved to the northward, near the Adjuntee pass, where they were joined by a detachment of regular infantry (under the command of M. Pohlman and M. Dupont,) consisting of sixteen battalions, with a large and well equipped train of artillery. The whole of the enemy's army was collected about Bokerdun, and between that place and Jaffierabad.

On the 21st of September the two corps under the command of major-general Wellesley and colonel Stephenson, met at Budnapoor, and it was determined that the two divisions should move separately towards the enemy, and attack them on the morning of the 24th. The disposition which the confederates had hitherto manifested to avoid an action and the necessity of making a vigorous effort against their main force, afforded no other means of effecting these important objects, than the plan adopted on this occasion by major-general Wellesley. With this view the two divisions marched on the 22nd, colonel Stephenson by the western rout, and major-general Wellesley by the eastern rout, round the hills between Budnapoor and Ialna.

The division under major-general Wellesley marched to Pangy on the 22nd of September, and on the 23rd to Naulnair, at which place intelligence was received that the combined armies of Scindiah and the rajah of Berar were encamped, at the distance of about six miles from the ground on which general Wellesley had intended to encamp.

General Wellesley immediately determined to attack the enemy, instead of waiting till the morning of the 24th for the arrival of colonel Stephenson. If general Wellesley had not adopted this judicious and spirited resolution, the enemy would probably have harassed him during the whole day of the 23rd; and, as he could afford no other security to the baggage of his army, than the intrenchments which he might be enabled to construct, it must have been exposed to loss if he had waited until the 24th : at all events he would have been obliged to leave more than one battalion for the protection of the baggage. By attacking on the 23rd, the enemy would be kept in ignorance respecting the position of the baggage of our army; and, in addition to these circumstances, there was every reason to believe that the enemy would learn that colonel Stephenson was on his march to attack them on the 24th, in which case it was extremely probable that they would withdraw their guns and infantry in the course of the night of the 23rd, in order that they might avoid the combined attack of the British armies on the 24th. The immediate attack of the enemy, therefore, was a measure of prudence as well as of courage.

Having provided for the security of his baggage and stores, which were left at Naulnair, under the protection of a battalion of sepoys and 400 men taken from the native corps, general Wellesley moved on towards the army of the confederates, which he found encamped between and along the course of two rivers, the Kaitna and the Juah, towards their junction. Their line extended east and west along the north bank of the Kaitna river, the banks of which are high and rocky, and are impassable for guns, excepting at places close to the villages.

The right of the enemy, which consisted entirely of cavalry, was posted in the vicinity of Bokerdun, and extended to their line of infantry, which was encamped in the neighbourhood of the fortified village of Assye. The British army had marched fourteen miles to Naulnair, and the distance from that place to the enemy's camp being six miles, it was one o'clock in the afternoon before the British troops came in sight of the combined army of the confederates.

Although major-general Wellesley arrived in front of the right of the enemy, he determined to attack their left, where the guns and infantry were posted, and accordingly marched round to their left flank, covering the march of the column of British infantry by the British cavalry in the rear, and by the Mahratta (the peishwah's) and Mysore cavalry on the right flank.

The British troops passed the river Kaitna at a ford beyond the enemy's left flank, near the village of Pepulgaon. Major-general Wellesley formed the infantry in two lines, with the British cavalry as a reserve in a third, in an open space between the Kaitna and, the Juah rivers, which run nearly parallel. The peishwah's and the Mysore cavalry occupied the ground beyond, or to the southward of the Kaitna river, on the left flank of the British troops, and kept in check a large body of the enemy's cavalry, which had followed general Wellesley's rout from the right of their own position. The first line of major-general Wellesley's infantry consisted of the advanced picquets to the right, two battalions of sepoys, and his majesty's 78th regiment; the second, of his majesty's 74th regiment and two battalions of sepoys; and the third, of his majesty's 19th dragoons, with three regiments of native cavalry.

The number of British troops engaged, appears to have amounted to about 1200 cavalry, European and native, 1900 Eu-

Sir Aurther Wellesley commanding at the Battle of Assye.

ropean infantry and artillery, and 2000 sepoys.; in all, about 4500 men. The force of the enemy consisted of 16 regular battalions of infantry, (amounting to 10,500 men,) commanded by European officers, a well equipped train of artillery, exceeding in number 100 guns, and some very large bodies of horse, consisting, it is stated, of between 30,000 and 40,000 men. The enemy commenced a cannonade, but with little effect, as the British troops advanced to the Kaitna river, and, having discovered general Wellesley's intention to attack their left, changed the position of their infantry and guns, while the British troops advanced under a severe fire from the enemy's cannon. The British artillery had opened upon the enemy at the distance of 400 yards ; but general Wellesley, finding that it produced little effect on the enemy's powerful and extensive line of infantry and guns, and that his own guns could not advance on account of the number of men and bullocks which had been disabled, ordered his artillery to be left behind, and the whole line to move on. At the same time colonel Maxwell, with the British cavalry, was directed to take care of the right of the infantry, as the line advanced towards the enemy, who were soon compelled, notwithstanding their tremendous cannonade, to fall back upon the second line, in front of the Juah river. The British cavalry, perceiving their confusion, having crossed the Juah river, cut in among their broken infantry, and charged the fugitives along the bank with great effect. General Wellesley's force was not equal in numbers to the importance of the enterprise : many of the enemy's guns which had been left in his rear, were turned upon the British troops by individuals who, having thrown themselves upon the ground, had been passed by the British line under the supposition that they were dead, and who availed themselves of this artifice, (which is often practised by the troops composing the armies of native powers in India,) to continue for some time a very heavy fire.

Lieutenant-colonel Maxwell was killed in charging with the British cavalry, who

had crossed the Juah river, a body of infantry which had retired and was again formed. Some time elapsed before the fire which the enemy kept up from the guns which they had manned in the rear of the British line, could be silenced, and general Wellesley himself was obliged to take the 78th regiment, and the 7th regiment of native cavalry to effect this object. In the course of the operation, the general's horse was shot under him. In a short time, however, the body of the enemy's infantry, which had been formed again, and had been charged by the British cavalry, gave way, and the enemy retreated, leaving 1200 men dead on the field of battle, the whole country covered with their wounded, and in possession of the British troops, 98 pieces of cannon, seven standards, their camp-equipage, a great number of bullocks and camels, and a large quantity of military stores and ammunition.

During the severe and brilliant action of ASSYE, the conduct of major-general Wellesley united a degree of ability, prudence, and of dauntless spirit, seldom equalled and never surpassed ; nor can any instance be adduced from the annals of our military glory of more exemplary order, firmness, discipline, and alacrity, than were manifested by the British troops in every stage of the arduous contest. Several officers in general Wellesley's army have declared that it is no disparagement to the French artillery to say, that cannon were never more admirably served even by the most skilful of their engineers, than by the enemy in the battle of ASSYE. But, notwithstanding this circumstance, and the appearance of large bodies of the enemy's cavalry, the British troops, animated by the gallant spirit of their general, and emulating the noble example of his zeal and courage, exhibited a degree of resolution, firmness, and discipline, which completely overawed the enemy's cavalry and infantry, and forced them to retire with the loss of 1200 men killed, besides a vast number of wounded, scattered over the country in the vicinity of the field of battle. Sciudiah's principal minister received a wound in the action, of which he afterwards died, and an European officer apparently of rank, was also cut down, and afterwards found dead on the scene of conflict.

After some ineffectual and delusive attempts at negotiation on the part of Scindiah, the confederates having collected the remains of their broken army, and moved to the westward along the bank of the Taptee, general Wellesley determined not to ascend the Adjuntee ghaut, with the division under his immediate command, but to remain to the southward and to regulate his movements by those of the enemy. In the mean time lieutenant-colonel Woodington of the Bombay establishment invaded the province of Guzerat, carried the fort of Baroach, and completed the conquest of the district of Champaneer.

A principal object of the governor-general's attention was directed to the formation of an arrangement for the occupation of the province of Cuttack. For this purpose a part of the northern division of the army under the presidency of Fort George, commanded by lieutenant-colonel Campbell of his majesty's 74th regiment, was ordered to be holden in readiness to proceed on that expedition from Ganjam; and a detachment consisting of two companies of his majesty's 22nd regiment, and a part of the 20th Bengal regiment was despatched from Fort William to reinforce the troops under lieutenant-colonel Campbell's command. The whole of that force consisted of 573 Europeans of his majesty's and the honorable company's troops, 2408 sepoys, and a party of native cavalry consisting of 60 men.

The governor-general had also directed a detachment consisting of 500 Bengal native volunteers to proceed by sea, under the command of captain Dick, for the purpose of occupying the post of Balasore. Previously, however, to the departure of this detachment from Fort William, intelligence was received, which induced the governor-general to consider it possible that the Mahratta forces in Berar had been reinforced, and that a vigorous opposition might be expected at the fort of Cuttack, as well as during the advance of the British troops from Ganjam.

This circumstance determined the governor-general to send captain Dick's detachment, with some additional battering-guns, direct to Ganjam, for the purpose of reinforcing the main body of the British troops advancing from that quarter; and the detachment accordingly embarked from Fort William on the 30th of August.

In consequence of a severe illness, lieutenant-colonel Campbell was rendered unable to proceed with the detachment from Ganjam. The governor-general therefore, at the express solicitation of lieutenant-colonel Campbell, then confined to his bed by a violent fever, despatched on the 28th of August his military secretary, lieutenant-colonel Harcourt, of his majesty's 12th regiment of foot, to Ganjam, for the purpose of taking the command of the troops assembled at that station. The governor-general also directed a second detachment of 500 native volunteers, a proportion of artillery-men, some field-pieces, and a proportion of stores, to embark under the command of captain Morgan of the Bengal establishment, on the 13th of September, from Fort William, and to occupy Balasore. Another detachment was at the same time formed at Jelasore, under the command of lieutenant-colonel Fergusson of the establishment of Bengal, consisting of 770 sepoys, and 84 men of the governor-general's body guard, with two galloper guns, for the purpose of advancing into the province of Cuttack, and forming a junction with the detachment at Balasore, when the state of the intermediate country, and the progress of the main division under lieutenant-colonel Harcourt, should favour that movement. This detachment was supported by a force of 800 sepoys, and some artillery, assembled at Midnapore, which was afterwards reinforced by about 500 native volunteers, who left Fort William for that purpose towards the end of the month of September.

The total number of troops assembled for the invasion of the province of Cuttack, therefore, amounted to 4916 men; of this number 3041 formed the main detachment, which was to advance from Ganjam under the command of lieutenant-colonel Harcourt, who was appointed to the general command of all the forces employed on this service; 500 men were on their way under captain Dick, to reinforce lieutenant-colonel Harcourt; 521, (including 21 artillerymen,) under the command of captain Morgan, were destined to occupy Balasore; 854 were stationed at Jelasore, ready to advance whenever that movement might be deemed advisable; and 1300 remained at Midnapore, to support the troops at Balasore and Jelasore, and to afford, at the same time, protection to the frontier of the company's territories, against the incursions of any of the rajah of Berar's predatory horse.

On the 8th of September, the troops under the command of lieutenant-colonel Campbell commenced their march from Ganjam. On the 11th of September, lieutenant-colonel Harcourt arrived at Ganjam, and took the command of the troops. Lieutenant-colonel Campbell, with the zeal and spirit which he has manifested on so many occasions, had endeavored, notwithstanding his illness, to proceed with the troops from Ganjam, but had been carried back after one day's march, in a state which menaced his life for several weeks, and rendered him utterly unable to move with the expedition.

On the 14th of September, the British troops conducted by lieutenant-colonel Harcourt, took possession of Manickpatam without any resistance on the part of the Mahrattas, who fled on the approach of colonel Harcourt's force.

From that station lieutenant-colonel Harcourt dispatched a letter to the principal brامins of the pagoda of Jaggernaut, encouraging them to place the pagoda under the protection of the British troops.

On the 16th, a favorable answer was received from the bramins, and a deputation was sent to the British camp to claim the protection that had been offered by lieutenant-colonel Harcourt; and, on the 18th, the British troops encamped at Jaggernaut, which was immediately evacuated by the Mahratta forces.

The inundated state of the country prevented the march of British troops from Jaggernaut until the 24th of September. Owing to a very heavy fall of rain, which had rendered the roads impassable, and the consequent rise of the rivers which intervene between Jaggernaut and the town of Cuttack, lieutenant-colonel Harcourt's progress was much retarded, and the British troops did not reach Cuttack until the 10th of October, when the town was immediately occupied on the part of the enemy.

Lieutenant-colonel Harcourt had been actively employed in preparations for the siege of the fort of Barabutty at Cuttack. This fort is of great strength, and has only one entrance by a narrow bridge over a wet ditch twenty feet in breadth, and varying in breadth according to the situation of the bastions, from 35 to 135 feet. The storming party, however, courageously passed the bridge, notwithstanding the efforts of the enemy to destroy it, and forty minutes elapsed before they succeeded in blowing open the wicket of the principal gate, the gate itself having been strengthened with thick masses of stone. Having effected their entrance into two additional gates, the British troops were completely victorious, and obtained possession of the fort, which was immediately abandoned by the enemy, whose loss was considerable. By these repeated successes, the province of Cuttack was annexed to the dominions of the company. It will now be necessary to revert to the transactions which had occurred on the north-west frontier of Oude, and to exhibit the result of the operations which were entrusted to the personal direction and command of general Lake.

With a view to occupy a position favorable to the early commencement of military operations in the event of hostilities with Scindiah, the commander-in-chief, general Lake, marched from Cawnpore on the 7th of August, and reached the vicinity of Coel on the 28th of the same month. By the direct order of the governor, he moved, on the next day, into the Mahratta territories, with the intention of attacking Monsieur Perron's force, which had been assembled in the neighbourhood of the fortress of Ally-Ghur. Monsieur Perron's troops were estimated to amount to about 15,000 horse, of which 4000 were regular cavalry. But he did not venture to dispute the advance of the British forces. Lord Lake took possession of the town of Coel, the army encamped to the northward, between the town and the fort of Ally-Ghur. This fort is of singular strength, it has a ditch from 100 to 200 feet in length, and 32 feet in breadth, with a fine glacis. The country for a mile round is levelled and completely exposed in every point to the fire of the fort. There is only one entrance, which is very intricate and over a narrow causeway, under which the enemy had commenced a mine, but had omitted to construct a draw-bridge, and our troops were thus enabled to pass the ditch on the causeway, and immediately to assail the body of the place. The fort was stormed on the morning of the 4th of September. The attack was conducted by lieutenant-colonel Monson, with the utmost degree of skill, judgment, gallantry, and fortitude. The troops moved down to within 600 yards of the sortie of the fort, and the only passage across the ditch into the fort, was followed by lieutenant-colonel Monson.

After waiting until the hour fixed for the assault, (half-past four o'clock,) the storming party moved on, (under cover of a heavy fire from the British batteries erected for the purpose,) and arrived within 100 yards of the fort before they were perceived; as soon, however, as colonel Monson saw that he was discovered, he endeavored, by pushing on with the flank companies of the 76th, to enter the fort along with the guard stationed outside the gates, behind a strong breast-work which covered the entrance. The colonel succeeded in passing the breast-work, but found the first gate shut. Two ladders were immediately applied, on which major Macleod, of the 76th regiment, with two grenadiers, attempted to mount, but they were forced to desist by a most formidable row of pikemen, who menaced every assailant with certain destruction. A twelve-pounder was then brought up,

but some time elapsed before it could be placed opposite the gate, which was situated in an inconvenient direction near the flank of a bastion. Four or five rounds were fired before any effect was produced on the gate; and, during this interval, which lasted about twenty minutes, the storming party was exposed to a most severe and raking fire of grape, wall-pieces, and match-locks. Our principal loss was sustained at this place. Colonel Monson was wounded here by a pike, discharged, it is thought, from a gun: at this spot were also killed the four grenadier officers and the adjutant of the 76th regiment, with lieutenant Furton of the 4th regiment native infantry.

As soon as the first gate was blown open, the troops advanced in a circular direction, (round a strong bastion of masonry, along a narrow road, and through two gate-ways, which were easily forced,) to a fourth gate-way, leading into the body of the place, during which time they were much annoyed by a heavy cross fire in every direction. It was a work of great difficulty to bring up the twelve-pounder, and when it arrived the gate was too strongly fastened to be forced. Major Macleod, however, pushed through the wicket, and entered the fort, after which, very little opposition ensued, and the place was completely carried. The general defence of this fort was very vigorous, and lasted for one hour, and our loss was extremely severe. The French commandant, M. Perron, was taken prisoner. As soon as the British troops had entered the body of the place, the garrison endeavored to escape in every direction: many jumped into the ditch, others were drowned. About 2000 were killed, some surrendered, and were permitted to quit the fort by the commander-in-chief, who was closely observing the result of his bold and well-planned attack. A large quantity of stores and ordnance was found in the fort, with some tumbrils of money, which the storming party divided on the spot.

The fall of the fort of Ally-Ghur was attended with the acquisition of most of the military stores belonging to the French party. This was the place of residence of

M. Perron, and it was the grand depôt of his military stores.

The necessary arrangements for the security of the fort of Ally-Ghur, and for the march of the army, having been completed on the 7th of September, the commander-in-chief moved on that day towards Delhi. A battalion of sepoys was left in Ally-Ghur, and a draw-bridge applied to the gate-way : the place might now be considered as impregnable to any native power.

On the 7th of September, the commander-in-chief received a letter, under date the 5th of September, from M. Perron, informing the commander-in-chief that he had resigned the service of Dowlut Rao Scindiah, and requesting permission to pass with his family, property, and the officers of his suite, to Lucknow, through the territory of the honorable company and of the Nawaub vizier. M. Perron also applied to the commander-in-chief for a sufficient escort, to be composed either of British troops or his own body guard. General Lake immediately complied with M. Perron's request, and permitted him to proceed through the British territories, attended by a British officer, who had been appointed to meet M. Perron to be escorted by his own body guard, and provided for his reception in the company's territories and those of the Nawaub vizier, with every mark of respect and honor.

On the 8th of September, the army reached Koorjah, a fort of some strength, about thirty miles distant from Ally-Ghur, which had been evacuated by the garrison on receiving the intelligence of the fall of that fortress. It is also probable that the capture of Ally-Ghur was one of the causes of M. Perron's determination to solicit the protection of the British government. M. Perron, however, stated that his reason for retiring proceeded from his having received intelligence that his successor had been appointed, and was actually on his way to take possession of his new charge. M. Perron also observed, that the treachery and ingratitude of his European officers convinced him that further resistance to the British arms was useless.

About this period the commander-in-chief received intelligence of the surrender to the enemy of a detachment of five companies of sepoys with one gun, under the command of lieutenant-colonel Coningham at Shekoabad. This small body of troops was attacked on the 2nd of September, by a numerous detachment of cavalry under the command of a Frenchman, named Fleury, and succeeded in compelling the enemy to retreat; but, being attacked on the 4th of September by the same superior force, and having nearly expended its ammunition, the party of British troops capitulated to the enemy. On receipt of this intelligence, the commander-in-chief immediately detached one regiment of European and two regiments of native cavalry, under colonel Macan, to join colonel Vandeleur, who was in the neighbourhood of Futty-Ghur with the 8th regiment of light dragoons and a detachment of infantry, with a convoy for the army. The 2nd brigade of infantry under colonel Clarke, was also ordered to reinforce colonel Vandeleur's detachment ; but, before these two parties could arrive at the place of their destination, the enemy recrossed the Jumna with great precipitation, and afterwards dispersed. Colonel Macan's detachment reached the fort of Firozeabad on the 7th of September, which the enemy immediately abandoned, leaving behind them nine guns, and several of the enemy's troops which had been wounded in the affair of Shekoabad. This is the only predatory incursion which the enemy had attempted on the company's frontiers.

The army under general Lake reached Secundra on the 9th of September. On the morning of the 10th, the commander-in-chief made a short march to the west of Secundra, and on the 11th, a march of eighteen miles beyond Soorajepoor. During the march, intelligence was received, that M. Louis Bourquien had passed the Jumna in the night with sixteen battalions of regular infantry, 6000 cavalry, and a considerable train of ordnance, for the purpose of attacking the commander-in-chief.

The British army reached its ground of encampment near the Jehuah Nullah (about six miles from Delhi) at eleven o'clock. The troops were much fatigued with the length of the march and the heat of the weather; and the tents were scarcely pitched when the enemy appeared in such force in front as to oblige the grand guard and advanced picquets to turn out. The number of the enemy continuing to increase the commander-in-chief proceeded in person to reconnoitre them with the whole of the cavalry (three regiments,) and found the enemy drawn up on rising ground in order of battle, and in full force. Their position was strong, each flank being covered with a swamp, beyond which was posted the cavalry. Their numerous artillery covered their front, which was further protected by a line of entrenchments; their front was the only direction in which the enemy could be attacked. As the British cavalry approached, the enemy began a very heavy cannonade.

As soon as the commander-in-chief had reconnoitred the enemy's position, orders were sent to camp for the infantry and artillery to join the cavalry. The line was ordered to fall in without delay, and move to the front by columns of grand divisions from each battalion. The camp was left standing; the advanced picquets increased by a part of the 17th regiment of native infantry, were brought in for its protection. The whole of the British troops who were engaged in this memorable action were his majesty's 76th regiment, seven battalions of sepoys, the artillery, the 27th dragoons, and two regiments of native cavalry, and amounted in number to about 4500 men. The number of the enemy amounted to about 13,000 infantry, and 6000 cavalry, in all 19,000 men.

Notwithstanding the alacrity and expedition with which the British troops got under arms, one hour elapsed before the infantry could join the cavalry, which had advanced about two miles in front, and was exposed to a severe and well directed cannonade, which occasioned a considerable loss of men and horses. During this interval the commander-in-chief's horse was shot under him.

Finding that it would be difficult to defeat the enemy in their actual position, general Lake determined to make a feint, by which they should be induced to quit their intrenchments, and to advance on the plain. With this view the British cavalry was ordered to retire, both for the purpose of drawing the enemy from his strong position, and of covering the advance of the British infantry; this retrograde movement was performed with the greatest order and steadiness, until the British infantry had effected their junction with the cavalry, when the latter immediately opened from the centre and allowed the infantry to pass on in front.

As soon as the cavalry began to retire, the enemy conceiving this movement to be a real retreat, immediately quitted their strong position, and advanced with the whole of their guns, shouting, and exhibiting every demonstration of perfect confidence in superior prowess. They halted however, on seeing the British infantry who were instantly formed into one line, with the cavalry in a second line, about forty yards in the rear of the right wing of the infantry. The whole of the British force then advanced towards the enemy, the commander-in-chief in person leading his majesty's 76th regiment. Notwithstanding a tremendous fire of round, grape, and chain-shot, the troops, led by general Lake, advanced with the greatest bravery and steadiness, and without taking their muskets from their shoulders, until they had reached within a hundred paces of the enemy, who commenced a heavy fire of grape from all their artillery. Orders were instantly given to charge them with bayonets, the whole British line fired a volley, and with their illustrious commander-in-chief at their head, rushed on with such impetuosity that the enemy gave way and fled in every direction. As soon as the British troops halted after the charge, general Lake, with his accustomed judgment, ordered the line to break into columns of companies ; which manœuvre being effected, the British cavalry (European and native) charged through the intervals with their galloper guns, and completed the victory by pursuing the enemy to the banks of the Jumna, and driving vast numbers into the middle of the river. The galloper guns attached to the cavalry were opened with considerable effect upon the fugitives in this situation. The commander-in-chief headed in person the 76th regiment, which exhibited under such a glorious example the most eminent proofs of valor and discipline.

While these operations took place to the right, under the immediate direction of the commander-in-chief, the left wing, under major-general St. John, attacked the enemy with great vigor, and the success of the British arms was complete in every point. The enemy left the whole of their artillery, 68 pieces of ordnance, and 37 tumbrils laden with ammunition, in our possession ; 24 tumbrils laden with ammunition were blown up in the field of battle; exclusive of which many tumbrils and ammunition carriages were left by the enemy in the Jumna, and in the Jehnah Nullah. Two tumbrils containing treasure were also taken on the field of battle.

The loss of the enemy was very considerable and has been estimated to amount to 3000 men. The exertions of the British were proportionate to the brilliant result of this glorious victory, and the whole army, with the commander-in-chief was under arms for seventeen hours. After the action they took up fresh ground nearer the river.

The battle was fought within view of the minorets of Delhi, and the whole army encamped the next day close to the Jumna river, opposite to that city. The unfortunate emperor Shah Aulum sent to general Lake immediately after the action, to express his anxious desire to place his person and authority under the protection of the victorious arms of the British government. On the 14th of September the army began to cross the Jumna ; and on the same day M. Bourquien who commanded the forces of the enemy in the late action of the 11th of September, together with four other French officers, surrendered themselves as prisoners to general Lake.

His excellency the commander-in-chief had the honor to pay his first visit to his majesty Shah Aulum on the 16th of September, and to congratulate his majesty on his emancipation from the control of the French faction, which had so long oppressed and degraded him.

From the commander-in-chief's despatches, and such accounts as have been received from private sources of intelligence, it appears that his majesty was graciously pleased to direct his eldest son and heir-apparent, the prince Mirza Akbar Shah, to conduct the commander-in-chief to his royal presence. The prince was to have arrived at the commander-in-chief's tent at twelve o'clock, but did not reach the British camp until half-past three o'clock, P. M. : by the time his royal highness had been received, remounted on his elephant, and the whole cavalcade formed, it was half-past four o'clock. The distance being five miles, the commander-in-chief did not reach the palace Delhi until sun-set. The crowd in the city was extraordinary ; and it was with some difficulty that the cavalcade could make its way to the palace. The courts of the latter were full of people anxious to witness the deliverance of their sovereign from a state of degradation and bondage. At length the commander-in-chief was ushered into the royal presence and found the unfortunate and venerable emperor—oppressed by the accumulated calamities of old age, degraded authority, extreme poverty and loss of sight—seated under a small tattered canopy, the remnant of his royal state, with every external appearance of the misery of his condition.

It is impossible to describe the impression which general Lake's conduct on this interesting occasion made on the minds of the inhabitants of Delhi, and of all the mussulmans who had an opportunity of being made acquainted with the occurrence of the 16th of September, 1803. In the metaphorical language of Asia, the native news-writers who describe this extraordinary scene, declared that his majesty Shah

Aulum recovered his sight from excess of
joy. In addition to many other marks of
royal favor and condescension, the emperor
was graciously pleased to confer on general
Lake the second title in the empire.

The result of the spirited and judicious
operations at Coel on the 29th of August,
of the gallant assault of Ally-Ghur on the
4th, and of the glorious battle of Delhi on the
11th of September, deeply affected the
French influence and authority, and secured to the British power the possession
of the doab of the Ganges and Jumna.

The French officers deprived of authority,
and finding themselves the objects of just
indignation to the people whom they had
governed, were compelled to solicit the
protection of the British government, while
the conquered country (rejoicing in the
change of masters, and deeply impresse'
with a just sense of the humane condu'
and orderly behaviour of the British troor
of the protection offered by general Lak'
the persons and property of the inhabit'
and of the mild treatment which the '
ish government extends to all its subj'
regarded the troops as friends an
liverers.

The army under general Lake ar'
Muttra on the 2nd of October.
formed a junction with colonel Va'
detachment, the commander-in-chi
on to the fortress of Agra, which
army reached at about two o'cl'
on the 4th of October. A sur'
immediately sent to the garri'
answer was returned. It app'
the European officers in the f
placed in confinement, and '
able confusion prevailed wit'
Seven battalions of th
gular infantry, with seve
encamped on the outside
occupied the town and f
of Agra, as well as some
through broken ground
camp on the south side
ditch and to the Delhi
it impossible to make
the fort of Agra as lo'
retained their positi
south-west of the fc

mined to
lodge the
With
10th of
encam'
direct
briga'
three
man
maj
ad'
at'
a'
t

impression was made on the walls by the fire
of the batteries, (which would soon have
effected a practicable breach,) and the fort
capitulated on the night of the 17th. The
garrison, consisting of about 5000 men,
marched out at noon on the following day;
when the place was immediately occupied
by the British troops under the command
of colonel Macdonald. A large quantity
of stores and many guns were found in the
fortress of Agra, together with several money tumbrils, containing twenty-four lacks
of rupees.

The British army marched from Agra
on the 27th of October, in pursuit of a
force of the enemy, composed of fifteen of
M. Perron's battalions, (which had been
detached by Scindiah from the Dekan in the
early part of the campaign, under the command of M. Dudernaigue,) and of two battalions which had effected their escape
from Delhi after the battle of the 11th of
September. During the siege of Agra this
force occupied a position about thirty miles
in the rear of the British army, but made
no attempt to interrupt the siege of that
important fortress. The commander-in-
chief was anxious to defeat this force,
because it was furnished with a numerous
artillery, and because its object was
to proceed towards Delhi for the purpose of attempting the recovery of that
important post. The existence of so large
a force of the enemy in Hindostan alarmed those native chieftains who were disposed
to unite with the British government, and
encouraged all those who might be adverse
to our interests.

A heavy fall of rain compelled the army
to halt on the 28th at Kerowly: on the
29th of October the army marched to the
northwest of Futtypore Sikree. On the
30th the army made a march of twenty
miles, leaving the heavy guns and baggage
in Futtypore, under the protection of two
battalions of native infantry from the 4th
brigade.

On the 31st of October the army marched twenty miles, and encamped a short
distance from the ground which the enemy
had quitted the same morning. Possessed
of this intelligence the commander-in-chief

determined to make an effort to overtake
the enemy with all the cavalry of the army,
intending to delay him by a light engagement until the British infantry should be
able to effect a junction with the cavalry
in advance, and to take advantage of any
confusion which might be occasioned by
this attack, to seize the enemy's guns and
baggage. With this view the commander-
in-chief with the whole of the cavalry advanced at twelve o'clock on the night of the
31st of October, and having performed a
march of twenty-five miles in little more
than six hours, came up with the enemy about
seven o'clock in the morning of the 1st of
November. The enemy's force amounted
to 17 regular battalions of infantry, (about
9000 men) 72 guns, and from 4000 to 5000
cavalry. Previously to the march of the
British cavalry, orders were given for the
infantry to follow at three o'clock in the
morning.

When the commander-in-chief at the
head of the cavalry reached the enemy
they appeared to be on their retreat, and
in such confusion, that the commander-in-
chief was induced to try the effect of an
attack with the cavalry alone, without waiting the arrival of the infantry. By cutting
the embankment of a large reservoir of
water, the enemy had rendered the road
difficult to pass, and had availed themselves of this circumstance (which caused
a considerable delay in the advance of the
cavalry,) to occupy an advantageous position, having their right in front of the village
of Laswaree, and thrown back upon a
rivulet (the banks of which were very high
and difficult of access,) their left upon the
village of Mohaulpoor, and their whole
front concealed by high grass and protected by a powerful line of artillery. A
cloud of dust, which had been raised by
the movements of the cavalry, completely
obscured the enemy, and prevented
the commander-in-chief from discovering this change in their position. General Lake, therefore, proceeded in the
execution of his original plan, (by which
he hoped to prevent the retreat of the
enemy and secure their guns,) and directed
the advanced-guard and the first brigade-

of cavalry to move upon the point where the enemy had been observed in motion, but which proved to be the left of their new position. The remainder of the cavalry was ordered to attack in succession, as soon as they could form, after passing the rivulet.

The charge of the advanced-guard under major Griffiths, of his majesty's 29th dragoons, (aid-de-camp to the governor-general,) and of the first brigade led by colonel Vandeleur of his majesty's 8th dragoons, was made with much gallantry. The enemy's line was forced, and the cavalry penetrated into the village, and took possession of several of the enemy's guns. The attacks of the brigades of cavalry, and particularly of the 3rd brigade under colonel Macan, were conducted with the same spirit and with equal success. The fire, however, from the other guns which the enemy still maintained, was so galling and destructive, that it was found necessary to withdraw the cavalry out of reach of the enemy's fire. The British cavalry retired in perfect order, retaining possession of a part of the enemy's artillery. Several guns, however, which had been captured by the British cavalry, were abandoned, from a want of draft bullocks.

Colonel Vandeleur, who had manifested the greatest skill, judgment, and gallantry, was killed in the charge. During his command of the detachment, which had been formed in the month of September, 1803, for the protection of the doab of the Ganges and Jumna; this brave and accomplished officer displayed considerable zeal and ability, and, by his judicious movements, compelled the enemy to make a precipitate retreat from the British territories. His death was universally deplored, and justly deemed a public loss.

The British infantry, having marched at three o'clock in the morning, arrived upon the banks of the rivulet about twelve o'clock at noon. After so long a march, (25 miles,) it was absolutely necessary to allow some time for the men to refresh themselves, during which the enemy sent a message to the commander-in-chief, offering, on certain conditions, to surrender their

guns. Anxious to prevent the further effusion of blood, the commander-in-chief directed a letter to be written, acquiescing in their proposals, and allowing the enemy one hour to fulfil the conditions of surrender proposed by themselves.

In the meanwhile the necessary arrangements were adopted for a general attack as soon as the prescribed time should elapse. The British infantry was formed into two columns on the left : the first composed of the right wing, under major-general Ware, was destined to assault the village of Mohaulpoor, and to turn the enemy's right flank, which since the 'morning had been thrown back, leaving a considerable space between it and the rivulet. The enemy had formed their infantry into two lines, with their right thrown back, the first line to the eastward and covering the village of Mohaulpoor, and the second to the westward of that village. Their cavalry was to the right of their position. The second column of British infantry, composed of the left wing, under major-general St. John, was ordered to support the first column. The 3rd brigade of cavalry, under colonel Macan, was directed to support the infantry. Lieutenant-colonel J. Vandeleur, with the 2nd brigade of cavalry, was detached to the right of the British army to watch the enemy's left, to avail himself of any confusion in the enemy's line, and to attack them upon their retreat. The 1st brigade of cavalry, under lieutenant-colonel Gordon, (who succeeded to the command on the death of colonel Vandeleur,) composed the reserve, and was formed between the 2nd and 3rd brigades. As many of the field-pieces of the British army as could be brought up, together with the galloper-guns attached to the cavalry, formed four different batteries to support the attack of the infantry.

At the expiration of the time which general Lake had allowed the enemy to determine on the surrender of their guns, no reply having been received, the British infantry advanced to the attack, moving along the bank of the rivulet through high grass and broken ground, which afforded cover. As soon as the British infantry became exposed to the enemy's guns, the four British batteries commenced their fire and continued to advance, notwithstanding the superiority of the enemy's artillery both in number and weight of metal. The cannonade on both sides was extremely severe, and maintained with great spirit and vigor. The enemy's artillery was exceedingly well served, and they threw grape from large mortars, as well as from guns of a very heavy calibre.

When the 76th regiment, which headed the attack, had arrived within 150 paces of the enemy, they were so much exposed to the enemy's fire, and were losing men so fast, that the commander-in-chief judged it preferable to proceed to the attack with that regiment, and as many of the native infantry, (the 2nd battalion of the 12th, and five companies of the 16th,) as had closed to the front, rather than to wait until the remainder of the column, which had been much impeded in its advance, should be able to form.

As soon as this small body of brave men arrived within reach of the enemy's cannister-shot, a most tremendous fire opened from the artillery of the latter. The loss sustained by the British troops was very severe, and the heavy cannonade from the enemy's line was sufficient alone to prevent a regular advance: at this moment the Indian cavalry also attempted to charge, but was repulsed by the fire of this gallant body of British infantry; they rallied at a short distance, and assumed so menacing a posture, that the commander-in-chief ordered an attack from the British cavalry. Major Griffiths having at that instant been unfortunately killed by a cannon-shot, this service was performed by his majesty's 29th dragoons, under captain Wade, with the greatest gallantry and success, in a manner highly honorable to every officer and trooper in that regiment. The remainder of the first column of the British infantry arrived in time to join in the attack of the enemy's reserve, which was formed in the rear of their first line, with its left upon the village of Mohaulpoor, and its right thrown back.

About this time major-general Ware

fell dead by a cannon-shot. He was a gallant officer, and his loss was deeply lamented. After this, the command of the column devolved upon colonel Macdonald, who, though wounded, continued to conduct himself in this important command in a manner which was highly satisfactory to the commander-in-chief.

The enemy opposed a vigorous resistance to the last, and did not abandon their position until they had lost all their guns. Even then their left wing attempted to retreat in good order, but was frustrated by his majesty's 29th regiment of dragoons, and the 6th regiment of native cavalry, under the command of lieutenant-colonel John Vandeleur, of the 8th light dragoons, who broke in upon the enemy's column, cut several to pieces, and drove the rest in prisoners, with the whole of the enemy's baggage.

The loss which the British troops sustained in the achievement of this complete victory was severe. Two thousand of the enemy were taken prisoners, and the remainder destroyed on the field of battle. They left in the possession of the British troops the whole of their bazars, camp-equipage, and baggage, with a considerable number of elephants, camels, and upwards of 1600 bullocks, 72 pieces of cannon of different calibres, 44 stands of colours, and 64 tumbrils completely laden with ammunition. Three tumbrils with money were also captured, together with 57 carts laden with match-locks, muskets, and stores, and some artificer's carts. Several tumbrils with ammunition were blown up during the action, and 5000 stand of arms, which had been thrown down by the enemy, were found in the field of battle. The whole of the ordnance taken, with the exception of eight guns, was in excellent order, and perfectly serviceable, and all the appointments of the enemy's corps were of the first quality.

The enemy displayed the most determined obstinacy, and called forth the utmost exertions of the steadiness and valor of the gallant 76th regiment, supported by the remainder of the infantry of the first column, and the repeated charges of the

4 F 2

cavalry. The resistance opposed by the enemy was more determined than any opposition which the army under general Lake had experienced since the commencement of the campaign. His majesty's 76 regiment, on this memorable day, maintained the high reputation which it had acquired on many former occasions, but especially in every occurrence of this glorious campaign.

The victory, however, must be principally attributed to the admirable skill, judgment, heroic valor, and activity of the commander-in-chief, general Lake, whose magnanimous example, together with the recollection of his achievements at Coel, Ally-Ghur, Delhi, and Agra, inspired general confidence and emulation. In the morning, general Lake led the charge of the cavalry, and in the afternoon conducted in person, at the head of the 76th regiment, all the different attacks on the enemy's line, and on their reserve posted in and near the village of Mohaulpoor. On this day, two horses were killed under the commander-in-chief. The shot showered around him in every direction : in the midst of the danger and slaughter which surrounded him, he displayed not only the most resolute fortitude and ardent valor, but the utmost degree of professional ability and knowledge, availing himself with admirable promptitude of every advantage presented by the enemy, and frustrating every effort of their obstinacy and boldness. His masterly plans of attack during the action were carried into instantaneous execution by his unrivalled personal activity ; and he appeared with matchless courage and alacrity in front of, every principal charge, which he had planned with eminent judgment and skill.

The staff of the army distinguished themselves greatly, and merited the highest commendation. Among these, one of the most distinguished was major G. A. F. Lake, of his majesty's 94th regiment, son to the commander-in-chief, who had attended his father in the capacity of aide-de-camp and military secretary, throughout the whole campaign, and whose gallantry

and activity in executing his father's orders, had been conspicuous in every service of difficulty and danger.

This promising young officer constantly attended his father's person, and possessed the highest place in his confidence and esteem. In the heat of the action, the commander-in-chief's horse, pierced by several shots, fell dead under him. Major Lake, who was on horseback close to his father, dismounted, and offered his horse to the commander-in-chief. This compliment was at first refused, but major Lake's earnest solicitations prevailed. The commander-in-chief mounted his son's horse, and major Lake mounted a horse from one of the troops of cavalry : in a moment a shot struck major Lake, and wounded him severely, in the presence of his affectionate father. At this instant the commander-in-chief found it necessary to lead the troops against the enemy, and to leave his wounded son upon the field. A more affecting scene never was presented to the imagination, nor has Providence ever exposed human fortitude to a more severe trial. General Lake, in this dreadful and distracting moment, prosecuted his victory with unabated ardor. At the close of the battle, the commander-in-chief had the satisfaction to learn that his son's wound, although extremely severe, was not likely to prove dangerous.

From the 8th of August, the day on which hostilities commenced, till the 1st of November, the British army conquered all the possessions of Scindiah in Guzerat, the city of Boorhanpoor in Candeish, the province of Cuttack in Orissa, the Mahratta dominions between the Jumna and the Ganges, the city of Delhi, and the right bank of the Jumna, the city of Agra and the adjoining territory ; reduced by storm, the fortified town of Ahmednuggur, the forts of Ally-Ghur, Baroach, and Cuttack ; and by capitulation, after having opened batteries, the forts of Ahmednugger, of Powanghur and Champoneer, the fort of Assurghur, denominated the key of the Dekan, and the fort of Agra, denominated the key of Hindostan ; and defeated the enemy in three general engagements at Delhi on the 11th of September, at Assye on the 23rd of September, and at Laswaree on the 1st of November; having taken according to the official returns, on the field of battle in those engagements and under the walls of Agra, 268 pieces of ordnance, 5000 stand of arms, 215 tumbrils, and 51 stand of colours, with a large quantity of stores, baggage, camp-equipage, and ammunition. The amount of the returns actually received of ordnance found in the several forts, exclusive of that taken on the field of battle, is 445 pieces of ordnance, exclusive of tumbrils, stores, &c. making the total number of ordnance, of which returns have been received, captured from the 8th of August to the 1st of November, 713.

The progress and result of these successful operations restored his highness the peishwah to his sovereign authority at Poonah, and cemented our alliance with that prince, secured the succession of the legitimate heir of the sovereign prince of the Dekan to the government of his deceased father, the late nizam; protected the British interest at Hyderabad from injury:

confirmed the stability of the treaties by which the French were expelled from the Dekan in 1798; and delivered the aged, venerable, and unfortunate emperor of Hindostan from misery and ignominy, from indigence and bondage, and from the hands of the French.

The achievements of general Lake and major-general Wellesley, combined with the admirable and exemplary conduct of the officers and troops during this campaign, more particularly in the signal and splendid victories of Delhi, of Assye, and of Laswaree, inspired a general sentiment of just confidence in the vigor of our military resources, and in the stability of our dominion and power. Our uniform success in frustrating every advantage of superior numbers, of powerful artillery, and even of obstinate resistance opposed by the enemy, constituted a satisfactory proof of the established superiority of British discipline, skill and valor; and demonstrated that the glorious progress of our arms, was not the accidental result of a temporary or transient advantage, but the natural and certain effect of a permanent cause.

CHAP. XXXVI.

Indisposition of George III.—Demeanor of Napoleon towards Lord Whitworth—His Allegations against England—Assassination of Pichegru—Banishment of Moreau—Execution of his Duke D'Enghien—Changes in the English Ministry—Capture of Four Spanish Frigates—Elevation of Buonaparte to the Throne of France—Naval Operations—Rise and Progress of a New Coalition—Buonaparte takes the Command of the Army—State of his Forces—Narrative of his Rapid and Masterly Movements—Commencement of the Campaign of 1803—Imbecility of Mack—Ulm is Invested—The Austrian General Capitulates—Buonaparte proceeds to further Victories.

IN the month of January, 1804, considerable agitation was excited by the recurrence of those symptoms which always preceded and accompanied his majesty's peculiar and lamentable malady. A day of prayer for his recovery was appointed, and the people at large testified the most lively interest in the affliction of their sovereign. But the national anxiety was soon relieved by a declaration of Mr. Addington, that no suspension of the exercise of the royal authority was necessary, and the discontinuance of the bulletins restored the public mind to its usual tranquillity. It is strongly suspected however, that during the temporary indisposition of the king, his name was affixed to many important documents, and his authority adduced in matters of which it was impossible that he should take the slightest cognizance.

Having proceeded to extremities, the British government lost no time in sending reinforcements to the West Indies, the troops in Malta being already sufficiently numerous for the protection of the island. The defensive force of the country was called forth in the regular and supplementary militia, and in the organization of a system of volunteering which testified by its success, the enthusiasm and loyalty of the people. Expeditions were despatched to reduce the islands of St. Lucia and Tobago, and preparations were made for attacking the other possessions of France in different quarters. France on the other hand was not inactive. A few days after the date of the king's message, admiral Linois sailed from Brest for the East Indies, and the army of Italy, strongly reinforced, pushed on to Tarentum, and threatened to occupy all the strong posts in the kingdom of Naples bordering on the Adriatic. On the 18th of May, *before* the English declaration of war, general Mortier summoned the Hanoverian electorate, to surrender to his army. The professions and the menaces of the French general were opposed by the exertions and proclamations of the duke of Cambridge, but with no decisive effect, and the troops of the electorate were obliged to capitulate, and enter into an engagement not to serve against France or her allies till regularly exchanged. The intelligence from Egypt was peculiarly gratifying to the French, as it imported that Alexandria had been evacuated by the English on the 17th of March, though Elfi Bey had embarked as

1803.

ambassador extraordinary from the beys in Egypt to the court of London. The consul in the mean time appeared to have lost the usual reserve and circumspection of his character. His ebullitions of caprice, and his bursts of passion were equally inconsistent with the dignity of his station, and with the dictates of rational policy. His demeanor towards the English ambassador at once betrayed the nature of his views and the bitterness of his enmity to England, and the letter of lord Whitworth to lord Hawkesbury, exhibits a singular picture of his manners and conversation.

Paris, Feb. 21st, 1803.
" My lord,

" My last despatch, in which I gave your lordship an account of my conference with M. de Talleyrand, was scarcely gone, when I received a note from him, informing me that the first consul wished to converse with me, and desired I would come to him at the Thuilleries, at nine o'clock. He received me in his cabinet, with tolerable cordiality ; and, after talking on different subjects for a few minutes, he desired me to sit down, as he himself did, on the other side of the table, and began. He told me that he felt it necessary, after what had passed between me and M. de Talleyrand, that he should, in the most clear and authentic manner, make known his sentiments to me, in order to their being communicated to his majesty ; and he conceived this would be more effectually done by himself, than through any medium whatever. He said, that it was a matter of infinite disappointment to him, that the treaty of Amiens, instead of being followed by conciliation and friendship, the natural effects of peace, had been productive only of continual and increasing jealousy, and mistrust ; and that this mistrust was now avowed in such a manner, as must bring the point to an issue.

" He now enumerated the several provocations which he pretended to have received from England. He placed in the first line, our not evacuating Malta and Alexandria, as we were bound to do by the treaty. In this, he said, that no consideration on earth should make him acquiesce ; and, of the two, he had rather see us in possession of the Fauxbourg, St. Antoine, than Malta. He then adverted to the abuse thrown out against him in the English public prints ; but this, he said, he did not so much regard, as that which appeared in the French papers published in London. This he considered, as much more mischievous, since it was meant to excite this country against him, and his government. He complained of the protection given to Georges, and others of his description, who, instead of being sent to Canada, as had been repeatedly promised, were permitted 'to remain in England, handsomely pensioned, and constantly committing all sorts of crimes on the coasts of France, as well as in the interior. In confirmation of this, he told me that two men had, within these few days, been apprehended in Normandy, and were now on their way to Paris, who were hired assassins, and employed by the bishop of Arras, by the baron de Rolle, by Georges, and by Dutheil, as would be fully proved in a court of justice, and made known to the world.

" He acknowledged that the irritation he felt against England increased daily, because every wind (I make use as much as I can of his own ideas and expressions,) which blew from England, brought nothing but enmity and hatred against him.

" He now went back to Egypt, and told me, that if he had felt the smallest inclination to take possession of it by force, he might have done it a month ago, by sending 25,000 men to Aboukir, who would have possessed themselves of the whole country, in defiance of the 4000 British in Alexandria. That instead of that garrison being a means of protecting Egypt, it was only furnishing him with a pretence for invading it. *This he should not do, whatever might be his desire to have it a colony, because he did not think it worth the risk of a war, in which he might, perhaps, be considered as the aggressor, and by which he should lose more than he could gain, vince, sooner or later, Egypt would belong to France, either by the falling to pieces of the Turkish empire, or by some arrangement with the Porte.*

"As a proof of his desire to maintain peace, he wished to know what he had to gain by going to war with England. A descent was the only means of offence he had, and that he was determined to attempt, by putting himself at the head of the expedition. But how could it be supposed, that, after having gained the height on which he stood, he would risk his life and reputation in such a hazardous attempt, unless forced to it by necessity, when the chances were that he and the greatest part of the expedition would go to the bottom of the sea. He talked much on this subject, but never affected to diminish the danger. He acknowledged that there were one hundred chances to one against him, but still he was determined to attempt it, if war should be the consequence of the present discussion; and that such was the disposition of the troops, that army after army would be found for the enterprise.

"He then expatiated much on the natural force of the two countries. France, with an army of 480,000; for to this amount it is, he said, *to be immediately completed,* all ready for the most desperate enterprizes: and England, with a fleet that made her mistress of the seas, and which he did not think he should be able to equal in less than ten years. Two such countries, by a proper understanding, might govern the world, but by their strifes might overturn it. He said, that, if he had not felt the enmity of the British government, on every occasion, since the treaty of Amiens, there would have been nothing that he would not have done to prove his desire to conciliate; participation in indemnities, as well as in influence, on the continent; treaties of commerce; in short, any thing that could have given satisfaction, and have testified his friendship. Nothing, however, had been able to conquer the hatred of the British government, and, therefore, it was now come to the point whether we should have peace or war. To preserve peace, the treaty of Amiens must be fulfilled; the

abuse in the public prints, if not totally suppressed, at least kept within bounds, and confined to the English papers; and the protection so openly given to his bitterest enemies, (alluding to Georges, and persons of that description,) must be withdrawn. If war, it was necessary only to say so, and to refuse to fulfil the treaty. He now made the tour of Europe, to prove to me that in its present state, there was no power with which we could coalesce, for the purpose of making war against France; consequently it was our interest to gain time, and if we had any point to gain, renew the war when circumstances were more favourable. He said it was not doing him justice, to suppose that he conceived himself above the opinion of his country or of Europe. He would not risk uniting Europe against him, by any violent act of aggression, neither was he so powerful in France, as to persuade the nation to go to war, unless on good grounds. He said that he had not chastised the Algerines, from his unwillingness to excite the jealousy of other powers, but he hoped that England, Russia, and France would one day feel that it was their interest to destroy such a nest of thieves, and force them to live rather by cultivating their land, than by plunder.

"In the little I said to him, (for he gave me in the course of two hours, but very few opportunities of saying a word.) I confined myself strictly to the tenor of your lordships instructions. I urged them in the same manner as I had done to M. de Talleyrand, and dwelt as strongly as I could on the sensation which the publication of Sebastiani's report had created in England, where the views of France towards Egypt must always command the utmost vigilence and jealousy. He maintained that what ought to convince us of his desire of peace was, on the one hand, the little he had to gain by renewing the war, and on the other, the facility with which he might have taken possession of Egypt, with the very ships and troops which were now going from the Mediterranean to St. Domingo, and that with the approbation of Europe, and more particularly of the

Turks, who had repeatedly invited him to join with them, for the purpose of forcing us to evacuate their territory.

"I do not pretend to follow the arguments of the first consul in detail : this would be impossible, from the vast variety of matter which he took occasion to introduce. His purpose was evidently to convince me, that on Malta must depend peace or war, and, at the same time, to impress upon my mind a strong idea of the means he possessed of annoying us at home and abroad.

"With regard to the mistrust and jealousy which, he said, constantly prevailed since the conclusion of the treaty of Amiens, I observed, that, after a war of such long duration, so full of rancour, and carried on in a manner of which history has no example, it was but natural that a considerable degree of agitation should prevail : but this, like the swell after a storm, would gradually subside, if not kept up by the policy of either party ; that I would not pretend to pronounce which had been the aggressor in the paper war of which he complained, and which was still kept up, though with this difference, that in England it was independent of government, and in France its very act and deed. To this I added, that it must be admitted that we had such motives of mistrust against France, as could not be alleged against us ; and I was going to instance the accession of territory and influence gained by France since the treaty, when he interrupted me, by saying, I suppose you mean Piedmont and Switzerland ; *" ce sont des bagatelles :"* and it must have been foreseen, whilst the negotiation was pending ; " *Vous n'avez pas le droit d'en parler a cette heure,*" I then alleged, as a cause of mistrust and of jealousy, the impossibility of obtaining justice, or any kind of redress, for any of his majesty's subjects—He asked me in what respect ; and I told him, that, since the signing of the treaty, not one British claimant had been satisfied, although every Frenchman, of that description, had been so within one month after that period ; and that since I had been here; and I could say as

much of my predecessors, not one satisfactory answer had been obtained, to the innumerable representations which we had been under the necessity of making in favor of British subjects and property, detained in the several ports of France, and elsewhere, without even a shadow of justice : such an order of things, I said, was not made to inspire confidence, but, on the contrary, must create mistrust. This, he said, must be attributed to the natural difficulties attending such suits, when both parties thought themselves right ; but he denied that such delays could proceed from any disinclination to do what was just and right. With regard to the pensions which were granted to French or Swiss individuals, I observed, that they were given as a reward for past services during the war, and most certainly not for present ones, and still less for such as had been insinuated of a nature repugnant to the feelings of every individual in England, and to the universally acknowledged loyalty and honor of the British government. That as for any participation of indemnities, or other accessions which his majesty might have obtained, I could take upon myself to assure him, that his majesty's ambition led him rather to preserve than to acquire. And that, with regard to the most propitious moment for renewing hostilities, his majesty, whose sincere desire it was to continue the blessings of peace to his subjects, would always consider such a measure as the greatest calamity ; but that, if his majesty was so desirous of peace, it must not be imputed to the difficulty of obtaining allies ; and the less so, as those means which it might be necessary to afford such allies for, perhaps, inadequate services, would all be concentrated in England, and give a proportionate increase or energy to our own exertions.

"At this part of the conversation he rose from his chair, and told me that he should give orders to general Andreossy to enter on the discussion of this business with your lordship ; but he wished that I should, at the same time, be made acquainted with his motives, and convinced of his sincerity, rather from himself than from his ministers. He then, after a conversation of two hours, during the greatest part of which he talked incessantly, conversed for a few moments on indifferent subjects, in apparent good humour, and retired.

"Such was, nearly as I can recollect, the purport of this conference.

"It must, however, be observed, that he did not, as M. Talleyrand had done, affect to attribute colonel Sebastiani's mission to commercial motives only, but as one rendered necessary, in a military point of view, by the infraction by us of the treaty of Amiens.

"I have the honor to be, &c.
"WHITWORTH."

This letter was almost immediately succeeded by the precipitate departure of lord Whitworth from the capital, and by the publication of a decree for the detention of every English subject resident in France. A measure so inconsistent with the law of nations and with the rights of humanity, was justified on the pretext that two French merchant vessels in the bay of Audierne, had been captured by the English without any previous declaration of war. The exertions of Buonaparte were commensurate with the importance of the emergency. He obtained from the Dutch legislative body at the Hague, a proclamation announcing that the Batavian army should be placed at the disposal of the French commander. The ship-builders and carpenters were placed in immediate requisition ; and the numbers of the army were extensively and rapidly augmented. The personal safety of the consul was in the mean time endangered by a conspiracy among the friends of royalty, in which, if we believe the evidence of the French journalists, the generals Pichegru and Moreau were deeply implicated. It is said that 150 men were to assemble in the uniform of guards, to seize Buonaparte at Malmaison while he was hunting, and to carry him off. The uniforms of this desperate band were discovered, in conse-

quence of the information of one of the conspirators. Georges, the chief of the Chouans, with difficulty effected his escape from the officers of police, who, having occasion to suspect madame——the mistress of an hotel, and determined to search her person, found beneath her glove a piece of English gold, resembling the badges worn by the rest of the conspirators. They then opened her drawers, and found a letter, directing her on a day specified, carry to a certain house in the Rue de Bourgoing au Morris, twenty dozen of wine, and to ring twenty times at the door. The police officers took the bottles and repaired to the house, where they rang, and found a number of persons, who made a desperate defence. Among the individuals arrested, were Mairn, an intimate friend of Georges, the cook of the latter, and a person named Victor. General Moreau was immediately arrested : a report was made to the French government, in which the grand judge asserted that the courier Jollais transmitted the sentiments of Moreau to Pichegru, when the latter was in London ; and that at a spot between Dieppe and Treport, the brigands of England were brought over in British ships, by captain Wright, to various positions on the coast, from whence they proceeded to Paris by nightly marches. After the report of the judge had been read in the tribunate, the brother of general Moreau made an indignant and energetic speech, declaring the whole accusation to be a malignant calumny, and demanding that his brother might be instantly brought to trial. General Pichegru and Georges, notwithstanding the latter had remained in concealment, since his escape, were now arrested. These two individuals, together with Moreau, were, after the mock formalities of a partial trial, pronounced to be guilty. Georges was executed, and died with great fortitude. Moreau was pardoned, on condition of transporting himself to America ; and Pichegru died in prison, by the hands of the emissaries of Buonaparte. At one o'clock in the morning of the 7th of April, four robust Mamelukes, at whose head were four officers of the high police, were introduced with the utmost secrecy into the interior of the *Conciergerie*, where care had been taken to remove from the scene of this horrible execution every subordinate observer. The chiefs of police were placed in the leading passages, in order to wait the result. Scarcely was the door of Pichegru's dungeon opened, before the Mamelukes, inflamed by intoxication, threw themselves upon the unfortunate general. He slept in his drawers and had risen at the noise of the bolts. Round his left thigh was the cravat which contained his papers. Though surprised by his assassins he struggled and they fell together, so that they had the utmost difficulty in passing the fatal noose; but their victim had scarcely uttered a cry, before they succeeded in strangling him. The principals now came in, and finding him dead, threw his corps upon the bed; they emptied the neckcloth in which his papers were concealed, and fastened it round his neck, tightening it with part of a chair, that it might appear as if the unhappy general had committed suicide. On the next morning the turnkey was terrified at finding the general strangled upon his bed, and immediately ran to inform the gaoler who feigned the utmost surprise, and instantly proceeded to communicate the catastrophe to those who were as well acquainted with the circumstances as himself. The event was then announced by a *proces-verbal,* which had been drawn up beforehand in a secret conference; and on the the same day the Parisians were informed in the newspapers, that general Pichegru had strangled himself in prison by means of his neck-cloth.

The secret resentment of the French people, and the astonishment of Europe at the precipitate and partial condemnation of Pichegru and Moreau, were still further inflamed by the extraordinary and atrocious murder of the duke D'Enghien, the heir presumptive to the rights and titles of the house of Bourbon. The duke resided, with a number of royalists, at Ettenheim in the German and neutral territory of the elector of Baden. Buonaparte despatched M. de Cauliucourt, his

aid-de-camp to the German side of the Rhine, and that general marched to Offenburg (March 14th) and ordered the commandant to point out the emigrants in that town, fifteen of whom were immediately arrested including the duke D'Enghien. No resistance was made by the elector of Baden, but he immediately despatched a courier to his son-in-law, the emperor of Russia, to inform him of the outrage. In the night of the 21st of March, the duke having arrived at Paris, under an escort of 50 *gens d'armes,* was conveyed to the castle of Vincennes, where he was tried and condemned by a military commission, and immediately conveyed for execution to the neighbouring wood. In one of the dark and secret recesses of the wood illuminated by torch light, a grave had been prepared which met the eyes of the unhappy victim, as they conducted him to the fatal spot. He would not suffer his eyes to be bound, and implored the indulgence of a few moments, while he supplicated the throne of eternal mercy. This request was brutally and peremptorily refused. The nine grenadiers by whom he was surrounded, fired in succession, and his body pierced by seven bullets, was committed to the grave and covered with quick-lime. Such was the untimely and lamented fate of a prince who united to all the graces of an elegant exterior, the most various and splendid accomplishments, and the most amiable and unobtrusive virtues; the victim of insatiable power, and lawless malignity.

About this period one the *Moniteurs* contained a voluminous report, consisting of a series of letters and papers designed to prove that Mr. Drake the British minister at Munich was employed in secret and atrocious designs against the existence of the French government, by promoting the disorganization of the armies, and by destroying the powder-mills through the medium of disaffected agents. This report was answered on the 30th of April, by a manifesto addressed to the ministers of foreign courts resident at the court of London, in which lord Hawkesbury contended for the right of belligerent powers to avail themselves of all discontents, which might exist in their enemy's dominions. He recriminated upon the French for keeping up a traitorous correspondence with his majesty's disaffected subjects in Ireland; alluded to a corps of rebels in the service of France, and stationed on the coasts of that kingdom; and stated that France had no right to be recognized as a civilized government, since it was evidently the interest of Europe to destroy her. Notwithstanding these indications of inveterate hostility, and notwithstanding the changes which occurred in the English ministry, the war languished on both sides. The parties of lord Grenville and Mr. Fox had now united, and Mr. Pitt became finally hostile to the administration which he had so lately patronised. It was the general wish of the country that a cabinet should be formed of men selected from every party for their talents and their virtue, and Mr. Pitt warmly recommended that measure to the notice of his majesty. Finding his representations on this subject to be wholly ineffectual, he agreed to resume his office in a new administration, which was formed in the month of May. The public expected

1804. on the return of Mr Pitt new vigor in the administration of affairs, but few events of importance occurred to justify their hopes. Goree was taken from the French, but in a short time recovered. General Green and commodore Hood with a force from Barbadoes, obtained possession of Surinam, and some attempts on the flotilla of the enemy stationed on his coasts for the pretended purpose of invasion, were made by single sloops and frigates, but the success was trifling. Much ridicule was excited by the partial execution of a plan suggested by Mr. (now sir Richard) Phillips a bookseller, for blocking up the harbors of France, by sinking stones and hulks, and by the employment of clockwork machinery. Since the recommencement of hostilities the preservation of her neutrality had been granted to Spain, but it being ascertained that active preparations were going on in her ports, and that the French troops were marching through Spain for the purpose of co-operating in the harbors of the Peninsula; a squadron

was sent from Britain to intercept the frigates belonging to Spain, which were employed in carrying her specie from South America to Cadiz. Captain Moore of the Indefatigable with three frigates, executed this commission with great promptitude. He came up with four Spanish frigates on the 5th of October, which he instantly engaged. One of the enemy's vessels blew up, and 240 lives were lost. The vessels taken were brought safely to Britain, but the injustice of the procedure previous to a declaration of war, excited the most deserved and general animadversion, and the transaction was pronounced by the duke of Clarence in the house of peers, to be an act of " piracy and murder."

The elevation of Buonaparte to the consulship for life, prepared the way for his accession to the highest object of his ambition, and he no longer affected to conceal his views and pretensions to the throne. His obsequious dependants obtained from the legislative bodies a resolution that the first consul be proclaimed emperor of the French, and be invested with the government of the French republic. The measure was carried by the acclamations of all the assembly except Carnot; and the consul Cambeceres, president of the senate, presented the act to Buonaparte on the 18th of May at St. Cloud, in a congratulatory speech; to which the emperor replied by assuring the legislative bodies " that he accepts the title because they think it necessary to the glory of the nation," and " that France will never have reason to repeat surrounding his family with honors." Joseph and Louis Buonaparte were created, by the senatus consultum, princes of France. His imperial majesty appointed Joseph grand elector; Louis grand constable; Cambeceres, arch-chancellor; and Lebrun, arch-treasurer of the empire. A number of celebrated generals were promoted to the rank of marshal; and the accession of the emperor was announced to the French bishops in a letter which concluded by commanding the Veni Creator and Te Deum to be sung in the churches. Preparations of the most costly and magnificent character were commanded for the approaching ceremony of coronation, and several military corps were ordered to re-main in readiness for marching to Paris, to assist in the spectacle.

On the 2nd of December, 1804, Napoleon was annointed and crowned emperor of the French by Pius VII. with great solemnity in the cathedral of Notre Dame. Thus did this great aspirer succeed in raising himself to an elevation which neither Cæsar nor Cromwell durst venture to ascend.

But the attention of the emperor and of Europe was soon diverted from the pomp and splendor of courtly ceremonials to the pride and circumstance of war.

The year 1805 commenced with an over-ture of peace from the newly created em-peror, who might reasonably expect that an ostensible effort to relieve his subjects from a burdensome war, would increase his popularity and confirm his power. He therefore addressed a letter to the king of Great Britain, expressing a desire for the termination of the contest, and the establish-ment of a permanent peace. To this over-ture his majesty returned for answer that there was no object which he had more at heart than to procure for his subjects the blessings of peace, founded on such a basis as would be consistent with the se-curity and interests of his dominions, but as these objects were closely connected with the general security, his majesty de-clined to enter into any particular expla-nations, without previous communication with his allies. Having been thus repulsed, Buonaparte resumed his plans and prepa-rations for the invasion of England. Fo-rests were cut down and conveyed to the coast, for the purpose of constructing ves-sels fit for the enterprise; shipwrights, carpenters, and other artisans, were placed in requisition, and the ports and harbors of France and her dependencies exhibited a bustle and activity before unknown. Soldiers were marched down in great numbers to the sea-side and practiced in naval tactics; and the harbor of Boulogne, contigu-ous to, and directly opposite the eastern shore of England being appointed the general rendezvous for the different vessels,

was strongly fortified and secured against attack.

Thither in a comparatively short space of time, swarmed numerous divisions of the enemy's flotilla; so that the immense num-ber of masts in the harbor made it resemble a forest. The construction of these ves-sels were peculiarly well adapted to the purposes for which they were intended, drawing little water they were able to creep along shore from the contiguous rivers and harbors in which they were built; and being protected by their batteries on land, to enter Boulogne in spite of the efforts of our cruizers to intercept them. The ease also with which they were built and ma-naged, rendered them in a little time familiar to the soldiers, and admitted with-out great loss of time or expence, their accumulation to almost any number; and their shape and dimensions were well calcu-lated for conveying troops a short distance and speedily gaining the shore.

Buonaparte who made frequent visits to Boulogne, occupied himself in giving sys-tem and activity to the immense mass of materials for invasion, which he had now collected. The flotilla still prodigiously increasing by the arrival of fresh divisions of vessels from the neighbouring harbors, was regularly exercised in manœuvering before the port; and the soldiers encamp-ed on the heights above Boulogne were frequently marched to the shore, and prac-tised in embarking, landing, rowing, and all the other movements necessary to render them expert and efficient in the projected expedition. This joint manœuvering of the vessels and troops soon gave their opera-tions a plan and daring well calculated to make them formidable. Divisions of the flotilla containing troops at length ventured outside their harbor, and, notwithstanding the interruption of a heavy fire from our ships, continued to manœuvre and fight with great intrepidity, and latterly their confidence had so increased, that they generally sent out a force for covering the arrival of any fresh division from the attack of our ships. On these occasions, smart actions ensued, and even the coasting division displayed great firmness ; but, having the advantage of a heavy fire from their batteries on shore, after some close fighting, in which several lives were lost, and great bravery shewn on both sides the enemy's vessels, for the most part succeeded in getting into Boulogne.

But Boulogne, though the great centre of operations against England, was not the only point whence attack was threatened, nor the flotilla which it harbored the only means of carrying that attack into execution. Buonaparte, when he projected the invasion of England, and devised the Boulogne flotilla for carrying his army across the Channel, also saw the necessity of having a powerful fleet, without which his flotilla could be of no use ; he therefore diligently applied himself to increase his navy, and in no great space of time, from the extraordinary exertions made, the marine of France was elevated to a respectable footing. The same creative energy was also communicated to Holland, where several ships of war were speedily equipped ; and Spain, lately precipitated into the war by a policy, the soundness of which is more than doubted, lost no time in joining her marine to that of France.

Thus, in little more than two years from the commencement of the war, the 1805. enemy found himself at the head of a powerful navy, which enabled him to commence offensive operations by sea, and to give an imposing aspect to his formidable preparations for invading England. His first efforts on the ocean were to injure and interrupt our commerce, and alarm us for the safety of our foreign possessions. This policy, besides diminishing the elements of our resources, would force us, he hoped, to detach a considerable portion of our military strength from home, and would also divide and distract our fleets. An uncommon activity was seen to prevail in all our enemy's ports, from the Texel to Toulon ; and, notwithstanding the principal harbours in this immense line of coast were blockaded and narrowly watched by our fleets, yet some strong squadrons of his ships contrived to slip out of port and form threatening junctions.

Of this description were the combined French and Spanish fleet, which sailed from Cadiz in April, and which, for the three following months, kept the British empire in anxious apprehension for their objects and destination. In July, this formidable fleet returned to Europe from the West Indies, fortunately without obtaining any object but that of alarming us, which appeared to be agreeable to their original plan. Steering, however, for the coast of Spain, which they now approximated, they were fallen in with on the 22nd of the same month, by a division of our ships, cruizing before Ferrol, under sir R. Calder, and, as the British admiral was between the enemy and the land, an action became unavoidable on the part of the combined fleet. Sir Robert commenced it by attempting to break the enemy's line, so as to cut off his rear ; but this manœuvre, so successful with the British fleet on former occasions, was defeated by a counter-manœuvre of the French admiral, who, perceiving the intention of sir Robert, tacked his fleet so as to render that intention nugatory. A smart action then took place between the two fleets, in which the British tars displayed their usual bravery, and the French and Spaniards shewed great courage. A fog, and night coming on, put an end to the engagement ; and, notwithstanding two Spanish line of battle-ships were captured during the action by our fleet, yet the enemy claimed the victory. For the two following days, the hostile fleets remained in sight of each other, but without renewing the engagement : on the 26th, the combined fleet was out of sight, and in a few days afterwards entered the ports, first of Vigo, and then of Ferrol.

The result of this engagement, though honorable to the British navy, was certainly far short of the expectations of the British nation, and of the brilliant victories which it was lately in the habit of seeing achieved by its fleets. The circumstances of the country too were calculated to give it peculiar interest at the moment; nor could the public well conceive how a British fleet, even though inferior in numbers to a combined French and Spanish fleet, had not succeeded in gaining a more complete victory.

The murmurs of disapprobation at the conduct of the British admiral, became so frequent and so unrestrained, that sir Robert Calder returned to England for the purpose of demanding an investigation of his proceedings, to which government having acceded, he was tried by a court-martial in Portsmouth harbor, on the 22nd of December, when, upon a full examination of the circumstances which took place posterior to the action of the 22nd of July, the court decided that the admiral had not done his utmost to take or destroy every ship of the enemy, which it was his duty to engage; but at the same time ascribed such conduct to error in judgment, acquitting him absolutely of any imputation of fear or cowardice, and therefore only sentencing him to be severely reprimanded.

This maritime enterprise of the enemy greatly increased his confidence: detached squadrons put to sea with a view of annoying our commerce; his large fleets seemed prepared to execute important movements, and a general and simultaneous effort of invading us from all his ports, began, not without the appearance of reason, to be seriously apprehended.

To meet the gathering storm, the British minister had, from the moment when invasion was first threatened, employed himself in taking measures of defence. The army was increased to the utmost, which the means resorted to were capable of producing: the navy was carried to a magnitude before unknown; and the people, sensible of the imminence of the danger, volunteered to arm in defence. In a few months, more than 300,000 volunteers appeared in arms, equipped and ready to take the field; and, although not bred up in camps, were fully determined to defend to the last, their country and their homes. Troops were marched down in great numbers to guard the coast opposite France; the necessary orders

were issued how to act in case of actual invasion; signal posts were erected along the coasts, and for some distance in the country, so as to give an early and extensive notice of the enemy's landing, that troops might be speedily collected from all quarters; a strong fleet was stationed in the Downs, to watch the movements of the enemy's flotilla in Boulogne, and to attack it in case it ventured out; and arrangements were also made for calling out, in case of necessity, the *levy en masse*.

It was resolved, should the enemy's armaments put to sea, and either by eluding our fleets or by an unlucky combination of other circumstances, succeed in gaining our shores, to abide the event of the contest on British ground. But just as this severe trial, in all probability approached, when Britain was about to be plunged in all the horrors of an exasperated war, carried on in her very bosom, and for her existence, events occurred on the continent which produced that co-operation for which the British ministry had so long and ardently sought, and which, by directing the forces of France to new objects of hostility, suddenly relieved England from the menaced invasion.

The capture and execution of the prince D'Enghein excited strong sensations throughout Europe. The young king of Sweden, son-in-law to the margrave of Baden, remonstrated with the French government on the violation of the independence of the German empire. Notes to the same purpose were transmitted from the Russian and other courts concerned in maintaining the rights of the Germanic body. The acquisitions of France at the close of the late war, exasperated the resentment of the powers at whose expense they had been obtained; and Austria, the principal sufferer, sighed for an opportunity of recovering her military fame and her wrested provinces. The emperor of Russia had lately shewn considerable dislike to the proceedings of the French government, and on the 11th of April, 1805, a treaty of alliance was concluded between the courts of London and St. Petersburgh, by which they mutually engaged to support all the great principles of European independence, and to obtain, as far as in them laid, in conjunction with Sweden and Austria, the evacuation of Sweden and of the north of Germany, the establishment of the independence of Holland and Switzerland, and other objects equally arduous and important.

Austria having acceded to this treaty, the confederated powers of the continent engaged to bring into the field a force of 500,000 effective troops, and Great Britain was to allow them a subsidy at the rate of £12 10s. per man. The subsidy was made payable to Austria from the 1st of October, 1804, with a further sum of 1,000,000 and a half as an earnest, or "*premiere mise en-campagne.*" Of the stipulated forces, Austria engaged to raise 320,000, and Russia 115,000, so that the whole quota of the two empires amounted to 435,000 men. The remaining 65,000 were to be supplied by the other confederates. It was also agreed that the continental powers should not withdraw their forces, nor Great Britain her subsidies, till a general pacification took place with the common consent of all the contracting parties.

The plan of this coalition, which was ably conceived, and promised the most brilliant results, may justly be called the master-piece of Mr. Pitt's policy. It was one of the greatest and most extensive schemes ever devised by any cabinet; but, through the precipitance of the Austrians, the tardiness of the Russians, and the vigor of the French emperor, its result was only productive of disappointment and dismay to the friends of liberty.

The hostile demonstrations of Russia were accelerated by the seizure of Genoa, and on the 31st of August, a declaration was officially made to the government of France, that the Russian court was willing to renew a former negotiation, terminated by the recal of M. Novosiltzof, but as a measure of precaution had caused two armies of 50,000 men each, to march to the Danube.

The preparations of Austria for war about the period when the rupture of the negotiation between Russia and France

took place, became too evident to be longer concealed under the pretence of merely exercising the troops. Buonaparte, who saw their true design, took the alarm, and declarations in the form of notes, were immediately passed between the French and Austrian ministers.

The first material note is from count de Cobentzel, (the Austrian minister at Paris,) to Talleyrand : it was delivered early in August, in consequence of a conference held between the two ministers. In this note, which expresses great moderation, and an ardent desire for the restoration of general tranquillity, the emperor of Austria, after regretting deeply the failure of the proposed negotiation, offers his mediation, and invites the court of St. Petersburgh and the Thuilleries immediately to renew the negotiation which was on the point of being opened, and to which he promises to lend his most earnest assistance.

To this note Talleyrand, by order of Buonaparte, then at Boulogne, returned on the 13th of August a long answer, in which the French emperor, after expressing how sensibly he was affected by the moderation of the aforesaid declaration, and the readiness of the emperor of Austria to interpose his mediation, yet declines the latter emperor's offer, alleging " that the present state of things, and the insults offered him by Russia, must render it wholly fruitless, and involve the dignity of the mediator." Buonaparte then proceeds to charge Russia with being averse to peace, and does not hesitate to say, that the expectation alone of co-operation from Austria, led England to continue the war ; that therefore the emperor of Austria had it in his power by making a declaration similar to that of Prussia, viz. " not to enter in any case into a hostile project against France," to restore peace to the world, in which case he (Buonaparte) would immediately fulfil his promise of separating the crowns of France and Italy for ever.

" But if, on the other hand," continues Buonaparte, " Austria, by indecision, leave a doubtful opinion, and authorise the English ministry to assert that she belongs to a coalition, and if she continues to keep 72,000 men in Italy, the emperor will be obliged to believe that she sees with a secret joy a war which weakens France, and that she thinks the moment favorable for resuming hostilities, of which the present generation must be made the victims."

The French note next takes notice of the military movements and preparations in Poland and Italy, and the formation of an army and magazines in the Tyrol ; and, after conjuring Austria to make a declaration of neutrality, and confirm it by reducing her army to the peace establishment, it emphatically says, " for the interests of Austria herself and the glory of her sovereign, his majesty wishes that the emperor of Germany may avail himself of the opportunity which is offered to him." The fate of his own states and that of Europe, is now in his hands. In one hand he holds the disturbances and revolutions, in the other the general peace. An important neutrality is sufficient to obtain for him what he desires, and to ensure the peace of the world. The most efficacious mediation for peace which Austria can make, consists in preserving the most perfect neutrality, in the cessation of armaments, in not obliging France to make a diversion, and in leaving no hope for England of bringing over Austria to her side."

Fresh intelligence of the movements and preparations for war on the part of Austria being received, Talleyrand, in three days after the communication of the above note, presented a second one to the Austrian minister, by order of Buonaparte.

In this note, which is of a very decisive nature, Buonaparte, after stating his disappointment at the movement of troops, and other hostile dispositions shewn by Austria, at a time when he was entirely occupied in a war with England, and had relied on the pacific and friendly assurances of the German emperor, declares, " that he is compelled to demand a categorical and speedy explanation of the objects of these movements, which (he states) already had the effect of forcing him to postpone his projects against England, and thereby made a most powerful diversion in her favor."

" Thus," continues the note, " Austria has done as much as if she had commenced hostilities." And, after particularizing the different warlike steps taken by the emperor of Germany, Buonaparte declares, " that protestations can no longer satisfy him ; that he cannot admit any intermediate state between that of war or of peace , that if Austria wanted peace, every thing in Austria must be restored to the peace-establishment ; but that, should Austria desire war, the French emperor would have no other alternative than to throw back upon the aggressor all the evils he would bring, not only upon the present generation, but also upon his own estates and his own family."

The French note then concludes by demanding,

" 1st, That the 21 regiments sent to the German and Italian Tyrol, shall be withdrawn, and those troops only allowed to remain who were there six months before.

" 2nd, That the camp-fortifications be discontinued.

" 3rd, That the troops in Stiria, Carinthia, Friali, and the Venetian territory, be reduced to the numbers at which they stood six months before.

" And lastly, That Austria declare to England her firm and unshaken determination to preserve an exact and scrupulous neutrality, without taking a part in the present dispute."

To this menacing note, which had the object of obtaining a categorical answer to the question, peace or war? and of affixing to the court of Vienna the ungracious part of having provoked the renewal of hostilities on the continent ; the Austrian cabinet transmitted to Paris early in September, a long and important reply.

In this answer, which sets out with declaring that the court of Vienna has no other motive in its preparations than the maintaining peace and friendship with France, and securing the general tranquility of the continent ; the German emperor, however, for the first time, speaks his unreserved sentiments ; he boldly charges France with having transgressed the treaty of Luneville, by forcing governments on the Italian, Helvetic, and Batavian republics, contrary to their free-will, and inconsistent with the maintenance of that real political independence, which was stipulated and guaranteed to these states, by one of the articles of the above treaty.

The Austrian note farther enumerates various other grounds of complaint against France, and observes " under such circumstances it becomes necessary for other powers to arm, to support each other, and to join in maintaining their own and the general security. Thus the military preparations of the court of Vienna are provoked by those of France, as well as by her neglect of all means of securing a true peace and future tranquillity.

The encroachments and innovations in Italy are then charged upon France, and after noticing the failure of the late overtures, towards a negotiation, the note says " The emperor arms not with hostile views; he arms not to operate a diversion against a landing in England ; the emperor arms for the maintenance of the peace existing between him and France."

This long note next adverts to the wishes of the emperor of Russia, as contained in a declaration, delivered at Vienna, by the Russian ambassador, count Rasoumowsky, on the 31st of August; and in which the emperor of Russia coincides with the emperor of Austria in the necessity of an immediate armament, and also proposes to march two armies of 50,000 men each, through Gallicia to the Danube, in order to combine the support of a powerful army with the negotiations for peace.

The Austrian answer concludes with the following important declaration in the name of the two imperial courts of Austria and Russia:

" That they are ready to enter into a negotiation with France, for maintaining the peace of the continent on the most moderate terms which are compatible with the general tranquillity and security.

" That whatever shall be the issue of the negotiations, and even should the commencement of hostilities become unavoidable, they, at the same time, pledge themselves to abstain from every proceeding tending to interfere with the internal concerns of France, or to alter the state of possession, and the legally existing relations in the German empire, or in the slightest degree to injure the rights or interests of the Ottoman Porte, the integrity of whose dominions they are, on the contrary, prepared to defend to the utmost of their power.

" Finally, that the sentiments of Great Britain are conformable to those herein expressed, and that she has displayed the same moderate disposition for the restoration of peace between her and France."

This bold and unexpected reply from Austria, disclosed to Buonaparte a formidable confederacy formed against him; and immediately determined him to make preparations to attack and disperse it.

Accordingly the French army in Italy, which continued to be reinforced from the moment the Austrians were perceived to make movements in that quarter, was now rapidly augmented ; the principal fortresses also were abundantly stored with provisions and ammunition; and the whole Italian kingdom was soon placed in a warlike attitude. From Italy Buonaparte quickly repaired to Boulogne, to direct the operations there in person, and no doubt to concert the plan of the future campaign. The immense flotilla which had been collected at this harbor with so much industry and effort for the invasion of England, was immediately ordered to be dismantled, and laid up, and the formidable army intended for the daring enterprise, received its rout without loss of time, for the Rhine, and had actually commenced its march for that river early in September. The troops also which had embarked at the Helder and other ports, speedily relanded and marched for the same destination, and the French emperor issued his decree, ordering the 60,000 conscripts for the year 14 to join the army without delay.

The British minister being thus freed by the appearance of approaching hostilities on the continent, from the menace of invasion by the French, actually prepared to become the assailant in his turn. The circumstances of the country for some time past, conspired to afford him a large dis-posable force, the regular army was well disciplined and appointed, and the militia and volunteers were fully equal to the de-fence of the empire at home. Accordingly vigorous preparations were made for fitting out a respectable force, to act against the enemy on the continent; transports for their conveyance were engaged by government, and besides 10,000 troops who had sailed from Cork in the latter end of August, on an expedition under general Baird, several regi-ments consisting of cavalry and infantry both in England and Ireland, together with strong detachments of artillery, received orders to hold themselves in readiness for immediate foreign service.

Russia who had been for some time busily employed in completing her army to the full war establishment, now resolved to augment it still more considerably; and with this view the emperor Alexander is-sued an ukase on the 1st of September, ordering that in the whole extent of the Russian empire, four recruits be taken from every 500 souls. A powerful Russian army passed, about the same time, the frontiers, and directed its march towards the Danube to join the Austrians; considerable rein-forcements had been sent by way of the Black sea, and straits of Constantinople, to increase the Russian force in the Seven Islands, and in conjunction with the Brit-ish troops already in the Mediterranean, to threaten Italy; while numerous transports were collecting in the Baltic, for conveying a joint Russian and Swedish army to Swed-ish Pomerania, which with the expedition preparing in England, was intended to re-cover Hanover and enter Holland, and thus to make a powerful diversion in the north, while the grand united armies of Austria and Russia reconquered Italy, and pressed France on the south and on the east.

Buonaparte viewed this awful preparation against him with a determined eye; he saw that if he waited till all its parts were join-ed and brought against him, in the whole, either its immense pressure must sweep him from his throne, or if, by dint of great and gigantic exertions in his favor, the French people enabled him to resist the attacks of his numerous adversaries, the struggle would be long and calamitous, and the results it might lead to be equally in-jurious to the safety of his crown with ac-tual defeat.

On the other hand by attacking the coali-tion while yet in embryo, he would escape those formidable evils, and with an army infinitely inferior to the aggregate of his enemies, (did he allow them time to meet in the field) he would be enabled by enter-prize and celerity of movement, to attack and overwhelm successively the different divisions of their yet disjointed force.

Perhaps no other conjunction of circum-stances could offer so grand and favorable an opportunity for displaying the genius and activity of the French chief and his followers. Whilst a mighty coalition threat-ened to wrest from him his conquests, and perhaps his crown, a bold and decisive conduct might not only succeed in averting the storm, but give him the brilliant eclat of having thrown back on his opponents the imminent danger they had prepared for him.

Accordingly Buonaparte redoubled his exertions to seize the favourable moment; besides the powerful army rapidly march-ing from Boulogne to the Rhine, the prin-cipal part of the French troops in Holland and Hanover were ordered to repair to the same point: extraordinary measures were had recourse to for compelling the whole of the conscripts to march to the army with the utmost despatch; and that the great body of the regular troops might be withdrawn from France in safety, the na-tional guards were called out, for the pur-poses of maintaining internal order, defend-ing the coasts and frontiers, securing the retreat of the active army, and opposing a strong barrier to the enemy in case of re-verse.

During these formidable preparations for war, Buonaparte ordered his charge d af-faires at Ratisbon, to induce the German diet to represent to the view of the emperor of Austria, the dangerous step he was about to take; and to endeavor to dissuade him from replunging Europe into the hor-rors of a new war. Bacher at the same time presented a note to the diet, which may be considered in the light of a manifesto against Austria. In this note Buonaparte makes a solemn declaration of the sentiments by which he is actuated, and, after again charging Austria with being the aggressor, and insinuating that her hostile intentions may in the end be directed against Bavaria and the German empire, he declares, "that he will consider as a formal declaration of war directed against himself, all aggressions which may be attempted against the German body, and especially against Bavaria."

This note, which had for its object the alienation of the German princes from the cause of the emperor, and drawing closer the ties of friendship between them and France, was presented to the diet, in consequence of demonstrations made by the Austrians for crossing the Inn and invading Bavaria.

In a few days afterwards, Austria caused a counter-declaration to be presented to the German diet.

In this note the emperor of Austria retorts upon France the charge of disinclination to restore peace, and repeats his willingness to promote that desirable end. He again asserts, that in arming in conjunction with Russia, he is not otherwise interested than to put a stop to the further encroachments of France, and to secure his own safety. The Austrian monarch next assures his co-estates, that, in case war should prove unavoidable, the legal state of the constitution and possessions of the German empire shall be maintained inviolable; and finally, in the event of war taking place, he calls upon the unanimity, fidelity, and courage of the majority of the states of the empire, to enable him to ward off from Germany the scene of hostilities, and to carry into effect the salutary views of Austria and Russia.

Whilst France and Austria were thus making mutual recriminations, and threatening each other, both powers were actively employed in collecting and maturing the means for hostile operations. The public prints were filled with accounts of the great preparations making by the emperor of Germany for war : they were reported

to be of a grand and imposing nature, and for a time it was supposed, that Buonaparte was really taken by surprise.

On the other hand, the French chief with more silence, and, as it afterwards appeared, with more effect, prepared for striking an important blow. The circumstances of France enabled him to collect a large army in a comparatively short period ; and, although for some time Buonaparte appeared inactive, as if disconcerted by the sudden and unexpected movements of Austria, he nevertheless in a few days, found himself strong enough to commence operations against his enemies, which the rashness and inability of their councils permitted him to do with dreadful effect.

Early in September, the elector of Bavaria received a commanding letter from the emperor of Russia, requiring that the Bavarian troops should be forthwith delivered up to the Austrian generals, for the purpose of being incorporated in separate divisions with the Austrian army. This letter was accompanied with a menace, that, in case of refusal, the electoral troops should be disarmed, and Bavaria no longer considered a friend. At the same time the Austrian army assembled on the Inn, made demonstrations for crossing that river and entering Bavaria with the view of enforcing the demand.

The elector, who at the time was endeavoring to negotiate at Vienna for his neutrality during the approaching contest, was no less surprised than confounded at this threatening and, as he supposed it, degrading demand ; but the Austrian army being at hand, and being unable to resist, he had recourse to negotiation with the Austrian cabinet, with the view of gaining time.

In the interim, however, the Austrian army crossed the Inn on the 8th of September, and entered Bavaria ; their first steps were marked by heavy contributions ; they demanded the administration of the country to be placed in their hands, began to force their paper money into circulation at its nominal value, while in their own land it had fallen to a discount of more than thirty per cent. in exchange for specie, and in short treated the electorate as a conquered country. These proceedings the emperor of Austria justified on the ground of political necessity

To evade the first bursts of the storm, the elector quitted Munich, and retired with his court to Wurtzburg, in Franconia: the Bavarian troops also, to escape capture, retreated in divisions, first into the Upper Palatinate, and afterwards into Franconia.

Intelligence of the invasion of Bavaria reaching Paris, Buonaparte immediately prepared for setting out to place himself at the head of the French armies now rapidly approaching the Rhine. Prior, however, to his quitting that capital, the French emperor, in order to give more force and solemnity to his proceedings, repaired, on the 23rd of September, to the hall of the senate. The minister for foreign affairs read a long exposition of the comparative conduct of France and Austria since the peace of Luneville. It commenced with expressing the sincere desire of the emperor Napoleon to have preserved the peace of the continent : it then reiterates charges, particularly against England and Austria ; and, after noticing the invasion of the elector of Bavaria's territories by the troops of Austria, it concludes with a declaration, "that the emperor of the French will never lay down his arms until he shall have obtained full and entire satisfaction, and complete security, as well for his own estates as for those of his allies."

At this sitting also, the senate passed a decree for raising 80,000 additional conscripts, "to ensure," (in the words of Regnauli, who presented the grounds of the decree,) "that our battalions and squadrons shall be always complete, and always renewed until the last victory." Buonaparte, in a short address to the senators, informed them, that he was about to leave the capital, to head the army, and bring speedy succour to his allies ; that the war had already commenced in the heart of Germany by the Austrians, who had invaded Bavaria, had already driven the elector from his capital, and possessed themselves of a great part of his territories.

Finally, he called upon the French people to exert themselves in support of their sovereign in the present unprovoked war, and concluded his address in the following words : " Frenchmen, your emperor will do his duty, my soldiers will do theirs, you will do yours."

These measures being taken, Buonaparte, having delegated his brother Joseph to govern in his absence, set out, accompanied by the empress, from Paris, for the army on the following day, the 24th of September, and arrived at Strasburg on the 26th, at five o'clock in the evening ; he was preceded by several carriages, containing Berthier and others of his ministers, and he was received by the mayor of Strasburg, who addressed him in a complimentory speech, to which the French emperor returned a short and suitable reply.

The French army, about 140,000 strong, was now rapidly hastening to pass the frontiers and enter Germany. It marched in six separate corps or grand divisions, in the following manner : the first corps under marshal Bernadotte, advanced from Hanover, about the same time that the army set out from Boulogne, and, taking the rout of Gottingen and Frankfort, arrived at Wurtzburg in Franconia, on the 23rd of September.

General Marmont, who had arrived from Holland at Mentz, at the head of the second corps, passed the Rhine by the bridge of Cassel, and advanced to Wurtzburg also, where he formed a junction with the Bavarian army, (25,000 strong,) which had retreated thither on the advance of the Austrians, and also with the corps under marshal Bernadotte.

A third corps, commanded by marshal Davoust, passed the Rhine on the 26th, at Manheim, and marched by Heidelberg and Necker-Eltz, on the Necker.

The fourth corps, under marshal Soult, passed the Rhine on the same day, by a bridge which had been thrown over it at Spires, and advanced towards Heilbronn on the Necker.

Marshal Ney, with the fifth grand division of the army, also crossed the Rhine on the 26th, by a flying bridge opposite

Durlach, and marched towards Stutgard on the Necker likewise.

The sixth corps under marshal Lasnes, passed the Rhine on the 25th at Kehl, and advanced towards Louisburg.

Prince Murat with the cavalry of reserve forming a separate body, also passed the Rhine at Kehl, and on the same day, and remained for several days in position before the defiles of the Black Forest, with the view of making the Austrians believe that the French army meant to penetrate by these defiles.

On the 30th of September, the great park of artillery passed the Rhine at Kehl, and advanced towards Heilbronn.

The whole of the French army being on the German side of the Rhine by the end of September, Buonaparte, after issuing a short proclamation to his troops, left the empress and court at Strasburg, and accompanied by his staff and a part of his imperial guards, passed the Rhine at Kehl, on the first of October, at eleven o'clock, to put himself at the head of his army. He slept that night at Ettlingen, where he received the elector and princess of Baden, and next day proceeded to Louisburg, to the elector of Wurtemburg, in whose palace he took up his abode.

The French emperor immediately on crossing the Rhine, commenced his operations; the Austrian army in Germany, 100,000 men strong, and commanded by general Mack, after overrunning Bavaria, had advanced by forced marches into Suabia, to seize the passes of the Black Forest, by which they supposed the French would endeavor, as before, to penetrate into Germany. Their right wing extended in front of Ulm, in which town they were busily employed in improving the works. Their centre was posted before Memmingen, which was the head-quarters, where they also strengthened the works; and their left stretched in the direction of Kempten and the Tyrol; while the advanced guard of 14,000 men under the command of general Klenau, took post between Stockach and Doneschingen, in the rear of the Black Forest, the passes of which the Austrian troops also occupied.

To render this position the stronger, the Austrians fortified the line of the Iller, which was in their rear, from Kempten to Ulm; and thus secured in front by the defiles of the Black Forest, and behind by a river and a strong chain of intrenchments which would oppose a formidable barrier to the career of a pursuing army. General Mack awaited the attacks of the French on his front, expecting also to be joined by the first Russian army, of 25,000 men, now rapidly approaching the Inn, under general Kutusof, by the way of Moravia and Bohemia.

To prevent this junction, which must render the united army more formidable, and particularly as its numbers would be soon after increased still further by the arrival of other Russian divisions following the first; and at the same time to capture or destroy the whole of the Austrian army under general Mack, now formed the bold and gigantic plan of the French chief. With this view Buonaparte determined that the French army should immediately cross the Necker, and together with the Bavarian and Wurtemburg troops advance as if intending to penetrate into Bohemia, but really for the purpose of suddenly turning the right wing of the Austrian army, and, by crossing the Danube below Ulm, to precipitate themselves into the rear of the Austrians, so as to cut off their retreat.

Accordingly, on the 2nd of October, the day after Buonaparte crossed the Rhine, all the corps of the French army were in full march, for that part of the Danube between Ulm and Ingolstadt: the united corps of marshal Barnadotte and general Marmont, together with the Bavarians who had joined them, began their march from Wurtzburg to Ingolstadt, to form the left wing of the army; and such was deemed the important necessity of arriving in time, to the success of the operations meditated, that the French emperor preferred risking the friendship of the king of Prussia, rather than not march these divisions through the neutral territories of Bareuth and Anspach in Franconia, so as to have their powerful co-operation sufficiently early for executing his grand plan on the Danube.

The other corps composing the centre and right wing of the French army, directed their course higher up that river, between Ingolstadt and Ulm, in the following order, viz.

The corps of marshal Davoust marched from Necker-Eltz, by the rout of Mackmulh, Ingelfingen, Chuilsheim, Dunkolsbuhl, Oetingen, and Harburg, towards Newburg on the Danube.

The corps of marshal Soult marched from Heilbronn, and advanced by Gehringen, Hall, Gaildroff, Aalen, and Nordlingen, towards Donawert, also on the Danube.

Marshal Ney's corps marched from Stutgard, and advanced by the rout of Erslingen, Goppingen, Weissentein, Heydenheim, Notlkeim, likewise towards Nordlingen and the Danube.

The sixth corps under marshal Lasnes, advanced towards Nordlingen also, having marched from Louisburg by Geneund and Aalen : the whole army advanced rapidly by forced marches for the Danube, and on the 6th occupied the following positions on and contiguous to the left bank of that river.

The corps under Bernadotte and Marmont, with the Bavarians, were at Weissenburg, on their rout for Ingolstadt.

Davoust's corps were at Oetingen and the banks of the Rednitz.

Soult with his corps marched on to Donawert, and prepared to seize the bridge.

Marshal Ney's corps was at Kneffingen ; that of Lasnes at Neresheim ; while prince Murat with his dragoons stood on the left bank of the Danube.

Thus, in the course of only a few days, this grand and unexpected movement of the French army brought them into Bavaria, enabled them to avoid the Black mountains, and the line of those rivers which running parallel, flow into the valley of the Danube, and what was of infinite consequence, provided against the difficulties of a state of operations, which would always have been flanked by the entrances into the Tyrol. This bold advance of the French by the plains of Bavaria, also was attended with other great advantages; it made the occupation of the Black Forest by the Austrians nugatory and dangerous; rendered their

extensive fortifications on the Iller wholly useless ; and finally, by placing the French army several marches in the rear of the Austrians, forced the latter to change their positions, and take measures for their safety. General Mack now seeing his right wing turned, and apprehending interruption to his retreat, immediately withdrew his advanced posts from the defiles of the Black Forest, changed the front of his army which he also concentrated, and falling back upon the Iller, leaned with his right wing on Memmingen, and his left on Ulm : here he expected to be shortly joined by an Austrian corps of 12,000 men advancing to his support from Austria, under general Kenmeier, and also by the first Russian army, now rapidly approaching the scene of action.

Buonaparte having now gained the left bank of the Danube, considerably below the Austrian positions, lost not a moment in executing his daring design of immediately crossing that river, and throwing himself with his whole army in the rear of the Austrians under Mack ; so that being interposed between the latter general and the expected Austro-Russian reinforcements, he would be enabled to prevent their junction and at the same time by cutting off general Mack's retreat, to attempt the destruction of his whole army.

Accordingly while the left wing of the French army under Bernadotte hastened to cross the Danube at Ingolstadt, its centre and right wing prepared to pass that river higher up and nearer the Austrians. With this view the second division of marshal Soult's corps of the army under the command of general Vandamme, having stopped but two hours on the 6th at Nordlingen continued its march and arriving in the evening at Donawert, proceeded to take possession of the bridge across the Danube. The regiment of Colloredo made a brave resistance to the French, but, overpowered by the latter, they were forced, after the loss of some lives on both sides, and, having partly destroyed the bridge, to retire to the right bank, leaving the command of the bridge with the enemy. On the following morning, at day break, prince Murat, with his body of dragoons, advancing before the army, arrived at the bridge which was re-established in the night, and passed it, supported by a body of troops under general Walter. The prince immediately advanced to the Lech, but, finding the bridge over that river also occupied by the Austrians, he ordered general Walter to pass at the head of 200 dragoons, who, after a smart charge, drove the Austrians from the bridge, of which the French took possession. Murat arrived in the night at Rain, and his advanced-guard was quickly followed by the corps of marshal Lasnes, which crossed the Danube at Donawert on the 7th of October, and advanced towards the Lech. On the following morning, prince Murat, with the advanced-guard, marched at day-break from Rain towards Wertingen, for the purpose of cutting off the rout from Ulm to Augsburg. On arriving at the above village, he fell in with a strong division of the Austrians which had been detached on the preceding evening from Guntzburg to Wertingen, to observe the French. This Austrian division, commanded by field-marshal Auffenburg, and consisting of twelve battalions of grenadiers and fusileers, supported by two squadrons of duke Albert's cuirassiers, and two troops of Latour's light horse, were immediately surrounded by Murat's dragoons ; and marshal Lasnes, who was marching in the rear of the French cavalry, coming up with Oudinot's division, an obstinate action ensued. The Austrians sustained for two hours, with great bravery, the furious attacks of the French ; but a column of their grenadiers, which had formed in a square of four battalions, being penetrated and cut down by the enemy's cavalry, and cut off at a considerable distance from the main body of the Austrian army, while the French continually increased in numbers around them, this brave but unfortunate division was compelled to give way, and only a small part of it saved themselves by flight. The French took eight standards, the whole of the Austrian cannon, two lieutenant-colonels, six majors, 60 officers of inferior rank, and 4000 soldiers. Murat, after this success, hastened to take post

at the village of Zumershausen, whither he was accompanied by marshal Lasnes with the grenadier division of Oudinot and the division of Suchet. On the same day the corps of marshal Soult, which had manoeuvred the day before on the left bank of the Danube to intercept the passages from Ulm, and to observe the division of the Austrian army stationed in that place, passing the Danube and the Lech, advanced towards Augsburg.

Early on the morning of the 9th, the remaining corps of the French army were in motion to cross the Danube. Marshal Ney's grand division, belonging to the right wing, ascended the Danube to force his passage at Guntzburg. The day before, a part of the Austrian army had advanced from Ulm to that town, for the purpose of collecting the regiments which had not yet joined, but were arriving from their cantonments. It encamped near Guntzburg, resting with its right on the village of Limpach, and its left on Riesersburg. The Austrians also occupied the bridges on the Danube as far as Leipheim, and detached general Von Aspres with a corps of light troops to the left bank of that river, for the purpose of sending out parties to procure information respecting the enemy.

This detached corps of Von Aspres was immediately attacked by Ney's advanced-guard, and forced to retreat with loss, to the right bank of the Danube. The marshal now made a furious assault upon the bridges, but was received with showers of grape-shot from the Austrians, who bravely defended them. The contest was long and obstinate ; but, towards evening, the French general Malher, at the head of a column, succeeded, notwithstanding the gallant resistance made by prince Ferdinand, in carrying the bridges of the causeway leading into the town, and ultimately the town itself. The Austrians having suffered considerably, retired by night to Ulm, leaving the French in quiet possession of the important position of Guntzburg. In this severe action, the Austrians lost near 2000 men killed and wounded, about 1000 prisoners, and all their cannon.

While this desperate attack was making on the right, the centre of the French army crossed the Danube lower down, at Donawert and Neuburg, and the left wing passed the river still further in the same direction at Ingolstadt. The great division of the army under marshal Bernadotte, took post at Psaffenhoven, on the road to Munich, while the main body of the French army marched back upon the Lech, and, crossing that river, proceeded in the direction of their advanced-guard, stationed under Murat at Zumershausen, to Augsburg, which town now became the French head-quarters. It was in this passage of the Lech by the French troops that the emperor Napoleon, being stationed on the bridge when general Marmont's division defiled, formed each regiment into a circle, and spoke to them of the critical situation of the enemy, and of his immediate expectation of a general action.

Buonaparte having thus, by his bold and rapid manœuvres, succeeded in placing the whole French army between the Austrians under general Mack, and Vienna, instantly proceeded to accomplish the remainder of his gigantic plan. Bernadotte's corps, together with the Bavarians, in all about 40,000 men, he ordered to advance under the command of that general, on the road to Munich, for the purpose of opposing the approach of the Russians and Austrians advancing to reinforce Mack; while with the rest of the army, the French emperor seized on that general's communications, and marched to attack his army in its positions.

Accordingly marshal Bernadotte, with the troops under his command, set out from Psaffenhoven, where he had been posted after crossing the Danube, and marched forward the whole of the 11th for the capital of Bavaria. In this march his light troops captured the baggage of several Austrian generals. On the next morning, (the 12th,) at eight o'clock, Bernadotte entered Munich, taking 800 prisoners. This general soon afterwards crossed the Iser, at that town, and advanced on the high road of Brannau, on the Inn, where the first Russian army

had already arrived, and formed a junction with the Austrian corps under general Kenmeier. On the 15th, the French advanced posts pushed on to Wasserbourg and Slaag, and, falling in with some Austrian detachments, took a few hundred prisoners and several pieces of cannon. Marshal Bernadotte then advanced and took a strong position with his army between Munich and the Inn, for the purpose of watching the Austro-Russian forces, who were posted on the other side of the latter river, and of attacking them, should they attempt to cross it and advance.

Thus secured in his rear by the advance of Bernadotte towards the Inn, Buonaparte was enabled to employ in security the main body of the French army in his operations against Mack. On the morning of the 10th, he detached marshal Soult, with his corps of the army from the left, to occupy Landsberg and cut off that great communication of the Austrians. The marshal arrived there at half past four on the 11th, and immediately attacked some of the enemy's cuirassiers who defended the place; but, after a smart resistance, in which the French took some prisoners and two pieces of cannon, the Austrians hastily retreated to Ulm, leaving the important pass of Landsberg in the hands of the enemy.

While Buonaparte's left wing was thus occupying the openings along the Lech, and extending itself opposite the right of the Austrians posted on Memmingen, the emperor himself, with a large portion of his army, took measures for surrounding the strong position of Ulm, which contained nearly one-third of the whole Austrian army, together with magazines of military stores, and also the general-in-chief Mack. With this view, Buonaparte proceeded from Augsburg to the neighbourhood of Ulm. On the 11th, he caused marshal Ney's corps of observation to make an attack on a part of the Austrians strongly posted before the town: the action was obstinate and bloody; but the French emperor, arriving with a reinforcement towards evening, ordered a fresh and general attack to be made on the enemy, when he succeeded in carrying their entrenchments on the heights near Ulm, and consequently surrounding all the posts within their compass.

During these operations for insulating Ulm, Soult pursued his plan successfully against the enemy's right wing: on the approach of the French to Landsberg, the archduke Ferdinand retired with the corps of the Austrian right wing under his command, from the neighbourhood of Memmingen towards Biberach: marshal Soult in consequence, marched on the 12th for the former town, and arriving at day-break on the 13th, immediately surrounded the place. On the next day (the 14th) Memmingen seeing no hope of relief, capitulated; when the Austrians which it contained, amounting to several thousands, surrendered themselves prisoners of war.

Soult on the day following (the 15th) advanced to Biberach, in pursuit of the archduke Ferdinand; but finding that he had quitted that place and retired still further towards Ulm, he directed his course towards Bregeng to intercept the road to the Tyrol.

Ulm being at length completely surrounded by Buonaparte, who took post himself at Elchingen, the archduke Ferdinand saw himself cut off from the main body of the Austrian army under Mack, and endeavored to retreat with the divisions under his command, by the rout of Nordlingen and Nuremburg, into Franconia. He was however quickly pursued by prince Murat with his dragoons, and by marshal Lasnes with his corps: these divisions of the French army came up with the Austrian prince on the 18th near Nordlingen, and succeeded in surrounding a considerable part of his force, when the whole of the Austrian division of Werneck, amounting to above 12,000 men, together with lieutenant-general Werneck himself; and several other generals were forced to capitulate, and lay down their arms. Several pieces of cannon, and the Austrian heavy baggage, fell likewise into the hands of the French. After sustaining this severe loss,

prince Ferdinand, with his remaining troops, pushed forward, and throwing himself into the Prussian territory, took the road of Guntzenhausen to Nuremburg: prince Murat still followed him closely and took the lead of him, which occasioned an action on the road from Furth to Nuremburg, on the evening of the 21st of October. The Austrians defended themselves bravely, but being overpowered by numbers, they were forced to retreat, leaving with the French some prisoners, together with the principal part of their remaining artillery and baggage. After driving prince Ferdinand beyond Nuremburg, the French relinquished any further pursuit, and returned towards their main army, having taken from the prince, during his retreat, about 15,000 prisoners (including the division of Werneck before mentioned,) several stands of colors and 18 generals.

Whilst the detached corps of the French army were thus successfully employed in routing and destroying the divisions which had formed the right wing of the Austrian army, Buonaparte was equally fortunate in his operations against Ulm: he had himself directed his measures for reducing this important town, containing a principal part of the Austrian army, together with the chief commander and his staff, and he superintended in person their execution. By having possessed himself of the entrenched heights near Ulm, he gradually approached and commanded that place; and occupying as he did all the principal passages leading from that town, he reduced general Mack to the alternative either of surrendering with his army, or of boldly marching out and endeavouring to open for himself a passage through the French.

This determination the Austrian general did not think proper to adopt, and Buonaparte wishing to hasten the surrender of the place, made preparations on the 15th as if intending to storm Ulm the next day, and issued an address to his troops accordingly. In this proclamation he tells them, that "The following day will be an hundred times more celebrated than that of Marengo; that the Austrian troops

were now placed in the same situation."—
" But" continues the address, " merely to
conquer the enemy, is doing nothing
worthy either of you, or your emperor;
it is necessary that not a man of the enemy's army shall escape; that that government which has violated all its engagements, shall first learn its catastrophe
by your arrival under the walls of Vienna."
On this day also Buonaparte sent in a
message to general Mack in Ulm, requiring him immediately to capitulate with his
army; and threatening in case of refusal,
to storm that town.

General Mack seeing all his communications cut off; so as to be left without
much hope of escape, perceiving no immediate chance of relief at hand; his provisions running short; and apprehending
the effects of an assault against an imperfectly fortified town, accepted, after some
deliberation, the terms of capitulation offered; and on the 17th of October agreed
to surrender the city of Ulm, with all its
magazines and artillery to the French
army, and that the garrison (consisting of
about 30,000 men,) after marching out with
all the honors of war, and filing off, should
lay down their arms, the field officers to
be allowed to return to Austria on their
parole, but the soldiers and subalterns to
be sent prisoners into France, where they
were to remain until exchanged.

The execution of this capitulation, however, was not to take place, until it pleased
the commander-in-chief of the Austrian
troops, provided it was not delayed beyond
twelve o'clock at noon on the ensuing
25th, and general Mack, still having some
hope that the Russians and other reinforcements might yet arrive to his relief,
further stipulated, " That if an Austrian
or Russian army arrived in sufficient force
to raise the blockade of Ulm, before
twelve at midnight on the 25th, the garrison should in that case, be considered
as released from the capitulation, and be
at liberty to act as it might think fit."

Buonaparte who wished to cut short
his delay at Ulm, that he might proceed
without loss of time with his army against
the Russians, and Austrians on the Inn,

granted an audience to general Mack
on the 19th; after which, that general
being assured on the honor of the French
marshal, Berthier, that there was no
possibility of succor arriving before Ulm,
signed an addition to the capitulation, by
which he agreed to evacuate Ulm and surrender the army the next day, the 20th,
on condition that the whole corps of marshal Ney, consisting of twelve regiments
of infantry and four regiments of horse,
should not go beyond the distance or
ten leagues from the city and its environs,
before the 25th at midnight, the period when
the former capitulation was to have expired.

What could have induced the Austrian
general to consent to these additional articles of capitulation, by which he enabled
the great body of the French army to
proceed against the Austro-Russians on
the Inn, several days sooner than it could
otherwise have done, is not easy to be
explained, except that being severely
pressed for want of provisions, and despairing of his own relief, he was willing
to free the inhabitants of Ulm, and the
neighbouring country, from the pressure
of two great armies.

But whatever were his motives for so
doing, the garrison marched out with all
the honors of war the next day (the 20th,)
agreeably to the new capitulation; and
after filing before the French emperor,
laid down their arms and surrendered
themselves prisoners of war. Buonaparte had taken, his proud station from
two o'clock in the afternoon till seven
in the evening, on the heights near Ulm,
to behold the captured Austrian army
march past him; the French army also
were posted on those heights. The emperor surrounded by his guards, sent for
general Mack and the other Austrian
generals, whom he received with much
distinction: while their troops were filing
off he is said to have addressed them in
the following words: " Gentlemen your
master carries on unjust war. I tell you
plainly, I know not for what I am fighting.
I know not what can be required of me.
It is not in this army (looking towards
the French army) that my resources consist,

though, were this the case, I should still be able to make head with it; but I shall appeal to the testimony of your prisoners of war, who will speedily pass through France, they will observe with their own eyes, the spirit which animates my people, and with what eagerness they flock to my standards. This is the prerogative of my nation and my condition. At a single word 200,000 volunteers crowd to my standard, and in six weeks become good soldiers; whereas, your recruits only march from compulsion, and do not become good soldiers but after several years.

"I would give my brother, the emperor of Germany, one further piece of advice—let him hasten to make peace. This is the crisis when he must recollect, all states must have an end. The idea of the approaching extinction of the dynasty of Lorrain must impress him with terror

"I desire nothing upon the continent; I want ships, colonies, and commerce; and it is as much your interest as mine that I should have them."

To this speech of Buonaparte, general Mack is reported to have replied, "That the emperor of Germany had not wished for war, but was compelled to it by Russia."—"If that be the case," said Napoleon, "then you are no longer a power." Several of the other Austrian generals also are stated to have expressed their dislike to the war, and how much they were affected at seeing a Russian army introduced into the heart of their country. The generals the French emperor treated with much civility, comforting them under their misfortunes, and telling them that "war has its chances, and that they who had frequently been conquerors might be conquered for once."

Thus by the premature councils of the allies, the bad combinations of their generals, and the superior genius and rapidity of Buonaparte, did this extraordinary warrior succeed, as it were, in an instant, and at a blow, in destroying an Austrian army of 100,000 brave men, in the heart of Germany, and in their chosen positions; not even suffering 20,000 to escape. That Buonaparte opposed to Mack, and

no doubt with an army superior to the Austrians under that general, should conquer, is not surprising; but [that in the short space of only a few days, he should have annihilated a whole army, and taken the Austrian commander-in-chief prisoner, astonishes and confounds. But a month before, the French troops were stationed on the heights of Boulogne, in Holland, and in Hanover; at the call of their chief, they fly from the coasts of the English Channel, the North Sea, and the northern extremity of Germany, and, proceeding by forced marches, in a fortnight cross the Rhine: in a week more, they pass with the same rapidity the mountains of Wurtemberg, the Iller, and appear on the left bank of the Danube. Their plan now developes itself; instead of wasting their strength before the formidable defiles of the Black Forest they left it on the right, and boldly and rapidly advanced by the plains of Bavaria. The deceived general Mack, apprehensive for his retreat, retires from his advanced positions near the Black Forest, and falls back on the Iller, there to wait the junction of the first Russian army, then rapidly advancing to reinforce him. Buonaparte, however, immediately crosses the Danube with his whole army below the Austrians, and, detaching his left wing, (the most conveniently situated for this service,) under Bernadotte, on the road to Munich and the Inn, to oppose the approach of the Russians who were expected to arrive by that rout; he, with the rest of his army, completely turns the positions of the Austrians on the Iller, and, seizing all the passes between it and Vienna, succeeds, in less than a week after passing the Danube, and after several smart actions with distinct corps of the Austrians, in destroying the whole of this fine army, consisting of 100,000 men, taking upwards of 60,000 of them prisoners, together with their park of artillery, and 90 generals, including Mack, the Austrian commander-in-chief.

Great and signal, however, as this destruction of the Austrian army might be, it yet had its cause not in any supernatural influence ; in no uncommon accident, nor sudden and general infliction by disease, but in one plain prominent circumstance, incapacity in the councils and generalship of one of the combatants, and great and extraordinary genius and activity in the other. Incidental causes, it is true, which I shall have occasion to notice in the course of these pages, gave interest to the general fate of the campaign, and indeed to the contest altogether ; but the difference in talent between the adverse parties alone sealed the destruction of the first and most numerous of the Austrian armies.

HISTORY OF THE WAR.

CHAP. XXXVII.

Buonaparte prepares to Attack the Austro-Russian Army—Proposals to Negotiate—Fatal Confidence of the Russians—The French Army retreats—The Russians prepare to attack and surround the French Army—Disposition of the French Army—Battle of Austerlitz—Armistice between France and Austria—The Russian Army retreats.

BUONAPARTE, to reward his troops for their great exertions in gaining the late signal successes, and with a view to animate them to fresh enterprise, decreed, on the day succeeding the surrender of Ulm and the Austrian army, that the month Vindemiaire, year 14, should be reckoned as a campaign to all the individuals composing the French grand army in Germany, and be so charged to the state in the valuation of subsistence and military services; and further, that the war contributions, as well as the ordinary contributions which were to be levied in Suabia, should go to the army, with all the magazines that might be taken from the enemy, excepting those of artillery and provisions. At the same time the French emperor issued a flattering address to his soldiers, in which, after boasting that they had made a campaign in fifteen days, and chased the Austrians from the territories of the elector of Bavaria, their ally, he says, " of 100,000 men which composed the Austrian army, 60,000 are prisoners; they will go to replace our conscripts in the labor of our fields." And again: " But we shall not stop here; you are impatient to commence a second campaign; we shall make the Russian army undergo the same fate."

" To this combat is more especially attached the honor of the infantry; it is here that is to be decided, for the second time, that question which has been already decided in Switzerland and Holland; whether the French infantry be the first or the second in Europe ? There are among them no generals over whom I can have any glory to acquire; all my care shall be to obtain victory with the least effusion of blood—my soldiers are my children."

Napoleon now ordered possession to be taken of all the states of the house of Austria in Suabia; and, having directed the march of the Austrian prisoners for France, and the demolition of the fortifications of the towns of Ulm and Memmingen, he set out with his army, excepting Ney's corps, from Elchingen, on the 21st, for Augsburg, on his rout to Munich. In passing the Lech, he gave orders that *têtes de pont* should be constructed on all the points of that river, and that magazines should be established beyond them. On the 24th of October, at nine in the evening, the French emperor arrived at Munich; the town was illuminated in compliment to him, and he gave audience immediately on his arrival, to the principal officers of the elector, the foreign ministers, and the magistrates, with whom he remained a considerable time in conversation. Prince Murat, who had exhibited so much activity and skill in his late pursuit of the

Austrians under prince Ferdinand, directed his march from Nuremburg straight to
Munich, which place he reached some time
before the emperor, after having left a division of his troops under general Mortier,
together with general Baraguay d' Hilliers
and his dragoons, on the left bank of the
Danube, near Ratisbon, to descend that
river and observe the movements of the
archduke Ferdinand and the Austrians in
Bohemia. The elector of Bavaria not being
yet returned to his capital, Buonaparte sent
his aid-de-camp, colonel Lebrun, to receive
him, and to offer him escorts of honor on
the road : and the French emperor being
informed of the commencement of the campaign in Italy by Massena, prepared to
put himself again at the head of the army,
now in full march for the Inn.

Buonaparte having completed his arrangements for further operations, quitted
Munich on the 27th of October, to advance
with his army, flushed with the remembrance of their late stupendous victory. To
protect his flanks and rear, while he proceeded himself to drive the Russians and
Austrians from the Inn, and afterwards
marched forward with the main body of the
grand French army, to seize upon Vienna,
and penetrate into the heart of the Austrian hereditary states, he ordered the division of Mortier to advance from near Ratisbon along the left bank of the Danube,
and at the same time directed marshal Ney,
with a body of Bavarians, to proceed with
his corps from Ulm ; and ascending the
Lech, to attack the Tyrol on the Bavarian
side, while marshal Augereau, who had
passed the Rhine at Huninguen on the
11th, after having crossed France with his
army from Brittany, coasted along the
banks of the lake of Constance, in order to
attack it on the Suabian and Swiss frontiers.

Thus secured on his left flank by general
Mortier's division, which would not only
keep the Austrians in Bohemia in check,
but also threatened to penetrate into that
country, and protected on his right flank
by the corps of Ney and Augereau ; which,
while they covered this flank of the army,
and were ready in case of necessity to
cover his rear, would also accelerate the

important conquest of the Tyrol, and en-
close on their side, the army of the archduke Charles in Italy, Buonaparte advanced for the Inn with the following generals
and their corps : viz. Bernadotte, Lasnes,
Davoust, Soult, and Marmont. Prince
Murat also marched forward with his dragoons, and marshal Bessieres, accompanied
by the imperial guard.

The combined Russian and Austrian
army, amounting to about 45,000 men, was
strongly posted on the right bank of the
Inn, where they appeared determined to
oppose the passage of the river. On the
28th the French head-quarters were advanced to Haag, on the high road to Brannau on the Inn, and on that day the French
troops commenced the passage of this
river in the following order : viz.

Marshal Bernadotte, who with his corps
had advanced by Wasserburg, proceeded
on the 27th to Altenmarkt, where finding
six arches of the bridge burnt down, he
halted that night. Count Manucci, colonel
of, the Bavarian army, advanced with a
body of French and Bavarians, from Roth
to Rothenheim, where he also found the
bridge burnt and the enemy on the opposite
side. After, however, a brisk cannonade,
the Austrians retired from the right bank,
when several battalions of French and Bavarians passed the Inn, and by the exertions
of colonels Morio and Somis of the engineers, by the afternoon of that day (the
28th) both the bridges were completely
repaired : as soon as a sufficient force of
the French troops could pass over, the
Austrians and Russians were quickly
pursued, and a few of their rear guard
were made prisoners.

The corps of Davoust, which marched
to Freysing on the 26th, and reached Muhldorf on the next day, found the bridge at
that place in like manner mostly destroyed,
and the enemy with some batteries advantageously posted on the right bank : the
latter opposed the passage of the river with
much determination, but towards evening
on the 28th, the French under Davoust
with difficulty succeeded in gaining the
right side. On this day also prince Murat
ordered a brigade of cavalry to pass over

the bridge of Muhldorf, and, having caused the bridges of Oeting and Marekiri to be repaired, he passed the Inn with his reserve.

The combined Russians and Austrians finding themselves unable to prevent the passage of the Inn by the French army, and apprehending that Buonaparte might succeed in turning their positions as he had done those of general Mack, began their retreat from the right bank of that river, and retired slowly through the strong country behind them, in the direction of Vienna, to cover, if possible, that capital, and give time for the execution of the measures adopted by the Austrian cabinet for saving the place.

Amongst other steps resorted to for defending the metropolis, a general levy was ordered by proclamation, of all persons in Vienna fit to carry arms; and, to counteract the despondency which the late disasters on the Danube and Ilier was calculated to induce, and also to rouse his subjects to a spirited resistance against the French, the emperor of Austria and Germany issued from Vienna, on the 28th, (the day on which the French were passing the Inn,) a firm and intrepid proclamation, in which, after charging the cause of the war on the vanity and injustice of Buonaparte, he boldly declares, that he will rest his cause on its justice, and depend for victory on the love and affection of his 25,000,000 of people, supported by the assistance of his powerful auxiliaries the Russians.

On the 29th, the Austro-Russian army having retreated from the greatest part of the right bank of the Inn, the remaining corps of the French army which had been stationed on the left bank of that river, ready to support the divisions that had advanced, also crossed; the corps of marshal Soult and Marmont on the bridges already passed by the army, and consequently without opposition; and that of marshal Lasnes at Brannau. This general had directed his march from Lanshut towards the latter town; but, on arriving at the left bank of the Inn, he found the bridge cut away: he instantly ordered

some men to embark in boats and proceed to the other side, and the enemy being at the same time attacked by prince Murat, who had passed the Inn higher up, retreated, leaving Brannau to be taken possession of by their pursuers. The French found in this important place, which is surrounded with a circumvallation, and fortified by bastions, draw-bridges, a half-moon, and ditches full of water, numerous magazines of artillery, in good condition. They also found large stores of provisions, which the French army wanted much, after its march through the barren tract of country between the Ister and the Inn, which consists of only a continued forest of fir-trees. The Russians, who had garrisoned Brannau, left behind them a considerable quantity of powder and other military stores; and Buonaparte, who arrived on the 30th, fixed his head-quarters there, and appointed general Lauriston, who lately joined the army from Cadiz, governor of the place.

Whilst the centre of the French army effected the capture of Brannau, and prepared to drive the Austro-Russian army from their strong positions on the road to Vienna, Buonaparte detached marshal Bernadotte with his corps, (which had before formed the left wing of the army,) to the right, to occupy Saltzburg; afterwards to march forward, and, by keeping himself interposed between the rear of the archduke Charles and the retreating Austro-Russians, to prevent their junction; and, at the same time that he threatened to cut off the retreat of the former, to be in readiness for turning the positions of the latter, and thus to hasten their flight. The marshal accordingly proceeded, soon after having crossed the Inn, for Saltzburg, where he arrived at ten o'clock on the morning of the 30th. The elector of Saltzburg, the brother of the emperor of Austria, had quitted it some days before, and retired with his court to Vienna; and a corps of 6000 men, which had been placed there, on hearing of the advance of the French, retreated precipitately, the evening before, and took the road in the direction of Wels. Immediately on Bernadotte's arrival, he detached general Kellerman at the head of the advanced-guard, in pursuit of this division, which took shelter under the fort of Pasling, in the defile of that name, and, notwithstanding the great strength of this position, the carabiniers of the 27th regiment of light infantry attacked it with impetuosity, and a detachment of the French force succeeding at the same moment in turning it by extremely difficult roads, the Austrians were forced to retreat, leaving a few hundred men prisoners with the French.

The intended operations of the main body of the French army under Buonaparte being greatly facilitated by this movement of Bernadotte to the right, the different corps, immediately after passing the Inn, began their march forward to attack the enemy and drive him from his positions, notwithstanding the weather had now set in as intensely cold as in the depth of winter, and the snow which had fallen rendered the roads extremely bad.

Prince Murat, with his cavalry, was the first to advance : he set out on the 30th, in pursuit of the enemy, and overtook their rear-guard, about 6000 strong, on the heights of Ried. The French cavalry instantly charged that of the enemy, who resisted bravely, but, being overpowered by numbers, was at length forced to retreat; it however again rallied, to protect the passage of its infantry through a defile, when the French cavalry, making another furious charge, entered the defile with them, and, after a very sharp contest, succeeded in putting them to flight, with the loss of between 400 and 500 prisoners. In this action great bravery was displayed on both sides : the Austro-Russians fought manfully, and the French shewed great devotion for their chief. A quarter-master of the 8th regiment of dragoons having had his wrist shot off, exclaimed, as prince Murat was passing, " I regret the loss of my hand, because I can no longer serve our brave emperor !" After the above affair, the advanced-guard of Murat took a position beyond Ried, whither also the remainder of the French army was in full march.

On the next day, the 31st, prince Murat, who continued to pursue closely the retreating Austrians and Russians, arrived before Lambach : some battalions of Russians who had advanced for the purpose of protecting the retreat of the combined army, but were repulsed by Murat's advanced-guard, which drove them to Lambach, taking about 400 prisoners, among whom were 100 Russians. The French also took in this affair a few pieces of cannon, and found the next day at Lambach, (which the Russians had evacuated,) magazines of salt, worth several millions of francs.

This day, the 1st of November, the combined army continued its retreat to take a strong position behind the Ens : the French followed up the pursuit, and were slightly opposed by the Austro-Russian rear-guard. Murat's advanced troops had taken Wels in the morning, and his reserve of cavalry, under general Milhaud, also entered Lenz on the same day : the latter town contained considerable magazines, which were highly serviceable to the French. The whole of the French army continued to advance on the 2nd, making some prisoners ; and next day, (the 3rd,) marshal Lasnes arrived with his division at Lenz ; and Davoust, who advanced by Lambach, pushed on towards Steyer on the Ens This day also, Buonaparte removed his head-quarters to Lambach, and made dispositions for driving the enemy from the banks of the Ens, the last line for defending the approaches to Vienna. With this view he ordered prince Murat with his dragoons, to advance from Lenz against Ens, on the river of that name, whilst marshal Davoust, with his corps of the army, marched to Steyer also on that river : and he at the same time detached general Marmont with his corps, on the right towards Leoben, as if to turn the enemy's position.

Accordingly next morning, the 4th, Murat set out from Lenz, on his march for Ens : the Austrians had left at Ebersberg 300 or 400 men, to retard the passage of the Traun ; but general Walter's dragoons, (of the advanced-guard,) threw themselves into boats, and, under protection of the artillery, attacked the town with impetuosity, forcing the Austrians to retreat: after which general Walter passed the bridge of Traun, and advanced towards Ens. General Milhaud's brigade also was opposed at the village of Asten, where it defeated the Austrian and Russian rearguard, and pursued it to the Ens. While these operations were taking place on the left, Davoust on the right had entered Steyer, and made some prisoners; and the Austro-Russian army seeing the enemy thus boldly advance in front, and apprehending that the troops under Marmont were marching to attack them in the rear, quitted the right bank of the Ens, and slowly retreated.

The French army having thus succeeded in driving the Austrians and Russians from the important position of the Ens, hastened to cross that river, and to press forward for the capital of their adversary: and letters intercepted by the French advanced posts, on couriers travelling from Vienna, betrayed the consternation and confusion which reigned in that town on the approach of the French army, and gave reason to be assured that no very formidable resistance could be made to the entrance of the French.

Prince Murat therefore after taking Ens, advanced on the following morning, the 5th, before the army in pursuit of the retreating enemy: the Russian army had taken a position on the heights of Amstetten, with a view of retarding the progress of the French. Murat immediately attacked it with general Oudinot's grenadiers: the battle was obstinate and bloody; the Russians frequently repulsing the desperate charges of the French cavalry, and resisting the furious attacks of their grenadiers; but at length after fighting severely for several hours, they were forced to retreat from the field, leaving behind them about 400 dead, and 1200 prisoners. The French also suffered considerably in killed and wounded in this sharp action, in which general Oudinot's aid-de-camp, Legrange, was wounded. The Russians who after this defeat at Amstetten, had hastened their retreat, cut down the bridges over the Ips, and retired towards St. Polten, on the direct road to Vienna, and only about thirty miles distant from that capital: in this strong position it was expected they would make a stand, and measures were accordingly concerted by the French for dislodging them from it.

Buonaparte, whose head-quarters had been advanced on the 5th to Lenz, received on the 7th at night, a message from the emperor of Germany, demanding, in the name of himself and his allies, an armistice for a few weeks, for the purpose of opening negotiations for a general peace: count Giulay was the bearer of the Austrian message. The French emperor held a long conference with the count, and returned for answer that he had no objection to agree to the armistice desired, provided the Austrian monarch would also agree to the return home of the allied troops; the disbanding of the Hungarian levy; and the evacuation of the duchy of Venice and the Tyrol, to the French armies. With this reply count de Giulay returned to his court, and Buonaparte and his army continued to execute with rapidity the plans they had concerted for pressing forward to the Austrian capital. Murat, the day after defeating the Russians at Amstetten, repaired the bridges of the Ips, and passing over with his cavalry, pushed forward his advanced posts towards Molk: the next day (the 7th) the general fixed his head-quarters at the abbey of Molk, and advanced his out-posts as far as St. Polten. This day also general Mortier, who with a part of the troops under his command on the left bank of the Danube, had kept pace with Buonaparte's advance on the right, manœuvred in such a manner, as greatly to assist the operations of Murat, and the other corps of the centre of the army; and Davoust with his division marched from Steyer on the right, to take the road by Naydhoffen, Marienzel, and Lilienfeld, with the view of uncovering the left of the enemy's army stationed at St. Polten; while Buonaparte with his advanced-guard under prince Murat and his centre, consisting of the corps of marshals Lasnes and Soult, together with his own imperial guards, advanced to attack it in front.

On the next day (the 8th,) Davoust's advanced-guard, still some leagues from Marienzel, met the córps of the Austrian general Meerfeldt, who was marching for Neufstadt to cover Vienna on that side. The general of brigade Hendelet, commanding the French advanced guard, immediately attacked the Austrians with great impetuosity. An obstinate and bloody action ensued, which lasted for some hours, and in which great bravery was exhibited on both sides. The French however succeeded in routing their opponents, taking three standards, 16 pieces of cannon, and 3000 prisoners. This victorious corps of the French army, after closely pursuing for several leagues, the remainder of Meerfeldt's division, which at length scattered and fled towards Hungary, commenced its march on the 9th, by a great carriage road directly for Vienna, leaving the corps of Bernadotte and Marmont (the latter of whom entered Leoben this day) still to manœuvre on the right, and to watch the rear of the archduke's army, now hard pressed by Massena in front, and retreating out of Italy by Carmola towards Hungary.

These well combined movements had the desired effect: the Russians seeing Buonaparte prepared to attack them in front, apprehending their left might be turned by Bernadotte, Marmont, and Davoust, whom they supposed to have been detached to the right of the French army for that purpose; and also dreading that their communication with Moravia would be cut off by the French corps under Mortier, who frequently manœuvred on the left bank of the Danube with the view of inspiring this fear, immediately resolved to repass that river, which they hastily effected on the 9th at Krems, burning down the bridge behind them.

All the strong posts where a defence might be made, being now resigned by the combined army, and Vienna itself being abandoned, Buonaparte made immediate preparations for possessing himself of that important capital. Davoust was hastening to approach it from the right, and Murat, who took post at St. Polten, on its evacu-

ation by the Russians, detached the brigade general of dragoons, Sebastiani, to proceed towards it by the direct road. Buonaparte this day, the 9th, advanced his headquarters from the Ips to the fine abbey of Molk. Here he was waited on by a deputation of the magistracy of Vienna, who came to supplicate the conqueror "to treat their city with kindness, as the unfortunate inhabitants were not the cause of the war," The French emperor, who immediately admitted them to an audience, replied, "That the inhabitants of Vienna must take care not to open their gates to the Austrians and Russians, but only to the French."

All the intercepted accounts from Vienna represented that metropolis as in the utmost consternation at the dispersion of the combined army, and the consequent approach of the French. The emperor of Austria, who on the 25th of October, received at Wels, the first intelligence of the destruction of his army at Ulm, and since that fatal period was unable, notwithstanding all his exertions, to recover that dreadful blow, prepared, now that the enemy was at the gates, to remove with his court to Brunn in Moravia, where he expected to be visited by the Russian emperor-Alexander, on his return from Berlin. Accordingly on the 7th, the day on which he demanded the armistice from Buonaparte, Francis II. emperor of Austria and Germany, and king of Hungary and Bohemia, &c. &c. was compelled to quit his capital, and with his family to fly into one of his provinces for refuge from the conqueror. As he stepped into his carriage, he could not help casting his eyes towards his palace, and exclaiming, "O God! O God!" a dreadful reverse for the contemplation of the rulers of empires! Besides the emperor, all the nobility, and those most concerned in having advised the war, quitted Vienna, to retire into Hungary; and so great was the crowd of fugitives flying into that province, as to cover the road to Presburg.

The great body of the inhabitants however were forced to await calmly in their homes the capture of their city, and trust to the generosity of the conqueror. The war had been undertaken contrary to their wishes, because they apprehended its unfortunate consequences ; and now that, the results had actually happened, they were not greatly astonished. The conduct also of the Russian privates was such as not to increase their regret at the disastrous events of the war ; and the distress occasioned by the depreciation of the bank paper money, which fell thirty per cent. and the consequent scarcity of provisions at Vienna, still further helped to lessen their disappointment at its failure. Without intending, therefore, to offer any resistance to the invader, a national guard was appointed to protect private property, and every other measure was taken to preserve the peace of the city.

On the 10th, the advanced-guard of the French army marched forward, and next day arrived before Vienna. Prince Murat took up his abode in the country palace of prince Lichtenstein, and the troops were quartered in the places around, which had been previously provisioned for their reception, from the capital. Next day the remainder of the French army arrived, and were lodged in the suburbs, where they conducted themselves peaceably ; and the French emperor fixed his head-quarters at Bukersdorff, a post station about two miles distant from Vienna.

All the Austrian troops had already evacuated their capital, and the national guard, which was well organised, did the duty. On the 13th, the French entered the town. Their advanced-guard under Murat, marched through it in the morning without halting, and observing the greatest order, and passed the Danube by the bridge of Vienna, taking the road for Moravia. The Austrian engineers had prepared to burn the bridge, but had been directed from their purpose by the French, who made them believe that a cessation of hostilities was about to take place. Next day, the 14th, at nine in the morning, the division of marshal Soult passed through Vienna, following the direction of the advanced-guard. Marshal Davoust soon after arrived with his corps, a part of which he detached down the Danube towards

Presburg in Hungary. On this day also, at two o'clock, Buonaparte made his entry into Vienna : he passed a great part of that night in visiting the advanced posts upon the left bank of the Danube, as well as the positions, and in satisfying himself that the duty was properly done. At daybreak next morning, he returned to the palace of Schoenbrunn, where he had taken up his residence.

This orderly conduct of the French troops prevented any great shock being given to the city ; and, notwithstanding its capture by the enemy, trade continued to be carried on nearly as usual. The French found in Vienna an immense quantity of military stores, which the Austrians had not been able to remove : there was left behind, ammunition sufficient for two or three campaigns, besides a vast number of pieces both of light and heavy artillery ; and this loss was the more severe to the house of Austria, as it had no other foundry, for casting cannon, nor any other arsenal than that at Vienna. Several thousand muskets were also found in the arsenal, 15,000 of which Buonaparte made a present to the elector of Bavaria, and he at the same time ordered all the artillery to be restored to him, which Austria had taken in the Bavarian states on former occasions. Buonaparte made large requisitions for his army. He had not yet received any of the authorities of Vienna, but only a deputation from the different corporate bodies, who, on the day of his arrival, went to meet him at Sigartskirschew. The French emperor received the deputation with much kindness, and told them that they might assure the people of Vienna of his protection.

On the next day, the 15th, Buonaparte, having appointed the general of division, Clarke, governor-general of Upper and Lower Austria, left Vienna to rejoin his army now advancing into Moravia in pursuit of the retreating Russians. It will be remembered that the Russian army under general Kutusof repassed the Danube on the 9th, at Krems. On the 10th, in the afternoon, with about 6000 men, approached the Russian advanced posts in the vicinity of Diernstein, and drove them back along the Danube, from Weisskirchen to Stein. The Russian general therefore prepared to attack the French next morning in three columns, preserving that disposition as much as possible in a country covered with vineyards. A more obstinate battle has been seldom fought, or a more brilliant defence sustained by a few thousand men against a large army. The action commenced at six in the morning, and continued with unabated fury till four in the afternoon. The French having repulsed the repeated attacks of the Russians, and obtained possession of the village of Loiben, imagined that they had terminated the labors of the day; but they were soon alarmed by the approach of the enemy in two columns, by difficult passes, with the purpose of out-flanking them, an object which they accomplished. Mortier endeavored to cut his way through the Austrian lines: the action commenced with redoubled fury; the carnage was horrible; but the French general, with a few of his followers, succeeded in opening a passage and effecting a retreat. The Russians sustained a considerable loss, and the French lost about 2000 prisoners, besides a considerable number killed and disabled. The day after the battle of Diernstein, general Kutusof quitted the Danube and continued his retreat in the direction of Brunn, the present residence of the Austrian court, and the rout by which he might await his junction with the second Russian army now advancing under general Buxhovden.

The French army having passed through Vienna on the 13th and 14th, crossing the Danube at that town, advanced into Moravia. While it proceeded to outflank the Russians on the right, Bernadotte, who had quitted Saltzburg on the 6th, and approached the frontiers of Hungary, marched back for the Danube near Vienna, and, crossing that river, advanced to co-operate with Buonaparte.

On the 15th of November, Murat and Lannes came up with the Russian army at Holbreinn, (spelt also Holbronn and Holbrunn.) The French cavalry charged the enemy, who abandoned their ground, leaving behind some of their baggage. The Russian general finding himself hard pressed, and desirous to gain a little time, had recourse to a stratagem of which the example had been set by the French in passing the bridge at Vienna. A flag of truce presented himself at the French advanced-posts, and Winzingerode, aid-de-camp to the emperor, demanded leave for the Russian army to capitulate, and separate from the Austrians. This offer appeared too specious not to demand attention; and Murat himself, the author of this species of deception, communicated the information to Buonaparte. It soon became suspected, and Buonaparte refused to agree to the proposed terms, on the ground that the Russian was not authorised to treat; but he declared that if the emperor would ratify the convention, he would likewise do it. The French army immediately advanced. The Russians, who, during this parley, had made some progress in their retreat, were attacked the next day near Guntersdorf. The Russians behaved with great bravery, and repulsed the enemy at the point of the bayonet. Marshal Lasnes attacked them in front, general Dupas, with a brigade of grenadiers turned their left, while marshal Soult was on their right, so that they were compelled to give way.

At the time of the junction of the two Russian armies near Wischau, they had only opposed to them the corps of prince Murat, part of which formed the advanced-guard, those of marshals Soult and Lasnes, the imperial guards under marshal Bessieres, and a corps of grenadiers drawn from these different troops, forming a reserve of 15,000 men, under general Duroc. This army, when near Bruun, was composed of eight divisions, each of which was about 7000 strong. The Russian army was so much fatigued with the continual marches it had been making, whether to fall back on the support, or the support to get forward in time, that it was decided at Wischau to take up the position of Olmutz, to give some days' rest to troops.

Opinions were at that time much

The Russian advanced-posts had no s
of information as to the position and fo
of the enemy; at one time, even pr·
Bagration was ignorant of the situatior
cupied by the French advanced g·
The Austrians also notwithstanding
facility they ought to have possess
procuring intelligence in the countr
only *very vague data* to act upon.

By *this* information, however, it
ed, that the French forces were (
only in small numbers near Br·
some generals of the combined s
their opinion at Wischau for ir
resuming the offensive. It is p(
moment might have been mor·
than that which was afterwr
The strength of the coalesced
from the 19th of November,
that of the enemy, who was ·
ed that the junction of the
armies had been effected,
could not expect an offen·
such as a manœuvre on eit·
would have been. The ar
near him to admit of hir
forcements from Brunn.
versity of opinion, perh
movement of Olmutz r
those in command did
decision, which can on·
military eye. ·

The Austrian genera
sent into Galicia, for th
ing the army of Bu
hereditary states. I
putation, who did n
who had inspired r
fidence. As soon (
united, he filled
master-general. '
previously select
this important t
man of superior
for the profou·
that tranquil ·
and deliberati
shewn himself
the confidenc
his life there
the hopes c
ther soldier

Bagration with his advanced guard, was at Prosnitz. General Keinmaer, with his upon the left, at Kralitz, pushed on detachments upon Krenowitz. The out-posts were at Predlitz. An Austrian partisan was sent along the March, on Tobitschau, Kogetein, and Kremsir, to observe that country. The French army had also sent a partisan from Goeding on Hradisch, and Kremsir; but the latter was repulsed and the Austrian detachments remained masters of the March. It will not escape the observation of the reader that this operation gave the allies the means of manœuvring by their left, while their right (which would then have rested on the March) was secured, and would have masked the movement so as to give them, at least two days' march in advance. The good understanding at that time subsisting with Prussia, appears to have been such, as to have made it expedient for the allied army, to think of establishing a communication with the archduke Charles. But in determining on offensive movements, nothing appears to have been thought of, but going straight forward.

M. de Kutusof had also sent some Austrian partisans, on his right flank, who marched upon Tribau and Zwittau, whither the archduke Ferdinand, who was at Czaslau, had sent some parties of light troops, to keep up the chain of communication.

Prince Murat arrived on the 18th of November, at Brunn. His advanced guard under general Sebastiani, pushed forward in the first instance, to Bausnitz, and afterwards entered Wischau, after prince Bagration had evacuated it. The emperor Napoleon established himself, on the 20th of November, at Brunn, and placed his army in concentrated cantonments, in the following manner:

The corps of guards, the grenadiers of the reserve, and the troops under marshal Lasnes, in Brunn and its vicinity. The cavalry under prince Murat, on the right and left of the great road, between Brunn and Posorsitz. Marshal Soult at Austerlitz: and the three divisions of which his army was composed, were divided between that place. Butzchowitz, Neuwieslitz, Stanitz, and the road to Hungary. At Gaja, was a strong detachment, which kept open the communication with that which observed the river March in order to secure the right of the army.

The 25th of November the grand-duke Constantine arrived at Olmutz, with the corps of guards, of which he had the command. After a long aud forced march from St. Petersburgh, this fine body of men was in the best order.

This corps was composed of 10 battalions, and 18 squadrons, the whole amounting to 10,000 men; of whom, however there were ouly 8,500 under arms. At this moment the army under M. de Kutusof may be computed to have amounted in all to above 80,000 men, as will be seen hereafter in detail.

A reinforcement of 10,000 men was still expected under general Essen; which accordingly arrived near Olmutz, at the moment when the allied army commenced its offensive operations. The corps of Essen was at Kremsir, the day of the battle of Austerlitz, and was of no kind of use. The army under M. de Kutusof was certainly stronger than the one opposed to it; but while the latter was concentrated towards a single point, and formed into masses, the former diffused its force as it advanced. It is not in numbers that the only, aud indeed the principal strength of an army consists; but there are emergencies and occasions, in which it is absolutely necessary to profit by that advantage; and the present was an instance of the kind. The allied army was under the necessity of advancing, for the reasons hereafter to be detailed. Had it commenced its movement from the day on which the grand duke Constantine arrived with his reinforcements forming the reserve of the centre; if at this epoch, it had manœuvred with rapidity and calculation; if the reserve under the grand duke had been augmented by the corps under general Essen; if less importance had been attached to the resting an army, which, after some days' inactivity could no longer be fatigued, there might perhaps have been found means, without risking a battle, to oblige the French army to abandon their positions, by turning one of its flanks; which, by threatening its communications, would have induced it to move upon Vienna or Bohemia. The former step would have been attended with danger. The corps of Bernadotte, which came from Iglau to reinforce the army in front of Brunn, the evening before the battle of Austerlitz, would not then have had time to make this movement, which was followed by such fatal consequences to the allies. It was only by means such as these, had the allies acted with prudence and vigor, that they could have hoped to make the French fall into their combinations; combinations which should have been calmly conceived and vigorously executed. But the quarter-master-general, it has before been mentioned, though an officer of great personal courage, had not that confidence in himself which could enable him to give advice at the head-quarters, where the greatest degree of wisdom was requisite. Without regarding the difficulties thrown in his way, this officer too easily abandoned his own opinions to adopt those of his coadjutors.

The astonishing rapidity with which the unfortunate events of this disastrous war succeeded each other; the excessive imprudence of Mack, which was only to be surpassed by his disgrace, and in which originated that succession of guilty errors which astonished Europe and calumniated a brave army; the folly of never anticipating a check, and of not establishing magazines in the rear, as a consequence of that presumption, were the immediate causes that the army, while in the position of Olmutz, was almost destitute of provisions. It had only been there one day before it was obliged to have recourse to forced requisitions, a violent expedient, which, by the disorderly manner in which it was executed, had much influence on the discipline of the army, into which a spirit of licentiousness began to insinuate itself from that day forward. In the then state of politics, the gaining time was at that moment nearly of equal importance with gaining a battle; and the instant it was decided, not to ma-

nœuvre, it became of the highest importance to be enabled to subsist in the position of Olmutz, for the purpose of maintaining it. There still remained countries from which it would have been possible to draw provisions, but they were at a distance, and the convoys were obliged to make a long circuit. To this it was necessary to apply a speedy remedy. The officers of the commissariat received orders, incessantly repeated, but never sufficiently urgent, to establish convoys of provisions with all possible despatch, upon the different roads; but some of this department wanted both activity and inclination; their systematic conception of military affairs not allowing them to feel the extent of the emergency, while others experienced great embarrassment, from the detention, by the Russians, of a great part of the horses belonging to the country, employed in the transport of provisions, and were, in consequence, at a loss for the means of conveyance. The bread was plundered on the road, both by the detachments appointed for its escort, and by a number of marauders who followed the army. The strict subordination that ought to have existed, was not vigorously maintained, under the pretext that the army was starving. Relaxation of discipline is always succeeded by excesses; and the licentiousness attendant upon it gives full latitude to the disaffected, and to all those who have not courage to sustain the numerous privations of modern warfare. It was thought impossible to subsist the army in the position in front of Olmutz, and it was resolved to abandon it for the purpose of attacking the enemy.

We have already seen the uncertainty in which M. de Kutusof found himself, as to the movements and force of the enemy, at the moment when it was decided to resume the offensive. The accounts derived from the people of the country were contradictory, and the out-posts gave no information whatever. The first disposition made for the advance, was not founded upon an exact knowledge both of the position of the enemy and the numbers to be contended with, but was solely adapted to the nature of the ground between Olmutz and Wischau. This disposition was given to the generals, the 24th of November. The 25th was the day on which it was fixed to march, but it was necessary to take two day's provisions, and these provisions could not arrive till the day after: When that day came, some of the generals had not sufficiently studied their dispositions, and thus another day was lost. The enemy profited by this time. The evening before the battle, as has been already mentioned, marshal Bernadotte, as well as part of the corps of marshal Davoust, reinforced the emperor Napoleon. It was necessary to recal the attention to these facts on which I shall yet have occasion still further to remark.

The 27th of November, at eight o'clock in the morning, the army was put in motion in five columns, to approach nearer the advanced-guard, under prince Bagration, who on that day made no movement whatever, in order that the manœuvre might be concealed from the enemy. This was done with a view of concentrating the troops, which, however, in the end, were diffused afresh. The five roads by which the army advanced, were parallel to each other. The two right columns marched along the foot of the mountains, to the right of the causeway, and were composed of infantry only. That of the centre was on the great road to Prosnitz; the fourth to the left of this, and very little distant from it; the fifth, composed entirely of cavalry, was in sight of the fourth. In front of this last, the country was entirely open.

The first column assembled at Nebotin, and marched upon Przebschein, Blumenau, and Kobelnizeek, where it formed in two lines.

The second column assembled at Olschan, and marched upon Studnitz, Czechowitz, and Ottaslowitz, where it formed, with its right supported by the left of the first column.

The third column assembled on the high road to Prosnitz, on which it marched, and formed in line with the two right columns.

The fourth column assembled at Nedwiis; and marched upon Wrahowitz and Do-

brochow, where it formed and established its communication with the centre column.

The fifth column assembled at Schabelin, and marched upon Kralitz and Bazesowitz, where it formed in two lines.

This last column not being covered by the outposts on the left, had an advanced-guard of its own, commanded by general Stutterheim, which communicated with the detachments observing the river March.

The army advanced with much precaution, because it was ignorant of the enemy's movements. It had orders to refuse the left, and to allow the right, which moved along the mountains to gain ground, in order to turn the enemy's left, in case of meeting with it. The corps under the grand duke marched upon Prosnitz, (where the two emperors and the head-quarters were established,) and formed the reserve. After four hour's march, the army arrived on its different points of formation without any obstacle.

Information was received, that the enemy had made no movement whatever, and that his advanced-guard at Wischau had neither been reinforced nor diminished. Preparations were in consequence made for its attack the next morning, and prince Bagration received orders to put it in execution. The army was to follow in the same order as before, the rout that should be opened for it by this general. On the 28th, at day-break, prince Bagration put his corps in motion in three columns; that of the centre remained on the causeway; the two others on the right and left, turned the town of Wischau, in which the enemy had a regiment of hussars and one of chasseurs. Two other regiments of cavalry were posted in reserve in rear of the town, while general Sebastiani was at Huluboschan with a regiment of dragoons. As soon as the Russians, with the cavalry under general Keinmaer, (composed of the hussars of Szechler and Hesse Homburg,) on their left, appeared before Wischau and on the heights of Brindlitz, the French cavalry, with the exception of about 100 men, precipitately abandoned the town.

The adjutant-general Dolgoruoky, took possession of the town with two battalions of infantry and made four officers and 100 men prisoners. The enemy's cavalry received considerable reinforcements in retiring upon Rausnitz, where there was a strong reserve. In the first instance they were pursued by four squadrons of Russian hussars and two of Cossacks; but afterwards all the cavalry under prince Bagration, reinforced by that of the fourth column, under the command of lieutenant-general Essen, (under whose orders were placed ten squadrons of hulans, five of cuirassiers, five of dragoons, and eight of Cossacks) passed through Wischau, to support the attack of the advanced-guard. To cover his right during this movement, prince Bagration had received orders to send a regiment of chasseurs, and one of cavalry, to the fright of Drissitz by Bustomirz, and Dietitz, upon Habrowan. This general prosecuted his march as far as the heights of Rausnitz, where he took up his position. The enemy was still master of this little town, and began to cannonade; but the Russian artillery which was more numerous, soon silenced the fire. In the evening two Russian battalions took possession of Rausnitz, in front of which were placed the outposts.

M. de Kienmaer, who with his cavalry, had supported the Russian advanced-guard on the left, took his direction upon Drasowitz, and there established his communication with prince Bagration.

The army on the 28th, moved, as before, in five columns, and followed up the movement of the advanced-guard.

Upon the movements of the allies, the French quitted their cantonments. By a signal made from Austerlitz, marshal Soult collected his corps there, which evacuated the villages it had before occupied.

The allies flattered themselves that the French would not risk the fate of a battle in front of Brunn. After the 28th, this hope became the prevailing opinion at headquarters. Then instead of hastening their movements, they wished to manœuvre at a period when too much had been risked, to enable them to avoid a decisive action. We have hitherto seen M. de Kutusof advancing his right, and refusing his left,

with the view of turning the enemy's num by the mountains, for which purpose he had disposed the greater part of his infantry on the right wing. At Wischau this disposition was changed. He wished to manœuvre on the right of the enemy. A march to the left was undertaken, which lost both time and the ground that might have been gained to the front. The 29th of November the combined army moved from Lutsch, and the heights of Noska upon those of Huluboschau and Kutscherau. It was not till the 1st of December that marshals Bernadotte and Davoust joined the emperor Napoleon; and on the 29th M. de Kutusof might have been at Austerlitz. After having passed Wischau, the allied army could no longer manœuvre with impunity. The time it then lost in making movements, which did not lead it directly towards the enemy, whilst it discovered their intentions to the French army, gave also the means of receiving such reinforcements as were within reach. A short flank movement could not answer the end proposed; while one that was longer, would have afforded the enemy an opportunity of attacking on the march.

While the army was moving on the heights of Kutcherau, prince Bagration pushed on his advanced-posts towards Pososrsitz: general Kienmaer marched upon Austerlitz, which the enemy had evacuated at ten o'clock, on the morning of the 29th; and general Stutterheim arrived at Butschowitz, whence he kept up the communication by Slanitz, with a detachment under lieutenant-colonel Scheither, who had driven the enemy's detachments from Gaja. The French army concentrated its forces, the same day, between Turas and Brunn; it occupied the villages of Menitz, Tellnitz, Sokolnitz, Kobelnitz, and Schlapanitz, which covered its front, and placed its outposts at Aujest, on the heights of Guchikowitz, and near Krug. On the 30th of November the combined army in consequence of its new plan, again marched to its left.

On the 1st of December there was a good deal of firing the whole of the morning, along the entire chain of outposts. The enemy, from day-break, was continually reconnoitring along the heights in front of Pratzen and Krug. He also for the like purpose, pushed parties from his left beyond the high road. M. de Keinmaer's outposts on the left were at Satchan; and he had a post near Menitz, a village which the French abandoned. Five battalions of frontier troops, under major-general Carneville, being a part of the Austrian infantry, arrived in the evening to reinforce M. de Kienmaer.

The combined army, the left of which was commanded by general Buxhovden, and the centre by the general-in-chief, after having dined, moved forwards in five columns.

At one moment during the night, the enemy evacuated the village of Tellnitz, in which outposts were placed by a half squadron of Austrian light cavalry of the regiment of O'Reilly: but two hours after, the French returned in force, and posted a regiment of infantry in this village, from the division of Legrand, forming a part of the right of marshal Soult. The outposts on the left of the allies, sent continually through the night, patrokes to their right, in order to establish a communication with the Russian advanced posts, but could never fall in with them.

This offensive movement had been made by the army in open day, and in sight of the enemy, who from the heights of Schlapanitz, and in front of Kobelnitz, had been able to remark it at his ease. The position occupied by the allies, at the moment when they crowned the heights between the Aujest, Pratzen, and Holubitz, was a strong one. The enemy, had he been well observed, would have found it difficult to advance for the purpose of attacking these heights, the defiles of Tellnitz, Sokolnitz, and Schlapanitz, which separated the two armies, offered the means of delay; and the very elevated points of these heights afforded strong means of defence. Here, as in the position, in front of Olmutz, the army was posted on a curtain, behind which massive columns might be posted, ready to act offensively. Its left was secured by the lakes of Menitz, and Aujest, while the right was refused. But the taking advantage of this position was never thought of, any more than the possibility of being attacked on these heights, or of finding the enemy on this side the defile. The French emperor took advantage in a masterly manner of the faults that were committed. He kept his troops concentrated in massive columns, ready to act according to circumstances. Marshal Bernadotte (who had joined the emperor Napoleon the day on which the allies shewed themselves on the heights of Pratzen,) had been posted in the first instance to the left of the high road. In the night the emperor caused his corps to pass this road, and posted it in rear of the village of Gitschicowitz, which was occupied in force. This corps, composed of the divisions of Rivaux and Drouet, formed the centre of the French army. Prince Murat's cavalry was in rear of marshal Bernadotte, and on his left. Marshal Lasnes formed the left wing with the division of Suchet and Caffarelli; this last was connected with the left of prince Murat. The right of the army commanded by marshal Soult, was placed between Kobelnitz and Sokolnitz; the division of Legrand forming the extreme right, was posted between Sokolnitz and Tellnitz, and occupied these villages with strong detachments of infantry. The division of Vandamme was on the left, and the division of St Helaire in the centre of marshal Soult's corps.

The reserve of the army, composed of the battalions of the imperial guard, and of ten battalions of general Oudinot's corps, the whole commanded by general Duroc, was near Turas. The division of Friant, belonging to the corps under marshal Davoust, which had just arrived from Presburg, was sent to the convent of Regern, on the Schwartza, to observe and keep the enemy in check, should he approach by the rout of Auspitz. The division of general Gudin (also arrived from Presburg,) with some dragoons belonging to marshal Davoust's corps, advanced from Nickolsbourg, on the right of the French army, to keep in check the corps of M. de Marveldt, who had penetrated through Hungary to Lundenburg. This general had with him his own regiment of hulans and the emperor's hussars, much weakened by the losses they had sustained during a difficult retreat, and six battalions of infantry, also very weak; the whole amounting to little more than 4000 men. A detachment of O'Reilly's light cavalry, and some cossacks, were sent to Gros-Niemchitz to observe that point.[1]

The disposition for the attack of the French army was delivered to the general officers of the Austro-Russian army, soon after midnight, on the morning of the 2nd of December. But the imperfect knowledge which was possessed of the enemy's positions, though scarcely out of the reach of musketry, rendered the plan of attack uncertain and indefinite. They supposed that the French army was weakened in its centre to reinforce its left. The combined army outflanked the enemy's right. It was imagined that, by passing the defiles of Lokolnitz and Kobelnitz, their right might be turned, and the attack be afterwards continued between Schlapanitz | and the wood of Turas, thus avoiding the defiles of Schlapanitz and Bellowitz, which it was conjectured, covered the front of the enemy's position. The French army was then to be attacked by its right, with great celerity and vigor. The valley between Tellnitz and Lokolnitz was to be passed with rapidity. The right of the allies was to cover this movement. With this view the five columns already mentioned received orders to advance, and at seven o'clock the next morning they put themselves in motion from the heights of Pratzen.

The movements of the allies were perfectly discernible to the French, who could not but perceive considerable intervals between their columns, in proportion as they approached the valleys of Tellnitz, Locolnitz, and Kobelnitz. At the dawn of day, Buonaparte had collected his generals on a commanding eminence: he waited until the sun had appeared above the horizon before he issued his last orders.

They then rode off at full gallop to join their respective corps, while Buonaparte himself passed with great rapidity along the whole line of his troops.

The action began on the left wing of the allies. The corps of general Kienmaer, posted in front of Aujut, was nearest the enemy, and destined to force the defile of Tellnitz, and to carry that village as soon as possible, in order to open a passage for the first column, which had a great circuit to make before it could arrive at the point which would bring it in a line with the second column.

After a desperate conflict, this column obtained possession of the hill that commanded the village, from which they dislodged the French. The latter, however, being reinforced, and availing themselves of a sudden fog, regained possession of the village and the hill beyond it. As soon as the fog dispersed, the allied troops again moved forwards, and the French abandoned the village. This being accomplished, the defile was passed without difficulty, and the plain occupied between Tellnitz and Turas. Here they waited to form a communication with the second column; but, this, and likewise the third column, had met with some opposition from a part of the division of Legrand, which occupied Locolnitz, and, in passing that village, they were further delayed by some confusion in their movements.

Soult, with the two divisions of St. Hilaire and Vandamme, traversed the villages of Kobelnitz and Puntswitz, to attack the heights and the village of Pratzen, while Buonaparte put in motion his massive columns, which he had kept together for the purpose of marching against the centre, and by that manoeuvre cutting off the left wing, which still continued to advance for the purpose of turning the French army in a position that it *did not occupy.* At the same time Bernadotte having crossed the rivulet at the village of Girschicowitz, with the division of Ribaud on his left, and that of Drouet on his right, took his direction on the heights of Blazowitz. The cavalry under prince Murat formed

In several lines on the left of Bernadotte, and marched between Girschicowitz and Krug. Lasnes having on his right the division of Caffarelli, and on his left that of Suchet, moved forward on the left of Murat. From that time the centre and right of the allies became engaged at all quarters.

We shall, however, dismiss the movements on the right, as they were only secondary, to more important evolutions, to trace the operations on the centre and left of the allies. The centre of the combined army had been very much weakened by the strong force which had been sent to such a distance on their left, with a view of turning the enemy's right, while the division on the right was not sufficiently strong to divide the French forces. Buonaparte, from the moment that he discovered the plan of the allies, brought a very superior force to act against their centre, which was thus perfectly insulated. However, according to the original plan, they prepared to advance about eight o'clock, the emperor Alexander having arrived at the head of the fourth column, commanded by general Kollourath. The action near Tellnitz had just begun, and the left was in motion, when the centre was formed and broke into platoons on the left. These measures had hardly been taken, before a massive column of French infantry, composed of the division of Vandamme and St. Helaire, was discovered in a bottom in front of Pratzen.

The commander-in-chief, general Kutusof, destined at no very distant period, to be hailed as the saviour of his country, felt the full importance of the heights of Pratzen, against which the enemy was moving. Attacked, himself, unexpectedly, in the midst of offensive operations, and perceiving these heights were to the Key, to the position his army had just quitted, he gave orders for shewing the enemy a front, and for occupying a height. After much skirmishing, the Russians made an attack; but they opened their fire at too great a distance, while the French continued to advance without firing a shot, till they came within 100 paces of the enemy, when they commenced a dreadful fire. The conflict was long and sanguinary, and, after an ineffectual charge with the bayonet, the fourth column, abandoned by the left wing, lost the heights of Pratzen, beyond the possibility of recovery, together with the greatest part of their artillery, which was entangled in the deep clay of the country.

In the mean time the first, second, and third columns continued to march upon the points fixed in the original plan of attack, without adverting to the enemy's movements, and without discretion. The French being in possession of the heights of Pratzen beyond the left of the allies, the Russians at Locolnitz, amounting to 6000 men, were surrounded and taken prisoners. The relics of the second column retreated upon Aujut in disorder, whence, after many mistakes and misfortunes, they were driven by the division of Vandamme, from the heights of Pratzen, with considerable loss. The centre and rear of the first column fell back upon the plain between Tellnitz and the lake. The only retreat left them was over a narrow dyke between two lakes, and under the protection of the Austrian cavalry; the Russian infantry marched all night in a heavy fall of rain, and thus effected their escape, leaving behind them all their artillery. The loss sustained on both sides was immense. By killed, wounded, and prisoners, the allied army was diminished more than one-fourth part. Forty standards, and the greatest part of their artillery were taken; and such was the number of wounded left upon the field, that they could not all be dressed till two days after the battle.

It will not have escaped the observation of the reader, that it is principally to the following causes that the loss of this battle is to be attributed. To the want of correctness in the information possessed by the allies, as to the enemy's army; to the bad plan of attack, supposing the enemy to have been entrenched in a position which he did not occupy; to the movement executed the day before the attack, and in sight of the enemy, in order to gain the right flank of the French; to the great interval between the columns, when they quitted the heights of Pratzen; and to their want of communication with each other. To these causes may be attributed the first misfortunes of the Austro-Russian army. But, in spite of these capital errors, it would still have been possible to restore the fortune of the day, in favor of the allies, if the second and third columns had thought less of the primary disposition, and attended more to the enemy, who, by the boldness of his manœuvre, completely overthrew the basis on which the plan of attack was founded: or, if the first column, (which possessed the means of doing so,) instead of retiring by Aujest, as before mentioned, had marched to the assistance of the two former, and, together with them, had moved upon the heights, of which the French had as yet but a precarious possession. Their extreme right, which made only feeble demonstrations, continued at Posorsitz.

No computation has been made in this work as to the loss of the two armies at the battle of Austerlitz. It is impossible for any one, though actually bearing a part in the action, to calculate with any degree of accuracy, the number of killed and wounded on each side.

The carnage made on the 2nd of December was very great. The few Austrian troops there yet remained were not collected to one point; but, as we have seen, they conducted themselves every where with constancy and animation. The sixth battalions of the regiments of Wurtemburg, and Reuss-Graitz, were the only corps in confusion at the time when the fourth column was defeated. The Russians, at the commencement, fought with intrepidity; and the guards and hulans distinguished themselves for their courage. The French infantry manœuvred with coolness and precision, fought with valor, and executed its bold movements with admirable concert. After having made some efforts without effect, the Russian battalions began to waver; confusion, and finally complete defeat, were the consequences of the imprudent conduct of the second and third columns.

The fourth column of the allies abandoned a part of its artillery. The first, second, and third columns, lost the whole of theirs, with the exception of general Keinmaer's corps, which saved its cannon. The guns were entangled in the sloughs, as before mentioned, and the Russian horses, which are more calculated for speed than for draft, could not drag them out of the deep clay into which they had sunk. The number of the Russian prisoners may be computed to 15,000 men; while their killed and wounded, must have been very considerable: in addition to these misfortunes they had a great number of soldiers missing.

The loss of the French army must, also, necessarily have been very considerable. The fire at the commencement of the action was too warmly kept up not to have done great execution; still, however, the French force was by no means diminished in the same proportion as that of the allies. The generals who were killed, wounded, or taken prisoners, were of the highest rank and most splendid reputation.

The Austro-Russian army had experienced so many difficulties in regard to its subsistence, on the line of operations it had followed previous to these offensive movements, that it was abandoned during the retreat, in order to direct its march upon Hungary. The allies quitted the position of Hodiegitz at twelve o'clock at night, and marched upon Czeitch, where they arrived on the morning of the 3rd of December. On the same day the column under general Dochtoroff arrived at Niskowitz, on the road to Hungary, where it found general Keinmaer, then forming the rear-guard of the allies. This Russian column continued its march for the purpose of rejoining the army at Czeitsch, but lost a considerable number of men during the night, who had straggled and lost themselves in the woods and villages. The Austrian cavalry which had protected, the retreat of these wrecks of the left wing of the combined army, and which was a part of the corps under M. de Keinmaer, halted at Niskowitz. Lieutenant-general prince Bagration was a

league in rear of this Austrian corps, occupying the heights of Urschutz. Between
Niskowitz and Urschutz is a large wood,
under cover of which, the French had it
in their power to surround and cut off
the corps under M. de Keinmaer, which
was thus too much pushed forward. He
therefore remained in this position no
longer than was necessary to give time to
the stragglers of the army, and to some
baggage, to fall back upon Urschutz, and
to obtain some knowledge of the enemy's
movements. As soon as the French who
had entered Austerlitz, in the morning,
began to advance, general Keinmaer fell
back upon general Bagration, and in front
of Saruschitz formed the support of that
prince's corps. A detachment of O'Reilly's
light cavalry, and some Cossacks, were
sent to Stanitz, to watch that road. The
corps under M. de Merveldt had received
orders to retire from Lunenburg, in the
direction of Goeding, to observe the country on the left, and principally the two
roads of Auspitz and Nicolsbourg.

. On the 3rd of December, the French
army advanced in the following manner :

The cavalry, under prince Murat, which
had pushed forward detachments upon
Rausnitz and Wischau (on the evening of
the same day on which the battle was
fought) pursued that rout, and made immense booty : it advanced beyond Prosnitz, and then sent out strong detachments
upon Kremsir.

Marshal Lasnes at first took the same
road, and then moved by his right, to
gain the right of the allies by Butschowitz
and Stanitz. Marshal Soult and Bernadotte, the imperial guards, and the grenadiers of the reserve, were posted on
the rout towards Hungary, as soon as
the emperor Napoleon had received information of the direction taken by the
allied army ; they advanced, however, but
slowly ; probably with a view to give
time for the extreme right of their army
to gain ground on the left of the allies.

Marshal Davoust marched upon the
left flank of the Austro-Russian army,
by the rout of Nicolshourg, (in which
was the division of Gudin,) and by
that of Auspitz, in which was the re-

mainder of that corps ; these two roads
unite within half a league of Goeding.

Prince Bagration had placed some outposts in the wood. of Urschutz. The
French, about two o'clock in the afternoon,
began to reconnoitre it, obtained possession
of the wood, and established themselves on
the skirts of it. A trifling affair ensued,
which lasted about two hours, and which
terminated by general Bagration maintaining his post, which, however he evacuated
that evening, retiring towards Czeitsch;
general Keinmaer posted himself in his
front, upon the heights of Nasedlowitz,
pushing forward his outposts in the direction of Urschutz.

On the 4th of December the allied army
crossed the river March, and arrived at
Hollitsch, much diminished in numbers,
and with very few effective men, compared
with the army to which it was opposed.
The emperor Alexander took up his quarters
in the castle of Hollitsch, while the emperor
of Germany remained at Czeitsch, to be
ready for the interview which was about
to take place with the emperor Napoleon.

On the 3rd at day-break, prince John of
Lichtenstein, who commanded the Austrian
army, came to the French emperor's head-
quarters in a barn, and obtained a long audience of Buonaparte. Next day the
French chief left Austerlitz, and proceeded
to the advanced posts near Suruchetz,
where he had fixed his night guard. Here
the emperor of Germany arrived soon afterwards, and the sovereigns had an interview
which lasted two hours ; during which they
agreed on an armistice, for the purpose of
negotiating the conditions of a separate
peace between Austria and France.

Agreeably to the terms of this armistice,
granted by the victorious French chief to
the unfortune Francis ; the French was to
continue in the possession of its conquests
in the emperor of Germany's dominions,
viz. a part of Moravia and Hungary ; all
Upper and Lower Austria, the Tyrol,
the state of Venice, Carinthia, Stiria, Carniola, the country of Goritz and Istria ;
and lastly, in Bohemia, the circle of Mon-
tabar, and the whole space to the eastward,
from Fabor to Lintz. This immense tract
of possession the French troops were to

bold until the conclusion of a definitive peace, or the rupture of the negotiations; in the latter of which cases it was stipulated, that hostilities should not recommence within fourteen days, and that the cessation of the armistice should then be announced to the plenipotentaries of both powers, at the head-quarters of their respective armies. It was further agreed upon in the armistice, that the Russian army should evacuate the Austrian states, with Austrian Poland, viz. Moravia and Hungary, within the period of fifteen days, and Gallicia within a month; the routs to be prescribed to the Russian army; that there should be no levy en masse, or insurrection, in Hungary, nor any extraordinary recruiting for troops in Bohemia; that no foreign army should be permitted to enter the territory of the house of Austria; and that the negotiations for both powers should meet at Nicolsbourg for the immediate commencement of a treaty, in order to effect, without delay, the re-establishment of peace and good understanding between the two emperors.

Accordingly the Russian army, which suffered considerably for want of provisions, and from the loss of a principal part of its baggage and stores, immediately after the signing of the armistice (on the 6th) between the emperors of France and Austria, commenced its retreat from the Austrian states. The negotiators, prince John of Lichtenstein on the part of the emperor of Austria, and Talleyrand for the French emperor, repaired to Nicolsbourg, to conclude a definitive treaty. Buonaparte returned to the palace of Schoenbronn near Vienna, to take up his residence, and the French army prepared to enjoy that repose in cantonments (in the countries they possessed,) which their active services during the campaign rendered so necessary.

In this manner terminated the terrible battle of Austerlitz; a battle which for the importance of its consequences, has perhaps never been exceeded. By this second great blow Buonaparte in effect annihilated the confederacy which had been formed against him: the emperor of Russia, it is true, refused to be comprehended in the negotiations proposed, and his troops continued to make common cause with the British and Swedes assembled in the north of Germany, and with a division of British troops in the Mediterranean; but now that Alexander was forced with the shattered remains of his principal army, to trace his steps out of the Austrian states, and retire into his own, leaving the house of Austria to its fate; all the great objects for which the confederacy had armed were necessarily abandoned, and the conqueror was left at full liberty to secure his conquests, and make such changes in the territories of his fallen opponents as would secure him against any future attempts at hostility.

To the great superiority of talent on the part of the French, must chiefly be attributed the success of the campaign. Buonaparte, spurning the rules of ordinary warfare, advanced with the rapidity of lightning, to precipitate himself with his whole army in the rear of the enemy; to cut off his supplies, seize his resources, and occupy favorable positions between him and the heart of his states from which he could force him to a decisive battle; or by manœuvring, divide his force and conquer him in detail. With this view he marched forward with scarcely any stores; the velocity of his advance surprised the depots of his enemies, and the French army found in the countries of their opponents which they invaded abundance for their subsistence. The able and comprehensive manner in which the French chief laid his plans, and the vigor with which they were executed, each part always assisted and supporting some other, whilst the whole bore on the enemy with unexpected and irresistible force; greatly accelerated the fate of the campaign. Nor must it be concealed that the inability of the councils and generals of the confederates, and the indifference of the people of Germany, materially contributed in affording Buonaparte an opportunity for achieving one of the most splendid, astonishing, and important series of victories that had ever been obtained even by the heroes of antiquity or since the time of Marlborough

HISTORY OF THE WAR.

CHAP. XXXVIII.

The Campaign in Italy—Position and strength of the Armies—The French force the Passage of the Adige—Battle of Caldiero—Retreat of the Archduke Charles—Movements of Massena—Conquest of the Tyrol.

ALTHOUGH Buonaparte by his bold and unexpected irruption into Bavaria, and his consequent successes in that direction, made Germany the grand theatre of the war; Italy it would appear, had been expected by the Austrian cabinet to be the principal scene of its operations. It was led to this supposition, partly from believing that the French chief would make his greatest efforts in the favourite tract of his former triumphs; and in part from the hope and desire of the Austrian cabinet itself, to be enabled with the assistance of the allies, to expel the French from that important country, and to restore it to its former condition.

With these expectations the emperor of Germany had sent large reinforcements early in the dispute with France, to augment his Italian army, the command of which he gave to the archduke Charles: and with a view of totally preventing the French in case of their success from piercing through the Tyrol, as they had done in the late war, and effecting a junction between their German and Italian armies; the principal posts in that important and almost inaccessible country were speedily fortified. On the 20th of September the archduke arrived at Padua, the head-quarters of his Italian army, and next day announced his having taken the command, in a short address to the troops.

Marshal Massena, whom Buonaparte placed at the head of the French Italian army, assumed the command early in September; and on the tenth of that month communicated his arrival to the army, in a proclamation, from his head-quarters at Valegio; from this time to the actual commencement of the campaign, both these generals employed themselves in making preparations for that part of the plan of operations entrusted to them by their respective sovereigns.

It was the intention that an army consisting of Englishmen, Russians, and Swedes should assemble in the north of Germany to recover Hanover and attack Holland; while a joint English and Russian force threatened Italy from the Mediterranean; and assisted the grand united armies of Austria and Russia, in reconquering that country and menacing France. With this view the emperor of Germany had formed a large army in Italy, and marched another towards the Rhine; and both waited only the junction of the Russians, then on their march, to commence these vast and formidable movements.

The unexpected and rapid successes, however, of Buonaparte on the Danube, totally and suddenly changed the plan of operations concerted by the allies. He had taken advantage of the premature advance of general Mack's army towards the Rhine, to effect its immediate destruction; the Austrian army in Italy lost its point of support in Germany, and was forced to abandon all offensive intentions, and to look only to its own safety, now endangered by the victorious advance of the grand French army into the heart of Germany in its rear.

Massena being advised of the critical situation of general Mack's army on the Iller, and of its probable and speedy destruction, prepared to commence his operations against the archduke Charles, with the view of driving him out of the Venetian territory; whilst Buonaparte, in his advance to Vienna, detached troops from his right, to intercept the archduke's rear. Accordingly the period agreed on between the two generals for commencing hostilities, having expired on the 17th of October, Massena immediately prepared to force the passage of the Adige; on the opposite banks of which river the adverse armies were posted; the Austrians amounting to about 75,000 men, and the French to 90,000.

With this view, at four o'clock the next morning, (the 18th,) the French general ordered a false attack to be made on his right, and at the same time caused an appearance of hostile movement to be made on his left, for the purpose of distracting the enemy by these various manœuvres; while from his centre he attacked the bridge at the old castle of Verona, and effected the passage of the Adige. The first object to be accomplished was to throw down the walls which barricaded the middle of the bridge, and which the French accomplished in a very gallant manner. The Austrians had made two cuts in the bridge; these the French rendered passable by means of planks, and immediately 24 companies of light troops, selected from the divisions of Gardanne and Duhesme, precipitated themselves from the other side of the river, under cover of the guns of the old castle, and were soon followed by the whole of the division commanded by general Gardanne. In a short time the walls on the bridge were levelled; and, notwithstanding the Austrians made a brave and obstinate defence, the French succeeded in forcing the passage: the remainder of their army now crossed the bridge, and pursued the Austrians to the entrenched heights, to which they retired at some distance from the Adige. Here the action was renewed with great vigor; and, although the archduke sent frequent reinforcements, which arrived in various directions, and the Austrian army continued to resist in the most determined manner till six in the evening, the French at length succeeded in forcing them from some of their positions, and in destroying some entrenchments: the latter, however, retired after the engagement, across the river to their former positions. The Austrians lost in this action seven pieces of cannon and 18 waggons, together with about 1200 prisoners: the loss in killed and wounded also was great on both sides.

Next day the French prepared to make a second attack upon the Austrians, who occupied positions a short distance behind their former ones. At five on the morning of the 20th, Massena put his army into motion for the purpose. Whilst on the left wing, the division of general Sesia passed the Adige at Polo: that of general Verdier manœuvred from Ronco to Albaro. At the same time the divisions of generals Gardanne and Duhesme extending themselves before the bridge of the old castle of Verona, attacked the heights of Val Pantena, and drew round the castle of San Felici; when the general-in-chief, availing himself of his position, obliged the Austrians to evacuate Veronette. The pallisades of the new bridge were immediately cut down, and the division of horse chasseurs under general Espagne, a division of grenadiers, the cavalry of reserve, and the division of general Molitor, marched through Veronette, and proceeded to the great road of St. Michael: here the Austrians opposed with their infantry and cavalry, supported by some pieces of artillery, their further progress.

The French cavalry were now ordered to make repeated charges, which they effected with great vigor against the Austrians, and were well supported by the grenadiers of the division of Molitor: in one of these charges the squadron of guides forced 500 Austrian infantry to lay down their arms: After a most desperate conflict, which lasted several hours, the Austrians were forced to retire from the village of St. Michael, and the French occupied Vago : the latter took 1500 prisoners and two pieces of cannon. The loss in killed and wounded was considerable in both armies.

After the action of the 20th, the French army advanced, and took a position within two miles of Caldiero, near which the archduke was strongly posted. Massena was now advised of the destruction of Mack's army at Ulm, and the consequent advance of the French grand army under Buonaparte, towards the Austrian capital : he therefore prepared to act with increased vigor. Hitherto his operations were studiously confined, with the view of not exposing or disconcerting the grand results of the plan of the campaign, by a premature execution of any of its parts : compelling the archduke Charles to retreat before the proper moment arrived, might only force him to fall back on succour, and perhaps form a junction with an Austrian or Russian army in Germany, which was an event not then to be desired by Buonaparte. Now, on the contrary, that the French chief had destroyed the main Austrian army in Germany, and was rapidly advancing to attack the Russians on the Inn, and force his way to Vienna, Massena could not press the archduke Charles too closely in front, whilst the advance of Buonaparte into the hereditary states was calculated to threaten and intercept his rear.

Marshal Massena immediately began to avail himself of this favorable condition of French operations, and, on the morning of the 30th, made a vigorous attack against the Austrian army, along its whole line. The division of Molitor forming the left, began the action ; that of general Gardanne attacked the centre, while general Duhesme moved on from the right. The different attacks were well conducted ; and the Austrians, who fought with great courage, were forced, after an obstinate conflict, to abandon the village of Caldiero, and to retire to the heights. At half-past four, the archduke ordered his reserve, consisting of 24 battalions of grenadiers, and several regiments, to advance : the battle

then became more general. Both armies displayed uncommon determination, and fought with great fury : the French cavalry made some successful charges, and several battalions of their grenadiers coming up at the same time, attacked the Austrians with the bayonet ; and, notwithstanding the latter made a desperate resistance, and were supported by the fire of 30 pieces of cannon planted in their entrenchments, they were at length driven from the field, with the loss of more than 3000 prisoners. Both the French and Austrians had a great number of killed and wounded in this action ; on the termination of which, prince Charles requested a truce to bury the dead.

A disastrous consequence of this action to the Austrians was the separation of one of their columns, amounting to 5000 men, from the corps of Rosembourg, and its being completely cut off : the French commander sent one of his aid-de-camps to summon it to surrender ; but the general officer, Hillinger, who commanded the Austrian column, not seeing any French troops near him, declared his intention to defend himself. A regiment of French light infantry was then ordered to advance from Veronette, when the Austrian column made a movement to approach, and forced the regiment to take a position under the walls of San Felici. Massena immediately repaired to the spot, and ordered four battalions of grenadiers to surround the Austrians. A fresh summons was then sent to general Hillinger, who, seeing himself surrounded, and no chance left of his escape, entered into a capitulation for laying down his arms.

The archduke Charles on his part, finding that a column of his army had been cut off, and being apprehensive that his positions might be turned, proceeded to effect his retreat, and marched on the night of 1st, for that purpose. Next morning break of day, the French reconnoitring parties sent to the different parts Austrian line, found they had quit retreated in the night, a division seurs on horseback, and the line of general Gardanne, immedi

4 M 2

ward in the pursuit of the Austrians, whom these troops harassed during the day, taking about 500 prisoners.

The Austrian commander-in-chief was also hastened in his retreat by the junction of the army under general St. Cyr, with that under Massena, which took place on the 30th, during the late action of Caldiero: that army, 25,000 strong, marched from Naples, where it had been stationed, in consequence of a treaty of neutrality entered into between Buonaparte and the Neapolitan king, towards the latter end of September. In this treaty the French emperor bound his Sicilian majesty to adhere to a strict neutrality during the present war, to shut his kingdom and ports against the troops and fleets of the belligerent powers, and not to confide the command of his army or places to any Russian, Austrian, or French emigrant officer: for these obligations the French chief agreed to evacuate Naples, and St. Cyr's army accordingly marched to reinforce Massena.

On the 2nd of November, the French Italian army being thus considerably augmented, pushed on in pursuit of the archduke Charles, and advanced its head-quarters to Montebello. Its stay here was not long; for, after a few hours' rest, it again set out, and marched in the direction of Vicenza. The gates of this city had been secured. Massena summoned it to surrender, but received a refusal; next morning, however, being determined to force a passage, he ordered some pieces of cannon and howitzers to be directed against the gates and the city itself; when the gates were thrown open, and the French army allowed to enter. They found in Vicenza 1000 wounded; and the remains of some magazines, which the Austrians had not time to remove.

The archduke Charles, with his army, retreated by the road of Bassano, whither Massena continued the pursuit, constantly galling the Austrian rear: by taking this direction, it seemed as if the archduke wished to assist the Tyrol; but, being no doubt informed by this time, of the rapid advance of Buonaparte towards the here-

ditary states, and of the approach of Augereau and Ney to the Tyrol, for the purpose of attacking it; he immediately altered his determination, and where the road branches off to Bassano and Treviso, he directed his march to the right for the latter city, after burning behind him the bridge over the Terrent. When the French arrived at the village of St. Pierre in Ger, they found it occupied by a corps of Austrians; these were immediately charged, and a sharp action ensued, in which the French succeeded in making about 500 prisoners, and driving their opponents, after a brave resistance, from the village.

The French next marched for the Brenta, at which river their advanced-guard arrived at the moment when the Austrians had crossed, and were endeavoring to destroy the bridge: a brisk cannonade was immediately commenced from both banks of the river, which was continued till night. Next day, the 14th, at four in the morning, Massena ordered several regiments of cavalry, with the light troops mounted behind them, to ford the river, whilst the bridge was repairing. The French army soon after crossed it, and advanced for Cittadella, where it arrived in time to cut off the rear-posts of the enemy. At five in the evening, Massena entered Castel-Franco, and his chasseurs, by pushing forward, took possession of Salvatrunda and Albaredo: in these positions the French general found it necessary to allow his army to take a few hours' rest, after the late incessant exertions. In this advance from Montebello, the French made 1500 prisoners.

On the 5th, the division of the right, which had directed its march against **1805.** this place, occupied Padua; and, on the next day, the 6th, the division of the left, which marched against Bassano, by the Sette Communi, also possessed itself of that town. The French levied heavy contributions from these large towns, after which they resumed their pursuit of the retreating Austrians. Massena met with only a slight opposition in his march from Brenta to the Piave, and he effected the passage of the latter river without much obstruction, in his further march for the Piave to the Tagliamento, he could only perceive rapidly retreating before him some corps of Austrian cavalry, which appeared to observe the French army, but fell back in such a manner as to avoid any action. It was behind the Tagliamento that prince Charles waited to make a serious resistance to the enemy.

He had assembled on the left bank six regiments of cavalry, and four of infantry, whose firm front led the French to suppose that the Austrians were determined obstinately to dispute the passage of the river. Massena at first only intended to reconnoitre their position with the cavalry: the division of chasseurs, commanded by general d'Espagne, that of dragoons and cuirassiers, under the orders of generals Meimet and Pully, were posted on the river, while the divisions of Duhesme and Séras marched by St. Vito; and those of generals Molitor and Gardanne took the direction of Valvasonne. General d'Espagne had received orders to push forward his patroles. On the 12th of November, a squadron which he had ordered to pass the river, was charged by a regiment of Austrian cavalry, but general d'Espagne coming to its assistance, compelled the Austrians to retire. A heavy cannonade then commenced from the opposite banks of the river, and continued during the whole day. Massena did not think proper to attempt any thing further till the following morning. In the evening the divisions of French infantry arrived, and their commander-in-chief contented himself with making dispositions for forcing the passage of the river next day: with this view he posted his divisions as they arrived at St. Vito and Valvasonne, from which two points he intended they should pass the river, turn the Austrians and cut them off.

But prince Charles, who no doubt anticipated the intentions of the French general, apprehensive for the consequences, retreated from the Tagliamento in the night by the road of Palma Nuova: next day the French army crossed that river, and found the left bank covered with men and horses, which the fire from the artillery on the preceding day had destroyed. Massena now continued his march in pursuit of the archduke, who in consequence of the alarming approach of Buonaparte with the grand French army to Vienna, and his having detached two corps of that army, under Bernadotte and Marmont, to watch the archduke's rear, directed his retreat towards Laybach, in Carniola.

The Austrians did not attempt to defend Palma Nuova, though a strong fortified town, and the French advanced some miles beyond it before they were able to come up with the enemy's last posts, when some trifling skirmishes took place. On the 15th the French army was formed into two columns, and advanced towards the Isonza; the advanced-guard under general d'Espagne, entered Gradisca about two hours before night-fall, after a feeble resistance on the part of the Austrians. The horse chasseurs then ascended the right bank of the river to Gorizia, and Seras' division established itself at the same time on the left bank, at Sagrado. The next day the divisions of Molitor, Gardanne, and Partonneaux, marched by the right bank of the Isonza, with the intention of passing the river below Gorizia; but the bridge of boats not being arrived, they could not pass the river at that point. The divisions of Seras and Duhesme marched on their side towards Rubia and Savogna; their advanced posts followed close after the Austrians, which brought on a smart action, after which the latter retired under the walls of Gorizia.

Massena made his dispositions for a general attack the next morning (the 17th,) but the archduke Charles, whose object was to effect his retreat with what force he could, for the purpose of endeavoring to succor the hereditary states, availed himself of the night to quit his position near Gorizia, and hastened his march towards Laybach; whither general d'Espagne, with the French cavalry and light infantry, pursued him. The magazines established at Udina and Palma Nuova fell into the hands of the French army which now took a position beyond the Isonza, the head-quarters being advanced to Gorizia.

The French general having thus succeeded in forcing the archduke Charles to
evacuate the Venetian territory in Italy,
determined to wait with the principal body
of his army in its present position, until the
whole of the Tyrol which was in his rear,
was entirely cleared of the Austrians, and
some of their detached corps which had
defended that country, or had retired to it,
after the destruction of the army at Ulm,
were captured or expelled. Marshal Ney
I had said, with his corps of the grand army,
together with a body of Bavarians, had been
detached from the neighbourhood of Ulm
towards the end of October, to attack the
Tyrol on the side of Bavaria ; while marshal
Augereau, with the seventh corps of the grand
French army, hastened to attack it on the
side of Switzerland and Suabia. Early in
November the latter general commenced
his operations ; and shortly after made
himself master of Lindau, Bregentz, and
Feldkerch, forcing the corps of generals
Iellachich and Walskehl, amounting to
about 6000 men, to capitulate on the 14th
of November, and to engage not to serve
against France for a year. After this success marshal Augereau proceed for some
distance in pursuit of the corps of prince
Rohan, but immediately after changed his
course ; and, marching by Memmingen in
Suabia, on the 26th, directed his rout for
Ulm, there to wait such further orders as
circumstances might dictate.

Marshal Ney on his side, was equally
in his operations against the Tyrol, and
was well supported by the Bavarians under
his command. On the approach of these
troops towards the Tyrol in the beginning
of November, they fell in with a strong
detachment of the Austrians, who occupied
beyond Lovers, a difficult defile, flanked
on the right and left by peaked mountains.
This position was further strengthened by
Tyrolean chasseurs, who covered the summit, and three stone forts secured the
mountains and commanded the access to
them. The Bavarians led on by their general Deroi, marched boldly to the attack of
this formidable position : they lost several
brave officers and men, and general Deroi
himself was wounded by a pistol ball, in

attacking the last of the fort ; all which,
however, after an obstinate resistance, the
Bavarians carried, making about 500 prisoners.

Soon after this success Ney succeeded
in turning the fortresses of Sharnitz and
Neuslack ; both of which he carried by
force of arms, taking one standard, 16
field-pieces, and about 1700 prisoners.
On the 16th of November at five in the
afternoon, he entered Inspruck, where he
found an arsenal, with a respectable artillery, 15,000 muskets, and a great quantity
of powder ; and on the same day he entered Hall, where he found very considerable magazines. Marshal Ney now continued to penetrate still further into the Tyrol,
and on the 20th fixed his head-quarters
at Botzen, pushing his advanced-guard as
far as Treut. The archduke John, who
had the command of the Tyrol, finding himself unable any longer to retain its possession against such superior forces, and
being uncovered by the retreat of the archduke Charles from the Venetian territory ;
he had determined to evacuate the Tyrol,
and try to effect his retreat towards Carniola. This arduous undertaking he accomplished, and he succeeded in joining
the archduke Charles with a part of his
army, when both brothers continued to
retreat for Hungary.

The remaining division of the Austrian
army in the Tyrol, under the prince de
Rohan, finding itself cut off by the movements of the above corps of the grand
French army, endeavored to escape by
crossing the mountains between the Tyrol
and Italy, with a view of gaining Venice.
Accordingly, on the 24th of November, that
corps consisting of about 7000 infantry
and 1000 cavalry, and commanded by
prince Rohan, appeared in the neighbourhood of Bassano, in the Venetian territory,
and proceeded to Castel Franco. General
St. Cyr, who had been left with his corps
from Naples, by Massena, near Padua,
to watch Venice, and be ready to oppose
the threatened descent at that place, of the
English and Russians ; on receiving information of the enemy's arrival, immediately marched to reconnoitre and stop him.

At the same time Massena, who had been apprised of the movements of prince Rohan, left the main body of his army in its position beyond the Isonza, and marched back himself towards Bassano, with the reserve, consisting of a corps of Poles commanded by general Peyri, a French regiment of cavalry, a battalion of French infantry under general Reguier, and with four pieces of cannon, escorted by a regiment of Italian infantry, with the view of surrounding the corps of Rohan, and forcing it to capitulate.

General Reguier was detached to Piombino, to prevent the march of the Austrians, who were inclining towards Venice. Prince Rohan attacked the French general on the 25th, at day-break, with great fury, and forced him, after a brave resistance, to retire three times from the field ; but general St. Cyr, coming up and falling on the Austrian rear, prince Rohan was at length compelled to give way, when the French succeeded in making the greater part of the Austrian division prisoners, including the prince himself and several other officers of distinction.

Italy on the Tyrol being now cleared of the Austrian forces, Massena detached some troops from his right to take possession of Trieste ; he also sent a division from his left to Villach and Ponteba Venata, to open a communication with marshal Ney's division of the grand army, which, after having garrisoned the Tyrol, directed its march forward, extending itself between Saltzburg and Carinthia, whilst marshal Massena, with the main body of his army, advanced to Laybach, from whence the archduke Charles had retired .

CHAP. XXXIX.

Committal of the Sheriffs of London to the Tower—Proceedings on the Delinquency of Lord Melville—General Despondency of the English People—Indisposition of Mr. Pitt—Dismissal of Lord Melville—Escape of the Combined Fleets of France and Spain, and their Pursuit by Lord Nelson—Battle of Trafalgar—Death of Lord Nelson—Memoirs of Lord Collingwood—The remains of the Discomfited Fleet Captured by Sir Richard Strachan—Conduct of Prussia—Gallantry and Wisdom of the Emperor of Russia.

ON the 6th day of April, Mr. Whit-- bread, in pursuance of a former notice, brought under the consideration of the house the subject of the tenth report of the commissioners of naval enquiry. He began by describing the origin of the commission, praised the integrity and perseverance of the commissioners themselves, and complimented the late board of admiralty, by which they were appointed; after which he passed on to the nature of the charge he had to bring against lord viscount Melville, and in which were implicated the conduct of Mr. Trotter, Mr. Wilson, and Mr. Mark Sprot. He then referred to the act, of which lord Melville was the supporter, in 1785, for regulating the department of treasurer of the navy, and the order of council by which his salary was advanced from £2000 to £4000 a year, in lieu of all profits, fees, or emoluments he might before have derived from allowances of the public money in his hands. Lord Melville was himself at that time treasurer of the navy, and though the act was passed in July, it was not till the subsequent January that the balances were paid into the bank, pursuant to the terms of the act, and this delay in the transfer could only be accounted for on the score of private emolument. He then stated his three heads of charges against the noble lord,—first, his having applied the money of the public to other uses than those of the naval department, in express contempt of an act of parliament, and in gross violation of his duty.—Secondly, his conniving at a system of peculation in an individual, for whose conduct, in the use of the public money, he was deeply responsible, and for this connivance he denounced him as guilty of a high crime and misdemeanour.—Thirdly, his having himself been a participator in that system of peculation; but as this only rested on suspicion, at present, he should not now much insist upon it; but, if the enquiry should be instituted, he pledged himself to follow it up, with moderation on his own part, but with firmness and steadiness for the country. He knew that, even at the utmost height of party spirit, charges such as these had seldom been preferred, and it was singular that the only instance of a similar charge, for a great number of years, was brought by lord Melville himself against sir Thomas Rumbold, for malversations in India. He then went to observe, that the commissioners had discovered deficiencies, for a number of years, in the treasurer's department, of £674,000 a year. It then became necessary to call lord Melville and Mr. Trotter before them, and there they had an opportunity of exculpating themselves if they could, which was a sufficient refutation of the argument that this report of the commissioners was only an *ex parte* proceeding. But lord Melville could not answer, because he destroyed the documents, and Mr. Trotter could only answer that there were some advances made to other departments, the amount of which he could not tell. Mr. Trotter, it appeared, opened five different accounts—his own account—his' account as paymaster of the navy—his first separate account—his broker's account—and Jellico's account, and when asked for what they were intended, he had the assurance to tell the commissioners that they had no right to interfere in his private affairs. Mr. Trotter was also found busy in buying all sorts of stock, to sell again to advantage, and lord Melville, on whom the responsibility attached, was never known to interfere in it, though, if he happened to have been disappointed in his speculations, the public money was lost, and inevitable ruin must have been the consequence. The broker, Mark Sprott, who might have given a clue to these transactions, said that he was advised by his lawyer (Mr. Serjeant Shepherd) to keep a religious silence, Lord Melville, however, owned that he knew of the transactions, but not the details, and if he knew of either, he held him to be equally criminal. Mr. Trotter was in the habit of making lord Melville pecuniary advances, to a large amount, and as the former had no fortune when the latter took him under his patronage, he must have known that the advances were made out of the public money. He here commented on the evidence of lord Melville and Mr. Trotter, observing that the other paymasters of the navy, since the act of parliament, lord Bayning, lord Harrowby, Mr. Bragge, and Mr. Tierney, had no hesitation in declaring, upon oath, that they had received no emolument from the application of the public money, while lord Melville alone was driven to evasive answers, and Trotter screening himself under a clause in the act of parliament, allowing witnesses to decline questions which might

VOL. I.

criminate themselves, refused to give any answer. After having exhorted gentlemen of all descriptions in that house to join with him in bringing such enormous delinquency to punishment, he concluded with reading thirteen resolutions, founded on the subject matter of his speech, but added that, for the present, he should only press the first eleven of them.

The chancellor of the exchequer observed, that, whatever else the report of the commissioners might contain, there was not a single word in it which could imply that any mischief had arisen to the public, or that the delay of even a single day had occurred in the discharge of any of the demands of the seamen. It was not therefore very fair in the honorable gentleman to endeavor to excite the passions, in a cause which ought rather to be examined with great coolness and deliberation. He admitted that the contents of the report were of a grave and serious nature, and that it was important to have them fully investigated, and that, with reference to any instance of irregularity, it was the duty of the house to set their mark upon the transaction, after a full and fair consideration of the case ; but at present he saw nothing to justify his consent. He thought the best course to be pursued would be to refer the report to a select committee, in order to decide upon the whole of the case. In judging of this transaction, the house was to take into its consideration the motives, the circumstances, and the necessity which led to it, although it might have been a violation of the law. If they should decide upon its merits, upon a consideration of whether any loss had arisen, and that it was not justifiable in the noble lord to connive at the practises of his paymaster, still much of that would depend on the circumstance, the extent, and the danger that had been incurred. It did not appear that lord Melville had been aware of the private purposes of profit to which his treasurer had applied the money ; the sums vested in the house of Messrs. Coutts and co. did not appear to have been lodged there for the benefit of the noble lord, or his paymaster, but in the course of business; and the same practice prevailed, of drawing in gross for small payments instead of detail. The paymaster had to advance from day to day to the sub-accountants, in order to afford the means of satisfying assignments, for which the parties had a right to demand immediate payment. After a variety of other observations, he moved, as an amendment, " that the tenth report of the commissioners of naval enquiry be referred to a select committee of the house," but afterwards, on the suggestion of Mr. Fox, he consented to move the previous question.

Lord Henry Petty supported the motion, and rested much upon the ground that lord Melville had acted in violation of the law.

The attorney-general spoke in favor of the amendment, and Mr. Tierney against it. The latter said, that, during the time he held the office of treasurer of the navy, he felt no inconvenience result from a compliance with the act of parliament, and that the report, like that of the committee on the Middlesex election, should be taken as conclusive evidence against lord Melville. He had already as fair a trial as the nature of the case would admit of, and no committee of that house could throw any more light upon the subject.

Mr. Canning thought the justice of the house must require of it to give an opportunity of examining whether the whole of the charge against the noble lord might not be done away; for there was no analogy between this case and that referred to, of the Middlesex election, where the parties were fully heard by themselves and counsel, and allowed to cross examine witnesses: but here the parties, instead of being fully heard, were not heard at all. The breach of the law, in this instance, was by no means clear; for the law could scarcely have meant that which was physically impossible. In several cases, where large sums of money were to be paid to numerous claimants, in the course of a few days, and the majority of these claims under twenty pounds, and many

as low as a few shillings, it was not to be expected that each individual should be paid by a draft upon the bank of England. If the doctrine laid down, in the report of the committee of 1782, was correct, the whole of the money in the hands of the treasurer was not that for which he was responsible to the public, but to the individuals to whom these sums belonged. Upon the whole, he did not think that this amounted to any thing more than a case of suspicion, and concluded a long and able speech by an explanation of his own conduct at the time that he was before the commissioners.

Mr. George Ponsonby thought that the delay of even ten years of enquiry would not enable the house to say that lord Melville did not connive at his paymaster's taking the money out of the bank, and applying it to purposes of private emolument. If this charge was only supported by ex parte evidence, it must be remembered that it was the evidence of the party accused, stating every thing he thought proper in his own defence. Lord Melville distinctly admitted, that he knew of Mr. Trotter's taking money from the bank, and placing it at his private banker's. Mr. Trotter was his general agent. As he allowed him to continue in the practice, it must be supposed there was some fellow-feeling between them. It was monstrous language to say that lord Melville was excusable, because no loss had accrued to the public. To forge any of those bills was felony, and if an expert forger was detected in having counterfeited one of them, it would be no defence for him, in a court of justice, to say, or even to prove, that he had the money to replace it when it became due. Similar to that was the case of Mr. Trotter, who, as an expert calculator, must know to what extent he could use the public money, before the demands for it could come round upon him. This might be a proof of his skill, but not of his innocence. He trusted that the house would adopt the original proposition, as he was sure it must be their general sentiment that lord Melville could not be defended; and he observed, that no gentleman-spoke for him that day, who had not been his colleague in office.

The master of the rolls was for an enquiry upon the principles of jurisprudence, which required the whole of the case to be gone into before any man could be pronounced guilty. The object of the naval commissioners was not to try criminals, or to convict men upon their own confession, but to inquire into abuses, and the house could not therefore, upon their mere report, convict a man without hearing evidence at their bar. It did not appear to him that any thing like personal corruption was proved against the noble lord.

Mr. Fox- contended that nothing could be more corrupt than to permit a man's own agent to convert the money of others to his own private purposes. This appeared from the noble lord's own confession, and, though further examination might shew him to be more guilty, it could not shew him less so than he acknowledged himself to be. If it was true that no loss accrued to the public from this malversation, it did not follow that there was no risk incurred. Lord Melville indeed might secure Mr. Trotter from any loss, because he knew the navy bills were likely to be funded. Mr. Trotter might act upon his information, and, by this sort of speculation, the public actually did suffer a loss of one per cent. upon the discount of the bills. That house had not any power to inflict an adequate punishment on such delinquents as lord Melville and Mr. Trotter; but if it should determine on any prosecution, with a view to punishment, he maintained that the confession of the party accused would be evidence to proceed upon, and the house was called upon to act as a grand jury to pronounce upon the guilt of the party. The guilt consisted in the violation of the law, and it never could be pretended that such a foundation was innocent. In many cases the most severe punishments attached to offences to which the charge of moral turpitude did not apply; such as many of the offences against our revenue laws: therefore the breach of the law was proof against lord Melville, and on this proof, which

arose out of the nature of the law, he had no hesitation to pronounce him guilty. He could not say there was any direct evidence that lord Melville participated in the profits of Trotter, but there certainly was strong grounds of suspicion. When he held at the same time the office of treasurer of the navy and secretary of state, and it was stated, on the other side of the house, that he only received the salary of the latter office, and nothing for his treasurership. He did not then, it seems, accept any thing of the legal salary; but did it not justify something more than suspicion that he fondly clung to the office of his friend, Mr. Trotter, and when there were so many, even of his own relations too, who would have been glad to accept the office of treasurer? It had been said that the house should proceed with the utmost delicacy in deciding upon character, but the character of lord Melville was already so completely destroyed, in the public estimation for ever, that were the vote of this night unanimous in his favor, it would not have the slightest effect in wiping away the stigma universally affixed to his name. What was the world to think of retaining a man at the head of the naval department, who, when asked if he derived any advantage from the use of the public money, was obliged equivocally to answer, " to the best of my recollection I never did ?" If a man were asked if he was not, on a particular night, in a particular room, with John a Noaks, it might be very well to answer that, to the best of his recollection, he was not there; but if he were asked whether John a Noaks did not charge him with an attempt to pick his pockets, what would be the inference if he were to answer that John a Noaks did not, to the best of his recollection ?

Lord Castlereagh exhorted the house not to be led away, by vociferation, into a premature decision, on a subject of so much magnitude, but to defer it to a deliberate enquiry.

Mr. Wilberforce did not see that any of the friends of lord Melville at all affected to deny the bare broad fact of his having borrowed ten or twenty thousand pounds, at a time, from one of his clerks, and had afterwards admitted, that he had allowed the same man to remove large sums of public money to his private bankers. Such a circumstance, in itself, afforded a strong ground of suspicion, and the loss and mischief such a practice might have brought upon the naval department, would have been incalculable. The house was now appealed to, as the constitutional guardian of the rights of the people, and he should ill discharge his duty to the public, if he did not give his most cordial and sincere support to the present motion.

After a few observations from lord Andover, Mr. Wallace, sir Charles Price, and lord Archibald Hamilton, the house divided: for Mr. Whitbread's motion, 216, against it, 216,—and the numbers being thus equal, the speaker gave his casting vote in favor of Mr. Whitbread. Some conversation afterwards occurred, upon amendments proposed by Mr. Pitt, in the wording the resolutions, which, however, suffered no material alteration. Mr. Whitbread then moved an address to his majesty, to remove lord Melville from his councils and presence for ever; but, on the suggestion of Mr. Pitt, it was agreed to postpone the consideration of this motion till the Wednesday following, and, at five o'clock in the morning, the house adjourned.

On Wednesday the chancellor of the exchequer, as soon as he entered the house, informed it, that lord Melville had resigned the office of first lord of the admiralty. Mr. Whitbread then moved, that the eleventh resolution, charging lord Melville with being privy to, and conniving at, the withdrawing, for proposes of private interest or emolument, sums issued to him as treasurer of the navy, be read, which being done accordingly, he again rose, and stated, that though the notice now given could not have been unexpected to any one, yet it could not satisfy either him, that house, or the public. Lord Melville had not been dismissed; he gave in his resignation, which was no more than any honorable man might do, from feelings of his own. The result of the proceedings on the last night had dif-

fused such universal joy through the country, that the representatives of the people may

" Read their history in a nation's eyes,"

but lord Melville might be restored to-morrow, and they would have no such cause of exultation, if they did not render it impossible for his majesty ever to call him to his councils. He thought it right to tell his majesty, in the most solemn manner, that it was necessary to remove lord Melville from all the offices he holds under the crown. He would go further, and though he understood, from the right honorable gentleman (Mr. Canning,) that Mr. Trotter had been dismissed, it was his intention, immediately after the holidays, to move, that his majesty's attorney-general be directed to proceed against lord Melville and Mr. Trotter, for the recovery of the profits so unjustly taken from the public purse. And it was also his intention to move, after the holidays, for a select committee, to enquire into the transfers from one service to another, and all the other transactions referred to in the report. He further observed, that the right honorable gentleman opposite him (Mr. Pitt,) was himself implicated, and it was in vain for him to exculpate himself. What he alluded to was, the *quietus* of £24,000 to Mr. Jellico. No satisfaction, he said, would be afforded to public justice, that lord Melville should quietly retire with his riches and his honors. He then entered into a statement of the emoluments arising from the several offices of lord Melville, and particularly dwelt upon the grant of £1500 a year to lady Melville out of the public money, and for which no service had been performed, and observed, that if any of those grants were revocable, they ought to be revoked. He then concluded with moving, " an humble address to his majesty, praying that he would be graciously pleased to remove lord Melville from all offices under the crown during pleasure, and from his councils and presence for. ever."

Mr. Canning did not think that the

case which, at the most, amounted to no more than a bare suspicion, warranted the severity of the proceedings now proposed. When he looked back to the proceedings in that house, in 1795, upon the serious charges then brought forward against two most eminent commanders, and that their most active defender, and most indefatigable advocate, was that very noble lord, who has now been the theme of the honorable gentleman's violence and invective, he little expected that, in his present defenceless state, attempts to hunt him down would have been made by the kindred of sir Charles Grey, and the friends of sir John Jervis.

Mr. Grey knew of no similitude in the two cases. When the two commanders alluded to returned home, distinguished by military success; instead of concealing their conduct, by any dishonorable subterfuge, they courted an enquiry. In that situation, the support given them by lord Melville, instead of being a favor, was doing them no more than justice. After declaring the noble lord had been guilty of a high breach of duty, it was necessary to follow it up with some corresponding measures. The resignation of the noble lord was a matter of course, as he dare not remain in power after the opinion of that house had been so solemnly expressed; but he was still a privy counsellor, and held several lucrative offices during pleasure, his removal from which would not be at all carrying punishment very improperly. For these, and other reasons, he supported the motion.

Mr. George Ponsonby thought the present motion inseparably connected with the former resolutions, unless an assurance was given, that the political life of lord Melville was for ever closed.

Mr. Samuel Thornton defended the conduct of the bank, and maintained, that no blame could attach to it in any of these transactions.

Mr. Bankes did not think there was any necessity for the eagerness shewn to follow up the blow already struck; as he thought there was no probability that the noble lord would again be restored to his majesty's councils. He also thought it contrary to precedent, as he never understood it to be the usage of the house, to address his majesty against persons out of office; therefore, though he voted for the motion of the former night, he should resist the present.

Mr. Windham thought it necessary to require a promise, or declaration, which would render it impossible to restore lord Melville; otherwise he had such a hold of those in power, and they were so linked and connected together, that an attempt might be made to counteract what the house had done. It would be a lamentable instance of the mutability of opinion, if that house should forfeit, by indifference, or languor, the high honors which their conduct, on the preceding evening, had obtained them from all sorts of people, honors

"Which should be worn now in their newest gloss."

If the house then valued its own consistency and honor, it was bound to pass this motion, as a corrollary from the resolutions of Monday last. The noble lord, it was true, might still be *carus amicis*, but he was no longer *idoneus patriæ* : it was fit that it should be declared so.

The chancellor of the exchequer said, that as some gentlemen seemed to require a specific declaration respecting the restoration of lord Melville, he had no hesitation at all in saying, that all idea of the noble lord's return to power was completely annihilated, and that no danger whatever need be apprehended on that head. In making this frank declaration, he wished it to be understood, that it was not to continue in force, in case the resolutions of Monday should, on future enquiry, be found to have been premature, and consequently be erased from the journals of the house : in any other case, he should think it absolutely impossible, that any minister could ever think of re commending the noble lord to a share in his majesty's councils. After this explanation, he thought it but an act of common liberality to the noble lord, not to persist in the present motion.

Mr. Fox, after descanting on the impropriety of retaining Mr. Trotter in the important office of paymaster of the navy, so many months after the report of the commissioners, and his sudden dismissal now, when nothing more appeared against him than was known before, proceeded to observe, what little ground there was for bestowing such extravagant panygerics. He asked, was it to be found in the eagerness he had ever shewn to heap up emoluments, and systematise corruption, of which he reported all the instances that occurred to him ? Was it in his freedom from party spirit, in refusing to receive the voluntary services of a body of loyal men at Tavistock, because they were to have been commanded by the late duke of Bedford ? or in his having used the whole weight of government to deprive the honorable Henry Erskine of the office of dean of the faculty at Edinburgh ? After adverting to a variety of topics, he said, that not wishing the house of commons to monopolise the whole gratitude of the nation, on this proceeding, but desiring that his majesty, and the house of lords might have their share of the credit, so universally attached to it, he should have no objection to the motion being withdrawn.

Mr. Wilberforce felt himself undecided in what manner he should feel inclined to vote, and strongly recommended to the gentleman to withdraw his motion.

Mr. David Scott thought this a measure of great severity, after forty years of merritorious services, to a man who never valued money, and who, though he might have made millions, if he had availed himself of the advantages he possessed, yet always thought himself very happy, if, at the end of the year, he could make both ends meet.

Mr. Kinnaird insisted, that lord Melville was known to have been, in Scotland, a very bitter political enemy, as was exhibited in the case he alluded to, of the dean of faculty.

The secretary at war, (Mr. W. Dundas,) did not think the honorable member, who spoke last, could have discovered that character of bitterness in the noble lord, in the frequent opportunities he took of partaking the conviviality of his mansion, for weeks and months at a time.

Mr. Kinnaird replied, that it was a proof of very bad taste to suppose, that, because he lived in the same country with lord Melville, and mixed in society with him, he ought now to be precluded from the faithful discharge of his duty, as a member of parliament.

Mr. Whitbread, after a short reply, to some of the preceding speakers, withdrew his motion, in lieu of which, he moved, " the resolutions of the former night be laid before his majesty," which resolution was carried unanimously ; as was also another,—" that they be laid before his majesty by the whole house."

On the 6th of May Mr. Whitbread rose to move that his majesty's answer to the communication made to him of the resolutions of that house be taken into consideration, when he was interrupted by the chancellor of the exchequer, who stated that he had felt it his duty to advise the erasure of lord Melville's name from the list of the privy council, to which his majesty had acceded. He was not ashamed to confess that, however anxious he might be to accede to the wishes of the house of commons, he felt a deep and bitter pang in becoming the unwilling instrument of his lordship's dismissal.

The election for the county of Middlesex in the preceding year had been warmly and severely contested ; and every artifice was employed by the rival candidates to obtain a majority. In the prosecution of their respective views, neither bribery nor intimidation were neglected, and a committee being appointed to examine the merits of the case, they reported that, on the 13th, 14th, and 15th days of the poll, on the first of which there was a considerable majority of votes in favor of W. Mainwaring, Esquire, the sheriffs R. A. Cox Esquire, and sir William Rawlins, Knight, wilfully and knowingly did admit to poll, for sir Francis Burdett, bart. upwards of 300 persons, claiming to vote under a fatitious right, by which a color-able majority was obtained in favor of sir Francis: and that they afterwards rejected persons tendering their votes under the same circumstances. On the question being put, that the house should agree to the resolutions of the committee Mr. Rose represented the partiality of the sheriffs to sir Francis Burdett, as so very glaring, and the insults offered to Mr. Mainwaring so very gross, that when this resolution was agreed to, he should propose another, for the proper punishment of those returning officers. After some conversation the following resolution was voted, " that the said R. A. Cox, Esq. and sir William Rawlins, Knight, by their conduct and practices at the said election, as stated in the foregoing resolutions, as well as by refusing to refer to the assessments of the land-tax, have acted in violation of their duty, contrary to law, and in breach of the privileges of the house of commons." It was then ordered on the motion of Mr. Rose, " that the said R. A. Cox, Esq. and sir William Rawlins, Knight, for their said offence be committed to Newgate, and that the speaker do issue his warrant for that purpose." They were accordingly escorted to their place of confinement amidst the acclamations of the populace.

On the 12th of January, of the present year, Mr. Addington was raised to the peerage, by the style and title of viscount Sidmouth, and two days afterwards succeeded the duke of Portland, as lord president of the council. The latter nobleman had long been considered as a minister in name only, his great age and infirmities having rendered him totally incapable of its functions. It was stated, however, in the gazette, that his grace retired on account of ill health. To the earl of Buckinghamshire, one of lord Sidmouth's most assured friends, was given the seals of the duchy of Lancaster, and other near connexions of his were admitted to the privy council.

The return of the Addingtons to a share in administration, did not cause much surprise either to the friends or enemies of that party ;—but that the minister should again ally himself to the man, whose conduct in office he had arraigned, in terms of the bitterest sarcasm, and severest invective, with reference to his general conduct of the public interests both at home and abroad ; whom he had repeatedly held up to view as ignorant and inefficient, and whom he had so recently exposed, with all the bitterness of the most reproachful scorn, indeed excited universal astonishment.

That there existed a strong necessity for ministers to call in parliamentary and political aid at this period, cannot be doubted, but we must be allowed to question the efficacy of the means adopted. What the terms of the convention were, which united parties recently engaged in the deepest hostility towards each other, the author cannot presume to conjecture ; but, had they even been such as would have ensured a stable and permanent union between them (and a very short period proved the contrary) still it must be considered an unfortunate measure for the interest of the existing administration, as, what it gained in point of numbers, it lost in credit and reputation ; its manifest weakness became notorious, and while it united and invigorated an opposition already too formidable, it added nothing to itself in point of ability or character. The event, which I have just recorded, was approaching which threatened, and in fact actually produced, a dissolution of this strange and ill-assorted connexion.

When the utmost efforts of administration failed, in screening lord Melville from the effect of the parliamentary resolutions, moved against him, we have seen that the mode of procedure against his lordship, as a delinquent, was warmly contested within the walls of the house of commons. The friends of the accused, who were at first adverse to the measure of impeachment, and had pledged the house to a prosecution in the courts of law : for reasons which it would be indelicate and imprudent to discuss, saw grounds for believing it would be more to the advantage of lord Melville to be tried by his peers, now therefore suddenly veered round, and moved that he should be impeached ; which measure, although with great difficulty, they carried. During the whole of these proceedings the new president of the council and his adherents, separated from the minister, and took an eager, and an active part, in bringing lord Melville to the bar of public justice :— conduct which must have been considered as a defection from the government, of which they formed a part, and, as such, must have been deeply resented by the minister.

It was also rumoured that other causes of distaste and disagreement existed between Mr. Pitt and lord Sidmouth, at this period ; that the former was jealous of the influence which the latter maintained in a CERTAIN QUARTER; which had lately been manifested in the conferring of high ecclesiastical dignities : and, that instead of gaining an useful ally Mr. Pitt had only exposed himself to the machinations of a dangerous rival.

Whether these reports were founded in truth, it is not my province to decide, but certain it is, that, on the 10th day of July, the viscount Sidmouth and the earl of Buckinghamshire resigned their respective offices, and were succeeded in them by earl Camden and the lord Harrowby. Some other changes took place in administration, too insignificant to be here noticed, but none conducive to its strength, and thus did the minister find himself, at a most arduous moment, deprived, in the cabinet, of the assistance of lord Melville, and, in parliament, of the aid of the members attached to the interests of lord Sidmouth, on both of which he had so much necessity to depend.

Every successive hour now bore evidence to the truth of the sentiment of lord Grenville, that, in a crisis like the present, " as large a proportion as possible of the weight, talents, and character, to be found in public men, of all descriptions, and without any exception," should be included in government. Aided by the brilliant talents, profound experience, and parliamentary weight and eloquence of a Grenville, a Fox, a Spencer, and a Windham, with their respective connexions, too numerous to be detailed, who, collectively, were the talent and weight of the country ; energy and activity would have pervaded every depart-

ment of the state, the confidence of the nation would have been raised ; the measures of government unimpeded and unembarrassed—prompt and efficacious assistance have been afforded to our allies—and, more than probably, France have been checked in her career of victory, if not humbled to a sense of the necessity of restraining her lust of conquest, and forced, in her turn, to tremble for her own safety ! What a mortifying reverse to this flattering picture does the close of this year offer to our view ; a reverse entirely due to the miscalculation of Mr. Pitt, when, confiding in his own abilities, great and mighty as I allow them to have been, he undertook alone to move the vast machinery of the British empire : at once to provide her resources at home, protect her interests abroad, conduct a war the most dangerous in which Britain was ever engaged, and lastly, and not the least arduous part of his task in a government like ours, defend his measures in parliament against a formidable phalanx of patriotism and ability. One great source of his mortification was the disgrace and public trial of his colleague, lord Melville, a circumstance which united with the discharge of his vast and complicated duties bowed down his mighty mind, and preyed upon a frame already enfeebled with care and disease; but the severest blow which this great man and true patriot received was from the successes of the French upon the continent. Immediately after the tidings of the surrender of general Mack at Ulm had reached England, Mr. Pitt was observed to droop. His health already much impaired became daily worse, and he was compelled however reluctantly to quit all public business and repair to Bath, the use of the waters, it being hoped rather than expected, might give a favorable turn to his disorder.

It is scarcely possible to conceive the dismay and despair of all ranks of people, upon the arrival of intelligence respecting the issue of the battle of Austerlitz, and its fatal consequences to the common cause. In the capital there was at this moment scarcely the appearance of a government The minister was dying at Bath, few of his colleagues remained at their posts, and the country seemed abandoned to its fate. Nor was the aspect of affairs improved by the circulation of certain accounts of successes gained by the allies posterior to the " battle of the three emperor's," by some of the subordinate officers of state ; a weak and impolitic attempt, which covered the fabricators with shame and disgrace, as a few days produced their entire confutation, and a full confirmation of the calamitous intelligence.

From these unpleasant subjects, the reader will return with pleasure to a more animating and grateful theme ; the naval exploits of the year, which, happily for Great Britain and her existence, as a nation equalled if not exceeded those of any similar period in her annals.

I have already noticed the invention and trial of the stone or catamaran experiment ; and the last action of the preceding year, the attempt on Fort Rouge, near Calais, by a machine of the latter designation, though conducted under the orders of the veteran lord Keith and sir Home Popham, completely failed in the design of blowing up the enemy's works, and exposed the enterprise to the contempt and derision of the French. As a contrast to this abortive attempt of quackery and innovation, an action occurred in the course of this year well worthy of the historic page. The Arrow sloop, and Acheron bomb-vessel, having convoy, were attacked by two of the largest sized French frigates, to which the commanders were obliged to surrender, after a desperate action, but not until they had the satisfaction of seeing the merchantmen they were in charge of in safety, and their own vessels sunk.

A squadron of six sail of the line and two frigates, which had remained strictly blockaded in Rochfort for more than two years, found means to elude the British force, and put to sea. About the same time, the Toulon fleet, of 11 ships of the line and two frigates, which had been long in a state of complete equipment, also pushed out of the harbor without being perceived by the squadron under lord Nelson, then cruizing at some distance,

conformably with the system of that great man, who, more than a twelvemonth in those seas, never strictly blockaded the port, but gave the French fleet every fair opportunity of putting to sea. The destination of the combined squadron was for some time a question of anxious conjecture ; but intelligence was received on the 6th of May, from the British commander-in-chief of the forces in the Windward and Leeward islands, that Dominica had been attacked on the 22nd of February, by a French armament of one three-decker, and four other line of battle ships, three frigates, two brigs of war, and a schooner, with about 4000 land-men on board. Brigadier-general Prevost, the governor of the island, immediately made the best dispositions for its defence, and resolutely opposed, with the small force under his command, the landing of the French. At length the whole of the enemy's troops, consisting of 4000 men, under cover of the tremendous fire of the Majestrieux, of 120 guns, and four seventy-fours, having landed, and threatened by their dispositions to cut off the retreat of the governor from the town and fort of Prince Rupert. General Prevost, with the utmost promptitude and presence of mind, directed the regular force under captain O'Connel, to make a forced march across the island, and join him at Prince Rupert, to which place he himself, attended only by his staff, repaired, and arrived in twenty-four hours. The governor immediately took the necessary precautions to place the fort in the best state of defence ; and the French commander-in-chief, after having in vain summoned him to surrender, thought proper, after levying contributions on the inhabitants of Roseau, which town had been set on fire on the moment of attack, to re-embark his whole force, and sail to Guadaloupe. In pursuance of the predatory system adopted by the French, their squadron again appeared on the 15th of March, in Basseterre roads, in the island of St. Kitts, where they landed, levied a contribution of £18,000 sterling, and burnt some merchantmen richly laden. Lord Nelson in the mean time traversed the Mediterranean with the utmost celerity, in search of admiral Villeneuve, who, unknown to his lordship, had taken refuge in Toulon for the purpose of refitting, and did not leave that port till the 30th of March. The designs of France were materially promoted, and the inertness of all the British fleets, except the squadron under lord Nelson, rendered indispensible by the negligence and inactivity of lord Melville, and above all, by his sacrifice of the dearest interests of the public to the pretence of economy, at a moment when he was committing various acts of indiscreet, if not criminal, peculation. He was succeeded by sir Charles Middleton, created lord Barham, a nobleman remarkable for his zeal, activity, and judgment, but deplorably ignorant at his accession to office, of the plans, resources, and stations of the enemy.

It would be impossible to trace within the limits of a work purely historical, the various evolutions of lord Nelson's fleet during his long and anxious pursuit of admiral Villeneuve. With 10 sail of the line, foul, and after a cruize of more than two years, he undertook to pursue across the Atlantic, or to whatever part of the globe they might have shaped their course, the enemy's combined squadrons of 18 sail of the line, in a state of the most complete equipment, fresh from their ports, with their full complement of sailors, and carrying 10,000 land troops. On the 20th of May, he found himself towards the eastward of Madeira, where he was joined by admiral Cockrane and two ships of the line; but, unable to find or to overtake the object of his search, he returned to Portsmouth, and in the month of August was offered the command of an armament to be prepared immediately, of sufficient force to cope with that of France in any quarter of the world, in which it should be destined to act. His lordship, without a moment's hesitation, embraced the opportunity of again bearing his country's flag triumphant over all opposition. To this situation the public suffrage universally called him, and on him all eyes were turned, with hope, at a moment when every other circumstance around appeared gloomy and unpromising. The successes of the French upon the continent were no longer equivocal, and serious apprehensions were entertained of the fate of the allied powers. It was in this crisis that lord Nelson hoisted his flag on board the Victory, which had been completely refitted, on the 14th of September, at Portsmouth, and put to sea on the following day. There were then at port, five ships of the line and a frigate, which were under orders to sail with him; but, not finding them in sufficient readiness, so anxious was he to repair to the scene of his future glory, where his duty called him, that he sailed with the Euryalus frigate only, in company. Off Plymouth he was joined by two ships of the line, the Ajax and Thunderer, and thence proceeded directly for the coast of Spain.

On the arrival of lord Nelson off Cadiz, he received the command of the British fleet from admiral Collingwood, which, having had reinforcements poured into it from every quarter, had become equal to the task of coping with the enemy, and of punishing his temerity should he venture out of port. As far as it could be ascertained, the combined fleet was nearly ready for sea, and its probable destination was the Mediterranean, where, if it could collect to itself the ships of war yet remaining in the different French and Spanish ports in that sea, it would form together an accretion of force, which might eventually overpower all opposition, for a time at least, to the great detriment of the British interests. Ever averse, however, to the system of blockade, as leading ultimately to the ruin of the navy, lord Nelson determined to give the enemy an opportunity of putting to sea, and even had recourse to stratagem to induce him to adopt a measure which his confidence in his officers, his sailors, and himself, led him to hope would end in the total destruction of the adversary.

At length, about the middle of October, lord Nelson having received certain information that he would be joined in a day or two by a reinforcement of seven sail of the line, from England, hesitated not.

as a means to induce the combined fleet to put to sea, to detach admiral Louis and six ships of the line, being a fourth of his then force, upon a particular service, and that in so open a manner, and so undisguisedly, that it became immediately known to the enemy and decided his conduct.

Admiral Villeneuve, deceived by this bold manœuvre, and believing that the English fleet was now reduced to 21 sail of the line, whilst that of France and Spain, thoroughly equipped and refitted, consisted of 33, resolved to take advantage of this great superiority of strength, and make one vast effort to humble the naval force of Great Britain. There were also it is said personal motives, which led the French admiral to this resolution. Since his return from the West Indies the French official paper, the Moniteur, had severely glanced at his conduct in that transaction! Buonaparte had also spoken sarcastically of him : he was upbraided by the Spaniards for his not having supported them better in the action off cape Finisterre, where the brunt of the fight was borne by them ; and finally, it was generally understood that his command was about to be taken from him, and conferred on admiral Rosily, then actually on his road from Paris for that purpose. Stung and mortified by all these circumstances united, he determined, contrary, it is said, to the wish of the Spaniards to give battle to lord Nelson. A victory over the greatest naval character of the age would redeem his character, and cover him with glory, while a defeat could add but little additional disgrace to his present state of humiliation.

Accordingly on the 19th day of October, the French and Spanish combined fleet, to the number of 33 sail of the line, 18 of which were French and 15 Spanish, sailed from Cadiz with light westerly winds ; which being communicated to lord Nelson, his lordship with the British fleet, having received the expected reinforcement, and therefore consisted of 27 ships of the line, three of which were of 64 guns, conceiving the Mediterranean to be the course of the enemy, immediately made all sail for the Straits, where he was informed by the fri-

gate stationed there, that the enemy had not yet passed them.

On Monday, at day-break, the 21st of October, 1805, a day which will be for ever memorable in the British annals, the combined fleet was descried about six or seven miles to the eastward, cape Trafalgar bearing E. by S. about seven leagues, there being very little wind and that westerly. The commander-in-chief immediately made the signal for the fleet to bear up in two columns, as they formed in the order of sailing, to avoid the inconvenience and delay in forming a line of battle in the usual manner, a mode of attack his lordship previously communicated to his officers, as that alone calculated, "to make the business decisive," in the last order he ever gave. They were dated on the 10th of October, in contemplation of the event which I am about to detail, and which exhibit in the strongest manner, the comprehensive mind of this great man, and his profound knowledge of his profession. Lord Nelson, in the Victory, led the weather column, and the Royal Sovereign, admiral Collingwood the lee.

It had originally been the intention of admiral Villeneuve, in the belief that the English fleet consisted only of 21 sail of the line, to have attacked them in the usual line of battle, with an equal number of vessels, whilst twelve of his select ships, forming a body of reserve to windward, were to bear down and double on the British line after the action had commenced, and thus place a great portion of it between two fires ; every other precaution had been taken by him to ensure success : nearly 5000 land troops were distributed throughout his fleet, and his ships were furnished with every species of combustibles and fire balls, in order to set the adversary on fire, or facilitate their boarding when opportunity should offer. On perceiving however, the real strength of the English, the French admiral abandoned his first plan, and formed his ships into one line, with great closeness and correctness ; but as the mode of attack was unusual, so the structure of his line was new, forming a crescent convexing to leeward. Admiral Villeneuve was in the

4 o 2

Bucentaure, of 80 guns, in the centre, and the Prince of Asturias, of 112 guns, bore the flag of the Spanish admiral Gravina, in the rear ; but the French and Spanish ships ' were intermingled without any regard to order of national squadron. The combined fleet thus situated, waited the attack with equal firmness and intrepidity.

About noon, the dreadful contest began by the leading ships of the columns breaking through the enemy's line, which was first effected by admiral Collingwood, in the Royal Sovereign, in so gallant a manner, as to excite the admiration of both fleets. He broke through about the twelfth ship from the rear of the enemy, leaving his van unoccupied ; the succeeding ships breaking through in all parts astern of their leaders, and engaging the enemy at the muzzles of their guns. At twenty minutes past twelve, the action became general. It had been the intention of lord Nelson to have penetrated the enemy's line, between the tenth and eleventh of his ships in the van ; but, finding it so close that there was no room to pass, he ordered the Victory, which bore his flag, to be run on board the ship opposed to him, and the Temeraire, his second, also ran on board of the next ship in the enemy's line, so that these four ships formed one mass, and were so close, that every gun fired from the Victory set the Redoubtable, to which she was opposed, on fire ; whilst the British sailors were employed, at intervals, in the midst of the hottest action, in pouring buckets of water on the flames in the enemy's vessels, least their spreading should involve both ships in destruction : an instance of cool and deliberate bravery not to be paralleled in antient or modern history. The action was equally severe around the Royal Sovereign and in several other quarters. The enemy's ships were fought with the greatest gallantry ; but the attack upon them was irresistible. About three in the afternoon, admiral Gravina, with ten sail of the line, joining the admiral's frigates to leeward, bore away to Cadiz : five more of their headmost ships in the van, under admiral Dumanoir, about ten minutes after, tacked and stood to the southward and to windward of the British line. They were engaged, and the sternmost taken. The remaining four escaped, leaving a noble prey to the British fleet of *nineteen* ships of the line, with the three flag officers, Villeneuve, the commander-in-chief, and the Spanish admirals D'Aliva and Cisneros. At forty minutes after four, all firing ceased, and a complete victory was reported to lord Nelson, who, having been wounded early in the action, survived just long enough to hear the joyful tidings, and died as he had lived, with the most heroic resolution.

The heroic commander-in-chief had been engaged in the *Victory* with the Redoubtable of 74 guns, and subsequently with his old antagonist, the Santissima Trinidada, of 140, for more than an hour, having, at the same time, the Bucentaure of 80 guns, carrying the French admiral Villeneuve on his quarter. At about fifteen minutes after one, standing on the quarter-deck, moving, as was his custom when much pleased, the shoulder and sleeve of his amputated arm, up and down, with great rapidity, he received a wound from a musket-ball, discharged by a marksman, on the poop of the Bucentaure, which entered his left breast, and which he immediately declared to be mortal. To the last moment of his life, which now ebbed fast, his solicitude for the event of the action never ceased ; every consideration was dormant, save an anxious wish for the glory of his country. He repeatedly, while below, demanded the news of the battle, and expressed the most lively satisfaction on being assured of immediate victory. About four, his anxiety became extreme, and he repeatedly sent for captain Hardy, who fought his ship. That officer could not consistently with prudence quit the deck : at length, however, seeing the enemy striking the colours on every side, or flying the scene of action in confusion, captain Hardy carried the glad tidings to the dying hero, who, after thanking God most fervently for the event, that he had survived to have it made known to him, and that he had been enabled once more to do his duty to his country, expired without a groan.

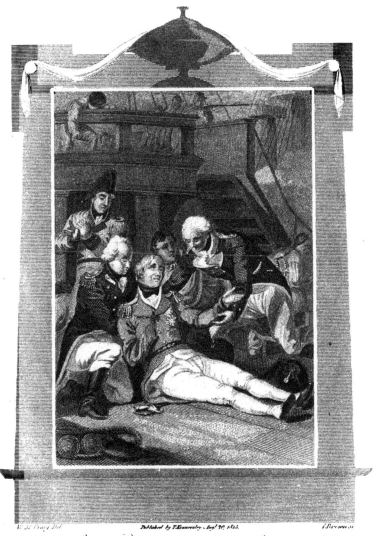

W. M. Craig Del.   Published by T. Kinnersley, Aug.t 20, 1813.   I. Brown sc.

*Admiral Lord Nelson mortally wounded on the quarter deck of
the Victory, in the Battle of Trafalgar.*

By a reference to the narrative of the French campaign on the continent, it will appear that the city of Ulm was entered in triumph on the 20th of October, the day preceding the battle of Trafalgar. In the dismay. and consternation produced by the misfortunes of Austria in the mind of the British public, intelligence of the battle of Trafalgar, opportunely arrived to cheer the spirits, and alleviate the despondency of the people. The misfortunes of our ally were forgotten in the enthusiasm of general exultation; and one consolation at least reanimated the hopes and the confidence of the nation, that England had secured the dominion of the seas, and that the example of lord Nelson would stimulate his successors to a glorious perseverance in the career of victory.

Where all were equally brave it would be difficult to point out individual merit in this well-fought day. Captain Harvey, who nobly seconded lord Nelson, having been boarded by a French line of battleship on one side, and a Spanish on the other, compelled both, after a vigorous contest, to strike their colours. A similar exploit was effected by captain Freemantle, of the Neptune. When five of the captured ships were engaged so closely that the muzzles of the lower deck guns of the antagonists touched each other, the French immediately lowered their ports, and deserted their guns upon the deck, while on the contrary, the English sailors were deliberately loading and firing their guns, with two, and often with three round shot, which soon reduced the enemy's ships to a perfect wreck.

Such a victory could not be gained without serious loss. Captains Cook, of the Bellerophon, and Duff, of the Mars, were deeply lamented. But every other feeling, even the unmingled joy which would have resulted from this glorious victory, were lost in the irreparable loss his country and the British navy sustained in the death of lord Nelson.

The total of killed and wounded was thus estimated in the official returns.

	killed.	wounded.
Royal Sovereign,	47	64
Dreadnought,	7	26
Mars,	29	69
Bellerophon,	27	123
Minotaur,	3	22
Revenge,	28	51
Leviathan,	4	22
Ajax,	2	9
Defence,	7	29
Defiance,	17	53
Total,	173	468

The action had scarcely terminated before a tremendous gale of wind arose, which not only placed the captured ships, but the captors, in a most dangerous situation. Both had suffered severely, and the wind increased to such a degree, that the whole fleet were most perilously circumstanced. Many were dismasted, all were shattered, and the whole fleet was in thirteen fathoms water, off the shoals of cape Trafalgar. In this dangerous state, the skill and experience of admiral Collingwood, the second-in-command, and whose conduct during the action was eminently conspicuous, were put to the utmost test, nor was he found unequal to the emergency. This brave warrior and amiable man, was born at Newcastle upon Tyne, of parents respectable, but not opulent. As his public despatches have been justly admired for the strength and beauty of their composition, it is but justice to the memory of a venerable man now no more, but who lived to witness the triumphs of his pupil to mention that he was educated under the tuition of the reverend Hugh Moises, of the grammar-school, Newcastle, who at the same time numbered among his pupils lord Elden, the present lord chancellor, and his brother sir W. Scott, the learned judge of the admiralty. The king, when lord Collingwood's account of the battle of Trafalgar reached England, observed, that his letter was an excellent one, and immediately added, "he was, however, bred at the same school as the chancellor." Lord Collingwood entered the service in the year 1761, under the protection of his maternal uncle, captain (afterwards admiral) Braithwaite. He spent *thirteen years* in the service without promotion, but in 1774 was raised to the rank of lieutenant, and served with a party of seamen in the memorable battle of Bunker's Hill. About this period his friendship with lord Nelson commenced, a friendship which only terminated with the death of that illustrious hero, and of which the survivor so feelingly expressed the value, when in his despatches to the admiralty he said " I have only to lament in common with the British navy and the British nation, in the fall of the commander-in-chief, the loss of a hero whose name will be immortal, and his memory ever dear to his country : but my heart is rent with the most poignant grief for the death of a friend to whom by many years intimacy, and a perfect knowledge of the virtues of his mind I was bound by the strongest ties of affection ; a grief to which even the glorious occasion on which he fell, does not bring that consolation which perhaps it ought."

It is a curious circumstance that from an early period Collingwood seemed destined to be the successor of Nelson. Whenever the one advanced a step in rank, the other succeeded to the station which his friend had left. In 1777, when Nelson, from master and commander of the Badger sloop was made post-captain in the Hinchinbrooke, Collingwood was promoted into the Badger; and again upon Nelson's promotion to a larger ship, Collingwood was made post-captain of the Hinchinbrooke. Towards the close of the year 1780, he was appointed to the command of the Pelican of 24 guns, and afterwards of the Sampson of 64, in which ship he served to the peace of 1783, and when he was paid off he was appointed to the Mediator, and sent to the West Indies, where he again met his friend Nelson, who at that time commanded the Boreas frigate. In the. letters of lord Nelson to captain Locker there are some passages which speak the closeness of the frinedship which subsisted between him and Collingwood. In one of them, dated on board the Boreas, he says " Collingwood is at Grenada which is a great loss to me, for there is nobody whom I can make a confidant of!" and, in another, " Collingwood desires me to say, he will soon write you such a letter, that you will think it a history of the West Indies. *What an amiable good man he is !*" Again he writes from St. Kitts, " What a charming good man ! He is a valuable member of society." From his station off Martinique in 1786, he observes, " This station has not been over pleasant ; had it not been for Collingwood, it would have been the most disagreeable I ever saw."

In this ship and on this station he remained until the latter end of April, 1786, when he returned to England, and his ship being paid off, he took the opportunity to visit his native country and renew his acquaintance with his family and friends. In 1790, when a war with Spain was threatened, he was drawn out of retirement and appointed to the Mermaid of 32 guns, in which he proceeded to the West Indies, but the dispute with Spain being adjusted without hostilities, he returned to Newcastle, and in this interval married Sarah, the eldest daughter of J. E. Blackett, Esq. one of the aldermen of that town. By this marriage he left two daughters, Sarah, and Mary Patience.

On the commencement of the revolutionary war, Collingwood was called to command the Barfleur, the flag-ship of rear-admiral Bowyer, with whom he served in the action of the 1st of June, 1794. The following year he was employed in the Hector, and afterwards in the Excellent, in which ship he had the honor to acquire fresh laurels in the brilliant victory off cape St. Vincent, on the 14th of February, 1797. Lord Nelson, who himself took a noble part on that memorable occasion, bore ample testimony to the conduct of his friend, and exclaimed to his officers as Collingwood was coming into action, " See here comes the Excellent, which is as good as two added to our number ;" and the support which he received from this ship in particular he gratefully acknowledged in the following laconic note of thanks. " Dear

ADMIRAL LORD COLLINGWOOD

Collingwood—A friend in need, is a friend indeed."

On the promotion of officers in 1799 captain Collingwood was raised to the rank of rear-admiral of the White, and was employed in the channel-fleet, but had no further opportunity of distinguishing himself during the remainder of the war. In the interval of the peace of Amiens, admiral Collingwood passed a year in the bosom of his family, on the recommencement of hostilities in 1803 resumed his station in the channel-fleet, and was for some time employed in the blockade of Brest. From this station he was called in May, 1805, to a more active service, having been detached with a reinforcement to the blockading fleet at Ferrol and Cadiz. In the immortal action of which I have just recorded the particulars, it fell to the lot of admiral Collingwood in the Royal Sovereign, to lead his own column into action, and first to break through the enemy's line; which he performed in a style commanding the admiration of both fleets, and drew from lord Nelson this warm and honorable testimony to the skill and bravery of the partner of his glory, " Look at that noble fellow! Observe the style in which he carries his ship into action." At this glorious moment admiral Collingwood with equal justice to the skill and valor of his friend, was enjoying the proud honor of his situation, and saying to those about him, " What would Nelson give to be in our situation?"

On the death of lord Nelson the command of his conquering fleet and the completion of the victory devolved on admiral Collingwood, who, as he had often done in the early part of his life, now succeeded to the rank and appointment of his friend.

His exertions immediately subsequent to the battle of Trafalgar, though little calculated to display the prowess and intrepidity of the accomplished seamen, were highly creditable to his talents, his prudence, and his tactical experience. On the 22nd the weather was still unfavorable, but on the following day the gale increased and the sea ran so high that many of the captured ships drifted on shore. Towards the afternoon, ten sail of the combined fleet, which

had not been much engaged, pushed out from Cadiz, in hopes of attacking with advantage, the damaged and scattered English ships. In this attempt however they were completely frustrated by the determined countenance of admiral Collingwood, who collecting the least injured of his fleet, not only protected his own disabled vessels but took possession of one (the El Rayo) belonging to the enemy. Admiral Gravina's own ship, the Prince of Asturias, being dismasted by the violence of the gale, he returned with his squadron to Cadiz. On the 24th and 25th the storm so much increased that orders were issued for the captured French and Spanish ships to be destroyed. Five of these vessels were sunk or burnt by the victors among which was the Santissima Trinidada of 140 guns, nine were entirely wrecked on different parts of the coast by the violence of the storm, many with their whole crews on board. L'Achille, a French 74, blew up during the action, and four by the almost incredible efforts of the British officers and seamen were carried into Gibraltar. The Santa Anne and nine more of the enemy's vessels escaped into Cadiz in a battered condition, and out of that number five had struck, but were abandoned by the English, in consequence of the violence of the gale.

In return for his important services, on the 9th of November, 1805, admiral Collingwood was created a peer of the realm, by the title of baron Collingwood of Caldburne and Hethpoole, in the county of Northumberland; and the two houses of parliament in addition to their vote of thanks, concurred in the grant of £2000 a year for his own life, £1000 of which descended to his lady, and £500 per annum to each of his two daughters. The corporation of London, the patriotic fund, and other public bodies voted him honorary rewards.

At the close of the battle of Trafalgar, the French admiral Dumanoir with four sail of the line escaped to the southward. Their respite however from sharing the fate of their companions was of short duration. On the night of the 2nd of November cruizing off Ferrol with four ships of the line and three frigates, rear admiral sir Richard Strachan fell in with the fugitives and pursued them all night, and during the whole of the next day. Early in the morning of the 4th, the Santa Margarita and Phoenix frigates, which had outsailed the ships of the line, gallantly commenced the action by firing upon the enemy's rear, and considerably retarded their flight. The action soon after became close and general, and continued nearly three hours and a half, the enemy fighting with the greatest resolution and obstinacy, when their four ships struck, after being rendered quite unmanageable. They proved to be the Formidable of 80 guns, captain Dumanoir, and the Duguai Truin, Mont Blanc, and Scipion, of 74 guns each. The loss of the French was severe : their admiral was wounded, and one of their captains killed : the loss on board the English ships was comparatively trifling. By this exploit of sir Richard Strachan, the last remnants of the French and Spanish combined fleets, amounting to 35 vessels of the line, were brought into an English port ; and of the whole of that formidable armament only three disabled ships remained to the enemy. A result so glorious to the skill, the courage, and the perseverance of our officers and seamen, contributed in a material degree to sooth the mortification and alleviate the depression excited by the contemplation of foreign affairs, and tended to counterbalance the effects of the mighty victories and splendid successes of the French on the continent of Europe. It was even hoped that the conduct of Prussia might cooperate with the glorious intelligence of the battle of Trafalgar, to reanimate the exertions of the minor powers, and give stability and effect to the measures adopted by the emperor of Russia.

1805.

The ministers of Austria, Russia, and England, at the court of Berlin, were not slow in representing the danger to what remained independent in Europe from the restless spirit of encroachment, by which the ruler of the French nation was constantly actuated, or to amplify the probabilities there existed of entire success,

should Prussia join her arms to those of the new confederacy. In vain, however was every art of persuasion to move the cold and selfish councils of the court of Berlin, to take any part but that of putting the troops upon a war establishment, filling the magazines, and providing the different corps with camp-equipage ; thus maintaining a neutrality indeed, but an armed and a suspicious one, ready to act on either side, as interest and opportunity should suggest. When hostilities were inevitable, and the Austrian and Russian forces had begun to move, the emperor Alexander made an effort, in person, to prevail upon the king to adopt a more generous and noble, and, perhaps, a wiser part : but, although the former was received at Berlin with every demonstration of personal respect and esteem, and with a splendor and consideration worthy of his exalted rank and character, the imperial guest was equally unsuccessful with the ministers of the allied powers, and he was obliged rapidly to return, baffled and disappointed, to place himself at the head of his armies, then advancing in aid of Austria.

But in the course of the campaign, an event occurred, which, had it produced those consequences which Europe had a right to expect, would have materially altered the face of affairs, and most probably have determined the war to a far different issue. I have already alluded to the direct violation of the Prussian neutrality, by a French corps, which marched through the Prussian territory of Anspach, from Wurtzburgh to the Danube. This step was totally unexpected by the Austrian commander-in-chief, who, conceiving that the force in question was destined for Bohemia, took his measures accordingly. Nor indeed was it to be supposed that at such a juncture, Buonaparte would run the risk of provoking the king of Prussia to hostilities, by an insult so pointed and glaring, as the infraction of one of the first laws of neutrality. This portion of country, however, which had devolved to the Prussian crown, by the act of the last margrave, was interposed between Wurtzburgh and the Dannbe, to which river it was of the utmost consequence to the success of his plans, that the corps assembled at the former place, should proceed the shortest way, and in the least possible time. Buonaparte, with that decision which marks his character, without the smallest hesitation, ordered the march of his army, which, after some slight show of opposition from the Prussian major Howen, at the head of 500 men, passed through the territory of Anspach without further molestation.

The surprise and indignation of all ranks of people throughout the Prussian dominions, at this bold and unprecedented step, was extreme, and vengeance for the insult was demanded from every quarter. The hopes of the allies were revived, and fresh solicitations were poured in upon the king, to declare himself a party in the war and thus avenge himself for so gross an injury. The British government lost no time in despatching lord Harrowby to the court of Berlin, on a special mission, to negotiate a treaty, and offer subsidies in case of co-operation. And even the government of Prussia itself seemed roused by this flagrant breach of public law, to some sense of its dignity and its wrongs. Immediate preparations were made for hostilities, the garrisons of Berlin and Potzdam were ordered to hold themselves in readiness to take the field, and the regular troops were ordered to the

frontiers. Scarcely however, had these demonstrations of energy been made, before the capture of Ulm, and the discomfiture of Mack, disposed the Prussian monarch to pass over the affront received; count Haugwitz, the strenuous advocate of France, was despatched to treat with Buonaparte at his head-quarters; and an accommodation was immediately effected.

The intervention of the Russian emperor in the cause of the degraded and insulted states of Europe originated in the purest and most disinterested motives, and his subsequent conduct was distinguished by every quality of the head and heart. Having superintended the arrangements and preparations necessary for sending three great armies into the field, he proceeded on the 26th of October to Berlin, where he gained all hearts by his affable and engaging manners. On the fatal day of the battle of the three emperors, on the plains of Moravia, he evinced the greatest personal courage and magnanimity. When the fortune of the day became decidedly adverse to the allies; he charged the enemy three times successively at the head of his guards, and by his gallantry not only secured the retreat of the remander of the army, which would otherwise have been cut to pieces, but rescued and carried off the whole of the Russian artillery, previously captured by the French.

CHAP. XL.

THE results of the last campaign in India were not more splendid than fallacious, and the treachery of the native powers, once more demanded the exercise of those extraordinary talents which equally characterised the viceroy of India and the generals to whom our armies were confided. It was well known to the British government, that previously to the late war between the company and the confederate Mahratta chiefs, Dowlut Rao Scindiah and the rajah of Berar, Scindiah had made important concessions to Jeswunt Rao Holkar, under an implied engagement to combine his troops with those of the confederate chieftains in hostility against the British government; while it was equally notorious that the exactions of Holkar from the city of Aurungabad (belonging to the old and faithful ally of the British power, the nizam) were of such a nature as would have completely justified the British government in demanding and enforcing a compensation in favor of his highness, whose territory the company was bound by treaty to defend against all enemies.

Subsequently to the conclusion of peace between the British power and the confederated Mahratta chieftains, Holkar despatched a vakeel or envoy to the court of Dowlut Rao Scindiah, the principal object of whose mission was to engage Scindiah to unite with Jeswunt Rao Holkar, in an attack upon the British possessions. This last proposal was communicated officially to the British resident at the court of Dowlut Rao, by the principal minister of that chieftain.

Notwithstanding these friendly overtures on the part of Holkar towards Scindiah, the former in the true spirit of his treacherous and predatory habits, about the same time, made a hostile attack upon Scindiah's fort and territory of Ajmere; in consequence of this aggression, a vakeel was despatched by Dowlut Rao for the purpose of expostulating with Holkar, and of obtaining the most accurate information as to the real designs of that chieftain.

Scindiah's vakeel was received by Holkar with marks of peculiar distinction, and the latter explicitly declared to him his intention to direct his predatory forces against the British possessions. With respect to the fort and territory of Ajmere, he stated, that he was compelled against his will, to that act by the peremptory requisitions of the rajah of Jodepoor, with whom he intended to leave his family, when he commenced his operations against the English; and he therefore hoped that Scindiah would excuse his conduct, in that instance, as it was a matter of necessity and not of choice, to which he had submitted, solely with a view to enable him to prosecute a war against the company, which involved the independence of the Mahratta empire.

The concurrent report of messengers who had been dispatched for intelligence from Nagpoor to the camp of Jeswunt Rao Holkar, corroborated this statement with respect to the declared intention of that chieftain to "carry on a predatory war against the British possessions."

In addition to these avowed intentions of hostility, Holkar had advanced, towards the frontiers of the ally of the company, the rajah of Jeynaghur, and occupied a position with the main body of his forces, which indicated a design of violating the territories of the rajah ; and which, from its menacing aspect, rendered it necessary to retain the British army in the field, under the personal direction of the commander-in-chief, although the most' important consideration of policy, and especially of economy, required at the same time, that the British army should, as early as possible, be established at the respective stations fixed for its permanent position.

The proofs, however, of Holkar's hostile designs, are not confined to the instances which have been already stated :—a letter was delivered to the British commander-in-chief by the rajah of Macherry, one of the company's allies, addressed to the rajah, by Jeswunt Rao Holkar, the object of which was to detach that chieftain from his alliance with the British government ; and a further correspondence of a nature hostile to the British interests, was discovered between Holkar and several persons owing allegiance to the British government ; while every previous instance of a hostile disposition on the part of Jeswunt Rao was aggravated by the deliberate and barbarous murder of three British subjects in his service, on a false charge of a correspondence between one of these officers and the commander-in-chief of the British forces.

Notwithstanding the equivocal conduct of Jeswunt Rao, towards the British government, and the depradations committed by him on the territories of the nizam, (the intimate ally of the company,) during the course of the war between the British power and the confederated Mahratta chieftains, Dowlut Rao Scindiah, and the rajah of Berar, no attempt was made, during that period, to molest Jeswunt Rao Holkar ; and the governor-general, the marquis Wellesley, in his instructions to the honorable major-general Wellesley, under date of the 12th of June, 1803, " positively prohibited" that officer from prosecuting hostilities against Holkar, merely for the purpose of obtaining indemnity for the depradations committed by that chieftain on the territory of the nizam, and for any other predatory incursion.

Subsequently, however, to the conclusion of peace between the British government in India and the confederated Mahratta chieftains, the menacing position which Holkar had assumed towards the British government and some of its allies, together with the numerous other indications of hostile designs, which have already been noticed in the foregoing pages, appeared to the governor-general to render it indispensibly necessary, either to adopt measures for the reduction of Holkar's force, or to frame some arrangement with him, which, without compromising the dignity of the British government, and without violating the general principles of justice, or the acknowledged rights of other states and chieftains, might render it the interest of Jeswunt Rao Holkar to abandon his predatory habits, and might preclude the necessity of an extensive military establishment for the defence of the British territories and those of our allies, against the incursions of that active and unprincipled freebooter.

The commander-in-chief, (on the 27th of February, 1804,) addressed a letter to Jeswunt Rao Holkar, stating generally the terms on which the British government was disposed to leave him in the unmolested exercise of his authority, and inviting him to despatch vakeels or envoys to the British camp, for the purpose of making known his wishes, and of effecting an amicable arrangement on the basis of the governor-general's propositions.

The vakeels of Holkar having at length, on the 16th of March, 1804, arrived in the

British camp, a conference was held between them and the commander-in-chief, at which it appeared that the vakeels possessed no powers to conclude any arrangement, but were simply instructed to state the propositions of Holkar, and to acquaint them with the terms that might in consequence be offered to the company. The demands brought forward by the vakeels in the name of their master, stipulated among a number of other extravagant requisitions, for a considerable portion of territory belonging to the company, to be ceded to Holkar, and that the country already usurped by him, should be held under the solemn guarantee of the company.

That the reader may judge of the propriety of the rejection of Holkar's propositions, I shall here insert them in substance.

Firstly, that he (Jeswunt Rao,) should be permitted to collect the choute, (or tribute,) agreeably to the custom of his ancestors.

Secondly, that the possessions formerly held by the family, such as Etawah, (which formed part of the possessions of the company previously to the Mahratta war,) twelve districts in the doab of the rivers Jumna and Ganges, (also a part of the British possessions,) and a district in Bundlecund should be ceded to him.

Thirdly, that the country of Hurriana, which was formerly in the possession of the family, should be given to him; and lastly, that the country then actually in his possession should be guaranteed by the company, and that a treaty should be concluded with him on the same terms as that lately concluded with Scindiah.

It will readily be granted, that these demands were of a nature so extravagant, and in every point of view, so entirely inadmissible, that they must have been, (as in fact they were,) positively rejected. The commander-in-chief referred the vakeels to the terms already offered by the British government, and insisted upon Holkar's immediate return within his own territories, as a preliminary to any negotiation.

Notwithstanding the positive promise of Holkar, contained in his letter to the commander-in-chief, that "he would immediately withdraw his troops from their actual position," the vakeels explicitly declared that their master "would not retire" with his troops unless the demands now brought forward were complied with. The whole language and deportment of the vakeels was indeed distinguished by an offensive spirit of arrogance and haughtiness, which seemed to betray an expectation on their part, that the British government might be intimidated by an exaggerated description of Holkar's power and resources.

Subsequently to the formal communication of these demands, the vakeels intimated to the commander-in-chief, that, although the propositions already stated were in conformity to their instructions, they were authorised to recede from them, and to accept any provision in lands or money, which the British government should think proper to assign to Holkar: the commander-in-chief replied to this proposal in the same terms as to the preceding requisitions. Shortly after this conference, the vakeels quitted the British camp, on their return to that of their master.

Notwithstanding the unfavorable result of the conference with Holkar's envoys, the commander-in-chief addressed a second letter to him, repeating the just and moderate terms on which that chieftain might remain at peace, and again desiring him to send to the British camp a confidential person, vested with sufficient powers to conclude a final arrangement.

About the time of these proceedings, a letter was addressed by Holkar to the honorable major-general Wellesley, commanding the British army in the Deccan, apparently written early in the month of February, 1804, demanding the cession of certain districts in that country, as the condition of peace, and adding that, in the event of war, although unable to oppose the British artillery in the field, "countries of many hundred coss should be overrun and burnt, that the British commander-in-chief should not have leisure to breathe for a moment, and that calamities should fall on laes, (hundreds of thousands,) of human beings in continued war by the attacks of his (Holkar's army,) which OVERWHELMS LIKE THE WAVES OF THE SEA."

Although this insolent and hostile declaration, combined with the other facts which have been stated relative to Holkar's conduct, would have abundantly justified immediate hostilities, the governor-general determined to await the result of the negotiation, which was still depending under his orders.

Jeswunt Rao Holkar, in his reply to the second letter of the commander-in-chief, evaded an answer to the proposition contained in it, and required a communication of the leading articles of the arrangement proposed by the British government, previously to his despatching a confidential agent to the British camp; a letter was at the same time received from the principal minister of Holkar by a British officer, who had been employed by the commander-in-chief in the negotiation, renewing the demands which had been formerly brought forward by the vakeels, and decidedly rejected.

The commander-in-chief, in reply to Holkar's second letter, received on the 4th of April, 1804, recalled the attention of the chief to the indulgence and forbearance already manifested towards him by the British government, and exhorted him to adopt the only line of conduct consistent with his true interests and with the preservation of peace.

The necessity of a new arrangement with Holkar was no sooner manifest to the British government, than it immediately adopted such measures as were best calculated to give weight to its just demands, in any negotiation with that chieftain, or in the event of unavoidable hostilities, to afford means of bringing the contest to an early and successful termination.

With a view to these combined objects, the British army, which had recently been employed against that of Scindiah and M. Perron, in Hindostan, was retained in the field, (under the personal command of the commander-in-chief, lord Lake,) in the

vicinity of the position assumed by Holkar and his forces; and instructions were issued to major-general Wellesley, commanding the British troops in the Deccan, for the purpose of securing, in the event of hostilities with Holkar, the most prompt and effectual co-operation between that officer and the commander-in-chief, against the forces of the enemy.

The merits of the military operations against this predatory chieftain, cannot be estimated by any reference to the extent of the period during which they continued; their protracted issue was in no degree owing to a want of zeal or energy, on the part of either the government or the army; every practicable effort was made by the former to facilitate the movements, and to promote the efficiency of the latter in the field; and the most distinguished zeal, courage, and ability, were manifested throughout the army, in every part of its operations, on the same occasion.

The obstacles opposed to military movements by the periodical rains in that part of India, the desultory operations of the enemy, the difficulty of compelling him to risk a general action in the field, and the unaccountable defection of the rajah of Burtpore, who, without any provocation on the part of the company, or any alleged cause of complaint, joined the enemy under circumstances of unexampled treachery, were the sole means by which Holkar was enabled to procrastinate his submission to the decided superiority of the British power.

Had not the most consummate judgment and energy been opposed to the difficulties which have been described, the contest might have continued even until this moment. The British government, as well as its chief officers in the field, fully aware of this truth, wisely resolved to sacrifice many temporary considerations of convenience, to the benefits which could only be expected to arise from an uncommon degree of exertion, in the contest in which they were engaged; and accordingly the energy, decision, and wisdom manifested by the government in its prompt and abundant supply of the army employed against Holkar, was in exact conformity to those memorable efforts, which so eminently distinguished the brilliant administration of lord Wellesley, in every crisis of difficulty and danger ; while at the same time the ardor, intrepidity, and perseverence, displayed by lord Lake, major-general. Wellesley, and the army in the prosecution of each successive advantage added increased lustre to their recent achievements, and became the ultimate means of securing to the British arms and power a brilliant and decided triumph.

It will be sufficient to observe that while the troops in the Deccan, under the able direction of major-general Wellesley, whose brilliant career in India was not yet terminated, were successfully employed in the reduction of the strong fortress of Chaudore, and of the other possessions of Holkar in that quarter, the indefatigable and heroic commander-in-chief of the British forces in India, lord Lake, had by the most rapid and able movements compelled the cavalry and infantry of the Mahratta chieftain to risk actions with the British troops, productive of the most disastrous consequences to their sovereign, and finally leading to his entire subjugation.

On the 13th day of November, 1804, general Fraser attacked the artillery and infantry of Holkar, near the fortress of Deeg, and obtained a signal victory. The force of the enemy amounted to 24 battalions of infantry, a body of irregular horse, and 160 pieces of ordnance. He was driven from a position of the greatest strength, and 87 pieces of artillery, won at the point of the bayonet, were left a prey to the conquerors.

This victory was however dearly purchased by the death of the brave and gallant general Fraser, who received a mortal wound in this memorable action, the result of almost unexampled skill, courage, and activity. General Fraser was interred at Muttra, on the 25th of November, 1804, the last sad honors due to his rank having been paid by that part of the army, which he had so lately led to victory and to glory.

During these operations, lord Lake, the commander-in-chief, with six regiments of cavalry, and the reserve of the army in the field after marching a distance of 400 miles in 18 days, succeeded on the 17th of November, 1804, in surprising the whole force of the cavalry of the enemy, under the personal command of Holkar, near the city of Ferruckabad and after a most rapid and extraordinary march of 70 miles without rest, obtained a glorious and complete victory. Vast numbers of the enemy's troops and horses were destroyed ; the whole of his draught bullocks and baggage captured ; and Holkar himself escaped from the disastrous field with the utmost difficulty.

Notwithstanding these successes, splendid in themselves and productive in their consequences of the greatest advantage to the British power and national character, the war in India was unexpectedly protracted, by the unaccountable, unwarrantable, and treacherous defection from the company of the rajah of Burtpore, who at this critical conjuncture, violated his alliance with the British power, and joined its enemy in the field. This conduct extraordinary as it was, was the less to be apprehended, as it was well known throughout India, that in addition to the many benefits that personage had received in consequence of his alliance with the company, the British government, as a mark of unconditional favor, had actually transferred to him a portion of the territories to the westward of the river Jumna, which had been conquered from the confederated Mahratta chieftains in the late war. Those cessions were equal in value to one third of the ancient possessions of the Burtpore rajah.

From the period of the month of November, 1804, Holkar and the rajah were in open and avowed confederacy, their interests were completely identified, and they carried on the war in conjunction. Indeed for the remainder of the campaign Holkar depended exclusive on the Burtpore chieftain for supplies of money, and every other branch of military resource. Lord Lake therefore allowed of no relaxation in his efforts, but continued his operations with undiminished activity and after a variety of the most brilliant achievements, the minute details of which are too voluminous for a work like this, he succeeded in compelling Holkar to yield to the decided superiority of the British arms, after having experienced all the perils and distress, which were the natural consequences of his temerity, in hazarding an unprovoked aggression against the company's government.

The defeat of Holkar's armies, the capture of his guns, forts, territories, and the reduction of his power and resources were effected, under circumstances equally calculated to augment the glory of the British name, and to perpetuate the important benefits which have resulted in every quarter of India, from the successful efforts of our counsels and arms.

For a considerable period of time, previously to the appointment of lord Cornwallis to the government of India, in the month of December, 1804, it was well known to his majesty's ministers and to the court of directors, that lord Wellesley was desirous of returning to England, his lordship having applied to the government for that purpose. In the year, 1802, lord Wellesley actually resigned the government of India and signified his intention of embarking for Europe, at the close of the year 1803, but at the special request of his majesty's ministers and of the court of directors, his lordship consented to postpone his departure, until the month of January, 1804. At that period of time however, the treaties of peace which had been recently concluded with the Mahrattas, by sir Arthur Wellesley, had not reached Calcutta and the settlement of the conquered territories, together with the consolidation of our new alliances in various quarters of India, required the superintendance of a vigorous and established authority, combining all the advantages of practical experience, with the confidence arising from the long and brilliant success of the tried administration. At the same time the principles of public duty, which in compliance with the request of the government and the court of directors, (conveyed to lord Wellesley, under date the 29th of September, 1802,) had induced his lordship to prolong his continuance in India after his resignation in 1802, appeared to lord Wellesley to demand his further residence in that quarter, while the state of public affairs was so unsettled as at the commencement of the year 1804.

Lord Wellesley therefore determined to remain in India until the year 1805; but the necessary preparations were made for his departure, at an early period of that year, and accordingly in the month of March, (which is a favorable season for leaving Bengal,) the St Fiorenzo frigate was actually detained in the river Hoogley, for the purpose of conveying lord Wellesley to England. The events however of the war in Hindostan, combined with the despatches, which, it is stated, and confidently believed in England, his lordship received at that time from his majesty's ministers, rendered it necessary for the marquis Wellesley again to postpone his departure, and the St. Fiorenzo frigate was accordingly ordered upon a cruise.

Lord Wellesley remained at Calcutta till the 22nd of August, when he embarked on board the frigate, 1805. which (under the orders of the admiralty, in consequence of the marquis Wellesley having particularly requested, as early as 1802, for one of his majesty's ships,) had been prepared for his accommodation. On the 29th of July, ten days after lord Cornwallis's arrival in India was publicly known, an address was voted to lord Wellesley by the inhabitants of Calcutta.

Peace with the rajah of Burtpore having been concluded, on the submission of that chieftain to the British power, on the 17th of April, lord Lake immediately pursued Holkar, who had fled from Burtpore, and who never, from the month of May 1805, ventured to approach within 100 miles of any of the British detachments. Holkar was left without territory or resources of any description, Scindiah's power was reduced to the lowest state, and Aumeer Khan, who was a common robber, never made any attempt against the company's possessions, after his expulsion from the doab, by general Smith, and his ignominious flight, followed for 40 days by the British cavalry

Previously to lord Wellesley's departure, orders were also issued by his lordship for the distribution of the army at its permanent stations, in different parts of the country, for the reduction of all extra expenses, and for every arrangement necessary to the final and entire consolidation of our alliances in every quarter of India ; not an enemy had appeared in the Deccan for many months, and the company's paper, which, on lord Wellesley's arrival, bore a discount of fifteen per cent. was nearly at par.

During the course of the administration of the marquis Wellesley, the general state of public credit in India was improved in a proportion of more than twelve per cent. at each of the three presidencies ; while the resources of India not only kept pace with the growing demands upon them, and she not only paid her own expenses, but actually contributed, (exclusive of the increase of commerce and duties,) upwards of 10,000,000 sterling, in aid of the mother country : the various sources of commerce also were materially extended and improved, the defective part of our frontier considerably strengthened, our political relations so defined and consolidated, as to preclude all probability of future war with any of the native states, and the permanent revenues of India raised from 7,000,000 to upwards of 15,000,000 sterling. The general condition of our power and resources was established on a firm basis, which bade defiance to the hostile projects of all our enemies, and which, under a firm system of government, equally conduced to the affluence of the parent country, and to the uninterrupted and progressive prosperity of our Indian empire

RIGHT HONORABLE WILLIAM PITT.

Published by I.Kennerley Jan 1, 1845

HISTORY OF THE WAR.

CHAP. XLI.

Indisposition of Mr. Pitt—His death—Honors paid to his Memory—His Political and Moral Character—Change of Administration—Conduct of the new Ministry—Mr. Windham's Militia-Bill—Parliamentary Proceedings on the Slave Trade—Trial and Acquittal of Lord Melville—Proposals to Mr. Fox for the Assassination of Buonaparte, and the consequent renewal of Negotiations between the French and English Governments—Treaty of Buonaparte with the Russian Ambassador—Conclusion of the Treaty of Presburg between France and Austria—Naval Operations—Proceedings in Italy and Sicily—Battle of Maida—Memoirs of Sir J. Moore.

THE English parliament met, after repeated prorogations, on the 21st of January, but the discussions of the session were chiefly devoted to the internal situation of the kingdom, the consideration of foreign politics having been postponed in consequence of the severe and fatal indisposition of Mr. Pitt. That celebrated statesman had left Bath on the 8th of January, and on his arrival at Putney Heath, he was advised to seclude himself entirely from business. The experiment was unsuccessful ; he was seized with symptoms of typhus fever, his pulse rose to 130, he became incapable of rational and coherent conversation, and early on the 23rd of January, he expired.

On the 27th of January, Mr. H. Lascelles moved in the house of commons that an humble address be presented to his majesty, that " he will be graciously pleased to give directions that the remains of the right honorable William Pitt be interred at the public expense, and that a monument be erected in the collegiate church of St. Peter, Westminster, to the memory of that excellent statesman, with an inscription expressive of the public sense of so great and irreparable a loss." The chief arguments for the motion, which was passed

by a large majority, were the splendid talents, and important public services, of the eminent character to whom it related. The objections of the opposition were founded on the plea, that it was not customary to confer public honors unless where merit was conjoined with success, and that in the only instance where such honors had been conferred on a statesman, (that of lord Chatham,) the success was not less indisputable than the merit. Mr. Windham, in a speech replete with his usual corruscations of wit, and vehemence of argument, dissented from the motion, alleging that the prolongation of the war and its consequent pressure on the English people, was to be attributed exclusively to the unskilfulness and pertinacity of the pilot who had assumed the direction of the helm of state. Mr. Fox contrasted the successful issue of lord Chatham's measures, with the disappointment and disgrace attaching to the administration of his son, and was answered by lord Castlereagh and Mr. Wilberforce, who attributed the stability of the throne and the salvation of the country to Mr. Pitt's prompt, continued, and energetic exertions against the aggressions of revolutionary violence, and the diffusion of republic principles.

The motion having passed by a great majority, Mr. Cartwright moved that a sum not exceeding £40,000 should be voted for the payment of Mr. Pitt's debts; a motion which passed without opposition. At a meeting of the common council of London, it was moved that a monument be erected in Guild-hall to perpetuate his memory, and after some debate the question was carried by a majority of only 77 to 71.

Such were the trivial and parsimonious honors paid to the memory of a statesman, who with all his faults, was entitled to the gratitude and admiration of his country: and whose hereditary claims to respect and confidence were not enfeebled by his personal conduct and career. Mr. Pitt derived many advantages from his birth and education. He was the darling of his father and designed to support, not the name and honors, but the fame and power of his family. Tutored by the penetrating observations of his father, he was an adept in politics even in his nonage, and an accomplished statesman before the laws regarded him as a man. He came into political life with every advantage. The people adored the representative of the great patriot who had breathed his last in the cause of freedom; and they fondly invested him with all the talents and virtues which they had associated with the name of Pitt. Even the court beheld him with comparative favor, and were willing to escape from the dreaded yoke of the aristocracy by the efforts of the people and the son of Chatham. The coalition of the aristocracy with the excluded tools of the court, whom they had hitherto branded as the basest of reptiles, overwhelmed all his adversaries with infamy, and when the dissolution of parliament had manifested the national sentiments, he set forward in his political career, with the agreeable assurance that the court and the people were equally his friends. At the moment of his accession to power, an unpopular war was just concluded. Men returned with eagerness to the pursuits of peace: agriculture, manufactures and commerce began to flourish anew, and to shoot forth blossoms more gay and fruitful than they had hitherto borne. The taxes became more productive yet were less felt, and while the necessities of the government were relieved, the people were visibly enriched. When they compared this happy state of affairs with the grievances and discontents from which they had just escaped, they naturally referred their new blessings to the presiding spirit who now stood at the head of the government, and while they estimated his talents by their own prosperity, and compared his years with his abilities, they felt grateful to Providence that he had now vouchsafed to an afflicted nation " *A heaven-born minister.*"

As his career proceeded, his good fortune kept pace with it. The flourishing state of the finances enabled him to resume the plans of Walpole. The scheme of the sinking fund was neither new nor complicated, but it had a splendid and most gracious appearance, and he had the virtue to excel his predecessor, by abstaining from the fund thus appropriated, even under his greatest difficulties.

The war of the French revolution presented him with a new scene, but under circumstances less fortunate. On the one hand by persevering in the course which he had hitherto pursued, he had before him the reputation of preferring the real felicity of the nation to the glittering temptations of ambition; of guiding the vessel of the state with skill through shoals and quicksands, in which others were perishing; of rendering his country rich, powerful, and happy, while neighbouring kingdoms were ravaged by intestine convulsions, and ruined by external wars. Not that I conceive, on a candid and impartial retrospect, that this would have been the result of a pacific system of policy. I am only estimating the motives by which Mr. Pitt was influenced. On the other hand the career of ambition was thrown wide before him: the glory of subduing enemies, of ruling allies, of calling forth the valor of his countrymen, and shining in the eyes of posterity, with the accompanying lustre of conquests and victories. He chose the latter, and in a moment of ferment and anxiety the feelings of the people responded to his own.

The atrocities of the French revolution, and the excesses of some infatuated persons, in our own country, who were fitter subjects for Bedlam than for Newgate, threw the people into a general panic. The great trembled for their honors, the wealthy for their riches, the numerous dependants of the court for their places and pensions. Every one seemed to feel the dagger of an assassin at his back, and the hand of a robber in his pocket. Every one felt himself called upon with his life and fortune to assist the minister who was destined to encounter these terrible calamities. He was met with full support, and encouraged by acclamations. When a due lapse of time had dispelled the panic, and men venturing to look round, found no dagger at their back, but the dagger of new penal statutes; no hand in their pockets, but the hand of the tax-gatherer; they thanked heaven for their miraculous escape, and amazed at their own security prostrated themselves before the saviour of their country.

His oratory was the grand pillar of his reputation. His deep-toned voice, his warm and forcible utterance, his slow, distinct, measured enunciation, his elevated and ornamented style, his long, involved, and apparently premeditated sentences, all impressed his hearers with an opinion of his profoundness and dignity. Every period was delivered with pomp, every sentiment breathed an air of importance. His declamation was always suited to the feelings of his audience, and was always received with bursts of applause. Their attention was still more forcibly attracted by the pointed sarcasm in which he delighted. His irony was keen, direct, and cruelly persevering. He never left his victim however contemptible till he had broken every limb on the wheel.

The impressions produced by the striking qualities of his oratory made its defects pass unperceived. The tritest idea acquired importance from the pomp with which it was announced; and amidst the miserable and abortive attempts at haranguing which usually disgrace the house of commons, half-sentencings, stammerings, provincialisms, tasteless repetitions, mutterings, and whispers, the oratory of Pitt shone like a comet amidst the twinkling stars.

There was a sternness and obstinacy in his character which often subdued opposition, but always excited enemies. It exasperated while it overawed the court, and it converted his political contests into private animositses. To those at a distance it bore the appearance of firmness, but several transactions dictated by this spirit drew on his character the reproach of boyish obstinacy and pitiful revenge. While his firmness bound to·him his partisans, his harshness often disgusted them, and it was observed that no man had more political or fewer private friends. Yet like the majority of statesmen he could become submissive and pliant, when the interests of his ruling passion, ambition, were at stake. His original principles dropped from him when he entered the threshold of the court, and all men smiled at his attempt to preserve an appearance of consistency in leaving to his dependants the task of opposing some popular questions, while he himself remained in the minority. He carried through his favourite measure, the union with Ireland, by promising emancipation to the catholics, and when the court refused to fulfil his promise, a sense of decency prompted him to resign. But the want of power was intolerable and he quickly gave up his pledge to recover his situation.

This last step caused his sun, long so brilliant, to set amidst impenetrable gloom. Untaught by his father's sorrows, he quarrelled with his most respectable friends, and threw himself defenceless into the arms of the court. Bereft of his independence, forsaken by the confidence of the nation, unsupported by the miserable dependants by whom he was surrounded, and unfortunate in his dearest enterprises, the agitation of a proud spirit overpowered the feebleness of an exhausted body and he fell at an early age, a victim to the pangs of disappointed ambition.

His figure was tall, his bones large, his habit spare. His features were prominent and coarse, and his mouth which was always open as he walked, expressed to those who met him, without knowing him, a conviction of his ideocy or imbecility. His gestures were ungraceful. Even when he harangued, he chiefly moved his head and his right arm, which he brandished with great violence, but in the same uniform direction. His private life was distinguished by few peculiarities, yet had considerable effect on his political reputation. Of a cool temperament he felt little inclination towards the female sex, and was considered wholly free from the vice of incontinence; a circumstance which procured him a high character for unspotted morality, and rendered him the idol of grave and religious persons throughout the nation. In his latter years, this impression was somewhat diminished by the discovery that he was much addicted to the pleasures of the bottle, a dereliction which was attributed to the example of his friend Mr. Dundas. He entrusted the whole management of his private fortune to his servants, and their careless profusion involved him in necessities. After his resignation, he expressed to some of his confidential friends his resolution of returning to his original profession, the bar, for the purpose of retrieving his ruined fortune; a design at once honorable to his courage, and to the disinterested honesty with which he had served his country

On the subject of his religious feelings at the point of death, the representations of his friends and servants are contradictory. An individual who knew him well, declares that his expiring moments were not those of confidence, while Mr. Canning declares that he did not neglect to prepare himself in silence for that higher destination, which is at once the incentive and reward of human virtue. " His talents, superior and splendid as they were, never, never made him forgetful of that eternal wisdom from which they emanated. The faith and fortitude of his last moments were affecting and exemplary." Lord Hawkesbury having declined the office of premier and accepted the wardenship of the Cinque-ports, and every attempt to form an administration from the wreck of the late ministry

having proved unsuccessful, his majesty was at length induced to call in the assistance of lord Grenville. His majesty acquiesced in the proposal of that nobleman to consult Mr. Fox on the possibility of " forming an administration, comprehending all the leading men of the country." The plan of the new ministry was submitted to the king on the 31st of January. His majesty fully acquiesced in all the appointments so far as regarded the persons of the individuals, but objected to certain intimations of the conduct about to be pursued by the new ministry, and particularly to a paper containing their avowal of dissatisfaction with the system of army regulation, and with the superintendence of the duke of York. The conference was broken off abruptly; but, on the 3rd of February, lord Grenville was **1806.** called to another audience, and the new administration was finally arranged. The cabinet was composed of the following members. Lord Erskine, lord high chancellor of England; earl Fitzwilliam, lord president of the council; viscount Sidmouth, lord privy-seal; lord Grenville, first lord of the treasury; lord Howick, first lord of the admiralty; earl of Moira, master-general of the ordnance; earl Spencer, Mr. Fox, and Mr. Windham, secretaries of state for the home, foreign, and war departments; lord Henry Petty, chancellor of the exchequer; and lord Ellenborough, lord chief justice. The office of lord of the treasury held by lord Grenville, was incompatible with that of auditor of the exchequer, which he held for life; and a bill was therefore passed to enable the possessor of the latter place to hold the former, provided he should name a trustee responsible to himself for the salary of auditor, and to the public for the execution of his office. This arrangement excited universal discontent among the great body of the people, who had looked forward to the accession of the new ministry as the æra of justice, retrenchment, and reform; but the appointment of lord Ellenborough to a seat in the cabinet, was a measure of still more doubtful policy. The functions of a counsellor of the king and of a judge, are obviously incompatible with each other: in cases of treason or of libel, the accused individual might justly object to the superintendence of a judge whose access to the royal presence, and whose duties as a counsellor must inevitably bias his opinions. The subject was debated in the house of commons with considerable vehemence, but on a division, a great majority remained in favor of the appointment.

Having animadverted with severity on the financial systems of their predecessors, and expressed on all occasions the most enthusiastic regard for the rights and interests of the people, it was expected that the members of the new administration would redeem their promises by an immediate effort to alleviate the national burdens. Great, therefore, was the surprise and disappointment of the public, when it appeared that they adopted exclusively, the principles of Mr. Pitt; that individuals who had deprecated in every form of reprehension the imposition of a tax on property, had raised that very tax from six and one-half to ten per cent. and levied it on incomes of 100 a year, that the houses of the people were subjected by these advocates of freedom to the scrutiny of a private excise on beer brewed in private families; and that the intrepid and strenuous advocate of the liberty of the press, lord Erskine, sacrificed the integrity of office to private friendship, and issued an injunction prohibiting the circulation of any judicial or legal reports which should not be published by Mr. Gurney.

These errors, however, on the part of the new ministers, were in some degree redeemed, by their prompt and decided exertions for the abolition of the slave trade. The last motion made by Mr. Fox was to propose a resolution couched in the strongest language against the African slave trade; and in his speech on that occasion he declared " that so fully was he impressed with the vast importance and necessity of attaining his object, that if, during the almost forty years of his parliamentary career, he had been so fortunate as to accomplish that and that only, he should think he had done enough, and should retire from public life with comfort and conscious satisfaction, that he had fulfilled his duty.

Soon after the formation of the ministry, the attorney-general brought in an important bill which passed both houses of parliament with some opposition, and afterwards received the royal assent. This bill prohibited the exportation of slaves from the British colonies after the 1st of January, 1807, and prohibited all subjects of this country residing at home or in foreign settlements, from trafficking in slaves, and from being accessary to the supply of foreign countries. The enactments of the bill were secured by heavy penalties; resolutions were passed declaring the African slave trade to be contrary to the principles of justice, humanity, and sound policy, and an address was presented to the king, imploring him to use his influence with foreign governments and states for the abolition of the trade, and the execution of the regulations adopted for that purpose.

The army bill of Mr. Windham was another beneficial and important measure, and relieved the country for awhile from the mode of raising the militia by ballot; a method in every respect the worst that could be devised, operating on those who can afford to pay substitutes as a tax by lottery: upon the poor as absolute compulsion, and impeding the regular recruiting service, by tending inevitably to raise the price of men. No preceding law was more beneficial to the peasantry and the poor. That part of the bill which substituted service during a limited term of years, for that indefinite and hopeless bondage to which our soldiery had hitherto been doomed, had long been called for by enlightened men. Its consequences, if they had been left to their natural operation, would have filled our towns, villages, and hamlets with men, who, having employed the restless activity of youth in seeing the world, and retired when that restlessness was abated, to calmer occupations, would at all times have been ready for the effectual defence of their country, and would by the stories of what they had seen, have excited the rising generation to follow the same course. The crimp and the recruiting serjeant might have been dispensed with, and the soldier's life, into which under former systems, the criminal was forced, the innocent inveigled, and only the dissolute and desperate voluntarily entered, would have become the deliberate and not imprudent choice, of young peasants and mechanics, so that once to have served would have been regarded as a regular part of national education.

An unsuccessful attack on the conduct of lord St. Vincent was succeeded by a series of charges against the marquis of Wellesley. Mr. Paul, a gentleman lately returned from India, obtained orders for the production of various papers relative to the wars of India, and he continued to urge his accusations with unabated constancy and perseverence. The firmness and intrepidity which he displayed would have entitled him to the highest praise had these qualities been accompanied with judgment, temper, or discretion: but fortunately for lord Wellesley Mr. Paul was eminently deficient in these qualifications, nor was he possessed of parliamentary knowledge, personal ability, or political influence. The charges of rapacity, cruelty, and injustice, were ordered to be printed and taken into consideration on a future day, but no further proceedings took place during the present session.

The trial of lord Melville commenced in Westminster hall on the 29th of April. Ten days were employed by the managers in bringing forward and examining their evidence, and in the speeches of Mr. Whitbread who opened the case, and of the solicitor-general. Three days were afterwards employed by the counsel for the defendant in their reply; two by Mr. Plumer, and the third by Mr. Adams. The fourteenth and fifteenth days of the trial were occupied by the managers in their reply on the part of the commons, the legal argument being conducted by the attorney-general, and the observations on the evidence being assigned to Mr. Whitbread. On the sixteenth day of trial the sentence

1806.

was pronounced. The articles of impeachment were ten in number, but were in substance as follows.

That lord Melville while treasurer of the navy did, previously to the 10th of January, 1786, take and receive out of the money entrusted to him from his majesty's exchequer the sum of £10,000, and fraudulently and illegally convert the same to his own use, or to some other corrupt and illegal purposes, and on the 11th of June, 1805, did refuse in the house of commons, to account for the application of the said sum.

That after the passing of an act of parliament in 1785, for better regulating the office of treasurer of the navy, he had in violation of that act, permitted Trotter his pay-master, illegally to take from the bank of England, for other than immediate application to naval purposes, large sums of money.

That he had fraudulently and corruptly permitted Trotter to apply the money so abstracted to purposes of private use and emolument, and had himself fraudulently and corruptly derived profit therefrom. On the 12th of June the house of peers having adjourned to Westminster hall, and being there resumed, the lord-chancellor put the question beginning with the junior baron, " Is Henry viscount Melville guilty or not guilty?" After numbering the votes his lordship declared to him, " that the lords had fully considered of his case, and had found him *not guilty* of high crimes and misdemeanors, charged on him by the impeachment of the house of commons."

About ten days after Mr. Fox came into office, he received a letter from a person calling himself Guillet de la Gevrilliére, stating that he was arrived at Gravesend without a passport, and requesting Mr. Fox to send him one, as he had very lately left Paris, and had something to communicate, which would give Mr. Fox satisfaction. On receiving this letter, Mr. Fox gave orders to the alien office to send for the man from Gravesend, and a private interview having been solicited, to bring him, on his arrival in London, to Mr. Fox's house in Arlington street. In consequence of these orders, the Frenchman was next morning carried to Mr. Fox's house, and there admitted to his closet ; when, after some unimportant conversation, he proceeded to declare the object of his journey, and to inform Mr. Fox that a plan had been arranged for the assassination of Buonaparte, and a house hired at Passy from which it would be carried into effect with certainty and without risk. Surprised and confounded at the audacity of the villain in making him the confidant of so execrable a design, Mr. Fox, without inquiring further, instantly dismissed him from his presence, and desired Mr. Brooke to send him, as soon as possible, out of the kingdom. But on reflection, he ordered him to be detained till such information might be given to the French government, as might prevent the perpetration of his crime. With that view he transmitted to M. Talleyrand a short and simple statement of the occurrence, and received an answer containing a natural and well turned compliment to the honor and generosity of Mr. Fox's character, and inclosing an extract from the emperor's speech to the legislative body, purporting that he was willing to make peace on the basis of the treaty of Amiens. Mr. Fox considered this communication as a distinct overture, and proceeded to answer it with his accustomed promptitude and frankness. A correspondence ensued of considerable length, and in consequence of the conciliatory manner in which it was conducted, Mr. Fox solicited as a personal favor, the release of several of his private friends detained prisoners at Verdun. Among the persons named by him was the earl of Yarmouth, (only son of the marquis of Hertford,) who, together with his wife and family, had resided in France since the commencement of the war. On lord Yarmouth's arrival in London, early in June, he communicated the substance of a conversation with M. Talleyrand, in which that minister states, as the basis of a treaty, the restoration of Hanover, and the possession of Sicily, conformably to the *vti possidetis*. The English ministry, on the representation of lord Yarmouth, renewed their assurances of anxiety to

negotiate, but in the mean time the circumstances of the two nations were materially changed by the victories of France, in favor of France. Talleyrand openly asserted the right to take advantage of this revolution in 'affairs, and in the first interview with lord Yarmouth on the return of the latter to Paris, departed entirely from his explicit offer of Sicily, indulged himself in vague allusions to further demands, and suggested the necessity of negotiating" with a formal plenipotentiary. The instructions to lord Yarmouth on this occasion, were distinct and peremptory. He was directed to insist generally on a recurrence to the original overtures, and to make the readmission of Sicily the *sine qua non* of the production of his full powers, which, " to avoid all pretence of cavil," were transmitted without delay. In the meanwhile the conduct and language of M. D'Oubril, the Russian ambassador at Paris, fully justified the expectations of Talleyrand. Such was the success of the French negotiators, that they intimidated the Russian into a belief that the delay of forty-eight hours in the signature of a separate treaty, would expose Germany and Europe to dismemberment and destruction. He accordingly signed a treaty on the 20th of July, and, without communicating to lord Yarmouth some of the most material articles to which he had consented, hastened, according to his own expression, to lay his work and his head at the feet of his imperial master. The French regarded the signature of this treaty in the light of an important victory, and so far succeeded in terrifying lord Yarmouth, that they prevailed upon him to produce his full powers before the stipulated basis had been recognised. The necessity of some other negotiator was immediately felt, and the important charge was entrusted to lord Lauderdale ; who, convinced even at the commencement of his diplomacy that the French were insincere, was detained under various pretences, till it became the policy of Britain as well as France, to await the decision of the court of St. Petersburgh, respecting the treaty with D'Oubril. On the 3rd of September, a courier brought the intelligence to Paris that the emperor had refused to ratify the act of his ambassador, and that event having been foreseen, lord Lauderdale was instructed, to consider the two courts as having reverted to their former situation, and to propose a joint negotiation with our Russian ally. To this last proposal Talleyrand replied in a note conceived in the language of remonstrance and reproach. Lord Lauderdale replied to this communication with equal coolness and spirit. In the meanwhile Buonaparte left Paris for the army of the Rhine, and general Clarke and Talleyrand, accompanied him upon his journey. M. Champagny who remained to conduct the negotiation was neither authorised to relinquish the claims of Joseph on Sicily, nor to acquiesce in such arrangements as would satisfy the court of Russia. The negotiation was therefore at an end, and lord Lauderdale peremptorily insisted on his passports.

The preliminaries of peace signed by D'Oubril contained the following articles. Russia gave up to France Cattaro and all the places occupied by her troops in Dalmatia. The French emperor restored Ragusa to its former state, and promised to abstain from hostilities against the Montenegrins. The republic of the Seven Islands was declared independent. The independence of the Ottoman Porte was recognized, and a wish was expressed on the part of Buonaparte for the arrangement and conclusion of a maritime peace. M. D'Oubril having not only violated his instructions, in the conclusion of this treaty, but acted directly contrary to their sense and spirit, was disgraced and exiled from court, but retained his rank and his appointments.

The armistice concluded at Austerlitz by prince John of Lichtenstein, and marshal Berthier, was followed by conferences for a separate peace between France and Austria. This negotiation which was intrusted to Talleyrand on the part of France, and conducted by prince John of Lichtenstein and count Ignaz de Gnylac on the side of Austria, was soon brought to a favourable issue. A definitive treaty of peace was signed by these plenipotentiaries, at Presburg, on the 26th of December and was next day ratified by the French emperor. Prince John of Lichtenstein, who was the chief adviser of the emperor of Germany in these pacific measures, is accused by the partisans of the coalition, of having betrayed his master into a system which they considered fatal to the interests and derogatory from the interests of his crown, for so trivial a consideration as the prospect of removing the pressure of war from his own private estates in Moravia. But however selfish the motives of the adviser, it is clear from all the events that have since occurred, that the advice was most salutary and judicious ; and that to the promptitude with which this treaty was concluded, and to the fidelity with which it was observed, Austria owed the privilege of being an independent state.

The terms however of the peace of Presburg were much less favorable to the emperor of Germany than those which in similar extremities, he had formerly obtained from the ruler of France. By the present treaty he was compelled to renounce his share of the Venetian territories, which at the peace of Luneville, had been reckoned no inadequate compensation for his loss of the Low Countries, and to consent that these valuable provinces should be annexed to the kingdom of Italy. He was also forced to cede the country of Tyrol and lordships of Voralberg, to the king of Bavaria, the hereditary enemy of his family ; and to abandon his possessions in Franconia, Suabia, and Bavaria to be divided among the kings of Bavaria and Wurtemburg, and the elector of Baden. The only territory bestowed upon him in compensation for so many losses, was the county of Saltzburgh and Berchsolgaden, which was taken from his brother the archduke Ferdinand, and formally incorporated with the empire of Austria ; while the archduke in return received the territory of Wurtzburg, from the king of Bavaria, accompanied by a promise of the emperor Napoleon's good offices, to obtain for him a full and entire indemnity in Germany. The grand-mastership of the Teutonic order, with all the rights, domains, and revenues belonging to it, was also transferred in perpetuity to the house of Austria, to be held as an hereditary dignity in the family of any one of its princes, whom the emperor of Germany and Austria should appoint. The total cessions of Austria have been estimated in extent of territory at 1297 square miles; in number of subjects, at 2,716,000 souls; and in loss of revenue, at 16,060,000 florins, at about £1,600,000.

While the plenipotentiaries at Presburg were settling the conditions of peace between France and Austria, a treaty was concluded at Vienna between France and Prussia, which led, at a subsequent period, to important consequences. The ostensible object of this treaty was to secure the tranquillity of the north of Germany, and prevent the revival of hostilities in that quarter. It stipulated that the French emperor should suspend the march of his army against Hanover, and send no more troops into that country, on condition that the blockade of Hameln should be raised, and its garrison supplied with provisions, and that the forces of the allies in Hanover should be withdrawn and replaced with Prussians. This treaty was signed at Vienna on the 15th of December by count Haugwitz and general Duroc, and such of its engagements as the contracting parties thought proper to make public were carried into immediate execution. The blockade of Hameln was raised, and its garrison supplied with provisions by order of the Hanoverian regency. The French armies advancing against Hanover were ordered back. The British forces under lord Cathcart retired to Bremen, and waited there for the arrival of transports to convey them to England. Bad weather prevented them from embarking till the beginning of February; but, owing to the protection of the armistice, they remained in perfect security, and without the smallest molestation from the French. The Russians, who had been left by their emperor at the entire disposal of the king of Prussia, were marched in the first instance, to the city of Hanover, and afterwards across the Elbe. The Swedes also withdrew to the other side of that river, and took up their quarters in Lauenburg and Mecklenburg,

VOL. I.

where they published a proclamation, declaring that the dominions of his Britannic majesty on the right bank of the Elbe were under the protection of Sweden. As the allies evacuated the country, the Prussians entered and took possession of it; and, notwithstanding the opposition of the Hanoverian minister, who protested in vain against their proceedings, they occupied, before the middle of February, the whole electorate of Hanover, except Hameln, where the French had still a garrison, and Lauenburg, which was held by the Swedes.

After the retreat of the Russians, and conclusion of treaties with Austria and Prussia, the French emperor had no remaining enemy within his reach, except the king of Naples, whose recent conduct had been such as to provoke the utmost fury of his indignation. A treaty of neutrality between France and Naples had been concluded at Paris on the 21st of September, by Talleyrand and the marquis of Gallo, and ratified at Portici by the king of Naples on the 8th of October. By this treaty, the French agreed to withdraw their troops from the Neapolitan territory, where they had been stationed, without any justifiable pretence, since the commencement of the war with England; and the king of Naples engaged in return, to remain neutral in the war between France and the allies, and to repel by force, every encroachment upon his neutrality. He more particularly became bound not to permit the troops of any belligerent power to enter his territories, not to confide the defence of his strong places or the command of his armies to any Russian or Austrian officer or French emigrant, or subject of any belligerent, and not to admit any belligerent squadron into his ports. But hardly had six weeks elapsed after the ratification of this treaty, when every one of its stipulations was violated by the court of Naples. On the 20th of November, a squadron of English and Russian ships of war appeared in the bay of Naples, and landed a body of forces in that city and its vicinity. It is still doubtful whether this expedition was undertaken by the allies in concert with the Neapolitan government; but, whether previously consulted or not, by not opposing the landing of the troops, nor even remonstrating against it, the latter made itself a party to the transaction, and forfeited the neutrality secured to it by the treaty recently concluded. Such at least was the interpretation of its conduct by the French ambassador at Naples, who instantly took down the arms of France from over the gate of his hotel, and demanded passports to enable him to leave the kingdom. Had the court of Naples been able to justify itself from a participation in the counsels that led to these proceedings, or been still desirous of maintaining its neutrality in the war between France and the allies ; this was the moment for explanation. But, instead of keeping open the door for accommodation, it suffered the French ambassador to depart without even attempting a vindication of its conduct ; and contented itself with issuing a decree, in which, after slightly alluding to the late transactions, but without even condescending to say, that the neutrality of its territory had been violated against its will, it promised to foreign merchants, subjects of the allies of France, and resident in the Neapolitan dominions, protection for their property and commerce.

The Russians, who amounted to 14,000 men, under general Lasey, landed at Naples, and were quartered in that city and its vicinity. The English, to the number of 10,000, embarked at *Castel-a-mare,* under the command of sir James Craig and sir John Stuart. Scarcely, however, had the court of Naples excited the resentment of Napoleon, by these hostile demonstrations, when the allies set the first example of flight, and the retreat of the Russians by the command of Alexander, rendered the retreat of the English on Sicily, unavoidable. This hasty retreat of sir James Craig excited the loud and persevering murmurs of his troops, and the repeated but ineffectual remonstrances of the court of Naples. In the mean time a French army under the command of Joseph Buonaparte, assisted by Massena,

Regnier, and other generals of reputation, was advancing towards Naples. The right, commanded by Regnier, advanced to Gaeta without opposition, and captured the redoubt of St. André ; the second division, under the command of Massena, met with no resistance on its march to Naples, which Joseph entered on the 15th of February, the king and queen having sought refuge a second time at Palermo. The misfortunes of the king excited the commiseration of his subjects ; the cruel, vindictive, and intriguing character of the queen rendered her absence the topic of general exultation. The forces of the duke of Calabria, heir-apparent of Naples, took a strong position at Lago Negro, whither they were followed by general Regnier, from Gaeta. Their efforts were unskilful and ineffectual. After two trivial skirmishes, magnified in the bulletins and proclamations of the French, into important battles, the whole kingdom of Naples, except Gaeta and Civitelle del Tranto, submitted to the enemy.

Buonaparte now issued a decree, conferring the crown of Naples upon his brother Joseph, an act which excited the warmest indignation at the court of Palermo ; and, instead of profiting by their past misfortunes, the queen and the duke of Calabria, entertained the quixotic, and, at that moment, hopeless design of recovering the kingdom. By the magnificence of their promises and by the loyalty of those who forgot the infamy of the queen in their affection for her husband, Abruzzo and Calabria, were delivered for a short time from the French yoke. But, though the insurgents fought with unparalleled courage and intrepidity, the numbers and discipline of the French at length prevailed ; so that, after a fruitless waste of blood and perpetration of atrocities, these provinces were again compelled to acknowledge Joseph Buonaparte for their sovereign.

In this extremity the court of Naples had once more recourse not only to the attachment but to the interests, the vices, and the prejudices of the Calabrians. The recollection of their former expedition to Naples, the plunder they had made, and the licence

W M Craig Del. Published by T. Kinnersley Sepr 20 1815. J Brown Sc.

The British storming the French Lines with the Bayonet
at the Battle of Salamanca

they enjoyed on that occasion, excited them to re-embark with willingness in an enterprise so congenial to their national habits. All their efforts, however, and all the exertions of the court might have proved abortive, had not an English army landed on the coasts of Calabria, and began its military operations by the important and splendid victory of Maida.

About the middle of April, sir Sidney Smith had arrived at Palermo, in the Pompee of 84 guns, and taken the command of the English squadron destined for the defence of Sicily, consisting of five ships of the line, besides frigates, transports, and gun-boats. With this force under his command, sir Sidney sailed to the coast of Italy, and began his operations by introducing into Gaeta supplies of stores and ammunition. After alarming the coast, and distributing arms, money, and ammunition among the Calabrians, he found that unless an English army should make its appearance in the country, there was little hope of exciting a *successful* insurrection against the French. Sir John Stuart, who succeeded to sir James Craig in the command of the English troops in Sicily, in compliance, therefore, with the urgent request of the exiled court, but in opposition to his own opinion, consented, at length, to land with part of the army on the continent, and arrived on the 1st of July, in a bay in the gulph of St. Eufemia, near the northern frontier of Lower Calabria. A proclamation was immediately issued, inviting the Calabrians to join the standard of their lawful sovereign, and offering them arms and ammunition for their defence. Few or none obeyed the summons. Disappointed in his expectations from the inhabitants, sir John Stuart determined to re-embark, when he received intelligence that general Regnier was encamped at MAIDA, about ten miles distant, with an army nearly equal to his own. Aware, at the same time, that the French general would be immediately joined by numerous reinforcements, he determined to advance and attack him before they arrived. The two armies were separated by a plain from four to six miles in breadth, extending

from sea to sea, and bounded on the north and south by chains of mountains. The French occupied a strong position on the sloping side of a woody hill, below the village of Maida, having the river Lamato in front, and their flanks strengthened by a thick impervious underwood. In numbers they were greatly superior to the English, having received the expected reinforcements before the battle. Their force is supposed to have been about 7000 men, while that of the English did not amount to 4800. Had Regnier remained upon the heights, the English must have attacked him under circumstances of great disadvantage : but, fortunately blinded by an excessive confidence, and an unbounded contempt of the enemy, he quitted his strong position, and drew up his army on the plain. The English, surprised at the number of his troops, but undismayed by their appearance, resolutely advanced to the attack. After some firing, both sides prepared to charge with the bayonet, and advanced with apparently equal resolution ; but the French, astonished at the firmness and intrepidity of the English, and struck with a sudden panic, gave way, after the bayonets of the two armies had begun to cross, and endeavored to save themselves by flight. They were overtaken with immense slaughter, and the left wing of their army was totally routed and dispersed. An effort was then made with the right to retrieve the honor of the day ; but they were resisted with great steadiness by the English left, and their cavalry was thrown into disorder, in attempting to turn the English flank. An unexpected fire from the 20th regiment, which landed during the action, and came up at this critical juncture, induced them to abandon the field of battle with precipitation, and to leave an undisputed victory to their opponents. About 700 French were buried on the ground, and 1000 prisoners taken, among whom were general Compere and several other officers of rank. Their total loss was estimated, (with little probability,) at 4000 men, while that of the English amounted only to 45 men killed, and 282 wounded.

The glorious victory of the 6th of July was the signal of general insurrection in both the Calabrias; in Lower Calabria, after committing every description of oppression and inhumanity, only 3000 men out of 9000 were able to escape the vengeance of the natives, and in Upper Calabria their losses were avowedly considerable. Sir John Stuart, however, reflecting on the smallness of his forces, disgusted by the imprudence of the court, who cherished the insurrection by the agency of galley-slaves, assassins, renegado priests, and the lovers of murder and rapine, returned to Messina, where he was succeeded in the chief command by general Fox, who immediately despatched him on a second expedition to Calabria, but when sir John Moore, his senior officer, joined the army with reinforcements from England, sir John preferred returning to his native country to remaining third-in-command in Italy.

Sir John Moore was born at Glasgow in the year 1760: he entered the army at a very early period of life, and from the connection which his father Dr. Moore, had formed with the families Hamilton and Argyle, he rapidly rose in the service. In 1790 he was promoted to the lieutenant-colonelcy of the 51st regiment of foot, and shortly after was actively employed in the Mediterranean.

The force under lord Hood having been obliged to evacuate Toulon in the latter part of the year 1793, and a place of arms being absolutely necessary for our troops and navy, general Pascal Paoli had determined to contend once more for the sovereignty of his native isle, and entered into correspondence with Great Britain, to which he made an offer of the sovereignty of Corsica.

Lieutenant-colonel Moore, and major Kœhler, were selected as the most proper officers, to inquire into the probability of success that would attend operations in that quarter. They landed secretly, obtained an interview of Paoli, and made a flattering report of his power and authority. This intelligence determined lord Hood to anticipate the French who had embarked a body of troops at Nice, for the subjugation of the island. Having anchored in a bay to the westward of Martella tower, a body of troops, amounting to about 14,000 men, was landed under lieutenant-general Dundas, and it was determined that this important post should be immediately seized, without which precaution the anchorage could not be deemed secure. A regular siege, however, was rendered necessary, and the garrison surrendered in two days. Lieutenant-colonel Moore was not present, he had been detached with two regiments, a howitzer, and a six-pounder, for the purpose of seizing on Fornelli, by a sudden and unexpected movement. Having advanced for several miles through a mountainous country, on reconnoitring the place, it was found that it could not be taken by a *coup-de-main*. Sir John Moore however reported that if artillery were brought up, the attack would be attended with success. Accordingly, after four days of incessant fatigue, a sufficient quantity of ordnance was advanced to an eminence elevated no less than 700 feet above the level of the sea. From this commanding height, a single eighteen-pounder so annoyed two French frigates in the adjacent bay of St. Fiorenza, that they were forced to retire, while one battery, consisting of three pieces of artillery, enfiladed the redoubt of the convention, and a second took it in reverse. A body of Corsicans amounting to 1200 men, now advanced to the support of the British troops, and the French commander having refused to capitulate, preparations were made for an assault, which commenced on the evening of the 17th of February. A column under lieutenant-colonel Moore advanced against the nearest part of the redoubt, while lieutenant-colonel Wanchope and captain Steward extended in the centre, and on the left, and having thus divided the attention of the enemy, drove them down a steep hill in the rear. The English now became masters of the town, as well as of the heights of St Fiorenza.

The possession of Calvi was the next object of the British general, and on the 9th of June, 1795, the troops having received considerable reinforcements under lieutenant-general Stewart, they encamped at Serra del Cappucine, distant three miles

from the object of their attack. But before
the body of the place could be assaulted,
it became necessary to carry two detached
forts, the latter of which lieutenant-colonel
Moore was directed to take. Day-break
was judged most proper for making the attempt, while to arrive there at the appointed
moment it became necessary to post the
troops among bushes, while false attacks
were made in other quarters. Colonel
Moore and major Brereton rapidly advanced to surprise the enemy, but were observed
from the ramparts, and a volley of grape-
shot was fired which did little execution.
The storming party now scrambled up
amongst the rubbish, regardless of the fire
of small arms, and the bursting of shells.
A variety of impediments occurred from
the nature of the ground and the desperate
resistance of the enemy. Lieutenant-colonel Moore received a contusion in the
head by the bursting of a shell, yet, notwithstanding the effusion of blood, entered the
place along with the grenadiers. On general Stewart quitting Corsica he recommended lieutenant-colonel Moore, now invested
with the rank of adjutant-general, as a proper person to succeed him. On his return
from this station he was appointed to serve
in the expedition to the West Indies, in
1795, under sir Ralph Abercrombie. In
1799, he accompanied the duke of York to
Holland, and afterwards shared in the danger and the glory of the expedition to
Egypt. In the battle of Aboukir *major-
general* Moore was wounded in the leg, but
refused to quit the field, and notwithstanding his misfortune, the further progress of the
army through a long and critical march
was committed to his direction. After the
campaign in Egypt he was placed for some
time on the staff of the southern military
district, from which he was called to join
the army in Calabria.

He soon discovered however that the
great object for which a British armament was stationed in the Mediterranean,
could not be sacrificed to the caprices of
the queen, and to the uncertain prospect
of recovering Naples. Kingdom after king
dom had been subdued, throne after throne
had been subverted without teaching the
Neapolitan government that there is no
solid security to any government but the affection of the people, and that the price of
affection is to deserve and return it. While
the queen and the duke of Calabria projected the recovery of Naples by force of
arms, the Sicilians, their only hope, were
neglected and despised; their grievances
remained unredressed; and to the disgrace
of England, her power instead of being extended to their relief, served only to support the arrogance and maintain the authority of their tyrants and oppressors.

THE violation of the Prussian territory of Anspach, in the preceding year, by the French troops under Bernadotte, had awakened Prussia from the apathy that for so many years had characterized her policy, and at a moment, when the evident danger of Austria might have been expected to confirm her prepossessions in favor of a rigid neutrality, an angry note was delivered by baron Hardenburg to the French mission at Berlin, which concluded with an intimation that the king of Prussia found himself compelled to order his armies to occupy such positions as might be necessary for the protection of his states. Had this intimation been followed up by a prompt and vigorous commencement of hostilities, Austria might have been saved, and Prussia preserved from future humiliation and discomfiture. But to temporize was the favourite policy of the court of Berlin, and a protracted negotiation at the headquarters of Buonaparte, conducted by the weak, the ignorant, and the dilatory count Haugwitz, was artfully prolonged till the battle of Austerlitz had been fought, the armistice concluded, and the coalition dissolved. Alarmed and confounded, the Prussian court despatched general Von Pfuhl, who was empowered to accept the very conditions which had been formerly rejected, but previously to the arrival of Von Pfuhl, Haugwitz had signed a definitive treaty at Vienna, by which Prussia from being the friend and ally of the combined powers, and almost the open and declared enemy of France, became the ally of the latter, and her associate in the spoils of the vanquished and baffled coalition. On the one side was stipulated a mutual guarantee of possessions, the ratification of whatever arrangements should be concluded at Presburg, and the inviolability of the Turkish territory ; and on the other (at a time when the Prussian court professed the most anxious and sincere participation in the views of Britain,) the annexation of Hanover to Prussia in return for the cession of three provinces. As some palliation of this latter act of injustice, articles were proposed by Prussia, which stipulated that the French should not return to Hanover, that the completion of the treaty respecting that electorate should be deferred till a general peace, and that the consent of his majesty, the king of Great

Britain should be obtained to the arrangement. Under pretence, however, of securing the electorate from the calamities of another ruinous war, the troops of the allies were withdrawn and replaced by Prussians. Yet even the reluctance displayed by the king of Prussia to enter Hanover without some regard to his connection with the court of St. James, was far from being acceptable to the emperor of France, and a new treaty was concluded, by which his Prussian majesty agreed to annex Hanover to his dominions, and exclude the British flag from the ports of that electorate, conditions which were promptly enforced. Measures of retaliation were immediately adopted by the British government. Notice was given to the ministers of neutral powers, that the necessary means had been taken for the blockade of the rivers Ems, Weser, Elbe, and Trave. A general embargo was laid upon all Prussian vessels in the harbors of the united kingdom, and this order was afterwards extended to all vessels belonging to the rivers Elbe, Weser, and Ems, vessels under the Danish flag alone excepted: the English mission at Berlin was recalled, and a message being sent to the two houses of parliament, addresses were presented in return.

Some suspicions, however, were entertained of the real intentions of France with respect to Hanover; the occupation of Cattero by the Russians had served as a pretext to the French emperor for retaining possession of Brannau, and for keeping on foot an immense army in Germany, which he maintained at the expense of the free towns and states of Suabia and Franconia : and the *confederation of the Rhine*, so memorable in the history of future wars, so destructive to the interests of the German empire, was signed on the 17th of July by princes and ministers, who were scarcely allowed time to read the deed to which they affixed their signatures. The members of this confederation were, the emperor of France, the kings of Bavaria and Wurtemburg, the archbishop of Ratisbon, the elector of Baden, the grand duke of Berg, the landgrave of Hesse, Darmstadt,

the princes of Nassau-Weilburg, of Nassau-Usingen, of Hohenzollern-Heschingen, Hohenzollern-Siegmaringen, Salm-Salm, and Salm-Kyrburg, Isenburg, Birchstein, and Lichtenstein, the duke of Aremburg, and the count of Lien. By their articles of confederacy, these princes separated themselves from the Germanic empire, and, renouncing all connection with it, appointed a diet to meet at Frankfort to conduct their public concerns ; established among themselves a federal alliance, and fixed the contingents which each should furnish in case any one of them was threatened or attacked. Among other stipulations, the imperial city of Nuremburg was given to the king of Bavaria, and that of Frankfort on the Maine, to the archbishop of Ratisbon. In compliance with a requisition from Buonaparte, the humiliated emperor of Austria, by a formal deed resigned his title of emperor of Germany, and annexed to his empire the remaining German provinces and states : the prince of Hesse was cut off from part of his own territories, and Prussia discovered that, after guaranteeing to her the possession of Hanover, her faithless ally had negotiated with England on the basis of restoring that electorate.

A determination to prosecute the war was now unavoidable, but the imbecility of the Prussian councils has seldom been more strikingly exemplified than by the mission of Paris of M. Kobelsdorf, a man so totally unqualified for his important task, that when Buonaparte left Paris to take the command of his army against Prussia, Kobelsdorf inquired with the greatest simplicity, whether he should not accompany his majesty the emperor to head-quarters, little suspecting against whom the march of Napoleon was directed. The French troops advanced with rapidity towards the future scene of action : on the 24th of September, Buonaparte left his capital to take the command of the army, and a note was presented to M. Talleyrand, which produced the just and mortifying retort, that, had France been willing to gratify the rapacious ambition of Prussia at the expense of her weaker neighbours, the flames of war would not have been rekindled on the continent. Prussia had in reality been as perfidious, as unprincipled in her ambition, as France, but she had conducted herself with less ability and less success. Her counsellors were weak, wavering, and corrupt, yet to individuals who had so evidently displayed during the late negotiations their treachery or incapacity, was committed the awful and responsible task of defending a country enured to peace, against the most formidable and successful warrior of modern times.

In this emergency the English minister lord Morpeth, at the humble and earnest request of the king of Prussia, whose policy was equally inconsistent with prudence, reputation, and dignity, proceeded to the head-quarters of the Prussian army at Weimar. This promptitude did not correspond with the views of the Prussian minister. They were on the eve of a great battle, which might decide the fate of the campaign, and indulged a hope that in the event of a decisive victory, Hanover might still be theirs, and Haugwitz, whose petty cunning was only equalled by his general incapacity, contrived, by various evasions, to avoid a meeting with lord Morpeth. Subsequently to the battle of Overstadt, but while the result was still unknown, his lordship having asked Lucchesini whether the court of Prussia was ready to enter into an immediate negotiation, the Italian unguardedly replied, that it would depend on the issue of the battle which had just been fought. At this very moment the English ministry were proving the sincerity of their endeavors to obtain a reconciliation by removing (September 25th,) the blockade of the Prussian ports and rivers, which had hitherto subsisted with great inconvenience to the north of Germany. Early in October, the Prussian head-quarters were at Naumburg, where they had collected their principal magazines, and their army extended itself in the country bordering on the Saal in Upper Saxony. On the 4th of that month, their head-quarters were removed to Erfurth, and on the 10th to Weimar. The whole force, Prussians and Saxons, under the command of the duke of Brunswick, did not amount to less than 150,000 men. While this immense army remained inactive on the banks of the Saal, the French were collecting their scattered troops, and concentrating their forces in the neighbourhood of Bamburg. On the 6th of October, Buonaparte arrived in that city, and on the 8th the French army was in motion to attack the Prussians, whose negligence in leaving their magazines unprotected was equally reprehensible with the slowness of their movements. Cut off from their depositories at Hof, Zwickau, Weissenfels, and Naumburg, they had no alternative but to fight or starve, in their formidable position. When their cavalry took the field on the morning of the battle of Averstadt, the horses had been without corn, and the men without food, for two nights and a day. Another fatal error in the disposition of the army, was its encampment on the left bank of the Saal, by which the electorate of Saxony, the chief fortresses of the Prussian states, and the capital itself, were laid open to the enemy, and the Prussians were cut off from Magdeburg, the only place of refuge in case of a defeat.

The French army advanced on the 8th, in three divisions, the right composed of the corps of marshals Soult and Ney, and of a division of Bavarians, set out from Amberg and Nuremburg, formed a junction at Bayreuth, and then marched against Hof. The centre, commanded by the grand duke of Berg, the prince of *Ponte Corvo*, (Bernadotte,) and marshal Davoust, marched from Bamburg to Cronack, and from thence to Saalburg and Schleitz. The left, composed of the corps of marshals Lasnes and Augereau, advanced from Scweinefurth upon Coburg, Graffenthal, and Saalfeld. By these means, the left wing of the Prussians, which stretched to a great distance from their centre, was exposed to the attack of the whole French army. Aware of their critical situation, the Prussians at Hof, who were at the extremity of the line, and in the greatest danger of being cut off, fell back upon

Schleitz before the arrival of marshal Soult. Some prisoners were taken and all the magazines. Soult, followed by Ney, pressed forward to Plauen in Upper Saxony, where he arrived on the 10th. The French centre passed the Saal at Saalburg, and advanced on the 9th to Schleitz, where a body of 10,000 Prussians was posted under the command of general Tauenzein. An action ensued in which the Prussians were worsted with considerable loss : on the next day the French advanced to Auma, and on the 11th to Gera, within a day's march of Naumburg, the grand depository of the Prussian magazines. The French left was equally successful with the other divisions of their army. Lasnes entered Coburg on the 8th, and advanced to Graffenthal on the 9th. On the 10th he attacked at Saalfeld the advanced-guard of prince Hohenlohe, commanded by prince Louis of Prussia, and gained over it a signal victory. Prince Louis, to whose rashness and disobedience of orders, in quitting his position at the bridge of Saalfeld, and advancing to attack the enemy, this misfortune was entirely to be attributed, fell in the action.

By the success of these operations the French, after turning the Prussian left, 1806. became masters of all their magazines, and placed themselves between their grand army, and the cities of Berlin and Dresden. On the 12th part of the French centre under marshal Davoust entered Naumburg, and took possession of the magazines which they set on fire. Their army now extended along the right bank of the Saal from Naumburg to Neustadt. Their first line was composed of the corps of Davoust at Naumburg, of the corps of Lasnes at Jena, and of that of Augereau at Kahla. In the second line was the grand duke of Berg between Zietz and Leipsic, the prince of Ponte Corvo at Zietz, the emperor and Soult at Jena, and Ney at Neustadt.

Notwithstanding the alarm excited by the death and defeat of prince Louis, so remiss were the Prussians in the most ordinary precautions, and so absurdly confident in the strength of their positions, that one of their patroles, sent from head-quarters

towards Naumburg to reconnoitre, returned without going to Naumburg, because they met a traveller on the road who told them that " no intelligence respecting the French had reached that city." From this state of blind security they were awakened on the night of the 12th by the blaze of their magazines. Immediate preparations were made for battle : the French remaining in nearly their former positions, and the Prussians being assembled between Averstadt, Weimar, and Jena. The two armies were separated by the heights of the Saal which seemed to present an impregnable position. to the Prussians, and to oppose an insuperable barrier to the French. But the inadvertence and treachery of the Prussian generals, overlooked these advantages, and they left the most important passes of the Saal entirely undefended. The French, perceiving their omission, were indefatigably employed on the ensuing night in securing these passes, and transporting cannon to defend them ; and, when the day broke, the Prussians saw themselves attacked in their apparently impregnable position. At break of day, the whole of the French army was under arms. The light troops of the centre, began the action, by opening a brisk fire on the Prussians, which enabled the French line to extend itself on the plain and draw up in order of battle. The Prussian left, amounting to about 80,000 men, were despatched early in the morning towards Naumburg to take possession of the impregnable defiles of Kœsen, but these were already occupied by Davoust, whom they attacked eleven times successively, but in vain attempted to dislodge. Their centre consisting of 80,000 men was opposed to the French centre at Jena, and these were the only two divisions of their army engaged in the heat of the action. Their right, under general Ruehel, amounting to 12,000 men, did not arrive till their centre was thrown into disorder, and their rear-guard, commanded by the duke of Saxe-Weimar, was still at Meinungen, 30 miles distant from the field of battle. A thick fog obscured the early part of the day, and when it cleared up the two armies beheld each other at less than the distance of cannon-shot. The action began by some French batallions taking possession of a small village from which the Prussians attempted to dislodge them. Lasnes advanced to support his countrymen, and Soult obtained possession of a wood on his right occupied by the enemy. In less than an hour the action became general. Two hundred and fifty thousand men with 700 pieces of artillery, scattered death in every direction. The Prussian infantry behaved with courage and firmness; but their cavalry worn out, fatigued, and disheartened, did not justify their antient reputation. Both armies manœuvred with the same exactness as on a field-day, but the rapidity of the French evolutions astonished and bewildered the slow and systematic Prussians. Soult having obtained possession of the wood after a combat of two hours, pressed forward, and at the same instant the French reserve of cavalry and infantry advanced to the front line, which being thus strengthened, compelled the Russians to retire. They rallied and returned to the action, which they maintained for an hour, but were again thrown into confusion by the advance of the second French reserve, composed of the dragoons and cuirassiers under the grand duke of Berg. The charge of this body of reserve, at the close of the day, in conformity with a system which I shall shortly have occasion to notice, was irresistible. Neither cavalry nor infantry could withstand the shock. The ranks of the Prussians were broken, the artillery, cavalry, and infantry were all put to the rout, and the French reached Weimar as soon as their fugitive enemies.

While the Prussian centre and right were thus completely defeated, their left repulsed by Davoust, in its repeated attempts to drive him from the defiles of Kœseu, was forced, after a combat of several hours, to fall back upon Weimar, at the moment when the broken corps which had reached that city were attempting to retreat in the direction of Naumburg. The confusion arising from these opposing currents may be easily imagined, and the innumerable baggage-waggons that blocked up all the roads to Erfurt, impeded the retreat of the

troops, and compelled them to consult their safety by a precipitate and desultory flight. The king himself quitted the high road, and escaped from the scene of disorder across the fields. According to the French accounts more than 20,000 Prussians were killed and wounded in this disastrous action, and from 13,000 to 14,000 were taken prisoners, while the loss on their own side amounted only to 1100 killed, and 3000 wounded, an absurd and incredible computation, which has since been refuted by respectable authorities, who estimate the loss of the two armies, to have been nearly equal. The duke of Brunswick was mortally wounded, and no commander-in-chief remained to issue general orders to the army, a circumstance which contributed to augment the disasters of the retreat.

The fugitives who arrived at Erfurt amounting to 14,000 men surrendered on the following day to the duke of Berg, and among these was the prince of Orange. Another division of the Prussian army under general Kalkreuth attempted to escape in a body over the Hertz mountains, but was pursued as far as the village of Greusen, and defeated with loss. On the other side of Weimar prince Eugene of Wurtemburg, who was advancing with the Prussian reserve from Custrin was defeated, with the loss of 5000 prisoners, by the prince of Ponte Corvo.

The unfortunate king of Prussia arrived at Charlottenberg near Berlin, on the 17th of October, and continued his rout to Konigsberg. He was followed to Custrin by the garrison of Berlin, which was withdrawn on the 21st, and a provisional administration appointed to maintain the public tranquillity. Buonaparte had arrived on the 24th at Putzdam, where he stopped to examine the apartment and visit the tomb of the great Frederic. He ordered the sword of that great man, his scarf, the ribbon of his order, the black eagle, and all the colors which he took in the seven years' war, to be sent to the hotel of the invalids at Paris, as a present to the old soldiers who had served in the Hanoverian war. On the 27th he made his public entry into Berlin, where he distributed his favors and his punishments as caprice and interest might dictate. While these unexpected scenes astonished the peaceable citizens, the wreck of the Prussian army, under prince Hohenlohe, amounting to 40,000 men, marched for Stettin, after sending forward detachments of cavalry to destroy the bridges over which the French must pass to intercept his march. After a variety of detours and occasional skirmishes, they were overtaken as they reached the heights of Prenzlau, and, after a severe conflict, all hopes of reaching Stettin were extinguished. That city was seven German miles from Prenzlau; the Prussians were without bread or forage, and almost without ammunition; the French were preparing to renew the attack, and were hourly receiving reinforcements. In this emergency, prince Hohenlohe was reduced to the deplorable necessity of surrendering with the whole force under his command, amounting to 17,000 men, a disaster which was followed on the succeeding day by the surrender of an additional body of 6000 men, belonging to his army, which had pushed forward by a different rout to Pasewalk.

The rear of prince Hohenlohe's army, commanded by general Blucher, and amounting to 15,000 men, had the good fortune to join in the neighbourhood of Strelitz the corps of the duke of Weimar, amounting to 10,000 men, but he received, at the same time, the unwelcome news that Soult had crossed the Elbe, and was between him and that river with his army. Harassed and observed by the forces of Ponte Corvo, of Soult, and of the duke of Berg, he had no alternative but to throw himself into Lubeck, the gate of which was immediately stormed by his indefatigable enemy. A combat ensued in the streets and squares of the city, in which the Prussians were worsted, many of their army cut in pieces, and 4000 taken prisoners. The inhabitants were abandoned for some hours to the lust, cruelty, and rapacity of the conquerors. Blucher, after a gallant resistance, made good his retreat from the scene of horror and devastation, and reached the frontiers of Danish Holstein with

10,000 men; but, less able than ever to hazard an engagement, and not daring to violate the neutrality of Denmark, he surrendered, on the 8th of November, at Swarten, with all his forces. A body of 1600 Swedes, on their way home from Lauenburg, who had been detained by contrary winds at the mouth of the Trave, were also compelled to lay down their arms.

The fortresses of Prussia: Spandau, a place of considerable strength; Stettin, garrisoned by 6000 effective men, and defended by 160 pieces of cannon; Magdeburg, occupied by 20,000 troops; and Hameln, containing forces to the amount of 9000 men, were, to the astonishment of Europe, and the disgrace of the Prussian commanders, surrendered almost without a struggle. The treachery of the generals combined with the panic of the troops, and the battle of Averstadt seemed to have deprived the principal generals of their honesty or understanding.

Immediately after the battle of Averstadt, the king of Prussia had applied to Buonaparte for an armistice, and Luchesine was despatched to the French head-quarters, where a negotiation was commenced between him and Duroc. At first the Prussian minister was amused by the hope of concluding an honorable peace, but the demands of the French became more exhorbitant in proportion to the progress of their arms, and the emperor Napoleon, at length, explicitly declared, that he would never quit Berlin nor evacuate Poland, till Moldavia and Wallachia should be yielded to the Porte, and till a general peace was concluded on the basis of restoring all the Spanish, French, and Dutch colonies taken by Great Britain during the war. With this declaration vanished all expectations of peace, and an armistice was concluded, so dangerous and disgraceful, that the king of Prussia refused his ratification, and determined to persevere in his resistance, supported and reanimated by the co-operation of his Russian ally.

During these negotiations, the various corps of the French army crossed the

Odet early in November; the one under the command of marshal Davoust entered Posen early in that month; the other, consisting of the troops of Wurtemburg and Bavaria, with Jerome Buonaparte at their head, undertook the conquest of Silesia. But the panic, which had materially contributed to the surrender of the Prussian fortresses, began to subside; few of the traitorous and the profligate were stationed in the more distant or insulated towns, and Great Glogaw and Breslau did not surrender till after a gallant resistance.

The efforts of the French emperor to excite insurrection in Poland were comparatively ineffectual. Notwithstanding the circulation of various inflammatory papers, scarcely any indication was displayed of opposition to the existing government. In Russian Poland, all classes were resigned to their chains, and the nobles sacrificed the rights and the freedom of their country to indulgence in the pomps and revelries of St. Petersburgh.

While the grand French army was proceeding in this uninterrupted career of victory, an inferior army assembled at Wesel, under the command of Louis Buonaparte, lately created king of Holland, overran the Prussian provinces of Westphalia, and penetrated into the electorate of Hanover. The prince of Hesse, on various frivolous pretences, was expelled from his capital and dominions by marshal Mortier and the duke of Mecklenburg Schwerin, a relative of the emperor of Russia: the houses of Brunswick, Lunenburg, and Brunswick Wolfenbuttel, shared the same fate. On the 11th of December, the elector of Saxony was elevated to the dignity of king, and the other princes of the house of Saxe were permitted to enter the confederation of the Rhine. From Hesse and Hanover Mortier proceeded to Hamburg, on the 19th of November, where he sequestrated all the English produce and manufactures; the British merchants were placed under arrest, and the magazines of corn were immediately conveyed to Berlin; from which city Buonaparte promulgated, on the 20th of November, his memorable decree, by which the British

islands were declared to be in a state of blockade; all subjects of England found in countries occupied by French troops, were declared prisoners of war; all letters addressed to Englishmen or written in English, were ordered to be stopped; all commerce in English produce and manufactures was prohibited, and *all vessels touching at England or at any English colony*, were excluded from every harbor under the control of France. It was declared, at the same time, that the regulations of the decree should be regarded as a fundamental law of the French empire, till England should recognise the law of war to be one and the same by sea and land, and in no case applicable to private property, or to individuals not bearing arms; and till she consented to restrict the right of blockade to fortified places actually invested by a sufficient force. It is singular that the imperial promulgator of this decree should have forgotten or chosen to forget his own system of confiscations or contributions, or that he should not have felt the discordance between his theory on the subject of blockade, and the conditions of his own decree. Had the blockade of the British ports affected in its principle the English alone, it might have been regarded as a just but intemperate act of pretended retaliation, but it equally tended to injure and insult as far as its theory extended, (for its execution was impossible,) the neutral powers for whom Napoleon avowed the most considerate regard.

On receiving intelligence of the treaty of M. D'Oubril with France, the Ottoman government, alarmed at the progress of the French power, consented to send a special embassy to France, and to receive an ambassador in return, of whom Buonaparte demanded that the passage of the Bosphorus should be shut against the Russian ships of war, and threatened the Porte, in case of refusal, with the advance of a formidable French force already stationed in Dalmatia. The Russian ambassador, Italinski, informed that the Sublime Porte, intimidated by the denunciations of Buonaparte, had complied with his demands, threatened in his turn to relinquish all discussion on the topics immediately concerning Russia and Turkey: and the government of the latter power, with their accustomed imbecility, yielded a second time to their fears, reversed their late orders, and acceded to all the demands of Italinski. Notwithstanding these concessions, the Russian troops, under general Michelson suddenly entered Moldavia. But so unwilling was the Turkish government to engage in hostilities with Russia, that more than thirty days were suffered to elapse, before war was declared. At length a Russian brig which attempted to pass through the straits of Constantinople, was stopped by the Turkish vessels, and Italinski was permitted to depart from Constantinople, contrary to the usual practice of the Ottoman government, without molestation. The progress of Michelson in Wallachia, his entrance into Bucharest, and his threatened junction with the revolted Servians, still further exasperated the resentment of the lanquid and indolent divan, and in the extremity of their distress Paswan Oglon, the pacha of Widdin, who had been lately pursued and besieged as a rebel, was selected to oppose the further progress of the invasion.

Towards the end of November an English fleet of three ships of the line, and four frigates commanded by admiral Louis, made its appearance off Tenedos, and two vessels, the Canopus of 74 guns, and Endymion of 44, passed through the Dardanelles, without opposition, and cast anchor before Constantinople. The Canopus was afterwards employed in carrying away from that city the Russian ambassador Italinski. The Endymion kept its station before the Seraglio point; at the end of this year, and in the beginning of the next rendered a similar service to Mr. Arbuthnot the English ambassador, who yielding to his fears of Turkish violence unfortunately determined on quitting Constantinople, and abandoning the field of diplomatic warfare to the more successful and dexterous Sebastiani.

Towards the close of the present year the courts of inquiry, which had been appointed to investigate the conduct of the Austrian officers during the late campaign, concluded their labors. Many officers were degraded and dismissed from the service; the prince of Aversberg who had neglected to burn the bridge at Vienna, though he had received positive orders to destroy it, was condemned to ten years' imprisonment, and general Mack received sentence of death by the unanimous verdict of his judges. But the emperor remitted the capital part of his punishment, and mitigated the severity of several of the other sentences.

On the dissolution of the Germanic constitution the king of Denmark formally annexed Holstein to his other dominions, as an integral part of the Danish monarchy, declaring it to be for ever separated from the Germanic empire, and to owe no allegiance but to himself. By these and similar changes the whole system of continental relations was completely disorganized, and even the Dutch republic was converted into an arbitrary monarchy. Louis Buonaparte a younger brother of Napoleon was created king of Holland, and unwillingly dragged from the delights and frivolities of Paris, to superintend, in a foggy climate, the concerns of a laborious, parsimonious, and impoverished people. While Buonaparte was pursuing the discomfited Prussians, the king of Holland overran Westphalia and penetrated without opposition into Hanover, and upon his return issued a proclamation enforcing and confirming the principles of the Berlin decree.

On his return to Paris Buonaparte sojourned at Munich for a fortnight in order to be present at the marriage of his stepson, Eugene Beauhernois, with a princess of Bavaria; and in honor of the nuptials, declared Eugene his adopted son, and appointed him his successor in the kingdom of Italy. On his arrival at Paris he announced to the senate his intention of marrying the princess Stephanie Beaubarnois, niece of the empress Josephine, to the hereditary prince of Baden. On the 31st of March he submitted to the senate a variety of decrees for its approbation. He annexed the Venetian territories to the kingdom of Italy, conferred the — 1806.

kingdom of Naples on'his brother Joseph, bestowed the duchies of Berg and Cleves on his brother-in-law Murat, and the principality of Guastalla on his sister Paulina and her husband prince Borghese. He gave to Berthier the principality of Neufchatel, united to Lucca the countries of Massa, Carrara, and Garragnana, and created in Italy a number of duchies with suitable revenues, to be distributed among his civil and military officers. Some time afterwards the duchy of Benevento was erected into a fief of the French empire, and given to Talleyrand with the title of prince and duke of Benevento, and Bernadotte received the duchy of Ponte Corvo. Cardinal Fesch, uncle of Buonaparte, was appointed at the same time to be coadjutor and successor of the archbishop of Ratisbon, arch-chancellor of the Germanic empire. A new order of knighthood was instituted for the kingdom of Italy, called the order of the Iron Crown, and established on the footing of 200 knights' companions, besides commanders and higher dignities.

The civil labors of the French emperor during the present year were terminated by the convocation of a Jewish sanhedrim, or meeting of rabbis, in which its members were prevailed upon to acknowledge, that their laws concerning marriage and divorce were subordinate to the regulations of the civil magistrate, that their precepts respecting diet might be dispensed with in military service, or absence from home occasioned by any other cause ; that their present form of church government might be lawfully changed, having its origin merely in views of expediency, and that their prohibition, and in other cases their permission of usury related to charitable loans and not to mercantile transactions. In return for these explanations and concessions, the French government undertook to pay stipends to the Jewish priesthood, and succeeded in giving such a form to their church establishment, as ensured to the state a decided influence and command over their clergy. By this innovation a fourth religion was added to the three already established by law, and pensioned by the state. The Catholic, the Reformed, the Lutheran, and the Jewish faith were equally tolerated throughout the empire, by a sovereign, who, indifferent to the truths and interests of religion, was influenced in these arrangements by no other motive than a regard to the stability of his power.

It would be vain to expect the annual occurrence of an action so splendid and important as that of Trafalgar, yet the accustomed superiority of the British navy was maintained during the present year. Sir Thomas Duckworth fell in with a portion of the Brest squadron consisting of five ships of the line, two frigates, and a corvette, commanded by admiral Leisseg-nes, and cruizing in the bay of Occa ; the squadron of admiral Duckworth amounted to seven ships of the line, and four frigates. Alarmed by this disparity of force, the French commander endeavored to effect his escape, but the English vessels pursued him with success, and an action commenced, in which three of the French line of battle were captured, and two were burnt. The two French frigates and corvette put to sea during the heat of the action. The loss of the English was 64 killed, and 294 wounded, that of the French killed and wounded in the three captured vessels amounted to 760 men. Another division of the Brest squadron, commanded by admiral Villaumez, after being watched and pursued successively by admiral Cochrane, sir John Borlase Warren, and sir Thomas Lewis, were ordered by their commander to disperse in different directions. The Veteran of 74 guns commanded by Jerome Buonaparte, reached in safety the small harbor of Concarneau, on the coast of Brittany, under the protection of batteries, where, though the vessel was stranded, the stores and guns were saved, and the captain and crew were conveyed to shore. The admiral's ship the Foudroyant of 80 guns reached the Havannah (September 14th) under jury-masts, after an action with the Anson frigate of 40 guns. The Impeteneux, after having lost her masts, bowsprit, and rudder in a storm, which endangered the whole fleet, was standing in for the Chesapeake under jury-masts, when she was descried by the squadron of sir

Richard Strachan, and having run aground as she attempted to escape, was burned by the boats of the Melampus, and her crew made prisoners. Two other seventy-fours which arrived safely in the Chesa-peake, were afterwards destroyed by the English on the American coast, and the Cassant arrived safely at Brest in the middle of October. The French admiral Linois, who had so long wandered about the Indian seas, and carried on a most destructive and predatory war against our commerce in the east, was this year inter-cepted with his booty on his return to France, by sir John Borlase Warren, and brought to England with the Marengo of 80 guns, and the Belle Poule of 40 guns, the only ships under his command. Five large frigates and two corvettes, with troops on board for the West Indies, having es-caped from Rochefort, were intercepted by sir Samuel Hood, and, after a running fight of several hours, four of the five frigates were compelled to strike.

An expedition against the Cape of Good Hope had sailed from England in autumn, 1805, at the moment when hostilities were breaking out on the continent, and when, from the plan of operations concerted be-tween the British government and its allies, it might have been expected that the whole of our disposable force would have been employed in some continental diversion, in-stead of being directed to an object which, however valuable and important in itself, should never have been permitted to inter-fere with the deeper and more important game, in which we were engaged nearer home. But it was the constant error of Mr. Pitt's administration, to be engaged in the pursuit of two objects at once, and his misfortune and that of his country, that, in attempting both, he often succeeded in neither, and was sure always to fail in the most important. In the present instance, though Europe was lost, the Cape of Good Hope was taken and reduced under sub-jection to Great Britain.

The force destined for this conquest consisted of about 5000 land troops under sir David Baird, with a proportional naval force commanded by sir Home Popham.

Having touched at San Salvador for re-freshments, the expedition sailed from that place on the 26th of November, and reached Table bay on the 4th of January, 1806. It was the intention of the commanders to have disembarked the troops without de-lay; but, when the fleet arrived at its anchorage, the evening was too far ad-vanced to attempt a landing; and, next morning, the surf ran so high, that it was found impracticable to land the troops where it was first intended; nor could any safer or better landing-place be dis-covered, after a close examination of the shore from Lospard's bay to Cape town. In this emergency it was determined to go northward to Saldahna bay, about eigh-teen or twenty leagues distant from Table bay, and, however difficult the march from thence to Cape town, it was judged better to submit to that inconvenience than to hazard any further delay in disembarking the troops. In consequence of this deter-mination, brigadier-general Beresford was sent to Saldahna bay with the 38th regi-ment and 20th light dragoons, the rest of the army being ordered to follow him; but the next morning the surf was so much abated, that it was resolved to land the army at Lospard's bay, as at first intended. The disembarkation was conducted with great order, under the protection of the fleet, and, though a few sharp-shooters ap-peared on the heights, and somewhat an-noyed the troops, only two persons were wounded by their fire, and the landing would have been attended with no greater loss than this, but for the accident of a boat upsetting, by which 35 soldiers were drowned. The whole of the army having landed on this and the following day, ex-cept the detachment sent to Saldahna bay with general Beresford, sir David Baird began his march to Cape town on the morning of the 8th, and, having reached the summit of the Blue mountains, he there descried the enemy drawn up in the plain, and prepared to receive him. They were commanded by general Jansseus, governor of the colony, and their force amounted to about 5000 men, chiefly cavalry. Their position was good, and strengthened by 23 pieces of cannon. The force under sir David Baird amounted to about 4000 men. The necessary dispositions having been made for the attack, the action was begun by Brigadier Ferguson's brigade, which advanced against the enemy's left, under a heavy but ill directed fire of musketry and grapeshot. The Dutch received the British fire without quitting their ground; but, at the moment of charging, they gave way, and fled from the field with precipitation. In this action, the loss of the enemy exceeded 700 killed and wounded, while that of the British army amounted to 15 killed, and 197 wounded and missing.

After this engagement, there remained no obstacles to impede the progress of the army under sir David Baird, except such as arose from the scarcity of water and want of provisions, or from the natural difficulties of the country through which they had to pass. They reached the Salt river on the 9th, where they proposed to encamp, but a flag of truce having arrived from the town with offers to capitulate, the articles were soon settled, and the troops put in possession of Fort Knocke the same evening. Next day the capitulation was signed, and the town surrendered.

After the battle of the 8th, general Janssens retired with a body of forces to Hottentot Holland's Kloof, a pass leading to the district of Zwellendam, and seemed disposed to maintain himself in the interior against the English. But general Beresford having caused a body of troops to be sent against him, he was prevailed to surrender upon terms by which the conquest of the colony was completed, and its internal tranquillity secured. By the articles of capitulation signed with general Beresford, it was settled that general Janssens and his army should be sent back to Holland, and not considered as prisoners of war, in return, for the complete surrender of the colony and its dependencies.

Sir Home Popham, the naval commander employed against the Cape, had contributed materially to the expedition being undertaken, by the intelligence he had communicated to his majesty's government of the defenceless state of that important colony, and of the probability that it would soon be reinforced from Europe. He had also, in common with other naval officers, been occasionally consulted by Mr. Pitt and lord Melville about their designs on South America, and, at their desire, he had conferred with general Miranda on that officer's views and projects in this quarter. The result of these communications had been his appointment to the command of the Diadem of 64 guns, in 1806, for the purpose of co-operating with general Miranda, to the extent of taking advantage of any of his proceedings, which might tend to our attaining a position on the continent of South America, favorable to the trade of this country. But he had been afterwards given distinctly to understand, that, from deference to Russia, all projects of that nature had been for the present abandoned. Forgetful, however, of his duty as an officer, he determined to employ the whole of the force stationed off the Cape in some important enterprise on the Rio Plata, and obtained from sir D. Baird a small body of troops under general Beresford, with which he sailed from the Cape about the middle of April, leaving that settlement without an armed vessel to protect it from insult, and directed his course to St. Helena, where he obtained a small reinforcement to his little army, which did not even now exceed 1600 men, including marines. With this force, so inadequate to the importance of his enterprise, he steered for the Rio Plata, and arrived before Buenos Ayres on the 24th of June. On the next day, he disembarked without resistance, at the Punta de Quilsnes, drove before him, the next morning, a body of Spaniards, and captured their artillery. No other obstacle occurred after this success, except the passage of a river between the army and Buenos Ayres; but this object being effected with the aid of rafts and boats, general Beresford entered the city on the 27th, the viceroy having previously fled to Cordova, with the small body of troops under his command. About 1,200,000 dollars of public money were found in the town and sent to England, and public property in quicksilver and Jesuit's bark, to the value of 2,800,000 dollars, was seized for the benefit of the captors, but before it was secured on board the English vessels, the place was retaken by the enemy.

I have already noticed the extravagant joy and delusive expectations, which the news of the capture of Buenos Ayres diffused through every part of the British empire. A circular manifesto from sir Home Popham to the principal mercantile cities announcing and certainly not under-rating the value of the market be had opened, spread widely and rapidly the most exaggerated notions of his conquest; and led, as was naturally to be expected from so unusual and unprecedented an address from such authority, to many rash and improvident mercantile speculations, in which the adventurers had reason afterwards deeply to lament their credulity. The delusion was universal, and allowing much for ignorance and want of reflection, incredibly and unaccountably great.

Long before the system proper to be followed came to be discussed in the British cabinet, that settlement was in the hands of the enemy. The Spaniards had been taken by surprise and beaten by a handful of men, because attacked where they were unprepared for resistance; but no sooner had they recovered from their panic and discovered the smallness of the number of of their opponents, than, ashamed of their defeat, they began to concert measures to expel their invaders. Emissaries from Buenos Ayres excited the country people to arms, and an insurrection was organized in the heart of the city, under the eye of the British commander-in-chief, which seems to have escaped his vigilance till it had arrived at maturity and was ripe for action. Liniers a French colonel in the Spanish service, crossed the river in a fog, unobserved by the English cruizers, and landed at Conchas, above Buenos Ayres, bringing with him about 1000 men from Monte Video and Sacramento. Encouraged by this reinforcement the armed levies from the country, which had been defeated by general Beresford in a sally, advanced again to the city and summoned the castle

to surrender. The whole inhabitants of the town were now in arms, and the danger appeared so imminent, that the English had determined to evacuate the place and retire to their ships; but they were prevented by the state of the weather, and assembled on the 12th in the streets and great square of the town, in which they were attacked with incredible fury, were annoyed by a destructive fire from the windows and balconies of the houses, and were compelled to lay down their arms. The terms on which they surrendered became afterwards a subject of dispute and recrimination between generals Beresford and Liniers, who acted as commander-in-chief of the Spaniards. This much only is certain, that the English, contrary to the articles of capitulation signed by Liniers, were detained prisoners of war, and marched up the country. The loss of the British in the action of the 12th amounted to 165 killed, wounded, and missing besides 1300 made prisoners. Thus terminated the first expedition to Buenos Ayres, and such were the bitter fruits of an enterprise undertaken without authority and originating in a breach of public duty, which, though alleviated by circumstances, was judged, by a court-martial, to be highly censurable, and for the general good of his majesty's service deserving of a severe reprimand.

Sir Home Popham, the author of all these calamities was on board of ship when the city was retaken; after which with the squadron under his command he continued to blockade the river, till the arrival of troops from the Cape of Good Hope, enabled him to recommence offensive operations. He then attempted in the first place to make himself master of Monte Video, but finding it impossible for his ships to get near enough to batter the walls, he was forced to desist from this enterprise. A body of troops was then landed at Maldonado, under colonel Vassal, and the Spaniards having been driven from that place, and from the isle of Goritti, a sufficient space was gained for the encampment of the troops, and a tolerably safe anchorage procured for the ships. In this situation an army in South America remained at the end of the present year, receiving successive reinforcements from England and the Cape, and preparing for further, and, as it proved, still more disastrous operations.

The United States of America continued to prosper under the pacific administration of Mr. Jefferson, and protected by their neutrality which in the midst of so many belligerent powers, they were still able, though with difficulty, to maintain. They extended their trade and navigation beyond all further example. From the 11th of October, 1805, till the 30th of September following, their exports were valued at 101,000,000 of dollars, of which 41,000,000 were in native commodities, and the rest in foreign goods re-exported. Their revenue arising almost entirely from the receipt of customs, which, in 1805, had not exceeded 13,000,000 of dollars, rose in 1806 to near 15,000,000. The reduction of their national debt proceeded as rapidly as the conditions upon which it had been contracted would permit, and at the close of the year the sum actually redeemed amounted to 23,000,000 of dollars, more than two-thirds of what remained due. The tranquillity of their interior frontier was secured by the wise and just policy of their government towards the native tribes, whose esteem and confidence it had gained by the unvarying rectitude of its conduct in all its transactions with them, and by its unceasing attention to promote their happiness and welfare. So successful had been its exertions in eradicating the prejudices, and softening the character of these savages, that many of their tribes were engaged in the pursuits of agriculture and household manufacture, and some had disposed of part of their territory, to purchase the means of improving the remainder, and enable them to subsist their families, while preparing their farms. In the prosecution of this wise and laudable policy, the brightest part by far of Mr. Jefferson's administration, he was powerfully seconded by his precursors in this beneficent work, the Quakers of Pennsylvania, who had been for some years diligently employed in inspiring the American savages with a taste for the comforts of civilized life, and

in teaching them arts which they had formerly rejected and despised. A treaty of peace between the regency of Tripoli and the United States had rendered the navigation of the Mediterranean more secure to the citizens of the latter, than it had been at any period since the declaration of their independence; and though a misunderstanding had arisen with the regency of Tunis, it served rather as an excuse for not withdrawing their squadron from the European seas, than as a ground of seriously apprehending the renewal of hostilities with that power. Nothing, then, seemed necessary to consolidate the pacific system of Mr. Jefferson, but an amicable adjustment of the disputes between the United States, and the governments of Spain and England. For as to France, great as were the outrages of her marauding squadrons on the ships and commerce of America, Mr. Jefferson never ventured to allude to them in his addresses to congress, though he expatiated largely on every species of injury sustained from England, and inveighed bitterly against the new principles of maritime law, which he accused her of having interpolated in the law of nations.

The differences between Spain and the United States arose partly from the illegal capture of American vessels by Spanish cruizers during the late war, and partly out of the uncertainty of the limits of Louisiana. The Spanish minister for foreign affairs, had signed a convention at Madrid in 1802, which admitted that the Americans were entitled to compensation for injuries done to their commerce by subjects of Spain, and settled that commissioners should be mutually named to investigate their claims. But, before this convention was sent back from Washington, the approbation of congress, the sale of Louisiana and other events had taken place, which determined the Spanish government to refuse to ratify it, without the insertion of additional articles to which the Americans would not accede. The sale of Louisiana to the United States contrary to the solemn promise of the French government, never to alienate that province without the knowledge and consent of Spain, had alarmed and offended the court of Madrid, and drawn from it some ineffectual remonstrances, which however, with its usual weakness and timidity, it addressed not to Paris but to Washington. While indisposed by this transaction towards the Americans, and jealous of their views on its colonies, it learned with surprise that congress had laid claim to a considerable port of Florida, as included in the cession of Louisiana, and had passed an act, empowering the president of the United States to erect fortifications, construct ports, and build custom-houses in districts, which, in the apprehension of the Spaniards, were clearly parts of the Spanish territory. It was at this moment that the convention of 1802 was brought back to Madrid for ratification; and in such circumstances it is not surprising that the Spanish government refused to confirm this agreement until all matters in discussion between the two nations were finally adjusted; nor does it appear to me that in the refusal they acted unwisely or unfairly. There could be no obligation on the Spaniards to make compensation to the Americans for past injuries, while the Americans were committing injuries on the Spaniards. If Spanish cruizers had illegally captured the vessels of Americans, the Americans had encroached on the territories of Spain, and this encroachment had not been the unauthorised act of a private individual, but the effect of a solemn enactment of the legislature. The reality of this injury, it is true, was denied by the Americans, who contended that the territory claimed by the Spaniards was part of Louisiana; but, till the limits of that province were settled, the Spaniards, who were in possession of debatable ground, were entitled to retain it, and to resent any attempts of the American government to dispossess them. It was clear from the language and conduct of the Americans, that the acquisition of one or both the Floridas was an object on which they were bent; and, having succeeded so well in obtaining Louisiana from France in exchange for a sum of money and an old debt of the national convention, there was but too much reason to suspect that they had formed a

similar project with respect to the Floridas; that, aware of the pecuniary embarrassments of the court of Madrid, they pressed forward their commercial claims, not for the purpose of procuring indemnification to the individuals who had been injured, but with a view of terrifying by the magnitude of their demands, and possibly of bribing, by the offer of an immediate supply of money, that needy and profligate court. It was quite consistent with such an indirect course of proceeding in the American government, that it raised pretensions to a considerable district in Florida; for, though its claim might not bear examination, it would facilitate a negotiation for the cession or purchase of the province, and keep out of sight the true nature of the transaction.

Such being the views of the Americans, it does credit to the penetration and address of Cevallos, the Spanish minister, that he detected and defeated their design, by refusing to proceed in the question of pecuniary compensation, till the territorial limits were first adjusted. In this state had the Spaniards and Americans continued since 1804, the Spaniards keeping possession of the river Mobile and other parts of West Florida claimed by the United States, and refusing to execute the convention of 1802, till the American government renounced its unjust pretensions upon Florida; while the president, in his annual reports in congress, contented himself with compliments to his own moderation, and contrasting it with the violence and obstinacy of Spain. At one time, indeed, in the course of the year, it seemed as if the disputes between the two countries were proceeding to extremities. A body of Spaniards entered Louisiana from the side of Mexico, and took a position in an old French settlement on the Red river, which clearly belonged to the United States. But in consequence of the remonstrances of the Americans against this aggression, accompanied by threats of more active hostility, the Spanish commander was induced to fall back upon the Sabine river, and this river was afterwards fixed upon by mutual consent, as the line of separation between the troops of the two nations, till the provinces should be settled by authority.

The complaints of the United States against Great Britain related to our practice of impressing British seamen found on board of their merchant-vessels upon the high seas ; to our violation of their neutral rights by seizing and condemning their merchantmen, though engaged in a lawful commerce ; and to our infringement of their maritime jurisdiction upon their coasts.

The third ground of complaint on the part of the Americans was of infinitely less importance than the others, and their demand to have their maritime jurisdiction defined and respected, was so just and reasonable, that no objection could be made to it. An unfortunate accident, in which an American seaman happened to be killed, within sight of New York, by a shot from the British armed vessel, the Leander, had drawn attention to this subject, and rendered some regulation indispensible ; but no difficulty could occur in settling a point which was already settled by the law of nations. The affair of the Leander having taken place during the elections at New York, great use was made of it by the federal party to excite odium against the president, and bring discredit upon his administration, on pretence that foreigners were encouraged to commit such outrages by their knowledge of the weakness and timidity of his government. To counteract these designs, Mr. Jefferson issued a violent proclamation, accusing of murder the captain of the Leander, and prohibiting that, and some other British vessels, from entering the harbors, or remaining within the jurisdictional limits of the United States. The captain of the Leander was afterwards tried in England for the murder of the American seaman, and acquitted.

As the conferences which were held in London for the adjustment of these differences by Mr. Mouroe and Mr. Pinkney, on the part of the United States, and by lord Holland and lord Auckland on the part of Great Britain, though brought to a conclusion before the close of 1807, terminated in a treaty, from which the president of the United States thought proper to withhold his ratification, it will be unnecessary to enter minutely into the results of the negotiation. It appears, however, from the papers since published and laid before parliament, that the commissioners on both sides were animated by a sincere desire of establishing a firm and lasting friendship between the two countries on terms the most advantageous to both. After many fruitless conferences, held in the hope of devising some adequate substitute for the practice of impressing on the high seas, they consented, contrary as it appears to their instructions, to proceed in the other articles of the treaty, without any further satisfaction upon this head, than an official paper from lord Holland and lord Auckland, pledging the government of Great Britain to issue instructions for the observance of the greatest caution in their impressment of seamen. In the other questions between the two countries, the negotiators were more fortunate in bringing their labors to a successful issue. On the subject of the circuitous trade permitted to the United States between the colonies of the enemy and other parts of the world, an article was framed which satisfied the American commissioners, by substituting a clear and precise rule for the regulation of that commerce, in place of the uncertain and changeable system under which it had hitherto been conducted. The principle of this article was taken from lord Hawkesbury's communication to Mr. Rufus King, defining the difference between a continuous and an interrupted voyage ; but, besides requiring as in that communication, that the goods should be landed, and the duties paid in the neutral country, this article expressly stipulated, that on re-exportation, there should remain after the drawback, a duty of one per cent. ad valorem on all articles of the growth, produce, and manufacture of Europe, and on all articles of colonial produce, a duty of not less than two per cent. ad valorem. The maritime jurisdiction of the United States was guaranteed by another article against the alleged encroachments and violations of his majesty's cruizers, and on account of the peculiar circumstances of the American coast, an extention of maritime jurisdiction to the distance of five miles from shore, was mutually conceded by both parties in the American seas, on certain conditions, and with certain limitations expressed in the treaty. On the other articles of the treaty, it is only necessary to add, that the commercial stipulations contained in it appear to have been framed on the fairest and most liberal principles of reciprocal advantages and utility to the two countries.

The appointment of marquis Cornwallis to be governor-general of Bengal, was calculated to produce the most beneficial and important consequences. At an advanced period of life, and with a constitution broken by infirmities, this excellent and respectable nobleman was induced to take a voyage to India, with little prospect of ever revisiting his native country. Holkar was still in arms, and Scindiah, dissatisfied with our conduct, or jealous of our designs, had imprisoned our resident, and only waited for a favorable opportunity to recommence hostilities. Lord Cornwallis immediately proceeded to take the command of the army, and had reached Gazypour in Benares, when death deprived his country of his services. He was succeeded in his functions by sir George Barlow, the second in council, who, after a short negotiation, concluded advantageous treaties with Holkar and Scindiah. But neither the talents nor the temper of this gentleman were adapted to the importance of his office, and his total indifference to the feelings of the population over which he was called to govern, was productive of the most injurious and alarming consequences. An attempt was made by his orders to change the shape of the sepoy turban into something resembling the helmet of European light infantry, and to prevent the native troops from wearing on their foreheads the marks of their respective casts. These innovations would in themselves have excited the indignation and alarm of the sepoys; but their resentment

knew no bounds when a report was industriously circulated, that the British government had determined, by forcible means, to convert them to Christianity. On the 10th of July, about two o'clock in the morning, the European barracks at Vellore, containing four complete companies of the 69th regiment, were surrounded by two battalions of sepoys in the company's service, who poured in a heavy fire of musketry at every door and window, upon the soldiers. At the same time the European sentries, the soldiers at the main guard, and the sick in the hospital, were put to death. The officer's houses were ransacked, and their unfortunate occupants murdered. Upon the arrival of the 19th light dragoons under colonel Gillespie, the sepoys were immediately attacked; 600 were cut down upon the spot, and 200 taken from their hiding-places and shot. Of the four European companies, 164 perished, including officers; and many British officers of the native troops were massacred by the insurgents. Subsequent to this explosion, there was a mutiny at Nundydroog, and in one day 450 Mahometan sepoys were disarmed and expelled the fort. A spirit of general and determined disaffection was visible at Bangalore, and prevailed throughout the adjacent country, to a degree which threatened the tranquillity and existence of our Indian empire.

The critical situation of our eastern dominions, and every other subject of foreign and domestic policy, were now absorbed in the general sensation excited by the death of Mr. Fox. Endowed by nature with unusual vigor of constitution, that illustrious statesman, notwithstanding his various and continued irregularities, had enjoyed uninterrupted health till about two years before his death. Having in the summer of 1804 made free use of the waters of Cheltenham, he was, soon after, seized with a pain in his right side, and was afterwards subject to a disorder of the bowels. In the beginning of 1806, he attended the funeral of lord Nelson, and, being then exposed for many hours to the cold, was seized with a return of his complaint, which was considerably aggravated by the fatigues and anxieties of his official station. It was at length thought necessary by his physicians to have recourse to a surgical operation for his relief, which was repeated after an interval of three weeks. On Monday the 7th of September, he sunk into an alarming state of insensibility and depression, in which he languished till the evening of Saturday the 13th, when he expired. He retained to the last his senses and understanding; and retained, till a short time before his death, confident hopes of his recovery. The latent cause of his death was a schirrus affection of the liver.

Thus died, a few months after his illustrious rival, one of the most eminent statesmen, and distinguished advocates of public freedom, that has appeared in England. He derived from nature a vigorous capacity which was early improved by a liberal education. His conceptions were rapid, his fancy brilliant, the indulgence of his father gave him an open and fearless address, and a continual intercourse with the circles of gaiety and fashion, rendered his expression fluent, unconstrained, and elegant. He seemed born an orator. His temper frank, candid, and generous, was calculated to gain him many friends, and to disarm the animosity of every enemy. There was nothing in it to inspire awe, or to excite distrust, no one was thrown to an uncomfortable distance. He was born " to write, converse, and live with ease," and to communicate the most agreeable feelings to all around him.

His more advanced education tended to discourage the sanguine expectations of his friends. His youth was a continued course of dissipation. . Those hours of vigor and ardor which ought to have been spent in the labors of the closet, were devoted to the gaming table, the amour, and the midnight debauch.

His introduction into political life was not peculiarly fortunate. His father enjoyed the reputation of abilities, yet had sunk under the talents and integrity of Chatham. But if Fox derived some stain from his parentage, his own conduct was not

calculated to remove the blot, and while the people admired the brilliance of his parts, they wondered and lamented that so much genius should be united with so little prudence or virtue.

During the American war he had derived much popularity from his resolute and violent opposition to lord North; but when this nobleman and his friends passed over to the party of Fox, and were by him received with his usual facility and frankness, the people regarded their patriot as guilty of the most unprincipled dishonesty, in cordially uniting with a man whom he lately pursued with the most opprobrious invective. When Great Britain interfered to oppose the conquering arms of Russia, the friends of monarchy were alarmed and incensed at the conduct of Mr. Fox, who not only opposed the measures of administration at home, but sent abroad an accredited agent to thwart the views of government. On the lamented illness of the sovereign, his activity was obnoxious to the people at large, and to many of his friends. At the commencement of the French revolution, Fox, in conformity with his principles, applauded the first movements of the Parisians. The excesses which ensued, changed the general opinion; the best principles became abhorred when found in the mouths of atrocious villains; and, in the ideas of the multitude, Fox became associated with those who spoke the same language, however different their intentions and actions. The consternation was diffused throughout the kingdom, and no one seemed worthy of the public trust who did not revile Fox as an enemy to his country. His own imprudence was indeed scarcely less fatal to his interests, than the arts of his adversaries. He gave too free access to men of profligate characters and dark designs, and degraded himself to a level with the lowest demagogues by haranguing motley mobs in the fields around London. His patriotism became more suspected when he declared his country to be in extreme danger, and then took the unmanly resolution of abandoning her councils, and retiring to ease and inactivity. These acts have been

THE RIGHT HONORABLE CHARLES JAMES FOX.

Published by I. Hinnersley Feb 1, 1815.

attributed to that facility of temper which led him to comply with the persuasions of men whom he ought to have despised, but this apology only defends his heart, at the expense of his head.

The same lamentable facility characterised his accession to unexpected power. His first act in the house of commons, as a minister, was the introduction of a bill to enable a colleague to possess at the same time two important, rich, and incompatible offices. He seemed to feel his own degradation; he seemed conscious that he was setting at defiance all his former professions, and trampling to dust the glory of his life. His countenance reddened, and his voice became choked with shame and anger, when his adversaries reminded him of his repeated inconsistencies; the worst measure of his predecessors, the property-tax, which he had reprobated as the most impolitic and oppressive of all exactions, he now supported as an ingenious device, and defended an augmentation of its injustice and oppression.

The general opinion of Fox's personal licentiousness was the greatest obstacle to his fortunes and his reputation, and he was believed to be the principal instrument in polluting that spring from which the nation expected its future happiness to flow. Even the moral act by which he closed his gayer career, (his marriage with Mrs. Armstead,) excited the most severe and general reprehension. However reclaimed and meritorious might be the object of his choice, yet it appeared too shocking for decorum, that the wife of a great statesman should be an improper companion for any honest matron.

His eloquence was the grand foundation of his fame. He had to struggle with the disadvantages of appearance. His figure was unpromising, his motions ungraceful, his voice shrill, and his enunciation at the commencement of his speech indistinct, and hesitating. But as he grew warm his words began to flow, his enunciation became clear and forcible, his countenance glowed with ardor, and every motion indicated the force of his feelings. He hastened directly to his subject. It seemed to occupy his whole soul, and to call forth every power of imagination and judgment. He was irresistibly hurried on by his emotions, and his hearers were hurried along with him. In whatever he said there was an air of candor and earnestness, which irresistibly impressed his audience with a conviction of his sincerity. By the rapidity and strength of his conceptions, he was enabled to place his subject in the clearest light, and he possessed an unusual facility of calling to his assistance the resources with which books or conversation had supplied him. His wit was very successful, and his sarcasms peculiarly poignant, but they were not delivered with bitterness, and were on most occasions as just as they were severe.

Yet his eloquence was not free from the vices to which it was naturally subjected by his habits. His orations were never regular or skilfully arranged. The hearer borne along by his warmth, did not discover his desultory transactions, but on recollection found it difficult to trace the maze which he had traversed. As he always trusted to the moment, his exhibitions depended much on the state of his spirits, and it was not uncommon to see him labor through a hesitating, devious discourse, which scarcely retained the attention of his hearers. His early dissipation, and the narrowness of his private fortune, involved him in perpetual difficulties which embarrassed his mind, and subjected him to the most humiliating dependance. The expedient of a general contribution of his friends, by which his difficulties were at length removed, gave an irrecoverable blow to his respectability. His most enthusiastic admirers, could not behold without some revolution of sentiment, the idol of their attachment, degraded into a suppliant for their alms.

His inviolable attachment to peace was the noblest trait in his public character. Even his most determined enemies lamented his death, when they saw the negotiations which had owed their birth entirely to him, expire *as our only, minister of peace* expired.

The account of his death was received

at court with coldness and indifference, and such inquiries into the particulars of that event, as curiosity dictated, were studiously addressed to those who, from their intimate connection with him, were the least likely to receive from them gratification, or consider them as marks of an interest in his fate. No haste was expressed to fill up the vacancy occasioned by his death. It was rather desired that due consideration should precede the formation of the new ministerial arrangements, which that event rendered necessary. But if expectations were harbored that lord Grenville, on whom the suggestion of the new arrangements naturally devolved, would take this opportunity of separating from Mr. Fox's friends, they were completely disappointed. That nobleman seems, on the contrary, to have taken pains to shew that his attachment to his new associates had been strengthened, instead of being impaired by their connection, and that even an event like this, which left him the choice of his future partners in the government, was insufficient to detach him from them. He recommended lord Howick to succeed Mr. Fox in the foreign office; Mr. Grenville to be first lord of the admiralty in the place of lord Howick; Mr. Tierney to be president of the board of control in the place of Mr. Grenville, who had succeeded to that office with a cabinet place, on the appointment of lord Minto to the government of Bengal; lord Sidmouth to succeed to the presidency of the council, from which lord Fitzwilliam, on account of bad health, was desirous to withdraw; and lord Holland to succeed lord Sidmouth, as lord privy-seal. In these appointments it is worthy of remark, that lord Holland, the nephew of Mr. Fox, was the only new member brought into the cabinet.

The returns to the new parliament were such as greatly to add to the weight and influence of the friends of administration in the house of commons. The Whig party,

which had been driven out of the representation of Yorkshire, in 1784, recovered one of the seats for that great and independent county. In Norfolk, after a hard-fought contest, both members returned were Whigs. One of the seats for Liverpool was carried by the abolitionists against the traffickers in human flesh. But, on the other hand, a friend of administration was turned out of the representation of Southwark, and another lost the city of Norwich. Westminster was the scene of a most violent contest between a friend of government and a discontented Whig; and one of the seats for Middlesex was lost to the popular party, by a wanton and personal attack of sir Francis Burdett on the memory of Mr. Fox.

Ireland enjoyed tranquillity during the greater part of the present year, under the mild and conciliatory government of the duke of Bedford. It may be questioned, indeed, whether the system of conciliation, pursued by that amiable and excellent nobleman, was not carried further than prudence justified, or popular discontent could bear. Since the catholics could not be gratified with the restoration of their privileges, they ought to have been soothed by the public and marked disgrace of their enemies, and relieved from future apprehension by purging, without delay, the magistracy of their oppressors and persecutors. Towards the close of the year, disturbances broke out in the north-west of Ireland, occasioned by a banditti, who went about in the night time, under the name of threshers, committing every sort of crime and outrage. Strong applications were made to the castle to have these disturbances put down by the insurrection law, the usual remedy in Ireland on such occasions; but the duke of Bedford refused to have recourse, without necessity, to so violent a measure; and, by proper use of the ordinary and regular authority of government, he succeeded in repressing and putting a stop to these excesses.

HISTORY OF THE WAR.

A comparative Estimate of the Russian, French, Prussian, and Austrian Armies, as far as relates to the Principle of their Manœuvres, and their qualifications for the Military profession—Character and Military System of Suwarrow—Illustration of Buonaparte's Principle of Reserves, and causes of his Extraordinary Success.

THE character of the Russian troops has been so little understood, and so unjustly calumniated, that an impartial statement of their manners, their discipline, and their military qualifications, and a comparison in these points between the organization of the Russian and the other armies of Europe, will at once do justice to a calumniated race of men, and assist the judgment while it gratifies the curiosity of the reader.

The Russian infantry is generally composed of athletic men, between the ages of eighteen and forty, endowed with great bodily strength, but generally of short stature, with martial countenance and complexion ; inured to the extremes of weather and hardship, to the worst and scantiest food, to marches for days and nights, of four hours' repose and six hours' progress ; accustomed to laborious toils, and the carriage of heavy burdens ; ferocious, but disciplined ; obstinately brave, and susceptible of enthusiastic excitements ; devoted to their sovereign, their chief, and their country.—Patient, docile, and obedient ; possessing all the energetic characteristics of a barbarian people, with the advantages engrafted by civilization.

The untrained Russian also, like the Briton, undaunted while he can front the danger, disdains the protection of favoring ground, or the example of his adversary, and presents his body exposed from head to foot, either to the aim of the marksman or the storm of the cannonade.

No carnage intimidates the survivors ; bullets may destroy, but the aspect of death awes not, even when a commander's evident error has assigned the fatal station. " Comrades, go not forward into the trenches !" cried out a retiring party to an advancing detachment; " retreat with us or you will be lost, for the enemy are in possession." " Prince Potemkin must look to that, for it was he that gave us the order : come on Russians," replied the commander. He and his men marched forward, and perished the victims of their courageous sense of duty.

The Russian, nurtured from earliest infancy to consider Russia as the supreme nation of the world, always regards himself as an important component part of the irresistible mass. Suwarrow professed the principle, and, profiting of the prejudice, achieved, with the most inadequate means, the most splendid success ; and, whilst he was more regardless of their blood than any of his predecessors or contemporaries, he was affectionately endeared to every soldier as his parent ; and national pride and personal admiration, have deified his memory as the presiding god of their battles

An acquaintance with the composition of his armies, a knowledge of their insignificant numerical strength, the assurance of the internal impediments that he had to encounter, so much augment the merit of his exploits, that he is entitled, to the reputation of one of the first captains of any age or nation. His very eccentricities were characteristics of his superiority of intelligence. They affected his estimation amongst superficial observers, but he disdained the sneer of the less enlightened, and steadily persevered in the course that his wisdom had traced for the attainment of his patriotic ambition. His unmerited disgrace broke a heart of which the vital principles were glory and loyalty, but neither the folly of the sovereign, nor the *vultus instantis tyranni* could restrain the tears or check the emotions of a soldiery who bewailed his loss as an irreparable affliction. Such was their enthusiastic affection for him, that when the coffin in which his body was conveying into the church of the citadel to be deposited near the remains of the great Catherine, was jammed in the doorway, and instruments were ordered to wrench a passage—one of the grenadier bearers, indignant at the check, exclaimed " What is all this? *Nothing* could resist Suwarrow *living*, and *nothing* shall resist him *dead*." The sentiment was hailed as a just tribute to the invincible character of their chief. That consciousness supplied strength to zeal, and the remains of Suwarrow were borne triumphant to the grave !

Amidst the Russian qualities the love of country is also pre-eminent, and inseparable from the Russian soldier. This feeling is paramount, and in the very last hour his gaze is directed towards its nearest confines. The wounded drag their mangled bodies over the field to expire with more satisfaction in the effort of approaching their native boundaries, and the principle of patriotism has sometimes superseded even the impulse of humanity.

When general Beningzen was retiring upon Eylau, considerable numbers of stragglers formed, what they denominated, corps of marauders, who placing themselves under the orders of chiefs chosen by themselves, lived by violence till an opportunity offered for a return to Russia. A party of Russian officers who had been taken at Landsberg, were marching to Prague on parole, but under the charge of some French

officers ; a corps of marauders surprised them and after some violence the Russian soldiers were indiscriminately proceeding to despatch the French, when their officers interfered, and endeavoured to explain that as these French were but an amicable escort to them, who had given their parole, their lives must not only be preserved, but that honor obliged the Russian officers to refuse the opportunity of release, and bound them to proceed as prisoners of war till regularly exchanged. The marauder captain stepped forward, " Will you" addressing himself to the Russian officers, " join and command us and conduct us to our country ? If so we are bound to obey you, but with this annexed condition, that you do not interfere with our intention of putting to death the French who are in your company." " No, we cannot," was the answer, and arguments were urged to justify the propriety of their decision. The marauders then assembled as a court-martial ; and after some deliberation the captain readvanced and delivered its sanguinary decree. " The French for their atrocious conduct to Russian prisoners on every occasion have merited death ; execute the sentence !" Obedience was immediate, and the victims were successively shot. This lawless assassination completed, silence was again ordered, and the leader resumed his harangue. " Now, degenerate Russians, receive your reward, you forgetting that you were born so, that your country has a prescriptive right to your allegiance, and that you have voluntarily renewed it to your sovereign, have entered into new engagements with their most hated enemies, and you have dared to advance in your defence that your *word* must be binding in their service when you violate the *oath* you have sworn against them. You are therefore our worst enemies; more wicked, more unnatural, than those whom we have just slain, and you have less claim upon our mercy. We have unanimously doomed you to death, and instant death awaits you." The signal was immediate, and fourteen officers were thus massacred for a persevering virtue, of which history does not record a more affecting and honourable trait. The fifteenth (colonel Arslnoeff, of the imperial guards) was supposed dead, the ball of the musquet having entered just above the throat. He was stripped and the body abandoned on the frozen and freezing snow. Towards night after several hours' torpor, sense returned, and whilst he was contemplating the horror of the past and present scene, identified, not only by his own condition, but still more painfully by the surrounding corpses of his mangled friends, and momentarily becoming more terrific, from the apprehension of a horrible and solitary death, he perceived a light towards which he staggered with joyous expectation, but when he approached the hut a clamor of voices alarmed his attention. He listened and recognized his carousing murderers! He withdrew from imminent destruction to a fate, as he then supposed, not less certain, but less rude and revolting. He had still sufficient strength to gain the borders of a no very distant wood, where he passed the night without any covering on his body, or any application to his open wounds. The glow of latent hope, preserved his animation, his fortune did not abandon him, and, as the day broke, he perceived passing, a peasant who gave him some milk, provided him shelter, and obtained him surgical relief. He recovered and went to Petersburgh. The emperor ordered him to pass the regiments in review that he might designate the offenders. He declined to do so, observing, that he thought it " unadvisable to seek an occasion of correcting such a notion of indefeasible allegiance; that it was better to bury in oblivion a catastrophe that could not be alleviated, than by an exemplary punishment hazard the introduction of a refined polity and manners, which by denationalising the Russian, prepared him for foreign conquest; that Russia was menaced by an enemy who could only triumph by the introduction of new theories, generating new habits; and although he had suffered from an effort of more liberal philanthrophy and respect for the laws of war, he would not, at such a moment, be accessary to innovations which removed some of the most

impregnable barriers to the designs of France."

The regular food of the Russian soldier is of the plainest and coarest quality, and their commissariat was so ill arranged, that even this issue was precarious, and their subsistence depended on their own diligence, or rather rapine, through a country where terror had induced every inhabitant to fly, and the anticipation of famine had buried many feet deep under snow and ground, the pittance destined for the future maintenance of the peasantry; but even with this miserable and uncertain provision they existed without murmur, and occasions were frequent in which they shared their insufficient meal with some starving wretch, whose humid eye implored what his power of utterance was almost too feeble to solicit.

The *wear and tear* however of a Russian army is enormous, in consequence of these bad arrangements; and the emperor might have increased his army one third solely by the establishment of an improved system. In this campaign such an addition would have been decisive of victory.

The recruiting of the Russian infantry is not by volunteer enrolment. The magistrates select the most efficient young men according to the required number. The day of nomination is passed in general grief, and each family is in unaffected affliction at the approaching separation of a son or a brother. But no sooner is the head of the reluctant conscript shaved, according to military habit, no sooner is he recognized as a defender of his country, than the plaints and lamentations cease, and all his relatives and friends present articles of dress or comfort to the no longer reluctant recruit: then revel, with the music and the dance takes place until the moment arrives when he is to abandon his native home, and the adored tomb of his fathers; the eternal farewell is mutually expressed in repeated cheers, and the exulting soldier devotes his future life to the glory and prosperity of his sovereign and his country.

The soldier however does not enter into a new state with which his domestic habits had been at variance. From the earliest infancy, he has been accustomed to sports of manly and warlike character; and his body has been hardened by exposition to the elements and the use of his national bath, whilst no intemperance has vitiated his constitution, no unhealthy employment has impregnated the germ of decay.

Religious, perhaps superstitious,—but not a bigoted intolerant, the Russian believes that heaven is a palace with many gates; and, while he respects his own faith, he gives himself no concern whether he shares his ration with a Mahomedan, a Protestant, or a Pagan. He professes no concern about any soul but his own; he invades not the right of option to any form of worship, and presumes not to select in the name of the Almighty, those who shall alone find favor in his sight.

The cossacks are a description of troop peculiar to the Russian army. Amalgamated in the Russian empire, the natives of the Don and the Volga still preserve a constitutional independence, which is possessed by none of the other provinces of Russia. Regulated by their own laws, exempt from taxes, and governed under the immediate authority of their own attaman, or chief, chosen from amongst themselves, they are relieved from all impositions; but the obligation of every male to serve gratuitously for five years with the Russian armies, and in some interior services connected with their own police. Blessed with a country of rich plains and noble rivers, which nature covers with the glorious canopy of a fine climate, and fills with redundant food, the cossack still retains his warlike character, and unites with the most enthusiastic admiration of his country, and a disposition to profit of its enjoyments, the ambition of martial service and an errant spirit of adventurous and foreign enterprise. On his native plains, he is the peaceful and civilized inhabitant, natural in his affections, and domestic in his habits; but in other countries he is the lawless Scythian, respecting neither property nor rights.

Proud of his comparative freedom, he bears himself as one conscious of superiority and privilege; and yet he tempers the haughty sense of these advantages with an Asiatic grace of manner that renders its expression inoffensive to his associates and grateful to the stranger. Of late years the attaman has lost some of his power and consequence at St. Petersburgh, but as yet no serious encroachment has been made on the independence and character of the nation. He was almost an independent prince; but is now more subject to the laws and will of the autocrat. He has been deprived of some of the apapnages of royalty, and is perhaps more pliable to the views of Russia, in the character of one of her generals; but still the cossacks remain a people with the worth to deserve, and the resolution to maintain, their freedom or sacrifice themselves in the effort.

In the qualities of private character, the cossack is to no man inferior—affectionate to his family, faithful to his friend, hospitable to the stranger, and generous to the distressed; with graceful simplicity of manners, and a candour that commands confidence. His military virtues are splendid in common with the Russian nation; but hereditary habits of war, and perhaps a natural talent for that species of it in which they are engaged, adds an acute intelligence and capacity that is not generally shared. By the stars, the wind, and an union of the most ingenious observations, the cossack travels over countries unknown to him; through forests almost impervious, and reaches his destination, or tracks some precurser that he is directed to pursue, with the ardor of the instinctive bloodhound. Nothing can elude his activity, escape his penetration, or surprise his vigilance. Irreparable disgrace would dishonor the cossack, whose negligence offered an advantage to the enemy. The crimes of the passions, cowardice itself, would not attach so fatal a stigma; for, in the words of their attaman, "this offence would not only sacrifice the army to the swords of the enemy, but entail a reproach on all, that no valor or service could retrieve." And such is the general impression of its base character, that no instance of a surprise is on record. Mounted on a very little, ill-conditioned, but well-bred horse, which can walk at the rate of five miles an hour with ease, or in his speed dispute the race with the swiftest; with a short whip on his wrist, (as he wears no spur,) armed with the lance, a pistol in his girdle, and a sword, he never fears a competitor in single combat.

Although the cossacks on some occasions, have discomfited regular cavalry by indirect attacks, it must not be supposed that they are calculated to act generally in line. Their service is of a different character, which requires a greater latitude and liberty of operation. They act in dispersion, and, when they do reunite to charge, it is not with a systematic formation, but *en masse*, or what in Germany is called the swarm attack ; a movement which is frequently the effect of a voluntary impulse that animates the whole body, and which is expressed by a yell of excitement more frightful and terrific than the war-whoop of the Canadian savage.

Dexterous in the management of a horse that is guided only by the snaffle, they can twist and bend their course through the most intricate country at full speed ; and Platoff, in front of Hulsberg, when Buonaparte was retiring on Parsarge at the head of his regiment, charged into a pinewood filled with French infantry, *en tirailleur*, (who had, during the whole day, disputed possession with 4000 Russian infantry,) carried it in an instant, and decided the affair.

Notwithstanding, however, their military services, the security which their vigilance assures their army, and the distress their enterprises and stratagems occasion the enemy, they are injurious in countries where the good will of the inhabitants is of immediate importance, or where regularity and moderation can alone provide the army with its subsistence. Then the cossacks are too frequently scourges of terror and desolation, more fatal to friends than foes ; sweeping and devastating in the lawless thoughtlessness of barbarian invaders, without any consideration of future necessities.

Such is the general character of the Russian armies ; and the conviction of their superiority in all the qualities requisite to success, might have stimulated the emperor Alexander to a still more early resistance to the power of France, had not the long and repeated successes of the French army thrown around them an air of invincibility. Were these victories, and the melancholly events which have followed them, matter of remote history, this romantic delusion would be of as little consequence as if its luminous, yet delusive halo, invested the brows of Cæsar or of Alexander ; but our safety as a nation, is unfortunately deeply implicated in the judgment which we may form of the French armies, the genius of their leader, and the causes of their success. Our part of the spell flung around them has been fortunately dissipated by repeated practical experiment. No one for a moment is now tempted to doubt, that man to man, and regiment to regiment, the French soldiers are, both in a moral and physical point of view, so decidedly inferior to the British, that the antient romantic proportion of two to one, has in some instances scarcely put them upon an equality. Still, however, another part of the charm hovers around us. The general is invested with a double portion of that merit which he formerly divided with his armies, and we now hear of nothing but the commanding genius of Buonaparte, which, supplying all deficiencies, making up for all disasters, conquering all obstacles, gathers victorious laurels, on the very fields from which every other general, antient and modern, must have retired with defeat and dishonor. With this is combined a fearful and inaccurate apprehension, or rather a superstitious terror, of some new discovered and irresistible system of tactics, devised and acted upon by this irresistible leader. Such opinions, were they generally entertained, would form a bad omen for a nation forced unto collision a second time, (March, 1815,) for all that they hold dear, with the very person of whose irresistible skill in arms such an ineffable idea is held forth. I am not, however, very apprehensive that this dispiriting creed will become general among those whose opinions in such subjects are of most consequence, among the victors of Alexandria, Maida, Vimiera, Talavera, Busaco, Barrosa, and Salamanca. The doctrine of French invincibility requires no confutation among those who retreated with Moore and advanced with Wellington; nor is it to them that, like the antient pedant in presence of Alexander, the author presumes to read his lectures on the art of war.

It is scarcely necessary to say that these observations only respect the French principle of distributing their forces upon the day of battle. Other advantages of a great and important nature, arise from the combination of the various corps of their invading armies maintaining their *liaison* or correspondence, by means of the *etats-majors* or staff-establishments attached to every division, whose communication with each other, and with the head-quarters of the emperor, is preserved at all risks, and with a consummate degree of accuracy and address. Thus orders are circulated and combined movements achieved in consequence of these orders, with the same ease and facility through various *corps d'armée* occupying positions or moving upon lines of march an hundred leagues asunder, as in other services through a single brigade. It is unnecessary to notice the unity, firmness, and consistency, which this regularity and facility of intelligence communicates to the whole plan of invasion. Another cause of success which may be shortly noticed is their attention to the commissariat and its dependencies. Every French general is qualified to provide for the subsistence of his army, every French soldier is accustomed to lighten the general's labor, by looking out for himself and his messmates, and it must be owned that if the united efforts of the general and soldier prove unsuccessful, the latter can sustain hunger and privation with great patience and firmness. None of these considerations are embraced in this inquiry, neither do I mean to investigate the still more powerful causes of success which the French will name *les grands*

moyens, which embrace *espionage*, bribery, and political intrigue. My present subject is limited to the consideration of Buonaparte and his troops, arrived on the field of battle and preparing for conflict.

The genius of Frederic of Prussia brought into practical use an improvement upon the antient order of battle, the effect of which whether applied to attack or defence, was to give the general the power of changing his array, and executing such movements, even during the heat of action, as must be decisive of the event, unless the same activity, pliability of disposition, and military talent, were displayed to counteract his purpose, as he brought to execution. This grand step in the art military consisted in subdividing the long line into a number of brigades, each of which could be easily moved and manœuvred without the risk of confusion or interference. By this simple principle of subdivision, to which his troops and his officers were heedfully and regularly trained, the king of Prussia instead of making his dispositions before the action, and then trusting the event to fortune and the valor of his troops, was enabled totally to change his arrangement in the very moment of advance, even in the battle itself, and to gain such positions as must ensure the defeat of the enemy, who frequently found themselves pressed on the very point, which at the commencement of the action, was least menaced, and which was proportionally ill provided for defence. This is the guiding principle of the Russian tactics, to facilitate which all their discipline tended, and which repeatedly gave Frederic conquest when employed against the most formidable armies, which however brave, numerous, and skilful, did not possess the principle of activity thus maintained by the Prussians. In a word, the method of subdividing extensive lines with a view to facilitate their movements, the principles and machinery by which these subdivisions, and consequently the whole order of battle can be accurately moved and reunited upon new ground, either in the former or in any new relation, were brought to perfection, if not in great measure invented by Frederic II

The Russian tactics were transferred to France by the writings of Guibert; and although modified, as we shall presently see, to the circumstances of their own armies, do at present form the leading principles of all their movements. So little do those know of the modern art of war, who are daily exclaiming against the sluggish and heavy tactics of Frederic, as incompatible with, and supplanted by, the vivacious movements and new discoveries of the modern French school of war. The Austrians also adopted the new principle of movement, but unfortunately they had not genius enough to discover, that like a mechanical power, it was capable of being applied in an endless variety of modes. They seem to have considered it as only applicable to the antient order of an extended line, and to have overlooked the obvious consideration, that having once divided the line of battle into moveable brigades, it became as easy to reduce it into a column of those brigades, as it is to form a regiment into a column of companies or half companies. About the year 1793, the Austrians might have been able to engage Frederic upon somewhat resembling his usual application of the principle which he had invented; but they were unfortunately unprepared for the tactics of a new enemy, who applied the same principle in a manner suited to the nature and resources of their own armies.

The king of Prussia whose troops were excellently disciplined, and whose numerical force was usually much inferior to that of his antagonist, applied his principle of manœuvre in the oblique order, inclining his line so as to turn his antagonist's flank. Thus his order though moving obliquely, retained the antient principle of extension, and continued to be a line though not drawn parallel to that of his enemy. It suited his purpose well, but it did not apply equally to that of the armies of France. These wanted (at least at the commencement of the revolutionary war,) the skill and discipline which the Prussian regiments possessed, and they had the numerical superiority which the Prussian monarch wanted. It was therefore, their object so to employ their armies, that they might derive the utmost advantage

from that superiority, and encounter the least possible risque from their deficiency in practice and discipline. It was plain that the subdivisons of Frederic might not only be arranged in line, but that they might be placed behind each other in *reserve*, by which it is not meant that the usual reserve used in all disciplined armies, which supports the troops in action, and is in fact very nearly engaged as soon as they; but a substitution and succession of several strong divisions, as, *corps d'armée*, placed at a considerable distance in the rear of each other, and none of which is brought into action till that in front of it has sustained the heat of the contest for some time, and by doing so, exhausted the strength of the enemy. An army so placed may be termed an open column of divisions, each of which in turn either makes or sustains attacks. In either case their advantage over the extended order, so pertinaciously adhered to by the Austrian tacticians is demonstrable.

In the case of attack, the numerical superiority and preponderating weight of a column impelled against an extended line, must undoubtedly break it. Now, an order of battle, consisting of a number of lines, short in extension, in proportion to the depth with which they are formed behind each other, is, upon the general and abstract view, an open column, moving on the principle, and possessing all the advantage and disadvantage of that order. The leading division, supported as it is by those behind it, and acting *de fort en foible*, probably breaks the extended line of the enemy. It is true that the manœuvre is a hazardous one, for the division that so penetrates an enemy's line is immediately exposed to a murderous cross fire from the divided portions betwixt which it has passed, and whom the slightest inclination or alteration will place on both its flanks, and such a body if unsupported, is almost certainly destroyed.

It is here that their system of reserve enables the French to avail themselves of the numerical superiority of their whole army. If that first division is defeated, those who escape throw themselves into the rear of the reserve, for the facilitating which, the French regiments are often exercised in the manœuvre of rallying upon a new position after total dispersion; the second reserve advances to support or to revenge it, and advances perhaps at the moment when the enemy, having made a flank movement upon the first line, are themselves exposed to be flanked by the second. If the enemy, by reinforcements, or obstinate valor, defeats the second reserve, a third advances to the charge, with all the advantage of fresh and unbroken strength, against a foe who has already undergone the loss, fatigue, and confusion of having sustained two desperate attacks. If the attack of the third reserve also is sustained, that of the fourth becomes irresistible, unless the system which exposes an extended line to the attacks of a concentrated succession of attacks, is in the mean time abandoned, and a similar concentration of force afford relief to the party attacked, and counteracts the movements of the French. But if, on the other hand, the centre of the army thus attacked be at length broken, while its wings, either by distance or being themselves occupied, are prevented from closing to its relief, total defeat may be considered as unavoidable. Its ranks are broken, its flanks exposed, and flight alone can save any part of it. It is for this advantage that the French are willing to make any sacrifice of lives; for they well know, that if it be once attained, valor and discipline are alike unavailing, and the best troops are exposed to be destroyed by those of a very inferior description, if the officers of the latter know but how to avail themselves of the position they have gained.

Hitherto I have supposed the simple case of the French divisions attacking in succession a stationary line; but the advantage of their disposition is the same, if the enemy had either originally begun the attack or has become the assailant, and advanced in pursuit, after sustaining and repelling the first charge of the French. In either case the attacking enemy has the disadvantage of encountering a succession of detached *corps d'armee*, each of which he finds drawn up in its own position, prepared with every advantage of freshness and good order to renew a combat, which his troops have sustained for the whole day. I have already detailed the incidents of the battle of Marengo, in which the Austrians were assailants, and where the French sustained the attack upon the principle, and solely by means of their numerous and powerful reserves.

In all the grand general actions of Buonaparte, the same principle can be discovered, namely, that of combining a prompt and vigorous mode of action with a concentrated order of battle, which it has been generally his good fortune to oppose to indecision, want of energy, and a prejudice in favor of an extended line. Where circumstances, as in the battle of Wagram, have, as it were, compelled his enemies to present a more collected front than usual, he has employed a still greater degree of concentration on his part, so as to ensure his having the last reserve which can be brought up. In short, he does not gain the battle by the perseverance of the soldiers engaged in it, but by renewing it by means of numerous reliefs. The perseverance is in the general and his plan of tactics, not in the troops; and the principle consists not in requiring it from the latter, but in making up for their want of it. It is a most admirable plan for a general, circumstanced as Buonaparte, whom extended means of every kind, as well as the great unity and promptitude of combining different marching columns upon a given position, enable always to appear in the field with a numerical superiority. The old mode by which a general used to avail himself of the advantage of numbers, was by extending his wings, so that their extremities might outflank and surround his enemy, as in the battle of Rosbach. But by this extension, the line is exposed to be attacked by the concentrated force of the enemy in any given point, as really happened at that battle. The system of Buonaparte is the very reverse of this, and consists, as we have seen, in condensing his line, leaving it in length barely equal at most, to the enemy's front, and often much less extended, but strengthening it in depth, by placing one division in rear of another. It is this system of repeated reserves which enables him to avail himself of the superiority of numbers to its fullest extent, and to compel the enemy to put forth their whole strength in struggling with a force equal to their own, while he can bring up at the chosen moment, reinforcements sufficient to throw the odds against them.' That moment he waits for with the utmost coolness and patience, and even partial success does not induce him to anticipate its arrival by a premature motion in advance.

The post of the emperor or *quarteir-general* is at the head of the strong and numerous reserve which supports the centre. From that point all orders are issued ; and to that point, with inexpressible celerity, all communications are made. In general, the French permit the enemy to commence the attack, and content themselves with maintaining a severe fire of musketry and artillery.' No regiment of infantry or cavalry is permitted to advance beyond the line of battle in order to charge ; for in French tactics they adhere strictly to the military rule, that the particular movement of each battalion must always bear reference to the general movement of the whole body,—a rule which is of course most easily attended to in a condensed and concentrated array, through which orders can be transmitted with accuracy and promptitude. On the other hand, they are ready to avail themselves of the partial and unsustained advance of any portion of the opposing force. Thus, at Austerlitz, the imperial horse-guards of Alexander precipitated themselves on the French line, and broke through it. But it was an unsupported movement of indignant impatience ; and no sooner were they in the rear of the line which they had broken, than they were themselves flanked and routed, or cut to pieces by the cavalry of Buonaparte's reserves. At Talavera too, the gallant impetuosity of the guards, endangered, by a rash advance, the victory of the day. But they were supported and covered by direction of a general whose eye nothing escapes. The French

Vol. L.

then do not hazard these partial and dangerous movements, especially in the commencement of an action, considering it, and justly, as of more importance to preserve the unity of their order, than to grasp hastily at any subaltern advantage.' They are aware, that, when the day is far advanced, the victory must remain with that party who can last bring into the field a strong force of fresh troops. It is often in the very moment in which the enemy suppose themselves victors, that this unexpected apparition turns the scale of battle. Their advantages cannot have been acquired without loss, tumult, and disorder ; and it is while they are in that state that they are suddenly pressed by fresh troops, who in this moment are permitted to indulge all their national vivacity of courage and enterprise. Thus, in one of Buonaparte's bulletins concerning the battle of Friedland, it is stated, that, after the conflict had continued a great part of the day, the emperor resolved to put an end to it, (a proof that he was rather apprehensive of the result,) and came up with a strong reserve.

It remains to shew in what manner the French masque their formation, and occupy the attention of the enemy along the full extent of their long order of battle, while in fact they only oppose a short and condensed front to the centre of their line This is accomplished by means of their numerous light troops, which were at first formed after the example of the irregular sharpshooters of America, as the readiest mode of training their conscripts. But the genius of the French soldier seems particularly adapted to this light and skirmishing species of warfare. The loose order, or rather the dispersion of these tirailleurs, enables a number comparatively small, to occupy the attention and harass the movements of the enemy's extended front, if unprovided with similar forces. Thus these numerous irregulars act as a screen to their own lines, while it is impossible for those who are assailed by them to discern whether they are supported by battalions, or in what order the French general is arraying his forces in the rear of this swarm of hornets. Thus they remain in complete ignorance of the French disposition, and dare not of course attempt to change their own; and while the wings waste their force, nay, sometimes sustain heavy loss in encountering this harassing, and, as it were, unsubstantial enemy, their centre has to sustain the full weight of the French line, concentrated as it has been described. This mode of warfare was peculiarly severe on the Austrians; for it happened by some unfortunate fatality, that in her passion for the Prussian discipline, that power judged it fit to convert the greater part of her croats, the finest light troops in the world, into heavy battalions, and thus diminished their strength of this particular description of force at the moment when the fate of battle was about to depend upon it. The excellence of those light corps which Austria retained, could not supply their great inferiority of numbers; and the French acquired a superiority which enabled them, without the least risque of being outflanked, to contract their own line within the extent necessary for employing the so often-mentioned principle of reserves. The French had been almost uniformly victorious, and how avails it to what their victories can be ascribed? The answer is two-fold. To the system of reserves, and the number of his armies. Such an investigation as I have attempted, leads us to due appreciation of the talents of Buonaparte, instead of blind terror, blinder admiration, or unjust censure.

I grant him,
——Strong, and skilful to his strength,
Fierce to his skill, and to his fierceness,
valiant.

But it will remain to be inquired whether his genius is of such a transcendent and overpowering nature as a distant contemplation of his exploits might induce us to believe. His plan, of which the author has endeavored to develope the principle, is indeed well fitted to ensure the most numerous of two encountering armies the full superiority of its numbers;

but there is no brilliant genius requisite to its formation. It is not an invention like Frederic's discovery of a new principle of moving an extended line. The latter is like the discovery of a mechanical power, and must, in one shape or other, be useful while armies are opposed to each other. The system of Buonaparte is only a peculiar mode of employing the same power previously discovered, which may be destroyed by any counteracting system, or superseded by any improvement of the application of the principle on which it turns. In all his great engagements, (that of Austerlitz perhaps excepted,) Buonaparte seems never even to have attempted manœuvring, that is, he never attempted to gain for his army a position which must give it an immediate and decided advantage over the enemy. Now this art is the consummation of military ability, as being that by which military skill applies the lack both of strength and of numbers. In the battles of the king of Prussia and other distinguished generals, we are led to augur the fortune of the day from the dispositions their ability enabled them to make relative to their enemy; and in the progress of the action we gradually observe our expectations realized. But Buonaparte's dispositions never authorise any conclusion as to his final success; and the imperfection of his positions, as well as the inferiority of his troops, is frequently conspicuous by the defeat of his army during the greater part of the day, until at length the fortune is turned by that in which his secret seems to consist; the appearance of a numerous reserve fresh and in order.

It may indeed be pleaded too justly, that the acknowledged imperfections in the Russian commissariat, the deficiencies of the staff, and above all, the deplorable neglect of their government to supply and reinforce their armies, deprived them of the fruits of victory; while the active energy of Buonaparte drained his whole requisitions of every soldier, or man who could be made such, to resume the field with a force superior to that which had foiled and defeated him. These considerations however, do not respect the present subject, which refers merely to the field of battle, on which the Russians have neutralized Buonaparte's favourite manœuvre. It may be briefly noticed with respect to the progress of future events that the inhabitants of the peninsula, less fortunate in the field, and who at Tudela experienced discomfiture from the effects of that system which has been detailed, have yet shewn, that when a general battle is lost, the advantages of the victory may be in a great degree intercepted. The inveterate and desperate hostility of the Spaniards and Portuguese, so widely diffused through the peasantry of the country, utterly destroyed the boasted system of intercourse and communication, by which the march of one French column was made to correspond with that of all who were acting in the same kingdom. Near as the events and positions were, it is almost impossible that Massena could have known the fall of Badajoz, when he broke up from Santarem, or that Soult anticipated the retreat of Massena when he himself fell back into Spain, instead of advancing into Alentejo to make a diversion, and afforded support to the *enfant gaté*,

(the spoiled child,) whom fortune was dropping out of her arms. But the general and inveterate enmity of the peasantry entirely annihilated all the fair system of unity and constant correspondence, which in Germany the French armies maintained at any given distance. Couriers, aids-de-camp, orderly men, and disguised spies, were alike the objects of suspicion to the Ordenanza, who, rather than miss securing their letters, would steadily rip up their bowels,—a sad interruption to a regular and friendly correspondence. And thus these two great generals seem to have known little more of each other's motions, than if they had been next-door neighbours in London. The self-devoting patriotism with which the Portuguese destroyed every part of their property, which could afford supply or assistance to the invading army, rendered the genius of the French for the commissariat department equally unavailing, and even *les grand moyens* themselves proved fruitless in a country where lord Wellington declared that none, even of the lowest description, forgot through any compulsory intercourse with the French, the duty which they owed to their country.

4 x 2

CHAP. XLIV.

Narrative of the Campaign in Poland from the Assumption of the Command by General Beningzen to the Termination of the Battle of Eylau.

WHEN general Beningzen arrived on the borders of the Vistula with his corps, he fixed his head-quarters [at Pultusk, and sent forward into the environs of Warsaw, Sedmorasky's division. One part remained at Prague, the rest composed of chasseurs, a regiment of huzzars, and some squadrons of cossacks and cavalry, passed the Vistula, and an advanced-guard proceeded to the river Bsura, but on the approach of the enemy, on the the 26th of October, 1806, it retired after some inconsiderable affairs, reached the Vistula, and burnt the bridge of Warsaw.

The enemy having occupied Warsaw, constructed several heavy batteries, which obliged general Sedmorasky to retire behind the Bug, where he took possession at Zsegz and Dembe, whilst the division of Galoun defended the tract between the confluence of the Narew and the Bug, and the Austrian frontier near the village of Areickow. The division of count Ostreman was at Makow; that of Zacheu between Ostrolenka and Pultusk.

General Beningzen proposed to remain on the defensive, until the junction of general Buxhowden's corps with his own was effected.

The enemy having passed the Vistula advanced to the Bug, the passage of which river was long disputed, but finally marshal Ney threw over a bridge near Nowidwoe, at the confluence of the Wkra, the Bug, and the Vistula, but the first detachments which passed were cut off by the Russians,

and general Beningzen, finding that the corps of Buxhowden was delayed, resolved, with his own corps, to attack the enemy at Modlin.

As the French had strongly fortified an height that commanded the left bank of the Wkra near Pomechowe, and as a column, from the badness of the roads, could not arrive at the appointed time, this plan was abandoned, and the position of Nowemiasto, Sochoczyn, and Czarnowo, was occupied for the defence of the Wkra. In the mean time marshal Soult passed the Vistula at Wysogrod, marshal Augereau with his corps between Zakroczn and Utrata, a little below the embouchure of the Bug into the Vistula, and the corps of marshals Ney, Bessieres, and Lasnes passed the Vistula at Thorn.

General Lesloeg having been ordered to retire by general Beningzen, obeyed after several remonstrances, when marshal Ney marched against the corps of Lesloeg, and Lasnes and Augereau upon Plonsk. The former joined Davoust and Modlin; the latter appeared before Nowemiasto on the right bank of the river Wkra.

General Beningzen finding that he could not resume the offensive with his single corps, resolved to fall back upon Pultusk, where there was a reserve of the army, his heavy artillery, and favorable ground, to which the enemy could only advance, from the state of the roads, with light guns. The arrival of general Kaminskoy occasioned the dereliction of this project, as the general imagined that he could force the enemy behind the Wkra, and made his dispositions accordingly; but Buonaparte having arrived on the Wkra on the 23rd, did not give him time to execute his movement, for he ordered his army to attack the Russians, on the same evening, and on the 24th, at the three' points of Czarnowo, Sochoczyn, and Nowemiasto.

For fourteen hours count Ostreman, with a part of his division, resisted the corps of Davoust, Lasnes, and the guards, bnt at length they succeeded in forcing the Wkra, when the count retired upon Nasielsk, without any serious loss, and afterwards to Strzegooin, where the division of Zachen, Barclay de Tolloy, and Sedmorasky having united, the whole marched to Pultusk. During this time prince Gallitzin, with several regiments of cavalry and infantry, had marched to the succor of the post at Nowemiasto, but did not advance farther than Lopaczin, on the river Sonna, when he was attacked by marshal Augereau's corps and a considerable number of cavalry which had passed the river Wkra at Kursomb, not far from Nowemiasto, and by whom he was compelled to retire on the road of Pultusk, but on which he fell in with a part of Zachen's division which was on march to rejoin its corps. Obliged to halt at Golmyn, the prince was there attacked by the corps of Augereau, and the cavalry under Murat, upon the same day on which the combat of Pultusk took place.

The troops which had assembled at Strzegooin, (composing 60 battalions and 55 squadrons without including the cossacks,) arrived in the environs of Pultusk on the 24th and 25th of December, and took up a position with the left appdied on the town, and the right thrown forward into a wood, commencing in front of the right between 200 and 300 paces, and extending along the front of the whole line, but towards the centre, retiring about 2000 paces. The right was the strongest part of the position,—there general Barclay de Tolloy commanded,—the centre was under the orders of general Zachen—the left was commanded by count Ostreman—the reserve by general Sedmorasky. General

Bagavont with two regiments of the line and a regiment of chasseurs, composing part of the advanced-guard, was posted 400 paces in front of count Ostreman, and near some houses on an elevation which formed part of the site of the town; the cavalry was placed between 1500 and 2000 paces in front of the line; and in their front some corps of chasseurs were pushed by general Barclay into the forest.

The position between Pultusk and the wood, was apparently one large plain, but was intersected in front with small defiles. Behind, the plain extended deep, but towards the right was divided by the river Narew, and on the left by the forest in part occupied by general Barclay.

In the evening of the 25th, the corps of Davoust approached and made a reconnoisance. On the 26th, at ten o'clock in the morning, the enemy consisting of the corps of Davoust and Lasnes, with the French guards, commenced the action by a cannonade from the centre neither brisk nor well maintained, as he had not been enabled to advance his cannon.

Towards mid-day, however, the attack was more vigorous on the left of the position, and the Russian fire of musketry was considerable. The Russian cavalry also had several opportunities to charge, which they did with complete success. The enemy making no impression on the left, notwithstanding repeated efforts, directed some attacks against the center, but there also being foiled he concentrated and threw nearly his whole force upon the right, and, by an overbearing and unexpected weight of fire, obliged the Russians to retire, (but not in any disorder,) upon their successive reserves and artillery. The enemy elated and confident from this retrograde movement, continued, notwithstanding heavy loss, to advance upon the Russian batteries in the wood, some of which being gallantly maintained to cover the retreat, they carried by assault.

General Beningzen however, having resolved on battle, was determined to sustain it, to oppose force to force, and manœuvre to manœuvre; he therefore directed general Barclay to recede, and throwing back the right of his line, and retiring the cavalry from his front, opened a well-directed fire of artillery from 120 pieces, which so confounded and destroyed the enemy, that they almost immediately gave way ; several regiments being sent to the support of general Barclay, he vigorously advanced, and the original ground was altogether recovered, a great number of the enemy killed, and the darkness of night alone preserved the remainder, for they fled in great confusion and consternation, augmented by the attack of the Russians on their right.

When general Kaminskoy had found his position behind the Wkra forced by the enemy, he resolved to retire the Russian army behind the Njemen river, and gave directions accordingly to the corps of Buxhowden and Beningzen, but his orders were given under such circumstances, that general Beningzen considered himself as authorized to use his own discretion, and therefore preferred to give battle at Pultusk, hoping that general Buxhowden or general d'Aurep would support him ; by some unfortunate misapprehension or disagreement, probably originating in the want of acknowledged superior direction and authority, neither of these officers had advanced to his assistance, he therefore thought it more prudent 'to retire during the night, notwithstanding his success, as Soult was on march for Ostrolenka, and as he feared to be surrounded by the whole French army, reuniting to revenge its partial disgrace, if he remained on the position of Pultusk ; and this determination was indeed almost indispensable, since he had not any provisions in his camp or in the neighbourhood.

The French force which had opposed him was so severely beaten, that their flight continued during the night, and they abandoned many guns, Buonaparte's equipage, &c. nor could the cossacks, who patrolled two German miles in front of Pultusk, on the 27th, find even a rear-guard of the enemy. The French did not readvance until the second day, and general Corbineau did not enter Ostrowiec until the 1st of January, 1807. The loss of the Russians was less than 500 men, and the French at the most moderate computation had 8000

killed and wounded, among whom were several generals and distinguished officers. Had Buxhowden or d'Aurep with his division but co-operated, the action at Pultusk might have decided the campaign, for the entire annihilation of the enemy would have then been certain.

But the result of this affair made a very favorable impression for the character of general Beningzen, and on the Russians. It was the first check that Buonaparte had experienced on the continent, a charm was broken and the French army foresaw that their future combats would be no longer chaces of pleasure. The Russian generals resumed confidence. The stain of Austrelitz was effaced from their escutcheons, and the soldiers recognised themselves as not unworthy of the companions of Suwarrow. It was in vain that Buonaparte denied the victory. It was in vain that he boasted the trophy of some cannon which the Russians had abandoned in consequence of the state of the roads, on their subsequent march. He could not deceive the army. He was not able even to resume his interrupted operations so as to pursue the offensive until he had possessed himself of what yet remained of Prussia ; and thus if he could not render the battle equivocal in history, diminish the mischievous consequences of its loss. It was in vain that he announced the entire destruction of the Russian army, and his consequent return to Warsaw there to remain till he chose to renew the campaign. His march had been arrested, all his enterprizes discomfited, and he had scarcely proclaimed that had he repelled the Russians eighty leagues, when the same Russians reappeared in the field to assure him with terrible evidence of their existence.

The affair of Golmyn, on the same day, contributed to animate the Russian courage and *amour propre.* Prince Gallitzin with 15 battalions and 20 squadrons, having found himself obliged to take post there, whilst count Pahlin, with the regiment of hussars of Somskoy, and general Laptow, with a regiment of chasseurs, effected their retreat upon him, was vigorously attacked by the whole corps of Angereau and the cavalry under the orders of Murat, but maintained his ground ; and, towards, the evening, being reinforced by the division of general Ducturof, and a part of the division of general Tutchikow, he advanced, and drove back from every point the enemy ; nevertheless, in consequence of general Kaminskoy's order for a retreat, and the uncertainty of the issue of the combat sustained by general Beningzen, it became necessary for him to retire upon Ostrolenka, which he did in perfect order, and there joined the corps of general Beningzen, who, on the 27th, had marched to Rozan, and on the 28th, to Ostrolenka. From thence he retired to Novogorod, with the united divisions of general Essen and d'Aurep ; and general Buxhowden, with his corps, marched to Kolno. The intention was to repass the Narew, but the state of the ice preventing the construction of a bridge, the army was obliged to fall back as far as Tykoczn, to cross the river. The enemy, aware of general Kaminskoy's order for the Russian army to retrograde, and unwilling, after the battle of Pultusk, to readvance it by any active operations, made their disposition of winter-quarters. Marshal Bernadotte went to Elbing, Ney to Güttstadt, Augereau to Thorn, Davoust to Przasnic, Lasnes to Markow, Soult to Pultusk, and Buonaparte with his guards to Warsaw. General Buxhowden, at Tykoczyn, was removed from the army, and general Beningzen received the supreme command. Desirous to profit of his success at Pultusk, and the confidence there acquired by his troops, he determined to continue the plan proposed by general Buxhowden, who had promised the king of Prussia to save Koningsberg, still menaced by the gradual approach of the corps of marshals Ney and Bernadotte.

The army, 70,000 strong, with 500 cannon, having passed the Narew, marched to the Bobra river, and crossed at Gonionetz and Innowa, except the corps of general Sedmorasky, 12,000 strong, which remained at Konionetz. The rout of march was directed upon Bialla, where the head-quarters were established on the 15th of January. On the 16th, they were transferred to Arys ; on the 18th, to Rhein, where the divisions of generals Ducturof and Tuchikof, which had been detached, joined general Beningzen's army ; and on the 19th, the advanced-guard fell upon several of the detachments of the enemy in their cantonments. From Rhein the troops marched to Heilige Linde, and then to Bischoffstein.

The general being informed that marshal Bernadotte was retiring with precipitation from Elbing, resolved to pursue him, and on the 24th marched to Arensdorf, and on the 25th to Liebstadt ; but on the same day, the advanced-guard under general Markof, commenced an attack on the village of Mohrungen, in which, to the great regret of the army, general d'Aurep was unfortunately killed. During the action, prince Dolgurowckey entered the town by the rear, surprised the enemy's guards, and took the whole baggage of marshal Bernadotte, while the marshal himself with difficulty escaped.

The grand army advanced on the 26th, to Mohrungen, which it reached the next day, from whence he removed, after many skirmishes, to Yankowo, and subsequently retreated upon Wolsdorf. He was supported in his retrograde movements by prince Bagration, Barclay de Tolloy, and Bagavont. Buonaparte conducted the pursuit in person, with the advanced-guard of his army, which, from the woody and intersected nature of the country, sustained considerable loss. The retreat of the Russians was much embarrassed by the peculiar temper of the subordinate officers and of the troops, who were equally unwilling and unaccustomed to retrace their steps in the presence of an enemy, and the severe and inclement night-marches, after the fatigues of the day, combined with the scarcity of food, would have been sufficient to conquer the discipline of better regulated troops. The soldiers were compelled, as the only relief from famine, to prowl and dig for the buried food of the peasantry ; they had no other bed than the snow, no shelter but the heavens, no covering but their rags.

After moving in the direction of Landsberg, Beningzen was attacked in that place by the corps of marshal Soult and Augereau, and was obliged to retire with the loss of 3000 men, among whom prince Gallitzin was mortally wounded, to the vicinity of Eylau.

By twelve o'clock on the 7th, the army had gained its position in rear of Preuss Eylau, but a division was left in the town to support the advanced-guard, and to maintain the town after the advanced-guard had retired into line as was proposed.

Two miles in front of Preuss Eylau the enemy pressed prince Bagration, when the regiment of Petersburgh dragoons, emulous to retrieve the misfortune of the previous day, charged a column of the enemy, cut to pieces the two battalions composing it, and captured two eagles. At the same time the Russian infantry charged two other columns advancing to storm the height, and put to death so considerable a number, that an elevation which the fugitives had attempted to gain, was for three weeks afterwards actually cased with their dead. The enemy's cavalry then attempted to turn the right wing; but four Russian regiments of infantry, and as many of cavalry, sustained and repelled these efforts with sanguinary execution on the assailants. This severe check daunted the enemy so, that the rear-guard retired, without further molestation, into Preuss Eylau ; but no sooner had it passed through, than the division which was stationed to defend the town, by a mistake of the order, commenced its march also upon the position, the centre of which was not more than 300 yards from the interior houses.

The general instantly ordered other troops to replace them ; but the vigilant and active enemy had already taken possession. They were, however, dislodged by a vigorous attack ; but Buonaparte threw in another division, and, as an encouragement, promised the sacking of the town, whilst at the same time he made a movement with his left to lodge some infantry in a village and an avenue of trees,

from which he could incommode the Russian right, and open a communication with marshal Ney, then momentarily expected by the rout of Schloditten.

As the heavy artillery had arrived the same afternoon by that village, general Beningzen was willing to abandon the contest for the town, and had directed a division which was advancing to support the Russians again retiring from the suburbs, to fall back ; but the ardor was so vehement, that the columns continued to move on with drums beating, and when they entered the streets, charged the enemy with the bayonet, and killed many of them in the attack, and afterwards in the houses, where they were committing the most infuriated excesses under the authority of Buonaparte's orders.

As the hillocks, however, on the French side were closed up to the houses, the enemy still hung under their cover, and fired into the streets. General Barclay de Tolloy, who commanded in the town, was severely wounded in the arm by one of their random shots, after it was dark, a circumstance which deprived the army of the services of a most valuable officer at an important crisis.

When general Beningzen had taken up his position on the morning of the 7th, he had chosen for the alignement of his army, an open space of uneven ground, of about two miles from right to left, and a mile deep. This ground was bounded by fir woods, except in rear of his right, and in a continuation of his left, where the open country extended. The town of Preuss Eylau, which had no species of work for its protection, lay in a hollow about 300 yards in front of the right of the Russian centre, which rose above it so as to overtop the roofs of the houses ; in front of the Russian left was the village of Serpallen. On this ground general Beningzen had formed his army, nearly 60,000 strong, which had concentrated, with the exception of Lesloeg's corps, on the evening of the 7th, notwithstanding the efforts of the French marshals and Buonaparte's bulletins.

Four divisions of infantry in small columns, and one division in a single column, formed the first and second lines, and two divisions the reserve.

The cavalry protected both flanks, and was partially distributed in the second alignement.

The rear-guard had orders to act according to circumstances; and, having suffered so heavily, it was proposed finally to relieve it, and draw it into the position, for which purpose the division had originally been sent into the town of Preuss Eylau to cover its retreat.

The enemy, on their arrival in front of Preuss Eylau, had taken up a position nearly parallel, but on ground that completely commanded the Russian position, so as to expose the minutest object to their fire, whilst the intervals between the elevations afforded shelter to their troops, and a concealment of their movement and force. There Buonaparte posted the corps of Soult on the right, Augereau on the left, and the guards and the cavalry under Murat, while Davoust manœuvred on his right to turn the Russian left; and Ney, on his arrival, was to form on Augereau's left: the total force, exclusive of Bernadotte's, certainly could not be less than 90,000 men.

The unoccupied space between the armies was open and flat, intersected by lakes, passable on the frozen surface in every direction.

About ten o'clock, the firing being diminished, and almost confined to the sentries, general Beningzen withdrew to a house situated about three quarters of a mile in rear of his position, where he had directed the general officers to assemble for their orders; but he had not arrived half an hour when the wounded general Barclay de Tolloy was brought in, and almost immediately afterwards an officer arrived with the intelligence that the Russian division stationed in the town of Preuss Eylau, had also withdrawn when their commander had been removed; and that the enemy, having possession of the town, had thrown out their sentries within half musket-shot of the Russian batteries. The general immediately directed that division, reinforced by one regiment, to take post between the town and

his position, to cover his alignement from surprise or insult; and, apprehending that an attempt might be made at day-break to pierce his centre from Preuss Eylau, directed, in a very perspicuous order, two divisions to be formed in columns of reserve behind his centre, and a third behind his left wing, and a brigade from the right to fill up the interval which was occasioned in the line by withdrawing one of the divisions for a division of reserve. The Prussians, momentarily expected, were directed to occupy the ground on the right, which the Russians by this movement weakened. But, notwithstanding the active superintendance of the general himself, this change could not be completed, on account of the darkness of the night, before day-break, and after that the fire of cannon and musketry had commenced from the Russian batteries, and the French and Russian tirailleurs in front of Preuss Eylau, and large vacancies continued in the alignement, even until an hour after the close of day.

Perhaps no night was ever more awful, no occasion ever excited a higher interest. The approximation—the contact of the adverse armies—the importance of their character and objects—the fortunes that awaited their achievements—the, events that depended on them—the presence of 150,000 men, undaunted at the aspect of battle's terrific preparations, but impatient for mutual slaughter—the wintry wildness of the scene, faintly cheered by the partial fires, on whose blaze the darkness of the storm rested, and whose flames, chilled by impenetrable icy beds, but exposed to view the shivering groups extended around—knowledge of the Russian sufferance—commiseration of their helpless distress—admiration of their heroism—anxiety for their fate, kept unclosed the wearied eye, and oppressed the mind with variety and weight of thought: but at early dawn, when the firing of small arms commenced, universal confidence dispelled all other cares but that of rendering the contest destructive to the enemy.

Soon after day-break, the Russian cannon opened, and played very heavily, but rather at hazard, as the French columns were principally concealed by the favoring swells of their ground and the town and suburbs of Preuss Eylau. The French cannon quickly replied with vigor and effect, as every man of the Russian army was exposed from head to foot.

About half an hour after the cannonade began, the French made an advanced movement with their left in column, supported by a strong body of cavalry, to turn the Russian right, and another strong column passed out of the town of Preuss Eylau by the church, with the intention of storming the centre, whilst 150 pieces of cannon covered their approach, and 40 pieces of the imperial guard played upon the centre Russian battery. These troops had not advanced above 300 yards, repelling the Russian tirailleurs, when the Russian cannon-shot, admirably directed, ploughed through the mass, and so shattered their order, that, after a minute's pause, they inclined for shelter behind a detached house, but, being still exposed, they rushed back in the wildest disorder to the town; while the other columns and the cavalry, also oppressed with bullets and grape, broke and fled, pursued by the Russian cavalry and light infantry, who again dislodged the enemy from the village and avenues of trees which they had sought to occupy the preceding evening.

The French repulsed in their first assaults, maintained a very heavy fire of artillery from their heights and the salient points of the town, and, as the whole Russian army was still exposed to their observation and fire, with much effect, as to the destruction of men.

Some time afterwards several French columns attempted to carry the village of Serpallen in front of the Russian left, and in advance of which village there had been, from day break a sharp fire of musketry, but general Baggavout, who was stationed there, having received a reinforcement of two regiments of cavalry, attacked the enemy and drove them with great loss back upon the wood which bordered the right of the French position. Animated by this success, they took several eagles, so that the enemy was obliged to reassemble his forces towards his own centre. The village of Serpallen however, had been set in flames during the contest.

Heavy snow storms obscuring the atmosphere, and driving with great violence in the faces of the Russians, had hitherto favored the approaches of the enemy, and a very heavy storm falling about mid-day, presented an occasion which the enemy did not omit to use, or the Russians to prepare against. When the darkness was clearing, six columns of the enemy, including the French guards, and supported by the cavalry and a numerous artillery, were discovered close upon the first line of the Russians. At that instant general Beningzen gallopped forward with his staff, directed the reserves to advance, and marched down to meet the enemy, whilst his exulting troops shouted acclaiming peals of victory.

The brave Russians (it is difficult to refrain from enthusiastic expressions of praise when their conduct at this awful moment is recollected) inclining inwards eagerly pressed on, indifferent to the shower of balls that plunged through their ranks, and uniting with the first line, the whole charged home upon the enemy, who, panic-struck by this unexpected attack, instantly gave way, abandoning their cannon and several eagles, and pursued, when the army ceased to advance, by the musketry-fire of one of the deploying columns, and the artillery of all the batteries.

The efforts of the French cavalry had been equally unsuccessful; the Russian cavalry overwhelmed them, pursued them to the French batteries, took two eagles and twenty cannon from the fugitive infantry rallying upon their heights, and extended the almost unparalleled carnage to their very reserves.

A regiment of the French cuirassiers had, during the storm, gained an interval in the Russian line between their centre and left wing, but the cossacks and some hussars immediately as they were perceived bore down upon them. The cuirassiers apparently like men stupified by the magnitude of their own enterprize, and unprepared for success, rushed with a considerable detour through the rear of the camp, and then turned towards the right of the Russian right wing, but their bodies successively tracked the course, and only 18 escaped alive.

The Russian army which had now advanced several hundred paces, was, if possible, more than ever exposed, but the columns remained as a rampart to be battered down, thus proving the superiority of their active and passive courage over an enemy who only advanced with a faultering step to be destroyed, or retired behind the cover that his position offered for shelter.

The enemy's attack having been thus completely baffled, measures were taken to secure the victory on general Lestocy's arrival, who was momentarily expected to appear, as officers had come from him, and orders had been sent for him to expedite his march, when a French corps was observed advancing from a wood to turn the Russian left, and almost immediately a very severe fire was directed upon the Russians, who endeavored to maintain Serpallen, but notwithstanding their gallantry and perseverance, were obliged to abandon it. Two regiments were then sent to extend the Russian left to Sausgarten, but the French advanced with such impetuosity that they rapidly gained ground towards the rear of the Russian army, and as another body of the enemy was seen advancing upon the right of the corps which was hitherto turning their position, the left wing and the greater part of the centre was thrown back almost at right angles with the right wing. In the circumstances under which this movement was executed, disorder could scarcely be avoided, and the enemy reached the farm-house behind the centre of the position, which had been general Beningzen's head-quarters on the previous evening, whilst their artillery posted on favorable eminences, played with great execution throughout the field.

Never was a change more sudden. The victors were yielding the field to the vanquished, and surprize and alarm were rapidly displacing confidence and paralizing exertion.

But whilst anxiety was at its height,

and a supporting movement of the enemy from Preuss Eylau was apprehended, as one division alone remained in the Russian right wing, at that critical moment general Lestocy, (whose approach had been so long announced, and whose arrival had been so long earnestly expected, but who had to perform his march pressed by marshal Ney's corps) entered the field by the village of Althoff, where a battalion of grenadiers and some cossacks were left to check the progress of marshal Ney, proceeded uninterrupted by the left of the enemy's army, to which his right flank was exposed, passed the Russian right, rapidly moved in three columns along the open tract in its rear, and advanced upon the village of Kutschitten, already occupied by the enemy.

After an able disposition for the attack of the village, and the prevention of succor, the two columns destined for the assault, and supported by a battalion of grenadiers, impetuously rushed forwards and were met by the enemy at the extremity of the village but the greater part of the French were instantaneously put to death by the bayonet, and the fugitives in vain endeavoured to rally on reserves in the street—every impediment was forced, and, as a last resource, they fired the village for the purpose of sheltering their flight. The precautions of general Lestocy had however environed them with destruction; the troops directed to intercept their retreat on Lampasch, or the wood between that village and Auklappen, charged as they sallied out, and not one man of the whole 800 who had originally defended Kutschitten escaped; one eagle was taken, and the three Russian guns abandoned on the retreat of the Russian left wing, were recovered by the Russian regiment of Wyburg. This service being achieved general Lestocy formed his corps in two lines, the cavalry forming the second line, and one regiment extended the left of the infantry, to keep in check the enemy's right, he then advanced in direction of the wood between Auklappen and Lampasch, with his rear towards the captured village of Kutschitten, upon the enemy, whose advanced line had been cannonaded during the storm of Kutschitten.

and driven back to the entrance of the forest. The corps of general Lestocy never fired a shot until within a few paces of the enemy, when a furious action with artillery and musketry commenced. The Prussian guns having an advantageous position, overwhelmed the fire of the French cannon, and at the same time occasioned their troops an unremitting heavy loss ; and the Prussian infantry, being at length less exposed than the enemy, in consequence of some broken ground, their fire occasioned such a carnage, that, notwithstanding the treble superiority, at least, of the French, the enemy were compelled, after half an hour's combat, to yield the ground and abandon between 3000 and 4000 killed or wounded. The Prussians, who had till that moment remained in the most regular alignement, now advanced forwards to close upon the enemy, and chased them through the forest towards Sausgarten, until night arrested their victorious career.

The Russian left had also rallied, under protection of the flying artillery judiciously posted ; and the columns being formed, readvanced, drove the enemy back as rapidly as he had proceeded, recovered the farm-house, expelled him from the wood, and, by a bold attack of cavalry, which destroyed an entire column, dispersed them in the greatest disorder.

Night had now closed in darkly, and only an occasional shot or shell was fired from the heights above Eylau ; but, as marshal Ney had driven the Prussian battalion and the cossacks from Althoff, (from whence they had retired with the most gallant and skilful conduct, so as to unite with the Russian right,) and had occupied Schloditten, which post menaced the communication with Koningsberg, general Beningzen ordered a division under general Kaminskoy to storm it, which order was executed about ten at night, with irresistible ardor ; and the hussars of the charging troops, being heard at Preuss Eylau, the enemy supposed that a general attack would be renewed, for which Buonaparte found his army so little prepared, that he sent off his heavy artillery, baggage, &c. to Landsberg, ordered Davoust to join him, and

withdrew his troops back upon the heights immediately in front of the woods, where he with difficulty reassembled the wreck of his shattered and dispirited army, and awaited information of the Russian movements.

About eleven o'clock the Russian generals assembled, (still on horseback,) when general Beningzen informed the circle that he had determined, notwithstanding his success, to fall back upon Koningsberg, for he had no bread to give the troops, and their ammunition was expended ; but, by a position in the neighbourhood of such a city, his army would be certain of every necessary supply, and be assured of the means of re-equipping itself so as to appear again in the field before the enemy could repair his losses.

All the Russian generals entreated general Beningzen to keep the field, and not render nugatory a victory so dearly bought. They assured him that the enemy was in retreat, that his own army was ready to advance at the moment, and general Knoring and general Tolstoy, (the quarter-master-general, and second in command,) offered to move forwards and attack whatever troops Buonaparte might have rallied, and thus complete the victory ; and at all events they pledged their lives, that, if he but remained on his ground, the enemy would retire altogether. General Lestocy also urged the same arguments ; but general Beningzen thought it his duty not to incur the hazard of a reinforcement of fresh troops enabling the enemy to cut off his communications with Koningsberg. He found the privations of his army now pressing heavy on their physical powers. He knew that his own loss was not less than 20,000 men, and he was not then aware of the full extent of the enemy's disorganization and loss, which was afterwards proved to exceed 40,000 men, including 10,000 who had quitted their colours, under the pretence of escorting the wounded, and who did not return for many days : he therefore persevered in his original determination, directed the order of the march, and, after thirty-six hours, passed on horseback, without any food, and being almost exhausted, placed himself in a house filled with several hundreds of dead and dying to obtain an hour's repose, amidst the groans and shrieks of the wretched sufferers.

About midnight, the army commenced its movements. The division of count Osterman continued its march without interruption, and the Russian head-quarters were fixed three leagues in front of Koningsberg, where they continued until the third day, when general Beningzen transferred them into the city, and withdrew his army to Mulhausen, while general Lestocy received directions to cover the Pregel and Aller at Friedland, to which he passed by the wood of Domnau, through Lampash, without any interruption from the enemy. Several skirmishes ensued ; and the cossacks, elated with their successes, allowed the enemy no repose by night or day. Fifteen hundred of the wounded French cavalry were deposited in the prisons and hospitals, and the slain amounted to an equal number : the Russians seldom granted quarter, and the emperor had been compelled to prevent the effusion of bloodshed by the gift of a ducat for every captive.

Buonaparte, convinced that his cavalry was unable to cover his army, apprehensive of still more daring opposition, baffled in his avowed expectation that Beningzen would retire behind the Pregel, unable to obtain an armistice, and repulsed in his offer of peace, resolved to retire upon the Vistula. On the 19th, Preuss Eylau was evacuated by his troops, but the houses remained filled with French and Russian wounded, and above 200 French tumbrils tracked the enemy's rout to Landsberg. In the latter town were abandoned 760 French soldiers, and a number of their officers, and above 20 pieces of cannon were discovered in the lakes about Eylau, which the enemy, unable to remove them, had forced through the ice for the purpose of concealment. The soldiery and peasantry had, since the battle, been continually employed in burying the dead ; the ground was still covered with human carcases, and many parts of the road to Landsberg, were literally paved with frozen and encrusted bodies, which the returning cannon-wheels had lacerated and deformed.

HISTORY OF THE WAR.

CHAP. XLV.

THE new parliament assembled according to appointment, on the 15th of December, 1806, and a speech was delivered by the commissioners, which descanted on the rupture of the late negotiation, lamented the ambition and injustice of the enemy which had kindled a fresh war in Europe, and congratulated the nation, that, notwithstanding the late calamities, the good faith of his majesty's allies had remained unshaken. The speech proceeded to declare the necessity of the public burdens, complimented the loyalty and energy of the people, recommended the most rigid economy in the administration of the public revenues, and expressed the firmest confidence in the discipline of our fleets and armies, the unimpaired resources of our prosperity and strength, and the general union of sentiment and action. It concluded by an assurance that with these advantages, and an humble reliance on the protection of divine Providence, his majesty was prepared to meet the exigencies of this important crisis, confident of receiving the surest support from the wisdom of his parliament, and from the affection, loyalty, and public spirit of his people.

The address was carried after a long debate, in which lord Castlereagh defended the conduct of sir Home Popham, accused the ministry of neglecting to send reinforcements to Buenos Ayres, and expatiated on their general negligence and imbecility. Thanks were voted by acclamation to sir John Stuart and the victors of Maida; and, on a motion of lord Howick, another address was presented to his majesty, expressive of decided coincidence with the ministry on the subject of the late negotiations, and the political arrangements with foreign powers. After long but frivolous discussions, the resolutions connected with the army bill of Mr. Windham were agreed to. A conversation took place on the motion for an addition of £5000 to the sum of £8000 already granted to the Roman Catholic college of Maynooth in Ireland, which was strenuously opposed by Mr. Wilberforce, on the ground that it would cramp the growth of Protestantism in Ireland: It would be cruel, he observed, to oppress or restrain the

Catholic religion, but its members could not reasonably expect that they should be favored to the injury of the protestant establishment. Notwithstanding these objections, the motion was unanimously passed with the warm participation of every friend of toleration and humanity.

The commission of military enquiry, which had been appointed in the latter year of Mr. Pitt's administration, after detecting the minor *inadvertencies* of lord Melville, discovered abuses of the most enormous and extensive kind in the barrack department. It appeared that general Delancey, barrack-master-general had been in the habit of drawing, through the medium of Mr. Greenwood, the army agent, immense sums of the public money long before they were wanted, and that in a part only of his accounts, (as the commissioners had not yet examined the whole,) there were overcharges and misstatements to the amount of no less a sum than £90,000.

The third report of the commissioners, made at an early period of the session, related to Mr. Alexander Davison, banker, and colonel of a regiment of volunteers. This man, who had been lately tried for bribery at elections, and imprisoned for that offence, soon after his liberation from prison, had been made treasurer of the ordnance, an office in which between 3,000,000 and 4,000,000 passed through his hands of the public money. It appeared from the report, that, in consequence of a bargain with general Delancey, Davison was to receive a commission of two and a half per cent. for supplying the articles of beds, bedding, sheets, blankets, towels, ironmongery, candles, beer, and forage; but as to coals he was to supply that article as a merchant.

It appeared also, from the report that the mode in which the public was injured by Davison, was two-fold. First, by following the example of Delancey in drawing immense sums of money long before they were expended for the public service, so that he always retained in hand 1,000,000 or more of the public treasure of which he embezzled the interest. Secondly, he imposed upon the public in the price of

the articles purchased. There did not appear to be any means of discovery respecting the articles on commission, but ample means of detection were found with respect to the coals. It appeared that Davison, by his contract was to buy the coals on his own account, and to sell them to the barrack office at the wholesale prices, and deliver them at the several places where the barracks were situated. That these prices might be ascertained in a regular way, Davison was to produce certificates from persons of perfect respectability, that his prices were fair. But it appeared that Delancey never made any enquiry into the character or responsibility of the persons who signed Davison's certificates, and among them was one individual named Walker, for some time the agent of Davison, who was found guilty of perjury and executed.

In the investigation of these delinquencies, it appeared that he charged in point of measure, as a retailer, not making the allowance expected from wholesale dealers, of one chaldron in twenty, so that, supposing his prices to have been fair, he thus gained one twentieth part more than would have been demanded by a fair wholesale dealer. The average price charged to the public was 81 shillings per chaldron, and the average price paid by Davison was 61 shillings. To this sum must be added, the one chaldron in twenty, making altogether a gain of £30 in every hundred. He was bound to make the deliveries in the most favorable season, instead of which he made nearly the whole of them in winter, when coals were dearest, though he had bought them at the cheapest seasons. The wealth accumulated by this person from the plunder of the public, must have been immense; nor was he at any pains to conceal his guilt, but seemed desirous to display it by the utmost splendor and magnificence. He was a purchaser of the most valuable pictures and estates, and was in the habit of giving splendid and expensive entertainments to the prince of Wales, the junior branches of the royal family, and the nobility.

The commissioners of barrack accounts

communicated to the lords of the treasury their opinion that Mr. Davison should be required to produce his cash-account with the barrack-master-general. Mr. Davison, after many delays, declared his readiness to give such information respecting his cash-account, as he could give, but stated, at the same time, that his cash-account was so mixed with *other accounts*, that it was impossible he could give a clear view of it ; he wrote at the same time to the lords of the treasury, stating that he would produce in his own defence, an account which would prove satisfactory. The commissioners, however, by the direction of the treasury, called for the cash-account, and directions were given for the recovery of the sums due.

The day appointed for the second reading of the bill for abolishing the slave trade, was Wednesday, the 5th of February, and it was carried by 100 voices against 36, a glorious and decisive victory to the persevering and indefatigable advocates of philanthropy. But the triumph of the friends of humanity was not obtained but after a severe contention with the sophistries and misrepresentations of the enemies of the bill. The reasoning of the anti-abolitionists, on the ground of policy or expediency, may be reduced to the following dilemma. Either the black population of the colonies could support itself, or it could not. If it could, it must increase : for population is never exactly stationary. The proportion of whites to blacks would be more and more diminished. And the horrors of St. Domingo proclaimed the fate of a colony, in which the power of the Africans predominated over that of the Europeans. But if it should not be able to support itself, hands would be wanting more and more for the cultivation of the soil, and the value of estates, and the commerce, naval power, and revenue of the empire, be more and more diminished. With regard to humanity, it was alleged, that if the prisoners taken in war, were not sold as slaves, they would be either put to death by their savage conquerors, or sacrificed to their gods, or at best retained in a state of the most rigorous and horrid

slavery in their own country.—As to justice, slavery was one of the conditions in which a very great portion of mankind had existed in all ages, and in Africa particularly. There are gradations of ranks or conditions of life, and that of the slave, though at the bottom of the scale, was one of them.—It was mentioned without either abhorrence or disapprobation in the sacred scripture.—But if slavery was allowed both by the order observed in the course of Providence, and by revelation, it was reasonable to infer, that a trade in slaves was allowed also. Was no advantage to be taken of any benefit that might be traced to the follies and vices of men ? This doctrine, carried into all its consequences, would throw society back into a state of wild, ferocious, and uncomfortable barbarism. The British legislature, in taking measures for the civilization of Africa, went entirely beyond the limits of their province. The general government of the world was in the hands of the Almighty Ruler, who had permitted evil, both physical and moral, to be blended with good, but who, by the operation of general laws, educed good out of evil, in his own time and way. The British government would find sufficient exercise for all their philanthropy and legislative wisdom at home. The *Scallags* in the Hebrides, the fishermen in the isles of the Shetlands, and the Orkneys were as much slaves as the negroes in our West India islands, and in circumstances far less comfortable.—The laboring poor, and other classes in England, Scotland, and Ireland, were also objects of great commiseration. The first attentions of the British legislature were due to these sufferers.—Their sufferings it might alleviate. But it was wholly beyond their power to prevent those evils which arise out of the ambition, the jealousy, the animosity, the rage and revenge which produce incessant war, and slavery among that multitude of chiefs and princes under whose dominion the vast peninsula of Africa is divided. The greatest good that Britain could do to Africa, would be to continue a trade, by which the condition of the captives taken in war is rendered so much better than what it would be if they remained in the hands of their most barbarous captors. It was clearly the interest of the masters to treat the slaves well. And measures had been recommended to the colonial assemblies, which if adopted, as they no doubt would be, would certainly effect, though gradually and progressively, the abolition of the slave trade.

It was argued on the other side, that the population of the negroes on our islands was capable of supporting itself, if they were treated with common humanity. Why should it be supposed that an universal law of nature should be resisted, opposed; and overpowered, only in the West Indies? and that there alone the human species should not continue, in obeying the call of nature, to increase and multiply? In fact, the population of our great settlement Jamaica had been found competent to support itself, notwithstanding many adverse circumstances, which, it might be expected, the abolition of the slave trade would remove. It had been ascertained by the most accurate calculations respecting the negro population of Jamaica, that from the year 1698 to 1730, the excess of deaths above the births amounted to 3½ per cent.; from 1730 to 1755, to 2½ per cent.; from 1755 to 1769, 1¼ per cent.; from 1769 to 1780, to 3-5ths per cent. And the average of three years ending in 1800, gave an excess of deaths of only 1-24th per cent.—It was remarkable also, that in Dominica, although a newer settlement, and although new lands were known to be inimical to population, there was an excess of population above the deaths, and so there was also in the Bermudas and Bahamas. Fresh importations of labourers, therefore, were not necessary to the cultivation of the islands, or those parts of the islands that were already under cultivation. And, with respect to the cultivation of new lands, the continuance of the slave trade for that purpose, would be to ruin the planters, who were now distressed by the accumulation of produce on their hands for which they could not find a market.—With respect to the general security of the islands, the

danger did not arise from those negroes who had been long settled in them, and used to their masters, but from those who had been freshly imported and were smarting under recent wrongs. The case of St. Domingo had been cited as an example of caution against the adoption of any measure that might tend to stir up, and agitate the passions of our negroes, or to unite them, by an *esprit de corps*, in a design to assert their liberty. But the events which had taken place in that island, ought to serve as a warning against successive importations: for it was well known that, just before the insurrections and commotions which prevailed in that ill-fated island, there had been unusually large importations from Africa. The passions of men had been let loose and inflamed at the commencement of the French revolution, throughout every part of the French empire, Hence St. Domingo became a prey to intestine commotions, and was divided into different political parties, each of which in their turn endeavored to avail themselves of the assistance of the blacks. And the fresh and large importations from Africa during that period, served as fuel to the flames of discord, insurrection, and all the fury of war: whereas among the old slaves, and such particularly as were natives of the island, there were a great many instances of faithful and attached slaves saving, at the expense of their own, the lives of their mistresses and masters. The newly imported African was much more dangerous than the man born in the island. It deserved to be remembered, that Dessalines himself was an imported African. It was admitted that St. Domingo in its present state was not a good neighbour, and that emissaries had been sent from thence to excite revolt in Jamaica. But emissaries would have been sent if the present question had never been agitated. And the effects of the abolition would be to counteract the attempts of such emissaries, by tending to make the situation of the negroes more comfortable.

It had been argued that this measure would tend to diminish the white population in the islands by discouraging those who go out from this country to the islands as book-keepers and overseers, with the hope of procuring plantations and making their fortunes. But the expectation of making large fortunes could not be considered as the main inducement for such persons to go from this country to the West Indies, but rather that they might obtain such a competent provision as they were not likely to meet with at home. But were no other modes of employment by which the white population might be kept up, and such a militia as might be necessary to control the negroes ? a great deal of what is now performed by blacks, might be performed by whites, or done by machinery : and encouragement might be given to Europeans to settle in the West Indies, and pursue such trades as those of coopers, wrights, carpenters, and other employments. Thus the proportion of whites to blacks would be increased : and by this increase, and treating the negroes kindly, there would be no reason to dread either intestine commotion or the attacks of a foreign enemy.

With regard to the national, and the individual interests connected with the slave trade considered by itself, and independently of its effects on the colonies, it was computed that the African tonnage was not quite 1-52nd part of the export trade of this country, (without including that of Ireland and the coasting trade) and the seaman employed not quite 1-23rd part, of the seamen in the general trade. Now it was not to be doubted but, in the flourishing state of our commerce, employment would be found for this shipping, when not embarked in the slave trade.—As to the capital embarked in the African trade, it did not exceed 1-110th part of the whole export capital.

Thus it appeared, that the abolition of the slave trade would contribute to both the security and prosperity of our West India islands without materially affecting the interests of individuals or the public revenue. But were these doubtful points, the abolition of that horrid traffic was imperiously demanded by justice. What right had we to deprive, by force, the

nations of Africa, of the means of laboring for their own advantage, and compelling them to labor for ours ? Was it to be endured, that the profits obtained by rapine and outrage were to be urged as an argument for the continuance of rapine and outrage ?—Greater indignation, if possible, still, was excited by the cold calculations of those who affected to defend the slave trade, even on the ground of humanity, and to maintain that greater evils would be created to the Africans, by an abolition of the slave trade, than any which it was proposed to remedy. War among the numerous and almost innumerable chiefs of Africa, it was said, would exist if there were not any trade in slaves, and but for the slave trade, prisoners taken in war would be put to death.—It was not supposed that slavery was the only cause of war among the savage tribes of Africa : but it was one cause, and on the sea-coasts the chief. Because wars spring out of ambition, hatred, revenge, and other evil passions ; was it nothing to add another motive to war, and that, one more constant and permanent in its operation, namely, avarice ? In the interior of Africa, population and civilization increased, and on the coast barbarity reigned with undiminished sway ; a contrast to be accounted for only by the slave trade. As to the alleged murder of prisoners of war, though human sacrifices had sometimes been made, it was known that the common fate of prisoners of war, as among all barbarous nations, was, to become domestic slaves to the captors. It had been objected, that " if we abandoned the slave trade, other nations would take it up."—They might say the same thing of us ; and the argument would go round in a circle, without ever leading to a satisfactory conclusion.—As to the argument that slavery had always been one of the states of existence in which man had been placed by Providence, it would be more correct to say that man had been placed in that state by the tyranny of man. If, however, through the abuse of reason and free-will, moral good was blended with evil, there was a principle of progressive civilization and humanity implanted in human nature by its gracious Author ; and, if many things were tolerated, as arbitrary divorcement among the Jews for a time, on account, as it is said in the scripture of " the hardness of men's hearts ;" the great, all-comprehending, and paramount law of the gospel, was charity :—" Whatsoever ye would that men should do unto you, do ye even the same unto them, for this is the law and the prophets." By the progress of civilization and of the influence of religion, slavery was gradually mitigated in the Roman empire, and finally abolished in almost the whole of modern Europe. This was the course of Providence : this was the progression of grace and good-will towards men. And it became men and Christians, to co-operate with this benevolent plan, not to counteract it. .

Lord Howick, on the 5th of March, in pursuance of previous notice, moved for leave to bring in a bill for securing to all his majesty's subjects the privilege of serving in the army or navy upon their taking an oath prescribed by act of parliament, and for leaving to them as far as convenience would admit, the free exercise of their respective religions. The motion was vehemently and successfully opposed by Mr. Perceval, and all further attention to it was postponed till the 18th of March, on which day lord Howick gave notice that he should not move for the second reading of the bill. Connected with this declaration, several animadversions were made in the discussion of the reversion bill on the cupidity of Mr. Perceval, who, it appeared, had been offered the chancellorship of the duchy of Lancaster, for life, on condition of his accepting a place in the new government. These remarks led to an explanation from Mr. Perceval, who, to the astonishment of the public, informed the house, that he had been offered not only the chancellorship of the duchy of Lancaster, but the post of chancellor of the exchequer, an appointment which implied a total revolution in the ministry. He assured the house at the same time, of his readiness to serve his majesty, even without the chancellorship of the duchy of Lancaster for life.

Lord Grenville in the house of lords, and, on the same day, lord Howick in the house of commons, detailed the circumstances of the late changes in his majesty's councils, and stated, at great length, the principles on which they were friends to the bill, for granting relief to the catholics and other dissenters. In the year 1778, a law passed in Ireland to enable the protestant dissenters in that country to hold employments of any kind, civil as well as military, and without any restriction. Here the law was quite different ; no dissenter could hold a place without taking the sacramental test within a certain time. And if the Irish law of 1793, by which the catholics were admitted to any rank in the army not above that of colonels, were not repealed, would not the English dissenter have a right to say, " On what principle of justice do you exclude me, while you are a friend to the catholic ?" A draft of the despatch to the lord-lieutenant of Ireland, relative to the communications to be had with the catholics, was submitted to his majesty by his ministers, and met with his approbation. They pointed out the difference between the law of 1793 and that which they meant to propose. After some objections, his majesty gave his consent that the measure should be proposed, and authority was given to the lord-lieutenant to communicate by his secretary to the heads of the catholics, that the army and navy would be opened to them. A meeting of the catholics was assembled for receiving this information, when Mr. Elliot, the Irish secretary, was asked by one of them, (Mr. O'Connor,) whether it was the intention of government merely to pass the law that was promised in 1793, or whether it was allowed the catholics to rise to all military offices, including the staff.—Mr. Elliot was not then able to answer the question. But the catholics understood by the despatch that they were not to be excluded from any situation in the army. A second despatch was drawn up, removing Mr. Elliot's doubt, and authorising him to give a decided answer to Mr. O'Connor's question in the affirmative. This second despatch was laid before his majesty, who returned it without any objection or comment ; it was therefore immediately forwarded to Ireland. Doubts, however, as to the extent of the measure, had been entertained by some members of the cabinet, who, being at last fully aware of it, expressed their dissatisfaction in the strongest terms ; and his majesty, apprised that the measure was of far greater extent than he had conceived it to be, declared a decided objection. The ministers then endeavored to modify the bill so as to reconcile it to his majesty's wishes without destroying the very essence of the measure. Failing in this attempt, they determined to drop the bill altogether, but at the same time, in vindication of their own character, to insert in the proceedings of the cabinet, a minute, reserving to lord Grenville and lord Howick, 1st, The liberty of delivering their opinions in favor of the catholic question ;—2nd, That of submitting this question, or any subject connected with it, from time to time, according to circumstances, to his majesty's decision. But the ministers were called upon not only to withdraw the latter reservation, but to substitute in its place a written obligation, pledging themselves never again to bring forward the measure they had abandoned, nor ever to propose any thing connected with the catholic question. To this they found it impossible to assent. They could not fetter themselves by a written engagement, inconsistent with what they might conceive to be their duty, which even by their oaths they were bound to perform. The two leading ministers having respectfully communicated to his majesty their sentiments on this subject, they on the next day received an intimation from his majesty, that he must look out for other ministers. Lord Howick was particularly solicitous to establish the point, " that whatever misunderstanding might have arisen, the fault was not with ministers, as his majesty was afforded every opportunity completely to ascertain the object of the bill." But it would appear that there must have been not a little obscurity in the details of the bill since the Irish secretary, Mr. Elliot, was unable to answer

Mr. O'Connor's question respecting the extent to which it was carried in favor of the catholics.

Both houses of parliament met on Wednesday, the 8th of April, pursuant to adjournment ; and in the mean time a new administration was formed, in which the duke of Portland was created first lord of the treasury, Mr. Perceval chancellor of the exchequer, lord Eldon lord chancellor, lord Liverpool secretary for the home department, lord Castlereagh secretary for the war department, Mr. Canning minister for foreign affairs, and lord Mulgrave first lord of the admiralty.

The state of domestic politics, after these arrangements, was remarkable. For the first time we were subjected to an administration without a name : its ostensible head, the duke of Portland, was a man who never appeared in parliament, and who was never spoken or thought of by the public. The other members held their places less by their own strength than by the weakness of their opponents. Of all the administrations, indeed that of " all the talents," had been the most unpopular. The two parties of which it was composed had been for many years engaged, not merely in opposition, but in absolute enmity and hatred of each other ; and their coalescence was like the combination of two chemical substances, each having a distinct character of its own, which, when they meet and are neutralized, is lost in both. The Grenville party suffered the least by this union, for it had less to lose, and had made fewer concessions of principle. The peace of Amiens had placed the talents of lord Grenville in a stronger light than they had been previously contemplated : the same prophetic foresight which Mr. Fox had displayed when the first unfortunate war was undertaken, he had manifested at its fallacious termination, and that too with a feeling of national honor, which all his opponents seemed in some degree to have laid aside. In another point also, his character stood higher than that of Mr. Pitt, for both of them equally favoring and being equally pledged to the measure of catholic emancipation, he had refused to abandon that measure as the means of coming into power, while Mr. Pitt thought proper to concede it.

Lord Grenville, therefore, when he re-entered the administration was looked up to with confidence, by the remains of that once numerous portion of the people, who, having formerly been duped by the anti-jacobin alarmists, regarded the old minority as the most dangerous enemies of their country, and relied upon *him* as their security against *them*. The most sanguine reliance on his integrity also distinguished that wiser class, who, however they had differed respecting the justice and necessity of the last war, were convinced that the present was unavoidable, and that England had no other danger to apprehend than that of being entrapped into a deceitful peace. To the catholics, and to a vigorous prosecution of the war, so long as war was essential to the safety and honor of the nation, lord Grenville and his friends were pledged, but to these points and these only. With the Foxites it was otherwise: their leader was bound, as strongly as professions could bind him, to obtain the repeal of the test act, and with the same reason a reform in the representation of the people was expected from lord Howick. It was demanded, and justly demanded, from these statesmen, now they were in power, that each should effect the measure which he had so strenuously and so often brought forward when in opposition; and from the whole party, as I have already observed, the removal, or at least the modification of the income tax was expected, since they had formerly resisted that impost as inquisitorial in its principle, iniquitous in its proportions, and oppressive in its operation. The promises of men in place have long been considered as proverbially worthless: the professions of those who are out of place are little better. Upon the death of Mr. Pitt, the government fell, as it were, by inheritance, to his opponents. The sinecure which he had vacated was secured by one of his colleagues, and then, without a struggle, they yielded to the influence and reputation of their successors.

Lord Castlereagh told them they had succeeded to a bed of roses, a phrase which became for a time, from its ridiculous inapplicability, a bye-word among the people. Great, however, as were the difficulties of the times, the uniform failure of their measures was to be attributed, at least, as much to misconduct as to misfortune. It was apprehended that the French would again seize upon Egypt, and occupy the whole of the Levant: the Egyptians, weary of the ignorant tyrants who degraded them, longed to be again under the dominion of a more enlightened power; and, having successively experienced the effect of French and of British protection, decidedly preferred the latter. It will appear from the subsequent narrative of several measures and enterprises projected during their possession of power, but of which intelligence did not arrive in England till after their dismissal, that their conduct was marked by the most culpable negligence and inadvertence. When it was at length determined to prevent the enemy from obtaining possession of Egypt, and information was required concerning the force that would be requisite, it was replied that 5000 men might secure Alexandria; but, if it was meant to conquer Egypt, 20,000 would be required. Five thousand were sent. They attempted to do that for which 20,000 were necessary, and the consequences were equally disgraceful and disastrous. At the same time an expedition was sent to Constantinople to overawe the porte, and we retreated with shame; our fleet narrowly escaping from the enormous stone balls of the Turkish artillery. But the heaviest loss, and the deepest dishonor, which the British arms sustained, was at Buenos Ayres. That city having been surprised without the knowledge, and against the wishes, of the late administration, their successors, in condescension to a popular cry, consented to conduct plans of conquest, of which, in their own better judgment, they disapproved: instead of establishing in those colonies an independent government, for which the occasion was so favorable, they began to dream of subduing South

America, and they assigned an important command to general Whitelocke, who by his gross incapacity occasioned the destruction of several hundred brave men, while the rest of the army were reduced, as we shall see, to a disgraceful capitulation. Every ministry will be judged by its contemporaries according to the success of its measures; nor is the criterion altogether false, for though wise measures may occasionally fail, it is seldom that foolish ones prosper. In such cases unfortunate is but another term for unwise, and as a general is responsible for the safety of his army, a minister ought to be answerable for the capacity of the ambassador or commander to whom he has intrusted the interests of the nation.

They sinned equally in what they attempted and what they performed. It was not possible to have assisted the Russians at Jena, for Prussia, whose final precipitance was not less remarkable, than her former endurance, had given us no time for effectual co-operation, and her king relying too confidently on the fortunes of the house of Brandenburg, upon his own popularity in the north of Germany, his untried strength, and the hereditary reputation of his armies, was playing an ambitious game, of which Hanover, and perhaps Holland with an imperial crown would have been the prize. A memorable lesson was afforded to posterity in that disastrous battle, when a single day sufficed for the overthrow of a power which it occupied a century of violent and iniquitous policy to establish. But with the Baltic open to our fleets we might have assisted Russia: an English force might have relieved Dantzic; an English army might have been present at Pultusk and at Eylau, and would probably have rendered either of those battles a *decided* victory over the French. An English army might have drawn off part of the strength of France from Russia, and, by a diversion, or by its presence, changed the fortune of many important battles. But instead of exerting the resources of the British nation at a period when the popular opinion upon the continent was in our favor, our

ministers stood aloof from the contest, leaving the continental powers to fight their own battles, and depend upon their own resources. The timorous character of their united policy, explained the nature of the concessions which the Grenville party had made to their colleagues, and the nation perceived, when it was too late, that the good which either party might have produced by acting wholly upon its own principles, was not to be expected from a coalition which paralized both.

The parliamentary conduct of the Foxites disappointed, still more poignantly, those who had fixed their hopes upon them. Catholic emancipation was adjourned till a more convenient season: the dissenters looked in vain to Mr. Fox for the repeal of the test act, and lord Howick, so many years the foremost advocate for reform in the representation, had now discovered that it was not the general wish of the people of England. Cruel and iniquitous as the income tax confessedly was in its principle, and severely as the people felt the late addition to its pressure, it was made as vexatious as possible by compelling those persons whose little incomes were below the standard of taxation to pay their full proportion, which they were afterwards to recover by producing proper testimonials: thus subjecting them to probable loss, and certain inconvenience, from their ignorance of the means by which restitution might be obtained, and the difficulty and expence of taking a journey to obtain it. The extension of the impost to so burdensome a degree, obtained for lord Henry Petty the name of the Rehoboam of taxation because his little finger was heavier than his predecessors loins: Such indeed were the proceedings of this party, when in possession of that power which had been for so many years the object of their wishes, that the sorrow and humiliation with which they filled their former advocates, could only be equalled by the pleasure of their enemies. Every debate afforded some instance of pliability; old doctrines were recanted, new ones advanced; and language which had formerly been used for the purpose of obtaining popularity, was explained away till no meaning was left which could gratify the mob, or offend the most submissive devotee of the crown. " What shall we hear *unsaid* to night?" was the triumphant sneer with which the new opposition were accustomed to enter the house of commons, and the general question was, " If these be the principles of the Foxites, what is it that has kept them out of place till now ?". To these causes of general disgust, other circumstances are to be added even more offensive to the public feeling. Never before had so total a displacement been made in the offices of state ; hitherto such changes had been confined to those great places which are the stakes for which the game of politics is played ; the revolution, in this instance, extended further, and men too humble, it might have been thought to be considered as belonging to any party, and who regarded themselves, and were regarded, as possessing a life-hold property in their respective situations were ejected to make room for a set of hungry partisans. The facetious complaint of the leader of the party that they lay three in a bed, became the topic of common conversation, and the people of England sorrowfully remembered the old fable of the Fox and the Flies.

The ministry however, deplorably as it disappointed the nation in other respects, had the merit of effecting the two most important measures of the present reign :— the army bill of Mr. Windham, and the abolition of the slave trade. The latter measure must be considered as an act of more certain, unmingled, permanent and extensive good, than it ever before devolved to any prince, statesman, or government, to effect. Thomas Clarkson is the man, whom this age, and all succeeding ages are bound to reverence as the principal cause and mover of the abolition. With him the work began, it was prosecuted by the unabating zeal of Mr. Wilberforce, and that excellent body of Christians the Quakers. Mr. Fox, as we have already seen, pledged the house of commons, by one of his last measures, to accomplish it, and the honor of carrying it into effect was reserved for

lord Grenville, who, from the time that the question was first agitated, had zealously and sincerely espoused the cause of humanity, and who had frequently declared in the bosom of his family, when the triumphant result was not to be foreseen, that, come death when it would, the remembrance of the part which he had taken would be his consolation.

The ministry were entitled to the higher praise, since they were obliged to contend with the greatest and most formidable influence. Neither all their political errors, nor their political sins, occasioned them such powerful enemies, as their most beneficial and salutary measures, and they were hated most for the good which they had done. The army-bill was regarded with horror, as an experiment, an innovation, and the abolition provoked the desperate hatred of all whose interests were involved in the trade of man-stealing ; a body of men who during the long struggle between good and evil which Clarkson had occasioned, frequently availed themselves of means scarcely less infamous than the cause which they defended. When the change of ministry rendered a new parliament necessary, no other place in England was disgraced by such riots as occurred in Liverpool. Their late member, Mr. Roscoe, was not less remarkable for his private virtues, than eminent for his literary productions. Born among them, and living among them, they who differed from him most widely in opinion, had hitherto respected his high and spotless character : yet, on his reappearance as a candidate, ruffians were posted to attack him : the horse of one of his friends was stabbed, a young man was killed, and to prevent further evils he withdrew from a contest which was conducted against him by force of arms.

The question upon which this ministry ventured to try their strength with the king, and in which they were compelled to yield, not only the measure in dispute, but their offices and authority, increased the load of unpopularity under which they labored. After the manner in which the subject of catholic emancipation, had previously been waived, they lost more credit by the want of sagacity thus displayed in bringing it forward, than they gained by adhering to their principles. Those who favored this emancipation were chiefly of two descriptions: dissenters who consider a repeal of the test act as its necessary consequence, and men whose readiness to tolerate any system proceeds from their indifference to all. A third class may be added, those who knowing, or supposing that they know the truth, and loving it sincerely and ardently, believe that pure religion may grant with safety toleration to every form of error. The majority of the nation had never thought of the question till an appeal was made to them concerning it by a general election: but they regarded popery as a bad thing, against which their forefathers had borne testimony at the stake, which had been subdued with great difficulty, and had long been considered as perilous to the state. Their natural conclusion from these premises, was, that it could not be right to encourage a religion which it had been so long our object to destroy.

The opponents of the measure, were of two classes: the first and loudest were a base crew, the hired retainers of party, and the noisy hunters after preferment. Their cry was, "the church is in danger;" they represented the fallen ministers as its enemies, and their clamors were dishonorably and dangerously fomented, by some of those who came into power upon the dismissal of their rivals. The second of these classes asserted that all emancipation would be useless at all times, and dangerous at present: dangerous because its immediate effect would be to introduce Irish priests, acting under orders from a church which Buonaparte had ostentatiously restored into our army and navy: useless because it would not satisfy those whom it was intended to conciliate.

While part of the falling administration declared themselves hostile to catholic emancipation, some of the members of the new ministry were friendly to the measure. Mr. Canning had always avowed this opinion, and lord Castlereagh had pledged his word to the Irish catholics. On the other hand, lord Erskine, connected as he had always been with the Foxites, reasoned on this occasion with the crown, and the same sentiments were entertained by lord Sidmouth and his friends, who, though the least powerful, were the most popular part of the discarded administration.

In the house of commons, Mr. Brand, on the 9th of April, after an introductory speech, in which he quoted the judgment of lord Coke, respecting the duty of a privy counsellor, moved "that it was contrary to the first duties of the confidential servants of the crown, to restrain themselves by any pledge, express or implied, from offering to the king any advice that the course of circumstances might render necessary for the welfare and security of any part of his majesty's extensive empire." The motion was ably opposed by Mr. Wharton, who, in a terse and energetic speech, descanted on the impropriety of entertaining in the house any abstract proposition. Mr. Osborne suggested an amendment; and, on the question being put, the ministers obtained a majority of 36. The debates which occurred previous to the division, were of a character more disgraceful than any which the house had witnessed. The opposition were exasperated by their unexpected fall, and by the success of rivals whom they despised: the ministry were provoked by the violence with which they were assailed; anger produced anger; abuse was answered by abuse, and accusation by recriminating charges. A new election gave the ministry a secure preponderance, but the temper of both parties remained the same.

There were two other parties in the house of commons, each more important from its influence with the people, than from its numbers, and each daily acquiring progressive influence over the opinions of the people. That which was denominated the Saints, or Evangelicals, was one. At the head of these was Mr. Wilberforce, a man of great, natural, and acquired endowments, and deservedly eminent for having, during so many years, attempted, and at last accomplished, the abolition of the slave trade. The principle of his party was to assist the existing government, but they supported it only upon principle. No administration could command their votes, and more than once, when their votes and opinions were of most weight, they were given against the minister. The other party were the radical reformers, whose leader, sir Francis Burdett, had for many years borne the brunt of political calumny : upon questions involving, no general principles, he now gave his support to the ministry, not because he approved of their talents, their character, or their domestic policy, but because there were no better to supply their place. The feeling which sir Francis expressed, was that of the people in general. They rejoiced in the fall of the late ministry, but it was with the joy of a vindictive temper, not of hope, and they preferred their successors for no other reason, than because they had supplanted men whom they so heartily disliked. As for talents, there was little to choose between them ; and so equally balanced were their virtues and their vices, that it became the general complaint that no man or set of men could be found who were entitled to the public confidence.

While the state was involved in these extraordinary circumstances, with a national debt of £626,000,000. and an annual expenditure of £72,000,000, England was engaged in a war against a military power more formidable than any of antient or modern times.

The measures of the late ministry with respect to the Ottoman government, were the subjects of just and vehement animadversion. Sebastiani, formerly a monk, now in the military order with the rank of general, labored with great assiduity to conciliate the favor of the divan, and of the sultan Selim. Finding that his flatteries and deceptions were ineffectual, he assumed a lofty tone, and presented a note to the Turkish government, stating in the most positive terms, that if the Turkish seas, and particularly the passage of the Dardanelles, and the canal of Constantinople, should be left open to the enemies of France, the grand signior must be re-

garded as the friend and ally of Russia and England. Mr. Arbuthnot, the English ambassador at the porte, observing the influence of these denunciations on the divan, communicated his sentiments to the British government, who immediately determined to send a British fleet with a military force, while they commenced a negotiation with the porte in conjunction with Russia. The fleet, consisting of seven ships of the line, besides frigates and bomb-ships, cast anchor about the middle of February, at the isle of Tenedos, where it was joined by the frigate on board of which Mr. Arbuthnot had made his escape. The fleet passed the Dardanelles on the morning of the 19th. A Turkish squadron, consisting of a 64 gun-ship, four frigates, and several corvettes, had been for some time at anchor within the inner castles. Orders were given to commodore sir Sidney Smith, to bear up with three ships of the line, and destroy the Turkish squadron should any opposition be made to his passage. The whole fleet passed the Dardanelles, and, as a token of forbearance, made no return to the fire of the Turks: But, while passing the narrow strait between Sestos and Abydos, they were under the necessity of answering a heavy cannonade, which was opened on them from the inner castles. Sir Sidney Smith destroyed a small Turkish squadron, and the marines spiked the cannon of a formidable battery. On the 20th of February, the English squadron came to anchor near the isles of Princes, at the distance of eight miles from Constantinople. From this station a flag of truce was immediately transmitted to the seraglio by Mr. Arbuthnot, containing assurances of the most cordial friendship should the porte accede to a negotiation, and denouncing the most rigorous measures in case of a resumption of hostilities. A letter in the same spirit was sent by admiral Duckworth to the Reis Effendi, but which stipulated, at the same time, that the Turkish government, as a condition of peace, should deliver into his hands all the ships and vessels of war belonging to the sublime porte. A proposal so arrogant and insulting, and compared with the force of the English squadron, so perfectly futile, only excited the derision of the mussulmans; but, after many notes and verbal propositions had been exchanged, the two parties assented to a conference on board the Royal George or the Endymion, and the admiral, for the purpose of receiving the Turkish plenipotentiary, moved the squadron four miles nearer the city, but continued beyond the reach of cannon-shot. In the mean time the fortifications, of which the English complained, were continued with unremitted activity and vigor. The grand signior himself, conducted by the French ambassador, general Sebastiani, superintended and encouraged the completion of the works. The Greek patriarch, and a number of his clergy, put their hands to the pick-axe and the wheel-barrow: men, women, and children, assembled from every quarter, and the members of the divan and other grandees, remained on the busy scene night and day, taking their necessary repose in small tents constructed for the purpose. At the end of four days, while the English were amused by pretended concessions and fallacious proposals, batteries were mounted with excellent breastworks, 500 pieces of cannon, and 100 mortars. The hostile disposition of the porte now became too evident and formidable to admit of further hesitation; and, on the 1st of March, after being prevented by unfavorable weather from obstructing or retarding the formidable preparations of the Turks, sir Thomas Duckworth repassed the Dardanelles. The fire of the two inner castles upon our ships on their inward passage had been severe, but its effects on their return were peculiarly formidable and alarming. Bullets, and blocks of marble of immense weight and size, were fired at our ships from huge mortars. One of these weighing 800 pounds, cut the main-mast of the Windsor man of war in two, and the ship was only saved by the most desperate exertions. Fortunately for the officers and seamen engaged in this inglorious expedition, they were able to avoid these masses, which were easily discovered in their course, by

stepping aside and opening a clear way for their passage. The loss sustained by the British admiral amounted to 250 in killed and wounded. The Dardanelles had by this time been so ably fortified by French engineers, that they could not be attacked by the most daring and powerful fleet with any hope of success; and, on the departure, therefore, of sir Thomas Duckworth, the strait was blockaded by a Russian squadron of ten sail of the line, and many frigates, under the command of admiral Siniavin. The Turkish captain, Bashaw Seid Ali, immediately set sail, and, having collected a force of eleven ships of the line, he bravely determined to risk an engagement with the Russian fleet, consisting of 22 ships of war, 10 of which were of the line. The action took place on the 1st of July, near the isle of Tenedos, and was continued for seven hours with great obstinacy on both sides. Four of the Turkish ships were carried by the wind out of the line of battle, a circumstance which rendered the skill and intrepidity of Seid Ali totally unavailing. Four of his ships of the line, including the vice-admiral's, were taken, three were burnt, and above 1000 Turks were killed or drowned.

The failure of our attempt on the capital of the Turkish empire was succeeded by an effort against the fortress of Alexandria in Egypt. On the 6th of March, a military force of about 5000 men was sent against that city, by general Fox, from Messina, under the command of major-general Mackenzie. The troops were landed on the 18th, and in the morning of the 19th, the general took up his position on the ground which the British troops had occupied on the 21st of March, 1801. After obtaining possession of Aboukir castle, and other advantageous positions, a truce was granted, which ended in the quiet surrender of the city: but unhappily from an unfounded dread of scarcity in the captured place, an attempt was likewise made to take Rosetta, and a large proportion of the British troops were cut off; 1000 men having been killed, wounded, or taken prisoners. The commanding officers at

Alexandria, now menaced with expulsion by the inhabitants, and harassed by repeated attacks from the enemy, gave up all idea of defending the place, and agreed to the evacuation of Egypt on condition that the Turks would restore the prisoners taken at Rosetta. These terms being obtained, the British troops returned to Sicily.

The result of sir Home Popham's unauthorised expedition to Buenos Ayres, had left the remainder of the British troops at the close of 1806, in possession of nothing more than the solitary post of Maldonado. The conduct of sir Home Popham was generally attributed to rapacity; and, notwithstanding the dexterous management of the newspapers, which profusely flattered him with the epithets of the *gallant* captain, the *gallant* commodore, and the *gallant* sir Home Popham, his conduct was declared, by a court-martial held in March, to be highly reprehensible, and leading to a subversion of all military discipline, and subordination to government. He was therefore reprimanded, at a moment indeed when the final result of 1807. his expedition to the Rio de la Plata was unknown, and when every prejudice was in favor of the enterprise.

A reinforcement of the British troops had been sent to La Plata in October, 1806, under the command of sir Samuel Auchmuty; and the conduct of sir Charles Stirling in the Ardent ship of war, who was appointed to supersede sir Home Popham. He there received intelligence of the recapture of Buenos Ayres, and of our having possession of Maldonado, near the mouth of the river. The general, on his arrival at Maldonado, found our troops without artillery, destitute of stores and of provision, and exposed to the insults of a corps of 400 horse, that hovered around the English to intercept supplies.

For a detailed account of the capture of Monte Video, the author cannot do better than refer to the despatches of sir Samuel Auchmuty, who, after announcing the landing of the forces about nine miles from the town, gives the following interesting account of the subsequent operations.

" The enemy came out of the town, and attacked us with their whole force, about 6000 men, and a number of guns. They advanced in two columns; the right consisting of cavalry, to turn our left flank, while the other, of infantry, attacked the left of our line; this column pushed in our advanced-posts, and pressed so hard on our out-picquet, of 400 men, that colonel Browne, who commanded on the left, ordered three companies of the 40th, under major Campbell, to their support: these companies fell in with the head of the column, and very bravely charged it; the charge was as gallantly received, and great numbers fell on both sides; at length the column began to give way, when it was suddenly and impetuously attacked in flank by the rifle corps, and light battalion, which I had ordered up, and directed to the particular point. The column now gave way on all sides, and was pursued with great slaughter, and the loss of a gun, to the town. The right column, observing the fate of their companions, rapidly retired, without coming into action.—The loss of the enemy was considerable, and has been estimated at 1500 men; their killed might amount to between 200 and 300; we have taken the same number of prisoners, but the principal part of the wounded got back into the town: I am happy to add, that ours was comparatively trifling.—The consequences of this affair were greater than the action itself. Instead of finding ourselves surrounded with horse, and a petty warfare at our posts, many of the inhabitants of the country separated, and retired to their several villages, and we were allowed quietly to sit down before the town.—From the best information I could obtain, I was led to believe that the defences of Monte Video were weak, and the garrison by no means disposed to make an obstinate resistance; but I found the works truly respectable, with 160 pieces of cannon; and they were ably defended.—The enemy, being in possession of the island of Ratones, commanded the harbor; and I was aware that their gun-boats would annoy us, as we apprehended. A two gun battery was constructed on the 23rd, to keep them in check, and our posts were extended to the harbor, and completely shut in the garrison on the land side. Their communication was still, however, open by water, and their boats conveyed to them troops and provisions. Even water for the garrison was obtained by these means; for the wells that supply the town were in our possession.

"On the 25th we opened batteries of four 24-pounders, and two mortars, and all the frigates and smaller vessels came in, as close as they could with safety, and cannonaded the town. But finding that the garrison was not intimidated into a surrender, I constructed, on the 28th, a battery of six 24-pounders, within 1000 yards of the south-east bastion of the citadel, which I was informed was in so weak a state that it might be easily breached. The parapet was soon in ruins, but the rampart received little injury, and I was soon convinced that my means were unequal to a regular siege; the only prospect of success that presented itself was, to erect a battery as near as possible to a wall by the south gate, that joins the works to the sea, and endeavor to breach it. This was effected by a six-gun battery, within 600 yards; and though it was exposed to a very superior fire from the enemy, which had been incessant during the whole of the siege, a breach was reported practicable on the 2nd instant. Many reasons induced me not to delay the assault, though I was aware that the troops would be exposed to a very heavy fire in approaching and mounting the breach. Orders were issued for the attack an hour before day-break the ensuing morning, and a summons was sent to the governor in the evening to surrender the town. To this measure no answer was returned.—The troops destined for the assault, consisted of the rifle corps upon major Gardener, the light infantry under lieutenant-colonel Brownrigg and major Trotter, the grenadiers under

majors Campbell and Tucker, and the 38th regiment under lieutenant-colonel Vassal and major Nugent.—They were supported by the 40th regiment under major Dalrymple, and the 87th under lieutenant-colonel Butler and major Miller. The whole were commanded by colonel Browne. The remainder of my force, consisting of the 17th light dragoons, detachments of the 20th and 21st light dragoons, the 47th regiment, a company of the 71st, and a corps of 700 marines and seamen, were encamped under brigadier-general Lumley, to protect our rear.

"At the appointed hour the troops marched to the assault. They approached near the breach before they were discovered, when a destructive fire from every gun that could bear upon it, and from the musketry of the garrison, opened upon them. Heavy as it was, our loss would have been comparatively trifling, if the breach had been open; but during the night, and under our fire, the enemy had barricaded it with hides, so as to render it nearly impracticable.— The night was extremely dark. The head of the column missed the breach; and when it was approached, it was so shut up, that it was mistaken for the untouched wall. In this situation the troops remained under a heavy fire for a quarter of an hour, when the breach was discerned by captain Renny, of the 40th light infantry, who pointed it out, and gloriously fell as he mounted it. Our gallant soldiers rushed to it, and, difficult as it was of access, forced their way into the town. Cannon were placed at the head of the principal streets, and their fire for a short time, was destructive; but the troops advanced in all directions, clearing the streets and batteries with their bayonets, and overturning their cannon. The 40th regiment, with colonel Browbe, followed.—They also missed the breach, and twice passed through the fire of the batteries, before they found it.—The 87th regiment was posted near the north gate, which the troops who entered at the breach were to open for them, but their ardor was so great that they could not wait. They scaled the walls, and entered the town as the troops within approached it. At daylight, every thing was in our possession except the citadel, which made a show of resistance, but soon surrendered; and early in the morning the town was quiet, and the women were peaceably walking the streets.

"The gallantry displayed by the troops during the assault, and their forbearance and orderly behaviour in the town, speak so fully in their praise, that it is unnecessary for me to say how highly I am pleased with their conduct. The service they have been engaged in since we landed has been uncommonly severe and laborious, but not a murmur has escaped them; every thing I wished has been effected with order and cheerfulness.—Our loss during the siege was trifling, particularly as we were not sheltered by approaches, and the enemy's fire of shot and shell was incessant. But it is painful for me to add, that it was great at the assault. Many most valuable officers are among the killed and wounded. Major Dalrymple, of the 40th, was the only field officer killed. Lieutenant-colonels Vassal and Brownrigg, and major Tucker, are among the wounded. I am deeply concerned to say, that the two former are severely so. The enemy's loss was very great, about 800 killed, 500 wounded, and the governor Don P. R. Huldobro, with upwards of 2000 officers and men, are prisoners. About 1500 escaped in boats, or secreted themselves in the town.

"From brigadier-general, the honorable W. Lumley, and from colonel Browne, I have received the most able and the most zealous assistance and support. The former protected the line from the enemy during our march, and covered our rear during the siege. The latter conducted it with great judgment and determined bravery.—The established reputation of the royal artillery has been firmly supported by the company under my orders; and I consider myself much indebted to captains Watson, Dickson, Carmichael, and Wilgress, for their zealous and able exertions. Captain Fanshaw, of the engineers, was equally zealous; and though

young in the service, conducted himself with such propriety, that I have no doubt of his proving a valuable officer.—The captains and officers of the navy have been equally zealous to assist us; but I feel particularly indebted to captains Donnelly and Palmer for their great exertions. They commanded a corps of marines and seamen that were landed, and were essentially useful to us with the guns, and in the batteries, as well as in bringing up the ordnance and stores.—I have the honor to be, &c.

S. AUCHMUTY.
Brigadier-general commanding

"P. S. I am extremely concerned to add, that lieutenant-colonels Vassal and Brownrigg both died yesterday of their wounds. I had flattered myself with hopes of their recovery; but a rapid mortification has deprived his majesty of two most able and gallant officers."

The loss of the English, which fell chiefly on the storming column, was 600.

When the ministry received intelligence of the recapture of Buenos Ayres, they ordered general Craufurd, who had been sent on an expedition to Chili, to relinquish that enterprise, and repair to the Rio de la Plata. After this junction between him and general Whitelocke, the whole British force in La Plata was computed at 9500 men. The latter general, through the friendly influence of Mr. Windham, had been selected for the direction of the new expedition, and set sail for his destination early in March, carrying along with him an additional force of 1630 men. The escape of general Beresford, on his rout from Buenos Ayres to his destined place of confinement, supplied him with much useful information. On the 11th, general Whitelocke took the command of the troops, and on the 28th of June, a force was assembled near Ensenada de Barragon, amounting to 7822 rank and file, including 150 mounted dragoons. It was provided with 18 pieces of field artillery, and 206 horses and mules for their conveyance. After some fatiguing marches, through a country much intersected by swamps and muddy rivulets, the army reached Reduction. Major-general Gower, with the right column, crossed the river at a ford called Passo Chico, and, falling in with a corps of the enemy, attacked and defeated it. Next day general Whitelocke, with the main army, having joined general Gower, formed his line by placing brigadier sir Samuel Auchmuty's brigade on the left, extending it towards the convent of the Recolletta, from which it was distant two miles. Two regiments were stationed on its right. Brigadier-general Craufurd's brigade occupied the central and principal avenues of the town, being distant three miles from the great square and fort; three regiments on his right extended in a line towards the Residentia. The town was thus nearly invested; and this disposition of the army, and the circumstances of the town and suburbs being divided into squares of 140 yards on each side, together with the knowledge that the enemy meant to occupy the flat roofs of the houses, gave rise to the following plan of attack: brigadier-general sir S. Auchmuty to take possession, with a regiment, of the Plaza de Toros, and the adjacent strong ground, and there to take post. Four other regiments, divided into wings, were ordered to penetrate into the streets directly in its front. The light battalion divided into wings, and each followed by a wing of the 95th regiment and a three-pounder, was ordered to proceed down the two streets on the right of the central one, and the 25th regiment down the two adjoining; and, after clearing the streets of the enemy, this latter regiment was to take post at the Residentia. Two six-pounders were ordered along the central street, covered by the carabineers and three troops of the 9th light dragoons, the remainder of which regiment was placed as a reserve in the centre. Each division was ordered to proceed along the street directly in its front, till it arrived at the last square of the houses next the river Plata, of which square it was to take possession, forming on the flat roofs, and there to wait for further orders. Two corporals, with tools, were ordered to march at the head of each column for the purpose of breaking open doors. The whole troops were unloaded, and no firing was to be permitted until the columns had reached their final points and formed. A cannonade in the central streets was the signal for the whole to come forward. The issue of the conflict which ensued, was such as was to be expected from a plan so weak, and indeed ludicrous. Our troops moving forward in the appointed order, with their unloaded muskets and iron crows, were assailed by a heavy and continued shower of musketry, hand-grenades, bricks and stones, from the tops of the windows of the houses, the doors of which were barricadoed in so strong a manner, as to render it almost impossible to force them. The streets were intersected by deep ditches; and cannon planted on the inside of these, poured volleys of grape-shot on our advancing columns. They were saluted also with grape-shot at the corners of all the streets. Every householder, with his negroes, defended his own dwelling, which was in itself a fortress. Yet, in the midst of all this assailance, and while the male population of Buenos Ayres, by the means of destruction just mentioned, was employed in its defence, sir S. Auchmuty, after a most spirited and vigorous attack, in which his brigade suffered much from grape-shot and musketry, made himself master of the Plaza de Toros, took 82 pieces of cannon, an immense quantity of ammunition, and 600 prisoners. This position served as a place of refuge to some other regiments that were overpowered by the enemy. Brigadier-general Cranford with his brigade, being cut off from all communication with any of the other columns, was obliged to surrender: so also was lieutenant-colonel Duff, with a detachment under his command. Still, however, the result of this day's action left general Whitelocke in possession of the Plaza de Toros,- a strong post on the enemy's right, and the Residentia, another strong post on his left; whilst general Whitelocke himself occupied an advanced post on his centre. But these advantages had cost about 2500 • men, in killed, wounded, and prisoners. This was the situation of our army in the morning of the 6th of July, when general Liniers addressed a letter to the British commander, offering to give up all his prisoners taken in the late affair, together with the 71st regiment, and others taken with brigadier-general Beresford, on the condition of his desisting from any further attack on the town, and withdrawing his majesty's forces from the river Plata; intimating, at the same time, that, from the exasperated state of the populace, he could not answer for the safety of the prisoners if he persisted in offensive operations. General Whitelocke, influenced by this consideration (which, he says, he knew from better authority to be founded in fact,) and reflecting of how little advantage would be the possession of a country, the inhabitants of which were so absolutely hostile, resolved to forego the advantages which the bravery of his troops had obtained, and acceded to a treaty of peace, on the basis that had been proposed by the Spanish commander.

At a general court-martial, held at the hospital of Chelsea, on the 28th of January, 1808, and continued by adjournments until the 18th of March, lieutenant-general John Whitelocke was tried upon the following charges:

First charge.—That lieutenant-general Whitelocke, having received instructions from his majesty's principal secretary of state, to proceed for the reduction of the province of Buenos Ayres, pursued measures ill calculated to facilitate that conquest: that when the Spanish commander had shewn such symptoms of a disposition to treat as to express a desire to communicate with major-general Gower, the second in command, upon the subject of terms, the said lieutenant-general Whitelocke did return a message, in which he demanded, amongst other articles, the surrender of all persons holding civil offices in the government of Buenos Ayres, as prisoners of war: that the said lieutenant-general Whitelocke, in making such an offensive and unusual demand, tending to exasperate the inhabitants of Buenos Ayres,

to produce and encourage a spirit of resistance to his majesty's arms, to exclude the hope of amicable accommodation, and to increase the difficulties of the service with which he was intrusted, acted in a manner unbecoming his duty as an officer, prejudicial to military discipline, and contrary to the articles of war.

Second charge.—That the said lieutenant-general Whitelocke, after the landing of the troops at Ensenada, and during the march from thence to the town of Buenos Ayres, did not make the military arrangements best calculated to ensure the success of his operations against the town; and that, having known, previously to his attack upon the town of Buenos Ayres, upon the 5th of July, 1807, as appears from his public despatch of the 10th of July, that the enemy meant to occupy the flat roofs of the houses, he did nevertheless, in the said attack, divide his force into several brigades and parts, and ordered the whole to be unloaded, and no firing to be permitted on any account, and under this order, to march into the principal streets of the town unprovided with proper and sufficient means for forcing the barricadoes, whereby the troops were unnecessarily exposed to destruction, without the possibility of making effectual opposition: such conduct betraying great professional incapacity on the part of the said lieutenant-general Whitelocke, tending to lessen the confidence of the troops in the judgment of their officers, being derogatory to the honor of his majesty's arms, contrary to his duty as an officer, prejudicial to good order and military discipline, and contrary to the articles of war.

Third charge.—That the said lieutenant-general did not make, although it was in his power, any effectual attempt, by his own personal exertion or otherwise, to co-operate with, or support the different divisions of the army under his command, when engaged with the enemy in the streets of Buenos Ayres, on the 5th of July, 1807; whereby those troops, after having encountered and surmounted a constant and well-directed fire, and having effected the purpose of their orders, were left without aid and support, or further orders; and considerable detachments, under lieutenant-colonel Duff and brigadier-general Craufurd, were thereby compelled to surrender: such conduct on the part of the said lieutenant-general Whitelocke tending to the defeat and dishonor of his majesty's arms, to lessen the confidence of the troops in the skill and courage of their officers, being unbecoming and disgraceful to his character as an officer, prejudicial to good order and military discipline, and contrary to the articles of war.

Fourth charge.—That the said lieutenant-general Whitelocke, subsequent to the attack upon the town of Buenos Ayres, and at a time when the troops under his command were in possession of posts on each flank of the town, and of the principal arsenal, with a communication open to the fleet, and having an effective force of upwards of 5000 men, did enter into, and finally conclude, a treaty with the enemy, whereby he acknowledges, in the public despatch of the 10th of July, 1807, " That he resolved to forego the advantages which the bravery of his troops had obtained, and which advantages had cost him about 2500 men, in killed, wounded, and prisoners ;" and by such treaty, he unnecessarily and shamefully surrendered all such advantages, totally evacuated the town of Buenos Ayres, and consented to deliver up to the shamefully abandon and deliver up to the enemy, the strong fortress of Monte Video, which had been committed to his charge ; and which, at the period of the treaty and abandonment, was well and sufficiently garrisoned and provided against attack, and which not, at such period, in a state of blockade or siege ; such conduct, on the part of lieutenant-general Whitelocke, tending to the dishonor of his majesty's arms, and being contrary to his duty as an officer, prejudicial to good order and military discipline, and contrary to the articles of war.

The court-martial found the general guilty of the whole of these charges, with

the exception of that part of the second charge, which related to the order. that " columns should be unloaded, and that no firing should be permitted on any account." The court was " anxious that it might be distinctly understood, that they attached no censure whatever to the precautions taken to prevent unnecessary firing during the advance of the troops to the proposed points of attack ; and did therefore acquit lieutenant-general Whitelocke against that part of the said charge." The court adjudged, " That the said lieutenant-general Whitelocke be cashiered, and declared totally unfit and unworthy to serve his majesty in any military capacity whatever." This sentence was confirmed by the king, who gave orders that it should be read at the head of every regiment in his service, and inserted in all regimental orderly books, with a view of its becoming a lasting memorial of the fatal consequences to which officers expose themselves, who, in the discharge of the important duties confided to them, are deficient in that zeal, judgment, and personal exertion, which their sovereign and their country have a right to expect from officers entrusted with high commands.

The plan of attack on Buenos Ayres adopted by general Whitelocke, it would appear, was not of his own contrivance, but proposed to him by lieutenant-general Gower. This was declared by the general himself in his defence. And general Gower admitted, in his evidence, that the basis of the plan adopted by general Whitelocke was very much like his. Indeed, general Whitelocke appears, from his trial, to have been very undecided and wavering in his conduct, and in that state of mind which reposes on the counsels of others. Towards the end of the trial, public curiosity was less excited to know its issue, than the interest on means by which general Whitelocke had obtained his important appointment.

HISTORY OF THE WAR.

CHAP. XLVI.

State of the Hostile Parties at the commencement of the Campaign of 1807—Movements of the various Armies, and the progress of the Campaign to the arrival of the Russians at Friedland—Buonaparte's critical situation—Alarm of the Parisians—Fall of Dantzic—Negotiations of the Emperor of France with Turkey—Promotion and aggrandisement of his favorite Generals.

DURING the early part of the present year every eye was fixed on the coast of the Baltic. A mighty contest was yet to be decided between the emperor of Russia and the king of Prussia, aided by the co-operation of Sweden and Great Britain on the one part, and on the other Napoleon Buonaparte, supported by the population and the resources of Italy, Spain, Holland, and a great part of Germany. The alleged defeat of the Russians at the battle of Eylau, was more than counterbalanced in the opinion of the enemies of France, by the facilities afforded to the manœuvres of a Swedish army between Dantzic and Hamburgh, through Lower Saxony. It was expected that the immense distance of Buonaparte from his resources, combined with the severity of an inclement and unhealthy climate would expose his army to the most fatal indisposition, and to insupportable privations. The Russians, on the contrary, were perfectly enured to the scene of action, and could receive stores and reinforcements by land and sea, from Russia, Sweden, and England.

The talent, intrepidity, and perseverance of the emperor of France overcame 1807. however the obstacles and the dangers, by which he was surrounded. The number and activity of his agents, and the admirable organization of his commissariat, so strikingly contrasted by the tardiness and negligence of the Russians in that important department, ensured the arrival to all parts of his army of ample and regular supplies. Owing to the mildness of the season and the rapidity of their movements few of the troops were afflicted with disease, and the absolute authority of Buonaparte gave him all the advantages that arise in council and in battle from unity of purpose, and firmness and celerity of decision.

The relative positions in which the French and Russians were placed after the battle of Eylau, were not misunderstood by Buonaparte, who according to his usual policy on every great crisis, despatched Bertrand, a general of division, to the Russian commander-in-chief with some overtures of a pacific nature. But general Beningzen, in the true spirit of a gallant soldier, replied that he " had been sent by his master not to negotiate, but to fight." Bertrand was then ordered to proceed from Koningsberg to Memel, with the same overtures to the king of Prussia, with whom he had not greater success than with the Russian chief. Buonaparte endeavored, however, after these repulses, to make it believed in Germany, that both the Prussians and Russians were desirous of peace, and that treaties were on the point of being concluded. It was asserted in his newspapers that Duroc had gone to St. Petersburgh, and that the king of Prussia was governed by the counsel of Lombard, Beyme, and Kockyriz, the men who together with Hareywitz and Lucchesini, managed as he wished the court of Berlin. He was desirous to spread a conviction that he possessed the same influence at the court of Memel. Thus he hoped to sow the seeds of jealousy among the allies, and to deter any of the German states from any reliance on powers with which he was likely very soon to be on terms of peace, amity, and alliance.

The Russians were not induced by the battle of Eylau, and the necessity their main army was under, of retreating behind the Pregel, to give up their original plan of acting on the offensive against the French, and harassing them without ceasing by all means and at all seasons. While the main army of the French still lay at Eylau, 3000 Russian prisoners were rescued by a squadron of cossacks, 1000 strong, at Wildenberg, from 15 to 20 leagues on this side of Eylau on the Omulcio, to the south-west of the lakes of Passenheim. General Van Essen, on February the 15th, at the head of 25,000 men advanced to Ostrolenka, along the two banks of the Narew. At the village of Flakis Lawowa he met the advanced-guard of general Savary, who commanded the 5th corps of the French army. On the 16th at day-break, general Gazan with a part of his division moving towards the advanced-guard, met with the enemy on the way to Novogorod, and attacked and defeated him. But at the same moment the Russians by the left bank attacked Ostrolenka, which was defended by general Campana, with a brigade of the division of general Gazan and general Ruffin, and a brigade of the division of general Oudinot. The Russian infantry advanced in several columns. They were suffered to come fairly within the town, as far as half the length of the streets; when they were charged by the French with fixed bayonets. Thrice did the Russians make an attack upon the French, and were as often repulsed, leaving the streets covered with the dead. Their loss was so great that

they were forced to abandon the town, and take a position behind the sand-hills which cover it. The divisions of general Suchet and Oudinot advanced, and at noon the heads of their columns arrived at Ostrolenka. General Savary drew up his army in the following manner. General Oudinot commanded the left in two lines; general Suchet the centre; and the general of division Reille, chief of the staff of the army, commanding a brigade of the division of Gazan, formed the right. He covered himself with all his artillery, and marched against the enemy. General Oudinot putting himself at the head of the cavalry made a successful charge, and cut in pieces the cossacks of the Russian rear-guard. A very brisk fire was kept up for a considerable time on both sides. The Russians at last gave way on all quarters, and were followed fighting for three leagues. The loss of the Russians was 1300 killed, among whom were two generals, above 1200 taken, seven pieces of cannon, and two standards. The French according to their accounts had only 60 men killed, and among these the general of brigade Campana, an officer of great merit, and a native of Marengo. At Guttenfield on the 12th of February, 500 French soldiers were made prisoners by Platoff, hetman or attaman of the cossacks. On the same day a division of the French corps marched to Marienwerder, situated on a small river called the Leibe, not far from its junction with the Vistula, thirty-four miles south from Dantzic and forty-four north-east of Thorn. Seven Prussian squadrons found at this place were attacked and routed, and 300 men with 250 horses taken. The rest of the Prussians making their escape, took refuge in Dantzic.

On the 16th of February, the day before Buonaparte began to march from Eylau, for the disposition of his troops in winter-quarters he thought it proper to counteract any impression that might be entertained of his being subjected to the necessity of a retreat, and to keep up the courage of his army by assuming a very lofty air of triumph, in the following proclamation, dated Eylau, February the 16th. " Soldiers we had begun to enjoy a little repose in our winter quarters when the enemy attacked the first corps and shewed themselves on the Lower Vistula. We broke up and marched against him, we have pursued him sword in hand 80 leagues, he has fled to his strong-holds, and retired beyond the Pregel. In the battles of Bergfried, Deppen, Hoff, and Eylau, we have taken from him 65 pieces of cannon and 16 standards, besides the loss of more than 40,000 men in killed, wounded, and taken prisoners. The heroes who on our side remain on the bed of honor, have died a glorious death. It is the death of a true soldier. Their relatives will always have a just claim to our care and bene-ficence. Having thus defeated all the en-terprises of the enemy, we shall return to-wards the Vistula, and resume our winter-quarters. Those who shall dare to disturb these quarters shall have reason to repent, for whether beyond the Vistula, or on the side of the Danube, whether in the middle of winter or the beginning of autumn, we shall still be found French soldiers, and soldiers of the grand army."

The first and leading consideration in the choice of positions for winter-quarters for the French army, was to cover the line of the Vistula, and to favor the reduction of Colberg, Grandenz, and above all of Dant-zic. It was therefore concentrated in cantonments, behind, that is, to the west-ward, of the Passarge, a small river which passing by the town of Braunberg dis-charges itself a little below this place, into the Frisch-haaf. The prince of Ponte Corvo with his corps lay at Prussian Hol-land and Braunsberg; marshal Soult with his at Leibstadt and Morungen; marshal Ney at Gutstadt; marshal Davoust at Allenstein, Hobenstein, and Deppen; a Polenese corps of observation, commanded by general Zayoncheek, at Niedenburg; marshal Le Febvre before Dantzic; the 5th corps of the French army, was station-ed at Omulew; and the 8th as a corps of observation, in Swedish Pomerania. There was a corps under prince Jerome Buona-parte employed in the reduction of the fortresses of Silesia. The Bavarian division, commanded by the heir apparent, or as the French style him, the crown prince of Ba-

varia, serving under Jerome, lay at this time at Warsaw, and was on its rout to join the French army. There was still a strong garrison at Thorn, where general Rapp, Buonaparte's aid-de-camp, was ap-pointed governor in the room of marshal Le Febvre, now employed in the siege of Dantzic. The head-quarters were at Osterode, nearly equidistant between Thorn (which formed as it were a bastion on the right of the French, supposing their eye still directed to the east,) and Marien-werder, and Elbing, with the isle of Nogat, which supported the left. And for main-taining a communication between the op-posite banks of the Vistula, as well as for securing a retreat, in case of any disaster, in the course of future operations, the têtes-du-pont, or fortified bridges at Praga, Mod-lin, Duchaw, in the palatinate of Ulm and Thorn, were put in a proper state of de-fence, and new ones constructed at Marien-burg and Marienwerder. From the country around Marienwerder and Elbing, which, particularly the isle of Nogat, is exceed-ingly fertile, the French army was abun-dantly supplied with provisions.

It was now the immediate object of Buonaparte, to refresh and recruit his army, and to secure the possession or command of the countries he had overrun, by redu-cing the Prussian fortresses that still held out on the Vistula, and the Oder. But the Russians determined and resolute in their purpose to give him no rest, engaged the French in continued skirmishes, and in some very sharp actions which were at-tended with considerable loss to both parties. The most serious of these it may be proper briefly to notice, though they were of little importance in comparison with the siege of the more important port and post of Dantzic, to which after the battle of Eylau, every eye was turned. A Russian detachment marched on the 26th of Febru-ary against Braunsberg, the head or the most advanced and easterly of the French cantonments. Buonaparte being informed of this movement, gave orders to the prince of Ponte Corvo, that the detachment should be attacked, the execution of which orders was committed to general Dupont, an officer of great merit, who on the same day, at two o'clock in the afternoon, attacked the Russian corps, which was 10,000 strong, overthrew it with fixed bayonets, drove it from the town and across the Passarge, took 16 pieces of cannon, and two stands of colours, and made 2000 prisoners.

On the side of Gutstadt, general Loger Belair, on receiving advice that a Russian column had arrived during the night at Peterswald, repaired to that village at day-break on the 25th, overthrew it, took the general, baron de Korf, who commanded it, with his staff, several lieutenant-colonels and other officers, and 400 men.

After the affairs of Brauensberg and Peterswald, which encouraged the military ardor of the conscripts, for the year, whose services were now to be called in, though six months before the time fixed by the constitution ; a statement was published of all the pieces of cannon taken from the enemy by the French, since their arrival on the Vistula. In the engagements of Pultusk and Golymin, they had taken 89 pieces of cannon ; at the engagement of Bergfried, 4 pieces ; in the retreat of Allenstein, 5 pieces ; at the engagement of Deppen, 16 pieces ; at the engagement of Hoff, 12 pieces ; at the battle of Eylau, 24 pieces ; at the engagement of Ostrolenka, 9 pieces ; and at that of Braunsberg, 6 pieces ; in all, 175 pieces of cannon. It must be owned that an account of the cannon taken from the enemy is a more satisfactory proof of success than any estimate of the numbers of the killed and wounded. The cannon may be produced as vouches of every military statement, and the French gazettes usually inform us in what manner each division has disposed of the captured artillery.

On the 29th of February, the head-quarters of the Russian army had reached Heilsberg, from whence the enemy, having been driven with loss, had fallen back upon the Passarge. Marshal Bernadotte was cantoned at Holland and Braunsberg. Marshal Soult at Leibstadt and Morungen. Marshal Ney in advance of the Passarge. Marshal Davoust at Allenstein, Hohen-

stein, and Deppen. The main body of the cavalry in the country about Elbing, and the head-quarters at Ostèrode. The Poles were at Neidenburg, and the 5th corps, which Massena now commanded, was cantoned upon the Oumlew. The corps of marshal Le Febvre was before Dantzic. A Bavarian division before Warsaw, and the 8th corps in Swedish Pomerania.

These corps were extremely weak, and, in addition to casualties of the field, sickness was so prevalent, that in Warsaw alone, there were 25,000 men in the French hospitals, and the French cavalry were entirely unfit for active service.—To repair these losses, Buonaparte raised the siege of Colberg, nearly evacuated Silesia, ordered, under the severest penalties, a new levy in Switzerland, marched troops from Dalmatia, Calabria, Italy, and the very invalids of Paris, to recruit his army in Poland ; and, in a message to the senate, dated Asterode, the 10th of March, demanded a new conscription, of the year 1808, which of course was granted : he then determined to check, by daring countenance and partial aggressions, the advance of the Russians, and to recover the *moral* of his army by the active character of his operations. By this time he had also discovered that he had advanced from the Vistula with too great temerity, and that the port and fortress of Dantzick offered to his enemies a débouchure on his rear, which might, under a vigorous direction, separate him from France, or oblige a retrograde movement to preserve his bridges and a passage over the Vistula, which would be ruinous to his army, if not fatal to himself. He therefore gradually approached Dantzic with his Polish, Saxon, and Baden levies ; and, after several affairs, drove the Prussians into the city, which was defended by 16,000 men, and two Russian garrison battalions under prince Tcherbatoff, with some cossacks. Consonant with this plan, he directed his marshals to make strong reconnoissances, to distract the Russian general and recal his parties, who had already reached Allenstein, Ortelsburg, Willenburg, and Passenheim ; and on the 3rd of February, the French reoccupied Allenstein and Guttstadt, and a considerable corps from Wormdit attempted to carry a Russian post between Wormsdorf and Arensdorf, but here the enemy were foiled with great loss, as a masked battery suffered them to approach close, and then poured rapid discharges of grape. This movement occasioned a general concentration of the Russian army, and the renewal of the campaign was expected, especially on the following morning, when a heavy cannonade commenced at Zechern, two leagues in front of Heilsberg, occasioned by the advance of a French corps who had pushed across the plain from the village, and lodged themselves in a deep wood, from whence they had annoyed the Russian advanced-posts. Fire attracted fire, and a serious action appeared probable, though not premeditated by either army. At length the Russians opened their guns, which were answered from the heights of Zechern, but the Russian cannon soon silenced that battery. Still the enemy's infantry hung in the wood, and already 500 Russians were wounded. General Zachen, who commanded, determined towards evening to finish this harassing contest, and ordered two regiments to charge into the wood, and two regiments of cossacks, headed by their attaman, were ordered to co-operate. Upon the signal being given, the cossacks rushed forward with their war yell, echoing terror, and killed or made prisoners in a few seconds, 160 men, with the loss of only 10 killed and 14 wounded. The remaining French escaped by some rugged ground; and, as the Russians menaced the storm of Zechern, the three French regiments and a regiment of cavalry that had sustained this affair, marched off rapidly on Guttstadt. Accurate intelligence was obtained from the prisoners, which exposed the enemy's views, and a particular, but private incident, further gave general Beningzen every information that he sought. Whether or not the enemy were suspicious of this incident, is not known ; but, on the 6th, the French expecting to be attacked,

drew out their forces along their line, and, by this demonstration of vigilance, preserved themselves from an attack that was projected for the following day.

The Russian reinforcements had now begun to arrive ; amongst them was a superb regiment of cuirassiers, (the Catherina Slaber,) commanded by general Kratof, and two cossack regiments, whose sumptuous wildness was novel and interesting ; and general Beningzen, having abandoned his plan of attack, removed his head-quarters to Bartenstein, for the convenience of his arrangements.

To cover his cantonments from insult, Buonaparte threw forward on the side of Willemburg, 15,000 Poles, and placed them under the orders of Massena ; these being new levies, did not add greatly to his real force, or inspire much respect among the Russians ; but general Platoff was directed to proceed on that side with 3000 cossacks, and act against them. In the mean time the siege of Dantzic continued ; and the enemy, being lodged on the Nehrung, all communication by the coast road, between Pillau and Dantzic, was cut off ; but an attempt was made to surprise and force the enemy's posts stationed there, which failed. The attacking corps was therefore obliged to return to Pillau, with some trifling loss to the Prussian advanced-guard. On the 12th, Murat was checked in his advance with seven regiments of cavalry, on Bischoffstein ; and general Zachen, in the neighbourhood of Wormdit, killed 100 dragoons, and sent in 200, of whom the greater part were severely wounded. On the 18th, general Platoff broke in upon the enemy's line of posts between Passenheim and Willemburg, made 300 Polish cavalry, with seven officers, prisoners, after a great slaughter of their corps; and, having induced the 15th and 22nd regiments of cavalry to charge in pursuit through a wood, where he had ambuscaded half his cossacks, he put to death or captured the whole.

On the 24th, the enterprising and active Platoff again marched from Passenheim, to attack the confederates at Kutzen, Malga and Omilow. The column directed

on Kutzen being wilfully misled, the guide
was executed. The second column advanced at dawn against three squadrons
posted in the village of Malga, and drove
them upon six supporting squadrons, when
the whole fell back upon the woods of
Mollendorf, where the Polish infantry
were stationed. The cossacks then feigned
to fly. The Polish cavalry pursued over
the plain, and, when sufficiently forward,
the cossacks turned, charged, and killed
300, making the colonel, lieutenant-colonel,
and 200 privates, prisoners. At Omilow
the Polish infantry lined the woods, and
kept the cossacks in check ; but a distinguished cossack, (colonel Karpoff) thought
that an opportunity presented itself to
attack some infantry in a more open space.
As he was advancing, the infantry formed
a hollow square, his cossacks hesitated ;
he, however, alone rushed on, pierced,
passed through, and was returning cheer-
ing on his cossacks, when a musket-ball
struck him dead. Platoff reproached his
party at the funeral for not having revenged his death and devoted themselves
to sacrifice the enemy ; and, when he
kissed the forehead, (according to custom,)
previous to the lid of the coffin being
closed, he could not refrain from tears :
wiping them away, he observed, " That
he did not weep for the lot of mortality,
but that friends could not go together out
of the world."

It appears that general Zyoncheck, the
commander of the Poles, had proposed to
attack the cossacks at Passenheim with
3000 infantry, 8 pieces of cannon, and 15
squadrons of cavalry, and that they were
actually on march for that purpose, when
the fortuitous enterprise of the attaman
discomfited their design ; but, on the
26th, the 300 cossacks stationed at Ortelsburg were driven out of that town. As
that post was of great importance, being
in the line of communication between
general Essen's right wing at Ostrolenka,
and general Beningzen ; general Tchapliz,
with his regiment of hussars, 6 guns, and
300 cossacks, immediately advanced upon
it, and, by a most able disposition and
gallant bearing, compelled 2000 Polish in-

fantry, with 4 guns, 800 French cavalry,
and 300 Polish cavalry, to retire with the
loss of 50 killed and some prisoners, which
the peasants murdered in revenge for outrages committed by the corps during the
night.

In the beginning of April, the French
made an assault upon Graudentz, but were
repulsed with great loss. It was said
that the governor gave the enemy reason
to suppose that he embraced a dishonorable
offer made to him, and [then suffered the
columns to approach close to his works
before he inflicted punishment. General
Platoff continued to send in prisoners, and
interrupt the foraging parties of the enemy,
whilst he maintained, notwithstanding frequent attacks, the post of Ortelsburg.
On requiring succors, he was reinforced
by a regiment of dragoons, one of hussars,
two battalions of infantry, and two of chasseurs. On the 17th, the emperor and the
king of Prussia arrived at Bartenstein, and
on the 22nd they inspected the advanced-
guard of prince Bagration in front of Heilsburg, which was found in admirable order,
and the huts, &c. arranged with an elegance that was quite unexpected. Their
majesties then advanced with three or four
persons, and closely reconnoitered the
enemy's posts, after which they returned
to Heilsburg, where troops daily arrived
from Russia, and amongst them the corps
of guards under the grand duke Constantine, at the head of which, as the regiments successively entered, the emperor
always marched through the town.

The siege of Dantzic continued to be
vigorously pressed : the Holme island at
the back of the city, on which the two
Russian battalions were lodged, had been
carried with the loss of 400 men on their
part. As the occupation of this island
by the enemy completed the investment
of the city, exposed every part to a bombardment, and intercepted all its communications with the Fair Wasser, and
Weickselmunde, (where there are two
forts at the mouth of the Vistula, about
four miles from Dantzic,) great anxiety
prevailed, for the place, then wanting ammunition, and having only a garrison of

inferior description, chiefly composed of recruits raised in the Polish provinces occupied by the enemy ; and, as the place itself, notwithstanding Buonaparte's bulletins in compliment to marshal Le Febvre, can scarcely be rated in the second order of fortresses.

General Kaminskoy, on the 7th of May, was therefore ordered, with 6000 men, to embark at Pillau, and proceed to the Fair Wasser, under convoy of the Falcon British sloop of war, and a Swedish ship of the line. To favor this operation, general Putchikof, who had replaced general Essen, was ordered to attract the enemy's attention, by demonstration of building bridges on the Narew and the Bug, and partial attacks ; and the emperor and the king, after reviewing the grand army, on the 14th of May, proposed an attack on marshal Ney's corps at Guttstadt.

The head of the column formed in the woods had already reached the débouchure on the plain in front of Peterswald, where the sovereigns and commander-in-chief rode on to reconnoitre. In about two hours the army received orders to retire into their cantonments, but the enemy alarmed, did not dismiss his troops for thirty-six hours. Accounts were received from general Tuchikof, that in conformity to his instructions, he had attacked the enemy by a corps under the command of general Wickenstein ; that the general had passed the Narew on the 13th, and taken two pieces of cannon, several French officers and 60 men : and general Platoff reported, that he had on the 12th, with the same motive, attacked the Poles at Malga, killed several, and made three officers and 100 men prisoners ; and that from thence to favor the attack on Guttstadt, he had on the 13th driven the enemy's posts into Allenstein, and cannonaded the town for the whole day. Further advices from general Putchikow stated, that the enemy having passed the Narew at Shiroz with several divisions of French and Bavarian troops, and some Polish horse, were immediately repulsed with the loss of several hundred killed, and three officers and 107 prisoners ; and that another column which had passed

the Narew in front of Pultusk had retired on the approach of general Tutchikof. On the 15th of May general Kaminskoy made his attempt to enter Dantzic. The absence of the Swedish man of war which had on board 1200 of his men had delayed his enterprize and afforded time for Buonaparte to reinforce marshal Le Febvre by the bridge of Marienwerder, with more troops under marshal Lasnes, amongst which was Oudinot's division.

The Russians 4400 strong, having to defile over the narrow bridge on the Vistula, which communicated to the Nehrung, were not ready to advance until two hours after day-break, when they moved forward in three columns, under a heavy cannonade, which immediately opened from the Holme island. The columns with the most daring resolution, entered the wood and stormed the enemy's treble line of entrenchment, defended by Saxons, Poles, and French, of whom they killed many, and took several pieces of cannon : they then advanced, but their order of formation being broken by the trees, they presented themselves on the plain at the extremity of the wood in disorder. Here they were attacked by a very considerable body of troops, every moment reinforced from the left bank of the Vistula, when marshal Lasnes found the point of attack was confined to the right bank. Unable to resist such a superiority, the Russians fell back, pressed by a large body of cavalry. Rallying at the wood, they, a second time, attempted to advance, but after some success were again driven back, and the enemy entered the wood: A third time impelled by desperation they pushed on with the bayonet, and cleared the wood; killing many of the grenadiers, but a tremendous cannonade then beat them back, nor had they a gun to sustain them, and unfortunately all the zealous exertions of the British naval officers and crews of the vessels destined to co-operate, were ineffectual, as their want of wind prevented their advance against the stream.

General Kaminskoy finding the force of the enemy so enormously superior, and their position impenetrable, ordered at eight o'clock his troops to retire, which movement was executed back to the range of the guns from Wieckselmunde, without any loss, but the Russian soldiers with great reluctance quitted the works which they had so gallantly carried. The loss of the Russians in killed and wounded was 45 officers and 1600 men, whilst the enemy stated their own to be but 25 killed, and 200 wounded. A whole Saxon battalion, (independent of the loss sustained by Oudinot's division, the French light infantry, Poles, &c.) had, however, been destroyed without mercy, and the French official report of the affair characterizes it as most daring on the part of the Russians,—for some time successful, and to the last obstinate. The British flotilla had been unable to co-operate in the action; yet the laborious exertions, the ardent zeal, the affectionate interest with which they had toiled, and which now assured the relief and comfort of the wounded, were not only dwelt upon by the Russian officers and soldiers as honourable to the individuals and the British nation, but as a splendid and grateful proof of national attachment and sincerity for the common cause.

Whilst general Kaminskoy was endeavoring to advance by the Vistula, 2000 Prussians moved along the Nehrung from Pillau. They proceeded as far as Kailsberg, but pausing at that place in consequence of some intelligence, they were attacked by a considerable body of the enemy's infantry, and a brigade of dragoons, and routed with the loss of 600 men, two guns, and two vessels with provisions at anchor. A reserve on the narrow part of the Nehrung preserved the remainder, and it was fortunate for them, that they had not pushed on beyond Kailsberg, as the enemy had prepared to cut off their retreat by crossing the Frisch Haaf with a considerable force, and lodging it at that post.—Thus terminated this impracticable expedition.

General Kalkreuth after general Kaminskoy's unsuccessful enterprize, having repeated by telegraph his urgent want of ammunition, an English vessel of 22 guns, armed with 32lb. cannonades, on the 18th, attempted the bold project of forcing her way into Dantzic, although the Vistula is a very rapid river, and not above 60 yards broad with a boom thrown across.—Laden with 150 barrels of powder, and having 50 chasseurs on board, she adventured; but she had scarcely gained the Holme, when a cannon shot injured her rudder, and her rigging being materially damaged, she became unmanageable and grounded,—every effort to get her off failed, and after a gallant defence against nine batteries she was compelled to surrender. Dantzic was now reduced to the last extremity, and general Kalkreuth had protracted the defence to a most extraordinary length, (52 days open trenches,) he had done all that ability and devotional loyalty could effect: he had applied, he had exhausted every resource, and could entertain no hope of succour. As therefore the enemy were preparing to storm the Hackelberg, he proposed to capitulate, if allowed to retire with his garrison and arms, on the condition of not serving, without being regularly exchanged, for one year, against France or her allies. As Buonaparte was fearful of being attacked whilst embarrassed with this siege, these terms were granted, and on the 27th, the garrison, reduced to 9000 men, marched out for Koningsberg. Marshal Le Febvre then summoned the Weickselmunde, and Fair Wasser, which being no longer of any advantage, and if once besieged incapable of being approached so as to save the garrison, were on the the 26th evacuated by the Prussians.—General Kaminskoy had previously returned with his division to the army.

Buonaparte announced the surrender of Dantzic as the first glorious result of the victory of Eylau, but that battle did not supply to him the means of laying siege to Dantzic. The surrender, *according to date*, followed, but was not by any means the consequence of operations on the 8th of February. Had his army never been disturbed in their original cantonments, the siege might still have been formed, and if he had really driven the Russians behind the Pregel, with far greater probability of success.

Accounts from Graudentz diminished the gloom of these ill tidings. The garrison had made a very successful sally—taken and disarmed two German battalions, and possessed themselves of several vessels laden with corn, rice, ammunition, and money, so that hopes were entertained of its being in a condition to hold out, notwithstanding its long investment, and the threatened siege of marshal Victor. On the 3rd of June, notwithstanding the surrender of Dantzic had disengaged 30,000 of the enemy's troops—notwithstanding the Russian means had not been subsequently augmented, general Beningzen proposed a plan of operations by which he hoped to cut off marshal Ney, and if successful, to fall on marshal Davoust at Allenstein. Circumstances retarded the attack until the 5th, when the Prussians 10,000 strong, and the Russians 10,000 strong, immediately under the command of general Beningzen, opened the campaign against an enemy that could oppose to that force 130,000 men, and who had re-collected, between the Vistula and the Meinel, by the most vigorous exertions that Buonaparte had ever occasion to make, (exertions unparalleled in the history of Europe,) 190,000 men, including the garrison of Dantzic; whilst his cavalry had been reinstated and almost renewed by considerable remounts, drawn from Silesia, and the country about Elbing.

The Prussians, on the 5th of June, feigned a serious attack on the bridge of Spanden over the Passarge, defended by the corps of marshal Bernadotte, and protected by a strong tête-du-pont. After an action that lasted the whole day, in which the Prussians shewed much gallantry, they desisted, according to the original plan of combined operation. At the same time two Russian divisions commenced an affair at the bridge of Lomitten, defended by the corps of marshal Soult, and, according to the same arrangement engaged the attention of the enemy during the day, but on each side several hundred men were killed and wounded. The real attack was directed against the posts of marshal Ney's corps; 24,000 strong, whose stations were Altkerken, Ammt, Guttstadt, and Wolsdorf, whilst general Platoff with 500 men, including the brigade of infantry under

Vol. I.

general Knoring, was directed to pass the Aller, between Allenstein and Guttstadt, to alarm the rear of marshal Ney, and keep the corps at Allenstein in check. Unfortunately the different columns were directed to connect operations and wait upon each other, instead of having orders to press vigorously and reach the Passarge with all possible expedition, so as to anticipate the arrival of the enemy, who, pursued by superior forces, could not deviate to undertake any operation that might delay his retreat. In consequence of this combined movement and mutual progress, marshal Ney was enabled to defend himself without any uneasiness for his flanks, and it was not until two o'clock that general Gartchikof could enter Guttstadt, where he took some magazines and 300 prisoners, but even then when marshal Ney was driven from the Aller, he was not urged back so as to throw his lines into confusion, but he was permitted to retire gradually till night interrupted the action, when he withdrew his main body across the Passarge at Deppen, (about six miles distant,) where there was no tête-du-pont, and which was completely commanded by heights along the right bank, so that if the execution had been as well achieved as the plan was projected, marshal Ney with all the ability and means he employed could not have prevented the complete loss of his corps.

Whilst marshal Ney had been defending Guttstadt, general Platoff passed the Aller near Bergfried, and surprized an enemy's post of 60 men. Count Strogonau then proceeding to Rezengaite, saw the enemy's baggage retiring, and charging the escort with a very inferior force, took 30 officers and 500 men prisoners and made a considerable booty. The next morning at six o'clock the Russian army readvanced, and the advanced-guard under prince Bagration drove the rear-guard of the enemy across the bridge, where the Russians, the rest of the day, maintained a sharp fire of musketry and cannon on the French position and the village of Deppen, which were completely commanded by the Russian guns. At six, the action ceased, when

5 c

part of the town had been consumed, and the bridge too much damaged for passage. During this action, a regiment of cossacks had swam the Passarge, penetrated eight miles in rear of the enemy, attacked and cut to pieces an escort of cavalry, broke the carriage of one gun, which, for want of horses, they could not take away, destroyed 30 baggage waggons, and brought off a howitzer, which they contrived to transport across the river and deliver into the Russian camp.

On the 7th, the Russian army was about to move on Allenstein, when the cossacks sent advice that they were in the town, and that Davoust had abandoned it to join Marshal Ney. Some musketry, and an occasional cannonade had occurred in the morning at the bridge of Deppen, but no enterprise of consequence was attempted by either side.

On the morning of the 8th, the French drew out their troops, and made demonstrations as if they would attack the Russians and pass at Deppen, which occasioned for two or three hours a very severe cannonade, and a partial fire of musketry continued through the whole day.

About mid-day, Buonaparte had been seen to arrive, and the shouts of his army were distinctly heard. After inspecting the divisions, various movements were made, and cavalry and guns appeared to defile towards Osterode; but, being attentively observed, they were seen to quit that rout under cover of a wood, and retake the road in the direction of Leibstadt. Towards the afternoon, general Ilavoiski, with some cossacks, sent in several hundred dragoons that he had made prisoners, after killing as many in an attack upon three regiments of French cavalry ; and, in consequence of information from the prisoners, general Beningzen determined to fall back with his army upon Heilsberg, leaving prince Bagration to cover the retreat of his left, and general Platoff his right. These movements were immediately commenced, and the cossacks traversed from the left of the line to the right ; but, on reaching Lignau, at day-break on the 9th, general Ouwarrow, with a brigade of heavy cavalry

was found there, checking the advance of a body of the enemy lodged in a small wood in front of Elditten, and into which wood he had the evening before driven a party of their horse, with the loss of 150 killed and wounded. From various indications, general Ouwarrow believed that the enemy were passing the bridge of Elditten in force, and covering their operations by the shelter of the wood, on the skirts of which, small detachments only were seen ; but, before he withdrew, according to his orders, no serious augmentation of force was visible, and as the enemy remained quiet, a small advanced party was only left, and the main body fell back about two miles to refresh their horses, as the movement upon Heilsberg was to be deferred as late as possible, that the army might not be interrupted in march so as to produce confusion.

Buonaparte, when he had heard of the serious attack upon marshal Ney, accompanied almost immediately by intelligence of his retreat upon the Passarge, directed his army to assemble, and, with the corps of marshals Ney, Davoust, and Lasnes, the guards, Oudinot's division, and the cavalry of reserve, passed at the bridge of Elditten, whilst the other marshals crossed at Wuhsen, Spanden, &c. The forces under the command of Buonaparte being formed in close columns within the small wood already noticed, concealed their operations until about mid-day, when the columns advanced upon the plain, (bordered with woods to the right and left,) in three lines, and with flanking columns, whilst a considerable part of the cavalry marched in front, and a part in rear of the left. Over the first two miles he experienced no resistance ; but, when general Platoff arrived and threw forward his cossacks, which were supported by prince Bagration's cavalry, the Russians resumed the offensive and charged ; the numerous skirmishes and supporting detachments that swarmed the plain, animated with success, pressed forward with so much vigor, that the French infantry halted, rapidly formed squares, and the whole cavalry, except such part as was driven in, consisting of the light brigades of generals Pajol, Bruyeres, and Durosnel, and the division of heavy cavalry of general Nansouty, at full speed, rushed to the right, in which direction the Russians were advancing, whilst volleys of artillery and musketry poured upon them, but with comparative little loss; for so soon as they found the effort of the mass no longer expedient, they broke and separated over the plain, whilst prince Bagration covered their retreat by his artillery and the judicious disposition of his infantry.

The Russian rear-guard, however, now nearly approached the extremity of the level ground, from whence an inclined plain descended to the town of Guttstadt, and to the Aller, over which river, and an arm of it, there were two bridges, in the town on which general Platoff directed his troops, and three pontoon bridges had been formed on the left of the town for the passage of prince Bagration's division. The greatest resolution alone could save the troops, and any disunion of movements between the rear-guards would infallibly have insured destruction. The cavalry seemed sensible of the importance of their exertions at this critical conjuncture; and, by gallantry and active manœuvre, so repelled the French advanced cavalry, that, after various rencontres, in which they were always worsted, the latter retired and paused, until their infantry approached to their support; but, during this time, prince Bagration had crossed his infantry and guns, except guards for the têtes-du-pont, and taken up a position to cover the retreat of the cavalry which now successively began to withdraw. From the direction of the river, general Platoff's distance from the town was not so great as prince Bagration's, and he was earlier driven back towards the Aller, where his cossacks being still hard pressed, began to retire with an irregular pace, and disorder was commencing. Platoff, sensible of his duty to the general safety, fearful of a rush upon the town and the bridges, which would be fatal to the fugitives from their own tumult, apprehending that the enemy would be encouraged to profit of the confusion, and carry the town, whilst his troops were unable to fight or fly in choked streets, dismounted from his horse, enforced order, and, with the tranquillity of parade exercises, retired his cossacks in small bodies with large intervals; and, when he found that he could, without detriment to prince Bagration, move upon the bridges, he with his own rear-guard, leisurely regained them, and remained until the whole were destroyed by the artificers stationed for that purpose.

Perhaps the enemy thought the town occupied by infantry, and feared to compromise themselves by an attack; for, instead of advancing boldly upon it, the cavalry halted, and only the skirmishers and some flying artillery fired upon the retiring cossacks, until the French infantry arrived upon the heights, when, deploying from columns, the lines continued for some time to fire heavy volleys, and the artillery taking position, inundated the town with shot and shells, as also the sand-hills beyond, on which the Russians had stationed artillery to cover the rear-guards, and through the fire of which, when the enemy perceived them ascending, the rear-guards had to pass. Prince Bagration, with that courage, conduct, and fortune, which characterized all his services, had also withdrawn his troops, and destroyed his bridges without any loss; but a post of 150 infantry, who had been thrown on the left, were charged, approaching the river, and 50 of them were drowned. Thus Buonaparte, with all his genius, vigor, and prodigious superiority of power, actually marching in the same field, suffered, in his very presence, the escape of a feeble rear-guard, which must have been overwhelmed if properly pressed and acted against. An escape far more extraordinary and reproachful than was that of marshal Ney on the 5th, to the Russian reputation, since marshal Ney had 24,000 men under his command, and was sustained on his left by marshals Soult and Bernadotte, who were actually engaged with the Russians, and by marshal Davoust on his right, whom it was necessary to watch with 4000 men.

The enemy, satisfied with possession of

Guttstadt, and the left bank of the Aller, did not cross any troops over the river to pursue, but continued a heavy fire, while the Russians remained on the opposite bank, during which cannonade, the main body of the French army moved along the left bank, in the direction of Launau. Towards night prince Bagration fell back about half way to Heilsberg, and the cossacks took post in his front.

On the 10th the French army being now concentrated (except the corps of Victor, which was manœuvring on the left,) and composed of the corps of marshals Ney, Lasnes, Davoust, Mortier, Oudinot's division, the imperial guards, and the cavalry under Murat, advanced upon Heilsberg, and drove in the advanced-posts stationed to observe their approach; but the ground from Launau, for about a league towards Heilsberg was broken by transverse lines of high ridges, and the Russians retired gradually under the protection of artillery posted on the elevations and disputed each tenable station, which gave time for the arrival of prince Bagration about mid-day with his advanced-guard, which general Beningzen had ordered to cross the river, when he found the enemy directed their march altogether on the left bank, but the prince had been obliged to fall back as far as Heilsberg before he could cross on the pontoon bridges, so that he reached his station on the left bank only as the enemy had gained the uneven ground, and were beginning to deploy on the plain which extended with partial interruption of wood on their left flank, to the position of Heilsberg. A corps of the enemy formed the advance, on the right of which two divisions drawn from the supporting corps marched, whilst another division extended the left to some commanding grounds bordered by woods.

Buonaparte seemed determined to retrieve his error on the 9th, and to crush the advanced-guard of the Russians by weight of fire and cavalry attacks. The Russians driven from the broken ground endeavored in vain to hold their position on the level; they were obliged to form alternate lines to sustain by fire their retrograde movements, yet the successive retreat of each was rapid, and the loss momentarily augmented. The Russian cavalry presented a good countenance, but being so out-numbered were unable to check the enemy. Prince Bagration sent for reinforcements. Some infantry were advanced to support him, and 15 squadrons of Prussian cavalry, with a battery of horse artillery, by their most gallant behaviour afforded him great relief, but still the enemy by reinforcing his advanced lines, proceeded, and about four in the afternoon, when prince Bagration sent for further aid, general Beningzen ordered forward more cavalry, and directed the prince to keep retiring and allure the enemy under the guns of this part of his position, armed with 150 pieces of cannon, and reinforced by all his troops, except the guards and some cavalry from the position on the right bank. About six the enemy had approached sufficiently near, when the allied cavalry withdrew by the flanks, and a cannonade of extraordinary fury commenced, which compelled the enemy to recede from the reach of grape, but they threw their left in a small wood about 500 yards in front of the Russian centre, and establishing their batteries played upon all parts of the Russian lines, which extended from the river to the right about half a mile, whilst as night approached swarms of tirailleurs advanced, and maintained an incessant and close fire.

About seven the French columns suddenly again moved forward, and charging rapidly, carried the advanced work of the Russian position, with three guns.—It was a critical moment, but Russia had officers and troops equal to the crisis. Prince Gartchikow commanding the right wing, instantaneously ordered the charge. The huzzas of his troops assured victory. They darted forward overwhelmed all opposition, captured two eagles, and pursued till they threw their right upon the wood which the enemy had occupied. Then the cannon again thundered, and the musketry rolled—illuminating the atmosphere with continued flame.—The combat relaxed gradually and the Russian lines reascended to their position.

A little before ten at night, a deserter came over to the Russians, through the fire, and informed the general that another assault was preparing from the wood. Suitable arrangements had scarcely been made when the dark bodies of the columns were seen sweeping forward. Again the batteries opened and the fury of the battle again raged; but the assailants, unable to force their progress, fled back wrecked and almost annihilated. The action became then more feeble, and about 11 o'clock, the enemy along their line of tirailleurs shouted *arretez le combat*, when this grand and peculiar scene was closed, and the massacre (for no other term can be so properly applied,) terminated; but the cessation of the tumultuous uproar of war was followed by a din still more melancholy—the groans of wounded who anticipating the morrow's renewal of the fight, or tortured by pain, in vain implored removal, relief, or even death.

Heavy rain fell in the early part of the night, and rendered the clayey ground behind the Russian batteries so slippery that the various arrangements of the night were greatly incommoded, and the troops experienced much distress. Before daybreak the Russians again stood to their arms, momentarily expecting fresh efforts on the part of the enemy.

When light broke, the French were arrayed in order of battle, but a spectacle, indiscribably disgusting, more engaged attention than the hostile dispositions. The ground between the wood and the Russian batteries about a quarter of a mile, was a sheet of naked human bodies, which friends and foes had during the night mutually stripped, although numbers of these bodies still retained consciousness of their situation. It was a sight that the eye loathed, but from which it could not remove. The position of the bodies proved the desperate ardor of the attack. The ditches, the glacis were filled with them, to which they now served as a protection, unless Buonaparte's columns would or could have marched upon this pavement of their fallen comrades.

Towards ten the French after some movements, a cannonade, and a faint musketry, declined battle, and dismissed their troops, and each army now felt assured of a day's interruption to the work of slaughter; but the mutual positions still continued within cannon-shot distance, and the interest consequent on the proximity of two such armies increased, whilst considerations of future movements and comparative means engaged serious attention.

The loss of the Russians during their retreat upon the position had been considerable. One general had been killed, and four wounded, three battalions of chasseurs were almost destroyed, and altogether 7000 men had been returned, as killed or wounded in the battle. The loss of the enemy had certainly amounted to not less than 10,000 men, for even in the advance they had not proceeded with impunity, and the result of their assaults was not dependant on doubtful intelligence, still the effective force of the enemy in front of Heilsberg, indisputably exceeded 100,000 men, and another corps was known to be manœuvring against the Prussians on the left, so that the Russians had no equality of strength in the field, and no reserves to supply losses, except 30,000 men who had not passed the Russian frontier. The enemy had indeed been repulsed in his attacks, and therefore been defeated in the object of his enterprise on Heilsberg, but the victory had not an influence beyond the moment, for the redundant power of the French was still unimpaired, and they could traverse by the right of the position, move on Konigsberg, or, by throwing bridges over the Aller, surround and blockade the Russian army, who had not two days' bread in their camp or in those magazines, whilst contagion from the putrid loads that tainted the atmosphere, would have augmented the evils of famine.

About mid-day a corps of the enemy (marshal Davoust's) was seen in march upon the Landsberg road, and general Beningzen conceived that the enemy were moving upon Konigsberg, and that general Lestocy, who had been ordered in the morning to Zinlen from Heiligenbeil, on which he had fallen back, might not be strong enough to resist the advance of the enemy, and cover Konigsberg; he therefore detached general Kaminskoy with 8000 men to join him, and ordered general Lestocy to fall back with all expedition upon Konigsberg, and to maintain that city, as he was moving upon Wehlau with the army to support the line of the Pregel.

Fortunately general Lestocy had intercepted a courier with the order from Buonaparte to marshal Victor, which directed him to attack general Lestocy on every point and march direct to Konigsberg; whereupon the general with that decision and judgment which has rendered his name illustrious amidst the wreck of his country's fame, immediately determined to anticipate the enemy's object, and throwing himself between Victor, already at Muhlsack, and the city, gained it notwithstanding the enemy's movements and numerous attacks; general Kaminskoy by extraordinary exertion joined him during the march, and reached Konigsberg, but a brigade on Lestocy's right, consising of four squadrons of cavalry, two battalions of light infantry, and a half battery of horse artillery, which had been posted to watch Braunburg, was, while marching, intercepted by the rout of Frischaf, and after a most gallant attempt to force a passage, was obliged to surrender, when within two miles of Konigsberg.

At night the Russian army began to cross the Aller, cheered by the assurance that they were not retiring, but moving to fight the enemy in a new position, for confident from their late victory, they still felt an abhorrence of retrograde operations, and recollected that Eylau had secured them a long and luxurious repose. Day broke and three divisions of infantry had still to pass the bridges, but the enemy, unaccountably supine, although the whole operation was under their view and within musket-shot, made no movement, and the cossacks did not retire until two hours afterwards, when they fell back upon the bridges. Here the attaman stood to permit the passage of wounded men, successively coming from the town until near seven o'clock, when some French yagers appearing, he ordered the first bridge to be cut

away—waited to see the order executed—and in the same manner superintended the destruction of the second and third; after which he retired unmolested, leaving the enemy but their mass of killed and wounded, and only those Russians who from loss of limbs were unable to move.

The army on the 12th occupied Bartenstein, and Buonaparte's head-quarters were directed on Eylau, but his army was not put in motion before mid-day. A division of dragoons, and two brigades of light cavalry had cautiously followed the Russians along the right bank of the Aller, acting rather as a corps of observation than of pursuit. On the 12th the Russian army moved on Shippenbeil, but some cavalry marched on the left bank of the Aller. As heavy rain had fallen, the roads were distressingly bad.

The French army on the 13th moved from Eylau. Murat was ordered to join marshal Victor with his cavalry, at Konigsberg, and marshal Davoust to support him. Marshal Soult marched upon Creutzburg, marshal Lasnes upon Domnau, the marshals Ney and Mortier upon Lampasch. When Buonaparte found that the Russians were marching upon Shippenbeil, he had directed Murat, with the marshals Soult and Davoust, to move upon Konigsberg; and with the corps of marshal Ney, Lasnes, Mortier, and Victor, Oudinot's division, and the imperial guard, he in person marched upon Friedland.

On the same day the Russian army reached Friedland in the evening. During the morning a body of French hussars had been in the town; (on the left bank of the Aller,) but had been driven out by a brigade of Russian cavalry. From the information of the prisoners, general Beningzen believed that Oudinot's corps so shattered at Heilsberg, was alone stationed at Posthenon, about three miles in front of Friedland, on the road to Konigsberg. Having occupied the town and thrown forward some cavalry to cover it from insult during the night, he determined at four o'clock in the morning to fall upon Oudinot with a division and complete his extinction: accordingly he ordered a division to cross the Aller and advance to the attack. The enemy at first shewed but a very small force, which encouraged perseverance in the enterprise, but, by degrees, resistance so increased, that another division was ordered to pass the Aller, and, in addition to the town bridge, the construction of three pontoon bridges was directed. A heavy cannonade soon commenced,—the enemy's tirailleurs advanced,—columns presented themselves,—cavalry formed on the Russian right flank,—and general Beningzen, instead of a rencontre with a crippled division, found himself seriously engaged, not only with Oudinot, but the two supporting corps of Lasnes and Mortier, sustained by a division of dragoons under general Grauchy, and by the cuirassiers of general Nansouty, whilst his own feeble army was lodged in a position that was untenable; from which progress could not be made against an equal force; nor retreat be effected without great hazard; and when no military object could be attained for the interests or reputation of the Russian army, whose courage had been sufficiently established, without tilting for fame, as adventurers who have nothing to lose, and every thing to win.

Previous to the battle of Friedland, a proposition was made either by Russia in concert with her allies, to the ruler of France, or by the ruler of France to Russia and her allies, for a congress of all the belligerent powers to be held for the purpose of a general pacification. The Russian governments keeping a steady eye on Constantinople, objected to the admission of the Turks into the congress. Buonaparte insisted on the admission of the grand signior, as the friend and ally of France, in return for which, Russia would be permitted to make common cause with England in the congress. The basis of negotiation proposed by Buonaparte, between what he called the two belligerent *masses*, was equality and reciprocity, and a system of compensations. Though the negotiation had been interrupted by a series

of hot actions, and the king of Prussia and the Russian generalissimo had declined to enter into any treaty for an armistice or peace, as above noticed, after the battle of Eylau, Buonaparte, on the fall of Dantzic, made a direct proposal for renewing the negotiation to the emperor Alexander, accompanied by a declaration that he was desirous of peace above all things, and ready to listen to any reasonable overture to that end. That the French chief was sincere in this declaration, there is little reason to doubt. The progress of his arms from the Elbe to the Oder, and from the Oder to the Passarge, beyond the Vistula, and the commanding position of his army, might enable him to treat with advantage, and to return to Paris with glory. On the other hand, the battle of Eylau, as well as that of Pultusk, and other engagements, proclaimed the uncertain issue of a decisive action with such an enemy; and in whose favor a powerful diversion might be occasioned by a combined Swedish and English army, landing in Pomerania, in his rear, and commanding the course of the Oder from Stralsund to Frankfort. The necessity too, which would be involved by a prolongation of the war, of drawing levy after levy, of unfortunate young men and boys, from their wretched families, could not be any other than a cause of most serious alarm and apprehension. Since the commencement of the war against Prussia, that is, in the course of six or seven months, three several levies of conscripts had been raised. The last of these, by which the conscripts of September 1808, were called for in March, 1807, created a melancholly bordering on despair. Although all correspondence relative to the position of the armies was rigorously interdicted, and no letters suffered to pass without scrutiny, it was impossible wholly to conceal the mortality and the hardships inseparable from the various movements of the troops, and the unaccustomed rigors of a northern winter. A third conscription was generally considered as an undertaking too bold for the internal administration, especially at a moment when a belief was current among all ranks, that the emperor would not be able to extricate himself from the embarrassments, in which, after the battle of Eylau, he was supposed to be involved. The government, apprehensive of the danger, endeavored to prepare the public mind for the event, by employing emissaries to announce their intention in whispers through the circles, and 3000 coffeehouses of the capital. But an impression of terror was visible, even to a cursory observer, on the countenances of those who were either exposed to the danger, or shuddered at the prospect of new revolutionary horrors; of suspicion and joy, but half disguised in the lowering brows of the most resolute of the disaffected, constantly on the alert to improve the concurrence of opportunity, and who hailed this desperate expedient as a confirmation of their hopes. The orator of the government, Renaud St. Jean D'Angely, shed tears whether of sorrow or joy, as he stated the necessity of the measure ; and the senate received it contrary to their usual practice; in silent acquiescence, and with every symptom of reluctance and dismay. In order to assuage the general grief, it was found advisable to qualify the new call for 80,000 men, with a clause enacting that they were then to be merely organized, and retained within the limits of the empire as a national guard. Circumstances enabled them to adhere to this condition, which most certainly would have been violated if the armies had sustained a defeat. In the midst of disquietude and fear, public festivals were multiplied, in order to give the administration at home an air of confidence ; and an unusual degree of splendor brightened the court of the empress, who remained in Paris, and took a principal share in these mummeries of despotism.

It was not to be wondered at, therefore, if all things considered, Buonaparte should be desirous of a pacification. There was no reception, no return for him to Paris, but in the character of a conqueror. Though after the fall of Dantzic, the main army was increased by a disposable force of more than 30,000 ; and, though there was neither truce nor armistice, he did not take any measures for immediately opening the campaign, and surprising the enemy according to his usual system, by the promptitude and the celerity of his movements, but manifested every symptom of a sincere and even somewhat earnest desire, that hostilities might be for the present terminated by negotiation. Till this negotiation should be brought to some issue, he seemed determined to remain on the defensive. The ambassadors attending his court at Finkenstein, were witnesses of the proud eminence on which he now stood, and abundant care was taken that they should fully understand the importance of his recent conquest, the great bulwark of the Vistula. When the ambassador of the port, (Seid Mahomed Vahid,) was presented, on the 28th of May, by the prince of Benevento, Maurice Talleyrand, to Buonaparte, he said to the ambassador, that he and the sultan Selim would be for ever after as inseparably connected as the right hand and the left. The offices and administration of the government were now transferred from Warsaw to Dantzic, which seemed at this time to be intended for the capital of the French dominions in those parts. This city was visited on the 30th of May, by Buonaparte, attended by the greater part of his staff, his minister for foreign affairs, and, in short, all his court. He reviewed his troops, and gave orders for the reparation of the works demolished in the course of the siege. General Rapp, a great favorite, was appointed governor, and Le Febvre created duke of Dantzic. Each soldier engaged in the siege received a gratuity of ten francs. From his imperial camp at Finkenstein, May 28th, Buonaparte wrote to the conservative senate, that he had instituted duchies, as rewards for eminent services done him, whether military or civil, and that in pursuance of this system of encouragement, he had created, by letters patent, the marshal Le Febvre hereditary duke of Dantzic, in consideration of his former attachment and late achievements. It was incumbent on him, he observed, to establish the fortunes of such families as devoted themselves to his service, and sacrificed to a sense of loyalty and public duty, their own particular interests in life.

HISTORY OF THE WAR.

CHAP. XLVII

History of the Campaign of 1807, from the Memorable Battle of Friedland, to the Treaty of Tilsit—Conditions of that Treaty—Humiliation of Prussia—Magnanimity of the King of Sweden—Disputes between Great Britain and Denmark—Protracted Negotiations—An English Fleet and Army are sent into the Baltic—Bombardment of Copenhagen—Surrender of the Danish Fleet—Evacuation of Zealand—Opinions of Political Partisans on the subject of the Expedition—Designs of Buonaparte on Spain and Portugal—Invasion of the latter Country—Lord Strangford's Mission—Escape of the Court of Portugal to their Brazilian Empire—Affairs of St. Domingo—Capture of Curacoa—Discomfiture of the Indian Chief, Dundie Khan.

FRIEDLAND is a considerable town situated on the left bank of the Aller; a long wooden bridge connects the town with the right bank—west of the town is a capacious lake—the country for a mile in the direction of Heilsberg forms a semicircle of apparent plain, but is cut by a deep and narrow ravine full of water, scarcely fordable, which runs from Domnau into the lakes. Near the town on the left of the plain, the ground abruptly descends, and woods border the Aller; a deep wood fringed the plain from the Aller to the village of Heinricksdorf, where there was a little interruption; but woods again closed round to the Aller, the banks of which were very steep, the fords subsequently used were unknown, and, when discovered late in the evening, scarcely pervious. In the open space of the semicircle between the Aller and the rivulet, and about half a mile in front of Friedland, general Beningzen at first formed his troops in column, the cavalry being to the right of the Heinricksdorf road, and, as the succeeding division passed the Aller, the right and part of the centre of his infantry, were posted between that road and the rivulet, and that part of the centre was covered by a branch of the rivulet which terminated in a broad piece of water : his army was thus entirely exposed to fire, and every movement distinctly seen; whilst the enemy were sheltered from aim, and their force and operations were concealed till they chose to expose them. Upon the right of the enemy's position, he had the advantage of some rising ground, which commanded both banks of the Aller as far as the town.

After a heavy cannonade and much musketry, which the French maintained with their troops dispersed *en tirailleur*, the French cavalry and a body of their infantry, attempted to turn the Russian right, by the occupation of Heinricksdorf. Thirty French squadrons bore down upon the twelve Russian squadrons stationed to the right of the village, advanced rapidly, charged, and obliged the Russians to break; but the Russian cannon, and some columns of infantry moving forward, checked their progress, and compelled the cavalry to retreat in confusion and with some loss; during the attack the enemy's chasseurs, with several pieces of cannon, had lodged themselves in Heinricksdorf, taken three pieces of cannon improperly advanced, and opened a battery from the village. Soon afterwards the enemy being anxious to profit of the feeble fire of the Russians, yet scarcely established in their positious, advanced from the village in a column composed of 2500 men to force the Russian right and gain Friedland. This column was suffered to approach close to the Russian cannon, when the Russians opened a destructive fire of grape, which was irresistible. The column hesitated and almost immediately gave way, the retreat commencing with the rear ranks, when the Russian infantry charged forward and captured the eagle of the 15th regiment. An attack on the Russian left had been attended with no better success, and the enemy was compelled to shelter their columns in the wood, but still they maintained in advance various batteries and an incessant tirailleur fire.

The Russian divisions had successively continued to pass, and about nine o'clock in the morning only one division remained on the right bank, and in its front about half a league the cossacks under general Platoff were still stationed. General Beningzen, who from some prisoners, was now acquainted with the force opposed to him, fearful that a corps of the enemy might be sent to seize the bridge of Allenburg, which would intercept his retreat on Wehlau, and defeat the original plan of movement concerted with general Lestocy, directed 8000 men of which a regiment of the imperial guards composed a part, to recross the Aller and march upon that town; this detachment added to general Kaminskoy's deprived his army of 15,000 of his best troops, and left him but 40,000 men to defend the two banks of the Aller, and the probable destinies of Europe—40,000 gallant warriors, but almost exhausted by fatigue and by want of sustenance.

About 11 o'clock the enemy gave way in every point, and great hopes were entertained that he was retiring altogether upon Eylau. General Beningzen therefore ordered the Siberian chasseurs of the guards to lodge themselves in the wood at the ex-

tremity of the French right wing. They moved forward under the command of colonel St. Priest in the most intrepid manner, drove or destroyed every thing before them, and pierced into the wood, but they could not long maintain themselves in that advanced position, for the enemy immediately moved his principal forces against them. Obliged to withdraw they fell back with most perfect order, to half musket-shot distance from the wood, where they threw their left upon the Aller and obtained the shelter of some farm houses.

The Russian cavalry had manœuvred on the right to gain the enemy's left, by gradually encroaching into a new alignment. Having succeeded, a part charged the French dragoons and cuirassiers stationed in advance, who at first fled, but on a French officer riding down to them, they rallied, readvanced, and met the Russians, who, daunted at this unexpected onset, receded until a Russian reserve moving to their succour, the French again yielded the ground. The remainder of the French cavalry then galloped forward, the residue of the Russian cavalry also rushed into the combat, and a general mêlé ensued, which terminated in considerable loss to the enemy, especially his cuirassiers, and the temporary recovery of the village of Heinricksdorf, which was again abandoned, as the enemy brought on a numerous artillery

Thus far all had prospered, not indeed as to the original project, which had been early abandoned, but as to the realization of a hope that had succeeded of maintaining the ground until night. Under this confidence no precautions had been taken against disaster; no works were constructed to defend the entrances into the town and cover the retiring troops, if prematurely forced to recross the Aller, precautions that were perfectly easy of execution, as well as eligible, and which would have discomfited the ultimate efforts of the enemy. About mid-day the enemy's fire, which had relaxed, resumed more vigor, the cannonade increased, the tirailleurs came forward greatly reinforced, and from that time the cannon and the musketry continued unremittingly a tremendous fire upon the Russians, who were totally exposed, standing in columns with some infantry thrown forward to act as tirailleurs, whilst the French columns still remained in the woods, and the supporting lines of the advanced infantry concealed themselves 'from direct aim by laying down in long grass, or behind the favoring ground. Never was resolution more heroic, or patience more exemplary, than that now displayed by the Russians—never was a sacrifice of such courage more to be deplored.

The enemy had continued to arrive with fresh succours, and the woods were now thronged by battalions which advanced upon the edge and there reposed. About four o'clock in the afternoon Buonaparte was first noticed by the bustle and movement amongst the French troops, and soon afterwards he was distinctly seen giving directions. A little before five the French army stood to their arms and the cavalry mounted. From the town of Friedland the masses appeared through the interstices of the trees and the partial interruption of the wood, of enormous power and extensive depth, but the eye could not distinguish where the weight of the force was directing. From the plain the horizon seemed to be bound by a deep girdle of glittering steel.

It was in vain that general Beningzen had notice, and saw with his own eyes the mighty preparation.—The ammunition of his artillery was exhausted, and not forty pieces could fire. He had not a single battalion in reserve, and as he had been obliged to pass the last division over the river, not a soldier but the cossacks remained on the right bank of the Aller, and they half a league in advance. His columns reduced by the loss of 12,000 men were now so thinly scattered over the position that they seemed rather advanced detachments than the army itself, and this impression deceived Buonaparte so far that he suspended ulterior efforts after the battle. It was now that he regretted the absence of the 6000 men detached in the morning to Allenburg—a detachment that the world has had cause indeed to deplore; for if these 6000 men had been present at this

moment on the left of the position, Russian courage would have maintained a victorious contest against the enormous superiority of hostile forces, and against their more ruthless destiny, which had seduced them into the plain of Friedland.

General Beningzen in this extremity did all that his means and the time permitted. He directed six guns to take post on the elevation at the right bank of the Aller, a little in front of his left, so as to flank the enemy's right in a forward movement. He closed up the wreck of his centre, and sent an order for his cavalry to quit the right wing of the position and support the centre and right of the infantry, orders which were under these circumstances most judicious; but before the officer could reach the cavalry, the enemy's proposed attack was in execution.

About five o'clock the French army had taken its order of battle; marshal Ney on the right, marshal Lasnes in the centre, marshal Mortier on the left, marshal Victor and the imperial guard in reserve, general Grouchy with his division of cavalry supported the left, general Lahoussaye's division of dragoons, and the the Saxon cuirassiers, the centre, general Latour Maubourg's division, the right.

At half past five o'clock, 20 pieces of cannon discharging *salvos* gave the signal of attack, whilst another battery of 30 pieces opened upon the Russian left. The report of the guns were scarcely heard when the French column started from the wood, and the right corps advanced in massy echellons at a quick step.

The chasseurs of the imperial guard greatly committed by an advanced station, fired some volleys and retreated. Several battalions of militia formed behind the chasseurs, and on the low garden ground near the banks of the Aller, also gave way and streamed to the bridges, while the six guns upon the elevation on the right bank, overpowered by fire, were beaten back out of action. Some cossacks and cavalry so soon as the French had quitted the wood, attempted to attack the rear of the right flank, but a division of French dragoons, sustained by infantry, repulsed them. The enemy quickened their pace, animating each other to the assault by loud cheers, and driving every thing before them, notwithstanding gallant efforts from a division of infantry in front of the guards, whilst the remaining French columns sallying from the wood could scarcely find space for the formation of their numbers. The Russian imperial guards impatient of the cannonade which tore them to pieces, rushed forward with fixed bayonets, reached the enemy, and pierced the leading column, but a reserve division advanced, obliged the guards to fall back, and, after a further obstinate contest in the streets, forced the town. During this contest the bridges were ordered to be fired. The flames rolled over them instantaneously; they were no longer passable for friends or foes, and were consumed notwithstanding the efforts of the enemy to preserve them, so that a great portion of the Russian infantry were obliged to plunge into the stream, and escape by a difficult and dangerous ford. The infantry of the centre and right wing, supported by the cavalry slowly retired, checking the progress of 50,000 men, and crossed to the right of the Aller at a ford, through which the infantry were obliged to wade breast high. The loss of the Russians in killed and wounded amounted to 10 generals, 500 subordinate officers, 12,000 men, 500 prisoners, and owing to the bravery of the troops only 17 cannon. The loss of the enemy at the lowest computation was 300 officers, 7000 men, and 400 prisoners.

At Wehlau the Russian army passed the Pregel without any loss or even annoyance, on a single bridge. A detachment of 4000 French troops watched their movements, but did not oppose their retreat. The bridge was then burnt, and the Russians continued their retrograde movement to Pepelkin, where they were rejoined by the Prussian corps, under general Lestocy, and a Russian corps under general Kaminskoy, who had been detached to Koningsberg on the 10th; for after the defeat of the main Russian army, Koningberg was untenable. At eight in the morning Buonaparte threw a bridge over the Pregel, and took a position there with the army. Almost all the magazines which the enemy had on the Aller, had been thrown into the river or burnt. At Wehlau however the French found more than 6000 quintals of corn—possession was taken of Koningsberg by the corps under marshal Soult. At this place also were found some hundred thousand quintals of corn, more than 20,000 wounded Russians and Prussians, and all the ammunition that had been sent to the Russians by England, including 160,000 muskets that had not been landed. The French bulletin (No. 79,) concluded as follows: "It was on the 5th of June that the enemy renewed hostilities. Their loss in the ten days that followed their first operations may be reckoned at 60,000 men, killed wounded, taken, or otherwise put *hors de combat.* They have lost a part of their artillery, almost all their ammunition, and the whole of their magazines on a line of more than 40 leagues. The French armies have seldom obtained so great advantage with so little loss."

On the 19th at two o'clock, p. m. Buonaparte with his guards entered Tilsit. The Russians pursued after the battle of Friedland by the grand duke of Berg, at the head of the greater part of the light cavalry, and some divisions of dragoons and cuirassiers, crossed the Niemen, burnt the bridge of Tilsit, and continued their retreat eastward. The emperor of Russia who had remained three weeks with his Prussian majesty at Tilsit, left that place along with the king in great haste. On the 19th an armistice was proposed to the *chief of the French army* by the Russian commander-in-chief. In consequence of this proposition, an armistice was agreed on at Tilsit, on the 22nd of June by which it was settled that hostilities should not be resumed on either side without a month's previous notice of such an intention. That a similar armistice should be concluded between the French and the Prussian armies in the course of five days. That plenipotentiaries should be instantly appointed by the different parties for the salutary work of pacification, and that there should be an immediate exchange of prisoners. The boundary between the French and Russian armies during the armistice, was the Thalwag or middle of the stream of the Niemen from the Kurischbaf, where it falls into the sea at Grodno; and a line from thence to the confines of Russia, between the Narew and the Bug. Such was the formidable position of the French, while nothing remained to the king of Prussia but the small town and territory of Memel. The first interview between Buonaparte and the emperor Alexander, took place on the 25th of June, on a raft constructed for the purpose, on the Niemen, where two tents had been prepared by the French for their reception. Alexander and Napoleon landed at the same time from their boats, and embraced each other. It was agreed that half the town of Tilsit should be considered as neutral ground, and be occupied by the emperor of Russia, with the officers of his household, and his body guards. Great were the mutual courtesies and expressions of kindness and respect that ensued among French, Russians, and Prussians, of all ranks; visiting, feasting, and all kinds of entertainment and festivity that could be invented. Human nature gladly relaxed from the miserable rage of war, and indulged, and was eager to acknowledge, and emphatically to express, every sentiment of social and generous affection. A magnificent dinner was given by Napoleon's guards, to those of Alexander and the king of Prussia. At this entertainment, they exchanged uniforms, and were to be seen in the streets in a motly kind of dress, partly Russian, partly Prussian, and partly French. It is much in the same spirit that the chiefs of so many islands in the south seas exchange names for a time, with persons to whom they wish to shew friendship, or pay a compliment. A stranger to the ways of Europe, witnessing, at Tilsit, such ardent love among those different tongues and nations, from the highest to the lowest, might have wondered what motives could possibly have impelled such good-natured and tender-hearted people to the most horrid scenes of war and bloodshed.

A treaty of peace was concluded between his majesty Napoleon; stiling himself emperor of the French and king of Italy, and his majesty the emperor of all the Russias, at Tilsit, July the 7th. As the contest between Russia and France related not to any direct interests of their own, but wholly to those of their respective allies, there was nothing to be adjusted between these powers on their own account, farther than that there should be henceforth perfect peace and amity between their imperial majesties, that all hostilities at all points by sea or land, should immediately cease, and that, for this purpose, couriers should be immediately despatched to their respective generals and other commanders. The great sacrifice to peace was of course the kingdom of Prussia, which was reduced from the rank of a primary power to the state in which it existed on the 1st of January, 1772, before the first partition of Poland. The greater part of those provinces which on that day formed a part of the kingdom of Poland, and had since, at different times, been subjected to Prussia, were annexed to the dominions of his majesty the king of Saxony, under the title of the duchy of Warsaw, and were to be governed by a new constitution or system of fundamental laws, that should secure the liberties and privileges of the people of the duchy, and be consistent with the security of the neighbouring states.— This constitution, framed on the model of that of France, was presented, approved by *Napoleon, by the grace of God and the constitution, emperor of the French, king of Italy, and protector of the confederation of the Rhine,* and signed by him, and counter-signed by his secretary of state, Maret, at Dresden, so early as the 22nd of July. The city of Dantzic, with a territory of two leagues around it, was restored to her former independence, under the protection of his majesty the king of Prussia, and his majesty the king of Saxony, was to be governed by the laws by which she was governed at the time when she ceased to be her own mistress. For a communication between the kingdom of Saxony and the duchy of Warsaw, his majesty

ALEXANDER EMPEROR OF RUSSIA.

While the British Lion is on the point of destroying the Gallic Cock;
the Russian Eagle breaks the Chains of Europe.

the king of Saxony, was to have the free use of a military road through the states of his majesty the king of Prussia : this road, the number of troops to be allowed to pass at once, and the resting places with magazines, to be fixed by a particular agreement between the two sovereigns, under the mediation of France. Neither his majesty the king of Prussia, his majesty the king of Saxony, nor the city of Dantzic, were to oppose any obstacle whatever to the free navigation of the Vistula, under the name of tolls, rights or duties. In order, as far as possible, to establish a natural boundary between Russia and the duchy of Warsaw, a certain territory, heretofore under the dominion of Prussia, to be for ever united to the empire of Russia.— This territory added two hundred subjects to those of the Russian empire.—Their royal highnesses, the dukes of Saxe Cobourg, Oldenburgh, and Mecklenburgh Schwerin, were each of them to be restored to the complete and quiet possession of their estates : but the ports in the duchies of Oldenburgh to remain in the possession of French garrisons till a definitive treaty should be signed between France and England ; for the accomplishing which, the mediation of Russia was to be accepted, on the condition that this mediation should be accepted by England in one month after the ratification of the present treaty. Until the ratification of a definitive treaty of peace between France and England, all the ports of Prussia without exception, to be shut against the English. His majesty the emperor of all the Russias, acknowledged the confederation of the Rhine; his majesty Joseph Napoleon, king of Naples; his majesty Lewis Napoleon, king of Holland ; and his imperial highness prince Jerome Napoleon, as king of Westphalia : a kingdom to consist of the provinces ceded by the king of Prussia on the left bank of the Elbe, and other states then in possession of his majesty the emperor Napopoleon. These were the most generally important articles in the treaties. There were others relating to private estates and other property, more interesting, no doubt, to individuals. The time and manner in which the different stipulations in the treaties were to be carried into execution, were fixed by a special convention between France and Prussia.

The Prussian fortresses in Silesia, that held out the longest against the besieging French, were Glatz and Silverberg. They capitulated at last about the end of the campaign, begun the 5th and ended on the 21st of June. Graudentz and Colberg, though vigorously besieged, still held out when a negotiation for peace was entered into at Tilsit. The siege of this last place was fatal to thousands of the French. If all the governors of Prussian fortresses, from the 14th of October 1806, to the 14th of June 1807, had been animated with the fidelity, and persevering courage of general Blucher, the issue of the war might have been very different. It was at this siege that colonel Schill, whose heroism, loyalty, and patriotism shone forth so conspicuously in the north of Germany in 1809, first attracted the attention and admiration of his countrymen. He was in the situation of a Prussian captain retired from service, when the misfortunes and dangers of his country called his courage and military skill into action. He was extremely successful, during the siege of Colberg, in harassing the French at the head of an irregular levy. It was this officer that took general Victor prisoner, on his way to Dantzic ; when he also intercepted a treasure of 100,000 ducats belonging to the enemy. The king of Prussia, as a reward for his services, raised him to the rank of colonel, and gave him the command of a regiment. Neither the loss of so extensive and so fine a territory, nor of revenue, nor of population, was so severe a wound, to the Prussian monarchy, as the degrading conditions on which he was suffered to retain what remained ; a military road across Silesia, for opening and maintaining a communication between the king of Saxony's German dominions, and his new duchy of Warsaw, and the shutting up of all the Prussian ports against England : those very ports through which he had just received arms, and other succours. The more attentively we consider the pacification of Tilsit, we shall the more perceive the Machiavelian policy and deep-laid designs of Buonaparte. The fine duchy of Silesia would not, it may be presumed, have been restored to Prussia, if, in the hands of the Prussians, it had not been calculated to serve as a constant source of hostility between the courts of Berlin and Vienna. The military highway across Silesia, was in like manner calculated to foment jealousy and discord between the courts of Berlin and Dresden; while it was to be at the same time wholly under the mediation, that is, the control of France. The confederation of the Rhine strengthened by the creation of the new kingdom of Westphalia, was rendered too powerful to be shaken by any aggression on the part of Austria on the one hand, or of Russia on the other. The kingdom of Westphalia, which it should seem was intended to be pre-eminent among the other members of the confederation, was to receive farther accessions of territory, by the annexation of any other states that might be thought proper by his majesty the emperor of France; and. the emperor of all the Russias engaged to recognise the limits whatever they might be that should be determined by Napoleon, in pursuance of these articles.

Sweden alone, after the battle of Friedland, remained faithful to her alliance with Britain. Russia, even before that period, had indicated various symptoms of secession, particularly by the nomination of count Romanzof, a man notoriously hostile to the interests of Great Britain, to the administration of foreign affairs. Denmark affected a neutrality, which she was incapable of maintaining. An apprehension for the safety of her German territory pervaded the cabinet, and when the combination was formed against France, in 1805, she collected a contemptible army which could answer no other purpose, than to watch the motions of Prussia, while the French were fighting on the banks of the Danube. France was the natural enemy of Denmark, yet alarmed by the menaces, or purchased by the bribes of Buonaparte, she had requested of the English government to be excused from receiving our packet-boats at the ports of Holstein or Sleswick.

We rejected the proposal with disdain, and our determination was confirmed by private information, that in the secret treaty of Tilsit, provisions had been made for a northern confederacy in which Denmark should become an active ally. The British government at length prepared to send into the Baltic a formidable naval and military force, consisting of 27 sail of the line and a considerable number of soldiers.

Lord Cathcart obtained the direction of the army, and admiral Gambier was appointed to the command of the fleet. Mr. Jackson was selected to conduct the negotiation, and was instructed to visit the residence of the prince-royal, to call upon his highness for an unequivocal explanation of the designs of Denmark, and if these designs were not inimical, for a pledge of his sincerity, in the surrender of the Danish fleet, till the termination of the war, when it should be restored. Should this proposal be refused Mr. Jackson was directed to assure him that the British armament already arrived in the Sound, would enforce its stipulations. In the event of compliance, the British government would liberally and honourably guarantee protection, security, and the enlargment of the Danish territories.

Mr. Jackson arrived at Kiel on the 6th of August. On the day subsequent to his arrival he intimated to count Bernstorf the import of his instructions, and requested an interview with the prince royal, which was immediately granted, and in which his highness expressed his surprise and indignation at the unjust and imperative demands of the British court. On the ensuing day the prince departed for Copenhagen, whither he was followed by the ambassador; who, on his arrival at the capital, was coldly informed that the prince had returned to Sleswick, and that the minister was not authorized, during his absence to comply with Mr. Jackson's proposals. The latter discovering all prospect of negotiation to be hopeless, took his leave and retired on board the advanced frigate, then at anchor a few miles from Copenhagen; and the commanders were given to understand that the most vigorous measures must be instantly adopted. The army accordingly landed without opposition, at the village of Vedbeck, on the morning of the 16th of August, and, after some ineffectual attempts of the enemy to annoy its left wing, it closely invested the town on the land side. The fleet removing to an advanced anchorage, formed an impenetrable blockade by sea, and a proclamation was issued in a tone at once menacing and conciliatory. On the evening of the 2nd of September, the land batteries and the bomb and mortar-vessels opened a tremendous fire upon the town, and with so much effect, that the city in a short time was visibly in flames. The ramparts of the town returned a feeble fire; and that of the English was for awhile remitted in the expectation of some proposals from the Danish government. But the assault was renewed with such terrible vigor and effect, that a trumpeter appeared at the British outposts, proposing a cessation of arms during twenty-four hours, as preliminary to a capitulation, which was not concluded till three days afterwards, when the citadel, dock-yards, and batteries, were taken possession of by the British army. The admiral immediately issued orders to rig and fit out the ships which filled the capacious basins, and had been laid up in ordinary. At the expiration of the time specified in the capitulation, they were conveyed to England, with the stores, timber, and every other article of equipment, found in the arsenals; and arrived in safety, with the exception of one ship stranded on the isle of Huen. Though the animadversions of the opponents of the ministry on the design and conduct of the expedition to Copenhagen were deferred to the early part of the ensuing year, it will be necessary, for the purpose of connection, to notice in this place, the animadversions of the popular, and the replies of the ministerial parties. The latter endeavored to defend the obnoxious measure, by observing that their foreign agents had communicated the intentions of the Danes to submit to France. It was maintained that Denmark was compelled to become a secret party to the treaty of

Tilsit, that Denmark was unable or averse to contend with France, that express overtures of the most dangerous tendency had been made to the prince regent of Portugal, who had communicated their stipulations to the British government, and that the Danish minister himself admitted the impossibility of defending Holstein, Sleswick, and Jutland, from a French invasion. These assertions have been since unexpectedly and decidedly corroborated by the unfortunate murder of the count D'Aintraigues, who, subsequent to that fatal event, has been declared the agent through whose connections and activity ministers obtained the secret articles of the treaty of Tilsit, and whose services were rewarded by a handsome pension. The system, however, on which the Danish war commenced, was not improved to the extent of which it was undoubtedly capable, and the abandonment of the island of Zealand, in conformity to the capitulation, but contrary to the secret wishes of the king and the administration, left the acquisition of that object to the mercy of a French army, and to the discretion of the prince of Denmark.

The treaty of Tilsit was scarcely concluded before Buonaparte turned his eyes towards the west of Europe, and resolved upon the subjugation of Spain and Portugal. While bodies of French troops poured into Spain, or advanced towards it, Buonaparte set out on a journey to Fontainbleau, November the 15th, and on the 21st arrived at Milan. At that city, he received the homage of the Italians in every part of the peninsula. The inhabitants of Tuscany swore allegiance to Napoleon; under whose influence it was stated in the gazette of Florence, Etruria might expect to be roused from that lethargy into which it had been sunk for some time. The aged elector, now king of Bavaria, including the Tyrol, came also with his spouse to Milan, thus doing homage to Napoleon as a kind of vassal. Eugene Beauharnois, the viceroy, was appointed Buonaparte's successor in the kingdom of Italy, under certain restrictions or reservations, in certain contingent cases, closely connecting that kingdom with the crown of France. Count Melzi was created duke of Lodi. From Naples Buonaparte went to Venice, where he gave orders for some improvements, both for the defence of the city and the promotion of commerce. He returned to Paris in January, 1808, by the way of Lyons, bringing in his train, the late queen regent of Etruria, and her young son.

After the peace of Tilsit, Buonaparte demanded of the court of Lisbon, 1st, To shut up the ports of Portugal against England. 2nd, To detain all Englishmen residing in Portugal. 3rd, To confiscate all English property; denouncing war in case of a refusal. And, without waiting for an answer, he gave orders for retaining all Portuguese merchant-men that were in the ports of France. The prince regent of Portugal hoping to ward off the storm, acceded to the shutting up of his ports, but refused to comply with the other two demands, as being contrary to the principles of the public law, and to the treaties subsisting between the two nations. The court of Portugal then began to concert measures for securing its retreat to the Portuguese dominions in South America. For that purpose the prince regent ordered all ships of war fit to keep the sea, to be fitted out; and also gave warning of what was intended to the English, directing them to sell their property and leave Portugal; in order thus to avoid an effusion of blood, which in all probability would have proved useless. He resolved also to comply, if possible, with the views of the French, in case he should not allow himself to be softened down to more moderate pretensions. But Buonaparte peremptorily insisted, not only on the shutting up of the ports, but on the imprisonment of all British subjects, the confiscation of their property, and a dereliction of the project of a retreat to America. The prince regent, when he had reason to believe that all the English not naturalized in the country had taken their departure from Portugal, and that all English property had been sold, and even its amount exported, adopted the resolution to shut up the ports against England, and even to comply with the other demands of France, declaring, however, at the same time, that, should the French troops enter Portugal, he was firmly resolved to remove the seat of government to Brasil, the most important and best defended part of his dominions.

It had been frequently stated to the cabinet of Lisbon by the English ambassador, lord Strangford, that the king of Great Britain, in agreeing not to resent the exclusion of British commerce from the ports of Portugal, had gone to the utmost extent of forbearance; that in making this concession to the peculiar circumstances of the prince regent's situation, his majesty had done all that friendship could justly require; and that a single step beyond this line of modified hostility, must necessarily lead to the extremity of actual war. Nevertheless, the prince regent, in the hope of preserving Portugal by conciliating France, on the 8th of November, signed an order for detaining the few British subjects, and the very inconsiderable portion of British property that yet remained at Lisbon. On the publication of this order, lord Strangford removed the arms of England from the gates of his residence, demanded his passports, presented a final remonstrance against the recent conduct of the court of Lisbon, and proceeded, on the 17th of November, to a British squadron commanded by sir Sidney Smith, who, immediately on the suggestion of lord Strangford, established a most rigorous blockade at the mouth of the Tagus. A few days afterwards, the intercourse between the court of Lisbon and the British ambassador was renewed. Lord Strangford, under the assurances of protection and security, proceeded to Lisbon on the 27th, when he found the prince regent wisely directing all his apprehension to a French army which had entered Portugal, and was on its march to Lisbon, and all his hopes to an English fleet. The object of this march, he was at no loss to understand; for Buonaparte had declared in his journals "that the house of Braganza had ceased to reign." Lord Strangford promised to his royal highness on the faith of his sovereign, that the British squadron before the Tagus should be employed to protect his retreat from Lisbon, and his voyage to the Brasils. A decree was published on the 28th of November, in which the prince regent announced his intention of retiring to the city of Janeiro until the conclusion of a general peace, and of appointing a regency to administer the government at Lisbon, during his royal highness' absence from Europe.

On the morning of the 29th of November, the Portuguese fleet set sail from the Tagus, with the prince of Brasil and the whole of the royal family of Braganza on board, together with many of his faithful counsellors and adherents, as well as other persons attached to his present fortunes. The fleet consisted of eight sail of the line, four large frigates, several armed brigs, sloops, and corvettes, and a number of Brasil ships; amounting in all to about 36 sail. While they passed through the British squadron, our ships fired a salute of 21 guns, which was returned with an equal number. The friendly meeting of the two fleets at a juncture so critical and important, was a most interesting and affecting scene. Four ships of the line were sent by the British admiral to accompany the royal family to Brasil.

The Portuguese fleet had not left the Tagus when the French, with their Spanish auxiliaries, appeared on the hills above Lisbon, under the command of general Junot, who had formerly resided for several years at the court of Portugal, in the character of an ambassador from France. Though the Portuguese had long apprehended a visit from the French, they were surprised at their sudden arrival. The court of Portugal had always considered the march of an army through the mountains of Beira, as a matter of extreme difficulty, if not impracticable, especially in the winter season. They never dreamt that their invaders would advance by any other rout than the course of the Tagus. The entrance of the French troops into Portugal was not known at Lisbon till

their advanced-guard had reached Abrantes. The retreat of the royal family from Lisbon, was, of course, with extreme precipitation. Junot did not meet with any more opposition, on his entrance into the capital, than when he passed on his march the Portuguese frontier. The greatest professions were made on the part of the French army and nation, of friendship and affection for the people of Portugal. Nevertheless the inhabitants of Lisbon were disarmed, they were prohibited from assembling together to the number of more than ten at a time; cannons were placed in all the streets and squares; very heavy contributions were imposed for the maintenance of the French, with their Spanish auxiliaries; and in a word, the French system of governing subdued countries, was completely established.

After Portugal had fallen under the dominion of France, the valuable island of Madeira was committed to the protection of British troops, to be restored to Portugal on the conclusion of a general peace.

The annals of France had been stained by the suspicious death of Touissaint L'Ouverture, who after a short but brilliant career in St. Domingo, fell into the hands of the French, and consequently was cast into a dungeon, where he died, as was supposed, of poison.

A commercial and friendly intercourse was at length established between Great Britain and general Christophe, who having defeated and destroyed the emperor Dessalines, governed a great part of the island of St. Domingo, under the more modest title of the president of Hayti. He had been long opposed in arms by Petion, at the head of the mulattoes. But in the decisive campaign of 1807, the mulatto party were broken and dispersed, and Christophe remained, though not without a competitor for the supreme power, without any formidable rival. Christophe appears to have possessed in a very eminent degree, the virtues of humanity, and a regard to the true interests of his country, as well as good sense and military skill and courage. He declared it to be the

great object of his government, to repair
the havoc and devastation of Hayti, by
the establishment of just laws, social
order, freedom of trade, and, above all,
by a friendly and commercial intercourse
with the only people that had stood
forth in support of regular government
and law, amid so many countries subverted, and every where shaken. He had
a strong predilection for the personal
character of the English. He spared the
lives of the crowds of prisoners who had
fallen into his hands, he took great care
of the sick and wounded, and assured
all men peaceably disposed, of his protection. This was his ultimate view, even
when mistaken conduct had reduced him
to the necessity of opposing it by force
of arms. " The friend of humanity,
(said he,) the man who loves his country
and is submissive to the laws, demands
to know what purpose the rebel Petion
meant to serve by exposing to massacre
the miserable tools of his ambition ? What
would have been the destiny of those
miserable people whom the fate of war
placed under the power of the president,
if his clemency had not spared even those
who pointed their weapons against his
person ? Why should that cannibal Petion shed such deluges of blood, if it
was not on a plan of destruction, purposely
conceived to diminish the population of
Hayti ? A plan in perfect unison with the
projects of their implacable enemies; a
plan favored by a faction that had never
made any account of the blood that was
spilt, when it was to be subservient to the
ambitious views of the commander."

- Christophe, with the assistance of men
of enlarged views, had been employed
for some time in the formation of a new
constitution for Hayti, which was proclaimed on the 17th of February, 1807,
the fourth year of the independence. It
was founded on a moral and religious
basis; it breathed a spirit of moderation,
justice, political wisdom, and enlarged
views of the true interest of Hayti, in its
foreign and internal concerns. Slavery
was for ever abolished in Hayti. Every
man was to find a sacred asylum in his

own house; his person and property
were secure, under the safeguard of the
law. Assassination was punished with
death. The first magistrate was invested
with the title and quality of *president and
generalissimo of the forces of Hayti by land
and sea.* And he was to appoint his successor out of the number of his general
officers. The whole of the articles or
clauses of the fundamental laws or constitution of Hayti, fifty-one in number,
were reduced under ten heads. I. The
condition of the citizens. II. Government. III. Council of state. IV. Superintendance of the finances. V. Secretary
of state. VI. Tribunals. VII. Religion.
VIII. Public education. IX. No attempts
to be made on the neighbouring colonies.
X. General regulation relating to service
in the national militia; security of the
persons and properties of foreign traders
resorting to Hayti; marriage, and a rigorous prohibition of divorce; the heritage
of children; agriculture, the first, noblest,
and most useful of all the arts; public
festivals for celebrating the national independence, and in honor of the president
and his spouses.—The proclamation of
the constitution was followed by an address from Henry Christophe, president
and generalissimo of the forces of Hayti
by sea and land, to the army and people.

A number of turbulent persons in the
southern parts of Hayti had formed designs of revolt and revolution in Jamaica;
but general Christophe, who had been informed of the plot, and who were the
principal individuals concerned in it, immediately denounced them, and they
were arrested. The British government,
in consideration of this service, issued,
in February 1807, an order of council,
authorising all British merchantmen bound
for Buenos Ayres, to proceed to any port
in the island of St. Domingo, not under
the power of France or Spain; a measure
wisely calculated to encourage the mutual trade of Hayti and Great Britain.
Another event still more favorable to the
national commerce, was the capture of Curacoa, which was reduced with little resistance, after storming the town of Amsterdam.

The affairs of India during the present year were comparatively unimportant. A chief named Dundie Khan, having murdered a subordinate officer of the law, and exhibited many instances of contumacy, was invested by the British in Comona, his principal fort. Trenches were dug, batteries erected, and a breach was reported to be practicable. On the 18th of November, 1807, the British made an attack upon a fortified garden, to the right of the fort, which was repelled with great loss to the storming party. When our men descended the head of the glacis they discovered a ditch 28 feet deep, and 44 broad, but were retarded by numerous obstacles from ascending to the breach, for at the bottom of the ditch the enemy had dug pits which they filled with powder, and on these they threw lighted choppers, by which numbers of the English were blown up. Exposed to this furnace while the bastions completely enfiladed the storming party, our troops after remaining two hours in this distressing situation, at last retired but not without difficulty. On the following night the enemy evacuated the fortress of Comona, and proceeded to that of Ghurnowrie. The loss of the British at Comona, in consequence of the negligence of general Dickers in not filling up the ditch, was 35 officers killed and wounded, and 700 men, of whom 147 were Europeans. On the 24th of November, regular approaches were begun against Ghurnowrie, and when these were sufficiently advanced shells were thrown, which so effectually annoyed the troops of Dundie Khan, who had no garrison to retreat to at Comona, that about seven in the evening of the 10th of December, they abandoned the fort and escaped across the Jumna.

1807.

HISTORY OF THE WAR.

CHAP. XLVIII

THE situation of Great Britain at the beginning of the year 1808, was more extraordinary than any that is exhibited in the history of former times. After a war which, with the short interval of the peace of Amiens, had continued 15 years, her last reliance on the continental government had failed, and all Europe was so humbled, that it was manifest the few states which still preserved a semblance of neutrality, would soon be compelled into a confederacy with France. The French military force and the English navy were opposed to each other without the apparent possibility of coming into conflict. Masters as the French were, of the continent of Europe, no propitious circumstances promised to enable us to attack them by land, and neither they nor their allies dared to shew their flag upon the seas. The threat of invasion had long been laid aside, and the gun-boats of Napoleon, were left to rot in the harbor of Boulogne. Secured against the apprehension of this enterprise by its confessed abandonment by our fleets, and by our internal strength, we were prosecuting the war equally without fear and without hope.

The new year began with an offer on the part of Austria to become the mediator of a general peace. On the 1st of January, prince de Starhremberg transmitted a note importing that he was charged by the orders of his court, which was anxious to conform with the desires of the emperor of France, to propose to the English ministry that they should immediately send plenipotentiaries to Paris: and added that to avoid every species of delay, he was authorized by France to give passports to the ministers who might be appointed. The reply (January 8th,) was becoming the spirit and dignity of the British nation. It noticed what could but be perceived, that the prince de Starhremberg when proposing that plenipotentiaries should be sent to Paris, had omitted to explain whether he had received the commission from his imperial majesty, or from the government of France: if from the former, his majesty was concerned that in framing this proposal so little reference should have been had to the correspondence which had already taken place between the courts of London and Vienna. So long ago as in April, the offer of mediation had been accepted, yet now the same offer was repeated without any notification of the acceptance of those conditions which were then stated to be indispensible prelimina-ries to a negotiation, and the present pro-posal extended only to the powers com-bined with France in the war against Great Britain, and not to the allies of Great Bri-tain. in the war with France. If, on the other hand, the prince de Starhremberg were only acting as an agent, authorized to re-ceive and convey whatever communications the government of France might think fit to entrust to him, the statement of some precise authority, and the production of some specific and authenticated documents were then necessary. The previous settle-ment of a basis of negotiation, (as had in-deed been suggested by the emperor of Austria in his first offer,) was indispensible, the experience of the last attempt at treat-ing with France having placed that ques-tion beyond controversy; but upon this subject no intimation was now given. His majesty was willing to treat with France, but it must be on a footing of perfect equality; he was ready to treat with the allies of France, but the negotiation must equally embrace the allies of Great Britain; as soon as the basis was settled he would be prepared to name plenipotentiaries, but he would not consent to send them again to a hostile capital. This frank and unequi-vocal exposition of his majesty's sentiments, was made to the minister of the emperor of Austria; but no authority was given to the prince de Starhremberg to speak in the name of England to the government of France. Four days after the date of this answer (on the 12th of June,) the prince de Starhrembeg demanded his passports:

This prelude to a declaration of war on the part of Austria, scarcely in the slighest degree excited the public attention. Sor-row and indignation had been felt at the conduct of the emperor Alexander, indig-nation at the baseness with which he had become a sharer in the spoils of Prussia; sorrow, that one whose natural disposition had discovered such rectitude of feeling, should have been deluded into measures so prejudicial to the interests of his country, and so fatal to his own reputation. When therefore he issued his hostile manifesto, the feelings of the British ministry were expressed in the following state paper, which is certainly the best that has pro-ceeded from the court during the progress of the war.

British Declaration.

The declaration issued at St. Peters-burgh, by his majesty the emperor of all the Russias, has excited in his majesty's mind the strongest sensations of astonishment and regret.

His majesty was not unaware of the nature of those secret engagements which had been imposed upon Russia in the con-ferences of Tilsit. But his majesty had entertained the hope, that a review of the transactions of that unfortunate negotiation, and a just estimate of its effects upon the glory of the Russian name, and upon the interests of the Russian empire, would have induced his imperial majesty to extricate himself from the embarrassment of those new counsels and connections which he had adopted in a moment of despondency and alarm, and to return to a policy more congenial to the principles which he had so invariably professed, and more condu-cive to the honor of his crown, and to the prosperity of his dominions.

This hope has dictated to his majesty the utmost forbearance and moderation in all his diplomatic intercourse with the court of St. Petersburgh since the peace of Tilsit.

His majesty had much cause for suspi-cion and just ground for complaint. But he abstained from the language of reproach. His majesty deemed it necessary to require specific explanation with respect to those arrangements with France, the conceal-ment of which from his majesty could not but confirm the impression already received of their character and tendency. But his majesty, nevertheless, directed the demand of that explanation to be made, not only without asperity, or the indignation of any hostile disposition, but with that conside-rate regard to the feelings and situation of the emperor of Russia, which resulted from the recollection of former friendship and from confidence interrupted but not destroyed.

The declaration of the emperor of Russia proves that the object of his majesty's forbearance and moderation has not been attained. It proves, unhappily, that the influence of that power, which is equally and essentially the enemy both of Great Britain and of Russia, has acquired a decided ascendency in the counsels of the cabinet of St. Petersburgh; and has been able to excite a causeless enmity between two nations, whose long established connection, and whose mutual interests, prescribed the most intimate union and co-operation.

His majesty deeply laments the extension of the calamities of war. But called upon, as he is, to defend himself against an act of unprovoked hostility, his majesty is anxious to refute in the face of the world the pretexts by which that act is attempted to be justified.

The declaration asserts that his majesty the emperor of Russia has twice taken up arms in a cause in which the interest of Great Britain was more direct than his own; and founds upon this assertion the charge against Great Britain of having neglected to second and support the military operations of Russia.

His majesty willingly does justice to the motives which originally engaged Russia in the great struggle against France. His majesty avows with equal readiness the interest which Great Britain has uniformly taken in the fates and fortunes of the powers of the continent. But it would surely be difficult to prove that Great Britain, who was herself in a state of hostility with Prussia when the war broke out between Prussia and France, had an interest and a duty more direct in espousing the Prussian quarrel than the emperor of Russia, the ally of his Prussian majesty, the protector of the north of Europe, and the guarantee of the Germanic constitution.

It is not in a public declaration that his majesty can discuss the policy of having at any particular period of the war effected, or omitted to effect, disembarkations of troops on the coasts of Naples. But the instance of the war with the porte is still more singularly chosen to illustrate the charge against Great Britain of indifference to the interests of her ally; a war undertaken by Great Britain at the instigation of Russia, and solely for the purpose of maintaining Russian interests against the influence of France.

If, however, the peace of Tilsit is indeed to be considered as the consequence and the punishment of the imputed inactivity of Great Britain, his majesty cannot but regret that the emperor of Russia should have resorted to so precipitate and fatal a measure, at the moment when he had received distinct assurances that his majesty was making the most strenuous exertions to fulfil the wishes and expectations of his ally, (assurances which his imperial majesty received and acknowledged with apparent confidence and satisfaction;) and when his majesty was in fact, prepared to employ for the advancement of the common objects of the war those forces which, after the peace of Tilsit, he was under the necessity of employing to disconcert a combination directed against his own immediate interests and security.

The vexation of Russian commerce by Great Britain is, in truth, little more than an imaginary grievance. Upon a diligent examination, made by his majesty's command, of the records of the British court of admiralty, there has been discovered only a solitary instance in the course of the present war, of the condemnation of a vessel really Russian; a vessel which had carried naval stores, to a port of the common enemy. There are but few instances of Russian vessels detained; and none in which justice has been refused to a party regularly complaining of such detention. It is therefore matter of surprise as well as of concern to his majesty, that the emperor of Russia should have condescended to bring forward a complaint which, as it cannot be seriously felt by those in whose behalf it is urged, might appear to be intended to countenance those exaggerated declamations, by which France perseveringly endeavors to inflame the jealousy of other countries, and to justify her own inveterate animosity against Great Britain.

The peace of Tilsit was followed by an offer of mediation on the part of the emperor of Russia, for the conclusion of a peace between Great Britain and France; which it is asserted that his majesty refused.

His majesty did not refuse the mediation of the emperor of Russia; although the offer of it was accompanied by circumstances of concealment, which might well have justified his refusal. The articles of the treaty of Tilsit were not communicated to his majesty; and specifically, that article of the treaty in virtue of which the mediation was proposed, and which prescribed a limited time for the return of his majesty's answer to that proposal. And his majesty was thus led into an apparent compliance, with a limitation so offensive to the dignity of an independent sovereign. But the answer so returned by his majesty was not a refusal. It was a conditional acceptance. The conditions required by his majesty were,—a statement of the basis upon which the enemy was disposed to treat; and a communication of the articles of the peace of Tilsit. The first of these conditions was precisely the same which the emperor of Russia had himself annexed not four months before to his own acceptance of the proffered mediation of the emperor of Austria. The second was one which his majesty would have had a right to require, even as the ally of his imperial majesty; but which it would have been highly improvident to omit, when he was invited to confide to his imperial majesty the care of his honor and his interests.

But even if these conditions (neither of which has been fulfilled, although the fulfilment of them has been repeatedly required by his majesty's ambassador at St. Petersburgh) had not been in themselves perfectly natural and necessary; there were not wanting considerations which might have warranted his majesty in endeavoring, with more than ordinary anxiety, to ascertain the views and intentions of

the emperor of Russia, and the precise nature and effect of the new relations which his imperial majesty had contracted.

The complete abandonment of the interests of the king of Prussia (who had twice rejected proposals of separate peace, from a strict adherence to his engagements with his imperial ally,) and the character of those provisions which the emperor of Russia was contented to make for his own interests in the negotiations of Tilsit, presented no encouraging prospect of the result of any exertions which his imperial majesty might be disposed to employ in favor of Great Britain.

It is not while a French army still occupies and lays waste the remaining dominions of the king of Prussia, in spite of the stipulations of the Prussian treaty of Tilsit; while contributions are arbitrarily exacted by France from that remnant of the Prussian monarchy, such as in its entire and most flourishing state, the Prussian monarchy would have been unable to discharge; while the surrender is demanded, in time of peace, of Prussian fortresses, which had not been reduced during the war; and while the power of France is exercised over Prussia with such shameless tyranny, as to designate, and demand for instant death, individuals, subjects of his Prussian majesty, and resident in his dominions, upon a charge of disrespect towards the French government;—it is not while all these things are done and suffered, under the eyes of the emperor of Russia, and without his interference on behalf of his ally, that his majesty can feel himself called upon to account to Europe, for having hesitated to repose an unconditional confidence in the efficacy of his imperial majesty's mediation.

Nor, even if that mediation had taken full effect, if a peace had been concluded under it, and that peace guaranteed by his imperial majesty, could his majesty have placed implicit reliance on the stability of any such arrangement, after having seen the emperor of Russia openly transfer to France the sovereignty of the Ionian republic, the independence of which his imperial majesty recently and solemnly guaranteed.

But while the alleged rejection of the emperor of Russia's mediation, between Great Britain and France, is stated as a just ground of his imperial majesty's resentment; his majesty's request of that mediation, for the re-establishment of peace between Great Britain and Denmark, is represented as an insult which was beyond the bounds of his imperial majesty's moderation to endure,

His majesty feels himself under no obligation to offer any atonement or apology to the emperor of Russia for the expedition against Copenhagen. It is not for those who were parties to the secret arrangements of Tilsit, to demand satisfaction for a measure to which those arrangements gave rise, and by which one of the objects of them has been happily defeated.

His majesty's justification of the expedition against Copenhagen is before the world. The declaration of the emperor of Russia would supply whatever was wanting in it, if any thing could be wanting to convince the most incredulous of the urgency of that necessity under which his majesty acted.

But until the Russian declaration was published, his majesty had no reason to suspect that any opinions which the emperor of Russia might entertain of the transaction at Copenhagen could be such as to preclude his imperial majesty from undertaking, at the request of Great Britain, that same office of mediator, which he has assumed with so much alacrity on the behalf of France. Nor can his majesty forget that the first symptoms of reviving confidence, since the peace of Tilsit, the only prospect of success in the endeavors of his majesty's ambassador to restore the antient good understanding between Great Britain and Russia, appeared when the intelligence of the siege of Copenhagen had been recently received at St. Petersburgh.

The inviolability of the Baltic sea, and the reciprocal guarantees of the powers that border upon it, guarantees said to have been contracted with the knowledge of the British government, are stated as aggravations of his majesty's proceedings in the Baltic. It cannot be intended to represent his majesty as having at any time acquiesced in the principles upon which the inviolability of the Baltic is maintained; however his majesty may, at particular periods, have forborne, for special reasons influencing his conduct at the time, to act in contradiction to them. Such forbearance never could have applied but to a state of peace and real neutrality in the north; and his majesty most assuredly could not be expected to recur to it, after France has been suffered to establish herself in undisputed sovereignty along the whole coast of the Baltic sea from Dantzic to Lubec.

But the higher the value which the emperor of Russia places on the engagements respecting the tranquillity of the Baltic, which he describes himself as inheriting from his immediate predecessors, the empress Catherine and the emperor Paul, the less justly can his imperial majesty resent the appeal made to him by his majesty as the guarantee of the peace to be concluded between Great Britain and Denmark. In making that appeal, with the utmost confidence and sincerity, his majesty neither intended, nor can he imagine that he offered, any insult to the emperor of Russia. Nor can his majesty conceive that, in proposing to the prince royal terms of peace, such as the most successful war on the part of Denmark could hardly have been expected to extort from Great Britain, his majesty rendered himself liable to the imputation, either of exasperating the resentment, or of outraging the dignity of Denmark.

His majesty has thus replied to all the different accusations by which the Russian government labors to justify the rupture of a connection which has subsisted for ages, with reciprocal advantage to Great Britain and Russia, and attempts to disguise the operation of that external influence by which Russia is driven into unjust hostilities for interests not her own.

The Russian declaration proceeds to announce the several conditions on which alone these hostilities can be terminated, and the intercourse of the two countries renewed.

His majesty has already had occasion to assert, that justice has in no instance been denied to the claims of his imperial majesty's subjects.

The termination of the war with Denmark has been so anxiously sought by his majesty, that it cannot be necessary for his majesty to renew any professions upon that subject. But his majesty is at a loss to reconcile the emperor of Russia's present anxiety for the completion of such an arrangement, with his imperial majesty's recent refusal to contribute his good offices for effecting it.

The requisition of his imperial majesty for the immediate conclusion, by his majesty, of a peace with France, is as extraordinary in the substance as it is offensive in the manner. His majesty has at no time declined to treat with France, when France has professed a willingness to treat on an admissible basis. And the emperor of Russia cannot fail to remember, that the last negotiation between Great Britain and France was broke off, upon points immediately affecting, not his majesty's own interests, but those of his imperial ally. But his majesty neither understands, nor will he admit, the pretension of the emperor of Russia to dictate the time, or the mode, of his majesty's pacific negotiations with other powers. It never will be endured by his majesty, that any government shall indemnify itself for the humiliation of subserviency to France, by the adoption of an insulting and peremptory tone towards Great Britain.

His majesty proclaims anew those principles of maritime law against which the armed neutrality, under the auspices of the empress Catherine, was originally directed, and against which the present hostilities of Russia are denounced. Those principles have been recognized and acted upon in the best periods of the history of Europe, and acted upon by no power with more strictness and severity than by Rus-

sia herself in the reign of the empress Catherine.

Those principles it is the right and the duty of his majesty to maintain; and against every confederacy his majesty is determined, under the blessing of divine Providence, to maintain them. They have at all times contributed essentially to the support of the maritime power of Great Britain; but they are become incalculably more valuable and important at a period when the martime power of Great Britain constitutes the sole remaining bulwark against the overwhelming usurpations of France; the only refuge to which other nations may yet resort, in happier times, for assistance and protection.

When the opportunity for peace between Great Britain and Russia shall arrive, his majesty will embrace it with eagerness. The arrangements of such a negotiation will not be difficult or complicated. His majesty, as he has nothing to concede, so he has nothing to require: satisfied, if Russia shall manifest a disposition to return to her antient feelings of friendship towards Great Britain; to a just consideration of her own true interests; and to a sense of her own dignity as an independent nation.

Westminster, Dec. 18, 1807.

The sentiments expressed in the above declaration were those of the nation, as well as the government. But when Prussia declared against England, and Austria prepared to join the same confederacy, the only sentiment which prevailed was pity for the abject state of subjection to which these courts were reduced, and the wretched thraldom which their mutual jealousy and mutual misconduct had brought on Germany.

During the last war the flourishing state of trade was the constant boast of ministers, and the custom-house books were referred to as proofs of national prosperity from which there could be no appeal. This wretched folly imposed upon the people, and even deceived the enemy, for while the English confounded the wealth of nations with their welfare, Buonaparte mistook it for their strength. He called us a nation of shopkeepers, and reasoning as if we were so, concluded that by ruining our trade he must destroy our prosperity. Upon this avowed principle he prohibited all trading in English manufacture, ordered every article of English merchandise belonging to England or coming from her colonies, to be seized as lawful prize, and declared, as we have seen, the British islands to be in a state of blockade. The tyrannical clauses affected others more materially than us; and it remained to be ascertained, whether America, the only nation which could properly be called neutral, would remonstrate against a measure so injurious to her trade. But in the government of America, there was a manifest disposition to crouch at the feet of France. After it had been vainly intimated therefore to the neutral powers, that, if they submitted to have their ships confiscated in France when bound to or sailing from an English port, we should seize and confiscate all British cargoes bound to or from France; the threat was followed by an order of council, (November 11th, 1807,) enacting, that all neutral ships, with neutral goods on board bound for France, or any of the countries under her control, should come into an English port, and there pay duty to an English custom-house, so that no goods should enter France which we had not previously taxed. This decree exasperated Buonaparte, and he immediately issued at Milan, an edict, declaring that every neutral vessel which submitted to be searched by a neutral ship, or paid any duty whatever to the English government, should be considered as denationalized, as having forfeited the protection of its own government, as having become English property, and in consequence as liable to be seized as lawful prize by French ships of war. The British islands were again declared to be in a state of blockade both by land and sea, the passion of Buonaparte not pausing to consider whether such a land-blockade were intelligible. Our orders in council were in fact seized upon as a pretext for new-wording and colouring a previous

commercial decree issued at Milan a few days after them, but before they could be known, (November 23rd.) For this previous decree enacted, that "All vessels, after having touched at England, entering the ports of France, shall be seized and confiscated, as well as their cargoes, without exception or distinction of commodities or merchandise." The orders in council, therefore, were now represented as the provocation and reason of enacting what had been before enacted.

Under these circumstances, America appeared to have only a choice of evils, to join with one of the hostile powers, to arm her vessels against both for defensive war, or to submit to both, and carry on her trade with England. But the president and the populace of America were alike under the influence of hostile feelings towards England. The first state papers of Mr. Jefferson were so strikingly contrasted, with all which it had been our fortune to see promulgated in Europe, that the feeling of delight which they occasioned in the heart of an Englishman, were more than counterbalanced by a sense of humiliation which he could not fail to experience. They spoke of plans for national improvement, of expense curtailed, and taxes remitted to the people, and they indicated a spirit of hope not less philosophical than generous, which promised to hasten the approach of happier ages. But when trying times came on, and the president was weighed in the balance, he was found wanting. His enmity to this country continued long after it behoved him as a minister and a statesman, to return to more natural sentiments. The war against the French republic undoubtedly contributed to this animosity, and something has been ascribed to wounded vanity. Mr. Jefferson had been received at Paris with the most flattering distinction; in London he was entertained with a reserve more consonant to our usual manners than his real merit would have justified, or policy dictated. The temper of the American people corresponded but too well with that of their president. The identity of language which in better times will restore the two nations to a state of mutual amity, gave occasion in the present agitated aspect of affairs to mutual provocations. Our seamen frequently deserted to the Americans, and their sailors were sometimes impressed on suspicion of being Englishmen. On both sides there was just cause of complaint. We endured most injury, but they received most insult. But it was the practice of searching merchant-vessels, which chiefly irritated the Americans. Accustomed during the last war, to enjoy the whole carrying trade of Europe, they forgot in their vexation at its loss, that France had begun this system of restriction, and their whole resentment was directed against England. Under the impression of this feeling they co-operated with Buonaparte, in his plan of commercial warfare. A non-importation act prohibiting many articles of English manufacture was passed in 1806, which was at various times suspended, but when Buonaparte and his ally the emperor of Russia, had endeavored by their edicts to close the ports of Europe against us, this act was once more brought forward to be enforced. The oppressive conduct of France at length extended to the Americans themselves, who reduced by the edicts of Milan and the orders in council, to a choice of difficulties, adopted the strange expedient of suspending their own commerce entirely, by laying an embargo on all exports. Encouraged by this event, Buonaparte now determined to proceed in his experiment. He had already sent an army into Portugal, which expelled the reigning family, occasioned their exile to Brasil, and shut the port of Lisbon against us. The king of Prussia in a melancholy declaration, prohibited all intercourse between us and his states, and the king of Spain, so long the tool, and destined to be the victim of the French emperor, added another proof of blind subservience to his treacherous ally, by adopting in all his dominions the measures which had been enacted by France. In consequence of these combined and cotemporary measures, the whole continent of Europe, with the exception of Sweden, was closed against British goods, and our import trade from America was suddenly suspended.

The power and the will of Buonaparte had occasioned this state of things. In England the immediate inconvenience which was felt occasioned a partial cry of peace, begun by some of those manufacturers whose trade was at a stand, and supported by others whose views were less selfish, though not more enlightened. The most strenuous advocate for peace at this inauspicious moment was Mr. Roscoe, a man not to be mentioned without respect even when his errors are noticed. His pamphlets were eagerly received, and the authority of so excellent and celebrated a man, was triumphantly quoted by the advocates of peace. But his pamphlets produced no other effect, and they persuaded no person who had not already adopted his opinion. If there was little cause of fear in pursuing this inevitable and apparently interminable war, the manner in which it had been, and was now conducted, precluded the hope of ultimate success. Every administration, this like the last, and the last like that before it, proceeded without any system, and trod the same beaten and uniform path of incorrigible fatuity. The same tardiness, the same indecision, the same half measures, the same waste of men and money in fruitless expeditions, characterized them all. Even now when it became us to appear, as in reality we were, the only supporters of morals, intellect, and freedom, we continued to obey the pleasure of corrupt courts, in opposition to the welfare and the wishes of their subjects, and to squander our resources in attempting to support the most atrocious and arbitrary governments.

Much time during the early part of the session was consumed in debates upon the expedition to Copenhagen, and the subjects which it implicated. The orders in council were not less obstinately contested. The present ministry when out of place had pursued a system of harassing and vexatious opposition, which was now fully retaliated upon them. Night after night the discussion was renewed, and upon every separate debate the lights in Westminster hall were to be seen burning till morning. What leisure can a ministry have for the important duties of their station whose whole time must be employed in haranguing about what they have done, instead of arranging what they are to do? His days occupied in the office with the business of such an empire, in such times, and his nights consumed in fruitless debates in parliament, the iron frame of Talus is as necessary for an actual minister of state, as his moral inflexibility for an ideal one. Many reforms in the constitution of parliament have been proposed, a regulation which should exempt the efficient ministers from this wasting fatigue, would be one of the most beneficial. They might present their reports to the house, and leave the house to discuss them.

Lord Grenville, in the debate upon the king's speech, had shown what ground would be taken in opposing these orders of council. He affirmed that the ministers could not on the king's authority, constitutionally decree such extraordinary prohibitions, and that they had actually violated an article of Magna Charta. No ministers, it was said, had ventured to give such advice to the crown, since the reign of James II. when that monarch was advised that he had a power to dispense with the laws of the country. The exercise of the prerogative was limited by fixed rules, and the court of privy council was subject to the law of nations, which law was broken by the present orders. These arguments were enforced with much ability by lord Grenville in the upper, and by lord Henry Petty in the lower house. But, alas! the law of nations was extinct. The law of the strongest, which had often been acted upon in its stead, was now proclaimed by the enemy; and to call up the ghost of Magna Charta against a ministry, is as hopeless as it is to oppose Puffendorf to Buonaparte; majorities are as little influenced by the one as armies by the other. All arguments from the law of nations were therefore futile; and the other objection amounted only to this, that ministers ought to come to parliament for a bill of indemnity, which, had they supposed their proceedings required any palliation, they would of

course have done, but this they absolutely denied. The statutes which were infringed, they said, related to a state of peace and not of war, and the measures in question were measures of war, which the king was entitled by his prerogative to adopt.

It was observed by lord Hawkesbury that when the French decree was published, there appeared two courses, either of which might be adopted; to consider the decree as wholly ineffective, and treat it with contempt, or to regard it as a substantial measure, calculated to injure the interests of the country, and justifying measures of retaliation. The former would have been least inconvenient to ourselves, most dignified, and most humiliating to the enemy. And this alternative lord Hawkesbury would have preferred, had not the contrary system been adopted by the late administration, which had exercised the right of retaliation, and distinctly avowed their determination to extend, if necessary, the principle of the orders in council issued on the 7th of January, 1807. " The principle was incontrovertible; we were completely justified in retaliating upon the enemy their own measure; if they declare that we shall have no trade, we have a right to declare that they shall have none, and we have the power to enforce our decrees."

The great body of the people and even the merchants were decidedly in favor of these orders in council, as they would have been of any measure which was thought necessary for supporting the honor of their country, and continuing the war against Buonaparte. But there were many persons whose interests were immediately affected to a material degree. A petition against the orders was brought up from Liverpool, and nearly fifty nights of the session were consumed in debates upon the policy of the measure. Even after the orders had been enacted by a large majority, licences were granted exempting ships from those very orders, and enabling them to trade with France; an inconsistency which was occasioned by the rapacity of the clerks belonging to the privy council office, who received for every licence a handsome perquisite.

Ministers found an easy task in the

department of finance. Here they had indeed succeeded to a bed of roses, the thorny business of which had been performed by their predecessors. The supplies voted in the session, amounted to £48,653,170. The ways and means for answering this demand, were £3,000,000 upon malt and pensions, £3,000,000 and a half advanced by the bank, the unappropriated surplus of the consolidated fund, war taxes, the lottery, and £4,000,000 on exchequer bills.

Among the changes produced by the new ministry in the military arrangements, was the substitution of a local militia in aid of the volunteers. This local militia was to be balloted for in different counties: the ages of limitation were eighteen and thirty-one, and no exemptions were granted but on the payment of a heavy pecuniary fine. The period of service was to be twenty-eight days annually, exclusive of the days for assembling, marching, &c. for which the officers and men were granted an allowance of pay. It was calculated by the minister, that the adoption of this measure would place at the command of government 400,000 men, in addition to the regular army of 200,000, which might, if necessary, be increased to 250,000. It was vehemently opposed by Mr. Windham, as founded on principles directly opposite to that of his own military bill, enacted in the preceding year; and, after a short reply from its projector, lord Castlereagh, it was censured by sir Francis Burdett in the most remarkable speech which he ever pronounced in parliament. Mr. Herbert of Kerry, who preceded him, had praised the plan as being worthy of the noble lord in whom it originated. Alluding to this, sir Francis began by saying, that the noble lord was indeed the fittest person to originate such a measure;—but was the honorable gentleman who complimented him for bringing it forward, aware of what that measure would render the people subject to? In times when the army was undisciplined, and the nation barbarous, when social order was trampled under foot, and liberty was but another name for licentiousness,—in such

times it might have been right to enact and to enforce that military code, the penalties of which were now the exclusive disgrace of the British army and the British nation. But when so great an amelioration had taken place in the discipline and composition of our military force, it was no longer excusable to continue those penal enactments. To a conscription in the full force of the word, he should not object; it never could be considered a hardship for a man to be called forth to defend his home and his country, or to qualify himself for that necessity. It was not, therefore, on that account that he objected to the measure; but, before he could consent to subject the British people to any general summons of this nature, he would call for an amendment in the military code. He could not consent to commit the whole people of England to what was dishonorable, and pernicious to the army itself; he never could allow them to be subject to the lash. Then bursting into a strain of the bitterest personality, he could not, he said, describe the indignation which he felt at beholding the minister of the day dare to stigmatize the representatives of the people, by offering such a measure for their adoption. It required audacity to propose what only folly could imagine efficient, that the reluctant conscripts of our oppressed population should be marshalled under the scourge of tyranny, and presented to the nation as her defence. When you want men for your defence, offer them a post fit for men to accept; when you propose a military code, let it be fit for Englishmen and freemen. What! did the noble lord suppose that the people would endure and bend beneath the sanguinary, remorseless, and ferocious despotism, which even slaves would turn upon? Did he suppose that the lash of tyranny,—the insults, the contumely, and scorn of overweening power, the *fœdum signum servitutis*, would be suffered by a free people with impunity? It was, however, in this part of the measure that the fitness of the noble lord to be its proposer, was particularly shewn. The features of the offspring intuitively bespoke the parent as with the appearance of the *fasces*, must be associated the idea of the *lictor*. Atrocious measures must be expected in age from him, whose youth had been familiarized in his native country to executions, and when the author of this bill had wrung the heart-strings of his own country, little delicacy could be expected from him, for the dignified feelings of another. Experience had shewn that he was the fittest man in the world to submit a whole people to the lash.

Another question of considerable importance, connected with our laws of war, was brought forward by sir Francis Burdett ; but the attention of the house and of the people was diverted from the proposed investigation into the justice and policy of the *droits* of the admiralty, by certain unexpected disclosures in the course of the debate. Mr. Lushington said he would state one instance of the misapplication of these funds. Sir Home Popham had, in the year 1787, being at that time a lieutenant in the naval service, obtained leave of absence on half pay. He went to Ostend, and there procured a ship of 500 tons, bearing the imperial flag, in which he freighted a cargo for the East Indies. There he exchanged his vessel for an American ship called the President Washington, of 950 tons, which he immediately christened by the name of his old ship, the Etrusco, and, without scruple, transferred the papers of the smaller vessel to that which was nearly double its size. In this he conveyed a cargo to Canton, and, having taken in a fresh cargo at that place, sailed for Dungeness in Ireland, where he landed goods, " or, in plain English," said Mr. Lushington, " smuggled them." Lieutenant Bowen, of the Brilliant frigate, captain Robinson, seized the ship in Ostend roads, after a person had escaped on shore with part of the goods. The vessel was brought to judgment in the admiralty court. During the proceedings, sir Home claimed his share of the cargo and freight ; but, when it became necessary to serve a process of the court upon him, he was not to be found. The ship was condemned ; but for all the

trouble, inconvenience, and loss of time, in the prosecution of the business, captain Robinson did not receive one shilling. Yet afterwards, in consequence of a treasury warrant signed by the marquis of Blandford, Mr. Long, and the advocate-general, £25,000, the amount of his claim, was restored to the honorable baronet. The truth of this statement was feebly contradicted by sir Home Popham in person ; and, notwithstanding these circumstances related, attested as they were by the records of the admiralty, the bill itself, and the discoveries to which it gave rise, were dismissed from the consideration of the house by a majority of 82 to 57.

On the subject of the catholic question, to which the attention of the commons was now directed, Mr. Grattan opened the debate in a speech replete with eloquence, moderation, and good sense. He was opposed chiefly on the ground of inexpediency, and of regard to the feelings and opinions of the sovereign. There have been few debates in which all parties were placed in so humiliating a situation ; for on the one part, the ministry insulted their opponents for having waived this question, when they themselves were in power, and the opposition in return, accused them of a breach of promise made at the union, a sacrifice of individual opinion to the desire of place, and a mean regard to personal and temporary interest. Fortunately for the reputation of Mr. Perceval, the lateness of his accession to power, secured him from the charge of political inconsistency, as no former opportunity had occurred of delivering, *ex cathedra*, his opinions on the subject.

The affairs of India, and the conduct of the marquis of Wellesley, were, as usual, the themes of endless and fruitless debate. The bill to prevent the granting of offices in reversion, after long and vehement discussions, was past by a small majority, and a variety of subordinate questions warmly contested, but terminating in no beneficial or satisfactory result, exhausted the patience of the members at large, and wearied the attention of the public.

The aspect of foreign affairs, and the

record of our naval exploits compensated in some degree to the busy, the patriotic, and the inquisitive, for the paucity of domestic events, and the unmeaning levity of parliamentary debate.

The destruction of the Dutch naval force in the East Indies, was completed by sir Edward Pellew.—On the 20th of November, 1807, he sailed from Malacca with a squadron of two seventy-fours, two frigates and four smaller vessels, and, on the 5th of the following month, arrived off Point Panke, at the eastern extremity of Java, where the Dutch ships were lying in a dismantled state at Grissee. The line of battle ships could not proceed beyond Sedaye, which is about ten miles up the straits of Madura, without being lightened : they anchored there and a commission under a flag of truce, consisting of captain Fleetwood Pellew of the navy, captain sir Charles Burdett of the 30th, and Mr. Locker, the commander-in-chief's secretary, were sent to treat with the commandant of the Dutch naval force, for the surrender of his squadron. The summons which they bore was suitable to the power and moderation of the British government. It stated that the English were the natural friends of the Dutch, but that it was become their duty to prevent Dutch ships of war from acting under the control of France against the British. If the commander would deliver up the Dutch ships and vessels of war, and all others under French colors which might then be lying there, they would forbear from any measures of violence against the settlements and their inhabitants, and peaceably retire, after having obtained the necessary provisions. The Dutch commandant at Grissee, M. Cowell, contrary to the law of nations arrested the commissioners, and sent back answer, that his duty as an officer in the service of the king of Holland, prevented him from suffering either the boat or people to return; and that whatever injury the chance of war might expose him and his countrymen to, would be miserably obviated by attending to the proposals which the English commander had thought proper to make.

Upon this sir Edward Pellew ordered

the line of battle ships to be lightened, and then proceeded with his whole squadron. A battery consisting of 12 nine and eighteen-pounders, at Sambelargan, on the island of Madura, hulled several of the ships with red-hot shot, but no injury was done and it was soon silenced. The battery of Grissee was silenced also, after a few ineffectual discharges. M. Cowell, as soon as he perceived the English approaching, scuttled his Dutch ships and sent his prisoners to Sourabaya, a town about 15 miles higher up the straits, to which Grissee is subject. This is a beautiful place, situated about a mile and a half from the sea, upon a river navigable for vessels of 100 tons, having a tracking path on the bank. The Chinese carry on a considerable trade here, and have a town on the opposite side of the river. The resident at Sourabaya has the rank of senior merchant, and the title of commander of the eastern district. When the English commissioners arrived here they complained to the commander of their unwarrantable detention, they were in consequence released, accompanied by a deputation of three members of the council, to disclaim all concurrence on the part of government with such a measure and to express their concern.

Sir Edward Pellew and colonel Lockhart now proposed the following terms to the government and council, stating, first, that M. Cowell by his violation of the flag of truce was excluded from all farther communication with the British.—The ships, they said, at Grissee were already in their hands, and must be destroyed, but the private property, provisions, and other stores should remain secure; the British force was not directed against individuals; and if the governor and council would declare, that there was no ship of war at Sourabaya, their word would be received a security for that settlement. They pledged their word, and accordingly the place was untouched. The battery of Sambelargan it was said, must be destroyed, but, to prevent the necessity of employing force, it was proposed that the governor and council should issue their orders for the purpose, a British officer and a party of troops being admitted into the fort for the completion of the same. "We are compelled," said the governor and council in their answer, " to acknowledge that the destruction of Sambelargan by the artillery of English ships, is in the power of your excellency, and that we are unable to oppose any resistance; but the generosity which has been shown towards Grissee, assures us that it cannot be your intention to give us any insult, by compelling us to submit to the destruction of the battery by your troops; we therefore request, that you will relax from this article, upon our engaging to disarm and demolish this battery at the same time." This was acceded to by the English commander, and the battery was accordingly destroyed by the Dutch, the commanding officer of artillery inspecting it after it was demolished. A supply of water was required, about 300 head of cattle, and fruit and vegetables, to be paid for immediately in Spanish dollars at the usual market prices. Upon these terms the security of the Dutch settlement was guaranteed.

Two seventy-gun ships were destroyed, which had been very fine vessels, but much neglected; a third which had been cut down to a hulk, a company's ship of 1000 tons, pierced for 40 guns, and a transport; and thus the entire destruction of the naval power of Holland in the East Indies, a power which had once been so formidable, was completed.

The Danish settlements of Tranquebar and Serampore were taken possession of without opposition, as soon as news arrived of the rupture with Denmark. The last intelligence of the year from India was of an action between the St. Fiorenzo and La Piedmontaise, one of the most glorious in the annals of the British navy. The St. Fiorenzo, originally a French forty-gun frigate, called La Minerve, had been captured and sunk in the Mediterranean, and afterwards weighed up, chiefly by the exertions of captain, now admiral Tylar, to whom the command of her was then given, and her new name was then imposed after the town and port so called in Corsica. Captain

George Nicholas Hardinge served on board her at that time as a midshipman; and thirteen years afterwards, during which he had distinguished himself by the most enterprising services, he was appointed to this same frigate at Bombay, when, after undergoing a repair she was in such a condition as to be described by himself " barely effective, but not eligible, and rather safe than sound." She carried 38 guns; and her crew consisted of 186 men chiefly invalids. The Piedmontaise mounted 50 long eighteen-pounders, and was manned with 566 men. This vessel had long annoyed our commerce in the Indian seas, and it had long been the wish of the English ships of war to fall in with her; because her second captain, Charles Moreau, had wounded the captain of the Warren Hastings, and some others of the crew with a dagger, after they had surrendered. In consequence of his barbarity orders had been issued by sir Edward Pellew to inflict upon him due punishment whenever he should be taken; but hitherto the Piedmontaise had outsailed every thing. The Frenchman having made many captures upon the cruize, learned from different accounts, that three Indiamen were about to sail from Bombay without convoy, and resolved to wait for them off cape Comorin. His plan was to run close along-side the first, and throw about 150 men on board, and then engage the second, by which he expected to secure two of the three at least.

On the 4th of March the St. Fiorenzo sailed from Ponte de Galle, in Ceylon; and on the morning of the 6th came in sight of the three Indiamen, just as the Piedmontaise was about to bear down upon them. It was nearly midnight before the English frigate could get near enough the enemy to engage; she then ranged along side him within a cable's length, but in a few minutes the Piedmontaise was out of the range of her shot. The St. Fiorenzo pursued all night; shortly after day light they recommenced firing at the distance of half a mile, gradually closing to a quarter: this was continued for about two hours, when the Frenchman again made all sail, having materially crippled his enemy's

rigging. The English repaired their damage, kept sight of the Piedmontaise during the night, bore down for action in the morning, and, about three o'clock, came up with her within a quarter of a cable's length. After an hour and twenty minutes, the Piedmontaise struck her colours. This victory, glorious as it was, was dearly purchased by the loss of captain Hardinge, who fell in the last action by a grape-shot, deeply and deservedly regretted by the British navy, which did not contain an officer of higher promise. The loss of the English was 13 killed, and 24 wounded; that of the French was 50 killed, and 122 wounded. Moreau, as was to be expected, fought desperately, and for some time prevented his men from striking; when he saw that the contest was hopeless, and that no friendly ball came to save him from a more ignominious fate, he shot himself, and that not proving effectual, was at his own request thrown overboard by his men, while yet living. Great honors were paid to the memory of captain Hardinge, in India, and the king granted an honorable augmentation to the armorial bearings of his family, the crest being a naval sword passing through a wreath of cypress, and another of laurel.

During the spring of the year, the hopes of the British people were excited by the unusual circumstance of a French squadron having put to sea. It escaped from Rochefort in the month of January, at a time when sir Richard Strachan had left that port for a few days, either from stress of weather or because his ships had not been duly supplied. Intelligence was soon given to sir John Duckworth, who, supposing they were bound for the West Indies, made all sail in that direction. He touched at Madeira, proceeded to the squadron which was blockading Martinique, ran down as far as Hayti, and then struck for America, and arrived off the Chesapeake on the 11th of March. Here the Americans enforced their inhospitable interdict, and refused to supply our ships with water and provisions. From thence the squadron sailed for the Western islands, where they were well sup-

plied; and then returned to England after an unsuccessful cruize of more than 13,000 miles. Sir Richard Strachan in the mean time, was, with as little success, seeking the same enemy in the Mediterranean. It was at last ascertained that they had taken refuge in Toulon.

The temper of the Americans was manifested by their conduct towards our squadron,—a method of displaying their enmity as base as it was contemptible. The same spirit appeared at their celebrations of the anniversary of their independence, when their toasts were levelled against the power of England with safe insolence. The embargo, was, however, severely felt; and, if the Americans had been as bold in actions as in words, discontent in some of the states must have burst out into civil war. A separation from the union was openly proposed by the newspapers in the New England state; combinations were formed for resisting the embargo, and the president issued a proclamation to put down such combinations by force of arms. But the Americans are too prudent a people to involve themselves hastily in war, when nothing can be gained; and a note was addressed by the American plenipotentiary to Mr. secretary Canning, in which it was proposed, that, if Great Britain would repeal her orders in council, America would suspend her embargo as far as it regarded Great Britain. A month elapsed before any answer to this proposal was returned, the English government waiting to discover the answer of France to a similar offer. France, however, did not think proper to reply; and the consequent silence of the English ministry produced a message from the president of the United States, which urged the continuance of the embargo, and in which he not only descanted with unusual acrimony upon the specific topics of debate, but described the pretension of England to the sovereignty of the seas, as an inadmissible preliminary, which all the resources of the United States would be strenuously exerted to resist.

In the month of February, a convention between his Britannic majesty and the king of Sweden was signed at Stockholm, in which Great Britain agreed to pay to Sweden £1,200,000 in twelve monthly payments, the king of Sweden engaging to employ that sum in supporting a respectable establishment by land and sea. Previous to the signature of this treaty, the Russian troops were already on their march to Finland; and, on the 10th of February, the emperor Alexander issued a declaration, expressive of the most decided hostility to her alliance with England, and of his determination to resort to those means which providence had placed in his hands for the purpose of protecting and securing his dominions. The Russian general Buxhovden circulated a similar manifesto on entering Finland, and Denmark issued a labored and violent declaration. To the denunciations and the sophistries of his united enemies, the replies of the king of Sweden were more rational and moderate than might have been expected from the impetuosity of his character; but they were preceded by an extraordinary act, which was barely justified by the law of nations. As the Russian troops had entered Finland before any communication had been made by M. Alopeus, the Russian ambassador, which could lead him to expect such intelligence, he ordered him to be placed under a military guard, considering him as deprived of his public character by the insidious aggressions of his court, as a dangerous enemy by the revolutionary principles with which that aggression was accompanied, and as a hostage for the Swedish ambassador at St. Petersburgh. Alexander acted upon this occasion with unusual prudence. He issued a declaration, expressing his astonishment at the conduct of the king of Sweden, and gave orders that the Swedish ambassador should be treated with increased respect, and permitted to depart whenever he thought proper. M. Alopeus was detained about three months, and then suffered to leave Stockholm.

The death of the king of Denmark, who died suddenly, occasioned no alteration in affairs: he had long been in a state of idiocy, and the crown prince, who now succeeded him by the name of Frederic VI. acquired only the regal title, having for many years exercised the sovereign authority. French troops were at this time pouring into Holstein. Ten thousand Spaniards, under the marquis de la Romana, were following them from Hamburgh;—Bernadotte was directing their operations, and it was expected that the Danes, with these allies, would make a descent upon Sweden. But Buonaparte had other views in marching the Spaniards to the Baltic; and the war with Sweden was to him a matter no otherwise important, than as it served to divert the attention and waste the strength of the northern powers. The people of Hamburgh experienced at this time another instance of military despotism. The French commandant in that city ordered the gates to be shut on Easter Tuesday at an earlier hour than usual, under pretence of preventing holiday excesses. In consequence of this, a number of inhabitants were shut out. They demanded entrance, which was refused. The people within the town became clamorous to have the gates opened, and at length began to pelt the soldiers, who then fired upon them; some were killed, and many wounded. The confusion was increased by the breaking out of an accidental fire and the ringing of the alarm-bell in consequence. The military soon quelled this disturbance, which their own conduct had provoked. More troops, however, were sent to overawe the people; and, on the following day, the commandant issued a proclamation, enacting, that if any person threw a stone at a French soldier, he should be tried by a military commission, and put to death; that if four or more persons were found talking together, the French soldiers on duty, were to require them to separate, and fire upon them unless they obeyed; and that if any person sounded the alarm-bell without instructions from the French, he should be shot upon the spot. Such was the miserable state of slavery to which the city of Hamburgh was reduced,

The Dey of Algiers consulting his council.

while its freedom and independence were still nominally acknowledged. Altona was treated with as little respect. The Danish guard refused admission to the Spanish troops; and the president of the senate protested, that he had no instructions from his sovereign to receive them; they however, pursuant to the French orders which had been given them, entered with fixed bayonets and quartered themselves upon the inhabitants.

Little alarm seems to have been excited at Stockholm, by the preparations on this side of the Baltic. Gustavus, indeed, was dreaming of conquests; and marched an army under baron Armfeldt into Norway, when all his efforts should have been directed to the defence of Finland. That service was entrusted to count Klingspor, a man who acquired far more honor in an unsuccessful campaign, than the victorious general who was opposed to him. For though unable to stop the progress of an army greatly superior in numbers to his own, assisted by French engineers, and led by Swedish traitors, who were well acquainted with the country, he effected his retreat in the face of the enemy, for more than 400 English miles, repeatedly fighting as he went, yet always avoiding a general engagement; he made no attempt to impede his pursuers by laying waste the land he was endeavoring to defend, and he brought off with him the whole of his magazines, artillery, baggage and stores. His men partook of the spirit of their general—not a desertion took place—not a murmur was heard among them. The Russians had expected that he would have no resource left,— the gulf was impassable on account of floating ice; and if he attempted to march by Touca, along the dreary coast of East Bothnia, his troops must perish with hunger,—he would, therefore, they concluded, have no alternative but to surrender. But their attempt to surround him totally failed, and he effected a junction with another detachment under count Cronstedt, which enabled him to make a stand, at a time when the Russians ceased the pursuit, and collected their forces at Wasa. Mean time in another quarter they were making con-

quests more easily than by the sword. Sweaborg, a place so strong, as to have been called the Gibraltar of the north, after a defence not sufficient to furnish cowardice, or corruption with a decent plea for surrendering it, was yielded by its governor admiral Cronstedt, with the whole flotilla in its harbor, consisting of above 300 gunboats and transports;—an absurd stipulation being inserted in the convention, that this was to be restored to Sweden after the conclusion of peace, in case England should restore the Danish fleet. Gustavus immediately dismissed Cronstedt with ignominy, from the service, and all the officers, of rank along with him who had not protested against the surrender. A heavier and more condign punishment would probably have been inflicted, had the culprit been within reach of justice. The Russians now pushed over to Gothland, and obtained possession of that island. But there fortune seemed to turn,—Gothland was recovered, and all the enemy who had landed there were taken prisoners. Buxhovden retreated for want of provisions, and Klingspor pursuing, twice engaged and defeated him; but the Swedish troops were too inferior in number to follow up the favorable opportunity thus presented to them in vain.

No race of princes except the Plantagenets have possessed so much genius as the royal family of Sweden; but there has been a leaven of insanity mingled with it, which manifested itself in Christiana and in Charles XII. and of which some indications appeared in Gustavus. Neither calculating his own strength nor that of his adversaries, he suffered Finland to fall while he was idly contemplating the conquest of Norway. General Armfeldt on invading that country, issued a proclamation, saying, that the Danish government had declared war against Sweden, without cause or provocation, and had spontaneously submitted to a foreign yoke; the Swedes, therefore entered Norway according to the laws of war. Their object was not to injure the Norwegians, but to open their ports, quicken their industry, and secure in the north an asylum for loyalty and honor. It is not from an invading army that a brave and honourable people will accept of commercial privileges and the gratuities of trade. A report prevailed that they offered to withdraw their allegiance from Denmark, remain neutral, and open their ports as usual to British ships, protesting that they would never submit to Sweden,—though they desired to be at peace with her;—that this proposal was made to sir John Moore and admiral Keates, by a deputation from the Norwegian nobility, but that they had no authority to negotiate such an arrangement. Ten thousand English troops, under the first of these distinguished officers, had been sent to the assistance of our ally; they arrived at Gottenburgh on the 17th of May; it was intimated that they were not to land there, and sir John Moore suppressing his resentment repaired to Stockholm, to communicate his orders and concert measures with the king. It has seldom been the fate of an English expedition to be despatched too soon. In this instance however, it appears that no previous plan had been arranged with Gustavus, and that ministers in their admiration for the noble spirit of that monarch, had overlooked the defects of his character. His first proposal to sir John Moore was, that the troops should remain in their ships till some Swedish regiments were collected at Gottenburgh; and that then the combined forces should land and conquer Zealand. A regular army, far superior to any that could possibly have been collected, was assembled in Zealand; there are several strong fortresses in that island, and the French and Spaniards in the isle of Funen could not have been hindered from crossing over in small bodies. Our general, with his characteristic mildness, respectfully represented, that these difficulties were too great to be surmounted by the bravest troops. Gustavus then proposed that the British should land in Russian Finland, storm a fortress and take a position there. This would have been to expose 10,000 Englishmen to the principal forces of the Russian empire. Notwithstanding the respectful manner and gentle nature of sir John Moore, the violence

of the king's temper broke forth and he actually arrested the British general. Sir John however, found means to escape, hastened to Gottenburgh, and brought back his army to England.

Some apprehensions were entertained that the king of Sweden would take advantage of this dispute, to make his peace with France, and purchase the forbearance of Russia, by shutting his ports against England, even if resentment did not hurry him into hostilities against us. But they who reasoned thus wronged Gustavus by their suspicions. There was a want of sanity in his conduct, which proceeded from the disease of his nature, but there was in him a sense of honor and an unyielding spirit, not unworthy of his illustrious ancestry. His own imprudence had now bereft him of that support which 10,000 British troops would have afforded; a force sufficient to have turned the tide of war in Finland,— and he was left to his own resources. The imprudence of his plan of operations was soon manifested. The Norwegians who had been unexpectedly attacked and made little or no resistance at first to their invaders, soon rallied. They were disciplined, it is said, by some Prussian officers, who had been made prisoners at Lubeck with general Blucher, a veteran whose activity, enterprise, and courage, deserved to have been better supported. These officers had entered into the Danish service. The Norwegians are a brave people, and their country strong and easily defended; Armfeldt, therefore, when they made head against him, was compelled to retreat as rapidly as he had advanced, and was driven out of Norway with considerable loss.

While part of the Swedish army was thus miserably misemployed, Klingspor was unable to take advantage of the distress of the Russians, or their temporary weakness, they were soon reinforced in such numbers, that he was no longer able to withstand them. Their admiral, Badisco, during the short time that he was in possession of the isle of Gothland, had honorably distinguished

CHARLES JOHN, CROWN PRINCE of SWEDEN

himself by the strict order which he enforced, and by his humanity towards the inhabitants. A different conduct was pursued in Finland. That country had been the happiest in the whole north of Europe, while all other nations of the same race suffer under the most brutal and brutalizing tyranny. While the Esthonian mother weeps over her infant, because slavery and wretchedness are its inheritance, while the Livonian nobles send their young greyhounds to be suckled by the female peasantry, the Swedish Finlanders were free, and enjoyed the produce of labor in comfort and security. Gustavus alluded to this contrast in his declaration against Russia. "Inhabitants of Finland," said he, "a people worthy of esteem, your king has, during the whole of his reign, attended to your instruction and to the cultivation and prosperity of your country. A faithless neighbour threatens to hurl you back to that state in which you were in past ages, and this because your neighbourhood is a reproach unto him." Well might Gustavus thus address them. There had been an increase of 60,000 in the population of this province during the last twenty years ; and Seume, a traveller, whose judgment is as sound as his feelings are excellent, declares the whole country was so highly cultivated, that he had seen nothing equal to it in Italy, Germany, or France, considering the difficulties that were to be surmounted. "I never" says this good man, "felt so much respect for human industry as during my tour through Swedish Finland."

This happy country fell under the yoke of Russia. The generals of that country resembled Suwarrow in barbarity, however unlike him in the nobler parts of his character. The town of Wasa was given up to be plundered ; and, while the soldiers were perpetrating every atrocity, in open day, their generals, Kniper, Demidof, and Emine, to whom the government of the town had been given on its capture, rode through the streets, hallooing these wretches on, and at all their enormities crying out, Well done !—Many of the officers imitated the conduct of their superiors,; and, when the work of havoc was over, they publicly divided the spoil with the common soldiers. The adjacent country presented only a scene of devastation and wretchedness ; villages in ashes, and houses in which nothing was left but such of their miserable inhabitants as had escaped death or captivity ; happy even then if they were not mangled or dishonored. General Rajewski repressed these horrors while he was present, expressing his utmost detestation of them ; and the official account published by the deputy lord-lieutenant of the province, acknowledges that some few! of the soldiers and even of the officers, without regard to their own danger, did all they could to protect the poor inhabitants. The officers were worse than the soldiers, as is generally the case in that great empire,—natural virtues are to be found in the lower ranks,—the higher ones have exchanged them for the vices of French refinement. Gustavus addressed a letter to the emperor Alexander, conjuring him to put a stop to these horrors, which, he said, could not fail of bringing down on his person and government, the curses of divine Providence. In consequence of this letter, Demidof was displaced from his command and ordered to Petersburgh.

Wasa, after it had thus been sacked, was evacuated by the Russians ; but Klingspor, who had advanced beyond that town, and endeavored to maintain a position which would cover the most fruitful part of East Bothnia, was unable to resist the increasing numbers that were brought against him. His line of operations extended from Lindalax and Omyssa to Lappfjerd, 28 Swedish miles. The corps at Lindalax was driven back ; and the Russians, after having been repulsed on three successive days, succeeded in cutting off the communication between Lappo and Lappfjerd. This latter post was now threatened ; and Klingspor was compelled to retreat. He effected his retreat as he had on the former occasion, with the greatest skill and courage, still facing a superior enemy, and bringing off all his baggage and artillery. An armistice for an unlimited time was concluded between the two armies at the end of September. It left each party in possession of the country which it occupied ; but the Russians were soon strong enough to resume offensive operations, and a second armistice, signed on the 20th of November, virtually surrendered Finland to Russia. The Swedes were to evacuate all their posts there, and retire beyond the river Keims, the limit of the province.

During this campaign, many unimportant actions took place between the flotillas of the contending powers, and our trade in the Baltic received considerable injury from the Danish gun-boats. The honor of the British flag, was, however, gallantly supported by that distinguished officer, sir Samuel Hood, who, having joined the Swedish admiral Nauckhoff with the Centaur and Implacable, two seventy-fours, sailed in quest of the Russian fleet, on the 25th of August. Next morning the enemy were discovered off Hangolldd. All sail was set in pursuit. The British ships out-sailed their allies ; and, about five o'clock on the following morning, the Implacable brought the Sewolod, of 74 guns, being the most leeward of the enemy's line of battle, to close action. The Russian admiral immediately bore up with his whole force. In the course of twenty minutes, the Sewolod was completely silenced, and her colours struck both ensign and pendant ; but sir Samuel was obliged to make signal for the Implacable to join him. The Russian admiral sent a frigate to take the disabled ship in tow, and again hauled his wind. As soon as the Implacable was ready to make sail, sir Samuel gave chace again,

and soon obliged the frigate to cast off her tow. This made the Russian again bear down with his main force, and it was hoped that a general action would be brought on, but the enemy availed themselves of a favorable slant of wind, and entered the port of Rogerswick.

The Sewolod, which had fallen to leeward, grounded on a shoal just at the entrance of the port ; she soon, however, rode at anchor, exertions were made to repair her damage, 100 men from the other ships were sent on board to replace her loss in the action, and at sun-set boats came out to tow her in. Upon this sir Samuel stood in with the Centaur to cut her off. She was just entering the port when he laid her on board. Her bowsprit took the Centaur's fore-rigging, and she swept along with her bow, grazing the muzzles of the British guns. When the bowsprit came to the mizen, it was lashed there. Sir Samuel now attempted to tow her out,—but an anchor had been let go from her. A severe contest for about half an hour ensued; when the Russians, after losing in this second conflict 180 men, struck. The Centaur and her prize now grounded, and two of the enemy's ships were seen under sail standing towards them ; but captain Martin, in the Implacable, anchored his ship so as to heave the Centaur off, and they then retreated. The prize was first on shore, and sir Samuel, finding it impossible to bring her off, burnt her. Hopes were entertained in England when this intelligence arrived, that the Russian fleet might be destroyed ; but the harbor was strongly fortified. They landed their men, and erected more batteries, and it was found impossible to make any impression upon the enemy.

HISTORY OF THE WAR.

CHAP. XLIX.

THE castle of Scylla in Calabria, which was held by an English garrison under lieutenant-colonel Robinson, was taken by the French general Regnier, early in the year. The town of Scylla lies partly on the shore, but the greater part on the rocks above, where nine rows of houses are seen, one immediately above the other : and above the highest of these, in an oblique direction, there are six or seven other rows. The castle is upon a cliff over the sea ; but, notwithstanding the advantages of its situation, it is not strong. There were between 400 and 500 armed Calabrians in the town, and about 200 British soldiers in the castle. The besieging force consisted of about 6000 men, who were now incessantly employed in forming roads to bring their heavy ordnance from Seminara : the besieged laboring on their part to render the approach difficult, and to harass the French outposts. The month of January was past in these preparations, when four Sicilian gun-boats, each carrying a 24-pounder, were taken by the enemy ; and thus all the endeavors which had been used to prevent him from bringing battering cannon into that part of Calabria

were rendered unavailing. The Delight sloop of war, in endeavoring to recover them, run on shore, several of her crew were killed, and the remainder made prisoners. In this unfortunate affair, captain Hanfield, her commander, fell; a man of so much professional and individual worth, that his death was a greater misfortune than the loss of Scylla and its castle. The sloop was burnt on the next day by our boats, it being impossible to get her off. The French were now enabled to bring five 24-pounders, five 18-pounders, and four mortars, besides field-pieces, against the works. They came down from the heights on the 6th of February, and made their approaches in form. The armed peasantry opposed them with great spirit for three days ; they were then obliged to yield to superior numbers, but the castle-guns covered their retreat, and they were sent to Messina, not a man falling into the enemy's hands. On the 14th, the batteries opened ; in three days the guns of the castle were buried in the ruins of the parapet, and the garrison could only defend themselves with musketry. Two breaching batteries had now been erected at 300 and 400 yards distance, and by the evening of the 16th they had battered the left bastion with so much success that in the course of the following day the breach would have been practicable. From the time the batteries opened, the weather had been so stormy that the gun-boats from which much assistance had been expected could not possibly be employed.

The situation of the castle being made known by telegraph to general Sherbrooke, who commanded in Sicily, boats were sent over from the Faros during a temporary abatement of the gale to bring off the garrison. Aware of the means of retreat, the enemy on the 15th, had pushed round the front of the rock, and attempted to destroy the sea staircase, but they were discovered and beat off with great slaughter. By this staircase the British effected their way to the boats through a tremendous fire; they embarked without leaving a man behind them, and before they were musket-shot distant, the French were in the fort, which they found only a heap of ruins. They purchased their success by the loss of 700 men; on the part of the garrison 11 were killed, and 31 wounded.

A few days after this event, a treaty of alliance with Sicily was signed by our envoy at Palermo, which stipulated the payment to his Sicilian majesty of an annual subsidy of £300,000 in monthly payments, commencing from the 10th of September, 1805. His Sicilian majesty engaged not to make peace with France separately from England, and his Britannic majesty on his part also engaged to conclude no treaty which did not embrace the interests of his ally.

An unexpected attack was made on the isle of Capri, by a body of troops under general Lamarque, and prince Pignutelli, second in command. The fort of Ancapri had been left to the defence of a Maltese regiment. These men, of whom four-fifths were married, would have been excellent soldiers on their own island, but it was now thought proper to unite them into one large regiment under English officers, contrary to their own entreaties, and to the judgment of sir Alexander Ball. Ac-

customed to be commanded on their native rock, by their own nobility, they were sent to serve where they had no interest at heart, and in the hour of trial they laid down their arms without resistance. The French obtained possession of the heights, and shortly afterwards compelled the English garrison to surrender as prisoners of war. They were to be transported to England, on condition that they should not serve until exchanged.

Buonaparte in the mean time was steadily pursuing the views of his restless and insatiable ambition. His first act was through the medium of the conservative senate to call out 80,000 conscripts born within the year 1789, who according to the laws should have belonged to the conscription of the succeeding year. By a decree of the same date the towns of Kehl, Wesel, Cassel, and Flushing, were united to the French empire. The kingdom of Etruria which he himself had created for one of his puppet kings was no longer to exist. It was now incorporated as an inseperable indivisible portion of the French dominions, and one usurpation was made a precedent for another. A junta, with general Menou at its head, was appointed to govern the new departments of the Arno, the Mediterranean, and the Ombrona, into which the states of Tuscany had been now divided. The same decree incorporated the dukedoms of Parma and Placentia under the title of the department of the Taro. The pope had long foreseen that these events were only a prelude to his own humiliation, and demeaned himself with unexpected dignity. He protested against the designs of the French government, and soon after the circulation of his remonstrance, French troops were marched to Rome, under pretence of freeing that city from the Neapolitans. They seized those cardinals who were attached to the pope, and forcibly carried them as prisoners, from the palace of the Quirinal; they took possession of the post-offices for the purpose of examining all correspondence; incorporated the papal troops into their own army, and set guards over all the printing-offices, that the pope might not avail him-

self of the influence of the press. The appearance of respect to the pope himself, who was now a prisoner in his own palace, was not long observed. A French detachment burst through the gates at six in the morning, and arrested those of the Swiss guards, who would not consent to receive their future orders from the French general. Against each of these acts the pope continued to protest, but was only answered through the medium of M. Champagny by insult and invective. The protests of the pontiff were succeeded by a memorial remarkable for its firmness, its intelligence; and its piety, in the publication of which he was evidently actuated by a determination not to concur in the usurpation of Spain, upon which Napoleon had determined. The consequences of his conduct were such as he had foreseen. Buonaparte issued from Ancona, a decree to incorporate the papal territories with the kingdom of Italy. Having thus secured the dependance of the latter country on France, he proceeded in the creation and establishment of his new nobility. The great dignitaries of the empire were to have the title of prince and of serene highness. Their eldest sons were to be dukes of the empire in their own right, as soon as their fathers should assign them an entail yielding an income of 200,000 francs, which title and entail were to pass to their descendants either lineal or adopted from male to male. The great dignitaries could assign to the eldest of two sons an entail with the title of count attached to it. Ministers, senators, counsellors of state holding their offices for life, presidents of the legislative body, and archbishops, were made counts, that title being also hereditary and descending from the archbishops to such nephews as they might choose. An income of 30,000 francs was required as a qualification for this title, and to the eldest of two sons these nephews might assign an entail with the title of baron. The presidence of the departmental electoral assemblies having presided during three sittings, the first presidents and attorneys-general of the courts of cassation, appeal, and accounts, having exercised their functions 10 years

to the emperor's satisfaction; and the mayors of 37 cities who have the right of being present at the coronation, and in like manner have held their offices for that term, were to be invested with the title of baron. The members of the legion of honor were to have the title of knights, made hereditary, with a qualification of 3000 francs. In case reasonable grounds should be assigned for alienating their landed property, it was only on condition that the estates should be replaced by others of the same size.

While Buonaparte thus artfully flattered the vanity of the French nation, he hinted at another part of his new project, which, however gratifying it might be to his own love of power, was pregnant with the most pernicious consequences. "Europe," said the arch-chancellor, "is covered with our trophies, and will receive with respect names to which our sovereign has graciously been pleased to add new lustre. Great models will impose great duties on future generations, and the exertion of power which this obligation will render necessary, will be for France a never failing stream of fame and prosperity. These considerations have induced the emperor no longer to defer the benefits of an institution, which unfolds all the dignity and greatness of his object." The titles which he conferred were taken from the countries he had overrun, and the obligation imposed on France, was that of maintaining the same authority which he at that time possessed over places so remote as Ragusa and Abrantes. The result of these changes, and of his attempt to render the advance and predominance of French ambition, certain and perpetual, is best exhibited by the following

King of Westphalia,—Prince Jerome Napoleon.

Viceroy of Italy,—Prince Eugene Beauharnois,—(4th corps,)

Princess of Borghese,—Paulina Buonaparte.

Grand duchess of Florence,—Eliza Buonaparte.

Grand duke of Berg,—Prince Charles Louis Napoleon.

Grand duke of Warsaw,—Frederic Augustus IV. king and elector of Saxony.

Archbishop of Lyons,—Cardinal Fesche.

Prince of Ponte Corvo,—Marshal Bernadotte, crown prince of Sweden.

Prince of Neufchatel,—Marshal Berthier.

Prince of Essling,—Marshal Massena.

Prince of Benevento,—Talleyrand.

Prince of Echmuhl,—Marshal Davoust.

Duke of Abrantes,—Marshal Junot, (dead.)

Duke of Albufera,—Count Suchet.

Duke of Averstadt,—Marshal Davoust.

Duke of Bassano,—Maret.

Duke of Belluno,—Marshal Victor.

Duke of Cadore,—Champagny.

Duke of Castiglione,—Marshal Augereau.

Duke of Cornegliano,—Marshal Money.

Duke of Dalmatia,—Marshal Soult.

Duke of Dantzic,—Marshal Le Febvre.

Duke of Elchingen,—Marshal Ney.

Grand duke of Florence,—General Bacchiochi.

Duke of Friuli,—Marshal Duroc.

Duke of Montebello,—Marshal Lasnes, (killed at Wagram.)

Duke of Istria,—Marshal Bessieres.

Duke of Otranto,—Fouché.

Duke of Padua,—General Argia.

Duke of Parma,—Cambaceres, arch-chancellor.

Duke of Placenza,—Marshal Le Brun, prince arch-treasurer.

Duke of Ragusa,—Marshal Marmont.

Duke of Reggio,—Marshal Oudinot.

Duke of Rovigo,—General Savary.

Duke of Tarento,—Marshal M'Donald

Duke of Treviso,—Marshal Mortier.

Duke of Valmy,—Marshal Kellerman.

Duke of Vicenza,—General Caulincourt.

Ex-Marshal Brune

Ex-Marshal Jourdan.

Marshal Penignon.

Marshal Serrurier.

General of Division,—Barons of the empire, to wit.

Andreossi.

Baraguay de Hilliers.

Belliards.

Bruyeres.

Gouvion St. Cyr.

Defrance.

Duc Tailles.

St. Germain.

Arnaud.

Rapp, (late governor of Dantzic, and first aid-de-camp to the emperor.)

Regnier.

Moraud.

Sebastiani.

Vandamme, (formerly commandant of Boulogne.)

Linois, vice-admiral.

Grouchy.

Hogendorp.

Hulin, governor of Paris.

Loison, (formerly governor of the imperial palace.)

Mauberg.

Montbrun.

Nansouty.

It soon became apparent, that the forces which Buonaparte was marching into Spain, were designed to effect some important revolution in that country, though of what nature that revolution would be, no reasonable conjecture could be formed. On the 30th of October, in the preceding year, a proclamation was issued from the escurial, in which the king of Spain accused his son, the prince of Asturias, of conspiring to dethrone him. "My life," he said, "which has so often been in danger, was too long in the eyes of my successor. Being informed that he had entered into a project to dethrone me, I thought proper to inquire personally into the truth of the fact, and, surprising him in my room, I found in his possession the cypher of my correspondence. In consequence of this discovery, I immediately convoked the governor and council in order that they might make the necessary investigation, the result has been the detection of several malefactors, whose imprisonment I have ordered, as well as the arrest of my son." Six days after the date of this extraordinary proclamation another was issued, containing two letters from the prince, in which he confessed his guilt, avowed repentance, and implored forgiveness.

In consequence of these letters, and at the entreaty of the queen, the king declared that he forgave him, "for the voice of nature unnerved the hand of vengeance."

The prince, he added, had declared the authors of this horrible plot, and the judges were commanded to continue the process already commenced; and submit their judgment to the king, who, at the request of his council, ordered a public thanksgiving for this interposition of divine Providence in his behalf. This mysterious affair has never been clearly elucidated.

The Spaniards imputed it to the machinations of Don Manuel Godoy prince de La Paz, or of the peace, an upstart, who, being in the most infamous sense of the word, the favorite of the queen, had obtained the highest power of the state. This man was completely subservient to France, and the real plot was in all probability concerted between him and Buonaparte, for the purpose of exciting divisions in the royal family.

After the adoption of these preparatory measures for the usurpation of Spain, the next step towards the accomplishment of the design, was to remove its best troops, and, in conformity to treaty, 16,000 men were marched into the north of Germany, under the marquis de Romana. At the very moment when the transaction of the escurial took place, a secret treaty for the partition of Portugal was signed at Fontainbleau, by which the king of Etruria, on ceding his Italian possessions in full, and entire sovereignty to Buonaparte, was to have the province of Entre Minho e Douro, with the city of Porto for its capital, erected into a kingdom, under the title of Northern Lusitania. Alentejo and Algarve we[re] in like manner to be given to Godo[y] entire property and sovereignty,

title of prince of the Algarves; and a other subordinate stipulations, the o Portuguese provinces were to be held sequestration till the conclusion of general peace. A secret convention d termined the means by which this n farious treaty was to be carried into effect and the quotas of troops in both sides destined for the invasion of Portugal, were explicitly stated. Aware of the integrity and acuteness of Don Cevallos, the Spanish secretary of state, Buonaparte and Charles entrusted the whole negotiation to the weak and treacherous Don Juan Isquierdo, whose instructions were never communicated to Cevallos, nor to that department of the ministry of which he was the head; In conformity to this treaty, a French army under Junot entered Portugal, and was joined by the stipulated Spanish force. Happily for the court of Portugal, the sentence of Buonaparte that "the house of Braganza had ceased to reign," was pronounced before the victims were in his power; and even those idolaters of the emperor of France, who have most enthusiastically admired his abilities, confess that in this instance his passions overpowered his policy.

One provision of the secret treaty having thus been fulfilled, Godoy was anxiously expecting to be put in possession of his new kingdom of the Algarves. He relied upon the good offices of Murat, the gra[nd] duke of Berg, with whom he com[muni]cated through his agent and c[...] Isquierdo; and, if a few milli[ons...] be necessary to expedite hi[...] treasure which he had [...] his infamous administr[...] to spare these at com[...] ever, informed [...] was now beco[...] the extraord[...] Spaniard[...] prince [...] to [...] th[...]

was favorable to the project of the marriage, made the king write to him, and request his consent to it. This alliance which he had so lately dreaded, and endeavored to prevent by means so perilous to the royal family, he would now have willingly promoted in hopes of sheltering himself. But Buonaparte chose at this time to keep all parties in suspense, that they might be confused by their own fears; he assumed an air of displeasure towards Isquierdo, and kept him at a distance in order to cut off the direct mode of communication; and he set off for Italy giving to his journey an affected importance which excited the expectations of all Europe. Carrying into execution those parts of the secret treaty which were to his own advantage, he expelled from Tuscany the queen regent and her children, and seized all the public funds of a court that was ignorant of the very existence of the treaty, in virtue of which they were called upon to surrender not only what he had given them, but those dominions which they had possessed, before he and his family were banished from Corsica.

From Italy he answered the king of Spain's letters, assured him that he had never received any communication from the prince of Asturias, nor had obtained the slightest information of the circumstances respecting him which those letters imparted; but he nevertheless consented to the proposed marriage. In a letter afterwards written to Ferdinand himself, he acknowledged the receipt of this letter which he now denied. Holding out these hopes to the prince, and yet, at the same time by his long silence, and his reserve towards Isquierdo, keeping him, his father, and the favorite, equally in suspense and alarm, he was, in the mean time, marching his armies into Spain. That they should enter it had been stipulated by the secret treaty of Fontainbleau, and the court was not in a condition to insist that the two contracting powers were to come to a previous agreement upon that point. It was essential to his views that he should make himself master of the principal fortresses, and his generals were instructed to obtain possession of them in whatever manner they could. The wretched court fearing they knew not what, were now punished by their own offences; the treaty into which they had entered for the destruction of Portugal was now turned against themselves; they had neither sense nor courage to take those measures for their own security which the people would so eagerly have seconded; they gave the most positive orders that the French should be received every where, and treated even more favorably than the Spanish troops, and the gates of Pampeluna, St. Sebastian, Figuieras, and Barcelona, were thrown open to the enemy. The next object of these treacherous guests was to obtain possession of the citadels. Early in the morning of the 16th of February, a party of about 30 French soldiers, with two officers, went to the citadel of Pampeluna with empty bags to receive rations as usual. A shower of rain gave them a pretext for taking shelter in the guard-room at the gate, and there watching their opportunity, they seized the arms of the guard, which consisted only of thirteen men and an officer, and knocked down the sentry, who attempted to resist them. Immediately they made their signal, 200 of their comrades hastened to their assistance, they entered the citadel, overpowered the advanced-guard, and took possession of all the batteries. The soldiers who were quartered in the fortress about 200 in number, were told that if they did not submit they might abide the consequences. About 100 were detained to do duty with them. More troops came in to support them, while others, according to their orders, made themselves masters of the bridges, and secured the powder magazine. When all was done, Darmagnac, the general of division, whom Buonaparte had chosen to perpetrate this act of treachery, addressed a letter to the magistrates, informing them that as he understood he was to remain some time in Pampeluna, he felt himself obliged to ensure its safety in a military manner, and he had therefore ordered a battalion to the citadel, in order to garrison it, and do duty with the Spanish troops. I beseech you, he added, to consider this as only a trifling change, incapable of disturbing the harmony which ought to subsist between two faithful allies.

Measures had been so concerted that Barcelona was surprised on the same day. About 10,000 French troops, under general Duhesme, arrived in the neighbourhood of that city, on the 13th of February, and requested permission to halt there and refresh themselves for a few days on their way to Valencia. The gates were opened to them, and they were received by the people as friends and allies. On the 16th, the *generale* was beat; they assembled on the parade as if to proceed upon their march; their hosts and acquaintances came to bid them farewell, and the idlers of the place gathered round to see them depart. On a sudden, they filed off in two divisions, one to the citadel, the other to Monjui, a fort upon a hill which commands the town. Here there was a garrison capable of resisting them; but, though the commander demurred at their summons, saying he must receive instructions from his government, he had not resolution enough to act up to his duty. The French general insisted that his orders were peremptory, and must be executed. To have resisted would have brought on an immediate attack; and, though the commander could have defended Monjui, he dared not venture upon an act which would have involved his country in a war with France. In this manner the French surprised Barcelona. A century ago it was taken by the earl of Peterborough, and his conduct presents a contrast too honorable and too characteristic to be forgotten on this occasion. Monjui had fallen, and he was treating in person with the governor at the gates;—the articles were agreed upon, but not yet completed, when an uproar was heard within the town, and the Spaniard accused Peterborough of betraying them; "while we were capitulating," said he, "with honor and sincerity, your troops have forced their way in, and are sacking the place." Peterborough replied, "They must be the prince of Darmstadt's troops, and that there was but one means of

saving the town, which was, to let him and the English enter,—he would drive them out, and return to finish the capitulation." Nothing was risked in assenting to this, even if the governor had for a moment doubted of a proposal, which was made with such evident sincerity of heart, and was so congenial with the character of our great Peterborough, a man who carried into modern warfare all the enterprise and all the virtues of the best ages of chivalry. He, with his English troops, accordingly entered the town, drove out the Germans and Catalans, made them restore their plunder, peaceably returned to the gate, and signed the terms of capitulation.

The government of Spain had not virtue enough to know the strength which it possessed in such a people as the Spaniards; feeling nothing but its own imbecility, it had not courage to prevent these aggressions, and consequently dared not resent them; and, as the French seized these places in the name of their emperor, on the score of alliance, this wretched court consented to the occupation of them upon the same plea. Symptoms of a far different spirit appeared in Barcelona; and the count Espeleta, captain-general of Catalonia, found it necessary, (February 29th,) to issue a proclamation, calling upon all fathers of families, and heads of houses, to preserve tranquillity, and thus co-operate with the intentions of their rulers, and declaring that the late transactions did in no way obstruct or alter the system of government, neither did they disturb public nor private order. His proclamation was posted in all parts of the city Duhesme, however, soon gave the inhabitants new cause for alarm, calling upon the captain-general to fill the magazines, and establish depôts for the subsistence of his troops. The count of Espeleta returned for answer, (March 18th,) to this requisition, "that the French general might consider the whole city as his magazine; that, as he had no enemy to dread, and was quartered there as an ally, the measures which he proposed to take could only serve to create suspicion and distrust;

and that the emperor would be ill pleased to hear that he had alarmed, with fearful forebodings, a city which afforded him so hospitable a reception. " Your excellency," he pursued, " will be pleased to request the opinion of his imperial majesty respecting your determination, before you carry it into effect, and to accompany your request with this explanation of mine, as I shall also lay the business before the king, my master, without whose orders I cannot give to your excellency what the forts in possession of the Spanish troops have not. Meanwhile I wish to impress upon your mind, that it will serve no good purpose to supply the forts with stores of provisions ; that such an intention is pointed and offensive, and that it will neither be in the power of your excellency nor of myself, to remedy the consequences of the sensation which such a measure may excite among the inhabitants."

It seems at this time to have been Buonaparte's intention that the royal family should fly to their American empire ; he might then take possession of the kingdom as left to him by their abdication ; and there were no means of ultimately securing Spanish America itself, so plausible as permitting this family to repair thither, as both countries would be desirous that the intercourse between them should continue. For the purpose of increasing the fear of Charles and his ministers, he wrote an angry letter, complaining in the severest terms of reproach, that no farther measures had been taken for negotiating the proposed marriage. The king replied that he was willing it should take place immediately. He probably considered Buonaparte to be sincere in his intentions of forming this alliance ; and never having been fit for business, and now, perhaps for the first time, really feeling its cares, a natural wish for repose began to arise, and a thought of abdication passed across his mind. " Maria Louisa," said he to the queen, in the presence of Cevallos, and of all the other ministers of state, " we will retire to one of the provinces, where we will pass our days in tranquillity, and Ferdinand, who is a young man,

will take upon himself the burden of the government."—This was a thought which the example of a predecessor would naturally suggest to a king of Spain. But it was not this which the Corsican desired ;—he perceived his victim was not yet sufficiently terrified, and therefore Isquierdo, who had been kept at Paris in a state of perpetual suspense and agitation, was now commanded to return to Spain. No written proposals were sent with him, neither was he to receive any ; and he was ordered not to remain longer than three days. Under these circumstances he arrived at Aranjuez, and was immediately conducted by Godoy to the king and queen. What passed in their conference has never transpired ; but, soon after his departure from Madrid, Charles began to manifest a disposition to abandon Spain and emigrate to Mexico. If he were capable of feeling any compunctious visitations, how must he have felt on reflecting, that he had assisted in driving his kinsman and son-in-law to a similar emigration ; that he was now become the victim of his own misconduct ; and, envying the security which that injured prince had obtained, was himself preparing, in fear and in peril, to follow his example.

Preparations for such a removal could not be so easily made at Madrid and Aranjuez as at Lisbon. There was also a wide difference between the circumstances of Spain and Portugal, making that a base action in the sovereign of the former kingdom, which, for the last half century, would have been the wisest measure that the house of Braganza could have adopted. The Spaniards were confident in the size and strength of their country ; and in the prince of Asturias and his party they had leaders to whom they were enthusiastically attached. Great agitation prevailed in the metropolis ; the French were rapidly advancing, the intentions of the royal family were soon suspected, and probably the prince's friends in the ministry, to whom those intentions were necessarily entrusted, spread the alarm abroad. It is said that the council of Castile was assembled, and that, after a deliberation of six hours, the answer of that assembly to the king was, that he ought not to leave the country, and that they would not allow him to do so. If such an answer was returned, it must have been under the fear of popular opinion. Aranjuez was as much disturbed as Madrid. A decree was posted up, (March 16th,) in which the king endeavoured to remove the suspicions of the people. " The army of his dear ally, the emperor of the French, were traversing his kingdom in peace and friendship, their object being to march to those points which were threatened by the enemy." The junction of his life-guards was explained by saying that they were only summoned to protect his person, not to escort him on a journey, which malice endeavored to represent as necessary. This explanation did not satisfy the public, the proofs of his intention were unequivocal. Carriages and carts had been placed in requisition, and relays of horses were stationed on the road to Seville. The people flocked to Aranjuez and found the baggage of the court packing up for removal. It was now beyond a doubt that their government was on the point of abandoning them, and they determined therefore to stop them by force, and to take vengeance on Godoy, to whom they imputed all their calamities. The favorite remained in the palace till late at night, and attempted to escape from his own house about one in the morning. The alarm was given by one of the life-guards, who fired a pistol; others of that company instantly assembled, and the people gathered round the house, and endeavored to force their way in. Godoy's own soldiers were faithful to him, and some of the life-guards fell in this attempt. His brother, Don Diego Godoy, came with his regiment of guards to his assistance, and ordered them to fire upon the people; but they refused to obey, and suffered him to be bound hand and foot. The tumult increased; it was reported that the royal family were about to fly; they were in bed at the time;—but when the house of Godoy was forced. it was found that he had

escaped, and a party of life-guards pursued at full speed, and overtook him at Ocana. The princess de la Paz and her daughter were with them ; and it is not improbable their presence preserved him from that vengeance which he had so righteously merited. They were conducted back and delivered by the populace to the prince of Asturias.

This took place during the night of the 17th. On the following morning the king issued a decree, saying that as he intended to command his army and navy in person, he released Godoy from his employments of generalissimo and admiral, and gave him leave to withdraw whither he pleased. The people were not to be satisfied with a measure, the obvious intent of which was to screen the favorite and give him an opportunity to escape. Their agitation still continued, and Charles the next day, by a public decree abdicated the throne. " The complaints," he said, " under which he labored would not permit him any longer to bear the heavy burden of government; and, as it was necessary for the recovery of his health, to enjoy the tranquillity of a private life in a more temperate climate, he had determined, after the most serious deliberation, to abdicate the crown in favor of his very dear son." He therefore by this decree of free and voluntary abdication, made known his royal will, that the prince of Asturias should be acknowledged and obeyed as king and natural lord of all his kingdoms and dominions.

The first act of Ferdinand the VII. was to reappoint the five secretaries of state, whose offices terminated with the former reign. Cevallos was thus confirmed in the same situation under the son which he had held under the father. Assuredly no inconsistency or want of principle ought to be attributed to him on this account; it was his duty to serve his country as he best could under any administration. Ministers in other kingdoms are not to be overthrown by opposition as they are in England. Those persons who are not employed must be in retirement, and the friends of Ferdinand would be more useful to him .

by acting under Godoy, than they possibly could be while unemployed. These reappointments were made public on the 19th of March, the day of abdication. Cevallos however, sent in his resignation; the reasons which he alleged for so doing have not been made public; perhaps he wished to withdraw as much as possible from increasing difficulties and dangers, against which no remedy appeared; perhaps some degree of unpopularity attached itself to him on account of his connexion with Godoy. The language in which Ferdinand, by a public decree refused his resignation, is of that import. It had, he said, been proved to him that though Cevallos had married a cousin of the prince de la Paz, he never participated in the projects of which that man was accused, and into which judicial inquiries had been instituted. This manifested a noble and loyal heart, he was therefore a servant of whom the king would not deprive himself. The day after the accession, the senior governor of the council published a proclamation at Madrid, whereby the king confiscated the whole of Godoy's property of every kind. He announced his intention of speedily coming to the metropolis, to be proclaimed, expressing however his wishes that the inhabitants would previously give him proofs of their tranquillity, since he had communicated to them this most efficient order against the late favorite. By the same proclamation the duke Del Infantado, a nobleman of the highest character, was appointed to the command of the royal Spanish guards, and to the presidency of Castile. All those persons who had been confined in consequence of the affair which happened in the escurial, (thus the pretended conspiracy was spoken of,) were recalled near his royal person. These various measures, it was said, were made public that they might come to the knowledge of all, and that the loyal inhabitants of Madrid might know how great an interest the king took in their happiness, and the gratification of their wishes. They were requested to retire to their homes, and remain there in tranquillity; thus giving to

their new sovereign, in the first moments of his reign, the best testimony of the sincerity of their sentiments, and the truth of their professions.

A proclamation of the following day informed the people, that the king had notified to the French emperor the happy event of his accession, assuring him at the same time, that animated by the same sentiments with his august father, and far from changing in the slightest degree, his political system with respect to France, he would endeavor by all possible means, to draw closer the bands of friendship and strict alliance, which so fortunately subsisted between Spain and the French empire. This communication, it was said, was made, in order that the council might act conformably to the king's sentiments, in taking measures to restore tranquillity at Madrid, as well as for receiving the French troops who were about to enter that city, and for administering to them every requisite assistance. They were to endeavor also to convince the people that these troops came as friends, for purposes advantageous to the king and to the nation. It is manifest that the people were too wise to believe these assurances. Their eyes were open to the danger; but owing to the imbecility of their former rulers, and the situation in which Ferdinand found himself on his assumption of regal power, they were delivered over, bound, as it were hand and foot, to their treacherous enemies.

The ministers of the foreign courts all congratulated the new king upon his accession, except the French ambassador, who declined it, because he had not been furnished with the necessary instructions. Murat was at this time advancing towards Madrid with his army. "Ney, supposing," says Cevallos, "that the royal family were already on the coast and at the point of embarking, and that the people would receive him with open arms as their deliverer; he conceived that the Spaniards were in the highest degree dissatisfied with their government, and never reflected that they were only dissatisfied with its abuses." The occurrences at Aranjuez were altogether unexpected, and he immediately hastened with his whole army towards the capital to profit by the occasion, and take such steps as might by any means make him master of Spain. The approach of such an 'army, the silence of the French ambassador, the mysteriousness of Buonaparte, and his journey to Bayonne, perplexed and alarmed Ferdinand. He had immediately communicated his accession to this emperor in the most friendly and affectionate terms—fear could suggest no other. Lest this should be deemed insufficient, he appointed a deputation of three grandees to proceed to Bayonne, and compliment him in his name ; and another grandee was sent in like manner, to compliment Murat, who had already reached the vicinity of Madrid. This worthy agent of such a master was fully in the Corsican's confidence ; he assured Ferdinand that Buonaparte might be every moment expected, and he spread this rumour on all sides. Orders were therefore given for preparing apartments in the palace suitable for such a guest ; and the king, whose fears made him restless, wrote again to Buonaparte, saying how agreeable it would be to him, to become personally acquainted, and to assure him with his own lips, of his ardent wishes to strengthen more and more the alliance which subsisted between them.

Murat, evidently for the purpose of displaying his forces, (March 23rd,) to intimidate the Spaniards, reviewed his whole army before the walls, then made his entrance into Madrid, preceded by the imperial horse-guards, and by his staff, and followed by all the cavalry, and by the first division of foot under general Mounier ; two other divisions were encamped without the city, and a detachment proceeded to take possession of Toledo. Ferdinand made his public entry on horseback the following day, with no other parade than that which, under happier circumstances, would have been the most grateful of all spectacles ; a concourse of all the people of the capital and its vicinity, rejoicing in his presence, and testifying by their acclamation, that they expected from him the regeneration of their country. But never before did a prince succeed to such a crown of thorns.

Murat spoke 'mysteriously upon the change of government which had been effected, declaring that, until the emperor had acknowledged Ferdinand VII. it was impossible for *him* to take any step which might appear like an acknowledgment ; he therefore must be under the necessity of treating with the royal father. As a farther indication of the course which would be pursued, he affected to take an interest in behalf of Godoy. A sort of military government was immediately established in the metropolis ; the French general 'Grouchy, being made governor of the city, and patroles instituted to preserve the police, under the joint superintendance of a French officer and a Spaniard.

No people in time of popular tumult, ever conducted themselves with such respect to the magistrates and the law, as the people of Madrid had done during this revolution. They do not seem to have injured the person of any individual ; even Godoy himself escaped unhurt. A party had assembled round the house of one of his creatures, when an alcayde came up, and inquired what they were about to do ?—To put to death a villain, was the answer. Who gave them authority to do so ? One of the crowd was ready with an answer, and replied, His crimes. Were there no courts of justice ? the spokesman was asked, and he answered by another question, Why then does he still live ? But, said the alcayde, Have you proved him to be guilty ? We know him to be so. But has the law pronounced his condemnation ? No. Well then, said the officer, he is my prisoner, and I will deliver him to justice. This satisfied the people, and they dispersed without committing any act of violence. An alcayde preserved another house from violence by fixing the royal arms in its front.

In the provinces, the news of the abdication was received with the utmost joy ; the imbecility of Charles was well known ; the queen was unpopular for her open profligacy, and nothing could exceed the hatred in which the favorite was held. Te deum was performed in several places, as a thanksgiving for his fall. At Salamanca, the monks and students are said to have testified their exultation by dancing in the market-place. The use which Ferdinand made of Godoy's treasures, increased the general satisfaction ; one of his earliest measures was to pay up the arrears due to the officers and widows on the pension list.

Murat's intention was to frighten Ferdinand into the toils ; an alarm that should have made him start would have ruined the plot. The interest which this grand duke affected for Godoy, his refusal to acknowledge the new government, and the respect which he paid to Charles, all tended to this end. The rumour of Buonaparte's coming was carefully spread abroad ; fresh couriers were said to have arrived ; the emperor had left Paris, and was to be expected speedily in Madrid. The soldiers were told that he would lose no time in putting himself at the head of his armies in Spain ; they were ordered to put themselves (April 2nd,) in a state to appear before him ; and in this proclamation, which appeared in a Madrid gazette extraordinary, the ominous notice was given, that they would immediately be supplied with cartridge. It was hinted that it would be a delicate compliment to the emperor, if the infante, Don Carlos, (Ferdinand's next brother,) would set off to receive him on the way. His highness, said Murat, could not fail to meet him before he had proceeded two days on his road. This was readily agreed to, and the infante, accompanied by the duke del Infantado, departed upon this fatal journey. Having secured the victims, Murat endeavored to entice Ferdinand himself into the snare, what had at first been hinted at, and advised, as a mark of attentive consideration, was now pressed upon him as a thing of importance ; a measure which would be attended with the happiest consequences to himself and the whole kingdom. The young king hesitated at this ; it was more than courtesy required, more than an ally

was entitled to expect ; and perhaps he felt it was more than a king of Spain ought to perform. Cevallos constantly advised him not to leave his capital till he had received certain intelligence that Buonaparte had actually passed the Pyrenees, and was approaching Madrid ; and even then he urged him to proceed so short a way, that it should not be necessary for him to sleep out of his capital more than a single night. This advice prevailed for a time against the repeated solicitations of Murat and the ambassador Beauharnois. It became necessary, therefore, to introduce a new actor in this detestable plot.

During the interval which elapsed before this agent could appear, Murat informed Cevallos, that the emperor would be gratified if the sword of Francis I. were presented to him ; and he desired that this might be intimated to the new king. It might be supposed that this was designed not [merely to gratify the French nation, but also to lower Ferdinand in the opinion of the Spaniards, if Buonaparte and his agents ever took the noble feelings of our nature into their calculation. But it was a mere trick for the Parisians, and neither they nor the tyrant himself would feel that France was far more dishonored by the circumstances under which the sword was recovered, than by the manner in which it had been lost. Accordingly this trophy of Pescara's victory, which had lain since the year 1525 in the royal armoury at Madrid, was carried, (March 31st,) with great ceremony to the lodgings of the grand duke ; he, it was said, having been brought up by the side of the emperor, and in the same school, and illustrious for his military talents, was more worthy than any other person could be, to be charged with so precious a deposit, and to transmit it into the hands of his imperial majesty. This base language appeared in the Madrid gazette. The people of this city passively beheld the surrender of the trophy ; it was the act, however compulsory, of this lawful king, the king of their choice, the compulsion was neither avowed on the one side, nor confessed on the other ; but, from the imputation of beholding it with indifference, they amply redeemed themselves. Murat, upon receiving it, pronounced a flattering eulogium on the Spanish nation,— that nation which he was in the act of plundering, and which he came to betray and to enslave.

Notwithstanding the patroles and rounds, and military government, the suspicions of the people began to manifest themselves more and more, and their poor prince was compelled, while he concealed his own fears, to exert his authority for suppressing theirs. By a new edict, (April 3rd,) it was enacted, that no liquors should be sold after eight in the evening, master-manufacturers and tradesmen were ordered to give notice to the police if any of their workmen or apprentices absented themselves from their work, fathers of families were enjoined to keep their children and families from mixing with seditious assemblies, and to restrain them by good example, good advice, and the fear of punishment. It was declared, at the same time, that the guilty would be most severely punished, without remission and without delay.

On the introduction of Savary, the French ambassador, to the closet of Ferdinand, he assured the unfortunate prince that the emperor was already near Bayonne, on his way to Madrid, and that it would be highly flattering to his imperial majesty, if the king would meet him on the road. Ferdinand, incapable of suspecting that the envoy was sent merely to deceive him, yielded to his solicitations; and, having issued a proclamation, in which he announced his departure to meet his "friend and mighty ally the emperor of France," and appointed the infante Don Antonio president of the high council of government, he began on the 11th of April, his unhappy journey. Savary affected the most zealous and assiduous attention, solicited the honor of accompanying him, and asserted that the emperor would certainly be found at Burgos on their arrival. When they reached Burgos, Buonaparte was not there, and Ferdinand hesitated whether to advance or return, but, again deceived by the flatteries of Savary, and afraid to refuse a favor so

earnestly required, proceeded to Vittoria, yet so reluctantly, that on their entrance into that town, thinking it would be useless to renew his solicitations, Savary left him there and continued his journey to Bayonne, there to arrange measures with his master for securing the prey which was now already in the toils. At Vittoria, Ferdinand received intelligence that Buonaparte had reached Bourdeaux, and was on his way to Bayonne. In consequence of this advice, the infante Don Carlos, who had been waiting at Tolosa, proceeded to Bayonne, whither the emperor had invited him, and when the modern Cæsar Borgia arrived there, he found one victim in his power. Don Carlos soon discovered the views of Buonaparte; and, having communicated his fears to Pignatelli, on whom he relied as a Spaniard and a man of honor, drew up with his advice a letter to Ferdinand, beseeching him to abandon his journey to Bayonne. Pignatelli was in Napoleon's interest, and intercepted the messengers. Their measures were soon resolved upon : Savary returned to Vittoria with a letter from Buonaparte to Ferdinand, couched in terms of mingled sarcasm, menace, and ardent friendship. Such a letter might well have intimidated Ferdinand from proceeding on his journey to Bayonne, but he had advanced too far to recede, and the French troops in the neighbourhood of Vittoria surrounded him, ready to intercept his retreat, should he attempt it. Cevallos, his other counsellors, and the people of Vittoria, besought him not to advance, while general Savary assured him with the most vehement protestations, that in a few minutes after his arrival at Bayonne, he would be recognised as king of Spain and of the Indies. Confused, terrified, and in the power of Buonaparte, the only relief he could find was in yielding implicit belief to these representations. His credulity can hardly be condemned. The treachery was too complicated, too monstrous to be suspected. Centuries had elapsed since any act of similar perfidy had stained the history of Europe.

He proceeded and crossed the stream

which divides the two kingdoms. Scarcely had he set foot upon the French territory before he remarked that no one came to receive him; a neglect more striking as he had travelled so far to meet the emperor. At St. Jean de Luz he was complimented by the simple and unsuspecting mayor, and shortly afterwards was met by his grandees, who had been sent to compliment the emperor. Their report was sufficiently discouraging, but he was now near Bayonne, and it was too late to turn back. The prince of Neufchatel, (Berthier,) and Duroc, the marshal of the palace, came out to meet him, and conduct him to the place which had been appointed for his residence, a place so little suited to such a guest, that he could not for a moment be insensible that it marked the most gross and wilful disrespect. Before he had recovered from his surprise and alarm, Buonaparte accompanied by several of his generals paid him a visit. Ferdinand, from motives of policy, went down to the street door to receive him, and they embraced with every token of friendship. The interview was short and merely complimentary. Buonaparte embraced him at parting. "The kiss of Judas Iscariot," says a Spanish patriot, "was not more treacherous than the Corsican salute."

Ferdinand was not long suffered to remain uncertain of his fate. Buonaparte, as if he derived a criminal pleasure from acting the part of the deceiver, invited him to dinner, sent his carriage for his conveyance, came to the coach steps to receive him, again embraced him and led him by the hand into the banquet room. Ferdinand sat at the same table with him as a friend, a guest, and an ally, and no sooner had he returned to his own residence, than general Savary came to inform him of the emperor's irrevocable determination that the Bourbon dynasty should no longer reign in Spain; that it was to be succeeded by the Buonaparte; and that Ferdinand was expected in his own name and that of all his family to renounce the crown of Spain, and of the Indies in their favor. Ferdinand for a while resisted the proposal, and through the agency of M. Cevallos, represented with

firmness but moderation its injustice to himself, to his family, and to Europe. Already he had sufficient reason to feel himself a prisoner, and determined to hazard the utmost vengeance of Napoleon, rather than passively submit to accumulated injuries, he announced his intention to return, in conformity with his solemn promise, to the Spanish nation, adding that he should be ready to treat in his own dominions on all convenient subjects, with any person whom it might please his imperial majesty to authorize. No answer was returned to this despatch, but the spies within the palace, and the guards without were doubled. A guard at the door even ordered the king and his brother, on their appearance at midnight, to retire to their apartments. The mind of Ferdinand was not yet so subdued, as to brook this insult. He complained bitterly of the humiliation to which he was subjected, and the governor endeavored to soothe his indignation by courteous language. The act however was repeated, and unwilling to expose himself a third time to insults which he had no means of resenting, he abstained from leaving his chamber.

In the mean time collateral measures were not neglected. The prisoner Godoy had been and would be the creature of of France, and Buonaparte was resolved to save him. Having recourse to direct falsehood, he sent information to Murat that the prince of Asturias had placed the prisoner entirely at his disposal, and ordered him to demand and obtain the surrender of his person. The marquis de Castellar to whom the custody of Godoy was committed, reluctantly complied with a note from the supreme junta, transmitted, in consequence of the assurances of Murat, by general Belliard, and demanding his liberation, and Godoy was removed by night. With a rapidity that eluded the vigilance of the exasperated people, he proceeded accompanied by a strong escort, to Bayonne. Godoy, as was expected, became one of the most useful and active instruments of Buonaparte. By his influence Charles was induced to treat his son as an enemy, a rebel, and a traitor, and to resume the crown for the purpose of transferring it to a despot and a stranger, from whose unprovoked aggression, he himself a few weeks before, attempted to abandon his kingdom and fly to America.

Ferdinand was now reduced to the necessity of choice between degradation and absolute destruction. He made however one effort in behalf of Spain and of himself, and addressed his father in a letter not less dignified than respectful, in which he asserted his right to the crown, and his readiness to restore it. In the answer to this letter, the style as well as the purposes of Buonaparte were apparent. The hatred of popular assemblies, the affectation of philosophy, the perpetual reference to brutal force, and the number and inconsistency of the falsehoods it contained were all characteristic of the bureau from which it originally proceeded. Ferdinand's answer to this extraordinary paper was highly honorable to himself and his advisers, and Buonaparte irritated and surprised by the firmness of his resistance, demanded an hour's conference with Charles, at the conclusion of which Ferdinand was called in by his father, to hear in the presence of Napoleon, and of the queen of Spain, expressions so indecent and disgusting, that I dare not record them. It may be mentioned however, that intimidated by the threats of Buonaparte, the queen declared Ferdinand to have been born in adultery, and authorised the emperor of France to assert that he had no other right to the crown than what he derived from his mother. While all the rest of the visitors were seated, Ferdinand was kept standing, and his father (May 6th) ordered him to make an absolute renunciation of the crown, under pain of being treated with all his household as a usurper and conspirator against the lives of his parents. For the sake of his adherents he submitted, and delivered in a renunciation couched in such terms as at once to imply compulsion, and reserve the condition of his father's return to Spain. He was not aware when he executed this form of renunciation that his father was no longer qualified to receive it. Napoleon had not waited for this pre-

liminary to conclude his mock negotiation with Charles. This wretched puppet addressed an edict on the 4th of May to the supreme junta of Madrid, in which he nominated Murat, lieutenant-general of the kingdom, and president of the government. The message was immediately succeeded by a resignation on the part of Charles, of the sovereignty of Spain to the emperor of France, in return for an asylum in France, and various pecuniary gratuities dependent on the punctuality and integrity of Napoleon. The agreement was signed by general Duroc, grand master of the palace, on the part of Buonaparte, and on the part of Charles, by Godoy, under his titles, Spanish and Portuguese, of prince de la Paz, and count of Evora Monte. Having executed his commission, the latter retired into the interior of France, there to remain for a while, neglected, and despised, and ultimately to leave behind him a name more infamous than any which Spanish history replete as it is with atrocious narratives, had yet recorded.

Ferdinand had hitherto renounced his right in reference to his father only. It was now demanded that he should cede his claims to the emperor of France, and he was told to choose between cession and death. That Ferdinand should at length have yielded is not to be severely condemned, it is rather to be admired that he should have resisted so long. Even had he been of a more heroic frame than from his family and education there is any reason to suppose, imprisonment and death were all that he could expect from further opposition. Thus intimidated he ordered his former tutor, Escoiquiz, to treat with Duroc for the surrender of his own rights, and those of his brothers and his uncle Don Antonio, who had now been sent from Madrid, rather as prisoners, than in any other character. The preamble declared that the emperor of the French and the prince of Asturias having differences to regulate had agreed to these terms : I. That Ferdinand acceded to the cession made by his father, and renounced as far as might be necessary the rights accruing to him as prince of Asturias. II. The title of royal highness with all the honors and prerogatives, personal and hereditary, which the princes of the blood enjoyed, should be granted him in France. III. The palaces, parks, and farms of Navarre should be given to him and his heirs in property for ever. V. VI. VII. Four hundred thousand livres of appanage rent, on the treasury of France, should be settled upon him with reversion to his heirs, and the prince himself should receive a life rent of 600,000 livres, while the infantes and their descendants should continue to enjoy the revenues of their commanderies in Spain, and an appanage rent of 400,000 livres in perpetuity, with reversion to the issue of Ferdinand. No mention was made in the treaty of the queen of Etruria, and her son, a boy of eight years old, who was to have been made, by the doubly treacherous treaty of Fontainebleau, king of northern Lusitania. Involved in the common destruction of their house, they were seized with the infantes at Madrid, and escorted to Bayonne. After this event, the whole of the unhappy family, now that the mockery of negotiation was at an end, were sent into the interior of France.

END OF THE FIRST VOLUME.

Brightly and Childs, Printers, Bungay.